C0-BJK-485

OREGON WASHINGTON

TourBook®

An annual catalog of selected travel information

American Automobile Association
1000 AAA Drive
Heathrow, FL 32746-5063

Valid through February 1996

Printed in the USA by Quebecor Printing Buffalo, Inc., Buffalo, NY

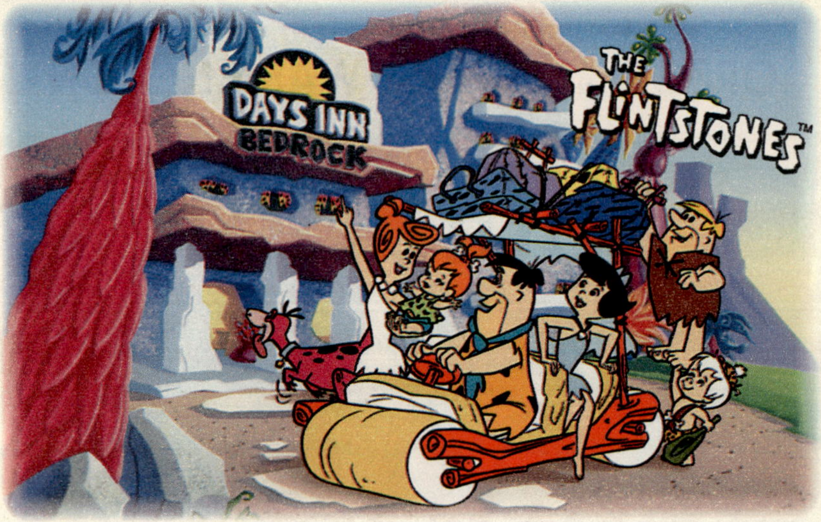

Head out on your own Great Days Inn Road Trip.

Staying at Days Inn can mean big savings on the road. Especially if you're a AAA member. You'll receive our low rates at over 1500 Days Inn locations worldwide. Not to mention plenty of Flintstones fun the whole family will enjoy. For more information or to make reservations, contact your travel agent or call **1-800-AAA-DAYS.**

Hanna-Barbera

DAYS INN®

The Best Value Under The Sun.℠

©1994 Days Inns Of America, Inc. ©1994 Hanna-Barbera Productions, Inc. The Flintstones™ and all related names and likenesses are trademarks of Hanna-Barbera Productions, Inc. All rights reserved.

CONTENTS

INTRODUCTION: USING YOUR TOURBOOK

TIPS FOR THE TOURBOOK TRAVELER

ATTRACTIONS

LODGINGS & RESTAURANTS

MAPS

FOR YOUR INFORMATION

INDEXES

AAA SUPERNUMBER 1-800-AAA-HELP

COMMENTS

Write: AAA Member Comments
Box 61, 1000 AAA Dr.
Heathrow, FL 32746-5063

ADVERTISING (407) 444-8280

published by **American Automobile Association**® 1000 AAA Drive, Heathrow, FL 32746-5063

Cover: *Mount Jefferson, Deschutes National Forest, OR* / Charlie Ott / SuperStock

4620

The publisher is not responsible for changes that occur after publication. Published for the exclusive use of members. Not for sale. Copyright AAA 1995 edition. All rights reserved.

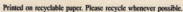

Printed on recyclable paper. Please recycle whenever possible.

USING YOUR TOURBOOK

This TourBook has one purpose: to make your trip as enjoyable as possible by providing reliable, detailed information about attractions, lodgings and restaurants in the area through which you are traveling.

Attractions and AAA rated lodgings and restaurants are listed in this book under the name of the city in which they physically are located. If the establishment is located in an unincorporated area, it is listed under the nearest recognized city. This policy—called geographical listing—ensures AAA books are consistent, specific and accurate. Use AAA maps in conjunction with this book when planning your trip.

No attraction, lodging or restaurant pays for a listing. Each is listed on the basis of merit alone after a AAA field inspector or a designated AAA representative has carefully evaluated it. AAA's unique network of local club travel specialists checks information dealing with attractions and touring areas annually. Road reporters and cartographic researchers keep maps current.

There are three components that comprise the book's information:

- Attractions
- Maps
- Lodgings & Restaurants

Knowing *about* these components—discussed here in the order in which you will discover them in the book—is your key to unlocking this TourBook, which AAA publishes to provide its members with the most accurate travel information available.

ABOUT ATTRACTIONS

The Attractions section of your TourBook serves as a guide to selected places rather than as a commercial, geographic or promotional encyclopedia. Communities or areas included offer something for you to do or see that sets them apart from others in the area or nation. We call these "points of interest."

Each state begins by introducing you to historical, geographic, economic and other factors that contribute to the state's character. The Recreation Areas chart lists facilities available in national and state parks and other areas; unusual or special features of a park are also mentioned.

SCHEDULES AND PRICES

All information was reviewed before publication for accuracy at press time. However, changes often occur between annual editions. We regret any inconvenience resulting from such instances, but they are beyond our control. Please use the phone numbers in the attraction write-ups if you wish to confirm prices.

READING THE LISTINGS

Any attraction with a separate heading has been approved by a AAA field inspector or designated AAA representative. An attraction's quality is reflected in the length and scope of its general description. We have placed a star (★) before attractions of exceptional interest and quality. An index to starred attractions appears with the orientation map. *(See ABOUT MAPS, page 6.)*

Attractions are listed alphabetically under the name of the nearest community; in most cases the distances given are computed from the center of town, unless otherwise specified, using the following highway designations: I (interstate highway), US (federal highway), SR (state route), CR (county road), FM (farm to market road), FR (forest road) and MM (mile marker).

Descriptive information about the attraction follows the location description. Next come the days, hours and seasons the attraction is *open.* These may be preceded by a suggested minimum visiting time. Following are admission prices quoted *without* sales tax; children under the lowest age specified are admitted free when accompanied by an adult. Days, months and age groups written with a hyphen are *inclusive.*

Credit cards accepted for admissions or fares may be indicated at the end of the listing as follows: AE, American Express; CB, Carte Blanche; DI, Diners Club; DS, Discover; ER, EnRoute; JCB; MC, MasterCard; VI, VISA. Minimum amounts that may be charged appear in parentheses when applicable.

ADMISSION DISCOUNTS

Your AAA membership card is the key to reduced prices at many attractions because they value your patronage and respect the AAA name. Whether or not a listing shows a discount, present your valid AAA or CAA card when purchasing tickets; some attractions not formally enrolled in the program may still give members a discount. A full list of participating attractions appears in the Indexes section of this book. Discounts are offered for the validity period noted on the title page of this book.

Participating attractions individually determine the terms of the discount they offer. The discount may not apply if any other price reduction is offered or if tickets are purchased through an outlet other than the attraction's ticket office.

ABOUT MAPS

Maps created specifically for this book have precise purposes and should be used in *conjunction* with the more complete sheet maps and Triptik maps provided by your AAA travel counselor. To ensure your complete satisfaction, use book maps as *supplementary* guides only. Not every book will contain every map type listed below.

State and province orientation maps appear before the Points of Interest listings in the Attractions section. Regional orientation maps appear with the description of the points of interest. Their purpose is to illustrate the relative positions of towns, recreation facilities and starred points of interest listed in the TourBooks. Only major road networks are portrayed on these maps.

Coordinates (for example: A-3) following the place or city names in the Points of Interest listings refer to this map; stars next to town names on the maps indicate the presence of highly recommended attractions. An index to starred attractions appears with or adjacent to each orientation map.

Accommodations orientation maps are used for large geographical areas that are attractions in themselves (for example: the Finger Lakes region in New York and Michigan's Upper Peninsula). These maps are located in the Lodgings & Restaurants section of your book. Because the maps are on such a small scale, lodgings and restaurants are not shown, but the towns that have these types of facilities are printed in magenta type so you can plan your trip accordingly.

Spotting maps assist you in locating the facilities listed in the Lodgings & Restaurants section of your book. These maps locate, or "spot," lodgings with a black-background numeral (20, for example); restaurants are spotted with a white-background numeral (20, for example). Indexes found near the map match the number symbol to the property.

Downtown spotting maps are provided when spotted facilities are more concentrated. Starred points of interest also appear on these maps.

City/Area spotting maps show the main roads required to find a dining or lodging facility, as well as the major landmarks that are near the lodgings and restaurants. Airports are also shown on city/area spotting maps. The names of cities that have AAA-rated properties are shown in magenta type.

City maps show metropolitan areas where numerous attractions are concentrated. While reading an attraction description, refer to this map to see where it is located in relation to major roads, parks, airports, etc.

Walking or Self-Guiding tour maps provide an exceptional level of detail, showing specific routes corresponding to text in the TourBooks. Well-known buildings are often outlined for easier identification. Routes are well-marked with beginning and ending points as well as directional arrows.

National park maps familiarize drivers with the area in and around the park. The main features depicted are mountains, streams, hiking trails, canyons, ice fields, etc. Some of the campground sites and lodges spotted on the maps do not meet AAA criteria, but have been listed as a service to members who wish to stay at these facilities.

Driving distance maps located in the For Your Information section of the book are intended to be used only for trip-distance and driving-time planning. Refer to more detailed AAA maps available from your club for actual route numbers.

ABOUT LODGINGS & RESTAURANTS

Lodging and restaurant listings appear after the attraction listings and are introduced by a title page. Both types of properties are listed alphabetically under the nearest town or city, with lodgings listed first. To help you plan your trips, these towns and cities are printed in red on AAA regional, state, provincial and Triptik maps. The TourBook includes special accommodation "spotting" maps to help you find lodgings and restaurants. *(See ABOUT MAPS.)*

AAA inspectors carefully evaluate every lodging establishment and restaurant listed in this publication at least once every year. Their rigorous inspection helps ensure that all properties meet AAA's exacting standards for quality.

AAA monitors member satisfaction through your comments and surveys. AAA rating criteria reflect your needs and expectations and the design and service standards determined by the lodging industry.

Additionally, we maintain an open dialogue with individual establishment operators, the American Hotel and Motel Association and most major lodging chains.

USING LODGING LISTINGS

To use this book most effectively, read the sample lodging listing along with the explanation of the terms appearing on page 9. The location is given from the center of town unless noted otherwise. Baths are not mentioned if all rooms have private baths. All showers are tub showers unless otherwise noted.

If parking is provided on the premises at no charge, it is not mentioned in the listing. Other parking conditions such as no parking available, off-site parking, street parking only or off-site valet parking, and any charges, are specifically noted in the listing. **Check-in** times are shown only if they are after 3 p.m.; **check-out** times are shown only if they are before 10 a.m. Service charges are not shown unless they are $1 or more, or at least 5 percent of the room rate.

GUEST SAFETY

AAA/CAA requires that all lodgings listed in the 1995 TourBooks for the United States and Canada must comply with AAA's revised guest room security requirements. In response to AAA/CAA members' concern about their safety at accommodations, AAA/CAA rated properties must have deadbolt locks on all guest room entry doors and connecting room doors. If the area outside the guest room door is not visible from inside the room through a window or door panel, viewports must be installed on all guest room entry doors. Bed and breakfast properties and country inns are not required to have viewports. Ground floor and easily accessible sliding doors must be equipped with secondary locks.

Verification that the required hardware was in place at each AAA/CAA rated property listed in the 1995 TourBooks was obtained by one of the following methods. Either the field inspector, on a random selection of inspected rooms, observed the correct hardware; or, AAA received a signed, notarized affidavit from the property, attesting that the appropriate locks were installed by a specified deadline. AAA field inspectors view a percentage of rooms at each property. Because it is not feasible for the inspectors to evaluate every room in every lodging establishment, AAA cannot guarantee that there are working locks on all doors and windows in all guest rooms.

Guest security is a significant concern for AAA/CAA members and all travelers. Research shows that 99% of members expect deadbolts on guest room doors. While safety can never be guaranteed, our revised security guidelines address this major issue.

Lodging Evaluation Criteria

Regardless of the diamond rating, properties listed by AAA are required to provide:

- Clean and well-maintained facilities throughout
- Hospitable staff
- A well-kept appearance

Regardless of the rating, each guest room is required to have:

- Comfortable beds and good quality bedding
- Locks on all doors and windows
- Comfortable furnishings and pleasant decor
- Smoke detectors
- Adequate towels and supplies
- At least one chair
- Adequate illumination at each task area

THE LODGING DIAMONDS

Before a property may be listed in this book, it must satisfy a set of minimum standards that reflect the basic lodging needs AAA members have identified. If a property meets those requirements, it is assigned a diamond rating reflecting the overall quality of the establishment. The ratings range from one to five diamonds and reflect the physical and service standards typically found at each diamond level.

Ratings are assigned according to the property's classification, which appears beneath the diamond rating in the lodging listing. The classification represents the physical design and level of services provided by the property. For example, a motel offers limited services and recreational facilities. A resort hotel offers extensive guest services and recreational facilities. Comparing a motel to a resort hotel would be like comparing an apple to an orange. By assigning ratings according to classification AAA compares apples to apples. A description of classifications is on pages 10 & 11.

Although one diamond is AAA's minimum rating, a one diamond property still is better than one-third of the lodgings in operation, since the majority of unlisted properties do not meet AAA's minimum standards.

Lodgings AAA rated ◆ provide good but modest accommodations. Establishments are functional, emphasizing clean and comfortable rooms. They must meet the basic needs of privacy and cleanliness. Rates are generally economical.

The ◆◆ lodging maintains the attributes offered at the one diamond level, while showing noticeable enhancements in decor and/or quality of furnishings. They may be recently constructed or older properties, both targeting the needs of a budget-oriented traveler.

Establishments rated ◆◆◆ offer a degree of sophistication. Additional amenities, services and facilities may be offered. There is a marked upgrade in services and comfort.

Excellent properties displaying a high level of service and hospitality are AAA rated ◆◆◆◆. Properties offer a wide variety of amenities and upscale facilities, both inside the room, on the grounds and in the public areas.

Lodgings awarded ◆◆◆◆◆ are renowned. They exhibit an exceptionally high degree of service; striking, luxurious facilities; and many extra amenities. Guest services are executed and presented in a flawless manner. The guest will be pampered by a very professional, attentive staff. The property's facilities and operation help set the standards in hospitality and service.

A few properties are listed without a rating. They were either under construction or undergoing such a substantial renovation at press time that it was impossible to assign an accurate rating.

RATE OPTIONS AND DISCOUNTS

Annually, lodging operators are asked to update rates, discounts and rate options for TourBook publication. Properties are not required to offer a discount to be listed in the book. But they commit to one of three rate options to offer AAA members. That option appears in the listing.

(1) Special Value Rates—The establishment not only guarantees rates will not exceed the maximum rates printed in the TourBook, they also offer a minimum discount of 10 percent off printed rates. This is the only rate option that contains a discount. Since these rates are discounted only for AAA members, you *must* identify yourself as a AAA member and request the **AAA Special Value Rate** when making reservations. Show your membership card at registration and verify the AAA Special Value Rate. *Note:* Members may take either the **Special Value Rate** or the **Senior Discount**, but not both.

(2) Guaranteed Rates—The establishment guarantees AAA members will not be charged more than the maximum rates printed in the TourBook. To receive these rates you *must* identify yourself as a AAA member and request the AAA guaranteed rate when making reservations. Show your AAA card at registration and verify the rate.

(3) Rates Subject To Change—The printed rates are the establishment's estimated charges for the periods noted. The actual rates charged may be reasonably higher or lower than those printed in the TourBook.

Exceptions: Lodgings may temporarily increase their room rates or modify their policies during a special event or for those traveling as part of a group or convention. Examples of such events range from Mardi Gras and the Kentucky Derby to college football homecoming games, holidays and state fairs. At these times the **Special Value** and **Guaranteed** rate options do not apply.

Senior Discount: Some establishments offer the senior discount with either the **Rates Guaranteed** option or the **Rates Subject to Change** option. Where the words "Senior Discount" are included in a listing, a minimum discount of 10 percent off the prevailing or guaranteed rate is available to AAA members who are 60 years of age or older. This discount is in effect whenever the establishment is open. You *must* identify yourself as a AAA member *and* request the Senior Discount when making reservations. Show your AAA card at registration and verify the rate and discount. Members may take this discount or the AAA Special Value Rate, but not both. Senior discounts might not apply during special events.

Rate lines: Rates are for typical rooms, not special units. Rates do not include taxes. Multiple rate lines are used to indicate a seasonal rate difference.

USING RESTAURANT LISTINGS

We strive to approve consistently good dining establishments. In metropolitan areas, where many are above average, we select some of those known for the superiority of their food, service and atmosphere and also those offering a selection of quality food at moderate prices (including some cafeterias and family restaurants). In small communities the restaurants considered to be the best in the area may be listed.

Restaurants are classified by major cuisine type (Italian, French, etc.). Some listings indicate the availability of a senior discount for members 60 years or older; some also indicate the availability of "earlybird specials" if they are offered at least 5 days a week. Phone ahead for details on discounts and specially priced meals.

The range of prices is approximate and reflects dinner (salad or appetizer, a main course, and a non-alcoholic beverage) for one person. Taxes and tips are not included.

Cafeterias, buffets and other self-service operations are rated only as compared to similar establishments. Listings in this category are suited to family dining.

THE RESTAURANT DIAMONDS

Restaurants rated ◆ provide good but unpretentious dishes. Table settings are usually simple and may include paper placemats and napkins. If alcoholic beverages are offered, wine and beer selections may be limited. The restaurants are usually informal, with an atmosphere conducive to family dining.

The AAA rated ◆◆ restaurant will usually have more extensive menus that represent more complex food preparation. A wider variety of alcoholic beverages will usually be available. The atmosphere is appealing and suitable for family or adult dining. Although service may be casual, host or hostess seating can be expected. Table settings may include tablecloths and cloth napkins.

Most ◆◆◆ restaurants have extensive or specialized menus and a more complex cuisine preparation that requires a professional chef. Cloth table linens, above-average quality table settings, a skilled service staff and an inviting decor should all be provided. Generally, the wine list will include representatives of the best domestic and foreign wine-producing regions. Restaurants in this category can offer a formal dining experience or a special family occasion.

AAA rated ◆◆◆◆ restaurants have appealing ambience, often enhanced by fresh flowers and fine furnishings. The overall sophistication and formal atmosphere create a dining experience more for adults than for families. A wine steward presents an extensive list of the best wines. A smartly attired, highly skilled staff will be capable of describing how any dish is prepared. Elegant silverware, china and correct glassware are typical. The menu will include creative dishes prepared from fresh ingredients by a chef who frequently has international training. Eye-appealing desserts will be offered at tableside.

The few restaurants that are awarded ◆◆◆◆◆ are world-class operations. They have the attributes of a four diamond restaurant with even more luxury and sophistication and feature exceptional, innovative cuisine. A proportionally large staff, expert in preparing tableside delicacies, will provide flawless service, with impeccable linens, silver and crystal glassware.

MARINA'S COVE AAA Special Value Rates **Phone:** 808/931-2311 **10**
Hotel
All Year [AP] 1P: $265- 430 2P/1B: $265- 430 2P/2B: $265- 430 XP: $45 F-17
Location: Oceanfront; 5 blks s of Kalakaua Ave via Kanekapolei St. 2199 Kapahulu Rd 96815 FAX 808/931-8004. **Terms:** Reserv deposit, 3 day notice; 4 night min stay, 12/28-1/1; no pets. **Facility:** 456 rooms. Distinctive hotel with refined atmosphere. Exceptional service. Spacious guest rooms & suites with simplistic elegance. Diamond Head & ocean backdrop from large lanai. 44 suites, $580-$3500; 6-22 stories; interior corridors; conference facilities; beach, pool; exercise room. **Dining & Entertainment:** 2 dining rooms; 7 am-10 pm; $20-$38; cocktails/lounge; 24-hour room service; afternoon tea; also, La Mer, see separate listing; entertainment. **Services:** secretarial services; valet laundry. childcare; massage, airport transportation; valet parking. **Recreation:** children's program 6/1-8/31; swimming. **All Rooms:** honor bars, refrigerators, safes, cable TV. **Some Rooms:** CP's. **Cards:** AE, CB, DI, JCB, MC, VI. A Preferred Hotel. Roll in showers. Ⓓ Ⓢ ⊗

① This section of the listing shows: whether the lodging is a AAA Official Appointment (see What The Means pg. 13), what the lodging's diamond rating is (see pg. 7), and under what classification the lodging was rated (see pgs. 10-11).

② This is the Rate Option the lodging has chosen to offer AAA members (see Rate Options and Discounts pg. 7).

③ This section of the listing is comprised of the rate lines, which show from left to right: dates the rates in that line are effective, any meal plan included in the rate (CP=Continental Plan of pastry, juice and another beverage; BP=Breakfast Plan of full breakfast; AP=American Plan of three meals daily; MAP=Modified American Plan of two meals daily), number of Persons/Beds allowed/provided for the rates shown, the rates charged, the extra person (XP) charge and, if applicable, the family plan indicator (F17=children 17 and under stay free; D17=discount for children 17 and under; F=children stay free; D=discounts for children). The establishment may limit the number of children to whom the family plan applies.

④ If present, this number locates the lodging on accommodations spotting maps provided for some communities (see About Maps pg. 6).

⑤ The Facility section lists all the key elements of the lodging's common areas, the physical attributes of the property all guests may experience—including pools and other recreation facilities. The list of facility elements for which there are charges is preceded by "Fee:".

⑥ The Dining section describes food and beverage services, including the hours of operation and price range for dinner.

⑦ The Services section iterates additional non-recreation types of assistance, equipment or benefits available from the lodging. The list of services for which there are charges is preceded by "Fee:".

⑧ The Recreation section inventories leisure opportunities and activities. The list of recreation options for which there are charges is preceded by "Fee:". Equipment available at a cost is preceded by "Rental:".

⑨ The All Rooms section shows the amenities offered within the guest rooms. Amenities with limited availability are listed after the words "Some Rooms:". Amenities available for a charge follow the word "Fee:".

⑩ Up to five symbols may appear in the lodging listing. As shown here they mean, from left to right: wheelchair and hearing impaired accessibility (see Access for the Disabled pg. 13), Ⓓ all rooms have smoke detectors, Ⓢ all rooms have fire protection sprinklers, and ⊗ non-smoking rooms are available. The words "Roll in showers" will appear before the symbols if such a facility is available for the disabled guest.

LODGING CLASSIFICATIONS

Lodgings are classified according to the physical design and services offered. The classification appears beneath the diamond rating in each lodging listing.

BED AND BREAKFAST (limited service)—Usually a smaller establishment emphasizing personal attention. Guest rooms are individually decorated with an **at home** feeling and may lack some modern amenities such as TVs, phones, etc. Usually owner-operated with a common room or parlor where guests and owners can interact during evening and breakfast hours. May have shared bathrooms. A Continental or full hot breakfast is served and is included in the room rate. Parking may be limited or on the street.

COMPLEX (service varies depending on type of lodgings)—A combination of two or more kinds of lodging classifications.

COTTAGE (limited service)—Individual bungalow, cabin or villa, usually containing one rental unit equipped for housekeeping. May have a separate living room and bedroom(s). Parking is usually available at each unit. Although basic cleaning supplies must be provided, cottages are not required to offer daily housekeeping service.

COUNTRY INN (moderate service)—Although similar in definition to a bed and breakfast, country inns are usually larger in size. Specialized decor may include antiques. Offers a dining room reflecting the ambiance of the inn. At a minimum, breakfast and dinner are served. Parking may be limited. Note: The Country Inns Index also lists establishments that are primarily restaurants and may not have lodging facilities.

HOTEL (full service)—A multistory building usually including a coffee shop, dining room, lounge, a pool and exercise equipment, room service, convenience shops, valet, laundry and full banquet and meeting facilities. Parking may be limited.

LODGE (moderate service)—Typically two or more stories with all facilities in one building. Located in vacation, ski, fishing areas, etc. Usually has food and beverage service.

MOTEL (limited service)—Usually one or two stories. Food service, if any, consists of a limited facility or snack bar. Often has a pool or playground. Ample parking, usually at the guest room door.

MOTOR INN (moderate service)—Usually two or three stories, but may be a high-rise. Generally has recreational facilities and food service. May have limited banquet and meeting facilities. Ample parking.

RANCH (moderate service)—may be any classification featuring outdoor, Western-style recreation. Accommodations and facilities may vary in size.

SUBCLASSIFICATIONS

The following are subclassifications that may appear along with the classifications on page 10 to provide more description about the lodging:

APARTMENT—Usually four or more stories with at least half the units equipped for housekeeping. Units typically provide a full kitchen, living room and one or more bedrooms, but may be studio-type rooms with kitchen equipment in an alcove. May require minimum stay and/or offer discounts for longer stays. Although basic housekeeping supplies must be available, apartments are not required to offer daily housekeeping service. This classification may also modify any of the other lodging types.

CONDOMINIUM—A destination property located in a resort area; may apply to any classification. Guest units consist of a bedroom, living room and kitchen. Kitchens are separate from bedrooms and are equipped with a stove, oven or microwave, refrigerator, cooking utensils and table settings for the maximum number of people occupying the unit. Although basic housekeeping supplies must be available, condominiums are not required to offer daily housekeeping service.

HISTORIC—May apply to any type of lodging. Accommodations in restored structures more than 50 years old, reflecting the ambience of yesteryear and the surrounding area. Antique furnishings complement the overall decor of the property. Rooms may lack some modern amenities and have shared baths. Usually owner-operated and food service is often available. Note: The Historical Lodgings and Restaurants Index also lists establishments that are primarily restaurants and may not have lodging facilities.

RESORT—May apply to any other type of lodging. Has a vacation atmosphere offering extensive recreational facilities for such specific interests as golf, tennis, fishing, etc. Rates may include meals under American or Modified American plans.

SUITE—One or more bedrooms and a living room, which may or may not be closed off from the bedrooms.

REMEMBER:

AAA inspectors assign diamond ratings by evaluating lodging establishments based on their classification. Thus, "Hotels" are rated in comparison with other "Hotels," and so on with all classifications.

TIPS FOR THE TOURBOOK TRAVELER

OUR CUSTOMERS ALWAYS WRITE

We encourage your communication to tell us what we need to improve and what we have done well. We respond through our products and services, and we reply to thousands of letters from members every year.

We encourage you to report both pleasant and unpleasant experiences by visiting your local AAA club for assistance in completing a form prepared for this purpose. Or, if you prefer, write directly to AAA Member Comments, 1000 AAA Dr., Box 61, Heathrow, FL 32746-5063.

PROTECT YOURSELF AND YOUR PROPERTY

Travelers are faced with the dual task of protecting their homes while away and protecting themselves while in a strange environment. There is no way to guarantee absolute insulation from crime. But the experts—law enforcement officials—advise travelers to take a pro-active approach to securing their property and ensuring their safety.

BEFORE YOU LEAVE:

- Many law enforcement departments offer free home security checks. Take advantage of them.
- Know your neighbors and ask them to take in your mail and newspapers. Do NOT stop delivery. Also, make sure neighbors know who should and who should not have access to your home.
- Fix any doors and windows that do not operate properly, making sure the locks are sturdy.
- Make arrangements to have your lawn mowed.
- Put lights and a television or radio on timers, or ask a neighbor to turn them on and off.
- Ask police to patrol past your home on a regular basis. Many departments offer free "homewatch" programs, but prior arrangements must be made.
- Use steel bars in the tracks of all sliding-glass doors and windows.
- Do not leave ladders or other objects outside your home that a burglar could use to gain access to a second floor.

Once you've secured your home and property, consider actions that will help prevent being victimized while on the road. Above all, do not leave your common sense at home. You are more vulnerable when in unfamiliar surroundings; do not be complacent. Your safety begins with you.

ON THE ROAD:

- Be aware of your surroundings. Watch who is watching you.
- If your car is bumped from behind or if someone says there is something wrong with your car don't stop. Go to a service station or a well lit area and call for help.
- Don't pull over for flashing headlights; police have red or blue lights.
- Make sure the hotel desk clerk does not announce your room number; if so, quietly request a new room assignment.
- Never count money or display expensive jewelry in public. Use credit cards and/or traveler's checks as much as possible. Leave unneeded credit cards (department store, gas, etc.) at home.
- Use room safes or safety deposit boxes provided by the hotel. Store all valuables out of sight, even when you are in the room.
- Use deadbolt and other locks provided by the hotel. Make sure adjoining room doors are securely locked and all sliding-glass doors and windows have steel bars in the tracks.
- Never leave room keys unattended or needlessly display your keys. If you plan to be at the pool, check your key at the front desk.
- Ask front desk personnel which areas of town to avoid and what, if any, special precautions should be taken when driving a rental car (some criminals target tourists driving rental cars).
- Never open the door to a stranger; use the peephole and request identification. If you are still unsure, call the front desk to verify the identity of the person and the purpose of his/her visit.
- Never leave video cameras, car phones or other expensive equipment visible in your car; lock them in the trunk.
- Carry money separately from credit cards or use a "fanny pack." Carry your purse close to your body and your wallet in an inside coat or front trouser pocket. Never leave luggage unattended, and use your business address, if possible, on luggage tags.
- Beware of distractions staged by would-be scam artists, especially groups of children that surround you or a stranger who accidently spills something on you. They may be lifting your wallet.
- Travel in groups when possible. Walk only in well-lit areas and fill the gas tank before dark.

- If using an automatic teller machine (ATM), choose one in a well-lit area with plenty of foot traffic, such as one at a grocery store. Machines inside establishments are the safest to use.
- Walk with a purpose, as if you know where you are and where you are going.
- Have your car keys in hand before walking to the car and check the back seat before entering it. Lock the doors as soon as you get in the car.
- Report suspicious persons or situations to police or the hotel front desk. If a situation "doesn't feel right," it probably isn't. Remove yourself from the area immediately.
- Avoid poorly lit parking lots, dark doorways and shrubbery.
- Law enforcement agencies consider card-key (electronic) door locks the most secure.
- Uniformed security personnel in and around the hotel often indicates that management is aware of the potential for crime and is taking positive steps to ensure guest safety.

ADVERTISING

All attractions, lodgings and restaurants are inspected and approved for listing for their inherent value to members. An establishment's decision to advertise has no bearing on its inspection, evaluation or rating. Advertising for services or products does not imply AAA endorsement.

WHAT THE MEANS

Lodgings and restaurants approved by AAA are eligible for our Official Appointment Program, which permits the display and advertising of the emblem. The preceding a listing printed in bold type identifies that property as an Official Appointment establishment with a special interest in serving AAA members. The sign helps traveling members—like you—find accommodations on which they can depend. These properties want AAA business.

ACCESS FOR THE DISABLED

Many lodging establishments and restaurants listed in this publication have symbols indicating that they are accessible to individuals with disabilities.

For lodging establishments, the ensures there is at least one fully accessible guest room and that an individual with mobility impairments will be able to park their vehicles, check-in, and use at least one food and beverage outlet. For restaurants, the symbol indicates that parking, dining rooms and restrooms are accessible.

The indicates that a lodging establishment provides closed caption decoders, text telephones, visual notification for fire alarms, incoming phone calls and door knocks, and phone amplification devices.

AAA does not evaluate recreational facilities, banquet rooms or convention and meeting facilities for accessibility. You should call a property directly to inquire about your needs for these areas.

The criteria used by AAA are consistent with, but do not represent the full scope of, the Americans with Disabilities Act of 1990. AAA urges members with disabilities to always phone ahead to fully understand accommodations offerings.

MAKING RESERVATIONS

Always make lodging reservations before leaving home. Your local club can make reservations for you and will provide written confirmation if you request it. Remember that a room is most likely to be held if a deposit accompanies your request. Establishments don't always allow you to guarantee reservations with a credit card, although the card may be used for final payment. The establishment might require you to submit a check to guarantee your reservations absolutely. As a rule, a room reserved without a deposit will be released if it is not claimed by a specified time (usually 4 p.m.-6 p.m.), unless the establishment agrees in advance to a late arrival time. Resorts invariably require a deposit.

When making reservations, you must identify yourself as a AAA member. Give all pertinent information about your planned stay. Request written confirmation to guarantee: type of room, rate, dates of stay, and cancellation and refund policies.

Most establishments give full deposit refunds if they have been notified at least 48 hours before the normal check-in time. However, when making reservations, confirm the property's deposit, cancellation and refund policies. Some properties may charge a cancellation or handling fee. When this applies, "cancellation fee imposed" will appear in the listing. If you cancel too late, you have little recourse if a refund is denied. When an establishment requires a full or partial payment in advance, and your trip is cut short, a refund may not be given.

When canceling reservations, call the lodging immediately. Make a note of the date and time you called, the cancellation number if there is one, and the name of the person who handled the cancellation. If your AAA club made your reservation, allow them to make the cancellation for you as well so you will have proof of cancellation.

When you are charged more than the rate listed in the TourBook, under the headings **Rates Guaranteed** or **AAA Special Value Rates**, or you qualify for the **Senior Discount** and did not receive it, question the additional charge. If management refuses to adhere to the published rate, pay for the room and submit your receipt and membership number to AAA *within 30 days (see address page 12)*. Include all pertinent information: dates of stay, rate paid, itemized paid receipts, number of persons in your party, the room number you occupied, and list any extra room equipment used. A refund of the amount paid in excess of the stated maximum will be made when our investigation indicates that unjustified charging has occurred.

When you find your room is not as specified, and you have written confirmation of reservations for a certain type of accommodation, you should be given the option of choosing a different room or finding one elsewhere. Should you choose to go elsewhere and a refund is refused or resisted, submit the matter to AAA *within 30 days* along with complete documentation, including your reasons for refusing the room and copies of your written confirmation and any receipts or canceled checks associated with this problem.

GOLDEN PASSPORTS

U.S. residents 62 and older can obtain Golden Age passports for a one-time $10 fee. Golden Access passports are free to the medically blind and permanently disabled. Both cover entrance fees for the holder and accompanying private party to all national parks and historic sites, monuments and battlefields within the national park system, plus half off camping and other fees. Apply in person at most federally operated areas.

The Golden Eagle Passport costs $25 annually and covers entrance fees for the holder and accompanying private party to all federally operated areas. Obtain the pass in person at any national park or regional office of the U.S. Park Service or Forest Service.

HOTEL/MOTEL FIRE SAFETY

The AAA inspection program is designed to provide you with the most useful information for selecting the lodgings best suited to your needs. Because of the highly specialized skills needed to conduct professional fire safety inspections, however, AAA inspectors cannot assess fire safety.

All listed establishments provide smoke detectors and/or automatic sprinkler systems in guest rooms. Lodgings that provide this added protection are identified with symbols (see the Sample Listing). At each establishment whose listing shows these symbols, a AAA inspector has evaluated a sampling of the rooms and verified that this equipment is in place.

For additional fire safety information read the page posted on the back of your lodging room door, or write the National Fire Protection Association at 1 Batterymarch Park, P.O. Box 9101, Quincy, MA 02269-9101.

AUTOMOBILE MAINTENANCE

A broken radiator hose or dead battery can put a damper on even the best planned vacation. In order to ensure a safe, hassle-free road trip, there are a few things you should do before setting out on the open road. AAA Automotive Engineering and Road Service offers the following suggestions for a pre-trip checkup and on the road maintenance.

- If your vehicle is due for a tune-up, have it done before you go; consult your car owner's manual for manufacturer's recommendations for maintenance.
- Normally, the oil level should be checked with every fill up, and the oil and oil filter should be changed every 3,000 miles or every 3 months.
- Make sure that your tires are properly inflated before you begin your trip. Also check for cuts, bulges and uneven or excessive tread wear. Tire pressure should be checked while the tires are cool. To achieve better fuel economy and tire life, 2 to 3 more pounds per square inch (psi) of pressure over the car manufacturer's recommendation can be safely added if the new pressure does not exceed the maximum indicated on the tire sidewall. Remember to also check the spare.
- Check the cooling system. Look for leaks in the radiator. Check both the coolant level and the antifreeze-water mixture in the radiator. The coolant level should be checked when the engine is cool. If your car has a coolant recovery tank, maintain the level indicated. Otherwise the coolant level should be 1 to 2 inches below the filler neck of the radiator. A 50/50 mixture of antifreeze and water is recommended.
- Also check the radiator and heater hoses for soft, spongy or swollen spots. A worn hose can burst at any time, especially during hot-weather driving.
- Loose belts reduce the efficiency of the devices that they operate. Worn belts can snap unexpectedly, so it is important to check the belts that drive the alternator, air conditioner, water pump, air pump and power steering. Make sure that the engine is turned off before inspecting any belts. Roll each belt between your thumb and forefinger, checking the sides and the bottom for cracks, splits, or contamination from grease or oil. A correctly tensioned belt has about half an inch of give or pull.
- It is important to check the brake pad linings, brake shoes and brake fluid levels before setting out. Also look for leaks.
- Do not forget to check the transmission and power steering fluid.
- Check all of the lights, including brake lights, turn signals, headlights and hazard lights, to ensure they are in proper working order.
- Finally, it is imperative that you be able to see clearly, so clean the windshield and top off the washer fluid with each fill-up.

Your local AAA club can assist in planning your trip and provide you with further information about auto maintenance.

HEALTH ON THE ROAD

Most travelers expect to have a carefree trip, leaving their worries and troubles behind. However, a minor illness or accident can turn a great vacation into one that you would rather forget. A few simple precautions can save a vacation.

BEFORE YOU LEAVE:

- If you are going on a long trip or traveling a far distance you might want to get a medical and dental check-up to ensure a clean bill of health.
- Read your medical insurance policies very carefully. Does your policy provide complete coverage during your travels?
- Take advantage of a CPR or first-aid course. Your local American Red Cross provides frequent courses for a minimal fee.
- Get ready to walk! Taking daily walks a few weeks before your trip can help eliminate fatigue and leg cramps.
- Bring a medical identification card that includes a list of persons to contact in the event of an emergency, specific medical needs, allergies, blood type, and your doctor's name, address and phone number.
- Update your prescription medicine and bring the instructions and dosage amounts. Be aware: You should never combine various medications into the same bottle.

WHAT TO BRING:

- Bring your medical insurance card and a claims form in case of an illness or injury.
- Pack comfortable clothing and shoes. Pack several pair of shoes that have already been broken in to avoid painful and blistered feet.
- Bring an extra pair of glasses or contact lenses and a copy of your prescription.
- A first-aid kit is essential. The American Red Cross advises that a basic kit include a pair of scissors, waterproof tape, antiseptic, cleansing wipes, a pair of latex gloves, a variety of bandages and a blanket. Customize your first-aid kit to fit your needs.

CLIMATE AND ALTITUDE:

- Protect yourself from the sun. If you are traveling in a hot or dry climate pack plenty of sunscreen. Try to avoid the midday sun, wear light and loose-fitting clothes, and drink a lot of liquids. Heat strokes and heat exhaustion can be very dangerous.
- If you are visiting a wet and humid climate, an insect repellent will prove to be invaluable. This type of climate tends to be the perfect breeding ground for mosquitos.
- Frostbite can occur in a matter of seconds if the temperature falls below 32 F and the wind is blowing (strongly). Wear layers of clothing—wool over cotton tends to provide the best insulation. Wear a hat.
- Traveling to a higher altitude can sometimes cause high altitude sickness or mountain sickness. Because of the change in oxygen intake you might experience some dizziness, shortness of breath, headaches and nausea. The symptoms usually strike at around 8,000 feet in altitude.

ON THE ROAD:

- Avoid alcohol, sedatives and tranquilizers.
- Rotate drivers to prevent drowsiness.
- Always wear your seatbelt.
- Take a break. AAA Traffic Safety suggests that a traveler stop every 3 hours to stretch and exercise. This will aid in preventing fatigue and loss of concentration.
- If you tend to get motion sickness, drive or sit in the front passenger seat and open a window for some fresh air. Don't read while the car is moving. If symptoms persist, consider taking a motion sickness medication.

Remember to think before you travel. Leave your worries behind but don't forget to pack your common sense. A little time and effort before your trip can go a long way—especially when you are far from home.

PLAN YOUR PET'S VACATION

The first decision to be made is whether to leave your furry friend behind or take him along. The American Society for the Prevention of Cruelty to Animals (ASPCA) maintains that pets are most comfortable in familiar surroundings and it is better, therefore, to leave them behind.

If you feel you must take your pet along due to the duration of the trip, or because you can't live without him, you should plan every detail of your pet's travel with his safety and comfort in mind.

A trip to the veterinarian, preferably one who has cared for him on a regular basis, is the first order of business. All vaccinations should be up-to-date and certificates obtained: Requirements differ among states, so it is best to contact the appropriate state or county department before beginning your trip.

PETS ON THE ROAD:

- Pets feel a sense of security when they are in a confined area; an animal crate or cat carrier is a wise investment. For information on appropriate carrier sizes, consult your veterinarian or the ASPCA, 441 E. 92nd St., New York, NY 10128; phone (212) 876-7700.
- Ask your vet for advice regarding your specific pet.
- Use motion sickness medication or a tranquilizer only if necessary.
- Make sure your pet is properly licensed and has collar tags or a permanent ID tattoo.
- Stop often for exercise and bathroom breaks, allowing your pet time to stretch. Always keep him on a leash.
- If you plan to stay in a hotel or motel, make arrangements in advance. AAA TourBook lodging

listings specify whether pets are allowed and whether there are fees or other restrictions attached. Phone all establishments prior to departure to verify the information and make reservations.

- Bring your pet's food and water dishes, as well as his bedding and a favorite toy.
- Bring a small amount of food and a jug of drinking water from home to help your pet become acclimated to new sources of food and water. Keep extra drinking water in the car.

TAKING CHILDREN ALONG

Taking children on a vacation can be rewarding and educational for the whole family, but it requires advance planning, flexibility and a positive attitude. Pediatricians, child psychologists and experienced parents offer the following helpful hints for a smooth vacation.

Involve children in the planning.

- Let them suggest where they would like to go on vacation.
- Point out the route and destination on a map. Let the kids have their own map and help them trace your route using bright markers.
- Read about what will be seen on the way to and at your destination. Make this a family affair and let each member plan a daily activity.
- Pack a change of clothes for everyone in a separate bag for the first overnight stop.
- For short trips take just what is needed, but be sure to include swimwear.
- Bring a first-aid kit—it's better to be safe than sorry.

Car rules must be obeyed.

- All passengers must utilize car seats or seat belts at all times.
- Feet, hands and head should always stay inside the vehicle, and do not distract the driver.
- Never play with the door locks and handles.

Travel on a schedule, but leave enough extra time for unexpected situations.

- Be aware of detours or construction along your route, and don't travel at rush hour.
- Keep the child's regular nap, meal and bedtimes as much as possible.

Keep kids occupied on the road.

- Practice alphabet skills with road signs or collect state names from license plates. Memory and counting games are other good activities.
- A tape recorder (with earphones), favorite tapes and blank tapes for recording themselves can be real lifesavers.
- Activity books and colored pencils—no crayons, they melt—or washable felt-tip pens can keep children occupied for hours. Don't forget a small pencil sharpener. Get a copy of the AAA Children's Travel Activity Book from your club.
- Let children be responsible for their own tote bag with books, toys, travel games and note pads. The bags can be hung around front seat headrests for easy accessibility.
- Take healthy snacks rather than junk food.
- Keep plenty of water available.
- Remember to take napkins, pre-moistened wipes and a bag for garbage.
- Try to stop when you sense the kids are getting irritable, before a real problem develops. Give them some time to stretch.

Provide reassurance on the road.

- When stopping at an unfamiliar place to sleep, make sure youngsters have something from home, such as their own pillow or special blanket, to comfort them.

Show appreciation for how well the children behave while traveling. Stop for an ice cream cone or other favorite treat. And remember that just being together is the most important part of your vacation.

TIPPING

Tipping is an accepted practice and many service industry personnel depend upon tips for a large part of their incomes. At airports 50¢ to $1 per bag is appropriate for skycaps if the service is to the curb, more if the bag handling is farther. Taxi drivers expect 15 percent. In hotels it is appropriate to tip the bellperson or porter no less than $1, and often $1 per bag; the maid is left $2 per day; the doorman receives $1 to $5 depending upon the difficulty of the service he performs; the garage attendant is given $1 to $2; bathroom attendants receive 50¢ to $1.

Since the job of the concierge is to help guests, he or she usually should not be tipped unless an unusual or very difficult task is performed; then a minimum of $5 is appropriate.

Tipping in restaurants depends upon the luxuriousness and sophistication of the establishment and, of course, upon the quality of the service. The standard for waiters and waitresses is 15 percent of the bill. If some person other than your server helps serve your meal, a 5 percent tip is appropriate. If you are paying by credit card it is acceptable and less awkward to put a 20 percent tip on the form and allow these personnel to sort out their portions.

When traveling away from home . . .

AAA **SUPERNUMBER®**

1-800-AAA-HELP
1-800-955-4TDD (Hearing Impaired)

a 24-hour toll-free Emergency Road Service information system.

It's easy to use Triple A's **SUPERNUMBER®** when traveling outside your local club area.

1. Look in the white pages of the telephone book for a listing under "AAA" in the United States or "CAA" in Canada, since road service is dispatched by the local club in many communities.
2. If there is no listing, have your membership card handy and call **SUPERNUMBER®** 1-800-AAA-HELP for the nearest road service facility. *Hearing impaired call 1-800-955-4TDD.*

SUPERNUMBER® available 24 hours a day, is only for Emergency Road Service . . . and only when traveling outside the area served by your home club. Questions regarding other club services should be directed to the nearest club office.

Travel Information System

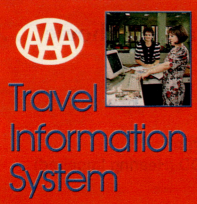

AAA TRAVEL COUNSELORS are a unique and vital element of AAA's travel information system. They offer what no other auto club can: personalized, top-quality service. Our trained professionals are especially knowledgeable about geography and popular vacation destinations. They can tell you the fastest or most scenic way to get where you're going and update you on highway construction projects and local weather conditions.

TOURBOOKS are annually revised catalogs of selected travel information. Listings include AAA-approved attractions, lodgings and restaurants, plus details on sightseeing and valuable AAA discounts.

TRIPTIK MAPS show your driving route mile-by-mile. Conveniently spiral-bound, the maps indicate exit numbers and stops for food and gas as well as capsule summaries of places along the way.

SHEET MAPS are large-scale regional and state maps, completely researched, revised and reprinted regularly. Our network of AAA clubs and our Road Reporters make AAA maps the most detailed and accurate road maps available.

CAMPBOOKS contain comprehensive regional listings of AAA-approved public and private campgrounds across the continent.

CITIBOOKS provide complete information about major travel destinations like San Francisco and New York City. Not all clubs carry these booklets, which are extractions from the TourBooks.

ATTRACTIONS

Whether your interests
are amusement parks
or historical monuments,
the attraction listings offer
a quick, concise overview
of descriptive information
on sightseeing destinations
throughout the United States
and Canada.

If you lose your cash, you hit rock bottom. If you lose your American Express® Travelers Cheques, you'll get a refund. That's why AAA offers its members fee-free American Express Travelers Cheques. *Don't leave home without them.®*

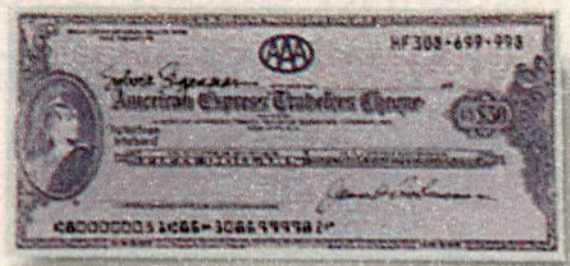

AAA American Express Travelers Cheques

©1994 American Express Travel Related Services Company, Inc.

OREGON

An introduction to the state's history, geography, economy and recreation

TRAVELING in oxen-drawn covered wagons, courageous pioneers made their way through perilous droughts and blizzards in hopes of reaching a land of plenty and open promises. They were not disappointed—the snowcapped peak of Mount Hood, the towering cliffs of the Pacific coast, the slopes and plateaus of the Cascade Range, the endless green pastures of the Willamette Valley and the fertile land surrounding the Columbia River were all there to greet the weary travelers.

HISTORY

In search of a northwest passageway to the Orient for trade purposes, English admiral Francis Drake discovered the territory now known as Oregon in 1579. He declared jurisdiction over the land and presented it as a gift to Queen Elizabeth I. At the time of Drake's discovery, more than 125 Indian tribes inhabited the remote area.

In 1804, President Thomas Jefferson persuaded Congress to fund the Lewis and Clark expedition. Departing from St. Louis, the expedition focused on forging a route between the Columbia and Missouri rivers for fur trading, establishing relations with Indian tribes and reporting on the geography and terrain. An unstated goal of the expedition was to lay the groundwork for future U.S. claims to the territory. Explorers Meriwether Lewis and William Clark made their famous 1805-06 journey to the Oregon country, and upon returning from their travels told many tales of the rich land that they had seen.

America and Great Britain raced to set up fur-trading companies in this new land of opportunity. Two English fur companies had already been established by the time American John Jacob Astor founded the Pacific Fur Co. in 1811. Astor built the trading post of Astoria and soon after witnessed an influx of American fur traders. But Great Britain's Hudson Bay Co. emerged as the dominant fur-trading operation. John

FAST FACTS

POPULATION: 2,842,300.

AREA: 97,073 square miles, ranks 10th.

CAPITAL: Salem.

HIGHEST POINT: 11,239 ft., Mount Hood.

LOWEST POINT: Sea level, Pacific coast.

TIME ZONES: Pacific/Mountain. DST.

MINIMUM AGE FOR DRIVERS: 16.

SEAT BELT/CHILD RESTRAINT LAWS: Required for driver and all passengers. Child restraints required for under 4 or under 40 pounds; applies to out-of-state if resident state has child restraint law.

HELMETS FOR MOTORCYCLISTS: Required for driver and passenger.

RADAR DETECTORS: Permitted.

FIREARMS LAWS: Vary by state and/or county. Contact Oregon State Police Patrol Division, 3700 S.E. 92nd, Portland, OR 97266; phone (503) 731-3020.

HOLIDAYS: Jan. 1; Martin Luther King Jr.'s Birthday, Jan. (3rd Mon.); Lincoln's Birthday, Feb. (1st Mon.); Washington's Birthday, Feb. (3rd Mon.); Memorial Day, May (last Mon.); July 4; Labor Day, Sept. (1st Mon.); Columbus Day, Oct. (2nd Mon.); Veterans Day, Nov. 11; Thanksgiving; Dec. 25.

TAXES: Oregon has no statewide sales tax.

STATE INFORMATION CENTERS: State border information centers are open Apr.-Oct. at the following locations: I-5 south of Ashland; on US 101 at Astoria; on US 101 n. of Brookings; on US 97 s. of Klamath Falls; at jct. US 395 and SR 40 in Lakeview; on I-84 at Ontario; off the I-5 bridge over the Columbia River at Portland; on US 101 in Seaside; and on I-82 in Umatilla. Another, in Salem, is open year-round. Hours vary with locations. In addition, 24-hour Travel Infocenter gazebos are in rest areas on I-5, I-84, US 97 and US 101.

McLoughlin, head of Hudson Bay, became a prominent figure and governed the region 1824-46.

During the 1830s, missionaries took the westward journey, settling along the Columbia River and in the Willamette Valley. Led by Jason Lee, Methodist missionaries founded the first permanent settlement in the Willamette Valley in 1834. Missions functioned as the educational and cultural centers of the new settlement. Abundant resources and successful farmlands encouraged others to migrate to the area.

One of the greatest migrations in the history of the world began in 1843. The 2,000-mile trek from Independence, Mo., along the Oregon Trail promised settlers a fresh start but instead was plagued with much hardship. More than 300,000 traveled the trail over a period of 3 decades, confronting Indian attacks, harsh weather and cholera epidemics.

The arrival of these pioneers led the way to land ownership rights. Married men were given 640-acre land plots when they arrived. A territorial government was created in 1849, claiming Oregon City for its capitol. Oregon's admission to the Union in 1859 as the 33rd state coincided with an expanding search for gold in northern California. As gold strikes were depleted in California, seekers continued north in search of riches. Portland developed into a major port and distribution center for supplies destined for inland mining operations.

Isolation was the chief deterrent to growth 1860-80. Not until 1883 did the Northern Pacific Railroad link Oregon with the rest of the nation. As railroads proliferated, new residents were attracted by subsidy land programs. Oregon's population doubled before 1890. In the late 1800s, fishing and energy resources began to be developed.

In 1905, the Lewis and Clark centennial brought many new settlers and investors to the area. World War I prompted the growth of Oregon's shipbuilding and lumber industries. In the mid-1930s, Depression-weary Americans flocked to the state seeking financial stability and refuge from hard times; however, opportunities were just as scarce in Oregon as in the rest of the nation.

The start of World War II brought an economic boost. Portland saw an influx of more than 150,000 people pursuing jobs at the local shipyards.

Since the 1950s, Oregon has become an advocate for environmental rights. Planned multi-use of the state's natural resources aims to preserve and protect them. In 1967, Oregon's coast became protected for "Free and Uninterrupted Use" by the public. This law set aside all beachfront property from the Columbia River on the north to the Oregon/California border on the south. Oregon's Bottle Bill, enacted in 1971, encourages recycling by offering refunds for glass and aluminum products. The bill was the first of its kind in the nation.

Oregon passed a law involving statewide land use planning in 1973. This law provides for the coordination of both conservation and development through planning goals set by the state, cities, counties and special districts.

1993 marked the 150th anniversary of the "Great Migration of 1843." The early pioneers that survived their journey along the Oregon Trail saw a land of bountiful resources and endless opportunities. Oregonians today subscribe to that same ideal and strive to ensure that those opportunities remain for decades to come.

FOR YOUR INFORMATION

FURTHER INFORMATION FOR VISITORS:

Tourism Division
Oregon Dept. of Economic Development
775 Summer St., N.E.
Salem, OR 97310
(800) 547-7842

RECREATION INFORMATION:

Oregon Dept. of Parks and Recreation
1115 Commercial St., N.E.
Salem, OR 97310-1001
(503) 378-6305

FISHING AND HUNTING REGULATIONS:

Oregon Dept. of Fish and Wildlife
2501 S.W. 1st St., P.O. Box 59
Portland, OR 97207
(503) 229-5403

NATIONAL FOREST INFORMATION:

Bureau of Land Management
P.O. Box 2965
Portland, OR 97208
(503) 280-7001

Pacific Northwest Region
333 S.W. First Ave., P.O. Box 3623
Portland, OR 97208
(503) 326-2877
(800) 280-CAMP (information and reservations)

SPECIAL REGULATIONS: Motorists are not permitted to pump their own gas at service stations in Oregon.

GEOGRAPHY

Oregon presents a variety of landscapes. A major feature is the Cascade Range, which divides the state into two distinct climatic regions. Sea winds warmed by the Japan Current and laden with moisture create the lush vegetation on the west while the east has a continental—and in some places semiarid—climate.

Isolated, perpetually snowcapped peaks tower high above the surrounding mountains: Mounts

Jefferson and the Three Sisters are more than 10,000 feet high, and Mount Hood reaches an elevation of 11,239 feet. These and other peaks of volcanic origin were the sources of the lava that formed the central and southeastern plateau.

The Coast Range, deeply folded and cut by narrow ravines, parallels the seashore, sometimes encroaching on it in a series of cliffs and headlands. It rises in average elevation in the south, where it finally blends with the Cascades. The coastline has several natural harbors that can accommodate oceangoing ships.

In the north, between the Coast Range and the Cascades, the Willamette River flows through its valley toward the Columbia. This area's mild climate and fertile soil made it the focus of early settlement.

The Blue, Wallowa and Umatilla ranges extend from the northeastern corner of the state into the central plateau. Altitudes rise to 10,000 feet above sea level in the Wallowas, not far from the spectacular 6,000-foot-deep Hells Canyon of the Snake River.

Southeastern Oregon is completely different. Geographically it is part of the range and basin province, a high, semiarid plateau marked by such sharply tilted fault-block mountains as Steens, which slopes gently upward on the west to about 9,000 feet, then drops in one colossal precipice to the Alvord Valley on the east.

Many of the rivers are short and often disappear into the porous lava and sandy soil; such lakes as Malheur frequently shrink to puddles during years of little rainfall. In years of abundant rainfall and snow melt from Oregon's east-central mountains, Harney and Malheur lakes join, forming the state's largest inland body of water.

The Snake River marks the northeastern boundary between Oregon and Idaho; the Columbia River delineates all but the eastern 100 or so miles of the northern border. The latter slices through the backbone of the Cascades in the Columbia River Gorge. Dozens of waterfalls plunge hundreds of feet over the solid rock walls from the Oregon side of the chasm. Multnomah drops more than 600 feet and is the fourth largest waterfall in the United States. With its many parks and overlooks, this is one of the more popular scenic corridors in the state.

In addition to the Snake, Columbia and Willamette, other major rivers are the white-water Rogue in the southwest; the John Day, which reaches the Columbia after a long loop to the west and north; the Deschutes in the northwest; and the Owyhee in the southeast. Though the waters of the Klamath River spring from Klamath Lake in the southwestern part of the state, most of its drainage is through the northern portion of California.

ECONOMY

With nearly half its land forested, the economy of Oregon has traditionally depended upon its forests. The vast timber resources once yielded huge amounts of lumber, making Oregon a national leader in lumber production. The recession of the 1980s influenced the industry, but forestry is still one of the leading industries.

Oregon does not rely as heavily on its forests as it once did. In recent years diversification has occurred, stablizing the economy.

Until lumbering took the lead around 1900, agriculture was the state's main economic contributor. Because of its mild climate, Oregon is said to be able to harvest every crop grown in regions north of the tropics. The Willamette River Valley and the Hood River Valley, as well as central and eastern Oregon, are the centers of most agricultural activity. The northern and central plateau region is especially noted for wheat and Portland ranks among the country's top wheat ports.

The numerous vineyards located throughout the western Oregon valleys from Medford to Portland attest to the economic importance of Oregon's expanding wine industry. Livestock industries also are important, particularly dairying. Other enterprises include flour milling, meatpacking and canning and freezing fruits, vegetables, juices and preserves. Wool from the sheep of southeastern Oregon often becomes fabric in the mills of Pendleton. Recently, plant nurseries and bulb farms have become important elements in Oregon's economy.

Long before dams and fish ladders were known on the Columbia, salmon struggled against the current while Indians netted them. With salmon as its most important commercial fish, the Columbia is still the country's major salmon stream. Astoria and Newport are major canning centers. Shrimp processing has been added to the list of industries.

Power provided by McNary, John Day, The Dalles and Bonneville dams on the Columbia, as well as by smaller projects on many other rivers, has encouraged development of nonagricultural industries. A fast-growing metal industry near Albany produces titanium and other rare metals. Oregon also has attracted a large number of software, high-tech and bio-tech industries; Portland has become the unofficial "Silicon Valley" of the north.

Portland, the largest city, is home to the Port of Portland, a gateway for trade between the United States and the Pacific Rim nations. Oregon's tourist industry continues to grow as national and international tourists discover the beauty and diversity of the state. Its mountains and beaches offer visitors recreational opportunities ranging from skiing to surfing.

RECREATION

Oregon's coastline, vast mountain ranges and high plateaus offer a wealth of recreational opportunities. The public beaches rank among the finest in the country. There are lake and mineral springs resorts in the mountain areas. Scenic Crater Lake, snowcapped Mount Hood, Oregon Caves and Wallowa Lake are other places of beauty. Oregon Dunes National Recreation Area contains extensive sand dunes.

Exceptional **fishing** and **hunting** are found on the open grasslands and within the boundaries of the 13 national forests that embrace much of the state's timber and mountain land. Oregon's lakes and streams are renowned for large mouth bass, catfish, crappie and coho salmon, as well as brook, rainbow and steelhead trout.

The Rogue River's spring and fall runs of Chinook salmon and steelhead trout are revered by serious anglers. Deep-sea and surf fishing bring in halibut, salmon, sea bass, several varieties of cod and other species.

The central and eastern uplands afford the best hunting for antelopes, chukar, grouse, pheasants and quails; lake and swamp margins harbor ducks and geese. Bears, deer and elks are found in the mountainous areas.

Numerous winter sports areas are scattered throughout the Cascade, Siskiyou and Blue mountain regions. Some of the more popular are in Mount Hood National Forest near Government Camp, Deschutes National Forest near Bend, Wallowa-Whitman National Forest near La Grande and Baker, and the Siskiyou Mountains near Ashland.

Oregon has one of the most extensive park systems in the western states. Most of the areas are open year-round, weather permitting, although some state parks do close for the winter. A few parks offer **camping** all year. A $3 entry fee is charged from early May through late September for day-use facilities at most state parks. State parks also charge varied overnight user fees; fees also are charged at some national forest campgrounds.

The Oregon Department of Transportation offers a bicycling guide and a coastal bicycle route map. Both publications are available free of charge from the Oregon Dept. of Transportation, Room 210, Transportation Building, Salem, OR 97310; phone (503) 986-3556.

Developed recreation areas in the national forests also provide a wide range of recreational opportunities. For detailed listings of camping and trailering areas, both public and private, *see the AAA Northwestern CampBook.*

RECREATION AREAS	MAP LOCATION	CAMPING	PICNICKING	HIKING TRAILS	BOATING	BOAT RAMP	BOAT RENTAL	FISHING	SWIMMING	PETS ON LEASH	BICYCLE TRAILS	WINTER SPORTS	VISITOR CENTER	LODGE/CABINS	FOOD SERVICE
NATIONAL PARK *(See place listing)*															
Crater Lake (F-7) 183 acres on the crest of the Cascade Range off SR 62.		•	•	•				•		•	•	•	•	•	•
NATIONAL RECREATION AREAS															
Hells Canyon (B-12) 603,150 acres off SR 82 near Joseph. Horse rental. *(See place listing)*		•	•	•	•	•		•		•			•		
Oregon Dunes (F-1) 32,000 acres between North Bend and Florence. *(See Siuslaw National Forest)*		•	•	•	•	•		•	•	•			•		
NATIONAL FORESTS *(See place listings)*															
Deschutes 1,602,609 acres in central Oregon 6 mi. s. of Bend via US 97. Horse rental.		•	•	•	•	•	•	•	•	•	•	•	•	•	•
Fremont 1,200,679 acres in south-central Oregon.		•	•	•	•	•		•	•	•	•	•			
Malheur 1,465,397 acres in eastern Oregon.		•	•	•	•	•		•	•	•	•	•			
Mount Hood 1.1 million acres in northwestern Oregon.		•	•	•	•	•	•	•	•	•	•	•	•	•	•
Ochoco 959,317 acres in central Oregon off US 26.		•	•	•	•	•		•	•	•	•	•			
Rogue River 629,088 acres in southwestern Oregon off I-5 from Medford. Horse rental.		•	•	•	•	•	•	•	•	•	•	•		•	•
Siskiyou 1,092,302 acres in southwestern Oregon.		•	•	•	•	•		•	•	•	•	•	•		
Siuslaw 629,460 acres in western Oregon.		•	•	•	•	•		•	•	•			•	•	
Umatilla 1,402,483 acres in northeastern Oregon. Horse rental.		•	•	•	•	•		•	•	•	•	•	•		
Umpqua 984,602 acres in southwestern Oregon 33 mi. e. of Roseburg on SR 138.		•	•	•	•	•	•	•	•	•	•	•	•	•	•
Wallowa-Whitman 2,396,049 acres in northeastern Oregon. Horse rental.		•	•	•	•	•	•	•	•	•		•			
Willamette 1,675,407 acres in western Oregon.		•	•	•	•	•	•	•	•	•	•	•		•	•
Winema 1,039,093 acres in south-central Oregon off US 97N or 140W from Klamath Falls.		•	•	•	•	•	•	•	•	•	•	•	•	•	•

RECREATION AREAS	MAP LOCATION	CAMPING	PICNICKING	HIKING TRAILS	BOATING	BOAT RAMP	BOAT RENTAL	FISHING	SWIMMING	PETS ON LEASH	BICYCLE TRAILS	WINTER SPORTS	VISITOR CENTER	LODGE/CABINS	FOOD SERVICE
ARMY CORPS OF ENGINEERS															
Applegate Lake (G-6) 205 acres 23 mi. s.w. of Medford via SR 238.	108	●	●	●	●	●		●	●	●					
Blue River Lake (D-7) 1,420 acres off SR 126 at Blue River. Water skiing.	109	●	●		●	●		●	●	●					
Bonneville Lock and Dam (B-7) 206,000 acres 40 mi. e. of Portland via I-84 exit 40. *(See Bonneville)*	110	●	●	●	●	●	●	●		●			●		
Cottage Grove Reservoir (F-3) 6 mi. s. of Cottage Grove via I-5.	98	●	●		●	●		●	●	●					
Cougar Lake (D-7) 1,280 acres s.e. of Blue River off SR 126 and West Side Rd. Water skiing.	111	●	●	●	●	●		●	●	●					
Detroit Lake (C-7) 3,500 acres off SR 22 at Detroit. Water skiing.	112	●	●	●	●	●		●	●	●					
Dexter Lake (F-3) Off SR 58 at Dexter. Water skiing.	113		●		●	●	●	●	●	●					
Dorena Reservoir (F-3) 5 mi. e. of Cottage Grove off I-5.	100	●	●		●	●	●	●	●	●					
Fall Creek Lake (E-3) 1,820 acres 16 mi. s.e. of Springfield via Jasper Lowell Rd. Water skiing.	114	●	●		●	●		●	●	●					
Fern Ridge Reservoir (E-3) 9,000 acres 12 mi. w. of Eugene off SR 126. Water skiing.	115	●	●		●	●	●	●	●	●					
Foster Lake (E-3) 1,220 acres off US 20 at Sweet Home. Water skiing.	116	●	●		●	●		●	●	●					
Green Peter Lake (D-4) 3,720 acres n.e. of Sweet Home off Quartzville Rd. Water skiing.	117	●	●		●	●		●	●	●					
Hills Creek Lake (F-4) 2,710 acres s.e. of Oakridge off SR 58 and Rigdon Rd. Water skiing.	118	●	●		●	●		●	●	●					
John Day Lock and Dam (B-8) 31,041 acres 2 mi. e. of Rufus off I-84 exit 109. Water skiing. *(See Rufus)*	119	●	●		●	●	●	●	●	●					
Lookout Point Lake (F-3) 4,360 acres just s. of Dexter off SR 58.	120	●	●		●	●		●		●					
Lost Creek Lake (F-6) 3,430 acres 30 mi. n.e. of Medford via SR 62. Water skiing.	121	●	●	●	●	●	●	●	●	●			●		
McNary Lock and Dam (B-10) 9,718 acres 1 mi. e. of jct. I-82 and US 730 at Umatilla. Water skiing. *(See Umatilla)*	122		●		●	●		●	●	●					
The Dalles Lock and Dam (B-7) 9,400 acres off I-84 exit 87 on the e. edge of The Dalles. Water skiing. *(See The Dalles)*	123	●	●		●	●		●	●	●			●		
STATE															
Ainsworth (B-7) 156 acres 37 mi. e. of Portland on US 30. Scenic.	2	●	●	●											
Armitage (E-3) 57 acres 5 mi. n. of Eugene on Coburg Rd.	4		●	●	●	●		●		●					
Beachside (E-1) 17 acres 4 mi. s. of Waldport on US 101.	6	●	●					●							
Ben and Kay Dorris (E-4) 92 acres 31 mi. e. of Eugene on US 126.	7		●	●	●			●		●					
Benson (B-7) 272 acres 30 mi. e. of Portland off I-84.	8		●		●	●		●	●						
Beverly Beach (D-1) 130 acres 7 mi. n. of Newport on US 101.	9	●	●	●				●							
Bullards Beach (G-1) 1,226 acres 1 mi. n. of Bandon on US 101. *(See Bandon)*	10	●	●		●	●		●	●						
Cape Arago (G-1) 134 acres 5 mi. s. of Charleston.	11		●	●				●							
Cape Blanco (F-4) 1,880 acres 9 mi. n. of Port Orford, then 6 mi. w. off US 101. *(See Port Orford)*	12	●	●	●				●							
Cape Kiwanda (C-2) 185 acres 1 mi. n. of Pacific City off US 101. Scenic.	13			●	●			●							
Cape Lookout (C-2) 1,974 acres 12 mi. s.w. of Tillamook off US 101. Clamming.	14	●	●	●				●		●					
Carl G. Washburne Memorial (E-1) 1,089 acres 14 mi. n. of Florence on US 101.	15	●	●	●				●	●	●					
Cascadia (E-4) 253 acres 14 mi. e. of Sweet Home on US 20.	16	●	●	●				●		●	●				
Casey (F-6) 80 acres 29 mi. n.e. of Medford on SR 62.	17		●		●	●		●	●						
Catherine Creek (C-11) 160 acres 8 mi. s.e. of Union on SR 203.	18	●	●					●		●					

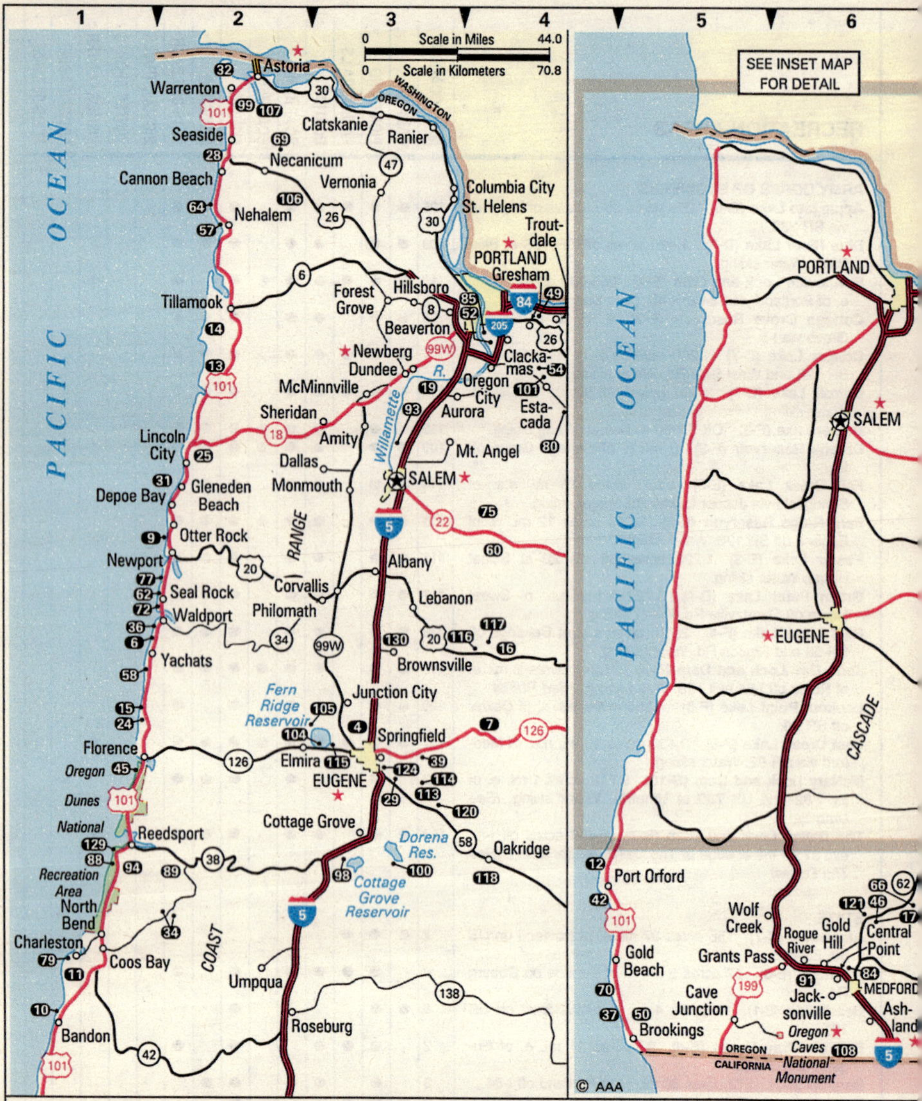

INDEX TO STARRED ATTRACTIONS

ATTRACTIONS OF EXCEPTIONAL INTEREST AND QUALITY

Astoria Column - see Astoria

Bonneville Lock and Dam - see Bonneville

Cascade Lakes Highway - see Bend

Champoeg State Park - see Newberg

Columbia River Scenic Highway - see Columbia River Gorge Nat'l Scenic Area

Columbia River Maritime Museum - see Astoria

The Cove Palisades State Park - see Madras

Crater Lake National Park - see place listing

Fort Clatsop National Memorial - see Astoria

Hells Canyon National Recreation Area - see place listing

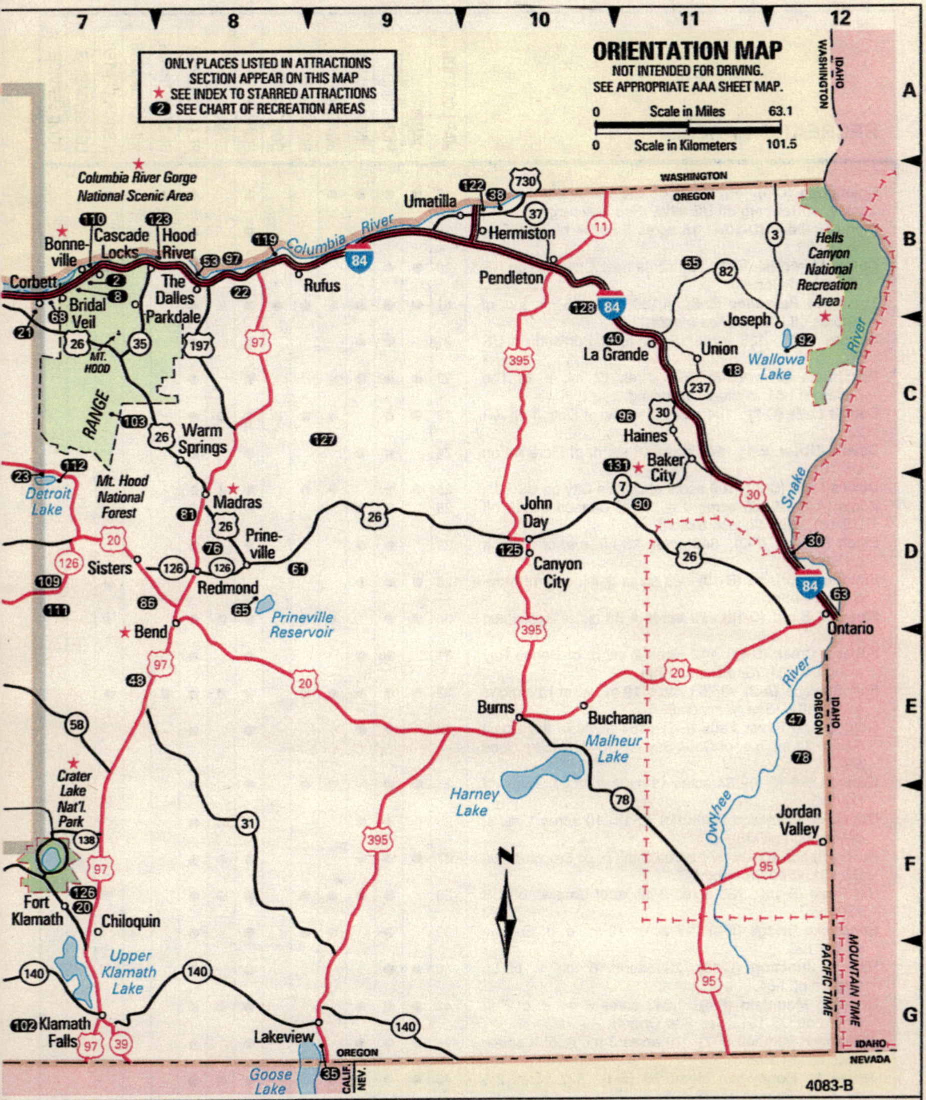

High Desert Museum - see Bend

Hult Center for the Performing Arts - see Eugene

Metro Washington Park Zoo - see Portland

National Historic Oregon Trail Interpretive Center - see Baker City

Oregon Caves National Monument - see place listing

Oregon History Center - see Portland

Oregon Shakespeare Festival - see Ashland

Portland Art Museum - see Portland

Rim Drive - see Crater Lake Nat'l Park

Sinnott Memorial Overlook - see Crater Lake National Park

State Capitol - see Salem

Washington Park - see Portland

RECREATION AREAS	MAP LOCATION	CAMPING	PICNICKING	HIKING TRAILS	BOATING	BOAT RAMP	BOAT RENTAL	FISHING	SWIMMING	PETS ON LEASH	BICYCLE TRAILS	WINTER SPORTS	VISITOR CENTER	LODGE/CABINS	FOOD SERVICE
Champoeg (C-3) 587 acres on the Williamette River 7 mi. e. of Newberg off US 99W. *(See Newberg)*	19	●	●	●	●			●		●	●		●		
Clyde Holliday (D-10) 15 acres 7 mi. w. of John Day on US 26.	125	●	●					●		●					
Collier Memorial (F-7) 655 acres near Chiloquin on US 97. *(See Chiloquin)*	20	●	●	●				●		●			●		
The Cove Palisades (D-8) 4,130 acres 15 mi. s.w. of Madras off US 97. *(See Madras)*	81	●	●	●	●	●	●	●	●	●					●
Dabney (C-7) 135 acres 19 mi. e. of Portland on US 30.	21		●	●				●		●					
Deschutes River (B-8) 515 acres 17 mi. e. of The Dalles off I-84. White-water rafting.	22	●	●	●				●		●					
Detroit Lake (C-7) 104 acres 2 mi. w. of Detroit on SR 22.	23	●	●		●	●	●	●	●	●					
Devil's Elbow (E-1) 545 acres 13 mi. n. of Florence on US 101.	24		●	●				●		●					
Devil's Lake (C-2) 109 acres at Lincoln City on US 101.	25	●	●		●	●		●	●	●					
Ecola (A-2) 1,303 acres 2 mi. n. of Cannon Beach off US 101. *(See Cannon Beach)*	28		●	●				●		●					
Elijah Bristow (F-3) 848 acres 15 mi. s.e. of Eugene on SR 58.	29		●	●				●		●					
Emigrant Springs (B-10) 23 acres 3 mi. n.w. of Meacham on I-84.	128	●	●	●									●		
Farewell Bend (D-12) 72 acres 4 mi. s. of Huntington off I-84.	30	●	●		●	●		●	●	●					
Fogarty Creek (D-2) 142 acres 2 mi. n. of Depoe Bay along US 101. *(See Depoe Bay)*	31		●	●				●		●					
Fort Stevens (A-2) 3,763 acres 10 mi. w. of Hammond on US 101. *(See Hammond)*	32	●	●	●	●	●		●	●	●	●		●		
Golden and Silver Falls (F-2) 157 acres in the Coast Range 24 mi. n.e. of Coos Bay off US 101. *(See Coos Bay)*	34		●	●				●		●					
Goose Lake (G-9) 64 acres 15 mi. s.w. of Lakeview off US 395.	35	●	●		●	●		●		●					
Governor Patterson Memorial (D-1) 10 acres 1 mi. s. of Waldport on US 101.	36		●	●				●		●					
Harris Beach (G-4) 171 acres 2 mi. n. of Brookings on US 101. *(See Brookings)*	37	●	●	●				●	●	●					
Hat Rock (B-10) 735 acres 9 mi. e. of Umatilla off US 730.	38		●	●	●	●		●	●	●					
Hendricks Bridge (E-3) 17 acres 13 mi. e. of Eugene on US 126.	39		●		●	●		●		●					
Hilgard Junction (C-10) 233 acres 8 mi. w. of La Grande off I-84.	40	●	●					●		●					
Humbug Mountain (F-4) 1,842 acres 6 mi. s. of Port Orford on US 101. *(See Port Orford)*	42	●	●	●				●	●	●					
Jackson F. Kimball (F-7) 19 acres 3 mi. n. of Klamath Falls off SR 232.	126	●	●	●				●		●					
Jessie M. Honeyman Memorial (E-1) 522 acres 2½ mi. s. of Florence off US 101.	45	●	●	●	●	●		●	●	●					
Joseph P. Stewart (F-6) 910 acres 35 mi. n.e. of Medford off SR 62.	46	●	●	●	●	●		●	●	●	●				
Lake Owyhee (E-12) 730 acres 33 mi. s.w. of Nyssa off SR 301.	47	●	●		●	●	●	●		●					
La Pine (E-7) 2,008 acres 8½ mi. n. of La Pine off US 97. *(See Bend)*	48	●	●		●	●		●		●					
Lewis and Clark (B-4) 56 acres 16 mi. e. of Portland off I-84.	49		●	●	●	●		●		●			●		
Loeb (G-5) 320 acres 8 mi. n.e. of Brookings off US 101. *(See Brookings)*	50	●	●					●	●	●					
Mary S. Young (C-4) 133 acres 3 mi. s. of Lake Oswego on SR 43.	52		●	●				●		●	●				
Mayer (B-8) 613 acres 10 mi. w. of The Dalles off I-84.	53		●		●	●		●	●	●					
Milo McIver (C-4) 937 acres 5 mi. w. of Estacada off SR 211.	54	●	●	●	●	●		●		●					
Minam (B-11) 602 acres 15 mi. n.e. of Elgin off SR 82.	55	●	●					●		●					

RECREATION AREAS	MAP LOCATION	CAMPING	PICNICKING	HIKING TRAILS	BOATING	BOAT RAMP	BOAT RENTAL	FISHING	SWIMMING	PETS ON LEASH	BICYCLE TRAILS	WINTER SPORTS	VISITOR CENTER	LODGE/CABINS	FOOD SERVICE
Nehalem Bay (B-2) 878 acres 3 mi. s. of Manzanita Junction off US 101.	57	●	●		●	●		●		●	●				
Neptune (E-1) 302 acres 3 mi. s. of Yachats on US 101.	58		●	●				●	●	●					
North Santiam (D-4) 120 acres 4 mi. w. of Mill City off SR 22.	60		●	●				●		●					
Ochoco Lake (D-8) 10 acres 7 mi. e. of Prineville on US 26. Cross-country skiing, snowmobiling.	61	●	●	●	●	●		●		●		●			
Ona Beach (D-1) 237 acres 8 mi. s. of Newport on US 101.	62		●		●	●		●	●	●					
Ontario (D-12) 35 acres 1 mi. n. of Ontario on I-84.	63		●		●			●		●					
Oswald West (B-2) 2,474 acres 5 mi. n. of Manzanita on US 101. Historic. Clamming.	64	●	●	●				●	●	●					
Prineville Reservoir (D-8) 365 acres 17 mi. s.e. of Prineville off US 26.	65	●	●	●	●	●		●	●	●		●			
Prospect Wayside (F-6) 6 acres 44 mi. n.e. of Medford off SR 62.	66		●	●				●		●					
Rooster Rock (B-7) 927 acres 22 mi. e. of Portland off I-84.	68		●	●	●	●		●	●	●					●
Saddle Mountain (A-2) 2,882 acres 8 mi. n.e. of Necanicum off US 26. *(See Necanicum)*	69	●	●	●						●					
Samuel H. Boardman (G-4) 1,473 acres 6 mi. n. of Brookings on US 101.	70		●	●				●		●					
Seal Rock Wayside (D-1) 7 acres 10 mi. s. of Newport on US 101.	72		●	●				●		●					
Shelton Wayside (C-9) 180 acres 10 mi. s.e. of The Dalles off SR 19.	127	●	●	●						●					
Silver Falls (D-4) 8,546 acres 26 mi. e. of Salem on SR 214. *(See Salem)*	75	●	●	●				●	●	●	●		●	●	●
Smith Rock (D-8) 623 acres 9 mi. n.e. of Redmond on US 97 to Terrebonne, then 3 mi. e., following signs. *(See Redmond)*	76		●	●				●		●					
South Beach (D-1) 411 acres 2 mi. s. of Newport on US 101.	77	●	●	●				●		●					
Succor Creek (E-12) 1,910 acres 30 mi. s. of Nyssa off SR 201.	78	●	●	●				●		●					
Sumpter Valley Dredge (D-11) 83 acres 29 mi. s.w. of Baker City on SR 7.	131		●	●				●	●	●		●			
Sunset Bay (G-1) 395 acres 2 mi. s.w. of North Bend.	79	●	●	●				●	●	●					
Tou Velle (G-6) 51 acres 9 mi. n. of Medford off SR 62.	84		●		●	●		●		●					
Tryon Creek (B-4) 627 acres 6 mi. s.w. of Portland off I-5 on Terwilliger Blvd.	85			●						●	●	●	●		
Tumalo (D-7) 320 acres 5½ mi. n. of Bend off US 20. *(See Bend)*	86	●	●	●				●	●	●					
Umpqua Lighthouse (F-1) 450 acres 6 mi. s. of Reedsport off US 101. *(See Reedsport)*	88	●	●	●	●			●	●	●					
Umpqua Wayside (F-2) 95 acres 7 mi. e. of Reedsport on SR 38.	89		●		●			●		●					
Unity Lake (D-11) 39 acres 5 mi. n. of Unity Junction on SR 7.	90	●	●		●	●		●		●					
Valley of the Rogue (G-6) 275 acres 3 mi. s. of Rogue River off I-5.	91	●	●		●	●		●		●					
Wallowa Lake (C-12) 166 acres 6 mi. s. of Joseph on SR 82.	92	●	●	●	●	●	●	●	●	●			●		●
Willamette Mission (C-3) 1,686 acres 8 mi. n. of Salem on Wheatland Ferry Rd.	93		●	●	●	●		●		●	●				
William M. Tugman (F-1) 560 acres 19 mi. n. of Coos Bay on US 101.	94	●	●		●	●		●	●						
OTHER															
Alton Baker (E-3) 490 acres on Centennial Blvd. off Coburg Rd. in Eugene. Birdwatching, canoeing.	124		●	●	●	●	●	●		●	●				
Anthony Lakes (C-11) 28 mi. w. of North Powder off I-84.	96	●	●	●		●		●	●	●		●			
Bastendorff Beach (F-1) 2 mi. w. of Charleston via Coos Rd. Playground. *(See Charleston)*	129	●	●					●	●						
Celilo (B-8) 16 mi. e. of The Dalles via I-84.	97		●		●	●			●	●					

RECREATION AREAS	MAP LOCATION	CAMPING	PICNICKING	HIKING TRAILS	BOATING	BOAT RAMP	BOAT RENTAL	FISHING	SWIMMING	PETS ON LEASH	BICYCLE TRAILS	WINTER SPORTS	VISITOR CENTER	LODGE/CABINS	FOOD SERVICE
Cullaby Lake (A-2) 165 acres 8 mi. s. of Astoria off US 101. Playground.	99	●	●	●	●	●		●	●	●	●				
Estacada Timber Park (C-4) 55 acres 1 mi. w. of Estacada on SR 224.	101		●		●	●		●	●	●					●
Howard Prairie Lake (G-7) 250 acres 22 mi. e. of Ashland.	102	●	●	●	●	●	●	●	●						
Perkins Peninsula (E-2) 87 acres 9 mi. w. of Eugene on SR 126.	104		●		●	●		●	●	●					
Pioneer Park (D-4) 18 acres off Main St. at the end of Park Ave. in Brownsville. *(See Brownsville)*	130	●	●	●				●	●						
Promontory (C-3) 37 acres 7 mi. e. of Estacada via SR 224.	80	●	●	●	●	●	●	●		●				●	
Richardson Point (E-3) 157 acres 17½ mi. n.w. of Eugene via the Prairie Rd. exit off the Beltline W., n. on Irving St., then 8 mi. w. on Clear Lake Rd.	105		●		●	●		●	●	●					●
Spruce Run (B-2) 128 acres on the lower Nehalem River 3 mi. s. of Elsie on FR 912.	106	●	●	●				●	●	●					
Timothy Lake (C-7) 1,500 acres 10 mi. s. of Mount Hood on US 26 to Skyline Rd., then 10 mi., following signs. *(See Mount Hood and Mount Hood National Forest)*	103	●	●	●	●	●		●	●	●	●				
Young's River Falls (A-2) 10 acres 15 mi. s. of Astoria on Young's River Loop Rd.	107		●	●				●	●	●					

Touring Oregon

For descriptions of places in bold type, see individual listings.

Central

Born of fire and in places shaped by ice, central Oregon extends from the lava fields south of **Bend** north to the Columbia River and from the Cascade summit eastward to the foothills of the Blue Mountains. The western one-fourth of the region is the east slope of the Cascades, heavily forested, studded with lakes and crowned with a gleaming succession of volcanic peaks.

The rest of central Oregon is the great central plateau, marked by juniper-peppered volcanic buttes and cinder cones, isolated ranges covered with ponderosa pine, and gorges cut through lava by relentless rivers.

The primary north-south highway through the region is US 97. After leaving the Klamath Basin, it crosses into the Deschutes River watershed, following the Little Deschutes through the **Deschutes National Forest.** The eastern part of the forest contains features that testify to the monumental forces that shaped central Oregon. SR 31 and several forest roads lead into the lava fields from La Pine and other points along US 97, but remember: this is forbidding country and you should check on road conditions locally before venturing off the main paved highways.

A few miles north of La Pine, Cascade Lakes national scenic byway heads west into the Cascades, offering (except in winter, when part of it closes) a 100-mile scenic loop through the western part of Deschutes National Forest. The drive winds around a series of large lakes and features a view of Mt. Bachelor. It rejoins US 97 at Bend.

At Bend US 97 intersects with cross-state US 20, which angles northwest to **Sisters.** Sisters is the gateway to two important Cascade passes, McKenzie and Santiam. The former is reached by SR 242, a summer-only, no-trailers road that ranks among the state's more scenic mountain drives. The Santiam Pass area is lower and tamer, but very popular for both summer and winter recreation.

North of Bend US 97 crosses an expanse of juniper and sage en route to the geographical center of the state, **Redmond.** From here trans-state SR 126 leads east to **Prineville** and US 26, which crosses the high desert and the Ochoco Mountains into the John Day country. The rimrock area around Prineville is rich in agate, jasper, petrified wood and thundereggs. Farther east, the Painted Hills and Sheep Rock units of **John Day Fossil Beds National Monument** tell much about the Oregon of 30 million years ago.

From Redmond US 97 runs north past the head of Crooked River Gorge—there are good views into the chasm from Smith Rock State Park and Ogden Scenic Wayside, both a few miles from Terrebonne—and across a part of Crooked River National Grasslands to **Madras.** Nearby lakes Simtustus and Billy Chinook are favorites for boating, fishing, houseboat vacationing and water skiing. White-water outfitters abound in Madras, because below Pelton Dam the Deschutes River is a designated state scenic waterway that ranks high in adventure as well.

US 26 west of Prineville intercepts US 97 a few miles south of Madras, then continues northwest into the Warm Springs Indian Reservation. **Warm Springs** is the headquarters of the vast reserve, which extends from the Cascade summit between Mount Jefferson and Abbot Pass eastward to the Deschutes.

From the potato and peppermint fields around Madras, US 97 traverses somewhat more open range country to a junction with US 197. US 197 continues north, crossing the Deschutes at Maupin and passing through such small towns as Tygh Valley (scene of the annual Pacific Northwest Championship All-Indian Rodeo) before reaching the Columbia River a few miles east of **The Dalles.** US 97 veers northeast across a high grassland punctuated by scattered ghost towns. Shaniko, with its weathered buildings and old vehicles, remembers its turn-of-the-20th-century heyday as a thriving railroad and sheep-raising center. Antelope, another once-lusty community, lies south of Shaniko off SR 218.

At Antelope SR 218 turns east toward the John Day River and the Clarno Unit of the John Day Fossil Beds National Monument. Beyond the John Day River, the plateau gives way to the hills of wheat country. SR 218 ends in Fossil at SR 19, an important trans-grain belt link between US 26 and the Columbia River. To the north roll wheat fields; to the south lie the broken buttes and domelike hills that have lured fossil hunters and gold seekers.

Until it meets US 30/I-84 at the Columbia River, US 97 intersects with only one other major route. At Wasco SR 206 turns southeast across 42 townless miles to SR 19 at Condon, the seat of wheat-rich Gilliam County; northwest of Wasco, it passes near the mouth of the Deschutes River en route to its terminus west of Biggs. US 97 proceeds to Biggs, where a bridge carries it across the Columbia to Maryhill, Wash. For more information on touring central Oregon phone the Central Oregon Recreation Association at (800) 800-8334.

Coast

Among the nation's more spectacular shorelines, the Oregon coast stretches some 400 miles from the California border near **Brookings** to Astoria at the mouth of the broad, gray Columbia River. In between, outlined by breakers, lie beaches protected by rocky headlands, miles of sand dunes, lighthouses and more than 50 state parks and waysides. With the fir-clad Coast Range shouldering in some places to the water's edge, this sparkling marine region offers photogenic scenery at every turn.

A trip along US 101, the Oregon Coast Highway, misses very little of the shoreline: only at **Coos Bay, Tillamook,** and from Florence to Reedsport does the highway take a somewhat inland tangent. In each case side roads lead to the seaside at such scenic spots as Cape Arago, Cape Meares and Cape Lookout. US 101 also is a doorway to one of the nation's best white-water rivers, the Rogue, which spills into the Pacific near **Gold Beach.**

Several of Oregon's rarities are found along this corridor. In the south, deep in a wilderness reserve in the **Siskiyou National Forest,** grows one of the world's rarest shrubs, the kalmiopsis. Stands of myrtle are found near Coquille and Myrtle Point, and the northernmost stand of redwoods can be seen in Loeb State Park just east of Brookings. A 40-mile ribbon of sand dunes between **North Bend** and **Florence** is set aside in Oregon Dunes National Recreation Area, part of the **Siuslaw National Forest.** A few miles north of Florence is the only year-round sea lion rookery on the U.S. mainland.

Towns and villages that bead the coast are often part fishing port, part resort and part industrial center. **Astoria** began with the Lewis and Clark expedition's encampment at Fort Clatsop in 1805-06 and the founding of John Jacob Astor's fur-trading post in 1811. While much of the town's charm stems from its 19th-century appearance, the treasury is supplied chiefly by canneries and the massive shipping industry.

Other venerable towns are **Seaside,** the state's oldest and largest ocean resort, and **Newport,** with its turn-of-the-20th-century waterfront and century-long standing as a lively resort community. For more information on touring the Oregon coast phone the Oregon Coast Association at (800) 858-8598. A detailed map of the Oregon coast can be obtained through AAA Oregon by contacting your local AAA office.

The Mount Hood Scenic Loop: Portland, Mount Hood and the Columbia River Gorge National Scenic Area

Few of Oregon's touring regions pack so much diversity into so small an area as the Portland-Mount Hood-Columbia Gorge area. The state's largest city, its highest mountain and one of its most magnificent rivers are all within 70 miles of one another, linked by the scenic Mount Hood Loop.

From **Portland,** where commerce, culture, environmental stewardship and industry are equally evident, US 26 leads through acres of orchards to **Mount Hood,** the centerpiece of **Mount Hood National Forest.** In addition to its beauty and geological significance—Mount Hood is a dormant volcano—the peak's prime attraction is year-round skiing: historic Timberline Lodge and Government Camp are the highlights of the area.

A short distance east of the Timberline cutoff, SR 35 turns north through the Hood River Valley, one of the country's more productive fruit-growing areas. The drive is especially rewarding in April, when the orchards blossom against the backdrop of forested hills and Mount Hood's glistening snows. Panorama Point, just east of the highway a few miles before it reaches the Columbia Gorge, offers an exceptional view of the valley.

SR 35 terminates at I-84/US 30 at **Hood River.** At this point in mid-gorge the winds are ideal for windsurfing, and all summer the Columbia River dances with the gaudy sails of surfboards. East of Hood River lies **The Dalles,** the true eastern gateway to the Columbia Gorge. Here began the series of rapids that marked the river's thunderous breaching of the Cascade Range, presenting a final hazard to pioneers bound for the Willamette Valley.

Dams at The Dalles and **Bonneville** temper, if not wholly tame, the river. It rolls westward between high, waterfall-laced walls, paralleled by I-84 (the low road) and the actual Historic Columbia River Highway, old US 30 (the high road). Particularly along US 30, numerous waysides, overlooks and state parks permit leisurely sightseeing.

The dams themselves are worth a visit, offering tours to their powerhouses, fish ladders and, at Bonneville, a large visitor center. A different perspective is available from a stern-wheeler that operates from **Cascade Locks** during the summer. The two highways emerge from the gorge at the Sandy River and enter Portland, completing the loop. For more information phone the Mt. Hood Information Center at (503) 622-4822.

Northeast

Roughly speaking, northeastern Oregon extends from the western foothills of the Blue Mountains to the Idaho border and from the mountains north of **Burns** to the Washington border. The western edge of the region is more or less delineated by US 395; the eastern boundary follows the Snake River north from **Ontario** through the continent's deepest gorge—Hells Canyon.

The Blue Mountains extend across the region from southwest to northeast, where they spill into Washington state. East of the Blues and separated from them by the Grande Ronde and Powder River valleys, are the Wallowa Mountains. South of the Blues lie mountains of a different character, the jagged Strawberry Range. The northwestern corner of the area is the Umatilla Basin, with its wheat fields, truck farms and lively capital, **Pendleton.**

Following nearly the same trace as its wagon-cut ancestor, today's Oregon Trail, I-84, bisects the region diagonally from southeast to northwest. After leaving the Snake River Valley near Huntington—pioneers dubbed the spot Farewell Bend for just that reason—the highway runs through hilly rangeland to **Baker City,** in the Powder River Valley.

In the 1860s, the mountains flanking Baker City teemed with prospectors; derelict towns and abandoned diggings are scattered throughout the **Wallowa-Whitman National Forest.** The Elkhorn Drive, a 106-mile route comprising SR 7 and a network of forest service roads west of Baker City, passes mining and logging towns and the Anthony Lakes recreation area before returning to the valley near North Powder.

East of Baker City SR 86 threads along the Wallowa foothills to Oxbow Dam and the southern gateway to **Hells Canyon National Recreation Area.**

The segment of I-84 between Baker City and Pendleton is especially scenic. After dipping into Grande Ronde Valley at **La Grande,** the highway climbs to the summit of the Blue Mountains. The view from the final grade down to Pendleton is spectacular.

La Grande also is the starting point for another of northeastern Oregon's scenic specials: the Hells Canyon Overlook at Hat Point via **Wallowa Lake.** SR 82 runs along the Grande Ronde River to Elgin, then curves east and southeast for a breathtaking run to Enterprise; the designated scenic route then follows SR 3 northward into Washington.

SR 82 ends at **Joseph,** near the north end of the lake; a paved road goes on to Imnaha, at the boundary of Hell's Canyon National Recreation Area. The last 24 miles to Hat Point are gravel. The drive from Imnaha to Hat Point takes approximately an hour.

Along the western edge of the region between US 20 at Burns and I-84 at Pendleton, US 395 illustrates the transition from semiarid range land to wheat country. North of Burns it traverses the Silvies and Bear valleys, passes the western shoulder of the Strawberry Mountain Wilderness in the **Malheur National Forest,** then drops into the John Day Valley. **Canyon City** and **John Day** both figured in the gold rush of 1862-64.

At John Day US 395 intersects with US 26. To the east US 26 crosses the Blue Mountains via Dixie Pass, a popular winter sports area; to the west it parallels the John Day River into central Oregon. A few miles west of John Day US 395 turns north again, traversing five mountain passes and interesting valleys en route to Pendleton. Northwest of Pendleton the highway travels through irrigated farmland around **Hermiston** and reaches the Columbia at **Umatilla,** where it crosses McNary Dam into Washington.

South

Three mountain ranges and two major river systems define southern Oregon. The region extends eastward from the Coast Range, across the valleys of the Umpqua and Rogue and over the Cascades to the lakes and pine lands of the Klamath Basin.

I-5, with its sometimes parallel, sometimes concurrent companion SR 99, traverses the Rogue and Umpqua River valleys. It is especially scenic between the California border and **Grants Pass** as it passes from the summit of the Siskiyous into Rogue River Valley, the state's chief pear-growing region. At **Ashland** I-5 runs into Renaissance England; Ashland is the home of the annual Oregon Shakespeare Festival.

Medford, the largest city and commercial hub of the valley, is the western terminus of SR 62, which arcs northeastward to **Crater Lake National Park,** then south to US 97 near **Chiloquin** in the Klamath Basin. Another facet of the Rogue valley lives in historic **Jacksonville.** Grants Pass is the starting point for the many raft trips that challenge the Rogue.

US 199, the Redwood Highway from California's redwood coast, joins I-5 at Grants Pass. The segment of US 199 between the border and O'Brien is particularly scenic. During the gold rush prospectors scoured these hills and streams for "color," with considerable success. **Cave Junction** is the access point for another treasure, **Oregon Caves National Monument.**

North of Grants Pass I-5 crosses three low passes and enters the rich Umpqua River valley, famous for fishing, logging, melon growing and wine producing. The largest town in the valley is **Roseburg,** a convenient base for visiting the local wineries and such towns as late 18th-century Oakland.

The 103 miles of SR 138 from Roseburg to **Crater Lake National Park** ranks among Oregon's most scenic highways. The route follows the North Fork of the Umpqua into the **Umpqua National Forest,** passes near many dramatic waterfalls and climbs to the summit of the Cascades along Diamond Lake, near the base of Mount Thielsen. At the entrance to the national park the scenic route continues south to Crater Lake; SR 138 heads due east to join US 97.

Running north-south through the central part of the state, US 97 very nearly marks the boundary between southern Oregon and the semiarid southeastern region. The chief town is sunny **Klamath Falls.**

Two highways turn west from Klamath Falls into the Cascade lake country. SR 66 meets I-5 at Ashland; SR 140 arches northwest and west, crossing the divide near Mount McLoughlin, and joins SR 62 just north of Medford. Both offer access to year-round recreation.

COVERED BRIDGES

Highwaymen used them for cover while awaiting their victims; moonshine whiskey was hidden in them; political rallies, church meetings and dances were held in them; and sweethearts secretly met in them. Oregon's covered bridges once served as more than just routes over the numerous waterways; they were part of Oregon's pioneer culture. As early as 1850 pioneers began constructing strong bridges made from the timber of Oregon's plentiful Douglas fir trees. Oregon's bridges were covered to protect them from the rainy weather, doubling their life span.

In the 1930s, there were more than 300 covered bridges in the state of Oregon. Today there are only 49 of these picturesque reminders of horse-and-buggy days. Although the oldest remaining covered bridge in Oregon was built as recently as 1914, they offer people a warm, nostalgic feeling of days-gone-by—a time when things were not so rushed. With the largest concentration of covered bridges west of the Mississippi, Oregon's many bridges vary in size, shape and design.

The longest covered bridge is Lane County's Office Bridge. Built in 1939, this 180-foot bridge, north of Oakridge on North Fork Road, spans the North Fork of the Willamette River and originally connected with a lumber mill and office—thus its name Office Bridge.

Jackson County is home to the shortest of Oregon's covered bridges—Lost Creek Bridge. Spanning just 39 feet, Lost Creek Bridge was built in 1919.

Originally built in 1926, the Chitwood Bridge, 18 miles east of Newport on Hwy. 20 in Lincoln County, was saved from demolition in 1982 and rebuilt—thus making it the newest covered bridge in Oregon.

Also in Lincoln County is the Upper Drift Creek Bridge, Oregon's oldest bridge. This 1914 structure, 2½ miles south of Lincoln City on Hwy. 101 then right 2½ miles on Upper Creek Road, is no longer open to traffic.

Several counties, including Benton, Douglas, Lane, Lincoln and Linn, offer brochures outlining the bridges in their area. Contact the chamber of commerce or the visitor center for more information.

North of Klamath Falls, attractions at Chiloquin and **Fort Klamath** explore Oregon's logging industry and life at a frontier army post. For more information phone the Southwest Oregon Visitors Association at (800) 448-4856.

Southeast

Consisting of two of the state's largest counties and most of a third, the sparsely populated southeastern region stretches from the California border to the foothills of the Strawberry Range north of **Burns,** and from the Gearhart Mountains of the **Fremont National Forest** eastward to the Idaho border.

Faulting, volcanism and erosion were—and are—the artists here, and they have created the setting for some of Oregon's most singular surprises: a geyser, colossal fault scarps, lava flows, lakes and canyons whose walls tell tales of unremembered time.

For all its acreage, southeastern Oregon has few major highways. Many of the most interesting features are reached only by gravel or dirt roads. Always check road and weather conditions locally before venturing off the main routes.

US 395, the north-south artery through the western part of the region, enters Oregon from California via the Goose Lake Valley. On the west a jumble of mountains and rims conceals the Gearhart Mountain Wilderness; on the east rise the commanding Warner Mountains. Goose Lake, like other lakes in the region, is a vestige of prehistoric Lake Chewaucan, whose ancient shorelines are visible on the surrounding mountainsides.

At **Lakeview,** the business center for the area, US 395 intersects the western leg of SR 140. Part of the route called the "Winnemucca to the Sea Highway," SR 140 slices along the Nevada-Oregon border, joins US 395 for a few miles to Lakeview, then resumes its westward course across the southern Cascades to **Medford.** (From Medford, follow I-5 north to **Roseburg** and SR 42 west to complete the "to the sea" part.)

At Valley Falls US 395 comes to a Y. The left arm is SR 31, the Fremont Highway, named for the young army lieutenant whose expedition came this way in 1843. SR 31 passes Summer and Silver lakes and connects with US 97 at the town of La Pine.

The Y's right arm is US 395, which threads along the base of one of the highest exposed fault scarps in North America, the Abert Rim. Besides being geologically and scenically awesome, the 2,000-foot-high escarpment is a favorite locale for hang gliding.

The rim separates Lake Abert from the Warner Valley, whose lakes and streams support large ranches and whose eastern wall is the massive volcanic ridge of Hart Mountain. The Warner Valley is reached by an unpaved road that cuts south from US 395 about 10 miles north of Lake Abert; it passes through Plush, from where another road enters the vast, game-rich Hart Mountain Refuge, then continues south to SR 140 east of Lakeview. East of the junction, off SR 140 near Adel, is Oregon's only spouting geyser.

Beyond Lake Abert, US 395 crosses some 90 miles of sage plains and alkali flats to Riley, where it meets US 20. Westbound, US 20 speeds across the silent miles to **Bend;** eastward it runs concurrently with US 395 to Burns.

Two roads head south from Burns. SR 78 skirts the state's largest lake, formed by the merger of Harney and Malheur lakes, then heads southeast to meet US 95. SR 205 runs south from Burns, passes the lake and follows the edge of the Malheur National Wildlife Refuge. Frenchglen, at the south end of the refuge, has changed little since the days of the cattle barons. Its eight-room hotel is preserved as a state historic wayside.

At Frenchglen an unimproved road loops to the summit of Steens Mountain, one of the largest fault-block mountains on the continent. On the west the mountain rises gently from the Harney Plain to the aspen-grown summit; on the east it plunges abruptly to the Alvord Valley thousands of feet below. The summit road is usually passable from mid-July through October, but not always for every kind of vehicle; and weather at 9,000 feet can deterioriate swiftly even in summer. You should stop at the Bureau of Land Management office in Burns for a map and current road information before undertaking the summit road, or consider taking one of the all-day van tours that are available in Burns.

A loop around the whole mountain follows SR 205 south from Frenchglen, then a gravel road to Fields. At Fields, which once prospered on freighting borax, another gravel road turns north along the eastern base of the mountain, traverses a semiarid sagebrush plateau and intersects with SR 78 some 100 miles southeast of Burns.

US 95, running from McDermitt on the Nevada border north to Burns Junction, then east through **Jordan Valley** to Idaho, holds within its arc the dry, desolate Owyhee country. Here rises the Owyhee River, whose spring white-water potential has only recently been widely recognized. North of Rome, where river trips usually begin, the river is a designated state scenic waterway. Also near Rome are the Pillars of Rome, the dramatically sheer, layered sides of a dry canyon. Northwest of Jordan Valley lie some of the more recent lava flows in the country.

Two miles before US 95 enters Idaho a scenic gravel road heads north, following part of an old stage route through Succor Creek Canyon. Like much of southeastern Oregon, the canyon is rich in thundereggs. The gravel road connects with SR 201, which drops into the agricultural Snake River Valley. At Owyhee a side road turns west along the Owyhee River to bass-rich Owyhee

Lake; SR 201 continues north through Nyssa to **Ontario.**

Willamette Valley

In the 1800s, the Willamette Valley was the end of the Oregon Trail—both the cause of and cure for the "Oregon Fever" that propelled thousands of pioneers westward. The region's excellent soils and long growing season quickly delivered on their promise of bountiful, diversified crops, which in turn attracted more and more settlers.

While retaining its agricultural importance, the valley is now home to more than 60 percent of Oregon's people and has eight of the 10 largest cities. From its headwaters, the Willamette River flows northward some 120 miles to the Columbia River; the valley, flanked by the heavily forested Cascades and Coast Range, is about 60 miles wide.

Although I-5 is the chief artery, speeding in an almost straight line from **Cottage Grove** to **Portland,** SR 99 (designated W or E depending on its position relative to the river) offers a closer view of the valley's charms. Among those charms is the largest concentration of covered bridges outside New England—testimony to the Yankee origins of many of Oregon's settlers. Five of the bridges are within a few miles of Cottage Grove, the southernmost major city in the valley.

The largest metropolitan area in the southern part of the valley is created by **Eugene,** home of the University of Oregon, and neighboring **Springfield,** an important forest products center and the gateway to the McKenzie River recreation area.

Farther north lie the mid-valley cities of **Albany,** appropriately named **Corvallis** (heart of the valley), and the gracious state capital, **Salem.** The region's industries range from grass seed, mint and wood products through high-tech research and manufacturing, to education: Oregon State University is in Corvallis; Willamette University is in Salem.

In the northern part of the valley the urban aspect becomes more noticeable. This was the first part of interior Oregon to be settled; such towns as **Oregon City,** the original capital of Oregon Territory, and **Newberg** have buildings dating from the early 1800s. Complementing the commerce and industry of the cities are the fruit and nut orchards and, most recently, the vineyards. Grapes grown in the Willamette Valley's soils have produced wines that have commanded international acclaim. For more information phone the Willamette Valley Visitors Association at (800) 526-2256.

POINTS OF INTEREST

ALBANY (D-3) pop. 29,500, elev. 210′

Albany was the home of the Calapooia Indians before being settled in 1848 by two brothers from Albany, N.Y. The town changed its name in 1853 to Takenah, an Indian word describing the depression, or large pool, created by the Calapooia River as it flows into the Willamette. Two years later the town was Albany again, because too many people insisted on translating Takenah as "hole in the ground."

Despite its brief identity crisis, Albany grew rapidly between 1851-1900, and its citizens erected hundreds of Victorian homes. More than 500 of the town's early structures remain and several can be toured during annual open houses the last Saturday in July and the second Sunday in December.

Guided heritage tours of Albany's historic homes and surrounding countryside are available. For information contact the Albany Visitors Association, 300 S.W. 2nd Ave., Albany, OR 97321; phone (503) 928-0911 or (800) 526-2256. The visitors association is open Mon.-Fri. 8-5, Sat. 9-5 (also Sun. 11-4, mid-May through Dec. 31).

In early July Albany celebrates Oregon's logging heritage with the World Championship Timber Carnival, featuring international competition in tree climbing and topping, ax throwing and birling—balancing upright on a floating log while spinning it.

A popular pastime is touring the area's numerous covered bridges. Oregon has the largest collection of covered bridges outside of New England, and a detailed brochure outlining their locations is available from the Albany Visitors Association.

Self-guiding tours: A self-guiding driving tour past many of the city's historic buildings, featuring such styles as Queen Anne, Italianate, French Second Empire and Classic Revival, is detailed on a map and brochure available from the Albany Visitors Association.

AMITY (C-3) pop. 1,200, elev. 159′

Deriving its name from the peaceful resolution of a dispute in 1849, Amity was the site of one of the earlier woolen mills in Oregon.

AMITY VINEYARDS, ¼ mi. e. on Rice Ln. from 99W to 18150 Amity Vineyards Rd. S.E., offers guided tours and tastings. Allow 1 hour minimum. Daily noon-5, May-Nov.; Sat.-Sun. noon-5, rest of year. Closed Dec. 24-Jan. 31. Free. Phone (503) 835-2362.

ASHLAND (G-6) pop. 16,200, elev. 1,868′

A crossroads for culture and outdoor activity, Ashland is home to the Oregon Shakespeare Festival and the Pacific Northwest Museum of Natural History. Annual events include the Old-fashioned July 4th Food and Fireworks Celebration and the Holiday Festival of Light which features a candlelight tour of historic homes tour and a parade.

Recreational opportunities at 100-acre Lithia Park include hiking, horseshoes, picnicking, tennis and volleyball. Mount Ashland, southwest of town within the Rogue River National Forest *(see Recreation Chart and place listing)*, is a popular skiing area in the winter. Numerous lakes in the region permit fishing and water sports.

A scenic stretch of I-5 passes through Ashland, intersecting with SR 66. Ashland Vineyards and Winery, 2 miles off I-5 exit 14 at 2775 E. Main St., offers guided tours and tastings year-round; phone (503) 488-0088.

ADVENTURE CENTER provides white-water and scenic rafting trips on nine rivers in southern Oregon and northern California, including the Rogue, Upper Klamath and North Upqua rivers, Mar.-Oct. Trips lasting from 4 hours to 9 days are available. Bicycle and ski tours also are available. Fee for 4-hour trips $55. Full-day trips which include lunch $95-$102. 2- to 9-day camp/lodge trips $275-$950. **Discount.** For further information and reservations contact Adventure Center, 40 N. Main St., Ashland, OR 97520. Phone (800) 444-2819.

NOAH'S WORLD OF WATER offers rafting and fishing trips lasting ½-day to several days on the Umpqua, Rogue and Klamath rivers. One-day trips include lunch. Transportation to and from Ashland motels is provided. Trips require varying degrees of agility, fitness and health. Minimum age restrictions may apply.

Half and one-day departures require a minimum of four persons. Departures daily at 8 or 10:30 and 1 for ½-day trips and 8 for trips lasting 1 or more days, Apr. to mid-Oct. Half-day trip $55; Full-day trip $95-$105. AE, MC, VI. Reservations are advised. Contact Noah's World of Water, P.O. Box 11, Ashland, OR 97520. Phone (503) 488-2811 or (800) 858-2811.

★**OREGON SHAKESPEARE FESTIVAL,** one of the oldest in the Western Hemisphere, presents matinee and evening performances in an outdoor Elizabethan stage house and two indoor theaters. An exhibit center featuring costumes, photographs and properties of the festival's past and present is open 10-4 every performance day. Backstage tours, which include admission to the exhibit center, are available at 10 a.m. every performance day except July 4; reservations are required.

Performances, including modern plays, are given Tues.-Sun., mid-Feb. through Oct. 31. Tickets $17.50-$26.50. Backstage tour $8. AE, MC, VI. Reservations are required. Contact OSF Box Office, Box 158, Ashland, OR 97520. Phone (503) 482-4331.

PACIFIC NORTHWEST MUSEUM OF NATURAL HISTORY, 1500 E. Main St., contains hands-on interactive exhibits describing the diverse ecosystems of the Pacific Northwest. Many of the exhibits are designed to appeal to all five senses. A re-creation of a lava tube complete with warm gusts of air and a glowing lava flow serves as the entrance to the main exhibit hall titled "Treasures of the Northwest." Ecosystems highlighted in the hall range from Oregon's lush coastal rain forests to the windswept expanses of the high desert.

Visitors to the museum are issued personal access codes to be used with interactive displays featuring videos, microscopes and computers. After completing their tour of the exhibits, visitors are presented with a record of their activities. The museum also features traveling exhibits, paintings and sculptures, and the exterior landscaping emphasizes the differences between prehistoric and contemporary plant life in Oregon.

Allow 1 hour minimum. Daily 9-5, Apr.-Oct.; 10-4, rest of year. Closed Thanksgiving and Dec. 25. Admission $6; over 62, $5; ages 5-15, $4.50.

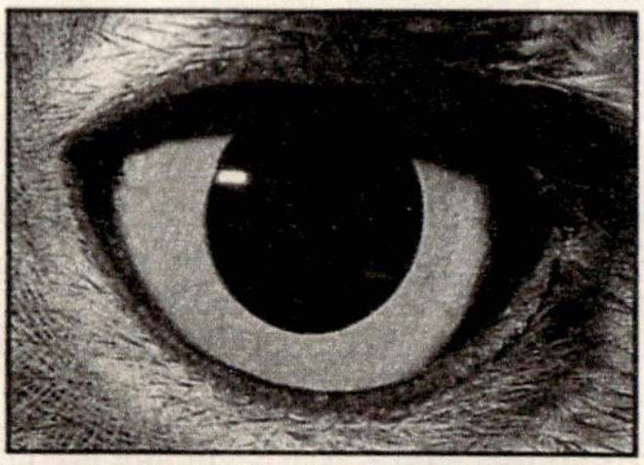

GET REAL

Touch the natural world through multi-sensory nature exhibits, interactive video adventures, hands-on games and experiments, and live animal shows. Open daily. Interstate 5, Exit 14. Call 1-800-637-8581 or (503) 488-1084.

PACIFIC NORTHWEST MUSEUM OF NATURAL HISTORY
1500 East Main St., Ashland, OR 97520

AE, DS, MC, VI. Phone (503) 488-1084. *See ad p. 36.*

WEISINGER'S WINERY AND TASTING ROOM, 3150 Siskiyou Blvd., is a family owned and operated winery. A glass-enclosed working beehive is of special interest. Tours of the facilities are conducted daily at 2, June-Sept. Allow 30 minutes minimum. Open daily 11-6, June-Sept.; Wed.-Sun. 11-5, Apr.-May and in Oct.; Thurs.-Sun. 11-5, in Mar.; Fri.-Sun. 11-5, rest of year. Closed Thanksgiving and Dec. 25. Free. Phone (503) 488-5989 or (800) 551-9463.

ASTORIA (A-2) pop. 10,100, elev. 16'

Astoria dates from the winter of 1805-06, when the Lewis and Clark expedition camped at Fort Clatsop. In 1811, Fort Astoria was built by a fur-trading company established the previous year by John Jacob Astor. In the following decades, Astoria was the destination of traders, explorers, missionaries and settlers.

A Scandinavian Midsummer Festival takes place the third week in June and features ethnic food, singing and dancing along with arts and crafts. The area's bountiful harvests are celebrated with the Astoria Regatta the second week of August during which parades, ship tours and tours of Victorian homes are offered.

Astoria is the northernmost Oregon city on US 101, a scenic highway that begins south of Santa Barbara, Calif., and runs along the Pacific Coast from Eureka, Calif., to South Bend, Wash., and then continues on a more inland course.

Shopping areas: Popular specialty stores are in Pier 11 at the foot of 11th Street.

★**ASTORIA COLUMN** was erected in 1926 to commemorate the discovery, exploration and settlement of the area. The 125-foot-high column stands on Coxcomb Hill, 635 feet above the Columbia River. An observation platform up 164 steps affords a view of the nearby mountains, river and ocean. Column open daily 8-dusk. Information booth open daily 11-6, June 1-Labor Day. Free. Phone (503) 325-6311.

BIG CREEK FISH HATCHERY is 15 mi. e. on US 30 to Knappa, then 2 mi. s. on Hillcrest Loop Rd. Operated by the Oregon Department of Fish and Wildlife, the hatchery offers views of adult chinook and coho salmon in the fall and steelhead and cutthroat trout in the winter. The best time to visit is in September when the salmon are spawning. Daily 7:30-4:30. Free. Phone (503) 458-6512.

★**COLUMBIA RIVER MARITIME MUSEUM,** 1792 Marine Dr., describes the maritime history of the Columbia River and Northwest coast through artifacts, ship models, graphic illustrations and photographs. Included are exhibits on the early exploration of the area, fur trading, navigation, marine safety, fishing, whaling, steam and motor vessels and U.S. naval history. Visitors can tour the lightship *Columbia,* the last seagoing lighthouse to serve on the West Coast.

Allow 1 hour minimum. Daily 9:30-5; closed Thanksgiving and Dec. 25. Admission $5; over 63, $4; ages 6-18, $2. MC, VI. **Discount.** Phone (503) 325-2323.

FLAVEL HOUSE MUSEUM, 441 Eighth St., is a restored Queen Anne Victorian mansion furnished in period. Built in 1885 by George Flavel, a bar pilot and entrepreneur, the elegant home contains displays of Victorian art and clothing. Allow 1 hour minimum.

Daily 10-5, May-Sept.; 11-4, rest of year. Closed Jan. 1, Thanksgiving and Dec. 25. Combination admission to house, Heritage Museum and The Uppertown Firefighters Museum $5; ages 6-12, $2.50. Phone (503) 325-2203.

FORT ASTORIA, Exchange and 15th sts., is a re-creation of one corner of the 1811 fort which was the first permanent American outpost west of the Mississippi. Daily 24 hours. Free. Phone (503) 325-2203.

★**FORT CLATSOP NATIONAL MEMORIAL,** 5 mi. s.w. near US 101, features a replica of the log fort built by the Lewis and Clark expedition in 1805. A living-history program portraying the clothing, equipment and lifestyle of the expedition is presented by park rangers daily 9:30-5:30, mid-June through Labor Day. Allow 1 hour minimum. Daily 8-6, mid-June through Labor Day; 8-5, rest of year. Closed Dec. 25. Admission $2, under 17 free. Phone (503) 861-2471.

HERITAGE MUSEUM, 1618 Exchange St., describes the region's history through artifacts and photographs housed in a restored neoclassic building. Changing exhibits also are featured. Allow 1 hour minimum. Daily 10-5, May-Sept.; 11-4, rest of year. Closed Thanksgiving and Dec. 25. Combination admission to museum, Flavel House Museum and The Uppertown Firefighters Museum $5; ages 6-12, $2.50. Phone (503) 325-2203.

THE UPPERTOWN FIREFIGHTERS MUSEUM, at 30th and Marine Dr., is in a historic 1896 fire station. Displays include vintage fire engines and firefighting equipment. Fri.-Sun. 10-5, May-Sept.; Fri.-Sun. 11-4, rest of year. Closed Thanksgiving and Dec. 25. Combination admission to museum, Flavel House Museum and Heritage Museum $5; ages 6-12, $2.50. Phone (503) 325-2203.

AURORA (C-3) pop. 600, elev. 130'

Founded as a self-sustaining religious colony in 1856, Aurora is virtually the same size today as it was then. Many historic buildings house antique shops.

Shopping areas: The Aurora Colony Historic District, downtown, includes a number of shops specializing in antiques, crafts and rugs.

OLD AURORA COLONY MUSEUM, 2nd and Liberty sts., is part of a five-building museum complex. The 1860 Ox Barn contains original furniture, musical instruments, quilts and tools. Behind it are the 1863 Kraus Colony Home, the 1876 Steinbach Log Cabin, a machine shed and a wash house, all of which have been restored.

Allow 1 hour, 30 minutes minimum. Tues.-Sun. 12:30-4:30, June-Aug.; Wed.-Sun. 12:30-4:30, Feb.-May and Sept.-Dec. Closed major holidays. Admission $3.50; ages 6-18, $1.50. MC, VI. **Discount.** Phone (503) 678-5754.

BAKER CITY (C-11) pop. 9,100, elev. 3,446'

The Baker Valley gave the Oregon Trail pioneers their first glimpse of the promise of the Oregon Territory. Five miles east of Baker City is the National Historic Oregon Trail Interpretive Center at Flagstaff Hill, built to preserve and intrepret the Oregon Trail heritage. At the site, 15 miles of wagon ruts left by the emigrants' wagons have been preserved.

In 1861, gold was discovered in Baker County by miners searching for the mythical Blue Bucket Mine. Subsequently, several mining towns sprang up throughout the county, many of which are now ghost towns. The Armstrong gold nugget, weighing 80.4 ounces, was found here and is now displayed in the U.S. National Bank *(see attraction listing)*. Many of Baker City's historic buildings are reminiscent of the ornate architecture of the early gold rush days.

In the heart of the ghost town area is Sumpter Valley State Park, the centerpiece of which is a 1,250-ton gold dredge built in 1935 and operated until 1954. More than $4.5 million in gold was extracted from the valley by the dredge.

The mountains that were once the miner's Eldorado are now an easily accessible recreational retreat. The Blue Mountains to the west and the Wallowa Mountains to the east are within the boundary of the Wallowa-Whitman National Forest *(see place listing)*. Another nearby highlight is Hells Canyon National Recreation Area *(see place listing)*, which lies east via SR 86.

A scenic stretch of I-84 begins just south of Baker City, running 93 miles northwest to Pendleton.

Self-guiding tours: Maps and brochures for self-guiding walking and driving tours are available Mon.-Fri. 8-6 and Sat. 8-4 at the Baker County Visitor and Convention Bureau, 490 Campbell St., Baker City, OR 97814; phone (503) 523-3356 or (800) 523-1235. Tours include the Baker City historic district, ghost gold-mining towns and the National Elkhorn Scenic Byway through the Blue Mountains.

★**NATIONAL HISTORIC OREGON TRAIL INTERPRETIVE CENTER,** on Flagstaff Hill 5 mi. e. of jct. I-84 and SR 86, features permanent and changing displays of historical artifacts and replicas illustrating the Oregon Trail journey and early life in the Northwest. The center has life-size exhibits, pioneer household articles, murals and living-history areas depicting a typical pioneer camp and mining operations.

Volunteers dressed in period costumes demonstrate pioneer arts and skills. Stage productions and outdoor programs are presented in an amphitheater. An indoor theater offers live performances and slide shows depicting the trail's development as well as the the hardships endured by families traveling westward.

A 4.2-mile trail system loops around Flagstaff Hill and passes a series of scenic views and historic sites. Interpretive exhibits allow visitors to experience the sights and sounds encountered by

Wherever you travel there's a Hilton waiting **Home Away From Home** in the United States, Hiltons across the U.S. to serve you. And many offer savings of 10% off room rates when you present your AAA membership card upon arrival. For reservations call the nearest AAA office or Hilton today at 1-800-HILTONS.

OREGON: Eugene Hilton, Portland Hilton. **WASHINGTON:** Bellevue Hilton Inn, Seattle Airport Hilton, Seattle Hilton.

Hilton

HILTON. SO NICE TO COME HOME TO.

Savings may vary. Subject to availability. Discount not valid for group or convention reservations; may not be used in combination with discounted room rates or other promotional offers and is subject to change without notice. The Hilton logo and logotype are registered trademarks of Hilton Hotels Corporation. ©1995 Hilton Hotels.

pioneers on the sagebrush plains. Allow 2 hours minimum. Daily 9-6, Apr.-Oct.; 9-4, rest of year. Closed Jan. 1 and Dec. 25. Free. Phone (503) 523-1843.

OREGON TRAIL REGIONAL MUSEUM, I-84 exit 304 at Campbell and Grove sts., has a comprehensive collection of rock, mineral and semiprecious stone specimens, as well as period clothing and memorabilia dating back to the 1840s. Allow 1 hour, 30 minutes minimum. Daily 9-5, May 1-late Oct. Admission $2; under 18, 50c; family rate $5. Phone (503) 523-9308.

SUMPTER VALLEY RAILROAD departs from the Dredge depot, 24 mi. s.w. on SR 7, and from the Sumpter depot, 29 mi. s.w. on SR 7. The railroad offers 5-mile, 40-minute one-way and round-trip tours through the historic gold-mining district west of Baker City and a wildlife habitat created after gold dredging left the land ill-suited for farming. Picnic facilities and nature trails are available in Dredge Depot Park.

Allow 2 hours minimum. Trains depart Dredge depot Sat.-Sun., and holidays at 10, 12:30 and 3, Memorial Day weekend-Sept. 30. Trains depart Sumpter depot Sat.-Sun. and holidays at 11, 1:30 and 4, Memorial Day weekend-Sept. 30. The last Sumpter depot trip is one-way only. Fare (round-trip) $8; ages 6-16, $6. Fare (one-way) $5; ages 6-16, $4. Phone (503) 894-2268.

U.S. NATIONAL BANK, 2000 Main St., has an exhibit of native gold in all its naturally occuring forms. The bank features the Armstrong Nugget, an 80.4-ounce gold nugget that was discovered on June 19, 1913. Daily 10-5 (also Fri. 5-6). Free. Phone (503) 523-7791.

BANDON (G-1) pop. 2,200, elev. 55′

Bandon is an important harbor and a popular vacation spot and artists' colony. The area's major industries include the export of cranberry products and cheese; many cranberry bogs can be seen north and south of town. Bandon's beaches, strewn with agates, jasper and other semiprecious stones, are very popular with rockhounds and sunbathers.

The renovated Oldtown Harbor District boasts art galleries, craft shops and cafes. Annual events in Bandon include the Seafood and Wine Festival and Sand Castle Contest both held Memorial Day weekend, the Coquille Indians' Native American Salmon Bake and Festival in June, the Cranberry Festival in September and the December Festival of Lights. For more information about the area contact the Bandon Chamber of Commerce, 300 S.E. Second, Bandon, OR 97411; phone (503) 347-9616.

BANDON HISTORICAL SOCIETY MUSEUM, W. 1st St. in the Old Coast Guard Building, has artifacts and historic photographs relating to Bandon, a marine exhibit and American Indian artifacts. Tues.-Sat. noon-4; closed Thanksgiving and Dec. 25. Admission $1, under 12 free. Phone (503) 347-2164.

BULLARDS BEACH STATE PARK is 1 mi. n. on US 101. The Coquille River Lighthouse, once known as the guardian of the "navigator's nightmare" (where river and ocean meet), is at the southern end of the spit. It is reached via a road through the picnic area and features a lighthouse exhibit. Camping is available. Daily dawn-dusk. Free. Phone (503) 347-2209. *See Recreation Chart and the AAA Northwestern CampBook.*

WEST COAST GAME PARK WALK-THRU SAFARI, 20 acres 7 mi. s. on US 101, features more than 75 species of animals and many tame exotic birds. Visitors are allowed to walk among, feed and pet the more than 450 creatures which may include bears, cougars, leopards, lions and tiger cubs. Allow 1 hour minimum. Daily 9-dusk, Mar.-Nov.; 9-5, rest of year. Closed Thanksgiving and Dec. 25. Admission $6.50; over 60, $5.50; ages 7-12, $5.25; ages 2-6, $4. MC, VI. **Discount.** Phone (503) 347-3106.

BEAVERTON (C-3) pop. 53,300, elev. 188′

Named for the abundance of beaver dams in the area, Beaverton was established in 1868 as a shipping point on the Oregon Central Railroad. Now it is an electronics, light industry and research center. Complementing the city's industry

Different faces, delightful places

Welcome to Washington County, Oregon

Just 10 minutes away from downtown Portland, Washington County is known as Oregon's cornucopia with something for everyone:

- Relax in full service accommodations
- Tour award winning wineries
- Meet heart warming alpacas
- Explore our historical museums
- Shop in tax free boutiques, malls and craft shops
- Ride the dinner train into the majestic Coast Range
- Bike or drive the scenic loop
- Golf at some of Oregon's finest courses!

For more information call or write:
Washington County Visitors Association
5075 SW Griffith Dr., Suite 120
Beaverton, OR 97005
(800) 537-3149

are its almost 300 acres of vineyards and a variety of recreational facilities. Seasonal activities include A Taste of Beaverton in late June and Good Neighbor Days in early September. For more information contact the Beaverton Area Chamber of Commerce, 4800 S.W. Griffith Dr., Beaverton, OR 97005; phone (503) 644-0123.

Ponzi Vineyards, 14665 S.W. Winery Ln. off Scholls Ferry Road, offers guided tours by appointment and wine tastings February through December; phone (503) 628-1227.

Shopping areas: The Beaverton Mall, on Cedar Hills Boulevard, has 80 stores. The local shopping area along 1st and Hall streets includes stores specializing in crafts and antiques. The Beaverton Antique Mall, 12905 S.W. Beaverdam Rd., features more than 70 dealers; phone (503) 626-3179.

WASHINGTON COUNTY MUSEUM, 17677 N.W. Springville Rd. on the Rock Creek campus of Portland Community College, has exhibits detailing the history of Washington County plus a research library. Guided tours are available by appointment. Allow 30 minutes minimum. Mon.-Sat. 10-4:30. Admission $1; ages 6-18, 50c; free to all Mon. Phone (503) 645-5353.

BEND (D-8) pop. 20,500, elev. 3,623′

Bordered by the Deschutes National Forest *(see place listing)* and the Cascade Mountains, Bend is surrounded by recreation areas. Tumalo State Park *(see Recreation Chart and the AAA Northwestern CampBook)* is 3½ miles north and La Pine State Park *(see Recreation Chart and La Pine in the AAA Northwestern CampBook)* is 27 miles south. Drake Park, along the Deschutes River, is known for its abundance of waterfowl.

Juniper Park on E. 6th Street has an aquatic center, horseshoe pits, picnic facilities and tennis courts. Nearby Pioneer Park provides a pleasant view of the Deschutes River. Mount Bachelor Ski Resort is 22 miles west of the city. Eleven miles south, ancient volcanoes and their lava formations can be seen.

★**CASCADE LAKES HIGHWAY** is an 87-mile scenic drive through Deschutes National Forest *(see place listing)*. The road runs west past Mount Bachelor before turning south, then east to Fall River and US 97, heading northward back to Bend. Along the highway are several lakes, including Cultus, Devil's, Elk, Lava, North and South Twin, Sparks and Todd, as well as Crane Prairie and Wickiup reservoirs. The highway also offers views of the Three Sisters, Mount Bachelor and Broken Top.

Recreational opportunities include boating, camping, fishing, hiking, horseback riding, sailing, swimming and windsurfing in the summer and alpine and Nordic skiing, ice skating and snowmobiling in the winter. The portion of the road between the Mount Bachelor Ski Resort and the Deschutes Bridge is usually closed October through March due to heavy snowfall. For more information contact the Deschutes National Forest at (503) 388-2715 or the Bend Ranger District at (503) 383-5664.

★**HIGH DESERT MUSEUM,** 6 mi. s. on US 97, is a living-history participation museum representing the natural and cultural history of the Pacific Northwest's arid intermountain region. Highlights of the museum's indoor and outdoor plant and animal exhibits include otters, porcupines and birds of prey demonstrations. A Desertarium features smaller regional animals in a natural setting.

Changing exhibits of American Indian artifacts, Western art and natural history materials are displayed in the Brooks Gallery. Western art and artifacts are displayed in the Earle A. Chiles Center. The walk-through "The Spirit of the West" exhibits cover 100 years of Western history. A visitor center and self-guiding trails with trail-side exhibits also are available. Allow 2 hours, 30 minutes minimum. Daily 9-5; closed Jan. 1, Thanksgiving and Dec. 25. Admission $5.50; over 64, $5; ages 5-12, $2.75. AE, MC, VI. Phone (503) 382-4754.

LAVA BUTTE AREA—
see Deschutes National Forest.

LAVA RIVER CAVE—
see Deschutes National Forest.

NEWBERRY CRATER—
see Deschutes National Forest.

PILOT BUTTE STATE PARK is e. on US 20. The 101-acre park contains Pilot Butte, a lone cinder cone rising 511 feet above the city. From the summit there is a magnificent view of the Cascade Range. No drinking water is available. Daily dawn-dusk. Free.

BONNEVILLE (B-7) elev. 52′

Bonneville was named for Capt. Benjamin L.E. Bonneville, whose life as an explorer in the Rocky Mountain country was documented in Washington Irving's "The Adventures of Captain Bonneville."

The Bonneville Dam spans the Columbia River from Oregon to Washington, a distance of 3,460 feet. A scenic portion of I-84 passes through Bonneville and parallels the Columbia River from Troutdale 150 miles east to Boardman.

BONNEVILLE FISH HATCHERY, off I-84 exit 40 adjacent to the dam, has display ponds with sturgeon and trout. The salmon spawn September through November. Daily 7:30-dusk. Office closed Jan. 1, July 4, Thanksgiving and Dec. 25. Free. Phone (503) 374-8393.

★**BONNEVILLE LOCK AND DAM,** in three sections separated by Bradford and Cascade Islands is part of a system of dams which produces power and creates a 465-mile navigable waterway. The Bradford Island Visitor Center, off I-84 exit 40, features an underwater viewing room from which visitors can see fish swimming up a fish ladder. Most species can be seen Mar.-Nov. Audiovisual presentations, powerhouse viewing and local history displays also are available. A navigation lock is located between the visitor center and the fish hatchery.

Picnicking and fishing are permitted. Access to the Washington facilities *(see North Bonneville, Wash.)* is via the Bridge of the Gods, 4 miles east at Cascade Locks. Allow 1 hour, 30 minutes minimum. Daily 9-5; closed Jan. 1, Thanksgiving and Dec. 25. Free. Phone (503) 374-8820. *See Recreation Chart.*

JOHN B. YEON STATE PARK, 2½ mi. w. off I-84 exit 35, includes picturesque Elowah Falls on McCord Creek Trail. Trails lead to viewpoints and falls. Daily dawn-dusk. Free. For more information phone the Columbia River Gorge District at (503) 695-2261.

BRIDAL VEIL (B-7) elev. 56′

Bridal Veil, a former lumber mill community in a valley along the historic Columbia River Scenic Highway *(see Columbia River Gorge National Scenic Area),* is surrounded by rocky cliffs and waterfalls. The Bridal Veil Post Office, near the I-84 interchange, was established July 7, 1887 and is one of the oldest post offices in Oregon.

BRIDAL VEIL FALLS STATE PARK, on scenic US 30, has a ⅓-mile trail to the falls and a ½-mile paved path to the gorge overlook. Daily dawn-dusk.

GUY W. TALBOT STATE PARK, 4 mi. w., contains Latourell Falls, a picturesque cataract along the Columbia River bluffs. Picnicking is permitted and hiking trails are available. Daily dawn-dusk. Free. For more information phone the Columbia River Gorge District at (503) 695-2261.

SHEPPERD'S DELL STATE PARK, about 3 mi. w. on US 30, has unusual rock formations, a historic bridge and a waterfall accessible by a trail. Parking is limited. Daily dawn-dusk. Free. For more information phone the Columbia River Gorge District at (503) 695-2261.

BROOKINGS (G-5) pop. 4,400, elev. 129′

Because of its unusually mild climate, Brookings is sometimes called "The Banana Belt of Oregon." Temperatures regularly reach around 70 degrees F. in winter. Flowers bloom all year—about 90 percent of the country's Easter lilies are grown locally. Commercial fishing, lumbering, making wood products and tourism are Brookings' largest industries.

The only aerial attack on the mainland United States by a Japanese war plane during World War II occurred just east of town near Mount Emily.

The port of Brookings-Harbor and the Chetco and Winchuck rivers provide popular fishing areas. Nearby streams offer abundant salmon and steelhead and cutthroat trout. Harris Beach and Loeb state parks are nearby *(see Recreation Chart and the AAA Northwestern CampBook).* Agate seeking, beach combing and crabbing also are popular activities.

Forest and trail maps and other recreational information on the Siskiyou National Forest *(see place listing)* are available Mon.-Fri. 7:30-4:30 from the Chetco Ranger Station, 555 Fifth St., Brookings, OR 97415; phone (503) 469-2196. Goat Island, a migratory bird sanctuary, is at the north edge of town.

The Azalea Festival is held Memorial Day weekend. Log Show by the Sea the third weekend in September features logging competitions, food and live music. Information on other local events is available from the Brookings-Harbor Chamber of Commerce, 16330 Lower Harbor Rd., Brookings, OR 97415; phone (503) 469-3181 or (800) 535-9469.

AZALEA PARK is downtown on US 101. Some of its many wild azaleas bloom in both late spring and early fall. A play area for children is available. Picnicking is permitted. Daily dawn-dusk. Free. Phone (503) 469-3181.

THE CENTRAL BUILDING, 703 Chetco Ave. off US 101, once served as the administrative building for a group of lumber companies that owned and operated the mill town of Brookings. The building now houses a museum, restaurant and small shops. Mon.-Sat. 9-5. Free. Phone (503) 469-3181.

BROWNSVILLE (E-3) pop. 1,300

Settled in 1846, Brownsville retains many homes dating 1850-1900 and several historic buildings. The community is the scene of Oregon's oldest annual celebration, the Pioneer Picnic, held in Pioneer Park *(see Recreation Chart)* the third weekend in June. Off Main Street at the end of Park Avenue, the park also offers camping, fishing, swimming and other recreational opportunities as well as picnic facilities mid-April to mid-October.

Self-guiding tours: Guide books for historical walking and driving tours are available at the Linn County Historical Museum *(see attraction listing)* or at the city hall on Main Street. City hall is open Mon.-Fri. 8-5; phone (503) 466-5666.

LINN COUNTY HISTORICAL MUSEUM, 101 Park Ave., includes a late 19th-century railroad depot, freight cars and a model of a circus train, as well as artifacts and photographs depicting life from the pioneer days to the 1940s. Allow 1 hour minimum. Mon.-Sat. 11-4, Sun. 1-5; closed Jan.

1, Easter, Thanksgiving and Dec. 25. Donations. Phone (503) 466-3390.

THE LIVING ROCK MUSEUM, 3 mi. e. on SR 228 off I-5 at the Brownsville exit, contain Biblical scenes portrayed in illuminated rock and wood carvings, oil paintings of Oregon wildlife, a mineral collection and an exhibit on the history of logging in Oregon. Allow 30 minutes minimum. Mon.-Sat. 10-3; evenings by appointment. Admission $2; ages 6-12, $1. Phone (503) 466-5814.

BUCHANAN (E-10) elev. 4,000′

OARD'S MUSEUM, 1604 Buchanan Rd., displays Native American art and artifacts. A complete costume worn by an Indian chief in 1890, an antique gun collection, an art gallery of Indian works and more than 100 antique clocks also are highlighted. Allow 2 hours minimum. Mon.-Sat. 8-7, Sun. 8:30-7. Free. Phone (503) 493-2535 or (800) 637-0252.

BURNS (E-10) pop. 2,900, elev. 4,148′

Few people associate the Old West and its cowboy legends with Oregon, but Burns was once the unofficial capital of the 19th-century cattle empires that staked claim to the grasslands of this high desert plateau. Henry Miller, who acquired a million acres and more than a million head of cattle, was typical of the cattle barons who settled the region.

The junction of US 20, which roughly follows the old Central Oregon Emigrant Trail, and US 395 in Burns have made the town a transportation hub. The Burns Paiute Indian Reservation is on the north edge of town.

About 70 miles south of Burns is 30-mile-long Steens Mountain, which slopes gradually away from Malheur Lake to its 9,733-foot summit, then drops abruptly to the Alvord Desert on the east. Aspen groves, lakes and meadows stud the area.

About 50 miles west of Burns off US 20, the Glass Buttes rise some 2,000 feet above the surrounding countryside. The buttes, one of the larger known outcroppings of iridescent obsidian, furnished generations of Native Americans with material for spear points and other implements. Together with the outcroppings found in Yellowstone National Park, they supplied most of the arrowheads for tribes as far east as Ohio.

The John Scharff Migratory Bird Festival in April is one of several special events held in Burns or nearby Hines. Summer events include Obsidian Days, a rock and mineral display, and the High Desert Hot Air Balloon Rally and Rock 'n' Rise Reunion in early July. The Harney County Fair, Rodeo and Race Meet is held in September. For more information contact the Harney County Chamber of Commerce, 18 W. D St., Burns, OR 97720; phone (503) 573-2636.

HARNEY COUNTY HISTORICAL MUSEUM, Broadway and D sts., exhibits wildlife displays, Fort Harney artifacts, photographs, pioneer items, old machinery and wagons, and Indian sandals and mats dating back 11,000 years. Allow 1 hour minimum. Tues.-Sat. 9-5, early May to mid-Oct. Admission $1.50; under 16, 50c; family rate $2.50. Phone (503) 573-5618.

MALHEUR NATIONAL WILDLIFE REFUGE, 26 mi. s. on SR 205, then 6 mi. e., encompasses 185,000 acres of desert, lakes, river bottom and wetland. Malheur Lake, a major nesting and feeding stop along the Pacific flyway, is at the northern boundary of the refuge. The refuge and surrounding area provides habitat for thousands of migratory birds. Prime bird season is mid-March through mid-June. More than 320 bird and 57 mammal species have been recorded.

Wildlife can be viewed along the 40-mile center patrol road that runs south from the refuge headquarters to Frenchglen. A museum at the refuge headquarters contains wildlife exhibits. The refuge office is open Mon.-Fri. 7:30-3:30. Refuge and museum open daily dawn-dusk; closed holidays. Free. Phone (503) 493-2612.

CANNON BEACH (B-2) pop. 1,200

Cannon Beach was named for the cannon that washed ashore from a schooner shipwrecked in 1846. The coastline includes one of the world's largest monoliths, Haystack Rock. The Cannon Beach Information Center at 2nd and Spruce streets is open daily 9-5; phone (503) 436-2623.

Shopping areas: Hemlock Street has a variety of specialty shops featuring glass-blowing, clothing and crafts.

ECOLA STATE PARK is 2 mi. n. on the coast off US 101. Sea lion and bird rookeries are on offshore rocks and a small herd of deer roams freely. A cliff trail offers scenic views. Daily dawn-dusk. Admission $3 per vehicle, mid-May through Aug. 31;pedestrians free. *See Recreation Chart.* Phone (503) 436-2844.

CANYON CITY (D-10) pop. 600, elev. 3,194′

The discovery of gold in nearby Canyon Creek prompted the overnight settlement of a mining camp in 1862. During the height of the gold rush, supplies and mail were brought into camp three times a week from The Dalles by pony express, later replaced by freight service over the old Dalles Military Road. Passions ignited by the gold rush were further heightened by clashes between the pro-Union Oregon miners and the Confederate Californians.

Canyon City evokes the excitement of its gold rush years during its '62 Day Celebration, held the second complete weekend in June.

GRANT COUNTY HISTORICAL MUSEUM, just n. of the post office, houses regional relics and artifacts. Guided tours are available by appointment. Allow 30 minutes minimum. Mon.-Sat. 9:30-4:30, Sun. 1-5, June-Sept.; otherwise varies in

May and Oct. Admission $2; over 62 and ages 13-18, $1; ages 6-12, 50c. Phone (503) 575-0362, June-Sept., or 575-0666, rest of year.

Joaquin Miller's Cabin, next to the museum, was the home of the Oregon poet and his family.

CASCADE LOCKS (B-7) pop. 900, elev. 102′

The town was named for the series of locks built in 1896 on the Columbia River, once the primary artery of transportation in the state. Before the locks were built, travelers along the river had to dock and make a rocky, treacherous portage around the dangerous cascades and whitewater rapids of this section of the Columbia.

The locks were submerged in 1938 by the rising backwaters of the Bonneville Lock and Dam *(see Bonneville).* Cascade Locks celebrates Sternwheeler Days the third weekend in June with music, dancing and food as the stern-wheeler *Columbia Gorge* returns from Portland for the summer months.

A scenic portion of I-84 passes near Cascade Locks, following the Columbia River from Troutdale 150 miles east to Boardman. The town also is an access point to the Pacific Crest National Scenic Trail.

PORT OF CASCADE LOCKS AND MARINE PARK, off Wa-Na-Pa St. on Marine Park Dr., is a scenic 20-acre riverfront park with historic locks, a marina, a museum and a visitor center. The museum has tools, photographs and other regional artifacts. Also of interest is the state's first locomotive, "The Oregon Pony." Fishing is permitted. The visitor center is open daily 8-6, June-Oct.; Mon.-Sat. 8-5, rest of year. The museum is open daily noon-5, May-Sept.; by appointment rest of year. Free. Phone (503) 374-8619 or 374-8427.

THE STERNWHEELER *COLUMBIA GORGE*, departing from Cascade Locks Marine Park, offers 2-hour narrated cruises through the Columbia River Gorge. Dinner cruises are available Wed.-Sat., brunch cruises Sat.-Sun. and a lunch cruise is at 12:30 on Fri. The MV *Columbia Gorge* operates out of Portland October to mid-June *(see Portland).* Two-hour cruise daily at 10, 12:30 and 3, mid-June to mid-Oct. Reservations are required for brunch, lunch and dinner cruises. Fare $11.95; over 55, $10.95; ages 4-12, $5.95. AE, MC, VI. For reservations phone (503) 223-3928 or 374-8427.

CAVE JUNCTION (G-5) pop. 1,100, elev. 1,325′

Cave Junction, a primary point of access to Oregon Caves National Monument *(see place listing),* was once known for its nearby rich gold fields. One prospector discovered a nugget that was worth $1,200 in the late 1850s. Most of the deserted mining camps have become overgrown by forest.

Several area wineries offer guided tours and tastings. Bridgeview Vineyard and Winery, 4210 Holland Loop Rd., offers guided tours of the vineyard November through April; phone (503) 592-4688. Foris Vineyards Winery, 654 Kendall Rd., also offers guided tours and tastings; phone (503) 592-3752 or (800) 843-6747. Siskiyou Vineyards, 6220 Oregon Caves Highway, offers a tasting room open daily 11-5, tours by appointment; phone (503) 592-3727.

JOSEPHINE COUNTY KERBYVILLE MUSEUM, 2 mi. n. on US 199, is in the 1871 Stith-Naucke House. Rooms are furnished in period. Displays include a collection of farm and mining machinery, some of which is handmade. An annex has antique guns and Indian and pioneer artifacts. Allow 1 hour, 30 minutes minimum. Mon.-Sat. 10-5, Sun. 1-5, May 15-Sept. 15. Donations. Phone (503) 592-2076.

CENTRAL POINT (G-6) pop. 7,500, elev. 1,272′

Central Point was named for the intersection of two stagecoach routes. It is the home of Jackson County Exposition Park, which is the site of county fairs, rodeos and festivals.

CRATER ROCK MUSEUM, 1 mi. n. and ½ mi. e. of SR 99 at 2002 Scenic Dr., displays a large collection of cut and polished rocks, most indigenous to the area, as well as Indian arrowheads and other artifacts. Guided tours are available by appointment. Allow 30 minutes minimum. Tues, Thurs. and Sat. 10-4. Donations. Phone (503) 664-6081.

DOGS FOR THE DEAF is off I-5 exit 32; take Biddle Rd. ¼ mi. e. to Table Rock Rd., then 8 mi. n. to Wheeler Rd., then ¼ mi. w. to 10175 Wheeler Rd. A non-profit agency which trains dogs to assist the hearing impaired, Dogs for the Deaf offers tours of its facilities. Training rooms are designed to look like home interiors, and visitors can watch actual training sessions during which dogs are taught to alert their masters when they hear smoke alarms, telephones, doorbells or babies crying. The tour includes the kennels where the dogs live during the 4-6 months of intensive training required to become a Hearing Dog. A 15-minute video explains the history of Dogs for the Deaf and includes interviews with several Hearing Dog recipients. A garden also is on the property.

Allow 1 hour, 30 minutes minimum. Tours depart on the hour Mon.-Fri. 10-2, May-Sept.; Mon.-Fri. at 10 and 2, rest of year. Closed major holidays. Free. Phone (800) 990-3647, or TDD (503) 826-9220.

CHARLESTON (F-1)

Deep-sea fishing is a way of life in Charleston. Halibut, snapper, tuna and other fish as well as oysters are abundant in the waters off Coos

Bay. Charter boats conduct fishing, whale-watching and scenic bay and ocean tours. Crabbing and clamming also are popular local recreational activities. The 91-acre Bastendorff Beach County Park is 2 miles west; *see Recreation Chart and the AAA Northwestern CampBook.*

SHORE ACRES STATE PARK AND BOTANICAL GARDENS, 743 acres, is 3½ mi. s. on Cape Arago Hwy. A former estate with 5 acres of formal gardens, this scenic park is landscaped with azaleas, roses, rhododendrons and other plants. A glass-walled shelter overlooking the ocean provides visitors with a view of seaside cliffs and possibly whales. The park hosts the Holiday Lights celebration in December. The celebration features 100,000 lights in the gardens and live entertainment (weather permitting). Daily dawn-dusk. Admission $3 per vehicle; pedestrians free. Phone (503) 888-3732.

SOUTH SLOUGH ESTUARINE RESERVE, off Cape Arago Hwy. on Seven Devils Rd. (SR 101), is a 4,400-acre freshwater and saltwater reserve. Hiking trails and canoe trails offer views of the area's plants, birds and other animals. A visitor center displays exhibits on the estuarine environment and offers educational programs. Allow 1 hour minimum. Daily 8-4:30, June-Aug.; Mon.-Fri. 8-4:30, rest of year. Closed holidays. Free. Phone (503) 888-5558.

CHILOQUIN (F-7) pop. 700

COLLIER MEMORIAL STATE PARK, near town on US 97, is an open-air museum with one of the larger collections of logging artifacts in the nation. Also on the grounds is a pioneer log-cabin village and a 1½-mile hiking trail. Daily dawn-dusk. Free. Phone (503) 783-2471. *See Recreation Chart and Klamath Falls in the AAA Northwestern CampBook.*

UPPER KLAMATH NATIONAL WILDLIFE REFUGE, 14,376 acres 20 mi. n. on US 97, harbors egrets, herons, white pelicans and other waterfowl. Canoe trails traverse the refuge. Allow 1 hour minimum. Refuge open daily dawn-dusk. Free. Phone (916) 667-2231.

CLACKAMAS (C-4) pop. 2,600, elev. 51'

NORTH CLACKAMAS AQUATIC PARK is off I-205 at the Sunnyside exit, then 1 mi. w. on Sunnyside Rd. to 7300 S.E. Harmony Rd. The park features a wave pool, lap pool and water slides. Food is available. Mon.-Fri. 10:30-6, Sun. noon-8, June 1-Sept. 11; closed Jan. 1 and Dec. 25. Admission $9; over 61 and ages 9-17, $6; ages 3-8, $4. Phone (503) 557-7873.

CLATSKANIE (A-3) pop. 1,600, elev. 20'

Named for a small tribe of Indians who once inhabited the region, Clatskanie is at the confluence of the Columbia and Clatskanie rivers. It is now a center for the processing of lumber and pulp into paper.

HISTORICAL FLIPPIN CASTLE, 620 Tichenor St., is a restored 19th-century gingerbread-style residence crowned by twin cupolas. Allow 1 hour minimum. Daily 10-2, Mar.-Dec. Admission $1; ages 6-12, 50c. Phone (503) 728-2026 or 728-3608.

COLUMBIA CITY (B-4) pop. 1,000, elev. 80'

CAPLES HOUSE, 1915 First St., was built in 1870 and now is a museum. On the grounds are a country store, the Pioneer Tool Shed and the Knapp Social Center. The Carriage House displays antique dolls, period clothing and toys. Allow 1 hour minimum. Wed.-Sun. 9-2, Feb.-Nov. Admission $2; under 13, 75c. **Discount.** Phone (503) 397-5390.

COLUMBIA RIVER GORGE NATIONAL SCENIC AREA (B-7)

Following the Columbia River in both Oregon and Washington, Columbia River Gorge National Scenic Area consists of 292,000 acres of sheer cliffs, mountainous coniferous forest, hilly deciduous woods and grassy plains. The Oregon section extends from the Sandy River near Troutdale about 80 miles east to the Deschutes River. Rain forests and waterfalls, characteristic of the area's western end give way east of the mountains to oak woods and grasslands.

Before settlement brought towns and dams, the rapids near The Dalles were impassable, requiring a difficult portage around the river and its enclosing cliffs. By 1913, plans were underway to create a scenic roadway similar to Charlemagne's winding roads through the Rhine Valley.

The Columbia provides a wide travel corridor and recreational playground. Through a collaboration of preservation and developmental interests, many public recreational areas have been set aside.

CROWN POINT STATE PARK, about 5 mi. e. of Corbett off I-84, encompasses 307 acres. The view from Crown Point offers a 30-mile vista of the Columbia River Gorge from 733 feet above sealevel. A panorama of the Columbia River Gorge can be seen from the Vista House overlook, built soon after the scenic highway was dedicated in 1916. The Vista House contains Columbia River Gorge exhibits. Park open daily dawn-dusk. Vista House open daily dawn-dusk, 8-6. Phone (503) 695-2261.

★**HISTORIC COLUMBIA RIVER HIGHWAY** offers scenic drives east of Portland. Portions of the highway split and become parallel roads: The upper level, old US 30, is the older, more scenic route; the lower level, I-84, is an interstate highway. For the best views of the gorge, enter the area from the east at I-84 exit 17 and leave on I-84W. The original 1915 highway, which was the first paved road in the state, was based on European highway systems that took into account an area's topography.

The highway provides panoramic views of the Columbia River Gorge at the Crown Point State Park *(see attraction listing)* and, near Portland, at Women's Forum State Park. East of the latter park, Larch Mountain Road runs 14 miles to another view at Sherrard Point, where a short trail accesses views of mounts Adams, Hood, Jefferson, Rainier and St. Helens.

The remaining 22-miles of this scenic road travel through the gorge, with cliffs 2,000 feet high, unusual rock formations and 11 waterfalls. The highest waterfall along the drive and one of the highest in the United States is 620-foot Multnomah, a slender stream falling from a steep, rocky cliff.

Near the base of the falls is an interpretive center with displays of the biology, geology and history of the area. Food is available. Between Hood River and The Dalles, the highway winds through more rugged, dry terrain and connects with the Mount Hood Loop Highway *(see Mount Hood and Mount Hood National Forest)*.

Note: A detailed map of the Columbia River Gorge area can be obtained through AAA Oregon by contacting your local AAA office.

COOS BAY (G-1) pop. 15,100, elev. 10′

The busy port of Coos Bay was founded in 1854 by J.C. Tolman of the Coos Bay Co. The town, originally named Marshfield after Tolman's hometown in Massachusetts, was renamed Coos Bay by referendum in 1944. Coos Bay is one of the world's largest ports for forest products. Wood chips account for a major portion of the port's export tonnage shipped to domestic and worldwide markets each year.

The Oregon Coast Music Festival, held the last two weeks in July, features a variety of music ranging from full symphony orchestra and chamber music to jazz, concert and dance bands **(discount).** For information contact the Oregon Coast Music Association, Box 663, Coos Bay, OR 97420; phone (503) 267-0938.

Coos Bay straddles scenic US 101, which winds past Oregon Dunes National Recreation Area *(see Siuslaw National Forest)* just north of town and continues along the Oregon coast to Florence.

Self-guiding tours: Brochures describing self-guiding hiking, biking, walking, driving and charter boat tours are available at the Bay Area Chamber of Commerce, 50 E. Central Ave., Coos Bay, OR 97420; phone (503) 269-0215 or (800) 824-8486. The chamber is open Mon.-Fri. 8:30-6:30, Sat. 10-4, Sun. 1-4, June 1-Labor Day; Mon.-Fri. 9-5, Sat. 10-4, rest of year.

Shopping areas: Coos Bay Village Shops on US 101 has a number of specialty stores.

COOS ART MUSEUM, 235 Anderson Ave., displays local, regional, national and touring exhibits. Collections include works by Frank Boyden, Red Grooms, Henk Pander, Robert Rauschenberg and Larry Rivers. Allow 30 minutes minimum. Wed.-Fri. 11-5, Tues. and Sat. 1-4; closed major holidays. Donations. Phone (503) 267-3901.

GOLDEN AND SILVER FALLS STATE PARK, is 24 mi. n.e. in the Coast Range. Two waterfalls, both about 100 feet high, and an old-growth myrtlewood forest highlight its 157 acres. Glenn Creek Road, the main road in the park, is not recommended for trailers and large motor homes. No drinking water is available. Daily dawn-dusk. Free. Phone (503) 888-3778 or (800) 824-8486. *See Recreation Chart.*

HOUSE OF MYRTLEWOOD, off US 101 at 1125 S. 1st St., offers a guided tour of its factory, where myrtlewood logs are used to manufacture various products. Allow 30 minutes minimum. Daily 8-6, June-Sept.; 9-5, rest of year. Closed Jan. 1, Thanksgiving and Dec. 25. Free. Phone (503) 267-7804 or (800) 255-5318.

CORBETT (B-7)

Corbett is east of the Sandy River, whose waters come from the melting glaciers on the south slope of Mount Hood. "The smelt are running in the Sandy" is a common refrain in the spring, when millions of the small oily fish ascend the river to spawn. Impromptu fishermen cast aside their poles in favor of buckets and other imaginative snares to catch the fish.

A scenic portion of US 30 passes through Corbett and Crown Point State Park *(see Columbia River Gorge National Scenic Area)*. Scenic I-84 parallels the Columbia River from Troutdale 150 miles east to Boardman.

CORVALLIS (D-3) pop. 44,800, elev. 273′

Located on the Willamette River between the Coastal Mountain range to the west and the Cascades to the east, Corvallis lives up to its Latin name meaning "heart of the valley." It is one of the state's leading centers of commerce, culture and education.

Oregon State University is the source of much of the city's cultural and intellectual wealth, while such industries as agriculture, high-technology and forest products contribute to its material resources. OSU offers a variety of athletic and cultural events throughout the year. Da Vinci Days, a festival of art, science and technology, is held in July, and the Fall Festival, held in late September, exhibits regional handmade arts and crafts.

Established in 1845, Corvallis has a variety of period homes in its historic district. Of particular interest is the 1888 Benton County Courthouse; it is one of the oldest courthouses in Oregon still in use.

The 5,300-acre William L. Finley National Wildlife Refuge, 6 miles south off SR 99W, provides habitat for a large population of migratory Canada geese, ducks and swans.

Self-guiding tours: Brochures outlining driving, bicycling and walking tours of the region and highlighting local wineries, covered bridges, historic sites and bird watching areas are available from the Corvallis Convention and Visitors Bureau, 420 N.W. 2nd St., Corvallis, OR 97330; phone (503) 757-1544 or (800) 334-8118. The bureau is open Mon.-Fri. 8-5. *See color ad.*

Shopping areas: The Old Cannery Mall, at the corner of 9th and Polk sts., and Avery Square, next door, feature a variety of speciality shops. Downtown is another popular area to find department and speciality stores.

COTTAGE GROVE (F-3) pop. 7,400, elev. 642′

Settled between two rivers, Cottage Grove is a recreation center for south Lane County. Area attractions include six covered bridges, two lakes, three golf courses, numerous streams, historic homes and the Bohemia gold-mining district. For information contact the Cottage Grove Area Chamber of Commerce, 710 Row River Rd., P.O. Box 587, Cottage Grove, OR 97424; phone (503) 942-2411.

COTTAGE GROVE MUSEUM, jct. H St. and Birch Ave., is in an octagonal structure built as a Roman Catholic church in 1897. The museum contains Indian artifacts, old mining tools, a working model of an ore stamp mill, 61 original Oregon covered bridge prints, a Titanic display and articles relating to pioneer domestic life, farming and industry. Allow 1 hour minimum. Wed.-Sun. 1-4, mid-June through Labor Day; Sat.-Sun. 1-4, rest of year. Free. Phone (503) 942-3963.

ALIVE & GREEN

Majestic mountains, ancient forests, meandering rivers & scenic routes, Corvallis, Oregon is a visual paradise. Enjoy bicycling, hiking, canoeing, golf. Each season has unlimited recreational opportunities. Come to Corvallis and you'll discover why the people who live here never want to leave.

CORVALLIS OREGON
1-800-334-8118
Corvallis Convention & Visitors Bureau
Dept. AAA 420 NW 2nd, Corvallis, OR 97330

★CRATER LAKE NATIONAL PARK (F-7)

Elevations in the park range from 4,250 ft. near the park's southern boundary to 8,929 ft. at Mount Scott. Refer to AAA maps for additional elevation information.

On the crest of the Cascade Range, Crater Lake National Park is 72 miles east of Medford off I-5 to SR 62, or from US 97 at Klamath Falls, take 97 north 21 miles then west on SR 62 for 29 miles. It's centerpiece is Crater Lake, noted for its deep, brilliant blue color. The lake is 6 miles long, 4½ miles wide and 1,932 feet deep. Its 26-mile shoreline is encircled by lava cliffs that rise 500 to 2,000 feet.

Until about 7,700 years ago, Mount Mazama, a 12,000-foot volcano, occupied the site of Crater Lake. Eruptions emptied the magma chamber beneath the mountain and caused the mountaintop to collapse, creating the caldera which now contains the lake.

Embracing three zones of vegetation, the park has more than 570 species of plants and a variety of trees, including several types of hemlock, fir, pine and spruce. The park also is known for its wildflowers.

Small game is abundant; among the large mammals are black bears, elks and mule deer. More than 200 species of birds have been identified. It is forbidden to feed, tease or in any way molest bears or other wildlife, as they are potentially dangerous.

General Information and Activities

The park is open daily 24 hours (weather permitting). Except during years of very heavy snowfall, the northern entrance road opens in mid-June; Rim Drive opens in early July. Both remain open until the first heavy snowfall.

Accommodations at Mazama Village, 7 miles south of Rim Village, and gasoline and are available from mid-May to mid-October. Food is available year-round. After being closed three years for rehabilitation, the 1915 Crater Lake Lodge at Rim Village will reopen in May 1995; for reservations phone (503) 594-2511.

There are more than 90 miles of maintained trails within Crater Lake National Park—snow usually blocks them from October to July. Mountain trails lead to the summits of several of the high points about the rim and down 670 feet to the lake. Trails to the rim ascend richly forested slopes that rise high above a lava plateau.

Near park headquarters is Castle Crest Wildflower Trail. The 1-mile Cleetwood Trail, a trail leading to the lakeshore, begins along Rim Drive 11 miles north of Rim Village Visitor Center. The Sinnott Memorial Overlook *(see attraction listing)* provides a view of Crater Lake.

The park has two visitor centers, Steel Information Center at park headquarters and Rim Village Visitor Center. Each visitor center has natural history displays and information on conducted trips, road conditions and points of interest.

All-weather roads are open to Steel Information Center, 4 miles north of SR 62 from the southern and western park entrances. The visitor center is open daily 9-5. Closed Dec. 25.

All-weather roads from the southern and western entrances also are open to Rim Village Visitor Center, on the south side of the lake, via SR 62. It is the focal point of park activities and the starting point of several trails. The visitor center is open daily June-Sept. (weather permitting). Visitors to the park are advised to prepare their cars for snowy conditions from mid-October to mid-May.

Back-country permits are required for overnight trips and are available free of charge at the visitor centers. Winter snowmobiling is allowed on the north entrance road only. No snowmobile facilities or ski tows are available, but cross-country ski equipment may be rented from the gift shop at Rim Village. Picnicking is permitted. *See Recreation Chart and the AAA Northwestern CampBook.*

ADMISSION to the park is $5 per private vehicle per day or by Golden Eagle, Golden Age or Golden Access passports.

PETS must be restricted at all times, either in vehicles or by leash, and are not allowed in public buildings or on trails.

ADDRESS inquiries to the Chief of Interpretation, Crater Lake National Park, Box 7, Crater Lake, OR 97604. Phone (503) 594-2211 for current road and weather information.

Points of Interest

CLOUDCAP, on the east rim, affords one of the better views of the lake. Its summit, almost 1,774 feet above the lake, is reached via a ¾-mile paved spur road off Rim Drive.

CRATER LAKE BOAT TOURS depart hourly from Cleetwood Cove Dock. Park naturalists explain the area's geological and natural history on the 2-hour trips. It should be noted that the trail from the parking area to the dock is steep and should not be attempted by those with respiratory or ambulatory problems. Daily 10-4:30, late June-early Sept. (weather permitting). Fare $10;

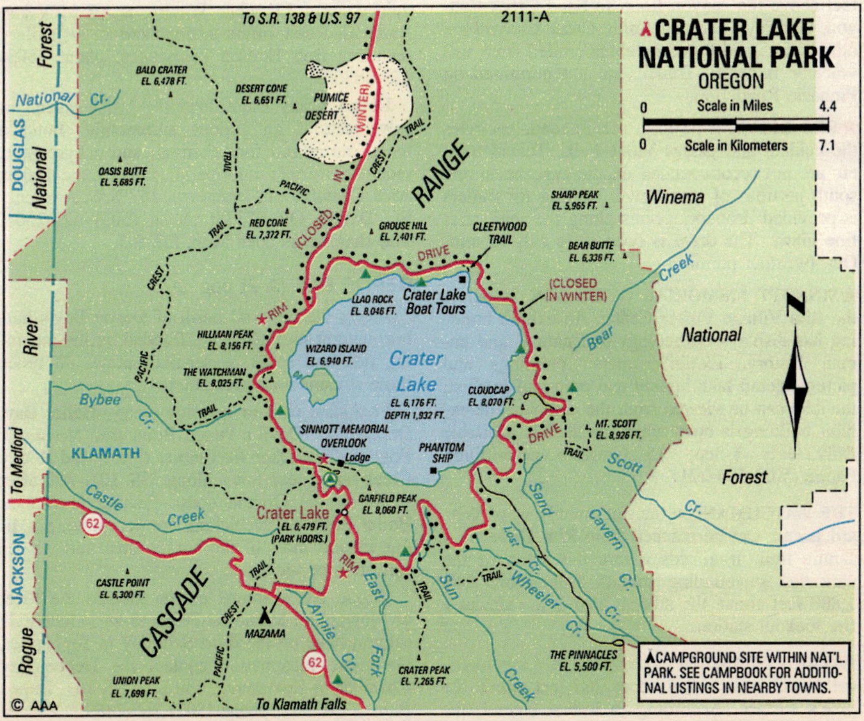

under 12, $5.50. MC, VI ($10). Phone (503) 594-2511.

GARFIELD PEAK is reached by a 1¾-mile trail from the lodge. The 8,060-foot summit provides views of the surrounding area.

HILLMAN PEAK, just n. of The Watchman, is the highest point on the rim, at 8,151 feet. Named for the first non-Indian to reach the rim of Crater Lake, it is a bisected satellite cone of Mount Mazama.

LLAO ROCK, a conspicuous feature on the north rim, is a lava flow filling an ancient explosion crater. Named for the Indian spirit Llao, Chief of the Below World, the formation rises more than 1,850 feet above the lake.

MOUNT SCOTT is the highest point in the park, at 8,929 feet. The easy 2½-mile trail from Rim Drive to a fire lookout station at the top offers extensive views.

PHANTOM SHIP, a lava dike rising about 160 feet above the lake's surface, resembles a ship under sail. The better views are from the launches and from Kerr Notch (Phantom Ship Overlook), 8 miles east of park headquarters on Rim Drive.

THE PINNACLES, along Wheeler Creek Canyon near the eastern boundary of the park, are spires of cemented pumice and scoria; some rise 200 feet above the canyon floor. In Sand Creek Canyon, Godfrey Glen and Annie Creek Canyon are other spires and fluted columns eroded from soft volcanic material. Trailers are not permitted on Pinnacle Road.

★**RIM DRIVE,** a 33-mile scenic road, encircles the caldera and passes Vidae Falls. Towed trailers are not recommended on the east, north and south portions of Rim Drive. Parking for trailers is provided. Lookout points along the road offer fine views. The drive is open early July to mid-Oct. (weather permitting).

★**SINNOTT MEMORIAL OVERLOOK** is below the Rim Village Visitor Center. An exhibit building has displays on geology and natural and human history. Exhibits, maps, paintings and pictures detail lake history and points of interest; the lake can be viewed from the parapet. The exhibit building is open when the staff is available daily, July 1-Sept. 15 (weather permitting). Phone (503) 594-2211.

THE WATCHMAN, on the rim directly w. of Wizard Island, can be reached from Rim Drive by a 1-mile trail. It affords a rare panorama of the park and surrounding country from more than 1,800 feet above the lake. It also is the site of a fire lookout station.

WIZARD ISLAND, in Crater Lake, is a symmetrical cinder cone rising about 760 feet above the lake's surface. According to Indian legend, the spirit Llao was quartered by an enemy spirit and thrown into the lake. Monsters devoured all except the head, which they recognized and would not eat, leaving it to form Wizard Island.

A trail from Cleetwod Cove parking area gives hikers access to regularly scheduled boats that carry hikers to the island during the summer. A 1-mile trail leads to the cone's crater from the island's shore. The hike is very strenuous and should not be attempted by those with respiratory or ambulatory problems.

There are no services on the island. Boats run on the hour daily 10-4:30, late June to mid-Sept. (weather permitting). Fare $10; under 12, $5.50. Phone (503) 594-2511.

DALLAS (C-2) pop. 9,400, elev. 326′

Settled in the 1840s and incorporated in 1874, Dallas was named for George Mifflin Dallas, U.S. vice president under James K. Polk. Among the town's historic buildings are the 1899 Polk County Courthouse and the 1863 Muir and McDonald Leather Tannery. The 35-acre Dallas City Park offers sightseeing and outdoor recreation opportunities; phone (503) 623-2338. The Delbert Hunter Arboretum and Botanic Garden in the park features native plants.

Baskett Slough National Wildlife Refuge is just northeast off SR 22. Chateau Bianca Winery, 17485 Hwy. 22, offers guided tours and tastings; phone (503) 623-6181. While it does not offer guided tours, Ellendale Winery, at SR 99W and Rickreall Road, offers tastings and an art gallery featuring Bob Hudson landscapes; phone (503) 623-6835.

Dallas Krazy Dayz, held the last weekend in July, features an antique automobile show; a wine, music and food festival; and a hydro-cart race. For further information contact the Dallas Area Chamber of Commerce, 167 S.W. Academy St., Dallas, OR 97338; phone (503) 623-2564. The chamber is open Mon.-Fri. 9-5.

DEPOE BAY (A-2) pop. 900

Along the sea wall north of Depoe Bay's harbor, natural rock tubes are flooded by the incoming tide and spout geyser-like sprays. At times these streams arch over US 101.

Five state park or wayside areas—Boiler Bay, Depoe Bay, Devil's Punch Bowl *(see Newport)*, Fogarty Creek *(see Recreation Chart)* and Rocky Creek—are near town along US 101. All offer views of the Oregon coast. Fishing (except at Boiler Bay) and picnicking are permitted. Sea lions inhabit most of the coastal area and whales can often be viewed.

Depoe Bay's annual events include the Fleet of Flowers on Memorial Day and an Indian-style salmon bake on the third Saturday in September. For more information contact the Depoe Bay Chamber of Commerce, 630 S.E. US 101, Depoe Bay, OR 97341; phone (503) 765-2889.

Shopping areas: The downtown area has a number of nautical gift shops.

DEPOE BAY AQUARIUM, jct. US 101 and Bay St., features an octopus and performing seals. Allow 30 minutes minimum. Daily 10-8, June 1-Sept. 15; 10-5, rest of year. Closed Dec. 25. Admission $2.25; ages 6-12, $1.75. AE, DS, MC, VI. Phone (503) 765-2259.

DESCHUTES NATIONAL FOREST

Elevations in the forest range from 2,150 ft. at Lake Bellychinook to 9,065 ft. at Mount Bachelor. Refer to AAA maps for additional elevation information.

Lying north of Crater Lake National Park *(see place listing)* on the eastern slope of the Cascades, Deschutes National Forest is 6 miles south of Bend on US 97. The third largest national forest in Oregon and one of the most popular, it is comprised of heavily forested land and volcanic landscapes. The forest's several areas of past volcanic activity are easily accessible from US 97.

The Newberry National Volcanic Monument area contains several volcanic features, including nearby Lava River Cave *(see attraction listing)*, one of the longest uncollapsed lava tubes in the Northwest. The cave was once the pathway of an underground stream of molten rock. Molten lava also formed the Lava Cast Forest *(see attraction listing)* as it engulfed a forest. Lava Lands Visitor Center sits at the base of Lava Butte Cone. The 6,000-year-old cone's lava flow once damned the Deschutes River.

To the south lies Newberry Crater; its two lakes, obsidian (black glass) lava flow and crater-rim waterfalls are part of a volcano that encompasses 500 square miles. The landscape of the volcano has been created over the last 500,000 years. Archeological excavations conducted in the crater led to the discovery of one of the oldest houses in the Western hemisphere. Studies show that the inhabitants hunted bear, deer, rabbit and bison.

The area's past volcanism provides numerous recreational opportunities for hikers and climbers, and the more than 200 lakes and miles of streams challenge anglers. Diamond Peak, Mount Jefferson, Mount Washington and Three Sisters wilderness areas offer hikers terrain ranging from rugged volcanic landscapes to alpine meadows and waterfalls.

Horses for pack and saddle trips are available locally. In the winter Mount Bachelor offers downhill skiing; a number of areas throughout the forest offer cross-country skiing and permit snowmobiling. A chairlift goes to the top of the 9,065-foot peak in the summer. For information and permits, phone the Forest Service at (503) 388-2715 or 388-5664. *See the Recreation Chart and the AAA Northwestern CampBook.*

★**CASCADE LAKES HIGHWAY**—*see Bend.*

LAVA BUTTE AREA is 11 mi. s. of Bend on US 97. Lava Butte, a 500-foot cinder cone, is one of more than 400 cinder cones in the Deschutes National Forest formed from volcanic eruptions. A surfaced road spirals to the top, where an observation/fire lookout is located. The lookout is closed when extreme fire danger or visible smoke is present.

Shuttle service is available on the half-hour daily 10-4, Memorial Day weekend through Labor Day. Fare $1.50; senior citizens and ages 6-12, $1. A ¼-mile signed hiking trail surrounds the rim.

The Lava Lands Visitor Center at the base of Lava Butte offers interpretive dioramas, trails, displays and information. Daily 10-4 (weather permitting). Phone (503) 593-2421.

LAVA CAST FOREST GEOLOGICAL AREA is 14 mi. s. of Bend on US 97, then 11 mi. e. on FR 9720. Along a self-guiding nature trail are the molds of pine trees that were engulfed by slow-moving lava 6,000-500,000 years ago.

LAVA RIVER CAVE, 11 mi. s. of Bend on US 97, was formed by lava flows and is about a mile long. Lantern rentals; fee $1.50. Picnicking is permitted, but no drinking water is available. The cave's temperature is 35-40 F; bring a jacket or sweater. Self-guiding tours are available May 15-Oct. 15. Admission $2; ages 13-17, $1.50; over 62, 75c. For more information contact the Bend/Ft. Rock Ranger District, (503) 388-5664, or the Lava Lands Visitor Center, (503) 593-2421.

METOLIUS RIVER RECREATION AREA, about 20 mi. n. of Sisters off US 20 and SR 126, is a scenic region of lush mountain meadows and ponderosa pine. The Metolius River, which flows from a large spring at the base of Black Butte, is popular for fly fishing.

NEWBERRY CRATER is 22 mi. s. of Bend and about 13 mi. e. of US 97 on CR 21. The huge caldera is the location of Paulina and East lakes. These lakes are separated by cinder cones and a large obsidian flow of more recent geological occurrence. They are popular areas for camping, hiking and fishing.

Visitors can drive or hike to 7,686-foot Paulina Peak and see the geological features of the crater and a panorama of central Oregon. Paulina Falls can be viewed from an observation point off CR 21. The Newberry Crater Visitor Center is open daily 10-4, last week of June-Labor Day. Phone (503) 593-2421.

DUNDEE (C-3) pop. 1,700, elev. 187′

Fertile soil and benevolent weather contribute to the proliferation of vineyards and groves in the Dundee area. Plums for prune production, filberts and English walnuts are the major area crops. Sokol Blosser Winery, 2 miles southwest on SR 99W to 5000 N.E. Sokol Blosser Ln., offers guided tours and tastings; phone (503) 864-2282 or (800) 582-6668. Argyle Winery, 691 Hwy. 99W, offers tastings and guided tours by appointment in a restored two-story farmhouse; phone (503) 538-8520.

ELMIRA (E-2)

Elmira serves as a midpoint for exploring the vineyards dotting the foothills of the Oregon Coast Range. Several local wineries offer tastings and guided tours.

ESTACADA (C-4) pop. 2,000

Estacada is known as the Christmas Tree Capital of the world. In a valley at the foot of the Cascade Mountains, the town is sheltered by the forested bluffs that overhang the Clackamas River. As the gateway to the Mount Hood National Forest *(see place listing)*, the area offers abundant recreational opportunities.

Built in 1883, the Philip Foster Historical Farm, 5 miles west of downtown, was the last stop on the Oregon Trail before pioneers reached Oregon City; phone (503) 630-5051.

The nearby Eagle Sports Center features many sports activities throughout the year. Milo McIver State Park *(see Recreation Chart and the AAA Northwestern CampBook)* hosts a Civil War re-enactment in April. The Clackamas River Canyon Marathon takes place in May. Timber Park hosts the July 4th Celebration and Fireworks, and in mid-July is the Clackamas River Family Heritage Festival. Trucks bring snow for sledding during the 3-week December Christmas Festival. The yuletide festivities also include an arts and crafts bazaar and a parade. For more information contact the Estacada-Clackamas River Area Chamber of Commerce, 477 S. Main St., P.O. Box 298, Estacada, OR 97023; phone (503) 630-3483.

EAGLE CREEK NATIONAL FISH HATCHERY is at 34288 S.E. Rainbow Rd. Salmon and trout can be seen swimming up fish ladders in nearby creeks in season. Adult salmon can be seen from late September through November and adult steelhead trout can be seen January through March. Mon.-Sat. 7:30-4. Phone (503) 630-6270.

EUGENE (E-3) pop. 112,700, elev. 422'

Located at the confluence of the Willamette and McKenzie rivers, Eugene is a major lumber and wood products center in the southern end of the Willamette Valley, a region that produces much of the nation's softwood plywood.

Surrounded by farmlands, forest and mountains, Eugene is noted for its fine parks, especially the nearby Spencer Butte Park. A

Lane County, Oregon...
Naturally

Imagine yourself on a spectacular adventure that takes you from rugged mountains through lush valleys and bustling cities to a magnificent coastline all in a matter of hours.

Lane County, OREGON

For your free Visitors Guide:

call: 800-547-5445

P.O. BOX 10286
EUGENE, OREGON 97440

Have the time of your life...Naturally

coniferous forest surrounds the park's South Hills Ridgeline Trail. The park also features 2,065-foot Spencer Butte, the highest point in the Eugene area, and a wide variety of plant and animal life. Hiking trails are available.

Miles of bicycle trails and opportunities for water sports can be found along the Willamette River. Riverfront picnic areas and meandering walkways thread through 5 acres of roses at Owens Memorial Rose Garden, along the south bank of the Willamette at N. Jefferson Street; phone (503) 687-5347.

In the east hills of Eugene is Hendricks Park Rhododendron Garden, graced by more than 6,000 rhododendrons and azaleas; phone (503) 687-5324. The Mount Pisgah Arboretum encompasses 118 acres of wooded hillsides and trails within the Howard Beauford Recreation Area. Alton Baker Park *(see Recreation Chart)* offers various developed recreational facilities. The McKenzie River white-water area is nearby.

Eugene and its sister city Springfield are at the head of a series of dams constructed by the Army Corps of Engineers for flood control in the Willamette River Basin. Lookout Point, Dexter and Fall Creek lakes *(see Recreation Chart),* formed by their namesake dams 20 miles southeast on SR 58, have picnic, fishing and boating facilities. The nearby Point Powerhouse lookout offers guided tours by appointment; phone (503) 937-2131.

Self-guiding tours: A brochure of the East Skinner Butte historic landmark area outlines a self-guiding walking tour of downtown focusing on several historic buildings dating 1855-1929. The landmark honors one of Eugene's founding fathers. Self-guiding tours of downtown also are among the featured activities during Historic Preservation Week in early May.

Maps and information can be obtained from the Convention and Visitors Association of Lane County Oregon, 305 W. 7th Ave., Eugene, OR 97401; phone (503) 484-5307. The association is open Mon.-Fri., 8:30-5, Sat. 10-4, Memorial Day-Labor Day. *See ad p. 50.*

Shopping areas: Two major area shopping malls are Valley River Mall on Valley River Way and the Oakway Plaza just northeast of downtown. Other popular shopping areas include the Fifth Street District at Fifth and High, with its specialty shops and the Saturday Market, downtown, where vendors sell crafts and food to the accompaniment of mimes and musicians March through December.

HINMAN VINEYARDS, 5 mi. s. on Bertleson Rd., then 2½ mi. e. on Spencer Creek Rd. to 27012 Briggs Hill Rd., offers 30-minute guided tours and wine tastings. Picnicking is permitted. Daily noon-5; closed major holidays. Free. Phone (503) 345-1945.

★**HULT CENTER FOR THE PERFORMING ARTS** is on Willamette St. between 6th and 7th aves.; from I-5 south, take exit 194, following signs to city center. The center, noted for its fine architectural and acoustical design, has two theaters—the 2,500-seat Silva Concert Hall and the 500-seat Soreng Theatre—which feature plays, concerts and other performances by national, regional and local talent.

Changing art exhibits are displayed in the lobby and in the Jacobs Room Gallery. Free guided 1-hour tours are available Thurs. and Sat. at 1. For tour information phone (503) 687-5087. Lobby and ticket office open Mon.-Fri. 11-5:30, Sat. 11-3 and 1 hour prior to performances. AE, DS, MC, VI. Phone (503) 687-5000 for ticket office, or 342-5746 for recorded information.

LANE COUNTY HISTORICAL MUSEUM, 740 W. 13th Ave., has displays interpreting Lane County history from its early settlement through the 1930s. Exhibits include 19th-century vehicles, logging history displays and period rooms. An Oregon trail display features diary quotes, artifacts, maps and photographs. Allow 1 hour minimum. Wed.-Fri. 10-4, Sat. noon-4. Admission $2; senior citizens $1; under 18, 75c. Phone 687-4239.

MAUDE KERNS ART CENTER, 1910 E. 15th Ave. next to the University of Oregon campus, has an arts and crafts school and several galleries. Allow 30 minutes minimum. Tues.-Fri. 10-5, Sat.-Sun. 1-5. Admission $2. Phone (503) 345-1571.

UNIVERSITY OF OREGON, bounded by Franklin Blvd., 11th and 18th aves., and Alder and Moss sts., has an enrollment of about 16,900 students. Campus guided tours depart from the information desk in Oregon Hall Mon.-Fri. at 10 and 2. Free. Phone (503) 346-3201.

Museum of Art, near the Knight Library at 1430 Johnson Ln., includes Asian and contemporary American art, photographic displays and changing exhibits. Metered parking is available on Kincaid. Allow 1 hour minimum. Wed.-Sun. noon-5; closed holidays. Donations. Phone (503) 346-3027.

Museum of Natural History, 1680 E. 15th Ave., features exhibits relating to Anthropology, Archeology and the natural sciences with an emphasis on the Pacific Northwest. Changing exhibits explore worldwide traditional cultures. Allow 30 minutes minimum. Wed.-Sun. noon-5; closed major holidays. Admission $1. Fee for special exhibitions. Phone (503) 346-3024.

WILLAMETTE SCIENCE AND TECHNOLOGY CENTER (WISTEC), 2300 Leo Harris Pkwy. next to Autzen Stadium, offers hands-on and changing exhibits. Wed.-Sun. noon-6. Admission $3; ages 4-16, $2. MC, VI. **Discount.** Phone (503) 687-3619 or 484-9027.

FLORENCE (E-1) pop. 5,200, elev. 11′

Between Florence and the ocean lies an extensive area of sand dunes that sometimes reach a height of 300 feet. A good view of the area is from the observation deck in nearby Harbor Vista County Park *(see the AAA Northwestern CampBook);* phone (503) 997-3128.

Other natural highlights include the freshwater lakes, sand dunes and beach that constitute Jessie M. Honeyman Memorial State Park *(see Recreation Chart and the AAA Northwestern CampBook)* just south of the town.

A scenic section of US 101 bisects Florence; several attractions can be seen along its route. Six miles north on US 101 is Darlingtonia Botanical Wayside, a sphagnum bog noted for cobra lilies; self-guiding walkways provide access to the bog. The Heceta Lighthouse, 12 miles north, contains Oregon's most powerful beacon.

Thousands of wild rhododendrons bloom in the late spring, and the town celebrates this event with a parade, carnival and other activities during the Rhododendron Festival the third weekend in May. For more information contact the Florence Area Chamber of Commerce, 270 Hwy. 101, P.O. Box 26000, Florence, OR 97439; phone (503) 997-3128.

Shopping areas: Old Town on Bay Street offers a variety of clothing, antique and other specialty shops and restaurants along the mouth of the Siuslaw River.

DOLLY WARES DOLL MUSEUM, on US 101 at 36th St., has a collection of more than 2,500 dolls, ranging from a crude pre-Columbian clay doll to glamorous dolls from France, Germany and Italy. Allow 30 minutes minimum. Tues.-Sun. 10-5; closed Jan. 1, Thanksgiving and Dec. 25. Admission $4; ages 5-12, $2.50. **Discount.** Phone (503) 997-3391.

SANDLAND ADVENTURES INC., 1 mi. s. on US 101, features dune buggy rides to the top of the South Jetty Dunes near the Siuslaw River. Odyssey dune buggies and four-wheelers are available. Under 16 must be with an adult. Drivers under 18 are not permitted on four-wheelers. All drivers must show proof of a valid driver's license or be accompanied by an adult with a valid driver's license. Dune buggy guided tours also are available. Bumper boats, miniature golf and a go-kart track are available for an extra fee. Allow 1 hour minimum. Daily 9-7:30, June 1-Labor Day; 9-5, rest of year. Closed Thanksgiving and Dec. 24-25. Rental fee $30-$35; tours $15-$25. DS, MC, VI. Phone (503) 997-8087.

SEA LION CAVES, 11 mi. n. on US 101, is the only year-round mainland home for wild Steller sea lions. Whether on the rocks outside or inside the cave, these mammals can be observed in their natural surroundings. Bring binoculars in the spring and summer to watch for grey whales and rare sea birds. A flight of stairs and pathway leading to an elevator, which descends 208 feet, provides access to the 1,500-foot-long cavern. A scenic path leads to the outdoor viewing area. Allow 30 minutes minimum. Daily 8-dusk, July-Aug.; 9-dusk, rest of year. Closed Dec. 25. Admission $6; ages 6-15, $4. MC, VI. Phone (503) 547-3111. *See ad p. A21.*

SIUSLAW PIONEER MUSEUM, 1 mi. s. on US 101, houses Indian and early pioneer artifacts. Memorabilia includes household items, furniture, clothing, photographs, a rope bed and a cider press. A research library is available by appointment. Allow 30 minutes minimum. Tues.-Sun. 10-4, Jan. 2-Nov. 30; closed Easter and Thanksgiving. Donations. Phone (503) 997-7884.

FOREST GROVE (B-3) pop. 13,600, elev. 169′

The town's founders aptly named Forest Grove for the surrounding white oak and fir forests. Nearby Pacific University, established as Tualatin Academy in 1849, is one of the oldest academic institutions in the Northwest. Kramer Vineyards, 7 miles south on SR 47 to Olson Road, offers guided tours and tastings; phone (503) 662-4545. Five other wineries and a sake brewery with a tasting room also are in the vicinity.

Forest Grove holds the All-Northwest Barber Shop Ballad Contest in March, the Concours d'Elegance antique car show in July and a Corn Roast in August. For further information contact the Forest Grove Chamber of Commerce, 2417 Pacific Ave., Forest Grove, OR 97116; phone (503) 357-3006.

PACIFIC UNIVERSITY MUSEUM, n. of SR 8 at 2043 College Way, is on the second floor of the 1850 Old College Hall. The museum exhibits photographs and memorabilia relating to the university's founders, school traditions, athletics and well-known graduates. Allow 1 hour minimum. Tues.-Fri. 1-4:30; closed university breaks and major holidays. Free. Phone (503) 359-2915.

TUALATIN VINEYARDS, w. on US 26 to SR 6, s.w. to Banks exit, right to SR 47, following signs, offers guided tours and tastings. The tasting room and picnic facilities overlook the vineyard and the Willamette Valley. A barrel tasting is held July 4 and a food and wine festival is held during the annual open house on Thanksgiving weekend. Allow 30 minutes minimum. Mon.-Fri. 10-4, Sat.-Sun. noon-5, Feb.-Dec.; closed holidays. Free. Phone (503) 357-5005.

FORT KLAMATH (F-7) elev. 4,200′

The Fort Klamath region, now a cattle-raising district, was the scene of frequent clashes between white settlers and the Modoc Indians during the 1870s. From 1863 to 1890 Fort Klamath was the Army post from which the federal government conducted its Indian campaign.

FORT KLAMATH HISTORICAL FRONTIER POST, on SR 62, was built in 1863 to protect wagon trains from Indian attacks. Exhibits depict frontier life and include American Indian artifacts and military medals. The graves of Captain Jack, a leader of the Modoc Indians, and three of his warriors are on the grounds. Allow 1 hour minimum. Thurs.-Mon. 10-6, June 1-Labor Day. Donations. Phone (503) 883-4208.

FREMONT NATIONAL FOREST

Elevations in the forest range from 4,699 ft. at Sprague Campground to 8,454 ft. at Crane Mountain. Refer to AAA maps for additional elevation information.

Extending over a high plateau broken by numerous faults and buttes, the Fremont National Forest in south-central Oregon presents a variety of landscapes, from sagebrush and juniper to pine forests and meadows.

So dramatic is this contrast, that Lt. John Fremont in his journal of 1843 described being snowbound on a ridge in December while summer conditions prevailed in the prairie below. Fremont named these neighboring areas Winter Ridge and Summer Lake, respectively.

Winter Ridge's topography is a familiar pattern in this forest where timbered slopes often rise sharply from sagebrush flatlands. Fremont National Forest offers small mountain lakes, the largest of which is the Thompson Reservoir.

Volcanism shaped both these national forests and left such features as Gearhart Mountain, one of Fremont National Forest's highest volcanic domes. This mountain is the centerpiece of the Gearhart Wilderness Area, which is characterized by high mountain meadows, U-shaped valleys and other glacial features.

The terrain of the Gearhart Wilderness makes it popular with hikers and cross-country skiers. Other favorite areas include forest camps and dispersed sites in the Warner Mountain Range, the Crane Mountain National Recreation Trail and the southern portion of Abert Rim, a favorite hang-gliding launch site. The forest encompasses a section of the National Recreation Trail which traverses the Silver Lake District. Skiing is available at the Warner Canyon Ski Area.

For further information contact the Forest Supervisor at 524 N. G St., Lakeview, OR 97630; phone (503) 947-2151. *See Recreation Chart and the AAA Northwestern CampBook.*

GLENEDEN BEACH (D-2)

Gleneden Beach lies south of Siletz Bay. Beachcombing for driftwood, agates and glass net floats is a popular activity, particularly early in the day during low tide or after storms.

Shopping areas: Salishan Marketplace, US 101, has a variety of galleries, craft and other specialty shops.

MAVEETY GALLERY, in the Salishan Marketplace on US 101, displays original arts and crafts by Northwestern artists. Changing exhibits include blown glass, furniture, jewelry, paintings, photography, pottery, prints and sculpture. Allow 30 minutes minimum. Mon.-Sat. 10-6, Sun. 10-5. Free. Phone (503) 764-2318 or (800) 764-2318.

GOLD BEACH (F-4) pop. 1,500, elev. 60′

Named for the placer mining prevalent until an 1861 flood swept the deposits out to sea, Gold Beach is a gateway for many activities in this popular coastal and river recreation area. The coastal vistas offer rewarding settings for photographers, especially along the 37-mile drive south to California via US 101. For more information contact the Gold Beach Chamber of Commerce, 1225 S. Ellensburg #3, Gold Beach, OR 97444; phone (503) 247-7526 or (800) 525-2334.

CAPE SEBASTIAN STATE PARK, 7 mi. s. on US 101, includes a group of park units covering 1,104 acres of open and forested land. Cape Sebastian is a towering headland rising 700 feet above sea level. Scenic views, wildflowers and hiking trails are among the park's attractions. Daily dawn-dusk. Free.

ROGUE RIVER JET BOAT TRIPS explore the scenic white-water section of the Rogue River and the wild river areas nearby. Reservations are recommended for all trips.

Court's White Water Jet Boat Trips depart from Jerry's Rogue Jet Dock at the s. end of the Rogue River Bridge, oceanside on US 101. A 6-hour, 64-mile trip and an 8-hour, 104-mile trip are available. The 8-hour trip includes lunch. The 6-hour trip departs daily at 8:30, May-Oct. (also at 2:30, July 1-Labor Day). The 8-hour trip departs daily at 8, May-Oct. (also at noon, July 1-Labor Day). Six-hour trip $27.50; ages 4-11, $10. Eight-hour trip $65; ages 4-11, $30. MC, VI.

For further information and reservations contact Court's White Water Jet Boat Trips, P.O. Box 1045, Gold Beach, OR 97444. Phone (503) 247-6504 or 247-6022 or (800) 525-2161.

Jerry's Rogue River Jet Boats & Whitewater Trips leave from the boat basin at Gold Beach, s. end of the Rogue River Bridge. A 6-hour, 80-mile white-water trip, an 8-hour, 104-mile white-water trip and a 6-hour, 64-mile jet boat trip are available. The 104-mile white-water trip includes a meal.

The 80-mile trip departs daily at 8:15 and 2:30, July 1-Labor Day; daily at 8:15, May-June and day after Labor Day-Oct. 31. The 104-mile trip departs daily at 8, May-Oct. (also at noon, July 1-Labor Day). The 6-hour jet boat trip departs daily at 8:30, May -Oct. (also at 2:30, July

Original Rogue River Jet Boat Tour
JERRY'S ROGUE JETS
Call Toll Free 1-800-451-3645
FREE ADMISSION
Open Year Around
ROGUE RIVER MUSEUM & GIFT SHOP
Located in Gold Beach, Oregon on the Southern Oregon Coast. Ideal for all ages, youngsters to seniors! Call or write for information and reservations.
Box 1011 • Gold Beach, OR 97444 Local Calls 247-4571

100th ANNIVERSARY
Mail Boat
HYDRO-JETS
Since 1895 we have been the Rogue River's original boat line. Help us celebrate by experiencing the unique wildlife, breathtaking scenery and extraordinary history of the Rogue River Canyon from the comfort of a powerful, modern hydro-jet.
Ask about our group rates. For Free color brochure or reservations, call or write:
ROGUE RIVER MAIL BOAT TRIPS
P.O. Box 1165-A, Gold Beach, OR 97444
Phone: (503) 247-7033
For reservations call toll free: 1-800-458-3511
MAIL BOAT
HYDRO-JETS
WILDCAT
MAIL BOAT

1-Labor Day). Eighty-mile trip $40; ages 4-11, $15. One hundred-four-mile trip $65; ages 4-11, $30. 6-hour jet boat trip $27.50; ages 4-11, $10. DS, MC, VI.

For reservations contact Jerry's Rogue River Jet Boats & Whitewater Trips, P.O. Box 1011, Gold Beach, OR 97444. Phone (503) 247-4571 or (800) 451-3645. *See ad.*

Rogue River Mail Boat Trips and White Water Trips leave from the Mail Boat dock, ¼ mi. upstream from the n. end of the Rogue River Bridge. A 64-mile jet boat trip and an 80-mile and a 104-mile, 8-hour white-water trip are available.

The jet boat trip departs daily at 8:30, May-Oct. (also at 2:30, July 1-Labor Day). The 80-mile trip departs daily at 8 and 2:45, July 1-Labor Day. The 104-mile trip departs daily at 8, May-Oct. Jet boat $27.50-$65; ages 4-11, $10-$30. The 104-mile trip includes a meal. Passengers are asked to arrive 30 minutes before departure. MC, VI.

For reservations contact Rogue River Mail Boat Trips and White Water Trips, P.O. Box 1165-A, Gold Beach, OR 97444. Phone (503) 247-7033 or (800) 458-3511. *See ad.*

GOLD HILL (G-5) pop. 1,000, elev. 1,085′

THE OREGON VORTEX, 1 mi. w. on SR 234, then 4 mi. n., is the site of The House of Mystery. Balls appear to roll uphill, short people seemingly get taller and visitors are unable to stand upright. Engineer John Litster conducted more than 14,000 experiments here and explained the strange phenomena as a whirlpool of invisible energy. Guided tours are available. Allow 1 hour minimum. Daily 9-5:30, June-Aug.; 9-4:30, Mar.-May and Sept.-Oct. Admission $6; senior citizens $5.50; ages 5-11, $4. Phone (503) 855-1543.

GRANTS PASS (G-5) pop. 17,500, elev. 951′

A stopping place on the California stage route, Grants Pass was named when settlers building the main road through town heard of Gen. Ulysses S. Grant's capture of Vicksburg in 1863. The town now is a central point in the Rogue River region and the departure point for many downriver raft trips. Numerous riverside parks offer boating, camping, fishing, and swimming *(see the AAA Northwestern CampBook)*.

A particularly scenic stretch of I-5 begins at the junction with US 199 in Grants Pass, running 60 miles southeast to the California line.

The Grower's Market, at 4th and F streets on the Southern Oregon lot, is one of the largest open-air markets in Oregon. Features include seasonal fruits and vegetables, a nursery and baked goods as well as musicans, artisans and craftspersons. The market is open Tues. and Sat. 9-1, Apr. 1-late Nov.; phone (503) 476-5375.

The town celebrates Amazing May with a multitude of special events culminating in the Boatnik Festival on Memorial Day weekend featuring skydivers, a carnival and an arts and crafts fair. The nostalgic Step Back in Time to the 50s Festival is held the last weekend in July. October events center upon Heritage Days which include a re-enactment of the founding of the Applegate Trail in 1846.

Hellgate Canyon, northwest of the city, marks the Rogue River's entrance into the Coast ranges. Guides can be hired for various trips along the Rogue River to Gold Beach. For further information about Rogue River trips as well as other area attractions contact the Grants Pass Visitors and Convention Bureau, 1501 N.E. 6th St., P.O. Box 1787, Grants Pass, OR 97526; phone (503) 476-5510 or (800) 547-5927.

GRANTS PASS MUSEUM OF ART in Riverside Park exhibits American art. Allow 30 minutes minimum. Tues.-Sat. noon-4. Free. Phone (503) 479-3290.

ROGUE RIVER BOAT TRIPS explore the Hellgate Canyon region. Minimum age restrictions may apply; phone for information. Reservations are recommended.

Galice Resort and Store Raft Trips depart from Galice Resort, 11744 Galice Rd., 15 mi. w. of I-5 Merlin exit 61. Full- and half-day guided raft tours are offered. Self-guiding trips also are available. Full-day trips include lunch. Full-day trip departs daily at 9, May-Sept. Half-day trips depart daily at 9 and 1, May-Sept. Full-day trip $50. Half-day trip $35. MC, VI. **Discount.** Phone (503) 476-3818.

Grants Pass Float Co. offers 2-hour, half-day and full-day excursions in inflatable kayaks or rafts departing from the Riverside Motel in downtown Grants Pass. Two-and three-day trips also are available. Full- and half-day trips depart daily at 8:15, May 15-Sept. 30. Full-day trip $50. Half-day trip with lunch $40. Half-day trip without lunch $35. Two-hour trip $20. AE, DS, MC, VI. **Discount.** Reservations are required. Contact Grants Pass Float Co., 209 Merlin Rd., Merlin, OR 97532. Phone (503) 479-2455 or (800) 63-KAYAK.

Orange Torpedo Trips offers 2-hour, half-day, full-day and multiday guided white-water trips in inflatable kayaks, rafts and paddle-rafts May-Sept. Two- and 3-day trips on the Rogue and 3-day trips on the North Umpqua and Klamath rivers also are available. The 3-day trip on the Rogue River is available Monday and Friday.

The 2-hour trip departs daily at 10:30 and 2:30. Half- and full-day trips depart daily at 8:30. Two-hour trip $20. Half-day trip $35. Full-day trip $50. Two-day trip $225. Mon. 3-day Rogue River trip $510. Fri. 3-day Rogue River trip $535. Three-day Klamath River trip $305-$435. AE, DS, MC, VI. **Discount.**

Reservations are required. Contact Orange Torpedo Trips, P.O. Box 1111, Merlin, OR 97532. Phone (503) 479-5061 or (800) 635-2925.

Rogue River Hellgate Jetboat Excursions to Hellgate Canyon depart from the Riverside Inn on the north bank of the Rogue River between 6th and 7th sts. Two-hour, 36-mile trips; 4-hour, 36-mile champagne brunch and dinner cruises; and 5-hour, 75-mile white-water trips are available.

Two-hour trip departs daily at 8:45 and 1:45, June 15-Aug. 31; at 8:45 and 12:45, in Sept.; and at 1:45, May 1-June 14. Brunch trip departs Sat.-Sun. at 9:15, May 8-Sept. 30. Dinner trip departs daily at 4:15, May 7-Aug. 31; at 3:15, in Sept. Five-hour white-water trip departs daily at 9:45 and 3:15, May 1-June 10; at 8:15 and 2:45, June 11-Aug. 31; at 8:45 and 2:45, in Sept. Two-hour trip $21; ages 4-11, $11. Brunch trip $32; ages 4-11, $19. Dinner trip $37; ages 4-11, $22. White-water trip $39; ages 4-11, $25.

Contact Hellgate Jetboat Excursions, 953 S.E. 7th St., Grants Pass, OR 97526. Phone (503) 479-7204 or (800) 648-4874. *See ad p. 56.*

Rogue River Raft and Fishing Trips, off I-5 in Merlin at 8500 Galice Rd., offers full-day guided fishing trips Sept. 1-Nov. 15 and 1-, 2- and 3-day white-water raft and 4-day camping trips from June 1 to mid-Sept. Two- and 3-day trips include accommodations in remote lodges. Fishing trip

NATURALLY
EXCITING

Fishing, rafting and jetboating on the famed Rogue River, plus golf, hiking and bike trails. With an historic downtown, and over 1000 quality rooms, Grants Pass is only one hour from California on I-5 or on Hwy. 199 from the coast.
FOR MOTEL, RV AND CAMPING INFORMATION: 1-800-547-5927.

GRANTS PASS
Oregon
Nature's Amusement Park

P.O. Box 1787, Dept. A5, Grants Pass, Oregon 97526

$190 per 2-person boat. One-day raft trip $240 per 6-person raft. Two-day lodge/raft trip $350 per person. Three-day lodge/raft trip $450 per person. Three-day camp/lodge/raft trip $425 per person. Four-day camping trip $425 per person.

Reservations are required. Contact Morrison's Rogue River Lodge, 8500 Galice Rd., Merlin, OR 97532. Phone (503) 476-3825 or (800) 826-1963.

SCHMIDT HOUSE MUSEUM, 508 S.W. 5th St., is a turn-of-the-20th-century, two-story structure built for the family of pioneer businessman Claus Schmidt. Most of the rooms contain the Schmidt's original furnishings and fixtures including an antique toy collection and an old hand pump. A research library also is available. Allow 30 minutes minimum. Tues.-Fri. 10-4 Memorial Day-Labor Day; 1-4, rest of year. Admission $1. Phone (503) 479-7827.

GRESHAM (B-4) pop. 68,200

Gresham was founded in 1852 by pioneers who cut a trail through the wilderness as they came over Mount Hood on their way to the Willamette Valley. Gresham is now the gateway to the Columbia River Gorge and the Mount Hood recreation area and offers abundant recreational activities including boating, fishing, hiking and skiing.

Music lovers flock to Gresham the last two weeks in July for the Windjam Northwest, and the first week in August for the Mount Hood Festival of Jazz which features international, national and regional artists.

ROGUE RIVER
Hellgate
JETBOAT EXCURSIONS
Hellgate EXCURSIONS
Reservations, Brochure & Information
1-800-648-4874
SOUTHERN OREGON
Breathtaking scenery & wildlife, fully interpreted tours through famous Hellgate Canyon.
• 2-hr Scenic, 4-hr Dinner or Brunch & 5-hr Whitewater Excursions.
• Daily Departures: May-thru-September
FROM $21 - $39
Hellgate JETBOAT EXCURSIONS
953 S.E. 7th St, Grants Pass, OR 97526 • (503) 479-7204
JUST OFF I-5
EXITS 55 - 58

HAINES (C-11) pop. 400, elev. 3,334'

EASTERN OREGON MUSEUM, 4 blks. off US 30, has a reconstructed blacksmith shop, kitchen, parlor, an old saloon bar, an 1880s train depot, a doll collection and pioneer relics including household, mining and farming artifacts. Allow 30 minutes minimum. Daily 9-5, Apr. 15-Oct. 15; by appointment rest of year. Donations. Phone (503) 856-3233.

★HELLS CANYON NATIONAL RECREATION AREA (B-12)

The 652,977-acre Hells Canyon National Recreation Area straddles the Snake River Canyon and encompasses parts of national forests in northeastern Oregon and western Idaho. The area is reached via SRs 82 and 86 in Oregon and US 95 in Idaho.

Confined within steep, eroded black basalt walls, the surging Snake River has carved North America's deepest gorge, measuring 7,913 feet from He Devil Mountain to Granite Creek below. White-water rapids alternating with deep pools characterize this 71-mile portion of the Snake River as it races north to meet the Columbia River.

The varied elevations of Hells Canyon support mixed plant communities sheltering such wildlife as bears, bobcats, bighorn sheep, cougars, elks, mule deers, mountain goats and many smaller birds, mammals and reptiles. Sturgeon, reputedly growing up to 11 feet long, inhabit the Snake River, sharing it with bass, catfish, salmon, steelhead and rainbow trout.

From the desert-like canyon floor to the alpine lakes of the Seven Devils region, the area presents a variety of recreational opportunities including boating, float trips and backpacking. From Pittsburg Landing, the Kirkwood Historic Ranch and Museum, once the home of Idaho governor and U.S. senator Len B. Jordan, is accessible by powerboat, floatboat or pack trail.

The Rapid River originates in the Seven Devils Mountains and eventually joins the Little Salmon River. The forks of the Rapid River provide quality water for raising Chinook salmon and therefore house the Rapid River Fish Hatchery.

The 214,000-acre Hells Canyon Wilderness, with its extensive trail system, protects a large portion of the canyon along the Oregon-Idaho border. If you plan to fish the lakes and the Snake River shoreline, you must acquire the appropriate state licenses *(see For Your Information box)*; both Oregon and Idaho licenses are valid for boat fishing on the river.

The Hells Canyon Scenic Byway is a series of routes to and through the Hells Canyon National Recreation Area. On the Oregon side, the best route is a two-lane paved loop which originates in Baker City. From Baker City follow SR 86 to Richland for approximately 41 miles. From Richland continue on SR 86 north for 11 miles to Halfway. Nine miles north of Halfway, SR 86 will intersect with FS 39N. Take FS 39N through the heart of Hells Canyon, high mountain country and through the town of Joseph to Enterprise. One mile west of Enterprise on SR 82 you will find the Wallowa Mountain Visitors Center. Continue along SR 82 west for approximately 64 miles and you will be back on I-84 at La Grande. The entire loop will take approximately 5 hours.

Another possible route from the Oregon side to the recreation area is via SR 82 to Enterprise and Joseph. From Joseph it is possible to go to Hat Point, a 6,982-foot ridge overlooking Hells Canyon, via Imnaha. The route to Hat Point follows FS 4240, a gravel, narrow road with steep grades

Another route from Imnaha, FS 3955, parallels the Imnaha River as it meanders through rims and benches similar to those along the Snake River. This route connects with the Wallowa Mountain Loop (FS 39), which leads back to Joseph or Halfway. FS 3955 and FS 39 are maintained for cars and trailers. FS 39 can be followed east to FS 3965 which leads to the Hells Canyon overlook. With an elevation of 6,000 feet, the overlook provides a spectacular view of the Wallowa mountains in Oregon and Idaho.

For maps and brochures of different drives contact the Baker County Visitors and Convention Bureau, 490 Campbell, Baker City, OR 97814; phone (503) 523-3356 or (800) 523-1235.

Buckhorn Springs, a scenic area overlooking the Imnaha drainage, can be reached from FS 46 off SR 3, a mostly gravel logging road.

On the Idaho side the best route to the canyon is SR 71. From Cambridge, Idaho, the road runs 29 miles northwest to Oxbow, crossing the Snake near Brownlee Dam. It crosses back into Idaho at Oxbow, then follows the river north to Hells Canyon Dam. The total distance is about 55 miles.

Note: It is advisable to check with the Hells Canyon Recreation Area regarding road conditions and construction. Some roads are gravel and caution should be exercised. Phone (503) 426-4978.

More than 30 outfitters provide float and jet boat trips down the Snake River from Hells Canyon Dam and jet boat trips upstream from Lewiston. For a list of local outfitters contact the Supervisor, Hells Canyon National Recreation Area, 2535 Riverside Dr., P.O. Box 699, Clarkston, WA 99403; phone (509) 758-0616 for information or 758-1957 for reservations. *See Recreation Chart and the AAA Northwestern CampBook.*

HELLS CANYON ADVENTURES, SR 86 to Hells Canyon Dam, offers guided 2-, 3- and 6-hour jet boat trips and white-water raft trips daily May through September as well as fishing and hunting excursions on the Snake River. Additional tours are available. Two-hour trip departs at 2. Three-hour trip departs at 10. Six-hour and white-water trips depart at 9. Two-hour trip $25; under 12, $10. Three-hour trip $30; under 12, $15. Six-hour trip $80; under 12, $30. White-water trip $95. Reservations are required. Contact Hells

Whitewater Rafting - RV Park & Campground
* Raft Trips from 1day to 1 week
* The Salmon "River of No Return"
* The Snake River in Hells Canyon
* Riverfront RV Park & Campground
* Open year round.* GOLD Panning
FULL SERVICE OUTDOOR CENTER
Northwest Voyageurs
Color Vacation Guide 1-800-727-9977 - PO Box 373 Lucile, Id 83542

ATTRACTION ADMISSION DISCOUNTS

Some attractions offer discounts to members upon presentation of a valid AAA or CAA membership card. The word **Discount** follows prices in the listings of attractions that have agreed to give reduced rates to members during the period that book is current. Participating attractions individually determine the terms of the discount they offer. The discount may not apply in cases where any other rate reduction is offered, or if tickets are purchased through an agent, rather than at the attraction's ticket office.

Canyon Adventures, P.O. Box 159, Oxbow, OR 97840. Phone (503) 785-3352 or (800) 422-3568. *See ad.*

HERMISTON (B-10) pop. 10,000

Crisscrossed with irrigation canals, Hermiston and the surrounding farmland were claimed from the desert as part of the Umatilla Irrigation Project. Fields of fruit, grain and vegetables now carpet land once hospitable only to sagebrush. Hermiston is regionally known for its fine desert honey, potatoes and watermelons. The nearby Columbia River provides hunting, fishing and other recreational opportunities.

HILLSBORO (B-3) pop. 37,500, elev. 174'

Hillsboro, founded in 1842, was home for several of the settlers who helped establish a civil government for the Oregon Territory. Hillsboro, 20 minutes west of Portland, is nestled in the Tualatin Valley half-way between the Cascade Mountains and the Pacific Ocean. The city is known as a center for high-tech industries such as computers and electronics.

The area produces thousands of gallons of berry and fruit wines annually; the climate is similar to the grape-growing region of France. Local wineries offer tastings and guided tours.

Every July as part of the Rose Festival, an air show draws 150,000 spectators to the Hillsboro Airport. Also during the summer, Hillsboro hosts the Washington County Fair, a rodeo, free Thursday night concerts in the park and a weekly farmers' market. For further information contact the Greater Hillsboro Area Chamber of Commerce, 334 S.E. 5th Ave., Hillsboro, OR 97123; phone (503) 648-1102.

OAK KNOLL WINERY, off SR 219 on Burkhalter Rd., offers self-guiding tours and tastings. In mid-May, The Bacchus Fest features live music, food booths and wine tasting. Allow 30 minutes minimum. Sun.-Fri. noon-5, Sat. 11-5. Free. Phone (503) 648-8198.

HOOD RIVER (B-8) pop. 4,600, elev. 154'

In addition to being one of Oregon's major apple-growing regions, the Hood River Valley is among the world's leading producers of winter pears. A 47-mile loop through the valley via SR 35 south to Parkdale, then north on SR 281 to Hood River, winds through the heart of fruit country.

The Mount Hood Loop Highway, SR 35, starts at the east edge of Hood River, off I-84 exit 64, and circles the eastern shoulder of Mount Hood *(see Mount Hood and Mount Hood National Forest).* Panorama Point, 3½ miles south on Eastside Road, gives a sweeping view of the Hood River Valley. I-84 also provides scenic vistas from Boardman to Troutdale.

The Mount Hood Railroad, departing from the Hood River Depot with a stop in Parkdale, provides 4-hour scenic trips through the Hood River Valley. For information and reservations contact Mount Hood Railroad, 110 Railroad Ave., Hood River, OR 97301; phone (503) 386-3556 or (800) 872-4661. Hood River Vineyards, 4693 Westwood Dr., offers guided tours and tastings March through November; phone (503) 386-3772.

The Hood River Expo Center, off I-84 exit 63, is the site of international sailboarding events. The sailpark also is available to amateur sailboarders.

For further information contact the Hood River County Chamber of Commerce, Port Marina Park, Hood River, OR 97031; phone (503) 386-2000 or (800) 366-3530.

Shopping areas: A variety of shops downtown caters to sailboarders, as well as those looking for crafts and antiques.

HOOD RIVER COUNTY HISTORICAL MUSEUM is in Port Marina Park; from I-84 exit 64 follow signs. The museum displays pioneer artifacts and exhibits on area history. Allow 1 hour minimum. Wed.-Sat. 10-4, Sun. noon-4, Mon. and Tues. by appointment, Apr.-Oct. Free. Phone (503) 386-6772.

LUHR JENSEN & SONS INC., 400 Portway, manufactures fishing lures and accessories. Allow 30 minutes minimum. Guided tours are available Mon.-Fri. at 11 and 1:30. Reservations are required for groups of five or more. Phone (503) 386-3811.

JACKSONVILLE (G-6) pop. 1,900, elev. 1,640'

Founded in 1852, Jacksonville encompasses a large assortment of preserved pioneer buildings—more than 80 of which have historical markers. This collection is the result of "gold fever"; it was here that the Pacific Northwest's first gold discovery occurred. A variety of museums reflects pioneer life in the 1800s.

The town is known for its Britt Festivals, held from mid-June through early September(**discount**). The series features festivals of internationally known classical, country, folk, jazz and pop music as well as dance and musical theater.

SEE HELLS CANYON
"the deepest part"
HCA
1-Day WHITE WATER RAFTING
JET BOAT TOURS
Hells Canyon Adventures, Inc.
Box 159, Oxbow, Oregon 97840
TOLL FREE
1-800-422-3568
or (503) 785-3352
Fax (503) 785-3353

Picnicking is permitted on the grounds. For ticket information and program schedules contact Britt Festivals, P.O. Box 1124, Medford, OR 97501; phone (503) 773-6077 or (800) 88-BRITT.

The community also celebrates Jacksonville Pioneer Days in June, and in December hosts a Victorian Christmas Celebration.

Self-guiding tours: Walking tours past historic sites in the downtown area are detailed on brochures available at the information center at the Rogue River Valley Railway Depot, Oregon and C streets. The depot is open daily 10-4, June-Aug.; Sat.-Mon. 10-4, rest of the year. Phone (503) 899-8118.

Shopping areas: California and Oregon streets offer a variety of specialty shops offering such items as crafts and antiques.

BEEKMAN BANK, 3rd and California sts., was the second bank in Oregon. Closed in 1915 at the death of founder C.C. Beekman, the bank contains all its original 1863 furnishings preserved behind glass. Allow 30 minutes minimum. Daily 1-5, Memorial Day-Labor Day. Free. Phone (503) 773-6536.

BEEKMAN HOUSE, 352 E. California St., is a well-preserved home reflecting the lifestyle of a well-to-do 19th-century businessman. The 1875 house contains original furnishings. Living-history programs on the life of the Beekman family are available Monday through Friday. Allow 30 minutes minimum. Daily 1-5, Memorial Day-Labor Day. Admission $2; ages 6-12, $1. Phone (503) 773-6536.

CHILDREN'S MUSEUM, 5th and D sts. in the old jail, portrays the daily life of Indians and settlers 1850-1930; many of the articles displayed may be handled. Allow 30 minutes minimum. Daily 10-5, Memorial Day weekend-Labor Day; Wed.-Sat. 10-5, Tues. and Sun. noon-5, rest of year. Closed Jan. 1, Thanksgiving and Dec. 25. Admission $2, under 6 free. Phone (503) 773-6536.

JACKSONVILLE MUSEUM OF SOUTHERN OREGON HISTORY, in an 1883 courthouse, displays an extensive collection of pioneer relics, Victorian exhibits, a railroad history exhibit and an early photography display. Allow 30 minutes minimum. Daily 10-5, Memorial Day weekend-Labor Day; Wed.-Sat. 10-5, Tues. and Sun. noon-5, rest of year. Closed Jan. 1, Thanksgiving and Dec. 25. Admission $2; under 6 free. Phone (503) 773-6536.

VALLEY VIEW VINEYARD, 8 mi. s. off SR 238, has guided tours and tastings. Allow 30 minutes

FISH HATCHERIES

Oregon's fish hatcheries produce 80 percent of all trout and 69 percent of all coho salmon harvested in the state each year; about 90 million fish are raised in hatcheries annually. The hatcheries provide anglers and the commercial fishing industry with sport and livelihood. Nearly 600,000 fishing licenses are sold annually, and revenue from commercial licenses and landing fees brings in $2 million a year. The commercial fishing industry nets around $200 million annually.

Hatcheries protect natural fish populations by breeding a supply of fish which can be harvested. By focusing the attention of commercial and sport fishing on hatchery fish, wild populations are allowed to proliferate. Fishing regulations also support this effort. For example, in some streams the release of hooked wild steelhead trout is required. Hatchery steelhead can be distinguished from wild steelhead by checking the adipose fins. Hatchery steelhead have the adipose fins—those on the back near the tail—snipped off before release into the natural environment.

Hatcheries became necessary as the human demand for fish exceeded the natural supply. The first Oregon hatchery was built in 1877 on the Clackamas River and operated by the federal government. Hatcheries support a renewed commitment to protect and restore wild fish.

Most hatcheries are open to the public free of charge. Visitors may watch the spawning process, see the fish being fed—and sometimes feed the fish themselves—and observe the fish in various stages of growth. Contact individual hatcheries for more specific information on seasonal fish raising activities.

Salmon and steelhead trout, after living most of their lives in salt water, return to spawn in the fresh waters where they were raised. When hatchery-raised fish spawn in the fall, the eggs are taken from the females and fertilized by the males. The eggs are then placed in incubation trays until they hatch. Wild specimens caught in hatchery nets are returned to the wild. Cutthroat and steelhead trout usually spawn from February through March; rainbow trout spawn from September through February. Coho and Chinook salmon spawn from August through December.

For more information contact the Oregon Dept. of Fish and Wildlife, 2501 S.W. 1st St., P.O. Box 59, Portland, OR 97207; phone (503) 229-5403.

minimum. Daily 11-5; closed Jan. 1, Thanksgiving and Dec. 25. Phone (503) 899-8468.

JEWELL (A-2)

JEWELL MEADOWS WILDLIFE AREA is 1½ mi. w. on SR 202. Divided among three land parcels totaling 1,200 acres, the Jewell Meadows Wildlife Area affords views of Roosevelt Elk and other native animals. Three marked viewpoints designate the area where the elk feed and rest. Daily 24 hours. Free. Phone (503) 229-5400.

JOHN DAY (D-10) pop. 1,800, elev. 3,083′

John Day, for whom the town was named, was a young Virginian and scout of the Astor overland expedition of 1811. During the gold-rush years of 1862-64, mail carried by horseback passed through town from Canyon City to The Dalles.

Besides transporting mail at the rate of 50c a letter, the daring riders often carried fortunes in gold dust. Attacks by bandits and hostile Indians were among the rigors of the job. By 1864, pony express riders were replaced by pack trains and freight wagons over The Dalles Military Wagon Road.

Modern John Day is a business community and trading center. Descendants of gold miners raise cattle and log the surrounding timberlands. For information on special events contact the Grant County Chamber of Commerce, 281 W. Main St., John Day, OR 97845; phone (503) 575-0547.

Lying in a broad valley, John Day is almost surrounded by the steep hills and rugged peaks of Malheur National Forest *(see place listing)*, whose headquarters and a district office are in town. The office provides maps and other information about recreational activities in the forest.

KAM WAH CHUNG & CO. MUSEUM, ½-blk. n. of US 26 next to the city park, was a Chinese doctor's office and store in the mid-1880s. Displays include relics, artifacts, more than 1,000 herbs, and western and Chinese medicines used by an herbal doctor. Allow 30 minutes minimum. Mon.-Thurs. 9-noon and 1-5, Sat-Sun. 1-5, May-Oct. Admission $2; senior citizens and ages 13-18, $1; under 12, 50c. Phone (503) 575-0028 or 575-0547.

JOHN DAY FOSSIL BEDS NATIONAL MONUMENT

Comprising 14,000 acres in east-central Oregon, the monument contains a variety of plant and animal fossils. The monument consists of three units: the Sheep Rock Unit, 7 miles northwest of Dayville on US 26; the Clarno Unit, 18 miles west of Fossil on SR 218; and the Painted Hills Unit, 9 miles northwest of Mitchell off US 26. Each unit displays different colored formations.

Fossil collecting is strictly prohibited, but many other activities are available. Hiking and picnicking are popular, and wildlife and wildflowers are abundant throughout the park. The John Day River offers trout fishing in season. Information centers with exhibits are 2 miles north of the junction of SR 19 and US 26 in the Sheep Rock Unit and at monument headquarters, 420 W. Main St. Allow 30 minutes minimum. Free. Phone (503) 575-0721 or 987-2333.

JORDAN VALLEY (F-12) pop. 400

In the center of Jordan Valley stands a *pelota fronton,* or ball court, which was built by the area's Basque settlers in 1915 for playing pelota, a game similar to American handball.

Driven by economic hardship and political oppression, thousands of Basques left their homeland in the Pyrenees in the late 1800s and settled in the western United States. Some became masons, fishermen or miners, but most became range sheepherders.

The Basques, independent people believed to be the oldest surviving race in Europe, lived a nomadic life herding flocks. They traveled across western ranges in search of better pastures, accepting sheep instead of wages. A few Basque sheepherders still roam the area, but most gradually assimilated into the country's urban culture.

Jordan Crater, which erupted just 2,500 years ago, is one of the youngest volcanoes in the continental United States. Antelope Reservoir, 10 miles southwest of town, offers trout fishing and boating. The Jordan Valley Big Loop Rodeo is held the third weekend in May.

JOSEPH (C-11) pop. 1,100, elev. 4,400′

The secluded town of Joseph, near Wallowa Lake State Park *(see Recreation Chart and the AAA Northwestern CampBook)* and the gateway to Hells Canyon National Recreation Area *(see place listing)*, is a popular vacation spot. Four bronze casting foundries and several art galleries specializing in bronze sculpture are in the vicinity.

Day-long pack trips, which include food, horses and guide, are available in the High Wallowas. Nearby Ferguson Ridge provides downhill skiing.

Joseph hosts a variety of events including the Vintage Car Mountain Cruise the first weekend in June and the Hot Air Balloon Rally in mid-June. The Chief Joseph Days Rodeo and the Jazz at the Lake Festival are held in July, and September is the month for both the Alpenfest and the Rattlesnake and Bear Feed. Further information is available from the Joseph Chamber of Commerce, P.O. Box 13, Joseph, OR 97848; phone (503) 432-1015.

WALLOWA COUNTY MUSEUM, on SR 82, exhibits historical artifacts from Wallowa County.

Allow 30 minutes minimum. Daily 10-5, Memorial Day weekend-late Sept. Donations. Phone (503) 432-6095.

JUNCTION CITY (E-3) pop. 3,700

Vast fields and fresh air continue to attract visitors to Junction City just as they once invited pioneers traveling the Oregon Trail to settle here.

The 4-day Scandinavian Fest is held in mid-August; each day is dedicated to a Nordic nationality—Danish, Finnish, Norwegian and Swedish. Festivities include native dances, clothing, crafts and food. For further information contact the Junction City-Harrisburg Area Chamber of Commerce, 565 Greenwood St., Junction City, OR 97448; phone (503) 998-6154.

KLAMATH FALLS (G-7) pop. 17,700

Upper Klamath Lake,bordered for 20 miles by US 97, is one of the largest bodies of fresh water in the state.

The Klamath Basin, on the Pacific flyway, contains six national wildlife refuges: Butte Valley Wildlife Area, Crater Lake National Park *(see place listing)*, Lower Klamath National Wildlife Refuge *(see attraction listing)*, Lava Beds National Monument, Modoc National Forest and Winema National Forest *(see place listing)*.

The white pelican is an interesting and familiar sight on nearby lakes and rivers. Protected by law, the bird often has a wingspan of 10 feet.

A local phenomenon in the city is the underground supply of geothermally heated water. Piped through radiators and grids, the water is used to heat homes, schools and businesses and melt snow from sidewalks, steps and the Esplanade St. Bridge. During the summer months an old-fashioned trolley winds through downtown.

For further information contact the Klamath County Chamber of Commerce, 507 Main St., Klamath Falls, OR 97601-6031; phone (503) 884-5193. The chamber is open Mon.-Fri. 8:30-5. The Klamath County Department of Tourism is in the Klamath County Museum *(see attraction listing)*; phone (503) 884-0666.

BALDWIN HOTEL MUSEUM, 31 Main St., contains original hotel furnishings from the early 1900s. Guided tours are available June through September. Tour options include first and second floors, third and fourth floors or all four floors. Allow 1 hour, 30 minutes minimum. Tues.-Sat. 10-4, June-Sept.; closed holidays. Fee for two-floor tour $2, over 55 and students $1.50, family rate $5. Four-floor tour $4, over 55 and students $3, family rate $10. Phone (503) 883-4207.

THE FAVELL MUSEUM OF WESTERN ART AND INDIAN ARTIFACTS, 125 West Main St., displays arrowheads, baskets, beadwork and stone carvings. Also shown are works by Western artists, coins, minerals, pioneer relics, rocks and a collection of miniature firearms. Allow 1 hour minimum. Mon.-Sat. 9:30-5:30. Admission $4; over 65, $3; ages 6-16, $2; family rate $12. DS, MC, VI. **Discount.** Phone (503) 882-9996.

KLAMATH COUNTY MUSEUM, 1451 Main St., depicts the history of Klamath County from the Modoc Indian Wars of the 1860s to the present. Exhibits focus on wildlife as well as Indian and pioneer history. Allow 30 minutes minimum. Mon.-Sat. 9-5:30, Sun. 9-5, June-Sept.; Mon.-Sat. 8-4:30, rest of year. Donations. Phone (503) 883-4208.

LOWER KLAMATH NATIONAL WILDLIFE REFUGE, 47,600 acres 20 mi. e. off US 97 on SR 161, provides shelter for large numbers of migratory waterfowl, including thousands of snow geese. Established by President Theodore Roosevelt in 1908, it is one of the nation's oldest waterfowl refuges. Not only waterfowl visit here—some 300-500 bald eagles arrive in November through April. Allow 1 hour minimum. Phone (916) 667-2231.

LA GRANDE (C-11) pop. 11,800, elev. 2,784′

La Grande, named in honor of the area's beauty, is on the western edge of the Grande Ronde Valley at the foot of the Blue Mountains. To the east rise the Wallowa Mountains. The area, which produces fruit, livestock and lumber products, also is rich in recreational opportunities, including fishing, hiking and skiing. The area's hot springs provide steam and mineral baths.

La Grande also is home to Eastern Oregon State College. A 93-mile scenic stretch of I-84 passes through Union County, intersecting with SR 82.

Annual events in La Grande include the Eastern Oregon Livestock Show in June; the Catherine Creek Junior Rodeo and Elgin Stampede and the Union County Fair in July; and Oregon Trail Days and the Blue Mountain Rodeo in August. For more information phone the La Grande-Union County Chamber of Commerce at 2111 Adams Ave., La Grande, OR 97850; phone (503) 963-8588 or (800) 848-9969.

LAKEVIEW (G-8) pop. 2,500, elev. 4,800′

One of the highest towns in Oregon and the county seat of Lake County, Lakeview is at the foot of the Warner mountains and on the edge of the southeast Oregon high desert. Towering 2,000 feet above Albert Lake and the surrounding plateau is Abert Rim, a 30-mile fault escarpment crowned with a sheer 800-foot lava cap. The lake is fed with fresh water from the Chewaucan River. Lt. John Fremont discovered the rim and lake in 1843 in his search for the mythical Buena Ventura River, which supposedly flowed from Klamath Lake to San Francisco Bay. Fremont named the scarp for his chief, Col. J.J. Abert.

Lakeview was established in 1876, some 30 years after Fremont's exploration. After the Indians were subdued, a land office was set up, and the vast rangeland surrounding the new community was opened to ranchers. From its days as a cow town, Lakeview has continued its role as the business center for the region. Industries center on agriculture, government services, lumber, tourism and wood products.

The town celebrates its Western heritage over Labor Day weekend during the Lake County Fair and Round-Up, one of the Northwest's oldest amateur rodeos.

Recreational activities are available around town and in the nearby Fremont National Forest *(see place listing)*. The national forest's desert country and mountains provide numerous opportunities for anglers, golfers, mountain bikers, hikers, hunters, rockhounds and skiers. Hang gliding also is a popular sport in this area. Warner Canyon Ski Area is 10 miles northeast off US 395. Native plants and wildlife can be seen along the Lakeview Nature Trail, which is entered through the Lakeview Park at Center and D streets.

One of the area's many natural features is the Old Perpetual Geyser, which is just north on US 395. Other interesting features are found along SR 31, which roughly follows Fremont's old route.

HART MOUNTAIN NATIONAL ANTELOPE REFUGE, 275,000 acres 65 mi. n.e., protects bighorn sheep, bobcats, golden eagles, mule deer, pronghorn antelope, sage grouse and other native wildlife. The natural focus of the refuge is Hart Mountain, a massive volcanic ridge which offers a range of landscapes from desert sagebrush and juniper to alpine streams and meadows.

Numerous canyons dot the terrain and shelter natural springs and hot springs. Primitive camping is available. Roads, often impassable November through April, are graveled and maintained throughout the tourist season.

SCHMINCK MEMORIAL MUSEUM, 1 blk. e. of US 395 at 128 S. E St., displays such relics of pioneer life as pressed-glass goblets and dishes. Fashions of the 1880s, including bustles, bows, hats and parasols, also are on display. Allow 30 minutes minimum. Tues.-Sat. 1-5, Feb.-Nov.; closed holidays. Admission $1; ages 12-18, 50c; ages 6-11, 25c. Phone (503) 947-3134.

LEBANON (D-3) pop. 11,000, elev. 333'

During the pioneer days of the 1800s, Lebanon was a stopping-off place on the Cascade Wagon Road. Some of the country roads found in Lebanon and the surrounding areas lead visitors to classic covered bridges and peaceful picnic sites.

The town is an agricultural center that celebrates nature's bounty with one of the world's largest strawberry shortcakes during the Lebanon Strawberry Festival in early June. For more information about the area contact the Lebanon Area Chamber of Commerce, 1040 Park St., Lebanon, OR 97355; phone (503) 258-7164.

LINCOLN CITY (C-2) pop. 5,900, elev. 114'

Lincoln City is a popular oceanside community offering 7½ miles of public beach. The town's recreational centerpiece is Devil's Lake State Park *(see Recreation Chart and the AAA Northwestern CampBook)*, which is favored by visitors who enjoy windsurfing, boating and other water sports. The nearby ocean, bay, estuaries and rivers provide excellent fishing, crabbing and mussel harvesting opportunities.

Built in 1914, Drift Creek covered bridge is one of the oldest bridges in Oregon. Favorite

WE'RE WITH YOU ALL THE WAY.

When you belong to AAA you're never alone. You have the security of AAA's Emergency Road Service behind you, plus the world's largest travel organization on hand. AAA does everything from booking airline tickets and lodgings to providing discounts on hotels and attractions, *fee-free* American Express® Travelers Cheques and free Triptik maps, TourBooks, CampBooks and CitiBooks. As a AAA member – you're in good company.

Contact your local AAA Club for more information.

pastimes include tidepooling, beachcombing, whale and bird watching, and golfing, with seven area courses. Cascade Head offers numerous hiking trails. Kite festivals are held in May, July and October. For more information contact the Lincoln City Visitor and Convention Bureau, 801 S.W. US 101, Lincoln City, OR 97367; phone (503) 994-8378 or (800) 452-2151. *See color ad.*

Shopping areas: Speciality shops fill a 7-mile stretch on US 101, offering items such as locally designed kites, antiques, beach bikes and handicrafts. Also located on US 101, Factory Stores At Lincoln City has more than 50 discount stores.

MADRAS (D-8) pop. 3,400, elev. 2,242′

Madras is surrounded by the high desert terrain and mountain peaks of the Mount Jefferson Wilderness Area. Warm Springs Indian Reservation is northwest via US 26. Rockhounding for thundereggs, the state rock, and agates is a popular activity, as is white-water rafting down the Deschutes River. Lake Billy Chinook, off US 97, offers water skiing and fishing. The Jefferson County Fair and Rodeo is held the last week of July.

Our cappuccinos aren't the only things that come with foam.
Call or write for a free vacation planning guide
1-800-452-2151
Lincoln City Visitor & Convention Bureau
801 SW Highway 101
Lincoln City, Oregon 97367
Or send $5 for our Lincoln City video brochure. It can't replace a visit, but it'll tide you over 'til you get here.
Lincoln City
Oregon
THE BEACH IS JUST THE BEGINNING

For a list of rockhounding locations and rafting operators, contact the Madras-Jefferson

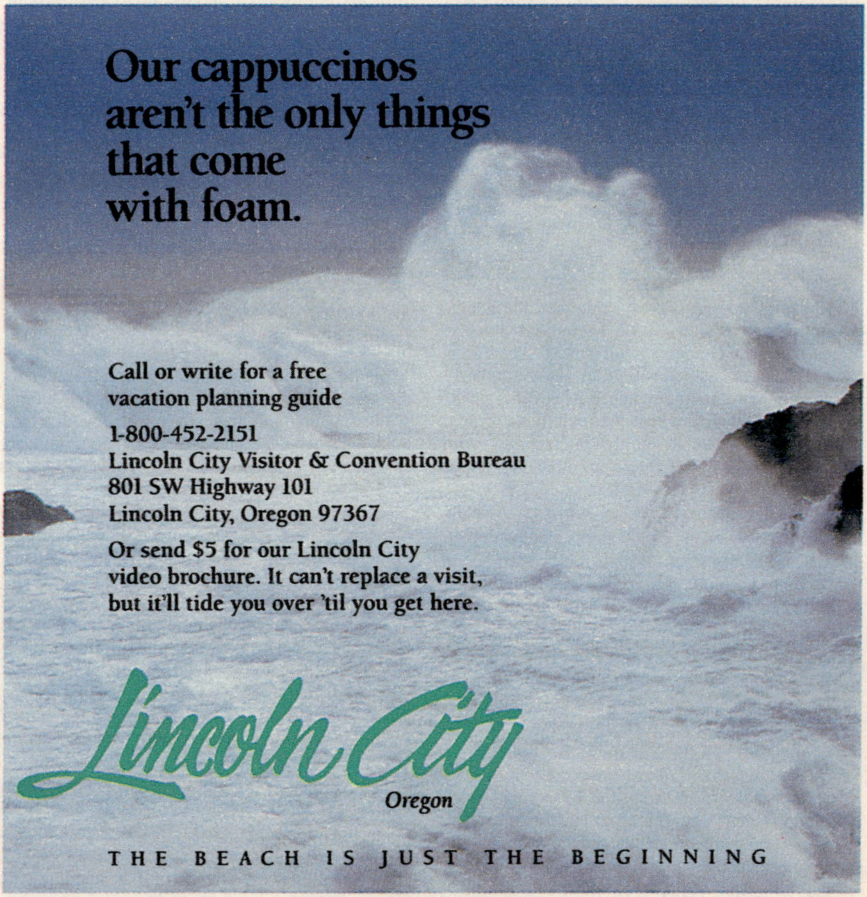

County Chamber of Commerce, 197 S.E. 5th St., P.O. Box 770, Madras, OR 97741; phone (503) 475-6975 or 475-2350.

★**THE COVE PALISADES STATE PARK,** 10 miles s.w. off US 97, encompasses Round Butte Dam and its reservoir, Lake Billy Chinook. Three geologically remarkable canyons have been carved by the Deschutes, the Crooked and the Metolius rivers, which meet in the park.

There are many developed recreational facilities, including those for water skiing. Houseboat rentals and fishing opportunities also are available. Park open Apr.-Oct. Phone (503) 546-3412. *See Recreation Chart.*

OREGON RIVER EXPERIENCES offers raft trips from Madras to Maupin to explore the Deschutes River. Trips range from 1 to 5 days. Other trips are available on several of Oregon's rivers. Fares begin at $65. For information and reservations contact Oregon River Experiences, 2 Jefferson Pkwy., #D7, Lake Oswego, OR 97035. Phone (503) 697-8133 or (800) 827-1358.

MALHEUR NATIONAL FOREST

Elevations in the forest range from 3,000 ft. near Fox Valley to 9,038 ft. at Strawberry Mountain. Refer to AAA maps for additional elevation information.

Malheur National Forest embraces the southwestern section of the Blue Mountains and extends south to Oregon's high desert. The forest reaches its highest elevation in the Strawberry Mountain Wilderness, which has several peaks over 8,000 feet. Elsewhere the mountains present rolling, forest-covered slopes interspersed with large meadows. Wildflowers brighten the slopes in season.

The Malheur River and the North Fork of the Malheur have their headwaters in the forest. These two rivers flow through rock canyons and provide opportunities for hiking, fishing and wildlife sightings.

Other major rivers in the forest include the headwaters of the Silvies and John Day rivers, as well as a number of smaller creeks. Of the several alpine lakes in the forest, the most popular is Magone, which is about 30 miles north of John Day; camping and picnicking are permitted.

Other areas of interest are the Strawberry Mountain Wilderness Area, the Monument Rock Wilderness and the Vinegar Hill-Indian Rock Scenic Area, with its abandoned gold mines and mountain meadows.

The extensive network of trails coupled with numerous forest roads make hiking a favorite activity, in addition to fishing, mountain biking, rockhounding and skiing, in season. Phone (503) 575-1731. *See Recreation Chart and the AAA Northwestern CampBook.*

McMINNVILLE (C-3) pop. 17,900, elev. 157′

Vineyards are scattered throughout Yamhill County, making McMinnville the center of Oregon's wine country. Yamhill Valley Vineyards, 16250 S.W. Oldsville Rd., offers guided tours and tastings mid-March through Thanksgiving.

Along with its more glamorous reputation as a wine-producing center, McMinnville is the home of Linfield College, established in 1857, as well as the HK-1 Flying Boat (formerly Howard Hughes' Spruce Goose). Points of interest on the 100-acre campus include the Renshaw Art Gallery and the Linfield Little Theater.

Locks used in the 1930s by steamboats towing log booms to Willamette sawmills are in Lafayette Locks County Park, northeast near Lafayette. Fort Yamhill Blockhouse, dating from 1855, is in nearby Dayton.

In early July McMinnville honors its agricultural heritage with the Turkey-Rama, which features a turkey barbecue, a street fair and an 8K run. Maps for historic walking tours are available at the Greater McMinnville Chamber of Commerce, 417 N. Adams St., McMinnville, OR 97128; phone (503) 472-6196.

Shopping areas: Layfayette School Antique Mall, on SR 99W, is in a restored 1910 schoolhouse. The mall features more than 100 antique dealers. Phone (503) 864-2720. Tanger Factory Outlet Center on SR 18 at Norton Lane has 25 stores. The downtown historic district is the location of art galleries in addition to specialty and retail stores.

MEDFORD (G-6) pop. 47,000, elev. 1,374′

Medford is a tourist and commercial center for the area's agricultural, manufacturing and lumber producing communities. Fruit growing is a primary industry—the city is known nationwide for its pears. An annual Pear Blossom Festival is held in mid-April.

Medford is headquarters for the Rogue River National Forest *(see place listing),* which offers opportunities for fishing, hunting and rafting. Points of interest in the immediate vicinity include the Butte Creek Mill, 10 miles north on SR 62, and Cole Rivers Fish Hatchery, north on SR 62 near Trail; the latter offers self-guiding tours.

Harry and David's Country Village at Southgate Mall, 2836 S. Pacific Rd., offers guided tours of a gift basket and plant packing house, including washing, sorting and packing; phone (503) 776-2121.

For further information on area attractions contact the Medford Convention and Visitors Bureau, 101 E. 8th St., Medford, OR 97501; phone (503) 779-4847. *See ad p. 65.*

A 60-mile scenic stretch of I-5, beginning in Grants Pass and running to the California state line, passes through Medford.

ADVENTURE CENTER—*see Ashland.*

HISTORY CENTER is at 106 N. Central Ave. Housed in a remodeled 1940s J.C. Penney Co.

Inc. department store building, the History Center houses historical exhibits describing the history of southern Oregon and a research library. Displays include quilts, furniture, clothing, tools, toys, appliances and American Indian artifacts. The research library contains books, maps and manuscripts; several photographs in the library's collection were taken by 19th-century pioneer photographer Peter Britt. Allow 1 hour minimum. History Center open Mon.-Fri. 9-5, Sat. noon-5. Research library Tues.-Sat 1-5. Closed major holidays. Free. Phone (503) 773-6536.

MONMOUTH (D-3) pop. 6,300

PAUL JENSEN ARCTIC MUSEUM, 590 W. Church St., on the campus of Western Oregon State College, displays extensive collections of arctic art and artifacts and an exhibit presenting the sights and sounds of an arctic day. Allow 1 hour minimum. Tues.-Sat. 10-4; closed Jan. 1, Thanksgiving and Dec. 25. Admission $2. Phone (503) 838-8468.

MOUNT ANGEL (C-4) pop. 2,800

Founded in 1880 as a German community, Mount Angel attracted Benedictine monks from Switzerland who built Mount Angel Abbey on a hilltop overlooking the present town.

In late July Mount Angel hosts a 3-day Bach Festival; wine and cheese or similar fare is served in the Abbey gardens. Oktoberfest takes place the third week of September and features German folk music, street dancing, a Biergarten and German foods. For more information contact the Mount Angel Chamber of Commerce, P.O. Box 221, Mount Angel, OR 97362; phone (503) 845-9440.

MOUNT HOOD AND MOUNT HOOD NATIONAL FOREST

Elevations in the forest range from 200 ft. at the Columbia River to 11,239 ft. at Mount Hood. Refer to AAA maps for additional elevation information.

The Mount Hood National Forest reaches from the Columbia River along the Cascades to Mount Jefferson and from the foothills east of Portland to the central Oregon plateau. From Portland, the forest may be entered either from SR 26 or I-205 to SRs 212 and 224. The Hood River entrance to the forest is off SR 35S.

Majestic Mount Hood rises 11,239 feet in splendid isolation, dominating the horizon for miles around. Many living glaciers extend to near the timberline on all sides. The peak is the highlight of the Mount Hood National Forest and the highest point in the state. Alpine meadows, waterfalls, glaciers, hot springs, and more than 4,000 miles of streams and 160 lakes grace the forest.

The Columbia River Gorge was formed by an ancient river of lava that also created nearby 620-foot Multnomah Falls. Spectacular scenic drives include the Mount Hood Loop and the Clackamas River Highway.

Forested acreage consists primarily of conifers—cedar, fir, hemlock, pine and spruce. Badger Creek, Bull of the Woods, Columbia, Mount Hood, Salmon Huckleberry and part of the Mount Jefferson Wilderness are specially preserved wilderness areas comprising 51,000 acres within the forest.

SOUTHERN OREGON'S VACATION HEADQUARTERS

MEDFORD

Located just across the California border on I-5, Medford is your vacation headquarters. 1500 quality rooms, delightful dining, shopping and super attractions; History, Culture, Recreation...

• World-renowned Crater Lake • Jazz Festival in October • Rafting on the Rogue River• Historic 1860's Mining Town - Jacksonville • The famous Oregon Shakespeare Festival • Winter and Summer Fun - fishing, skiing, hiking • Warm Hugs and Sunny Skies - 240 sunny days a year

WE HUG VISITORS IN MEDFORD

Visit the Visitor Information Center at the South Gateway Country Village by the clock tower. Take I-5 Exit 27 and follow the signs. Call or write: Medford Visitors Bureau, 101 E. 8th, Medford, OR 97501, **(503) 779-4847(HUGS)**

Recreational activities are varied; there are picnic areas, campgrounds and a 1,200-mile network of trails. Several downhill skiing areas, including year-round skiing at Timberline, are in the Government Camp area; cross-country skiing and snowshoeing can be pursued in other areas. For additional information contact the Forest Supervisor at 2955 N.W. Division St., Gresham, OR 97030; phone (503) 666-0771. *See Recreation Chart and the AAA Northwestern CampBook.*

MOUNT HOOD LOOP HIGHWAY permits scenic views from Government Camp to Hood River. The loop begins in Portland on I-84 and travels east through the canyon carved by the Columbia River. At Hood River, take SR 35 south to view the orchards and forested Hood River Valley. US 26 passes Barlow Pass, which was used by pioneers traveling the Old Oregon Trail from The Dalles to the Willamette Valley. The loop also crosses White River, which flows out of White River Glacier. For more information contact the Mount Hood Information Center, P.O. Box 342, Welches, OR, 97067. Phone (503) 622-4822.

TIMOTHY LAKE is 15 mi. s.w. of US 26 on Skyline Rd. This 1,400-acre lake has five separate camping and picnic areas open from mid-June to mid-September. Four of the five—Gone Creek, Hood View, Oak Fork and Pine Point—are on the south shore of the lake. Meditation Point is near the north shore and can be reached by trail or boat. *See Recreation Chart.*

NECANICUM (A-2)

SADDLE MOUNTAIN STATE PARK, 8 mi. n.e. off US 26, extends around Saddle Mountain, at 3,287 feet, the highest point in the north end of the Coast Range. There are panoramic views. The park is a deer and elk refuge; tent camping is permitted. *See Recreation Chart.*

NEHALEM (B-2) pop. 200

Nehalem, on the northern Oregon coast between Seaside and Tillamook on US 101, is the site of Nehalem Bay State Park *(see Recreation Chart).* Nehalem is an Indian word for "place of peace": *ne,* the prefix for "place" and *halem,* the word for "peace."

NEHALEM BAY WINE CO., 1 mi. off US 101 on SR 53, is the sixth oldest winery in Oregon and offers wine tastings. From 1909-69 this was the site of the Tillamook Cheese Factory. Allow 30 minutes minimum. Daily 10-5; closed Thanksgiving and Dec. 25. Free. Phone (503) 368-5300.

NEWBERG (C-3) pop. 13,100, elev. 286′

Newberg was the first community in Oregon granted permission to hold formal Quaker services. Herbert Hoover, who as a child lived in Newberg with his uncle, was in the first graduating class of Pacific Academy, established by the Quakers and later renamed George Fox College, for the English founder of The Society of Friends.

There are displays about Newberg's Quaker settlers in the north wing of Brougher Hall and Hoover memorabilia in the Herbert Hoover Academic Building. Campus guided tours can be arranged.

Some of Oregon's older and larger wineries are in and around Newberg. Rex Hill Vineyards, 30835 N. SR 99W, offers self-guiding tours and

WINERIES

More than 350 vineyards dot the Oregon landscape, illustrating the growth and popularity of this major statewide industry. Wineries are located throughout the state's western valleys from Medford north to Portland. The "Discover Oregon Wine" brochure published by the Oregon Wine Center describes five distinct viticultural regions: Columbia Valley, Rogue Valley, Umpqua Valley, Walla Walla Valley and Willamette Valley.

Oregon's marine climate, dominated by the tempering effect of the Pacific Ocean, provides a long, mild and gentle growing season—ideal for the cultivation of noble wine grapes and berries. Cabernet Sauvignon, Chardonnay, Gewürztraminer, Müller-Thurgau, Pinot gris, Pinot noir, Riesling and Sauvignon blanc are among the region's award-winning wines.

Most Oregon wineries are small, family-owned farms. Individual attention to producing and caring for wines is a hallmark of the dedicated Oregon winemaker. The devotion and commitment of both owners and workers is evident as they engage in the craft of producing fine wines.

Almost all of Oregon's wineries welcome visitors throughout the year for tours and tastings. A touring guide to Oregon wineries that includes area and local maps and visiting hours for each establishment can be obtained free of charge from the Oregon Wine Center, 1200 N.W. Front Ave., Suite 400, Portland, OR 97209; phone (503) 228-8403. Information also can be obtained through the AAA Oregon.

tastings April through December; phone (503) 538-0666. Bald Peak State Park, 9 miles northwest, has picnic areas and views of the Cascade Mountains and the Coast Range.

Popular events include boat races on the Willamette River during Memorial Day weekend and the Old-Fashioned Festival the last weekend in July. The Vintage Festival, held the Saturday after Labor Day at Sportsman Airpark, features vintage aircraft, classic cars and boats, local wines, food and fine arts. For more information contact the Newberg Area Chamber of Commerce, 115 N. Washington St., Newberg, OR, 97132; phone (503) 538-2014.

★**CHAMPOEG STATE PARK** is on the Willamette River 5 mi. s.w. of I-5 exit 278. Champoeg State Park was the site of the 1843 vote to form the provisional government for the first American commonwealth in the Pacific Northwest and the gateway to early Willamette exploration and settlement. The park has scenic views and picnic facilities. Admission $3 per vehicle, May-Sept.; free rest of year. Phone (800) 238-7488. *See Recreation Chart and Aurora in the AAA Northwestern CampBook.*

"Champoeg!"—Official Pageant of Oregon Statehood depicts the area's pioneer history in a 2,500-seat amphitheater. Performances are given Wed.-Sat. at 7:30 in July; gates open at 5:30. Tickets $7; over 65, $6; ages 5-16, $5. MC, VI. Tickets can be purchased at the gate; or by telephone or mail order to Friends of Historic Champoeg, 8239 Champoeg Rd. N.E., St. Paul, OR 97137. Phone (503) 678-1649.

Champoeg State Park Visitors' Center has exhibits on Champoeg history and the origins of Oregon's government. Daily 9-4; closed holidays. Phone (503) 678-1251.

D.A.R. Pioneer Mothers' Memorial Cabin was built in 1931 as a memorial to pioneer mothers. It is furnished with pioneer artifacts. Wed.-Sun. noon-5, Feb.-Nov. Admission $1.50; under 12, 75c. Phone (503) 633-2237.

Robert Newell House, on a hillside w. of the park entrance, is a reconstruction of a house built in 1852. Indian artifacts, gowns of Oregon governors' wives and an antique quilt collection are displayed. On the grounds is an 1850 Butteville jail and a pioneer school. Sat.-Sun. 1-5, Feb.-Nov. Admission $2; under 12, 75c. Phone (503) 678-5537.

HOOVER-MINTHORN HOUSE MUSEUM, S. River and E. Second sts., is where Herbert Hoover spent 4 years of his boyhood. The restored 1881 house contains original furnishings, photographs and mementos of Hoover's residency. The Hoover-Minthorn House also is the site of a quilt show in May and a Victorian Christmas celebration during the first weekend in December. Allow 30 minutes minimum. Wed.-Sun. 1-4, Mar.-Nov.; Sat.-Sun. 1-4, in Feb. and Dec. Closed holidays. Admission $2; over 65, $1.50; ages 5-11, 50c. Phone (503) 538-6629.

NEWPORT (D-1) pop. 8,400, elev. 68'

Spread across a blunt, ridged peninsula between the Pacific Ocean and Yaquina Bay, Newport has been a resort community for more than 100 years. The charm of the turn-of-the-20th-century era is preserved in The Old Bay Front, a waterfront section of the town.

The Lincoln County Vietnam Commemorative Walk Memorial is in the Donald A. Davis Park and is dedicated to war veterans. A sculpture is placed at 19 degrees northeast to cast its shadow across the granite each April 30th, a reminder of the day the Vietnam War ended.

The Newport Performing Arts Center hosts performances by local and visiting artists including ballets, concerts and plays. For ticket and schedule information phone (503) 265-9231.

Newport's location at the entrance of Yaquina Bay has made fishing an important industry. Clamming, crabbing and fishing are popular recreational pursuits; charter and rental boats are available. Newport celebrates its heritage the first weekend in May during the Loyalty Days and Sea Fair Festival and holds a Seafood and Wine Festival the last full weekend in February.

A number of nearby day-use areas and campgrounds are scattered along US 101, a scenic highway that bisects Newport and extends along the entire Oregon coast.

Shopping areas: Popular shopping areas include Sea Towne and US 101N. The Historic Bay Front, Bay Boulevard, has open-air fish markets, restaurants and galleries.

DEVIL'S PUNCH BOWL STATE PARK, 8 mi. n., has a bowl-shaped rock formation that at high tide fills from below with a roar. Ocean views can be seen from the park. Daily dawn-dusk.

HATFIELD MARINE SCIENCE CENTER, Marine Science Dr. on Yaquina Bay, is reached by access roads from the southern end of the Yaquina Bridge. This is the coastal research, teaching and marine facility for Oregon State University. The science center sponsors whale-watching programs during the winter and spring. Also of interest are the aquarium and museum. Allow 1 hour minimum. A public wing is open daily 10-6, Memorial Day weekend-Labor Day; 10-4, rest of year. Donations. Phone (503) 867-0226.

LINCOLN COUNTY HISTORICAL SOCIETY MUSEUMS, 545 S.W. 9th St., consists of a log cabin museum containing Indian artifacts, pioneer farm equipment, logging and maritime exhibits, as well as the 1895 Victorian Burrows House, which contains period furniture, clothing and pioneer exhibits. An herb garden is on the grounds. Allow 30 minutes minimum. Tues.-Sun.

10-5, June-Sept.; 11-4, rest of year. Donations. Phone (503) 265-7509.

NEWPORT VISUAL ART CENTER, at the Nye Beach turnaround, features handicrafts, paintings, photographs and changing exhibits. Next door, the Yaquina Art Center features the works of its members. Allow 30 minutes minimum. The Newport Visual Art Center open daily noon-4, May-Sept.; 11-3, rest of year. The Yaquina Art Center open daily 11-4. Free. Phone (503) 265-5133.

OREGON COAST AQUARIUM, 2820 S.E. Ferry Slip Rd., has indoor and outdoor marine exhibits. The 4 acres of outdoor exhibits include a nature trail, an aviary, an underwater cave with an octupus and a rocky pool with sea lions and seals. Two videotapes feature gray whales and Oregon's sharks. Food is available. Allow 2 hours minimum. Daily 9-6, mid-Mar. to mid-Oct.; 10-4:30, rest of year. Closed Dec. 25. Admission $7.75; over 60 and ages 13-18, $5.50; ages 4-12, $3.30. DS, MC, VI. Phone (503) 867-3474 or (800) 615-3474. *See color ad.*

RIPLEY'S BELIEVE IT OR NOT!, 250 S.W. Bay Blvd., displays bizarre and unusual mysteries of nature and technology. Allow 30 minutes minimum. Daily 9-8, June 15-Labor Day; 10-5, rest of year. Closed Dec. 25. Admission $5.50; ages 5-11, $3.50. MC, VI. Phone (503) 265-2206.

UNDERSEA GARDENS, 250 S.W. Bay Blvd., offers views of marine plants and animals in their natural habitat through large underwater windows. Scuba-diving shows are presented regularly. Allow 30 minutes minimum. Daily 9-8, June 15-Labor Day; 10-5, rest of year. Closed Dec. 25. Admission $5.50; ages 5-11, $3.50. MC, VI. Phone (503) 265-2206.

THE WAX WORKS, 250 S.W. Bay Blvd., features wax figures, some animated. A 5-minute film is presented on the 1980 eruption of Mount St. Helens. Allow 30 minutes minimum. Daily 9-8, June 15-Labor Day; 10-5, rest of year. Closed Dec. 25. Admission $5.50; ages 5-11, $3.50. MC, VI. Phone (503) 265-2206.

YAQUINA BAY LIGHTHOUSE, in Yaquina Bay State Park, was one of the first navigational aids built on the Pacific Northwest coast. The 1871 lighthouse is furnished in period. Daily 11-5, June 1-Labor Day; Sat.-Sun. noon-4, rest of year. Donations. Phone (503) 867-7451 or 265-5679.

NORTH BEND (F-1) pop. 9,600

On a peninsula jutting into the Coos Bay, North Bend thrives on commercial fisheries,

Not just another fish story.
Birds that fly underwater. Seals that doze upside down.
A mother with 80,000 kids.
Jellyfish that aren't really even
fish. Sea otters that use their chests as tables.
Sound like we're telling fish stories? Come find out for
yourself. Just bring this ad along for
a free gift. And by the way, wait until you see the fish.
Oregon Coast Aquarium
Sea Life Up Close.
Off Hwy. 101, South of Newport's Yaquina Bay Bridge. 503-867-3123
A

lumbering and manufacturing. The town straddles US 101, a scenic route that runs along the Oregon Coast from California to Washington. North Bend also is the gateway to the Oregon Dunes National Recreation Area *(see Suislaw National Forest).*

Brochures describing bay, dune and whale watching tours are available at the Bay Area Chamber of Commerce, 50 E. Central Blvd., Coos Bay, OR 97420; phone (503) 269-0215 or (800) 824-8486 and at the North Bend Information Center, 1380 Sherman, North Bend, OR 97459; phone (503) 756-4613.

COOS COUNTY HISTORICAL SOCIETY MUSEUM, in Simpson Park on US 101, displays a 1922 steam locomotive, a pioneer display, American Indian artifacts, and logging and farming exhibits. Allow 30 minutes minimum. Mon.-Sat. 10-4, Memorial Day-Labor Day; Tues.-Sat. 10-4, rest of year. Closed Thanksgiving and Dec. 25. Admission $1, children 25c. Phone (503) 756-6320.

PACIFIC COAST RECREATION, 6 mi. n. on US 101 at 4121 Coast Hwy. in Oregon Dunes National Recreation Area, offers narrated dune excursions in vintage World War II military vehicles. Allow 1 hour, 30 minutes minimum. Daily 9-5; closed Jan. 1, Thanksgiving and Dec. 25. Fare $12; under 14, $8. MC, VI. Phone (503) 756-7183.

OAKRIDGE (F-4) pop. 3,100

Lookout Point and Hills Creek reservoirs provide water sports in their recreation areas. Salt Creek Falls, one of the highest waterfalls in Oregon, is 16 miles east on SR 58. Green Waters Park, located in the center of town, has picnic facilities.

The Aufderheide Scenic Byway begins 3 miles west of Oakridge off SR 58 and continues north to SR 126. In nearby Westfir is the Office Bridge, the longest covered bridge in Oregon.

Oakridge celebrates the Tree Planting Festival the weekend before Mother's Day with a parade, quilt show, tree planting, crafts and a children's mini-Olympics. The fourth weekend in July is the Fat Tire Festival with mountain bike events, crafts, food and music.

OCHOCO NATIONAL FOREST

Elevations in the forest range from 3,500 ft. at the forest's boundary to 7,163 ft. atop Snow Mountain. Refer to AAA maps for additional elevation information.

Divided into three sections, the Ochoco National Forest covers 847,938 acres of pine, fir and larch. Under the same administration is the Crooked River National Grassland, with 111,379 acres of juniper-dotted rangeland north of Redmond. Access to the forest is provided by US 26 from Prineville. US 26 cuts through the grassland to Madras.

Within the forest's boundaries are three designated wilderness areas: Mill Creek, Bridge Creek and Black Canyon. These areas provide ample opportunities for hiking and back-country camping. Some geological areas of interest are Steins and Twin Pillars, volcanic tufts that jet upward through the high desert landscape.

Other areas of interest are the Mayflower Mining Settlement, off US 26, and the Wild Horse Range, also off US 26, named for the small bands of wild horses roaming the area. Some camping areas do not have water.

Antelope, elk and mule deer are some of the animals found on the forested and open land. Beneath the soil lie deposits of petrified wood, jasper, quartz and the Oregon state rock, the thunderegg, a geode containing opal or agate.

For further information and maps contact the Forest Supervisor, P.O. Box 490, Prineville, OR 97754; phone (503) 447-9641. *See Recreation Chart and the AAA Northwestern CampBook.*

ONTARIO (E-12) pop. 9,400, elev. 2,153′

The Ontario area, in an agricultural belt along the Snake River, has many reservoirs with good fishing and hunting, including Bully Creek Reservoir to the west. The agate, jasper, fossils, thundereggs and petrified wood make the region particularly popular with rockhounds. Thirty miles west of Ontario is Keeney Pass, on the main wagon-train route of the Oregon Trail.

Summer events held in or near town include the Japanese Obon Festival in mid-July and the Malheur County Fair the first week of August. The Ontario Winter Wonderland Parade is held the first Saturday in December. For further information contact the Ontario Visitor and Convention Bureau, 88 S.W. 3rd Ave., Ontario, OR 97914; phone (503) 889-8012.

LAKE OWYHEE, 40 mi. s.w., is reached by SR 201 and a county road winding through 10 miles of erosion-sculpted canyons along the Owyhee River. Lake Owyhee, one of the state's longest lakes, provides 60 miles of scenic, canyon-skirted waterway; Hawaiians, or Sandwich Islanders, who were employees of the Hudson's Bay Company, named the lake. Along the lake's eastern shore spectacular red-tinted cliffs rise 1,000 feet above water level.

East of Lake Owyhee is Succor Creek Canyon, where Indian artifacts have been found. Hunting and fishing are permitted. Succor Creek State Park *(see Recreation Chart),* popular with rockhounds for its thundereggs, agates and picture rock, provides camping and picnic areas. Inquire locally about road conditions before driving into canyon.

★OREGON CAVES NATIONAL MONUMENT (G-6)

Oregon Caves National Monument is in the Siskiyou Mountains, 20 miles east of Cave Junction on SR 46. Its access road winds through the dense forests that are southwest Oregon's trademark. Trailers and large recreational vehicles are discouraged.

In the marble heart of Mount Elijah at the 4,000-foot level, nature has carved and decorated the Marble Halls of Oregon. Pillars, stalactites and canopies of calcite line passageways and hang from the vaulted domes of the cavern's many galleries.

Paradise Lost has flowstone on the walls of a room 60 feet high. The largest room, about 250 feet in length, was created by underground streams. A 7-foot calcite column, a large flowstone cascade and an imprint resembling a whale's spine are a few of the cave's features.

There are marked trails in the park for day hikers; connecting trails lead into nearby Siskiyou National Forest *(see place listing)*. It is best to check trail conditions with park rangers before hiking in winter and spring.

The 75-minute cave tour is strenuous with more than 500 stairs; visitors must be accompanied by a guide. Comfortable walking shoes and protective clothing are recommended. Pets are not allowed inside the cave or on trails.

Tours are offered at intervals or as groups of 16 people form. Daily 8-7, mid-June through Labor Day; 9-5, May 1 to mid-June and day after Labor Day-Sept. 30; at 8:30, 10, 11:30, 1, 2:30 and 4, rest of year. Closed Thanksgiving and Dec. 25. Admission $5.75; ages 6-11, $3.50. Under 6 must be over 42 inches tall and pass a stair test; children may not be carried through cave. Infants and toddlers are not allowed in the cave under any circumstances. MC, VI. Phone (503) 592-3400.

OREGON CITY (C-4) pop. 14,700, elev. 55′

Oregon's first capital and the end of the Oregon Trail, Oregon City is on the Willamette River's east bank where the river plunges 40 feet over a basaltic ridge at Willamette Falls. Falls Vista Viewpoint, on SR 99E near the southern entrance into town, reveals a fine view of the falls. Across the river in West Linn are the Willamette Falls Locks, which opened the upper Willamette to navigation.

The Municipal Free Elevator, Seventh Street and Railroad Avenue, lifts pedestrians 90 feet up the face of a cliff to a residential-business district. An observation deck at the top overlooks the downtown area and the falls. Mount St. Helens can be seen on a clear day.

In Mountain View Cemetery on Hilda Street, off SR 213, is the grave of Peter Skene Ogden, a British fur trader who explored much of western America in the 1820s.

Riverfest is celebrated the second weekend in July. The outdoor musical drama "Oregon Trail Pageant" is held mid-July through August.

Self-guiding tours: Historical guidebooks for walking and driving tours are available for 75c at the Oregon City Chamber of Commerce, 1795 Washington St., Oregon City, OR 97045; phone (503) 656-1619.

Shopping areas: Oregon City Shopping Center, at McLoughlin Boulevard and I-205 bridge, and the downtown area offer a variety of popular shops.

CLACKAMAS COUNTY HISTORY MUSEUM is ½ mi. s. on US 99E to 211 Tumwater Dr., following signs. The center features permanent and

The Oregon Trail

The lure of the Oregon country unleashed one of the greatest peacetime migrations in the history of the world. The "Great Migration" began in 1843 when 1,000 pioneers, 120 wagons and 5,000 head of livestock left Independence, Mo.

These early pioneers, with their possessions and dreams for a new beginning, were ill-prepared for the trail's dangers: drought, blizzards, disease, wild animals and hostile Indians. One out of ten emigrants died along the trail, but this did not deter the mass overland emigration that continued for nearly three decades.

The gateway to the northwest was actually several major emigrant trails starting at the Missouri River and ending in Oregon City. The Barlow Road route dropped south at The Dalles past Mt. Hood and Timberline Road. The Applegate Trail opened in 1846 and crossed the southern Oregon Cascade Mountains through Grants Pass, Medford and Klamath Falls. The Meek-Elliott-Macy route was established in 1854 after 9 years of unsuccessful attempts to find passage from the Malheur River across Oregon's desert to Eugene. In all, the trail extended 2,000 miles and stretched across six states. Traffic along this highway was so relentless, swelled by lengthy wagon trains, that ruts as deep as 6 feet scarred the fragile prairie. Many of the ruts are still visible. It is estimated that more than 300,000 people crossed the route 1840-60.

For brochures contact the AAA Oregon at 600 S.W. Market St, Portland, OR 97201; phone (503) 222-6700.

changing exhibits on Clackamas County history. A research library housing county historical documents also is available. Allow 1 hour minimum. Mon.-Fri. 10-4, Sat.-Sun. and holidays 1-5; closed Jan. 1, Thanksgiving and Dec. 25. Combination admission to center and the Stevens-Crawford Museum $3; senior citizens $2; ages 6-12, $1.50; family rate (up to five persons) $7.50. MC, VI. Phone (503) 655-5574.

END OF THE OREGON TRAIL INTERPRETIVE CENTER, off I-205 exit 10 at 1726 Washington St. , houses artifacts and displays recalling the difficult journey over the Oregon Trail made by 300,000 pioneers. Also featured is an audiovisual portrayal of the Oregon Trail. Allow 1 hour minimum. Mon.-Sat. 10-4, Sun. noon-4; closed Thanksgiving and Dec. 25. Admission $4; senior citizens and ages 6-17, $2. Phone (503) 657-9336.

JOHN INSKEEP ENVIRONMENTAL LEARNING CENTER, 19600 S. Molalla, is a 15-acre environmental study area which was once an industrial site. The area is composed of ponds, creeks and pathways, all of which have an abundance of wildlife.

Featured are a fish-raising facility, one of the largest telescopes in the northwest, a birds of prey exhibit and a recycling demonstration facility with recycled plastic lumber used for picnic tables and park benches. Guided tours and interpretive programs are available Tuesday through Friday. Allow 1 hour minimum. Daily 9-dusk. Admission $2; senior citizens and ages 6-18, $1. Phone (503) 657-6958, ext. 2351.

JOHN McLOUGHLIN HOUSE NATIONAL HISTORIC SITE is at Seventh and Center sts. The restored residence was built in 1845 by Dr. McLoughlin, a Hudson's Bay Company representative who helped the settlers. The home contains original and period furnishings. Allow 1 hour minimum. Tues.-Sat. 10-4, Sun. 1-4, Feb.-Dec.; closed holidays. Admission $3; senior citizens $2.50; ages 6-17, $1. Phone (503) 656-5146.

STEVENS-CRAWFORD MUSEUM, 603 Sixth St., offers 1-hour guided tours of the 1907-08 home. Exhibits include many original furnishings, including dresses, dolls, china and kitchen implements. Tues.-Fri. 10-4, Sat.-Sun. 1-4, Feb.-Dec.; closed Thanksgiving and Dec. 25. Combination admission to museum and the Clackamas County History Museum $3; senior citizens $2; ages 6-12, $1.50; family rate (up to five persons) $7.50. MC, VI. Phone (503) 655-2866.

OTTER ROCK (D-2)

MARINE GARDENS, n. of Devil's Punchbowl, is off B St. At low tide, pools and caves of the rocky area reveal sea urchins and other forms of tidal pool life. Inquire locally for current tide tables. Daily dawn-dusk. Free.

OTTER CREST WAYSIDE, 1 mi. n., is on Cape Foulweather. Otter Crest, a bold, flat-topped rock rising 453 feet above the tide, offers views of the rocky shore where sea otters once dwelt. It is now inhabited by seals, sea lions and birds. Gray whales can be seen year-round.

PARKDALE (B-8)

This small community on the northeast edge of Mount Hood National Forest *(see place listing)* was established in 1910 and is the southern terminus of the Mount Hood Railroad *(see Hood River)*, one of the few remaining U.S. railroads operating on a switchback, permitting the train to climb from the Hood River canyon to the valley.

PENDLETON (B-10) pop. 15,100, elev. 1,068′

One of the West's prominent rodeos is the Pendleton Round-Up begun in 1910. Held the second full week in September, the 4-day event includes daily afternoon rodeos and the Happy Canyon Indian Pageant. The Westward Ho Parade features pack trains, stagecoaches and Indians dressed in traditional regalia. A tepee village occupied by tribes from throughout the Pacific Northwest is assembled for the celebration. Beneath the arena grandstand is the Round-Up Hall of Fame *(see attraction listing)*.

Downtown, visitors can view the restored 1889 Seth Thomas Clock Tower located outside the courthouse on the corner of Court Avenue and S.E. 4th Street. The 57-foot clock symbolizes the growth and prosperity of the 1880s. Visitors can view the glass-enclosed clock works at eye level.

A scenic stretch of I-84 begins at Pendleton, intersecting with US 395 before continuing 93 miles southeast to Baker City.

For further information contact the Pendleton Chamber of Commerce, 25 S.E. Dorion Ave., Pendleton, OR 97801; phone (503) 276-7411.

Shopping areas: Melanie Square Shopping Center, in the 1700 block of Court Place, has a variety of shops.

McKAY CREEK NATIONAL WILDLIFE REFUGE, 1,836 acres 7 mi. s. off US 395, harbors large numbers of waterfowl, primarily ducks and geese. Hunting is permitted. Daily 5 a.m.-10 p.m. Free. Phone (503) 922-3232.

PENDLETON UNDERGROUND TOURS, downtown at 37 S.W. Emigrant, offers a 1½-hour guided tour of the historical underground tunnels built by Chinese immigrants in the late 1800s. The first part goes through the old Shamrock Cardroom, the laundry and the meat market; the second part includes the Chinese jails, living quarters and the bordellos or "cozy rooms." Reservations are required. Allow 1 hour, 30 minutes minimum. Tours daily 10-4; office hours 9-5. Closed Thanksgiving and Dec. 25. Fee $10; ages 3-12, $5. MC, VI. **Discount.** Phone (503) 276-0730.

PENDLETON WOOLEN MILLS, 1307 S.E. Court Pl., offers guided tours of its facility for manufacturing woolen products. Allow 30 minutes minimum. Mon.-Fri. at 9, 11, 1:30 and 3; closed holidays. Free. Phone (503) 276-6911.

ROUND-UP HALL OF FAME, e. I-84 exit 207 to the Round-up Grounds underneath the south grandstand, exhibits Pendleton Round-Up memorabilia, Western items, photographs and Indian artifacts. Allow 30 minutes minimum. Daily 10-4, Memorial Day-Sept. 30. Donations. Phone (503) 276-2553.

UMATILLA COUNTY HISTORICAL SOCIETY MUSEUM, 108 S.W. Frazer, is in a refurbished 1909 railway depot. Exhibits depict the history of Umatilla county and include a display devoted to the area's sheep industry and Pendleton Woolen Mills, a railroad telegraph system and Indian and pioneer artifacts. Allow 1 hour minimum. Tues.-Sat. 10-4; closed holidays. Donations. Phone (503) 276-0012.

PHILOMATH (D-2) pop. 3,000, elev. 295′

Meaning "lover of learning," Philomath was named after Philomath College, started in 1867 by the United Brethren Church and closed in 1929. The town was incorporated in 1882. Many residents of Philomath are employed at Hewlett-Packard's Advanced Products Division, makers of computers and calculators.

During the second weekend of July, Philomath celebrates its Frolic and Rodeo Festival, a tradition that began in 1916 with the first Philomath Rodeo. The Pee Wee Rodeo is held the third weekend in August.

BENTON COUNTY HISTORICAL MUSEUM, 1101 Main St., is in the Philomath College Building, an 1867 Georgian-style brick structure. Permanent and changing exhibits interpret regional history. Monthly exhibits feature works by Oregon artists. A reference library is available by appointment. Allow 30 minutes minimum. Tues.-Sat. 10-4:30. Free. Phone (503) 929-6230.

MARY'S PEAK, 14 mi. w. on SR 34, is the highest peak in Oregon's Coast Range. This scenic area is often snow-covered in the winter. A 9-mile paved road climbs within ½ mile of the 4,097-foot summit and visitors can walk to the peak for a spectacular view of the Pacific Ocean to the west and the Cascade Range to the east. Four trails of moderate difficulty cover approximately 9 miles. Picnicking is permitted. Sno-Park Permit required Nov. 15-Apr. 30. Phone (503) 487-5811.

TRIPLE A-O.K. VACATION

Get out of the starting gate with plans for your vacation. Let the world's largest travel organization, AAA Travel—make it a winner. Fly to the ends of the Earth, cruise the oceans, or tour by motorcoach —your AAA Travel office can make all your arrangements.

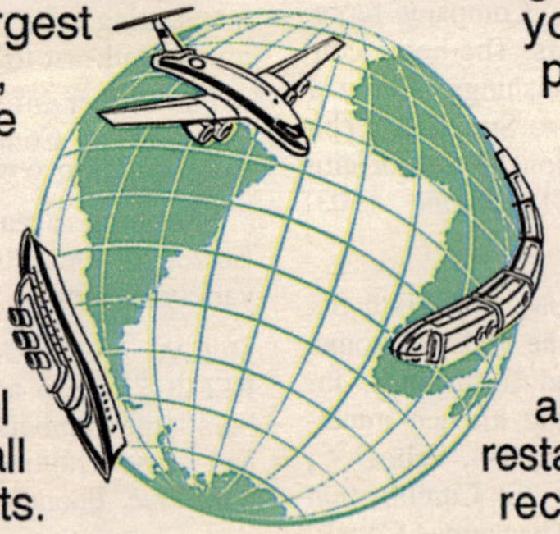

And of course, if you're traveling by car, AAA offers you money saving packages throughout the U.S. and Canada plus you get personal Triptik® maps and TourBooks® brimming with AAA approved lodgings, restaurants, attractions, recreation areas and much more.

As you plan your next trip make everything Triple A-O.K.

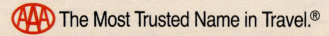

AAA The Most Trusted Name in Travel.®

Portland

Nature has endowed Portland with many gifts—majestic mountain vistas, a mild climate and a deep-water harbor—and these in turn have created an almost inspired devotion in its citizens. Though extreme, the sentiment of Portland's mayor, who proposed in 1905 that every other street be stripped of its buildings and planted with shade trees and roses, is characteristic of Portlanders.

Historic brick buildings complement modern glass and steel structures; parks replace old industrial areas; and art is tucked into playgrounds and office towers. As the city grew, it adopted the rose as a symbol of its renewal and growth. Christening itself the "City of Roses," Portland has made roses the centerpiece of both its major park and its most important annual celebration, the Rose Festival.

The deep-water confluence of the Columbia and Willamette rivers was first used by the Chinook Indians as a stop on their trading route. Over the years, as their campfires consumed more firewood, a 1-acre clearing took shape in the forest, known as "The Clearing."

Asa Lovejoy and Francis Pettygrove set out to build a city on this site in 1844, calling it "Stumptown" for the tree stumps that littered the site. The town was renamed in 1845 by a flip of the coin: Lovejoy and Pettygrove each wanted to name the site after his hometown—the former, Boston, Mass., and the latter, Portland, Maine.

Growing steadily, the community had added churches, schools and stores to its original blacksmith shop, tannery and sawmill by 1850. The California gold rush, Indian wars and the discovery of gold in eastern Oregon kept the town's merchants busy until the Civil War. With the end of the war, the coming of the railroad in 1883 and the Lewis and Clark Centennial Exposition in 1905, Portland shed its pioneer adolescence and entered the new century as a mature city.

Having expanded to straddle the Willamette River, greater Portland stretches from the foothills of Mount Hood to the western plains of the

THE INFORMED TRAVELER

POPULATION: 437,300; metro 1,477,900 **ELEVATION:** 77 ft.

Whom to Call

Emergency: 911

Police (non-emergency): (503) 230-2121

Time and Temperature: (503) 222-6721 and 236-7575

Hospitals: Bess Kaiser Medical Center, (503) 285-9321; Emanuel Hospital and Health Center, (503) 280-3200; Good Samaritan Hospital and Medical Center, (503) 229-7711; Oregon Health Science University Hospital, (503) 494-8311; Portland Adventist Medical Center, (503) 257-2500; Providence Medical Center, (503) 230-1111; St. Vincent Hospital and Medical Center, (503) 291-2115.

Where to Look

Newspapers

Portland's daily paper is *The Oregonian,* with morning and evening editions.

Radio and TV

Portland radio station KXL (750 AM) is an all-news/weather station; KOPB (91.5 FM in northern Oregon, 550 AM and 103.1 FM in southern Oregon) is a member of National Public Radio.

The major network TV channels are 2 (ABC), 6 (CBS), 8 (NBC), 10 (PBS) and 49 (FOX). For a complete list of radio and television programs, consult the daily newspaper.

Visitor Information

The *Willamette Week* and *The Downtowner* report on weekly entertainment, shopping specials and current events. In addition, the weekly *Portland Guide,* available at most local hotels, has tourist information.

The Portland Oregon Visitors Association offers self-guiding tour brochures and city maps. For further information contact the Portland Oregon Visitors Association, 25 S.W. Salmon, Portland, OR 97204; phone (503) 222-2223 or (800) 962-3700.

What to Wear

Portland's weather is mild with little or no snow in the winter. The city's average mean temperatures are 61 during summer and 44 during winter. Humidity averages about 60 percent for the year, and the city's average annual rainfall is 37 inches.

Coast Range and encompasses a four-county area. The city is one of the country's leaders in the export of wheat and lumber products, and its freshwater port ranks third on the Pacific coast in ocean-borne shipping.

Donald Macleay and other farsighted Portlanders conserved a portion of the city's former wilderness. Macleay bequeathed 107 forested acres to the city in 1900 and stipulated that no wheeled vehicle ever enter the property. The city has kept its promise to Macleay and has increased its holdings to encompass more than 200 parks, ranging from the 4,800 acres of Forest Park to Mill Ends Park, which measures just 24 inches across. The greenery of these parks is set against a majestic backdrop of mountains, a vista protected by an ordinance forbidding buildings over 40 stories.

Parks also were woven into the fabric of downtown as early as 1852, when townspeople planted a 25-block boulevard between Park and 9th avenues with trees and grass. Today this oasis, known as the South Park Blocks, is graced with statues and gardens, and alive with activities. This area offers a refuge to downtown shoppers, tourists and workers.

Portlandia, a post-modern statue in front of the Portland Building, stands 35 feet tall and represents an earth-mother kneeling among sculpted forest animals. In a downtown renewal effort, the city reclaimed its waterfront heritage by plowing under a four-lane highway along the west bank of the Willamette and transforming it into the Tom McCall Waterfront Park. Runners and rollerbladers mingle with strollers along this landscaped promenade. This park is the site of concerts and festivals, as well as a showplace for noontime picnics and major community events.

Within several of the city's parks are fountains which serve as refreshing oases in the summer. The Ira Keller Fountain in front of the Civic Auditorium and the Salmon Street Springs in Tom McCall Waterfront Park are particularly popular.

Some of Portland's other parks offer magnificent views. At 1,073 feet, Council Crest Park is the city's highest point. Reached by Fairmont Boulevard, it presents a vista of downtown and five Cascade peaks. Panoramic views also are found at Mount Tabor Park, one of the few extinct volcanoes within a U.S. city, and Rocky Butte, 1,000 feet above the city.

Portland has kept its air and water clean despite its big city status. Most area industries operate on electricity generated from mountain rivers, thus producing little soot or smoke. The Willamette River, the object of a vigorous decades-long cleanup campaign, is now fit for fishing, boating and water skiing.

With one hand outstretched to greet the future and the other protecting the past, Portland shaped itself into a naturally beautiful, progressive city. With such an attractive appearance, it's understandable why so many visitors have become residents, and why many Portlanders like to keep their city a well-guarded secret.

Approaches

By Car

The major north-south route to Portland is I-5, which originates in southern California and extends through Seattle and to the Canadian border. I-5 parallels the Willamette's east bank through Portland, affording access to bridges connecting the West Side.

Most traffic from the east follows I-84, which becomes Banfield Freeway on the East Side, then intersects I-5 and Burnside Street, a major downtown artery traversing both sides of the city via Burnside Bridge. East-west thoroughfares are US 26 and US 30. Both funnel traffic into Portland from points along the Pacific on the west; from the east US 26 skirts Mount Hood on its approach, while US 30 parallels the Columbia River, frequently following the I-84 alignment.

Bypass routes are provided by I-405, which skirts the western downtown area, and I-205, which swings in a wider arc through the eastern environs. Both interchange with major routes and streets en route.

By Plane, Bus and Train

Portland International Airport, 9 miles east of I-5, is served by most domestic airlines. I-84 East/Portland International Airport signs direct travelers to the airport.

Transportation from downtown to the airport is available by airport buses, which run between the airport and major downtown hotels every 30 minutes daily 5 a.m.-midnight; one-way fare is $7; ages 6-12, $1. Phone (503) 246-4676.

The public bus system, TRI-MET, also serves the airport; phone (503) 238-7433 Mon.-Fri. from 7:30-5:30 for schedules.

Limousine service is available from the Oregon Limousine Service, (503) 283-2275 or (800) 548-2563; the Portland Limousine Service, (503) 771-3344 or (800) 826-1431; and the Classic Chauffeur, (503) 238-8880 or (800) 245-8880. Reservations are required and fares average $60. Taxi fares average $20 one-way.

The Greyhound Lines Inc. terminal is at 550 N.W. 6th St.; phone (800) 231-2222. The Amtrak passenger train terminal is at 800 N.W. 6th Ave.; phone (800) 872-7245 or 273-4866.

Getting Around

Street System

Portland is divided into five sections—S.W., S.E., N., N.W. and N.E.—with the Willamette River dividing east from west and Burnside Street separating north from south. A series of 11 bridges connects the east and west sides. Street addresses are keyed to each of the sections—121 N.E. 21st Ave., or 200 S.W. Taylor St.

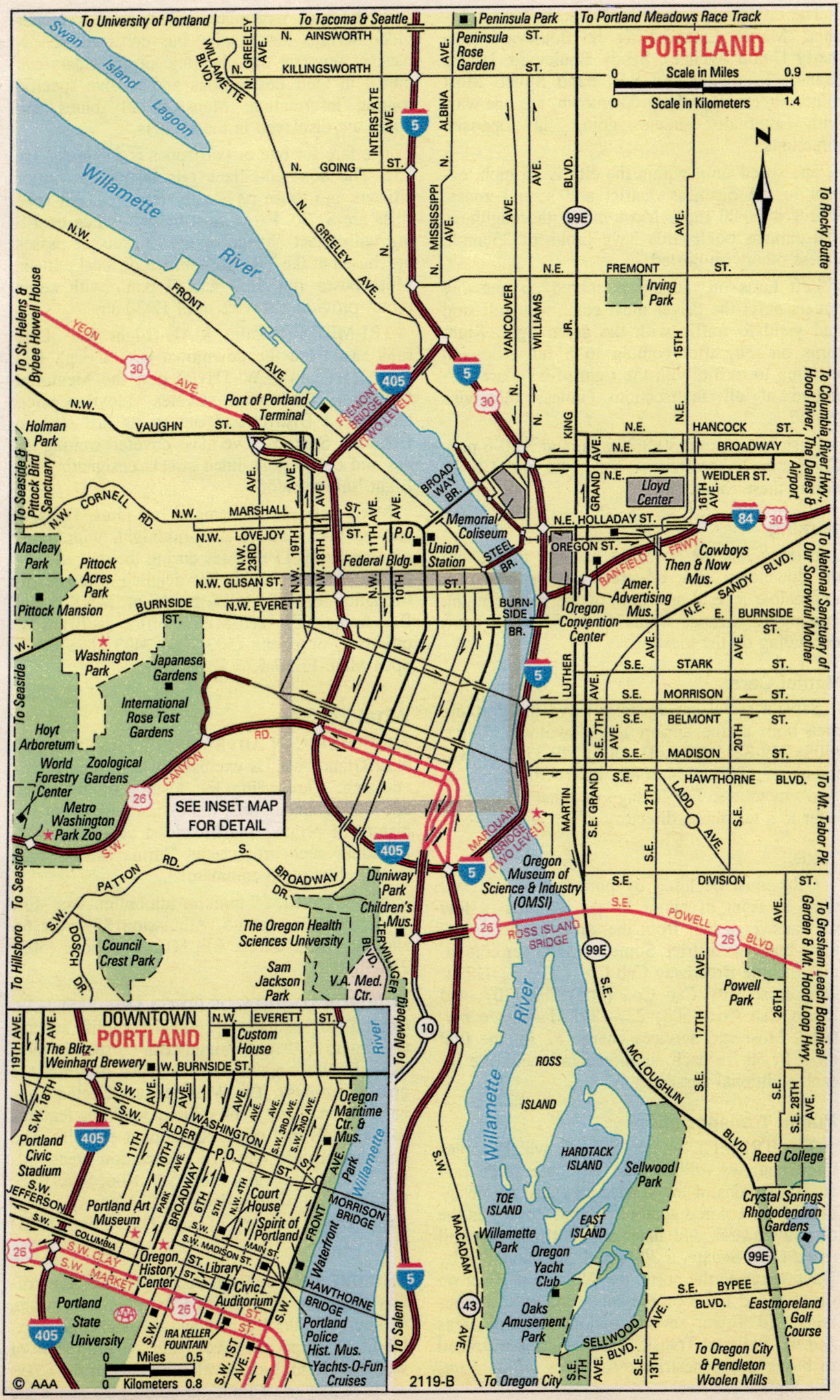
PORTLAND
Scale in Miles
0
0.9
0
Scale in Kilometers
1.4
N
To University of Portland
To Tacoma & Seattle
Peninsula Park
To Portland Meadows Race Track
Swan Island Lagoon
N. AINSWORTH
Peninsula Rose Garden
ST.
KILLINGSWORTH
ST.
WILLAMETTE BLVD.
N. GREELEY AVE.
INTERSTATE AVE.
ALBINA AVE.
N. GOING ST.
N. MISSISSIPPI AVE.
N. GREELEY AVE.
VANCOUVER AVE.
WILLIAMS AVE.
MARTIN LUTHER KING JR. BLVD.
N.E. FREMONT ST.
15TH AVE.
Irving Park
To Rocky Butte
Willamette River
N.W. FRONT AVE.
YEON AVE.
To St. Helens & Bybee Howell House
Port of Portland Terminal
FREMONT BRIDGE (TWO LEVEL)
BROADWAY BR.
N.W. VAUGHN ST.
Holman Park
To Seaside & Pittock Bird Sanctuary
N.W. CORNELL RD.
N.W. MARSHALL ST.
N.W. LOVEJOY ST.
N.W. 23RD
N.W. 19TH
N.W. 18TH AVE.
N.W. 11TH AVE.
10TH
P.O.
Union Station
Federal Bldg.
Memorial Coliseum
STEEL BR.
N.W. GLISAN ST.
N.W. EVERETT
BURNSIDE ST.
BURNSIDE BR.
Macleay Park
Pittock Acres Park
Pittock Mansion
N.E. HANCOCK ST.
N.E. BROADWAY
N.E. WEIDLER ST.
GRAND AVE.
Lloyd Center
16TH AVE.
N.E. HOLLADAY ST.
OREGON ST.
BANFIELD FRWY
Cowboys Then & Now Mus.
Amer. Advertising Mus.
Oregon Convention Center
N.E. SANDY BLVD.
E. BURNSIDE ST.
To Columbia River Hwy., Hood River, The Dalles & Airport
To National Sanctuary of Our Sorrowful Mother
W.
To Seaside
Washington Park
Japanese Gardens
International Rose Test Gardens
Hoyt Arboretum
World Forestry Center
Zoological Gardens
Metro Washington Park Zoo
CANYON RD.
S.W.
SEE INSET MAP FOR DETAIL
S.E. STARK ST.
S.E. MORRISON ST.
S.E. BELMONT ST.
S.E. MADISON ST.
S.E. 7TH AVE.
20TH AVE.
S.E. HAWTHORNE BLVD.
LADD AVE.
12TH
S.E. GRAND
To Mt. Tabor Pk.
MARQUAM BRIDGE (TWO LEVEL)
Oregon Museum of Science & Industry (OMSI)
S.E. DIVISION ST.
S.E. POWELL BLVD.
ROSS ISLAND BRIDGE
To Gresham Leach Botanical Garden & Mt. Hood Loop Hwy.
To Hillsboro
To Seaside
PATTON RD.
S.W. BROADWAY DR.
S.W. DOSCH DR.
Council Crest Park
Duniway Park
Children's Mus.
The Oregon Health Sciences University
Sam Jackson Park
V.A. Med. Ctr.
TERWILLIGER BLVD.
To Newberg
Powell Park
17TH AVE.
26TH
S.E. 28TH AVE.
MC LOUGHLIN BLVD.
Willamette River
ROSS ISLAND
HARDTACK ISLAND
TOE ISLAND
EAST ISLAND
Willamette Park
Oregon Yacht Club
Oaks Amusement Park
Sellwood Park
Reed College
Crystal Springs Rhododendron Gardens
S.E. BYPEE BLVD.
Eastmoreland Golf Course
SELLWOOD BLVD.
S.E. 7TH AVE.
S.E. 13TH AVE.
To Oregon City & Pendleton Woolen Mills
S.W. MACADAM AVE.
To Salem
To Oregon City
2119-B
DOWNTOWN PORTLAND
19TH AVE.
AVE.
N.W. EVERETT ST.
Custom House
The Blitz-Weinhard Brewery
W. BURNSIDE ST.
River
S.W. 18TH
Portland Civic Stadium
S.W. JEFFERSON
11TH
10TH AVE.
ALDER
WASHINGTON
PARK
BROADWAY
6TH
5TH
N.W. 4TH
S.W. 3RD AVE.
S.W. 2ND AVE.
P.O.
Court House
Spirit of Portland
Oregon Maritime Ctr. & Mus.
Willamette Park
MORRISON BRIDGE
FRONT AVE.
Waterfront
Portland Art Museum
COLUMBIA
S.W. CLAY
S.W. MARKET
S.W. MADISON ST.
MAIN ST.
Oregon History Center
Library
Civic Auditorium
HAWTHORNE BRIDGE
Portland State University
IRA KELLER FOUNTAIN
Portland Police Hist. Mus.
Yachts-O-Fun Cruises
S.W. 1ST AVE.
Miles 0 0.5
Kilometers 0 0.8
© AAA

The city's major thoroughfares are Grand Avenue, Martin Luther King Jr. Boulevard (formerly Union Avenue), Sandy Boulevard, US 26 (Sunset Highway) and S.E. 82nd Street. Most minor streets, especially downtown, are one-way, with alternate streets going in opposite directions.

The speed limit within the city is 25 mph, except in the business district and school zones, where it is 20 mph. Most major thoroughfares and express boulevards have limits of 35 mph, unless otherwise posted.

Left turns on red are permitted on one-way streets only; the driver must come to a full stop and yield to traffic with the green light. Right turns on red, after coming to a full stop and yielding to traffic with the right-of-way, are permitted at all intersections, unless otherwise posted.

Rush hours are 6:30-8:30 a.m. and 3:30-6 p.m. Congestion is greatest on I-5, I-84 and US 26 during these times.

Parking

Parking lots are scattered liberally throughout the downtown area; on-street parking is almost impossible to find any time of the day or night. Parking rates range from 75c to $2.50 an hour, depending on the location.

Rental Cars

Several rental car agencies serve the Portland area both at the airport and downtown. Hertz, (503) 249-8216 (airport), (503) 249-5727 (downtown) or (800) 654-3080, offers discounts to AAA members. For listings of other companies refer to a telephone directory.

Taxis

Cabs must be hired by phone or at taxi stations in front of major hotels, although a few will answer a hail from the street in the downtown business district. Some of the larger companies include Broadway Cab Co., (503) 227-1234; New Rose City Cab Co., (503) 282-7707; and Radio Cab Co., (503) 227-1212. Fares are metered. Most taxi services charge $2 for the first mile, $1.50 for each additional mile and 50c for each additional passenger.

Public Transportation

The TRI-MET transit agency, which serves three counties, divides the city into three fare zones; sections of the service area also are designated by a colored symbol. Within Zone 1 is the downtown area and inner-city Portland, as well as Fareless Square, a 300-block area bounded by Hoyt Street on the north, the Willamette River on the east and I-405 on the south and west. It contains Old Town, several major shopping areas and the Portland Transit Mall, which is restricted to buses and pedestrians. All rides within Fareless Square are free.

At the mall, passenger shelters have computer video screens that display bus departure schedules; at separate trip-planning kiosks, riders can punch in their destinations and receive specific routing information. Maps of all routes and zones are displayed in the shelters.

The fare for one or two zones is $1; under 19, 75c. The honored-citizen rate is 50c for senior citizens and those physically impaired. All-zone rides are $1.30. Fares must be paid when boarding with exact change or with tickets or passes purchased at the TRI-MET office or local outlets. Most buses run 5:30 a.m.-9 p.m., with some routes providing service until 12:30 a.m.

TRI-MET's 15-mile MAX Light Rail Line runs east from the downtown core though Old Town (1st and N.W. Davis) past the Memorial Coliseum, Convention Center, Lloyd Center, Hollywood District and out to its last stop in Gresham. Stations have glass-covered waiting areas and cobblestone-lined streets designating the Light Rail corridor.

MAX fares are the same as bus fares. The system operates daily 5 a.m.-midnight, with trains running every 15 minutes during the day and every half-hour at night. For detailed schedule information on TRI-MET buses or MAX Light Rail trains, visit TRI-MET's office at 701 S.W. 6th Ave., or phone (503) 238-7433. The office open Mon.-Fri. 9-5.

What To See

THE AMERICAN ADVERTISING MUSEUM, 600 N.E. Grand Ave., is exclusively dedicated to advertising. Chronicling the history of American advertising since 1683, the exhibits highlight the history of printed and broadcast advertisements, including such artifacts as Burma Shave signs and the first radio commercial.

Allow 1 hour, 30 minutes minimum. Wed.-Fri. 11-5, Sat.-Sun. noon-5. Admission $3; over 65 and ages 6-12, $1.50. AE, MC, VI. Phone (503) 230-1090.

AUDUBON SOCIETY OF PORTLAND, 5151 N.W. Cornell Rd., includes a 160-acre wildlife sanctuary, where birds and animals can be seen in their natural environment. Several miles of trails are open dawn-dusk. The Wildlife Care Center, a rehabilitation facility for injured wildlife, features live animals and other educational exhibits. The Audubon House has bird observation areas. Allow 1 hour minimum. Mon.-Sat. 10-6; Sun. 10-5. Wildlife Care Center daily 10-5, Memorial Day-Labor Day; 10-3, rest of year. Free. Phone (503) 292-6855.

CHILDREN'S MUSEUM, 3037 S.W. 2nd Ave., offers hands-on fun in Kid City, a grocery store, children's cultural center and other changing exhibits. Children can investigate the properties of water in H2 Oh! and work with clay in the Clayshop. A playground and an infant play space are provided. Allow 1 hour minimum. Daily 9-5; closed major holidays. Admission $3.50. Phone (503) 823-2227.

COWBOYS THEN AND NOW MUSEUM is at 729 N.E. Oregon St. From I-5 take Coliseum exit, turn on Weidler, then right on 7th, then e. on Oregon; or Lloyd Center exit off I-84 onto Lloyd Blvd., then right on Oregon St. The museum features a chuck wagon and hands-on tack room exhibits. Other highlights include displays depicting cowboy movie and television heroes, a videotape on past and present ranching methods and a research library. Allow 1 hour minimum. Wed.-Fri. 11-5, Sat.-Sun. noon-5; closed holidays. Donations. Phone (503) 731-3200.

CRYSTAL SPRINGS RHODODENDRON GARDENS are next to Eastmoreland Golf Course, 28th Ave. S.E., 1 blk. n. of Woodstock. More than 4,000 rhododendrons and azaleas start blooming in February and continue through June. Daily 6 a.m.-9 p.m., Apr.-Sept.; 6-6, rest of year. Admission (10 a.m.-6 p.m.) $2, otherwise free; free to all Tues.-Wed. Phone (503) 771-8386.

THE GROTTO (National Sanctuary of Our Sorrowful Mother) is a 62-acre park and religious shrine on Sandy Blvd. at N.E. 85th Ave. Erected in 1924, the shrine is maintained by the Servite Friars and Sisters as a place of reflection for all faiths. A grotto in a 10-story cliff serves as an outdoor cathedral. This natural gallery features flower-lined pathways under towering firs, running streams, a reflection pond, and sculptured bronze, marble and wood shrines. The Grotto's upper level of manicured gardens offers views of Mount St. Helens and the Cascade Range.

During December The Grotto presents the Christmas Festival of Lights featuring lighting displays, choral concerts and family entertainment.

Allow 1 hour, 30 minutes minimum. Daily 9-8, May-Sept.; 9-5, rest of year. An elevator operates 9-8. Elevator fee $1.50, under 6 free. AE, MC, VI. Phone (503) 254-7371.

HOYT ARBORETUM, 175 acres US 26 exit Washington Park Zoo, in Washington Park, contains more than 800 varieties of coniferous and flowering trees and shrubs. A visitor center provides displays and brochures detailing self-guiding tours along 10 miles of trails, including two mile-long loop trails and a wheelchair-accessible trail. A picnic shelter is across from the visitor center. Guided tours are available Sat.-Sun. at 2, Apr.-Oct. Grounds open daily 6 a.m.-10 p.m. Visitor center open daily 9-4. Donations. Phone (503) 823-3655.

IRA KELLER FOUNTAIN, 3rd and S.W. Clay sts., is one square block of sparkling waterfalls, pools, streamlets, trees and grass. Every minute 13,000 gallons of water flow. The water runs Thurs.-Tues.

JAMES F. BYBEE HOUSE is in Howell Park; go n. on US 30 then east over the Sauvie Island Bridge, follow signs. The restored 1858 house and its furnishings reflect life in mid-19th-century Oregon. On the grounds are an agricultural museum with farm tools, an exhibit explaining the history of farming and an orchard with specimens of the more than 100 varieties of apples brought west by pioneers. On the last Saturday in September, the house is the setting for Wintering In which features cider presses, 19th-century crafts, living history demonstrations and guided tours of the house.

Allow 1 hour minimum. House and museum open Sat.-Sun. noon-5, June 1-Labor Day. Grounds open daily dawn-dusk. Admission $2, ages 6-12, $1. Phone (503) 222-1741 or 621-3344.

LEACH BOTANICAL GARDEN, 6704 S.E. 122 Ave., encompasses 1,500 species of flowers along with native and non-native ornamentals. One-and-a-half-miles of trails wind through the 9-acre garden. Guided tours of the former estate grounds and a rustic stone cabin are offered Wednesday at 2 and Saturday at 10. A manor house on the property also is open for viewing. Self-guiding brochures are available. Tues.-Sat. 10-4, Sun. 1-4. Donations. Phone (503) 761-9503.

★**METRO WASHINGTON PARK ZOO,** 3 mi. w. on US 26, specializes in breeding programs for rare and endangered species such as the Asian elephant, Humbolt penguin and snow leopard. Major exhibits simulate the animals' natural environments. The Alaska Tundra exhibit is home to grizzly bears, wolves and other Alaska natives. An African exhibit features zebras, giraffes, DeBrazza monkeys and black rhinos.

Local animals such as beaver and otter are found in the Cascade Stream and Pond exhibit. The Penguinarium features natural ocean waves and realistic nesting sites. The African Rain Forest features rain, thunder, lightening and fog as well as crocodiles, mongooses, bats, monkeys and tropical birds.

The Afri-Cafe allows diners to view colorful tropical birds in an adjoining aviary. The zoo train winds its way along a 4-mile route through wooded hillsides to the International Rose Test Gardens and Japanese Gardens *(see Washington Park)*, which can be visited before returning to the zoo. Special events include summer concerts for adults and children in the outdoor amphitheater; ZooBloom, a floral display in the spring; ZooBoo, a two-week Halloween event featuring the zoo train; and the ZooLights Festival in December.

Allow 3 hours minimum. Trains operate daily, spring through fall (weather permitting). Zoo opens daily 9:30; closing times vary by season. Admission $5.50; over 65, $4; ages 3-11, $3.50. Railway (with zoo admission) $2.50; over 65 and ages 3-11, $1.75. MC, VI. Phone (503) 226-1561.

THE OLD CHURCH, 1422 S.W. 11th Ave., is one of the city's oldest existing church buildings. An example of Carpenter Gothic architecture, it is maintained as a landmark and community center, housing a collection of Victorian furniture and original stained-glass windows. Free sack-lunch concerts, often featuring the church's 1883 pipe organ, are offered Wednesday at noon. Allow 30 minutes minimum. Mon.-Fri. 11-3. Free. Phone (503) 222-2031.

★**OREGON HISTORY CENTER,** 1200 S.W. Park Ave., has 8-story-high trompe l'oeil murals of western themes by Richard Hass. The center's museum presents permanent and changing exhibits on Oregon history. The library is the primary resource center for information on the history of Oregon. Allow 2 hours minimum. Museum open Tues.-Sat. 10-5, Sun. noon-5. Library open Tues.-Sat. noon-5. Admission $4.50, students ages 6-18 with ID $1.50; free to senior citizens Thurs. Phone (503) 222-1741.

OREGON MARITIME CENTER AND MUSEUM, 113 S.W. Front St., contains a collection of ship models and permanent and changing exhibits of navigation instruments, a variety of ship hardware, paintings and photographs, and such artifacts as those from the USS *Oregon.* A guided tour of the *Steamer Portland,* a steam-powered, sternwheeler tugboat, is available. Maritime educational programs are presented periodically. Allow 1 hour minimum. Wed.-Sun. 11-4, Memorial Day weekend-Labor Day; Fri.-Sun. 11-4, rest of year. Admission $4; over 62 and ages 8-18, $3; family rate $10. **Discount.** Phone (503) 224-7724.

★**OREGON MUSEUM OF SCIENCE AND INDUSTRY (OMSI),** 1945 S.E. Water Ave., offers hands-on exhibits, planetarium presentations and classes. Planetarium shows are given daily. The 330-seat OMNIMAX® theater features a large movie projector, a five-story domed screen and a state-of-the-art sound system. Theater shows are given daily; phone for schedule. Laser shows in the planetarium are held Tuesday through Sunday evenings. Matinee shows also are available. Visitors can tour the USS *Blueback,* the last diesel-electric submarine built by the Navy. The submarine was used in the filming of "The Hunt for Red October."

Allow 2 hours minimum. Museum open daily 9:30-7 (also Thurs.-Fri. 7-9 p.m.), Memorial Day-Labor Day; 9:30-5:30 (also Thurs.-Fri. 5:30-9), rest of year. Closed Dec. 25. Admission $7; over 62, $6; ages 3-17, $4.50. MC, VI. Phone (503) 797-4000, or 797-4640 for show schedule.

OREGON RIVER EXPERIENCES, offers full-day and overnight raft trips that explore the Deschutes, John Day, Grande Ronde, McKenzie, North Santiam, Owyhee and Rogue rivers. Minimum age or weight restrictions may apply; phone for information. Departure points vary. Fees range from $65-$550 depending on the length of the trip. For reservations, contact Oregon River Experiences, 2 Jefferson Pkwy. #D7, Lake Oswego, OR 97035. Phone (503) 697-8133 or (800) 827-1358.

PENINSULA ROSE GARDEN, N. Ainsworth and N. Albina sts. in Peninsula Park, is one of the largest sunken rose gardens in America. It is landscaped in Elizabethan style with plantings of floribunda and tea roses. Blossom season is late May into fall. Daily dawn-dusk. Free. Phone (503) 823-3636.

PITTOCK MANSION, 3229 N.W. Pittock Dr., off W. Burnside, is the focal point of Pittock Acres Park. The restored French Renaissance mansion, furnished with 17th- and 18th-century European and American antiques, was built about 1914 by Henry Pittock, the founder of *The Daily Oregonian.* The mansion is nearly 1,000 feet above Portland and has a panoramic view of the city and five distant mountains.

Allow 1 hour, 30 minutes minimum. Grounds open daily 7 a.m.-9 p.m.; closed holidays. House open daily noon-4; closed holidays. House admission $4.50; over 65, $4; ages 6-18, $2. Grounds free. Phone (503) 823-3623.

★**PORTLAND ART MUSEUM,** 1219 S.W. Park at Jefferson, was founded in 1892 and is the region's oldest visual and media arts center. The museum's treasures span 35 centuries of art including Asian, European and American works, as well as collections of Native American art and regional and contemporary art. The film center features the annual Portland International Film Festival and Northwest Film Festival.

Allow 1 hour minimum. Tues.-Sat. 11-5, Sun. 1-5 (also 4-9 the first Thurs. of the month). Admission $4.50; senior citizens $3.50; students with ID and ages 6-12, $2.50; free to senior citizens on Thurs.; free to all 4-9 the first Thurs. of the month. AE, DS, MC VI. Phone (503) 226-2811, or 221-1156 for film schedule.

PORTLAND POLICE HISTORICAL MUSEUM, 1111 S.W. 2nd Ave., pertains to local police history. Exhibits include uniforms, handcuffs, guns and photographs. Allow 30 minutes minimum. Mon.-Thurs. 10-3. Free. Phone (503) 823-0019.

★**WASHINGTON PARK,** s. from Burnside Rd., has its main entrance at the head of Park Place. The crown jewel of the city's extensive park system, Washington Park encompasses almost 145 acres of hills and dales and offers a variety of activities, ranging from quiet contemplation to jogging and tennis. Commemorating Portland's past are the statues "Coming of the White Man" and "Sacajawea," which were dedicated by Susan B. Anthony at the opening of the 1905 Lewis and Clark Exposition. Phone (503) 823-2223.

International Rose Test Gardens, in the park, were established in 1917 as an outgrowth of the efforts of the Portland Rose Society. Covering more than 4 acres and encompassing 400 varieties, these gardens are a vivid and vibrant display of Portland's love affair with the rose. Some 10,000 bushes are planted in three terraces, which offer a sweeping view of the city. Roses bloom late May into fall. Free.

Japanese Gardens are on S.W. Kingston, above the International Rose Test Gardens; the main gate is reached by a path or, during the summer, a shuttle bus. Five traditional styles of gardens open onto a view of Portland and the mountains surrounding the city. Allow 1 hour minimum. Daily 9-8, June-Aug.; 10-6, Apr.-May and in Sept.; 10-4 rest of year. Closed Jan. 1, Thanksgiving and Dec. 25. Admission $5, over 62 and students with ID $2.50. Phone (503) 223-4070.

WORLD FORESTRY CENTER, 4033 S.W. Canyon Rd., in Washington Park off US 26, contains recreational and educational exhibits on forestry. Highlights include a 70-foot "talking tree," exhibits depicting Northwest old-growth forests and global tropical rainforests, a petrified wood collection and a multi-media presentation on "Forests of the World" as well as free outdoor exhibits. Allow 1 hour minimum. Daily 9-5, mid-June through Labor Day; 10-5, rest of year. Closed Dec. 25. Admission $3; over 61 and ages 6-18, $2. AE, MC, VI. **Discount.** Phone (503) 228-1368.

Industrial Tours

BLITZ-WEINHARD BREWERY, I-5 or I-405 City Center exit to 1133 W. Burnside St., offers a guided ½-hour tour and a hospitality room with free beer samples. The tour includes a 15-minute videotape depicting the history of the brewery and of the beer-making process. Allow 1 hour minimum. Tours Tours Thurs. and Fri. at noon, 1:30 and 3; closed holidays. Free. Phone (503) 222-4351.

PENDLETON WOOLEN MILLS, offers guided factory tours at two locations. Under 12 must be with an adult.

Foundation Weaving Plant, 4 mi. s. on SR 99E to 8550 S.E. McLoughlin, offers 30-minute guided tours demonstrating the processes involved in the production of woolen cloth. Tours leave from the store next door Tues.-Fri. Reservations are required. Free. Phone (503) 273-2786.

Milwaulkie Garment Factory, 6 mi. s. on SR 99E to 10505 S.E. 17th Ave., offers 45-minute guided tours showing the manufacturing of shirts and blouses. Tours Mon.-Fri. at 10 and 2; closed holidays, 2 weeks in mid-summer and the week of Dec. 25. Free. Phone (503) 273-2588.

What To Do

Sightseeing

Bus Tours

Gray Line offers various guided bus tours of Portland, as well as Mount St. Helens, the Columbia River Gorge, the Mount Hood loop and the northern Oregon coast. The tours operate mid-April through October 31. Phone (503) 285-9845 or (800) 422-7042 for schedules and reservations.

The public bus system, TRI-MET, can be used for a self-guiding tour of the city.

Boat Tours

SPIRIT OF PORTLAND**,** departing from Waterfront Park at the end of Salmon St., offers 2 and 2½-hour cruises on the Willamette River. Lunch and dinner cruises are offered in addition to special holiday and extended excursions. Lunch cruise departs Wed.-Fri. at noon. Dinner cruise departs Tues.-Sat. at 7 p.m., Sun. at 6 p.m. Lunch cruise $19.95. Dinner cruise $34.95 Tues.-Thurs., $39.95 Fri.-Sat., $29.95 Sun. MC, VI. Reservations are required. Phone (503) 224-3900 or (800) 224-3901.

THE STERNWHEELER *COLUMBIA GORGE*, departing from Waterfront Park, offers 2-hour narrated cruises of the Portland harbor area. Mid-June through Sept. 30 the MV *Columbia Gorge* operates out of Cascade Locks *(see place listing)*. Departures Fri. at noon, Sat. at 11:30, Sun. 11:30, Apr. 1 to mid-June and in Nov.; Sun. at 10 and 1, in Dec. Fares range from $11.95-$33.95, children $5.95-$23.95. AE, MC, VI. Reservations are recommended. Phone (503) 223-3928.

YACHTS-O-FUN CRUISES, departing from the RiverPlace Marina, offers boat excursions on the Willamette River. Dinner, harbor, moonlight, historical and Sunday brunch cruises are available. Reservations are required for brunch and dinner cruises and recommended for excursions. Fares range from $9-$30.95. AE, DS, MC, VI. Phone (503) 289-6665.

Plane Tours

Tours of Mount St. Helens are offered by several air charter companies; cost varies with the size of the plane and the number of passengers. For more information contact your local AAA club office.

Walking Tours

Maps to historic buildings, sculptures and fountains that can be visited on foot are available from the Portland Oregon Visitors Association, 25 S.W. Salmon St., Portland, OR 97201; phone (503) 222-2223.

Sports and Recreation

Portland offers a wide variety of sports, ranging from sailing to mountain climbing. The city's extensive system of parks provides jogging trails, bicycle paths, swimming pools, tennis courts and nature trails. Nearby state parks also have recreational and camping facilities.

Boating is available at many marinas on the Columbia and Willamette rivers, as well as at the state parks; most marinas have many types of craft for rent in the spring and summer.

Fishing opportunities abound on the Willamette, as well as in state parks and in area lakes and streams. Chinook salmon are plentiful in the lower Willamette March through early May, while steelhead trout run throughout the year in the Clackamas and Sandy rivers. For more information phone the Oregon Dept. of Fish and Wildlife at (503) 229-5403.

White-water rafting and **float trips** are offered throughout the state, usually April through September. Rates for such trips vary, but the average fee is $60 for a full-day excursion, $280-$525 for 3-, 4- and 5-day trips.

Reservations for trips can be made through the following Portland area agencies: C & J Lodge, P.O. Box 130, Maupin, OR 97037, (503) 395-2404; River Drifters, 13570 N.W. Lakeview Dr., Portland, OR 97229; River Trails, 336 E. Columbia, Troutdale, OR 97060, (503) 667-1964; and Whitewater Adventure, 38 N.W. Lake, White Salmon, WA 98672, (509) 493-3121 or (800) 366-2004.

Hunting opportunities abound in the mountains and forests surrounding Portland. For information on hunting and fishing areas and licenses, phone the Oregon Dept. of Fish and Wildlife at (503) 229-5403.

Hiking and **horseback riding** enthusiasts have miles of trails to explore in nearby state parks and national forests. Forest Service maps and other details are available from the U.S. Forest Service; phone (503) 666-0700. Check a telephone directory or call a local AAA office for a list of area horse stables that provide rentals.

Mountain climbing and **skiing** are possible in the hills bordering Portland. Mount Hood, about an hour's drive from the city, is said to be one of the most climbed mountains in the world. Information on ski resorts and conditions is available from AAA Oregon; phone (503) 222-6700. Information on mountain climbing is available from the U.S. Forest Service; phone (503) 666-0700.

For the less adventurous, **bicycle trails** wind through city parks; most connect with the statewide network of paths. Maps and route information can be obtained from the Oregon Parks and Recreation Division, 1115 Commercial St. N.E., Salem, OR 97310-1001.

Tennis players have the choice of the city's indoor courts or outside facilities. The indoor courts must be reserved. Phone the Portland Tennis Center at (503) 823-3190.

Golf fans can play at any of the 18 public courses, including Eastmoreland at 2425 S.E. Bybee St., (503) 775-2900; Rose City at 2200 N.E. 71st Ave., (503) 253-4744; Heron Lakes at West Delta Park off I-5, (503) 289-1818; and Progress Downs at 8200 S.W. Scholls Ferry Rd., (503) 646-5166. Prices average $18 for 18 holes, $9 for 9 holes.

Swimming is possible early June through August at several parks in the metropolitan area, including Sellwood Park at S.E. 7th Avenue and Miller Street, Mount Scott Park at S.E. 72nd Avenue and Harold Street, U.S. Grant Park at N.E. 33rd Avenue and Thompson Street and Columbia Park at 7701 N. Chautauqua St. Nominal admission fees may be charged; phone (503) 823-2223 for schedules and information.

Spectators will find there is much for them to watch. The Rose Garden, at 1 N. Center Ct., hosts most of the city's sporting expositions and events. The Trail Blazers play professional **basketball,** and the Winter Hawks play semiprofessional **hockey** from early winter through mid-spring. Next door, the Memorial Coliseum serves as a second site for spectator sports.

Auto racing can be seen in the summer at the Portland International Raceway in West Delta Park at N. Victory, (503) 285-6635; and at the Portland Speedway, 9727 N. Martin Luther King Jr. Boulevard, (503) 285-2883.

Horse racing with pari-mutuel betting takes place at Portland Meadows, 1001 N. Schmeer Rd., October through April; phone (503) 285-9144.

Greyhound racing is held Tuesday through Saturday nights May through September at the Multnomah Kennel Club, 12 miles east in Fairview, at N.E. 223rd Avenue and Glisan Street.Third Ave.; phone (503) 667-7700.

Note: Policies vary concerning admittance of children to pari-mutuel betting facilities. Phone for information.

Where To Shop

With the largest collection of cast-iron-fronted structures outside New York City, Portland has preserved a majority of them in two historic districts: Skidmore/Old Town and Yamhill. The two areas blend historic preservation with modern commerce, as many of these landmarks are filled with shops, galleries and restaurants.

The Skidmore/Old Town District straddles West Burnside Street between Davis and Stark streets. The focus of the area, and an outstanding example of cast-iron architecture, is the New Market Theatre building. The majestic former playhouse and produce market has been recast as a collection of shops and restaurants known as the New Market Village.

Under the Burnside Bridge and across from New Market Theatre is the open-air Portland Saturday Market where craftspersons, artists, entertainers, cooks and farmers come to sell their works and/or entertain the public. Open Sat. 10-5 and Sun. 11-4:30 March 1 through Dec. 24, the

Market sells only handcrafted (or locally grown) items; phone (503) 222-6072.

Other notable buildings in this area include the former Globe Hotel, which markets international goods in its Import Plaza, and the Skidmore-Fountain Building, a marketplace that has kept its late 1800s character.

A few blocks south of the Skidmore/Old Town District is the smaller Yamhill District. Its centerpiece is the Yamhill Marketplace, a contemporary version of the markets that were in this area around 1900.

In stark contrast to these historic buildings are the World Trade Center Buildings I, II and III, which houses the Portland Oregon Visitors Association, restaurants and galleries.

The nearby waterfront between the Hawthorne and Marquam bridges has reverted from freeway to a pleasant strip of grass and trees, with an esplanade bordered by the shops, restaurants and residences of RiverPlace.

Before the restoration of the historic areas, many businesses had moved uptown to an area between S.W. 4th and 10th avenues. Such department stores as Meier & Frank and Nordstrom are here. One former department store has been transformed into the Galleria—three levels of shops around a 75-foot atrium. Pioneer Place offers several specialty shops as well as a department store.

There are other downtown places of note as well: Morgan's Alley is an underground group of stores and eatery with a European piazza flavor; Powell's Books, one of the country's largest bookstores, covers two entire city blocks. Nearby on the West Side is N.W. 23rd, also known as Nob Hill, an eclectic collection of shops, boutiques, galleries and restaurants, some within restored Victorian houses.

Outside the downtown area are several places of interest. On the East Side, at Grand Avenue and N.E. Weidler, is one of Portland's oldest and largest urban malls, the Lloyd Center, offering an indoor skating rink. To the north of downtown off I-5 at the Interstate Bridge is the Jantzen Beach Center, whose 100 stores include five department stores.

South of the city center is the Water Tower at John's Landing, a 1903 furniture factory that now houses a variety of shops along its winding hallways. The Old Sellwood Antique Row, southeast of downtown along S.E. 13th Avenue beyond the east end of the Sellwood Bridge, features some 50 antique and craft shops in a well-preserved community where decades-old buildings are marked with signs labeling past owners and building dates.

Shopping centers in the suburbs include the Clackamas Town Center, with more than 180 stores, a library and an indoor ice rink, off I-205 and S.E. Sunnyside Road; and Washington Square, off I-5 south on SR 217 in Tigard.

Where To Dine

"Fresh" and "grown in Oregon" are the two defining characteristics of Portland's restaurants. The Yamhill Marketplace, where wines, fruits, vegetables, seafood and other foodstuffs are sold, provides a vivid display of Oregon's bounty. This emporium also offers rooftop dining.

Some other local landmarks offering regional foods include the Dan and Louis Oyster Bar, 208 S.W. Ankeny; Jake's Famous Crawfish Restaurant, 401 S.W. 12th Ave.; and McCormick & Schmicks Seafood Restaurant, 235 S.W. 1st Ave. Established in 1879, Huber's restaurant, at 411 S.W. 3rd, features an arched stained-glass skylight, solid mahogany paneling and a terrazzo floor and is famous for its turkey sandwich.

Portland's environs also harbor fine restaurants, and many offer panoramas of the distant Cascades and the nearby river. Floor-to-ceiling windows highlight the elegant setting of the Esplanade restaurant, 1510 S.W. Harbor Way, overlooking the Willamette River.

Other restaurants with river views are the Harborside Restaurant and Pilsner Room, 0309 S.W. Montgomery; and the Willamette Anchorage, 513 S.E. Marion St. Newport Bay Restaurant, 0425 S.W. Montgomery, is surrounded by water on all sides; it floats in the Willamette River.

For an all-encompassing view of the Portland region try Atwater's Restaurant and Lounge, atop the U.S. Bancorp Tower at 111 S.W. 5th, whose cuisine accents Northwest products, or The Chart House, 5700 S.W. Terwilliger Blvd. Of the city's many fish specialists, the Couch Street Fish House, 105 N.W. 3rd, is probably the most popular. Visitors can enjoy high tea or dinner amid the antiques that decorate the Victorian John Palmer House at 4314 N. Mississippi Ave.

Dining in Portland can also be an artful experience, as in the Heathman Hotel, next to Portland's Center for the Performing Arts. This historic hotel also is an art gallery. Andy Warhol's Endangered Species series hangs in the dining room, and works by Northwest artists also

LAFAYETTE SCHOOL ANTIQUE MALL • 100 DEALERS

Historic Lafayette, 30 miles west of Portland on old Hwy. 99W, is nestled in the center of Oregon's Wine Country. The white steepled church is now the county museum; the most prominent home a bed & breakfast; and the old schoolhouse an antique mall.

Open 7 Days

748 Hwy. 99W
Lafayette, OR
(503) 864-2720

OREGON'S LARGEST ANTIQUE DISPLAY

find a place to complement the restaurant's elegant regional cuisine.

Art is not the only cultural aspect of city dining, for ethnic restaurants are sprinkled throughout Portland. The most distinctive ethnic area is Chinatown, which overlaps Old Town and embraces a host of restaurants such as Marco Polo Garden, 19 N.W. 5th. Greek specialty dishes, including Mad Greek and Lumberjack sandwiches, are available at the Downtown Deli Greek Cusina, 404 S.W. Washington.

For a flavor of Italy, Angelo and Roses at 11051 S.W. Barbur Blvd., Delphina's Pasta and Pizza at 2112 N.W. Kearney, or Mazzi's at 5833 S.W. Macadam, provide a range of Mediterranean dishes. Pazzo Ristorante, at 627 S.W. Washington St.on the ground floor of the Hotel Vintage Plaza, also offers Italian cuisine.

Classic French dishes are created at L'Auberge, 2601 N.W. Vaughn. Specialty restaurants include the Bread & Ink Cafe at 3610 S.E. Hawthorne Boulevard, Moxie on N.W. 21st Street, and Papa Haydn on N. W. 23rd Street. Nearby streets offer a variety of eating experiences, ranging from fresh French pastries and chocolates to Oregon wines by the glass.

Nightlife

Nightlife in Portland offers a variety of entertainment, from small quiet lounges to rowdy rock 'n' roll bars. Within a few blocks of downtown you can satisfy a craving for jazz, rock, reggae and blues or just sit back and enjoy a breathtaking panorama of the city in one of the many rooftop lounges.

A popular spot for jazz is Brasserie Montmartre at 626 S.W. Park St. Karaoke can be performed at Harrington's Bar & Grill, at the corner of S.W. 6th and S.W. Main. The Rock 'n' Rodeo, 220 S.E. Spokane at the base of the Sellwood Bridge, offers dance music and occasional live country bands.

Hotel lounges, such as Alexander's on the Hilton's rooftop, Atwater's in the Bancorp Tower and Trader Vic's at the Westin Benson, offer somewhat quieter atmospheres.

Current schedules for live music can be found in such local publications as *Willamette Week* and *The Downtowner,* available at various locations in and around the city center. For complete entertainment listings consult the local newspaper, especially the Friday arts and entertainment sections or phone (503) 233-3333.

Note: The mention of any area or establishment in the preceding sections is for information only and does **not** imply endorsement by AAA.

Theater and Concerts

The Portland Center for the Performing Arts is the focal point for the city's major cultural events. Unlike many such centers, this is a decentralized complex with three buildings in separate locations. They include the Arlene Schnitzer Concert Hall, the Civic Auditorium and the New Theatre Building.

The Arlene Schnitzer Concert Hall, a restored 1928 vaudeville house, is home to the Oregon Symphony Orchestra and the venue to other musical concerts, dance and touring shows.

Across the street the New Theatre Building encompasses two performance spaces: the 292-seat Dolores Winningstad Theater and the 916-seat Intermediate Theater. These theaters are the hosts for performances by the Oregon Ballet Theater, the Portland Center Stage and a number of choral and orchestral groups.

Several blocks away, at 222 S.W. Clay St., the Civic Auditorium showcases performances by the Portland Opera and the Oregon Ballet Theater, as well as various national touring groups. For ticket and schedule information for the entire complex phone (503) 248-4335.

The Portland Repertory Theater, (503) 224-4491, whose plays are staged in the World Trade Center 2 Building, is one of the city's most renowned companies. Another notable ensemble is Chamber Music Northwest, (503) 223-3202, which performs concerts during June and July at Reed College and the Catlín Gabel School.

In addition, the city has many other smaller performing theaters and several colleges that produce plays and concerts. For current schedules phone (503) 222-2223.

Especially for Children

Portland offers the young traveler a variety of attractions. The Metro Washington Park Zoo, with more than 700 exotic and domestic animals, has petting areas and educational exhibits of particular interest to children.

The Children's Museum has games, toys, stuffed animals, artwork, fossils and other goodies to fascinate youngsters. The participatory exhibits at the Oregon Museum of Science and Industry will interest any budding scientist, as will the recreational and educational exhibits of the World Forestry Center.

For lighter entertainment, the Oaks Amusement Park in southeast Portland on the Willamette River, offers rides and roller skating. Many city parks are available for entertainment and recreation.

Special Events

Of the several events and celebrations in the Portland area, the Rose Festival in early June tops the list. The festival lasts 3-4 weeks and includes a band competition, exhibits, one of the country's largest children's parades, the Grand Floral Parade, the Starlight Parade, the Indy Car World Series Race, the Hot Air Balloon Classic and a traditional rose show. For information on tickets and the schedule of events, phone (503) 227-2681.

Other summer events in Portland include the The Rose City Blues Festival in early July which features both international and Oregon's finest blues artists. The Portland Scottish Highland Games are held in mid-July; phone (503) 293-8501. The Multnomah County Fair, which offers agricultural and horticultural exhibits and live entertainment, is held at the County Expo Center late July through early August.

The Mount Hood Jazz Festival, held in August on the campus of the Mount Hood Community College, features renowned jazz musicians from all over the country. In early August, the Obon Spirit Festival takes place in the Japanese Rose Gardens. In the middle of the month Portland's restaurants present The Bite: A Taste of Portland, a food extravaganza on the waterfront.

The annual festival of the arts, the ArtQuake Festival in early September showcases theater, dance, music, storytelling, literature and the visual arts. The Portland Oktoberfest, held in mid-September at Holladay Park near the Lloyd Center, offers a wide variety of entertainment, displays and activities. With its large tents, German oom-pah-pah bands and festive atmosphere, the Horst Mager Oktoberfest at Oaks Park resembles the Oktoberfest celebrations in Germany. It takes place in late September. At the end of the month "Wintering-In" is celebrated at the James F. Bybee House on Sauvie Island, as local farmers sell their harvest goods.

Rodeos, horse shows and exhibits are features of the Pacific International Livestock Show, which draws large crowds to the Washington County Fairplex in October. For further information contact your local AAA club or the Portland Oregon Visitors Association; phone (503) 222-2223 or (800) 962-3700.

PORT ORFORD (F-5) pop. 1,000, elev. 60′

The bluffs overlooking the Pacific Ocean were first sighted in 1792 by Capt. George Vancouver, who named the area for England's Earl of Orford. Port Orford, settled in the 1850s, became a shipping center for cedar. One of the early methods of transporting the logs was to lower them by rope over the bluffs onto ships anchored in the bay below. Cedar logging remains the area's primary industry.

A natural deep-water port, Port Orford is Oregon's only coastal port that required few man-made adaptations. The fishing fleet is hoisted from the water onto a dry dock and stored on rolling cradles to escape the rough seas whipped up by southwesterly winds.

Recreational opportunities include scuba diving, whale watching, fishing and crabbing. For additional information contact the Port Orford Chamber of Commerce, P.O. Box 637, Port Orford, OR 97465; phone (503) 332-8055. Humbug Mountain State Park, 6 mi. s. on US 101, offers camping, picnicking, hiking and fishing; phone (503) 332-6774. *See Recreation Chart and the AAA Northwestern CampBook.*

CAPE BLANCO STATE PARK, 5 mi. n., then 6 mi. w. off US 101, was named by Spanish explorers for its chalky appearance due to a concentration of fossilized shells. A large sea lion colony occupies the offshore rocks, and an 1870 lighthouse still functions. Daily 24 hours. Phone (503) 332-6774. *See Recreation Chart and the AAA Northwestern CampBook.*

The Hughes House, 8 mi. n.w., was built in 1898. The Eastlake Victorian-style ranch house contains collections of photographs and a variety of antiques. Allow 30 minutes minimum. Mon. and Thurs.-Sat. 10-5, Sun. noon-5, May-Sept. Donations. Phone (503) 332-0248 or 332-2975.

PREHISTORIC GARDENS, 12 mi. s. on US 101, presents life-size replicas of dinosaurs in a rain forest setting. Allow 30 minutes minimum. Daily 8-dusk. Admission $5; over 65 and ages 12-18, $4; ages 5-11, $3. MC, VI. Phone (503) 332-4463.

PRINEVILLE (D-8) pop. 5,400, elev. 2,868′

The rimrocks that almost encircle Prineville, as well as the region's other unusual geological features, make it a favorite place for rockhounds. The chamber of commerce has information about areas where thundereggs, agate and petrified wood can be found. In late June collectors gather to swap tales and rocks at the town's annual Rockhound Pow Wow.

Other recreational activities, including cross-country skiing, snowmobiling, hiking, boating and fishing, are found nearby at Prineville Reservoir as well as at Ochoco National Forest *(see place listing); see Recreation Chart and the AAA Northwestern CampBook.*

Maps and information can be obtained from the Prineville-Crook County Chamber of Commerce, 390 N. Fairview, Prineville, OR 97754; phone (503) 447-6304. The office is open Mon.-Fri. 9-5, Sat.-Sun. 11-4, Memorial Day-Labor Day; Mon.-Fri. 9-5, rest of year.

RAINIER (A-3) pop. 1,700, elev. 23′

This historic mill town, founded in 1851, was named for Mount Rainier, visible to the northeast. The town was an important river port in its early days. A bridge connects it to Longview, Wash.

REDMOND (D-8) pop. 7,200, elev. 3,007′

Surrounded by an abundance of juniper trees, Redmond is an industrial and lumbering center. One of the city's leading industries is the Redmond Air Center, a Forest Service smokejumping, firefighting and training installation at the

Redmond Airport. Arrangements can be made for a free guided tour of the facilities. Local recreational opportunities include rock climbing, swimming, golfing, fishing and whitewater rafting in addition to Nordic and Alpine skiing.

Operation Santa Claus,a ranch that raises the reindeer used by many communities during the Christmas season, is 2 miles west on US 126. For more information on area attractions contact the Redmond Chamber of Commerce, 106 S.W. 7th St., Redmond, OR 97756; phone (503) 923-5191 or (800) 574-1325.

PETERSEN'S ROCK GARDENS, 7 mi. s.w. off US 97, embraces several colorful acres. Bridges, terraces and replicas of historic structures are built of rock and petrified wood. A museum displays rare rock specimens. Picnicking is permitted. Allow 1 hour minimum. Museum open daily 9-6. Gardens open daily 9-9, Memorial Day weekend-Labor Day; 9-dusk, rest of year. Admission $2; ages 12-17, $1; ages 6-11, 50c. Phone (503) 382-5574.

PETER SKENE OGDEN STATE PARK, 98 acres 9 mi. n. on US 97, flanks the Crooked River Gorge. The park encompasses both highway bridge approaches. Picnicking is available. Daily dawn-dusk.

SMITH ROCK STATE PARK, n. on US 97 to Terrebonne, then 3 mi. e., affords scenic views of colorful cliffs above the Crooked River. Rock climbing, hiking and picnicking are popular activities. Daily dawn-dusk. Parking $3, mid-May to mid-Sept. *See Recreation Chart.*

REEDSPORT (F-2) pop. 4,800

Water was once the bane of existence for Reedsport, built on marshy tideland filled in with clay taken from the hills behind town. Flooding was so frequent that most of the town's early buildings and sidewalks had to be elevated 3 to 8 feet above ground. A devastating flood in 1964 resulted in the construction of a dike to protect the lower part of town.

Reedsport's watery surroundings evoke images of the salmon, steelhead trout and striped bass that abound. Adjacent Winchester Bay, at the mouth of the Umpqua River, is among Oregon's most productive sport-fishing harbors.

US 101 is a scenic highway that passes through Reedsport and stretches along the Oregon coast. It features such nearby scenic areas as Oregon Dunes National Recreation Area *(see Suislaw National Forest)* along its route. SR 38 from I-5 to US 101 parallels the scenic Umpqua River valley. Dean Creek Elk Viewing Area offers more spectacular scenery 3 miles east of Reedsport. Hiking, camping, beach combing and whale watching are popular activities near town.

For further information contact the Lower Umpqua Chamber of Commerce, 805 US 101 Ave., P.O. Box 11, Reedsport, OR 97467; phone (503) 271-3495 or (800) 247-2155.

ANTARCTIC RESEARCH VESSEL *HERO*, e. on SR 38 to 3rd St., then follow signs to Riverfront Dr., allows visitors to experience what it was like to explore the desolate continent of Antarctica. Powered by 720-horsepower, twin-diesel engines, the *Hero* accommodated a crew of 19, plus seven researchers. The oak-hull ship was designed to withstand the frozen conditions of the Antarctic, allowing researchers to conduct scientific experiments for months at a time.

The vessel is equipped with two laboratories that were used for oceanographical, geological and biological studies. Sails were used for silent tracking of whales and other marine life. Daily 10-4, May 15-Sept. 30; 10-4, rest of year. Admission $3; ages 5-12, $1.50. Phone (503) 271-4816.

UMPQUA LIGHTHOUSE STATE PARK, 5 mi. s. off US 101, embraces 2½ miles of shoreline with sand dunes that rise about 500 feet; it is next to the Oregon Dunes National Recreation Area. The 1892 lighthouse has a red beam that is visible for 20 miles. The lighthouse is west of the park but is not open to the public. The park is open daily dawn-dusk. *See Recreation Chart and the AAA Northwestern CampBook.*

ROGUE RIVER (G-6) pop. 1,800

JET BOAT RIVER EXCURSIONS, on the Rogue River off I-5 exit 48, offers 1- and 2-hour tours on the river mid-May through Sept. 30, as well as dinner excursions. Age or weight restrictions may apply. One-hour trips depart daily at noon and 2. Two-hour trips depart daily at 9. Dinner excursions depart daily at 4:30, May 1-Sept. 1; at 4, Sept. 2-Oct. 1. Office open 9-5:30. One-hour trip $10; ages 4-11, $6. Two-hour trip $18; ages 4-11, $9. Dinner excursion $34; ages 4-11, $16. DS, MC, VI. **Discount.** Reservations are advised. Phone (503) 582-0800.

PALMERTON ARBORETUM is off I-5 Rogue River city exit, following signs. Featured are a variety of labeled plants, shrubs and trees, as well as a duck pond, playground and picnic area. Allow 30 minutes minimum. Daily 8-dusk. Phone (503) 582-4401.

ROGUE RIVER NATIONAL FOREST

Elevations in the forest range from 1,300 ft. in Applegate Valley to 9,495 ft. at Mount McLoughlin. Refer to AAA maps for additional elevation information.

Rogue River National Forest encompasses 629,088 acres in two separate units in southwestern Oregon. The main entrance from the south is I-5 from Medford. The forest's western unit includes Mount Ashland, the highest point in Oregon west of the Cascade Range, and the headwaters of the Applegate River in the Siskiyou Mountains. Its many environments include open woodlands, conifer forests and rocky ridgetops with many botanical specimens.

The eastern unit contains the upper reaches of the Rogue River and Mount McLoughlin, a 9,495-foot volcanic cone. The Upper Rogue is generally too difficult for float trips, but it is still popular for other recreational pursuits and for its scenery in the volcanic terrain of the Cascade Range. The area's forest of Douglas fir, ponderosa pine and other conifers is enhanced by meadows, lakes and streams.

The forest is the western gateway to Crater Lake National Park *(see place listing)*. Two fascinating geological interpretive sites, Natural Bridge and Rogue Gorge, are located along Crater Lake Highway. The forest features developed campgrounds and opportunities for snowmobiling, sledding and cross-country and downhill skiing.

The Pacific Crest National Scenic Trail follows the southern Oregon Cascades and Siskiyou Mountains from Crater Lake into California. This and other forest trails provide access for hiking or pack-and-saddle trips.

Within the Applegate Valley region is Dutchman's Peak Lookout, which was built in 1927. It is one of the last cupola-topped lookout buildings still in use to detect forest fires. The lookout, 33 miles from Ashland via I-5, affords a panoramic view.

Also in the gold-rich Applegate Valley are remnants of hydraulic mining operations carried out by Chinese miners in the mid-19th century; one such site is along the Gin Lin Trail near the popular recreation facilities at Applegate Lake.

For further information contact the Forest Supervisor at 333 W. 8th St., Medford, OR 97501; phone (503) 858-2200. *See Recreation Chart and the AAA Northwestern CampBook.*

ROSEBURG (G-3) pop. 17,000, elev. 479'

Once known for its rich timber industry, Roseburg is a recreation seeker's delight. Centrally located, Roseburg is only 70 miles from the ocean and 70 miles from snow-capped mountains; Mount Nebo is visible across the Umpqua River. A scenic drive east of Roseburg via SR 138 follows the North Umpqua River to Diamond Lake and Crater Lake National Park *(see place listing)*. For more information contact the Roseburg Area Chamber of Commerce, 410 S.E. Spruce St., Roseburg, OR 97470; phone (503) 672-2648 or (800) 444-9584.

Roseburg also is the home of La Garza Cellars and Gourmet Kitchen, 491 Winery Ln.; phone (503) 679-9654. This winery offers guided tours Memorial Day weekend through Labor Day and tastings February to mid-December.

DOUGLAS COUNTY MUSEUM, off I-5 at exit 123, exhibits dioramas, more than 15,000 photographs, artifacts and natural specimens relating to the history, natural environs and growth of Douglas County. A research library is provided. Allow 1 hour minimum. Daily 10-5; closed Jan. 1, Thanksgiving and Dec. 25. Admission $3.50; ages 3-17, $1. Phone (503) 440-4507.

HILLCREST VINEYARD is 10 mi. n.w. of I-5 Garden Valley Blvd. exit 125, left on Melrose Rd., following signs to 240 Vineyard Ln. Guided tours and tastings are offered. Picnicking is permitted. Allow 30 minutes minimum. Daily 11-5. Free. Phone (503) 673-3709.

WILDLIFE SAFARI, 5 mi. s. off I-5 Winston-Coos Bay exit 119, is a 600-acre drive-through zoological park featuring exotic animals roaming freely in natural surroundings. Live animal programs and elephant and train rides are featured seasonally. Safari Village offers a petting zoo; food is available. No convertibles are permitted in the lion or bear drive-throughs; rental cars and pet kennels are available.

Allow 1 hour, 30 minutes minimum. Daily 9-7, Memorial Day weekend-Labor Day; 9-dusk, rest of year. Admission $9.95; over 65, $8.50; ages 4-12, $6.75; $1 per private vehicle entering park. AE, DI, DS, MC, VI. **Discount.** Phone (503) 679-6761 or (800) 355-4848.

RUFUS (B-9) pop. 300

JOHN DAY LOCK AND DAM, off I-84, offers guided tours encompassing all aspects of dam operation. The tour includes the navigation lock,

JUST IN CASE

Minor emergencies frequently occur on the road when there's no drugstore for miles around. Be on the safe side – always travel with a first-aid kit containing a first-aid booklet, assorted bandages, cotton, tweezers, aspirin, antihistamines, motion sickness pills and insect repellent.

spillway, powerhouse and fish ladder. Underwater windows allow visitors to see fish bypassing the dam. Allow 2 hours minimum. Daily 9-6, Memorial Day-Labor Day; Wed.-Sun. 10-5, day after Labor Day-Sept. 30; Wed.-Sun. 10-3, Apr. 8-day before Memorial Day. Free. Phone (503) 296-1181. *See Recreation Chart.*

ST. HELENS (B-4) pop. 7,500, elev. 98′

On the Oregon side of the Columbia River, St. Helens lies southwest of its supposed namesake, Mount St. Helens. From its inception, the town's position on the river made it a port. There is a historic district on the waterfront which includes a museum housed in the 1906 courthouse.

SALEM (C-3) pop. 107,800, elev. 171′

Salem is the capital of Oregon and the state's third largest city. The city was founded in 1841 by Methodist missionary Jason Lee, whose goal was to gather the Indians together and "teach them to cultivate the ground and live more comfortably than they could by hunting, and as they do this, teach them religion."

After limited success, Lee became discouraged. He decided to lay out a town and sell lots to finance the Oregon Institute, which developed into the present-day Willamette University, the oldest institution of higher learning west of Missouri.

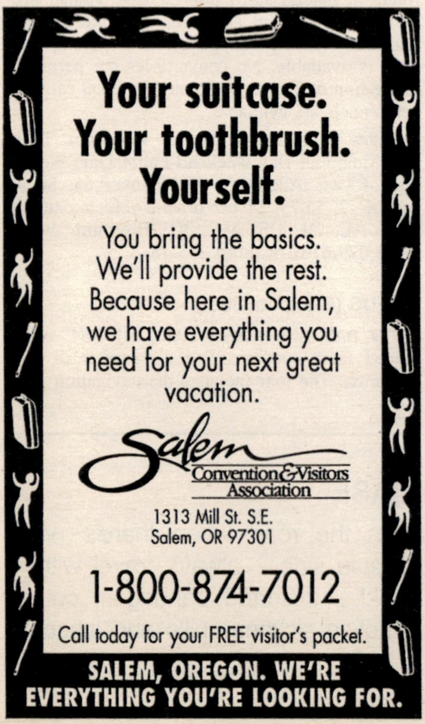
Your suitcase.
Your toothbrush.
Yourself.
You bring the basics.
We'll provide the rest.
Because here in Salem,
we have everything you
need for your next great
vacation.
Salem
Convention & Visitors Association
1313 Mill St. S.E.
Salem, OR 97301
1-800-874-7012
Call today for your FREE visitor's packet.
SALEM, OREGON. WE'RE
EVERYTHING YOU'RE LOOKING FOR.

Salem had only one house when it was plotted, and the Calapooya Indian name Chemeketa, or "place of rest," was proposed for the town's name. Missionaries, however, preferred the Biblical word "salem," which means peace.

Bethel Heights Vineyard, 6060 Bethel Heights Rd. N.W., offers guided tours and tastings Tues.-Sun. 11-5, June-Aug.; Sat.-Sun. 11-5, Mar.-May and Sept.-Dec.; phone (503) 581-2262. Orchard Heights Winery, 6057 Orchard Heights Rd. N.W., offers guided tours and tastings year-round; phone (503) 363-0375. Willamette Valley Vineyards, 2½ miles south off I-5 Turner Road exit 248, offers guided tours by appointment and a tasting which is open daily 11-6; phone (503) 588-9463 or (800) 344-9463. Other local wineries offer guided tours and tastings throughout the year, and a wine festival brings together more than 20 winemakers the first weekend in November.

The landscaped grounds of the Civic Center on Liberty Street contain foot and bike trails, fountains, Austrian black swans and sculptures. Schreiner's Iris Gardens on Quinaby Road N.E. offers a spectacle of blooming iris in the spring. Other facets of the city include an antique woolen mill, historic homes, a missionary settlement and Western Baptist College, which has an archeology museum at 5000 Deer Park Dr. S.E.

The third weekend in July the Salem Art Fair and Festival is held in Bush's Pasture Park *(see attraction listing)*, and mid-August brings the West Salem Waterfront Festival, with arts and crafts, a parade and fireworks. In late August the Oregon State Fair comes alive with rodeos, wine competitions and farmers markets. Further information about the area is available from the Salem Convention and Visitors Association, 1313 Mill St. S.E., Salem, OR 97301; phone (503) 581-4325 or (800) 874-7012. *See ad.*

Shopping areas: Lancaster Mall, off I-5 at Market Street and Lancaster Drive, has department stores such as Montgomery Ward, The Bon and The Emporium. Another popular area is the Mission Mill Village *(see attraction listing)*, 1313 Mill St. S.E., with the Thomas Kay Textile Museum and antique and craft stores in a historic village setting. Downtown, the Salem Centre Mall, connected with sidewalks to JCPenney, Meier & Frank, Mervyns and Nordstroms, has speciality shops and restaurants.

BUSH'S PASTURE PARK, 600 Mission St., is a 100-acre city park planted with several varieties of rare trees, shrubs and roses. Activities possible include baseball, tennis and picnicking. The Salem Art Fair and Festival, the third weekend in July, features more than 200 artists and craftspersons, performing arts exhibitions, children's activities and a parade.

Bush Barn Art Center (Salem Art Association), next to the Bush House Museum, features monthly exhibitions and a gallery. Tues.-Fri. 10-5, Sat.-Sun. 1-5. Free. Phone (503) 581-2228.

Bush Conservatory, built in 1882, has been restored. Mon.-Fri. 8-4, Sat.-Sun. noon-5, May-Sept.; Mon.-Fri. 8-4, Sat.-Sun. 2-5, rest of year. Free.

Bush House Museum, the former home of a pioneer banker and newspaper publisher, contains most of its original 1877 furnishings. Tues.-Sun. noon-5, May-Sept.; Tues.-Sun. 2-5, rest of year. Admission $2.50; senior citizens and students with ID $2; ages 6-12, $1. Phone (503) 363-4714.

DEEPWOOD ESTATE, 1116 Mission St. S.E. at 12th St., is an 1894 Queen Anne home known for its stained glass, ornate carriage house and 5½ acres of formal, informal and wildflower gardens. Allow 1 hour minimum. Sun.-Fri. noon-4:30, May-Sept.; Sun.-Fri. 1-4, rest of year. Admission $2.50; senior citizens and students with ID $2; under 12, $1. Phone (503) 363-1825.

ENCHANTED FOREST, 7 mi. s. on I-5 exit 248 to 8462 Enchanted Way, has storybook characters in a wooded setting, plus a re-created early mining town, Old World village, bobsleds, a log flume ride, a haunted house, summer comedy theater and a water/light show. Allow 2 hours minimum. Daily 9:30-6, Mar. 15-Sept. 30. Admission $4.95; ages 3-12, $4.25. Admission to the haunted house $1 per person; log flume $2 per ride; bobsleds $1 per ride. MC, VI. Phone (503) 363-3060.

THE GILBERT HOUSE CHILDREN'S MUSEUM, 116 Marion St. N.E., comprises two historic Victorian homes, the 1887 Gilbert House and the 1883 Rockenfield House, on Salem's downtown riverfront. Inside both are hands-on and interactive exhibits in the sciences, arts and humanities. The Discovery Garden allows visitors to plan and plant a garden in the spring and harvest it in the fall. Allow 2½ hours minimum. Mon.-Sat. 10-5, Sun. noon-4, Mar.-June; Tues.-Sat. 10-5, Sun. noon-4, rest of year. Closed holidays. Admission $4; over 60, $3. Phone (503) 371-3631.

HONEYWOOD WINERY, 1350 Hines St. S.E., is one of the state's oldest and largest wineries. Allow 1 hour minimum. Guided group tours are available by appointment. Winey Wine tastings are offered Mon.-Fri. 9-5, Sat. 10-5, Sun. 1-5. Free. Phone (503) 362-4111.

MARION COUNTY HISTORICAL SOCIETY MUSEUM, 260 12th St. S.E., interprets the history of the county from its Calapooyan Indian days to the present. A 19th century dugout canoe is a highlight. Changing exhibits and a research library also are available. Allow 30 minutes minimum. Tues.-Sat. 9:30-4:30; closed major holidays. Admission $1; over 65 and under 13, 50c. Phone (503) 364-2128.

MISSION MILL VILLAGE, I-5 exit 253 at 1313 Mill St. S.E., is a 5-acre park complex of historic buildings surrounded by Old Mill Stream. Visitors can experience the architecture, industry and lifestyles of the 19th-century pioneer settlers in the village. Daily 10-4; closed Jan. 1, Thanksgiving and Dec. 25. Phone (503) 585-7012. *See ad.*

Jason Lee House, the Parsonage and John D. Boon House, dating from the 1840s, are restored and furnished in period. The three houses were built as a Methodist mission for the Indians. Costumed interpreters offer various demonstrations. Allow 1 hour minimum. Combination ticket for the houses and the Thomas Kay Textile Museum $5; over 65, $4.50; ages 6-18, $2. MC, VI. **Discount.**

Thomas Kay Textile Museum includes a restored, operating water-power turbine. Established during the height of the Civil War in 1863, the mill demonstrates the process of converting fleece into woolen material and the importance of the mill to the community. Allow 1 hour minimum. Combination ticket for the museum and the Jason Lee House, the Parsonage and John D. Boon House $5; over 65, $4.50; ages 6-18, $2. MC, VI. **Discount.**

PREWITT-ALLEN ARCHAEOLOGICAL MUSEUM, 5000 Deer Park Dr., on the Western Baptist College campus, exhibits Middle Eastern and Biblical artifacts including replicas of the Rosetta Stone, the Code of Hammurabi of Babylon and the Assyrian Obelisk. Mon.-Fri. 8 a.m.-9 p.m., Sept.-May; 8-4, rest of year. Free. Phone (503) 375-7016.

SILVER FALLS STATE PARK, 26 mi. e. on SR 214, is Oregon's largest state park, 8,302 acres. Of its 10 waterfalls, six are more than 100 feet high. Admission (summer weekends and holidays) $3 per private vehicle. *See Recreation Chart and the AAA Northwestern CampBook.*

★**STATE CAPITOL,** between Court and State sts., is a marble structure of modern design with murals portraying historical events. The building is topped with a golden statue symbolic of the Oregon pioneers. Guided tours are available on the hour Mon.-Sat. 9-noon and 1-4, Sun. 1-3,

Discover the Valley, visit Salem's

Mission Mill Village

mid-June through Labor Day. Allow 30 minutes minimum. Building open Mon.-Fri. 8-5, Sat. 9-4, Sun. noon-4. Free. Phone (503) 986-1388.

SEAL ROCK (D-2)

The small community of Seal Rock is known for craft shops that carry such wares as jewelry, ceramics and large chainsaw-carved wood sculptures. Nearby Seal Rock Wayside State Park *(see Recreation Chart)* offers clamming, surf fishing, hiking and picnicking in a scenic setting.

SEA GULCH, s. on US 101, has more than 400 chainsaw-sculpted human and animal figures lining a ¼-mile trail in a Western theme park. Allow 30 minutes minimum. Daily dawn-6 p.m., June 1-Labor Day; 9-5, rest of year. Closed Dec. 25. Admission $4.50; senior citizens $3.50; ages 6-12, $3. Phone (503) 563-2727.

SEASIDE (A-2) pop. 5,400, elev. 15′

Oregon's largest and oldest ocean resort, Seaside lies at the end of the Lewis and Clark Trail. Near the southern end of the Promenade on Lewis and Clark Way is a replica of a salt cairn built by the Lewis and Clark party to extract salt from sea water.

A monument at the foot of Broadway commemorates the explorers' journey. Lewis and Clark's hazardous journey is the subject of the Lewis and Clark Historical Drama staged in late July and early August. The second weekend in August draws volleyball players from around the country to compete in the Annual Beach Volleyball Tournament. Further information about the area is available from the Seaside Chamber of Commerce, P.O. Box 7, Seaside, OR 97138; phone (503) 738-6391 or (800) 444-6740.

Shopping areas: Broadway has a variety of specialty shops offering such items as crafts, kites and clothing.

SEASIDE AQUARIUM, 2nd Ave. at the Promenade, exhibits marine life from the Oregon coast. Visitors can feed the seals and touch marine life in the touch tanks. Allow 30 minutes minimum. Daily 9-6 (also Fri.-Sat. 6-8 p.m.), June 15-Aug. 31; daily 9-6, Mar. 1-June 14 and Sept.-Oct.; Wed.-Sun. 9-5, rest of year. Admission $5; ages 6-11, $2.50. MC, VI. Phone (503) 738-6211.

SEASIDE MUSEUM AND HISTORICAL SOCIETY, 570 Necanicum Dr., 4 blks. n. of 1st. Ave., offers displays depicting the history of Seaside. Exhibits include Clatsop Indian items, logging memorabilia and a working 1920s Linotype. The restored Butterfield Cottage behind the museum depicts a 1912 beach cottage and rooming house. Daily 10:30-4:30; closed Thanksgiving and Dec. 25. Admission $2; over 65, $1.50; ages 13-18, $1. Phone (503) 738-7065.

SHERIDAN (C-2) pop. 4,000, elev. 186′

LAWRENCE GALLERY, n. on SR 18, displays changing exhibits of arts and crafts from Oregon and nearby states as well as an outdoor sculpture garden. There also is a wine-tasting room featuring wines from more than 35 Oregon wineries. Food is available. Allow 1 hour minimum. Daily 10-5:30 (also Fri.-Sun. 5:30-6:30); closed Dec. 24-25. Free. Phone (503) 843-3633.

SISKIYOU NATIONAL FOREST

Elevations in the forest range from 200 ft. near the Pacific Ocean to 6,480 ft. at Whiskey Peak. Refer to AAA maps for additional elevation information.

Siskiyou National Forest, 1.1 million acres on Oregon's southern coast, may be accessed on the east by US 199, on the west by US 101 and on the north and south by I-5. It has rugged scenery and varied recreational facilities. Known as the "Botanist's Paradise," the forest contains large numbers of plant species, including Brewer/weeping spruce and Port Orford cedar.

The Rogue River, which traverses the forest, is famous for catches of salmon and cutthroat and steelhead trout, in addition to its challenging white-water rafting. Hiking and backpacking are popular in the spring and fall, but high temperatures in late summer may discourage some hikers from hiking the entire 35-mile Rogue River Trail.

The Wild Rogue Wilderness is along the Rogue River between Mule Creek and Watson Creek; the area is accessible only by river or by foot trail. Boat trips are available up the Rogue River from Gold Beach and downriver from Grants Pass *(see place listings)*.

Kalmiopsis Wilderness covers 180,000 acres, with shallow, rocky canyons and mountain streams. It is accessible only by foot or by horseback. This is the principal range of the rare Port Orford cedar and the Brewer, or weeping, spruce. The kalmiopsis, a small rhododendron-like plant considered to be one of the world's rarest shrubs, also can be found in the wilderness.

The Grassy Knob Wilderness, 17,200 acres, lies in steep, rugged tree-covered canyons 7 miles east of Port Orford. Two roads provide access to the area and offer vistas of the wilderness and the Pacific.

The Red Buttes Wilderness, 3,414 acres southeast of Cave Junction, extends north from the California border. Eleven miles of trails, including the Boundary National Recreation Trail, are within the small wilderness area, which ranges in elevation from 3,600 to 6,300 feet. Wildflowers and open ridgetop meadows characterize this subalpine wilderness area.

More information can be obtained from the Galice Ranger District, 1465 N.E. 7th St., Grants Pass, OR 97526; phone (503) 476-3830. *See Recreation Chart and the AAA Northwestern CampBook.*

SISTERS (D-7) pop. 700

The area around Sisters was a crossroads for American Indian travelers long before settlers from the Midwest and East arrived in the 19th century. John C. Frémont, guided by Kit Carson, passed through the region in 1843.

The snowcapped Three Sisters Peaks, originally called Faith, Hope and Charity, form the backdrop for the town of Sisters and the Deschutes National Forest *(see place listing)*. Western facades provide a frontier town flavor. The Hotel Sisters, one of the few original buildings still standing, was restored to serve as a Western-style saloon and restaurant.

On the edge of the high desert, the community is the major recreational crossroads of US 20 and SRs 126 and 242 connecting the Willamette Valley and central Oregon. Nearby areas include Black Butte Ranch, a recreational development; the surrounding national forest lands; and two ski areas, Hoodoo Ski Area and Mount Bachelor.

Llamas are a frequent sight on the edge of town at the Patterson Ranch, which reputedly has the largest llama herd in North America.

Events in Sisters include the June Rodeo, an Outdoor Quilt Show in July, the High Mountain Dixieland Jazz Festival in September and an October Harvest Faire. For more information contact the Sisters Area Chamber of Commerce at P.O. Box 430, Sisters, OR 97759; phone (503) 549-0251.

The McKenzie Pass Scenic Highway *(see Willamette National Forest)* begins just west of town off US 20/SR 126. The road, open from early July through early October, offers panoramic views of the Cascades and nearby lava fields.

SIUSLAW NATIONAL FOREST

> *Elevations in the forest range from sea level at the Pacific Ocean to 4,097 ft. at Mary's Peak. Refer to AAA maps for additional elevation information.*

The timbered slopes of the 630,000-acre Siuslaw National Forest meet the ocean and extend along Oregon's shore in sections from Tillamook to Coos Bay. Beachcombing and fishing are allowed on 46 miles of public beach, and there are lakes and streams in the wooded areas. Hunting, boating, camping and picnicking are favorite pastimes. *See Recreation Chart and the AAA Northwestern CampBook.*

CAPE PERPETUA VISITOR CENTER, 3 mi. s. of Yachats off US 101, offers a 15-minute movie "Discovery at the Edge," which describes the natural forces that helped to shape the Oregon coast. Other displays include interpretations of the ecology and history of the area including early Indians, discovery and settlement, logging and Civilian Conservation Corps activities.

Nearby are the Devil's Churn and Cook's Chasm. Cape Perpetua Overlook, 2 miles off US 101, the highest point on the Oregon coast, provides an excellent view of the coast. Camping is available.

Allow 30 minutes minimum. Daily 9-5, Memorial Day-Labor Day; otherwise varies. Free. Phone (503) 547-3289.

OREGON DUNES NATIONAL RECREATION AREA, 32,000 acres, encompasses a 40-mile stretch of sand dunes between North Bend and Florence. The dunes average 250 feet in height. At its widest point the area extends inland about 2½ miles. The Oregon Dunes Overlook, midway between Reedsport and Florence, provides access to dune observation platforms, picnic sites, hiking trails and restrooms. Freshwater lakes for boating and fishing are easily accessible in the recreation area.

The Oregon Dunes National Recreation Area headquarters is in Reedsport and provides displays and a movie on the formation of sand dunes. Phone (503) 271-3611. *See Recreation Chart.*

SPRINGFIELD (E-3) pop. 44,700, elev. 472'

Springfield, separated from its sister city of Eugene by the Willamette River, is a major center for the state's forest products industry. It also is an access point to the McKenzie River, which offers fishing and white-water rafting amid striking scenery. Island Park on the Willamette River and Willamalane Park are popular picnicking spots.

Springfield Museum, 550 Main St., offers changing and permanent exhibits pertaining to regional and local history; phone (503) 726-2300.

The Weyerhaeuser Company conducts guided tours of its pulp and paper manufacturing facility; phone (503) 746-2511.

Annual events include the Broiler Festival in July, the Filbert Festival on Labor Day weekend and the Christmas Parade on the first Saturday in December. For further information contact the Convention and Visitors Association of Lane County Oregon, 305 W. 7th Ave., Eugene, OR 97401; phone (503) 484-5307. The association is open Mon.-Fri. 8:30-5, Sat.-Sun. 10-4, Memorial Day-Labor Day; Mon.-Fri. 8:30-5, rest of year.

LIVELY PARK SWIM CENTER, 6100 Thurston Rd., is an indoor water theme park with a wave pool, an open-flume waterslide, innertubes, a lap pool, a kiddie pool and a hydro-jet spa. Sun.-Fri. noon-5 (also Mon.-Fri. 6:30-9 p.m.), Sat. 6:30-9 p.m., mid-June through Labor Day; Mon.-Sat. 6:30-9 p.m., Sun. noon-5, rest of year. Closed Dec. 25. Admission $4, family rate $9, under 3 free. MC, VI. Phone (503) 747-9283.

OREGON WHITEWATER ADVENTURES, 660 W. Kelly Blvd., provides paddle raft and inflatable kayak trips on the Deschutes, Grande Ronde, Lower Klamath, McKenzie, Owyhee and Umpqua rivers. Half-day, full-day and multiday guided trips are available Apr.-Oct. Food is available. Departure times vary. Half-day trip $45; full-day trip $55-$70; 2- to 5-day trips $155-$470. MC, VI. Reservations are required. Contact Oregon Whitewater Adventures, 660 Kelly Blvd., Springfield, OR 97477. Phone (503) 746-5422 or (800) 820-RAFT.

THE DALLES (B-7) pop. 11,100, elev. 96′

Lying on a great crescent bend of the Columbia, The Dalles was an outgrowth of its location. The river narrows and once spilled over a series of rapids, which the French voyageurs christened *les dalles,* or the trough.

Indians and later fur traders found this natural break in navigation a convenient place for trade, a fact Lewis and Clark mentioned when describing it as "the great Indian mart of all this country."

Until 1845, when a wagon road was built, emigrants on the Oregon Trail could continue their journey only by floating their wagons down the treacherous Columbia. The rapids have since been submerged by the backwater of The Dalles Dam. A marker in City Park at 6th and Union streets commemorates the area where the overland route of the Oregon Trail ended 1843-46.

Much of The Dalles' past lingers in its many 19th-century homes and churches and in its museums. Scenic drives include a section of Historic Highway 30 between Mosier and The Dalles, and scenic I-84 bordering the Columbia from Troutdale to Boardman.

Recreational activities are available at nearby Deschutes River State Park *(see Recreation Chart and the AAA Northwestern CampBook),* where white-water rafting and fishing are popular. The Columbia at The Dalles is a favorite area for sailboarding and fishing.

Self-guiding tours: Maps detailing a 45- to 60-minute self-guiding walking tour through historic downtown and residential areas are available from The Dalles Convention and Visitors Bureau, 404 W. 2nd St., The Dalles, OR 97058; phone (503) 296-6616 or (800) 255-3385.

FORT DALLES MUSEUM, 15th and Garrison sts., is in the last remaining building of the fort established in 1850. Allow 30 minutes minimum. Mon.-Fri. 10:30-5, Sat.-Sun. 10-5, Mar.-Oct.; Wed.-Fri. noon-4, Sat.-Sun. 10-4, rest of year. Admission $2, students with ID free. Phone (503) 296-4547.

ORIGINAL WASCO COUNTY COURTHOUSE, 406 W. Second St., presents films on the history of Wasco County, the Columbia Gorge and attractions in The Dalles area. Self-guiding walking tours of the downtown area begin at the 1859 building. Allow 30 minutes minimum. Tues.-Sat. 10-4, mid-Apr. through Labor Day. Free. Phone (503) 296-4798.

ST. PETER'S LANDMARK, 3rd and Lincoln sts., is an 1897 red-brick Gothic church. Its 176-foot steeple topped by a 6-foot-tall rooster weather vane, 36 stained-glass windows and Madonna carved from the keel of a ship are of interest. Allow 30 minutes minimum. Tues.-Fri. 11-3, Sat.-Sun. 1-3; closed major holidays. Donations. Phone (503) 296-5686.

THE DALLES ART CENTER, 220 E. 4th St., was formerly the Carnegie Library. The 1910 building contains changing exhibits and the work of local artists. Trees, brick patios, planters and benches adorn the grounds around the building. Allow 30 minutes minimum. Tues.-Sat. 11-5. Free. Phone (503) 296-4759.

THE DALLES DAM, e. edge of town, is a vital link in the development of the Columbia River and the Pacific Northwest. Allow 1 hour minimum. Guided tours and a train ride to the powerhouse, fish ladder, lock and dam depart daily 9-5, June 1-Labor Day; Wed.-Sun. 10-4 (self-guiding tours Mon.-Tues., 8-4), second weekend in Apr.-day before Memorial Day and day after Labor Day-Sept. 30; Mon.-Thurs. 8-4, rest of year. Train not in operation October through March or on Monday and Tuesday in April, May and September. Free. Phone (503) 296-9778. *See Recreation Chart.*

WONDER WORKS CHILDREN'S MUSEUM, 419 E. 2nd St., is a hands-on learning-by-doing museum for children. Included are a playhouse, grocery store, creative building toys and an infant and toddler room. Allow 30 minutes minimum. Tues.-Sat. 10-5, Memorial Day-Labor Day; Wed.-Sat. 10-5, rest of year. Closed holidays. Admission $2, under 1 free. Phone (503) 296-2444.

TILLAMOOK (B-2) pop. 4,000, elev. 22′

Tillamook's lush grasses, nurtured by up to 72 inches of rain a year, sustain the herds that compose Oregon's dairy industry. Much of the county's annual milk production of 25 million gallons is made into natural cheddar cheese.

In addition to its agricultural importance, Tillamook is a major recreation center. Charter boats for crabbing and deep-sea fishing are available. Beachcombing, clamming, and jetty, river and surf fishing are popular activities at the beach areas 9 miles west of town. Hiking, hang gliding, scuba diving, windsurfing and canoeing also are among the area's recreational opportunities.

The Dairy Festival and Rodeo is held the fourth weekend in June. One event held at the Tillamook County Fair is a pig and Ford race in which participants race Model T's while holding a pig in their laps. For further information contact the Tillamook Chamber of Commerce at

3705 Hwy. 101 N., Tillamook, OR 97141; phone (503) 842-7525.

A scenic section of US 101 passes through Tillamook and connects with SR 6, which runs through the Tillamook State Forest from Portland.

THREE CAPES ROAD is a 38½-mile drive west, embracing the towns of Oceanside, Netarts, Tierra del Mar, Pacific City and Capes Meares, Cape Lookout and Cape Kiwanda. The Cape Meares Lighthouse and the Octopus Tree, a large Sitka spruce used by Indians as a burial tree, are along the route at Cape Meares.

TILLAMOOK COUNTY CREAMERY ASSOCIATION (Tillamook Cheese Factory), 2 mi. n. on US 101, features an observation area and an audiovisual presentation. Food is available. Allow 1 hour minimum. Daily 8-8, Memorial Day-Labor Day; 8-6, rest of year. Free. Phone (503) 842-4481.

TILLAMOOK COUNTY PIONEER MUSEUM, 2nd and Pacific Ave., has three floors of exhibits that include wildlife dioramas, a mineral room, a logging display, a blacksmith shop and items of pioneer, Indian and natural history. A steam donkey, a large steam engine used for logging operations, also is on the grounds. Allow 1 hour, 30 minutes minimum. Mon.-Sat. 8-5, Sun. noon-5, Mar. 15-Oct. 1; Tues.-Sat. 8-5, Sun. noon-5, rest of year. Closed Thanksgiving and Dec. 25. Admission $2; over 62, $1.50; ages 12-17, 50c; family rate $5. Phone (503) 842-4553.

TROUTDALE (B-4) pop. 7,800, elev. 73′

McMENAMINS EDGEFIELD WINERY, I-84 Woodvillage exit at 2126 S.W. Halsey St., offers 3 acres of vineyards, a brewery, an herb garden in addition to guided tours and free tastings. Food is available. Allow 1 hour minimum. Daily noon-10, Memorial Day-Labor Day; Sun.-Thurs. noon-8, Fri.-Sat. noon-10, rest of year. Closed Jan. 1 and Dec. 25. Free. Phone (503) 669-8610.

UMATILLA (B-9) pop. 3,000, elev. 294′

Founded as Umatilla Landing in 1864, Umatilla sprang up virtually overnight as an important trade and shipping center during the gold rush. This was primarily due to its key location at the confluence of the Umatilla and Columbia rivers. Local records report that at one time during the rush, 13 buildings were erected within 4 days. Just 6 months after its founding, Umatilla had more than 100 buildings, 25 stores and two hotels.

The town remained a major shipping center until the 1880s, when the construction of the Oregon Railway and Navigation Line diverted traffic and trade. The Columbia River provides fishing opportunities year round and is host to the Governor's Cup Fishing Tournament on Labor Day weekend. For further information contact the Umatilla Chamber of Commerce, 1300 6th St. #A, P.O. Box 59, Umatilla, OR 97882; phone (503) 922-4825 or (800) 542-4944.

McNARY LOCK AND DAM, 1 mi. e. of I-82/US 730 jct., is part of the vast inland waterway system of the Columbia and Snake rivers. Of interest are the visitor center, Pacific Salmon Visitor Information Center, locks, fish ladder, fish-viewing room and nature trail. A boat ramp is available; fishing is permitted. Guided tours of the powerhouse depart from the visitor center; guided tours of the Pacific Salmon Visitor Information Center also are available. Self-guiding tours of the grounds can be taken daily dawn-dusk. Visitor center and Pacific Salmon Visitor Information Center open daily 8:30-5, Memorial Day weekend-Aug. 31; by appointment rest of year. Free. Phone (503) 922-4388. *See Recreation Chart.*

UMATILLA NATIONAL WILDLIFE REFUGE is reached by US 730 between the towns of Irrigon and Boardman, n. 2 mi. on Paterson Ferry Rd. The refuge's 22,885 acres attract large concentrations of waterfowl. Allow 1 hour minimum. Daily 5 a.m.-10 p.m. Free. Phone (503) 922-3232.

UMATILLA NATIONAL FOREST

Elevations in the forest range from 1,600 ft. in Troy to 8,131 ft. at Vinegar Hill. Refer to AAA maps for additional elevation information.

The Umatilla National Forest encompasses 1,402,483 acres in four ranger districts extending from northeast Oregon into the southeastern corner of Washington. The highest point in the forest, at 8,131 feet, lies within the Vinegar Hill/Indian Rock Scenic Area. A drive to Indian Rock Lookout offers a view of the subalpine area.

Trips along the summit of the Blue Mountains on the primitive Kendall-Skyline, the paved Blue Mountain National Scenic Byway and the gravel Summit Road offer panoramic views. More than 1,000 miles of other forest roads offer wildlife viewing opportunities for visitors. Although these roads provide roadside viewpoints into the wildernesses, travel within the areas is served by many trails and can be toured only by foot or horseback.

There are ample opportunities for winter sports, as well as fishing, hunting, hiking and pack-and-saddle trips. Many picnic and camping areas are provided.

The Wenaha-Tucannon Wilderness, 177,465 acres astride the Oregon-Washington border in the northern Blue Mountains, is characterized by rugged basaltic ridges and deep canyons. Two additional wilderness areas are the North Fork Umatilla Wilderness which encompasses 20,144 acres, and the North Fork John Day Wilderness, which stretches over 121,800 acres.

For further information contact the Forest Supervisor, 2517 W. Hailey Ave., Pendleton, OR 97801; phone (503) 278-3716. *See Recreation Chart and the AAA Northwestern CampBook.*

UMPQUA (G-2)

HENRY ESTATE WINERY, I-5 exit 136 at 687 Hubbard Creek Rd., offers guided tours and free tastings. Picnic facilities are available. Allow 1 hour minimum. Daily 11-5. Free. Phone (503) 459-5120.

UMPQUA NATIONAL FOREST

Elevations in the forest range from 1,120 ft. where the North Umpqua River leaves the forest to 9,182 ft. at Mount Thielsen. Refer to AAA maps for additional elevation information.

The 984,602-acre Umpqua National Forest has something for nearly every outdoor enthusiast. Miles of trails wind through hills and valleys covered with Douglas fir and western hemlock; the Pacific Crest National Scenic Trail runs from Windigo Pass to Crater Lake.

The Diamond Lake Recreation Area is dominated by Diamond Lake, flanked to the east by Mount Thielsen and to the west by Mount Bailey. The Rogue Umpqua Scenic Byway (SR 138), which parallels the North Umpqua River, provides a scenic drive from Roseburg to Diamond Lake.

The three wilderness areas in the forest are Boulder Creek Wilderness, a 19,100-acre area important as an old-growth, timbered watershed of the North Umpqua River; the Rogue-Umpqua Divide Wilderness, a 26,350-acre area noted for its interesting geologic formations and extensive trail system; and the Mount Thielsen Wilderness, part of the Oregon Cascade Recreation Area totaling 21,593 acres.

Fishing for steelhead trout is popular in the forest's many streams and rivers. Saddle trips can be taken. Cross-country skiing and snowmobiling trails are open in the winter. For further information contact the Forest Supervisor, 2900 N.W. Stewart Pkwy., P.O. Box 1008, Roseburg, OR, 97470; phone (503) 672-6601. *See Recreation Chart and the AAA Northwestern CampBook.*

UNION (C-11) pop. 1,800, elev. 2,717′

Many Victorian homes have been preserved in Union, including Wildwood, an 1869 Gothic mansion at Main and Bryan streets. Several 19th-century red brick buildings line Main Street.

UNION COUNTY MUSEUM, 311 S. Main St., has collections relating to the natural history, settlement and development of northeast Oregon. The museum complex includes an 1881 building and early post office. Guided tours are available by appointment. Daily 11-5, May 1 to mid-Oct. Donations. Phone (503) 562-6003 or (800) 848-9969.

VERNONIA (B-3) pop. 1,800, elev. 620′

Founded in 1873 on the banks of Rock Creek where it meets the Nehalem River, Vernonia is a logging and recreational center. Lake Vernonia, formerly the mill pond for the lumber mill, is stocked with trout, blue gills, perch, bullheads, crappie and bass while the shore features a paved walking/biking trail. During the first full weekend in August, the town celebrates the Veronia Friendship Jamboree and Logging Show.

COLUMBIA COUNTY HISTORICAL SOCIETY MUSEUM, 511 E. Bridge St., features exhibits about the logging industry and contains locally found fossils, gems, American Indian artifacts and pioneer memorabilia. Allow 30 minutes minimum. Thurs.-Sat. noon-4, Sun. 1-4, June-Sept.; Fri.-Sat. noon-4, Sun. 1-4, rest of year. Free. Phone (503) 429-3713.

WALDPORT (D-2) pop. 1,600

At the mouth of the Alsea River, Waldport is popular with saltwater and freshwater anglers. The coastline on both sides of Alsea Bay varies from smooth sandy beaches to rugged rocky formations.

Several nearby state parks offer hiking, agate hunting, clamming and crabbing. Many of these parks can be found along the scenic stretch of US 101, which travels along the Oregon Coast from California to Washington. Just east of Waldport is Drift Creek Wildnerness Area which offers untouched old-growth forest for hikers.

WALLOWA LAKE (C-11)

Rich in Indian lore and legend, beautiful Wallowa Lake is at the foothills of the steep, forested mountains at the upper end of Wallowa Valley. Near the north end of the lake is the grave of Chief Joseph, leader of the Nez Perce, whose son Joseph battled the U.S. Army after the elder Joseph's death.

The 4-mile-long lake is the center of a popular recreational region. Horseback pack trips in the High Wallowas can be arranged. At the lake's southern tip is Wallowa Lake State Park *(see Recreation Chart and Joseph in the AAA Northwestern CampBook).*

WALLOWA LAKE TRAMWAY, on Hwy. 82 at Wallowa Lake, climbs to the 8,200-foot level on Mount Howard. It is among the steepest tram rides in the United States. From this point, the peaks of the Eagle Cap Wilderness Area, the Seven Devils of Idaho and the rim of Hell's Canyon are visible. Allow 1 hour minimum. The tramway departs daily 10-4, June 5 to mid-Sept.; 10-4, May 20-21 and 27-29; 1-3, June 1-4; Thurs.-Fri. 12-3, Sat.-Sun. 10-4, mid-Sept.

through Sept. 30 (weather permitting). Fare $10; over 62, $9; under 11, $5. MC, VI. Phone (503) 432-5331.

WALLOWA-WHITMAN NATIONAL FOREST

Elevations in the forest range from 800 ft. at the Hell's Canyon portion of the Snake River to 9,938 ft. at Sacajawea Peak. Refer to AAA maps for additional elevation information.

Varied scenery characterizes the Wallowa-Whitman National Forest, which encompasses 2,392,160 acres. In two divisions, it extends from the Blue Mountains in the southwest to the Grande Ronde and Powder rivers, over the Wallowa Mountains to the Snake River and over the Seven Devils Mountains in western Idaho.

The area contains snowcapped peaks, rushing mountain streams, timbered slopes and canyons. Travel in the Eagle Cap Wilderness Area, 358,461 acres of rugged beauty, is limited to foot or horseback. The Hells Canyon National Recreation Area *(see place listing)* is within the forest.

Skiing, fishing, boating, hunting, camping and picnicking opportunities are available. Horses can be rented through many outfitters. For further information phone (503) 523-1205. *See Recreation Chart and the AAA Northwestern CampBook.*

WARM SPRINGS (C-8) elev. 1,574′

Warm Springs is on SR 26 in the Warm Springs Indian Reservation. The 640,000 acres of the Warm Springs Indian Reservation are occupied by the Warm Springs, Paiute and Wasco tribes. Self-guiding tours of the Warm Springs National Fish Hatchery, 13 miles northwest on Indian Highway, are available.

Rich in culture, several festivals take place in Warm Springs including a powwow in June, a Huckleberry feast in August and an Indian Thanksgiving in November.

THE MUSEUM AT WARM SPRINGS, 2189 SR 26, contains exhibits from the Wasco, Paiute and Warm Springs Indian tribes. Displays include ceremonial clothing, drums, tools, murals, reconstructed mat houses and an art gallery featuring American Indian art. Demonstrations of beadwork and various crafts also are given. Allow 1 hour minimum. Daily 10-5; closed Jan. 1, Thanksgiving and Dec. 25. Admission $5; over 60, $4.50; ages 5-12, $2.50; family rate $15. MC, VI. Phone (503) 553-3331.

WARRENTON (A-2) pop. 2,700, elev. 7′

Platted in 1891 through the efforts of founder Daniel Knight Warren, Warrenton was built mostly on tidal flats. A system of dikes constructed by Chinese laborers keeps the town dry. Many boats moored nearby offer charter fishing trips and tours of the Columbia River.

The Greater Astoria/Warrenton Crab and Wine Festival is held to celebrate the maritime history of the area with arts and crafts, food and wine. Specialty retail and gift shops can be found at Youngs Bay Shopping Center near US 101 and Harbor Road.

FORT STEVENS STATE PARK, 10 mi. w. on US 101, is a coastal lake area near the mouth of the Columbia River. Fort Stevens protected the entrance to the Columbia River from the Civil War through World War II. The *Peter Iredale,* a schooner wrecked in 1906, is visible at low tide. Clamming is permitted. Daily dawn-dusk. Free. *See Recreation Chart.*

Fort Stevens Historical Area and Military Museum includes a war games building, gun batteries and a guardhouse. Guided tours of the installation in military trucks are offered, as well as underground battery tours. Allow 1 hour, 30 minutes minimum. Daily 10-6, May-Sept.; Wed.-Sun. 10-4, rest of year. Museum accepts donations. Underground bunker tour $3; ages 3-12, $1. Military truck tour $2.50; ages 3-12, $1.25. Parking $3, mid-May to mid-Sept. Phone (503) 861-2000.

WILLAMETTE NATIONAL FOREST

Elevations in the forest range from 1,155 ft. at Winberry Creek to 10,358 ft. at South Sister Peak. Refer to AAA maps for additional elevation information.

Covering 1,675,407 acres of high mountain country, the Willamette National Forest is often the top timber producer in the nation. Access is limited to horse or foot travel in some parts, including the Mount Jefferson, Mount Washington, Three Sisters, Middle Santiam, Waldo Lake, Menagerie, Bull of the Woods and Diamond Peak wildernesses.

Four wilderness areas have extensive volcanic formations. The Pacific Crest National Scenic Trail winds along the summit of the Cascades.

With more than 1,400 miles of trails and over 80 campgrounds, the forest provides ample recreational opportunities, including hiking and camping. The forest is open to hunting and fishing in regular seasons. Big game animals include elk, bear and deer; fishing enthusiasts can find several varieties of trout in the many lakes and streams.

Self-guiding tour cassette tapes of the Aufder Heide National Forest Scenic Byway are available free of charge from the Oakridge Ranger District office on SR 58 and the McKenzie River or Blue River ranger districts on SR 126. The drive is about 70 miles in length. Phone (503) 465-6521 or 822-3381.

The Hoodoo and Willamette Pass ski areas provide many skiing opportunities and snowmobile areas are located near Willamette Pass on

Waldo Lake Road and near Big Lake just off Santiam Pass on Highway 20. For further information phone the Forest Service at (503) 465-6521. *See Recreation Chart and the AAA Northwestern CampBook.*

McKENZIE PASS SCENIC HIGHWAY (SR 242) snakes across 5,324-foot McKenzie Pass between Belknap Springs and Sisters. The road, open early July through early October only, is not suitable for trailers. Lava fields at the summit constitute one of the larger, more recent flows in the United States.

There are excellent views of the Three Sisters, Mount Washington, Mount Jefferson and other volcanic formations from the Dee Wright Observatory at the summit. The Lava River Interpretive Trail, a ½-mile loop with signs, explains the geological phenomena of this area.

McKENZIE RIVER AREA, e. of Springfield, is noted by anglers for its rainbow trout. About 1½ miles east of McKenzie Bridge is the 26-mile McKenzie River National Recreation Trail with easy access from several points off SR 126.

From McKenzie Bridge, SR 126 veers northward at Belknap Springs and follows the Upper McKenzie River to its headwaters at Clear Lake, named for its transparent water. At its north end is a submerged forest, inundated more than a millennium ago when a lava flow dammed the canyon. Boat rental (motors prohibited) and campsites are available.

WALDO LAKE RECREATION AREA lies 70 mi. e. of Eugene, with access by a 12-mile paved road from SR 58. The 6,420-acre lake has three campgrounds on the east shore. Waldo Lake Wilderness Area, 37,157 acres, is to the north, west and south of the lake. The area is normally accessible July-October.

WINEMA NATIONAL FOREST

Elevations in the forest range from 4,000 ft. at Klamath Falls to 8,266 ft. at Aspen Butte. Refer to AAA maps for additional elevation information.

Established in 1961, the Winema National Forest embraces more than 1,038,986 acres extending from the high mountain country of the Cascade Crest north and south of Crater Lake eastward to the pine-timbered Klamath Basin.

Part of the Pacific Crest National Scenic Trail threads along the west edge of the forest. Horseback riding, hiking and cross-country skiing are popular diversions. The Mountain Lakes, Sky Lakes and Mount Thielsen wilderness areas preserve nature in its primitive state. Resorts are at Lake of the Woods and Rocky Point. For further information contact the Forest Supervisor, 2819 Dahlia, Klamath Falls, OR 97601; phone (503) 883-6714. *See Recreation Chart and the AAA Northwestern CampBook.*

LAKE OF THE WOODS, 36 mi. n.w. of Klamath Falls, is reached by paved road. Near the base of 9,497-foot Mount McLoughlin, the lake is surrounded by dense woodlands at an elevation of about 5,000 feet. Fishing and waterskiing are permitted, and snowmobiling and cross-country skiing are popular in winter. Camping areas and a Visitor Information Center are open early June through Sept. 30. Phone (503) 949-8800.

WOLF CREEK (F-5) elev. 1,293′

WOLF CREEK TAVERN, off I-5 exit 76 in the center of town, has been in almost continuous operation since it was built as a stagecoach inn on the Oregon Territorial Road in the early 1870s. The classical revival-style building has been restored and furnished in different periods to reflect the changing character of the tavern over the decades. Food is available. Allow 30 minutes minimum. Mon.-Sat. 11-8:30, Sun. 10-8. Free. Phone (503) 866-2474.

YACHATS (E-2) pop. 500

Yachats (YAH-hahts) is popular with anglers who come primarily for the smelt season, which occurs every year between April and October. This is one of the few areas in the world where hundreds of these sardinelike fish come to shore to spawn. The town celebrates the annual smelt run with the Smelt Fry in July.

Besides smelt fishing, the nearby Yachats River is a popular spot for salmon and steelhead fishing. Other popular pastimes include beachcombing, rockhounding, birdwatching and painting. The Arts and Crafts Fair is held in March and a Kite Festival takes place in October. For further information contact the Yachats Area Chamber of Commerce, P.O. Box 728, Yachats, OR 97498; phone (503) 547-3530.

Just south of town is Cape Perpetua *(see Siuslaw National Forest)*. The highest point on the Oregon coast, it offers a dramatic ocean view from its 800-foot headland.

LITTLE LOG CHURCH is 1 blk. w. of US 101 at 328 Pontiac. The church, the first constructed in Yachats, was begun in 1927. The present structure was rebuilt in 1993, retaining the original pews, pulpit and pump organ. Period clothing, American Indian baskets and artwork are displayed. Allow 30 minutes minimum. Daily 10-4. Donations.

When you visit a new city, be a cautious pedestrian.

WASHINGTON

An introduction to the state's history, geography, economy and recreation

LAND OF EXTREMES, Washington's majestic face has been shaped by the opposing forces of fire and ice: Volcanos drastically altered the land in mere moments, while glaciers carved their paths over hundreds of years. Opposing forces of the human variety also have left an indelible imprint. Native cultures led a simple existence on the eastern plains and along the coast, while American pioneers created a vital state out of the wilderness.

HISTORY

Although settled relatively recently, Washington's human habitation dates back thousands of years. Tools and early human skeletal remains have been found in the state's eastern region, while the Ozette of the western Olympic Coast left behind a perfectly preserved record of their existence when a mudslide buried their village.

European exploration of the area began as early as 1542, when a Spanish expedition led by Bartolemé Ferrelo, in search of the western opening of the Northwest Passage, sighted the southern coast of present-day Oregon. English explorer Francis Drake reached the northwest coast in 1578. Spain and England thus laid claim to the virgin territory, although neither country continued exploration until late in the 18th century.

Englishman James Cook's 1778 voyage to Cape Flattery rekindled interest in the area, and Capt. George Vancouver was sent to find the Northwest Passage and map the area. He met American captain Robert Gray at the Strait of Juan de Fuca and then continued northward, claiming Vancouver Island for Britain. Gray, also seeking the elusive waterway, turned south and discovered Grays Harbor and the mouth of the Columbia River. Gray's discoveries established a solid American claim to the area.

By now a waning power, Spain relinquished all claims to the Northwest, leaving the United

FAST FACTS

POPULATION: 4,866,700.

AREA: 66,511 square miles; ranks 20th.

CAPITAL: Olympia.

HIGHEST POINT: 14,411 ft., Mount Rainier.

LOWEST POINT: 5 ft. below sea level, Ebey Island, Snohomish County.

TIME ZONE: Pacific. DST.

MINIMUM AGE FOR DRIVERS: 16 with driver training, otherwise 18.

SEAT BELT/CHILD RESTRAINT LAWS: Seat belts required for driver and all passengers; child restraints required for under 2.

HELMETS FOR MOTORCYCLISTS: Required for driver and passenger.

RADAR DETECTORS: Permitted.

FIREARMS LAWS: Vary by state and/or county. Contact Professional Licensing Services, P.O. Box 9649, Olympia, WA 98507; phone (206) 753-6909.

HOLIDAYS: Jan. 1; Martin Luther King Jr.'s Birthday, Jan. (3rd Mon.); Lincoln's Birthday, Feb. 12; Washington's Birthday, Feb. (3rd Mon.); Memorial Day, May (last Mon.); July 4; Labor Day, Sept. (1st Mon.); Election Day; Veterans Day, Nov. 11; Thanksgiving, Nov. (4th Thurs.); Dec. 25.

TAXES: Washington's statewide sales tax is 6.5 percent, with cities and counties each allowed to add increments of 0.5 percent. Qualified areas also may impose increments of 0.1 percent up to 0.6 percent. Cities and counties may levy lodgings taxes of up to 2 percent—except in Seattle where the rate is 7 percent on lodgings within city limits and 2.8 percent in King County outside Seattle.

STATE INFORMATION CENTERS: Welcome centers at Blaine, Oroville, Spokane (Greenacres), Megler and Maryhill are open May through September. The Seattle-Tacoma International Airport and Vancouver information centers are open throughout the year.

States and Great Britain in a contest for ownership of the vast territory. The English soon established a thriving fur trade, but the Lewis and Clark expedition blazed a path from the east 1804-06, establishing American outposts and strengthening the U.S. claim.

John Jacob Astor sold his Pacific Fur Co.—the sole American venture—to the British during the War of 1812, leaving British companies the predominant economic influence. However, American traders and missionaries continued to stream into the region. Growing displeasure with English control led the settlers to establish a provisional government in 1843; "Fifty-four Forty or Fight!"—a reference to the proposed northern border—became their rallying cry. The fight was averted when England agreed to the present U.S.-Canadian border at the 49th parallel in 1846.

The Oregon Territory was established by Congress 2 years later. The difficulties of maintaining such a large area with one territorial capital soon became apparent, and settlers in the north began to campaign for separation. The Washington Territory, which included parts of northern Idaho and western Montana, was created in 1853.

As the establishment of the Oregon Trail in the 1840s increased white settlement, native cultures were slowly crowded out of their ancestral lands. A series of unfairly negotiated treaties, combined with the constant pressures of overly zealous missionaries, led to a string of wars between the settlers and various tribes throughout the mid-19th century.

The hostilities ended in the late 1850s, just as a dispute with England was brewing over possession of the San Juan Islands. The islands were awarded to the United States in 1872, ending the era of conflict and allowing settlers to turn their attention to statehood. Washington's increasing economic vitality could not long be overlooked, and thus the territory was admitted to the Union on Nov. 11, 1889.

The final decade of the 19th century brought the event that would forever change the fledgling state: the Klondike gold rush of 1897. Washington's boom resulted not from the mining of the precious ore, but from serving as an outfitting point for those heading north to make their fortunes. Following the boom was a heightened awareness of social issues; women were granted the vote in 1909, more than a decade before the rest of the nation followed suit.

The economic fortunes that accompanied World War I did not keep Washingtonians from feeling the effects of the Great Depression of the 1930s, but federal irrigation projects increased the amount of land available for agriculture, setting the stage for future economic growth. The Grand Coulee Dam is one of the more famous accomplishments of this period. World War II helped complete the economic recovery, as production increased in the shipbuilding, aircraft manufacturing and lumber industries and farmers prospered.

The future came to Washington in 1962, when Seattle hosted the Century 21 Exposition. The World's Fair celebration highlighted Washington's importance in commerce as well as its most important modern industries: aerospace technology, electronics and transportation.

Natural beauty and clean cities have attracted many newcomers to the state. These same qualities also have attracted television producers: The short-lived but groundbreaking television series "Twin Peaks" was filmed in Snoqualmie, while Roslyn serves as the exterior filming site for the series "Northern Exposure."

Washington's pioneer heritage is not forgotten—many towns preserve their past in downtown squares and plazas, while the region's oldest cultures are experiencing a renaissance of sorts, as their art and traditions are celebrated in many fine museums and galleries.

FOR YOUR INFORMATION

FURTHER INFORMATION FOR VISITORS:

Travel Development Division
Department of Commerce and Economic Development
General Administration Bldg.
Olympia, WA 98504
(360) 586-2088 or 586-2102

Seattle-King County Convention and Visitors Bureau
800 Convention Pl.
Seattle, WA 98101
(206) 461-5840

RECREATION INFORMATION:

State Parks and Recreation Commission
7150 Clearwater Ln.
Olympia, WA 98504
(360) 753-2027
(360) 664-3133 (hearing impaired)

FISHING AND HUNTING REGULATIONS:

Department of Fish and Wildlife
600 Capitol Way North
Olympia, WA 98501
(360) 753-5700

NATIONAL PARKS & FOREST INFORMATION:

Outdoor Recreation Information Office
915 Second Ave., Room 442
Seattle, WA 98174
(206) 220-7450
(800) 280-CAMP
(information and reservations)
(800) 879-4496 (hearing impaired)

GEOGRAPHY

A seeming paradox, part of Washington exhibits a panorama of deep canyons with rushing streams, towering mountains, fertile valleys, dense forests and shimmering bays, while scarcely 50 miles away are broad sagebrush plains, productive farmlands and rolling wheat country. The dividing line is the jagged, snowy crest of the Cascade Range, which separates a mild coastal climate from the interior continental climate.

The Cascades form the greatest of seven physiographic regions. The average elevation ranges from 5,000 to 8,000 feet, but above this level soar four isolated peaks of volcanic origin: Mount Rainier, 14,411 feet; Mount Adams, 12,276 feet; Mount Baker, 10,778 feet; and remote Glacier Peak, 10,568 feet. No longer in their company, Mount St. Helens was reduced to 8,364 feet by the catastrophic explosion of May 1980.

Along the Pacific shore the Coast Range rises from the 3,000-foot Willapa Hills in the south to the precipitous, ice-bound crags of the Olympic Mountains, which nearly fill the Olympic Peninsula. Mount Olympus, the loftiest, attains 7,923 feet. On the southwestern slopes of the Olympics some of the heaviest annual rainfall in the country—150 to 200 inches—has created dim, mysterious rain forests, yet agriculture on parts of the peninsula's northeastern coast requires irrigation.

Between the Cascades and the Coast Range lies the Puget Sound Lowland. The sound extends inland nearly 80 miles from the Strait of Juan de Fuca, with numerous arms and bays creating a fine harbor system. Its more than 300 islands include the San Juan group and Whidbey, one of the largest islands in the 48 contiguous states.

Except for the Okanogan Highlands, the Selkirk Mountains and the Blue Mountains, eastern Washington is a vast basaltic tableland. Through it the mighty Columbia River, born in a British Columbia lake, carves the great arc called the Big Bend and gives verdant life to an otherwise barren landscape. Interpretive markers along the Columbia River Gorge on SR 14 provide a historical and geological background of the region.

ECONOMY

Farmland occupies about 40 percent of the state's area. Washington produces more apples than any other state, as well as great quantities of cherries, peaches, pears and plums. In addition to orchard fruits, the valleys of western and central Washington yield berries, bulbs and seeds, peas, hops, potatoes, lettuce and asparagus. Beans and onions are important eastern Washington crops.

Dairying predominates in the west and northeast; beef cattle are raised extensively on the good range of central Washington. Lumbering ranks third as an economic factor; its associated industries place high among manufactured goods with an output of sash and doors, pulp, paper and paper products. Washington is second only to California in the production of premium vinifera wine and has three wine-producing regions.

With more than 200 edible species of fish and shellfish passing through its ports, Washington leads the West Coast in the processing and distribution of seafoods. The five types of salmon—chinook, sockeye, coho, pink and chum—are among the most prized. Much of the halibut caught in Alaskan waters is processed in Seattle and Bellingham. Such delicacies as oysters and clams also are abundant.

Not all of the state's manufactures derive from its natural resources, however. The manufacture of transportation equipment, particularly aircraft, is a key cog in the gears of the state's economy. Washington ranks first in aluminum production. Chemicals, steel, iron and machinery also figure prominently. Tourism is the fourth largest industry in the state. Today the most important products mined are sand, gravel and stone, silver, zinc and lead.

RECREATION

With the nation's first national volcanic monument, as well as more than 100 state parks, 26 wilderness areas, three national parks, six national forests and three national recreation areas, Washington offers magnificent scenery and diverse recreational opportunities. The state also maintains seven multiple-use areas—large tracts of state land with basic facilities for camping, hiking and other outdoor activities. *See Recreation Chart.*

Mountain climbing in the Cascades or Olympics provides adventure for the hardy, while **yachting** enthusiasts on Puget Sound enjoy some of the best inland boating waters in the world. Weaving through many of Washington's national forests and parks, the Pacific Crest National Scenic Trail offers excellent sightseeing and **hiking.**

Clamming is popular on the Puget Sound beaches of Alki, Carkeek and Golden Gardens, as well as the ocean beaches. Long Beach Peninsula boasts a 28-mile stretch of sand, one of the longest beaches in the country. Driving is allowed on designated sections of this and some other coastal beaches.

Scuba diving in Puget Sound, Lake Washington and the San Juan Islands area is enjoyed all year. There are underwater parks at Edmonds, Keystone and other coastal areas. **White-water rafting** and bald eagle sightseeing trips are popular on both sides of the Cascades and within Olympic National Park on the Olympic Peninsula. Raft and float trips can be booked directly through the outfitter or through one of the numerous booking agencies in Seattle.

Fishing for trout and bass is excellent in the many lakes and streams of the Cascades and the northeastern counties. Lake Chelan, a 55-mile-long glacial lake, has especially good fishing.

Salmon and other ocean fish are caught in Puget Sound and the Strait of Juan de Fuca, as well as off the coast.

Hunting is ample, given the state's abundance of wildlife. Bears, deer and elk are common in the mountain regions. Ducks, geese, grouse, pheasants and chukar are the primary game birds, the last two being most plentiful in the open country of eastern Washington.

Winter sports are extremely popular; some sections of the Cascades receive more than 200 inches of snow a year. There are developed ski areas at Bluewood, Crystal Mountain, Mission Ridge, Mount Baker, Mount Spokane, Snoqualmie, and Stevens and White passes. Both alpine and cross-country **skiing** are enjoyed in the Colville, Gifford Pinchot, Mount Baker-Snoqualmie, Okanogan and Wenatchee national forests.

About 233,000 acres are set aside in the state park system for scenic, historic or recreational value. Most parks offer fishing, **boating** and **swimming;** most also offer **camping** facilities, for which a user fee is charged. In addition, there are numerous camping areas in the national forests. However, during periods of extreme fire hazard, certain forest areas are often closed. For detailed listings of tent and recreational vehicle sites, both public and private, *see the AAA Northwestern CampBook.*

RECREATION AREAS	MAP LOCATION	CAMPING	PICNICKING	HIKING TRAILS	BOATING	BOAT RAMP	BOAT RENTAL	FISHING	SWIMMING	PETS ON LEASH	BICYCLE TRAILS	WINTER SPORTS	VISITOR CENTER	LODGE/CABINS	FOOD SERVICE
NATIONAL PARKS *(See place listings)*															
Mount Rainier (E-7) 378 square miles.		●	●	●				●				●	●	●	●
North Cascades (A-8, B-8) 505,000 acres.		●		●				●					●		
Olympic (B-4, C-5) 923,000 acres.		●	●	●	●	●	●	●	●			●	●	●	●
NATIONAL RECREATION AREAS *(See place listings)*															
Coulee Dam (C-11) 100,059 acres. Northeastern Washington. Water skiing.		●	●		●	●	●	●	●	●			●		●
Lake Chelan (C-9) 62,000 acres. Northwestern Washington. Horse rental.		●	●	●	●		●	●				●	●	●	●
Ross Lake (A-8) 118,000 acres. Northwestern Washington.		●	●	●	●	●	●	●					●	●	●
NATIONAL FORESTS *(See place listings)*															
Colville 1,100,000 acres. Northeastern Washington.		●	●	●	●	●		●	●		●	●			
Gifford Pinchot 1,299,546 acres. Southwestern Washington. Mountain climbing; horse rental.		●	●	●	●	●	●	●	●	●	●	●	●		●
Mount Baker-Snoqualmie 1,700,000 acres. Northwestern Washington.		●	●	●	●	●	●	●	●		●	●	●	●	●
Okanogan 1,745,054 acres. North-central Washington.		●	●	●	●	●		●	●		●	●	●		
Olympic 632,324 acres. Northwestern Washington.		●	●	●	●	●		●	●	●	●	●	●	●	●
Wynoochee Lake (D-5) 2,777 acres 1 mi. w. of Montesano on US 12, then 37 mi. n. on FR 22 (Old Wynoochee Valley Rd.).	125	●	●	●	●	●		●	●						
Wenatchee 2,100,000 acres. Central Washington.		●	●	●	●	●	●	●	●		●	●	●		●
ARMY CORPS OF ENGINEERS															
Chief Joseph Dam (C-10) 864 acres off SR 17 in Bridgeport.	126		●		●	●		●					●		
Ice Harbor Lock and Dam (F-10) 13,046 acres 12 mi. e. of Pasco off US 12/395, then 5½ mi. e. on SR 124 and 2½ mi. n. on Ice Harbor Dam Rd.	121	●	●	●	●	●		●	●				●		
Little Goose Lock and Dam (E-11) 16,364 acres 8 mi. n.e. of Starbuck off US 12 on Little Goose Dam Rd.	122	●	●		●	●		●	●				●		
Lower Granite Lock and Dam (E-12) 14,863 acres 37 mi. n.e. of Pomeroy on Kirby-Mayfield Rd.	123	●	●		●	●		●	●				●		
Lower Monumental Lock and Dam (E-11) 14,726 acres 6 mi. s. of Kahlotus on Devil's Canyon Rd. *(See Kahlotus)*	117	●	●		●	●		●	●				●		
STATE															
Alta Lake (C-9) 177 acres 2 mi. s.w. of Pateros of SR 164. Scuba diving, snowmobiling, water skiing.	1	●	●	●	●	●		●	●	●		●			
Battle Ground Lake (G-6) 279 acres 3 mi. n.e. of Battle Ground off SR 502. *(See Battle Ground)*	2	●	●	●	●	●		●	●	●	●				●

RECREATION AREAS	MAP LOCATION	CAMPING	PICNICKING	HIKING TRAILS	BOATING	BOAT RAMP	BOAT RENTAL	FISHING	SWIMMING	PETS ON LEASH	BICYCLE TRAILS	WINTER SPORTS	VISITOR CENTER	LODGE/CABINS	FOOD SERVICE
Bay View (C-3) 25 acres 7 mi. w. of Burlington via SR 20. Scuba diving.	3	●	●		●			●		●					
Beacon Rock (G-6) 4,482 acres 35 mi. e. of Vancouver via SR 14.	4	●	●	●	●	●		●		●	●				
Birch Bay (A-2) 193 acres 1 mi. s. of Birch Bay off SR 548. *(See Birch Bay)*	6	●	●	●				●		●					
Blake Island Marine (F-3) 473 acres 4 mi. w. of Seattle via boat. Clamming, scuba diving, water skiing. *(See Seattle)*	7	●	●	●		●		●		●					●
Bogachiel (C-4) 119 acres 6 mi. s. of Forks at Bogachiel on US 101.	8	●	●	●	●		●	●		●					
Bridgeport (C-9) 758 acres ¾ mi. n. of Bridgeport via SR 17. Golf, water skiing.	9	●	●		●	●		●	●	●					●
Brooks Memorial (F-8) 700 acres 12 mi. n.e. of Goldendale off US 97. Snowmobiling.	10	●	●	●				●		●		●	●		
Camano Island (D-3) 134 acres 14 mi. s.w. of Stanwood on Camano Island. Scuba diving.	11	●	●	●	●	●		●	●	●				●	
Central Ferry (E-11) 185 acres 22 mi. n.w. of Pomeroy on SR 127. Water skiing.	12	●	●	●	●	●		●	●	●				●	
Chief Timothy (F-12) 282 acres 8 mi. w. of Clarkston on US 12. Water skiing.	13	●	●	●	●	●		●	●	●			●	●	●
Conconully (B-9) 80 acres 18 mi. n.w. of Omak off US 97. Snowmobiling, water skiing.	14	●	●	●	●	●		●		●		●	●	●	
Crow Butte (G-9) 740 acres 30 mi. w. of McNary Dam on SR 14. Water skiing.	15	●	●	●	●	●		●	●	●					
Curlew Lake (B-10) 123 acres 10 mi. n.e. of Republic on SR 21. Snowmobiling, water skiing.	16	●	●	●	●	●		●	●	●					
Daroga (D-9) 47 acres, 6 mi. n. of Orondo. Tennis, water skiing; ballpark.	134	●	●	●	●	●		●	●	●	●				
Dash Point (G-3) 397 acres 5 mi. n.e. of Tacoma on SR 509 exit 143.	17	●	●	●				●		●					
Deception Pass (C-2) 2,477 acres 18 mi. w. of Mount Vernon on Whidbey Island. Scuba diving. *(See Oak Harbor)*	18	●	●	●	●	●		●	●	●			●		●
Dosewallips (F-1) 425 acres at Brinnon off US 101.	19	●	●	●	●			●		●	●				
Dougs Beach (G-7) 31 acres, 2 mi. e. of Lyle. Kayaking, windsurfing.	135							●	●	●					
Fay Bainbridge (F-3) 17 acres 4 mi. n. of Winslow on SR 305. Scuba diving.	21	●	●		●	●		●		●					
Fields Spring (F-12) 456 acres 5 mi. s. of Anatone off SR 129. Snowmobiling.	22	●	●	●						●		●			
Flaming Geyser (D-7) 2,008 acres 1¾ mi. s. of Black Diamond on SR 169, then 2¾ mi. w. on S.E. Green Valley Rd. *(See Black Diamond)*	23		●	●				●		●					
Fort Canby (E-4) 1,882 acres 3 mi. s.w. of Ilwaco off US 101. Historic. Lewis and Clark Center. *(See Ilwaco)*	24	●	●	●		●		●		●			●		●
Fort Casey (D-2) 411 acres 3 mi. s. off SR 20. Scuba diving; interpretive center. *(See Whidbey Island)*	25	●	●	●	●	●		●		●			●		
Fort Ebey (D-2) 228 acres 8 mi. s. of Oak Harbor off SR 20. Scuba diving.	26	●	●	●				●		●					
Fort Flagler (D-2) 783 acres 20 mi. s.e. of Port Townsend on Marrowstone Island. Historic. Scuba diving. *(See Port Townsend)*	27	●	●	●	●	●		●		●	●				
Fort Simcoe (E-8) 200 acres 27 mi. w. of Toppenish via SR 220. *(See Toppenish)*	28		●	●						●			●		
Fort Ward (D-7) 137 acres 4 mi. s.w. of Winslow on Pleasant Beach Dr. Historic. Crabbing, scuba diving.	118		●	●		●		●		●					
Fort Worden (D-2) 444 acres 1 mi. n. of Port Townsend on SR 20. Historic. Scuba diving. *(See Port Townsend)*	29	●	●	●	●	●		●		●	●		●	●	●
Grayland Beach (E-4) 411 acres on SR 105 in Grayland.	30	●		●				●		●	●				
Horsethief Lake (G-7) 338 acres 17 mi. e. of White Salmon off SR 14. Indian petroglyphs.	31	●	●	●	●	●		●		●					
Ike Kinswa (E-6) 454 acres 5 mi. n.w. of Mossyrock via US 12. Water skiing.	32	●	●	●	●	●		●	●	●	●				●

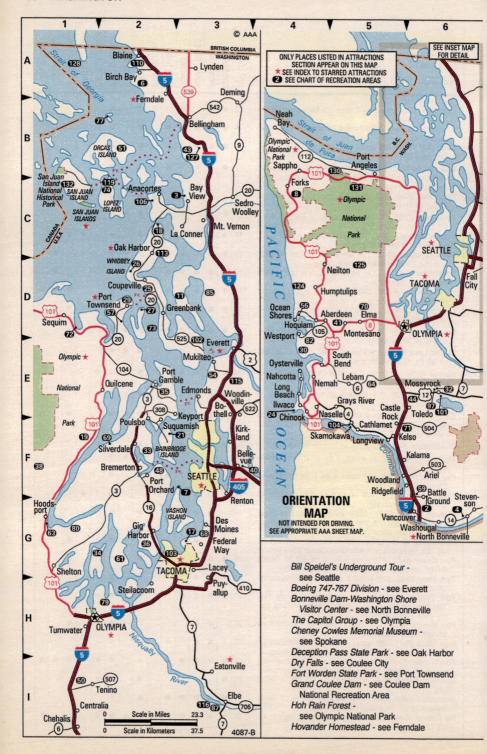

Bill Speidel's Underground Tour - see Seattle
Boeing 747-767 Division - see Everett
Bonneville Dam-Washington Shore Visitor Center - see North Bonneville
The Capitol Group - see Olympia
Cheney Cowles Memorial Museum - see Spokane
Deception Pass State Park - see Oak Harbor
Dry Falls - see Coulee City
Fort Worden State Park - see Port Townsend
Grand Coulee Dam - see Coulee Dam National Recreation Area
Hoh Rain Forest - see Olympic National Park
Hovander Homestead - see Ferndale

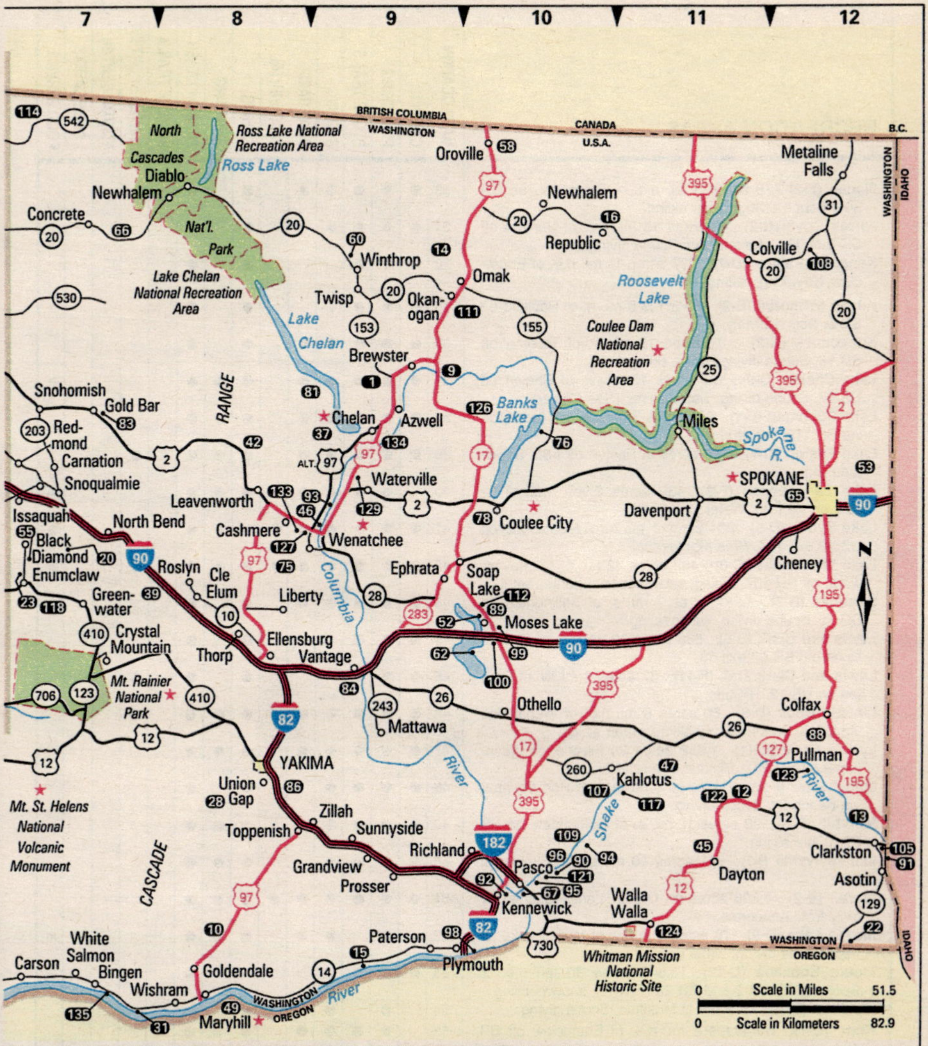

INDEX TO STARRED ATTRACTIONS

ATTRACTIONS OF EXCEPTIONAL INTEREST AND QUALITY

Hurricane Ridge - see Olympic National Park
Lake Chelan - see Chelan
Lake Washington Ship Canal and Hiram M. Chittenden Locks - see Seattle
Manito Park - see Spokane
Maryhill Museum of Art - see Maryhill
Mount Rainier National Park - see place listing
Mount St. Helens National Volcanic Monument - see place listing
Museum of Flight - see Seattle
Northwest Trek - see Eatonville
Ohme Gardens County Park - see Wenatchee
Olympic National Park - see place listing
Pike Place Market - see Seattle
Pioneer Square Historic District - see Seattle
Point Defiance Park - see Tacoma
Port Townsend - see place listing
Riverfront Park - see Spokane
Rocky Reach Dam - see Wenatchee
San Juan Islands - see place listing
Seattle Art Museum - see Seattle
Seattle Center - see Seattle
Space Needle - see Seattle
State Capitol Museum - see Olympia
Tillicum Village - see Seattle
Washington State Historical Society Museum - see Tacoma

RECREATION AREAS	MAP LOCATION	CAMPING	PICNICKING	HIKING TRAILS	BOATING	BOAT RAMP	BOAT RENTAL	FISHING	SWIMMING	PETS ON LEASH	BICYCLE TRAILS	WINTER SPORTS	VISITOR CENTER	LODGE/CABINS	FOOD SERVICE
Illahee (F-2) 75 acres 3 mi. n.e. of Bremerton on SR 306. Scuba diving, water skiing.	33	●	●	●	●	●		●		●					
Jarrell Cove (G-2) 43 acres 15 mi. n.e. of Shelton off SR 3 on Hartstene Island. Scuba diving.	34	●	●	●	●			●		●					
Kanaskat-Palmer (D-7) 297 acres 11 mi. n.e. of Enumclaw. Kayaking, rafting.	20	●	●	●				●		●					
Kitsap Memorial (E-2) 58 acres 6 mi. n. of Poulsbo off SR 3. Scuba diving.	35	●	●	●				●		●					
Kopachuck (G-2) 109 acres 16 mi. w. of Tacoma on SR 16. Scuba diving, water skiing.	36	●	●	●	●	●		●		●					
Lake Chelan (C-9) 127 acres 13 mi. w. of Chelan off US 97. Scuba diving, water skiing. *(See Chelan)*	37	●	●	●	●	●		●	●	●					●
Lake Cushman (F-1) 603 acres 7 mi. n.w. of Hoodsport via SR 119. Water skiing.	38	●	●	●	●	●		●	●	●					
Lake Easton (D-7) 196 acres at Easton off I-90. Snowmobiling.	39	●	●	●	●	●		●	●	●		●			
Lake Sammamish (F-3) 432 acres 2 mi. n.w. of Issaquah via I-90. Water skiing.	40		●	●	●	●		●	●	●					●
Lake Sylvia (D-5) 234 acres 1 mi. n. of Montesano off US 12 exit 104. *(See Montesano)*	41	●	●	●	●	●	●	●	●	●					●
Lake Wenatchee (C-8) 489 acres 22 mi. n. of Leavenworth off SR 207. Skiing, snowmobiling; horse rental.	42	●	●	●	●	●	●	●	●	●		●			●
Larrabee (B-3) 1,981 acres 7 mi. s. of Bellingham on SR 11. Scuba diving, water skiing.	43	●	●	●	●	●		●		●					
Lewis and Clark (E-6) 533 acres 12 mi. s.e. of Chehalis on old SR 99 exit 68.	44	●	●	●				●		●					
Lewis and Clark Trail (F-11) 37 acres 4 mi. w. of Dayton on US 12. Historic.	45	●	●	●				●		●		●			
Lincoln Rock (D-8) 80 acres 6 mi. n.e. of Wenatchee via US 2. Cross-country skiing, water skiing.	46	●	●	●	●	●		●	●	●		●			
Lyon's Ferry (E-11) 1,282 acres 20 mi. s.e. of Washtucna off SR 261. Historic. Water skiing.	47	●	●	●	●	●		●	●	●					
Manchester (F-2) 111 acres 6 mi. n.e. of Port Orchard via Beach Dr. Scuba diving.	48	●	●	●	●			●		●					
Maryhill (G-8) 98 acres 12 mi. s. of Goldendale on US 97. Water skiing.	49	●	●	●	●			●	●	●					
Millersylvania (I-1) 841 acres 10 mi. s. of Olympia off I-5.	50	●	●	●	●			●	●	●					
Moran (B-2) 4,606 acres on Orcas Island, reached by ferry from Anacortes.	51	●	●	●	●	●	●	●	●	●					
Moses Lake (D-9) 78 acres 5 mi. w. of Moses Lake off I-90. Scuba diving, water skiing.	52		●		●	●		●	●	●					●
Mount Spokane (C-12) 13,643 acres 30 mi. n.e. of Spokane via US 2 and SR 206. Skiing, snowmobiling.	53	●	●	●						●		●			●
Mukilteo (E-3) 18 acres at Mukilteo. Scuba diving.	54		●		●	●		●		●					
Nolte (D-7) 117 acres 6 mi. n.e. of Enumclaw off SR 169.	55		●	●	●	●		●	●	●					
Ocean City (D-4) 112 acres at the s. edge of Ocean City off SR 109. Scuba diving.	56	●	●	●				●		●			●		
Old Fort Townsend (D-2) 377 acres 3 mi. s. of Port Townsend off SR 20. Historic. *(See Port Townsend)*	57	●	●	●				●		●					
Osoyoos Lake (A-10) 46 acres 1 mi. n. of Oroville on US 97. Ice skating, water skiing.	58	●	●		●	●		●	●	●					●
Pacific Beach (D-4) 9 acres, in Pacific Beach. Clamming.	124	●	●	●				●	●	●					
Paradise Point (F-6) 88 acres 19 mi. n. of Vancouver off I-5 exit 16.	59	●	●	●	●	●		●		●					
Pearrygin Lake (B-9) 578 acres 5 mi. n.e. of Winthrop off SR 20. Snowmobiling.	60	●	●	●	●	●		●	●	●		●			
Penrose Point (G-2) 152 acres 3 mi. n. of Long Branch SR 302.	61	●	●	●	●	●		●		●					
Potholes (E-9) 640 acres 10 mi. s.e. of Moses Lake on SR 17, then 14 mi. w. on SR 170.	62	●	●	●	●	●		●		●					
Potlatch (G-1) 57 acres n. of Shelton off US 101. Scuba diving, water skiing.	63	●	●	●	●	●		●		●					
Rainbow Falls (E-5) 125 acres 18 mi. w. of Chehalis on SR 6.	64	●	●	●				●		●					

RECREATION AREAS	MAP LOCATION	CAMPING	PICNICKING	HIKING TRAILS	BOATING	BOAT RAMP	BOAT RENTAL	FISHING	SWIMMING	PETS ON LEASH	BICYCLE TRAILS	WINTER SPORTS	VISITOR CENTER	LODGE/CABINS	FOOD SERVICE
Riverside (D-12) 7,469 acres 6 mi. n.w. of Spokane off SR 291. Historic. Snowmobiling; horse rental.	65	●	●	●		●		●		●		●	●		
Rockport (B-7) 457 acres w. of Rockport off SR 20.	66	●	●	●											
Sacajawea (F-10) 284 acres 2 mi. s.e. of Pasco off US 12. Historic. Water skiing. *(See Pasco)*	67		●		●	●		●	●	●			●		●
Saltwater (G-3) 90 acres 1½ mi. s. of Des Moines off Marine View Dr. Scuba diving.	68	●	●	●				●	●	●					●
Scenic Beach (F-2) 88 acres 12 mi. n.w. of Bremerton at Seabeck. Scuba diving.	69	●	●	●				●		●					
Schafer (D-5) 119 acres 8 mi. n. of Satsop on the Satsop River.	70	●	●	●				●		●					
Seaquest (F-6) 296 acres 5 mi. e. of Castle Rock off I-5 exit 49.	71	●	●	●				●		●					
Sequim Bay (D-1) 92 acres 7 mi. s.e. of Sequim off US 101. Scuba diving.	72	●	●	●	●	●		●		●					
South Whidbey (D-2) 85 acres 10 mi. s. of Coupeville on Whidbey Island. Scuba diving.	73	●	●	●				●		●					
Spencer Spit (C-2) 130 acres on the e. side of Lopez Island. Scuba diving.	74	●	●	●	●			●		●					
Squilchuck (D-8) 288 acres 7 mi. s. of Wenatchee on Squilchuck Canyon Rd. Snow skiing.	75	●	●	●						●		●			
Steamboat Rock (C-10) 3,523 acres 11 mi. s. of Grand Coulee on SR 155. Scuba diving, water skiing.	76	●	●	●	●	●		●	●	●		●			●
Sucia Island (B-2) 564 acres 2½ mi. n. of Orcas Island. Accessible only by boat.	77	●	●	●	●			●		●					
Sun Lakes (D-10) 4,024 acres 6 mi. s.w. of Coulee City off SR 17. Golf; horse rental.	78	●	●	●	●	●	●	●	●	●			●		●
Tolmie (H-2) 106 acres 8 mi. n.e. of Olympia off I-5. Scuba diving; underwater park.	79		●	●				●		●					
Twanoh (G-1) 182 acres 5 mi. e. of Union on SR 106. Water skiing.	80	●	●	●	●	●		●	●	●					●
Twenty-five Mile Creek (C-9) 235 acres 25 mi. w. of Chelan on 25 Mile Creek Rd.	81	●	●	●	●	●		●		●					●
Twin Harbors (E-4) 172 acres 3 mi. s. of Westport on SR 105.	82	●	●	●				●		●					
Wallace Falls (C-7) 678 acres 2 mi. n.e. of Gold Bar off US 2. *(See Gold Bar)*	83	●	●	●				●		●					
Wenatchee Confluence (D-9) 91 acres 3 mi. n. of Wenatchee. Tennis, water skiing; ballparks.	127	●	●	●	●	●		●	●	●	●				
Wanapum (E-9) 451 acres 3 mi. s. of Vantage on the Columbia River. Water skiing.	84	●	●	●	●	●		●	●	●			●		
Wenberg (D-3) 46 acres 4 mi. n. of Marysville via US 5, then 8 mi. w. off SR 531. Water skiing.	85	●	●	●	●	●		●	●	●					●
Yakima Sportsmen's (E-8) 251 acres 1 mi. e. of Yakima off I-82.	86	●	●	●				●		●					
OTHER															
Alder Lake Park (I-3) 385 acres 5½ mi. s.w. of Elbe off SR 7 on Pleasant Valley Rd.	87	●	●		●	●		●	●	●					
Boyer Park (E-12) 40 acres s.w. of Colfax.	88	●	●		●	●		●	●	●				●	●
Carl Precht Memorial RV Park (B-10) 73 acres ¼ mi. w. of Main St. on Omak Ave. in Omak.	111	●	●		●			●	●				●		
Cascade Park (D-10) On Valley Rd. near Moses Lake. Water skiing; playground.	89	●	●		●	●		●	●						
Charbonneau Park (F-10) 34 acres 8 mi. e. of Burbank on SR 124, then 2 mi. n. on Sun Harbor Dr.	90	●	●		●	●		●	●	●					
Chief Looking Glass (F-12) 5 mi. s. of Clarkston on SR 129.	91		●	●	●	●			●		●				
Columbia Park (F-10) 434 acres at Kennewick along Lake Wallula. Archery, golf, tennis; ballpark.	92	●	●	●	●	●	●	●	●	●	●				
Connelly Park (D-10) 5 mi. n. of Moses Lake, w. of SR 17 on McConihe Rd. Playground.	112		●		●	●		●	●						
Entiat Park (D-9) On US 97A in Entiat.	93	●	●		●	●		●	●						
Fishhook Park (F-10) 29 acres 15 mi. e. of Burbank on SR 124, then 4 mi. n. on Page Rd.	94	●	●		●	●		●	●	●					
Hood Park (F-10) 50 acres 3 mi. s. of Pasco on US 12/395 at SR 124.	95	●	●		●	●		●	●	●					

RECREATION AREAS	MAP LOCATION	CAMPING	PICNICKING	HIKING TRAILS	BOATING	BOAT RAMP	BOAT RENTAL	FISHING	SWIMMING	PETS ON LEASH	BICYCLE TRAILS	WINTER SPORTS	VISITOR CENTER	LODGE/CABINS	FOOD SERVICE
Lake Gillette (B-12) 46 acres 35 mi. e. of Colville via SR 20.	108	●	●		●			●	●						
Lake Sacajawea (F-10) 9,200 acres 12 mi. e. of Pasco off US 12.	109	●	●		●			●	●						
Levey Park (F-10) 24 acres 10½ mi. e. of Pasco on Pasco-Kahlotus Rd., then 1 mi. s. on Levey Rd.	96		●		●	●		●	●	●					
Lighthouse Marine Park (A-1) 22 acres on s.w. corner of Point Roberts at 811 Marine Dr. Clamming, whale watching; boardwalk, observation tower.	119	●	●		●	●		●							
Mayfield Lake County Park (E-6) 51 acres 3 mi. w. of Mossyrock on US 12.	97	●	●	●	●	●		●	●						●
McNary Lock and Dam (F-9) 15 acres 1½ mi. e. of Umatilla, Ore., on US 730, then 1 mi. n. on McNary Dam Rd.	98		●		●	●		●					●		
Montlake Park (E-10) Beaumont and Linden aves. in Moses Lake. Water skiing.	99		●	●	●	●		●	●			●			
Moses Lake R.V. Park (E-10) 4 mi. s. from Moses Lake off Division St. Water skiing.	100		●	●	●			●	●						
Mossyrock Park (E-6) 272 acres 3 mi. e. of Mossyrock via Aljune Rd. and Swofford Rd.	101	●	●	●	●	●		●	●	●					●
Oak Harbor Beach Park (C-2) 40 acres ¼ mi. e. of SR 20 in Oak Harbor on Whidbey Island.	113	●	●		●	●		●	●						
Odlin County Park (B-2) 80 acres on n. side of Lopez Island. Birdwatching, clamming.	128	●	●	●	●	●		●	●	●					
Orondo River Park (D-9) 6 acres 2 mi. n. of Orondo. Water skiing	129	●	●		●	●			●	●					
Phil Simon Park (E-3) In Langley on Whidbey Island.	102		●		●	●		●	●						
Pillar Point County Park (B-4) 4 acres 35 mi. w. of Port Angeles. Clamming.	130	●	●		●	●		●		●					
Point Defiance Park (G-2) 698 acres in Tacoma off Pearl St. Scuba diving, tennis. *(See Tacoma)*	103		●	●	●	●	●	●	●		●				●
Salt Creek County Park (B-5) 196 acres 15 mi. w. of Port Angeles.	131	●	●	●				●		●					
Samish Park (B-3) 39 acres 10 mi. s. of Bellingham off I-5 exit 246 on North Lake Samish Dr. Canoeing.	120		●	●	●		●	●	●						
San Juan County Park (C-1) 15 acres on w. side of San Juan Island. Scuba diving.	132	●	●	●	●	●			●	●	●				
Semiahmoo County Park (A-2) 300 acres at the entrance to Semiahmoo Spit on the w. side of Drayton Harbor in Blaine. Clamming, sailing, water skiing. *(See Blaine)*	110		●		●			●	●				●		
Silver Lake County Park (A-7) 411 acres 4 mi. n. of Maple Falls off SR 542. Horse rental.	114	●	●	●	●	●	●	●	●			●	●	●	
Skamokawa Vista Park (F-5) 28 acres ½ mi. w. of Skamokawa on SR 4. Baseball, basketball, tennis. *(See Skamokawa)*	104	●	●		●	●		●	●						
Sunny Beach Point (I-3) 9 acres on Alder Lake off SR 7. Water skiing.	116		●		●			●	●						
Swallows Park (F-12) 1 mi. s. of Clarkston on SR 129.	105		●	●	●	●		●	●	●	●				
Thornton A. Sullivan Park (E-3) 27 acres 5 mi. s. of Everett on 112th St., S.E. Nature trails.	115		●		●		●	●	●						
Washington Park (C-2) 220 acres 4 mi. w. of Anacortes on Anacortes Sunset Ave. Scenic drive.	106	●	●	●	●	●		●	●						
Wenatchee River County Park (D-8) 10 acres 10 mi. n.w. of Wenatchee. Ballparks.	133	●	●		●	●		●		●					
Windust Park (E-10) 12 acres 10 mi. n.e. of Pasco on Pasco-Kahlotus Rd., then 5 mi. s.e. on Burr Canyon Rd.	107	●	●		●	●		●	●	●					

Carelessness is responsible
for more than 90 percent of all fires
in our national forests.

Touring Washington

For descriptions of places in bold type, see individual listings.

Columbia River Gorge

Rimmed by sheer cliffs separating Washington and Oregon, the Columbia River Gorge is hailed as one of the most scenic areas in the state. Tamed by hydroelectric projects, the once rogue river now provides a wide corridor for tourism and trade. The gorge runs from the moist forests near **Washougal,** through the Cascades, and out into drier, more open country east of **Bingen-White Salmon.**

A journey along 150-mile-long SR 14 from **Vancouver** to Plymouth parallels the river, covering a spectrum of changes in topography and vegetation. Bridges cross the river near **Stevenson,** Bingen, Dallesport, **Maryhill** and Plymouth. The Columbia River Gorge National Scenic Area covers 253,500 acres on both the Washington and Oregon banks between Washougal and Maryhill.

Beacon Rock State Park, 5 miles west of Stevenson, provides a sweeping view of the gorge. Bonneville Dam has bridled the Columbia's waters since 1938, providing a wider waterway for lumber and port towns like nearby Stevenson. **Carson,** 5 miles west of Stevenson, and Underwood, 5 miles west of Bingen, provide easy access to the **Gifford Pinchot National Forest.** Bingen, a logging town, also is known for its wineries. Dougs Beach State Park, just east of Lyle, is a windsurfing mecca.

Some 20 miles east of Bingen, US 197 turns south across the river to **The Dalles, Ore.** A few miles past the junction is the Dalles Dam; its impoundment extends to the US 97/SR 14 intersection in Maryhill. The next 80 miles to Plymouth is typical of the dry, hilly country sandwiched between the Cascades and the Blue Mountains.

Between Whitcomb and **Paterson** SR 14 parallels the northern edge of the Umatilla National Wildlife Refuge, which occupies wetlands and arid grasslands on both sides of the river. SR 14 ends at I-82 just outside Plymouth. McNary Dam is nearby.

North-central

To put it simply, north-central Washington is the northern Cascades. Bounded on the west by the Puget Sound Basin, on the east by the Columbia and Okanogan rivers, on the north by Canada and on the south by I-90, this is the roughest part of the range. It is a welter of peaks, crags and ridges, scored by deep ravines and crowned by two snowy volcanoes: sporadically restive Mount Baker, at the northwestern edge of the range, and dormant Glacier Peak, in the center.

Most of the region lies within the **Mount Baker-Snoqualmie, Okanogan** and **Wenatchee national forests, North Cascades National Park** and two national recreation areas, **Ross Lake** and **Lake Chelan.**

Three routes link the west and east slopes, and all three are designated scenic highways. The one north-south route, negotiable only by horses and hikers, is the Pacific Crest National Scenic Trail.

Snoqualmie Pass is the conduit for heavily traveled transcontinental I-90; at 3,022 feet the lowest pass, it is the first to be plowed after a snowfall. It is the state's busiest winter sports development, with four ski areas at the summit. The scenic section begins near **North Bend,** tops the summit and coasts along the Yakima River to **Cle Elum** and **Ellensburg.** Another scenic drive, SR 903, goes deeper into the summit country via **Roslyn** and Cle Elum Lake; it is reached from Cle Elum or via SR 10 from Ellensburg.

US 2 crosses the center of the region through dramatic 4,061-foot Stevens Pass, also kept open—for the most part—in winter. The route enters the Cascades foothills at Startup—named, incidentally, for a settler named Startup, not because it's where visitors start up into the mountains. Beginning at **Gold Bar,** the scenic segment twists east, skirting such picturesque towns as Index and Skykomish.

After cresting the pass and its adjoining ski area, the route runs through several small resort communities and the cutoff to Wenatchee Lake, then penetrates the dramatic Tumwater Canyon. A few miles east of Bavarian-style **Leavenworth** US 2 is joined by US 97 the rest of the way through **Cashmere** to **Wenatchee,** traversing the Wenatchee Valley, one of the nation's prime apple-growing regions.

The northernmost cross-Cascades route is SR 20, crossing 4,860-foot Rainy Pass and 5,477-foot Washington Pass through North Cascades National Park. Designated as scenic all the way from the Puget Sound Basin, the route travels the length of the Skagit Valley before clambering into the summit country east of Marblemount. From December into April, winter snows usually close the road between **Diablo** and Mazama.

From Mazama SR 20 follows the Methow River through **Winthrop** to **Twisp.** There it bears east over 30 townless, mountainous miles to US 97 at **Okanogan,** while SR 153 continues along the Methow to meet US 97 at Pateros.

There is one more way to reach the heart of the northern Cascades: by boat, up fiordlike Lake Chelan between **Chelan** and Stehekin.

Northeast

From the Okanogan Valley eastward to the Idaho border, and from the Canadian border south to I-90, northeastern Washington presents variety on a grand scale. The northern part is the Okanogan Highlands, whose mountains, the Kettles and the Selkirks, are an extension of the northern Rockies.

In the south spreads the vast basaltic plateau, formed by lava flows and scoured by the rushing meltwaters of the last ice age. The most prominent feature, however, is the mighty Columbia River, which curves down from Canada and furnishes irrigation, power and recreation to much of eastern Washington.

Except between **Ellensburg** and **Wenatchee,** US 97 delineates the western edge of the region as it snakes northward between the Columbia and the Cascades foothills. Basalt cliffs keep the river in bounds, as do the Rock Island and Rocky Reach dams, both near Wenatchee. The landscape to the east opens out as the highway nears Entiat, but the hills crowd close on the west all the way to **Chelan.**

After passing another dam at **Azwell,** the highway continues along the west bank of the Columbia to Pateros, where SR 153 turns northwest into the Methow Valley. A few miles east of **Brewster** US 97 forsakes the Columbia and heads north along the Okanogan River Valley; SR 17 branches south, leading to Chief Joseph Dam at Bridgeport, and thence into coulee country.

The deep, steep-walled coulees were ancient channels of the Columbia before melting ice allowed it to resume its original course. Some again contain water, thanks to dams; Grand Coulee Dam and **Coulee Dam National Recreation Area** are reached from SR 17 via SR 174.

The dam is the northern end of a particularly scenic route through this dramatic area. SR 155 passes the Grand Coulee Dam. At **Coulee City** US 2, which spans the farming country between Wenatchee and **Spokane,** carries the scenic route west to a junction with SR 17. In turn SR 17 heads south past Dry Falls, once three times the size of Niagara. The highway passes many lakes and huge farms en route to **Soap Lake,** where the road branches onto SR 28 to **Ephrata.** SR 17 continues south to meet I-90 at **Moses Lake.**

When it turns north into the Okanogan, US 97 enters Washington's Old West. The route parallels the Cariboo Trail, which funneled cattle between **Pasco** and Canada in the 1860s and was a highway for goldseekers later in the century. The valley is still largely devoted to ranching.

Running along the western edge of the Colville Indian Reservation, the route passes **Okanogan** and **Omak.** At the former, SR 20 from **Twisp** joins US 97 and runs concurrently with it to Tonasket. At Tonasket US 97 proceeds north to **Oroville** and the Canadian border, but SR 20 turns east, embarking on one of the state's least known scenic mountain drives.

Passing through the **Okanogan** and **Colville national forests,** it crosses the highest pass in the state highway system—5,575-foot Sherman Pass—and descends to the Columbia River and US 395 near Kettle Falls. At this point, US 395 heads north to the Canadian border and south toward Spokane; the scenic route follows it south to **Colville,** then branches east through the Selkirks.

At the Pend Oreille River SR 31 turns north toward **Metaline Falls** and Canada, and SR 20 bears south through slightly less scenic but still interesting mining country. SR 20 ends at US 2 at Newport, east of Spokane on the Idaho border.

I-90 is the main corridor across Washington. It leaves the Cascades at Ellensburg, leaps the Columbia at **Vantage,** then climbs the cliffs lining the edge of the gorge to a town whose name suggests the presence of a wag in its past: George. It then runs virtually curveless to Ritzville, intersecting en route with SR 283/28 to Ephrata and SR 17 at Moses Lake. At Ritzville US 395 joins I-90 for another nearly straight run to Spokane. Throughout, the route traverses the productive cropland that is the essence of the Inland Empire.

Olympic Peninsula

Contrasts and extremes distinguish the Olympic Peninsula. The Olympic Mountain Range divides it into two distinct worlds: the wild, sparsely populated western side, with its wave-racked coast, ancient glaciers and the largest temperate-zone rain forests in the world, and the sheltered eastern side, with its irrigated plains, picturesque mill towns and the Kitsap Peninsula's mosaic of islands, peninsulas and bays.

Making a loop along the Olympic Peninsula's edge, US 101 connects these disparate realms and provides access into **Olympic National Park** and the **Olympic National Forest.**

From **Olympia,** at the southern tip of Puget Sound, US 101 passes shallow Oyster Bay en route to the old logging town of **Shelton,** where SR 3 begins its trek along the Kitsap Peninsula's spine. Bounded by Hood Canal on the east and Puget Sound on the west, the peninsula is marked by such towns as **Bremerton,** a major Navy shipyard, and **Poulsbo,** noted for its Norwegian character.

SR 106 provides a scenic alternate route back to US 101, which borders oyster- and clam-rich Hood Canal. Inland, side roads lead into the high country of the Olympic National Forest. Meadows, woodlands and banks of rhododendron straddle US 101 as it continues north to the SR 20 junction to historic **Port Townsend.**

US 101 then turns westward along the Strait of Juan de Fuca. The only sizable towns on this narrow, remote coast are **Sequim** and **Port Angeles;** the latter offers one of the best approaches into the lofty heights of Olympic National Park. Such viewpoints as Hurricane Ridge offer panoramas of the park's jagged peaks, lowland lakes and wildflower meadows. Mountain goats, bears, marmots and chipmunks are but a few of the animals that can be seen; the Elwha River, just west, is noted for steelhead.

From Port Angeles SR 112 continues the coastal route and links towns and resorts geared to sport fishing. The busiest, **Neah Bay,** at the end of SR 112, boasts fishing resorts run by the Makah Tribe. The beaches next to these salmon ports yield agates and driftwood. Cape Flattery, the very northwestern tip of the peninsula, presents spectacular cliffs bounded by wave-battered offshore rocks.

To the south lie the wild beaches of Olympic National Park, most of which can only be approached by muddy hiking trails through moss-canopied forests and small meadows. Shipwrecks are common sights along these narrow headlands.

By contrast, few trails penetrate the dense rain forests on the inland side of US 101. In the Hoh, Queets and Quinault river valleys, Sitka spruce and Douglas fir with 8-foot trunks grow to heights of 275 feet, and mosses and ferns carpet the forest floor. Roads off US 101 venture into all three valleys and lead to high-country trails and campgrounds of the national park.

At Ruby Beach, a scenic section of US 101 rejoins a tamer coast, known for sandy beaches, driftwood, razor clams and smelt runs. Turning inland again, the highway borders the Quinault Reservation en route to Lake Quinault, one of the park's most developed recreational areas. Scenic vistas continue to unfold as US 101 runs south to **Aberdeen.** At **Hoquiam** SR 109 heads west to the seashore resort towns north of Grays Harbor.

US 12/SR 8, the final leg of the loop, affords views of the least rugged, yet most remote, side of the Olympics as it returns to Olympia.

Puget Sound and the San Juan Islands

Puget Sound cleaves southward from the Strait of Juan de Fuca nearly two-thirds of the way through the state. As the crow flies, the sound is about 140 miles long, but its indented eastern shore wriggles much farther than that between **Olympia** and the Canadian border.

One of the world's great embayments, the sound shelters in its many harbors not only fishing fleets and countless pleasure craft, but also, at such ports as **Everett, Seattle** and **Tacoma,** the giant vessels of the international tradeways. **Whidbey Island** and the **San Juan Islands,** in the northern half of the sound, remain in many ways a world apart.

On the narrow belt separating the sound and the Cascades foothills, 55 percent of the population lives and works in a sprawling conurbation that includes five of Washington's largest cities and its heaviest concentration of business and industry.

The chief corridor through this busy area is I-5. It reaches the sound at Olympia, which is almost as famous for the beer brewed at adjoining **Tumwater** as for its own august status as state capital. From Olympia the route speeds northeast toward Tacoma; a side road leads to venerable **Steilacoom,** the oldest incorporated town in the state.

Just south of Tacoma I-5 intersects with SR 512 which, with SR 167, forms an inland route to Seattle via the increasingly industrial Green River Valley. Near **Puyallup** SR 161 branches south along a high ridge that offers some stunning views of Mount Rainier. Beyond the old farming and logging town of Graham, SR 161 is part of the scenic route to Paradise in **Mount Rainier National Park.** Another road, SR 410, leaves SR 167 at Sumner; it leads to **Enumclaw,** east of which it provides a scenic drive to Sunrise in the eastern side of the park.

Development, industry and traffic increase as I-5 continues north through Seattle. Glimpses of Lake Washington and the sound, with their respective mountain backdrops, intersperse views of the hilly city. I-405 bypasses downtown by skirting the eastern shore of Lake Washington; it connects with I-90, the scenic Snoqualmie Pass highway, then continues through **Bellevue** to rejoin I-5 between Seattle and Everett.

North of Everett, towns become farther apart as I-5 traverses farming and dairy country. There are often views of the Cascades, which become increasingly rugged as they roll north. Mount Baker, the northernmost of Washington's volcanoes, shimmers above its bed of forested peaks in the **Mount Baker-Snoqualmie National Forest.**

A few miles west of Everett is **Mukilteo,** the mainland slip for the ferry to Whidbey Island. SR 525/20 along the island's spine earns its "scenic" designation when clear weather permits views of the sound, wooded islands, the Olympic Mountains and the Cascades. SR 20 leaps Deception Pass to reach the mainland between **Anacortes** and **Mount Vernon.**

Anacortes is the ferry port for the San Juan Islands. State ferries call at **Lopez,** Shaw, **Orcas** and **San Juan;** Lummi Island is reached via **Bellingham.** Boat charters, available at harbors all along the sound, allow exploration of the waterways off the ferry lanes.

Between Everett and Burlington I-5 connects with several highways that become designated scenic routes as they enter the Cascades. US 2 runs east from Everett, through the Skykomish Valley and over Stevens Pass; its scenic segment begins at **Gold Bar.** The Mountain Loop Highway, a route comprising SR 92, several county and forest service roads (one segment is closed in winter) and part of SR 530, loops east from Everett and returns to I-5 near Arlington.

At Burlington SR 20 turns east through **Sedro Woolley** to **North Cascades National Park.** Leading east from Bellingham the scenic Mount Baker Highway (SR 542) follows the Nooksack

River into the high cascades between Mount Baker and Mount Shuksan; the final 2 miles climbing up to the viewpoint at Artist Point are open only in the summer months.

Burlington also is the southern terminus of SR 11, the Chuckanut Drive, which hugs a bluff high above Samish Bay all the way to Bellingham. North of the city I-5 travels through farming country before entering Canada at **Blaine.**

South-central

Rolling northward from the Columbia River Gorge to I-90 and eastward from the western slopes of the Cascades to the Columbia River, the mountains and valleys of south-central Washington present a variegated picture indeed. The region has three of the state's great isolated volcanoes. Mount St. Helens, a less benign presence since its eruption in 1980, is the westernmost; it is the focus of **Mount St. Helens National Volcanic Monument.**

Some 35 miles due east of St. Helens, glacier-girt Mount Adams sits amid the broad, lake-strewn meadows of the Cascade crest. And in the north, looming some 8,000 feet above its forested foothills in **Mount Rainier National Park,** is the mighty peak that Washingtonians simply call "The Mountain." Almost all of the Cascades are within the **Gifford Pinchot National Forest.**

The mountains in the eastern part of the region are different. The forested granite peaks of the Cascades blend into the more rounded, bare ridges and basalt outcrops of the Simcoe Mountains, Rattlesnake Hills and Horse Heaven Hills.

The third major feature of the area is the rich Yakima Valley, a wide streak of green and gold slicing southeastward between the dun hills to the Columbia River. The valley is widest around **Yakima,** its largest city and chief commercial center.

Other than I-90 *(see North-central),* there is only one all-year highway through the Cascades—US 12. A designated scenic route from Morton through the Cowlitz River Valley, over 4,500-foot White Pass to Naches, it is doubly important since it connects with every other major highway in the region. It also links with a network of forest roads that rambles through the back country to the Columbia Gorge. Scenic highlights of the route include the Palisades and Clear Creek Falls bracketing White Pass and Rimrock Lake.

Several miles north of Packwood, US 12 junctions with scenic SR 123, which runs north through the eastern edge of Mount Rainier National Park to SR 410, thus creating a scenic loop highway around all but the west side of the mountain. The Stevens Canyon Road (closed in winter) through the southern portion of the park meets SR 123 a few miles above the US 12 junction.

SR 410, the northern arc of the loop, begins at **Enumclaw;** after intersecting with SR 123, it twists over 5,440-foot Chinook Pass and descends the eastern slope, ending at US 12 west of Naches. Both Chinook Pass and 4,694-foot Cayuse Pass at the junction of SRs 410 and 123 are closed in winter.

At Yakima US 12 is joined by I-82/US 97 from **Ellensburg** on I-90. SR 821 offers a 27-mile alternate through the scenic Yakima Canyon. US 12 and I-82 run concurrently along the north bank of the Yakima River, through **Zillah, Sunnyside, Grandview** and **Prosser.** US 97 follows the south bank of the river to **Toppenish,** then turns south on a scenic trip over 3,107-foot Satus Pass to **Goldendale** and **Maryhill.**

Prosser, on I-82/US 12, is the northern end of an important shortcut to Pendleton. SR 221 climbs south into the Horse Heaven Hills, where vineyards and wheatfields have supplanted mustangs, then follows SR 14 to Plymouth and McNary Dam. Just west of **Richland** I-82 also veers south toward McNary Dam. US 12 continues through the Tri-Cities area to southeastern Washington.

Southeast

Southeastern Washington seems to contain a little of everything. From the Columbia River it extends eastward across lava plateau and productive valleys, over the curious Palouse wheat country and the rugged northern end of the Blue Mountains to the Idaho border. The Oregon state line marks the southern boundary; I-90 delineates the northern. The Snake River, having emerged from Hells Canyon *(see Oregon),* arches westward to meet the Columbia at **Pasco.**

Two primary highways cross the region south to north: US 395 through the center and US 195 along the eastern edge. Besides I-90, west-to-east routes are US 12 in the south and SR 26 across the middle. There are numerous connecting routes as well, some of them especially scenic.

From Pasco, the smallest of the Tri-Cities (the other two being **Kennewick** and **Richland**), US 395 speeds northeast across miles of farmland toward Ritzville, where it joins I-90 for the remainder of the distance to **Spokane.** En route it intersects with SR 17, which heads north toward the Pothole Lakes country and I-90 at **Moses Lake,** and SR 26.

US 12 turns south from Pasco along the Columbia, then veers east along the Walla Walla River. The valley is rich in both crops and history: Acres of sweet onions bring the Walla Walla name to tables throughout the west; **Whitman Mission National Historic Site** commemorates the culmination of some unhappy circumstances in 1847. At **Walla Walla** US 12 begins its winding course between the Snake River and the foothills of the Blue Mountains; Waitsburg, **Dayton** and Pomeroy are the largest towns the route meets before it descends to **Clarkston.**

From Clarkston scenic SR 129 follows the Snake to **Asotin,** then heads toward Oregon's Wallowa Mountains, joining scenic SR 3 in Oregon.

US 195 actually branches north into Washington from Clarkston's Idaho sibling, Lewiston. It travels into the Palouse country, closely bypassing **Pullman.** At **Colfax** the highway connects with SR 26, an important corridor through the heart of eastern Washington's granary. Buttes rise to the east of US 195; Steptoe is reached via SR 271, which leaves US 195 north of Colfax and rejoins it near Rosalia. The rest of the way to Spokane the route traverses farming and grazing lands.

Vantage, on the Columbia River, is the starting point of two of the major routes across the region—I-90 *(see Northeast)* and SR 26—as well as for SR 243. SR 26 arrows almost due east, reaching the Palouse country and US 195 by way of **Othello** and a few other widely separated towns. SR 243 follows the east bank of the river past Wanapum and Priest Rapids dams; the section between Vantage and Beverly is scenic, hugging the cliff-lined Columbia River.

Southwest

The southwest corner of Washington is a green, rainy land extending from the Pacific shore across the coastal mountains and the inland valleys to Mount St. Helens and the foothills of the Cascades. The Columbia River is the southern boundary; the northern is marked by SR 8/US 12 between **Olympia** and the Grays Harbor cities of **Aberdeen** and **Hoquiam.** With its long beaches and excellent clamming and fishing, the coast is the chief vacation area; elsewhere farming, logging and dairying prevail.

Coastal US 101 and inland I-5 funnel traffic between western Oregon and Puget Sound. Only three paved highways link these arteries: SR 4, SR 6 and US 12.

US 101 merits the "scenic" designation that applies from the Columbia to Raymond. It threads between the river and the Willapa Hills to the stem of the Long Beach Peninsula, then veers north along Willapa Bay. Oysters farmed in the bay, cranberries and the recreation offered by **Ilwaco,** Seaview, **Long Beach** and other resort villages on the peninsula sustain the area's economy.

At Johnson's Landing SR 4 leaves US 101, branching southeast for a scenic drive through **Grays River, Skamokawa** and **Cathlamet** to I-5 at **Kelso.** US 101 continues north to **South Bend** and Raymond.

At Raymond US 101 proceeds north across woods and farmlands toward Aberdeen. SR 105 ends at Aberdeen too, but only after making a long loop along the bay and ocean shores to the fishing center of **Westport.** Raymond also is the western end of SR 6, which rambles through some towns with interesting names—**Lebam,** Pe Ell and Boistfort—and meets I-5 at **Chehalis.**

I-5 begins its beeline northward through Washington at **Vancouver,** the state's oldest settlement. North of Vancouver, I-5 passes **Kalama** and **Woodland** before turning away from the river at the twin cities of **Longview** and Kelso. Pretty farms and such busy little cities as **Toledo,** Chehalis and **Centralia** fall behind as the highway speeds toward Puget Sound.

One constant presence, though it can be seen from only a few places along I-5, is the burly hulk of Mount St. Helens, centerpiece of **Mount St. Helens National Volcanic Monument.** Two scenic roads approach the area. SR 503 leaves I-5 at Woodland and follows the Lewis River through **Ariel** and Cougar to the southern edge of the monument.

The 43-mile extension of the Spirit Lake Memorial Highway (SR 504) leads from I-5 at **Castle Rock** to Coldwater Ridge in Mount St. Helens National Volcanic Monument.

POINTS OF INTEREST

ABERDEEN (D-4) pop. 16,600, elev. 10′

Named for the Scottish city, Aberdeen wraps around the head of expansive Grays Harbor at the mouths of the Chehalis and Wishkah rivers. The settlement grew up around a sawmill established in 1884. By 1910 dozens of lumber and shingle mills lined the harbor and the population rose to 17,000.

Handsome Victorian homes grace Aberdeen's hillside residential district north of downtown. Samuel Benn Park, E. 9th and N. I streets, offers tennis courts, a playground, a rose garden and a network of pathways through landscaped rolling hills.

For additional information about the area contact the Grays Harbor Chamber of Commerce, 506 Duffy St., Aberdeen, WA 98520; phone (360) 532-1924 or (800) 321-1924.

Shopping areas: South Shore Mall, 1¼ miles south of downtown on SR 105 (S. Boone Street), features JCPenney, Kmart and Sears. Wishkah Mall, ½ mile east on US 12, features Lamonts.

ABERDEEN MUSEUM OF HISTORY, 111 E. 3rd St., uses period furnishings to re-create scenes from the town's pioneer days. Of particular note are photographs, a slide show and a collection of antique firefighting equipment. Allow 1 hour minimum. Wed.-Sun. 11-4, June 1 to mid-Sept.; Sat.-Sun. noon-4, rest of year. Closed Jan. 1, July

4 and Dec. 25. Donations. Phone (360) 533-1976.

ABERDEEN TROUT HATCHERY is ¾ mi. n. of US 12 on Lake Aberdeen Rd. More than 1 million fish are artificially spawned and raised at the hatchery annually. The summer steelhead run is June through September; the winter steelhead run is January through May. Guided tours are available by appointment. Daily 8-4:30. Free. Phone (360) 533-1663.

GRAYS HARBOR HISTORICAL SEAPORT is ½ mi. e. on US 12 at 813 E. Heron St. A former shipyard and lumber mill, the seaport has exhibits about the shipbuilding process and a replica of Capt. Robert Gray's ship, the *Columbia Rediviva,* on which he explored the Northwest coast and established the U.S. claim to the Oregon country in 1792. Daily 9-5; closed Dec. 25. Ship $3; over 64 and students with ID $2; ages 2-12, $1. Phone (360) 532-8611.

ANACORTES (C-2) pop. 11,500, elev. 75′

At the tip of Fidalgo Island, Anacortes is connected to the mainland by bridges and by daily toll ferry service with other points in the San Juan Islands and with Sidney on Vancouver Island, British Columbia.

Mount Erie is 5 miles south via Heart Lake and Mount Erie roads. The road is paved to the 1,270-foot summit, the highest point on Fidalgo Island. From this vantage point Mount Baker, Mount Rainier, the Olympic Mountains, the Cascade Range and the San Juan Islands are visible. At the base of this vista is Lake Campbell, with its unusual "Island on an Island." Washington Park *(see Recreation Chart)* is 4 miles west on wooded Fidalgo Head.

Self-guiding tours: A map outlining a self-guiding driving tour of Anacortes and Fidalgo Island is available from the Anacortes Chamber of Commerce, 819 Commercial Ave., Anacortes, WA 98221; phone (360) 293-3832.

ANACORTES MUSEUM, 1305 8th St., includes a Victorian parlor, cannery office, photographs and period furnishings among its displays of local history. Allow 30 minutes minimum. Thurs.-Mon. 1-5, Apr.-Sept.; Fri.-Sun. 1-5, rest of year. Donations. Phone (360) 293-1915.

W.T. Preston is at 7th St. and R Ave. The *Preston* was the last snag boat to operate on Puget Sound. Retired in 1981, the stern-wheeler is now a maritime museum showing the vessel's mechanism. Allow 30 minutes minimum. Fri.-Mon. noon-5, June 1-Labor Day. Donations. Phone (360) 293-1916.

ARIEL (F-6)

Ariel is most commonly associated with Ariel Dam, one in a string of huge power-development units on the Lewis River. It forms crescent-shaped Lake Merwin, which offers excellent fishing, boating and swimming. Merwin Park Recreation Area, off SR 503 half a mile south on Merwin Village Road, offers day-use recreational facilities on the north shore of Yale Lake.

LEWIS RIVER HATCHERY is at 4404 Lewis River Rd. Mature coho and chinook salmon are captured and artificially spawned; their young are then incubated and raised at the facility. Daily 8-4:30. Free. Phone (360) 225-7413.

SPEELYAI STATE HATCHERY, 11001 Lewis River Rd., uses mature fish trapped in the Lewis River to spawn and raise nearly 1 million coho and 1 million chinook salmon per year. Best salmon viewing is June through October. Daily 8-4:30. Free. Phone (360) 231-4210.

ASOTIN (F-12) pop. 1,000, elev. 760′

Originally named Has-Hu-Tin (meaning eel), the town of Asotin got its present spelling by an act of the legislature in 1886. Because of its mild climate, Asotin, at the confluence of the Snake River and Asotin Creek, is part of the "banana belt" of eastern Washington. The Asotin County Fair is held the last Friday and Saturday in April.

Boat trips in Hells Canyon National Recreation Area *(see place listing in Oregon)* are available by reservation through the Clarkston Chamber of Commerce, 502 Bridge St., Clarkston, WA 99403; phone (509) 758-7712.

For further information contact the Asotin Chamber of Commerce, P.O. Box 574, Asotin, WA 99402; phone (509) 243-4411.

ASOTIN MUSEUM, 3rd and Filmore sts., depicts early Western life through American Indian and pioneer artifacts, a Salmon River barge, preserved log cabin, pole frame barn, schoolhouse, blacksmith shop, working windmill and shepherd's cabin. Allow 30 minutes minimum. Tues.-Sat. 9-5. Donations. Phone (509) 243-4659.

AZWELL (C-9)

In the early 20th century camels were brought to the Azwell area for use as pack animals, but because they were unable to traverse rocky or marshy ground, their use was abandoned. Azwell was a stop on the Great Northern Railroad, which served the orchard industry along the Columbia River.

WELLS DAM, ½ mi. n. on US 97, is a large "hydrocombine," incorporating hydroelectric generators, fish passages, spillways, an electrical switchyard and a hatchery where more than 1.5 million chinook salmon and 1.5 million steelhead trout are raised annually. A 6,000-foot spawning channel, an exhibit about the life cycle of the salmon and a viewing window to a fish ladder are featured.

Other displays deal with American Indian and pioneer history and Fort Okanogan. Also available for viewing are the 160-ton spillway gates, the 230,000-volt switchyard and the turbine generators that can produce more than 840 megawatts of electricity. Exterior walkways provide views of water rushing through the spillgates, although during much of the year water is diverted into the powerhouse. Allow 30 minutes minimum. Daily 8-4:30. Free. Phone (509) 923-2226.

BAINBRIDGE ISLAND (F-2) pop. 3,100

The Bainbridge Island community of Winslow, consolidated with Bainbridge Island in 1991, traces its beginnings to the late 19th century, when it was a shipbuilding center for tall-masted schooners. Eagle Harbor still hums with the activities of the Washington State Ferries maintenance yard; daily ferries connect the community to nearby Seattle.

The Walkabout, a mile-long foot path, parallels the Winslow waterfront. A footbridge leads to Eagle Harbor Waterfront Park and a fishing pier. Seven miles north is Fay Bainbridge State Park *(see Recreation Chart)*, a well-known Puget Sound recreation area. The entire island is popular with bicyclists, despite its hilly terrain. Guided van tours are available.

For further information contact the Bainbridge Island Chamber of Commerce, 590 Winslow Way E., Bainbridge Island, WA 98110; phone (206) 842-3700.

Shopping areas: The Landing, a short walk from the ferry dock at 190 Madison Ave. N., has more than 100 booths offering antiques and arts and crafts works.

BAINBRIDGE ISLAND VINEYARDS AND WINERY, ¼ mi. n. of the ferry dock on SR 305, produces all its wines from its own island-grown vinifera grapes, raspberries and strawberries. An extensive collection of antique wine glasses includes specimens from Germany, France and England, an Egyptian pouring vessel dating to 3,000 B.C. and wine bottles dating to 1690. Guided tours of the vineyards and winery allow visitors to watch the wine-making process. Tastings are available. Picnicking is permitted. Wed.-Sun. noon-5. Free. Phone (206) 842-9463.

BLOEDEL RESERVE is 6½ mi. n. on SR 305, then 1 mi. e. to 7571 N.E. Dolphin Dr. This 150-acre former private estate with a bird marsh, English landscape, moss garden, reflection pool, Japanese garden and woodlands displays the influence of different cultures and styles on Northwest garden design. Allow 1 hour minimum. Wed.-Sun. 10-4; closed holidays. Admission $4; over 65, $2; under 5 free. Reservations are required. Phone (206) 842-7631.

BATTLE GROUND (F-6) pop. 3,800

In 1855 a group of American Indians being detained at Fort Vancouver escaped and their chief was accidentally killed. A band of volunteer soldiers permitted the escapees to give their chief a traditional burial; the volunteers were later chided by soldiers at the fort for not waging a battle against the fugitives. Although there never was a "battle ground," the name was nevertheless adopted by the town that was established in 1902.

Three miles northeast of town off SR 502 is Battle Ground Lake State Park *(see Recreation Chart)*. The site is believed to be a caldera formed by the collapse of a volcanic cone.

Self-guiding tours: Heritage loops I and II, scenic drives beginning in town, feature regional parks and points of interest. A brochure outlining the drives is available from the Battle Ground Chamber of Commerce, 1012 E. Main St., Battle Ground, WA 98604; phone (360) 687-1510. The chamber is open Mon.-Fri. 9:30-noon and 1-3:30.

LEWIS & CLARK RAILWAY, 1000 E. Main St., provides a scenic 2½-hour rail excursion along the Lewis River to Moulton Falls. Christmas excursions also are available; reservations are suggested. Trains depart the Battle Ground depot Sat.-Sun. at 10 and 1:30, Memorial Day weekend-Labor Day. Fare $10; over 59, $9; ages 3-15, $5. Phone (360) 687-2626.

BAY VIEW (C-3)

PADILLA BAY NATIONAL ESTUARINE RESEARCH RESERVE AND INTERPRETIVE CENTER, ¼ mi. n. of Bay View State Park at 1043 Bay View-Edison Rd., is a 10,600-acre reserve designed to protect habitats ranging from open marine waters, tideflats, marshes and beaches to wooded uplands and open fields. The reserve supports a variety of fish, mammals and birds, including nearly 250 visiting bird species.

The interpretive center displays photographs, artifacts and dioramas that focus on the variety of wildlife habitats native to Padilla Bay. The center also includes simulated environments, marine aquariums and a hands-on room for children. More than 3 miles of trails provide access to beach, shoreline and upland areas. Educational programs are presented periodically.

Allow 1 hour, 30 minutes minimum. Center open Wed.-Sun. 10-5. Trail open daily 24 hours. Beach access trail open Tues.-Sun. 10-4:30. Free. Phone (360) 428-1558.

BELLEVUE (F-3) pop. 86,900

In the eastern area of metropolitan Seattle, Bellevue is a center for distribution, light manufacturing and high-tech industries. Kelsey Creek Park has hiking trails, a playground and a barnyard zoo. In late July Bellevue stages its Pacific Northwest Arts and Crafts Fair.

For further information contact the East King County Convention and Visitors Bureau, 515 116th N.E., #111, Bellevue, WA 98004; phone (206) 637-9809.

Shopping areas: The city's original business district, Old Bellevue, has several restored shops and galleries. Major local shopping malls include Bellevue Square, N.E. 8th Street and Bellevue Way N.E., which features The Bon, JCPenney and Nordstrom; and Factoria Square, just southeast of the I-90/I-405 junction, with a Lamonts and a Mervyns.

BELLEVUE ART MUSEUM, 301 Bellevue Sq., displays works of local, regional and national significance. Mon.-Sat. 10-6 (also Tues. and Fri, 6-8 p.m.), Sun. 11-5. Admission $3, over 62 and students with ID $2, under 13 free; free to all Tues. **Discount.** Phone (206) 454-3322 or 454-6021.

BELLEVUE BOTANICAL GARDEN is at 12001 Main St. in Wilburton Hill Park; from I-405 take N.E. 8th St. exit ¾ mi. e., then ½ mi. s. on 124th Ave. N.E. to Main St. A ½-mile nature wends through this 36-acre tract of rolling hills, native woodlands, meadows and bogs. Demonstration gardens illustrate the use of groundcovers, alpine plants, perennials, drought tolerant plants, ferns and Northwest native plants. A Japanese garden honors Yao, Bellevue's sister city in Japan.

The visitor center contains a library. Guided tours are available upon request. Allow 1 hour, 30 minutes minimum. Garden open daily dawn-dusk. Visitor center daily 10-6, May-Sept.; daily 10-4, rest of year. Free. Phone (206) 462-2749 or 451-3755.

LAKE HILLS GREENBELT, 15416 S.E. 16th St., is a 150-acre reserve featuring a ½-acre wildlife habitat demonstration garden. Habitats include upland edges, hummingbird and butterfly gardens, a pond and a cedar haven. A 1-mile gravel trail leads to a pond that attracts ducks, geese and blue herons. Free 1-hour nature walks are offered Saturdays at 10, May through September. A visitor center has displays of native animals.

Grounds open daily dawn-dusk. Visitor center open Wed.-Sun. noon-6, June 1-Labor Day; Sat.-Sun. noon-4, rest of year. Closed holidays. Free. Phone (206) 451-7225.

ROSALIE WHYEL MUSEUM OF DOLL ART, 1116 108th Ave. N.E., traces the history of dolls through a collection of some 2,000 examples, including Victorian-era and one-of-a-kind items. Allow 1 hour minimum. Mon.-Sat. 10-5 (also Thurs. 5-8), Sun. 1-5; closed Jan. 1, Easter, July 4 and Dec. 25. Admission $5; over 64, $4.50; ages 5-17, $4; family rate $20. Phone (206) 455-1116. *See color ad.*

BELLINGHAM (B-3) pop. 52,200, elev. 60′

Bellingham overlooks Bellingham Bay, discovered in 1792 by English explorer Capt. George Vancouver. Beyond the sheltered harbor lie the 172 picturesque islands of the San Juan archipelago *(see San Juan Islands).* Bellingham also is within view of the Olympic and Cascade mountains.

The city's numerous parks and three nearby lakes offer a variety of outdoor activities; Mount Baker National Recreation Area is within easy driving distance. For those who prefer watching to participating, the Bellingham Mariners play class-A baseball at Civic Field; for information phone (360) 671-6347.

Bellingham is the southern terminus of the Alaska Marine Highway. Ferries depart the Bellingham Cruise Terminal at the foot of Harris Avenue for ports in southeast Alaska; for further information phone (800) 642-0066. San Juan Island Shuttle Express offers daily passenger boat service and whale watching excursions from Bellingham Cruise Terminal to Orcas Island and Friday Harbor, Memorial Day weekend through September; phone (360) 671-1137.

Additional visitor information is available at the Bellingham/Whatcom County Visitors Bureau, 904 Potter St., Bellingham, WA 98226; phone (360) 671-3990 or (800) 487-2032. *See ad p. 114.*

Shopping areas: Fairhaven, the restored business district along 11th Street between Mill and

Magic, just around the corner…
A world-class experience awaits in downtown Bellevue—the best in antique and contemporary dolls, displayed in an award-winning environment.
Monday thru Wednesday: 10 to 5;
Thursday; 10 to 8;
Friday & Saturday: 10 to 5;
Sunday: 1 to 5. Admission charged
Rosalie Whyel MUSEUM of DOLL ART
1116 108th Ave. N.E. • Bellevue, WA 98004 • (206) 455-1116

Larrabee avenues, sells books, cards, crafts and spices; there also is an art gallery. Bellis Fair, at I-5 exit 256, has more than 125 stores, including The Bon, JCPenney, Mervyn's and Sears.

CHILDREN'S MUSEUM NORTHWEST, 227 Prospect St., provides educational and career-oriented experiences through interactive exhibits and displays. Highlights include a medical center and a walk-through train. Allow 1 hour minimum. Thurs.-Sat. 10-5, Tues.-Wed. and Sun. noon-5. Admission $2. Phone (360) 733-8769.

CHUCKANUT DRIVE is n. on I-5 to exit 231 or s. on I-5 to exit 250. The drive (SR 11) winds along the Samish Bay shoreline, offering magnificent views of Puget Sound and the offshore San Juan Islands. At its intersection with Hawthorn Road is Fairhaven Park, where a large rose garden blooms from mid-June through September.

GARDENS OF ART, 2900 Sylvan St. in Big Rock Garden Nursery, displays the works of international and regional artists in a 2½-acre garden setting. The sculptures are in a range of styles from classical to contemporary and represent a variety of media, including metals, glass and stone. The surrounding gardens blend Japanese maples, rhododendrons and azaleas with native flora. Allow 1 hour minimum. Wed.-Sun. 10-5:30, May-Oct. Free. Phone (360) 671-1069.

MARITIME HERITAGE CENTER, 1600 C St., is on the site of an 1852 sawmill. A seven-station interpretive path explores the life cycle of salmon and demonstrates how young salmon are incubated and raised at hatcheries. Some 3 million chinook, coho and chum salmon are released every spring. Best viewing time is mid-October to mid-December. Picnic facilities are available. Allow 1 hour minimum. Daily dawn-dusk. Free. Phone (360) 676-6806.

ROEDER HOME, 2600 Sunset Dr., houses a cultural arts center. Built 1903-08, the home features interior oak paneling, hand-painted murals and a state-of-the-art built-in vacuum cleaning system. A gallery displays changing exhibits of regional arts. Tours of the home are available on request. Allow 30 minutes minimum. Mon.-Thurs. 9-4, Sat.-Sun. by appointment; closed holidays. Free. Phone (360) 733-6897.

SEHOME HILL ARBORETUM, on a wooded ridge in the center of Bellingham, is accessible by footpath from the Western Washington University campus or by car from the Bill McDonald Pkwy. Two miles of trails lead through the 165-acre reserve, which displays native flora. Panoramic views include the city, Bellingham Bay, the San Juan Islands, Mount Baker and the mountains of southern British Columbia. Daily 8-7. Free.

SQUALICUM HARBOR, 1 mi. n.w. on Roeder Ave., is one of the largest marinas on Puget Sound. Of interest are promenades, a 2,500-gallon marine life tank and a variety of shops and restaurants. A boat launch and visitor moorage are available. Daily dawn-dusk. Free. Phone (360) 676-2500.

***Island Mariner* Cruises,** 5 Harbor Esplanade at Squalicum Harbor, offers 7½-hour narrated whale search and nature watch cruises of the San Juan Islands. Bald eagles, harbor seals, porpoises, tufted puffins and orca and minke whales are some of the wildlife that can be seen on the 90-mile island tour. A sunset cruise of Bellingham Bay features a narrated history of the area.

Nature cruises depart Mon., Wed., and Sat. at 10, July-Aug.; Sat. at 10, May 22-June 30 and Sept. 1-11. Sunset cruise departs Wed. at 7 p.m., July 14-Aug. 18. Nature cruise $45. Sunset cruise $15. MC, VI. **Discount.** Phone (360) 734-8866. *See ad p. 114.*

VICTORIA/SANJUAN GRAY LINE CRUISES & TOURS, 355 Harris St., Suite 104, offers narrated passenger boat service to Victoria, British Columbia, through the San Juan Islands. Tours depart from the Bellingham Cruise Terminal daily at 9:30 a.m., late May-Oct. 15. Fare $74; ages 6-18, $37. MC, VI. Phone (360) 738-8099 or (800) 443-4552. *See color ad.*

WESTERN WASHINGTON UNIVERSITY OUTDOOR SCULPTURE COLLECTION, I-5 exit 252, then 1 mi. n.w. on Bill McDonald Pkwy. to E.

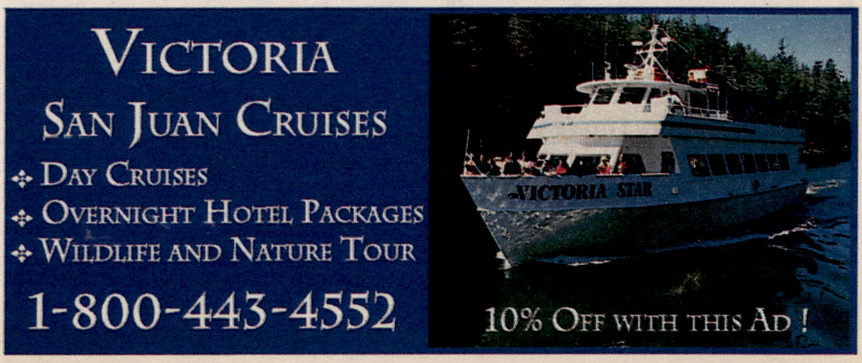

College Way, features a collection of works by regional, national and international artists focusing on the themes of nature, culture, human scale, personal perceptions and spatial dynamics. Representing the period 1960-present, the sculptures are displayed from the Western Gallery Plaza throughout the campus. A self-guiding tour brochure and audiophone are available from the visitor center.

Allow 1 hour minimum. Mon.-Fri. 10-4, Sat. noon-4. Free. Parking 50c per 4 hours. Phone (360) 650-3963.

WHATCOM MUSEUM OF HISTORY AND ART, 121 Prospect St., is housed in a late-19th-century Victorian building that was once the city hall.

Killer Whale Search Cruise

- 90 mile cruise in 172 San Juan Islands
- Narrated by our own "Captain Trivia"
- #1 success rate due to spotters
- Bellingham departures
- 110 foot "Island Caper"
- $45/person; ask about AAA discount

Write or call for 1994 schedule

Island Mariner
5 Harbor Esplanade
Bellingham, WA 98225
(206) 734-8866

FAST,
FREE,
FACTS

- Accommodations
- AAA Discounts
- Arts & History
- Sightseeing
- Activities
- Festivals
- Maps

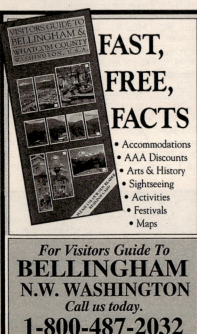

For Visitors Guide To
BELLINGHAM
N.W. WASHINGTON
Call us today.
1-800-487-2032
Local: 206-671-3990 I-5 Exit 253

First-floor displays depict regional history. Galleries on the second floor contain contemporary art, while third-floor exhibits include woodworking tools, toys and period clothing.

The nearby former fire hall houses the Syre Educational Center, featuring bird displays, logging equipment, pioneer items, period rooms and an extensive collection of Northwest Indian art. Changing displays are offered at the Arco Exhibits Building annex across the street.

Allow 1 hour minimum. Tues.-Sun. noon-5; closed Jan. 1, Thanksgiving and Dec. 25. Donations. Arco Exhibits Building only $2, over 64 and students with ID $1, under 6 free. Phone (360) 676-6981.

BINGEN-WHITE SALMON (G-7) pop. 2,600

The neighboring communities of Bingen and White Salmon overlook the Columbia River south of Mount Adams. Because Bingen is a sister city to Bingen, Germany, both Bingen and White Salmon have several buildings of Germanic design; one is the Glockenspiel Tower in White Salmon.

West on SR 14 is the Broughton Log Flume, which was the last operating log flume in the country. The 9-mile flume, which closed in 1987, floated lumber from Willard to Underwood, a drop of 1,000 feet.

SPRING CREEK NATIONAL FISH HATCHERY is 3 mi. w. of Hood River-White Salmon Bridge on SR 14. One of the oldest salmon hatcheries on the Columbia River, it has a visitor center, rearing ponds and a fish ladder. Mature chinook salmon can be seen in September; fingerlings are released in spring. Allow 30 minutes minimum. Mon.-Fri. 7:30-4; closed holidays. Free. Phone (509) 493-1730.

BIRCH BAY (A-2) elev. 20'

A waterfront resort community near the British Columbia border, Birch Bay is particularly popular with summer vacationers. Birch Bay State Park *(see Recreation Chart)* is 1 mile south on the coast.

For further information contact the Birch Bay Chamber of Commerce, 7387 Jackson Rd., Birch Bay, WA 98230; phone (360) 371-0334.

WILD 'N' WET is 3 mi. w. of I-5 exit 270 on Birch Bay-Lynden Rd. W. The park features four 400-foot warm-water flumes which descend in loops and curves to receiving pools. Also featured are three children's flumes and one ramp slide, an inner tube ride, whirlpool, picnic facilities and beach areas. Food is available.

Daily 10:30-7:30, mid-June through Labor Day; Sat.-Sun. and holidays 10:30-7:30, mid-May to mid-June. Admission $8.75 ($5.75 after 4:30); ages 3-5, $5; over 60, $4.25. MC, VI. Phone (360) 371-7911.

BLACK DIAMOND (D-7) pop. 1,400, elev. 628′

Black Diamond is named for the Black Diamond Coal Co. of California, which by 1895 was the primary developer of a major vein found in the region 5 years earlier. Among the area's natural assets is the Green River Gorge State Park Conservation Area, which includes Nolte State Park *(see Recreation Chart)*.

BLACK DIAMOND HISTORICAL MUSEUM, Railroad Ave. and Baker St., is in an 1883 Columbia-Puget Sound Line depot. Exhibits of 19th-century Americana include antique machinery, a Western jail and replicas of a country doctor's office, coal mine entrance, coal car and a caboose. Allow 30 minutes minimum. Thurs. 9-4, Sat.-Sun. noon-3. Donations. Phone (360) 886-2142.

FLAMING GEYSER STATE PARK, 1¾ mi. s. on SR 169, then 2¾ mi. w. on S.E. Green Valley Rd., is named for an old coal test hole that has an 8-inch methane flame. The Steelhead Trout Imprinting Project holds young fish in a series of ponds to instill the habit of homing. A playground is available. Daily 6:30 a.m.-dusk, Apr.-Sept.; 8-dusk, rest of year. Free. Phone (206) 931-3930. *See Recreation Chart.*

BLAINE (A-2) pop. 2,500, elev. 77′

Blaine is a port of entry on Drayton Harbor just south of the British Columbia border. First settled in 1856, it enjoyed a fleeting boom during the Fraser River gold rush. After the Homestead Act began attracting farmers to the area about 1870, Blaine became a dairy supply center and fishing port.

Nearby Peace Arch State and Provincial Park commemorates more than 100 years of harmony between the United States and Canada. The inscriptions on the arch read "Children of a Common Mother" and "Brothers Dwelling Together in Unity."

For further information contact the Blaine Community Chamber of Commerce, 865 Peace Portal Dr., P.O. Box 1718, Blaine, WA 98231-1718; phone (360) 332-6484.

Shopping areas: Peace Arch Factory Outlets, 5 miles south at I-5 exit 270, features 28 stores.

SEMIAHMOO COUNTY PARK, at the entrance to Semiahmoo Spit on the w. side of Drayton Harbor, contains three 19th-century bunkhouses. One houses the Semiahmoo Park Museum, which features a restored Bristol Bay sailboat and exhibits that illustrate local history and explain salmon fishing and canning.

Allow 30 minutes minimum. Grounds open daily dawn-dusk. Museum open Wed.-Sun. 1-5, Mar. 1-Labor Day; Wed.-Sun. 1-4, day after Labor Day to mid-Dec. Closed Easter and Thanksgiving. Donations. Phone (360) 371-5513. *See Recreation Chart.*

BOTHELL (E-3) pop. 24,500, elev. 27′

Bothell, named for pioneer founder David Bothell, dates back to 1884. The settlement prospered as a lumbering and agricultural center on the Sammamish River. The Canyon Park high-tech corridor parallels I-405 north of the city. The *Seattle Times* offers narrated 1-hour tours of its North Creek plant Monday, Wednesday and Friday by reservation; phone (206) 489-7015.

BREMERTON (F-2) pop. 38,100, elev. 10′

Named for German immigrant William Bremer, who made his home at Point Turner in 1891, Bremerton is on a hilly site indented with bays and inlets. The Puget Sound Naval Base is the northern home of the Pacific Fleet. Within the base is the city's largest industry—the Puget Sound Naval Shipyard.

Daily toll ferry service connects Bremerton with Seattle; phone (800) 843-3779 in Wash. A passenger toll ferry also links Bremerton to Port Orchard; phone (360) 876-2300. Daily May through October, Kitsap Harbor Tours offers 45-minute Naval Shipyard/Mothball Fleet boat tours, plus passenger ferry service to Keyport and Poulsbo. Both trips depart the Bremerton Boardwalk, on the waterfront north of the ferry terminal; phone (360) 377-8924 or 792-1008.

For further information contact the Bremerton Area Chamber of Commerce, 837 4th St., P.O. Box 229, Bremerton, WA 98310; phone (360) 479-3579.

BREMERTON NAVAL MUSEUM, near the ferry terminal at 130 Washington Ave., illustrates U.S. naval history with displays of ships models, naval weapons, photographs and memorabilia from naval vessels and the Puget Sound Naval Shipyard. Allow 1 hour minimum. Mon.-Sat. 10-5, Sun. and holidays 1-5, Memorial Day weekend-Labor Day; Tues.-Sat. 10-5, Sun. and holidays 1-5, rest of year. Donations. Phone (360) 479-7447.

***USS TURNER JOY* (DD-951),** n. of the ferry terminal on the Bremerton Waterfront at 300 Washington Beach Ave., serves as an educational facility and naval exhibit honoring the US. Navy. The *Turner Joy* was commissioned in 1959 and served as the flagship for Destoyer Squadron 13 and Destroyer Division 131, seeing action in the Gulf of Tonkin incident of 1964. Decommissioned in November 1982, the ship remains close to its original configuration. A self-guiding tour explores most of the ship.

Allow 1 hour minimum. Daily 10-5, Memorial Day-Labor Day; Mon. and Thurs.-Fri. 11-4, Sat.-Sun. 10-4, rest of year. Closed Jan. 1 and Dec. 25. Admission $5; over 62 and active military with ID $4; ages 5-12, $3; family rate $15. MC, VI. Phone (360) 792-2457.

BREWSTER (C-9) pop. 1,600

In 1896 a steamboat company bought a landing site at the confluence of the Okanogan and Columbia rivers from John Bruster; the resulting town bears his name in spirit, if not spelling. The Colville Indian Reservation is just east of town.

For further information contact the Brewster Chamber of Commerce, P.O. Box 1087, Brewster, WA 98812; phone (509) 689-3464.

FORT OKANOGAN STATE PARK, 5 mi. e. on US 97, ½ mi. e. on SR 17, then ¼ mi. s., covers 48 acres at the confluence of the Okanogan and Columbia rivers. In 1811 John Jacob Astor's Pacific Fur Co. built Fort Okanogan, the area's first fur-trading center, near this site. An interpretive center, jointly operated by the park and the Colville Confederated Tribes, displays artifacts of the Confederated Tribes and items from the fur trade. Fort Okanogan Overlook is 3 miles east on US 97. Wed.-Sun. 10-6, mid-May through Sept. 15. Free. Phone (509) 689-2243 or 923-2473.

CARNATION (C-7) pop. 1,100, elev. 75′

Settled in 1865 by Scandinavian farmers, Carnation took the name of a neighboring dairy farm that was famous for its superior dairy herds.

The Camlann Medieval Faire is a month-long celebration on weekends from mid-July through late August. The rich European cultural heritage of ideas, customs, arts, crafts and cuisine is explored through the re-creation of a medieval setting. For further information phone (206) 788-1353.

The daily activities of a working farm can be observed at Remlinger Farms, half a mile south on SR 203, then a quarter of a mile east on N.E. 32nd Street. Other highlights include animal viewing and petting, seasonal festivals and entertainment as well as pony, wagon and steam train rides; phone (206) 451-8740.

CARNATION FARMS is 3½ mi. n.w. on Carnation Farms Rd. Self-guiding tours of the farm feature a milking parlor, calf barn, petting area, gardens, a collection of carriages, a maternity barn, a kitty barn and kennels. A calf-birthing video is presented. Allow 1 hour minimum. Mon.-Sat. 10-3, Apr.-Oct.; closed holidays. Free. Phone (206) 788-1511. *See color ad.*

CARSON (F-7) elev. 242′

WIND RIVER DISTRICT AND NURSERY, 8 mi. n. on Wind River Hwy., then 1 mi. w. on Hemlock Rd., is one of the largest tree nurseries on the West Coast, where more than 17 million bareroot conifer seedlings are produced annually. The arboretum was established in 1912 to test how exotic tree species from Europe, Asia, Scandinavia and regions of the United States would adapt to the Northwest. Twenty-six species of trees are grown on about 180 acres of cultivated land.

Interpretive trails wind through the arboretum. Self-guiding tours of the seed extractory, tree-processing plant, bed houses and seedbeds are available. Activity is greatest February through April, when seedlings are pulled and packaged, and September through October, when cones are processed to extract seeds for the next crop. Allow 1 hour minimum. Daily 8-4:30. Free. Phone (509) 427-5645.

CASHMERE (D-8) pop. 2,500, elev. 795′

Named for south Asia's fabled "Vale of Kashmir," Cashmere, in the heart of Wenatchee Valley, is surrounded by fruit orchards. The town's roots can be traced back to a Roman Catholic mission established in 1863. The central business district has an early American look with its lampposts and covered sidewalks. The sandstone towers of Peshastin Pinnacles State Park, 2 miles northwest on US 2/97, are a popular rock climbing area.

For further information contact the Cashmere Chamber of Commerce, P.O. Box 834, Cashmere, WA 98815; phone (509) 782-3513.

ARRASTRA, identified by a roadside historic marker 10 mi. s. of US 2 on US 97, is an unusual 1861 water-powered ore-grinding device of

Carnation Farm

Nestled in the scenic Snoqualmie Valley, Carnation Farm has been known for decades as the "Home of Contented Cows." On your free tour you will see the maternity and calf barn, "The Birth of a Calf" video, petting area, milking parlor, beautiful formal gardens, Kitty Barn and Labrador kennels. This 40-minute walking tour is suitable for all ages. **Self-Guided Tours: April-Oct. Mon.-Sat. 10 A.M. - 3 P.M. Closed Sundays & Holidays**

ATTRACTION ADMISSION DISCOUNTS

The word **Discount** after the prices in attraction listings indicates the attraction has agreed to give a discount to members upon presentation of a valid AAA or CAA membership card.

Spanish design. The machine ground gold-bearing ore to powder until the 1880s.

CHELAN COUNTY HISTORICAL MUSEUM AND PIONEER VILLAGE, at the eastern entrance to Cashmere, re-creates the history of the Columbia River Indians before the arrival of the first pioneers. Its collection of artifacts is considered among the best in the Northwest.

Within Pioneer Village are restored pioneer rooms, a replica of the mission building, a blacksmith shop, hotel, school, gold mine, saloon, grocery store, doctor's and dentist's offices, three pioneer homes and an assay office. A working water wheel is on the bank of the Wenatchee River. Apple Days is celebrated the first weekend in October.

Allow 1 hour minimum. Mon.-Sat. and holidays 10-4:30, Sun. 1-4:30, Apr.-Oct. Admission $3; under 12, $1; family rate $5. Phone (509) 782-3230.

LIBERTY ORCHARDS CO. INC., 117-123 Mission St., across from the Burlington Northern Depot, offers 15-minute tours through its candy factory, including the kitchen and packaging area. The company produces fruit and nut confections covered with powdered sugar. Tours do not always coincide with production times.

Allow 30 minutes minimum. Mon.-Fri. 8-5:30, Sat.-Sun. 9-5, May-Dec.; otherwise varies. Free. Phone (509) 782-2191. *See color ad.*

CASTLE ROCK (E-5) pop. 2,100, elev. 59′

The town's namesake, a 150-foot-high rock, was a landmark for Cowlitz Indians and Hudson's Bay Co. traders as early as 1832. Castle Rock prospered as a Cowlitz River steamboat port and trading center for valley farms. A local sawmill was the first to produce cedar shingles, using the Western red cedar, which grows in abundance in the region.

Castle Rock marks the beginning of the Spirit Lake Memorial Highway (SR 504), a scenic route that leads past the areas affected by the eruption of Mount St. Helens in 1980. The Mount St. Helens National Volcanic Monument Visitor Center *(see place listing)* is 5 miles east of I-5 exit 49.

For further information contact the Castle Rock Chamber of Commerce, 147 Front Ave. N.W., P.O. Box 721, Castle Rock, WA 98611; phone (360) 274-6603.

CASTLE ROCK EXHIBIT HALL, 147 Front Ave. N.W., features displays that convey the impact of the Mount St. Helens eruptions on the area. Recordings offer oral histories from eyewitnesses. Other exhibits include logging equipment and historical photographs. Allow 30 minutes minimum. Daily 9-6, May-Sept.; otherwise varies. Donations. Phone (360) 274-6603.

MOUNT ST. HELENS CINEDOME THEATER, off I-5 exit 49 at 1238 Mount St. Helens Way, N.E. (SR 504), depicts the 1980 eruption of Mount St. Helens on a three-story, 55-foot-wide screen. The film progresses from the eruption to the immediate aftermath, concluding with a recent look at the return of life to the devastated area. Allow 1 hour minimum. Continuous screenings are presented daily 9-7. Admission $4.50; over 60 and ages 5-12, $3.50. DS, MC, VI. Phone (360) 274-8000.

CATHLAMET (F-5) pop. 500

Cathlamet is a picturesque riverside settlement linked with rural Puget Island and known as Little Norway for its largely Scandinavian population. Of interest is the 1895 Pioneer Church, built into a rock outcropping that overlooks the village. The last remaining ferry service on the lower Columbia River operates between Puget Island—accessible by bridge from town—and Westport, Ore.

A once-endangered population of white-tailed deer, thought to be extinct in the 1930s, lives within the Julia Butler Hansen National Wildlife Refuge. The refuge covers 4,400 acres on the mainland and several islands in the Columbia River below Cathlamet. Wildlife often can be seen from Steamboat Slough and Brooks Slough roads, especially in the morning and evening when the deer feed in the pastures. Motorists should watch for animals in or near roadways.

WAHKIAKUM COUNTY HISTORICAL MUSEUM, 65 River St., has displays from the county, including farm implements, artifacts from various

TOUR THE FAMOUS APLETS & COTLETS CANDY KITCHEN.

Sample the taste of Washington, just off Highway 2 in Cashmere. We're the perfect stop in your tour of the Cascade Loop, the perfect souvenir for family and friends. Come taste a delicious, freshly made sample. They're free.

TOUR HOURS — May through December:
Monday-Friday 8 a.m. to 5:30 p.m.
and Saturday-Sunday 10 a.m. to 4 p.m.
January through April: most weekdays.

Liberty Orchards
117 Mission, Cashmere, Washington
(509) 782-2191

Northwest Indian tribes, guns and logging equipment. Allow 1 hour minimum. Tues.-Sun. 11-4, June-Sept.; Thurs.-Sun. 1-4, rest of year. Admission $1. Phone (360) 795-3954.

CENTRALIA (I-2) pop. 12,100, elev. 188′

Along with neighboring Chehalis, Centralia forms the commercial center of the rich Chehalis Valley farmland and nearby timberlands. A black pioneer named George Washington founded Centralia in 1875 after his Missouri master freed him and adopted him as a son. Outdoor murals depicting late-19th-century Centralia grace downtown buildings.

Fort Borst Park, off Belmont Road, includes an arboretum, small rhododendron gardens and recreational facilities. The Borst Family Homestead is off Johnson Avenue near the park. Because the wood and joints were hardened and dipped in white lead for waterproofing, the 1860s home is well preserved. It features original furnishings.

For further information contact the Lewis County Visitors and Convention Bureau, 500 N.W. Chamber Way, Chehalis, WA 98532; phone (800) 525-3323.

Shopping areas: The Centralia Factory Outlet Center *(see ad p. 144)* and the Outlet Marketplace, I-5 exit 82, have more than 50 stores. The Centralia Square Antique Mall, 201 S. Pearl St., contains some 100 antique shops.

CHEHALIS-CENTRALIA RAILROAD—
see Chehalis.

CHEHALIS (I-1) pop. 6,500, elev. 196′

Chehalis was formed in 1873 when the Lewis County seat was moved from Claquato. First named Saundersville, the town's name was changed to Chehalis in 1879. The Claquato Church on Stern Road is one of the oldest churches in the state. The 1858 structure functioned for a time as Claquato Academy; the bronze bell in the belfry was cast in Boston in 1857 and shipped around Cape Horn.

For further information contact the Lewis County Visitors and Convention Bureau, 500 N.W. Chamber Way, Chehalis, WA 98532; phone (800) 525-3323.

CHEHALIS-CENTRALIA RAILROAD, e. of I-5 exit 77 on Main St., offers steam train excursions to Centralia and Ruth. Dinner trains also are available; phone for schedule. Allow 1 hour minimum. Trips to Centralia depart Sat.-Sun. at 1 and 3, Memorial Day weekend-Labor Day; trips to Ruth depart Sat. at 5, Memorial Day weekend-Labor Day. Centralia trip $6.50; under 16, $4.50. Round trip to Ruth $10.50; under 16, $8.50. Phone (360) 748-9593.

JOHN R. JACKSON HOUSE STATE HISTORIC SITE, 3 mi. e. of I-5 exit 68, or 4 mi. s. on Jackson Hwy., features one of the oldest pioneer structures north of the Columbia River. An important meeting place during the organization of the Washington Territory, the small 1845 log cabin also was a stopover for pioneer travelers. The structure, which served as the Jackson Courthouse as early as 1850, is in a small grassy park on Jackson's Prairie; its sparsely furnished interior can be viewed through the windows. Daily 24 hours. Free.

LEWIS COUNTY HISTORICAL MUSEUM, 1 mi. s.e. off I-5 exit 79 at 599 N.W. Front St., is in the former 1912 Burlington Northern Depot. Among the displays are a blacksmith shop, saw-filing shop, general store, pioneer kitchen, Chehalis Indian artifacts, firefighting equipment and logging and farming tools. There also is an extensive research library focusing on Lewis County history. Allow 1 hour minimum. Tues.-Sat. 9-5, Sun. 1-5; closed major holidays. Admission $2; over 64, $1.50; ages 6-18, 50c. Phone (360) 748-0831.

CHELAN (C-9) pop. 3,000, elev. 1,238′

In the heart of Washington and at the southern tip of Lake Chelan National Recreation Area *(see place listing),* Chelan lies in the midst of beautiful mountain and lake scenery in prime apple-growing country. Roads following the south and north shores of Lake Chelan offer pleasant scenic drives.

Although outdoor recreation is the primary pastime, history buffs will enjoy a stroll around downtown Chelan to see several preserved early-20th-century buildings. For further information contact the Lake Chelan Chamber of Commerce, P.O. Box 216, Chelan, WA 98816; phone (509) 682-3503 or (800) 4-CHELAN.

CHELAN AIRWAYS, 1328 W. Woodin Ave., 1 mi. w. on US 97 Alt., offers seaplane sightseeing tours and air taxi service to Stehekin at the north end of Lake Chelan or to points beyond in the Cascade Mountains. Passengers must check in at least 30 minutes prior to departure. Flights depart daily 8-6; closed Dec. 25. Fares $80-$100; ages 2-11, $40-$50. MC, VI. Reservations are recommended. Phone (509) 682-5555.

★**LAKE CHELAN,** one of the most scenic lakes in the Pacific Northwest, is in a glacial trough extending 55 miles into the Cascade Mountains. More than 1,500 feet deep, the lake bottom drops to 400 feet below sea level at its deepest point. This clear blue lake is fed by 27 glaciers and 59 streams.

Passenger excursion boats, the *Lady of the Lake* and *Lady Express,* provide round-trip service to Stehekin and Lake Chelan National Recreation Area. The *Lady of the Lake* departs daily at 8:30, May 1 to mid-Oct. The *Lady Express* departs daily at 8:30, June 16-Sept. 30; daily at 10 in Apr.; Mon., Wed. and Fri.-Sun. at 10, Nov.-Mar.; Sat.-Sun. at 8:30, May 15-June 15.

Lady of the Lake fare $21; ages 6-11, $10.50. *Lady Express* fare May 15-Sept. 30, $39; ages 2-11, $19.50. *Lady Express* fare Nov.-Apr., $21; ages 2-11, $10.50. Pets are not permitted on the boats. Reservations are suggested for the *Lady Express.*

For information write Lake Chelan Boat Co., P.O. Box 186, Chelan, WA 98816; phone (509) 682-2224 or 682-4584.

Lake Chelan State Park *(see Recreation Chart),* 9 miles west on the south shore of the lake off US 97 Alt., is open daily dawn-dusk, Apr.-Oct.; Sat.-Sun. and holidays dawn-dusk, rest of year. Free. Phone (509) 687-3710.

LAKE CHELAN MUSEUM, Woodin Ave. and Emerson St., displays natural and historical items relating to American Indian culture and pioneer life. Of interest is a large collection of apple box labels. Allow 30 minutes minimum. Mon.-Sat. 1-4, Memorial Day-Oct. 1; by appointment, rest of year. Donations. Phone (509) 682-5644.

CHENEY (D-12) pop. 7,700, elev. 2,373′

Cheney is on a rise of land that is one of the highest elevations in the state. Home of Eastern Washington University, Cheney has been a college town since 1890. A rodeo and parade highlight Rodeo Days, held in mid-July.

For further information contact the Cheney Chamber of Commerce, 1849 First St., P.O. Box 65, Cheney, WA 99004; phone (509) 235-8484 or (800) 545-8343.

TURNBULL NATIONAL WILDLIFE REFUGE is off I-90 exits 257 or 270 to SR 904, then 4½ mi. s. on Cheney Plaza Rd. to Smith Rd. The 15,468-acre refuge is an important breeding area for numerous species of waterfowl; tundra swans can be seen occasionally in spring. A public use area includes a self-guiding driving tour. Daily dawn-dusk. Admission $2 per private vehicle. Phone (509) 235-4723.

CHINOOK (E-4)

On May 12, 1792, thousands of American Indians witnessed Capt. Robert Gray's dramatic entrance into the mouth of the Columbia River in his great winged ship, the *Columbia Rediviva.* The historic landing established a strong U.S. claim to all country drained by the Columbia River. Chinook's past also is distinguished by Meriwether Lewis and William Clark, who camped in town with members of their expedition in November 1805, just prior to the culmination of their 2½-year transcontinental journey.

Before fixed gear was outlawed in Washington waters in 1934, Chinook's fishing industry brought such prosperity that the town enjoyed the highest per capita wealth of any settlement of its size in the country.

FORT COLUMBIA STATE PARK, 1¾ mi. e. on US 101, is one of three military posts established at the mouth of the Columbia River during the Spanish-American War. The 600-acre area encompasses 12 old structures, including bunkers, lookouts, searchlight stations, a hospital, a theater and 8-inch gun batteries. A museum features historical displays. Self-guiding tours include a ½-mile stroll past some of the most interesting historic installations of the fort and a hiking trail at Scarboro Hill. Picnic facilities are available.

Park open Wed.-Sun. 8 a.m.-dusk. Interpretive center open Wed.-Sun. 10-5, mid-May to late Sept.; by appointment, rest of year. Museum

Yet another way to play at Lake Chelan.

Your favorite casino games and great food at our Coyote Cafe, all in a beautiful setting at scenic Lake Chelan.

For special casino room rates, please contact these AAA motels:

MT. VIEW LODGE 1-800-967-8105

CARAVEL 1-800-962-8723

MILL BAY CASINO

(509) 687-2102

455 E. Wapato Lake Road, Manson, WA 98831

For general travel information on the Lake Chelan resort area, please contact the Lake Chelan Chamber of Commerce at 1-800-4-Chelan.

Blackjack!

Roulette!

Craps!

open Wed.-Sun. 9-5, May-Sept. Free. Phone (206) 777-8221 mid-May to late Sept., or (206) 642-3078 rest of year.

CLARKSTON (F-12) pop. 6,800

In 1902, after several name changes, the townspeople named their home Clarkston after William Clark, just as their neighbors in Lewiston, Idaho, named their town for Meriwether Lewis. The noted explorers spent time at the confluence of the Snake and Clearwater rivers where they were assisted by the Nez Percé. Six-thousand-year-old petroglyphs are accessible from River Road. Directions are available at the Clarkston Chamber of Commerce, 502 Bridge St., Clarkston, WA 99403; phone (509) 758-7712 or (800) 933-2128.

A series of dams on the Snake River has made Clarkston a shipping center. The town's once-barren landscape now offers a variety of recreational opportunities, including boating, camping, fishing and swimming.

Several companies, including Beamer's Hell's Canyon Tours (509) 758-4800, offer 1- and 2-day jet boat excursions and 3- and 5-day river float trips through Hell's Canyon. *See ad.*

BOAT TRIPS UP THE GRAND CANYON OF THE SNAKE RIVER are spectacular journeys into the main part of Hell's Canyon, the deepest river gorge in North America. Due to a lack of roads in the area, it is better to view the canyon by river. Various types of craft are used. Some trips return the same day while others require an overnight stop; all include one or more meals and frequently some type of refreshment. All depart in the early morning, usually before 8 a.m.

Rates vary according to craft and length of trip. Reservations are required. For further information contact the chamber of commerce; phone (509) 758-7712 or (800) 933-2128.

CLE ELUM (D-8) pop. 1,800

Meaning "swift water" in the Kittitas Indian tongue, Cle Elum aptly describes the Yakima River, which tumbles down from Lake Cle Elum, 8 miles to the northeast. The town originated as a gold claim in 1883. Three years later coal was discovered and Cle Elum gained a sawmill, a school and a stop on the Northern Pacific Railroad. Coal mining in Cle Elum ended in 1963.

The town is known as the entrance to a vast recreation area: the Wenatchee and Mount Baker-Snoqualmie national forests *(see place listings).* Nearly every conceivable sport can be enjoyed in the forests. A popular local activity is a 3- to 4-hour raft trip down the 16-mile stretch of the Yakima between Cle Elum and Thorp. Big rubber rafts and canoes are available for rent in town, as is transportation back to the launch site.

For further information contact the Cle Elum Chamber of Commerce, P.O. Box 43, Cle Elum, WA 98922; phone (509) 674-5958.

CLE ELUM HISTORICAL TELEPHONE MUSEUM, 221 E. First St., displays old telephones, switchboards and other telecommunications equipment. Allow 30 minutes minimum. Tues.-Fri. 9-4, Sat.-Mon. noon-4, Memorial Day weekend-Labor Day; Tues.-Fri. 9-4, rest of year. Donations. Phone (509) 674-5958.

IRON HORSE STATE PARK, 213 acres 1 mi. s. at the foot of 4th St. in South Cle Elum, offers a 25-mile hiking and horse trail along the scenic Yakima River. The John Wayne Pioneer Trail winds through the fir and pine forests of Easton to the rolling farmlands and canyons of the Upper Yakima River valley. Cross-country skiing is popular in winter. Picnicking is permitted. Daily 6:30 a.m.-10 p.m., Apr. 1 to mid-Oct.; 8-5, rest of year. Free. Phone (509) 656-2230.

COLFAX (E-12) pop. 2,700, elev. 1,974′

STEPTOE BUTTE STATE PARK, 150 acres 12 mi. n. on US 195, includes the 3,612-foot butte first known as Pyramid Peak. In 1858 Lt. Col. Edward J. Steptoe and 156 men suffered one of the worst defeats of the regular Army by a contingent of Nez Percé, Coeur d'Alene and Spokane Nation Indians, sending Steptoe and his forces into an after-dark retreat past the butte that now bears his name. In the 1870s a large hotel and ballroom were built atop Steptoe Butte, but they burned in 1911.

The butte, one of a series of volcanic projections that mark the area, is accessible by road and affords a 70- to 80-mile view in all directions. Geologists now refer to all such geologic features as steptoes. Parking and picnic facilities are available, but drinking water is not. Daily 6:30 a.m.-10 p.m., Apr. 1 to mid-Oct.; 8-5, rest of year. Free. Phone (509) 549-3551.

★COLUMBIA RIVER GORGE NATIONAL SCENIC AREA—*see place listing in Oregon.*

COLVILLE (B-11) pop. 4,400, elev. 1,917′

Old Fort Colville, originally near Kettle Falls, was the chief inland post of the Hudson's Bay

Exciting Hells Canyon jet boat tours

The greatest thing to do while in the Clarkston area is take a trip with us up the famous Hells Canyon on the Snake River. Our powerful jet boats get you to places in the canyon you'll never forget.

We offer all types of trips including the historic "Mail Boat Run". No group too big or small. All ages welcome.

Call toll free (800) 522-6966.

BEAMER'S

Co. for 30 years before it became the target of a gold rush in 1855. Great quantities of ore, including silver and iron, were extracted from the Colville mining district. Mining remains one of the area's primary industries. Fort Colville Monument on SR 20 commemorates the military post responsible for the area's development.

For further information contact the Colville Chamber of Commerce, 309 S. Main St., P.O. Box 267, Colville, WA 99114; phone (509) 684-5973.

KELLER HISTORICAL PARK, 700 N. Wynne St., comprises an early-20th-century residence, a museum of pioneer items, Colville's first schoolhouse and a machinery building with antique farming equipment and tools. Museum open Mon.-Sat. 10-4, Sun. 1-4, June-Sept.; daily 1-4, in May. House tours are offered Wed.-Sun. 1-3, May-Sept. Donations. Phone (509) 684-5968.

ST. PAUL'S MISSION, 12 mi. n.w. at US 395 and the Columbia River, is in the Coulee Dam National Recreation Area *(see place listing).* Built as a chapel by American Indians in 1845, the mission operated until the 1870s. The log church has been restored to its 1847 appearance. An interpretive hiking trail winds through the area; the road is not plowed in winter. Daily 24 hours (weather permitting). Free. Phone (509) 738-6266.

COLVILLE NATIONAL FOREST

Elevations in the forest range from 7,309 ft. at Gypsy Peak to 1289 ft. at the Columbia River Dam. Refer to AAA maps for additional information.

Covering about 1,100,000 acres in northeastern Washington, Colville National Forest possesses varied attractions. In the center of the forest is Roosevelt Lake; Grand Coulee Dam *(see Coulee Dam National Recreation Area)* is to the south. Through the middle of the forest courses the Columbia River. Gardner Cave, in the forest's eastern half, offers tours of its stalagmite and stalactite formations.

In the northeast corner of the forest, east of Metaline Falls, is the 41,000-acre Salmo-Priest Wilderness Area. To preserve this wilderness, no motorized vehicles are allowed. However, FRs 22, 20 and 270 and Sullivan Creek Road, south of Metaline Falls off SR 31, lead to trailheads where visitors can continue into the wilderness area on foot. The roads are closed due to weather from mid-November to early or mid-June.

Brochures and maps outlining several of the forest's self-guiding automobile and hiking tours are available at the Forest Supervisor's office, 765 S. Main St., Colville, WA 99114; phone (509) 684-3711. Lake Gillette Recreation Area near Colville offers developed recreational facilities as well as amphitheater programs; phone (509) 684-4557. *See Recreation Chart and the AAA Northwestern CampBook.*

CONCRETE (B-7) pop. 700

PUGET POWERPLANT VISITORS CENTER, 102 E. Main St., contains replicas of the Upper and Lower Baker dams and area relief maps, as well as mounted native fish and an outdoor fish trap used in the center's stocking program. The best viewing time is July through October. Allow 1 hour minimum. Mon.-Fri. 7-3:30; closed federal holidays. Free. Phone (360) 853-8341.

COULEE CITY (D-10) pop. 600, elev. 1,584'

Once nicknamed "Engineers' Town," Coulee City is the former junction of railroad and stagecoach lines running along the Columbia River. According to Guy Waring, a 19th-century pioneer and author, the trains and coaches were deliberately scheduled *not* to connect with each other, forcing passengers to spend the night in town. Coulee City still gets many passers-through; it is the only place between Soap Lake *(see place listing)* and Coulee Dam where those traveling on US 2 between Seattle and Spokane can cross the Grand Coulee.

For further information contact the Coulee City Chamber of Commerce, P.O. Box 896, Coulee City, WA 99115; phone (509) 632-5713.

★**DRY FALLS** is 4 mi. s.w. off SR 17. Huge floods rushing across eastern Washington during the last ice age carved a network of gashes, the largest of which is Grand Coulee. Dry Falls, Grand Coulee's central feature, was once a 3½-mile-wide cataract over which water plunged about 400 feet. For those not wishing to attempt the moderately rough road through the park, Dry Falls is visible from both SR 17 and the interpretive center.

Allow 1 hour minimum. Park open daily 6:30 a.m.-10 p.m., Apr. 1 to mid-Oct.; 8-5, rest of year. Interpretive center open daily 10-6, May-Sept. Free. Phone (509) 632-5583.

COULEE DAM NATIONAL RECREATION AREA (C-10)

Encompassing 100,059 acres in northeastern Washington, Coulee Dam National Recreation Area stretches from the Grand Coulee Dam along Franklin D. Roosevelt Lake toward the Canadian border. Geologic formations in much of the region are the result of intense volcanic activity followed by cataclysmic ice age floods. Numerous wildflowers grace the southern lava flows and terraces on Roosevelt Lake. Deer are common; beavers and muskrats frequent the lakeshores.

Franklin D. Roosevelt Lake, an 81,000-acre storage reservoir, is a rapidly developing recreational center. Fine beaches at 34 developed recreation areas provide swimming, boating and water skiing; motorboats cruise the reservoir's 130-mile waterway. Rangers conduct programs at some of the campgrounds in summer; phone (509) 633-9441.

Points of interest in the recreation area include St. Paul's Mission *(see Colville)* and Fort Spokane *(see Miles). See Recreation Chart and the AAA Northwestern CampBook.*

★**GRAND COULEE DAM** harnesses the Columbia River for irrigation, power and flood control. The dam is said to be the most massive concrete structure in the world: It is 550 feet high, 500 feet wide at its base and 5,223 feet long.

Allow 2 hours minimum. Self-guiding tours are available in summer when conditions permit. A visitor center on the west bank below the dam is open daily 8:30 a.m.-10 p.m., Memorial Day weekend-Labor Day; 9-5, rest of year. Closed Jan. 1, Thanksgiving and Dec. 25. The dam's spillway is illuminated by a free, hour-long laser light show presented nightly at 10, Memorial Day weekend-July 31; at 9:30, in Aug.; at 8:30, in Sept. Free. Phone (509) 633-9265.

COUPEVILLE (D-2) pop. 1,400, elev. 2′

Coupeville, on Whidbey Island, was established in 1853, making it one of the oldest cities in the state. Three old blockhouses built to defend Puget Sound and settlers' homes from the Coast Salish Indians can be visited. West of town is Madrona Drive, a 4-mile scenic route that winds along the shore of Penn Cove.

Self-guiding tours: Maps outlining a walking tour featuring nearly 30 historic buildings are available at the Central Whidbey Chamber of Commerce, 5 S. Main St., P.O. Box 152, Coupeville, WA 98239; phone (360) 678-5434.

Shopping areas: Antique shops, art galleries, crafts stores and souvenir shops line Front Street between Alexander and Center streets downtown.

ISLAND COUNTY HISTORICAL MUSEUM, at the foot of Coupeville Wharf, Alexander and Front sts., has displays depicting the culture of the Skagit Indians and other tribes of northern Puget Sound, maritime and agricultural history, and pioneer lifestyles. "Sails, Steamships and Sea Captains" chronicles the maritime history of Puget Sound 1850-1900.

Mon.-Fri. 11-5, Sat.-Sun. 10-5, Apr.-Oct.; Fri.-Mon. 11-4, rest of year. Admission $2, over 59, military and students with ID $1.50, under 6 free, family rate $4.50. Phone (360) 678-3310.

CRYSTAL MOUNTAIN (D-7) elev. 7,012′

Located northeast of Mount Rainier, Crystal Mountain is a resort community offering year-round recreation. Activities include alpine and nordic skiing, mountian biking, hiking, tennis and swimming. A visitor center at the junction of SR 410 and Crystal Mountain Blvd. offers additional information about the area; phone (360) 663-2656.

CRYSTAL MOUNTAIN CHAIRLIFT, in Crystal Mountain Resort, 1 Crystal Mountain Blvd., transports visitors to the 7,000-foot level of Crystal Mountain, where trails for hiking and mountain biking fan out. The summit offers panoramas of Mount Rainier. Food service and mountain bike rentals available. Chairlift runs Mon.-Fri. 10-8:30, Sat.-Sun. and holidays 9-8:30, July-early Sept. Fare $7; ages 62-69 and ages 6-17, $5; over 69, $3; under 6 free. AE, DS, MC, VI. Phone (360) 663-2300.

DAVENPORT (D-11) pop. 1,500, elev. 2,430′

LINCOLN COUNTY HISTORICAL MUSEUM, jct. Park and Seventh sts., contains Colville and Spokane Indian artifacts, photographs and old farm machinery, as well as pioneer furniture, clothing and tools. Allow 1 hour minimum. Mon.-Sat. 9-5, May-Sept.; by appointment, rest of year. Donations. Phone (509) 725-6711; for appointment phone (509) 725-2603, 725-7631 or 725-6342.

DAYTON (F-11) pop. 2,500, elev. 1,606′

At the center of a prosperous farming region, Dayton claims the oldest courthouse and railroad depot in the state. Built by the Oregon Railroad and Navigation Co. in 1881, the depot operated for 93 years. It is now restored and furnished with railroad memorabilia, antique furniture and photographs.

For further information contact the Dayton Chamber of Commerce, 163 E. Main, P.O. Box 22, Dayton, WA 99328; phone (509) 382-4825.

Self-guiding tours: The depot has walking-tour maps describing Dayton's two historic districts; phone (509) 382-2026.

DEMING (A-3) pop. 400, elev. 207′

MOUNT BAKER VINEYARDS, ½ mi. w. on SR 542 at 4298 Mount Baker Hwy., is in the picturesque Nooksack Valley at the foot of Mount Baker. All grapes, both classic and pioneer varieties, are grown on the property to produce 21 specialty wines. Tours and tastings are available on request. Allow 30 minutes minimum. Daily 11-5, July-Aug.; Wed.-Sun. 11-5, rest of year. Closed Jan. 1 and Dec. 25. Free. Phone (360) 592-2300.

DES MOINES (G-3) pop. 17,300

Located on the eastern shore of Puget Sound, Des Moines was settled in 1867. The city was named for the Des Moines City Improvement Co. and prospered as a major sawmilling center in the late 1800s.

The Des Moines Marina, west of SR 509 on South 227th Street, has a 670-foot public fishing pier. Guest moorage, boat launch facilities and gasoline are available; phone (206) 824-5700.

Two miles south of town on SR 509 is the very popular Saltwater State Park, with a 1,500-foot beach and a deep, forested ravine, offering opportunities to camp, picnic, hike and scuba dive *(see Recreation Chart and the AAA Northwestern CampBook)*. In late July the city celebrates its saltwater heritage during the Waterland Festival.

For further information contact the Greater Des Moines Chamber of Commerce, 22236 Dock Ave. S., P.O. Box 98672, Des Moines, WA 98198; phone (206) 878-7000.

DES MOINES BEACH PARK, 4 blks. w. of SR 509 via S. 223rd St., is a 20-acre reserve with meadows, woodlands, 635 feet of saltwater beach and a salmon-bearing stream that empties into Puget Sound. The park includes the Covenant Beach Historic District—20 buildings that operated as a church retreat 1931-87. The rustic camp reflects its Swedish architectural heritage. Picnicking is permitted. Daily 8-dusk. Free. Phone (206) 878-4595.

DIABLO (B-8)

SKAGIT TOURS—SEATTLE CITY LIGHT focus on the hydroelectric facilities around SR 20 in Newhalem and Diablo; follow SR 20 to the tour center in Diablo. The entire complex, which centers on the source of Seattle's electricity supply, lies within the Ross Lake National Recreation Area *(see place listing)*.

Visitors in Newhalem can see the 1926 steam locomotive, Gorge Powerhouse, Ladder Creek Falls and Rock Gardens or stroll along the Trail of Cedars Nature Walk. Between Newhalem and Diablo, the Gorge Creek Overlook offers views of a waterfall and the Gorge Dam and Lake.

The main tour departs from the Diablo tour center and lasts 4½ hours. Highlights include a 560-foot mountain ascent and descent on an antique railway lift, a slide show, a boat cruise on Diablo Lake and a tour of the massive generating facilities of Ross Powerhouse followed by an optional dinner. Additional 90-minute tours include the slide show, Diablo powerhouse and lift ride.

Main tours depart Thurs.-Mon. at 10, 12:30 and 3, mid-June through Labor Day; Sat.-Sun. at noon, weekend after Labor Day- early Oct. Ninety-minute tours depart Thurs.-Mon. at 11 and 1:15, July 1-Labor Day. Main tour (including dinner) $25; over 62, $22; ages 6-11, $10. Main tour (without dinner) $18; over 62, $15; ages 6-11, $5. Ninety-minute tour $5, under 6 free. Antique railway lift ride 25c. Reservations are recommended for meal tours. Contact Skagit Tours, 1015 3rd Ave., Seattle, WA 98104; phone (206) 684-3030.

EATONVILLE (I-3) pop. 1,400

★NORTHWEST TREK, 6 mi. n. on SR 161, is a 635-acre wildlife park featuring animals native to the Northwest. A guided tram tour through the preserve allows visitors to see moose, caribou, elk, bison and other animals in their natural habitats. Highlights include a grizzly habitat and several walk-through animal exhibits, a children's nature discovery center and a theater.

Allow 3 hours minimum. Park opens at 9:30, closing times vary. Tours depart daily on the hour Mar.-Oct.; Fri.-Sun. and holidays on the hour, rest of year. Admission $7.75; over 62, $6.75; ages 5-17, $5.25; ages 3-4, $3.25. MC, VI. **Discount.** Phone (360) 832-6117, or (800) 433-8735 in Wash. and Ore.

PIONEER FARM MUSEUM is 1½ mi. w. of SR 161 or ¾ mi. e. of SR 7 on Ohop Valley Rd. E. The 1880s farm offers guided tours with such hands-on activities as milking, grain milling and other household and farm chores similar to those the pioneers performed some 100 years ago. Guides conduct 1½-hour tours and explain pioneer life. Hour-long, hands-on guided tours of the Ohop Indian Village also are available.

Allow 2 hours minimum. Daily 11-5:30, mid-June to early Sept.; Sat.-Sun. 11-5:30, Mar. 1 to mid-June and early Sept. to mid-Nov. Ohop Indian Village tours are conducted Sat.-Sun. at 1 and 2:30, mid-June to Labor Day. Last tour departs at 4. Admission $5; over 61 and ages 3-16, $4. **Discount.** Phone (360) 832-6300.

EDMONDS (E-3) pop. 31,000

Legend has it that when logger George Brackett petitioned to establish the town of Edmonds in 1890, he added the names of his two oxen to the list to achieve the required number of petitioners. He named the town for Vermont Sen. George Franklin Edmunds but misspelled the name.

Edmonds' Puget Sound waterfront has beaches, a marina and a public fishing pier; the Olympic Mountains can be seen in the distance. Brackett's Landing Beach, just north of the ferry dock, includes Edmonds Underwater Park for scuba diving. Washington State Ferries provide frequent daily service to Kingston; phone (206) 464-6400.

For further information contact the Edmonds Chamber of Commerce, 120 5th Ave. N., P.O. Box 146, Edmonds, WA 98020; phone (206) 776-6711.

Shopping areas: Art galleries, antique shops, specialty stores and restaurants form Old Mill Town, a 22-store complex downtown at 5th Avenue S. and Dayton Street.

EDMONDS MUSEUM, 118 N. 5th Ave., chronicles the settlement and growth of Edmonds and southern Snohomish County. Special exhibits include a working model of a shingle mill and a marine room displaying the city's maritime heritage. The museum, which occupies the former 1910 Carnegie Library/City Hall, also offers changing regional history exhibits. Allow 1 hour minimum. Tues., Thurs. and Sat.-Sun. 1-4; closed holidays. Donations. Phone (206) 774-0900.

ELBE (I-3) elev. 1,211′

First called Browns Junction, residents changed the town's name to honor pioneer settler Henry Lutkens' birthplace, the Elbe Valley in Germany. The diminutive Little White Church on SR 7 was built in 1906 for the German-speaking Lutheran congregation.

MOUNT RAINIER SCENIC RAILROAD, on SR 7, is a steam-powered excursion train that travels 14 miles through tall timber and over high bridges to Mineral Lake. Trains feature restored coaches, open cars and live music. A dinner train also is available.

Allow 1 hour, 30 minutes minimum. Departures daily at 11, 1:15 and 3:30, mid-June through Labor Day; Sat.-Sun. at 11, 1:15 and 3:30, Memorial Day to mid-June and day after Labor Day-Sept. 30. Sightseeing fare $7.50; over 60, $6.50; ages 12-17, $5.50; ages 2-11, $4.50. DS, MC, VI. Reservations are required for dinner trains. For further information contact Mount Rainier Scenic Railroad, P.O. Box 921, Elbe, WA 98330; phone (360) 569-2588.

ELLENSBURG (D-8) pop. 12,400, elev. 1,577′

The Kittitas Valley was once a neutral area in which the mutually hostile Wenatchee, Nez Percé and Yakama Indians hunted and fished together in peace. For its first several years the settlement was named after a store called "Robber's Roost" by its puckish owners. The Ellensburg Rodeo recalls the town's early days every Labor Day weekend at Kittitas County Fairgrounds.

Self-guiding tours: Maps outlining a walking tour featuring nearly 35 sites in the town are available at the Ellensburg Chamber of Commerce, 436 N. Sprague, Ellensburg, WA 98926; phone (509) 925-3138.

CLYMER ART MUSEUM, 416 N. Pearl St., exhibits the works of Western artist John Clymer. The collection includes cover illustrations for the *Saturday Evening Post* and oils depicting Western themes. The gallery also features changing exhibits of Northwestern artists. Allow 30 minutes minimum. Mon.-Fri. 10-5, Sat.-Sun. noon-5; closed Jan. 1, Easter, July 4, Thanksgiving and Dec. 25. Admission $2; over 60 and ages 6-12, $1; family rate $5. Phone (509) 962-6416.

KITTITAS COUNTY HISTORICAL MUSEUM, 114 E. 3rd St., is in the 1889 Cadwell building, which has unusual horseshoe-shaped windows. Among the exhibits are Kittitas Indian artifacts and pioneer tools and articles, as well as a display of petrified wood and the Rollinger Rock and Mineral Collection. Tues.-Sat. 10-4, May-Aug.; Tues.-Sat. 10-3, rest of year. Closed holidays. Donations. Phone (509) 925-3778.

ELMA (D-5) pop. 3,000, elev. 70′

SATSOP POWERPLANT, 5 mi. s.w. off US 12, is the site of a future Pacific Northwest electrical generating station. The information office features a scale model and displays. Allow 1 hour, 30 minutes minimum. Visitor center open Mon.-Sat. 8-5, July-Aug.; Mon.-Fri. 8-5, rest of year. Tours are conducted Fri. at 10 and Sat. at 10, 12:30 and 2:30, July-Aug. Closed holidays. Free. Phone (360) 482-4428, ext. 5052.

ENUMCLAW (D-7) pop. 7,200, elev. 742′

Enumclaw, or "place of the evil spirits," is the name the Duwamish Indians allegedly gave a nearby mountain after they were frightened by a severe thunderstorm while camping there. The town, established in 1885, was named for the mountain. The community celebrates the King County Fair in mid-July.

The pastureland surrounding Enumclaw is a noted horse-raising area, producing more than 20 breeds, including Thoroughbreds, Morgans, paso finos and paints. January through June are the best months to see foals romping in their paddocks. For more information conatact the Enumclaw Area Chamber of Commerce, 1421 Cole St., Enumclaw, WA 98022; phone (360) 825-7666.

MUD MOUNTAIN DAM, 5½ mi. e. on SR 410, then 2½ mi. s. on Mud Mountain Dam Rd., is an earth-and-rock flood-control dam. Of interest are a cableway tower and samples of rock cores drilled with a 36-inch calyx drill. A park includes overlooks, a children's wading pool, hiking trails and a playground. Daily 9-8, June 1 to mid-Sept.; daily 9-4, Mar.-May; Sat.-Sun. 9-8, rest of year. Free. Phone (360) 825-3211.

EPHRATA (D-9) pop. 5,300, elev. 1,277′

GRANT COUNTY HISTORICAL MUSEUM AND PIONEER VILLAGE, 742 N. Basin St., contains a collection of old pictures, tools, farm equipment, rocks, Wanapum and Sinkiuse Indian artifacts, cowboy paraphernalia, clothing, documents and household furnishings from the homestead era. Exhibits are arranged chronologically from prehistoric times to the start of the Columbia Basin project.

Part of the museum is a 26-building pioneer village comprising authentic and reconstructed units. Included are a saloon, dress shop, printing office, barber shop, blacksmith shop, bank, school and livery stable. Allow 2 hours minimum. Tours are conducted Mon.-Tues. and Thurs.-Sat. 10-5, Sun. 1-4, May-Sept. Admission $1.50, under 6 free. Phone (509) 754-3334.

EVERETT (E-3) pop. 70,000, elev. 21′

Everett is on Port Gardner Bay, a natural landlocked harbor at the mouth of the Snohomish River. Across Puget Sound loom the snowy crags of the Olympic Range; to the northeast and southeast, Mount Baker and Mount Rainier dominate the Cascades. Once owned by timber barons, the mansions on Rucker and Grand avenues still grace the north section of town.

Jetty Island lies off the northern end of Everett's waterfront at the channel entrance of the Snohomish River. The man-made island is 2 miles long by 200 yards wide and is home to 45 species of birds and a herd of California sea lions from October to June. The island is accessible by private boat year-round. Free ferry service is available from Everett Marina Village. Phone (206) 259-0304.

A display of firefighting equipment can be seen through the windows of the Firefighters Museum on the 13th Street dock, west of Marine View Dr. The Everett Area Chamber of Commerce occupies the restored Weyerhaeuser Office Building at 1710 W. Marine View Dr., P.O. Box 1086, Everett, WA 98206; phone (206) 252-5181.

The sea and the sky are the themes of some of Everett's summer festivals: the Salty Sea Days in early June, the Silver Lake Triathlon in mid-July and the Washington State International Air Fair in mid-August.

The Everett Giants play class A Northwest League baseball at Memorial Stadium, 39th and Broadway; phone (206) 258-3673.

Shopping areas: A downtown public market at 2804 Grand Ave. contains antique and craft shops. The Everett Mall, 5 miles south of downtown off I-5 exit 189 on S.E. Everett Mall Way, has The Bon, Payless and Sears. Everett Marina Village, on the waterfront at the foot of 18th Street, is a renovated portion of the waterfront district that resembles an 1890s village.

★**BOEING 747-767 DIVISION,** I-5 exit 189, then 3½ mi. w. on SR 526 following signs, offers 90-minute tours which include a slide/film presentation and a visit to the assembly plant. Children under 8 and video cameras are not permitted on the plant tour. Tours reach capacity quickly during summer months. Tour center open Mon.-Fri. 8:30-4; phone for schedule. Closed holidays. Free. Phone (206) 342-4801.

EVERETT MUSEUM, 2915 Hewitt Ave., is housed in one of Everett's oldest commercial buildings, built in 1906. Exhibits depict Pacific Northwest history and its impact on Everett and Snohomish County with a series of thematic dioramas, artifacts and photographs. Wed.-Sun. 1-4. Free. Phone (206) 259-8849 or 259-8873.

FOREST PARK, 1 mi. w. of I-5 exit 192 on Mukilteo Blvd., includes a heated pool, a children's zoo and various recreational facilities. Park open daily 24 hours. Zoo open daily 9-6, mid-June through Labor Day. Free. Phone (206) 259-0300, or 259-0303 for the zoo.

LEGION PARK, 144 Alverson Blvd., is a recreation area featuring the Everett Area Arboretum, with a collection of native and exotic plants. Daily 24 hours. Free. Phone (206) 259-0300. ,

MOSQUITO FLEET San Juan Islands and sea life cruises depart from 1724-F W. Marine View Dr.; from I-5 exit 193 go 2½ miles n.w. via Pacific Ave., then w. on Marine View Dr. Round-trip bus transportation from major downtown Seattle hotels is available. The vessel arrives at Friday Harbor at noon and passengers may choose to disembark and explore the town at their leisure for 3 hours, or remain aboard and cruise the island in a 3-hour Orca spotting cruise. Whale sightings are not guaranteed, but reportedly a large majority of the trips are successful. Following a return to Friday Harbor, the ship arrives in Everett in the early evening.

Inquire about refund and weather policies, and where to park. Food is available. Allow a full day. Boarding daily at 7:30, mid-May through mid-Sept.; Sat.-Sun., late Sept.-Oct. 31. Departure is at 8. Fare mid-June through mid-Sept. $69; over 55 and under 18, $59. Fare mid-May to mid-June and late Sept.-Oct. 31, $49; over 55 and under 18, $44. AE, DI, MC, VI. Phone (206) 252-6800.

RIVER QUEEN, 1712 W. Marine Dr., is a sidewheeler providing a variety of sightseeing and meal cruises on the Snohomish River and Snohomish Delta, where sloughs and estuaries harbor and form the largest wetland area in the state.

Trips depart Everett Marina Village; phone for exact departure times and days. Dinner cruises $29.95; Sunday breakfast cruise $24.95; lunch cruise, $19.95; scenic nature cruises $15.95. Over 64, 10 percent reduction; under 12, half price. MC, VI. **Discount.** Reservations are recommended. Phone (206) 259-2743.

SNOHOMISH COUNTY MUSEUM AND HISTORICAL ASSOCIATION, 1 mi. w. of I-5 exit 194 at 2817 Rockefeller Ave., features changing exhibits illustrating the history of Snohomish County. The museum's collection includes photographs, telephones, textiles and furniture. Allow 30 minutes minimum. Thurs.-Sat. 1-4. Donations. Phone (206) 259-2022.

FALL CITY (D-6) pop. 64,000, elev. 378′

HERBFARM, 32804 Issaquah-Fall City Rd., is 3 mi. n. of I-90 exit 22, then ½ mi. n. on 328th Ave. The farm features 17 gardens and greenhouses that display hundreds of varieties of herbs, sedums and succulents. A Shakespearean theme garden features flowers and trees mentioned in his works. Other gardens include edible and fragrance flowers. Allow 1 hour minimum. Daily 9-6. Guided tours are offered Sat.-Sun. at 1. Closed Jan. 1, Thanksgiving and Dec. 25. Free. Phone (206) 784-2222.

FEDERAL WAY (G-3)

The large suburban community of Federal Way, part of the Seattle-Tacoma metropolitan area, covers a series of wooded ridges above Puget Sound. Its name comes from the federal highway built through the area in 1929. The Fall

Foliage Festival is held in mid-October at the Rhododendron Species Botanical Garden *(see attraction listing).*

For further information contact the Greater Federal Way Chamber of Commerce, 344004 16th Ave. S., Suite 105, P.O. Box 3440, Federal Way, WA 98063; phone (206) 838-2605.

Shopping areas: Sea-Tac Mall, 1 mile west of I-5 exit 143 at the southeast corner of SR 99 and S. 320th Street, contains The Bon, Lamonts, Mervyns and Sears.

ENCHANTED PARKS, w. of I-5 exit 142B to SR 161, then s. to 36201 Enchanted Pkwy. S., is a 50-acre family amusement park. Phone (206) 661-8000 or 925-8000. *See ad p. 167.*

Enchanted Village, features 16 rides, live entertainment, a 1906 carrousel and picnic areas. Daily 11-7, late May-Labor Day; Sat.-Sun. 11-6, early May through mid-May. Admission $10; ages 3-9, $8. DS, MC, VI.

Wild Waves Water Park, next to Enchanted Village, contains four waterslides, a 24,000-square-foot wave pool, two speed slides, a children's activity pool and warming spas. Daily 11-6, May 22-Labor Day. Admission (includes Enchanted Village) $18; ages 3-9, $16; over 49, $10. DS, MC, VI. *See ad p. 167.*

PACIFIC RIM BONSAI COLLECTION, ¼ mi. e. of I-5 exit 142A via SR 18, then ¼ mi. n. on Weyerhaeuser Way, is a 1-acre facility established as a symbol of the importance of trading relationships with Pacific Rim countries. The collection includes more than 50 bonsai trees from the United States, Canada, Japan, Korea, China and Taiwan. Several of the trees are more than 500 years old. Allow 30 minutes minimum. Fri.-Wed. 10-4, Mar.-May; Sat.-Wed. 11-4, rest of year. Free. Phone (206) 924-5206.

RHODODENDRON SPECIES BOTANICAL GARDEN is ¾ mi. e. of I-5 exit 142A via SR 18, then ½ mi. n. on Weyerhaeuser Way. This 24-acre garden features more than 2,000 varieties of rhododendron from around the world. The Alpine Garden displays rhododendrons and other plants adapted to survive the harsh growing conditions of high altitudes, while a Study Garden arrays species of rhododendron for comparison.

Allow 1 hour minimum. Fri.-Wed 10-4, Mar.-May; Sat.-Wed. 11-4, rest of year. Admission $3.50, over 64 and students with ID $2.50, under 12 free. **Discount.** Phone (206) 661-9377.

FERNDALE (B-2) pop. 5,400, elev. 30′

Ferndale, in the northwest corner of the state, was so named in 1872 when the area's first schoolteacher noticed clumps of ferns surrounding the schoolhouse. The town is now a trade center for area farms. The Scottish Highland Games celebrates Scottish cultural heritage in early June. The International Folk Dance Festival is held the third weekend of July, and the Old Settlers Pioneer Days Picnic in late July commemorates the area's pioneer heritage.

For further information contact the Ferndale Chamber of Commerce, 5640 Riverside Dr., Ferndale, WA 98248; phone (360) 384-3042.

★**HOVANDER HOMESTEAD,** is 1 mi. s. via Hovander Rd. The 1903 restored home is part of a large park encompassing an interpretive center, barn, milkhouse, children's farm zoo, gardens and picnic sites. The home and barn are furnished with antiques and vintage equipment. Allow 1 hour minimum. Grounds open daily 8:30 a.m.-9 p.m., Memorial Day weekend-Labor Day; 8:30-dusk, rest of year. Home open Thurs.-Sun. noon-4:30. Grounds $3 per private vehicle. Home $1; ages 5-12, 50c. Phone (360) 384-3444.

PIONEER PARK is 1 mi. w. of I-5 exit 262 at 1st and Cherry sts. Buildings dating 1870-95 form a pioneer village of 12 log structures, including a post office, church, granary, schoolhouse, stagecoach inn, veteran's museum and homesteads. Relics illustrate life during the pioneer era. Allow 1 hour minimum. Park open daily 24 hours. Guided and self-guiding tours are available Tues.-Sun. 11:30-4, May-Sept. Donations. Phone (360) 384-6461.

TENNANT LAKE NATURAL HISTORY INTERPRETIVE CENTER, 1¼ mi. s.w. of I-5 exit 262, offers displays interpreting the seasons, a nature walk and a boardwalk trail around a bog. The Fragrance Garden is specially designed for the visually impaired—plants have singular smells and textures and are signed in braille. Grounds open daily dawn-dusk. Center open Thurs.-Sun. 9-5, late June-Labor Day. Free. Phone (360) 384-3444.

FORKS (C-4) pop. 3,000, elev. 375′

This important Olympic Peninsula logging community takes its name from the forks of the three nearby rivers: the Bogachiel, Calawah and Soleduck. The westernmost incorporated city in the contiguous United States, Forks began in the late 1870s as an agricultural community; commercial logging followed a decade later. In addition to providing the town's name, area rivers support spectacular runs of steelhead trout during the summer and winter, attracting anglers.

For further information contact the Forks Chamber of Commerce, P.O. Box 1259, Forks, WA 98331; phone (360) 374-2531 or (800) 44-FORKS.

FORKS TIMBER MUSEUM, 1 mi. s. on US 101 across from the airport, has a variety of items from the late 1800s. Displays include a pioneer kitchen, farm equipment, vintage newspapers and photographs. Logging equipment and a fire lookout tower document Fork's role as an important logging community. Allow 30 minutes minimum. Tues.-Sat. 10-5, Sun. 1-5, late Apr.-Dec. 31;

closed Thanksgiving and Dec. 25. Donations. Phone (360) 374-9663.

GIFFORD PINCHOT NATIONAL FOREST

Elevations in the forest range from 80 ft. at an island in the Columbia River, to 12,276 ft. at Mount Adams. Refer to AAA maps for additional information.

Straddling the Cascade Range from Mount Rainier to the Columbia River, Gifford Pinchot National Forest covers 1,299,546 acres of mountains, meadows, caves, canyons and streams. On opposite edges of the forest, restless 8,364-foot Mount St. Helens and glacier-clad 12,276-foot Mount Adams tower above the lesser peaks; the fields of wild huckleberries scattered through the forest and surrounding Mount Adams lure thousands of pickers in late summer.

Forest roads are usually open from late May through November; however, many are narrow and winding and should be traveled with care. Check current road and weather conditions carefully. For information about Mount St. Helens phone the Forest Supervisor's office at (360) 750-5001 or Mount St. Helens National Volcanic Monument *(see place listing)* at (360) 750-3900.

Of the forest's seven wilderness areas, Goat Rocks and Mount Adams are the largest. Permits are required to enter the Indian Heaven, Mount Adams, Goat Rocks, Trapper Creek, Tatoosh and Glacier View wilderness areas. The forest is home to many species of animals; common birds are ducks, grouse, ravens and Steller and Canada jays. Salmon and trout inhabit the many streams.

Of particular interest are the Big Lava Beds 14 miles west of Trout Lake on FR 60. The unusual formations originated from a 500-foot-deep crater in the northern part of the lava bed. Ice Cave, 6 miles southwest of Trout Lake on SR 141, is one of numerous lava tubes in an area known as the Big Trench Cave System.

Ice usually remains in the 400-foot cave until late summer. Another interesting volcanic feature is the Palisades, which is visible from US 12, 2½ miles east of the SR 123 junction. The Clear Fork of the Cowlitz River has cut a deep gorge into an ancient lava flow, exposing an impressive 486-foot-high cliff of columnar basalt. Trails can be followed on foot or horseback.

The Pacific Crest National Scenic Trail traverses the forest on its passage from Mexico to Canada. Canoes and boats with small motors are permitted on some lakes; watch for speed restrictions. Snowmobiling, snowshoeing and cross-country skiing are popular winter pastimes. Fishing and hunting are permitted in season.

Recreation information is available at ranger stations in Amboy, Carson, Packwood, Randle and Trout Lake, or by writing the Forest Supervisor's Office, Gifford Pinchot National Forest, P.O. Box 8944, Vancouver, WA 98668-8944; phone (360) 750-5001. *See Recreation Chart and the AAA Northwestern CampBook.*

LLAMA TREE RANCH offers guided llama pack trips in the northern portions of the Gifford Pinchot National Forest and near Mount Rainier National Park. Lunch trips depart Sat.-Sun. at 11, May-Oct. Phone for other trip schedules. Prices start at $35 per person; meals are included. MC, VI. Package rates and customized trips are available. Reservations are suggested. Phone (360) 491-5262.

GIG HARBOR (G-2) pop. 3,200

Located on a small bay, Gig Harbor's bayfront business district retains the flavor of a fishing village. The bay was discovered by chance by members of the 1841 Wilkes expedition seeking refuge from a storm. They named the bay for their "gig," a type of boat. Weekends and by appointment the Puget Sound Mariner's Museum, 3311 Harborview Dr., depicts the nautical history of the region; displays include the 1903 German-built two-masted ketch the *Krestine,* moored behind the museum. For further museum information phone (206) 858-9395 or 858-7258.

Five miles northwest of Tacoma over the Narrows Bridge, Gig Harbor still provides shelter—not for explorers, but for commercial fishing boats and pleasure craft. Fishing boat charters, as well as rentals of fishing and other power boats, sailboats, sea kayaks, paddle boats and jet skis are available locally.

For further information contact the Gig Harbor/Peninsula Area Chamber of Commerce, 3125 Judson St., Gig Harbor, WA 98335; phone (206) 851-6865.

Shopping areas: Downtown along Harborview Drive are several dozen specialty shops and art galleries.

GOLD BAR (C-7) pop. 1,000, elev. 204′

A former prospector's camp, Gold Bar is a logging headquarters which also serves the needs of small farms in the region. During construction of the Great Northern Railroad, anti-Chinese sentiment in this area was so strong in camp agitators that Chinese laborers were forced to flee the camp hidden in hastily built coffins.

WALLACE FALLS STATE PARK, 678 acres, is 2 mi. n.e. off US 2. A 2½-mile trail ascends 880 feet through wooded parkland to the crest of 250-foot Wallace Falls. Excellent views of the Skykomish Valley can be had from the top of the falls. Picnic and camping facilities are available. Daily 6:30 a.m.-dusk, Apr. 1 to mid-Oct.; Wed.-Sun. 8-5, rest of year. Park admission free. Phone (360) 793-0420. *See Recreation Chart.*

GOLDENDALE (F-8) pop. 3,300, elev. 1,509′

GOLDENDALE OBSERVATORY STATE PARK, 1 mi. n. on Columbus Ave., has a 24½-inch Cassegrain reflecting telescope, one of the largest of its kind in the country available for public use. There also are an 8-inch Celestron telescope for viewing the sun and various small telescopes available. Wed.-Sun. 2-5 and 8-midnight, Apr.-Sept.; Sat. 1-5 and 7-9, Sun. 1-5 and by appointment, rest of year. Free. Phone (509) 773-3141.

KLICKITAT COUNTY HISTORICAL MUSEUM, 127 W. Broadway in the Winthrop B. Presby Mansion, was built in 1902. Displays of household items include a large coffee mill collection. A pioneer exhibit features branding irons and brands. Allow 30 minutes minimum. Daily 9-5, Apr.-Oct.; by appointment, rest of year. Admission $3; ages 12-18, $1. Phone (509) 773-4303, 773-4426 or 773-4195.

★GRAND COULEE DAM—

see Coulee Dam National Recreation Area.

GRANDVIEW (F-9) pop. 7,200, elev. 790′

Grandview, in the lower Yakima Valley, takes its name from the spectacular westward view of Mount Rainier and Mount Adams. The fertile soil of the valley enhances the bounty of such local crops as apples, asparagus, corn, hops, grapes, peaches and cherries. A chronology of area history is presented in the Ray E. Powell Museum on Division Street. Grandview hosts the Yakima Valley Junior Fair in August.

For a brochure listing several dozen wineries in the surrounding area contact the Yakima Valley Wine Growers Association, P.O. Box 39, Grandview, WA 98930.

For further information contact the Grandview Chamber of Commerce, 103 W. 5th St., P.O. Box 666, Grandview, WA 98245; phone (206) 376-2273.

CHATEAU STE. MICHELLE, W. 5th St. and Ave. B, is the oldest operating winery in Washington. The rare open-top fermenters are used to create premium red wines. Allow 30 minutes minimum. Tastings daily 10-4:30; closed Jan. 1, Easter, Thanksgiving and Dec. 25. Free. Phone (509) 882-3928.

GRAYS RIVER (E-5) elev. 27′

GRAYS RIVER COVERED BRIDGE, 1¾ mi. s. off SR 4, was built in 1905. The 158-foot span is considered the oldest remaining covered bridge in the Northwest, and the only one of its kind in the state.

GREENBANK (D-3) elev. 158′

MEERKERK RHODODENDRON GARDENS is 1½ mi. s. on SR 525, then ¼ mi. e. on Resort Rd. The gardens contain 53 acres of more than 2,000 plants. Allow 1 hour minimum. Wed.-Sun. 9-6, Mar. 1-Labor Day. Admission $2, under 12 free. Phone (360) 678-1912.

WHIDBEY'S GREENBANK LOGANBERRY FARM, ¼ mi. n. on SR 525, then e. on Wonn Rd., is one of the world's largest loganberry vineyards. A visitor center chronicles the history of the 125-acre farm and illustrates the process of distilling loganberry liquor. Picnic grounds and a wine-tasting room are available. Allow 30 minutes minimum. Daily 10-5; closed major holidays. Free. Phone (360) 678-7700.

GREENWATER (D-7)

FEDERATION FOREST STATE PARK, 1 mi. w. on SR 410, consists of 619 acres of virgin woodlands with nature trails and picnic areas. Exhibits at the Catherine Montgomery Interpretive Center illustrate the state's seven contrasting life zones. Park open daily 6:30 a.m.-dusk, mid-Apr. to mid-Oct. Interpretive center open Wed.-Sun. 10-5, mid-Apr. to mid-Sept.; by appointment, rest of year. Free. Phone (360) 663-2207.

HOODSPORT (G-1) pop. 1,100, elev. 70′

First settled in 1880, Hoodpsort lies at the base of the Olympic Mountains on the shore of Hood Canal, the westernmost arm of Puget Sound. Clams, oysters and shrimp are harvested from area waters. SR 119 leads west to Lake Cushman, a popular recreation area in the southeast corner of Olympic National Park *(see place listing)*. The Forest Service and National Park Service operate an information center 1 block west of US 101 on SR 119; phone (360) 877-5254.

HOODSPORT WINERY, N. 23501 US 101, specializes in fruit and varietal grape wines. Allow 30 minutes minimum. Fifteen-minute guided tours are conducted daily 10-6. Tasting room open daily 9-7, Memorial Day-Labor Day; 10-6, rest of year. Closed Thanksgiving and Dec. 25. Free. Phone (360) 877-9894.

HOQUIAM (D-4) pop. 9,000, elev. 10′

Forest products have been a staple of Hoquiam's economy since its first sawmill opened in 1882. The city's name derives from the Chehalis Indian word "Ho-qui-umpts," meaning "hungry for wood." Grays Harbor is a natural outlet for the area's prime export.

The Seventh Street Theatre, 313 7th St., was built 1927-28 and was the first theater in the state to show talking motion pictures. The tideflats lining the harbor west of town host migrating shorebirds in spring and fall. Bowerman Basin, part of the Grays Harbor National Wildlife Refuge, offers excellent birdwatching in late April, when more than a million shorebirds gather.

For additional information about the area contact the Grays Harbor Chamber of Commerce, 506 Duffy St., Aberdeen, WA 98520; phone (360) 532-1924 or (800) 321-1924.

F. ARNOLD POLSON PARK AND MUSEUM is on US 101 at 1611 Riverside Ave. The 26-room mansion belonged to lumber entrepreneur Arnold

Polson. The museum provides a pictorial history of the Grays Harbor communities, as well as special exhibits throughout the year. A rose garden is featured in the park. Wed.-Sun. 11-4, mid-June to mid-Sept.; Sat.-Sun. noon-4, rest of year. Admission $2; under 12, 50c. Phone (360) 533-5862.

HOQUIAM'S CASTLE, 515 Chenault Ave., was built in 1897 as the home of lumber industry magnate Robert Lytle. Restored in 1971, the turreted 20-room mansion contains antique furnishings and chandeliers. A re-created early-20th-century saloon also is featured. Allow 30 minutes minimum. Daily 10-5, mid-June to early Sept.; Sat.-Sun. 11-5, Jan. 1 to mid-June and early Sept.-Nov. 30. Admission $4; under 16, $1. Phone (360) 533-2005.

HUMPTULIPS (D-5)

Humptulips, a farming community above the Humptulips River, once served as the logging outlet for the largest stand of Douglas fir in the Northwest. The stand was so dense that loggers had little choice but to fell all timber in the same direction.

HUMPTULIPS SALMON HATCHERY, 1½ mi. w. of US 101, raises chinook, steelhead and coho salmon. Self-guiding tours are available. Daily 8-dusk. Free. Phone (360) 987-2215.

ILWACO (E-4) pop. 800

Protected by tall headlands to the west, Ilwaco lies northeast of Cape Disappointment, regarded as one of the most treacherous river bars in the world. Before jetties were erected to control its sandbar, the mouth of the Columbia River was known as the "Graveyard of the Pacific."

Cape Disappointment Coast Guard Station and Lighthouse, 3¾ miles southeast off US 101, is the home of one of the largest search and rescue facilities in the state; it also houses the Coast Guard's only heavy-weather Motor Lifeboat School. The Cape Disappointment Light Station, commissioned in 1856, is the oldest lighthouse in the Pacific Northwest. North Head Lighthouse, built in 1898, stands on a nearby promontory above Beard's Hollow.

ILWACO HERITAGE MUSEUM, 1 blk. e. of US 101 at 115 S.E. Lake St., depicts frontier life in southwest Washington. Exhibits include Chinook Indian and pioneer artifacts. Displays feature a scale model of an early 20th-century seaside town, a working replica of the local narrow-gauge railway and a working model of the Columbia estuary. Other exhibits portray area shipwrecks, horse sein fishing, and Western and American Indian art.

Mon.-Sat. 9-5, Sun. 10-4; closed Thanksgiving and Dec. 25. Admission $2; over 54 and students with ID $1.75; ages 6-12, 75c. Phone (360) 642-3446.

LEWIS AND CLARK INTERPRETIVE CENTER, 3 mi. s.w. off US 101 in Fort Canby State Park *(see Recreation Chart),* traces the 2½-year, 8,000-mile trek led by Meriwether Lewis and William Clark, with emphasis on the human and historical aspects of the expedition. These exhibits portray medical treatment, foods, entertainment, discipline and the contributions of the Chinook and other tribes toward the trip's success.

Sketches of the explorers and artifacts collected on the expedition are displayed, and a multimedia presentation depicts the highlights of the journey. There is a 200-yard uphill walk to the center. Allow 1 hour minimum. Daily 10-5. Free. Phone (360) 642-3029.

WILLAPA NATIONAL WILDLIFE REFUGE has its headquarters 8½ mi. n. of jct. US 101 and US 101 Alt. The refuge encompasses 11,200 acres of marshland, upland forests, pastures and tidal estuaries. Forested Long Island has a virgin stand of 1,000-year-old red cedars and tidal marshes that support deer, bears, elks, coyotes, beavers, smaller mammals and birds.

More than 180 species of migratory birds have been sighted among the salt marshes and shifting dunes of the Leadbetter Point Unit at the tip of Long Beach Peninsula. Also part of the refuge are the adjoining tidal flats at the southern tip of Willapa Bay. Camping is permitted on the Long Island Unit but accessible by private boat only. Allow 4 hours minimum. Daily 24 hours. Free. Phone (360) 484-3482.

ISSAQUAH (D-7) pop. 7,800, elev. 98′

The Seattle Pacific and Lakeshore Railroad's extension to nearby Squak Mountain in the late 1800s triggered a major coal-mining boom and the settlement of the community of Gilman. The town's name was changed to Issaquah, a Duwamish Indian word meaning "snake," in 1899.

Further information is available from the Greater Issaquah Chamber of Commerce, 155 N.W. Gilman Blvd., Issaquah, WA 98027; phone (206) 392-7024.

Shopping areas: Gilman Village, south of I-90 exit 17 at Gilman Boulevard and Juniper Street, is a complex of restored pioneer houses that contains restaurants and specialty shops. Hand-dipped chocolates are made at Boehm's Chocolate Factory, 255 N.E. Gilman Blvd.

ISSAQUAH STATE SALMON HATCHERY, 125 W. Sunset Way, offers self-guiding tours. Grounds open daily dawn-dusk. Lobby exhibits open daily 8-4:30. Free. Phone (206) 392-3180.

WASHINGTON ZOOLOGICAL PARK, s. of I-90 exit 15 at 19525 S.E. 54th St., is a 16-acre facility that focuses on threatened and endangered species. This teaching zoo houses almost 300 animals representing 30 species of mammals and birds. Tues.-Sat. 10-5, Sun. 11-5, Mar.-Oct.; Tues.-Sat. 10-4, Sun. 11-4, rest of year. Closed Jan. 1, Thanksgiving and Dec. 24-26 and 31. Admission $4.50; over 64, $4; ages 4-15, $3.50; ages 2-3, $2.50. MC, VI. Phone (206) 391-5508.

KAHLOTUS (E-11) pop. 200, elev. 896′

LOWER MONUMENTAL LOCK AND DAM, 6 mi. s. on Devil's Canyon Rd., has a 100-foot navigational lock, fish ladder, powerhouse overlook, picnic sites and a visitor center with a fish-viewing room. Allow 30 minutes minimum. Daily dawn-dusk, Apr.-Oct. Free. Phone (509) 547-7781. *See Recreation Chart.*

KALAMA (F-6) pop. 1,200

Founded in the 1840s, Kalama is named for Hawaiian native John Kalama, who settled in the area after marrying the daughter of a Nisqually chief. In addition to being a busy shipping center, Kalama claims two superlatives: a 140-foot single-tree totem pole, in Marine Park, and the first fish hatchery in the state. The latter has been replaced by two newer hatcheries. Nearly 100 antique dealers are in malls and individual shops on N. 1st Street.

Hart Brewing Co./Pyramid Ales, 101 W. Marine Dr. at the south end of the Port of Kalama Marina, specializes in hand-crafted ales brewed in the Northwest style. Free informal 20-minute tours are offered. Phone (360) 673-2962.

For further information contact the Kalama Chamber of Commerce, P.O. Box 824, Kalama, WA 98825; phone (360) 673-6299.

KELSO (F-6) pop. 11,800, elev. 26′

The dramatic and much-lauded run of smelt up the Cowlitz River in January and February has earned Kelso the title "Smelt Capital of the World." Also plentiful are steelhead and sturgeon, making Kelso an important fishing and canning center.

For further information contact the Kelso Chamber of Commerce, 105 Minor Rd., Kelso, WA 98626; phone (360) 577-8058.

Shopping areas: Kelso's major shopping center is Three Rivers Mall, just west of I-5 exit 39 at Allen Street and SR 4. The mall contains The Bon, The Emporium, JCPenney and Sears.

COWLITZ COUNTY HISTORICAL MUSEUM, 405 Allen St., recounts the history of the area in its reproductions of pioneer rooms and a general store. The main gallery contains the exhibit "Cowlitz Corridor: Footpath to Freeway," portraying settlement and transportation from the period prior to European settlement to the present.

Other exhibits include portions of a loggers' bunkhouse, a railroad depot, a 1925 Model "T" truck, a reassembled log cabin with period furnishings, an Cowlitz Indian canoe and other Cowlitz artifacts. One gallery is devoted to temporary exhibits. Allow 30 minutes minimum. Tues.-Sat. 9-5, Sun. 1-5; closed holidays. Free. Phone (360) 577-3119.

KELSO VOLCANO TOURIST INFORMATION CENTER is off I-5 exit 39 at 105 Minor Rd. The information center documents the 1980 eruption of Mount St. Helens. Displays include photographs, rock and pumice samples, a memorial list of those who perished in the eruption and a 15-foot scale model of the volcano and the Toutle River Valley with a recorded narrative. Allow 30 minutes minimum. Daily 8-6, May-Oct.; Wed.-Sun. 9-5, rest of year. Free. Phone (360) 577-8058.

KENNEWICK (F-10) pop. 42,200, elev. 362′

Meaning "winter paradise" in the Yakama Indian tongue, Kennewick was surrounded by a bunchgrass wasteland until the late 1800s, when the first of a series of irrigation projects began to convert the sagebrush into farmland. Promoted by a brief winter season, the fertile land became the best grape-producing area in the state. The 1957 Kennewick Highland irrigation project supplies water to 20,500 acres of alfalfa, corn and beans.

Reinforced by the huge hydroelectric dams harnessing the lower bend of the Columbia River, Kennewick's economy also is supported by chemical and agricultural processing. Kennewick, Pasco and Richland *(see place listings)* form the urban Tri-Cities area.

Near the confluence of the Columbia, Snake and Yakima rivers, Kennewick is the departure point for various scenic and recreational cruises on the Columbia River. Lake Wallula features developed recreational facilities at Columbia Park *(see Recreation Chart).* Tuesday through Sunday, youngsters can experience a variety of hands-on learning and play experiences at the Three Rivers Children's Museum at 873 Columbia Center; phone (509) 783-6311.

For further information contact the Kennewick Chamber of Commerce, 3180 W. Clearwater, #F, P.O. Box 6986, Kennewick, WA 99336; phone (509) 736-0510.

Shopping areas: Kennewick's major shopping mall is Columbia Center, 3 miles north of I-82 exit 109 on Badger Road. Stores include The Bon, JCPenney, Lamonts and Sears.

EAST BENTON COUNTY HISTORICAL MUSEUM, 205 Keewaydin Dr., contains historical photographs and displays illustrating the area's beginnings in agriculture, business and education. Allow 30 minutes minimum. Tues.-Sat. noon-4; closed major holidays. Donations. Phone (509) 582-7704.

OASIS WATERWORKS, 6321 W. Canal Dr., is a 9-acre amusement park with waterslides, a river ride, swimming pools, basketball and volleyball courts, batting cages, a game arcade, spa and picnic sites. Sun.-Thurs. 10-6:30, Fri.-Sat. 10-9:30, Memorial Day weekend-Labor Day (weather permitting). All-day admission $12.50, over 55 and under 3 free. Reduced admission daily from 2:30-6:30 and Fri.-Sat. from 6:30-9:30 p.m. Phone (509) 735-8442.

KEYPORT (F-2) pop. 300, elev. 43′

NAVAL UNDERSEA MUSEUM PREVIEW CENTER, 3 mi. e. of SR 3 on SR 308 to the main access road to Naval Warfare Ct., uses audio and visual effects to create the atmosphere of the undersea world. Mythology, legends and a historical timeline illustrate the development and innovations of sea exploration. A 15-minute slide presentation is shown in the orientation theater. The museum facility itself is scheduled to open in the fall of 1995. Allow 30 minutes minimum. Tues.-Sun. 10-4, June-Sept.; Tues.-Sat. 10-4, rest of year. Closed Jan. 1, Thanksgiving and Dec. 25. Free. Phone (360) 396-4148.

KIRKLAND (F-3) pop. 40,100, elev. 100′

Kirkland, the city with more public waterfront than any other in the state, has capitalized on its prime location by evolving into a major boating center. The many lakefront beaches and accompanying activities—sailing, windsurfing, swimming and fishing—add to Kirkland's appeal.

For further information contact the Greater Kirkland Chamber of Commerce, 356 Parkplace Center, Kirkland, WA 98033; phone (206) 822-7066.

Shopping areas: Kirkland Parkplace, 1 mile west of I-405 exit 18, contains specialty shops and clothing stores. Totem Lake Mall, northeast of I-405 exit 20B, is the major local shopping center and features a Lamonts.

LAKE WASHINGTON CRUISES depart from Kirkland Marina Park, 1¼ mi. w. off I-405 exit 18. The 1½-hour narrated tours of the Lake Washington shoreline offer a glimpse of luxurious waterfront homes and mountain scenery.

Shoreline cruises depart daily at 11, 1, 3 and 5, Memorial Day-Labor Day; at 1 and 3, May 1-Day before Memorial Day and in Sept.; otherwise varies. Fare $14.80; over 64, $11; ages 5-12, $5.30. MC, VI. Phone (206) 623-4252.

PETER KIRK BUILDING, ¼ mi. n. at 620 Market St., was built in 1891. The Kirkland Arts Center and Fine Arts School displays a variety of works by Northwestern artists. Tues.-Fri. 11-6, Sat. 11-4. Free. Phone (206) 822-7161.

KLONDIKE GOLD RUSH NATIONAL HISTORICAL PARK—*see Seattle.*

LACEY (H-3) pop. 24,300, elev. 185′

Lacey, a suburban community just east of Olympia, was first called Woodland, honoring pioneer Isaac Woods who settled here in 1852. By the 1890s Lacey boasted a sawmill, resort hotel and the region's major horse racing track. To avoid confusion with a like-named town in southern Washington, the name was changed to Lacey.

Tudor-style buildings dominate the campus of St. Martins College, founded in 1895 by the Order of St. Benedict. Tolmie State Park *(see Recreation Chart),* 4½ miles west of I-5 exit 111, features 1800 feet of shoreline on Puget Sound, a saltwater marsh and a 2½-mile nature trail. The near shore waters are popular with scuba divers.

For further information contact the Lacey Thurston County Chamber of Commerce, 701 Sleater-Kinney S.E., #7, Lacey, WA 98503; phone (360) 491-4141.

LACEY MUSEUM, 829½ Lacey St., occupies a renovated farmhouse that has served as a fire station, police station and town hall. Exhibits include a pioneer schoolroom, kitchen, early clothing and historical photographs illustrating farming, logging and fishing industries. Allow 30 minutes minimum. Thurs.-Sat. 10-4; closed Jan 1, Easter, Thanksgiving and Dec. 25. Free. Phone (360) 438-0209.

NISQUALLY NATIONAL WILDLIFE REFUGE, 7 mi. e. to I-5 exit 114, then ½ mi. n. on Brown Farm Rd., protects the Nisqually delta and the plant and animal life dependent upon it. The combination of salt- and freshwater marshes, tideflats, forests, grasslands and streams provides habitats for a variety of birds, mammals and reptiles.

The refuge is accessible only by foot trail; 8 miles of trails, varying in length from ½ to 5½ miles, wind through the refuge. A birdwatching platform, interpretive center, fishing facilities and refuge literature are available. Pets and bicycles are not permitted. Daily dawn-dusk. Admission $2, under 15 free. Phone (360) 753-9467.

LA CONNER (C-3) pop. 700

La Conner's docks, bait shops, galleries and museums embody the classic sights and sounds of a late-19th-century fishing port. Many historic buildings remain intact, including a log cabin built in 1869 by Magnus Anderson, one of the area's first settlers. Boats offering fishing and sightseeing cruises are available for charter at the La Conner Marina.

For further information contact the La Conner Chamber of Commerce in the Maple Center Building on Main St., P.O. Box 1610, La Conner, WA 98257; phone (360) 466-4778.

Self-guiding tours: Maps outlining a walking tour of the historic district are available at the Skagit County Historical Museum *(see attraction listing).*

Shopping areas: Clothing stores, art galleries and a variety of specialty shops can be found downtown on 1st Street between Morris and Douglas Hill streets.

GACHES MANSION, 2nd and Calhoun sts., is a restored 1891 Victorian house partially furnished in period. Fri.-Sun. 1-5, Apr.-Sept.; 1-4, rest of year. Admission $2. Phone (360) 466-4288.

The Valley Museum of Northwest Art, on the second floor of the mansion, displays a fine collection of paintings and sculpture characteristic of the Northwest School. Phone (360) 466-4446.

SKAGIT COUNTY HISTORICAL MUSEUM, n. of Benton St. at 501 S. 4th St., displays farm implements, logging equipment, pioneer relics and other items from the early settlement period. Also featured are a model blacksmith shop, a recreated general store, and a farmhouse kitchen, parlor and bedroom. In addition to the Hands on History permanent exhibit, the east wing offers special changing exhibits. The museum's balcony affords panoramas of the Skagit River Valley.

Allow 1 hour minimum. Tues.-Sun. 11-5; closed Jan. 1 and Dec. 25. Admission $2; over 64 and ages 6-12, $1; family rate $5. Phone (360) 466-3365.

VIKING CRUISES, 109 N. 1st, offers a 2-hour cruise through Deception Pass in a rigid-hulled inflatable jet boat. Sights along the way may include working tug boats, commercial fishing boats and a variety of wildlife, including eagles and harbor seals. A 3-day cruise to the San Juan Islands is available. Allow 2 hours minimum. Trips depart Wed.-Sun. at noon and 3, June-Sept. Fare $49; ages 6-12, $39. MC, VI. Phone (360) 466-2639.

LAKE CHELAN NATIONAL RECREATION AREA (B-8)

Accessible only by boat or charter float plane from Chelan *(see place listing)* or by trail, Lake Chelan National Recreation Area forms the southern tip of the North Cascades National Park Service complex. The approximately 62,000-acre area is at the northern end of Lake Chelan, one of the deepest lakes in the country and one of Washington's largest inland bodies of fresh water.

Deer, bears and marmots are among the animals that live in the mountains surrounding the Stehekin Valley. The only town within the recreation area is remote Stehekin, whose name means "the way through" in the Chelan Indian tongue. Free camping permits and recreation information are available at the ranger station Mon.-Fri. 8-4:30.

The Golden West Visitor Center, open daily 10-5, June-Sept., uses exhibits to explain local history. Park rangers lead naturalist walks and conduct evening slide presentations. Recreational opportunities range from short day hikes to overnight camping to strenuous mountain climbing; boating and fishing are popular in Lake Chelan and nearby streams.

Several trails traverse the area; most follow the creeks that flow into the Stehekin River. A particularly spectacular site is Rainbow Falls; rafting trips and trail rides are offered by Cascade Corrals, 3 blocks from Stehekin Landing.

The National Park Service provides shuttle bus service from the North Cascades Lodge in Stehekin to various trailheads. For information about trail conditions, transportation and recreation opportunities contact the Superintendent's Office, Lake Chelan National Recreation Area, P.O. Box 549, Chelan, WA 98816; phone (509) 682-2549. *See Recreation Chart.*

LEAVENWORTH (D-8) pop. 1,700, elev. 1,164'

Modeled after a Bavarian village, Leavenworth serves as a year-round recreation area. Local events include the Maifest in early May, the Washington State Autumn Leaf Festival in early October and the Christmas Lighting Festival in early December. Art displays are featured in City Park on weekends from May to October. A bridge in Waterfront Park leads to nature trails on 15-acre Blackbird Island.

The Wenatchee River between Leavenworth and Monitor is one of Washington's most popular rafting streams. Relatively calm stretches alternate with class III and IV rapids. Several outfitters offer all-inclusive white-water trips from May to early July, including Adventures with Wenatchee Whitewater, (509) 763-3307 or (800) 395-7238; Alpine Whitewater, (509) 548-4159 or (800) 926-7238; Leavenworth Outfitters, (509) 763-3733; Northern Wilderness River Riders, (509) 548-4583 or (206) 485-7238; and Osprey Rafting Co., (509) 548-6800 or (800) 743-6269.

A mile northwest of Leavenworth, US 2 parallels the Wenatchee River through the scenic Tumwater Canyon, which blazes with color in the fall.

For further information contact the Leavenworth Chamber of Commerce, 894 US 2, P.O. Box 327, Leavenworth, WA 98826; phone (509) 548-5807. *See ad p. A96.*

Shopping areas: Dozens of specialty shops line Front Street in downtown Leavenworth.

LEAVENWORTH NATIONAL FISH HATCHERY is 2 mi. s. on Icicle Rd. The hatchery is part of the Grand Coulee Dam project. More than 2.5 million chinook salmon are raised at the hatchery annually. Allow 30 minutes minimum. Daily 7:30-4. Free. Phone (509) 548-7641.

LEBAM (E-5)

Just east of the Willapa Hills and the Willapa River, the former logging town of Lebam got its name from founder J.W. Goodell, who simply took his daughter Mabel's name and spelled it backwards.

WILLAPA SALMON HATCHERY, 2 mi. w. on SR 6, raises more than 2 million chinook and 700,000 coho salmon a year. Especially interesting are a trap for adult fish, open September through November, and the incubation facilities, open October through March. Allow 30 minutes minimum. Daily 8-4:30. Free. Phone (360) 934-5457.

LIBERTY (D-8) elev. 2,417′

One of the oldest mining towns in the state, Liberty was established as Williams Creek in 1880. It flourished, reaching a population of 200 in its heyday. Today Liberty consists of only a small store and gift shop. Several small mines still operate in the area, and agate beds are found on Red Top Mountain.

LONG BEACH (E-4) pop. 1,200

A popular oyster farming and vacation center, Long Beach is at the southern end of Long Beach Peninsula, known for 28 miles of hard sand beach. Area sports include surf fishing, swimming, boating and deep-sea fishing. Among the peninsula's scenic viewpoints are Cape Disappointment and North Head lighthouses *(see Ilwaco),* North Jetty and Beard's Hollow. About 230 ships have been wrecked near Cape Disappointment.

A 12-foot-wide elevated boardwalk extends along 2,300 feet of beachfront. It has three observation platforms with telescopes and interpretive displays of natural history. The main access point is at the foot of Bolstad Street, off SR 103. The Washington State International Kite Festival is held in late August.

For further information contact the Long Beach Peninsula Visitors Bureau at the junction of US 101 and SR 103, P.O. Box 562, Long Beach, WA 98631; phone (360) 642-2400 or (800) 451-2542.

CLARKE RHODODENDRON NURSERY is 1¼ mi. n. on SR 103, then 1½ mi. e. on Pioneer Rd. and 2¼ mi. n. on Sandridge Rd. The nursery specializes in rhododendrons and azaleas; the peak blooming season is in May. Daily 8-5; closed Thanksgiving and Dec. 25. Free. Phone (360) 642-2241.

WORLD KITE MUSEUM & HALL OF FAME, jct. SR 103 and 3rd St., displays more than 600 kites from around the world. A special collection features elaborate hand-made kites from China and Japan. Allow 30 minutes minimum. Daily 11-5, June-Aug.; Sat.-Sun. 11-5, rest of year. Closed Dec. 25. Admission $1; over 61 and under 17, 50c; family rate $3. Phone (360) 642-4020.

LONGVIEW (F-5) pop. 31,500, elev. 13′

Founded in 1923, Longview is a planned city and a leading industrial port. Monticello Convention Site, a small park at 18th, Maple and Olympia avenues, commemorates the place where Cowlitz Valley and Puget Sound settlers met in 1852 to petition for the creation of a separate territory north of the Columbia River. Their wish was granted; the Washington and Oregon territories were divided by an act of Congress in 1853.

The Nutty Narrows Bridge is a 60-foot skybridge specially designed to provide squirrels a safe passage over Olympia Way near Longview's Civic Center.

For further information contact the Longview Chamber of Commerce, 1563 Olympia Way, Longview, WA 98632; phone (360) 423-8400.

PORT OF LONGVIEW, 2 mi. s. off SR 433 on Port Way, offers guided tours of port facilities, including ship-loading, cargo-moving and warehouse operations. Tours depart the port office Mon.-Fri. at 10:30 and 1:30, July 1-Labor Day; by appointment, rest of year. Free. Reservations are required. Phone (360) 425-3305.

LYNDEN (A-3) pop. 5,700, elev. 103′

First settled in the 1860s, Lynden became home to miners returning from the gold rush of 1858. Other homesteaders followed and together they turned the valley into fertile farmland. This attracted many Dutch immigrants at the beginning of the 20th century, and Lynden evolved into a prosperous agricultural region and one of the largest dairy centers in the nation. Other important crops include berries, potatoes and peas.

For further information contact the Lynden Chamber of Commerce, 444 Front St., #252, P.O. Box 647, Lynden, WA 98264; phone (360) 354-5995.

LYNDEN PIONEER MUSEUM, 217 Front St., focuses on early-20th-century life. A pioneer street includes a railroad depot, hotel, drugstore, barn, barnyard and farmhouse with period furnishings. Other displays include antique cars, buggies, farm equipment and Coast Salish Indian artifacts. Allow 1 hour minimum. Mon.-Sat. 10-5, Apr.-Oct.; Mon.-Sat. 10-4, rest of year. Donations. Phone (360) 354-3675.

MARYHILL (G-8)

Maryhill was founded in 1907 by Samuel Hill, who thought the sunny site had the makings of an agricultural utopia. An eccentric lawyer and pacifist Quaker, Hill also was a talented road and monument builder; his works include the International Peace Arch in Blaine *(see place listing)* and the Columbia River Scenic Highway on the Oregon side of the Columbia River Gorge.

★**MARYHILL MUSEUM OF ART,** on SR 14, 2¾ mi. w. of US 97, is in the castle-like former home of Northwest entrepreneur Samuel Hill. Dedicated by Queen Marie of Roumania in 1926, the museum opened in 1940. European and

American paintings are complemented by a collection of Auguste Rodin sculptures and watercolors, 19th-century French art glass and 18th-century Russian icons.

Other highlights include Hill photographs and memorabilia, American Indian basketry and artifacts, the Théâtre de la Mode French mannequin gallery, international chess sets and personal items and royal furnishings donated by Queen Marie. The works displayed in the Contemporary Northwest Artists Gallery are changed during the season. A visible storage gallery allows visitors a glimpse of the museum's weapons collection, Hill's death mask and busts of famous figures throughout history. Three or four special exhibitions are staged each season. Special events, including lectures, film sreenings and concerts, are offered throughout the season.

Picnicking is permitted. Food is available. Allow 1 hour minimum. Daily 9-5, Mar. 15-Nov. 15. Admission $4; over 62, $3.50; ages 6-16, $1.50. MC, VI. **Discount.** Phone (509) 773-3733.

STONEHENGE, 1 mi. e. of jct. US 97 and SR 14, then ¾ mi. s., is on a cliff overlooking the Columbia River. A 1918 concrete replica of the 4,000-year-old Stonehenge in Wiltshire, England, this is a memorial to the men of Klickitat killed in World War I. Because it was built 40 years before the position of Stonehenge was decoded for astronomical measurement, this reproduction is not exact. The crypt of the monument's builder, Maryhill founder Samuel Hill, is a short walk southwest of the replica. Daily 7 a.m.-10 p.m. Free.

MATTAWA (E-9) pop. 900, elev. 777′

Priest Rapids and Wanapum *(see Vantage)* dams, two major hydroelectric dams built on the Columbia River in the 1950s, created Priest Rapids and Wanapum lakes. Both reservoirs feature several public recreation areas.

For further information contact the Mattawa Area Chamber of Commerce, P.O. Box 1446, Mattawa, WA 99344; phone (509) 932-5015.

PRIEST RAPIDS DAM, 5½ mi. s. on SR 243, then 1½ mi. w., can generate nearly 800,000 kilowatts of power. Picnicking is permitted. Free.

METALINE FALLS (A-12) pop. 200

Prospectors who settled on the west bank of the Pend Oreille River founded Metaline Falls in 1909. Just east of town is the Colville National Forest's Salmo-Priest Wilderness Area.

BOUNDARY DAM, n. off SR 31, houses a huge underground powerhouse. Seattle City Light's vista house offers excellent views of the dam. Allow 1 hour minimum. Daily 9:30-3:45. Tours are offered Thurs.-Mon. 10:30-4:30, Memorial Day weekend-Labor Day. Free. Phone (509) 446-3073.

GARDNER CAVE, 11 mi. n. in Crawford State Park, has 1,055 feet of passageway and is reputed to be the second largest limestone cavern in the state. Picnic facilities are available. Allow 1 hour minimum. Guided tours are given Sat.-Sun. and holidays at 10, noon, 2 and 4, May-Sept. (weather permitting). Free. Phone (509) 446-4065 or 456-4169.

MILES (C-11)

FORT SPOKANE, just s. off SR 25, is in the Coulee Dam National Recreation Area *(see place listing)*. The 19th-century military outpost was built to ensure peaceful relations between the Colville and Spokane Indians and the white settlers. A visitor center and museum are in the brick guardhouse, one of four remaining outpost buildings. A self-guiding trail follows the old parade grounds. Historical interpretive programs are offered in the summer.

Allow 1 hour, 30 minutes minimum. Daily 9:30-5:30, July 1-Labor Day; Sat.-Sun. 9-4, mid-Mar. through June 30 and day after Labor Day to mid-Nov. Free. Phone (509) 725-2715.

MONTESANO (D-5) pop. 3,100

Founded in the 1850s near the confluence of the Chehalis and Wynoochee rivers, Montesano is a trading center for regional farming and lumber businesses. The Grays Harbor County Court House's indoor murals depict area history, including Capt. Robert Gray's discovery of Grays Harbor in 1792. Saturday and Sunday afternoons, the Chehalis Valley Historical Museum, 7 blocks w. of Main St. at 703 W. Pioneer Ave., documents the role of the area's forest products industry; phone (360) 249-5800.

Montesano is known as the birthplace of commercial forestry's tree-farm system. Weyerhaeuser established the Clemons Tree Farm in 1941; today the farm sprawls over 200,000 acres. Lake Sylvia State Park *(see Recreation Chart)*, 1 mile north of town off US 12 exit 104, is the site of the county's first sawmill. Along the park's 2-mile Sylvia Creek Forestry Trail, 15 interpretive markers describe management of a working forest.

For further information contact the Montesano Chamber of Commerce, P.O. Box 688, Montesano, WA 98563; phone (360) 249-5522.

MOSES LAKE (D-10) pop. 11,200

With the completion of Grand Coulee Dam, recreational facilities developed in the region south of Moses Lake. The porosity of the underlying lava rock permitted water to seep from the reservoirs and reappear miles away, forming lakes in almost every depression.

For further information contact the Moses Lake Chamber of Commerce, 324 S. Pioneer Way, Moses Lake, WA 98837; phone (509) 765-7888.

ADAM EAST MUSEUM AND ART CENTER, 122 W. 3rd Ave., contains American Indian artifacts and exhibits that highlight local history. Art exhibits are displayed in the gallery. Tues.-Sat. 11-5. Free. Phone (509) 766-9395.

MOSSYROCK (E-6) pop. 500

COWLITZ SALMON HATCHERY is 12 mi. w. on US 12, then 1½ mi. s. on Fuller and Spencer rds. Facilities for raising chinook and coho salmon include incubation equipment, salmon-sorting and fish-loading machinery, a fish ladder and a barrier dam. About 15 million salmon are released annually to accommodate the spring and fall runs. Visitors can view spawning salmon from September to mid-January. Hatchery open daily 8-4:30. Free. Phone (360) 985-2655.

MAYFIELD DAM, 5½ mi. w. on US 12, then 1¼ mi. s. on Gershick Rd., crosses a gorge along the Cowlitz River to form 13-mile-long Mayfield Lake. An overlook offers fine views. Mayfield Lake County Park and Ike Kinswa State Park *(see Recreation Chart)* border the lake.

MOSSYROCK DAM, 3 mi. e., forms 23-mile-long Riffe Lake. Hydrovista offers an overlook and interpretive displays of the hydroelectric project. Picnicking is permitted. Mossyrock Park *(see Recreation Chart)* is on the southwest corner of the lake. Daily 24 hours. Free.

MOUNT BAKER-SNOQUALMIE NATIONAL FOREST

Elevations in the forest range from 280 ft. along the Skykomish River east of Gold Bar, to 10,778 ft. at the summit of Mount Baker. Refer to AAA maps for additional information.

The 1,700,000-acre Mount Baker-Snoqualmie National Forest covers the western slopes of the Cascades from the Canadian border to the northern boundary of Mount Rainier National Park.

Some of the state's most primitive regions are within the forest. Mount Baker, at 10,778 feet, dominates the northern section and is the site of Sherman Crater's thermal activity, which began in 1975. The Mount Baker Wilderness surrounds the volcano. Glacier Peak, at 10,568 feet, towers over the central part of the forest; the Glacier Peak Wilderness lies between Stevens Pass and North Cascades National Park. In the high country between Snoqualmie Pass and Stevens Pass is Alpine Lakes Wilderness.

Four east-west highways provide scenic drives—I-90, US 2, SR 20 and SR 410. National Scenic Byways include the Mount Baker Highway (SR 542) from Glacier to Artist Point, and the Stevens Pass Highway (US 2) east from Gold Bar to Leavenworth. Mountain Loop Highway also is a National Scenic Byway leading into the heart of the western Cascades. From Granite Falls it parallels the South Fork of the Stillaguamish River past Mount Pilchuck, numerous forest service campgrounds and old mine sites.

Silverton, 22 miles east, is a former gold- and silver-mining center. The road beyond is closed from November until April or May. Four miles past Silverton a 1-mile trail leads to the Big Four Ice Caves.

From Barlow Pass the partly gravel road leads north to Darrington. The road to Monte Cristo, an important 1890s gold-mining town, is closed indefinitely due to washouts but is accessible to hikers. Check road conditions at Darrington Ranger Station; phone (360) 436-1155.

Wildlife abounds and fish are plentiful. Pack trips and hiking are popular, particularly along the Pacific Crest National Scenic Trail, the Washington portion of which runs along the north-south crest of the Cascades for more than 500 miles from the Columbia River to the British Columbia border. Camping and winter sports also are available. Crystal Mountain Ski Resort *(see Crystal Mountain)*, 41 miles east of Enumclaw off SR 410, runs its Midway Shuttle and Rainier Express chairlifts daily, July to early September.

Four other ski areas are at Snoqualmie Pass Summit on I-90; still more are at Mount Baker at the end of SR 542 and Stevens Pass on US 2. Visitor information is available at ranger stations in Darrington, Enumclaw, North Bend, Sedro Woolley and Skykomish; public service centers at Glacier and Verlot and a visitors center at Snoqualmie Pass are open late May to late September.

For further information contact the Forest Supervisor's Office, Mount Baker-Snoqualmie National Forest, 21905 64th Ave. W., Mountlake Terrace, WA 98043; phone (206) 775-9702. For recreation information contact the Outdoor Recreation Information Center, 915 2nd Ave., Room 442, Seattle, WA 98174; phone (206) 220-7450. *See Recreation Chart and the AAA Northwestern CampBook.*

★MOUNT RAINIER NATIONAL PARK (E-7)

See map page 136.

Elevations in the forest range from 1,760 ft. at the Carbon River entrance station, to 14,411 ft. at the summit of Mount Rainier. Refer to AAA maps for additional information.

Mount Rainier National Park has four entrances: the Nisqually, off SR 706 in the southwest; the Carbon River, on Carbon River Road in the northwest; the White River, on White River Road off SR 410 in the northeast; and the Stevens Canyon Road entrance in the southeast.

Mount Rainier, a towering, ice-clad volcano rising 14,411 feet, is a striking landmark in the Pacific Northwest. The cap of glacial ice that conceals all but a few crags and ridges makes it doubly impressive. Although Mount Rainier currently is dormant, it is not considered extinct. It belongs to the class of exploding volcanoes, much like recently awakened Mount St. Helens, and quite conceivably could one day erupt in a similar manner.

Although mere remnants of their former size, Rainier's 34 square miles of glaciers constitute the largest single-peak glacial system in the contiguous United States: 26 glaciers extend down the mountainside. Six of them—Nisqually, Ingraham, Emmons, Winthrop, Kautz and Tahoma—originate in the summit ice cap. Many other major glaciers are born of snows in valley heads, or cirques, between 10,000 and 12,000 feet; the most notable of these are Cowlitz, Carbon, Russell, North and South Mowich and Puyallup glaciers.

Forests cover the mountainsides up to 5,000 feet, where alpine meadows of wildflowers and grass contrast with masses of ice at higher elevations. The timberline is at about 6,500 feet. Deer, bears and mountain goats inhabit the forests, meadows and ridges. Park animals, either large and small, should not be fed; all food should be kept locked up or out of the reach of wildlife.

Flowers in the high meadows bloom from late June to mid-August. Huckleberries, vine maple and mountain ash grow throughout the park; fall colors are at their best from late September to early October.

General Information and Activities

The park is open daily. Only the Nisqually (southwest) entrance and Nisqually-Paradise Road are open all year, unless storms or avalanches threaten passage. All other roads are closed from late October or the first snowfall, whichever comes first, to somewhere between late April and early June, depending upon the occurrence of snowfalls. Cayuse Pass, between the northern boundary on SR 410 to Ohanapecosh, is usually closed from early December to early May. The road between Chinook Pass and Cayuse Pass is closed from mid-November to late May.

Naturalists conduct free guided and illustrated talks from late June through Labor Day at Longmire, Paradise, Sunrise, Carbon River and Ohanapecosh; schedules are posted at visitor centers.

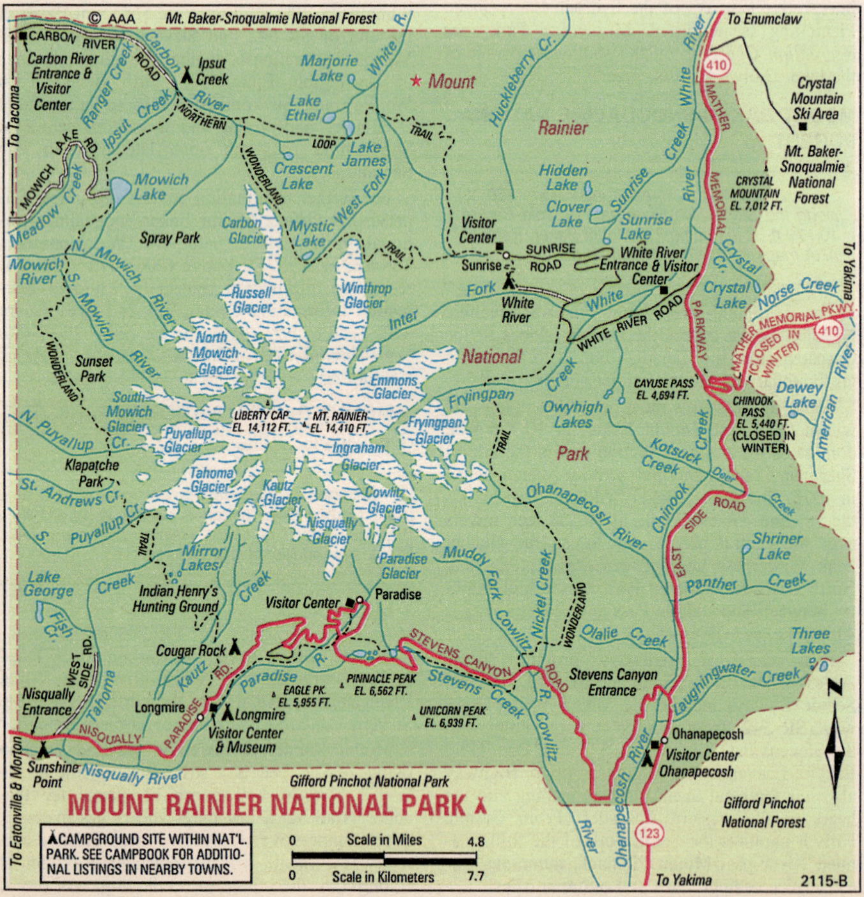

Snowshoe walks are conducted at Paradise from late December to early April. Self-guiding nature trails and wayside exhibits are found throughout the park. Hiker information centers are at Longmire and White River.

Permits are required for overnight backpacking. Sightseeing flights can be arranged through private operators in Morton and Puyallup. Information concerning roads, camps and programs can be obtained by contacting the Park Superintendent's office. For information about the park's inns write Mount Rainier Guest Services, Box 108, Ashford, WA 98304; phone (360) 569-2275. *See color ad p. 179.*

Special regulations apply to climbers; details are available from the Park Superintendent. Rainier Mountaineering Inc., at Paradise, conducts climbing schools and seminars as well as guided climbs. For details write Rainier Mountaineering Inc., 535 Dock St., Suite 209, Tacoma, WA 98402; from June through September, write Mount Rainier National Park, Rainier Mountaineering Inc., Paradise, WA 98398. June through September phone (360) 569 2227.

Trout fishing is permitted without a license; check at a ranger station for special regulations. Hunting is prohibited. Winter sports and a snow play area are available at Paradise from late December into early April (weather permitting). Snowmobiles are permitted only on designated roads. *See Recreation Chart and the AAA Northwestern CampBook.*

VISITOR CENTERS offer a variety of free information and exhibits.

Henry M. Jackson Visitor Center at Paradise has exhibits, audiovisual programs and an observation deck. Daily 9-7, mid-June through Labor Day; daily 9-6, mid-May to mid-June and day after Labor Day-Oct. 31; Sat.-Sun. 10-5, rest of year.

Longmire Museum has interesting rock, flora and fauna and history exhibits. Daily 9-5:30, June-Sept.; Sat.-Sun. 9-4:30, rest of year.

Ohanapecosh Visitor Center has exhibits about forest ecology and the history of the park. Daily 9-6, mid-June through Sept. 30; Sat.-Sun. 9-5, Memorial Day weekend to mid-June and Oct. 1-late Oct.

Sunrise Visitor Center presents geological displays. Daily 9-6, July 1 to mid-Sept.

ADMISSION to the park is by weekly pass, which costs $5 per private vehicle or $3 per person on foot or bicycle. Annual passes cost $15. Campground fees are $6-$10 per private vehicle.

PETS are permitted only if they are on a leash or are otherwise physically restrained at all times. Dogs and cats are not allowed on the trails or in buildings.

ADDRESS general inquiries to the Superintendent, Mount Rainier National Park, Tahoma Woods—Star Route, Ashford, WA 98304; phone (206) 569-2211.

Roads and Trails

More than 140 miles of roads and 300 miles of trails are open to the public. Trail maps are available at all visitor centers. Permits are required for back-country camping.

CARBON RIVER ROAD is a secondary road through virgin forests. It ends at Ipsut Creek Campground, which has limited camping facilities and access to back-country trails.

EAST SIDE ROAD (SR 123) extends across the eastern section of the park from Ohanapecosh to SR 410 at Cayuse Pass. The Stevens Canyon Road intersection is 2 miles north of Ohanapecosh. Tipsoo Lake and Chinook Pass are 5 miles east of Cayuse Pass on SR 410; excellent panoramas of Mount Rainier, Governors Ridge, the Pacific Crest National Scenic Trail and the high country of the Cascade Mountains are available from this site.

MOWICH LAKE ROAD, dirt and gravel surfaced, is open from early July to late October (weather permitting). Although it is not a through road, the lake road serves as a trailhead for those taking trips into the back country. Camping is permitted at a designated campsite along the lake, but campfires are prohibited.

NISQUALLY-PARADISE ROAD, from the s.w. entrance, connects with West Side Rd., 1 mi. from the park entrance. On the way to Paradise Valley are the Kautz Mudflow area; a museum at Longmire; Christine Falls; the trail to 320-foot Comet Falls, accessible only in summer; and 168-foot Narada Falls. The road is open all year but chains may be required in winter months.

NORTHERN LOOP TRAIL runs 17½ mi. from Carbon River to Sunrise. It climbs through rugged Windy Gap, intersects with a trail leading to Natural Bridge and passes Lake James, Grand and Berkeley parks and Frozen Lake. By combining the section of the Wonderland Trail from Sunrise past Mystic Lake and the Winthrop Glacier, this trail can be extended to a 36-mile loop back to Carbon River. The trail is free of snow only from late July to mid-September.

STEVENS CANYON ROAD, furnishing an east-west connection in the park, leaves Nisqually-Paradise Rd. about 1 mi. beyond Narada Falls. The effects of glacial and water erosion are apparent at the Box Canyon of the Cowlitz River. Picnicking is permitted a half-mile west.

There are excellent views of Mount Rainier, Mount Adams and the Tatoosh Range along this route, which intersects East Side Road 2 miles above Ohanapecosh; the best views are westbound. The road is open Memorial Day to mid-Oct. (weather permitting).

WEST SIDE ROAD, improved but not surfaced, leaves Nisqually-Paradise Road 1 mile from the park entrance, providing access to the west side trailheads. The road is closed indefinitely at milemarker 3; beyond that point the right-of-way is accessible to hikers. It is not a through road and is often closed due to bad weather or high water damage. Check locally for conditions.

WHITE RIVER ROAD, from the n.e. entrance to the Sunrise area, passes Fryingpan Creek; White River Campground and the trail to the moraine of Emmons Glacier; and Sunrise Point, offering a panorama of the crest of the Cascades. The road is open early July-late Oct. (weather permitting).

WONDERLAND TRAIL, which encircles the mountain, is divided into different portions. The 30-mile section from Paradise to Sunrise passes lakes, falls and Box Canyon, which is noted as one of the most unusual river canyons in America. From Sunrise to Carbon River—16½ miles—hikers enter the primitive area of the park to see Winthrop Glacier, Mystic Lake and Carbon Glacier.

From Carbon River to Longmire, a 39-mile stretch, the trail passes Mowich Lake, Golden Lakes, Sunset Park, Klapatche Park, Indian Henry's Hunting Ground and other points of interest. The 6½-mile section from Longmire to Paradise passes Carter, Madcap and Narada falls. Travel on the Wonderland Trail is recommended only from mid-July to mid-Sept.

Note: Until further notice, West Side Road is closed 3 miles north of Nisqually-Paradise Road; beyond that point the right-of-way is accessible to hikers.

★MOUNT ST. HELENS NATIONAL VOLCANIC MONUMENT (F-7)

Mount St. Helens National Volcanic Monument, covering 110,000 acres, contains the volcano and the surrounding area devastated by the 1980 eruption. Access to the area is limited; local roads only skirt the region, ending in overlooks providing scenic views. Southeast of the crater FR 25 branches off from FR 90 and continues north, becoming SR 131, then meeting US 12 at Randle. Northeast of the volcano FR 99 branches west off FR 25 to the Windy Ridge viewpoint, from which Mount St. Helens crater and Spirit Lake can be seen.

The roads are open from mid-June to late October (weather permitting); check on the current condition of FR 25. The Spirit Lake Memorial Highway extends 43 miles from I-5 at Castle Rock to Coldwater Ridge. This road is kept open year-round, although chains or winter traction devices may be required.

Until May 18, 1980, Mount St. Helens was one of Washington's snowcapped crown jewels. Spirit Lake, at its northern base, was a primary recreation center. The surrounding hills of the Gifford Pinchot National Forest *(see place listing)* beckoned hikers and outdoors enthusiasts, as well as loggers whose livelihoods its timber provided.

Then at 8:32 a.m. an explosion of incredible force blew the top 1,313 feet and much of the bulging north face off Mount St. Helens, shot a dense plume of smoke and ash 80,000 feet into the air, and released a mile-wide avalanche which raised Spirit Lake by more than 200 feet and laid over forests as if they had been combed. Mud and logs surged down the Toutle and Cowlitz rivers, temporarily clogging the Columbia River shipping lanes with silt. The pall of ash turned morning into midnight as it fell, halting traffic for a hundred miles and covering parts of three states with a fine gray powder.

The cataclysm was not wholly unexpected. Since the initial puff of steam and ash appeared on March 27, signaling the end of the mountain's 123-year-long sleep and announcing the first volcanic activity in the contiguous 48 states since the eruption of California's Mount Lassen 1914-21, Mount St. Helens had become one of the world's most closely monitored volcanoes.

Weeks before the great explosion, increasing seismic phenomena, heat and the swelling north slope had changed "*if* the mountain blows" to "*when* the mountain blows." Despite the renewal of life in the area since the 1980 blast, the watch continues as subsequent, but subtle, episodes suggest that the volcano might not yet be ready for another nap.

General Information and Activities

If you're planning to travel in southwestern Washington, you might wish to check with your home AAA club for the latest highway and recreation area information, then update that information by checking with clubs once you arrive in the Pacific Northwest. Many roads within the Gifford Pinchot National Forest are usually closed from November until April or May; you should check at Forest Service offices before driving on these roads.

More information about the volcanic area can be obtained from the Mount St. Helens National Volcanic Monument Headquarters, 42218 N.E. Yale Bridge Rd., Amboy, WA 98601; phone (360) 750-3900. *See color ad p. 164.*

Sightseeing tours by helicopter or airplane are available from many area airports, including Centralia-Chehalis, Cougar, Kelso-Longview, Morton, Silver Lake, Toledo Yakima and Vancouver. Flights also leave daily from Seattle *(see What To Do, Sightseeing).*

Scenic flights range from 30 to 90 minutes in length and start at about $40-$70 per person; some operators have a minimum passenger requirement. Check with local information centers, chambers of commerce or AAA Washington or Auto Club of Oregon offices for operators and schedules.

A growing network of hiking trails is becoming accessible around the volcano. It is possible to climb the southern flank of Mount St. Helens, allowing about 10 hours for the rigorous trek to the summit. For reservations on the summit climb and information about the hiking trails contact monument headquarters.

Two information stations are administered by the Forest Service. The Pine Creek Information Station, 18½ miles east of Cougar on FR 90, provides up-to-date information about volcanic activity and road conditions. There also is an information station at Woods Creek, 6 miles south of Randle on FR 25. From Memorial Day through Labor Day, stations generally are open daily at 9 and close at either 4 or 6.

Points of Interest

APE CAVE GEOLOGIC SITE is on FR 8303, 1 mi. w. of FR 83. Thought to be the longest lava tube in the Western Hemisphere, the 12,810-foot tunnel was found within a massive lava flow that oozed from the volcano almost 2,000 years ago. Flowing downhill, the stream of lava cooled and formed a hard crust atop the hot lava. In time the lava drained and left an intricate, winding lava cave behind. The cave was first explored in 1946 by the St. Helens Apes—the local Boy Scout troop for whom the cave is named.

Visitors should have three light sources, sturdy shoes and a jacket; the temperature is about 42 degrees Fahrenheit. The Ape Cave Information Station is open daily 10-5:30, mid-May to Sept. Free. Lanterns can be rented for $3.

COLDWATER RIDGE VISITOR CENTER, 43 mi. e. of Castle Rock via SR 504, is on a ridge offering spectacular views of the Upper Toutle River Valley, Coldwater Lake, Johnson Ridge and the crater and lava dome of Mount St. Helens, 7 miles in the distance. Interactive exhibits and a 6-minute multimedia presentation relate the eruption of the volcano and the return of life to the devastated region.

A ¾-mile trail leads to Coldwater Lake; the trail traverses a 700-foot altitude change. Guided walks along the Winds of Change trail and interpretive programs are offered. Pets are not permitted. Allow 1 hour minimum. Daily 9-6, Apr.-Sept.; 9-5, rest of year. Closed Thanksgiving and Dec. 25. Free. Phone (360) 274-2131.

MOUNT ST. HELENS NATIONAL VOLCANIC MONUMENT VISITOR CENTER is on the shore of Silver Lake, 5 mi. e. of I-5 exit 49 on SR 504. A walk-in model of the volcano illustrates its composition; pictorial and interpretive material and films highlight other features. A ⅛-mile trail outside the center leads to a viewpoint overlooking Silver Lake and, 34 miles east, Mount St. Helens. Allow 30 minutes minimum. Daily 9-6, Apr.-Sept.; 9-5, rest of year. Closed Thanksgiving and Dec. 25. Free. Phone (360) 274-2100. *See color ad.*

SCENIC DRIVES are provided by a network of state and forest roads connecting with I-5 and US 12, but Mount St. Helens is visible on clear days from Chehalis to Salem, Ore. A series of Forest Service roads forms a 60-mile link between Cougar and Randle, the principal western and northern gateways into the forest. FR 90, along the southern edge of the volcanic area east of Cougar, is paved as far as its intersection with FR 25, a paved road extending north to Randle.

A number of paved and gravel forest service roads branch off FRs 90 and 25, with viewpoints within the volcanic area. Many forest service roads are closed from October through June, depending on snow conditions. A concession stand and portable toilets are available at Cascade Viewpoint. Gasoline and groceries are available at the east end of Swift Reservoir.

Roads, some unpaved, leading into the volcanic area include Cougar Creek Road (FR 8303) from FR 83 to Ape Cave, which crosses a 1,900-year-old lava field with numerous caves and tubes; the first 10 miles of FR 81 from Cougar, which passes Merrill Lake and Kalama Falls; and FR 26, which reaches the awesome blast zone in the Ryan Lake area.

A particularly scenic road is the Spirit Lake Memorial Highway (SR 504), which follows the north fork of the Toutle River to the Coldwater Ridge Visitor Center *(see attraction listing).* Overlooks along the highway provide views of the crater and northwest lava dome, the blast

EXPERIENCE "THE
ERUPTION
OF MOUNT ST. HELENS!"
on our GIANT SCREEN
Standard Theater Screen
★★★★ ACADEMY AWARD NOMINEE
SPECIAL $1.00 DISCOUNT TO AAA MEMBERS
SUPER 70MM / SURROUND SOUND
MOUNT ST. HELENS CINEDOME THEATER
EXIT 49 CASTLE ROCK, WASHINGTON
(206) 274-8000

zone, Castle Lake, Coldwater Lake and Johnston Ridge.

FR 99 branches off FR 25 and travels west past Meta Lake to within 5 miles of the volcano at Windy Ridge. There, at the road's end, visitors have a fine view of the devastation stretching from Mount St. Helens' crater to Spirit Lake. For other viewpoint locations contact the monument headquarters; phone (360) 750-3902.

MOUNT VERNON (C-3) pop. 17,700, elev. 23′

West of Mount Vernon is one of the nation's largest commercial bulb-growing regions. Bulb farms cluster along county roads branching north and south from SR 20; follow SR 536 west from I-5 exit 226.

Area information is available from the Mount Vernon Chamber of Commerce, 200 E. College Wy., P.O. Box 1007, Mount Vernon, WA 98273; phone (360) 428-8547. The chamber also houses a visitor information center.

Daffodils bloom from mid-March to early April, tulips during the first half of April and irises in early May. The Skagit Valley Tulip Festival is held during April. Maps pinpointing the location of various flower fields and dates of festival events are available from the chamber of commerce.For recorded information during the blossom season phone (800) 4-TULIPS.

Shopping areas: Cascade Mall, off I-5 exit 229, has 84 stores, including Bon Marche, Emporium, JCPenney and Sears. The adjacent Pacific Edge Outlet Center has 34 stores.

LA CONNER FLATS DISPLAY GARDENS is w. of I-5 exit 226 on Kincaid St., right on S. 3rd St. to Division, then w. ½ mi. to Wall; right on McClean left 1 blk. to Rd., then 5½ mi. w., then 1½ mi. s. (left) on Best Rd. Or take I-5 exit 230 and continue w. 5 mi. on SR 20, turn left onto Best Rd. and continue south for 2 mi. Perennials, roses, vegetables and alpine plants are among the variety found in this 11-acre garden. Tues.-Sun. 10-6, Mar.-Oct. Donations. Phone (360) 466-3190.

ROOZENGAARDE is w. of I-5 exit 226 on Kincaid St., right on S. 3rd St. to Division, then w. ½ mi. to Wall; left 1 blk. to McLean Rd., then 3 mi. w., then s. on Beaver Marsh Rd. The 2½-acre display garden is filled with tulips, irises, daffodils and other flowering bulbs. Roozengaarde is a division of the Washington Bulb Co., one of the world's largest growers of tulips, daffodils and irises. The main blooming season is late February to late July. Picnic facilities are available. Mon.-Sat. 9-5:30, Sun. 10-5, Mar.-May; Mon.-Sat. 9-5, rest of year. Free. Phone (360) 424-8531.

WEST SHORE ACRES, 7 mi. w. via SR 536 and SR 20, then 2 mi. s. on La Conner-Whitney Rd., then 1½ mi. w. on Downey Rd., contains a 1½-acre flowering bulb display garden surrounding an 1896 Victorian farmhouse. Daily 10-6, mid-Mar. through Apr. 30; Mon.-Sat. 10-5, day after Labor Day-late Oct. Free. Phone (360) 466-3158.

MUKILTEO (E-3) pop. 11,900, elev. 12′

Mukilteo, named for the Suquamish word meaning "good camping ground," was the site of the Point Elliott Treaty of 1855. The document, signed by the leaders of 22 local tribes, relinquished land claims to white settlers. A lighthouse built in 1905 is open to visitors. Toll ferry service connects the mainland with Clinton on Whidbey Island; phone (800) 843-3779 in Wash.

NAHCOTTA (E-4) elev. 19′

Located on the Willapa Bay shore of the Long Beach Peninsula, Nahcotta is an important oystering center. Oystering on the bay dates back to the mid-19th century and huge mounds of oyster shells line th bayfront. Established in 1888 as the terminus of a norrow-gauge railroad linking the bay with Ilwaco on the Columbia River, its name commemorates a Chinook chief who befriended early settlers. The Willapa Bay Interpretive Center just east of SR 103 traces the history of oystering on the bay.

NASELLE (E-5)

NASELLE SALMON HATCHERY, 1¾ mi. e. of SR 4 on North Valley Rd., has information displays and self-guiding tours of its coho and chinook salmon facility. It is most interesting during spawning season, October through November. Daily 8-4:30. Free. Phone (360) 484-7716.

NEAH BAY (B-4) elev. 50′

Washington's first European settlers, the Spanish, landed in Neah Bay, which they called Núñez Gaona, in 1791. They established a fort which lasted 5 months. A Japanese ship brought new settlers from the Orient to the area in 1834; the wreck of that ship is off the coast of Cape Flattery.

Panoramas of Neah Bay Harbor, Vancouver Island and the Strait of Juan de Fuca extend from Koitlah Point, 3 miles west of Neah Bay off SR 112. Farther west off SR 112 at the tip of the peninsula is Cape Flattery, where a 30-minute hike takes visitors to the northwesternmost point in the contiguous United States.

Neah Bay's American Indian heritage is preserved at the Makah Indian Reservation and headquarters. Seasonal wildlife viewing opportunities abound on the reservation: Eagles, falcons and hawks migrate across the area in March; gray whales migrate along the Pacific coast in April and May; and trumpeter swans appear in November. Charters for fishing and wildlife viewing are available.

Of particular interest are Shi-Shi beach, the Cape Flattery Trail, and other Pacific Ocean and

Strait of Juan de Fuca trails. No alcohol is permitted. Visitors are welcome on the tribe's beaches but shellfish and shell gathering are restricted to tribal members. The tribe celebrates its citizenship grant during Makah Days in late August, with traditional dances, salmon bakes, bone games and canoe races.

MAKAH CULTURAL AND RESEARCH CENTER, on SR 112, contains exhibits pertaining to Makah history and culture, as well as flora, fauna and wilderness habitat and sport fishing. Some items are 500-year-old finds from one of the Makah's ancestral village of Ozette, which was buried in a catastrophic mudslide. The Ozette Archeaological Collection is the largest pre-contact Northwest Coast Indian collection in the country. Replicas of a 60-foot cedar longhouse and oceangoing canoes are displayed.

Daily 10-5, May 31 to mid-Sept.; Wed.-Sun. 10-5, rest of year. Closed Jan. 1, Thanksgiving and Dec. 25. Admission $4, over 62, military in uniform and full-time students with ID $3, under 4 free. MC, VI. Phone (360) 645-2711.

NEILTON (D-5)

QUINAULT NATIONAL FISH HATCHERY, 3 mi. s., then 4¾ mi. w. on Moclips Hwy., was built to replenish fish populations reduced by logging. More than 8 million salmon and trout are spawned and raised at the hatchery annually. An interpretive center explains the operation of the hatchery. Travel within the Quinault Indian Reservation is limited to designated roads. Allow 30 minutes minimum. Daily 8-3:30. Free. Phone (360) 288-2508.

NEMAH (E-4)

NEMAH SALMON HATCHERY, 2½ mi. e. on N. Nemah Rd., releases more than 5 million chinook, coho salmon and chum. Heavy runs are between September and mid-November, when mature fish are diverted into holding ponds. Allow 30 minutes minimum. Daily 8-4:30. Free. Phone (360) 875-6147.

NEWHALEM (B-10) elev. 525′

Derived from a Native American word meaning goat snare, Newhalem is a company town of frame homes and well-tended yards built to house employees of the Skagit River Hydroelectric Complex. A visitor center on SR-20 has displays and interpretive material on the Skagit River project and area recreation opportunities *(also see Diablo)*. Nearby is a 1926 Baldwin steam locomotive which operated on the Seattle City Light Railway. Also of interest are the Trail of Cedars nature walk and Ladder Creek Falls and Rock Garden, where summer evening illumination makes for a pleasant stroll.

NORTH BEND (D-7) pop. 2,600, elev. 445′

The chief agricultural center for the upper Snoqualmie Valley, North Bend straddles the South Fork of the Snoqualmie River. The town's proximity to Snoqualmie Pass and the western slopes of the Cascade Range makes it a good starting point for trips to both areas.

Mountains have influenced local architecture, much of which sports an alpine motif. Nearby Mount Si (SIGH) reaches an altitude of 4,167 feet; a 4-mile trail to the summit ascends 3,500 feet and affords spectacular views. The television series "Twin Peaks" was filmed in North Bend and neighboring Snoqualmie.

For further information contact the Upper Snoqualmie Valley Chamber of Commerce, P.O. Box 357, North Bend, WA 98045; phone (206) 888-4440.

Shopping areas: Great Northwest Factory Stores, I-90 exit 31, offers discount shopping in more than 35 stores.

PUGET SOUND AND SNOQUALMIE VALLEY RAILROAD—*see Snoqualmie.*

SNOQUALMIE VALLEY HISTORICAL MUSEUM, ½ mi. n. of I-90 exit 31 at 320 S. North Bend Blvd., contains Snoqualmie Indian artifacts and pioneer memorabilia and furnishings, including a vintage 1910 kitchen and parlor. Highlights include a 28-foot cedar dugout canoe, a farm shed with antique farming equipment and historical photographs. A diorama depicts the beginnings of the logging industry. Tours are available upon request. Allow 30 minutes minimum. Thurs.-Sun. 1-5, Apr.-Oct. Admission $1. Phone (206) 888-3200.

NORTH BONNEVILLE (G-6) pop. 400, elev. 74′

North Bonneville is named for Capt. Benjamin Louis Eulalie Bonneville, a French-born American army officer who explored a large portion of the Northwest in the early 1830s. Bonneville's travels were chronicled in Washington Irving's book "Adventures of Captain Bonneville, U.S.A., in the Rocky Mountains and the Far West," published in 1837.

The town was established in 1933 to house construction workers on the Bonneville Dam. It was relocated to its present site in 1976 to make way for a new powerhouse.

★**BONNEVILLE DAM—WASHINGTON SHORE VISITOR CENTER,** at n. end of dam off SR 14, offers self-guiding tours of the massive hydroelectric facility on the Columbia River. The orientation building contains a staffed information center and access to Bonneville Dam's second powerhouse. The Fish Viewing Building contains underwater windows and regional history displays that cover such topics as early history, development of the fishing industry and fish life cycles.

The power generators and turbines also are noteworthy. Access to the Oregon facilities is via the Bridge of the Gods, about 2 miles east.

Guided walks are offered daily. Allow 1 hour minimum. Daily 9-5. Free. Phone (509) 427-4281.

NORTH CASCADES NATIONAL PARK (A-7, B-8)

Elevations in the forest range from 400 ft. at the western entrance of the park, to 9,127 ft. at the summit of Mount Shuksan. Refer to AAA maps for additional information.

North Cascades National Park can be reached via trails off the North Cascades Highway (SR 20), from Marblemount on the western side and from Mazama through Okanogan National Forest on the eastern side. The highway is closed between Diablo Lake and Mazama from the first snowfall until late spring or early summer. From Marblemount, Cascade River Road leads east for 22 miles and is the only accessible road into the park. The park also can be reached by boat via Lake Chelan or from Canada via Ross Lake.

The park embraces 505,000 acres in north-central Washington. Its northern and southern sections, separated by Ross Lake National Recreation Area, are bordered by Okanogan National Forest to the east, Lake Chelan National Recreation Area to the southeast, Wenatchee National Forest to the south and Mount Baker-Snoqualmie National Forest to the west *(see place listings and Recreation Chart).*

Park terrain is the result of glaciation; more than 315 glaciers remain active. Jagged peaks, sheer canyons and many rivers and lakes characterize the landscape.

Mountain goats, deer and black and grizzly bears are among the most common animals in the park. Rarely visible but present are cougars and wolverines. Smaller mammals and a host of birds, including white-tailed ptarmigans, also inhabit the area. Hunting is prohibited. Several varieties of trout live in park waters.

General Information and Activities

North Cascades National Park is open daily 24 hours year-round. Highway access is non-existent in winter; however, SR 20 is passable from mid-April to mid-November (weather permitting).

Hiking access and roadside views of the northwest corner of the park are offered from SR 542 east from Bellingham. A passenger ferry provides round-trip service between Stehekin, in Lake Chelan National Recreation Area, and Chelan, at the southern end of Lake Chelan *(see Chelan).* Shuttle bus service transports visitors from Stehekin to High Bridge and Cottonwood in the remote southeast portion of the park, mid-May through September.

Trails suitable for hiking and climbing wind through the back country. Primitive campsites are available by free permit issued at most ranger stations; the most developed sites are off SR 20 in the Ross Lake National Recreation Area. Summer naturalist activities, including evening programs and guided walks, are featured at campgrounds in both recreation areas.

An information center adjoining SR 20 in Sedro Woolley is open daily 8-4:30 (also Fri. 4:30-6), mid-June through Labor Day; Mon.-Fri. 8-4:30, rest of year. Weather forecasts, trail conditions and free permits for back-country camping are available at the Chelan, Marblemount, Newhalem and Stehekin ranger stations; phone (509) 682-2549 in Chelan, (360) 873-4500 in Marblemount or (360) 386-4495 in Newhalem for details. *See Recreation Chart and the AAA Northwestern CampBook.*

ADMISSION to the park is free.

PETS are permitted in the Lake Chelan and Ross Lake national recreation areas only if they are on a leash or otherwise restricted at all times. Dogs and cats are not permitted on the trails or in buildings.

ADDRESS inquiries to the Park Superintendent's Office, North Cascades National Park, 2105 SR 20, Sedro Woolley, WA 98284; phone (360) 856-5700.

OAK HARBOR (C-2) pop. 17,200, elev. 84'

The largest town on Whidbey Island *(see place listing),* Oak Harbor takes its name from the white oak trees in the area. Many of the first settlers were Dutch; as a result, such events as April's Holland Happening are popular. Holland Gardens in Holland Park, with its windmill and flowerbeds, and the Dutch windmill in Oak Harbor Beach Park are other reflections of the Dutch influence.

North of Oak Harbor is Whidbey Island Naval Air Station. A seaplane base lies just east of the community.

For further information contact the Greater Oak Harbor Chamber of Commerce, 5506 SR 20, P.O. Box 883, Oak Harbor, WA 98277; phone (360) 675-3535.

★**DECEPTION PASS STATE PARK,** 9 mi. n. of Oak Harbor on SR 20, was named in 1792 by Capt. George Vancouver for the cliff-lined channel that separates Whidbey and Fidalgo islands. Within its 3,640 acres are freshwater lakes, tracts of forest, marshland, sand dunes, offshore islands and almost 15 miles of saltwater shoreline. The coastal landscape includes cliffs, rocky shores, beaches of gravel and sand, tide flats and hidden coves.

The Deception Pass Bridge offers a panorama of the channel. More than 25 miles of hiking trails meander through the park. Daily 6:30-dusk, Apr.-Sept.; 8-5, rest of year. Free. Phone (360) 675-2417. *See Recreation Chart.*

Civilian Conservation Corps Interpretive Center, 1 mi. n. of the Deception Pass Bridge, documents the story of the Civilian Conservation

Corps—a federal program that helped support the newly established state park system in the 1930s by building picnic shelters, residences, restrooms and hiking trails in state parks. Sat.-Sun. and holidays 9-6, mid-May to mid-Sept. Free. Phone (360) 355-5578.

OCEAN SHORES (D-4) pop. 2,300, elev. 43′

Occupying a sandy peninsula separating Grays Harbor from the Pacific Ocean, Ocean Shores is a popular resort area. Recreational activities include swimming, surf fishing, clamming, kayaking, horseback riding and golf. Charter fishing trips are avaliable from the Ocean Shores Marina at the southeastern tip of the peninsula. A daily passenger ferry service runs from the marina to Westport during the summer months; for further information phone (360) 289-3391.

For further information contact the Ocean Shores Chamber of Commerce, 899 Pt. Brown Ave. N.W., Suite A, P.O. Box 382, Ocean Shores, WA 98569; phone (360) 289-2451. *See color ad.*

OCEAN SHORES ENVIRONMENTAL INTERPRETIVE CENTER, 4 mi. s. at 1013 Catala Ave. S.E., features exhibits on the natural and human history of the peninsula and Grays Harbor. Displays depict native fish, shellfish, birds, animals, plants and land use concerns. Allow 30 minutes minimum. Wed.-Fri. 11-5, Sat. 11-6, Sun. 11-4, Memorial Day-Thanksgiving weekend. Free. Phone (360) 289-4617.

OKANOGAN (B-9) pop. 2,300

While exploring the Pacific Northwest in 1883, Gen. G.W. Goethals, a military man and chief engineer of the Panama Canal, camped in what is now one of Okanogan's two city parks. The town itself was established as Alma in 1888; it was renamed Pogue in 1905, and finally dubbed Okanogan in 1907. Its commercial growth was thwarted by the fact that the Okanogan River was only deep enough for steamboats to reach the town during May and June.

An irrigation system in 1906 attracted new settlers and businesses; a few years later a railroad line and a bridge over the river gave the town an added boost. Its primary industries are agriculture and cattle ranching. Apple orchards extend along the Okanogan River from the Canadian border to the Columbia River.

For further information contact the Okanogan Chamber of Commerce, P.O. Box 1125, Okanogan, WA 98840.

OKANOGAN COUNTY HISTORICAL MUSEUM, 1410 Second Ave., exhibits items pertaining to local history, including a reproduction of a 19th-century Main Street. Daily 10-4, mid-May to mid-Sept. Donations. Phone (509) 422-4272.

OKANOGAN NATIONAL FOREST

Elevations in the forest range from 778 ft. at Pateros to 8,105 ft. at the summit of Jack Mountain in the Pasayten Wilderness. Refer to AAA maps for additional information.

Most of the 1,745,054-acre Okanogan National Forest is in a rough triangle formed by the Canadian border, the Cascade Range and the Columbia and Okanogan rivers. Smaller sections are east of Oroville and Tonasket. Farther to the north is Pasayten Wilderness, containing 529,607 acres. Trails include 63 miles of the Pacific Crest National Scenic Trail. The Lake Chelan-Sawtooth Wilderness contains 145,667 acres.

One of the great scenic attractions in this area is the North Cascades Highway (SR 20), which connects Winthrop and Marblemount and is open mid-April through November (weather permitting). The Washington Pass Scenic Overlook, 32 miles west of Winthrop at an elevation of 5,500 feet, offers a short loop trail to an overlook, picnic sites and a small information booth.

Also on the North Cascades Highway is the Rainy Lake Trail at Rainy Pass. The 1-mile trail is paved and is open July through September.

A narrow gravel road leads to Slate Peak, 19 miles northwest of Mazama. Reaching an elevation of 7,400 feet, the road offers a top-of-the-world panorama of the North Cascades. The road is open from July until the first snowfall; it is not suitable for trailers.

Reached from the north and south by US 2 and US 97 and from the east and west by scenic North Cascades Highway (SR 20), the national forest offers winter sports, hunting and fishing. Rock hounding also is popular. The Early Winters Visitor Information Center, 17 miles northwest of Winthrop on SR 20, is open daily 9-5, June 1-Labor Day. Ranger stations are in Tonasket, Twisp *(see place listing)* and Winthrop *(see place listing)*.

Information about any of the forest's areas can be obtained by writing the Okanogan National Forest Supervisor's Office, P.O. Box 950, Okanogan, WA 98840; phone (509) 826-3275. *See Recreation Chart and the AAA Northwestern CampBook.*

OLYMPIA (H-2) pop. 33,900, elev. 36′

Settlers first arrived at Budd Inlet at the southern end of Puget Sound in the 1840s. Their community, Smithfield, became the site of the first U.S. customhouse in the Northwest and was renamed Olympia for the magnificent mountains to the west. The town flourished; it is capital of the state and an important commercial center.

Olympia is the starting point of the Olympic Highway (US 101), which circles the Olympic Peninsula and continues along the coast into northern California. Passing many beach and lake resorts, this highway provides access to Olympic National Park and Olympic National Forest *(see place listings)*.

The well known Olympia oyster is taken from Puget Sound in this vicinity. The beds in Mud, Oyster and Big and Little Skookum bays can be visited.

In September and October salmon can be observed from the 5th Street Bridge as they go into Capitol Lake; the fish also can be seen going up the fish ladders on the Deschutes River in Tumwater Falls Park. Olympia's Japanese Garden, on Plum Street north of Union Avenue, commemorates the sister city relationship with Yashiro, Japan. Among Olympia's special events are the Capitol Lakefair, held Wednesday through Sunday of the second weekend July, and Harbor Days, which takes place Labor Day weekend.

For further information contact the Olympia/Thurston County Chamber of Commerce, 1000 Plum St. S.E., P.O. Box 1427, Olympia, WA 98507; phone (360) 357-3362 or (800) 753-VISIT.

Shopping areas: Capital Mall, 2 miles west of downtown on Black Lake Boulevard off US 101, is the area's major shopping center. Stores include The Bon, JCPenney and Lamonts.

★**THE CAPITOL GROUP** includes buildings housing the legislative, judicial, insurance, labor and industries, Social Security, public lands, transportation, and general administration offices.

Guided tours of the Legislative Building are offered daily 10-3. Tours of the Supreme Court Temple of Justice are available by appointment; phone (360) 586-8687. Tours of the Governor's Mansion are available by appointment Wed. 1-2:30; phone (360) 586-8687. The State Library is open Mon.-Fri. 8-5; closed state holidays. Phone (360) 753-5590.

Self-guiding tours of the Greenhouse Conservatory are available daily 8:30-3:15, Memorial Day weekend-Labor Day; Mon.-Fri. 8-3:15, rest

I-5 EXIT 82 CENTRALIA, WA

50 FACTORY OUTLETS line I-5 Exit 82, offering the wares of major manufacturers at bargain prices. Downtown CENTRALIA SQUARE and the new ANTIQUE MARKET display the treasures of over 100 dealers along with specialty shops and a unique dining experience in the ANTIQUE MALL CAFE.

OPEN 7 DAYS 1-800-831-5334

THE NORTHWEST'S SHOPPING CENTER

of year. Visitor center open Mon.-Fri. 8-5. Free. Phone (360) 753-1752.

MIMA MOUNDS NATURAL AREA PRESERVE, 445 acres, is 10 mi. s. of Olympia off I-5 exit 95; take Maytown Rd. 3 mi. w. to Waddell Creek Rd., then ¾ mi. n.w. at the fork in the road. The preserve encompasses a curious topography of regularly spaced hills approximately 7 feet high.

An interpretive center details the natural history of the area and presents the various theories of the mounds' origins. Self-guiding trails traverse the open prairie and forests; wildflowers are at their peak April through June. Daily 8-dusk. Free. Phone (360) 586-8761.

OLYMPIA BREWING CO. is e. of I-5 exit 103 in Tumwater at Custer Way and Schmidt Pl. Olympia is a division of Pabst Brewing Co. Under 16 must be with an adult. Allow 30 minutes minimum. Tours are offered daily 8-4:30; closed Jan. 1, Thanksgiving and Dec. 25. Free. Phone (360) 754-5177.

★**STATE CAPITAL MUSEUM,** 211 W. 21st Ave., is in an Italian Renaissance revival mansion that was originally the home of Olympia banker Clarence Lord. The 32-room house has photographs and historical documents pertaining to Washington territorial and state governments, pioneer settlement and Northwest Coast Indians. A gallery displays changing exhibits of art and history. Outdoor highlights include the Pioneer Herb Garden and Native Plant Garden. **Note:** The museum is scheduled to reopen in June 1995, following renovations.

Allow 30 minutes minimum. Tues.-Fri. 10-4, Sat.-Sun. noon-4; closed major holidays. Admission $2; over 64 and under 19, $1; family rate $5. Phone (360) 753-2580.

OLYMPIC NATIONAL FOREST

Elevations in the forest range from sea level at Hood Canal to 6,988 ft. at Buckhorn Mountain. Refer to AAA maps for additional information.

Covering 632,324 acres on the Olympic Peninsula, Olympic National Forest is noted for its rugged mountain terrain, lush rain forests and glacial streams. Deer and bear are plentiful, and the Roosevelt elk population is the largest anywhere. Douglas fir, Western red cedar, Western hemlock, bigleaf maple, rhododendron and wildflowers are among the forest's prominent flora.

More than 200 miles of trails wind through the forest, with some overlapping into Olympic National Park. Pets are permitted on forest trails. Steelhead and trout fishing are popular; hunting is permitted in season. Most recreation sites are open May through October. Evidence of early mining activities, railroad logging and exploration remains.

Of special interest is the Quinault Rain Forest; 2 miles off US 101 at Lake Quinault, two loop trails into the rain forest begin at the nature trail parking lot off South Shore Road. Five wilderness areas encompass thousands of acres; Buckhorn is the largest. Permits are not needed to enter the wilderness areas; however, motorized vehicles are not permitted.

Panoramas of the Olympics, Hood Canal and Puget Sound can be had from Mount Walker viewpoint, reached by a gravel road off US 101 south of Quilcene. Also especially scenic is Seal Rock Beach, along the Hood Canal 2 miles north of Brinnon. For descriptions of areas near the national forest, *see Olympia and Olympic National Park.*

For further information contact the Olympic National Forest Supervisor's Office, 1835 Black Lake Blvd. S.W., Olympia, WA 98512; phone (360) 956-2400. *See Recreation Chart.*

★OLYMPIC NATIONAL PARK (B-4, C-5)

See map page 146.

Elevations in the forest range from sea level along 60 miles of beach, to 7,965 ft. at Mount Olympus. Refer to AAA maps for additional information.

Olympic National Park can be reached via US 101, which forms an inverted "U" shape around the park and the adjacent Olympic National Forest. Paved entrance roads include Hurricane Ridge Road, off Race Street in Port Angeles; Elwha Road, 8 miles southwest of Port Angeles; Soleduck Road, west of Lake Crescent; Hoh Road, 13 miles south of Forks; and North and South Shore roads, on either side of Lake Quinault.

Unpaved roads off US 101 include Deer Park Road, east of Port Angeles, not for use by trailers or recreational vehicles; Queets Road, east of Queets; Staircase Road, west of Hoodsport; and Dosewallips Road, west of Brinnon. All of these roads end fewer than 20 miles into the park; to preserve the wilderness, no roads pass through the park's interior.

Olympic National Park is a scenic wilderness of 923,000 acres extending from glacier-clad mountains to ocean shore. Ranging between these borders are coniferous rain forests, glaciers, lakes and streams, as well as 57 miles of unspoiled coastline. The wilderness area encompasses the interior of the Olympic Peninsula, between Hood Canal on the east and the Pacific Ocean on the west.

Mount Olympus, at 7,965 feet, is the highest of the park's mountains, which rise within a few miles of the sea. The range is extremely rugged, with spectacular cliffs and crags and deep, forested valleys. On the upper slopes are glaciers unusual for their formation at a comparatively low elevation.

Magnificent stands of Sitka spruce, Douglas fir, Western hemlock and Western red cedar cover the lower mountainsides. On the upper slopes near the timberline, Alaska cedar, mountain hemlock and subalpine fir intermingle in alpine meadows. More than 600 miles of trails run through virgin forests and along stream banks in narrow valleys to ridgetops and mountain passes.

Snowfall might make passage on some trails difficult; check with the visitor centers and ranger stations in the park. Only experienced mountain climbers should attempt to scale the park's challenging peaks. The Olympic high country can be reached by car only from the north side, where roads lead to subalpine meadows at Deer Park and Hurricane Ridge.

Rainfall averages 140 inches in the rain forests in the western valleys of the park. Sitka spruce, Western red cedar and Douglas fir are abundant. The most interesting of the centuries-old forests are found in the valleys of the Hoh, Quinault, Bogachiel and Queets rivers.

The area teems with wildlife. Of the 6,500 elk estimated to inhabit the peninsula, 5,000 are in the park, chiefly on the western slope of the mountains. Blacktail deer and many smaller mammals are common throughout the park. Hunting is prohibited. Among the great variety of birds in the park is the majestic bald eagle.

General Information and Activities

Though the park is open all year, parts of the high country are usually closed by snow from early fall until July. The streams of the Olympic Mountains offer fine fishing; salmon fishing is excellent in the Strait of Juan de Fuca and the

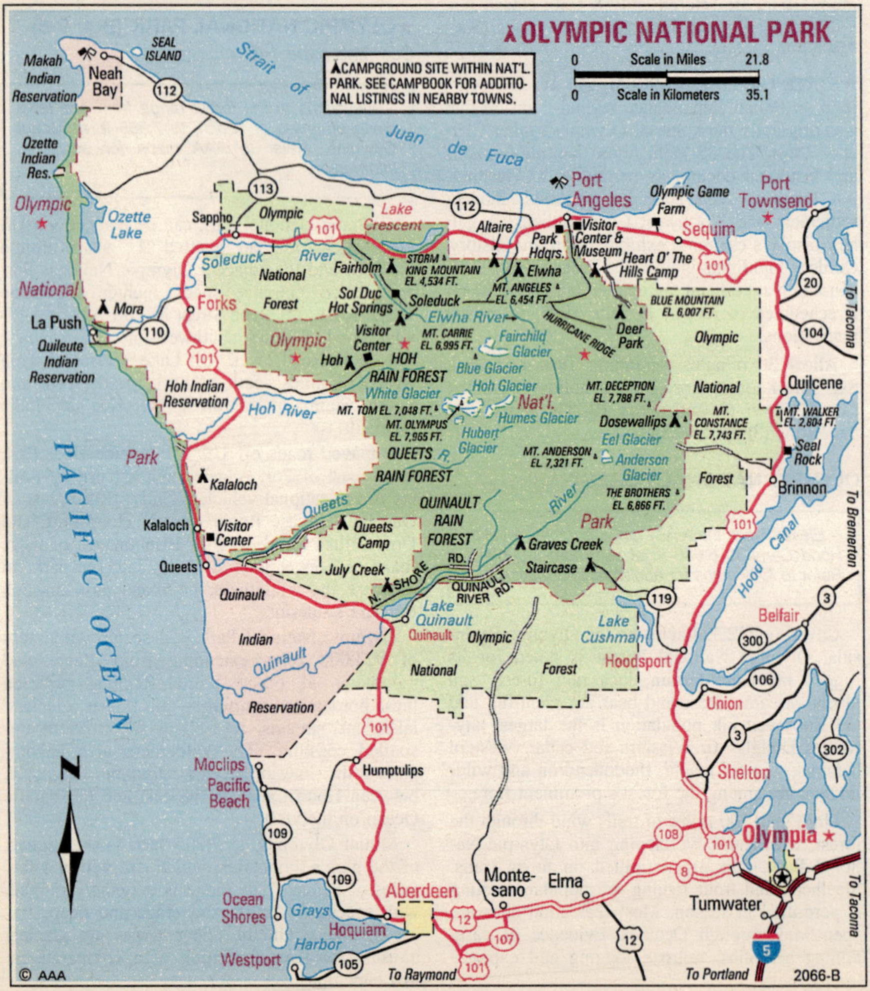

ocean. No license is required for fishing within the park boundaries, but steelhead and salmon punch cards are required in season. Sol Duc Hot Springs is in the Soleduck Valley, 12 miles southeast of US 101 *(see attraction listing).*

A number of self-guiding nature trails have been developed throughout the park. Rangers/naturalists give illustrated talks July 1 through Labor Day. Visitor centers are open all year at Port Angeles and the Hoh Rain Forest; the Kalaloch and Storm King (Lake Crescent) centers are open daily, July 1 through Labor Day. The Hurricane Ridge Center is open daily late April to late September. Road conditions prohibit the passage of trailers in some areas of the park. *See Recreation Chart and the AAA Northwestern CampBook.*

ADMISSION is free late Sept. to mid-May; a $5 entrance fee, good for 7 days anywhere in the park, is charged at Elwha, Heart o' the Hills, Hoh and Soleduck entrances from mid-May through late Sept. A $8 camping fee is charged at the major campgrounds.

PETS may only be carried in a car or led on a leash up to 6 feet in length in parking areas, on paved roads at Rialto Beach to Hole in the Wall, on the Kalaloch beaches and on the Shady Lane trail at Staircase. Pets may not be left unattended or tied to a stationary object.

ADDRESS inquiries to the Park Superintendent's Office, Olympic National Park, 600 E. Park Ave., Port Angeles, WA 98362; phone (360) 452-0330.

OLYMPIC RAFT AND GUIDE SERVICE operates through Olympic National Park on the Elwha and Hoh rivers. Overnight trips on the Queets River also are available. Allow 2 hours, 30 minutes minimum. Elwha River trips depart from the Elwha Resort, 8 miles west of Port Angeles on US 101, daily at 9:30 and 1:30, Apr.-Sept. Hoh River trips depart from the R&R Sports Center, 6 mi. e. of US 101 on Upper Hoh River Rd., daily at 10 and 2, Apr.-Sept. Elwha River fare $35; under 15, $20. Hoh River fare $35. MC, VI.

For information and reservations contact Olympic Raft and Guide Service, 239521 US 101 W., Port Angeles, WA 98363; phone (360) 452-1443.

PORT ANGELES PIONEER MEMORIAL VISITOR CENTER is s. of US 101 via Race St., at 3002 Mount Angeles Rd. The visitor center provides park information and presents a slide program. Museum displays relate to wildlife, plants, geology and Northwest Coast Indian culture. A nature trail is available. Daily 8:30-6, July 1-Labor Day; 8:30-4, rest of year. Closed Thanksgiving and Dec. 25. Free. Phone (360) 452-0330.

Points of Interest

DEER PARK, a subalpine meadow featuring endemic plants, can be reached via a 17-mile, mountainous, mostly unpaved road 5 mi. e. of Port Angeles; not recommended for trailers. A short trail leads to the summit of 6,007-foot Blue Mountain, which affords views of the Dungeness Valley and Olympic Mountains. Daily 24 hours. The access road is usually closed Oct.-July; check locally for conditions.

ELWHA RIVER VALLEY, 40 miles long from the river's headwaters near Mount Olympus to its outlet into the Strait of Juan de Fuca, is accessible via a paved road off US 101, 8 mi. w. of Port Angeles. After 5 miles, the road reaches dam-impounded Lake Mills, then climbs to an observation point and continues along tributary Boulder Creek. At road's end a 2-mile trail leads to primitive Olympic Hot Springs.

★**HOH RAIN FOREST** can be reached via a 19-mile-long paved road off US 101, 13 mi. s. of Forks. A visitor center features informative displays and serves as a departure point for several self-guiding nature trails, including the much-photographed "Hall of the Mosses" trail. Allow 1 hour minimum. Daily 9-7, July 1-Labor Day; 9-5 rest of year. Free. Phone (360) 374-6925.

★**HURRICANE RIDGE,** more than 5,200 feet above sea level, is accessible via Hurricane Ridge Rd., a 7-percent-grade highway from Port Angeles. Hurricane Ridge Lodge, open for day use only, provides striking views of the Olympic Mountains, the Strait of Juan de Fuca and Vancouver Island. Nature trails wind through the meadows, where wildflowers bloom from late June through October.

Naturalist programs are held daily July 1 through Labor Day. During the ski season rentals and rope tow service are available on weekends (weather permitting). The winter use area also features cross-country ski and snowshoe trails. For winter road conditions and activities phone (360) 452-0329.

KALALOCH AND RUBY BEACHES, reached by short trails off US 101 n. of Queets, are two of the park's most accessible beach areas. Kalaloch, southernmost of the two, has a campground and offers cliff-top views of the coast. Ruby Beach, with its sea arches and offshore islands, is more of a wilderness beach. Smaller beaches in the vicinity are designated by numbers.

LAKE CRESCENT, 17 mi. w. of Port Angeles on US 101, is a deep freshwater lake named for its shape. Surrounded by high mountains, including 4,534-foot Storm King Mountain, the lake is 10 miles long and 624 feet deep. Near the midpoint along US 101 is the trailhead for a 1-mile trail that leads to 90-foot Marymere Falls. Narrated excursions of the lake aboard a paddlewheeler depart several times daily mid-May through early October; phone (360) 452-4520.

SOL DUC HOT SPRINGS is in the Soleduck Valley, 30 miles w. of Port Angeles and 12 miles southeast of US 101. Natural mineral water flows from the springs at a temperature of 128 F and is piped into three large outdoor swimming pools ranging in temperature from 101 F to 105 F. Lodging, campsites and food are available. The pools are open daily 9-9, mid-May through Aug.; 9-8, in Sept. Admission $5.50; over 61, $4.50; under 4 free. AE, DS, MC, VI. Phone (360) 327-3583.

OMAK (B-10) pop. 4,100

A sister city to Okanogan *(see place listing)*, Omak is a lumber town whose name derives from the Salish word *omache*, meaning "good medicine." Apple orchards are a prime business, as is the growing of baby's breath, a florist industry staple.

Carl Precht Memorial RV Park *(see Recreation Chart)*, a quarter-mile west of Main Street on Omak Avenue, is the site of the Omak Stampede and Suicide Race in early August. Traditional American Indian foods and celebrations are featured at the Sunflower Festival in late May. Other nearby attractions reminiscent of the past are several ghost towns that harken back to the gold-rush days.

Additional information about the area is available from the Omak Chamber of Commerce, Route 2, Box 5200, Omak, WA 98841; phone (509) 826-1880 or (800) 225-6625.

ST. MARY'S MISSION is 4 mi. e. via SR 155, then 1½ mi. s. Father Etienne de Rougé founded this Jesuit mission in 1886 to minister to the 11 bands of the Colville Federation. The present church dates from 1910. The adjacent Paschal Sherman Indian School, the state's only American Indian boarding school, is managed by the Colville Confederated Tribes. The church and grounds are open daily 24 hours. Visitors can register at the main office. Free. Phone (509) 826-2097.

OROVILLE (A-9) pop. 1,500, elev. 913′

Set in a deep valley flanked by high ridges, Oroville takes its names from the Spanish word for gold for good reason: A strike found near the mouth of the Similkameen River in 1861 resulted in the establishment of the boom town. The arrival of the railroad in 1914 and the construction of irrigation works eventually turned the town's economic focus to commerical orchards, the first of which was planted in 1858 by prospector Hiram Smith. Most of the town's "gold" is now found in the form of locally grown apples.

The former Great Northern Depot, at 12th and Ironwood streets, contains exhibits about Oroville's history. Nearby Osoyoos Lake State Park *(see Recreation Chart)* offers several recreational facilities. The Oroville Visitor Information Center is open daily 8-6, May through September. For additional information contact the center at 1730 Main St., P.O. Box 536, Oroville, WA 98844; phone (509) 476-2739.

OLD MOLSON MUSEUM, 10 mi. e. on Oroville-Chesaw Rd., then 5 mi. n. on Molson Rd., contains a complex of early-20th-century buildings, including a bank, an assay office and two homestead cabins. Allow 1 hour minimum. Daily dawn-dusk, May-Oct. Donations. Phone (509) 485-3292.

Molson School Museum, several blks. n. of Old Molson Museum, contains several schoolrooms, a library and displays of various pioneer household articles and tools. Allow 1 hour minimum. Daily 10-5, Memorial Day-Labor Day. Donations.

OTHELLO (E-10) pop. 4,600

COLUMBIA NATIONAL WILDLIFE REFUGE, 735 E. Main St., is a 23,100-acre refuge used as a nesting area by numerous species of waterfowl and wildlife. Blue-winged, cinnamon teal, redhead, ruddy and mallard ducks nest in the summer. The ledges and cracks in the cliffs provide a nesting habitat for red-tailed hawks, swallows, ravens, and great-horned and barn owls.

Wildlife viewing is best during the spring and summer. A public use area offers a self-guiding driving tour. Allow 1 hour, 30 minutes minimum. Mon.-Thurs. 7-4:30, Fri. 7-3:30. Free. Phone (509) 488-2668.

OLD HOTEL ART GALLERY, 33 E. Larch St., displays folk art and handicrafts produced by Northwestern artists. Paintings, sculpture and other works are exhibited in the rooms of a former railroad-era boarding house built in 1912. Mon.-Sat. 9-5; closed holidays. Donations. Phone (509) 488-5936.

OYSTERVILLE (E-4) elev. 10′

It was the discovery of oysters, not gold, that created the boom town of Oysterville in the late 1800s. Town founders Clark and Espey, with the aid of Chief Nahcati, discovered the oyster beds of Willapa Bay in 1854. The demand for this delicacy grew rapidly; a plate of Shoalwater Bay oysters in San Francisco sold for about $50 in gold. Many of Oysterville's oldest homes and churches are in the historic district at the end of Peninsula Road.

PASCO (F-10) pop. 20,300, elev. 380′

Its location at the confluence of the Yakima, Snake and Columbia rivers has made Pasco a transportation center since its founding in the late 1800s. With its sister cities, Kennewick and Richland, Pasco dominates commercial development at the southern entrance to the Columbia River Basin. Wine production is a profitable industry; fruits of local vineyards grace the Northwest Wine Festival, held the first weekend in November.

Sacajawea State Park is 3 miles southeast off US 12 at the confluence of the Snake and Columbia rivers. Occupying the site of the late-19th-century railroad town of Ainsworth, the park is named for the Shoshone woman guide of the Lewis and Clark expedition. The party camped here in October 1805 on the westward leg of their journey. Phone (509) 545-2361. *See Recreation Chart.*

For further information contact the Greater Pasco Area Chamber of Commerce, 1600 N. 20th St., P.O. Box 550, Pasco, WA 99301; phone (509) 547-9755.

FRANKLIN COUNTY HISTORICAL MUSEUM, downtown at 305 N. Fourth Ave. in the former Pasco Carnegie Library Building, presents displays relating to agriculture, railroading, river and air transportation and local history. Also featured are artifacts of the Spokane, Wanapum, Yakama, Umatilla, Nez Percé, Palouse and Waiilattpu Indians. Tues.-Sat. 1-5. Free. Phone (509) 547-3714.

ICE HARBOR DAM, 12 mi. e., is one of four dams on the lower Snake River that extend river barge navigation from the Pacific Ocean to Lewiston, Idaho. Lake Sacajawea, formed by the dam, covers 9,200 acres. Self-guiding tours of the dam, powerhouse, fish ladders and navigation locks are available; a 30-minute slide show can be seen as well. Camping, boating, water skiing, fishing, swimming and picnicking are permitted. Allow 1 hour minimum. Visitor center open daily 9-5, Apr.-Oct. Free. Phone (509) 547-7781.

McNARY NATIONAL WILDLIFE REFUGE headquarters are ¼ mi. n. of US 12 near Burbank. The refuge covers about 3,600 acres on a part of the McNary Lock and Dam project on the Columbia River. One in a chain of refuges along the Pacific flyway, this is an important resting and feeding place for thousands of migrating waterfowl. Portions of the refuge are open for hunting in season. Fishing is permitted February through September. State hunting and fishing licenses are required.

Refuge open daily dawn-dusk. Headquarters open Mon.-Fri. 7-4:30. Free. Phone (509) 547-4942.

PRESTON PREMIUM WINES, 5 mi. n. on SR 395, offers self-guiding tours and wine tastings. Picnic facilities and a park are available. Allow 30 minutes minimum. Daily 10-5:30; closed Jan. 1, Easter, Thanksgiving and Dec. 25. Free. Phone (509) 545-1990.

PATERSON (F-9) elev. 377′

COLUMBIA CREST WINERY, 1 mi. n. of SR 14 on SR 221, is reputedly the largest winery in the Pacific Northwest. It consists of 9 acres of underground processing, fermenting, aging, filtering and bottling areas. Tours cover many facets of the wine-making process and end in the wine-tasting room. Most activity occurs during harvest time, late September to early November. Landscaped picnic grounds are available.

Allow 1 hour minimum. Self-guiding tours daily 10-4:30. Half-hour guided tours are given Sat.-Sun. at 11, 1, 2:30 and 4. Closed major holidays. Tours and tastings free. Phone (509) 875-2061.

PLYMOUTH (F-10)

McNARY LOCK AND DAM—*see Umatilla, Ore.*

PORT ANGELES (B-5) pop. 17,700, elev. 20′

In 1791 Spanish captain Francisco Eliza sailed into the natural harbor of what is now Port Angeles and became the first European to see this area. He named the site Puerto de Nuestra Señora de Los Angeles, "Port of Our Lady of the Angels," from which the current name is derived. The 4½-mile sandbar that forms the harbor is called Ediz Hook, which offers a panorama of the city and the Olympic Mountains.

Black Ball Transport operates passenger and automobile ferry service daily between Port Angeles and Victoria, 18 miles across the strait; phone (360) 457-4491. Victoria Express offers passenger ferry service to Victoria from mid-May to mid-October; phone (360) 452-8088, or (800) 633-1589 in Wash.

The waters of the Strait of Juan de Fuca are a rich fishing ground. Several charter operations offer fishing cruises for salmon and bottom fish; all-inclusive rates begin at $75. The Port Angeles Salmon Derby, one of the oldest in the state, celebrates the city's fishing bounty in mid-July. Van tours into the Olympic National Park are available in Port Angeles. For more information contact the Visitor Information Center, 121 E. Railroad Ave., Port Angeles, WA 98362; phone (360) 452-2363.

ARTHUR D. FEIRO MARINE LABORATORY, city pier at foot of Lincoln St., presents displays and a large touch tank of local intertidal marine flora and fauna. Daily 10-8, mid-June to early Sept.; Sat.-Sun. noon-4, rest of year. Admission $1; ages 6-12, 50c. Phone (360) 452-9277, ext. 264.

CLALLAM COUNTY MUSEUM, Lincoln and E. 4th sts., is in the 1914 former Clallam County Courthouse. Displays deal with local history, the port and fishing industries, genealogy and Clallam and Makah Indian artifacts. Of special interest are the country store and the works of the four-faced tower clock. Historical walking tours and guided tours of the museum are offered by appointment. Mon.-Sat. 10-4, June-Aug.; Mon.-Fri. 10-4, rest of year. Donations. Phone (360) 452-7831, ext. 364.

PORT ANGELES FINE ARTS CENTER, ¼ mi. e. of Race St. on E. Lauridsen Blvd., features changing exhibits of contemporary paintings, sculpture, photographs, drawings and functional arts. The center also hosts lectures, concerts and other performances. The 5-acre grounds have walking trails and offer a panorama of the city, harbor and Strait of Juan de Fuca. Allow 30 minutes minimum. Thurs.-Sun. and holidays 11-5; closed Thanksgiving and Dec. 25. Free. Phone (360) 457-3532.

PORT GAMBLE (E-2)

Founded in 1853, Port Gamble retains the atmosphere of a 19th-century company town. Established in conjunction with Pope & Talbot's, both the company and the town flourished. Logging continues to play a role: One of the oldest sawmills in the country still operates. The Cyrus T. Walker Nursery and Forest Research Center offers self-guiding tours. More than 30 Victorian-style homes, churches and buildings have been restored; electric street lamps have been replaced with gas-lamp duplicates.

OF SEA AND SHORE MUSEUM, on SR 104 in the country store building, has a large shell collection and displays depicting area marine life. Allow 30 minutes minimum. Tues.-Sun. 11-4, mid-May to mid-Sept.; Sat.-Sun. 11-4, rest of year. Closed Jan. 1 and Dec. 25. Free. Phone (360) 297-2426.

PORT GAMBLE HISTORIC MUSEUM, in town on SR 104, is in the basement of Port Gamble Country Store. Exhibits trace the development of the town's lumber industry 1853-present. Allow 30 minutes minimum. Daily 10-4, Memorial Day weekend-Labor Day. Admission $1, over 60 and students with ID 50c, under 6 free. Phone (360) 297-3341.

PORT ORCHARD (F-2) pop. 5,000, elev. 13'

The first settlers in the area built homes on the wooded shores of Sinclair Inlet in 1854 and named their community Sidney. Sawmills and shipyards formed a sound base for the town's economy, and in 1903 Sidney was renamed Port Orchard and made the seat of Kitsap County.

Port Orchard is largely unspoiled by modern growth. Antique and specialty shops operate near the marina, and the waterfront park is the scene of outdoor concerts in summer. The Log Cabin Museum, 416 Sidney Ave., features an 1880s vintage log house with period furnishings; phone (360) 876-3693.

Port Orchard's residents gather the week before July 4 to celebrate Fathoms O' Fun, a community festival. Daily passenger ferry service links Port Orchard to nearby Bremerton; phone (360) 876-2300 for schedule.

For further information contact the Port Orchard Chamber of Commerce, 839 Bay St., Port Orchard, WA 98366; phone (360) 876-3505.

Shopping areas: Antique shopping is popular in Port Orchard. Olde Central Antique Mall, 801 Bay St., has 70 shops. Sidney Village and The Backdoor Mall, Bay and Frederick streets, have several dozen stores.

SIDNEY MUSEUM AND ARTS ASSOCIATION, 202 Sidney Ave., is housed in a 1908 Masonic Lodge and exhibits the paintings and crafts of Northwestern artists. Displays include a pioneer post office, doctor's office, schoolhouse and mercantile and hardware stores. Other exhibits highlight the local pottery and logging industries. Allow 30 minutes minimum. Tues.-Sat. 11-4, Sun. 1-4 (also Sun. 4-5, Mar.-Dec.); closed Jan. 1, Thanksgiving and Dec. 25. Free. Phone (360) 876-3693.

★PORT TOWNSEND (D-2) pop. 7,000

Port Townsend's strategic location at the entrance to Puget Sound made it a port of entry and an active trade city in the late 19th century. Because Port Townsend is one of the oldest cities in the state, there are numerous examples of Victorian architecture, complete with turrets, towers and Carpenter Gothic trim.

An excellent example of the town's architectural eclecticism is the Jefferson County Courthouse on Walker Street. Built in 1892, it combines Romanesque and Gothic idioms as well as elements of a fairytale castle. Perhaps the most unusual of the town's attractions is the Tree of Heaven; it reputedly was a gift from a Chinese emperor in the 1860s, but the story remains unverified.

St. Paul's Church, Tyler and Jefferson streets, was built in 1865, making it the oldest Episcopal church in the diocese of Olympia. The bell in the tower was donated by a cutter captain on the condition that it would be rung on foggy days to help guide sailing vessels into the bay. The fire bell tower at Tyler and Jefferson streets dates from 1885.

Port Townsend's Victorian Homes Tour, held the first weekend in May and the third weekend in September, is an opportunity to tour many private restored homes. The Rhododendron Festival is held in mid-May just after the homes tour. Fall brings hundreds of classic boats to port for the Wooden Boat Festival.

Nearby Old Fort Townsend State Park *(see Recreation Chart)* includes the site of a U.S. Army post built in 1856 to protect settlers. The fort was abandoned in 1895 after it was destroyed by fire, and the site is now a wildlife sanctuary.

Washington State Ferries offers daily service from Port Townsend to Keystone on Whidbey Island; phone (800) 843-3779 in Wash. Puget Sound Express provides passenger service to the San Juan Islands from mid-May to mid-October; phone (360) 385-5288. For the more adventurous, sea kayaking trips are available locally.

Self-guiding tours: Information about a self-guiding driving tour is available at the Port

Townsend Chamber of Commerce Visitor Center, 2437 E. Sims Way, Port Townsend, WA 98368; phone (360) 385-2722.

Shopping areas: Lining the bay along Water Street, former sailors' saloons distinguished by handsome facades are now occupied by antique shops, restaurants, art galleries and specialty shops.

FORT FLAGLER STATE PARK, 20 mi. s.e. on Marrowstone Island, was established in 1890 as a part of the strategic coastal defense known as "Devil's Triangle." The fort possessed 6-inch disappearing guns; trails connect the gun batteries. The park contains historical displays and offers scenic views of Puget Sound and the Cascade Mountains. Daily 6:30 a.m.-dusk, mid-Apr. through Sept. 30; 8 a.m.-dusk, rest of year. Free. Phone (360) 385-1259. *See Recreation Chart.*

★**FORT WORDEN STATE PARK,** 444 acres 1 mi. n. via Cherry St., was part of an important system of coastal fortresses guarding the entrance to Puget Sound during Theodore Roosevelt's presidency. The large, grassy parade ground remains, and the handsome Victorian houses along Officers' Row have been restored. Daily 6:30 a.m.-dusk, Apr. 1 to mid-Oct.; 8-dusk, rest of year. Free. Phone (360) 385-4730. *See Recreation Chart.*

The Centrum Foundation in the park presents creative and performing arts from mid-June to early September. For schedule information contact The Centrum Foundation, P.O. Box 1158, Port Townsend, WA 98368; phone (360) 385-3102 or (800) 733-3608.

Coast Artillery Museum, in the park, commemorates the Army's 14th Coast Artillery Regiment and the 248th Regiment of the Washington National Guard with exhibits of uniforms, guns and historic photographs. Allow 30 minutes minimum. Daily 11-5, Memorial Day-Labor Day; Sat.-Sun. and holidays noon-4, Presidents Day-day before Memorial Day and day after Labor Day to mid-Nov. Donations.

Commanding Officer's House, in the park, was built in 1904 in the Jeffersonian style and features a slate roof and decorated boxed cornices. The nearly 6,000-square-foot home has been restored and furnished with period Victorian furnishings. Allow 30 minutes minimum. Daily 10-5, Apr. 1 to mid-Oct. Admission $1, under 12 free.

Marine Science Center, in the park, features exhibits and touch tanks displaying local marine life. Daily guided walks and special programs are offered in the summer. Tues.-Sun. noon-6, June 16-Labor Day; Sat.-Sun. noon-4, Apr. 1-June 15 and day after Labor Day-Oct. 31. Admission $2; under 12, $1. Phone (360) 385-5582.

JEFFERSON COUNTY HISTORICAL MUSEUM, in the 1891 city hall building at Madison and Water sts., exhibits Coast Salish Indian artifacts, military and maritime memorabilia, Victorian furnishings, an unusual bedroom display and 5,000 photographs. Author Jack London supposedly spent a night in the jail in the basement, which was in use as recently as the 1950s.

Allow 30 minutes minimum. Mon.-Sat. 11-4, Sun. 1-4, Feb.-Dec.; Sat.-Sun. 1-4, rest of year. Closed Jan. 1, Thanksgiving and Dec. 25. Donations. Phone (360) 385-1003.

ROTHSCHILD HOUSE, Jefferson and Taylor sts., is a fully restored 1868 Victorian home with original period furnishings, a restored herb garden and a flower garden with many early varieties of roses, peonies and lilacs. Daily 10-5, Apr.-Oct.; Sat.-Sun. 10-5, rest of year. Admission $2; ages 5-11, $1. Phone (360) 385-2722.

SIDEWALK TOURS, depart from Water and Madison sts. outside the Jefferson County Historical Museum *(see attraction listing).* The Waterfront Tour provides an overview of the town's history through anecdotes and an informative narrative. The Homes Tour covers two of the town's historic houses.

Allow 1 hour minimum. Waterfront Tour departs daily at 10 and 2, May 20-Oct. 2; by appointment, rest of year. Homes Tour departs daily at noon. Fee $4-$6; under 17, $2-$4. **Discount.** Phone (360) 385-1967.

POULSBO (F-2) pop. 4,800

Poulsbo's name is derived from a Norwegian word meaning "Paul's place." Norwegians settled at the head of fiordlike Liberty Bay in 1882 and developed a fishing and farming community. Poulsbo celebrates its Nordic heritage with the Vikingfest in mid-May, the Skandia Midsommarfest in mid-June and the Yule Log Festival in late November. May through October, Kitsap Harbor Tours offers daily passenger ferry service between Keyport and Poulsbo; phone (360) 377-8924 or 792-1008.

For further information contact the Greater Poulsbo Chamber of Commerce, 19131 8th Ave. N.E., P.O. Box 1063, Poulsbo, WA 98370; phone (360) 779-4848. A visitor information center is at 19003 Front St; phone (360) 779-9199.

KEMPER BREWERY, 22381 Foss Rd. N.E., offers 20-minute guided tours of the facility, including the brewing and bottling processes and the taproom. Tours are given Mon.-Fri. at 2:30 (also Sat. at 1 and 4, May-Sept.); closed Jan. 1, Thanksgiving and Dec. 25. Free. Phone (360) 697-1446.

MARINE SCIENCE CENTER, 18743 Front St. N.E., has educational exhibits and live marine specimens. Mon.-Sat. 10-5, Sun. noon-5, June-Aug.; Mon.-Sat. 10-4, Sun. noon-4, rest of year. Closed holidays. Admission $2; ages 3-11, $1. Phone (360) 779-5549.

PROSSER (F-9) pop. 4,500, elev. 662′

Part of the Yakima Valley's fruit-growing district, Prosser also is a shipping point for cattle and sheep. The treeless Horse Heaven Hills, where wild horses once roamed, rise to the south. Horse Heaven Vista, 2½ miles southeast via SR 221, offers a panorama of the lower Yakima Valley, the Cascades and the Yakima River. Vineyards are plentiful in the area; their harvest period is generally the last 2 weeks in September.

For further information contact the Prosser Chamber of Commerce and Economic Development, 1230 Bennett, Prosser, WA 99350; phone (509) 786-3177.

BENTON COUNTY HISTORICAL MUSEUM is in the city park at 7th St. and Paterson Ave. The museum has more than 20,000 items, including pioneer and American Indian artifacts, a natural history diorama, Edison phonographs, a cut glass and porcelain collection and reconstructions of a Victorian parlor and an early homestead. A collection of gowns dates 1843-1920. Allow 1 hour minimum. Tues.- Sat. 10-4, Sun. 1-5; closed Thanksgiving and Dec. 25. Admission $1; under 18, 50c. Phone (509) 786-3842.

HINZERLING VINEYARDS, 1 mi. from I-82 at jct. Wine Country Rd. and Sheridan Ave., is a limited-production winery offering informal tours and tastings. Mon.-Sat. 11-5, Sun. 11-4. Free. Phone (509) 786-2163.

PULLMAN (E-12) pop. 23,500, elev. 2,500′

Pullman is the home of Washington State University, founded in 1890. Points of interest on the campus include museums with special collections dealing with anthropology, modern art, veterinary medicine and zoology. Holland Library houses several historical collections. Campus tours are offered from room 442 in the French Administration Building Monday through Friday at 1.

For further information contact the Pullman Chamber of Commerce, North 415 Grand Ave., Pullman, WA 99163; phone (509) 334-3565 or (800) 365-6948.

PUYALLUP (H-3) pop. 23,900, elev. 48′

After crossing the plains in a covered wagon, Ezra Meeker arrived at a site just east of what is now Tacoma *(see place listing)* and named it for the Puyallup tribe; the name means "generous people."

Puyallup is the home of a lucrative flower bulb industry based on the irises, daffodils and tulips that thrive in the area's soil and climate; the Daffodil Festival is held in early April in Puyallup and nearby Tacoma, Sumner and Orting. Puyallup also hosts the Western Washington State Fair in mid-September.

For further information contact the Puyallup Area Chamber of Commerce, 322 2nd St. S.W., Puyallup, WA 98371; phone (206) 845-6755 or (800) 634-2334.

Shopping areas: South Hill Mall, ¼ mile south of SR 512 on Meridian Avenue E., features The Bon, JCPenney, Lamonts, Mervyns and Sears.

"JESUS OF NAZARETH" AT THE AMPHITHEATRE, 4½ mi. s. on SR 161 at 1422 Meridian E., offers performances of one of the largest passion plays in the United States, with more than 600 cast and crew members. Inquire about weather policies. Allow 2 hours, 30 minutes minimum. Performances are given Fri.-Sat. at 8, early July to early Sept. Tickets $10-$12; over 62, $8-$9.60; ages 1-12, $5-$6. Phone (206) 848-3411.

MEEKER MANSION, 312 Spring St., is a 17-room Victorian house that was the home of Ezra Meeker, an entrepreneur and Puyallup's first mayor. Guided tours of the 1890 mansion reveal ceiling art, handcrafted fireplaces, leaded glass windows and period furnishings. Allow 30 minutes minimum. Wed.-Sun. 1-4, Mar. 1 to mid-Dec.; closed holidays. Admission $2; over 62 and ages 12-18, $1.50; under 12, $1. Phone (206) 848-1770.

VAN LIEROP BULB FARMS INC., is 1½ mi. e. of SR 512/161; take E. Pioneer Ave. exit to 13407 80th St. E. A spring display garden with a variety of daffodils, tulips and hyacinths is featured. Allow 30 minutes minimum. Daily 9-5, Feb.-May; Mon.-Fri. 9-4:30, mid-Sept. through Oct. 31. Free. Phone (206) 848-7272.

QUILCENE (E-2)

Quilcene, at the head of Quilcene Bay off Hood Canal, is known for oysters. The State Shellfish Laboratory, 10 miles south of town, researches and raises shellfish indigenous to Puget Sound. The Quilcene National Fish Hatchery, 2 miles south of town, raises many varieties of salmon. The Olympic Music Festival, held on an early 20th-century farm 7½ miles north via Quilcene-Center Road, offers chamber music concerts weekends from late June through early September; phone (206) 527-8839, or (360) 732-4000 concert weekends.

MOUNT WALKER VIEWPOINT, 4½ mi. s. on US 101, then 4 mi. e. via a gravel road, offers panoramas of Puget Sound, the Olympics and the Cascades from its 2,804-foot summit. A hiking trail to the summit begins 300 yards from the beginning of the gravel road. The access road is not suitable for trailers or motor homes; it is sometimes closed in winter. Free. For road conditions phone (360) 765-3368.

REDMOND (C-7) pop. 35,800, elev. 50′

East of Seattle via I-405, Redmond's economy is based on light industry and electronics; the town is the headquarters for both Microsoft and Nintendo of America. Redmond's cultural background is commemorated in the Heritage Festival, held in early July, with arts and crafts and entertainment. Local recreation areas include Lake Sammamish State Park *(see Recreation Chart)* and Farrel-McWhirter Park.

For further information contact the Greater Redmond Chamber of Commerce, 16201 N.E. 80th St., P.O. Box 791, Redmond, WA 98073; phone (206) 885-4014.

MARYMOOR PARK, ½ mi. s. on W. Lake Sammamish Pkwy., is a 486-acre recreation area on the site of Seattle banker James Clise's estate. The 1904 mansion contains the Marymoor Museum, which has exhibits about local history. Guided tours are offered by appointment; phone (206) 885-3684.

The park provides facilities for picnicking, tennis, rock climbing, horseback riding, softball and bicycling; the velodrome is the scene of international-class cycling events. Park open daily 8-dusk. Museum open Tues.-Thurs. 11-4, Sun. 1-4, June-Sept.; Tues.-Thurs. 11-4, Sun. noon-4, rest of year. Park and museum free. Phone (206) 296-2964.

RENTON (G-3) pop. 41,700, elev. 45′

Originally a Duwamish Indian encampment, Renton has evolved into an important industrial city at the southern end of Lake Washington; production of jet aircraft and railroad cars is especially important. Boeing rolled out its first commercial jet, the 707, at its Renton plant, which now produces 737 and 757 aircraft.

Gene L. Coulon Memorial Beach Park, 2 miles north on Lake Washington Blvd., offers freshwater fishing, swimming, boating and a nature trail. Renton River Days, held in August, features arts and crafts, entertainment, rides, games and athletic events.

For further information contact the Greater Renton Chamber of Commerce, 300 Rainier Ave. N., Renton, WA 98055; phone (206) 226-4560.

RENTON HISTORICAL MUSEUM, 235 Mill Ave. S., features exhibits that trace the city's growth from a Duwamish Indian encampment through its late-19th-century coal-mining and lumbering days to its current status as a major manufacturing center. Displays focus on Boeing's Renton plant, pioneer lifestyles and education. The collection includes a 1927 fire engine and a Ford Model A coupe. Allow 30 minutes minimum. Tues. 9-4, Wed. and Sat.-Sun. 1-4; closed holidays. Donations. Phone (206) 255-2330.

***SPIRIT OF WASHINGTON* DINNER TRAIN,** 625 S. 4th St., offers 3½-hour round-trip excursions along the eastern shore of Lake Washington and through Bellevue to Woodinville. Trips include brunch, lunch or dinner served aboard the train and a 45-minute stop at the Columbia Winery in Woodinville *(see place listing).*

Dinner train departs Tues.-Sat. at 6:30 p.m., Sun. at 5:30 (also Mon. at 6:30 p.m., June 1 to mid-Sept.). Lunch train departs Sat. at noon. Brunch train departs Sun. at 11. Dinner train $57; lunch or brunch train $47. A seat in the dome car is $12 extra. MC, VI. Reservations are required. Phone (206) 227-7245 or (800) 876-7245.

REPUBLIC (B-11) pop. 900

Nestled in the Kettle River Range, Republic was incorporated in 1900 and named after the Republic Mine—the major gold claim in the area. For decades the town was one of the nation's largest gold producers. The town's economy relies on agriculture, lumber, mining and outdoor recreation.

Prospector's Days, held the second weekend in June, highlights the importance of logging and mining to the area with a parade and competitions.

For further information contact the Republic Area Chamber of Commerce, P.O. Box 502, Republic, WA 99166; phone (509) 775-3222.

STONEROSE INTERPRETIVE CENTER, 61 N. Kean St., provides a look at life on Earth 50 million years ago. Fossils of plants, insects and fish discovered at a nearby site are displayed. Visitors are encouraged to tour the site and dig for and keep fossils. Chisels and hammers are recommended for digging; tools are available for a fee at the center. Tues.-Sat. 10-5, May-Oct. Guided tours depart the center at 10 and 2. Donations. Phone (509) 775-2295.

RICHLAND (F-9) pop. 32,300

In 1944, along with Oak Ridge, Tenn., Los Alamos, N. Mex., and the Argonne Laboratory in Chicago, Richland was designated as a development site for the atomic bomb. From a hamlet of 250 people, Richland was gradually transformed into a major center of technological industries, among them Boeing Computer Services, Exxon, the Hanford Works of the Department of Energy, Rockwell, United Nuclear Industries and Westinghouse.

Richland also has been involved in less venturous pursuits. Irrigation from the Grand Coulee Dam helped develop the area's lush vineyards, fields and orchards.

For further information contact the Richland Chamber of Commerce, 515 Lee Blvd., P.O. Box 637, Richland, WA 99352; phone (509) 946-1651.

FAST FLUX TEST FACILITY VISITOR CENTER, 11½ mi. n. on Stevens Dr., interprets the functions of the adjacent sodium-cooled nuclear reactor through photographs, models and an audiovisual presentation. Thurs.-Fri. 11-4, Sat.-Sun. noon-5. Free. Phone (509) 376-6374.

HANFORD MUSEUM OF SCIENCE AND HISTORY, next to the Federal Building at 825 Jadwin, has displays, interactive exhibits, and videotapes. Themes include the development of the U.S. Department of Energy's Hanford Project, progress in environmental cleanup, and plans for Hanford's future. Allow 1 hour minimum. Mon.-Fri. 8-5, Sat. 9-5; closed major holidays. Free. Phone (509) 376-6374.

PLANT 2 VISITORS CENTER, 12 mi. n. in the Hanford Site, describes the workings of a nuclear power plant through a video tour, interactive exhibits and informational displays. Highlights include an exhibit explaining the atom-splitting and power-generation process, a comparison of nuclear energy with other sources of electric power and an energy-generating bicycle. Guided tours of the partially completed nuclear plant are available with advance notice.

Allow 30 minutes minimum. Thurs.-Fri. 11-4, Sat.-Sun. noon-5; closed major holidays and the day after Thanksgiving. Free. Phone (509) 372-5860.

RIDGEFIELD (F-5) pop. 1,300

RIDGEFIELD NATIONAL WILDLIFE REFUGE, 3 mi. w. of I-5 exit 14, is divided into two sections. The northern portion features the 2-mile self-guiding Oaks to Wetlands Wildlife Foot Trail through open pasture and oak groves, and around ponds. The southern unit consists of ponds, fields and pasture. Both units support sandhill cranes, songbirds and waterfowl. Canada geese, tundra swans and a variety of ducks are numerous in the winter months. Allow 2 hours minimum. Daily dawn-dusk. Free. Phone (360) 887-4106.

ROSLYN (D-8) pop. 700, elev. 2,266'

Roslyn, founded in 1886, at one time contained some of the most extensive coal fields on the West Coast. Although the last of the coal mines closed in the mid-1960s, Roslyn retains vestiges of its 1920s heyday, when the population peaked at 4,000. The television series "Northern Exposure" is filmed in town; filming of exterior scenes is done on selected weekdays from July through April. The Roslyn Cemeteries, half a mile west of town, is a 15-acre site with 25 separate cemeteries reflecting the town's ethnic diversity.

ROSLYN MUSEUM is at 403 Pennsylvania Ave. The museum displays historic documents and photographs, old mining equipment and a variety of pioneer relics. Daily 10-4:30. Donations. Phone (509) 649-2776.

ROSS LAKE NATIONAL RECREATION AREA (A-8)

Shaped like a backwards "L," Ross Lake National Recreation Area lies between the north and south sections of North Cascades National Park *(see place listing)*. For access from the east, west and south, SR 20 parallels the Skagit River through the southern half of the area, continuing southeast into Okanogan National Forest *(see place listing)*. Access from the north is possible only through Canada via a secondary road that begins in Hope, British Columbia.

Ross, Diablo and Gorge lakes are formed by Ross, Diablo and Gorge dams on the Skagit River. The dams are part of a hydroelectric project that supplies Seattle with electricity; a tour center is in Diablo *(see place listing)*. The 3½-mile Diablo Lake Trail, beginning near Diablo Lake Resort, leads to Ross Dam. From the south, access to Ross Lake is limited to trail and water routes. Seven major trails lead outward from Ross Lake into the back country.

Surrounding the lakes are 107,000 acres of glaciers, mountain peaks and forested valleys, which provide habitat for a variety of wildlife. Fishing season for Ross Lake, one of the few remaining large lakes in Washington not artificially stocked, is mid-June to late October; state fishing regulations apply, and a license is required.

For further information write the Park Superintendent's Office, North Cascades National Park, 2105 SR 20, Sedro Woolley, WA 98284; phone (360) 856-5700. Ranger stations are on SR 20 at Marblemount, phone (360) 873-4590, and Newhalem, phone (360) 386-4495. *See Recreation Chart and the AAA Northwestern CampBook.*

★SAN JUAN ISLANDS (C-1)

The glaciers that covered northwest Washington approximately 15 million years ago created the San Juan Archipelago between the mainland and Vancouver Island. As part of this archipelago, the San Juan Islands consist of 172 islands ranging in size from small rocky islets to Orcas Island, with its 57 square miles of picturesque bays and steep, forested ridges.

Spanish captain Francisco Eliza charted and named the islands in 1791, 16 years after a previous expedition discovered them. In 1792 Capt. George Vancouver claimed the islands for Britain, and in 1841 Capt. Charles Wilkes declared them American soil.

The ensuing dispute over ownership of the islands nearly brought the two nations to blows during the infamous "Pig War" of 1859, in which a stray British pig was shot in an American potato patch. The opposing sides occupied the islands for the next 13 years, but the conflict was solved peacefully through arbitration by German Kaiser Wilhelm I, who ruled in favor of the United States. What remains of the British and American forts are now part of San Juan Island National Historical Park *(see attraction listing)*.

Fidalgo, Lopez, Orcas and San Juan islands are the largest and most populated. San Juan Islands National Wildlife Refuge comprises 48 of the remaining rocks and islands, and all but Matia and Turn islands are closed to the public. The

San Juan Islands contain more bald eagles than any other region in the 48 contiguous states. Great horned owls, tufted puffins and a variety of other birds and mammals inhabit the islands; salmon, seals, dolphins and orcas (killer whales) thrive in the waters.

Recreational opportunities abound: Boating, swimming, scuba diving, fishing, hiking, bicycling and camping are among the main activities.

State ferries provide daily service between the ports of Friday Harbor, Anacortes, Lopez, Shaw and Orcas, as well as to Sidney, British Columbia, north of Victoria; phone (800) 843-3779 in Wash., *see color ad p. 156.* Seasonal passenger ferry service is available from Bellingham to Orcas Island via San Juan Island Shuttle Express *(see ad),* (360) 671-1137, and from Friday Harbor to Port Townsend via Puget Sound Express, (360) 385-5288, and to Seattle via Clipper Navigation, (800) 888-2535.

Sightseeing flights are available from Kenmore Air in Seattle; phone (206) 486-8400 or (800) 543-9595. Scheduled air service also is available from Bellingham, Seattle-Lake Union or Seattle-Tacoma International Airport. For further information contact AAA Washington or the San Juan Islands Visitor Information Service, P.O. Box 65, Lopez Island, WA 98261; phone (360) 468-3663.

Lopez Island (C-2)

One of the least visited of the San Juan Islands, Lopez Island offers miles of back roads leading through farms and rolling woodlands and a rugged coast marked with steep cliffs and isolated coves. The village of Richardson on Mackeye Harbor, now quiet, was a bustling fishing port at the turn of the 20th century.

The flat and rolling landscape has made the island particularly popular with cyclists. Camping and beach access is available at Odlin County Park and Spencer Spit Park; Agate Beach County Park also provides beach access.

LOPEZ HISTORICAL MUSEUM, 6 mi. s. of ferry dock on Weeks Rd. in Lopez Village, chronicles pioneer life on the island. Maritime exhibits include reef net boats, a captain's gig, a fish trap and steamboat models. Among the pioneer displays are kitchen utensils, horse-drawn farm machinery and what is believed to be the first car in San Juan County. Wed.-Sun. noon-4, July-Aug.; Fri.-Sun. noon-4, May-June and in Sept. Donations. Phone (360) 468-3447.

Orcas Island (B-2)

The largest and most rugged of the San Juan Islands, Orcas Island covers 57 square miles. Ferries dock at the Orcas village on the southern shore. Eastsound, at the head of Orcas' largest bay, is the island's major settlement. Historic buildings now house local commerical enterprises, including the Outlook Inn, which incorporates parts of a fur trappers cottage built in 1838. The Emmanuel Episcopal Church dates from 1886.

MORAN STATE PARK, on the e. side of Orcas Island, 8 mi. s.e. of Eastsound, was donated to the state in 1926 by former Seattle mayor and shipbuilding magnate Robert Moran. The 4,934-acre park includes hiking trails, mountain lakes and 2,409-foot Mount Constitution. A steep 6-mile road—not recommended for trailers or motorhomes—leads to a 50-foot lookout tower at the summit; the road is closed at dusk. Daily 6 a.m.-dusk. Free. Phone (360) 376-2326. *See Recreation Chart.*

ORCAS ISLAND HISTORICAL MUSEUM, in the village of Eastsound, contains Lummi and Sammish Indian artifacts, pioneer artifacts and documents contained in six homestead cabins built in the 1880s. Mon.-Sat. 1-4, Memorial Day-Labor Day; by appointment, rest of year. Admission $1; ages 6-12, 50c. Phone (360) 376-4849.

San Juan Island (C-1)

Westernmost of the major islands, San Juan Island covers 55 square miles. Rolling hills accented with small farms and patches of forest in the east give way to rugged terrain in the west, where Mount Dallas rises to 1,000 feet. Friday Harbor, the island's largest town and a bustling port, is a port of call for ferries and other boats.

Lime Kiln State Park, 10 miles west of Friday Harbor, is a good vantage point for watching pods of orcas and minke whales in summer. On the island's northwest corner is Roche Harbor, a resort town and popular yachting destination. In a peaceful glen nearby is the Afterglow Vista Mausoleum, which commemorates John S. McMillan, founder of the local limeworks.

EMERALD SEAS AQUATICS, downtown Friday Harbor at the ferry landing at 2A Spring St., at Spring St. Landing, provides scuba diving and kayaking adventures around the San Juan Islands. Visitors may see orcas (killer whales), sea otters, seals, sea lions and sea anemone; divers

San Juan Islands
Friday Harbor...
Whales...
Cruise from Bellingham Daily
(360) 671-1137
San Juan Island Shuttle Express Inc.
Bellingham Cruise Terminal (Exit #250 off I-5)

Capture the spirit of the great Northwest aboard the Washington State Ferries. Sparkling waters, snow-capped mountains, cityscapes, leaping orcas and salt air await you on our ten beautiful routes

Capture the spirit

throughout Puget Sound and the San Juan Islands.

For a free copy of our 14-page color brochure, call **1-800-84-FERRY**. Or write WSF, Public Affairs Office, Colman Dock/Pier 52, 801 Alaskan Way, Seattle, WA 98104. Bon voyage!

Washington State Ferries

can view a variety of rock fish, octopus, scallops and abalone. The center offers scuba diving and snorkeling classes, charter diving boats and rental gear, kayak rentals and professional guides.

Daily 9-6; closed Thanksgiving and Dec. 25. Group scuba classes $180; private classes $450. Dive gear rental $50-$70. Half-day diving charters $55. AE, CB, DS, MC, VI. Phone (360) 378-2772.

SAN JUAN ISLAND NATIONAL HISTORICAL PARK, on San Juan Island, commemorates the struggle for possession of the San Juan Islands by British and American settlers—a dispute that culminated in the "Pig War" of 1859. The lone casualty of the war was a stray pig, and in 1872 arbitration sustained the American claim to the San Juans. The British Camp is 10 miles northwest of Friday Harbor on a cove known as Garrison Bay. The blockhouse, commissary, hospital and barracks are restored.

The American Camp is on the southeastern tip of the island, 6 miles from Friday Harbor. Vestiges of the principal American defense work are preserved. East of the camp is the site of Old San Juan town, destroyed by fire in 1890. The officers' quarters and laundress' quarters have been restored.

Rangers are at the sites Memorial Day weekend-Labor Day and at the National Park Service office in Friday Harbor all year. Picnic areas, beaches and trails are available; hunting and camping are not permitted. The grounds are open daily dawn-11 p.m. Visitor centers at both camps are open daily 8-6, Memorial Day weekend-Labor Day; American Camp visitor center also open Thurs.-Sun. 8-4:30, rest of year. Free.

For additional information contact the Park Superintendent's Office, San Juan Island National Historical Park, 125 Spring St., P.O. Box 429, Friday Harbor, WA 98250; phone (360) 378-2240.

***WESTERN PRINCE* CRUISES,** departing from Port of Friday Harbor, offer 4-hour excursions of the San Juan Islands. An emphasis is on locating orca whales, but eagles, porpoises, harbor seals and birds also may be seen. Under 4 are not permitted. Allow 4 hours minimum. Trips depart Wed.-Mon. at 2, early June-early Sept.; at 1, early May to early June and mid-Sept.-early Oct. Occasionally morning trips are offered. Fare $43; ages 4-12, $31. AE, MC, VI. Phone (360) 378-5315; for reservations only, phone (800) 757-6722 in the U.S. Or write Western Prince Cruises, P.O. Box 418, Friday Harbor, WA 98250.

WHALE MUSEUM, 3 blks. n.w. of the ferry landing at 62 First St. N. in Friday Harbor, occupies one of the island's oldest buildings. Exhibits depict the biology, behavior and sounds of whales. Included are a display comparing the skeletons of a human, an otter and a dolphin; genealogy exhibit of local resident whales; and two videotapes. Complete skeletons of a baby gray whale and an adult killer whale also are displayed. Carvings, paintings, lithographs and photographs highlight other whale-related exhibits.

Allow 1 hour minimum. Daily 10-5, Memorial Day weekend-Oct. 1; 11-4, rest of year. Closed Jan. 1, Thanksgiving and Dec. 25. Admission $3; over 62 and students with ID $2.50; ages 5-11, $1.50. Phone (360) 378-4710.

SAPPHO (B-4)

SOLEDUCK HATCHERY INTERPRETIVE CENTER, 1½ mi. e. of US 101 on Pavel Rd., depicts the life cycle, production and harvest of salmon. Also of interest are the salmon trap and pen. Allow 30 minutes minimum. Daily 8-4:30. Free. Phone (360) 327-3246.

Be Especially Watchful at Night for Highway/Rail Grade Crossing Warning Signs.

At night it is particularly difficult to judge speed and distance. If you have any doubts, it is always better to be overly cautious than sorry.

OPERATION LIFESAVER®

Seattle

Blue water, not yellow brick, surrounds the so-called "Emerald City" of Seattle. Cupped between the jagged Olympic Mountains to the west and the volcanic peaks of the Cascade Range to the east, the city sets on a narrow strip of land between Puget Sound and 18-mile-long Lake Washington. Just north of downtown these bodies are united by a system of locks and a ship canal feeding into Lake Union, which bisects the city. Frequent rains and mists keep the surroundings cleaner and greener than most other cities of similar size.

Although early maritime expeditions sighted the Washington area before the close of the 18th century, Seattle itself was settled comparatively late. With an entire continent to cross, the first families did not reach what was to be Seattle until 1851, when they settled at Alki Point. The windswept town was soon moved around the point next to the protected waters of Elliott Bay. The city was named for Sealth, a friendly chieftain of the Duwamish and Suquamish tribes who was paid $16,000 for the use of his name.

The expanse of virgin timberland combined with the fine natural harbor to make an ideal setting for the first industry, Henry Yesler's sawmill. The mill cut timber for export, and the "road" down which logs were rolled gave birth to the expression "skid road," which later evolved into "skid row."

The population grew as the forested wilderness areas and their fur-bearing inhabitants drew lumberjacks, trappers and traders; the prospect of converting neighboring American Indians lured migrant missionaries.

The city prospered, but by 1865 a noticeable void remained: The busy bachelors had no brides. Asa Mercer, founder of the Territorial University, went East and recruited 11 brave and eligible young ladies to return with him; a second group of 57 women included the soon-to-be Mrs. Mercer. A hundred years later the saga became the basis for the 1960s television series "Here Come The Brides."

Built almost entirely of wood, the young city was destroyed in 1889 when a painter's glue pot boiled over and started the Great Fire. Seattle was soon rebuilt using more stone, iron and concrete. By 1893 the first transcontinental railroad

THE INFORMED TRAVELER

POPULATION: 516,300; metro 2,559,200 **ELEVATION:** sea level to 510 ft.

Whom to Call

Emergencies: 911

Police (non-emergency): (206) 386-1234

Time: (206) 361-8463

Temperature: (206) 464-2000, ext. 9902

Hospitals: Swedish Medical Center-Ballard, (206) 782-2700; Swedish Medical Center-Seattle, (206) 386-6000; University of Washington Medical Center, (206) 548-3300; VA Medical Center, (206) 762-1010.

Where to Look

Newspapers

The Seattle area has two daily newspapers, the *Post-Intelligencer* in the morning and the afternoon *Seattle Times.* There also is a daily Japanese paper, the *North American Post.*

Radio and TV

Seattle radio station KIRO (710 AM) is an all-news/weather station; KUOW (94.9 FM) is a member of National Public Radio.

The major TV channels are 4 (ABC), 5 (NBC), 7 (CBS), 9 (PBS) and 13 (FOX). For a complete list of radio and television programs, consult the daily newspapers.

Visitor Information

Further information is available from the Seattle-King County Convention and Visitors Bureau, 800 Convention Pl., Seattle, WA 98101; phone (206) 461-5840. The bureau is open Mon.-Fri. 8:30-5, Sat.-Sun. 10-4, Memorial Day-Labor Day; Mon.-Fri. 8:30-5, rest of year.

What to Wear

Seattle's summers have pleasant temperatures in the high 60s and low 70s; daily maximums in winter range from 45 F to 52 F. January and February are coldest, with average lows around 35 F; wear woolens and moisture-proof boots. The city receives about 80 percent of its rainfall October through April; keep rain gear handy.

had reached Seattle, and maritime trade had been established with the Orient and points east.

Swift growth followed the 1897 Klondike gold rush, for which the city served as a jumping-off point. Seattle's population increased sixfold from 1890 to 1910; tideflats were filled and steep slopes were leveled to create more liveable areas. In 1909 the city was host to its first world's fair, the Alaska-Yukon-Pacific Exhibition; the University of Washington now occupies the site.

Much of modern Seattle began in 1962 with the Century 21 Exposition, the last U.S. World's Fair to turn a profit. In addition to creating the Space Needle, the Seattle Center, the Coliseum and other city landmarks, the fair prompted the further development of parks, roads and transportation systems. Development was achieved with the preservation of the natural surroundings in mind.

The mainland U.S. port closest to the Orient, Seattle is a major trade center for exporting agricultural products, transportation equipment, seafood and forest products. Natural gas and lumber are imported from Canada; cars and electronic equipment are brought in from Japan; and petroleum arrives from numerous oil-producing nations.

Approaches

By Car

The major north-south route is I-5 from the Canadian border through Seattle to Portland and California. East-west traffic generally follows I-90, which crosses the Cascade Mountains and approaches Seattle over Lake Washington from Spokane and the East. During rush hours (7 a.m.-9 a.m. and 4 p.m.-6 p.m.), highway lane directions on I-5 and I-90 are adjusted to accommodate traffic flows going into and out of the city.

SR 520, which becomes the Evergreen Point Floating Bridge, runs east-west in the city from I-405. I-405 also runs north around Lake Washington and connects to I-5, which runs through the city.

By Plane, Bus, Boat and Train

Most domestic airlines, as well as some foreign ones, have regularly scheduled flights to Seattle-Tacoma (Sea-Tac) International Airport, midway between Seattle and Tacoma on SR 99. Closer to Seattle is Boeing Field, south of the city center on Airport Way. This is a smaller airport generally used by private and charter planes; all scheduled services use Seattle-Tacoma International Airport. For Sea-Tac airport parking and other information phone the Skyline, (206) 431-4444 or (800) 544-1965.

Gray Line Airport Express operates express buses every 30 minutes between Seattle-Tacoma International and 14 downtown hotels. Fare from the airport is $7; ages 2-12, $5.50; round trip is $12 and $9, respectively. For pick-up service information phone (206) 626-6088.

Shuttle Express offers door-to-door van service to and from Seattle-Tacoma International within the Seattle-Everett-Tacoma metropolitan area. Fares range from $16-$30. For information and reservations phone (206) 622-1424, or (800) 487-7433 out of Seattle.

Metro Transit buses link Seattle-Tacoma International with various points throughout the city; fare is $1.10 ($1.60 during rush hours). Phone (206) 553-3000.

The major nationwide busline in the Seattle area is Greyhound Lines Inc. The station is at 8th Avenue and Stewart Street. Phone (206) 628-5526.

Washington State Ferries, Colman Dock (Pier 52) at the foot of Marion Street, link Seattle with the Olympic Peninsula via Bremerton and Bainbridge Island; passenger-only ferries link Colman Dock with Bremerton and Vashon Island. State ferries leave Fauntleroy Pier in West Seattle for Vashon Island and Southworth. State ferry service also is available from Edmonds to Kingston. Phone (206) 464-6400 or (800) 843-3779.

Clipper Navigation provides daily round-trip passenger catamaran service between Seattle's Pier 69 and Victoria, and seasonal service to Friday Harbor in the San Juan Islands. For schedule information write Clipper Navigation, 2701 Alaskan Way, Seattle, WA 98121; phone (206) 448-5000 or (800) 888-2535. *See ad.*

Amtrak passenger trains arrive and depart the King Street Station at 3rd Avenue S. and S. King

Victoria, BC
via The
Victoria Clipper
Direct Service From Seattle
- Jet to Victoria in as lttle as 2-1/2 hours from Downtown's Pier 69
- Schedule allows up to 8-1/2 hours in Victoria
- Affordable hotel packages available
- Inner Harbour terminal close to attractions
- Visit the world-famous Butchart Gardens
- Explore the Royal BC Museum
- Tour the Parliament Building
- Enjoy many shops and restaurants

Ask About Our Many Hotel Packages

(206)448-5000
(800)888-2535

SEATTLE VICTORIA CLIPPER VICTORIA

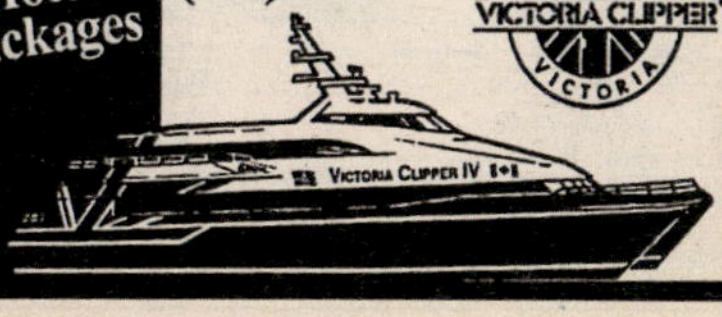

Street. For schedule information and reservations phone (800) 872-7245.

Getting Around

Street System

Seattle's avenues run north and south; they are designated by both numbers and names. Streets, also both numbered and named, run east and west. Most addresses also have area designations—N., S., E., W., N.E., N.W., S.E. or S.W.—which are important in determining correct locations. The downtown section south of Denny Way, north of Yesler Way and west of Melrose Avenue and Broadway, has avenues running parallel to Elliott Bay and streets going perpendicular to it.

Many downtown streets are one way. Synchronized traffic lights on northbound 4th Avenue and southbound 2nd Avenue make crossing the city easier. The speed limit is 30 mph or as posted. Right turns are permitted at red lights after a complete stop, unless signs indicate otherwise. Rush hours, 7-9 a.m. and 4-6 p.m., should be avoided if possible.

Portions of I-5 and I-90 have express lanes whose traffic flow changes during certain times; be aware of highway signs indicating times and directions.

Parking

On-street parking in downtown Seattle is metered, 25c for 15 minutes. During rush hours, however, parking is prohibited on certain streets; northbound 4th Avenue and southbound 2nd Avenue have a transit-only lane. There are 24-hour garages in the downtown business district at 5th Avenue and Seneca Street, 601 Olive Way, and 1st Avenue and Union Street. Garage rates range from $3 per hour to $10 per day.

Rental Cars

There are numerous automobile rental agencies in Seattle. Hertz, (206) 682-5050 or (800) 654-3080, offers discounts to AAA members. Check the local telephone directory for additional listings.

Taxis

Taxis must be ordered by telephone or hired while stopped at cab stands. Major companies

are Farwest Taxi, (206) 622-1717; Gray Top Taxi, (206) 282-8222; and Yellow Cabs, (206) 622-6500. Check the local telephone directory for further information.

Public Transportation

Seattle Metropolitan Transit System (Metro) operates a full schedule of bus and trolley service within the city and to the outlying suburbs. Passengers must have the exact fare: 85c in the city, $1.10 in King County. These fares increase to $1.10 and $1.60, respectively, during rush hours. Passengers pay as they board on in-bound and crosstown services and as they exit on outbound routes.

Free bus service is provided daily from 6 a.m. to 7 p.m. within the downtown area bordered by Battery Street on the north, Jackson Street on the south, 6th Avenue on the east and the waterfront on the west. For route information phone (206) 553-3000.

A 1.3-mile transit tunnel beneath Pine Street and 3rd Avenue offers fast trolley service through the downtown area. Station entrances are located at Convention Place (9th and Pine streets), Westlake, University Street, Pioneer Square and the International District (5th Street S. and S. King Street).

The transit authority operates streetcars along the waterfront between S. Main Street and Broad Street and to the International District on S. Main Street between Alaskan Way and 5th Avenue South. Fare is 85c, $1.10 during rush hours; cars run daily every 20-30 minutes. For times and information phone (206) 553-3000.

The Monorail, which whisks passengers from its terminal at 4th Avenue and Pine Street to Seattle Center in 95 seconds, operates daily 9 a.m.-midnight, Memorial Day weekend-Labor Day; Sun.-Thurs. 9-9; Fri.-Sat. 9 a.m.-midnight, rest of year. Fare is 90c; over 64, 35c; ages 5-12, 70c; under 5 free.

The Kingdome Shuttle transports passengers to the stadium south along 2nd Avenue from Pine Street, for football games and major concerts. Service begins 60 to 90 minutes before the event starts; fare is 50c. For further information phone (206) 553-3000.

What To See

BLAKE ISLAND MARINE STATE PARK, 473 acres 4 mi. w., is accessible only by boat; departures are from Pier 56. The park offers 16 miles of hiking trails, beach access, panoramas and exhibits. Clamming and other recreational activities are available. Deer and bald eagles are among the wildlife found in the park, which also contains Tillicum Village *(see attraction listing).*

Daily 24 hours. Round-trip boat fare $20.50; over 61, $20; ages 13-19, $9.50; ages 6-12, $7.50. For departure times phone (206) 443-1244; for park information phone 731-0770. *See Recreation Chart.*

BURKE MUSEUM, 17th Ave. and N.E. 45th St. entrance of the University of Washington campus, focuses on the natural and cultural history of the Pacific Rim and displays artifacts of the Northwest Coast Indians, including totem pole replicas, canoes, art and baskets. Other exhibits pertain to fossils, gems and minerals and dinosaurs. Allow 30 minutes minimum.

Daily 10-5; closed Jan. 1, July 4, Thanksgiving and Dec. 25. Admission $3; over 61 and students over 18 with ID, $2; ages 6-18, $1.50. Phone (206) 543-5590.

CENTRAL FREEWAY PARK, also known as Ellis Park, is a 5-acre plaza commemorating the Bicentennial. Dotted with greenery and water cascades, the park spans Seattle's eight-lane freeway (I-5) and connects downtown to First Hill and the Washington State Convention and Trade Center. Among the park's features is Naramore Fountain, a towerlike arrangement of bronze by George Tsutakawa. Daily 6 a.m.-10 p.m. Free.

COAST GUARD MUSEUM NORTHWEST, Pier 36 at 1519 Alaskan Way S., displays nautical items, ships models, Coast Guard memorabilia and more than 15,000 photographs dating from the mid-1800s. Other highlights include pieces of wood from the USS *Constitution* and HMS *Bounty.* Allow 1 hour minimum. Mon., Wed. and Fri. 9-3, Sat.-Sun. 1-5. Guided tours of Coast Guard cutters are offered Sat.-Sun. 1-4:30. Free. Phone (206) 217-6993.

DISCOVERY PARK, entered at W. Government Way and 36th Ave. W., covers 534 acres that include deep wooded ravines, tracts of forest, grassy meadows and 2 miles of beach at the base of Magnolia Bluff. On the beach behind West Point, archeologists have excavated an Indian shell dump site dating back 4,000 years, the oldest evidence of human habitation in the Seattle area. Nature trails are available. Free guided nature walks are offered. Park open daily 6 a.m.-11 p.m. Visitor center open daily 8:30-5. Nature walks depart Sat. at 2. Free. Phone (206) 386-4236.

The Daybreak Star Indian Cultural Center, which includes the Sacred Circle Indian Art Gallery, features contemporary American Indian art. Wed.-Sat. 10-5, Sun. noon-5. Free. Phone (206) 285-4425.

EVERGREEN POINT FLOATING BRIDGE, 3 mi. n., is the world's longest floating bridge. Consisting of 33 separate pontoon units, it has a total length of 7,578 feet.

FISHERMEN'S TERMINAL is off 15th Ave. W. (Emerson/Nickerson exit) at 3919 18th Ave. W. The terminal is home port to Puget Sound's fishing fleet. There are many fishing vessels and a harborfront plaza with a 30-foot-tall bronze and concrete memorial to fishermen lost at sea. Daily 24 hours. Free. Phone (206) 728-3395.

FRYE MUSEUM, 704 Terry Ave., displays 19th-century European and American paintings and changing exhibits of contemporary art. Allow 1 hour minimum. Mon.-Sat. 10-5, Sun. noon-5; closed Thanksgiving and Dec. 25. Free. Phone (206) 622-9250.

HENRY ART GALLERY, on 15th Ave. N.E. at N.E. 41st St. on the University of Washington campus, is the oldest public art museum in the state. The gallery presents changing exhibits of historical and contemporary art. **Note: The museum is scheduled to be closed for renovations from April 1995 to the summer of 1996.**

Tues.-Sun. 11-5 (also Thurs. 5-9). Admission $3.50, over 64 and students with ID $2, University of Washington students with ID and under 13 free; by donation Thurs. **Discount.** Phone (206) 543-2280.

KINGDOME, 2nd Ave. S. and S. King St., houses sporting events, concerts, trade shows and other activities. Tours, which include the press area, the playing field, a dressing room and the Kingdome Sports Museum, are offered Mon.-Sat. at 11, 1 and 3, Apr.-Sept.; at 11, rest of year. Tours enter through Gate D. Fee $4; over 65 and ages

6-12, $2. Special events might cancel some tours; phone to verify times. Phone (206) 296-3128 or 296-3111.

KLONDIKE GOLD RUSH NATIONAL HISTORICAL PARK, 117 S. Main St. in Pioneer Square Historic District, commemorates the city's role in the Klondike gold rush. Ignited by the return in 1897 of the steamship *Portland,* laden with 2 tons of solid gold from the Yukon River wilderness, a goldseeking mania swept the United States. Thousands of would-be prospectors, each equipped with a year's supply of goods, crammed aboard any available steamer bound for Alaska. Less than a year later, Seattle merchants had sold about $25 million in merchandise.

The Union Trust Annex building houses a visitor center which contains photographic murals, a slide show of old-time photographs, and displays of hardware, clothing and mining relics from the gold-rush era. Gold-panning demonstrations take place mid-June through Labor Day, and by request other times.

Feature-length films depicting the era are shown. National Park Service personnel provide interpretive services. Charlie Chaplin's classic silent film "The Gold Rush" is shown the first Sunday of the month at 3. A guided tour of the Pioneer Square Historic District is available Sunday at 10 during the summer. Allow 2 hours minimum. Park and visitor center open daily 9-5; closed Jan. 1, Thanksgiving and Dec. 25. Free. Phone (206) 553-7220.

★LAKE WASHINGTON SHIP CANAL AND HIRAM M. CHITTENDEN LOCKS, in Ballard in the n.w. part of the city, 4 mi. w. of I-5 exit 169, connect saltwater Puget Sound with the large freshwater harbor comprising Salmon Bay, Lake Union and Lake Washington. The locks are among the busiest in the Americas and are complemented by 7 acres of botanical gardens.

The visitor center explains the history and operation of the canal and locks with historical photographs and exhibits. Also featured is a 15-minute audiovisual presentation, "Lake Washington Ship Canal, Where the Activity Never Stops," every half-hour. Summer concerts are offered Sundays at 2.

The Administration Building displays historical photographs showcasing the construction of the locks and some of the more unusual vessels which have passed through them.

Trout and salmon fish ladders can be seen from a viewing window. The heaviest salmon runs occur mid- to late June through September. Allow 1 hour minimum. Lock operations can be viewed daily 7 a.m.-9 p.m. Administration Building open Mon.-Fri. 7:30-4; closed holidays. Visitor center open daily 10-7, June-Sept.; Thurs.-Mon. 11-5, rest of year. Closed Jan. 1, Thanksgiving and Dec. 25. All facilities free. Phone (206) 783-7059.

Carl S. English Jr. Botanical Garden, at Hiram M. Chittenden Locks, 3015 N.W. 54th St., encompasses 500 species of trees, shrubs and plants. Exotic species from around the world have been combined with plants indigenous to the Pacific Northwest. These include magnolias, crabapples, flowering cherries, rhododendrons, evergreen oaks, pines and camellias.

A self-guiding walking tour winds through the garden. A 1-hour guided tour includes the gardens, locks and fish ladder. Allow 30 minutes minimum. Daily 7 a.m.-9 p.m. Guided tours depart daily at 1 and 3, June-Sept.; Sat.-Sun. at 2, rest of year. Free. Phone (206) 783-7059.

MARITIME HERITAGE CENTER, S. Lake Union, is a 3-acre park that highlights the maritime history of the Pacific Northwest. Nautical tours, an education center and a restored shipyard are featured.

Center For Wooden Boats, 1010 Valley St., S. Lake Union, displays more than 100 wooden vessels ranging from replicas to boats more than 100 years old. The collection includes dugout canoes from American Indian and Polynesian cultures. Allow 30 minutes minimum.

Daily noon-6; closed Jan. 1, Easter, Thanksgiving and Dec. 25. Free. Sailboat, kayak, canoe and rowboat rentals are available at $8-$15 per hour; some exhibit boats also are available for rent. Phone (206) 382-2628.

Northwest Seaport, 1002 Valley St., S. Lake Union, features tours of the sailing schooner *Wawona.* The 1897 schooner typifies the ships that became the backbone of the Pacific Northwest lumber and fishing fleets. A 36-man crew operated the 165-foot vessel throughout the 6-month fishing season. Allow 1 hour minimum. Mon.-Sat. 10-5, Sun. noon-5, Memorial Day weekend-Labor Day; Mon.-Sat. 10-4, Sun. noon-4, rest of year. Closed Jan. 1 and Dec. 25. Donations. Phone (206) 447-9800.

MERCER ISLAND FLOATING BRIDGES, spanning Lake Washington, carry I-90 traffic over Lake Washington between Seattle and Mercer Island. The south span opened in 1940, but was

OLYMPIC NATIONAL PARK
Scenic Historical Cruise

(360)452-4520
Official Interpretive Program of the National Park Service
MOSQUITO FLEET

destroyed by a storm in 1990. It reopened in 1993. The north span, one of the world's largest floating bridges, opened to traffic in 1989.

★**MUSEUM OF FLIGHT,** ½ mi. n.w. of I-5 exit 158 at 9404 E. Marginal Way S., showcases the history of aviation technology. Exhibits in the restored Red Barn, Boeing's first manufacturing plant, document flight from the 13th century through the late 1930s.

The Great Gallery Complex contains more than 40 aircraft, more than 20 of which are suspended from the ceiling. Among those exhibited are a DC-3, a supersonic MD-21 Blackbird and drone, a restored World War II Corsair, a 1929 Boeing Model 80A-1, a 1926 Swallow, an Apollo command module and a full-scale model of an S/A-18 jet fighter.

The Hangar is a specially designed, hands-on exhibit area where children can interact with equipment and learn a variety of skills involving designing, building, maintaining and flying aircraft. Located on Boeing Field is a World War II-era B-29.

"The Dream" is an 8-minute audiovisual presentation focusing on the fulfillment of man's desire to fly. One-hour guided tours and 30-minute barnstorming tours also are available.

Allow 3 hours minimum. Daily 10-5 (also Thurs. 5-9); closed Thanksgiving and Dec. 25.

OMNIDOME
Mount St. Helens Then and Now!
The Eruption of Mount St. Helens
See it in 70mm OMNIMAX®
EXPERIENCE
OMNIDOME
Pier 59 • 622-1868
Next to the Seattle Aquarium

One-hour tours are given daily at 10:30, 12:30 and 2:30. Barnstorming tours are conducted daily at 11, noon, 1 and 1:30. Admission $6; ages 6-15, $3. AE, DS, MC, VI. **Discount.** Phone (206) 764-5720.

MUSEUM OF HISTORY AND INDUSTRY, 2700 24th Ave. E. in McCurdy Park on Lake Washington, has thousands of items dealing with the growth of Seattle and the Puget Sound region. Photographs and artifacts trace the city from its frontier settlement days to its growth as a lumbering and shipbuilding center. The collection includes nautical and aviation equipment, antique cars and costumes. A hands-on area contains period clothing, hats and toys.

Daily 10-5; closed Jan. 1, Thanksgiving and Dec. 25. Admission $5.50; over 64, physically impaired and ages 6-12, $3; ages 2-5, $1. **Discount.** Phone (206) 324-1126.

NORDIC HERITAGE MUSEUM, 3014 N.W. 67th St., focuses on Scandinavian cultural contributions to life in the Pacific Northwest from the 18th century to the present. Displays trace immigrants' journeys from Europe to America. Large galleries re-create the immigrants' small town settlements, the lumber and fishing industries and contributions from each of the five Nordic groups. Exhibits include handicrafts, textiles, personal effects and changing art exhibits from Scandinavia.

Allow 1 hour minimum. Tues.-Sat. 10-4, Sun. noon-4; closed Jan. 1, Thanksgiving and Dec. 24-25. Admission $3; over 65 and students with ID $2; ages 6-16, $1. **Discount.** Phone (206) 789-5707.

PIER 59, on Alaskan Way at the foot of Pike St., is a highlight of Seattle's waterfront development. From Pike Place Market the pier can be reached via a terraced walkway.

Omnidome Film Experience shows the updated 10th anniversary production of "The Eruption of Mount St. Helens." The OMNIMAX® film takes the audience on a simulated helicopter ride into the crater during the 1980 eruption and then returns for a comparative look a decade later. The film is presented in a 70-millimeter 180-degree format which virtually surrounds the audience. Other OMNIMAX® films are shown throughout the year

Allow 1 hour minimum. Daily 10-9, May-Sept.; 10-5, rest of year. Admission $6; over 65 and ages 13-18, $5; ages 3-12, $4. A combination ticket for Omnidome and Seattle Aquarium is available. DS, MC, VI. Phone (206) 622-1868. *See color ad.*

Seattle Aquarium, 1483 Alaskan Way, features more than 360 species of birds, fish, invertebrates and marine mammals. Highlights include the 400,000-gallon Underwater Dome, Pacific coral reef, a tide pool exhibit and discovery lab, and a giant monitor lizard. Also available for viewing are a salmon ladder and fish hatchery. Educational activities emphasizing natural history include whale- and eagle-watching trips; for further information phone (206) 386-4353.

Allow 1 hour, 30 minutes minimum. Daily 10-7, Memorial Day-Labor Day; 10-5, rest of year. Admission $6.75; over 64, and physically impaired $5.25; ages 6-19, $4.25; ages 3-5, $1.75. A combination ticket for Omnidome and aquarium is available. Phone (206) 386-4320.

★**PIKE PLACE MARKET**—*see Where To Shop.*

★**PIONEER SQUARE HISTORIC DISTRICT**—*see Where To Shop.*

PUGET SOUND VESSEL TRAFFIC SERVICE, ½ mi. s. at Pier 36 on Alaskan Way S., provides 24-hour traffic and weather information for vessels operating on Puget Sound and the Strait of Juan de Fuca. A slide show and 15-minute guided tour of the traffic center are offered. Allow 30 minutes minimum. Daily 8-6. Free. Phone (206) 217-6050.

★**SEATTLE ART MUSEUM,** 100 University St., houses a world-renowned collection of Asian, African and Northwest Coast Indian art. The collection also contains European decorative, 20th-century American, ancient Mediterranean and Egyptian arts; traveling exhibits are scheduled throughout the year. Food is available.

Allow 2 hours minimum. Tues.-Sun. 10-5 (also Thurs. 5-9); closed Jan. 1, Thanksgiving and Dec. 25. Admission $6; over 61, students with ID and ages 13-19, $4; under 13 free with adult; free to all first Tues. of the month. AE, MC, VI. Phone (206) 654-3100 or 654-3137 (TDD).

SEATTLE ASIAN ART MUSEUM is at 1400 Prospect St., in Volunteer Park at 14th Ave. E. and Prospect St. Renovated in 1993, this 40,000-square-foot museum houses one of the top seven collections of Asian art in the country. Six galleries are devoted to Chinese art, with more 2,500 works including paintings, sculpture, calligraphy, jades, bronzes, textiles, lacquers and ceramics. Six galleries of Japanese art range from prehistory to the present, and include a 17th century ink-gold screen, the "Crows," ceramics, textiles and extensive archeological materials. Korean art includes large-scale Buddhist paintings, folk art, porcelains and tomb pieces.

Other galleries display works from India, the Himalayas and Southeast Asia. The Garden Court features stone sculptures. Allow 1 hour minimum. Tues.-Sat. 10-5 (also Thurs. 5-9); closed Jan 1, Thanksgiving and Dec. 25. Admission $6, over 61 and students with ID $4, under 13 free; free to all first Tues. of the month. AE, MC, VI. Phone (206) 654-3100.

★**SEATTLE CENTER,** 74 acres 1 mi. from downtown near Elliott Bay, occupies the site of Century 21 Exposition, the 1962 World's Fair. Many of the fair buildings now house civic and cultural attractions, including the Pacific Northwest Ballet, Seattle Children's Theatre, Seattle Opera, Seattle Repertory Theatre and the Seattle Symphony. A striking feature is the architectural concept designed for life in the 21st century. Life-size dinosaur topiary is another highlight. Phone (206) 684-7200.

The Children's Museum, Center House, lower level, encourages children and adults to participate in hands-on, innovative and educational activities. Exhibits include a child-size neighborhood, drop-in art studio, toddler play center and a bubble area for play. Interpretive workshops complement the exhibits.

Allow 1 hour minimum. Tues.-Sun. 10-5; closed Jan. 1, Easter, Thanksgiving and Dec. 25. Admission $3.50, under 1 free. AE, DS, MC, VI. **Discount.** Phone (206) 298-2521.

Fun Forest Amusement Park features 18 rides. Mon.-Thurs, noon-11, Fri.-Sat. noon-midnight, Sun. noon-8, mid-June through Labor Day; Fri. 7 p.m.-midnight, Sat. noon-11, Sun. noon-8, mid-Mar. to mid-June and day after Labor Day-Oct. 31 (weather permitting). Each ride requires 2-4 tickets. Tickets 85c; eight tickets, $5.50; 18 tickets, $11. Phone (206) 728-1585.

Pacific Science Center presents science to children as an experience rather than a subject. Displays include full-size dinosaur models; Kids' Works, a multifaceted, interactive exhibit area focusing on sound, video and other science-related

Words to the Wise.

No matter how far you travel, you never will escape totally the need to guard against theft and personal crime. In a new locale, use the same prudence that you would at home. Be aware of your surroundings, and don't invite petty thievery by careless actions. Leave valuables in your hotel safe; use travelers checks instead of cash. Always lock your car, even when you are in it. And do your on-foot sightseeing in daylight hours, preferably with two or more companions.

subjects; Body Works, which explores the human body; Water Works, an outdoor exhibit with pumps, a propeller and a water wheel; a planetarium; and a laser light show. TechZone features experiments with technology, from virtual reality, to robots, to new computer software. An IMAX® theater also is featured; for schedule phone (206) 443-4629.

Allow 3 hours minimum. Daily 10-6, mid-June through Labor Day; Mon.-Fri. 10-5, Sat.-Sun. and holidays 10-6, rest of year. Closed Thanksgiving. Exhibits admission $6.50; over 65 and ages 6-13, $5.50; ages 2-5, $4.50; physically impaired free; over 65 free on Wed. Combination exhibits admission and IMAX or laser matinee, $8; over 64 and ages 6-13, $7; ages 2-5, $5.50. **Discount.** Phone (206) 443-2001.

★**Space Needle,** 605 feet high, has been Seattle's most visible landmark since it was built as the centerpiece for the 1962 World's Fair. An observation deck at the 520-foot level provides panoramas of the city, Puget Sound and the Cascade and Olympic mountains. The Compass Northwest exhibit offers information on major points visible from the observation deck. Telescopes are available on the outside deck walkway. Two restaurants atop the needle turn full circle every 58 minutes.

Allow 1 hour minimum. Daily 7 a.m.-midnight. Elevator $6.50; over 64, $5.75; ages 5-12, $4; free to restaurant patrons. AE, CB, DI, DS, MC, VI. Phone (206) 443-2100. *See ad.*

SMITH TOWER is on 2nd Ave. and Yesler Way. This 42-story building was the tallest building west of the Mississippi River when it was built in 1914. Of interest is the Chinese Room, where intricately carved Chinese characters tell the story of the Puget Sound area. An observation deck offers views of Seattle, the Olympics, Mount Rainier and the Cascades. Daily 10-10. Admission $2; over 60 and under 12, $1. Tickets are available at the first floor cigar store. Phone (206) 622-4004.

★**TILLICUM VILLAGE,** 8 mi. w. on Blake Island *(see Blake Island Marine State Park)*, features a Northwest Coast Indian longhouse where Northwest Coast Native American art and artifacts are displayed. An interpretive North American Coast Indian program, "Dance on the Wind," is performed, and a traditional baked salmon dinner is served.

Allow 4 hours minimum. The village is accessible by a 1-hour charter narrated cruise departing from Pier 56 daily at 11:30, 4:40 and 6:30, May 1-Oct. 15; Sat.-Sun. at 11:30, Oct. 16-Dec. 16 and in Apr.; Sat. at 11:30, Jan. 1-Mar. 31. Village admission (including cruise and Blake Island Marine State Park) $46.50; over 61, $43; ages 13-19, $30; ages 6-12, $18.50; ages 4-5, $9.25. AE, DS, MC, VI. **Discount.** Reservations are strongly suggested. Phone (206) 443-1244.

VOLUNTEER PARK, entered at E. Galer and 15th Ave. E. and E. Prospect and 14th Ave. E., encompasses 44½ acres of formal gardens and extensive lawns on Capitol Hill. The Conservatory has a large collection of cactuses, orchids and subtropical plants. Nearby, a statue of Secretary of State William H. Seward commemorates the 1867 Alaska Purchase. A spiral stairway leads to the top of the 75-foot Water Tower for an excellent view of the city, its lakes and nearby mountains.

Park open daily dawn-dusk. Conservatory open daily 10-7, May 1 to mid-Sept.; 10-4, rest of year. Free. Phone (206) 684-4743.

WASHINGTON PARK ARBORETUM, in Washington Park, contains 200 acres of plants from

THREE POPULAR THINGS TO DO IN SEATTLE:

1. *Visit the Space Needle's Observation Deck.*
2. *Experience the taste of Seattle--a delicious Tully's Coffee drink.*
3. *Duck the flying fish at the Pike Place Market.*

Present this ad at the Tully's Coffee shop on the Space Needle's 520-foot high Observation Deck and receive a complimentary 8 oz. latte (the Seattle espresso drink!) with the purchase of one pound of Tully's famous Space Needle Blend coffee.

Experience Seattle...and watch out for those fish!

Not valid with any other promotional offer, discount or group.
Offer requires Observation Deck ticket or restaurant reservations.
EXPIRES February 29, 1996

throughout the world. Lake Washington Boulevard E., which runs through the arboretum, is open daily 24 hours; the more scenic Arboretum Drive is open daily dawn-dusk. Guided tours are offered by appointment. Visitor center open Mon.-Fri. 10-4, Sat.-Sun. noon-4. Free. Phone (206) 543-8800.

Japanese Garden , n. of Madison St. in the arboretum, represents a compressed world of mountains, forests, lakes, rivers, tablelands and a village. Designed in Japan and built under the direction of Japanese landscape architects, the 3½-acre garden features azaleas, Japanese rhododendrons, camellias, evergreens, mosses and ferns. A tea house, a pond and an *azumaya,* or resting place, are integral parts of the garden. Nonparticipatory demonstrations of Chado, a Japanese tea ceremony, are presented the third Saturday of the month at 1:30.

Daily 10-8, June-Aug.; 10-7, in May; 10-6, Mar.-Apr. and Sept.-Oct.; 10-4, in Nov. Admission $2, over 64, ages 6-18 and physically impaired $1. Phone (206) 684-4725.

WING LUKE ASIAN MUSEUM, 407 7th Ave. S., presents a variety of cultural exhibits contributed by Asian communities in the Northwest. Examples of folk art, calligraphy and photography are displayed, as well as historical items and changing exhibits. The museum commemorates Seattle's first Asian city councilman, killed in an airplane crash, who was active in the city's International District.

Allow 30 minutes minimum. Tues.-Fri. 11-4:30, Sat.-Sun. noon-4; closed holidays. Admission $2.50; over 62 and ages 13-18, $1.50; ages 5-12, 75c; free to all Thurs. Phone (206) 623-5124.

WOODLAND PARK ZOO is at 5500 Phinney Ave. N. between N. 50th and N. 59th sts. Take I-5N exit 169 (50th St.), go w. 1⅓ mi. on 50th St. to s. entrance at N. 50th and Fremont Ave. N. The 92-acre zoo contains animals and reptiles representing almost 300 species. The Tropical Rain Forest features 50 animal species, 800 plant species and a gorilla exhibit, while Tropical Asia offers an elephant forest. The African Savanna has hippopotamuses, giraffes, monkeys and a variety of birds. The Temperate Forest is a marsh/swamp exhibit which includes waterfowl. A pheasant exhibit and the Family Farm petting zoo also are on the grounds.

Allow 2 hours minimum. Daily 9:30-6, Mar. 15-Oct. 14; 9:30-4, rest of year. Admission $7; over 64, $5.25; ages 6-17, $4.50; ages 3-5, $2.25. Parking $1-$2 for 4 hours. Phone (206) 684-4800, or TDD (206) 684-4026.

Industrial Tours

RAINIER BREWING CO., 3100 Airport Way S., offers tours of the brewing rooms and aging cellar as well as an audiovisual presentation about packaging; tastings are available. A sweater is

recommended; shoes are required. Children must be with an adult and be able to walk up stairs. Under 5 are not permitted. Allow 1 hour minimum. Mon.-Sat. 1-6; closed holidays. Tours and tastings free. Phone (206) 622-2600.

RED HOOK ALE BREWERY, 3400 Phinney Ave. N., offers 45-minute tours explaining the brewing and bottling processes, as well as free tastings. Under 21 are not permitted. Tours are given Mon.-Thurs. at 11 and 4, Fri. at 11, 4 and 6, Sat.-Sun. at 1:30, 2:30, 3:30 and 4:30, July 5-Labor Day; Mon.-Fri. at 3, Sat.-Sun. at 1:30, 2:30, 3:30 and 4:30, rest of year. Closed Jan. 1, July 4, Thanksgiving and Dec. 25. Fee $1. Phone (206) 548-8000.

SAN JUAN ISLANDS SEALIFE CRUISE
Orca Performances Daily

(206) 252-6800
The Seattle Aquarium's choice for San Juan Orca Searches
MOSQUITO FLEET

Seattle-Victoria Car Ferry

It's the most scenic distance between two points! Reserve your passage today and sail May through September on the *Royal Victorian* through some of the most beautiful scenery on the coast while you enjoy our buffet, duty free shopping and more. For recorded information, call 1-800-668-1167.

VICTORIA LINE.

Reservations (206) 625-1880 Seattle
(604) 480-5555 Victoria

What To Do

Sightseeing

Visitors may tour Coast Guard ships Sat.-Sun. 1-4 when in port; phone (206) 217-6993.

Bus, Limousine, Carriage or Train Tours

Gray Line Tours conducts bus trips through Seattle and its environs, including a "Northern Exposure/Twin Peaks"-Snoqualmie Tour. Other tour areas include Mount Rainier, the Olympic Peninsula, Vancouver and Victoria. Contact Gray Line of Seattle for further information; phone (206) 626-5208 or (800) 426-7532.

Gray Line's Seattle Trolley Tours offers narrated loop trips through the downtown area and Seattle Center in a motorcoach outfitted to resemble a trolley. Trolleys make seven scheduled stops at 30-minute intervals daily 9:30-5:50, June-October. Ticket booths are located on Pine Street opposite Westlake Center and on Alaskan Way at Pier 57. The all-day pass is $11; over 64, $10; ages 13-18, $9; ages 5-12, $7. Phone (206) 626-5212.

Seattle Tours offers 3-hour narrated, interactive van tours of the city's highlights, including the waterfront, Pioneer Square and and various neighborhoods. A stop to experience one of the popular espresso beverages is included in the tour. Tour size is limited to ten passengers. For reservations and information phone (206) 660-8687.

***SPIRIT OF WASHINGTON* DINNER TRAIN**—*see Renton.*

Bicycle Tours

TERRENE TOURS, offers 1-day guided bicycle excursions in the Seattle-Puget Sound area. Customized tours and bicycle rentals also are available. All tours depart at 9 and 5; fee includes bicycle rental, accessories, lunch and ferry transportation.

Puget Sound-Bainbridge Island tour departs from Myrtle Edwards Park Wed. and Sat. Lake Washington-Gasworks Park tour departs from Gasworks Park Mon. and Fri. Cascades-Snoqualmie Falls tour departs Thurs. and Sun. Afternoon sunset rides also are offered. A shuttle is available for pick-up one hour prior to the tour. Puget Sound and Lake Washington tours $109. Afternoon sunset tour $79. AE, MC, VI. Reservations are required. Phone (206) 325-5569.

Boat Tours

GLACIER BAY TOURS AND CRUISES offers narrated, 12-hour boat trips to the San Juan Islands. The 150-passenger excursion yacht cruises the protected waters of Puget Sound, including a port call at Roche Harbor on San Juan Island. Return trips traverse Deception Pass. Cruises depart Shilsole Marina daily at 7:30, mid-June through Nov. 30. Sat.-Sun. and holidays $54;

over 64, $49; ages 3-12, $29. Mon.-Fri. fare $49; over 64, $44; ages 3-12, $24. MC, VI. Reservations are required. Phone (206) 292-9606.

GRAY LINE WATER SIGHTSEEING cruises depart Pier 57 at the foot of University St. The 2½-hour narrated trips traverse the downtown waterfront, Elliott Bay, the Lake Washington Ship Canal and Lake Union via the Hiram Chittenden Locks. Departures daily at 10, 11:30, 1, 2:30, 4 and 7, July 1-Labor Day; daily at 10, 1, 4 and 7 Memorial Day-June 30 and day after Labor Day-Sept. 30; daily at noon and 3:30, Apr. 1-day before Memorial Day and in Oct.; Fri.-Mon. at noon, rest of year. Fare $19.95; ages 5-12, $9.75. AE, MC, VI. Phone (206) 623-4252.

MOSQUITO FLEET—*see Everett*

SEATTLE HARBOR TOURS, Pier 55 at the foot of Seneca St., offers 1-hour narrated trips along the waterfront and past the shipyards. Departures daily at 11, 12:15, 1:30, 2:45, 4 and 5:15, Memorial day weekend-Sept. 30; at 12:15, 1:30, 2:45 and 4, Apr.-May and in Oct.; at 2:45, rest of year. Fare $11.55; ages 5-12, $5.30. AE, MC, VI. Phone (206) 623-4252.

SPIRIT OF PUGET SOUND, Pier 70 on Alaskan Way at the foot of Broad St., offers 2- and 3-hour excursion cruises on Elliott Bay. Cruises include buffet lunch or dinner and entertainment. The 2-hour lunch cruise departs Mon.-Sat. at noon. The 2-hour brunch excursion departs Sun. at noon. The 3-hour dinner cruise departs daily at 7. The 2½-hour moonlight party cruise departs Fri.-Sat. at 11:30 p.m.; under 21 are not permitted. All cruises begin boarding 30 minutes prior to departure.

Mon.-Sat. lunch cruise $28.15. Sun. brunch cruise $30.45. Sun.-Thurs. dinner cruise $48.45, Fri. $50.45, Sat. $53.10. Moonlight party cruise $15.95. Ages 3-12 half price on all cruises. AE, MC, VI. Reservations are required. Phone (206) 443-1442.

Plane or Helicopter Tours

Seaplane sightseeing flights over the Seattle area depart daily from Kenmore Air Harbor at the north end of Lake Washington. Flights last approximately 20 minutes; phone Kenmore Air, (206) 486-8400, 364-6990 or (800) 543-9595.

Walking Tours

Chinatown Discovery Tours offers a cultural experience including a leisurely guided walking tour of Seattle's Chinatown/International District, a seven-course Dim-Sum lunch and a Chinese tea time with cakes and pastries. The evening tour includes an eight-course dinner. Tours without meals also are available. For reservations phone (206) 236-0657. City Hunt provides a clue and riddle guide to lead patrons on a 2-hour, self-guiding walking tour of the city; phone (206) 625-0607.

★**BILL SPEIDEL'S UNDERGROUND TOUR** explores the five-block area around Pioneer Square, with its 19th-century storefronts. The tour includes subterranean sidewalks and storefronts created when street levels were raised 8 to 35 feet following a fire in 1889. The tongue-in-cheek guided tour highlights Seattle's history in the aftermath of the fire that destroyed 30 blocks of downtown Seattle as well as 10 piers on the wharf. Comfortable walking shoes and appropriate clothing are recommended.

Allow 2 hours minimum. Tours depart numerous times daily from Doc Maynard's Public House in the Pioneer Building at 1st Avenue and James Street in Pioneer Square Park; departure times vary. Visitors should arrive at the departure point 25 minutes before scheduled tour time. Fee $5.50; over 59, $4.50; ages 13-17, $4; ages 6-12, $2.50. Reservations are strongly recommended. For departure times and reservations phone (206) 682-4646. *See ad.*

SEATTLE'S BEST WALKING TOURS depart from Westlake Plaza at 4th and Pine; meet outside the SBC shop between Nordstrom and The Bon Marche. These year-round guided 2½-hour walking tours of downtown Seattle offer a street-level overview of Seattle, its art, architecture and history. Reservations are suggested. Departures Tues.-Sat. at 10:15; closed major holidays. Fee $10. Phone (206) 226-7641.

Sports and Recreation

Seattle offers sports from skin diving to mountain climbing; its residents boast that its location and climate make it possible to sail in the morning and ski that afternoon. The extensive city park system includes more than 5,000 acres of parkland and boulevards. The many state parks in the vicinity provide recreational and camping facilities.

A variety of local outdoor recreation books and maps are sold in the Travel Store at the AAA Washington office.

SEATTLE'S HISTORY IS DEEP!

The underground is dry but its history is not. Tours start in a turn-of-the-century pub (lunches & snacks available). Guides take you into three abandoned underground areas on an unusually entertaining walking tour.

UNDERGROUND TOUR

For more information call (206)682-4646.

Spectator sports run the gamut in Seattle. There is **automobile racing** at three major raceways in the area; the racing schedule varies. The Kingdome features **football** by the NFL's Seahawks and major league **baseball** by the Mariners during their respective seasons.

Usually the Sonics play NBA **basketball** in the Seattle Center Coliseum, but renovations during the '94-'95 season have forced them to thrill their fans in the Tacoma Dome. The Seattle Thunderbirds play **hockey** in the Seattle Center Arena and the coliseum. Area college teams participate in all major sports. During the August Seafair, Lake Washington provides a course for **hydroplane races.**

Boating is available on freshwater Lake Washington, saltwater Puget Sound or both, thanks to the locks and canal connecting the two. A multitude of marinas provides moorage facilities. Any type of craft can be rented, from small sailboats or canoes to large seagoing yachts. Rental boats also are available at the Center for Wooden Boats at the Maritime Heritage Center *(see attraction listing).*

Golf courses, both municipal and commercial, are plentiful, as are driving ranges and pitch-and-putt courses. Some private clubs extend reciprocal privileges to visitors who are members of certain out-of-town golf clubs. The Seattle Park Department can furnish information about locations and greens fees; phone (206) 684-4075.

Hiking and **horseback riding** enthusiasts will find miles of forest trails in nearby areas and mountains. The U.S. Forest Service and Park Service, (206) 220-7450, can provide information about trails. The local telephone directories contain listings of stables and academies.

Fishing opportunities are plentiful. Freshwater fishing is available from piers at Green Lake and Lake Washington, in county parks and in area lakes and streams. The Washington State Department of Fish and Wildlife, (206) 775-1311, is the best source for freshwater license requirements and information.

Sport Fishing of Seattle, Pier 54 on the Elliott Bay waterfront off Alaskan Way, offers 6- and 7-hour salmon and bottom fishing cruises daily; phone (206) 623-6364. Spot Tail Salmon Guides offers offers private salmon fishing trips twice daily; phone (206) 283-6680. Piers 57 and 86 are public fishing piers on Elliott Bay. Charters for Puget Sound or deep-sea fishing off the coast can be arranged; consult the local telephone directories.

White-water rafting, float trips and bald eagle sightseeing tours are offered on rivers in the Cascades and Olympics. The season for white-water rafting is April through September; bald eagle sightseeing tours take place December through February. Rates for such trips are commensurate with offerings, but the average fee for a full-day excursion is $40-$75.

Reservations for trips can be made through the following Seattle agencies: Downstream River Runners, 12112 N.E. 195th St., Bothell, WA 98011, (206) 483-0335 or (800) 234-4644; Northern Wilderness River Riders, 77th Ave. S.E., Woodinville, WA 98072, (206) 448-7238 or 485-7238; and Orion River Expeditions Inc. 4739 Thackeray Pl. N.E., Seattle, WA 98105, (206) 547-6715 or (800) 553-7466 **(discount).**

Other agencies include River Recreation Inc., 13 211th Pl. S.E., Redmond, WA 98053, (206) 392-5899 or (800) 464-5899; and Zig Zag Expeditions, 1 Etruria St. #6, Seattle, WA 98109, (206) 282-2840. Most agencies' offices are open weekdays during working hours.

Mountain climbing and **skiing** are possible at many challenging spots in the Seattle area. Guided trips to the summit of Mount Rainier, as well as instructions in climbing techniques, are available *(see Mount Rainier National Park).* Major ski areas within a short drive of the city are noted under the listings for Mount Baker-Snoqualmie and Wenatchee national forests *(see place listings).* For ski reports phone (206) 634-2754 or 634-0071. Cross-country skiing also is available in several areas; for a cross-country ski report phone (206) 632-7787.

Swimming and **scuba diving** are favorite summertime sports. There are saltwater beaches at Alki and Golden gardens and freshwater beaches on Lake Washington and Green Lake, as well as several public swimming pools within the city. The local telephone directory provides information about scuba diving instruction and equipment rental.

Since the 1890s **bicycling** has been a popular sport in Seattle. The city has an assortment of asphalt and concrete routes for cycling enthusiasts. The Burke-Gilman Trail, designed for bicycling and hiking, extends 15½ miles from 8th Ave. N.W. and Leary Wy. to Tracy Owen Station Park at 61st Avenue and SR 522. The trail skirts the University of Washington campus and offers good views of the area. North of Lake Washington it connects with the Sammamish River Trail,

Note

AAA Washington's office at 330 6th Ave. N. is immediately west of Aurora Avenue (SR 99). It is illegal as well as extremely dangerous for pedestrians to cross Aurora Avenue. Members planning to stop at the club should arrange to park west of Aurora Avenue.

which then continues another 12 miles to Marymoor Park *(see Redmond)*.

One of Seattle's most popular bicycle paths is the 3-mile paved trail bordering Green Lake in the park of the same name. Many other routes connect with the city parks; others are along the waterfront. For further information phone (206) 522-BIKE.

Facilities for **tennis** and other sports also are available. The city park department maintains nearly 100 public courts, some of which are lighted for night matches; several private tennis clubs extend reciprocal privileges to travelers. Commercial ranges for **rifle** and **skeet shooting** are listed in the local telephone directory. City parks have facilities for both **jogging** and **lawn bowling.** For further information phone (206) 684-4075.

Where To Shop

Many downtown department stores and specialty shops are in an area bounded by 1st and 6th avenues, University Street and Olive Way. Center House at Seattle Center includes the Food Circus Court and the International Bazaar, which deal in the foods and products of many nations. International shops can be found in the University District along University Avenue between N.E. 41st and 55th streets.

The Broadway area in the Capitol Hill District and Rainier Square between 4th and 5th streets contains dozens of specialty shops. Visitors can watch artisans at work at the Northwest Craft Center on the Seattle Center grounds and at Pottery Northwest at 226 First Ave. N., just west of Seattle Center. Pier 70, at the foot of Broad Street on Alaskan Way, has blossomed into an array of shops and restaurants.

The Bon has branches in Seattle's many suburban shopping centers. Nordstrom is at 5th and Pine. Westlake Center at 5th and Pine has shops on four levels.

Recreational Equipment Inc. (REI), on 11th Avenue between East Pine and East Pike streets, is a well-known sporting goods store. Another well-known establishment is Shorey's Book Store, on the atrium level at 1411 1st Ave., which has more than 1 million old, rare and used books.

Artwork and crafts created by American Indians of the Northwest and other regions are sold at the Daybreak Star Indian Cultural Center in Discovery Park *(see attraction listing)*. A permanent art collection also is displayed.

The International District, one of the city's oldest sections, is bordered roughly by 4th and 12th avenues and Main and Lane streets. This area, which is mainly Asian, has restaurants and a number of unusual shops offering a variety of items from the Orient. Particularly notable is Uwajimaya, 519 6th Ave. S., which offers a wide selection of exotic products.

Waterfront areas along Puget Sound feature interesting curio shops. Ye Olde Curiosity Shop at Pier 54, Alaskan Way, has been a waterfront landmark since 1889; the shop contains a wide variety of articles, including American Indian and Eskimo crafts, carvings and novelties from around the world. Other import shops with such goods as clothing, gourmet foods, decorator items, pottery and antiques also are in the waterfront area.

Major shopping malls are Alderwood Mall in nearby Lynnwood, one of the largest shopping malls in the state; Northgate, 6 miles north of downtown just east of I-5 exit 173; and Southcenter, east of I-5 exit 153.

Antiques are the specialty in the Greenwood District, along Greenwood Avenue N. from N. 67th to N. 87th streets. There are two major factory outlet malls in Tukwila: Parkway Plaza, 17000 Southcenter Pkwy., and Pavilion Outlet, 17900 Southcenter Pkwy. The former has retail stores in addition to factory outlet establishments.

★**PIKE PLACE MARKET,** at Pike St. and 1st Ave., is a diverse marketplace that first opened as a farmers' market in 1907. The complex features fresh produce, seafood, arts and crafts, street musicians, shops and restaurants. The Pike Street Hillclimb, a skywalk with elevators and stairs, connects the market with the waterfront. Parking is available in a garage linked to both the market and the waterfront by elevator. Mon.-Sat. 9-6, Sun. 11-5; closed Jan. 1, Memorial Day, July 4, Labor Day, Thanksgiving and Dec. 25. Phone (206) 682-7453.

★**PIONEER SQUARE HISTORIC DISTRICT,** just s. of downtown between the waterfront and the International District, is a 30-block area of restored historic buildings. Most of the structures were built after the Great Fire of 1889; the district's architecture is notably harmonious, since most of the buildings were designed by one architect. The original Pioneer Square was actually a triangle between 1st Avenue and James Street. Today it features a totem pole carved by Tlingit Indians, as well as a statue of Chief Sealth.

Contemporary Pioneer Square consists of art galleries, antique shops, boutiques, nightclubs, restaurants and sidewalk cafes. Extending between S. Washington and S. Jackson streets is Occidental Park, a landscaped pedestrian mall.

Waterfall Park, at 2nd and S. Main streets, has a central waterfall and a stream around its perimeter. The distinctive 42-story Smith Tower at 2nd and Jefferson streets was for many years one of the tallest buildings west of the Mississippi River.

Where To Dine

From seafood stands on the water's edge to a revolving dining room 500 feet in the sky, Seattle offers dining choices to answer every craving. Seafood, particularly salmon, clams, shrimp, oysters and crabs, is excellent. Many restaurants along the waterfront specialize in fresh fish and seafood dishes; several delight patrons by serving salmon in the American Indian style, broiled over open fires.

Italian cuisine is popular: Prego, on the top floor of the Stouffer Madison Hotel, features Italian dining with a Northwest flair, while Saleh al Lago, 6804 E. Greenlake Ave. N., serves central Italian fare. For a taste of eastern Europe, the Labuznik at 1924 First Ave. serves Czechoslovakian favorites. At Nikko, 5th Avenue and Stewart Street in the Westin Hotel, Japanese food is the specialty.

Rare dining experiences where the scenery rivals the menu are found in the revolving restaurant atop Seattle Center's Space Needle and at Canlis, 2576 Aurora Ave. N., overlooking Lake Union and the Cascades.

Nightlife

Seattle offers a full range of nightlife spots from quiet lounges to splashy waterfront nightclubs. Most establishments are downtown, along the waterfront and Shilshole Bay, in Pioneer Square, around Lake Union or in the University District.

The regional music scene has spawned several bands that have attained national recognition, including Nirvana, Pearl Jam and Soundgarden. Seattle's "grunge" sound can be sampled at The Colourbox, 113 1st Ave. S.; Crocodile Cafe, 2200 2nd Ave.; Downunder, 2407 1st Ave.; Moe's Mo'Roc'N Cafe, 925 E. Pike St.; Off Ramp, 109 Eastlake Ave. E.; RKCNDY, 1812 Yale Ave.; and Swan Cafe, 608 1st Ave. The refurbished Paramount Theatre, 907 Pine St., presents popular bands and entertainers in concert; for schedules phone (206) 682-1414.

The large downtown hotels have elegant bars, including the Garden Court in the Four Seasons Olympic Hotel and the Lobby Bar at the Westin. You'll be missing a great opportunity if you don't mix your cocktails with a view at such rooftop lounges as the Camlin Hotel's Cloud Room or the Stouffer-Madison's Visions Lounge.

Some of Seattle's waterfront seafood restaurants become dance spots in the evening. Top-40 bands and video clubs are popular at Shilshole Bay and Lake Union. The Ballard District has a collection of popular nightspots, including The Backstage at 2208 N.W. Market St., and the Ballard Firehouse at 5429 Russell Ave. N.W.

A touch of history enhances the establishments in Pioneer Square: The J & M Cafe at 201 First Ave. S. recalls the early-20th-century gold rush saloons. Merchant's Cafe at 109 Yesler Way is one of the city's oldest restaurants; it now features local lounge acts and occasional jazz and blues bands. Jazz and blues also enliven Dimitriou's Jazz Alley, 2033 Sixth Ave., and the Old Timer's Cafe, 620 First Ave. New Orleans Restaurant, 114 1st Ave. S., features jazz, Dixieland, zydeco and rhythm and blues acts.

For those who prefer tickled funny bones to tickled ivories, the Comedy Underground at 222 S. Main in Pioneer Square and Giggles at 53rd and Roosevelt offer standup comedians.

Note: The mention of any area or establishment in the preceding sections is for information only and does **not** imply endorsement by AAA.

Theater and Concerts

Seattle Center is the cultural focus of metropolitan Seattle. Its Opera House is the headquarters of the Seattle Opera Association, which presents several full-scale operatic productions during its September through May season.

When not the scene of operas, the Opera House plays host to the Pacific Northwest Ballet, artists, theatrical productions, modern dance performances and concerts by the Seattle Symphony. The orchestra schedules evening concerts regularly Monday and Tuesday, September through April; Sunday matinees and family concerts also are offered.

The Bagley Wright Theatre at the Seattle Center houses the nationally acclaimed Seattle Repertory Theatre Company, which presents six plays from late October through May. Ticket prices range from $6 to $23.50; for curtain times phone (206) 443-2222.

Broadway shows are the attraction at the 5th Avenue Theatre, 1308 5th Ave.; phone (206) 625-1900. Popular with summer playgoers are A Contemporary Theater (ACT), near Seattle Center at 1st Avenue W. and W. Roy, (206) 285-5110; and Intiman at the Seattle Center Playhouse, (206) 626-0782.

Other performances are given at the Bathhouse Theater, the Empty Space Theatre, Glen Hughes Playhouse, the Penthouse and other small theaters.

Check the newspapers for full listings. Ticketmaster Northwest Entertainment Hotline has recorded information about a variety of events and activities; phone (206) 292-5444.

Especially for Children

Seattle offers a variety of attractions and experiences to interest even the most travel-weary youngsters. Bathtub sailors enjoy the bustle of dockside activity and tours of the harbor, locks and floating bridges. Budding fishermen will be interested in the city's aquarium and Fisherman's Terminal. Seattle's parks provide acres of play space; Gasworks Park has a playbarn and an area with ropes, towers and slides.

Woodland Park features a zoo. The totem pole in Pioneer Square Park intrigues many children. Designed exclusively for youngsters, The Children's Museum at Seattle Center features interesting hands-on displays. The Seattle Center's children's program includes puppet shows and other amusements for youngsters. The Seattle Children's Theatre presents fairy tale classics and contemporary productions; phone (206) 441-3322.

Special Events

Seattle hosts a wide variety of festivals and programs throughout the year. The city celebrates the coming of spring with the opening day of yachting season on the first Saturday in May, when a parade of boats sails from Lake Union to Lake Washington. Festivities continue through mid-May with street fairs held in the University District. Norwegian Constitution Day is celebrated May 17 in the city's Ballard district.

The Northwest Folklife Festival, held over Memorial Day weekend, is a showcase of traditional and folk arts of more than 100 countries. Music, dancing, crafts exhibits and demonstrations are among the activities, some of which are participatory.

The 23-day Seattle Seafair, held from mid-July to early August, heads the summer schedule with street parades and hydroplane races on Lake Washington. Bumbershoot, a festival of the arts, takes place at Seattle Center on Labor Day weekend. Entertainment and arts and crafts are featured at the Harvest Festival, a celebration of autumn held in late November. The Christmas Cruise, noted for its fleet of colorfully illuminated boats, takes place in early December.

SEDRO WOOLLEY (C-3) pop. 6,000, elev. 55′

Thick stands of Western red cedar covering the Skagit River valley first attracted logging interests to Sedro—from the Spanish word *cedro,* meaning "cedar"—in the late 1800s. Prospectors soon followed, on their way to the Mount Baker region during the gold rush. After developing into the head of navigation on the Skagit River, Sedro merged with the town of Woolley, a junction for the Great Northern and Northern Pacific railroads.

Fertile farmlands have replaced the valley's dense forests, although lumbering remains important. Sedro Woolley celebrates its lumbering heritage during the Loggerodeo in early July with competitions demonstrating logging skills.

For further information contact the Sedro Woolley Chamber of Commerce, 116 Woodworth St., P.O. Box 562, Sedro Woolley, WA 98284; phone (360) 855-1841.

LAKE WHATCOM RAILWAY, 10 mi. n. on SR 9 at the former Northern Pacific depot at Wickersham, provides a scenic 1½-hour train trip through the countryside. A steam-powered train departs Tues. and Sat. at 11 and 1, late June-Aug. 31. Special Santa Claus train rides run Sat. at 11, 1 and 3, in Dec. Specially decorated trains also operate on selected holidays and during the fall foliage season. Fare $10; ages 2-18, $5. Reservations are required for the Santa Claus train. Phone (360) 595-2218.

SEQUIM (D-1) pop. 3,600

Sequim (SKWIM), a Klallam Indian word meaning "calm waters," is a popular retirement area, with its dry sunny climate and varied recreational opportunities. Developed facilities are found at Sequim Bay State Park *(see Recreation Chart).* Dungeness Recreation Area in Clallam County Park, 6 miles northwest, provides camping facilities as well as access to Dungeness National Wildlife Refuge. The John Wayne Marina occupies land donated by the legendary actor to allow others to enjoy his favorite fishing spot.

A 3-hour parade and the crowning of the Irrigation Queen highlight the Irrigation Festival, held in early May; it is considered Washington's oldest continuing community festival.

For further information contact the Sequim/Dungeness Valley Chamber of Commerce, P.O. Box 907, Sequim, WA 98382; phone (360) 683-6197.

DUNGENESS NATIONAL WILDLIFE REFUGE, 4½ mi. w. on US 101, then 3 mi. n. on Kitchen Dick Rd., contains one of the longest natural sandspits in the United States. Dungeness Spit is about 6 miles long—and growing—and juts into the Strait of Juan de Fuca. It forms a saltwater lagoon that is used as a rest stop by thousands of migratory waterfowl. It also is the home of more than 250 species of birds.

The 63-foot-high New Dungeness Lighthouse at the end of the spit is open for free guided tours 9-4 daily. The lighthouse is only accessible by boat or by hiking the length of the spit. The 1927 lighthouse replaced an earlier one built in 1857.

Clamming, crabbing and fishing are permitted in season but are subject to state regulations. Refuge regulations prohibit fires, pets, bicycles, guns and camping. Other restrictions apply; see the refuge manager. No vehicles are allowed; visitors must park near the refuge entrance and hike in. Daily dawn-dusk. Admission $2 per family. Phone (360) 457-8451.

MUSEUM AND ART CENTER IN THE SEQUIM-DUNGENESS VALLEY, 1 blk. n. off US 101 at 175 W. Cedar, has exhibits on natural and human history, farming, Coast Salish Indian and pioneer life, works by local artists and a display on Dungeness Spit and its lighthouse. Highlights include specimens from the Manis mastodon site. Tours are available by appointment. Allow 30 minutes minimum. Daily 9-4; closed holidays. Donations. Phone (360) 683-8110.

NEUHARTH WINERY, ½ mi. e. on US 101, then ¼ mi. s. on Still Rd., offers free tastings and an observation area for viewing the winemaking process. Daily 9:30-5:30; closed Jan. 1, Easter, Thanksgiving and Dec. 25. Free. Phone (360) 683-9652.

OLYMPIC GAME FARM, 5 mi. n.w. on Ward Rd. following signs, is a 90-acre preserve for animals used in television commercials. Visitors can drive two loop roads through large fields containing bears, bison, deer, elk, sheep and zebras. Such predators as lions and wolves can be seen in the central compound. Also featured are movie sets, man-made dens, an aquarium, a studio-barn and a petting area.

Walking-tour guides discuss the animals in residence, describe filming procedures and explain the goals of research into the preservation of certain endangered species.

Self-guiding driving tours are available daily starting at 9; closing times vary. Guided walking tours are offered daily 9-3, May 15-Labor Day. Closed Jan. 1, Thanksgiving and Dec. 25. Admission $6; over 60 and ages 5-12, $5. Combined walking and driving tour $8; over 60 and ages 5-12, $6. Phone (360) 683-4295 or (800) 778-4295.

SHELTON (G-1) pop. 7,200, elev. 41′

Shelton, on an inlet of South Puget Sound, is known for Christmas trees and succulent oysters. The Oysterfest celebrates this bounty in early October with an oyster-shucking contest, a cook-off and arts and crafts and boating exhibits.

Between November and mid-December, 3 million Christmas trees are cut, packed and shipped from this area. A list of packing sheds that can be visited is available from the Shelton-Mason County Chamber of Commerce, P.O. Box 666, Shelton, WA 98584; phone (360) 426-8678.

The Mason County Historical Museum, downtown in the former library building, has exhibits pertaining to Shelton's logging industry. "Tollie," a 90-ton Shay locomotive that operated in the woods near Shelton 1924-58, is displayed at Railroad Avenue and Third Street. Its caboose houses the chamber of commerce.

SILVERDALE (F-2) elev. 25′

At the head of Dyes Inlet, Silverdale is 3 miles south of the Trident Submarine Base. Seabeck Highway leads west from Silverdale to Seabeck and Scenic Beach State Park *(see Recreation Chart)*. Rhododendrons bloom in early May.

For further information contact the Silverdale Chamber of Commerce, 9729 Silverdale Way, P.O. Box 1218, Silverdale, WA 98383; phone (360) 692-6800.

Shopping areas: The major shopping center in Silverdale is Kitsap Mall, just south of SR 3 at the Clear Creek Road interchange, featuring The Bon, Lamonts and Sears.

KITSAP COUNTY HISTORICAL MUSEUM, at 3343 N.W. Byron St. near Waterfront Park in the old Silverdale State Bank building, houses local archival material and pioneer and Coast Salish Indian artifacts. Tues.-Sat. 10-5; closed holidays. Admission $1, students with ID 50c, family rate $2. Phone (360) 692-1949.

SKAMOKAWA (E-5) pop. 200, elev. 26′

Settled in 1844, Skamokawa (skah-MOCK-away) is among the best preserved of the river boat communities along the lower Columbia River. Homes dating from the late 19th century line the sloughs and creeks, recalling the era when waterways formed the lanes of commerce and communication. The town's name honors a Wahkiakum chief whose name translates to "smoke on the water," a reference to the area's early morning fogs.

Skamokawa Vista Park *(see Recreation Chart)*, west of town on SR 4, offers a good vantage point for watching giant freighters navigate the Columbia River shipping channel. Beachcombers may find pumice from the eruption of Mount St. Helens.

RIVER LIFE INTERPRETIVE CENTER AT REDMEN HALL, 1394 W. SR 4, contains displays depicting the 1894 building's past as a pioneer schoolhouse and a fraternal lodge. Historic photographs and artifacts document life along the lower Columbia River 1850-1930. A bell tower provides vistas of the river. Allow 30 minutes minimum. Tues.-Sat. 11-5, Sun. and holidays 1-5, June-Sept.; Wed.-Sat. noon-4, Sun 1-4, rest of year. Admission $2; ages 6-18, $1. Phone (360) 795-3007.

SNOHOMISH (C-7) pop. 6,500, elev. 64′

Founded in 1859 at the confluence of the Pilchuck and Snohomish rivers, Snohomish preserves a Victorian-era flavor reflected in its homes and commercial buildings. Many substantial dwellings in the residential area north of 2nd Street are Victorian treasures; many 19th-century

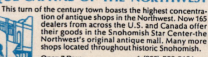

SNOHOMISH
FREE COPY
ANTIQUE QUARTERLY
Your Guide to Antique Shopping in the Northwest. Write:
Star Center Mall
829 2nd Street
Snohomish, WA 98290

ANTIQUE CAPITAL OF THE NORTHWEST
This turn of the century town boasts the highest concentration of antique shops in the Northwest. Now 165 dealers from across the U.S. and Canada offer their goods in the Snohomish Star Center-the Northwest's original antique mall. Many more shops located throughout historic Snohomish.
Open 7 Days 1-(360)-568-2131

buildings also have been restored along 1st Street and the riverbank.

Vintage homes are open to visitors during the Historic Homes Tour in late September or early October. East of Snohomish on US 2 is the town of Monroe, which is the scene of the Evergreen State Fair in late August and early September.

Self-guiding tours: Driving or walking tour maps of Snohomish are available from the Snohomish Chamber of Commerce, 116 Ave. B, P.O. Box 135, Snohomish, WA 98290; phone (360) 568-2526.

Shopping areas: Snohomish's historic business district, on 1st Street between Union Avenue and Avenue D, contains several dozen specialty shops in restored buildings. The Snohomish Star Center, 829 2nd St., offers displays from more than 165 antique dealers. *See ad p. 174.*

BLACKMAN MUSEUM, 118 Ave. B, was built in 1878 by Snohomish's first mayor, Hyrcanus Blackman. Subsequently enlarged and remodeled in 1895, the home and its furnishings have been restored to reflect the Victorian period. Allow 30 minutes minimum. Daily noon-4, June-Sept.; Wed.-Sun. noon-4, Mar.-May; Sat.-Sun. noon-4, rest of year. Admission $1; over 62 and under 12, 50c. Phone (360) 568-2526.

PIONEER VILLAGE, behind Pilchuck Landing on Pine Ave. and 2nd St., contains buildings representative of early Snohomish. Daily noon-4, June-Sept. Admission $1; over 62 and under 12, 50c. Phone (360) 568-2526.

SNOQUALMIE (D-7) pop. 1,500, elev. 423′

Snoqualmie Falls Park, on SR 202 between Snoqualmie and Fall City, is at the site of an underground power plant to which water from the falls is sometimes diverted. An observation platform overlooks the 268-foot falls; a trail leads down to the river at the base of the falls.

PUGET SOUND AND SNOQUALMIE VALLEY RAILROAD, on SR 202 off I-90 exit 27 or 31, is an operating railroad/museum that makes a 7-mile round trip through Snoqualmie, North Bend and the Snoqualmie Falls vicinity. Antique equipment includes steam engines and diesels. A collection of old railroad rolling stock stands west of the station. Trains run Sat.-Sun., Apr.-Oct.; departure times vary. Fare $6; over 62, $5; ages 3-12, $4. Phone (360) 746-4025.

SOAP LAKE (D-10) pop. 1,100, elev. 1,075′

Formerly called *Smokiam,* an American Indian word meaning "healing waters," Soap Lake has a mineral content that is believed to be of therapeutic value. Settlers later changed the name to Soap Lake in an effort to characterize the soapy texture of the water; the minerals and salts whip into a froth which covers the shoreline on a windy day. Black basalt cliffs along the shore highlight the lake's volcanic origin. Hot mineral baths also provide a dose of the allegedly medicinal waters. The semiarid climate of the area is conducive to the development of solar energy.

For further information contact the Soap Lake Chamber of Commerce, P.O. Box 433, Soap Lake, WA 98851; phone (509) 246-1821.

SOUTH BEND (E-5) pop. 1,600, elev. 11′

The development of rich timberland established South Bend as the key point in the water and stagecoach transportation system of Washington Territory in the late 1800s. Determined not to relinquish the title of county seat to its rival town of Oysterville during an election dispute in 1892, South Bend citizens abruptly removed all books and records from the Oysterville courthouse.

A descriptive marker 7¾ miles west on US 101 defines the site of Bruceville, settled in 1851 by the crew of the oyster schooner *Robert Bruce,* which burned near the site. The settlement enjoyed a lively oyster industry 1857-80, when enormous quantities of native oysters were gathered by Chinook Indians and loaded aboard schooners for San Francisco.

For further information contact the South Bend Chamber of Commerce, P.O. Box 335, South Bend, WA 98586; phone (360) 875-5231.

PACIFIC COUNTY COURTHOUSE is 2 blks. s. of US 101 on Memorial Dr. Once described as a "gilded palace of extravagance," the 1911 courthouse is an excellent example of Second Renaissance Revival architecture. The rotunda is lit by a stained-glass dome 29 feet in diameter. Waterfalls and a duck pond are on the grounds. Mon.-Fri. 8-5. Free. Phone (360) 875-9300.

PACIFIC COUNTY HISTORICAL SOCIETY MUSEUM, 1008 W. Robert Bush Dr., displays Chinook Indian crafts and artworks, photographs, local historical relics and items depicting the lumbering and fishing industries of the area. The museum also is a tourist information center for southwest Washington. Daily 11-4; closed Thanksgiving and Dec. 25. Free. Phone (360) 875-5224.

SPOKANE (C-12) pop. 177,200, elev. 1,898′

See map page 176.

Early settlers quickly spread the word that a trip to Spokane (spo-CAN) House meant warm hospitality as well as profitable business dealings. The active little trading post was the first non-Indian habitation of the Pacific Northwest. Spokane has since grown into the state's second largest city without losing its pioneering spirit.

The Northwest Fur Co. operation, established in 1810 soon after the Lewis and Clark expedition, was actually alongside Little Spokane River about 10 miles from the present city. It was not until 1872 that the nucleus of today's Spokane was established at Spokane Falls. Grain and lumber mills replaced fur trading as the major business; the appearance of railroads coincided with a gold rush to the Coeur d'Alene district.

After fire destroyed more than 30 city blocks in 1889, the burst of rebuilding spurred development which has continued unabated. One of Spokane's most convenient features is its system of enclosed skywalks that allows pedestrians to visit many downtown establishments without having to brave the winter cold.

A spectacular night view of the city can be seen from Cliff Park off 13th Avenue on the site of an old volcanic cone. Spokane Falls, at their best during the spring and early summer runoff periods, are best seen from the Monroe Street bridge just west of Riverfront Park. Three local wineries offer tours and tastings; contact one of the local AAA offices for details.

American Indian petroglyphs northwest of town near Rutter Bridge can be seen by following SR 291 (Francis Avenue) 2 miles west off US 395 (Division Street) and turning north onto Indian Trail Road for 4 miles.

Spokane welcomes spring with such events as the Lilac Bloomsday Run in early May and the Lilac Festival in mid-May. The city kicks off fall with the Interstate Fair in early September. Playfair Racecourse offers Thoroughbred racing mid-April through mid-November; phone (509) 534-0505.

Note: Policies concerning admittance of children to pari-mutuel betting facilities vary. Phone for information.

For further information contact the Spokane Convention and Visitors Bureau, 926 Sprague Ave., Spokane, WA 99204; phone (509) 624-1431.

Shopping areas: Major shopping centers are Northtown Mall, 4 miles north of I-90 and US 2/395 at Wellesley and Division; and University City, exit 287 off I-90, then 2 miles south and 1 mile east. Northtown Mall contains JCPenney and Sears; University City has JCPenney and Lamonts. Specialty items can be found in the Flour Mill, downtown at W. 621 Mallon.

Fifteen blocks of downtown Spokane are connected by enclosed skywalks, providing climate-controlled access to stores in the city center. Major department stores so reached include The Bon and Nordstrom.

CATHEDRAL OF ST. JOHN THE EVANGELIST (Episcopal), 12th and Grand, is an outstanding example of Gothic architecture. The carillon's 49 bells range in weight from 17 to 5,000 pounds; concerts are given Thursdays at noon and Sundays at 10:30. Allow 30 minutes minimum.

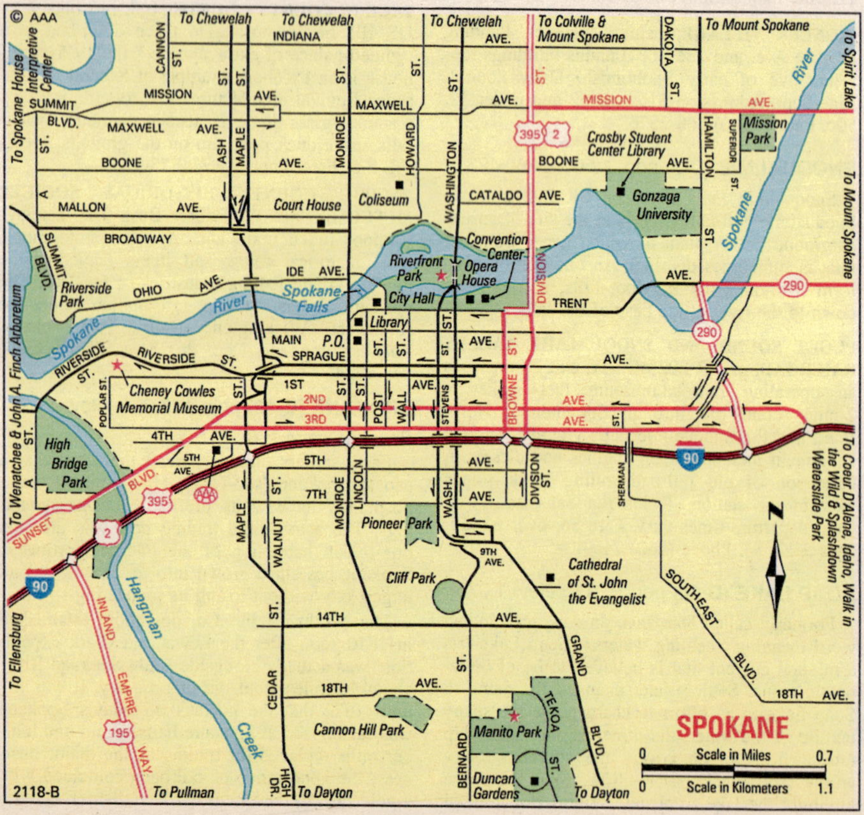

Guided tours are offered Mon.-Tues., Thurs. and Sat. noon-3, Sun. following morning services. Free. Phone (509) 838-4277.

★**CHENEY COWLES MEMORIAL MUSEUM,** 2316 W. First Ave., contains exhibits relating to the historical development of the Inland Empire, including displays on mining, timber and farming. Particularly noteworthy is the museum's extensive collection of Plateau Indian arts and handicrafts. The museum's art gallery features changing exhibits of regional, national and international scope.

The restored Campbell House, next to the museum, is representative of Spokane's turn-of-the-20th-century "age of elegance." Allow 2 hours minimum. Tues.-Sat. 10-5, Sun. 1-5. Admission $3; over 64, students with ID and ages 6-16, $2; family rate $7.50; half-price admission to all on Wed. Phone (509) 456-3931.

CROSBY STUDENT CENTER LIBRARY, E. 502 Boone Ave. at Gonzaga University, contains a collection of Bing Crosby's records and other memorabilia; he was an alumnus. Allow 1 hour minimum. Mon.-Fri. 8:30-4:30, Sat.-Sun. 11:30-4:30, Sept.-Apr.; Mon.-Fri. 9-4:30, rest of year. Free. Phone (509) 328-4220, ext. 4297.

JOHN A. FINCH ARBORETUM, w. on Second Ave., then s.w. on Sunset Blvd. to 3404 Woodland Blvd., cultivates a diverse collection of shrubs and trees on 65 acres along Garden Springs Creek. Highlights include a rhododendron glen, a maple section, a conifer section and a nature trail with interpretive signs in print and in Braille. Allow 2 hours minimum. Daily dawn-dusk. Free.

★**MANITO PARK** is on Grand Blvd. between 17th and 25th aves. The park features a conservatory, Japanese garden, perennial garden, rose garden, lilac garden and formal garden for the display of bedding plants. Flowering season for the formal and perennial gardens is May through October; the rose garden blooms June through September. Allow 2 hours minimum. The conservatory is open 8 a.m.-dusk. The Japanese garden is open 8 a.m.-dusk, May-Oct. Free. Phone (509) 456-4331.

MOUNT SPOKANE is 30 mi. n.e. in Mount Spokane State Park *(see Recreation Chart).* An improved road leads to the 5,878-foot summit. Chairlifts to the summit operate during the winter sports season.

★**RIVERFRONT PARK** is off I-90 along the Spokane River in downtown Spokane. The site of Expo '74 has been transformed into a beautiful 50-acre city park, featuring the cascading Spokane River and Spokane Falls. Some original attractions from the world exposition remain. Included are Canada Island, amphitheaters, the Opera House and Convention Center, the U.S. Pavilion, a carrousel and the IMAX® Theatre, with a five-story screen.

Allow 2 hours minimum. Park attractions open Fri.-Sat. 11-10, Sun.-Thurs. 11-9, Memorial Day-Labor Day; Fri.-Sat. 11-9, Sun. 11-4, Apr. 1 to Memorial Day and day after Labor Day-Sept. 30. Limited attractions and Ice Palace skating rink open daily, Oct.-Mar.

All-inclusive admission $11.95; over 62, and children over 42 inches tall, $10.95; children under 42 inches tall, $8.95; family rate (2 adults, 2 children) $32.95. IMAX Theatre $7.50-$5; over 62, $6.25-$4.50; under 17, $5-$4. Phone (509) 456-4FUN or 625-6600 (Pacific Time); or (800) 336-PARK in Idaho, Ore., Mont., Wash., Alberta or British Columbia.

Carrousel, on the s. side of the park, is a hand-carved antique built in 1909 by Charles Looff, who made the first carrousel for Coney Island in New York. Fare $1.

Gondola Ride, leaves from the w. edge of the park and carries visitors over the Spokane River and Falls and under the Monroe Street Bridge. Daily 11-dusk. Round-trip fare $3; over 62 and ages 3-17, $2.50. Phone (509) 625-6600.

SPLASHDOWN WATERSLIDE PARK is off I-90 exit 289, then s. to Mission Ave. in Valley Mission Park. Five water slides help visitors of all ages beat the heat; two hot tubs also are available. Mon.-Sat. 10-7, Sun. noon-7, Memorial Day-Labor Day. Admission $10.50; ages 3-11, $9.50; spectators $5. MC, VI. Phone (509) 924-3079.

SPOKANE HOUSE INTERPRETIVE CENTER is 9 mi. n.w. on Aubrey White Pkwy. in Riverside State Park *(see Recreation Chart).* The center is on the site of a trading post that was the first structure built in the Northwest by non-natives. Displays trace the development of the site. Allow 1 hour minimum. Wed.-Sun. 9-6, Memorial Day-Labor Day. Free. Phone (509) 466-4747.

WALK IN THE WILD is 8 mi. e. on I-90 to exit 289, then n. 1 mi. on Pines Rd. to Euclid Ave. The 80-acre wooded park is home to more than 100 animals in 30 separate exhibits. Big cats, range animals, bears, birds pf prey, endangered species and a children's zoo are on the premises. Allow 1 hour minimum. Daily 10-5, Mar.-Nov.; 9-4, rest of year (weather permitting). Admission $3.75; over 60 and ages 13-17, $3.25; ages 3-12, $2.25. Phone (509) 924-7220.

STEILACOOM (H-2) pop. 5,700, elev. 50′

Steilacoom, founded in 1854, was the site of the state's first library, courthouse and territorial jail. Many other structures in the town are more than a century old, including the first Protestant church in the state. The Roman Catholic Immaculate Conception Church, dating from 1856, is one of the oldest churches still in use in the state.

Bair Drug and Hardware Store, Wilkes and Lafayette streets, is a late-19th-century working museum that still dispenses sarsaparilla from its 1906 soda fountain. The restored 1857 Nathaniel Orr Home and pioneer orchard, 1811 Rainier St., features original furnishings.

Self-guiding tours: Maps outlining a walking tour of Steilacoom's historic attractions can be obtained at Steilacoom Historical Museum *(see attraction listing).*

For further information contact the Steilacoom Chamber of Commerce, P.O. Box 88584, Steilacoom, WA 98388.

STEILACOOM HISTORICAL MUSEUM, 112 Main St. in the basement of the town hall, features exhibits that focus on Washington pioneers 1860-1900. Displays include historical photographs, pioneer furnishings and original volumes from Washington Territory's first library. Allow 30 minutes minimum. Tues.-Sun. 1-4, Mar.-Oct.; Fri.-Sun. 1-4 in Feb. and Nov.-Dec. Closed holidays. Free. Phone (206) 584-4133.

TRIBAL CULTURAL CENTER AND MUSEUM, 1515 Lafayette St., occupies a former church built in 1903. The museum documents the history of the Steilacoom Tribe with exhibits ranging from the pre-Columbian era to the present. The permanent collection includes clothing made from cedarbark and deerskin, baskets, tools and adornments and other archeological artifacts. The statue of a Northwestern Indian was made from a body cast for the 1893 Chicago World's Columbian Exposition. Food is available.

Allow 1 hour minimum. Tues.-Sun. 10-4; closed major holidays. Admission $2; over 62 and ages 6-18, $1. Phone (206) 584-6308.

STEVENSON (F-6) pop. 1,100

The Upper Cascades of the Columbia River, 2 miles west of Stevenson on SR 14, were the site of a portage where pioneers reassembled their wagons after rafting down the river from The Dalles, Ore. After steamboats began to ply the upper river, the town of Upper Cascades served as the transfer point from steamboat to portage for all traffic between Portland and the Inland Empire.

For further information contact the Skamania County Chamber of Commerce, P.O. Box 1037, Stevenson, WA 98648; phone (509) 427-8911.

BEACON ROCK, 8 mi. w. of Stevenson in Beacon Rock State Park *(see Recreation Chart),* is believed to be the core of an extinct volcano; it is one of the largest geological formations of its kind in the world. A 1-mile trail with many switchbacks and bridges winds to the top of the 848-foot monolith. The summit affords an excellent view of the Columbia Gorge.

CASCADE STERNWHEELERS, 3 blks. off SR 14, offer 2-hour narrated tours on the Columbia River. The 600-passenger vessel departs from Stevenson daily at 11:15 and 1:45, mid-June to early Oct.; from the Bonneville Dam Visitor Center *(see North Bonneville)* at 10:30 and 1; and from Cascade Locks, Ore., at 10, 12:30 and 3. Fare $11.95; ages 4-12, $5.95; over 54, $5.95 on Mon. Tickets are available at Cascade Locks, Ore., daily 8-6. AE, MC, VI. Phone (503) 374-8427.

COLUMBIA RIVER GORGE INTERPRETIVE CENTER, 990 S.W. Rock Creek Dr., features displays on the natural and human history of the region. Exhibits depict Native American lifestyles, the fur trading era and the harnessing of the resources of the gorge. The collection includes a full-scale replica of a fish wheel and a diorama of a Native American dip-net fisher. Formerly the Skamania County Historical Museum, the facility is scheduled to move from Vancouver Ave. in the courthouse annex to 990 S.W. Rock Creek Dr. in May of 1995.

Allow 30 minutes minimum. Tues.-Thurs. and Sun. noon-5, Fri.-Sat. noon-6. Admission $5; over 64 and students with ID $4; ages 6-12, $3.50. To verify location and schedule, phone (509) 427-5141, ext. 235, or 427-9435 Sat.-Sun. before May 1995. After April 1995 phone (509) 427-8211 or 427-8210.

SUNNYSIDE (F-9) pop. 11,200, elev. 311'

Boasting one of the state's first irrigation projects of more than 100,000 acres, Sunnyside is known as the asparagus capital of the Northwest. Local farms and orchards produce more than 50 other crops as well. Settlement by the Christian Cooperative Movement has contributed to Sunnyside's growth into a busy trade center for the lower Yakima Valley.

Local attractions include the Sunnyside Historical Museum, which contains Yakama Indian artifacts and a pioneer kitchen and dining room; the 1859 Ben Snipes Cabin, reputedly the oldest homestead in the Yakima Valley; the Yakima Valley Cheese Co., where European-style cheese is prepared; and the Sunnyside Wildlife Recreation Area, a haven for waterbirds and shorebirds, which is south of the city along the Yakima River.

For further information contact the Sunnyside Chamber of Commerce, 812 E. Edison St., P.O. Box 329, Sunnyside, WA 98944; phone (509) 837-5939.

TUCKER CELLARS, 1 mi. s. on Yakima Valley Hwy., is a limited-production winery offering informal tours and tastings and a nearby picnic area. Daily 8-6, Memorial Day weekend-Labor Day; 9-5, rest of year. Free. Phone (509) 837-8701.

SUQUAMISH (F-2) pop. 1,500, elev. 202'

Suquamish Memorial Cemetery is the burial site of one of the most important American Indian leaders of the Northwest—Chief Sealth.

Known as Tsu-Suc-Cub to his people, Chief Sealth died in 1866 at the age of 80. In honor of his friendship, settlers named a community after him that later developed into the city and seaport of Seattle.

An interpretive marker at the west end of Agate Pass off SR 305 marks the former site of The Old Man House, which once housed eight Indian chiefs and their families.

SUQUAMISH MUSEUM, 2 mi. s. on SR 305 at the w. end of Agate Pass Bridge at 15838 Sandy Hook Rd., portrays the lifestyle of the Puget Sound Indians before and after the coming of non-native settlers. Features include photographs, artifacts and recorded interviews. Guided tours are available with 48 hours notice. Allow 30 minutes minimum. Daily 10-5, Memorial Day weekend-Labor Day; Fri.-Sun. 11-4 or by appointment, rest of year. Admission $2.50; over 60, $2; under 12, $1. Guided tour $15 per hour. **Discount.** Phone (360) 598-3311, ext. 422.

TACOMA (G-3) pop. 176,700, elev. 87′

Tacoma was shaped by a series of booms and busts that began after Swedish settler Nicholas de Lin started the first business in 1852. De Lin's sawmill was the first major means of employment for the settlers who braved harrowing conditions to reach this area, discovered by Capt. George Vancouver in 1792.

As the lumber industry prospered and the Puyallup Indians were coerced into leaving the region, the pioneers' settlement grew. Gen. Morton Matthew McCarver bought a large tract of land nearby in hopes that the Northern Pacific Railway would establish its terminus there. McCarver encouraged increased settlement and called the town Tacoma, a derivation of *Tahoma,* the Puyallup Indian name for Mount Rainier.

Tacoma is supported by a variety of industries, with wood products and shipping still at the top. Among the city's numerous cultural attractions is Fireman's Park, at the foot of S. Ninth Street, with one of the tallest totem poles in the nation. Carved from a single cedar by Alaskan Indians, the totem pole is 105 feet high.

Another lofty city landmark is the clock tower of Old City Hall, a fine example of Italian Renaissance architecture. Public fishing piers are available on McCarver Street, on Ruston Way and at the boat house in Point Defiance Park.

Spectator sports in Tacoma include professional baseball and ice hockey. The Tacoma Tigers play class-AAA Pacific Coast League baseball at Cheney Stadium; phone (206) 752-9161. The Tacoma Dome is home to the Western Hockey League Rockets; phone (206) 627-3653. For information about other events phone the Tacoma Dome Ticket Office at (206) 572-3663.

For further information contact the Tacoma-Pierce County Visitors and Convention Bureau,

Fife: half way, half price.

Vancouver, B.C.
Seattle
Fife
Tacoma
Portland, Ore.

Whether you're halfway there or halfway back, remember we're about 1/2 price.* Spend the night in Fife and go easy on your budget with 13 lodging choices and over 22 restaurants. Located on I-5 between Seattle & Tacoma. Just a short drive to Mt. Rainier, Point Defiance Zoo & Aquarium. Minutes from 2 major shopping malls.

Discounts to AAA members at participating properties.

Stay in Fife. Spend the money you save on fun!

Fife 1/2 price.

Lodging Hotline
1-800-577-0773
Extension 4
1-5 Exits 136A & 137.
Fife Chamber of Commerce

*Based on comparison of downtown Seattle average room rates.

906 Broadway, P.O. Box 1754, Tacoma, WA 98401-1754; phone (206) 627-2836.

Shopping areas: Old Town, the original business district at McCarver Street and Ruston Way, also has shops and restaurants. Tacoma Center, Court C between S. 11th and S. 13th streets, has specialty shops. Tacoma Mall, west of I-5 exits 130 and 131 on Tacoma Mall Boulevard, is the area's major shopping center. The Bon, JCPenney, Nordstrom and Sears are the major department stores.

Lakewood Mall, 2 miles northwest of I-5 exit 125 features The Emporium, Gottschalks, Lamonts and Mervyn's. Freighthouse Square, 1 block north of the Tacoma Dome at 25th and E. D streets, is a public market that features restaurants, specialty stores and a full calendar of special events.

CHILDREN'S MUSEUM OF TACOMA, 925 Court C, features hands-on displays, including arts and crafts. "Body Basics, the Inside Story" explores the human body. Allow 1 hour minimum. Tues.-Sat. 10-5, Sun. noon-4, Sept. 1 to mid-June; Tues.-Fri. 10-5, Sat. 10-4, Sun. noon-4, rest of year. Admission $3.50, under 2 free. Phone (206) 627-2436.

FORT LEWIS MILITARY MUSEUM is 16 mi. s., off I-5 exit 120, in Bldg. 4320 at one of the Army's largest permanent posts—Fort Lewis. The museum galleries specialize in military and Pacific Northwest history. The fort was the first military installation created as the result of a gift of land by private citizens to the federal government. Visitors must obtain an automobile pass at the visitors office located on the east side of the interstate near the entrance. Allow 1 hour minimum. Wed.-Sun. noon-4; closed holidays. Free. Phone (206) 967-7206.

LAKEWOLD GARDENS, is 9 mi. s. on I-5 to exit 124, then 1 mi. w. to 12317 Gravelly Lake Dr. S.W. Guided tours explore the gardens' highlights, including groves of native trees, Japanese maples and rhododendrons. A giant Douglas fir which creates its own shade garden, an 18th-century sculptured lion fountain, a medieval Knot Garden with a variety of unusual plantings, and a Georgian-style family home also are featured on the tour.

Allow 1 hour, 30 minutes minimum. Thurs.-Mon. 10-4, Apr.-Sept.; Thurs.-Fri. and Mon. 10-4, rest of year. Closed holidays. Admission $6; over 64, $5. MC, VI. Reservations are required. Phone (206) 584-3360.

McCHORD AIR MUSEUM, 1 mi. e. of I-5 exit 125 to main gate of McChord Air Force Base, contains memorabilia and military aircraft from the 1930s to the present. Allow 30 minutes minimum. Tues.-Sun. noon-4; closed holidays. Free. Phone (206) 984-2485.

NARROWS BRIDGE is one of the largest suspension bridges in the world. The center span is 188 feet high and 2,800 feet long. The present bridge replaced "Galloping Gertie," an architectural failure nicknamed for the way it swayed in the wind; it collapsed 4 months and 7 days after it opened in 1940. Parks adjoining the east and west ends of the bridge have interpretive displays and overlooks.

★**POINT DEFIANCE PARK,** almost 700 acres, has miles of woodland trails through old growth forest and gardens, scenic views and a waterfront. Recreational facilities include a public fishing pier and picnic area. Rental boats and fishing gear are available at the boathouse. Daily dawn-dusk. Free. *See Recreation Chart.*

Camp Six Logging Museum is a replica of an early-20th-century logging camp. The museum contains relics and historic photographs of early Tacoma. Camp open Wed.-Sun. and holidays 10-6, Memorial Day-Sept. 30; 10-4, rest of year. Donations. Logging train ride $2; over 65 and ages 3-12, $1. Phone (206) 752-0047.

Fort Nisqually, the first outpost of the Hudson's Bay Co. on Puget Sound, features the oldest standing structure in the state. Changing exhibits describe Washington's fur-trading era. Daily 11-6, June 1-Labor Day; Wed.-Sun. 1-4, rest of year. Admission $1; ages 5-12, 50c; free to all Mon.-Tues., June-Labor Day. Phone (206) 591-5339.

Never Never Land depicts 30 scenes from children's literature in a wooded 10-acre setting. Daily 11-6, mid-June through Labor Day; daily 11-5, May 1 to mid-June; Sat.-Sun. 11-5, Mar.-Apr.; Sat.-Sun. 11-6, day after Labor Day-Sept. 30. Admission $2; over 61 and ages 13-17, $1.50; ages 3-12, $1. Phone (206) 591-5845.

Point Defiance Zoo and Aquarium, 5400 N. Pearl St., features animals from the Pacific Rim area, including polar bears, beluga whales, sharks, sea otters and walruses. The North Pacific Aquarium provides a glimpse of the marine life of Puget Sound. The Discovery Reef Aquarium displays tropical fish and sharks. December evenings bring the Zoolights display, with more than 450,000 lights arranged in life-size replicas of zoo animals.

Allow 2 hours, 30 minutes minimum. Daily 10-7, Memorial Day-Labor Day; 10-4, rest of year. Closed Thanksgiving and Dec. 25. Admission $6.50; over 62, $6; ages 5-17, $4.75; ages 2-4, $2.50. MC, VI. **Discount.** Phone (206) 591-5335. *See color ad p. 179.*

TACOMA ART MUSEUM, at 12th and Pacific aves., features a permanent collection of American and French paintings, a children's gallery, an Early American room and collections of Chinese jade. Traveling national and international exhibits also are presented. Tues.-Sat. 10-5 (also Thurs. 5-7), Sun. and holidays noon-5. Admission $3; over 61, students with ID and ages 6-12, $2. Phone (206) 272-4258.

★WASHINGTON STATE HISTORICAL SOCIETY MUSEUM, 315 N. Stadium Way, depicts Washington's geographic diversity and human history from indigenous peoples through European exploration and immigration until the 20th century. A seven-minute multimedia presentation provides an overview of the state's history.

A diorama representing the state's environmental zones leads into an area illustrating the American Indian lifestyle, including exhibits about home-building and food-and reed-gathering. Also featured are such artifacts as baskets, carved masks, tools and clothing.

The pioneer era is documented through a diorama of a westward-bound immigrant family and maps, ships models, trade goods, weapons and related pioneer relics. Other highlights include displays on the beginnings of the railroad and lumbering industries, the development of agriculture, the impacts of the Depression and the New Deal, World War II homefront activities and commonplace items of the last half of the 20th century.

Allow 1 hour minimum. Tues.-Sat. and holidays 10-5, Sun. 1-5; closed Jan. 1 and Dec. 25. Admission $2.50; over 62, $2; ages 6-18, $1; family rate $6. MC, VI. Phone (206) 593-2830.

WRIGHT PARK, S. 3rd and G St., has the Seymour Botanical Conservatory, a 1908 Victorian structure with a large collection of tropical plants. Floral displays change monthly, with special exhibits at Easter and Christmas. Daily 8-4:20. Free. Phone (206) 591-5330.

TENINO (I-2) pop. 1,300, elev. 280

In the 1930s Tenino gained national attention when it issued wooden dollars after a local bank failed. This unusual solution worked and the dollars have since become collectors' items. A more durable local resource is the sandstone quarried nearby, which has been used in public buildings throughout the region. The importance to the area of quarrying, logging and the railroads is documented mid-March to mid-October in the Tenino Depot Museum in the city park; phone (360) 264-4321.

For further information contact the Tenino Chamber of Commerce, P.O. Box 506, Tenino, WA 98589; phone (360) 264-5075.

WOLF HAVEN INTERNATIONAL, 3¼ mi. n. on US 99 and e. on Offut Lake Rd., is a sanctuary for more than 30 wolves, an endangered species. Narrated tours describe the wolf's role in the wild. During the summer, "howl-ins" are held Friday and Saturday evenings with music, storytelling and the evocative wolf cry. Daily 10-5, May-Sept.; Wed.-Mon. 10-4, rest of year. Admission $5; ages 5-12, $2.50. Howl-ins $6; ages 5-12, $4. MC, VI. **Discount.** Phone (360) 264-4695 or (800) 448-9653.

THORP (D-8) pop. 400, elev. 1,635′

THORP MILL, 3 mi. w. from I-90 exit 101, is a pioneer industrial site built in 1883. A 17-minute multimedia presentation illustrates the milling process and the high level of automation at the mill, which operated until 1946. The full set of turn-of-the-20th-century machinery used to operate the mill is displayed. Picnic facilities are available. Allow 1 hour minimum. Sun., Tues. and Thurs. 1-4, Fri. 11-4, Sat. 10-4; other times by appointment. Donations. Phone (509) 964-9640.

TOLEDO (E-6) pop. 600, elev. 118′

ST. FRANCIS XAVIER MISSION, 2 mi. n.e. on Jackson Hwy., then ¼ mi. s. on Spenser Rd., was founded in 1838 by fathers Blanchet and Demers. It is the site of both the first Catholic church in the state and one of the oldest missions in the Northwest. Daily dawn-dusk. Free. Phone (360) 864-4126.

TOPPENISH (F-8) pop. 7,400, elev. 757′

Toppenish is the headquarters of the Yakama Indian Nation, which covers more than a million acres. The Treaty Day Powwow Encampment is held the second weekend in June, the Toppenish Powwow and Rodeo is held July 4th weekend, while the Yakama Nation Powwow takes place the third weekend in September. All powwows feature war dances, stick games, dance contests, hand games and a memorial for tribal members. For further information phone (509) 865-2800.

Toppenish is becoming known as the "City of Historical Murals." Artists are transforming the outside walls of many buildings with colorful scenes depicting pioneer life in the area. Walking and drawn vehicle tours are available; phone (509) 865-6516.

For further information contact the Toppenish Chamber of Commerce, A-11 S. Toppenish Ave., P.O. Box 28, Toppenish, WA 98948; phone (509) 865-3262.

AMERICAN HOP MUSEUM, 22 S. B St., is housed in a building whose exterior is is trompe l'oeil. Exhibits trace the history of the hop industry from its international commercial beginning in New York state in 1805 to the present in the Yakima Valley, where it is an important crop. Displays include historical photographs, publications, hop equipment, memorabilia and antiques. Displayed on the exterior of the building are several murals depicting various phases of the hop industry and the uses of hops. Wed.-Sun. 10-3. Admission $2; over 60 and ages 6-17, $1; family rate $5. Phone (509) 865-4677.

FORT SIMCOE STATE PARK, 200 acres, 27 mi. w. via SR 220, was one of the two interior Washington Territory army posts established as a result of hostilities between the settlers and Yakama Indians in the fall of 1856. Five original buildings have been restored and furnished in period; two blockhouses and a barracks have been reconstructed. Picnic facilities are available.

Park open daily 6:30 a.m.-dusk, Apr.-Sept.; Sat.-Sun. and holidays 8 a.m.-dusk, rest of year. Museum and interpretive center open Wed.-Sun. 9-4, Apr.-Sept.; by appointment, rest of year. Free. For further information contact the Park Supervisor's Office, Fort Simcoe State Park, 5150 Fort Simcoe Rd., White Swan, WA 98952; phone (509) 874-2372. *See Recreation Chart.*

TOPPENISH HISTORICAL MUSEUM, 1 S. Elm St., includes the Estelle Reel Meyer collection of American Indian basketry and beadwork. Meyer collected the items on visits to federal Indian schools during her tenure as superintendent of Indian Affairs 1898-1910. Also displayed are an exhibit on the cattle industry, antique firefighting equipment, school memorabilia 1930-50 and works by local artists. Allow 30 minutes minimum. Tues.-Sat. 2-4:30; closed holidays. Admission $1; ages 6-14, 25c. Phone (509) 865-4510.

TOPPENISH NATIONAL WILDLIFE REFUGE, 4¾ mi. s. on US 97, then ½ mi. w. off Pump House Rd., is in the lower Yakima Valley. Nearly 250 species of birds have been sighted on the refuge. A nature trail traverses the area. An interpretive center provides descriptions of the trails and features stuffed birds and other natural history exhibits. Refuge open daily dawn-dusk. Interpretive center open daily 6-2:30, mid-Oct. to mid-Jan.; Mon.-Thurs. 6-3:30, Fri. 6-2:30, Feb.-Sept. Free. Phone (509) 865-2405.

YAKAMA NATION CULTURAL CENTER, ½ mi. n. on US 97, includes a winter lodge/meeting hall, museum, theater, library and research center. The 76-foot-high lodge, a stylized version of the ancient Yakama winter lodge, dominates the center. Dioramas and exhibits in the 12,000-square-foot museum chronicle the history of the Yakama Indians. Allow 1 hour minimum. Daily 9-6, June-Sept.; 10-5, rest of year. Admission $4; over 55 and ages 11-18, $2; ages 7-10, $1; under 7, 75c; family rate $10. MC, VI. Phone (509) 865-2800.

YAKIMA VALLEY RAIL AND STEAM MUSEUM, is at 10 E. Asotin St., in the restored 1911 Northern Pacific Depot. The museum displays historical photographs of trains and other railroad related scenes and memorabilia, and an early 20th-century telegrapher's office. Some Saturdays and/or Sundays from May through mid-October, 2-hour, round-trip passenger train excursions are offered from nearby Harrah to White Swan; phone for schedule and fare. Museum open daily 10-5, May-Oct.; Sat. 10-5, Sun. 1-5, rest of year. Admission $2; over 60 and under 18, $1. For museum and excursions information, phone (509) 865-1911.

TUMWATER (H-1) pop. 10,000, elev. 115′

Founded in 1845, Tumwater was the first American settlement north of Fort Vancouver. Waterpower harnessed from the Deschutes River for a brewery, mills and other industries was the key to Tumwater's prosperity in the early 1900s. The original townsite, off Deschutes Way at the foot of Grant Street, is now Tumwater Falls Historical Park.

For further information contact the Tumwater Chamber of Commerce, 488 Tyee Dr., Tumwater, WA 98512; phone (360) 357-5153.

HENDERSON HOUSE, 602 Deschutes Way, depicts the history of the area. The 1905 house holds photographs, domestic tools and equipment and items from the town's original post office. Also in the historic district is the 1858 Crosby House, at Grant and Deschutes Way. Allow 30 minutes minimum. Henderson House open Thurs.-Sun. noon-4; closed holidays. Crosby House open Thurs. 2-4 and by appointment. Donations. Phone (360) 753-8583.

TWISP (B-9) pop. 900, elev. 1,590′

Twisp is in the Methow Valley, at the junction of the Twisp and Methow rivers. The valley had a mining boom in the 1890s, but most economic efforts now center on logging, apple production and farming. West of Twisp the North Cascades Highway (SR 20) begins its climb into scenic Okanogan National Forest and North Cascades National Park *(see place listings).*

For further information contact the Twisp Chamber of Commerce, P.O. Box 686, Twisp, WA 98856; phone (509) 997-2926.

NORTH CASCADE SMOKEJUMPER BASE, 5 mi. n. on East County Rd., offers 30-minute guided tours of the facility, including the parachute loft, firefighting equipment and aircraft. Visitors can view jumps during training sessions, usually held in early June. Daily 9-1 and 2-6, June 1-Oct. 1. Free. Phone (509) 997-2031.

OSPREY RIVER ADVENTURES offers 3-hour white-water rafting and scenic float trips on the Methow and Skagit rivers. Safety equipment is provided; wetsuit rentals are available. Inquire about age restrictions, refund and weather policies. Methow River trips are offered mid-Apr. to mid-Aug. Skagit River trips are offered mid-Apr. to mid-Oct. Phone for departure times and places. White-water trip $60 (includes wetsuit). Scenic trip $50; under 12, $45. Reservations are suggested. Phone (509) 997-4116.

UMATILLA NATIONAL FOREST—

see place listing in Oregon.

UNION GAP (E-8) pop. 3,200, elev. 980′

Union Gap takes its name from the natural pass or "gap" which the Yakima River has carved through high, barren hills. The gap divides the Yakima Valley into its upper and lower portions. Yakima City was established here in 1861. In 1884 the Northern Pacific Railroad convinced most of the town's businesses to relocate to its proposed station site 4 miles north. These relocated businesses formed the nucleus of the new town of North Yakima. In 1918 the state legislature dropped "North" from the new town's name and renamed old Yakima to Union Gap.

CENTRAL WASHINGTON AGRICULTURAL MUSEUM, 4508 Main St. in Fulbright Park, features outdoor displays of farm machinery and equipment. The museum also houses the Magness Hand Tool collection of more than 6,000 implements. Another highlight is a restored 1915 log cabin. Allow 2 hours minimum. Grounds open daily 7 a.m.-9 p.m. Museum open daily 9-5. Free. Phone (509) 457-8735.

VANCOUVER (G-5) pop. 46,500, elev. 42'

At the head of deep-water navigation on the Columbia River, Vancouver is the oldest city in the state. It was founded in 1824 as Fort Vancouver by the Hudson's Bay Co. During the 1860s the young town prospered from the gold rushes to eastern Washington and Idaho. Connections with the Northern Pacific from Kalama and increased river traffic furthered the town's development into a busy shipping center.

The Kaiser Co. shipyard, constructed in 1942 after the United States entered World War II, built about 100 vessels that were used in Pacific warfare. Today Vancouver's port accommodates both ocean and river commerce. Aluminum, pulp and lumber mills also contribute to the city's economy.

Esther Short Park was the property of the first Americans to file a land claim in the area and is at the corner of Columbia and W. 8th streets. The park includes the 1867 Slocum House, a "Rhode Island"-style home now used as a community theater; a massive woodcarving of an American Indian; Avard Fairbanks' bronze monument to the pioneer woman; and a restored 500,000-pound steam locomotive.

Providence Academy, 400 E. Evergreen Blvd., was the first permanent Catholic school in the Northwest. Erected in 1873 under the direction of Mother Joseph, it is constructed from about 300,000 handmade bricks. Today small specialty shops occupy the building.

For further information contact the Vancouver and Clark County Convention and Visitors Bureau, 404 E. 15th St., Suite 11, Vancouver, WA 98663-3451; phone (360) 693-1313.

Shopping areas: Vancouver Mall, just west of I-205 exit 30 on SR 500, is the major shopping center for Vancouver. The largest department stores are JCPenney, Meier & Frank, Mervyns, Nordstrom and Sears.

CLARK COUNTY HISTORICAL MUSEUM is at 1511 Main St. Displays of pioneer life include an early doctor's office, a printshop, a country store and exhibits of Clackamas Indian artifacts. The museum includes a genealogy library. Allow 30 minutes minimum. Tues.-Sun. 1-5; closed holidays. Donations. Phone (360) 695-4681.

S.P. & S. Railway Museum, in the basement of the Clark County Historical Museum, displays railroad memorabilia, including a reconstructed train compartment and railway telegrapher's office. A model depicts the railroads in the Columbia River Gorge. Tues.-Sat. 1-5; closed holidays. Donations. Phone (360) 695-4681.

COVINGTON HOUSE is at 4201 Main St. The house is an 1846 log cabin that purportedly was the first schoolhouse north of the Columbia River. Tues. and Thurs. 10-4, June-Aug. Free. Phone (360) 695-6750.

FORT VANCOUVER NATIONAL HISTORIC SITE, 165 acres on E. Evergreen Blvd., ½ mi. e. off I-5 exit 1C at Mill Plain Blvd., was the center of the Hudson's Bay Co.'s vast fur-trading empire 1825-49. In 1849 the first U.S. military post in the Pacific Northwest was founded nearby. The fort continued operation until it was deactivated in 1860.

The Hudson's Bay Co. stockade and several buildings have been reconstructed. Exhibits include beads, ceramics and iron items from the fur-trade era, as well as a replica of the Northwest's first formal garden. A visitor center has a museum and an audiovisual program.

Allow 1 hour minimum. Fort and visitor center open daily 9-5, day after Memorial Day-Labor Day; 9-4, rest of year. Closed Jan. 1, Thanksgiving and Dec. 25. Admission $2, over 61 with Golden Age Passport and under 16 free, family rate $4. Phone (360) 696-7655.

OFFICER'S ROW, e. of I-5 on E. Evergreen Blvd., preserves 21 stately Victorian homes built 1849-1906. Formerly the residences of officers at the U.S. Army post, they now house a variety of retail and office functions.

The 1886 Marshall House, 1301 Officers Row, is named for Gen. George C. Marshall, author of the post-World War II recovery plan. The tour includes a 20-minute slide show about Officer's Row and the history of the military in Vancouver since 1850. Allow 30 minutes minimum. Mon.-Fri. 9-5; closed holidays. Donations. Phone (360) 693-3103.

PEARSON AIR MUSEUM, 1 mi. s.e. of I-5 exit 1C at 1105 E. 5th St., features exhibits, photographs and relics that relate the history of aviation at Pearson—the oldest operating airfield in the United States. Guided tours are available.

A monument on SR 14 next to Pearson Air Park marks the site where three Soviet aviators completed the first non-stop flight from the Soviet Union to the United States in 1937; the aviators were forced to land when they ran out of fuel, short of their goal of San Francisco. The transpolar flight from Moscow to Vancouver covered 5,288 nautical miles in 63 hours and 16 minutes.

Allow 30 minutes minimum. Wed.-Sun. noon-5; closed Jan. 1 and Dec. 25. Admission $2, ages 6-17 and students with ID $1. Phone (360) 694-7026.

VANTAGE (E-9)

At Wanapum Lake, formed by the Wanapum Dam in 1959, are several recreation areas, including Wanapum *(see Recreation Chart)* and Ginkgo state parks. The monumental sculpture "Grandfather Cuts Loose the Horses" stands on a mesa overlooking the Columbia. The sculpture is best viewed from the Wanapum Vista viewpoint on eastbound I-90, 3 miles east of Vantage.

GINKGO PETRIFIED FOREST STATE PARK, 1 mi. n. of I-90 exit 136 on Vantage Hwy., includes 7,500 acres of fossilized trees dating back some 15 million years. Unlike most other petrified forests, the trees were entombed in once-molten lava. It is the only known place where petrified wood of the ginkgo tree has been found. The museum in the interpretive center contain exhibits. Several miles of hiking trails include a ¾-mile interpretive trail; another trail leads from the interpretive center to rocks with petroglyphs. Picnic facilities are available.

Allow 1 hour minimum. Park open daily 8-dusk. Interpretive center open Fri.-Sun. 10-6, mid-June to mid-Sept.; by appointment, rest of year. Free. Phone (509) 856-2700.

WANAPUM DAM AND HERITAGE CENTER is 5 mi. s. of I-90 exit 137 on SR 243. The center offers a fish-viewing room, a powerhouse and self-guiding tours of fish ladders. Exhibits depict the culture of the Wanapum Indians and life along the Columbia River. Guided tours of the powerhouse are available on request. Center and fish-viewing room open daily 9-5, Apr.-Nov.; otherwise varies. Closed Jan. 1, Thanksgiving and Dec. 25. Free. Phone (509) 754-3541, ext. 2571.

VASHON ISLAND (G-2)

Ice Age glaciers shaped the topography of Vashon Island, today a mosaic of woodland, small farms and settlements. Its first inhabitants were Shomamish Indians who visited the 12-mile by 5-mile island on hunting and gathering forays. In 1792, Capt. George Vancouver named the island for his friend James Vashon, an admiral in the British Navy. Homesteading began in the mid-19th century; farming, fishing, logging, brick making and shipbuilding flourished. In the 1890s the town of Dockton grew up around a large drydock. Several structures including a general store, hotel and row of company houses remain from this period. Point Robinson, at the island's eastern tip, features beach access and a 38-foot lighthouse built in 1915.

K-2 Corporation, 6 miles south of the Vashon ferry landing, at 19215 Vahon Hwy. S.W., offers free 1-hour tours. Visitors see the full range of ski and snowboard production, from design and manufacturing through shipping. Tours depart Tuesday and Wednesday at 10 and 1, May through October. Make reservations 1 day in advance. Phone (206) 463-3631.

WALLA WALLA (F-11) pop. 26,500, elev. 949′

Walla Walla, named after the Walla Walla Indians that inhabited the valley, means "many waters" or "small rapid stream." In 1836 Dr. Marcus Whitman and his wife, Narcissa, established the first permanent settlers' home in the Pacific Northwest. The valley is noted for its rich agricultural productivity.

Pioneer Park, Division and Alder streets, is a 47-acre recreation area with duck ponds, bandstands, an exotic bird display, a playground, a swimming pool and tennis courts.

For further information contact the Walla Walla Area Chamber of Commerce, 29 E. Sumach, P.O. Box 644, Walla Walla, WA 99362; phone (509) 525-0850.

DEPARTMENT OF VETERANS AFFAIRS MEDICAL CENTER, 77 Wainwright Dr. on the s. end of town off SR 125, offers guided tours of the grounds and the exterior of historic buildings that once were part of Fort Walla Walla. Mon.-Fri. 8-4:30. Free. Reservations are required. Phone (509) 525-5200.

FORT WALLA WALLA MUSEUM COMPLEX, on Myra Rd. on the s. end of town off SR 125, features 14 buildings depicting pioneer life. Pioneer farm exhibits are displayed in five agricultural buildings. Special events take place in summer. Allow 1 hour minimum. Tues.-Sun. 10-5, Apr.-Sept.; Sat.-Sun. 10-5, in Oct. Admission $2.50; ages 6-12, $1. Phone (509) 525-7703.

WHITMAN MISSION NATIONAL HISTORIC SITE—*see place listing.*

WASHOUGAL (G-6) pop. 4,800

In 1792 the crew from the HMS *Chatham,* led by Lt. William R. Broughton, claimed the Columbia River for Great Britain at Reed Island, 2¾ miles east of Washougal. Not until 1846 was this claim to the river relinquished under the terms of the U.S.-Canada boundary treaty.

Washougal's woolen mills have attracted expert weavers from New England and Europe. Of historical significance is the Mount Pleasant

Grange Hall, 6½ miles east on SR 14, the oldest continuously used grange hall in the state.

For further information contact the Camas-Washougal Chamber of Commerce, 422 N.E. 4th Ave., P.O. Box 919 Camas, WA 98607; phone (360) 834-2472.

PENDLETON WOOLEN MILL, at 2 17th St. off SR 14 Washougal exit, demonstrates raw wool processing. One-hour tours depart Mon.-Fri. at 9, 10, 11 and 1:30, Sept.-July. Closed week of Dec. 25. Free. Phone (360) 835-1118.

WATERVILLE (C-9) pop. 1,000, elev. 2,622′

Waterville lies near the base of Badger Mountain on a wheat-growing plateau. The town's compact business district contains 17 historical brick buildings dating to the late 1800s. Glacial erratics, or haystack rocks, a geological oddity, were deposited during the last ice age and can be seen 26 miles northeast along SR 172.

Waterville hosts the North Central Washington District Fair in mid-September. For further information contact the Waterville Chamber of Commerce, P.O. Box 628, Waterville, WA 98858; phone (509) 745-8871.

DOUGLAS COUNTY HISTORICAL MUSEUM, 124 W. Walnut St., displays pioneer household utensils, furnishings, farm implements and the former Withrow Post Office. Sinkiuse Indian exhibits include personal items belonging to Chief Moses. Also displayed is the Schluenz Rock Collection, which includes gems, minerals, thundereggs, petrified wood and meteorites. The 73¼-pound iron and nickel Waterville Meteorite, discovered in 1917, was the first recovered in the state.

Allow 1 hour minimum. Wed.-Sun. and holidays 11-5, Memorial Day weekend-late Sept. Donations. Phone (509) 745-8435.

WENATCHEE (D-9) pop. 21,800, elev. 651′

Despite its rich volcanic soil, the Wenatchee Valley was too arid for farming until the Highline Canal was built in 1903. Once irrigated, the land was planted with apple trees, and Wenatchee emerged as one of the world's largest producers of the fruit. In celebration of this important crop, the Apple Blossom Festival is held from the last week in April through the first weekend in May.

Wenatchee's proximity to the Wenatchee National Forest *(see place listing)* makes it a prime area for outdoor recreation, including skiing; Mission Ridge Ski Area is 13 miles southwest of Wenatchee via Squilchuck Canyon Road. Wenatchee Riverfront Park, at the foot of Orondo Avenue, offers a paved walking and bicycling trail along the Columbia River.

For further information contact the Wenatchee Area Chamber of Commerce, 2 S. Chelan, P.O. Box 850, Wenatchee, WA 98807-0850; phone (509) 662-2116.

Shopping areas: Shoppers will find specialty stores at Victorian Village, half a mile south of downtown at 611 S. Mission St. The major local shopping center is Wenatchee Valley Mall, at US 2 Business Route and SR 28 in East Wenatchee. Stores include Lamonts and Sears.

NORTH CENTRAL WASHINGTON MUSEUM, 127 S. Mission St., depicts pioneer and Native American life in north-central Washington through exhibits, demonstrations and cultural programs. Special exhibits include a pioneer trading post, "Mainstreet Wenatchee," "The River Sings," an operating model of the Great Northern Railway, a fully operational 1919 Wurlitzer pipe organ and changing exhibits in the art gallery. "Pioneer in Aviation" documents the first non-stop trans-Pacific flight. Other displays depict natural history and the cultural heritage of the Wenatchee Band of the Colville Confederated Tribes.

An archeological exhibit interprets the archeological heritage of the region, including the Clovis discovery in a nearby orchard which represents the earliest known human habitation in the state, about 11,500 years ago.

The Apple Industry Exhibit, connected to the main museum by a skybridge gallery, has audiovisual and other displays pertaining to the state's apple industry. Of special interest is a working antique apple-sorting and packing line containing an apple wiper and catapult sorter. Guided tours are offered by appointment. Mon.-Fri. 10-4, Sat.-Sun. 1-4, Feb.-Dec.; Mon.-Fri. 10-4, rest of year. Closed holidays and day after Thanksgiving. Admission $2; ages 6-12, $1; family rate $5. Guided tours $3. Phone (509) 664-3340.

★**OHME GARDENS COUNTY PARK,** 3 mi. n. off US 97 Alt., offers 9 acres of alpine-type gardens built on a rocky bluff overlooking the Wenatchee Valley and Columbia River. Evergreen trees and low-growing plants blend with rugged rock formations to create effects ranging from the lush growth of a rain forest to the variegated patterns of an alpine meadow. Stone pathways connect the garden levels, leading to such features as fern-bordered pools, rustic shelters, a wishing well and a lookout.

Allow 1 hour minimum. Daily 9-7, day after Memorial Day-Labor Day; 9-6, mid-Apr. through Memorial Day and day after Labor Day to mid-Oct. Admission $5; ages 7-17, $3. Phone (509) 662-5785.

★**ROCKY REACH DAM,** 7 mi. n. on US 97 Alt., is an L-shaped structure 5,000 feet long. A viewpoint enables visitors to watch migrating fish ascend the 1,700-foot-long fish ladder. In the powerhouse are the Gallery of the Columbia, which traces life along the river beginning 10,000 years ago; the Gallery of Electricity, which tells the story of man's use of electric power; a history of local railroads; and displays of flowers and arts and crafts.

The information center has history exhibits and displays on dam building. Gardens, a playground and a picnic area are available. Free guided 30- to 40-minute tours take visitors down to and below the generator floor. Allow 1 hour, 30 minutes minimum. Daily 8-8, mid-June through Labor Day; 8-6, mid-Feb. to mid-June and day after Labor Day-Dec. 31. Guided tours at 11, 12:30, 2, 3:30, 4 and by request. Free. Phone (509) 663-7522.

WASHINGTON STATE APPLE COMMISSION VISITOR CENTER, 2900 Euclid Ave., presents displays and a film illustrating the history and science of apple growing. A variety of apples and juices can be sampled. Mon.-Fri. 8-5; Sat. 9-5; Sun. and holidays 10-4, May 1-Dec. 25; Mon.-Fri. 8-5, rest of year. Free. Phone (509) 663-9600. *See color ad.*

WENATCHEE NATIONAL FOREST

Elevations in the forest range from 1,000 ft. in Swakane Canyon to 9,511 ft. at Bonanza Peak. Refer to AAA maps for additional information.

Extending from the Cascades' peaks to the Columbia River Basin and from North Cascades National Park and Lake Chelan National Recreation Area to the Yakama Indian Reservation, Wenatchee National Forest occupies 2,100,000 acres. US 2 over Stevens Pass and US 97 over Blewett Pass are the main routes. The Pacific Crest National Scenic Trail generally follows the western boundary line.

Parts of seven wilderness areas lie within the forest: Glacier Peak and Lake Chelan-Sawtooth in the north; Alpine Lakes and Henry M. Jackson in the central portion; and Norse Peak, William O. Douglas and Goat Rocks in the south. Permits are required to enter the Enchantments area of the Alpine Lakes Wilderness.

Hyak and Ski Acres ski areas are off I-90 on the east side of Snoqualmie Pass; Mission Ridge Ski Area is 13 miles southwest of Wenatchee; and White Pass ski area, off US 12, is 50 miles west of Yakima. The forest has 2,500 miles of recreation trails for hiking, horseback riding and bicycling. Popular recreation areas include Lake Wenatchee north of US 2, 20 miles north of Leavenworth; lakes Cle Elum, Kachess and Keechelus, near I-90 west of Cle Elum; Bumping Lake, off SR 410 and Rimrock Lake on US 12.

Ranger stations are located at Chelan, Cle Elum, Entiat, Lake Wenatchee, Leavenworth and Naches. For information write Wenatchee National Forest, 301 Yakima St., Wenatchee, WA 98801; phone (509) 662-4335. *See Recreation Chart and the AAA Northwestern CampBook.*

WESTPORT (E-4) pop. 1,900

Noted for its salmon, bottom and tuna fishing fleets and whale watching, Westport also has an 18-mile-long beach popular for surf fishing, clam digging, crabbing or just wading. An 1,800-foot walk and bridge enables fishermen to fish from the breakwater area as well as from the jetties. Passenger-only ferry service to Ocean Shores *(see place listing)* is available. For further information phone (360) 268-0047.

South of Westport near Grayland, cranberry bogs bloom in mid-June and are harvested in mid-October. Grayland also is noted for its beaches.

Visitor information can be obtained from the Westport-Grayland Chamber of Commerce, 2985 S. Montesano Ave., P.O. Box 306, Westport, WA 98595; phone (360) 268-9422 or (800) 345-6223.

WESTPORT HISTORICAL MARITIME MUSEUM, 2201 Westhaven Dr., features displays of Lower Chehalis and other Coast Salish Indian artifacts, pioneer household items, Coast Guard memorabilia and whale skeletons. Allow 30 minutes minimum. Daily 10-5, memorial Day weekend-Labor Day; Mon.-Fri. 10-5, Sat.-Sun. noon-5day after Labor Day-Nov. 30 and Mar. 1 to Memorial Day weekend; by appointment, rest of year. Donations. Phone (360) 268-0078, for appointments phone 268-9692.

WHIDBEY ISLAND (C-2)

Capt. George Vancouver discovered Whidbey Island in 1792, naming it after Joseph Whidbey,

Washington Apple Commission Visitor's Center

509-663-9600
Weekends: 509-662-3090

WASHINGTON®

The Washington Apple Commission Visitor's Center offers an in-depth look at the state's largest agricultural industry. You can see a 15-minute video, sample three varieties of apples and some cold apple juice, all on the house, of course. Tour Groups welcome. Bring this ad and get a free lapel pin* One per family.

JAN.–APRIL:
Mon.-Fri. 8 a.m.-5 p.m.
MAY–DEC.:
Mon.-Fri. 8 a.m.-5 p.m.
Sat. 9 a.m.-5 p.m.
Sun. 10 a.m.-4 p.m.

2900 Euclid Avenue, Wenatchee, WA 98801

*Offer expires 8/31/95

his sailing master. Whidbey proved the island was not a peninsula by navigating Deception Pass. The largest island in Puget Sound, Whidbey contains extensive tracts of farmland and forest, scenic shoreline vistas and parks. Its numerous bays and coves are popular with boaters and fishermen.

Deception Pass Bridge and ferries from Mukilteo and Port Townsend give access to Whidbey Island; for ferry information phone (800) 843-3779 in Wash. Whidbey Island has several notable towns, including Coupeville, one of the oldest towns in the state, Greenbank and Langley, a picturesque town which retains a historic atmosphere *(see place listings)*. Oak Harbor *(see place listing)* is the largest town on the island.

Ebey's Landing National Historical Reserve, which encompasses 17,000 acres in central Whidbey, protects a variety of natural and historic sites. SR 20, SR 525 and county roads link eight major areas: Coupeville, Smith Prairie, Crockett Lake and Uplands, Ebey's Landing, Grassers Hill and Lagoon, Monroe Landing, and Fort Casey and Fort Ebey state parks *(see Recreation Chart)*. A self-guiding driving tour map is available at the Island County Historical Museum in Coupeville *(see place listing)*.

The preserved buildings, farms, parks, scenic drives and military fortifications present a historical record of the area's exploration and settlement. For further information contact Ebey's Landing National Historical Reserve, P.O. Box 774, Coupeville, WA 98239; phone (360) 678-6084.

Fort Casey State Park, 3 miles south off SR 20, features late-19th-century fortifications. The two 10-inch "disappearing guns" on display are thought to be the only ones of their size still in existence; phone (360) 678-4519.

WHITMAN MISSION NATIONAL HISTORIC SITE (F-11)

Whitman Mission National Historic Site, 98 acres 7 miles west of Walla Walla off US 12, memorializes a mission established in 1836 by Dr. Marcus Whitman and his wife. Called Waiilatpu, "place of the people of the rye grass," this was one of the first mission stations of its kind in the old Oregon country. It operated until 1847, when deepening cultural differences and an outbreak of measles resulted in the Indians' killing of the Whitmans and 11 others.

The area has been excavated and the sites of the early buildings, which were burned after the massacre, have been outlined. The visitor center contains a museum. A 10-minute slide presentation is shown daily every half-hour in summer. Other demonstrations, including such pioneer crafts as butter churning, trail cookery, candle dipping and wool dyeing, and such American Indian crafts as cornhusk finger weaving, tule mat construction and cooking, are given on weekends in summer.

A 1-mile paved self-guiding trail leads to the former building sites, restored millpond, apple orchard, irrigation ditch, a portion of the Oregon Trail, the Whitman Memorial Shaft and the Great Grave. Audio stations explain the significance of the area. Picnic facilities are available.

Allow 1 hour minimum. Daily 8-6, June-Aug.; 8-4:30, rest of year. Closed Jan. 1, Thanksgiving and Dec. 25. Admission $2, under 16 free, family rate $4. Phone (509) 522-6360 or 529-2761.

WINTHROP (B-9) pop. 400, elev. 1,765′

Winthrop has recaptured the spirit of the Old West with a colorful main street. Rows of false-fronted buildings, wooden sidewalks and old-fashioned streetlights are reminiscent of the 1890s, when a mining boom brought many settlers to the area. Poet and author Owen Wister lived in Winthrop in the early 1900s and described some of Winthrop's sites and citizens in his novel "The Virginian."

For further information contact the Winthrop Chamber of Commerce, P.O. Box 39, Winthrop, WA 98862; phone (509) 996-2125.

SHAFER MUSEUM, off SR 20 downtown, includes several pioneer structures. The log cabin built by town founder Guy Waring in 1897 contains period furnishings. A general store displays 1890-1935 merchandise. A print shop, the former Mazama post office and a millinery shop display an eclectic collection of pioneer relics and oddities. A doctor's and dentist's office contains antique medical equipment. The collection includes an outdoor display of early 1900s mining and farm equipment and a 1913 Model "T" touring car.

Fascinated by Fossils?
Galvanized by Gardens?
Wild about Waterfalls?
Intrigued by Islands?

The Points of Interest Index will lead you to them.

Allow 1 hour minimum. Daily 10-5, Memorial Day weekend-late Sept. Donations. Phone (509) 996-2712.

WINTHROP NATIONAL FISH HATCHERY, 1 mi. s. on Twin Lakes Rd., annually raises 1 million spring chinook salmon. Allow 30 minutes minimum. Daily 7:30-4:30. Free. Phone (509) 996-2424.

WISHRAM (G-8)

The site now occupied by Wishram had been a major food-trading area for American Indians for centuries when Lewis and Clark arrived in 1805. Tribes from various regions would come to trade such items as seafood, vegetables, grains and fish.

The site also was a prime fishing area; local tribes speared salmon from scaffolds anchored on the Columbia River's basalt cliffs, then smoked and stored the fish in leaf-lined baskets for consumption throughout the year. Celilo Falls, 1 mile east of town, was a major fishing spot until it was flooded by the reservoir of The Dalles Dam in 1957 *(see The Dalles, Ore.).*

WOODINVILLE (E-3) elev. 39′

Woodinville contains one of the largest nurseries in Washington: Molbak's, 13625 N.E. 175th St., has a conservatory of tropical plants.

For further information contact the Woodinville Chamber of Commerce, 13205 N.E. 175th St., Woodinville, WA 98072; phone (206) 481-8300.

CHATEAU STE. MICHELLE, 2 mi. s. on SR 202, is a major producer of premium table wines. Resembling a French country estate, the winery is on 87 landscaped acres. Allow 1 hour minimum. Tours and tastings daily 10-4:30; closed major holidays. Free. Phone (206) 488-3300.

COLUMBIA WINERY, 2 mi. s. on SR 202 at 14030 N.E. 145th St., offers 20-minute guided tours illustrating the steps of the winemaking process. Free tastings are available. Allow 30 minutes minimum. Tours offered Fri.-Sun. 10-4:30. Free. Phone (206) 488-2776.

FRENCH CREEK CELLARS, 17721 132nd Ave. N.E., offers a tasting room and informal tours of the winery upon request. Picnicking by a creek is permitted. Wed.-Mon. noon-5; closed holidays. Free. Phone (206) 486-1900.

WOODLAND (F-5) pop. 2,500, elev. 25′

Settled in the mid 1800s, Woodland soon developed into a bustling center for the surrounding farming, dairying and poultry-raising area. Logging was a major industry in the early 20th century. An interpretive marker on Finn Hall Road describes the Old Finn Hall, a community center built in 1916 by Finnish immigrants.

For further information contact the Woodland Chamber of Commerce, 1225 Lewis River Dr., P.O. Box 1012, Woodland, WA 98674; phone (360) 225-9552.

HULDA KLAGER LILAC GARDENS, 4½ acres 1½ mi. w. off I-5 exit 21, is the former estate of the renowned hybridizer Hulda Klager, whose work with lilacs brought her acclaim. A variety of plants, trees and shrubs grow in the gardens. Lilacs bloom from approximately late April to mid-May. Allow 30 minutes minimum. Tours of the 1889 farmhouse are offered 10-4 daily during the Lilac Festival in late April or early May. Gardens open daily dawn-dusk. House open only during festival. Admission $1. Phone (360) 225-8996.

YAKIMA (E-8) pop. 54,900, elev. 1,065′

Yakima (YACK-i-mah) occupies the west bank of its namesake river. The valley's irrigated fields provide a verdant contrast to the surrounding arid foothills; Yakima is the northern gateway to the Yakima Valley wine country with more than 20 wineries. The Central Washington Fair takes place in late September.

Year-round attractions include American Indian petroglyphs, 5 miles west on US 12, scattered along an old trail leading to the Wenas Mountains. Yakima Canyon, north to I-82 exit 26, then north on SR 821, is popular with rockhounds and offers fine trout fishing along the Yakima River. About 6 miles north the Fred G. Redmon Memorial Bridge, one of the longest concrete arch spans in the nation, carries I-82 over the Selah Creek Canyon.

Adjacent viewpoints offer a panorama of the 330-foot-deep gorge and distant views of Mount Rainier and Mount Adams. The Yakima Greenway, which extends 10 miles along the Yakima River from Selah Gap on the north to Union Gap on the south, features a 7-mile paved walking and bicycling path. Concerts are presented in the summer; phone (509) 453-8280. Yakima Brewing and Malting offers 20-minute tours by advance appointment; phone (509) 575-1900.

Spectator sports in Yakima include the Bears, who play class-A Northwest League baseball at Parker Field; phone (509) 457-5151. The Sun Kings play CBA basketball in the Sun Dome; phone (509) 248-1222. Thoroughbred horse racing is offered at Yakima Meadows; phone (509) 248-3920.

Note: Policies concerning admittance of children to pari-mutuel betting facilities vary. Phone for information.

For further information contact the Yakima Valley Visitors and Convention Bureau, 10 N. 8th St., Yakima, WA 98901; phone (509) 575-1300.

Shopping areas: Track 29 features a dozen shops in railroad cars. The major local shopping centers are Valley Mall, 3 miles south of downtown via S. 1st Street, and Yakima Mall, between Yakima Avenue, A Street, 3rd Street and Naches

Avenue. Yesterday's Village and Farmers' Market, 15 W. Yakima Ave., has more than 100 specialty and craft shops. A historic district on N. Front Street houses specialty shops.

BOISE CASCADE CORP., 1 mi. s. off I-82 exit 31 on N. 1st St., then ½ mi. e. on H St. to 805 N. 7th St., is a state-of-the-art plywood and sawmill complex. Guided 2-hour tours are available. Children under 8 are not permitted. Long pants and boots or tennis shoes must be worn. Tours are offered Mon.-Fri. at 9 and 1, day after Labor Day-day before Memorial Day weekend; at 9, rest of year. Closed major holidays. Free. Reservations are required 2 days in advance. Phone (509) 453-3131.

YAKIMA AREA ARBORETUM, ⅛ mi. e. of I-82 exit 34 on Nob Hill Rd., is a 40-acre reserve containing native and non-native plants and vegetation. The flowering tree collection is at its peak in April and May. Daily dawn-dusk. Free.

YAKIMA INTERURBAN LINES offers rides on its 1906-model trolleys. Free self-guiding tours of a 1910 trolley shop are available at S. 3rd Avenue and Pine Street. Trips depart Mon.-Fri. at 7 p.m., Sat.-Sun. and holidays at 10, noon, 2 and 4, early May to mid-Oct. Fare $4; over 60, $3.50; ages 6-12, $2.50; family rate $14; under 6 free on lap of adult. **Discount.** Phone (509) 575-1700.

YAKIMA VALLEY MUSEUM, 2105 Tieton Dr. in Franklin Park, features a large collection of carriages, coaches and wagons. Other exhibits include Yakama Indian artifacts; agricultural equipment; a re-created blacksmith shop, dental office and general store; and a hands-on children's exhibit. The William O. Douglas Memorial Exhibit includes the United States justice's Supreme Court office. On the other side of the park at 2109 W. Yakima Ave. is a furnished 1890s farmhouse that is open for tours Fridays 10-3.

Allow 1 hour minimum. Mon.-Fri. 10-5, Sat.-Sun. noon-5; closed major holidays. Admission $2.50; over 60 and ages 10-21, $1.25; family rate $5. **Discount.** Phone (509) 248-0747.

ZILLAH (F-9) pop. 1,900, elev. 821′

Zillah, incorporated in 1911 and named for the daughter of the president of the Northern Pacific Railroad, is located in the heart of the Yakima Valley's orchard and vineyard district. Several local wineries offer tours or wine tastings, including Bonair Winery, (509) 829-6027; Hyatt Vineyards Winery, (509) 829-6333; and Portteus Vineyards, (509) 829-6970.

An architectural oddity in Zillah is the Teapot Dome gas station, off I-82 exit 54, which was built to parody the Wyoming oil lease scandal of the early 1920s.

For further information contact the Zillah Chamber of Commerce, P.O. Box 1294, Zillah, WA 98953; phone (509) 829-5055.

COVEY RUN, 1 mi. n. on Vintage Rd. via Roza and Highland drs., produces high-quality Yakima Valley wines. The tasting room overlooks the cellar and vineyards. Tours and tastings are available Mon.-Sat. 10-5, Sun. noon-5, Apr.-Nov.; Mon.-Sat. 11-4:30, Sun. noon-4:30, rest of year. Free. Phone (509) 829-6235.

Further Reading

The following sampling of books has been selected for the pleasure and enrichment of our members who wish to discover more about the region they are visiting. This list is not intended to be a complete survey of works available, nor does it imply AAA endorsement of a particular author, work or publisher.

Oregon:

Hill, William. "The Oregon Trail." Photographs, maps, drawings and diary and journal entries trace the history of the trail.

Kesey, Ken. "Sometimes a Great Notion." A dramatic story of life in a small Northwest lumbering town.

Parkman, Francis. "The Oregon Trail." A historical look into the adventures of the people who traveled along the famous northwestern trail.

Ross, Dana Fuller. "Oregon!" A dramatic adventure following the lives of pioneering men and women as they blaze their way across the untamed land of America. Other novels by Ross include "Oregon Legacy," "Texas!" and "Illinois!"

Washington:

Combs, Ann. "Helter Shelter." A humorous look at the adventures of the Combs family as they renovate their dilapidated house and adjust to rural living on Bainbridge Island.

Holbrook, Stewart. "The Columbia." A story about the people who traveled the river that was first opened to a vast flood of settlers in 1805 when Lewis and Clark discovered it.

Jones, Nard. "Seattle." The author, a lifetime Seattle resident, recounts the colorful history of the boisterous frontier town.

Prater, Yvonne. "Snoqualmie Pass." The author takes a look at the history and development of the road that began as a narrow Indian trail and progressively grew into a multilane highway.

Ross, Dana Fuller. "Washington!" The continuing multigenerational saga of a family's search for a new life on the wild frontier in the Washington timberland. Other works by Ross include "Oregon!," "Colorado!" and "Utah!"

Four Names Everyone Says Yes To

AAA is the most trusted name in travel. And, VISA and MASTERCARD are the most accepted names in credit cards. Put AAA on each credit card and there's only one name missing—*yours.* Increase the advantages of your AAA membership by using the new, exclusive AAA/VISA or AAA/MASTERCARD credit card for all your purchases. Ask your AAA club about the many benefits. They're two cards everyone says "yes" to. Why don't you? Call your local AAA office now to apply.

The AAA/VISA and AAA/MASTERCARD credit cards are owned and issued by sponsoring VISA and MASTERCARD issuers and are available only to members of participating AAA clubs. Both cards are accepted in over 160 countries worldwide in over 10 million locations.

©1989 American Automobile Association.

The Most Trusted Name in Travel.

AAA

LODGINGS & RESTAURANTS

The Five Diamond designation assures AAA's most discriminating members that they will experience definitive luxury, service and style. AAA congratulates the lodgings and restaurants listed in this book that have met or exceeded our highest standards of excellence.

Five Diamond Award

LODGINGS

Four Seasons
Olympic Hotel .... SEATTLE, WASHINGTON

AAA Members

#1
Hertz
The Hertz/AAA partnership saves you money!

When you're planning your next trip, whether it's a day, week-end or week, Hertz has your wheels. Hertz offers AAA members special discounts and benefits all year long. For more information call your AAA office or Hertz at 1-800-654-3080.

Hertz rents Fords and other fine cars.
®REG. U.S. PAT. OFF. ©HERTZ SYSTEM INC. 1994/418-94

AAA
Show Your Card & Save

Hertz

OREGON

ALBANY—29,500

LODGINGS

BEST WESTERN PONY SOLDIER MOTOR INN Rates Subject to Change **Phone:** 503/928-6322
AAA ◆◆◆ Motel
All Year [CP] 1P: $62- 72 2P/1B: $64- 74 2P/2B: $69- 79 XP: $5 F12
Location: On I-5; southbound exit 234A, northbound exit 234. 315 Airport Rd SE 97321. Fax: 503/928-8124. **Terms:** Sr. discount; reserv deposit; small pets only. **Facility:** 72 rooms. Exceptionally well kept, attractive units. 2 stories; exterior corridors; meeting rooms; heated pool, whirlpool; exercise room. **Dining:** Restaurant nearby. **Services:** data ports; guest laundry. **All Rooms:** free movies, refrigerators, cable TV. **Cards:** AE, CB, DI, DS, JCB, MC, VI. *(See ad below)* Ⓓ ⊗

COMFORT INN Rates Subject to Change **Phone:** 503/928-0921
AAA ◆◆ Motel
4/16-2/29 [CP] 1P: $62 2P/1B: $69 2P/2B: $75 XP: $7 F18
3/1-4/15 [CP] 1P: $58 2P/1B: $65 2P/2B: $70 XP: $7 F18
Location: On I-5; southbound exit 234A, northbound exit 234. 251 Airport Way SE 97321. Fax: 503/928-8055. **Terms:** Sr. discount; credit card guarantee; pets. **Facility:** 48 rooms. Tastefully appointed & well kept units. 2 stories; interior corridors; meeting rooms; heated indoor pool, sauna, whirlpool; exercise room. **Dining:** Restaurant nearby. **Services:** Fee: coin laundry. **All Rooms:** free movies, cable TV. **Some Rooms:** honor bars, coffeemakers, 3 kitchens, microwaves. Fee: refrigerators, whirlpools. **Cards:** AE, CB, DI, DS, JCB, MC, VI. *(See color ad below)* Ⓓ ⊗

MOTEL ORLEANS Rates Subject to Change **Phone:** 503/926-0170
AAA ◆◆ Motel
All Year 1P: $40 2P/1B: $45 2P/2B: $47 XP: $4 F12
Location: E of jct I-5 & Hwy 20; I-5 exit 233. 1212 SE Price Rd 97321. Fax: 503/967-3283. **Terms:** Sr. discount; reserv deposit; small pets only, $25 dep req. **Facility:** 78 rooms. Generous size units. 3 two-room units for up to 6 persons, from $53; 2 stories; exterior corridors; meeting rooms; indoor/outdoor pool; airstrip. **Dining:** Restaurant nearby. **Services:** Fee: coin laundry. **All Rooms:** combo & shower baths, cable TV. **Some Rooms:** microwaves, refrigerators. Fee: VCP's. **Cards:** AE, CB, DI, DS, MC, VI. Ⓓ ⊗

RESTAURANT

NOVAK'S HUNGARIAN PAPRIKAS **Dinner:** $11-$20 **Phone:** 503/967-9488
AAA ◆ Ethnic
Location: Off I-5 exit 233; w on Santiam Hwy. 2835 Santiam Hwy SE 97321. **Hours:** 11 am-9 pm, Sat 4 pm-9 pm. Closed: 1/1, 11/23, 12/24 & 12/25. **Reservations:** suggested. **Features:** No A/C; children's menu; health conscious menu items; carryout. Excellently prepared authentic Hungarian entress & desserts. Family owned & operated. Inviting atmosphere. Smoke free premises. **Cards:** MC, VI. ⊗

ASHLAND—16,200

LODGINGS

ASHLAND VALLEY INN Rates Subject to Change **Phone:** 503/482-2641
AAA ◆◆ Motel
5/29-10/15 1P: $68- 72 2P/1B: $72- 82 2P/2B: $82 XP: $6
3/16-5/28 1P: $39- 49 2P/1B: $44- 49 2P/2B: $49 XP: $6
3/1-3/15 & 10/16-2/29 1P: $32 2P/1B: $36- 40 2P/2B: $40 XP: $6
Location: 1/2 mi s on Hwy 99; from I-5, exits 14 or 19. 1193 Siskiyou Blvd 97520. Fax: 503/482-0139. **Terms:** Reserv deposit, 3 day notice; small pets only, $6, with credit card deposit. **Facility:** 64 rooms. 3 two-bedroom units. 2 stories; exterior corridors; heated pool. **Dining:** Restaurant nearby. **All Rooms:** free movies, combo & shower baths, cable TV. **Cards:** AE, DI, DS, MC, VI. Ⓓ ⊗

PONY SOLDIER MOTOR INNS
Best Western
Oregon • Washington • Idaho
1-800-634-PONY
PONY SOLDIER MOTOR INNS

WHEN YOU'RE LIVING OUT OF A SUITCASE...
Comfort Inn
In Albany/Corvallis
Comfort Inn
251 Airport Road S.E.
Albany, OR 97321
• Indoor Pool • Sauna • Spa
• Kitchenettes • Spa Suites
• Laundry • Meeting Room
• Free Cable TV • Free Continental Breakfast • Near Museums, Covered Bridges, Country & Timber Carnival
For reservations call 503-928-0921 or toll free 800-4-CHOICE

BEST WESTERN BARD'S INN MOTEL Rates Subject to Change **Phone:** 503/482-0049

◆◆ Motel

4/15-10/15	1P: $88- 90	2P/1B: $95	2P/2B: $118	XP: $10
3/1-4/14 & 10/16-2/29	1P: $48- 52	2P/1B: $58	2P/2B: $78	XP: $10

Location: 4 blks n on Hwy 99; from I-5, southbound exit 19, northbound exit 14. 132 N Main St 97520. Fax: 503/488-3259. **Terms:** Reserv deposit; pets, $10. **Facility:** 79 rooms. Very attractively decorated & well-maintained units. 3 two-bedroom units. 2-3 stories; interior/exterior corridors; pool, whirlpool. **Dining:** Breakfast only 7-11 am, 4/1-10/31. **All Rooms:** free movies, refrigerators, cable TV. **Some Rooms:** microwaves, radios, whirlpools. **Cards:** AE, DI, DS, MC, VI. Roll in showers. Ⓓ ⊗

BEST WESTERN HERITAGE INN Rates Subject to Change **Phone:** 503/482-6932

◆◆ Motel

6/24-10/8 [CP]	1P: $82	2P/1B: $91	2P/2B: $98	XP: $7 F18
6/1-6/23 [CP]	1P: $64	2P/1B: $74	2P/2B: $81	XP: $7 F18
3/1-5/31 & 10/9-2/29 [CP]	1P: $55	2P/1B: $62	2P/2B: $71	XP: $7 F18

Location: 3 mi n, I-5 exit 19. 434 Valley View Rd 97520. Fax: 503/482-8905. **Terms:** Sr. discount; reserv deposit, 3 day notice; pets. **Facility:** 53 rooms. Attractive, very well kept units. 6 large units with whirlpool, wet bar & refrigerator , $143, $98 off-season; 2-3 stories; interior corridors; meeting rooms; heated indoor pool, whirlpool. **Services:** data ports. Fee: coin laundry. **All Rooms:** free movies, combo & shower baths, cable TV. **Some Rooms:** 25 efficiencies. Fee: VCP's. **Cards:** AE, CB, DI, DS, JCB, MC, VI. *(See color ad below)* Ⓓ Ⓢ ⊗

CHANTICLEER INN AAA Special Value Rates **Phone:** 503/482-1919

◆◆ Bed & Breakfast

4/1-10/31 [BP]	1P: $125- 160	2P/1B: $125- 160	2P/2B: $160	XP: $25 F5
3/1-3/31 & 11/1-2/29 [BP]	1P: $90- 100	2P/1B: $90- 100	2P/2B: $100	XP: $25 F5

Location: Center; s of Hwy 99 (Siskiyou St) on Gresham St; from I-5 take exit 19. 120 Gresham 97520. **Terms:** Credit card guarantee, 21 day notice; no pets. **Facility:** 6 rooms. Charming country style guest room decor. 3 stories; interior corridors; smoke free premises; lawn games. **Dining:** Breakfast served 8:30-9:30 am in dining room or on patio; champagne breakfast Sun. **All Rooms:** combo & shower baths, no TVs. **Cards:** MC, VI. Ⓓ ⊗

COUNTRY WILLOWS BED & BREAKFAST INN Guaranteed Rates **Phone:** 503/488-1590

◆◆ Bed & Breakfast

5/1-10/31 [BP]	1P: $85- 160	2P/1B: $90- 165	XP: $30
3/1-4/30 & 11/1-2/29 [BP]	1P: $68- 128	2P/1B: $72- 132	XP: $30

Location: I-5 exit 14, 1/2 mi w on Ashland St, then 1 mi s on Clay St. 1313 Clay St 97520. Fax: 503/488-1611. **Terms:** Reserv deposit, 14 day notice; package plans; 2 night min stay, 6/15-10/15; no pets. **Facility:** 7 rooms. 1800's style farm house on spacious grounds in attractive, country setting. Comfortably appointed guest rooms. Large room with fireplace, wet bar, microwave, refrigerator & deck $165; $132 off season; 2 stories; interior corridors; smoke free premises; heated pool, whirlpool; access to forested walking trails. **Services:** airport transportation. **Recreation:** bicycles. **All Rooms:** combo & shower baths, no phones, no TVs. **Some Rooms:** coffeemakers, 3 efficiencies. **Cards:** MC, VI. Ⓓ

KNIGHTS INN MOTEL Rates Subject to Change **Phone:** 503/482-5111

◆ Motel

5/27-10/9	1P: $54- 62	2P/1B: $62	2P/2B: $62	XP: $6
3/1-5/26 & 10/10-2/29	1P: $33- 42	2P/1B: $37- 42	2P/2B: $42	XP: $6

Location: 1/4 mi w of jct I-5 & Hwy 66, off exit 14. 2359 Hwy 66 97520. **Terms:** Reserv deposit, 3 day notice; small pets only, $6. **Facility:** 40 rooms. 2 stories; exterior corridors; heated pool, whirlpool. **Dining:** Restaurant nearby. **All Rooms:** combo & shower baths, cable TV. **Some Rooms:** refrigerators. **Cards:** AE, DI, DS, MC, VI. Ⓓ ⊗

MT ASHLAND INN Guaranteed Rates **Phone:** 503/482-8707

◆◆◆ Bed & Breakfast

Fri & Sat & Sun-Thurs 5/1-10/31 [BP]	1P: $75- 125	2P/1B: $80- 130	XP: $20
Sun-Thurs 3/1-4/30 & 11/1-2/29 [BP]	1P: $67- 112	2P/1B: $72- 117	XP: $18

Location: 8 mi s to I-5 exit 6, 6 mi w on Mt Ashland Rd. 550 Mt Ashland Rd 97520. **Terms:** Reserv deposit, 10 day notice; no pets. **Facility:** 5 rooms. In scenic forest mountain setting. Charming handcrafted lodge-like building with very comfortable common areas & guest rooms. Suite avail; 2 stories; interior corridors; smoke free premises. **Dining:** 11/1-3/31 dinner avail by advance reservation, $15-$22. **Services:** complimentary evening beverages. **All Rooms:** combo & shower baths, no A/C, no phones, no TVs. **Some Rooms:** microwaves, refrigerators, whirlpools. **Cards:** MC, VI. Ⓓ ⊗

Budget Host International

Something Better...at A Budget Rate

Locations in 37 states and Canada. For Reservations or a FREE Directory, call: 1 800 BUD-HOST

IN ASHLAND

DO YOUR MIDSUMMER NIGHT'S DREAMING WITH US!

Ashland ... home of the famous Shakespeare Theatre and Festival

- Year-round Indoor Pool • Spa • Free In-room Cable TV and Movies
- Free Continental Breakfast • Kitchenettes • Spa Suites
- Meeting Rooms

Best Western Heritage Inn
434 Valley View Rd., Ashland, OR 97520
I-5 Exit 19
503-482-6932

BEST WESTERN RESERVATION: 800-528-1234

OAK HILL COUNTRY BED & BREAKFAST Guaranteed Rates **Phone:** 503/482-1554

AAA ◆ Bed & Breakfast	5/1-10/31 [BP]	1P: $70	2P/1B: $80	2P/2B: $80	XP: $25
	Fri & Sat 3/1-4/30 [BP]	1P: $65	2P/1B: $75	2P/2B: $75	XP: $25
	Sun-Thurs 3/1-4/30 & 11/1-2/29 [BP]	1P: $50	2P/1B: $60	2P/2B: $60	XP: $25

Location: 3/4 mi s of jct Hwy 99 & Hwy 66. 2190 Siskiyou Blvd 97520. **Terms:** Reserv deposit, 5 day notice; package plans; no pets. **Facility:** 5 rooms. 1910 Craftsman-style home. Attractive dining room & outdoor deck area. Color TV's avail on request; free movies. 2 stories; interior corridors; smoke free premises; yard games. **Dining:** Breakfast served at 8:30 am. **Recreation:** bicycles. **All Rooms:** combo & shower baths, no phones. **Cards:** MC, VI. (S) ⊗

QUALITY INN FLAGSHIP Guaranteed Rates **Phone:** 503/488-2330

AAA ◆◆◆ Motel	6/1-9/30 [CP]	1P: $65- 80	2P/1B: $75- 85	2P/2B: $90	XP: $6
	3/1-5/31 & 10/1-10/31 [CP]	1P: $45- 55	2P/1B: $50- 55	2P/2B: $60	XP: $6
	11/1-2/29 [CP]	1P: $40	2P/1B: $40- 50	2P/2B: $50	XP: $6

Location: 1 mi s; 1 blk e of jct I-5 & Hwy 66, exit 14. 2520 Ashland St 97520. Fax: 503/482-1068. **Terms:** Credit card guarantee, 4 day notice; pets, $6 dep req. **Facility:** 60 rooms. Very comfortably furnished & especially well-kept units. 1 bedroom suite with efficiency from $94; 2 stories; exterior corridors; heated pool. **Dining:** Restaurant nearby. **Services:** Fee: coin laundry, airport transportation. **All Rooms:** free movies, cable TV, VCP's. **Some Rooms:** 5 kitchens, microwaves, refrigerators. **Cards:** AE, CB, DI, DS, JCB, MC, VI. *(See color ad below)* (D) ⊗

REGENCY INN Rates Subject to Change **Phone:** 503/482-4700

AAA ◆ Motel	5/15-9/30	1P: $45	2P/1B: $48	2P/2B: $55	XP: $5
	3/1-5/14 & 10/1-2/29	1P: $35	2P/1B: $38	2P/2B: $43	XP: $5

Location: 3 mi n; I-5 exit 19. 50 Lowe Rd 97520. **Terms:** Reserv deposit; no pets. **Facility:** 44 rooms. Very neatly furnished nicely kept units. Hospitably operated. 1 two-room unit with refrigerator, microwave & wet bar, $89; 2 stories; exterior corridors; heated pool. **Dining:** Restaurant nearby. **All Rooms:** combo & shower baths, cable TV. **Cards:** DS, MC, VI. *(See ad below)* (D) ⊗

ROMEO INN Guaranteed Rates **Phone:** 503/488-0884

AAA ◆◆◆◆ Bed & Breakfast	All Year [BP]	1P: $115- 175	2P/1B: $115- 175	2P/2B: $115- 175	XP: $30

Location: Northbound I-5 exit 11; s on Sherman to Iowa & 1 blk w to Idaho; southbound I-5 exit 19; s on Main to Gresham; s 4 blks to Iowa & 1 blk e to Idaho. 295 Idaho 97520. Fax: 503/488-0817. **Terms:** Reserv deposit, 30 day notice; no pets. **Facility:** 6 rooms. Cape cod-style house in quiet residental area. Large, attractively decorated rooms some with fireplace. Attractively landscaped courtyard area. Off season rates for 3 guest rooms. 1-bedroom suite with whirlpool & efficiency, $185; 2 stories; interior corridors; smoke free premises; heated pool, whirlpool. **Dining:** Breakfast served 8:30 am-9:30 am. **All Rooms:** combo & shower baths, no TVs. **Cards:** MC, VI. (D) ⊗

REGENCY INN **1-800-482-4701**
I-5, EXIT 19 (Valley View Road) Ashland, OR
• 5 Min from Shakespearean Theatres • Heated Pool • Queen Sized Beds & Sofas • Color Cable TV • Large Rooms • Free Local Calls • Complimentary Morning Coffee, Tea, & Cocoa • Non-Smoking & handicap Rooms

Stratford Inn Ashland
555 Siskiyou Blvd.
(503) 488-2151
• 5 Blocks to Shakespearean Theatres • 20 Miles to skiing at Mt. Ashland • Indoor Pool • • Whirlpool • Kitchenettes • Handicap Rooms • Free Ski Lockers • Non-Smoking Facility • • Free Morning Coffee & Tea • Air-Conditioned • Queen-Size Beds • Color Cable TV • • In-Room Refrigerators
TOLL FREE RESERVATIONS (800) 547-4741

In Ashland
QUALITY INN Flagship
2520 Ashland Avenue
(OFF I-5, Exit 14)
Ashland, OR 97520
● Home of Shakespeare Festival ● Restaurant adjacent ● Mins. from golf course & river rafting ● All rooms have refrigs., dec. fireplaces, 2 phones, video players & satellite TV, remote control ● Comp. Continental breakfast ● Heated Pool ● Limo service
⇨ **1-800-334-2330** ⇦

STRATFORD INN — Rates Subject to Change — **Phone:** 503/488-2151

AAA ◆◆ Motel

6/15-9/30	1P: $87	2P/1B: $92	2P/2B: $92	XP: $5
3/1-6/14 & 10/1-10/31	1P: $51	2P/1B: $56	2P/2B: $56	XP: $5
11/1-2/29	1P: $41	2P/1B: $46	2P/2B: $46	XP: $5

Location: 1/4 mi s on Hwy 99; from I-5, exit 14 or 19. 555 Siskiyou Blvd 97520. **Terms:** Reserv deposit; no pets. **Facility:** 55 rooms. Very nicely kept, comfortable units. 2 one-bedroom suites, each with efficiency, 1 with whirlpool, $120-$130; 3 stories; interior corridors; smoke free premises; heated indoor pool, whirlpool. **Services:** guest laundry. **All Rooms:** refrigerators, combo & shower baths, cable TV. **Some Rooms:** 4 kitchens, microwaves, VCP's. **Cards:** AE, CB, DI, DS, MC, VI. *(See ad p A5)*

TIMBERS MOTEL — Rates Subject to Change — **Phone:** 503/482-4242

AAA ◆ Motel

6/1-10/14	1P: $51- 56	2P/1B: $56- 60	2P/2B: $60	XP: $5
3/1-5/31 & 10/15-2/29	1P: $35- 42	2P/1B: $35- 42	2P/2B: $42	XP: $5

Location: 3/4 mi w on Hwy 66, 1 blk e of jct Hwy 99; I-5 exit 14. 1450 Ashland St 97520. Fax: 503/482-8723. **Terms:** Reserv deposit, 4 day notice; no pets. **Facility:** 29 rooms. 2 two-bedroom units. 2 efficiencies, $12 extra; 2 stories; exterior corridors; small heated pool. **Dining:** Restaurant nearby. **All Rooms:** cable TV. Fee: VCP. **Cards:** AE, DS, MC, VI.

WINDMILL'S ASHLAND HILLS INN AND SUITES — Rates Subject to Change — **Phone:** 503/482-8310

AAA ◆◆◆ Motor Inn

6/1-9/30	1P: $75- 105	2P/1B: $75- 105	2P/2B: $85- 105	XP: $6	F17
3/1-5/31 & 10/1-10/31	1P: $65- 75	2P/1B: $65- 75	2P/2B: $65- 75	XP: $6	F17
11/1-2/29	1P: $45- 55	2P/1B: $45- 55	2P/2B: $45- 55	XP: $6	F17

Location: 1 mi s; 1 blk e of jct I-5 & Hwy 66, exit 14. 2525 Ashland St 97520. Fax: 503/488-1783. **Terms:** Check-in 4 pm; credit card guarantee; pets. **Facility:** 231 rooms. Spacious very comfortably furnished units, some with balcony. Attractive grounds & central courtyard. 7 one-bedroom suites, with wet bar & refrigerator $100-$225; 3 stories; exterior corridors; conference facilities; heated pool, whirlpool; 2 tennis courts; exercise room. **Dining & Entertainment:** Dining room, coffee shop; 7 am-9 pm; $8-$20; cocktails/lounge. **Services:** data ports; valet laundry; area transportation, to Shakespearian Theatre, airport transportation. **Recreation:** bicycles. **All Rooms:** microwaves, free movies, cable TV. Fee: VCP. **Some Rooms:** refrigerators. **Cards:** AE, DI, DS, MC, VI. *(See ad below)*

THE WOODS HOUSE BED & BREAKFAST INN — Guaranteed Rates — **Phone:** 503/488-1598

AAA ◆◆ Bed & Breakfast

6/1-10/31 [BP]	1P: $100- 107	2P/1B: $105- 112	2P/2B: $105- 112	XP: $35	F11
3/1-5/31 & 11/1-2/29 [BP]	1P: $65- 85	2P/1B: $65- 85	2P/2B: $65- 85	XP: $35	F11

Location: 1/2 mi n on Hwy 99 from I-5, exits 14 or 19. 333 N Main 97520. Fax: 503/482-7912. **Terms:** Check-in 5 pm; reserv deposit, 21 day notice; no pets. **Facility:** 6 rooms. 1908 Craftsman style house; very charming especially well-kept guest rooms. 2 stories; interior corridors; smoke free premises. **Dining:** Breakfast served 9 am. **All Rooms:** combo & shower baths, no phones, no TVs. **Cards:** MC, VI.

RESTAURANTS

CHATEAULIN — **Dinner:** $21-$30 — **Phone:** 503/482-2264

◆◆◆ French

Location: Center. 50 E Main 97520. **Hours:** 5 pm-10 pm; 11/1-5/30 5:30 pm-9:30 pm. Closed: 12/25. **Reservations:** suggested. **Features:** children's menu; cocktails & lounge; street parking; a la carte. 1 blk from Shakesperian Theatre. Small, charming, intimate, bistro-like atmosphere. Variations of beef, poultry, duck, seafood, veal & vegetarian dishes. Large wine list. **Cards:** AE, CB, DI, MC, VI.

MONET — **Dinner:** $21-$30 — **Phone:** 503/482-1339

AAA ◆◆ French

Location: Center. 36 S Second 97520. **Hours:** Open 2/1-12/31; 11:45 am-1:45 & 5:30-9 pm, Sun & Mon 5:30 pm-9 pm; 11:45-1:45 & 5:30-8:30 pm Tues-Sat 10/1-5/31. Closed: Jan. **Reservations:** suggested; in summer. **Features:** cocktails; a la carte. Tastefully appointed dining room with quiet, intimate atmosphere. Delicately prepared light French dishes. Dining on outdoor patio in summer. Smoke free premises. **Cards:** MC, VI.

OMAR'S FRESH FISH & STEAKS — **Dinner:** $11-$20 — **Phone:** 503/482-1281

AAA ◆◆ American

Location: 3/4 mi s at jct Hwy 99 & Hwy 66; 1 1/2 mi w of I-5 exit 14. 1380 Siskiyou Blvd 97520. **Hours:** 11:30 am-2 & 5-10 pm, Fri-10:30 pm, Sat 5 pm-10:30 pm, Sun 5 pm-10 pm. Closed: 12/25 & 1st Sun in Dec. **Features:** children's menu; senior's menu; health conscious menu; cocktails & lounge. Long established & locally popular. Fresh seafood, chicken & steak dishes. Popular sandwiches & salads. **Cards:** AE, DS, MC, VI.

PRIMAVERA — **Dinner:** $11-$20 — **Phone:** 503/488-1994

◆◆ Continental

Location: Center. 241 Hargadine 97520. **Hours:** 5 pm-8:30 pm. Closed: Jan, 11/23, 12/25, Mon & Tues 6/1-9/30 & Mon-Wed 10/1-5/31. **Reservations:** required. **Features:** cocktails; street parking; a la carte. Located below Oregon Cabaret Theatre. Roomy dining room with art decor. Daily changeable menu with limited selection of very tastefully prepared dishes with French-Italian influence. Smoke free premises. **Cards:** MC, VI.

WINDMILL INN
Ashland Hills Inn & Suites

Nestled Against the Cascade Foothills

159 Deluxe Rooms plus *72 Spacious 2-Room Suites
Restaurant • Lounge • Swimming Pool • Whirlpool
Tennis Courts • Gift Shop • Beauty Salon
12,000 sq ft of Meeting Space • Resort Amenities

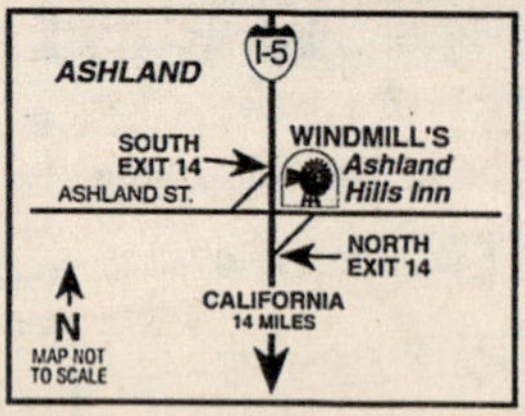

*Suites opening Early 1995

1-800-547-4747

Hospitality Guaranteed!

2525 Ashland Street • Ashland, Oregon • 97520 • 503-482-8310

ASTORIA—10,100

LODGINGS

BAYSHORE MOTOR INN Rates Subject to Change **Phone:** 503/325-2205
AAA 4/15-10/14 1P: $50- 55 2P/1B: $55- 60 2P/2B: $60- 65 XP: $5 F10
3/1-4/14 & 10/15-2/29 1P: $40 2P/1B: $45 2P/2B: $50 XP: $5 F10
◆◆ Motel **Location:** On Hwy 26 & 101, at e end of Young's Bay Bridge. 555 Hamburg 97103. Fax: 503/325-5550. **Terms:** Credit card guarantee; small pets only, $5. **Facility:** 37 rooms. Immaculately kept units, some with view of river. 1 kitchen unit $75; $65 low season; 2 stories; interior corridors. **Services:** Fee: coin laundry. **All Rooms:** combo & shower baths, cable TV, no A/C. **Some Rooms:** refrigerators. **Cards:** AE, DI, DS, MC, VI. Ⓓ ⊗

CREST MOTEL Guaranteed Rates **Phone:** 503/325-3141
AAA 5/15-10/15 2P/1B: $46- 79 2P/2B: $66- 79 XP: $10 F12
3/1-5/14 & 10/16-2/29 2P/1B: $46- 73 2P/2B: $59- 73 XP: $5 F12
◆◆ Motel **Location:** 4 mi e of Astoria Bridge on Hwy 30. 5366 Leif Erickson Dr 97103. **Terms:** Pets. **Facility:** 40 rooms. Attractive grounds overlooking Columbia River. Exceptionally maintained, many large units most with river view, some with deck. 2 two-bedroom units. 2 stories; exterior corridors; whirlpool. **Services:** Fee: coin laundry. **All Rooms:** coffeemakers, free movies, combo & shower baths, cable TV, no A/C. **Some Rooms:** refrigerators. **Cards:** AE, CB, DI, DS, MC, VI. *(See ad below)* Ⓓ ⊗

DUNES MOTEL Rates Subject to Change **Phone:** 503/325-7111
AAA 5/15-9/30 1P: $48- 65 2P/1B: $58- 64 2P/2B: $68- 74 XP: $7
3/1-5/14 & 10/1-2/29 1P: $40- 48 2P/1B: $48- 52 2P/2B: $48- 60 XP: $7
◆ Motel **Location:** 3/4 mi w on Hwy 30; 2 blks e of jct Hwy 101. 288 W Marine Dr 97103. Fax: 503/325-0804. **Terms:** Reserv deposit; no pets. **Facility:** 58 rooms. Neatly furnished units, some with river view. 2 stories; exterior corridors; heated indoor pool, whirlpool. **Services:** Fee: coin laundry. **All Rooms:** coffeemakers, free movies, cable TV. **Some Rooms:** A/C, refrigerators, whirlpools. **Cards:** AE, CB, DI, DS, MC, VI. Ⓓ ⊗

RED LION INN Rates Subject to Change **Phone:** 503/325-7373
◆◆◆ 5/1-10/1 1P: $68- 73 2P/1B: $83- 88 2P/2B: $83- 88 XP: $15 F17
Motor Inn 3/1-4/30 & 10/2-2/29 1P: $63- 68 2P/1B: $70- 79 2P/2B: $71- 81 XP: $15 F17
Location: 1 mi w at jct Hwy 30 & 101. 400 Industry St 97103. Fax: 503/325-8727. **Terms:** Sr. discount; reserv deposit, 3 day notice; pets. **Facility:** 124 rooms. Picturesque view of marina at river's edge. Comfortably furnished units, many spacious, with balcony. 1 two-bedroom unit. 2 stories; exterior corridors; meeting rooms. **Dining:** Also, Red Lion Seafare Pacific Grill & Chowder House, see separate listing. **All Rooms:** combo & shower baths, cable TV, no A/C. Fee: movies. **Cards:** AE, CB, DI, DS, JCB, MC, VI. Ⓓ ⊗

RESTAURANTS

PIER 11 FEED STORE RESTAURANT & LOUNGE **Dinner:** $11-$20 **Phone:** 503/325-0279
AAA ◆◆ American **Location:** On the pier at foot of 10th St. 77 11 th St 97103. **Hours:** 7 am-10 pm; 10/16-3/31, 7 am-9 pm, Fri & Sat-10 pm. Closed: 11/23 & 12/25. **Reservations:** suggested; in summer. **Features:** No A/C; children's menu; early bird specials; salad bar; cocktails & lounge. In former feed mill & store on dock along Columbia River. River view dining. Comfortable rustic atmosphere. Good variety of seafood; also steaks, chicken, pasta & sandwiches. **Cards:** DS, MC, VI. ⊗

RED LION SEAFARE PACIFIC GRILL & CHOWDER HOUSE **Dinner:** $11-$20 **Phone:** 503/325-7373
◆◆ American **Location:** At Red Lion Inn. 400 Industry St 97103. **Hours:** 6 am-10 pm, Sun-9 pm. **Reservations:** suggested. **Features:** Sunday brunch; children's menu; early bird specials; senior's menu; carryout; cocktails & lounge. Nautical theme dining room with view of marina. Popular seafood, steak and pasta dishes. **Cards:** AE, DI, DS, JCB, MC, VI. ⊗

SHIP INN **Dinner:** $11-$20 **Phone:** 503/325-0033
◆ Seafood **Location:** 1/2 mi w, 1 blk n off Hwy 30. 1 2nd St 97103. **Hours:** 11:30 am-9:30 pm. Closed major holidays. **Features:** No A/C; children's menu; carryout; salad bar; cocktails & lounge. Fish & chip house with casual atmosphere & river view. Also, some English specialties, salads & popular sandwiches. **Cards:** DS, MC, VI. ⊗

BAKER CITY—9,100

LODGINGS

BEST WESTERN SUNRIDGE INN Guaranteed Rates **Phone:** 503/523-6444
◆◆◆ All Year 1P: $52- 61 2P/1B: $56- 65 2P/2B: $62- 72 XP: $4
Motor Inn **Location:** I-84 at exit 304. One Sunridge Ln 97814. Fax: 503/523-6446. **Terms:** Sr. discount; reserv deposit, 3 day notice; no pets. **Facility:** 156 rooms. Large units, some with balconies or patios facing very attractively landscaped courtyard. 2 suites with whirlpool, $135; 2 stories; exterior corridors; heated pool, whirlpool. **Dining:** Restaurant; 5 am-midnight; $8-$16; cocktails. **Services:** area transportation, limited, airport transportation. **All Rooms:** free movies, cable TV. **Some Rooms:** microwaves, refrigerators. **Cards:** AE, CB, DI, DS, MC, VI. *(See ad p A8)* Ⓓ ⊗

Crest
MOTEL
Astoria, Oregon 97103

Picturesque hilltop setting, quiet surroundings, 40 lovely rooms, and spacious lawns overlooking the Columbia River and City of Astoria offer a unique motel experience. Coin Laundry. Non-smoking building. Whirlpool.

Call for Winter Rates

Located on U.S. 30 at the East edge of Astoria.

Phone (503)325-3141

Reservations Only 1-800-421-3141

QUALITY INN — Rates Subject to Change — **Phone:** 503/523-2242

AAA ◆◆ Motel

All Year [CP]	1P: $45	2P/1B: $49	2P/2B: $52	XP: $5 F18

Location: 3 blks s of I-84, exit 304. 810 Campbell 97814. Fax: 503/523-2242. **Terms:** Sr. discount; reserv deposit, 3 day notice; pets, $2. **Facility:** 54 rooms. Very attractive Spanish architectural style & grounds. 2 stories; exterior corridors. **All Rooms:** cable TV. **Some Rooms:** refrigerators. **Cards:** AE, DI, DS, JCB, MC, VI. (D) ⊗

ROYAL MOTOR INN — Rates Subject to Change — **Phone:** 503/523-6324

AAA ◆ Motel

All Year [CP]	1P: $32	2P/1B: $36	2P/2B: $39	XP: $5 F15

Location: W on Hwy 30; I-84 exit 304. 2205 Broadway 97814. **Terms:** Sr. discount; reserv deposit, 3 day notice; small pets only. **Facility:** 36 rooms. Long established very well-kept, comfortable units. 2 stories; exterior corridors; heated pool. **All Rooms:** cable TV. **Cards:** AE, CB, DI, DS, MC, VI. (D) ⊗

SUPER 8 MOTEL BAKER CITY — Rates Subject to Change — **Phone:** 503/523-8282

AAA ◆◆ Motel

Fri & Sat 5/16-9/30 [CP]	1P: $53	2P/1B: $53	2P/2B: $57	XP: $4
Sun-Thurs 5/16-9/30 [CP]	1P: $49	2P/1B: $51	2P/2B: $55	XP: $4
3/1-5/15 & 10/1-2/29 [CP]	1P: $39	2P/1B: $44	2P/2B: $49	XP: $4

Location: Off I-84 exit 304. 250 Campbell St 97814. Fax: 503/523-9137. **Terms:** Sr. discount; credit card guarantee, 10 day notice; no pets. **Facility:** 72 rooms. Immaculate, very well maintained units. 1 two-bedroom unit. Suite with efficiency $69; 4 one-room units with whirlpool $85, off-season $70 & $81; 2 stories; interior corridors; heated indoor pool, whirlpool; exercise room. **Services:** Fee: coin laundry. **All Rooms:** free movies, combo & shower baths, cable TV. **Some Rooms:** 2 efficiencies, no utensils, microwaves, refrigerators. Fee: VCP's. **Cards:** AE, CB, DI, DS, MC, VI. Roll in showers. (D) (S) ⊗

BANDON—2,200

LODGINGS

CAPRICE MOTEL — Rates Subject to Change — **Phone:** 503/347-4494

AAA ◆ Motel

5/15-10/15	1P: $34- 40	2P/1B: $37- 42	2P/2B: $48	XP: $5
3/1-5/14 & 10/16-2/29	1P: $25- 32	2P/1B: $30- 33	2P/2B: $36	XP: $4

Location: 1/4 mi s on Hwy 101. 97411 (Rt 1, Box 530). **Terms:** Sr. discount; reserv deposit, 3 day notice; small pets only. **Facility:** 15 rooms. Excellently kept & well maintained units. Located at south end of town. 2 two-bedroom units. 2 kitchen units, $7 extra; 1 story; exterior corridors. **All Rooms:** free movies, combo & shower baths, cable TV, no A/C. **Some Rooms:** coffeemakers. **Cards:** AE, DS, MC, VI. (D) ⊗

HARBOR VIEW MOTEL — Rates Subject to Change — **Phone:** 503/347-4417

AAA ◆◆ Motel

7/1-9/30 [CP]	1P: $64- 82	2P/1B: $69- 83	2P/2B: $72- 76	XP: $5
5/15-6/30 [CP]	1P: $59- 74	2P/1B: $63- 79	2P/2B: $66- 70	XP: $5
3/1-5/14 & 10/1-2/29 [CP]	1P: $49- 61	2P/1B: $53- 66	2P/2B: $56- 60	XP: $5

Location: Center, on Hwy 101. 355 Second St 97411 (PO Box 1409). Fax: 503/347-3616. **Terms:** No pets. **Facility:** 59 rooms. On bluff overlooking harbor. Units with balcony & view. 1 two-bedroom unit. 3 stories, no elevator; exterior corridors; whirlpool. **All Rooms:** coffeemakers, free movies, refrigerators, combo & shower baths, cable TV, no A/C. **Some Rooms:** kitchen. **Cards:** AE, CB, DI, DS, MC, VI. *(See ad below)* (D) ⊗

RESTAURANTS

BANDON BOATWORKS — **Dinner:** $11-$20 — **Phone:** 503/347-2111

◆ American

Location: 1 1/2 mi w off Beach Loop Rd to S Jetty Rd. 275 Lincoln 97411. **Hours:** 11:30 am-2:30 & 5-9 pm, Sun noon-8:30 pm. Closed: Mon & 12/31-2/14. **Features:** No A/C; children's menu; senior's menu; carryout; salad bar; beer & wine only; a la carte. Cozy restaurant with view of jetty. Very good selection of fresh seafood, beef & combination dishes. **Cards:** AE, DI, DS, MC, VI. ⊗

LORD BENNETT'S RESTAURANT & LOUNGE — **Dinner:** $11-$20 — **Phone:** 503/347-3663

AAA ◆◆ American

Location: 3/4 mi w on 11th from Hwy 101 to Beach Loop Rd. 1695 Beach Loop Rd 97411. **Hours:** 11 am-3 & 5-10 pm; in winter 5 pm-9 pm. Closed: 12/25. **Reservations:** suggested. **Features:** Sunday brunch; children's menu; carryout; cocktails & lounge. Attractive restaurant with ocean view. Features selected seafood, steaks, lamb, veal & chicken dishes. **Cards:** AE, DS, MC, VI. ⊗

I-84 EXIT #304 • *ALONG THE OREGON TRAIL*

Best Western

Non-smoking rooms • Large indoor spa pool • Heated outdoor pool • Coffee shop/dining/lounge • Cable TV • Close to hunting/fishing/skiing/OR Trail Interpretive Ctr.

Best Western Sunridge Inn — AAA ◆◆◆

One Sunridge Lane • Baker City, OR 97814 • (503) 523-6444

Toll Free Direct (800) 233-2368 • Best Western Worldwide reservations: (800) 528-1234

Spectacular Coastal View!

1-800-526-0209

"Beautiful Bandon-by-the-Sea"

HWY 101 • P.O. BOX 1409 • BANDON, OR 97411

HARBOR VIEW MOTEL

TRAVEL WITH CONFIDENCE: CONFIRM YOUR RESERVATIONS.

BEAVERTON—53,300 (See PORTLAND ACCOMMODATIONS spotting map page A47; see index starting on page A46)

LODGINGS

COURTYARD BY MARRIOTT Guaranteed Rates **Phone:** 503/641-3200 73

◆◆◆ Motor Inn

Sun-Thurs	1P: $86	2P/1B: $96	2P/2B: $96	XP: $10	F12
Fri & Sat 5/1-10/10	1P: $86	2P/1B: $86	2P/2B: $86	XP: $10	F12
Fri & Sat 3/1-4/30 & 10/11-2/29	1P: $69	2P/1B: $69	2P/2B: $69	XP: $10	F12

Location: N SR 217 to Scholls Ferry Rd, w 2 blks to Hall Blvd, s to Nimbus Ave; southbound on 217; Progress exit to Hall Blvd, w to Nimbus Ave. 8500 SW Nimbus Ave 97008. Fax: 503/641-1287. **Terms:** Sr. discount; no pets. **Facility:** 149 rooms. Immaculate rooms, most with balcony. Attractively landscaped courtyard & gazebo. 3 stories; interior corridors; meeting rooms; heated indoor pool, whirlpool; exercise room. **Dining & Entertainment:** Restaurant; 6 am-10 & 4-11 pm, Sat & Sun 7 am-noon; $6-$10; cocktail lounge; limited dinner menu. **Services:** data ports. Fee: coin laundry, airport transportation. **All Rooms:** Fee: movies. **Some Rooms:** refrigerators. **Cards:** AE, CB, DI, DS, MC, VI.
(See color ad p A44) D S

GREENWOOD INN Rates Subject to Change **Phone:** 503/643-7444 71

◆◆◆ Motor Inn

5/1-9/30	1P: $77- 82	2P/1B: $87- 92	2P/2B: $87- 92	XP: $10	F18
3/1-4/30 & 10/1-2/29	1P: $62- 72	2P/1B: $72- 82	2P/2B: $72- 87	XP: $10	F18

Location: 3/4 mi s; at jct SR 217 & Allen Blvd; 4 mi nw of jct I-5 & SR 217. 10700 SW Allen Blvd 97005. Fax: 503/626-4553. **Terms:** Sr. discount; reserv deposit; pets, $10. **Facility:** 251 rooms. Very attractively landscaped courtyard & grounds; & especially well maintained units. 24 one- & two-bedroom kitchen suites with deck, 8 with fireplace, 5 with whirlpool, from $145; 2 stories; interior/exterior corridors; conference facilities; 2 heated pools, sauna, steamroom, whirlpool; exercise room. **Dining & Entertainment:** Restaurant; 6:30 am-10 pm, Fri & Sat-11 pm; $7-$16; cocktails; entertainment. **Services:** data ports; area transportation, to Washington Square. Fee: airport transportation. **All Rooms:** free movies, combo & shower baths, cable TV. **Some Rooms:** coffeemakers, microwaves, refrigerators. **Cards:** AE, CB, DI, DS, MC, VI. *(See ad p A49)* Roll in showers. D

RAMADA INN BEAVERTON AAA Special Value Rates **Phone:** 503/643-9100 72

◆◆ Motel

6/1-8/31 [CP]	1P: $90	2P/1B: $90	2P/2B: $100	XP: $10	F18
3/1-5/31 & 9/1-2/29 [CP]	1P: $85	2P/1B: $85	2P/2B: $95	XP: $10	F18

Location: On SR 8; 1/2 mi w of Beaverton. 13455 SW Canyon Rd 97005. Fax: 503/643-0514. **Terms:** Reserv deposit, 3 day notice; no pets. **Facility:** 143 rooms. Properly equipped guest rooms. 1 two-bedroom unit. 17 efficiency units, $95. 1 suite with efficiency & microwave up to 4 persons $125; 3 stories; interior corridors; meeting rooms; heated pool; exercise room. **Dining:** Restaurant nearby. **Services:** data ports. Fee: coin laundry, airport transportation. **All Rooms:** free movies, cable TV. **Some Rooms:** coffeemakers. **Cards:** AE, CB, DI, DS, JCB, MC, VI. D

SHILO INN BEAVERTON Rates Subject to Change **Phone:** 503/297-2551 70

◆◆ Motor Inn

All Year	1P: $69- 89	2P/1B: $69- 89	2P/2B: $74- 84	XP: $10	F12

Location: On SR 8, 1/4 mi e of jct 217. 9900 SW Canyon Rd 97225. Fax: 503/297-7708. **Terms:** Sr. discount; pets, $7. **Facility:** 141 rooms. Attractive public rooms & very attractively landscaped central courtyard with gazebo. Many guest rooms with balcony & deck. 3 one- & two-bedrooms suites each with wet bar, $95-$175; 2-3 stories; interior corridors; conference facilities; heated pool, whirlpool; exercise room. **Dining & Entertainment:** Dining room; 6 am-11 pm; $8-$25; cocktails/lounge; entertainment. **Services:** data ports; airport transportation. Fee: coin laundry. **All Rooms:** microwaves, free movies, refrigerators. **Some Rooms:** Fee: VCP's. **Cards:** AE, CB, DI, DS, JCB, MC, VI. D

RESTAURANTS

OLIVE GARDEN ITALIAN RESTAURANT **Dinner:** $11-$20 **Phone:** 503/644-0607 44

◆◆ Italian

Location: On SR 8, 1 1/2 blks w of jct SR 217. 11650 SW Canyon Rd 97005. **Hours:** 11 am-10 pm, Fri & Sat-11 pm. Closed: 11/23 & 12/25. **Features:** children's menu; health conscious menu items; carryout; cocktails & lounge; a la carte. Warm, friendly atmosphere. Good selection of hearty traditional dishes. Classic desserts. **Cards:** AE, CB, DI, DS, MC, VI.

SAYLER'S OLD COUNTRY KITCHEN **Dinner:** $11-$20 **Phone:** 503/644-1492 45

◆◆ Steakhouse

Location: 2 blks w of jct SR 217, Beaverton-Hillsdale Hwy. 4655 SW Griffith Dr 97005. **Hours:** 4 pm-11 pm, Fri-midnight, Sat 3 pm-midnight, Sun noon-11 pm. Closed: 7/4, 11/23, 12/24 & 12/25. **Features:** children's menu; senior's menu; carryout; cocktails & lounge. Attractive & comfortable. Very good service. Broad selection of complete steak dinners; also, seafood & chicken. **Cards:** AE, DS, MC, VI.

BEND—20,500

LODGINGS

BEST WESTERN ENTRADA LODGE Rates Subject to Change **Phone:** 503/382-4080

◆◆ Motel

All Year [CP]	1P: $49- 79	2P/1B: $55- 89	2P/2B: $59- 89	XP: $5	F18

Location: 4 mi w on Cascade Lakes Hwy enroute to Mt. Bachelor ski area; 17 mi e of Mt. Bachelor ski area. 19221 Century Dr 97702. Fax: 503/382-4080. **Terms:** Credit card guarantee; pets, $5. **Facility:** 79 rooms. Very attractive, quiet wooded area. Very well kept units. 1 room with whirlpool & sauna, extra charge; 1 story; exterior corridors; pool, whirlpool. **Services:** Fee: coin laundry. **Recreation:** nature program; jogging. **All Rooms:** cable TV. **Some Rooms:** microwaves, radios, refrigerators. **Cards:** AE, CB, DI, DS, MC, VI. D

BEST WESTERN WOODSTONE INN Rates Subject to Change **Phone:** 503/382-1515

◆◆ Motel

All Year [CP]	1P: $49- 79	2P/1B: $55- 89	2P/2B: $59- 89	XP: $5	F18

Location: On Hwy 97; 3 blks s of jct Hwy 20. 721 NE 3rd 97701. Fax: 503/382-1515. **Terms:** Credit card guarantee, 14 day notice, 12/24-1/1; pets, $5. **Facility:** 102 rooms. Attractive, very well kept units. 1 two-bedroom suite with refrigerator; 2 stories; exterior corridors; meeting rooms; heated pool, whirlpool. **Services:** data ports. **All Rooms:** cable TV. **Some Rooms:** microwaves, refrigerators. Fee: whirlpools. **Cards:** AE, CB, DI, DS, MC, VI. D

COMFORT INN Rates Subject to Change **Phone:** 503/388-2227

◆◆ Motel

6/11-9/5 [CP]	1P: $61- 75	2P/1B: $69- 79	2P/2B: $75- 85	XP: $10	F18
4/16-6/10 [CP]	1P: $45- 56	2P/1B: $65- 75	2P/2B: $69- 79	XP: $10	F18
9/6-2/29 [CP]	1P: $44- 59	2P/1B: $49- 65	2P/2B: $67- 75	XP: $10	F18
3/1-4/15 [CP]	1P: $43- 53	2P/1B: $48- 65	2P/2B: $67- 75	XP: $10	F18

Location: 2 1/2 mi s on Hwy 97. 61200 S Hwy 97 97702. Fax: 503/388-8820. **Terms:** Sr. discount; reserv deposit, 3 day notice; pets. **Facility:** 65 rooms. Comfortable units. 6 room with whirlpool, $110-$130; 2 stories; interior corridors; meeting rooms; heated indoor pool, sauna, whirlpool. **Dining:** Restaurant nearby. **Services:** Fee: coin laundry. **All Rooms:** free movies, combo & shower baths, cable TV. **Some Rooms:** 31 efficiencies, refrigerators. Fee: VCP's. **Cards:** AE, CB, DI, DS, JCB, MC, VI. *(See color ad p A10)* D

DUNES MOTEL Rates Subject to Change **Phone:** 503/382-6811

AAA ◆ Motel

Fri & Sat 6/1-9/15	1P: $44- 69	2P/1B: $49- 69	2P/2B: $59- 79	XP: $3-5 F12
Sun-Thurs 6/1-9/15	1P: $40	2P/1B: $45	2P/2B: $50	XP: $3-5 F12
3/1-5/31 & 9/16-2/29	1P: $38	2P/1B: $43	2P/2B: $47	XP: $3-5 F12

Location: On Hwy 97; 5 blks n of jct Hwy 20E. 1515 NE 3rd St 97701. **Terms:** Sr. discount; no pets. **Facility:** 30 rooms. 2 stories; exterior corridors; whirlpool. **Dining:** Restaurant nearby. **All Rooms:** free movies, cable TV. **Cards:** AE, CB, DI, DS, MC, VI. (D) ⊗

HAMPTON INN Rates Subject to Change **Phone:** 503/388-4114

AAA ◆◆◆ Motel

All Year [CP]	1P: $50- 59	2P/1B: $60- 69	2P/2B: $65- 69	XP: $10 F18

Location: 1 1/2 mi n on Hwy 97. 15 NE Butler Rd 97701. Fax: 503/389-3261. **Terms:** Sr. discount; check-in 4 pm; small pets only. **Facility:** 99 rooms. Attractively equipped units; some compact units. 2 stories; exterior corridors; meeting rooms; heated pool, whirlpool. **Services:** data ports. **All Rooms:** free movies, cable TV. **Some Rooms:** refrigerators. **Cards:** AE, CB, DI, DS, MC, VI. *(See color ad inside front cover)* (D) ⊗

INN OF THE 7TH MOUNTAIN AAA Special Value Rates **Phone:** 503/382-8711

AAA ◆◆◆ Resort Motor Inn

6/5-9/30 & 12/19-1/2	1P: $65- 139	2P/1B: $65- 139	2P/2B: $99- 215
3/1-6/4, 10/1-12/18 & 1/3-2/29	1P: $59- 129	2P/1B: $59- 129	2P/2B: $89- 199

Location: 7 mi w on Cascade Lakes Hwy en route to Mt. Bachelor Ski area; 15 mi e of Mt. Bachelor ski area. 18575 S Century Dr 97702. Fax: 503/382-3517. **Terms:** Check-in 5 pm; reserv deposit, 7 day notice, 30 day refund notice 12/15-1/2; package plans; no pets. **Facility:** 327 rooms. Scenic mountain area. Extensive recreational facilities. 1- to 3-bedroom condominiums & units. Many fireplaces & balconies. 3 stories; exterior corridors; conference facilities; miniature golf; 2 heated pools, wading pool, sauna, whirlpools; 7 tennis courts; playground. Fee: 18 holes golf; roller skating 4/15-10/31. **Dining & Entertainment:** Dining room, restaurant, coffee shop, deli; 7 am-10 pm; $8-$18; cocktails/lounge. **Services:** Fee: coin laundry, area transportation, to Mt Bachelor ski area, airport transportation. **Recreation:** children's program, nature program, recreation program; canoeing, fishing; hiking trails, jogging. Fee: river rafting trip; ice skating 11/15-4/15; horseback riding. Rental: bicycles. **All Rooms:** combo & shower baths, cable TV. Fee: movies. **Some Rooms:** coffeemakers, 190 efficiencies, microwaves, refrigerators. Fee: VCP's. **Cards:** AE, CB, DI, DS, MC, VI. *(See ad below)* (D) ⊗

MOUNT BACHELOR VILLAGE Rates Subject to Change **Phone:** 503/389-5900

AAA ◆◆◆ Condo Motor Inn

All Year	1P: $68	2P/1B: $68	2P/2B: $97

Location: 6 mi w on Cascade Lakes Hwy in route to Mt. Bachelor ski area; 18 mi e of Mt. Bachelor ski area. 19717 Mt Bachelor Dr 97702. Fax: 503/388-7820. **Terms:** Check-in 5 pm; reserv deposit, 14 day notice, cancellation fee imposed; no pets. **Facility:** 100 rooms. Quiet setting on extensive, beautifully landscaped grounds. 1- & 2-bedroom condominiums, some with panoramic view, fireplace & balcony. 39 two-bedroom units for 2-6 persons, 28 two & three-bedroom units beautifully appointed with outdoor whirlpool & river view, $110-$275; 2 stories; exterior corridors; meeting rooms; heated pool, wading pool, whirlpools; 6 tennis courts (2 lighted). Fee: health club. **Dining & Entertainment:** Dining room, coffee shop; 11:30 am-10 pm, closed Mon; $5-$20; cocktail lounge. **Services:** Fee: coin laundry. **Recreation:** fishing; jogging. Fee: river rafting trips, nature trail along river. **All Rooms:** cable TV. **Some Rooms:** A/C, whirlpools. **Cards:** AE, MC, VI. (D) ⊗

WHEN YOU'RE LIVING OUT OF A SUITCASE...

Comfort Inn

In Bend

Comfort Inn
61200 S. Hwy 97
Bend, OR 97702

- Indoor Pool • Sauna • Spa
- Meeting Room • Cable TV
- Free Continental Breakfast
- Near Lava Butte, High Desert Museum, Mt. Bachelor Ski Area, Golf Course • Golf & Ski Pkgs. Avail.

For reservations call 503-388-2227 or toll free 800-4-CHOICE

"Oregon's Warmest Welcome"

- Nearest Resort to Mt. Bachelor
- Bedrooms
- Condominiums
- Sauna & Whirlpools
- Free Tennis
- 2 Restaurants
- Roller Skating/Ice Skating
- Whitewater Rafting
- Hiking/Fishing
- Heated Outdoor Pools
- Convention/Banquet Facilities
- 18 Hole Golf Course

THE INN of the SEVENTH MOUNTAIN
Bend, Oregon

18575 S.W. Century Drive
Bend, OR 97702
(503) 382-8711
1-800-452-6810

RED LION INN/NORTH AAA Special Value Rates **Phone:** 503/382-7011

◆◆◆ Motel

All Year 1P: $59- 69 2P/1B: $69- 79 2P/2B: $69- 79 XP: $10 F12

Location: On Hwy 97; 4 blks n of jct Hwy 20. 1415 NE 3rd St 97701. Fax: 503/382-7934. **Terms:** Credit card guarantee; pets. **Facility:** 75 rooms. Most large, very well appointed units; some smaller units. 2 two-bedroom units. 2-3 stories; exterior corridors; meeting rooms; heated pool, saunas, whirlpool. **Dining:** Restaurant; 6 am-11 pm; in winter 6 am-10 pm, Fri & Sat-11 pm; $5-$10. **Services:** data ports. **All Rooms:** free movies, combo & shower baths, cable TV. Fee: VCP. **Cards:** AE, CB, DI, DS, JCB, MC, VI. Red Lion Inns.

RED LION INN/SOUTH Rates Subject to Change **Phone:** 503/382-8384

◆◆ Motel

All Year [CP] 1P: $59- 69 2P/1B: $69- 79 2P/2B: $74- 84 XP: $10 F18

Location: On Hwy 97; 1 blk s of jct US 20. 849 NE 3rd St 97701. Fax: 503/382-9180. **Terms:** Sr. discount; pets. **Facility:** 74 rooms. Large units. Conveniently located on hwy 97. 2 stories; exterior corridors; heated pool, whirlpool; pavillion picnic area. **Dining:** Restaurant nearby. **Services:** data ports. **All Rooms:** free movies, cable TV. **Cards:** AE, CB, DI, DS, JCB, MC, VI. Red Lion Inns.

THE RIVERHOUSE MOTOR INN Guaranteed Rates **Phone:** 503/389-3111

◆◆◆◆ Motor Inn

All Year 1P: $52- 58 2P/1B: $61- 72 2P/2B: $67- 72 XP: $5 F6

Location: 1 1/2 mi n on Hwy 97. 3075 N Hwy 97 97701. **Terms:** Check-in 4 pm; reserv deposit; pets, $5 dep req. **Facility:** 220 rooms. Overlooking Deschutes River. Many spacious units with balcony or patio; some overlooking river. Few units with fireplace. 1 three-bedroom unit, 9 two-bedroom units. 44 kitchens, $71-$98; suites avail $75-$150, some with spa; 3 stories; interior corridors; conference facilities; 2 pools (2 heated, 1 indoor), saunas, whirlpools; 2 tennis courts; exercise room. Fee: 18 holes golf; rafting, guided tours of area attractions. **Dining & Entertainment:** 2 restaurants; 7 am-2 & 5:30-10 pm; $9-$18; cocktails/lounge; cafe 11 am-7 pm; 24-hour room service; entertainment. **Services:** data ports. Fee: coin laundry. **Recreation:** fishing; jogging. **All Rooms:** free & pay movies, cable TV. **Some Rooms:** refrigerators, whirlpools. **Cards:** AE, CB, DI, DS, MC, VI. *(See ad below)*

SHILO INN SUITES HOTEL Rates Subject to Change **Phone:** 503/389-9600

◆◆◆ Motor Inn

Fri & Sat 3/1-5/31, 6/1-9/30 & Fri & Sat 10/1-2/29	1P: $67- 93	2P/1B: $67- 93	2P/2B: $93- 104	XP: $10	F12
Sun-Thurs 3/1-5/31 & 10/1-2/29	1P: $62- 83	2P/1B: $62- 83	2P/2B: $83- 93	XP: $10	F12

Location: 1 1/2 mi n on Hwy 97. 3105 O B Riley Rd 97701. Fax: 503/382-4310. **Terms:** Sr. discount; check-in 4 pm; reserv deposit, 10 day notice; pets, $7. **Facility:** 121 rooms. Tastefully appointed, many large units with riverview, balcony & fireplace; some compact units. Units with whirlpool, $125-$135; 2 stories; interior/exterior corridors; meeting rooms; 2 pools (2 heated, 1 indoor), sauna, whirlpools; exercise room, steamroom. **Dining & Entertainment:** Dining room; 7 am-10 pm; $8-$20; cocktail lounge; entertainment. **Services:** data ports; airport transportation. Fee: coin laundry. **All Rooms:** free movies, cable TV. **Some Rooms:** coffeemakers, 54 efficiencies, microwaves, refrigerators. Fee: VCP's. **Cards:** AE, CB, DI, DS, JCB, MC, VI. *(See ad below)*

RESTAURANTS

LE BISTRO **Dinner:** $11-$20 **Phone:** 503/389-7274

◆◆ French

Location: On Hwy 97; 1/4 mi n of jct Hwy 20. 1203 NE 3rd St 97701. **Hours:** 5:30 pm-10 pm; 11/1-6/1 from 5 pm. Closed: Sun. **Reservations:** suggested. **Features:** carryout; cocktails; a la carte. Attractive dining room in former church building. Very good cuisine, including selected beef, shellfish & chicken dishes. Smoke free premises. **Cards:** AE, DI, DS, MC, VI.

PINE TAVERN RESTAURANT **Dinner:** $11-$20 **Phone:** 503/382-5581

◆◆ American

Location: Downtown; 1/2 mi w of Hwy 97. 967 NW Brooks St 97701. **Hours:** 11:30 am-2:30 & 5:30-9:30 pm, Sun 5:30 pm-9:30 pm. **Reservations:** suggested. **Features:** children's menu; health conscious menu items; cocktails & lounge. Very popular hospitably-operated restaurant; dining room overlooking park-like grounds & pond. Salad bar during lunch. Petite menu items avail for dinner. Smoke free premises. **Cards:** AE, DI, DS, MC, VI.

TUMALO FEED COMPANY **Dinner:** $11-$20 **Phone:** 503/382-2202

◆ American

Location: 3 mi w on Hwy 20. 64619 W. Hwy 20 97701. **Hours:** 5 pm-9 pm, Fri & Sat-9:30 pm, Sun 4 pm-9 pm; in summer 5 pm-9:30 pm, Fri & Sat-10 pm, Sun 4 pm-9:30 pm.Closed: 1/1, 11/23, 12/24 & 12/25. **Reservations:** suggested. **Features:** children's menu; early bird specials; cocktails & lounge. Generous meals with western flavor in historical building. **Cards:** DS, MC, VI.

The Riverhouse Lodging & Dining

LOCATED ON THE DESCHUTES RIVER

Rates $61.00 - $72.00 For Two

Golf and Ski Packages

CALL TOLL FREE: in Oregon **1-800-452-6878**
all other **1-800-547-3928**

AAA FOUR DIAMOND AWARD

Shilo Inns "AFFORDABLE EXCELLENCE"

SHILO INN - BEND SUITES HOTEL

Full service suites hotel nestled on the banks of the scenic Deschutes River. Fine dining Restaurant & Lounge. Outdoor and indoor pools, spas; steam room, sauna, fitness center. Guest laundromat. Meeting/banquet space. Guestrooms feature microwaves and refrigerators. Satellite TV with premium channels; VCR/movie rental. Free local airport shuttle and transportation to ski shuttle.

3105 O.B. RILEY ROAD - HWY 97 - BEND, OR 97701

(503) 389-9600 NATIONWIDE RESERVATIONS 1-800-222-2244

BIGGS

LODGING

BEST WESTERN RIVIERA MOTEL Rates Subject to Change **Phone:** 503/739-2501

AAA ◆◆◆ Motel

All Year [CP] 1P: $49 2P/1B: $55 2P/2B: $60 XP: $5

Location: On Hwy 30; w of jct I-84 & Hwy 97; from I-84 take exit 104 at Biggs jct. 91484 Biggs-Rufus Hwy 97065. Fax: 503/739-2091. **Terms:** Sr. discount; reserv deposit, 3 day notice; no pets. **Facility:** 40 rooms. Attractively decorated, especially well-maintained units. 2 two-bedroom suites $85; 1 one-bedroom suite $75; 1-2 stories; exterior corridors; heated pool. **Dining:** Restaurant nearby. **All Rooms:** free movies. **Some Rooms:** refrigerators. **Cards:** AE, CB, DI, DS, MC, VI. (D) ⊗

BLUE RIVER

LODGING

SLEEPY HOLLOW MOTEL Guaranteed Rates **Phone:** 503/822-3805

◆◆ Motel

4/1-10/31 1P: $36 2P/1B: $38 2P/2B: $40- 48 XP: $10

Location: 6 mi e on Hwy 126; 3 mi w of McKenzie Bridge. 54791 McKenzie Hwy 97413. **Terms:** Open 4/1-10/31; reserv deposit; no pets. **Facility:** 19 rooms. Very well kept units. 1-2 stories; exterior corridors. **Dining:** Restaurant nearby. **All Rooms:** refrigerators, combo & shower baths, no phones. **Some Rooms:** cable TV. **Cards:** MC, VI. (D)

BOARDMAN—1,400

LODGING

NUGGET INN Rates Subject to Change **Phone:** 503/481-2375

AAA ◆◆ Motel

All Year 1P: $38 2P/1B: $43 2P/2B: $48 XP: $5 F12

Location: S of I-84; off Boardman, exit 164. 97818 (PO Box 762). Fax: 503/481-2600. **Terms:** Sr. discount; reserv deposit, 3 day notice; pets. **Facility:** 51 rooms. Neat units. 1 story; exterior corridors; heated pool. **Dining:** Restaurant nearby. **All Rooms:** free movies, refrigerators, cable TV. **Some Rooms:** microwaves. Fee: whirlpools. **Cards:** AE, CB, DI, DS, MC, VI. (D) ⊗

BROOKINGS—4,400

LODGINGS

BEST WESTERN BEACHFRONT INN Rates Subject to Change **Phone:** 503/469-7779

AAA ◆◆◆ Motel

5/26-9/30	1P: $74- 84	2P/1B: $79- 89	2P/2B: $79- 89	XP: $5	
4/1-5/25	1P: $64- 84	2P/1B: $69- 89	2P/2B: $69- 89	XP: $5	
3/1-3/31 & 10/1-2/29	1P: $59- 74	2P/1B: $64- 79	2P/2B: $64- 79	XP: $5	

Location: 1 1/2 mi s of Brookings on Hwy 101, then 3/4 mi w on Lower Harbor Rd. 16008 Boat Basin Rd 97415 (PO Box 2729, HARBOR). Fax: 503/469-0283. **Terms:** Reserv deposit; pets, $5. **Facility:** 78 rooms. On beachfront adjacent to Port of Brookings Harbor. Large units, each with balcony. 6 efficiencies, $5 extra. 3 especially well furnished 1-bedroom suites with whirlpool & kitchen $160, $140 off-season; 3 stories, no elevator; exterior corridors; oceanview; meeting rooms; beach, heated pool, whirlpool; sun deck. **Services:** Fee: coin laundry. **All Rooms:** cable TV, no A/C. **Some Rooms:** 6 efficiencies, microwaves, refrigerators. **Cards:** AE, DI, DS, MC, VI. *(See color ad below)* (D) (S) ⊗

BEST WESTERN BROOKINGS INN AAA Special Value Rates **Phone:** 503/469-2173

AAA ◆◆◆ Motor Inn

6/16-9/15	1P: $59- 69	2P/1B: $64- 90	2P/2B: $69- 79	XP: $5	F12
3/1-6/15 & 10/16-2/29	1P: $50- 60	2P/1B: $55- 80	2P/2B: $60- 70	XP: $5	F12
9/16-10/15	1P: $50- 60	2P/1B: $55- 80	2P/2B: $55- 65	XP: $5	F12

Location: 1/4 mi n on Hwy 101. 1143 Chetco Ave 97415 (PO Box 1139). Fax: 503/469-2996. **Terms:** Credit card guarantee, 5/16-10/15; no pets. **Facility:** 68 rooms. Large units. Located at north end of town. 5 two-bedroom units. 2 units with whirlpool & refrigerator, $90; $80 off season; 2 stories; exterior corridors; meeting rooms; whirlpool, 4 pm-9 pm. **Dining & Entertainment:** Restaurant; 6 am-10 pm; $6-$13; cocktail lounge. **All Rooms:** free movies, cable TV, no A/C. **Cards:** AE, CB, DI, DS, MC, VI. *(See color ad below)* (D) ⊗

Best Western

- Barrier free rooms
- Family units
- Free HBO/ESPN
- All-Weather Spa
- No pets
- AAA special value rates

Flying Gull Restaurant & Lounge on Premises

Brookings Inn

P.O. Box 1139-HWY. 101 North Brookings, Oregon 97415 • Reservations 1-800-822-9087

Best Western

BEACHFRONT INN

At the Port of Brookings-Harbor

ON THE OCEAN

- BROOKINGS AREA'S ONLY OCEAN-FRONT MOTEL
- 78 DRAMATIC BEACHFRONT UNITS WITH PRIVATE DECKS
- ALL ROOMS WITH REFRIGERATORS AND MICROWAVES
- SUITES WITH OCEAN VIEW WHIRLPOOL TUBS
- KITCHENETTES • SWIMMING POOL & SPA
- JUST STEPS AWAY TO THE BEACH

AAA

FOR RESERVATIONS CALL

(503) 469-7779 OR 1-800-468-4081

16008 Boat Basin Road • P.O. Box 2729 • Harbor, Oregon 97415

HARBOR INN MOTEL Guaranteed Rates **Phone:** 503/469-3194

5/15-10/14	1P: $45		2P/2B: $55	XP: $5
3/1-5/14 & 10/15-2/29	1P: $35		2P/2B: $42	XP: $5

◆◆ Motel

Location: 2 mi s of Brookings on Hwy 101. 15991 Hwy 101S 97415. Fax: 503/469-0479. **Terms:** Sr. discount; reserv deposit, 3 day notice; pets, $5. **Facility:** 30 rooms. Few units with distant ocean view. 2 stories; exterior corridors. **Dining:** Restaurant nearby. **All Rooms:** free movies, cable TV, no A/C. **Cards:** AE, CB, DI, DS, MC, VI.

PACIFIC SUNSET INN Rates Subject to Change **Phone:** 503/469-2141

5/15-9/30	1P: $38	2P/1B: $47	2P/2B: $52	XP: $5 F8
3/1-5/14 & 10/1-2/29	1P: $32	2P/1B: $36	2P/2B: $44	XP: $5 F8

◆ Motel

Location: 1/4 mi n on Hwy 101. 1144 Chetco Ave 97415 (PO Box AL). Fax: 503/469-7837. **Terms:** Sr. discount; reserv deposit; pets, $5. **Facility:** 40 rooms. Nicely maintained units, most with covered parking. 2 two-bedroom units. 3 efficiencies from $52, $42 off-season; 1-2 stories; exterior corridors; playground. **Dining:** Restaurant nearby. **All Rooms:** free movies, cable TV, no A/C. **Some Rooms:** Fee: microwaves. **Cards:** AE, CB, DI, DS, MC, VI.

SPINDRIFT MOTOR INN Rates Subject to Change **Phone:** 503/469-5345

5/16-9/30	1P: $39- 42	2P/1B: $48- 52	2P/2B: $55- 59	XP: $5
3/1-5/15 & 10/1-2/29	1P: $32- 34	2P/1B: $36- 38	2P/2B: $42- 45	XP: $4

◆◆ Motel

Location: 1/4 mi n on Hwy 101. 1215 Chetco Ave 97415 (PO Box 6026). Fax: 503/469-5213. **Terms:** Credit card guarantee; no pets. **Facility:** 35 rooms. Attractive units with traditional-style furnishings. Some distant ocean views. 2 stories; exterior corridors. **Dining:** Restaurant nearby. **All Rooms:** free movies, refrigerators, cable TV, no A/C. **Cards:** AE, CB, DI, DS, MC, VI.

RESTAURANT

O'HOLLERAN'S RESTAURANT & LOUNGE **Dinner:** $11-$20 **Phone:** 503/469-9907

◆ American

Location: 1/4 mi n on Hwy 101. 1210 Chetco Ave 97415. **Hours:** 5 pm-10 pm. Closed: 12/24 & 12/25. **Reservations:** suggested; in summer. **Features:** children's menu; cocktails & lounge. Long established small casual dining room. Beef & seafood specialties. **Cards:** AE, DI, DS, MC, VI.

BURNS—2,900

LODGINGS

BEST WESTERN PONDEROSA Rates Subject to Change **Phone:** 503/573-2047

All Year	1P: $36	2P/1B: $42	2P/2B: $46	XP: $5

◆◆ Motel

Location: On Hwy 395 & 20; 1/4 mi w of jct SR 78. 577 W Monroe 97720. Fax: 503/573-3828. **Terms:** Sr. discount; reserv deposit; pets. **Facility:** 52 rooms. Attractively decorated & comfortable units. 4 two-bedroom units. 2 stories; exterior corridors; pool. **All Rooms:** free movies, cable TV. **Some Rooms:** refrigerators. **Cards:** AE, CB, DI, DS, JCB, MC, VI.

ROYAL INN Rates Subject to Change **Phone:** 503/573-5295

5/1-10/31	1P: $38	2P/1B: $42	2P/2B: $46	XP: $4 F12
3/1-4/30 & 11/1-2/29	1P: $36	2P/1B: $40	2P/2B: $44	XP: $4 F12

◆◆ Motel

Location: On Hwy 395 & 20, 1 mi w of jct SR 78. 999 Oregon Ave 97720. **Terms:** Reserv deposit; small pets only, $20 dep req. **Facility:** 38 rooms. Comfortable units. 2 stories; interior/exterior corridors; heated indoor pool, sauna, whirlpool. **Services:** Fee: coin laundry. **All Rooms:** free movies, combo & tub baths, cable TV. **Some Rooms:** whirlpools. **Cards:** AE, CB, DI, DS, MC, VI. *(See color ad below)*

RESTAURANT

PINE ROOM CAFE **Dinner:** $11-$20 **Phone:** 503/573-6631

◆ American

Location: On Hwy 20 & 395; 1/4 mi w of jct SR 78. Monroe & Egan sts 97720. **Hours:** 5 pm-10 pm; in winter -9 pm. Closed major holidays, Sun & Mon. **Reservations:** suggested. **Features:** children's menu; cocktails & lounge. Popular Restaurant. Well prepared dinners. Family owned & operated. **Cards:** MC, VI.

CANNON BEACH—1,200

LODGINGS

BEST WESTERN SURFSAND RESORT Rates Subject to Change **Phone:** 503/436-2274

6/7-9/3	1P: $129- 149	2P/1B: $129- 149	2P/2B: $129- 149
3/1-6/6 & 9/4-2/29	1P: $124- 139	2P/1B: $124- 139	2P/2B: $124- 139

◆◆◆ Motor Inn

Location: 1 blk w of Beach Loop Rd, at foot of Gower St. Ocean Front & Gower 97110 (PO Box 219). Fax: 503/436-9116. **Terms:** Sr. discount; check-in 4 pm; reserv deposit, 3 day notice; pets, $5. **Facility:** 74 rooms. Variety of 1 & 2-bedroom units, most with fireplace. Many with ocean view & balcony. 1- & 2-bedroom housekeeping apartments $159-$218, $109-$184 off season; 3-night minimum stay 6/5-9/13, 2 night minimum on weekends 9/4-6/30; 3 stories; exterior corridors; beachfront; meeting rooms; beach, heated indoor pool, whirlpool. **Dining:** Restaurant; 8 am-10 pm; $10-$20; cocktails. **Services:** Fee: coin laundry. **All Rooms:** free movies, cable TV, VCP's, no A/C. **Some Rooms:** refrigerators, whirlpools. **Cards:** AE, CB, DI, DS, JCB, MC, VI.

Royal Inn
ROYAL INN
Burns
INDOOR SWIM POOL
SAUNA
SPA
AAA ◆◆
• Comfortable, Spacious & Quiet Rooms • Restaurant & Lounge Nearby
• Senior, Commercial & Group Rates • 36 Ch. Cable with HBO & ESPN
FOR RESERVATIONS (503)573-5295 999 OREGON AVE. BURNS, OR 97720

MAJOR MOTEL Rates Subject to Change **Phone:** 503/436-2241

(AAA) ◆ Apartment Motel

Fri & Sat & Sun-Thurs 3/15-10/31	2P/1B: $89- 109	2P/2B: $79- 109	XP: $10
Sun-Thurs 3/1-3/14 & 11/1-2/29	2P/1B: $69- 89	2P/2B: $65- 89	XP: $10

Location: 1 mi s; 1/4 mi n of Tolovana exit off Hwy 101. 2863 Pacific St 97110 (PO Box 457). **Terms:** Reserv deposit, 7 day notice; no pets. **Facility:** 24 rooms. Comfortable, rustic 1 & 2-bedbroom units. Most with fireplace, efficiency & deck or patio. 9 two-bedroom units. 3-night minimum stay in summer & holidays, 2-night weekends off season; 2 stories; exterior corridors; beachfront; beach. **All Rooms:** combo & shower baths, cable TV, no A/C. **Some Rooms:** refrigerators. **Cards:** MC, VI. (D) ⊗

SCHOONER'S COVE Rates Subject to Change **Phone:** 503/436-2300

(AAA) ◆◆◆ Motel

5/15-9/30	2P/1B: $109- 129	2P/2B: $119- 129	XP: $5
3/1-5/14 & 10/1-2/29	2P/1B: $75- 95	2P/2B: $89- 95	XP: $5

Location: Center, 4 blks w of Hwy 101; 1 blk w of Beach Loop Rd, off 2nd St. 188 N Larch 97110 (PO Box 86). **Terms:** Reserv deposit, 7 day notice; no pets. **Facility:** 30 rooms. 1- & 2-bedroom units with kitchen or efficiency & balcony; most units with fireplace. 2 stories; exterior corridors; beachfront; meeting rooms; beach, whirlpool. **Services:** Fee: coin laundry. **All Rooms:** free movies, combo & shower baths, cable TV, VCP's, no A/C. **Cards:** AE, DI, DS, MC, VI. (D) ⊗

STEPHANIE INN Rates Subject to Change **Phone:** 503/436-2221

◆◆◆ Country Inn

All Year [BP]	1P: $129- 239	2P/1B: $129- 239	2P/2B: $195- 239	XP: $25

Location: 1 1/4 mi s off Hwy 101 Beach Loop. 2740 S Pacific 97110 (PO Box 219). Fax: 503/436-9711. **Terms:** Age restrictions may apply; reserv deposit, 3 day notice; no pets. **Facility:** 46 rooms. Charming New England atmosphere in beach front setting with convenient beach access. Very tastefully decorated guest rooms & suites with ocean or mountain view, whirlpool, deck & fireplace. Comfortable library with view. 2 two-bedroom suites, $360; 2 one-bedroom suites, $260; 3 stories; interior corridors; smoke free premises; oceanfront; meeting rooms. **Dining:** Dining room; by reservations only 7:30 am-10:30 am, Fri & Sat at 6 pm & 8 pm, 11 am Sun breakfast buffet; $25-$30; cocktails. **Services:** complimentary evening beverages; area transportation, downtown. Fee: massage. **All Rooms:** free movies, combo & shower baths, cable TV, VCP's, whirlpools, no A/C. **Some Rooms:** refrigerators. **Cards:** AE, CB, DI, DS, MC, VI. Roll in showers. (D) (S) ⊗

TOLOVANA INN Rates Subject to Change **Phone:** 503/436-2211

(AAA) ◆◆ Apartment Motel

6/15-10/15	1P: $68- 145	2P/1B: $68- 145	2P/2B: $154- 225	
3/1-6/14 & 10/16-2/29	1P: $61- 114	2P/1B: $61- 114	2P/2B: $134- 185	

Location: 2 mi s; off Hwy 101 beach loop. 97145 (PO Box 165, TOLOVANA PARK). Fax: 503/436-0134. **Terms:** Check-in 4 pm; reserv deposit, 3 day notice; 2 night min stay, weekends 7/1-9/1; pets, $9. **Facility:** 176 rooms. Many large, very good 1 & 2 room kitchen units with fireplace & ocean view. 3 stories, no elevator; exterior corridors; beachfront; meeting rooms; beach, heated indoor pool, wading pool, sauna, whirlpool. **Dining:** Restaurant nearby. **Services:** data ports. Fee: coin laundry. **Recreation:** recreation program. **All Rooms:** cable TV, no A/C. Fee: movies, VCP. **Some Rooms:** coffeemakers. **Cards:** AE, DS, MC, VI. *(See color ad below)* (D) ⊗

CANYONVILLE—1,200

LODGING

LEISURE INN Rates Subject to Change **Phone:** 503/839-4278

(AAA) ◆ Motel

3/1-9/30	1P: $35	2P/1B: $39	2P/2B: $45	XP: $4
10/1-2/29	1P: $33	2P/1B: $37	2P/2B: $43	XP: $4

Location: Center; off I-5, exit 98. 544 SW Pine Street 97417 (PO Box 869). **Terms:** Sr. discount; credit card guarantee, 3 day notice; no pets. **Facility:** 37 rooms. Generous size rooms. 10 Kitchens, $5 extra; 2 stories; interior corridors; small heated pool. **All Rooms:** cable TV. **Cards:** AE, DS, MC, VI. (D) ⊗

CASCADE LOCKS—900

LODGING

SCANDIAN MOTOR LODGE Rates Subject to Change **Phone:** 503/374-8417

(AAA) ◆ Motel

5/1-10/31	1P: $35	2P/1B: $43	2P/2B: $48	XP: $6
3/1-4/30 & 11/1-2/29	1P: $32	2P/1B: $38	2P/2B: $43	XP: $5

Location: On Hwy 30; off I-84 exit 44 Cascade Locks. 25 Oneonta St 97014 (PO Box 217). Fax: 503/374-8926. **Terms:** Reserv deposit; small pets only, $5. **Facility:** 30 rooms. Units with wood pannelled walls & Scandinavian-style bathrooms. 2 stories; exterior corridors. **Dining:** Restaurant nearby. **All Rooms:** shower baths, cable TV. **Cards:** AE, DI, DS, MC, VI. (D) ⊗

CHARLESTON

RESTAURANT

THE PORTSIDE SEAFOOD RESTAURANT **Dinner:** $11-$20 **Phone:** 503/888-5544

(AAA) ◆◆ American

Location: 1/4 mi w at Charleston Small Boat Basin. 8001 Kingfisher Rd 97420. **Hours:** 11:30 am-11 pm. Closed: 12/24. **Reservations:** suggested. **Features:** children's menu; senior's menu; carryout; cocktails & lounge; a la carte. View of boat basin. Extensive fresh seafood & shellfish dishes; also beef, poulty & pasta dishes. Friday seafood buffet. **Cards:** AE, DI, MC, VI. ⊗

Beautiful Oceanfront Resort Suites
Fireplaces · Kitchens · Balconies
1 mile south of Cannon Beach
Tolovana Inn 1-800-333-8890

CLACKAMAS—278,900 (See PORTLAND ACCOMMODATIONS spotting map page A47; see index starting on page A46)

LODGINGS

BEST WESTERN SUNNYSIDE INN Rates Subject to Change **Phone:** 503/652-1500 66
AAA ◆◆ Motel
All Year [CP] 1P: $59- 62 2P/1B: $65- 68 2P/2B: $68 XP: $7 F12
Location: 1 blk se of jct I-205 & Sunnyside Rd, exit 14. 12855 SE 97th Ave 97015. Fax: 503/786-4191. **Terms:** Sr. discount; check-in 4 pm; no pets. **Facility:** 141 rooms. Attractive grounds. Conveniently located near Clackamas Town Center. Cozy lobby. 12 rooms with fireplace, $74-$96; 3 stories, no elevator; exterior corridors; meeting rooms; heated pool, whirlpool. **Dining:** Restaurant nearby. **Services:** data ports; guest laundry; airport transportation. **All Rooms:** cable TV. Fee: movies. **Some Rooms:** refrigerators, whirlpools. **Cards:** AE, DI, DS, MC, VI.

CLACKAMAS INN Rates Subject to Change **Phone:** 503/650-5340 61
AAA ◆◆ Motel
All Year [CP] 1P: $49 2P/1B: $54 2P/2B: $59 XP: $5 F12
Location: Jct I-205 & SR 212; from I-205 southbound exit 12A, northbound exit 12. 16010 SE 82nd 97015. Fax: 503/657-7221. **Terms:** Sr. discount; reserv deposit; pets, $5. **Facility:** 44 rooms. Immaculate, tastefully decorated units. Some large units, $69-$89; 3 stories; interior corridors; meeting rooms; heated pool. **Services:** guest laundry. **All Rooms:** microwaves, free movies, refrigerators, cable TV. **Some Rooms:** Fee: whirlpools. **Cards:** AE, CB, DI, DS, MC, VI.

CYPRESS INN-CLACKAMAS AAA Special Value Rates **Phone:** 503/655-0062 62
◆◆ Motel
All Year [CP] 1P: $65- 69 2P/1B: $72- 77 2P/2B: $72- 77 XP: $7 F12
Location: Jct I-205 & SR 212; from I-205 northbound exit 12, southbound exit 12A. 9040 SE Adams 97015. Fax: 503/655-1861. **Terms:** Reserv deposit; small pets only, $7. **Facility:** 105 rooms. Comfortably furnished large lobby. Compact rooms. 4 stories; interior corridors; meeting rooms; whirlpools. **Dining:** Restaurant nearby. **Services:** guest laundry; airport transportation. **All Rooms:** free movies, refrigerators, cable TV. **Some Rooms:** whirlpools. **Cards:** AE, CB, DI, DS, MC, VI.

DAYS INN Rates Subject to Change **Phone:** 503/654-1699 63
AAA ◆◆ Motel
All Year [CP] 1P: $53- 75 2P/1B: $60- 82 2P/2B: $75- 82 XP: $7 F13
Location: At I-205 exit 14. 9717 SE Sunnyside Rd 97015. Fax: 503/659-2702. **Terms:** Sr. discount; reserv deposit, 3 day notice; no pets. **Facility:** 111 rooms. Near Clackamas Town Center. Very neat, especially well maintained rooms. 1-bedroom apartment with VCP, $120; 3 stories; interior corridors; meeting rooms; heated pool, sauna, whirlpool. **All Rooms:** free movies, combo & shower baths, cable TV. **Some Rooms:** kitchen, refrigerators. **Cards:** AE, CB, DI, DS, JCB, MC, VI. Roll in showers.

MONARCH HOTEL & CONFERENCE CENTER Rates Subject to Change **Phone:** 503/652-1515 64
AAA ◆◆◆ Motor Inn
All Year 1P: $82- 92 2P/1B: $92- 102 2P/2B: $92- 102 XP: $10 F12
Location: 1/2 mi s of jct I-205 & Sunnyside Rd, exit 14. 12566 SE 93rd Ave 97015. Fax: 503/652-7509. **Terms:** Sr. discount; reserv deposit; no pets. **Facility:** 193 rooms. Near Clackamas Town Center & Clackamas Promenade shopping mall. Very tastefully appointed units. Large, attractive courtyard. 2 parlor suites, $149-$159; 4 stories; interior corridors; conference facilities; heated pool, whirlpool. **Dining & Entertainment:** Restaurant; 6 am-10 pm, Fri & Sat-11 pm; $10-$20; cocktail lounge; entertainment. **Services:** data ports; area transportation, to selected areas, airport transportation. Fee: coin laundry. **Recreation:** jogging. **All Rooms:** cable TV. Fee: movies. **Some Rooms:** refrigerators, whirlpools. **Cards:** AE, CB, DI, DS, JCB, MC, VI.

RESTAURANT

OLIVE GARDEN ITALIAN RESTAURANT **Dinner:** $11-$20 **Phone:** 503/652-1200 40
◆◆ Italian
Location: I-205 exit 14; w on Sunnyside Rd. 8700 SE Sunnyside Rd 97015. **Hours:** 11 am-10 pm, Fri & Sat-11 pm. Closed: 11/23 & 12/25. **Features:** children's menu; health conscious menu items; carryout; cocktails & lounge; a la carte. Warm, friendly atmosphere. Good selection of hearty traditional dishes. Classic desserts. Located in Clackamas promenade area. **Cards:** AE, CB, DI, DS, MC, VI.

COOS BAY—15,100

LODGINGS

BEST WESTERN HOLIDAY MOTEL Rates Subject to Change **Phone:** 503/269-5111
AAA ◆◆ Motel
6/10-9/23 [CP] 1P: $64- 79 2P/1B: $64- 79 2P/2B: $64- 79 XP: $5
4/29-6/9 & 9/24-10/21 [CP] 1P: $58- 70 2P/1B: $58- 70 2P/2B: $58- 70 XP: $5
3/1-4/28 & 10/22-2/29 [CP] 1P: $50- 62 2P/1B: $52- 64 2P/2B: $52- 64 XP: $5
Location: On Hwy 101 n & southbound. 411 N Bayshore Dr 97420. Fax: 503/269-5111. **Terms:** Sr. discount; credit card guarantee; no pets. **Facility:** 77 rooms. Nicely equipped units. 3 two-bedroom units. 4 kitchens, $71-$105; $55-$105 off season; 2 stories; interior/exterior corridors; heated indoor pool, whirlpool; exercise room. **Dining:** Restaurant nearby. **Services:** Fee: coin laundry. **All Rooms:** free movies, cable TV. **Some Rooms:** A/C, refrigerators, whirlpools. **Cards:** AE, CB, DI, DS, MC, VI. *(See ad below)*

EDGEWATER INN Rates Subject to Change **Phone:** 503/267-0423
AAA ◆◆◆ Motel
All Year [CP] 1P: $67 2P/1B: $67 2P/2B: $72 XP: $5
Location: 2 blks e of Hwy 101. 275 E Johnson St 97420. Fax: 503/267-4343. **Terms:** Sr. discount; check-in 4 pm; reserv deposit, 3 day notice; pets, $6. **Facility:** 82 rooms. Large units. Most with balcony or patio. 7 units with whirlpool, $95. 2 units with microwave $71, 1 suite with whirlpool, VCP, stereo & kitchen, $105; 2 stories; interior corridors; meeting rooms; heated indoor pool, whirlpool; exercise room. **Services:** airport transportation. **All Rooms:** coffeemakers, cable TV. Fee: movies. **Some Rooms:** refrigerators. Fee: VCP's. **Cards:** AE, DI, DS, MC, VI.

Best Western
HOLIDAY MOTEL
DIRECT RESERVATIONS 1-800-228-8655 OR (503) 269-5111
For Business or Pleasure
• INDOOR POOL & SPA
• FITNESS CENTER
• GUEST LAUNDRY
• SPA UNITS • HBO
• SUITES • KITCHENS
• 24 HR. RESTAURANT ADJ.
411 N. BAYSHORE DR., COOS BAY, OR 97420

RED LION INN Rates Subject to Change **Phone:** 503/267-4141
◆◆◆ All Year 1P: $67 2P/1B: $82 2P/2B: $84 XP: $15 F18
Motor Inn **Location:** 1/2 mi n on Hwy 101. 1313 N Bayshore Dr 97420. Fax: 503/267-2884. **Terms:** Sr. discount; reserv deposit, 3 day notice; pets. **Facility:** 143 rooms. Attractively appointed, mostly spacious units. 10 two-bedroom units, from $85; 2 stories; exterior corridors; conference facilities; heated pool. **Dining & Entertainment:** Dining room; 6 am-9 pm; 6 am-10 pm in summer; $6-$18; cocktails/lounge. **Services:** health club privileges; airport transportation. **All Rooms:** cable TV. Fee: movies. **Cards:** AE, CB, DI, DS, MC, VI.
(D) ⊗

COQUILLE—4,100

LODGING

MYRTLE LANE MOTEL Guaranteed Rates **Phone:** 503/396-2102
AAA All Year 1P: $30- 35 2P/1B: $35- 37 2P/2B: $40 XP: $4 F13
◆ Motel **Location:** 1/4 mi n of jct SR 42 & Central Ave. 787 N Central 97423. **Terms:** Reserv deposit; pets, $4 dep req. **Facility:** 25 rooms. Long established. Immaculately kept & maintained units on neat grounds. 4 two-bedroom units. 1 kitchen unit, $10 extra; 1 story; exterior corridors; basketball court. **All Rooms:** combo & shower baths, cable TV, no A/C. **Some Rooms:** coffeemakers. **Cards:** DS, MC, VI.
(D) ⊗

CORVALLIS—44,800

LODGINGS

BEST WESTERN GRAND MANOR INN Rates Subject to Change **Phone:** 503/758-8571
AAA All Year [CP] 1P: $65- 88 2P/1B: $70- 93 2P/2B: $70- 100 XP: $5 F12
◆◆◆ Motel **Location:** 1 1/2 miles n, 1/8 mi w on SR 99W. 925 NW Garfield 97339. Fax: 503/758-0834. **Terms:** Credit card guarantee; no pets. **Facility:** 55 rooms. 1 1/2 mi to Oregon State University. Colonial style bulding with very inviting lobby & continental breakfast room. Large units with traditional furnishings. Some rooms with patio & balcony. 2 one-bedroom suites, $85-$90; 3 stories; interior corridors; heated pool, sauna, whirlpool; exercise room. **Services:** data ports. **All Rooms:** refrigerators, cable TV. **Some Rooms:** microwaves. Fee: VCP's. **Cards:** AE, CB, DI, DS, MC, VI.
(D) (S) ⊗

HARRISON HOUSE BED & BREAKFAST Rates Subject to Change **Phone:** 503/752-6248
◆◆◆ All Year [BP] 1P: $45- 60 2P/1B: $50- 65 XP: $15 F
Bed & Breakfast **Location:** 1 mi w of jct SR 34 & Hwy 20. 2310 NW Harrison 97330. **Terms:** Sr. discount; reserv deposit, 3 day notice; pets, with innkeepers approval. **Facility:** 3 rooms. 1939 Dutch Colonial style home. Elegantly furnished with tasteful family antiques. Conveniently located near OSU campus in a quiet location. Immaculately kept. Smoke free premises. **Recreation:** bicycles. **All Rooms:** free movies, cable TV, no A/C, no phones. **Cards:** AE, MC, VI.
(D) ⊗

MOTEL ORLEANS Rates Subject to Change **Phone:** 503/758-9125
AAA All Year 1P: $44 2P/1B: $50 2P/2B: $52 XP: $6 F12
◆◆ Motel **Location:** 1 1/2 mi n; 1/8 mi w of SR 99W. 935 NW Garfield 97339. Fax: 503/758-0544. **Terms:** Sr. discount; reserv deposit; no pets. **Facility:** 61 rooms. Comfortable units. 1 1/2 miles to Oregon State University. 3 stories, no elevator; interior corridors; whirlpool, swimming pool is located at The Grand Manor Motel next door. **Services:** Fee: coin laundry. **All Rooms:** combo & shower baths, cable TV. **Some Rooms:** microwaves, refrigerators. **Cards:** AE, CB, DI, DS, MC, VI.
(D) (S) ⊗

RAMADA INN Rates Subject to Change **Phone:** 503/753-9151
AAA All Year 1P: $74- 84 2P/1B: $84- 92 2P/2B: $96 XP: $10 F18
◆◆ Motor Inn **Location:** 1 1/2 mi n; 1/8 mi w of SR 99W. 1550 NW 9th St 97330. Fax: 503/758-7089. **Terms:** Sr. discount; reserv deposit, 3 day notice; no pets. **Facility:** 120 rooms. 1 1/2 mi to Oregon State University. 12 two-bedroom units. 19 suites with kitchen, $87-$115; 4 stories; interior corridors; conference facilities; heated pool. **Dining & Entertainment:** Restaurant; 6:30 am-2 & 5-9 pm; $8-$16; cocktails/lounge. **Services:** Fee: coin laundry. **All Rooms:** free movies, cable TV. **Some Rooms:** coffeemakers. **Cards:** AE, CB, DI, DS, JCB, MC, VI.
(D) ⊗

SHANICO INN Rates Subject to Change **Phone:** 503/754-7474
AAA All Year [CP] 1P: $44 2P/1B: $49 2P/2B: $51 XP: $5 F12
◆◆ Motel **Location:** 1 1/4 mi n; 1/8 mi w of SR 99W. 1113 NW 9th Ave 97330. Fax: 503/754-2437. **Terms:** Sr. discount; reserv deposit; pets, $3-$5. **Facility:** 76 rooms. Well back from the highway. 1 1/4 miles from Oregon State University. Comfortable units. 3 stories; interior corridors; heated pool. **Dining:** Restaurant nearby. **All Rooms:** free movies, cable TV. **Some Rooms:** microwaves, refrigerators. **Cards:** AE, CB, DI, DS, MC, VI.
(D) ⊗

RESTAURANTS

THE GABLES **Dinner:** $11-$20 **Phone:** 503/752-3364
AAA ◆◆ Steak and Seafood **Location:** 1 mi n; 1/8 mi w of SR 99W. 1121 NW 9th 97330. **Hours:** 5 pm-9 pm, Sun-8 pm. Closed major holidays. **Reservations:** suggested. **Features:** children's menu; early bird specials; health conscious menu items; cocktails & lounge; a la carte. Long established popular dinner house featuring prime rib, fresh seafood & steaks. Very good service. **Cards:** AE, CB, DI, DS, MC, VI.
⊗

MICHAEL'S LANDING **Dinner:** $11-$20 **Phone:** 503/754-6141
◆◆ American **Location:** On Hwy 20; 3 blks n of jct SR 34. 603 NW Second St 97330. **Hours:** 11:30 am-9 pm, Fri-9:30 pm, Sun 9:30 am-8:30 pm. Closed: 12/25. **Reservations:** suggested. **Features:** Sunday brunch; children's menu; early bird specials; carryout; cocktails & lounge; a la carte. In former train station. Good selection of popular seafood, beef, chicken & pasta dishes. **Cards:** AE, DI, DS, MC, VI.
⊗

COTTAGE GROVE—7,400

LODGINGS

BEST WESTERN VILLAGE GREEN RESORT HOTEL Rates Subject to Change **Phone:** 503/942-2491
◆◆◆ Motor Inn

8/1-8/31	1P: $76	2P/1B: $82	2P/2B: $89	XP: $5	F12
Fri & Sat 3/1-7/31 & 9/1-2/29	1P: $76	2P/1B: $82	2P/2B: $89	XP: $5	F12
Sun-Thurs 3/1-7/31 & 9/1-2/29	1P: $59	2P/1B: $59	2P/2B: $64	XP: $5	F12

Location: Off I-5; Cottage Grove-Dorena Lake exit 174. 97424 (725 Row River Rd). Fax: 503/942-2386. **Terms:** Pets. **Facility:** 96 rooms. Spacious, attractively landscaped grounds. Very tastefully appointed & especially well kept units. 10 one & two-bedroom suites, some with fireplace, from $99; 1 story; exterior corridors; meeting rooms; golf course & bowling nearby; heated pool, whirlpool; 2 tennis courts; playground, airstrip adjacent. **Dining & Entertainment:** Cocktail lounge; also, Copper Rooster Coffee Shop & Cascadia Dining Room, see separate listing; entertainment. **Services:** Fee: coin laundry. **Recreation:** jogging. **All Rooms:** coffeemakers, free movies, cable TV. **Some Rooms:** refrigerators. Fee: VCP's. **Cards:** AE, CB, DI, DS, MC, VI. *(See color ad p A17)*
(D) ⊗

COMFORT INN Rates Subject to Change **Phone:** 503/942-9747

Motel

6/1-10/31 [CP]	1P: $47	2P/1B: $52	2P/2B: $54	XP: $5	F17
3/1-5/31 & 11/1-2/29 [CP]	1P: $43	2P/1B: $48	2P/2B: $50	XP: $5	F17

Location: Off I-5 exit 174. 845 Gateway Blvd 97424. Fax: 503/942-8841. **Terms:** Sr. discount; check-in 4 pm; pets, $5-$15. **Facility:** 58 rooms. Very neat & tastefully decorated units. 2 units with whirlpool, $70-$74; 2 stories; exterior corridors; meeting rooms; heated pool, whirlpool. **All Rooms:** free movies, cable TV. **Some Rooms:** microwaves, refrigerators, VCP's. **Cards:** AE, CB, DI, DS, JCB, MC, VI.

ECONO LODGE Rates Subject to Change **Phone:** 503/942-1000

Motel

All Year [CP]	1P: $48	2P/1B: $52	2P/2B: $55	XP: $6	F18

Location: 2 blks w of I-5 exit 174. 1601 Gateway Blvd 97424. Fax: 503/942-1077. **Terms:** Sr. discount; reserv deposit; pets, $10, small dogs only. **Facility:** 41 rooms. Neatly furnished & arranged units. 2 stories; interior corridors. **Dining:** Restaurant nearby. **Services:** data ports. Fee: coin laundry. **All Rooms:** combo & shower baths, cable TV. **Some Rooms:** microwaves. **Cards:** AE, DI, DS, JCB, MC, VI.

RESTAURANTS

COPPER ROOSTER COFFEE SHOP & CASCADIA DINING ROOM **Dinner:** $11-$20 **Phone:** 503/942-2491

American

Location: At Best Western Village Green Resort Hotel. 725 Row River Rd 97424. **Hours:** 6:30 am-10 pm, 5 pm-10 pm in dining room. Closed: dining room closed Mon & Tues. **Reservations:** suggested; Cascadia Room. **Features:** Sunday brunch; children's menu; carryout; cocktails & lounge; entertainment; a la carte. Variety of popular dishes in coffee shop. Dining room features Northwest food. **Cards:** AE, CB, DI, DS, MC, VI.

COVERED BRIDGE RESTAURANT **Dinner:** $11-$20 **Phone:** 503/942-1255

Continental

Location: Downtown. 401 E Main St 97424. **Hours:** 11 am-9 pm, Fri & Sat-9:30 pm. Closed: Sun, 1/1 & 12/25. **Reservations:** suggested. **Features:** carryout; cocktails; a la carte. Small, quiet dining room. Selected steak, seafood, chicken & pasta dishes. Public parking lot nearby. **Cards:** MC, VI.

CRATER LAKE

LODGING

CRATER LAKE LODGE Guaranteed Rates **Phone:** 503/594-2511

Lodge	5/20-10/15	1P: $89- 119	2P/1B: $89- 119	2P/2B: $89- 119	XP: $10	F6

Too new to rate; **Location:** At Rim Village. (PO Box 128). Fax: 503/594-2622. **Terms:** Open 5/20-10/15; check-in 4 pm; reserv deposit, written cancellation notice, fee imposed; no pets. **Facility:** 71 rooms. Rating withheld pending completion of construction. Scheduled to open May, 1995. 4 one-bedroom loft units, $169; 4 stories; interior corridors; smoke free premises. **Dining:** Dining room, restaurant; 7 am-10 pm; $12-$18; cocktails. **Recreation:** Fee: boat tours of Crater Lake 10 am-4 pm, 6/15-9/15. **All Rooms:** combo & tub baths, no A/C, no phones, no TVs. **Cards:** MC, VI.

CRESCENT

LODGING

WOODSMAN MOTEL Guaranteed Rates **Phone:** 503/433-2710

Motel

All Year	1P: $31	2P/1B: $35	2P/2B: $37	XP: $4

Location: Center, On Hwy 97. Hwy 97 97733 (PO Box 54). Fax: 503/433-2917. **Terms:** Credit card guarantee; pets, $5. **Facility:** 15 rooms. Comfortable units with simple decor. Most units with small deck. 1 story; exterior corridors; horseshoe pit. **Dining:** Restaurant nearby. **All Rooms:** free movies, refrigerators, cable TV, no A/C. **Some Rooms:** 2 kitchens. **Cards:** MC, VI.

CRESWELL—2,400

LODGING

MOTEL ORLEANS Rates Subject to Change **Phone:** 503/895-3341

Motel

All Year	1P: $34	2P/1B: $40	2P/2B: $42	XP: $6	F12

Location: Off I-5, exit 182. 345 E Oregon 97426 (PO Box 988). **Terms:** Sr. discount; reserv deposit; no pets. **Facility:** 70 rooms. Comfortable units with unpretentious decor. 2 suites from $56; 2 stories; exterior corridors; pool; playground. **Dining:** Restaurant nearby. **All Rooms:** cable TV. **Some Rooms:** Fee: microwaves, refrigerators, whirlpools. **Cards:** AE, CB, DI, DS, MC, VI.

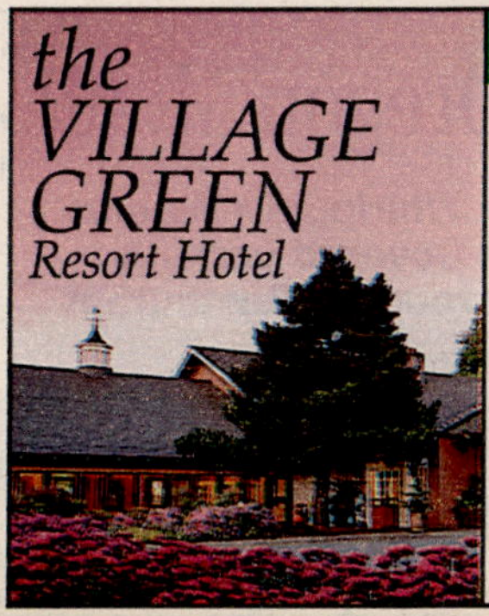

JUST SOUTH OF EUGENE/SPRINGFIELD

- 16 Garden Like Acres.
- Golf Course, Hot Tub and Heated Pool.
- Coffee Shop, Dining Room and Lounge.
- Meeting and Banquet Facilities.
- Jogging Trails and Shopping Nearby.

725 Row River Rd., Cottage Grove, Oregon 97424
Take exit 174, directly off of I-5
1-800-343-ROOM (7666)

Best Western

DEPOE BAY

LODGING

GRACIE'S LANDING BED & BREAKFAST INN — Rates Subject to Change — **Phone:** 503/765-2322

◆◆◆ Bed & Breakfast

6/1-9/30 [BP] 1P: $75- 100 2P/1B: $80- 105
3/1-5/31 & 10/1-2/29 [BP] 1P: $70- 95 2P/1B: $75- 100

Location: From Hwy 101, 1/4 e of jct SE Bay St. 235 SE Bay View Ave 97341 (PO Box 29). **Terms:** Check-in 3:30 pm; reserv deposit, 7 day notice; no pets. **Facility:** 13 rooms. Cape Cod style buildings overlooking harbor. Tastefully appointed guest room with balcony or patio & view, 9 with fireplace. Very comfortable library, guest lounge & dining room with view. 3 stories; interior corridors. **Dining:** Breakfast 7:30-10:30 am, complimentary cookies & beverages 2-5 pm. **All Rooms:** cable TV, VCP's, no A/C. Fee: movies. **Some Rooms:** whirlpools. **Cards:** AE, CB, DI, DS, MC, VI. (D) ⊗

RESTAURANT

SEA HAG RESTAURANT & LOUNGE — **Dinner:** $11-$20 — **Phone:** 503/765-2734

◆ Seafood

Location: Center on Hwy 101. 58 E Hwy 101 97341. **Hours:** 4:30 am-10 pm; 9/1-6/30, 7 am-10 pm. Closed: 12/25. **Features:** children's menu; health conscious menu items; carryout; salad bar; cocktails & lounge; entertainment; street parking. Long established & popular. Casual atmosphere. Nice selection of seafood & steak dishes. Fri seafood buffet 5 pm. **Cards:** AE, DI, DS, MC, VI. ⊗

ENTERPRISE—1,900

LODGING

PONDEROSA MOTEL — Rates Subject to Change — **Phone:** 503/426-3186

◆◆ Motel

4/1-11/30 1P: $32 2P/1B: $42 2P/2B: $44 XP: $2-6

Location: 1/2 blk e of SR 82. 102 SE Greenwood 97828. **Terms:** Open 4/1-11/30; reserv deposit, 10 day notice; small pets only. **Facility:** 25 rooms. Very pleasant units. 1 two-bedroom unit. 2 stories; exterior corridors. **All Rooms:** cable TV. **Cards:** AE, DI, DS, MC, VI. (D) ⊗

EUGENE—112,700

LODGINGS

BEST WESTERN GREENTREE MOTEL — AAA Special Value Rates — **Phone:** 503/485-2727

AAA ◆◆◆ Motor Inn

6/16-10/15 [CP] 1P: $48- 58 2P/1B: $63- 73 2P/2B: $61- 71 XP: $2
3/1-6/15 & 10/16-2/29 [CP] 1P: $46- 56 2P/1B: $61- 71 2P/2B: $59- 69 XP: $2

Location: 1 mi se on Hwy 99; from I-5 southbound exit 194B to I-105 exit 1 to University of Oregon route; northbound Eugene exit 192. 1759 Franklin Blvd 97403. Fax: 503/686-2094. **Terms:** Reserv deposit; pets. **Facility:** 65 rooms. Nicely furnished & very well kept & maintained units well off the hwy. 1 two-bedroom unit. 3 stories; interior corridors; meeting rooms; heated pool, whirlpool; exercise room. **Dining & Entertainment:** Restaurant; 11:30 am-3 & 5:30-10:30 pm, Sun 9 am-3 & 5-9:30 pm, Sat & Sun breakfast 11 am-2 pm only; $7-$14; cocktail lounge. **Services:** data ports. **All Rooms:** free movies, cable TV. **Some Rooms:** 3 kitchens, refrigerators. **Cards:** AE, CB, DI, DS, MC, VI. (D) ⊗

BEST WESTERN NEW OREGON MOTEL — Rates Subject to Change — **Phone:** 503/683-3669

AAA ◆◆◆ Motel

6/16-10/15 1P: $48- 58 2P/1B: $63- 73 2P/2B: $61- 71 XP: $2
3/1-6/15 & 10/16-2/29 1P: $46- 56 2P/1B: $61- 71 2P/2B: $59- 69 XP: $2

Location: 1 mi se on Hwy 99; I-5 southbound exit 194B, to I-105 then exit 1 to University of Oregon route; northbound Eugene exit 192. 1655 Franklin Blvd 97440 (PO Box 18). Fax: 503/484-5556. **Terms:** Sr. discount; reserv deposit; pets, $25 dep req. **Facility:** 129 rooms. Well appointed units, some with balcony. Located opposite University of Oregon campus. 8 two-bedroom units. 2 stories; exterior corridors; heated indoor pool, saunas, whirlpool; racquetball courts. **Dining:** Restaurant nearby. **Services:** data ports; guest laundry. **All Rooms:** free movies, refrigerators, combo & shower baths, cable TV. **Cards:** AE, CB, DI, DS, MC, VI. *(See ad below)* (D) ⊗

EUGENE HILTON — Rates Subject to Change — **Phone:** 503/342-2000

AAA ◆◆◆ Hotel

All Year 1P: $114- 182 2P/1B: $129- 207 2P/2B: $129- 207 XP: $15

Location: Downtown; from I-5 southbound, exit 194B then exit 1 to City Center-Mall; northbound exit 192 to Hwy 99 & City Center; adjacent to performing arts center. 66 E 6th & Oak sts 97401. Fax: 503/342-6661. **Terms:** Sr. discount; reserv deposit; pets, $25. **Facility:** 270 rooms. Very hospitably operated & well-maintained guest rooms & public areas. 6 suites each with refrigerator & wet bar, $185; 12 stories; interior corridors; conference facilities; whirlpool, small heated indoor pool; exercise room. **Dining & Entertainment:** Dining room, restaurant; 6:30 am-10 pm; $5-$22; cocktail lounge; Sun brunch; entertainment. **Services:** PC; airport transportation, 5 am-midnight; valet parking. **All Rooms:** cable TV. Fee: movies. **Some Rooms:** coffeemakers, whirlpools. **Cards:** AE, CB, DI, DS, MC, VI. *(See ad p 38)* (D) (S) ⊗

Best Western

Best Western New Oregon Motel

• Indoor heated pool • Sundeck • Whirlpool • Saunas
• Free guest racquetball courts • Covered parking
• King beds • Refrigerators in all rooms • Restaurant

Follow Univ. of Oregon Hwy. Signs from I-5
So. Bound Take Exit 194-B—No. Bound Take Exit 192

1655 Franklin Blvd. • P.O. Box 18
Eugene, OR 97440 • 1-503-683-3669

AAA

Make reservations at any Best Western or call toll-free 1-800-528-1234

HOLIDAY INN OF EUGENE Rates Subject to Change **Phone:** 503/342-5181
◆◆ 6/1-10/31 1P: $53- 55 2P/1B: $59- 61 2P/2B: $59- 61 XP: $6 F16
Motor Inn 3/1-5/31 & 11/1-2/29 1P: $48- 55 2P/1B: $54- 59 2P/2B: $54- 59 XP: $6 F16
Location: Near jct I-105 & Coburg Rd; from I-5 exit 194B to I-105, exit 1 to Coburg Rd. 225 Coburg Rd 97401. Fax: 503/342-5181. **Terms:** Sr. discount; credit card guarantee, 3 day notice; pets, $15 dep req. **Facility:** 148 rooms. Comfortably equipped rooms & large recreation area. 2 two-bedroom units. 2 stories; interior/exterior corridors; meeting rooms; heated indoor pool, whirlpool. **Dining:** Dining room; 6:30 am-2 & 5-10 pm; $9-$15; cocktails; dancing Fri & Sat. **Services:** data ports; guest laundry; airport transportation. **All Rooms:** free movies, cable TV. **Cards:** AE, CB, DI, DS, JCB, MC, VI.

PHOENIX INN Guaranteed Rates **Phone:** 503/344-0001
Motel All Year [CP] 1P: $49 2P/1B: $54 2P/2B: $52 XP: $5 F17
Too new to rate; **Location:** On Hwy 99; I-5 northbound Eugene exit 192; southbound exit 194B, to I-105 then exit 1 to University of Oregon route. 850 Franklin Blvd 97401. Fax: 503/686-1288. **Terms:** no pets. **Facility:** 99 rooms. Rating withheld pending completion of construction. Scheduled to open Oct, 1994. 4 stories; interior corridors; meeting rooms; heated indoor pool, whirlpool; exercise room. **Services:** data ports; guest laundry. **All Rooms:** microwaves, free movies, refrigerators, combo & shower baths, cable TV. **Some Rooms:** whirlpools. **Cards:** AE, CB, DI, DS, MC, VI.
(See color ad below)

RED LION INN Rates Subject to Change **Phone:** 503/342-5201
◆◆◆ All Year 1P: $66- 68 2P/1B: $81- 114 2P/2B: $83- 114 XP: $15 F18
Motor Inn **Location:** Near jct I-105 & Coburg Rd; from I-5 exit 194B to I-105, then exit 1 to Coburg Rd. 205 Coburg Rd 97401. Fax: 503/485-2314. **Terms:** Sr. discount; pets. **Facility:** 138 rooms. Very attractively appointed units, some with balconies. 2 stories; exterior corridors; conference facilities; heated pool. **Dining & Entertainment:** Dining room, coffee shop; 6 am-10 pm; $6-$14; cocktails; entertainment. **Services:** airport transportation. **All Rooms:** cable TV. Fee: movies. **Cards:** AE, CB, DI, DS, JCB, MC, VI. Roll in showers.

THE VALLEY RIVER INN AAA Special Value Rates **Phone:** 503/687-0123
AAA ◆◆◆ All Year 1P: $110- 140 2P/1B: $125- 155 2P/2B: $125- 155 XP: $15 F12
Motor Inn **Location:** I-5 exit 194B, Santa Clara exit 3, Valley River Center route. 100 Valley River Way 97440 (PO Box 10088). Fax: 503/683-5121. **Terms:** Pets. **Facility:** 257 rooms. Spacious guestrooms, many with balcony facing river or landscaped courtyard. Inviting lobby. Dining rooms & outdoor veranda dining with river view. 10 suites, 1 with whirlpool $160-$300; 3 stories; interior corridors; conference facilities; heated pool, wading pool, saunas, whirlpool. **Dining & Entertainment:** Dining room; 6:30 am-2 & 5:30-9:30 pm, Sun from 7:30 am; $13-$20; cocktails; entertainment. **Services:** data ports; airport transportation. **Recreation:** jogging. Fee: bicycles. **All Rooms:** coffeemakers, cable TV. Fee: movies. **Some Rooms:** Fee: VCP's. **Cards:** AE, CB, DI, DS, MC, VI.
(See ad below) Roll in showers.

RESTAURANTS

CHANTERELLE **Dinner:** $11-$20 **Phone:** 503/484-4065
◆◆ **Location:** 207 E 5th 97401. **Hours:** 5 pm-10 pm. Closed major holidays, 3/19-3/31, 8/27-8/31, 9/1-9/9 &
Continental Sun-Mon. **Reservations:** suggested. **Features:** cocktails; street parking. In 5th St Public Market. Small, intimate & very inviting dining room. Very tastfully prepared classic entrees & desserts. Smoke free premises. **Cards:** AE, MC, VI.

NORTH BANK RESTAURANT **Dinner:** $11-$20 **Phone:** 503/343-5622
◆◆ **Location:** I-5 to I-105; Autzen Stadium exit to Country Club Rd then s on Club Rd. 22 Club Rd 97401.
American **Hours:** 12:30 pm-9:30 pm, Fri & Sat-10:30 pm, Sun 4 pm-9 pm. Closed: 12/25. **Reservations:** suggested. **Features:** children's menu; early bird specials; cocktails & lounge; a la carte. Attractive interior with river view. Emphasis on fresh seafood, steaks, prime rib & combination dishes. Smoke free premises. **Cards:** AE, CB, DS, MC, VI.

PHOENIX INN
MINI-SUITES
850 Franklin Blvd.
Eugene, OR • 97401
503-344-0001 or 1-800-344-0131
▼ Near the University of Oregon
▼ Free Continental Breakfast
▼ Free Local Calls
▼ Indoor Pool & Spa
Southbound exit 194B
Northbound exit 192

Imagine If You Could Package Everything Good About Oregon.
We did. Call us for river rafting, fishing, wine tasting and music festival packages. We're nestled on the banks of the beautiful Willamette River and next door to the 140+ stores of Valley River Center. Give yourself a gift and come to the Valley River Inn.
Everything Good About Oregon Is Near.
1-800-543-8266
Ask about our AAA Special Value & Senior Rates.
Valley River Inn
1000 Valley River Way
Eugene, Oregon 97401

OREGON ELECTRIC STATION — **Dinner:** $11-$20 — **Phone:** 503/485-4444

◆◆ Steak and Seafood

Location: Downtown, 1 blk n of Holt Center, I-5 southbound exit 194B, then exit 1 to city center, I-5 northbound exit 192 to Hwy 99 & city center. 27 E 5th 97401. **Hours:** 11:30 am-2:30 & 5-10:30 pm, Sun 9:30 am-2 pm. Closed: 7/4 & 12/25. **Reservations:** accepted. **Features:** casual dress; Sunday brunch; children's menu; health conscious menu items; carryout; salad bar; cocktails & lounge. Located in former railroad station, dining available in authentic passenger cars. Prime rib & seafood selections. Live jazz Fri & Sat night. **Cards:** AE, DI, MC, VI. ⊗

WILLIE'S ON 7TH STREET — **Dinner:** $11-$20 — **Phone:** 503/485-0601

AAA ◆◆ American

Location: 388 W 7th 97401. **Hours:** 11:30 am-2 & 5-9 pm, Fri & Sat 5 pm-10 pm. Closed major holidays & Sun. **Reservations:** suggested. **Features:** carryout; cocktails & lounge. Dignified dining rooms in converted house. Varied seafood, chicken, veal & steak selection. **Cards:** AE, DI, DS, MC, VI. ⊗

FLORENCE—5,200

LODGINGS

BEST WESTERN PIER POINT INN — Rates Subject to Change — **Phone:** 503/997-7191

AAA ◆◆◆ Motor Inn

6/16-9/3 [CP]	1P: $79- 89	2P/1B: $79- 99	2P/2B: $89- 99	XP: $8
5/18-6/15 & 9/4-9/30 [CP]	1P: $59- 69	2P/1B: $59- 79	2P/2B: $69- 89	XP: $8
3/1-5/17 & 10/1-2/29 [CP]	1P: $49- 59	2P/1B: $49- 69	2P/2B: $55- 69	XP: $8

Location: 1 mi s on Hwy 101, near south end of bridge. 85625 Hwy 101 97439 (PO Box 2235). Fax: 503/997-3828. **Terms:** Check-in 4 pm; credit card guarantee, 3 day notice; no pets. **Facility:** 55 rooms. Most units with balcony & view of bay. 3 stories; interior/exterior corridors; meeting rooms; sauna, whirlpools. **Dining & Entertainment:** Restaurant; 5 pm-9 pm, Sun 4 pm-8 pm; $10-$20; cocktail lounge. **All Rooms:** free movies, cable TV, no A/C. **Cards:** AE, CB, DI, DS, MC, VI. *(See color ad below)* Ⓓ ⊗

DRIFTWOOD SHORES RESORT & CONFERENCE CENTER — Rates Subject to Change — **Phone:** 503/997-8263

AAA ◆◆ Apartment Motor Inn

6/1-9/30	1P: $73	2P/1B: $95	2P/2B: $110	XP: $15 F13
3/1-5/31 & 10/1-2/29	1P: $68	2P/1B: $89	2P/2B: $100	XP: $10 F13

Location: 4 mi n; w of Hwy 101 along Heceta Beach Rd. 88416 First Ave 97439. Fax: 503/997-8263. **Terms:** Sr. discount; check-in 4 pm; reserv deposit, 7 day notice; no pets. **Facility:** 136 rooms. Many adjoining units with kitchen. Most units with balcony. 3-bedroom apartments with fireplace, for up to 4-8 persons, $195; $130 low season; 4 stories; exterior corridors; oceanfront; meeting rooms; beach, heated indoor pool, saunas, whirlpool. **Dining & Entertainment:** Restaurant; 7 am-10 pm; $10-$20; cocktails/lounge. **Services:** Fee: coin laundry. **All Rooms:** free movies, cable TV, no A/C. **Some Rooms:** coffeemakers, 71 kitchens, refrigerators. Fee: VCP's. **Cards:** AE, CB, DI, DS, MC, VI. *(See ad below)* Ⓓ Ⓢ ⊗

BEST WESTERN PIER POINT INN

Best Western

Most rooms with
River View and Private Balcony
FREE Continental Breakfast • HBO • Spa & Sauna • 1/2 mile to Sand Dunes • 11 miles to Sea Lion Caves • 2 Golf courses within 4 miles

85625 U.S. 101 • FLORENCE • (503) 997-7191
Reservations: (800) 4-FLORENCE (356736)

ON HECETA BEACH
Driftwood Shores
RESORT & CONFERENCE CENTER
Surfside Restaurant and Lounge
ALL ROOMS OCEAN VIEW
136 Ocean View Rooms - 88 Kitchen Units
Ocean View Restaurant - Indoor Heated Pool
Conference Facilities
800-422-5091 88416 First Ave. Florence, Oregon 97439

HOLIDAY INN EXPRESS Rates Subject to Change **Phone:** 503/997-7797
Motel
7/14-9/3 [CP] 1P: $65- 75 2P/1B: $75- 85 2P/2B: $75- 85 XP: $10 F18
5/20-7/13 & 9/4-9/30 [CP] 1P: $55- 65 2P/1B: $59- 69 2P/2B: $69- 79 XP: $10 F18
3/1-5/19 & 10/1-2/29 [CP] 1P: $49- 59 2P/1B: $49- 59 2P/2B: $52- 62 XP: $10 F18
Location: 1 mi n on Hwy 101. 2475 Hwy 101 97439 (PO Box 2235). Fax: 503/997-7895. **Terms:** Credit card guarantee, 3 day notice; no pets. **Facility:** 51 rooms. Very inviting. Generous size units. 2 stories; interior corridors; meeting rooms; whirlpool; exercise room. **Services:** data ports; guest laundry. **All Rooms:** free movies, combo & shower baths, cable TV. **Cards:** AE, CB, DI, DS, MC, VI. *(See ad below)* Roll in showers.

LE CHATEAU MOTEL Rates Subject to Change **Phone:** 503/997-3481
Motel
7/1-9/30 1P: $45 2P/1B: $55 2P/2B: $60 XP: $5
3/1-6/30 & 10/1-2/29 1P: $36 2P/1B: $40 2P/2B: $45 XP: $5
Location: On Hwy 101, 1 blk n of jct SR 126. 1084 Hwy 101 97439 (PO Box 98). **Terms:** Reserv deposit; no pets. **Facility:** 48 rooms. Unpretentious units. 2 stories; exterior corridors; heated pool, sauna, whirlpool. **Dining:** Restaurant nearby. **Services:** guest laundry. **All Rooms:** cable TV, no A/C. **Some Rooms:** refrigerators. Fee: VCP's. **Cards:** AE, CB, DI, DS, MC, VI.

LIGHTHOUSE INN Rates Subject to Change **Phone:** 503/997-3221
Motel
6/1-9/30 [CP] 2P/1B: $50- 60 2P/2B: $70- 85 XP: $5
3/1-5/31 & 10/1-2/29 [CP] 2P/1B: $35- 40 2P/2B: $45- 55 XP: $5
Location: 3/4 mi s on Hwy 101. 155 Hwy 101 97439 (PO Box 187). Fax: 503/997-8256. **Terms:** Reserv deposit; no pets. **Facility:** 28 rooms. Cozy, compact units in well-maintained long established motel. Comfortable, inviting lobby. 4 two-bedroom units from $75, off-season $46; 2 stories; interior/exterior corridors. **Dining:** Restaurant nearby. **All Rooms:** combo & shower baths, cable TV, no A/C. **Cards:** MC, VI.

MONEY SAVER MOTEL Rates Subject to Change **Phone:** 503/997-7131
Motel
6/1-9/30 1P: $46 2P/1B: $50 2P/2B: $56 XP: $6
3/1-5/31 & 10/1-2/29 1P: $32 2P/1B: $36 2P/2B: $40 XP: $6
Location: 3/4 mi s on Hwy 101. 170 Hwy 101 97439. **Terms:** Reserv deposit; small pets only, $20 dep req. **Facility:** 40 rooms. Especially well maintained units. 2 stories; exterior corridors. **Dining:** Restaurant nearby. **All Rooms:** cable TV, no A/C. **Cards:** AE, DS, MC, VI.

PARK MOTEL Rates Subject to Change **Phone:** 503/997-2634
Motel
6/1-9/30 1P: $45 2P/1B: $47- 57 2P/2B: $57- 62 XP: $5
3/1-5/31 & 10/1-2/29 1P: $30 2P/1B: $34- 39 2P/2B: $39- 44 XP: $5
Location: 1 1/2 mi s on Hwy 101. 85034 Hwy 101 97439. **Terms:** Reserv deposit; pets, $5. **Facility:** 15 rooms. Very well kept cozy units. Set back from Hwy 101 in wooded area. 2 one-bedroom suites with kitchen, $66; $46-$48 low season; 1 story; exterior corridors. **Dining:** Restaurant nearby. **All Rooms:** combo & shower baths, cable TV, no A/C. **Some Rooms:** Fee: microwaves, refrigerators. **Cards:** AE, CB, DI, DS, MC, VI.

RIVER HOUSE MOTEL Rates Subject to Change **Phone:** 503/997-3933
Motel
6/1-9/30 1P: $58- 72 2P/1B: $64- 78 2P/2B: $70- 84 XP: $6
3/1-5/31 1P: $46- 60 2P/1B: $52- 66 2P/2B: $58- 72 XP: $6
10/1-11/30 1P: $40- 54 2P/1B: $48- 62 2P/2B: $52- 66 XP: $6
12/1-2/29 1P: $38- 52 2P/1B: $42- 62 2P/2B: $48- 62 XP: $6
Location: 3/4 mi s near n end of bridge; in Old Town, off Hwy 101. 1202 Bay St 97439. **Terms:** Reserv deposit; no pets. **Facility:** 40 rooms. Very neat & well-kept units, some with balcony & river view. Attractive whirlpool area. 2 large units with whirlpool $120, $95 off-season; 2 stories; exterior corridors; whirlpool. **Dining:** Restaurant nearby. **Services:** Fee: coin laundry. **All Rooms:** combo & shower baths, cable TV, no A/C. **Some Rooms:** radios. **Cards:** AE, DS, MC, VI.

RESTAURANTS

LOTUS SEAFOOD PALACE **Dinner:** $11-$20 **Phone:** 503/997-7168
Chinese
Location: 3/4 mi s near n end of bridge, in Old Town off Hwy 101. 1150 Bay St 97439. **Hours:** 11 am-10 pm, Sun 8 am-10 pm. Closed: 12/24. **Reservations:** accepted. **Features:** children's menu; carryout; cocktails & lounge; entertainment. Bayfront location. Broad selection of Northern Chinese dishes & popular American dishes with emphasis on seafood. **Cards:** AE, DS, MC, VI.

FLORENCE
2475 HWY 101 N. • (503) 997-7797

Holiday Inn EXPRESS®
STAY WITH SOMEONE YOU KNOW.®

New Facility in Florence with Beautiful new rooms. FREE HBO
FREE continental breakfast, Exercise room, Spa. Close to Golf Courses, Sand Dunes, Lakes and Ocean. NO PETS.
RESERVATIONS 1-800-HOLIDAY

"SUPERIOR COASTAL CUISINE & WINE"
Excellent selection of fresh, local seafood and extensive wine list featuring Oregon wines. A tradition on the Oregon coast since 1932. Recommended or featured by AAA, *Travel-Holiday Magazine* and *Oregon Magazine*. Serving Breakfast, Lunch, and Dinner. Beautiful "Courtyard" Lounge. Two blocks to "Sandpines".

Windward Inn Restaurant
3757 Highway 101 North
Florence, Oregon 97439
(503) 997-8243
(See our Listing)

Nature's Wildlife Special ...
Sea Lion Caves
World's Largest Sea Cave
There's no other place like it. Anywhere.
Midway on Oregon's Fabulous Coast
91560 Hwy. 101, Florence, OR 97439. Tel. (503) 547-3111

THE WINDWARD INN RESTAURANT **Dinner:** $11-$20 **Phone:** 503/997-8243
◆◆ Seafood
Location: 1 mi n on Hwy 101. 3757 Hwy 101N 97439. **Hours:** 7 am-9 pm, Fri & Sat-9:30 pm. Closed: 12/24 & 12/25. **Reservations:** suggested. **Features:** children's menu; early bird specials; senior's menu; carryout; cocktails & lounge; a la carte. Popular, attractive restaurant. Very good selection of fresh seafood, poultry & meat dishes. Also light dinners avail. **Cards:** AE, DI, MC, VI. *(See ad p A21)*

FOREST GROVE—13,600

LODGING

FOREST GROVE INN Rates Subject to Change **Phone:** 503/357-9700
◆ Motel

4/1-10/1	1P: $41	2P/1B: $46	2P/2B: $49	XP: $7 F12
3/1-3/31 & 10/2-2/29	1P: $35	2P/1B: $39	2P/2B: $42	XP: $7 F12

Location: 2 mi w on SR 8. 4433 Pacific Ave 97116. **Terms:** Reserv deposit; no pets. **Facility:** 20 rooms. Comfortably appointed units. 4 kitchen suites $65, $56 low-season; 2 stories; exterior corridors. **Dining:** Restaurant nearby. **All Rooms:** free movies, cable TV. **Some Rooms:** coffeemakers, microwaves, refrigerators. **Cards:** AE, CB, DI, DS, JCB, MC, VI. *(See color ad below)*

GLENEDEN BEACH

LODGINGS

CAVALIER CONDOMINIUMS Rates Subject to Change **Phone:** 503/764-2352
◆◆◆ Condo Motel

5/1-9/30	1P: $160	2P/1B: $160	2P/2B: $160	XP: $15
3/1-4/30 & 10/1-2/29	1P: $143	2P/1B: $130- 143	2P/2B: $130- 143	XP: $10

Location: 1 1/2 mi s, 3 blks w of jct Hwy 101 & Lancer St. 325 Lancer St 97388 (PO Box 58). **Terms:** Reserv deposit; no pets. **Facility:** 25 rooms. Secluded beach front location. Spacious, very comfortable, attractively appointed units, each with ocean view, living room, fireplace, kitchen, 2 bedrooms & bathrooms & balcony. 3 stories; exterior corridors; oceanfront; heated indoor pool, saunas; recreation room. **Services:** Fee: coin laundry. **All Rooms:** cable TV, no A/C. **Some Rooms:** VCP's. **Cards:** MC, VI.

SALISHAN LODGE Rates Subject to Change **Phone:** 503/764-2371
◆◆◆◆ Resort Motor Inn

5/1-10/31	2P/1B: $164- 236	2P/2B: $164- 236	XP: $15 F12
3/1-4/30 & 11/1-2/29	2P/1B: $109- 201	2P/2B: $109- 201	XP: $15 F12

Location: On Hwy 101. 7760 Hwy 101 N 97388 (PO Box 118). Fax: 503/764-3681. **Terms:** Sr. discount; check-in 4:30 pm; reserv deposit; pets, $10 per pet. **Facility:** 205 rooms. Distinguished. Extensive, beautifully landscaped grounds on wooded hillside. Excellently maintained units, many spacious, with fireplace, balcony & view of grounds. Library. Covered parking. 2 two-bedroom units. 2-3 stories; exterior corridors; business center, conference facilities; putting green; beach access, heated indoor pool, saunas, whirlpool; 4 tennis courts(Fee: 3 indoor); exercise room, playground, running loops. Fee: 18 holes golf. **Dining & Entertainment:** Dining room, restaurant; 7 am-9 pm; $8-$24; cocktail lounge; Sun brunch 9:30 am-1:30 pm; also, The Dining Room at Salishan Lodge, see separate listing; entertainment. **Services:** secretarial services; valet laundry. Fee: childcare; massage. **Recreation:** nature trails. Fee: horseback riding. **All Rooms:** honor bars, coffeemakers, cable TV, VCP's, no A/C. **Cards:** AE, CB, DI, DS, MC, VI.

RESTAURANTS

CHEZ JEANNETTE **Dinner:** $21-$30 **Phone:** 503/764-3434
◆◆◆ Continental
Location: 1/2 mi s of Salishan jct, on Gleneden Beach Loop Rd. 7150 Old Hwy 101 97388. **Hours:** 5:30 pm-9 pm, Fri & Sat-10 pm. Closed major holidays & Sun, Mon & 1 month in winter. **Reservations:** suggested. **Features:** No A/C; cocktails. Tastefully presented & prepared Continental cuisine with French influence. Vegetarian entrees on request. Charming intimate atmosphere. Smoke free premises. **Cards:** AE, MC, VI.

THE DINING ROOM AT SALISHAN LODGE **Dinner:** $21-$30 **Phone:** 503/764-3635
◆◆◆◆ Continental
Location: At Salishan Lodge. 7760 Hwy 101 N 97388. **Hours:** 5:30 pm-10 pm, Fri & Sat-11 pm. **Reservations:** required. **Features:** Sunday brunch; children's menu; cocktails & lounge; entertainment. Dignified dining room with quiet decor & view of Siletz Bay. Excellent regional cuisine with emphasis on locally harvested fish & produce. Excellent service with some tableside preparation. Extensive wine list. Smoke free premises. **Cards:** AE, DI, DS, MC, VI.

GOLD BEACH—1,500

LODGINGS

BEST WESTERN INN OF THE BEACHCOMBER Rates Subject to Change **Phone:** 503/247-6691
◆◆◆ Motel

5/16-10/17	1P: $79	2P/1B: $86	2P/2B: $79- 89	XP: $6 F12
3/1-5/15 & 10/18-2/29	1P: $49	2P/1B: $57	2P/2B: $51- 59	XP: $6 F12

Location: 1/2 mi s on Hwy 101. 1250 S Hwy 101 97444. Fax: 503/247-7981. **Terms:** Sr. discount; reserv deposit; small pets only. **Facility:** 49 rooms. Attractively appointed, immaculately kept units, many with ocean view. 5 units with fireplace, 2 with balcony $95, $65 off-season; 3 stories; beach, heated indoor pool, whirlpool; small picnic area. **All Rooms:** free movies, cable TV, no A/C. **Some Rooms:** coffeemakers, kitchen, refrigerators. **Cards:** AE, CB, DI, DS, MC, VI.

FOREST GROVE INN
4433 Pacific Avenue, Forest Grove
✓ Special Rates for AAA Members!
✓ Spacious Rooms with HBO
✓ Friendly & Affordable
✓ Clean & Comfortable
✓ In-Room Fridge, Microwave, Coffee
For Reservations Call
1-800-240-6504

CHECK-IN TIME? It is noted in the listing if it is after 3 p.m.

CLEAR SKY LUXURY LODGING Rates Subject to Change **Phone:** 503/247-6456

AAA ◆◆◆ Cottage

5/1-10/31		2P/1B: $100	2P/2B: $100	XP: $15
3/1-4/30 & 11/1-2/29		2P/1B: $70	2P/2B: $70	XP: $15

Location: 2 blks e of Hwy 101, exit 10th St. 268 10th St 97444. **Terms:** Check-in 4 pm; reserv deposit, 5 day notice, in season; monthly rates; 2 night min stay; no pets. **Facility:** 8 rooms. In residential area. Very comfortably equipped 2- & 3-bedroom townhouses, each with kitchen garage & carport. 6 two-bedroom units, 2 three-bedroom units. Sauna, whirlpool. **All Rooms:** cable TV. **Some Rooms:** VCP's. Ⓓ ⊗

GOLD BEACH RESORT Rates Subject to Change **Phone:** 503/247-7066

AAA ◆◆◆ Motel

5/15-9/30	1P: $79	2P/1B: $98- 99	2P/2B: $99	XP: $8
3/1-5/14 & 10/1-2/29	1P: $49	2P/1B: $49- 59	2P/2B: $69	XP: $8

Location: 1/2 mi s on Hwy 101. 1330 S Ellensburg Ave 97444. Fax: 503/247-7069. **Terms:** Reserv deposit; no pets. **Facility:** 39 rooms. Large very well maintained units with balcony. 2-3 stories, no elevator; exterior corridors; oceanview; meeting rooms; beach access, heated indoor pool, whirlpool. **Dining:** Restaurant nearby. **All Rooms:** free movies, refrigerators, cable TV, no A/C. **Some Rooms:** Fee: VCP's. **Cards:** AE, DI, DS, MC, VI. *(See ad below)* Roll in showers. Ⓓ ⊗

INN AT GOLD BEACH Rates Subject to Change **Phone:** 503/247-6606

AAA ◆ Motel

6/1-9/4	1P: $49- 79	2P/1B: $59- 79	2P/2B: $69	XP: $6
3/1-5/31 & 9/5-2/29	1P: $39- 49	2P/1B: $39- 49	2P/2B: $59	XP: $6

Location: 3/4 mi s on Hwy 101. 1435 S Ellensburg 97444 (PO Box 1036). Fax: 503/247-7046. **Terms:** Reserv deposit; pets, $5. **Facility:** 41 rooms. On hill facing ocean. Excellently well-kept & maintained units. Attractive outdoor deck with view. 1 two-bedroom unit. 3 kitchens, $15 extra; 1-2 stories. **Dining:** Restaurant nearby. **All Rooms:** free movies, combo & shower baths, cable TV, no A/C. **Some Rooms:** microwaves, refrigerators. **Cards:** AE, DI, DS, MC, VI. *(See color ad below)* Ⓓ ⊗

- Free HBO & Showtime movies
- 39 Oceanfront units w/balconies on the beach
- Non-Smoking Rooms
- Refrigerators In Room

TOLL FREE RESERVATIONS
1-800-541-0947
1330 S. Ellensburg on Hwy 101
Gold Beach, OR 97444

GOLD BEACH Resort

- King & Queen Beds
- Indoor Pool & Spa
- Conventional/Banquet Facilities
- Restaurant • Handicapped Rooms
- No Pets

BEACHFRONT
FAX # 503-247-7069
☎(503) 247-7066

GOLD BEACH OREGON
Secluded, Picturesque Golf • Fine Dining & Lodging
Rogue River Boat Tours • Year Round Fishing
Call 1-800-525-2334 for your travel packet

THE INN AT GOLD BEACH

AAA

1435 S. Ellensburg
P.O. Box 1036
Gold Beach, OR 97444
(503) 247-6606

Come Stay With Us!

All Ocean View Rooms

- Beach Access
- King and Queen Beds
- Non-Smoking Rooms
- All Major Credit Cards
- Airport/Bus Shuttle
- Restaurant & Lounge Adjacent
- Rogue River Jet Boat Trips
- Salmon & Steelhead Charters
- Whale Watching Deck
- Pets Welcome

TOLL FREE RESERVATIONS
1-800-503-0833

You're one in 36 million, but the most important.

IRELAND'S RUSTIC LODGES Rates Subject to Change **Phone:** 503/247-7718

AAA ◆ Cottage

6/1-9/30 1P: $56- 61 2P/1B: $56- 61 2P/2B: $45- 50 XP: $5
3/1-5/31 & 10/1-2/29 1P: $30- 47 2P/1B: $30- 47 2P/2B: $35- 40 XP: $5

Location: 1/4 mi s on Hwy 101. 1120 S Ellensburg 97444 (PO Box 774). **Terms:** Reserv deposit; pets, $5. **Facility:** 40 rooms. On beautifully landscaped park-like grounds. Rustic units most with balcony & ocean view & cozy cottages with fireplace. 9 two-bedroom units. 8 efficiencies $40-$55, $35-$40 off season, 2 room units $76, $62 off season; 2 stories; exterior corridors; beach access. **All Rooms:** free movies, comb, shower & tub baths, cable TV, no A/C, no phones. **Some Rooms:** 4 kitchens. (D) ⊗

JOT'S RESORT Rates Subject to Change **Phone:** 503/247-6676

AAA ◆◆◆ Motor Inn

6/1-9/30 2P/1B: $80- 90 2P/2B: $80- 90 XP: $3-5 F12
5/1-5/31 & 10/1-10/31 2P/1B: $65- 75 2P/2B: $65- 75 XP: $3-5 F12
3/1-4/30 & 11/1-2/29 2P/1B: $50- 60 2P/2B: $50- 60 XP: $3-5 F12

Location: W of Hwy 101, off n end of bridge on North Bank Rd. 94360 Wedderburn Loop 97444 (PO Box J). Fax: 503/247-6716. **Terms:** Check-in 4 pm; pets, $10. **Facility:** 100 rooms. Attractive riverfront setting. Balconies & river view. 2 two-bedroom units. 1 three-bedroom unit, $175-225; 2 stories; meeting rooms; 2 pools (1 heated, 1 indoor), sauna, whirlpool; marina. Fee: boat dock. **Dining & Entertainment:** Restaurant; 6 am-10:30 pm; 11/1-4/31, 7 am-10 pm; $9-$24; cocktails; entertainment. **Services:** Fee: coin laundry. **Recreation:** fishing. Fee: daily river excursion boat pick-up, fishing supplies. Rental: boats; bicycles. **All Rooms:** combo & shower baths, cable TV, no A/C. **Some Rooms:** 25 efficiencies, 30 kitchens. Fee: VCP's. **Cards:** AE, DI, DS, MC, VI. (D) ⊗

RIVER BRIDGE INN Rates Subject to Change **Phone:** 503/247-4533

AAA ◆◆ Motel

7/1-9/30 1P: $49 2P/1B: $59 2P/2B: $69 XP: $6 F12
3/1-6/30 & 10/1-10/31 1P: $36 2P/1B: $49 2P/2B: $49 XP: $6 F12
11/1-2/29 1P: $32 2P/1B: $38 2P/2B: $42 XP: $6 F12

Location: S end of Rouge River Bridge. 1010 Jerry's Flat Rd 97444 (PO Box 1336). Fax: 503/247-0467. **Terms:** Reserv deposit, 3 day notice; pets, $5, on leash. **Facility:** 50 rooms. Neatly appointed units, most with river view. 8 efficiencies, $5 extra. 2 units with balcony, whirlpool & wet bar, $65; 2 stories; whirlpool. **Services:** Fee: coin laundry. **All Rooms:** free movies, cable TV, no A/C. **Cards:** AE, CB, DI, DS, MC, VI. (D) ⊗

SHORE CLIFF INN Rates Subject to Change **Phone:** 503/247-7091

AAA ◆◆ Motel

7/1-10/15 1P: $55- 75 2P/1B: $55- 75 2P/2B: $72 XP: $8-9
5/27-6/30 1P: $49- 69 2P/1B: $53- 69 2P/2B: $56 XP: $8-9
5/16-5/26 1P: $42- 58 2P/1B: $42- 58 2P/2B: $55 XP: $8-9
3/1-5/15 & 10/16-2/29 1P: $41- 52 2P/1B: $49- 52 2P/2B: $49 XP: $8-9

Location: On Hwy 101. 1100 S Hwy 101 Hwy 97444 (PO Box 615). **Terms:** Reserv deposit; no pets. **Facility:** 38 rooms. Especially well kept units. Many with balcony. 2 stories; exterior corridors; oceanview; beach access. **All Rooms:** free movies, cable TV, no A/C. **Cards:** AE, CB, DI, MC, VI. (D) ⊗

TU TU' TUN LODGE Rates Subject to Change **Phone:** 503/247-6664

AAA ◆◆◆◆ Resort Country Inn

5/1-10/31 2P/1B: $120 2P/2B: $120- 155 XP: $10 F4
3/1-4/30 & 11/1-2/29 2P/1B: $75 2P/2B: $75

Location: 7 mi e on n bank of Rogue River; from Hwy 101, at n end of bridge, e on North Bank Rogue. 96550 North Bank Rogue 97444. Fax: 503/247-0672. **Terms:** Reserv deposit, 14 day notice; no pets. **Facility:** 19 rooms. Especially hospitable resort in secluded scenic area along the Rogue River. Very tastefully appointed units with balcony or patio overlooking river. 6 rooms with fireplace, 5 with outdoor soaking tubs. In room phone upon request. 1 three-bedroom unit. 2 one-bedroom suites with kitchen, $165-$175; $90 off-season. Garden house with fireplace & deck, from $190; $90 off-season; 2 stories; exterior corridors; pitch & putt; Heated lap pool; boat dock, boat ramp; library, daily river excursion boat pick-up. Fee: guided fishing. **Dining:** Dining room; 5/1-10/31, 7:30-9:30 am, lunch at 12:30 pm, registered guests only, dinner at 7 pm, non-guest dining by reservation; $29; cocktails. **Services:** airport transportation, from Gold Beach Airport. **Recreation:** fishing; hiking trails. **All Rooms:** combo & shower baths, no A/C, no TVs. **Cards:** MC, VI. *(See color ad below)* (D)

RESTAURANTS

THE CHOWDERHEAD RESTAURANT **Dinner:** $11-$20 **Phone:** 503/247-0588

AAA ◆ Seafood

Location: On Hwy 101. 910 S Ellensburg 97444. **Hours:** 11 am-10 pm, 9 pm in winter. Closed: 1/1, 11/23 & 12/25. **Reservations:** suggested. **Features:** No A/C; children's menu; early bird specials; salad bar; cocktails. Very good selections of fresh seafood dishes & specialties; few beef dishes. Casual dining room with view of the ocean. **Cards:** AE, DS, MC, VI. ⊗

NOR' WESTER SEAFOOD RESTAURANT **Dinner:** $11-$20 **Phone:** 503/247-2333

AAA ◆◆ Steak and Seafood

Location: W of Hwy 101, at Port of Gold Beach. #10 Harbor Way 97444. **Hours:** 5 pm-10 pm. Closed: 11/23, 12/24 & 12/25. **Features:** No A/C; children's menu; cocktails & lounge. Overlooking harbor. Fresh seafood & steaks. **Cards:** AE, MC, VI. ⊗

"NESTLED ON THE BANKS OF THE ROGUE RIVER"

- Experience our cordial personal attention.
- Sit on your private patio or balcony and watch the ever-changing Rogue.
- Enjoy madrone wood fires on the terrace at dusk.

503-247-6664

AAA ◆◆◆◆

ROD 'N REEL — **Dinner:** $11-$20 — **Phone:** 503/247-6823

AAA ◆◆ American

Location: W of Hwy 101 off n end of bridge. **Hours:** 6 am-10 pm; 11/1-4/31, 7 am-10 pm. Closed: 12/24 & 12/25. **Reservations:** suggested. **Features:** No A/C; children's menu; senior's menu; carryout; cocktails & lounge; a la carte. Long established, inviting dining room. Good selection of popular seafood, beef & combination dishes. Live entertainment Fri & Sat in lounge. **Cards:** AE, CB, DI, MC, VI. ⊗

GOVERNMENT CAMP

LODGING

MT. HOOD INN — Guaranteed Rates — **Phone:** 503/272-3205

AAA ◆◆◆ Motel

3/1-9/15 & 11/15-2/29 [CP]	1P: $90	2P/1B: $90	2P/2B: $90	XP: $10 F12
9/16-11/14 [CP]	1P: $65	2P/1B: $65	2P/2B: $65	XP: $10 F12

Location: Center; on Government Camp Loop Rd. 87450 E Government Camp Loop 97028 (PO BOX 400). Fax: 503/272-3307. **Terms:** Sr. discount; check-in 4 pm; reserv deposit; small pets only, $5. **Facility:** 56 rooms. In winter recreation area. Large comfortably furnished & immaculately kept units. Limited covered parking. 8 units with whirlpool, $135; 3 stories; interior corridors; meeting rooms; whirlpool. **Services:** Fee: coin laundry. **All Rooms:** free movies, combo & shower baths, no A/C. **Some Rooms:** 8 efficiencies, microwaves, refrigerators. Fee: VCP's. **Cards:** AE, CB, DI, DS, MC, VI. *(See ad below)* Ⓓ Ⓢ ⊗

GRANTS PASS—17,500

LODGINGS

BEST WESTERN GRANTS PASS INN — Guaranteed Rates — **Phone:** 503/476-1117

AAA ◆◆ Motel

5/15-9/30	1P: $69	2P/1B: $75	2P/2B: $79	XP: $5 F18
3/15-5/14	1P: $62	2P/1B: $69	2P/2B: $74	XP: $5 F18
3/1-3/14 & 10/1-2/29	1P: $54	2P/1B: $59	2P/2B: $65	XP: $5 F18

Location: Off I-5 exit 55. 111 NE Agness 97526. Fax: 503/479-4315. **Terms:** Credit card guarantee; small pets only, $5. **Facility:** 84 rooms. Very attractive lobby. Well kept units. Apartment units, $110-$165; 2 stories; exterior corridors; heated pool, whirlpool. **Dining:** Restaurant nearby. **Services:** data ports. **All Rooms:** free movies, combo & shower baths, cable TV. **Some Rooms:** coffeemakers, refrigerators. Fee: VCP's, whirlpools. **Cards:** AE, CB, DI, DS, MC, VI. *(See color ad below)* Roll in showers. Ⓓ ⊗

HOLIDAY INN EXPRESS GRANTS PASS — Rates Subject to Change — **Phone:** 503/471-6144

AAA ◆◆ Motel

5/15-9/30 [CP]	1P: $74	2P/1B: $79	2P/2B: $84	XP: $5 F18
3/1-5/14 & 10/1-2/29 [CP]	1P: $59	2P/1B: $64	2P/2B: $69	XP: $5 F18

Location: Off I-5 exit 55. 105 NE Agness 97526. Fax: 503/471-9248. **Terms:** Sr. discount; pets, $5. **Facility:** 81 rooms. Very attractive exterior & public areas. 1-bedroom suites with wet bar $129; off season $110; 4 stories; interior corridors; meeting rooms. **Dining:** Restaurant nearby. **Services:** data ports; guest laundry. **All Rooms:** free movies, combo & shower baths, cable TV. **Some Rooms:** microwaves, refrigerators, whirlpools. Fee: VCP's. **Cards:** AE, CB, DI, JCB, MC, VI. *(See ad below)* Roll in showers. Ⓓ Ⓢ ⊗

MOTEL ORLEANS — Rates Subject to Change — **Phone:** 503/479-8301

AAA ◆◆ Motel

5/15-11/1	1P: $45	2P/1B: $50	2P/2B: $52	XP: $5 F12
3/1-5/14 & 11/2-2/29	1P: $34	2P/1B: $39	2P/2B: $41	XP: $5 F12

Location: 3/4 mi n on Hwy 99, s of jct I-5, exit 58. 1889 NE 6th St 97526. **Terms:** Sr. discount; reserv deposit; no pets. **Facility:** 61 rooms. Nicely furnished & immaculately kept units. 2 stories; exterior corridors; pool. **Dining:** Restaurant nearby. **Services:** Fee: coin laundry. **All Rooms:** cable TV. **Some Rooms:** microwaves, refrigerators. **Cards:** AE, CB, DI, DS, MC, VI. Ⓓ ⊗

Mt. HOOD INN
•Ski Packages •Guest Laundry •Spa Bath Units
•Complimentary Continental Breakfast •Free Ski Lockers
•All Rooms With A Mountain View •In the Center of Mountain Recreation Activities (next to Ski Bowl)
For Reservations, call: 1-800-443-7777
MT. HOOD INN 87450 E. Government Camp Loop. Government Camp, OR 97028 (503) 272-3205

Best Western Grants Pass Inn
84 Guest Rooms & Suites • HBO & ESPN
Heated Pool & Jacuzzi
Elmer's Restaurant & Lounge
For Reservations: (800) 553-ROOM
I-5 at Exit 55
111 N.E. Agness • (503) 476-1117

Holiday Inn EXPRESS
81 Guest Rooms & Suites • HBO & ESPN
Pool & Spa Pool
Complimentary Breakfast Bar
For Reservations: 1-800-838-7666
I-5 at Exit 55
105 N.E. Agness • (503) 471-6144

REDWOOD MOTEL Guaranteed Rates **Phone:** 503/476-0878

AAA ◆ Motel

5/1-9/30 1P: $45 2P/1B: $50 2P/2B: $52 XP: $5
3/1-4/30 & 10/1-2/29 1P: $39 2P/1B: $43 2P/2B: $44 XP: $5

Location: 1/4 mi n on Hwy 99S; 1 mi s of I-5, exit 58. 815 NE 6th St 97526. Fax: 503/476-1032. **Terms:** Reserv deposit; small pets only, $5. **Facility:** 26 rooms. Nicely furnished & very well-kept units. Attractively landscaped tree-shaded grounds. 9 two-bedroom units. 6 kitchens, $10 extra. 9 two-room units, $5 extra. 1 one-room units & 1 two-room unit with kitchen from $65, off-season from $45; 1 story; exterior corridors; heated pool, whirlpool; playground. **Dining:** Restaurant nearby. **Services:** Fee: coin laundry. **All Rooms:** free movies, combo & shower baths, cable TV. **Some Rooms:** microwaves, refrigerators. **Cards:** AE, CB, DI, DS, MC, VI. *(See color ad below)* Ⓓ ⊗

RIVERSIDE INN AAA Special Value Rates **Phone:** 503/476-6873

AAA ◆◆ Motor Inn

All Year 1P: $55- 100 2P/1B: $60- 105 2P/2B: $85- 100 XP:$5-10 F12

Location: On Hwy 99 at n end of bridges; southbound, 2 1/2 mi s of jct I-5 exit 58; northbound, 2 1/2 mi w of I-5 exit 55. 971 SE 6th St 97526. Fax: 503/474-9848. **Terms:** Check-in 4 pm; reserv deposit, 5/15-9/30; pets, $15. **Facility:** 174 rooms. Nicely located along Rogue river. Most units overlooking river. Many balconies. 8 fireplaces. Jet boat launch site. 11 two-bedroom units. 6 parlor suites, 2 with fireplace $105-$175; 2-3 stories; exterior corridors; meeting rooms; 2 heated pools, whirlpools. **Dining & Entertainment:** Restaurant; 7 am-10 pm, Fri & Sat-11 pm; 10/15-5/14 6:30 am-9 pm; $7-$17; cocktails/lounge. **Services:** data ports. **All Rooms:** combo & shower baths, cable TV. Fee: movies. **Some Rooms:** coffeemakers, radios, refrigerators. **Cards:** AE, CB, DI, DS, MC, VI. Ⓓ ⊗

SWEET BREEZE INN Rates Subject to Change **Phone:** 503/471-4434

AAA ◆◆ Motel

5/15-9/30 1P: $39- 43 2P/1B: $43- 48 2P/2B: $50- 56 XP: $4
3/1-5/14 & 10/1-2/29 1P: $32- 36 2P/1B: $36- 38 2P/2B: $40- 42 XP: $4

Location: 1/2 mi n on Hwy 99 southbound; south of jct I-5, exit 58. 1627 NE 6th St 97526. **Terms:** Sr. discount; credit card guarantee, 3 day notice; no pets. **Facility:** 21 rooms. Very attractively decorated units. 2 stories; exterior corridors; smoke free premises. **All Rooms:** free movies, combo & shower baths, cable TV. **Cards:** MC, VI. Ⓓ Ⓢ ⊗

RESTAURANT

YANKEE POT ROAST Historical **Dinner:** $11-$20 **Phone:** 503/476-0551

AAA ◆◆ American

Location: On Hwy 99 southbound. 720 NW 6th 97526. **Hours:** 5 pm-9 pm. Closed: Tues, also Mon Jan-Apr. **Reservations:** suggested. **Features:** children's menu; cocktails; a la carte. In converted historic house with charming early 1900's atmosphere. Nice selection of standard dinners. Smoke free premises. **Cards:** MC, VI. ⊗

GRESHAM—68,200

LODGINGS

BEST WESTERN PONY SOLDIER MOTOR INN Rates Subject to Change **Phone:** 503/665-1591

AAA ◆◆◆ Motel

All Year [CP] 1P: $69- 74 2P/1B: $72- 77 2P/2B: $78- 83 XP: $5 F12

Location: At Cleveland & E Burnside; from I-84 eastbound, Wood Village-Gresham exit 16A, then s on NE 238th to Division, then right to Cleveland. 1060 NE Cleveland Ave 97030. Fax: 503/669-7265. **Terms:** Sr. discount; reserv deposit, 6/1-9/30; no pets. **Facility:** 75 rooms. Very attractively appointed units. Comfortable lobby with courtyard view. 3 kitchens, $81-$85; 2 stories; interior corridors; meeting rooms; sauna, whirlpool, small heated pool; exercise room. **Dining:** Restaurant nearby. **Services:** data ports; guest laundry. **All Rooms:** microwaves, free movies, refrigerators, cable TV. **Cards:** AE, CB, DI, DS, JCB, MC, VI. Ⓓ ⊗

HOLIDAY INN EXPRESS Guaranteed Rates **Phone:** 503/492-4000

AAA ◆◆◆ Motel

5/1-8/31 [CP] 1P: $61- 73 2P/1B: $68- 80 2P/2B: $75 XP: $7 F18
3/1-4/30 & 9/1-2/29 [CP] 1P: $55- 69 2P/1B: $62- 76 2P/2B: $69 XP: $7 F18

Location: 1/4 mi s of I-84 eastbound exit 13. 2323 NE 181 St 97230. Fax: 503/492-3271. **Terms:** Sr. discount; reserv deposit, 3 day notice; pets. **Facility:** 71 rooms. Attractive units & especially well-kept guest facilities. 3 units with whirlpool, refrigerator & wet bar $101, off season $92; 2 stories; interior corridors; meeting rooms; heated indoor pool, sauna, whirlpool. **Dining:** Restaurant nearby. **Services:** data ports; guest laundry. **All Rooms:** free movies. **Some Rooms:** 10 efficiencies, 3 kitchens. **Cards:** AE, CB, DI, DS, JCB, MC, VI. *(See color ad p A49)* Ⓓ Ⓢ ⊗

QUALITY INN Rates Subject to Change **Phone:** 503/666-9545

AAA ◆◆ Motel

All Year [CP] 1P: $50 2P/1B: $54 2P/2B: $61 XP: $4 F18

Location: I-84 eastbound, Wood Village-Gresham exit. 1545 NE Burnside 97030. Fax: 503/666-7171. **Terms:** Sr. discount; credit card guarantee; small pets only, $8. **Facility:** 73 rooms. 2 stories; interior corridors; meeting rooms; heated pool. **Dining:** Restaurant nearby. **Services:** Fee: coin laundry. **All Rooms:** free movies, cable TV. **Some Rooms:** microwaves, refrigerators. Fee: VCP's. **Cards:** AE, CB, DS, JCB, MC, VI. Ⓓ ⊗

Large Heated Pool & Spa
2-Room Family Units
Shaded Grounds
815 N.E. Sixth Street
Grants Pass, OR 97526
REDWOOD MOTEL
Air-Conditioned
Color Cable / HBO
Complimentary Coffee Service
Coin-Op Laundry
Phone: (503) 476-0878 • Fax: (503) 476-1032
All major credit cards gladly accepted.

REQUEST THE BEST IN SOUTHERN OREGON
Best Western Inn at the Rogue
See our listing under Rogue River, OR
I-5 Exit 48 • Adjacent to the World Famous Rogue River
Sparkling Heated Pool & Spa • HBO/Cable TV • Deluxe Fitness Center • AAA Discount • Free Continental Breakfast • Non-Smoking Rooms • Jacuzzi Suites • Fishing • Boating • Ballooning
8959 Rogue River Hwy • (503) 582-2200
Grants Pass, OR 97527 • (800) 238-0700

HAINES—400

RESTAURANT

HAINES STEAK HOUSE — **Dinner:** $11-$20 — **Phone:** 503/856-3639

◆ American

Location: 10 mi n of Baker City on Hwy 30. 97833. **Hours:** 5 pm-10 pm, Sat from 4 pm, Sun 1 pm-9 pm. Closed: Tues, 11/23 & 12/25. **Reservations:** accepted. **Features:** children's menu; cocktails; a la carte. Western frontier atmosphere, memorabilia & game trophies. Steaks, seafood, prime rib, roasted chicken & hamburgers. **Cards:** AE, DS, MC, VI.

HILLSBORO—37,500

LODGINGS

BEST WESTERN HALLMARK INN-HILLSBORO AIRPORT — Rates Subject to Change — **Phone:** 503/648-3500

AAA ◆◆◆ Motor Inn

All Year	1P: $61	2P/1B: $61	2P/2B: $70- 85	XP: $5	F12

Location: Opposite Hillsboro Airport; from Hwy 26 take Cornelius Pass-Hillsboro exit, 2 mi s to Hillsboro Airport. 3500 NE Cornell Rd 97124. Fax: 503/640-2789. **Terms:** Sr. discount; reserv deposit, 3 day notice; pets, $5. **Facility:** 123 rooms. Near Hillsboro Airport & Washington County Fairgrounds. 3 suites with wetbar & microwave, $105-$115; 2 stories; interior corridors; conference facilities; heated pool, whirlpool; exercise room. **Dining & Entertainment:** Restaurant; 6:30 am-9 pm, Fri & Sat-10 pm; $10-$15; cocktails/lounge. **Services:** data ports. Fee: coin laundry. **All Rooms:** coffeemakers, free movies, cable TV. **Some Rooms:** refrigerators, whirlpools. Fee: VCP's. **Cards:** AE, CB, DI, DS, JCB, MC, VI.

THE DUNES MOTEL — AAA Special Value Rates — **Phone:** 503/648-8991

AAA ◆ Motel

All Year	1P: $34	2P/1B: $38	2P/2B: $40

Location: 1/2 mi e on SR 8. 452 SE 10th 97123. Fax: 503/693-6710. **Terms:** Reserv deposit, 3 day notice; no pets. **Facility:** 40 rooms. Generous size rooms. 2 stories; interior corridors. **All Rooms:** free movies, cable TV. **Some Rooms:** refrigerators. **Cards:** AE, CB, DI, DS, MC, VI.

PARK DUNES MOTEL — Rates Subject to Change — **Phone:** 503/640-4791

AAA ◆◆ Motel

6/1-9/30	1P: $44	2P/1B: $44	2P/2B: $50	XP: $7	F6
3/1-5/31 & 10/1-2/29	1P: $39	2P/1B: $39	2P/2B: $45	XP: $7	F6

Location: 1/2 mi e on SR 8. 622 SE 10th 97123. Fax: 503/640-8127. **Terms:** Sr. discount; check-in 4 pm; reserv deposit; no pets. **Facility:** 58 rooms. 2 stories; exterior corridors. **Dining:** Restaurant nearby. **Services:** Fee: coin laundry. **All Rooms:** coffeemakers, refrigerators, cable TV. **Cards:** CB, DI, DS, MC, VI.

(See color ad below)

HOOD RIVER—4,600

LODGINGS

BEST WESTERN HOOD RIVER INN — Guaranteed Rates — **Phone:** 503/386-2200

AAA ◆◆◆ Motor Inn

6/9-9/30	1P: $83- 93	2P/1B: $89- 99	2P/2B: $89- 99	XP: $12	F18
10/1-10/31	1P: $59- 69	2P/1B: $65- 75	2P/2B: $65- 75	XP: $12	F18
4/1-6/8	1P: $55- 65	2P/1B: $61- 71	2P/2B: $61- 71	XP: $12	F18
3/1-3/31 & 11/1-2/29	1P: $49- 59	2P/1B: $55- 65	2P/2B: $55- 65	XP: $12	F18

Location: 1/2 mi e; ne of jct I-84 & SR 35, exit 64. 1108 E Marina Way 97031. Fax: 503/386-8905. **Terms:** Check-in 4 pm; small pets only, $12. **Facility:** 149 rooms. Located along Columbia River. Many rooms with balcony & river view. 12 compact units. 4 two-bedroom units. 4 two-bedroom units with fireplace & whirlpool $125-$165; 2-3 stories; interior corridors; conference facilities; beach access, heated pool, whirlpool; boat dock. **Dining:** Dining room, coffee shop; 6 am-10 pm; $7-$18; cocktails. **Services:** data ports; health club privileges. Fee: coin laundry. **All Rooms:** coffeemakers, cable TV. Fee: movies. **Some Rooms:** microwaves, refrigerators, whirlpools. **Cards:** AE, CB, DI, DS, MC, VI.

(See color ad p A28)

LOVE'S RIVERVIEW LODGE — Guaranteed Rates — **Phone:** 503/386-8719

AAA ◆◆ Motel

6/1-9/15	1P: $65	2P/1B: $69	2P/2B: $72	XP: $4-6	F11
4/1-5/31 & 9/16-10/31	1P: $55	2P/1B: $59	2P/2B: $62	XP: $4-6	F11
3/1-3/31 & 11/1-2/29	1P: $45	2P/1B: $49	2P/2B: $52	XP: $4-6	F11

Location: On Hwy 30, 1 mi e of jct I-84, exit 62. 1505 Oak 97031. **Terms:** Reserv deposit; no pets. **Facility:** 15 rooms. Neat, compact & very well-maintained 1 & 2-bedroom units; some with partial river view. 2 stories; interior/exterior corridors. **Services:** area transportation, locally. **All Rooms:** coffeemakers, free movies, refrigerators. **Some Rooms:** microwaves. **Cards:** AE, CB, DI, DS, MC, VI.

VAGABOND LODGE — Rates Subject to Change — **Phone:** 503/386-2992

AAA ◆◆ Motel

4/15-10/15	1P: $39- 52	2P/1B: $44- 65	2P/2B: $48- 68	XP: $6-7
3/1-4/14 & 10/16-2/29	1P: $36- 47	2P/1B: $39- 57	2P/2B: $43- 59	XP: $6-7

Location: 1 1/4 mi w off I-84 & Hwy 30, exit 62 (1/3 mi w of overpass). 4070 Westcliff Dr 97031. **Terms:** Reserv deposit; small pets only. **Facility:** 40 rooms. Attractive spacious grounds. Some large units. Many rooms overlooking Columbia River. 5 two-bedroom units. 5 large 2-bedroom suites with fireplace from, $75 for 2 persons, $65 off-season; 1-2 stories; exterior corridors; playground. **Dining:** Restaurants nearby. **All Rooms:** combo & shower baths, cable TV. **Some Rooms:** A/C, kitchen, refrigerators. **Cards:** AE, CB, DI, MC, VI.

"Clean Rooms - Friendly Service"

THE PARK DUNES
622 S.E.10th
HILLSBORO, OR 97123
(503) 640-4791
Res: 1-800-548-0163

Park Dunes Motel
"Affordable - Hospitality"
15 miles W. of Portland

Value For Your $
RESTAURANT ADJACENT
FAX: (503) 640-8127

★ Air Cond./Refrigerators/Microwaves
★ Queen-Size Beds - Waterbeds
★ 24-Hour Desk/Credit Cards
★ Commercial/Group/Wkly Rates

AAA

★ Cable TV/HBO/D.D. Phones
★ In-Room & Lobby Coffee
★ Coin Laundry/Sr. Discount
★ Shopping Center close by

RESTAURANT

STONEHEDGE INN Dinner: $11-$20 Phone: 503/386-3940

AAA ◆◆ American

Location: 1 1/4 mi w; s of jct I-84 & Hwy 30, exit 62. 3405 Cascade Dr 97031. **Hours:** seating at 5 pm. Closed major holidays, Mon & Tues. **Reservations:** suggested. **Features:** No A/C; cocktails & lounge; a la carte. Dining room with country atmosphere in converted house built in early 1900's. Very good traditional beef, fowl & seafood dishes. Smoke free premises. **Cards:** AE, DI, DS, MC, VI. ⊗

JACKSONVILLE—1,900

LODGINGS

JACKSONVILLE INN AAA Special Value Rates Phone: 503/899-1900

AAA ◆◆ Historic Hotel

All Year [BP] 1P: $60- 100 2P/1B: $80- 125 XP: $10

Location: 175 E California St 97530 (PO Box 359). Fax: 503/899-1373. **Terms:** Credit card guarantee, 3 day notice; no pets. **Facility:** 9 rooms. Hotel built in 1863. Very charming, restored guest rooms, few compact, with historic ambience. Very attractively decorated & furnished in period style. 1-bedroom cottage with whirlpool/sauna, VCR & coffeemaker, $175; 2 stories; interior corridors; smoke free premises. **Dining:** Cocktails; dining room, see separate listing. **Recreation:** bicycles. **All Rooms:** refrigerators, shower baths, cable TV. **Some Rooms:** microwaves, whirlpools. **Cards:** AE, DI, DS, MC, VI. (D) ⊗

THE STAGE LODGE Guaranteed Rates Phone: 503/899-3953

AAA ◆◆ Motel

5/15-9/30 [CP]	1P: $65	2P/1B: $69	2P/2B: $74	XP: $5 F12
3/1-5/14 & 10/1-2/29 [CP]	1P: $53	2P/1B: $58	2P/2B: $63	XP: $5 F12

Location: West side on SR 238. 830 N 5th 97530 (PO Box 1316). **Terms:** Reserv deposit, 5 day notice; no pets. **Facility:** 27 rooms. Generous size units, very tastefully decorated & furnished in traditional motif. 2 suites with wet bar, microwave, whirlpool & fireplace $125; $99 low season; 2 stories; exterior corridors. **Services:** data ports. **All Rooms:** free movies, combo & shower baths, cable TV. **Cards:** AE, DI, DS, MC, VI. Roll in showers. (D) ⊗

TOUVELLE HOUSE BED & BREAKFAST Guaranteed Rates Phone: 503/899-8938

◆◆◆ Historic Bed & Breakfast

4/1-9/30 & 12/1-12/31 [BP]	2P/1B: $90- 95	XP: $25
3/1-3/31, 10/1-11/30 & 1/1-2/29 [BP]	2P/1B: $80- 85	XP: $25

Location: 2 1/2 blks n. 455 N Oregon St 97530 (PO Box 1891). Fax: 503/899-3992. **Terms:** Reserv deposit, 7 day notice; no pets. **Facility:** 5 rooms. 1916 craftsman style home. Charming and stately decor. Small English garden. Porch & veranda sitting areas. Full house rental $470, $430 off season; 1 suite $145; 3 stories; interior corridors; smoke free premises; pool, whirlpool; small library with TV, stereo & VCR for guest use; guest phone & fax avail. **Dining:** Afternoon refreshments. **Services:** airport transportation. **Recreation:** bicycles. **All Rooms:** shower & tub baths, no phones. (D) ⊗

RESTAURANT

JACKSONVILLE INN DINNER HOUSE Dinner: $21-$30 Phone: 503/899-1900

AAA ◆◆◆ American

Location: Center. 175 E California St 97530. **Hours:** 7:30 am-10 & 11:30-10 pm, Sun 7:30 am-9 pm. Closed: 11/23, 12/24 & 12/25. **Reservations:** suggested. **Features:** Sunday brunch; children's menu; health conscious menu; cocktails & lounge; a la carte. In restored historic Jacksonville Hotel building. Very attractive, intimate dining rooms. Well-prepared seafood, veal, poultry, prime rib & steaks. Patio dining in summer. Also cafe menu, $6-$14. Smoke free premises. **Cards:** AE, DI, DS, MC, VI. ⊗

If You Try To Escape

We've Got You Surrounded

Surrounded, that is, by the beauty of the Columbia River Gorge and the Cascade Mountains. Riverfront rooms, dining, lounge, and our heated outdoor pool will make your stay the ultimate escape.

We're an incredibly scenic hour drive east of Portland, Exit 64 off I-84.

Best Western Hood River Inn

For Reservations Call **1-800-828-7873**

◆ **Diamonds** are a guest's best friend. ◆

JOHN DAY—1,800

LODGINGS

BEST WESTERN INN Rates Subject to Change **Phone:** 503/575-1700

(AAA) ◆◆ Motel

5/28-10/15 1P: $49 2P/1B: $55 2P/2B: $63 XP: $6 F12
3/1-5/27 & 10/16-2/29 1P: $45 2P/1B: $49 2P/2B: $53 XP: $6 F12

Location: 2 blks w on Hwy 395 & 26. 315 W Main 97845. Fax: 503/575-1558. **Terms:** Reserv deposit, 14 day notice; small pets only, $3.50, in designated rooms. **Facility:** 39 rooms. Very attractively appointed units. 2 two-bedroom units. 2 stories; exterior corridors; heated indoor pool, whirlpool; exercise room. **Services:** Fee: coin laundry. **All Rooms:** coffeemakers, free movies, refrigerators, cable TV. **Some Rooms:** microwaves. Fee: whirlpools. **Cards:** AE, CB, DI, DS, JCB, MC, VI. (D) ⊗

DREAMERS LODGE Rates Subject to Change **Phone:** 503/575-0526

(AAA) ◆ Motel

5/15-10/15 1P: $38- 40 2P/1B: $42- 44 2P/2B: $44- 46 XP: $2-4
3/1-5/14 & 10/16-2/29 1P: $36- 38 2P/1B: $40- 42 2P/2B: $42- 44 XP: $2-4

Location: 1/2 blk n of jct Hwy 26 & 395. 144 N Canyon Blvd 97845. Fax: 503/575-2733. **Terms:** Credit card guarantee; pets. **Facility:** 25 rooms. Located well back from highway. 3 two-bedroom units. 2 stories; exterior corridors. **All Rooms:** coffeemakers, free movies, refrigerators, combo & shower baths, cable TV. **Some Rooms:** 2 kitchens. **Cards:** AE, CB, DI, DS, MC, VI. (D) ⊗

KLAMATH FALLS—17,700

LODGINGS

BEST WESTERN KLAMATH INN AAA Special Value Rates **Phone:** 503/882-1200

(AAA) ◆◆ Motel

All Year [CP] 1P: $56- 60 2P/1B: $62- 66 2P/2B: $66 XP: $8 F12

Location: 2 1/2 mi e on SR 140 & 39 at jct Hwy 97; northbound on Hwy 97 take Lakeview SR 140 exit to Summers Ln, then to SR 39-140; southbound to jct SR 39-140. 4061 S 6th St 97603. Fax: 503/882-2729. **Terms:** Small pets only. **Facility:** 52 rooms. Attractive, very well kept units. 2 stories; exterior corridors; meeting rooms; heated indoor pool. **Dining:** Restaurant nearby. **Services:** data ports; health club privileges. **All Rooms:** microwaves, free movies, refrigerators, combo & shower baths, cable TV. **Some Rooms:** Fee: whirlpools. **Cards:** AE, CB, DI, DS, MC, VI. *(See ad below)* (D) ⊗

BEST WESTERN OLYMPIC INN Rates Subject to Change **Phone:** 503/882-9665

(AAA) ◆◆◆ Motel

7/1-9/3 [CP] 1P: $77 2P/1B: $77 2P/2B: $77 XP: $10 F18
3/1-6/30 & 9/4-2/29 [CP] 1P: $69 2P/1B: $69 2P/2B: $69 XP: $10 F18

Location: 1/2 mi e on SR 140/39; northbound on Hwy 97, Lakeview SR 140 exit to Washburn Way, then to S 6th; southbound to Hwy 97 Business Rt to Washburn Way. 2627 S 6th St 97603. Fax: 503/884-3214. **Terms:** Sr. discount; credit card guarantee, 14 day notice; no pets. **Facility:** 75 rooms. 1 spacious unit with wet bar, $99-$110; 3 stories; interior corridors; meeting rooms; heated pool, whirlpool. **Dining:** Restaurant nearby. **Services:** health club privileges; valet laundry. **All Rooms:** free movies, cable TV. **Some Rooms:** microwaves, refrigerators. **Cards:** AE, DI, DS, MC, VI. (D) (S) ⊗

COMFORT INN AAA Special Value Rates **Phone:** 503/884-9999

(AAA) ◆◆◆ Motel

All Year [CP] 1P: $56- 64 2P/1B: $64- 68 2P/2B: $68 XP: $8 F12

Location: 1 1/2 mi e on SR 140 & 39; northbound on Hwy 97 take Lake View SR 140 exit to Washburn Way, then to SR 39-140; southbound to Washburn Way. 2500 S 6th St 97601. Fax: 503/882-4020. **Terms:** No pets. **Facility:** 57 rooms. Comfortable rooms. Tastefully decorated. 10 suites with wet bar & 4 with whirlpool from $90; 2 stories; interior corridors; meeting rooms; heated indoor pool, whirlpool; exercise room. **Services:** health club privileges. Fee: coin laundry. **All Rooms:** free movies, cable TV. **Some Rooms:** microwaves, refrigerators. **Cards:** AE, DI, DS, MC, VI. (D) (S) ⊗

KLAMATH MANOR BED & BREAKFAST Guaranteed Rates **Phone:** 503/883-5459

(AAA) ◆◆ Bed & Breakfast

2/1-1/1 [BP] 1P: $50- 65 2P/1B: $55- 70 XP: $10

Location: Hwy 97S, w on Esplanade to 3rd St then n, w on Pine; Hwy 97N City Center exit, n on 2nd St, e on Pine. 219 Pine St 97601. **Terms:** Open 2/1-1/1; credit card guarantee, 5 day notice; no pets. **Facility:** 3 rooms. 1921 Victorian-style house with charming rooms. Oak floors and trim throughout. Afternoon beverages & snacks. Extensive video library. 1 room with fireplace & private bath $70; 2 stories; interior corridors; smoke free premises; street parking only. **Dining:** Breakfast on patio weather permitting; afternoon tea. **Services:** airport transportation. **All Rooms:** no A/C, no TVs. **Some Rooms:** combo & shower baths, shared bathrooms, phones. **Cards:** DS, MC, VI. (D) ⊗

Best Western

Best Western Klamath Inn

Best Western Hotels are independently owned and operated

AAA

- Indoor Heated Pool
- HBO - FAX Service
- Color Cable TV
- FREE Buffet Breakfast
- Non Smoking Rooms Available
- Bicycle Fitness Trail

Phone (503) 882-1200 or (800) 528-1234 • FAX (503) 882-2729

4061 South Sixth Street • Klamath Falls, Oregon 97603

MOLATORE'S MOTOR INN AAA Special Value Rates **Phone:** 503/882-4666
AAA ◆◆ Motor Inn
All Year 1P: $46- 64 2P/1B: $48- 64 2P/2B: $51- 64 XP: $6
Location: On US 97 business rt & SR 140; 1/4 mi s of jct SR 39. 100 Main St 97601. Fax: 503/883-8795. **Terms:** Reserv deposit, 3 day notice; no pets. **Facility:** 81 rooms. Some spacious newer units; few compact units. 4 one-bedroom suites, with wet bar & refrigerator, $82; 2 stories; exterior corridors; meeting rooms; heated pool. **Dining:** Restaurant; 6 am-11 pm, Sun-2:30 pm; $5-$23; cocktails. **Services:** health club privileges. Fee: coin laundry. **All Rooms:** cable TV. **Some Rooms:** microwaves, radios. Fee: VCP's, whirlpools. **Cards:** AE, CB, DI, DS, MC, VI. (D) ⊗

OREGON MOTEL 8 Guaranteed Rates **Phone:** 503/883-3431
AAA ◆ Motel
All Year 1P: $28- 35 2P/1B: $33- 39 2P/2B: $39 XP: $4 F5
Location: 3 mi n on Hwy 97N. 5225 Hwy 97 N 97601. **Terms:** Sr. discount; reserv deposit; pets. **Facility:** 29 rooms. Very neat, especially well maintained units. 5 two-bedroom units. 1 story; exterior corridors; heated pool. **All Rooms:** free movies, combo & shower baths, cable TV. **Some Rooms:** coffeemakers, 7 kitchens. **Cards:** MC, VI. (D) ⊗

RED LION INN Rates Subject to Change **Phone:** 503/882-8864
AAA ◆◆◆ Motor Inn
All Year 1P: $69 2P/1B: $74 2P/2B: $79 XP: $10 F18
Location: 2 1/2 mi e on SR 140 & 39; nourthbound on Hwy 97, take City Ctr exit to S 5th st, e on 5th merges 6th, s bound on Business Rt 97 to s 6th. 3612 S 6th St 97603. Fax: 503/884-2046. **Terms:** Reserv deposit; small pets only. **Facility:** 108 rooms. Spacious, very comfortable units. Located across from the Klamath County Fairgrounds. Complimentary coffee & danish each morning. 7 two-bedroom units. 2 stories; exterior corridors; meeting rooms; heated pool, whirlpool. **Dining & Entertainment:** Restaurant; 6 am-11 pm; $6-$11; cocktails/lounge; 24-hour room service. **Services:** data ports; health club privileges; valet laundry; airport transportation. **All Rooms:** free movies, combo & shower baths, cable TV. **Some Rooms:** refrigerators, whirlpools. Fee: VCP's. **Cards:** AE, CB, DI, DS, MC, VI. Red Lion Inns. (D) ⊗

THOMPSON'S BED & BREAKFAST Rates Subject to Change **Phone:** 503/882-7938
◆ Bed & Breakfast
All Year [BP] 1P: $60- 65 2P/1B: $65- 70 XP: $10 D12
Location: 3 mi nw; Hwy 97 take Lakeshore Dr/Oregon Ave exit, 1 1/2 mi w on Lakeshore Dr to Lynnewood; s on Lynnewood to Vista Way. W on Wild Plum Ct. 1420 Wild Plum Ct 97601. **Terms:** No pets. **Facility:** 4 rooms. Built against wooded hill in residential area. Large common room with picturesque view of Upper Klamath Lake. Outdoor deck. 2 rooms with view of lake. Lower level common room with microwave, VCP refrigerator coffeemaker & phone. 2 stories; interior/exterior corridors; smoke free premises. **Services:** guest laundry; airport transportation. **All Rooms:** combo & shower baths, cable TV. **Some Rooms:** A/C, radios. (D) ⊗

RESTAURANTS

CHEZ NOUS RESTAURANT **Dinner:** $11-$20 **Phone:** 503/883-8719
AAA ◆◆ Continental
Location: 1 1/2 mi e on SR 140 & 39. 3927 S 6th 97603. **Hours:** 5 pm-10 pm; 6/1-8/31, Sun 4 pm-9 pm. Closed major holidays, Mon & Sun 9/1-5/31. **Reservations:** suggested. **Features:** cocktails & lounge. Warm atmosphere in former residence. Very well prepared dishes include beef, veal, seafood, poultry & lamb. Very good wine selection. **Cards:** AE, CB, DI, MC, VI. ⊗

FIORELLAS ITALIAN RESTAURANTE **Dinner:** $11-$20 **Phone:** 503/882-1878
◆◆ Northern Italian
Location: 3 1/2 mi e on 140 & 39 (s 6th), northbound on Hwy 97 to city center exit to 5th St-merges with s 6th, southbound on Business Rt 97 to s 6th then e 1 mi. 6139 Simmers 97603. **Hours:** 5 pm-9 pm. Closed: Sun, Mon & 12/25. **Features:** children's menu; health conscious menu; cocktails & lounge. Charming authentic Italian family owned & operated restaurant. Nice selection of pasta, chicken, veal & seafood dishes prepared with homegrown herbs. **Cards:** MC, VI. ⊗

LA GRANDE—11,800

LODGINGS

BEST WESTERN PONY SOLDIER MOTOR INN Rates Subject to Change **Phone:** 503/963-7195
AAA ◆◆◆ Motel
All Year [CP] 1P: $60- 70 2P/1B: $62- 72 2P/2B: $67- 77 XP: $5 F12
Location: On SR 82; 1 blk e of I-84, exit 261. 2612 Island Ave 97850. Fax: 503/963-4498. **Terms:** Sr. discount; reserv deposit; small pets only. **Facility:** 148 rooms. Very attractively appointed units. Some with balcony. 2 stories; interior/exterior corridors; meeting rooms; heated pool, sauna, whirlpool; exercise room. **Dining:** Restaurant nearby. **Services:** guest laundry. **All Rooms:** free movies, refrigerators, cable TV. **Some Rooms:** Fee: VCP's. **Cards:** AE, CB, DI, DS, JCB, MC, VI. (D) ⊗

ROYAL MOTOR INN AAA Special Value Rates **Phone:** 503/963-4154
AAA ◆ Motel
All Year 1P: $37 2P/1B: $42 2P/2B: $44 XP: $3 F17
Location: On US 30; 1 1/2 blks n of jct SR 82, La Grande exit off I-84. 1510 Adams Ave 97850. Fax: 503/963-3588. **Terms:** Credit card guarantee; no pets. **Facility:** 44 rooms. Long established. Very well-maintained units. 2 stories; exterior corridors. **All Rooms:** coffeemakers, free movies, cable TV. **Some Rooms:** Fee: refrigerators. **Cards:** AE, DI, DS, MC, VI. (D) ⊗

STANG MANOR INN Guaranteed Rates **Phone:** 503/963-2400
◆ Bed & Breakfast
All Year [BP] 1P: $65 2P/1B: $70 2P/2B: $70 XP: $15
Location: Eastbound I-84 exit 259, e on Adams then s on Walnut 3 blks; westbound I-84 exit 264, w on SR 82 to Washington St, w on N Ave to Walnut then n. 1612 Walnut St 97850. Fax: 503/963-2400. **Terms:** Credit card guarantee, 7 day notice; no pets. **Facility:** 4 rooms. 1923 Georgian Colonial-style home. Located in residential neighborhood with convenient access to the hospital & Eastern Oregon State College. Spacious common room with sun room. Themed rooms. 3 two-bedroom units. 1 fireplace suite, $90; 2 stories; interior corridors; smoke free premises; street parking only. **Dining:** Afternoon tea. **Services:** area transportation, to train station. **All Rooms:** no A/C. **Some Rooms:** VCP's. **Cards:** MC, VI. (S) ⊗

SUPER 8 MOTEL LA GRANDE Rates Subject to Change **Phone:** 503/963-8080
AAA ◆◆ Motel

Fri-Sun 5/13-9/30	1P:	$55	2P/1B:	$55	2P/2B:	$55	XP:	$4	F12
Mon-Thurs 5/13-9/30	1P:	$51	2P/1B:	$51	2P/2B:	$51	XP:	$4	F12
3/1-5/12 & 10/1-2/29	1P:	$39	2P/1B:	$44	2P/2B:	$49	XP:	$4	F12

Location: Off SR 82; take Watson St, e of I-84 exit 261. 2407 E R Ave 97850. Fax: 503/963-2925. **Terms:** Sr. discount; reserv deposit; no pets. **Facility:** 64 rooms. Nicely equiped units. 5 one-bedroom suites with whirlpool, from $72.88; 2 stories; interior corridors; meeting rooms; heated indoor pool, whirlpool; exercise room. **Dining:** Restaurant nearby. **Services:** Fee: coin laundry. **All Rooms:** free movies, refrigerators, cable TV. **Some Rooms:** kitchen, microwaves. Fee: VCP's. **Cards:** AE, CB, DI, DS, MC, VI. (D) ⊗

LAKE OSWEGO—30,600 (See PORTLAND ACCOMMODATIONS spotting map page A47; see index starting on page A46)

LODGINGS

BEST WESTERN SHERWOOD INN Rates Subject to Change **Phone:** 503/620-2980 (28)
AAA ◆◆ Motor Inn
All Year 1P: $50- 60 2P/1B: $55- 65 2P/2B: $58 XP: $5 F12
Location: off I-5 exit 291; 10 mi s of Portland. 15700 SW Upper Boones Ferry Rd 97035. Fax: 503/639-9010. **Terms:** Sr. discount; reserv deposit, 3 day notice; small pets only, $5. **Facility:** 101 rooms. Very well maintained units & guest facilities. Some spacious, units. 3 one-bedroom suites with wet bar & refrigerator, $70; 3 stories; interior corridors; meeting rooms; heated indoor pool, sauna; exercise room. **Dining & Entertainment:** Restaurant; 6 am-11 pm, Sun 6:30 am-11 pm; $7-$12; cocktails/lounge. **Services:** data ports. Fee: coin laundry. **All Rooms:** free movies, combo & shower baths, cable TV. **Some Rooms:** Fee: whirlpools. **Cards:** AE, CB, DI, DS, MC, VI. (D) ⊗

HOLIDAY INN CROWNE PLAZA Rates Subject to Change **Phone:** 503/624-8400 (27)
AAA ◆◆◆ Hotel
6/1-9/6 1P: $90- 115 2P/1B: $105- 130 2P/2B: $105- 130 XP: $15 F18
3/1-5/31 & 9/7-2/29 1P: $85- 110 2P/1B: $100- 125 2P/2B: $100- 125 XP: $15 F18
Location: Off I-5, exit 292 at jct SR 217. 14811 Kruse Oaks Blvd 97035. Fax: 503/684-8324. **Terms:** Sr. discount; pets. **Facility:** 161 rooms. In suburban location. Attractive contemporary exterior. Very nicely appointed & comfortably equipped guest rooms. 12 one-bedroom suites, $110-$195; 6 stories; interior corridors; conference facilities; luxury level rooms; heated indoor/outdoor pool, sauna, whirlpool; exercise room. **Dining & Entertainment:** Restaurant; 6 am-10 pm; $8-$15; cocktails/lounge. **Services:** data ports. Fee: airport transportation. **All Rooms:** free movies, cable TV. **Some Rooms:** refrigerators. Fee: VCP's. **Cards:** AE, CB, DI, DS, JCB, MC, VI. (D) (S) ⊗

PHOENIX INN Guaranteed Rates **Phone:** 503/624-7400 (29)
AAA ◆◆◆ Motel
All Year [CP] 1P: $56 2P/1B: $62 2P/2B: $64 XP: $5 F17
Location: Off I-5 exit 292, s of Jct SR 217. 14905 SW Bangy Rd 97034. Fax: 503/624-7405. **Terms:** No pets. **Facility:** 62 rooms. Attractively decorated guest rooms. 4 suites with whirlpool; 4 stories; interior corridors; meeting rooms; heated indoor pool, whirlpool; exercise room. **Dining:** Restaurant nearby. **Services:** data ports. Fee: coin laundry. **All Rooms:** microwaves, free movies, refrigerators, cable TV. **Cards:** AE, CB, DI, DS, MC, VI. (D) (S) ⊗

RESTAURANTS

AMADEUS **Dinner:** $11-$20 **Phone:** 503/636-7500 (18)
AAA ◆◆ Continental
Location: 2 blks w of SR 43 on B Ave. 148 B Ave at 2nd 97034. **Hours:** 11 am-2:30 & 5-10 pm, Sun 10 am-2 & 5-10 pm. Closed: 12/25. **Reservations:** suggested. **Features:** Sunday brunch; children's menu; early bird specials; senior's menu; carryout; cocktails. Dining room with charming intimate atmosphere. Classic seafood, lamb, poultry & beef dishes. Pianist accompaniment. Balcony dining in-season. **Cards:** AE, MC, VI. ⊗

OLIVE GARDEN ITALIAN RESTAURANT **Dinner:** $11-$20 **Phone:** 503/684-3160 (16)
◆◆ Italian
Location: I-5 exit 292; s of jct SR 217. 6355 SW Meadows Rd 97035. **Hours:** 11 am-10 pm, Fri & Sat-11 pm. Closed: 11/23 & 12/25. **Features:** children's menu; health conscious menu items; carryout; cocktails & lounge; a la carte. Warm, friendly atmosphere. Good selection of hearty traditional dishes. Classic desserts. **Cards:** AE, CB, DI, DS, MC, VI. ⊗

RICCARDO'S **Dinner:** $11-$20 **Phone:** 503/636-4104 (17)
◆◆ Northern Italian
Location: 16035 SE Boones Ferry Rd 97035. **Hours:** 11:30 am-2:30 & 5-10 pm, Fri & Sat-10:30 pm; in winter-9:30 pm, Fri & Sat-10 pm. Closed major holidays & Sun. **Reservations:** suggested. **Features:** carryout; cocktails. Very tastefully prepared pasta, veal, free range chicken, lamb & seafood dishes. Cozy, colorfully decorated restaurant. Also attractive outside patio dining. Smoke free premises. **Cards:** AE, CB, DI, MC, VI. ⊗

LAKEVIEW—2,500

LODGING

BEST WESTERN SKYLINE MOTOR LODGE Rates Subject to Change **Phone:** 503/947-2194
AAA ◆◆ Motel
4/1-10/1 [CP] 1P: $50- 54 2P/1B: $56- 60 2P/2B: $62- 68 XP: $6
3/1-3/31 & 10/2-2/29 [CP] 1P: $44- 48 2P/1B: $50- 54 2P/2B: $56- 58 XP: $6
Location: At jct US 395 & SR 140. 414 N G St 97630. Fax: 503/947-3100. **Terms:** Credit card guarantee, 3 day notice; pets, $50 dep req. **Facility:** 38 rooms. Attractively decorated units. 2 stories; exterior corridors; heated indoor pool, whirlpool. **Dining:** Restaurant nearby. **Services:** Fee: coin laundry. **All Rooms:** coffeemakers, free movies, refrigerators, cable TV. **Some Rooms:** microwaves. **Cards:** AE, CB, DI, DS, JCB, MC, VI. (D) ⊗

LINCOLN CITY—5,900

LODGINGS

BEST WESTERN LINCOLN SANDS INN Rates Subject to Change **Phone:** 503/994-4227
AAA ◆◆◆ Motel
7/1-8/31 [CP] 1P: $120- 140 2P/1B: $130- 160 2P/2B: $130- 160 XP: $10
5/1-6/30 & 9/1-10/31 [CP] 1P: $80- 120 2P/1B: $90- 130 2P/2B: $90- 130 XP: $10
3/1-4/30 & 11/1-2/29 [CP] 1P: $70- 100 2P/1B: $85- 115 2P/2B: $85- 115 XP: $10
Location: 1 blk w of US 101 off NW 6th. 535 NW Inlet 97367. **Terms:** Check-in 4 pm; credit card guarantee; small pets only. **Facility:** 33 rooms. Large 1- & 2-bedroom suites with balcony or patio & ocean views. 2 two-bedroom loft units, $250; 3 stories; exterior corridors; beachfront; heated pool, whirlpool. **Dining:** Restaurants nearby. **All Rooms:** free movies, combo & shower baths, cable TV, no A/C. **Cards:** AE, DI, MC, VI.
(See color ad p A32) Roll in showers. (D) ⊗

BEST WESTERN RAMA INN Rates Subject to Change **Phone:** 503/994-6060
AAA ◆◆◆ Motel
6/1-9/15 [CP] 1P: $80 2P/1B: $80- 120 2P/2B: $80- 120 XP: $5 F12
3/1-5/31 & 9/16-2/29 [CP] 1P: $60 2P/1B: $65- 80 2P/2B: $65- 80 XP: $5 F12
Location: South side on Hwy 101. 4430 SE Hwy 101. Fax: 503/994-6066. **Terms:** Sr. discount; credit card guarantee, 3 day notice; no pets. **Facility:** 60 rooms. Attractive units, many with balcony or patio. Inviting lobby. 8 one-bedroom suites, 3 with fireplace, $100, $77 off-season; 2 with whirlpool $125, $100 off-season; 3 stories; interior corridors; meeting rooms; heated indoor pool, sauna, whirlpool; exercise room. **Services:** data ports. Fee: coin laundry. **All Rooms:** free movies, cable TV. **Some Rooms:** microwaves, refrigerators. Fee: VCP's. **Cards:** AE, CB, DI, DS, JCB, MC, VI. (D) (S) ⊗

COHO INN — Rates Subject to Change — **Phone:** 503/994-3684

AAA ◆◆ Motel

6/15-9/30	1P: $64- 68	2P/1B: $64- 68	2P/2B: $68	XP: $6	
4/1-6/14	1P: $54- 58	2P/1B: $54- 58	2P/2B: $58	XP: $6	
3/1-3/31 & 10/1-2/29	1P: $44- 48	2P/1B: $44- 48	2P/2B: $48	XP: $6	

Location: 3 blks w of Hwy 101, exit N 17th St. 1635 NW Harbor 97367. **Terms:** Check-in 4 pm; reserv deposit; small pets only, $6. **Facility:** 50 rooms. Excellently maintained. 1- & 2-room units, some with efficiencies. Some 1-bedroom units with sitting room & fireplace. Beach access 1/2 blk. 2-room units, most with efficiencies, some with fireplace $70-$82, 6/15-9/30; 3 stories; exterior corridors; oceanview; sauna, whirlpool. **All Rooms:** coffeemakers, free movies, combo & shower baths, cable TV, no A/C. **Some Rooms:** radios, refrigerators. **Cards:** AE, DS, MC, VI. Ⓓ ⊗

DOCK OF THE BAY MOTEL — Rates Subject to Change — **Phone:** 503/996-3549

AAA ◆◆ Motel

All Year	1P: $75- 98	2P/1B: $75- 98	2P/2B: $119- 149	XP: $10	D9

Location: S side, w of Hwy 101, exit SW 51st St. 1116 SW 51st St 97367. **Terms:** Sr. discount; credit card guarantee, 3 day notice; small pets only, $5 per pet. **Facility:** 30 rooms. Along bayshore. 1-bedroom suites with sitting room, bay view, balcony or patio & fireplace, kitchen. Also, 6 one-room units. Some covered parking. 11 two-bedroom units. 11 two-bedroom loft units, from $149; 3 stories; exterior corridors; sauna, whirlpool. **Dining:** Restaurant nearby. **All Rooms:** coffeemakers, combo & shower baths, cable TV, no A/C. **Some Rooms:** Fee: VCP's. **Cards:** MC, VI. Ⓓ ⊗

D-SANDS CONDOMINIUM MOTEL — Rates Subject to Change — **Phone:** 503/994-5244

AAA ◆◆◆ Condo Motel

Fri & Sat & Sun-Thurs 5/21-9/15	1P: $91	2P/1B: $99- 109	2P/2B: $99- 109	XP: $8	F8
Sun-Thurs 3/1-5/20 & 9/16-2/29	1P: $50- 70	2P/1B: $50- 70	2P/2B: $50- 80	XP: $8	F8

Location: On US 101 next to D River Wayside. 171 SW Hwy 101 97367. Fax: 503/994-7484. **Terms:** Sr. discount; check-in 4 pm; reserv deposit; no pets. **Facility:** 63 rooms. All ocean view with balcony or patio. Comfortable 1-room units & 1 bedroom suites with kitchen, 24 with fireplace. Some covered parking. 42 two-bedroom units. 3 stories; exterior corridors; beachfront; heated indoor pool, whirlpool. **Dining:** Restaurant nearby. **All Rooms:** free movies, cable TV, no A/C. **Cards:** AE, DI, DS, MC, VI. Ⓓ ⊗

THE INN AT SPANISH HEAD — Rates Subject to Change — **Phone:** 503/996-2161

AAA ◆◆◆ Condo Motor Inn

All Year	1P: $99- 168	2P/1B: $99- 168	2P/2B: $99- 168	XP: $15	F16

Location: S side on US 101. 4009 SW Hwy 101 97367. Fax: 503/996-4089. **Terms:** Check-in 4 pm; reserv deposit, 5 day notice; no pets. **Facility:** 120 rooms. Against cliff on oceanfront with outstanding ocean view. Guest rooms & 1- & 2-bedroom suites, each with balcony & efficiency or kitchen. 10 stories; interior/exterior corridors; conference facilities; beach access, heated pool, saunas, whirlpool; recreation room. **Dining & Entertainment:** Dining room; 8 am-10 pm, Fri & Sat-11 pm; $8-$22; cocktails/lounge; 24-hour room service. **Services:** guest laundry; valet parking. **All Rooms:** cable TV, no A/C. **Some Rooms:** 36 efficiencies. **Cards:** AE, CB, DI, DS, MC, VI. *(See ad below)* Ⓓ ⊗

Best Western
LINCOLN SANDS INN
All Suites - On the Beach
Private patio, ocean view, living room, fully equipped deluxe kitchen, heated pool and spa, HBO, handicap rooms, elevator and restaurants nearby.
Call (503) 994-4227 *or*
Toll FreeNumber
1 (800) 445-3234
535 N.W. INLET STREET • LINCOLN CITY • OREGON 97367

Every room has an ocean view with a story to tell of lost treasure and found romance. Some say when the sun sets just right you can see mermaids playing in the surf.

Scenic dining, heated pool, spa.
Inn At Spanish Head
4009 S.W. Highway 101
Lincoln City, OR 97367
1-800-452-8127

LINCOLN SHORES MOTEL Guaranteed Rates **Phone:** 503/994-8155

◆◆ Motel

5/1-10/1 1P: $50- 80 2P/1B: $50- 100 2P/2B: $55- 110 XP: $5
3/1-4/30 & 10/2-2/29 1P: $40- 70 2P/1B: $40- 70 2P/2B: $45- 75 XP: $5

Location: On Hwy 101 near D River. 136 NE Hwy 101 97367. Fax: 503/994-5581. **Terms:** Sr. discount; check-in 4 pm; reserv deposit; no pets. **Facility:** 30 rooms. Alpine exterior style, on trim grounds. Roomy, neatly appointed units, most with balcony. Kitchen units $15 extra; 3 fireplace units $5 extra; 2 stories; interior/exterior corridors. **Dining:** Restaurant nearby. **All Rooms:** combo & shower baths, cable TV, no A/C. Fee: movies. **Some Rooms:** coffeemakers. **Cards:** AE, DI, DS, MC, VI.

NORDIC MOTEL Rates Subject to Change **Phone:** 503/994-8145

◆◆ Motel

Fri & Sat & Sun-Thurs 5/22-10/3 2P/1B: $61- 79 2P/2B: $65- 79 XP: $4
Sun-Thurs 3/1-5/21 & 10/4-2/29 2P/1B: $51- 69 2P/2B: $55- 69 XP: $4

Location: 4 blks w of US 101, exit NW 21st St. 2133 NW Inlet 97367. Fax: 503/994-2329. **Terms:** Check-in 4 pm; reserv deposit; no pets. **Facility:** 52 rooms. Overlooking ocean. Very good, immaculately kept units, some with fireplace. 1-bedroom suites with efficiency & fireplace. Sun deck facing beach. 6 one-bedroom suites with fireplace, kitchen & 1 with efficiency; 3 stories; exterior corridors; beachfront; meeting rooms; beach access, heated indoor pool, saunas, whirlpool. **All Rooms:** cable TV, no A/C. **Some Rooms:** coffeemakers. **Cards:** CB, DI, DS, MC, VI.

RESTAURANTS

BAY HOUSE **Dinner:** $21-$30 **Phone:** 503/996-3222

◆◆◆ Continental

Location: 3 1/2 mi s on US 101, on Siletz Bay. 5911 SW Hwy 101 97367. **Hours:** 5:30 pm-9:30 pm, Sat from 5 pm. Closed major holidays, Mon & Tues 9/6-5/1. **Reservations:** suggested. **Features:** children's menu; health conscious menu; cocktails. Contemporary atmosphere overlooking Siletz Bay. Excellently prepared & artistically presented entrees, featuring Northwest cuisine with emphasis on seafood, meat & pasta. Smoke free premises. **Cards:** AE, DS, MC, VI.

DORY COVE **Dinner:** $11-$20 **Phone:** 503/994-5180

◆◆ American

Location: 1 mi n of jct US 101 & Logan Rd. 5819 Logan Rd 97368. **Hours:** 11:30 am-9 pm, 10/1-5/14 to 8 pm, Fri & Sat-9 pm, Sun noon-8 pm. Closed: 11/23 & Dec. **Features:** No A/C; children's menu; senior's menu; health conscious menu; beer & wine only. Popular, long-established. Very pleasant atmosphere & friendly service. Generous lunch & dinner entrees, emphasis on seafood; also large selection of sandwiches & hamburgers. Smoke free premises. **Cards:** MC, VI.

LONG CREEK—300

LODGING

LONG CREEK LODGE Rates Subject to Change **Phone:** 503/421-9212

◆◆ Motel

All Year 1P: $36 2P/1B: $40 2P/2B: $44 XP: $5

Location: 1/2 blk w of Hwy 395 & Main St. 171 W Main 97856 (PO Box 428). **Terms:** Reserv deposit; no pets. **Facility:** 9 rooms. Spacious units with hunting & logging decor in the lobby. 2 stories; interior corridors. **Services:** Fee: coin laundry. **All Rooms:** refrigerators, combo & shower baths, cable TV, no A/C, no phones. **Some Rooms:** microwaves, radios. **Cards:** MC, VI.

MADRAS—3,400

LODGINGS

LEISURE INN Rates Subject to Change **Phone:** 503/475-6141

◆ Motel

Fri & Sat [CP] 1P: $50 2P/1B: $55 2P/2B: $60 XP: $5 F12
Sun-Thurs 5/16-9/30 [CP] 1P: $45 2P/1B: $45 2P/2B: $51 XP: $5 F12
Sun-Thurs 3/1-5/15 & 10/1-2/29 [CP] 1P: $39 2P/1B: $44 2P/2B: $49 XP: $5 F12

Location: On Hwy 97 & Hwy 26 southbound. 12 SW 4th 97741. Fax: 503/475-2982. **Terms:** Sr. discount; credit card guarantee; no pets. **Facility:** 48 rooms. 2 stories; exterior corridors; heated pool. **Dining:** Restaurant nearby. **All Rooms:** free movies, cable TV. **Some Rooms:** refrigerators. Fee: VCP's. **Cards:** AE, DI, DS, MC, VI.

SONNY'S MOTEL Rates Subject to Change **Phone:** 503/475-7217

◆◆ Motor Inn

All Year [CP] 1P: $41 2P/1B: $48 2P/2B: $48 XP: $6 F6

Location: 1 mi s on Hwy 97. 1539 SW Hwy 97 97741. Fax: 503/475-6547. **Terms:** Sr. discount; reserv deposit, 3 day notice; pets, $7. **Facility:** 44 rooms. Comfortable units. 2 two-bedroom units. 2 one-bedroom suites with whirlpool, $65-$75; 2 stories; exterior corridors; heated pool, whirlpool. **Dining & Entertainment:** Restaurant; 4 pm-10 pm, Sun 7:30 am-12:30 & 4-9 pm; $8-$15; cocktail lounge. **Services:** Fee: coin laundry. **All Rooms:** free movies, cable TV. **Some Rooms:** 2 kitchens, refrigerators. **Cards:** AE, CB, DI, DS, MC, VI.

MCMINNVILLE—17,900

LODGINGS

BEST WESTERN VINEYARD INN AAA Special Value Rates **Phone:** 503/472-4900

◆◆ Motel

All Year [CP] 1P: $57- 65 2P/1B: $62- 70 2P/2B: $72- 80 XP: $6 F12

Location: 1 mi s on Hwy 99W. 2035 SW 99W 97128. Fax: 503/472-6399. **Terms:** Reserv deposit, 3 day notice; small pets only, $10. **Facility:** 65 rooms. Very comfortable rooms with decor reflecting grape harvest theme. 3 units with whirlpool $95; 4 stories; interior corridors; meeting rooms; heated indoor pool, whirlpool; exercise room, small game room. **Dining:** Restaurant nearby. **Services:** Fee: coin laundry. **All Rooms:** microwaves, free movies, refrigerators, cable TV. Fee: VCP. **Some Rooms:** coffeemakers. **Cards:** AE, CB, DI, DS, MC, VI.

SAFARI MOTOR INN Guaranteed Rates **Phone:** 503/472-5187

◆◆ Motor Inn

All Year 1P: $40 2P/1B: $44- 49 2P/2B: $46- 48 XP: $3

Location: 1 mi n on Hwy 99W. 345 N Hwy 99W 97128. Fax: 503/434-6380. **Terms:** Sr. discount; credit card guarantee, 3 day notice; no pets. **Facility:** 90 rooms. Spacious, very comfortably equipped units. 2 stories; exterior corridors; meeting rooms; whirlpool. **Dining:** Restaurant; 6:30 am-9 pm, Sun 7 am-3 pm; $4-$10; cocktails. **All Rooms:** free movies, cable TV. **Cards:** AE, CB, DI, DS, MC, VI.

MEDFORD—47,000

LODGINGS

BEST WESTERN MEDFORD INN Rates Subject to Change **Phone:** 503/773-8266
AAA 5/1-9/30 1P: $48- 52 2P/1B: $54- 58 2P/2B: $58- 64 XP: $6 F12
3/1-4/30 & 10/1-2/29 1P: $42- 46 2P/1B: $48- 52 2P/2B: $52- 58 XP: $6 F12
◆◆◆ Motel
Location: On Hwy 99; 2 blks w of I-5 exit 27. 1015 S Riverside 97501. Fax: 503/734-5447. **Terms:** No pets. **Facility:** 112 rooms. Very attractively furnished & decorated units. 5 two-bedroom units. 2 stories; exterior corridors; meeting rooms; pool. **Dining:** Restaurant nearby. **Services:** data ports. **All Rooms:** coffeemakers, combo & shower baths, cable TV. **Some Rooms:** refrigerators, whirlpools. **Cards:** AE, CB, DI, DS, MC, VI. Roll in showers. (D) ⊗

BEST WESTERN PONY SOLDIER MOTOR INN Rates Subject to Change **Phone:** 503/779-2011
AAA 5/15-9/30 [CP] 1P: $71- 76 2P/1B: $73- 78 2P/2B: $78- 83 XP: $5 F12
3/1-5/14 & 10/1-2/29 [CP] 1P: $65- 70 2P/1B: $67- 72 2P/2B: $72- 77 XP: $5 F12
◆◆◆ Motel
Location: 2 mi n on SR 62; 1 blk e of I-5 exit 30. 2340 Crater Lake Hwy 97504. Fax: 503/779-7304. **Terms:** Sr. discount; reserv deposit; small pets only. **Facility:** 72 rooms. Very tastefully appointed & well-furnished units. 2 stories; exterior corridors; meeting rooms; heated pool, whirlpool. **Dining:** Restaurant nearby. **Services:** data ports; guest laundry; airport transportation. **All Rooms:** free movies, refrigerators, cable TV. **Cards:** AE, CB, DI, DS, JCB, MC, VI. (D) ⊗

CEDAR LODGE MOTOR INN Rates Subject to Change **Phone:** 503/773-7361
AAA 5/1-10/31 1P: $37- 40 2P/1B: $45- 52 2P/2B: $49- 62 XP: $5 F12
3/1-4/30 & 11/1-2/29 1P: $32- 38 2P/1B: $40- 45 2P/2B: $46- 51 XP: $5 F12
◆ Motel
Location: On Hwy 99N; off I-5 northbound exit 27, southbound exit 30. 518 N Riverside 97501. Fax: 503/776-1033. **Terms:** Sr. discount; credit card guarantee, 3 day notice; pets, $10 dep req. **Facility:** 79 rooms. Very hospitably operated. 2 two-bedroom units. 2 stories; exterior corridors; heated pool. **Dining:** Restaurant nearby. **All Rooms:** free movies, combo & shower baths, cable TV. **Some Rooms:** kitchen, microwaves, refrigerators. **Cards:** AE, CB, DI, DS, MC, VI. (D) ⊗

HOLIDAY INN MEDFORD Rates Subject to Change **Phone:** 503/779-3141
AAA 5/27-9/3 1P: $75 2P/1B: $75 2P/2B: $75 XP: $5 F19
9/4-2/29 1P: $62 2P/1B: $62 2P/2B: $62 XP: $5 F19
◆◆ 3/1-5/26 1P: $58 2P/1B: $58 2P/2B: $58 XP: $5 F19
Motor Inn
Location: 2 mi n on SR 62; jct I-5 exit 30. 2300 Crater Lake Hwy 97504. Fax: 503/779-2623. **Terms:** Sr. discount; pets, $25 dep req. **Facility:** 164 rooms. Many attractively refurbished units. Poolside restaurant. 3 one-bedroom suites with refrigerator & wet bar, $120; 2 stories; interior corridors; conference facilities; putting green; heated indoor pool, wading pool; indoor recreation area. **Dining & Entertainment:** Restaurant; 6:30 am-2 & 5-10 pm, Sat & Sun 6:30 am-2 & 5-10 pm; $8-$15; cocktails/lounge. **Services:** airport transportation. Fee: coin laundry. **All Rooms:** cable TV. **Cards:** AE, CB, DI, DS, JCB, MC, VI. (D) ⊗

HORIZON MOTOR INN Rates Subject to Change **Phone:** 503/779-5085
AAA All Year 1P: $52- 61 2P/1B: $57- 61 2P/2B: $60 XP: $6 F17
◆◆ Motor Inn
Location: 1 blk e of I-5 on Barnett Rd; exit 27. 1150 E Barnett Rd 97501. Fax: 503/779-5085. **Terms:** Credit card guarantee; pets, $10. **Facility:** 128 rooms. Very attractive exterior layout, nicely decorated units. 2 two-bedroom units. 2 suites, 1 with whirlpool, $90-$150, 3 large units with refrigerator, wet bar & microwave, $70; 2 stories; exterior corridors; meeting rooms; heated pool, sauna, whirlpool. **Dining:** Restaurant; 24 hours; $6-$11; cocktails. **Services:** airport transportation. **Recreation:** bicycles. **All Rooms:** free movies, cable TV. Fee: VCP. **Cards:** AE, DI, MC, VI. *(See ad below)* (D) ⊗

PEAR TREE MOTEL Rates Subject to Change **Phone:** 503/535-4445
AAA 4/1-9/30 1P: $59 2P/1B: $59 2P/2B: $68 XP: $6 F13
3/1-3/31 & 10/1-2/29 1P: $49 2P/1B: $49 2P/2B: $55 XP: $6 F13
◆◆◆ Motel
Location: 3 mi s on I-5, exit 24. 3730 Fern Valley Rd 97504. Fax: 503/535-3960. **Terms:** Credit card guarantee; no pets. **Facility:** 46 rooms. Large, very attractive & comfortably furnished units. 2 stories; exterior corridors; meeting rooms; heated pool, whirlpool; playground. **Dining:** Restaurant nearby. **Services:** Fee: coin laundry. **All Rooms:** combo & shower baths, cable TV. Fee: movies. **Some Rooms:** refrigerators. Fee: VCP's. **Cards:** AE, DI, DS, MC, VI. (D) (S) ⊗

RED LION INN AAA Special Value Rates **Phone:** 503/779-5811
◆◆◆ 6/15-9/15 1P: $74- 89 2P/1B: $89- 104 2P/2B: $89- 104 XP: $15 F18
Motor Inn 3/1-6/14 & 9/16-2/29 1P: $69- 79 2P/1B: $79- 89 2P/2B: $79 XP: $15 F18
Location: On Hwy 99N; off I-5 northbound exit 27, southbound exit 30. 200 N Riverside 97501. Fax: 503/779-7961. **Terms:** Credit card guarantee, 3 day notice; pets. **Facility:** 186 rooms. Very attractively decorated units, some with balcony. 2 one-bedroom suites with whirlpool, wet bar, microwave & refrigerator $250; 2 stories; exterior corridors; conference facilities; 2 heated pools. **Dining:** Dining room, coffee shop; 6 am-11 pm; $7-$21; cocktails. **Services:** data ports; health club privileges; airport transportation. Fee: coin laundry. **All Rooms:** combo & shower baths, cable TV. Fee: movies. **Some Rooms:** Fee: VCP's. **Cards:** AE, CB, DI, DS, MC, VI. (D) ⊗

M · E · D · F · O · R · D
130 beautiful rooms (2 exec. suites) ■ Color TV w/movies, clock radios, direct dial phones, heated pool, jacuzzi and sauna ■ Restaurant, lounge, meeting and banquet rooms ■ FREE airport shuttle
10% commission paid promptly
HORIZON MOTOR INN
1154 E. BARNETT ROAD, MEDFORD OREGON 97504 (503) 779-5085
Nationwide: 1-800-452-2255

ROGUE REGENCY INN
MEDFORD, OREGON
• Close to all attractions • 124 mini-suite rooms w/refrigerators, microwaves, coffee makers, hair dryers, bar sinks and free HBO • Pool & spa • Regency Grill with full-service cocktail lounge.
1-800-535-5805

ROGUE REGENCY INN AAA Special Value Rates **Phone:** 503/770-1234

◆◆◆ Motor Inn

All Year 1P: $71 2P/1B: $81 2P/2B: $81 XP: $10 F18

Location: Off I-5, exit 30. 2345 Crater Lake Hwy 97501 (PO Box A). Fax: 503/770-2466. **Terms:** Credit card guarantee; no pets. **Facility:** 124 rooms. Large attractive rooms. 9 suites with whirlpool & fireplace, $145-$250; 4 stories; interior corridors; conference facilities; heated pool, whirlpool. **Dining & Entertainment:** Dining room; 6 am-10 pm; $9-$16; cocktail lounge. **Services:** data ports; area transportation, to Rogue Valley Mall, airport transportation. **All Rooms:** coffeemakers, microwaves, free movies, refrigerators, cable TV. **Some Rooms:** Fee: VCP's. **Cards:** AE, CB, DI, DS, JCB, MC, VI. *(See ad p A34)* (D) (S) ⊗

WINDMILL INN OF MEDFORD AAA Special Value Rates **Phone:** 503/779-0050

◆◆◆ Motel

6/1-9/30 [CP]	1P: $65	2P/1B: $65	2P/2B: $75	XP: $6	F18
3/1-5/31 & 10/1-2/29 [CP]	1P: $55	2P/1B: $55	2P/2B: $65	XP: $6	F18

Location: 2 mi n; 1 blk s of jct I-5, exit 30. 1950 Biddle Rd 97504. Fax: 503/779-0050. **Terms:** Credit card guarantee, 3 day notice; pets. **Facility:** 123 rooms. Large, especially well kept rooms. 2 stories; interior corridors; meeting rooms; heated pool, sauna, whirlpool. **Dining:** Restaurant nearby. **Services:** data ports; area transportation, to Rogue Valley Mall, airport transportation. **Recreation:** bicycles. **All Rooms:** free movies, combo & shower baths, cable TV. **Some Rooms:** efficiency, kitchen, whirlpools. **Cards:** AE, DI, DS, MC, VI.
(See ad below) Roll in showers. (D) ⊗

MILWAUKIE—18,700 (See PORTLAND ACCOMMODATIONS spotting map page A47; see index starting on page A46)

LODGING

ECONO LODGE SUITES INN Rates Subject to Change **Phone:** 503/654-2222 (79)

◆◆ Motel

6/16-9/30 [CP]	1P: $54- 64	2P/1B: $60- 72	2P/2B: $64- 78	XP: $8	F12
3/1-6/15 & 10/1-2/29 [CP]	1P: $54- 60	2P/1B: $54- 64	2P/2B: $64- 72	XP: $6	F12

Location: 3 1/2 mi s on Hwy 99E; 2 mi n of Oregon City; 1 1/2 mi n of Jct I-205 exit 9 & Hwy 99E. 17330 SE McLoughlin Blvd 97267. Fax: 503/654-1300. **Terms:** Sr. discount; reserv deposit, 7 day notice; no pets. **Facility:** 25 rooms. Nicely furnished & decorated units. Suite with whirlpool, $75; Fri & Sat, $85; 2 stories; exterior corridors; heated pool, whirlpool. **Dining:** Restaurant nearby. **Services:** Fee: coin laundry. **All Rooms:** free movies, refrigerators, cable TV. **Some Rooms:** microwaves. **Cards:** AE, CB, DI, DS, MC, VI. *(See ad below)* (D) (S) ⊗

RESTAURANT

AMADEUS AT THE FERNWOOD **Dinner:** $21-$30 **Phone:** 503/659-1735 (47)

◆◆ Continental

Location: Off Hwy 99E, take River Rd. 2122 SE Sparrow Rd 97222. **Hours:** 11 am-2:30 & 5-10 pm, Fri & Sat-11 pm, Sun 10 am-2:30 & 5-10 pm. Closed: 1/1 & 12/25. **Reservations:** accepted. **Features:** Sunday brunch; children's menu; early bird specials; senior's menu; cocktails & lounge. In former chateau-style home in forested hillside with some view of the Willamette River. Seafood, lamb, poultry & steak selections. Piano accompaniment. Smoke free premises. **Cards:** AE, MC, VI. ⊗

WINDMILL INN of Medford
1950 Biddle Rd • Medford, OR 97504
Toll Free 800-547-4747
Hospitality Guaranteed!

- Complimentary Morning Coffee, Muffin and Newspaper Delivered to Your Room
- Free Airport & Mall Shuttle
- Free Coffee, Iced Tea, Fresh Apples in Lobby
- Indoor Whirlpool & Sauna, and Outdoor Pool
- Use of Guest Bicycles
- Use of "Best Seller" Lending Library
- Free Local Telephone Calls
- Free Movie Channels
- Children Under 18 Stay Free In An Adults Room
- AAA Discount

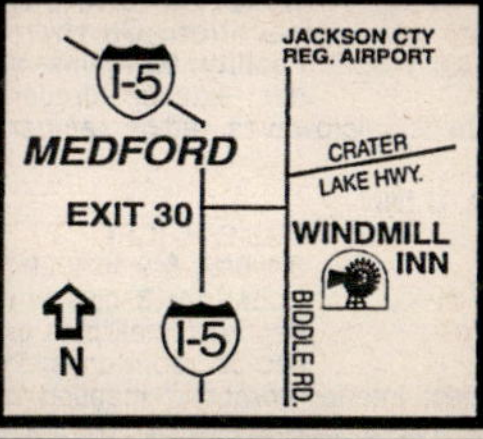

WHEN YOU'RE LIVING OUT OF A SUITCASE...

Econo Lodge

In Milwaukie/ Portland
Econo Lodge
17330 S.E. McLoughlin Blvd.
Milwaukie, OR 97267

- Indoor/outdoor heated pool & spa
- In-room Jacuzzi
- HBO
- Free continental breakfast
- All suites with microwaves & refrigerators

For reservations call 503-654-2222, fax 503-654-1300 or toll-free 1-800-4-CHOICE

MYRTLE POINT—2,700

LODGING

MYRTLE TREES MOTEL Rates Subject to Change **Phone:** 503/572-5811

AAA ◆ Motel

All Year 1P: $32- 39 2P/1B: $36- 39 2P/2B: $41 XP: $5

Location: 1/2 mi e on SR 42. 1010 8th St-Hwy 42 97458. **Terms:** Credit card guarantee; small pets only, $5. **Facility:** 29 rooms. Exceptionally well-maintained units. Outdoor lawn area with picnic tables. 8 two-bedroom units. 2 stories; exterior corridors; city park nearby. **All Rooms:** combo & shower baths, cable TV, no A/C. **Some Rooms:** Fee: microwaves, refrigerators. **Cards:** AE, DS, MC, VI. Ⓓ ⊗

NEWBERG—13,100

LODGING

SHILO INN Rates Subject to Change **Phone:** 503/537-0303

◆◆◆ Motel

5/1-9/30 [CP] 1P: $65- 71 2P/1B: $65- 71 2P/2B: $65- 71 XP: $10 F12

3/1-4/30 & 10/1-2/29 [CP] 1P: $59- 62 2P/1B: $59- 62 2P/2B: $59- 62 XP: $10 F12

Location: 3/4 mi e on Hwy 99W. 501 Sitka Ave 97132. Fax: 503/537-0442. **Terms:** Sr. discount; pets, $7. **Facility:** 60 rooms. Large, very well equipped units. 2 efficiencies, $78; 3 stories; interior corridors; meeting rooms; sauna, whirlpool, heated small pool; exercise room. **Dining:** Restaurant nearby. **Services:** data ports. Fee: coin laundry. **All Rooms:** free movies. **Some Rooms:** microwaves, refrigerators. Fee: VCP's. **Cards:** AE, CB, DI, DS, JCB, MC, VI. Ⓓ Ⓢ ⊗

NEWPORT—8,400

LODGINGS

BEST WESTERN HALLMARK RESORT Rates Subject to Change **Phone:** 503/265-8853

AAA ◆◆ Motel

5/1-9/30 [CP] 1P: $90- 120 2P/1B: $95- 125 2P/2B: $107- 147 XP: $5 F12

3/1-4/30 & 10/1-2/29 [CP] 1P: $70- 80 2P/1B: $75- 95 2P/2B: $85- 105 XP: $5 F12

Location: 3 blks w of Hwy 101. 744 SW Elizabeth St 97365. Fax: 503/265-9449. **Terms:** Sr. discount; reserv deposit; small pets only, $5. **Facility:** 72 rooms. Well-equipped units, some with fireplace. 6 two-bedroom efficiency loft units with fireplace from $95-$110 in season; 3 stories; exterior corridors; oceanfront; beach access. **Dining & Entertainment:** Cocktail lounge; restaurant nearby. **Services:** Fee: coin laundry. **All Rooms:** free movies, cable TV, no A/C. **Some Rooms:** coffeemakers, refrigerators. Fee: VCP's, whirlpools. **Cards:** AE, CB, DI, DS, JCB, MC, VI. Ⓓ ⊗

EMBARCADERO RESORT HOTEL & MARINA Rates Subject to Change **Phone:** 503/265-8521

AAA ◆◆◆ Resort Motor Inn

Fri & Sat 1P: $86- 116 2P/1B: $86- 116 2P/2B: $86- 116

Sun-Thurs 1P: $67- 99 2P/1B: $67- 99 2P/2B: $67- 99

Location: 1 mi e of Hwy 101 & n end of bridge, on Yaquina Bay. 1000 SE Bay Blvd 97365. Fax: 503/265-7844. **Terms:** Sr. discount; check-in 4 pm; no pets. **Facility:** 80 rooms. Very attractive bayfront location & grounds. Near picturesque fishing village. Rooms & apartments with fireplace & balcony with view of bay. 2-bedroom suites, $163, off season $148; 3 stories; exterior corridors; conference facilities; heated indoor pool, saunas, whirlpools; marina. **Dining & Entertainment:** Dining room, restaurant, cafeteria; 7 am-10 pm; $10-$16; cocktails/lounge. **Services:** Fee: coin laundry. **Recreation:** charter fishing, bait shop, fishing & crabbing piers & cooking facilities. Fee: boating. **All Rooms:** cable TV, no A/C. Fee: movies. **Some Rooms:** 50 kitchens. Fee: VCP's. **Cards:** AE, DI, DS, MC, VI. *(See ad below)* Ⓓ ⊗

PUERTO NUEVO INN Rates Subject to Change **Phone:** 503/265-5767

AAA ◆◆ Motel

5/15-10/15 [CP] 1P: $42- 45 2P/1B: $42- 45 2P/2B: $45 XP: $5

3/1-5/14 & 10/16-2/29 [CP] 1P: $38- 42 2P/1B: $38- 42 2P/2B: $42 XP: $5

Location: On Hwy 101. 544 SW Coast Hwy 97365. **Terms:** Reserv deposit, 3 day notice; no pets. **Facility:** 32 rooms. Very neatly appointed units. Units with whirlpool, efficiency & fireplace, $70-$100; 2 stories; exterior corridors; whirlpool. **All Rooms:** cable TV, VCP's, no A/C. **Some Rooms:** coffeemakers, 2 kitchens, microwaves, radios, refrigerators. **Cards:** AE, CB, DI, DS, MC, VI. Ⓓ ⊗

VAL-U INN Guaranteed Rates **Phone:** 503/265-6203

AAA ◆◆ Motel

6/15-9/15 [CP] 1P: $72 2P/1B: $72 2P/2B: $82 XP: $5 F12

3/1-6/14 & 9/16-2/29 [CP] 1P: $45 2P/1B: $45 2P/2B: $55 XP: $5 F12

Location: 3 blks w of Hwy 101. 531 SW Fall St 97365. Fax: 503/265-6623. **Terms:** Sr. discount; reserv deposit; small pets only, $5. **Facility:** 71 rooms. Very attractively furnished & traditionally decorated units. 5 two-bedroom units. 11 kitchens $78-$92, $73-$88 off season; 4 units with whirlpool $120, $98 low-season; 3 stories; interior corridors; meeting rooms. **Services:** Fee: coin laundry. **All Rooms:** cable TV, no A/C. **Some Rooms:** Fee: VCP's. **Cards:** AE, CB, DI, DS, MC, VI. *(See ad below)* Ⓓ ⊗

Resort Hotel & Marina
EMBARCADERO

- BEAUTIFUL YAQUINA BAY VIEW FROM ALL ROOMS
- PATIO GUESTROOMS, 1&2 BEDROOM SUITES W/KITCHEN & FIREPLACE
- INDOOR SWIMMING POOL, SAUNAS, JACUZZI
- EXCELLENT FISHING, CRABBING, BOATING
- SEAFOOD RESTAURANT & LOUNGE OVERLOOKING THE BAY

1000 S.E. BAY BLVD., NEWPORT, OR 97365
TOLL FREE NATIONWIDE 1-800-547-4779
OR CALL (503) 265-8521

VAL-U INN MOTEL
NEWPORT

•Guest Laundry •Spa Bath Units •Complimentary Continental Breakfast •Kitchen Units Available •15% Senior Citizen Discount (Sun.-Wed.)

For Reservations, call: 1-800-443-7777

531 S.W. Fall Street. Newport, OR 97365 (503) 265-6203

WHALER MOTEL Rates Subject to Change **Phone:** 503/265-9261

AAA ◆◆ Motel

All Year [CP] 1P: $85- 119 2P/1B: $85- 119 2P/2B: $95- 129

Location: 4 blks w of Hwy 101. 155 SW Elizabeth 97365. Fax: 503/265-9515. **Terms:** Sr. discount; reserv deposit, Sat & 7/1-9/30; small pets only, In designated rooms. **Facility:** 73 rooms. Exceptionally well-maintained, comfortable units. 6 units with efficiency & fireplace, 12 balcony junior suites; 2 stories; exterior corridors; oceanview; beach access. **Services:** Fee: coin laundry. **All Rooms:** free movies, cable TV, no A/C. **Some Rooms:** coffeemakers, microwaves, refrigerators. **Cards:** AE, DI, DS, MC, VI. *(See ad below)*

RESTAURANT

CANYON WAY **Dinner:** $11-$20 **Phone:** 503/265-8319

◆◆ American

Location: 1216 SW Canyon Way 97365. **Hours:** 11 am-3 & 5-9 pm; Sun 6/19-9/5, 5-9 pm. Closed major holidays. **Reservations:** suggested. **Features:** No A/C; children's menu; early bird specials; cocktails. Popular comfortable, informal atmosphere. Varied menu of fresh seafood, prime rib, steak & pasta. Also patio dining. Attractive book store. **Cards:** AE, DS, MC, VI.

NORTH BEND—9,600

LODGING

PONY VILLAGE MOTOR LODGE Rates Subject to Change **Phone:** 503/756-3191

AAA ◆ Motor Inn

All Year 1P: $42- 52 2P/1B: $53- 59 2P/2B: $55- 61 XP: $5 F12

Location: 8 blks w of Hwy 101 on Virginia Ave, at Pony Village Shopping Center. Virginia Ave 97459. Fax: 503/756-5818. **Terms:** Sr. discount; credit card guarantee, 3 day notice; pets, $3, in designated rooms. **Facility:** 119 rooms. Average to large size units. Some with covered parking. 1 two-bedroom unit. 1 family 2-room suite, $73; 2 stories; interior/exterior corridors; conference facilities. **Dining & Entertainment:** Dining room; 6 am-9 pm, Fri & Sat 10 pm; $6-$23; cocktails/lounge. **Services:** health club privileges. **All Rooms:** cable TV, no A/C. Fee: movies. **Some Rooms:** efficiency, microwaves, refrigerators. Fee: VCP's. **Cards:** AE, CB, DI, DS, MC, VI.

RESTAURANT

HILLTOP HOUSE RESTAURANT **Dinner:** $11-$20 **Phone:** 503/756-4160

AAA ◆◆ American

Location: 1 3/4 mi n off Hwy 101, near n end of bridge. 166 N Bay Dr 97459. **Hours:** 11:30 am-2:30 & 4-10 pm, Sun 10 am-2:30 & 4-9 pm. **Reservations:** suggested. **Features:** Sunday brunch; children's menu; early bird specials; carryout; cocktails & lounge; a la carte. Located on hilltop. Very pleasant dining with some view of bay. Nice selection of seafood, steaks & veal dishes. **Cards:** AE, MC, VI.

OAKLAND—800

RESTAURANT

TOLLY'S **Dinner:** $11-$20 **Phone:** 503/459-3796

◆◆ American

Location: Off I-5, exit 138. 115 Locust 97462. **Hours:** 9 am-9 pm. Closed major holidays. **Reservations:** suggested. **Features:** children's menu; health conscious menu items; cocktails; street parking. Located in "Old Town" in former Mercantile building. Original soda fountain. Turn-of-the century motif with antiques displayed. Moderate selection of beef & chicken entrees. Seasonal patio area noon-8:30 pm. **Cards:** AE, MC, VI.

OAKRIDGE—3,100

LODGING

BEST WESTERN OAKRIDGE INN Rates Subject to Change **Phone:** 503/782-2212

AAA ◆◆ Motel

All Year [CP] 1P: $45 2P/1B: $56 2P/2B: $60 XP: $5 F12

Location: 1/2 mi w on Hwy 58. 47433 Hwy 58 97463. Fax: 503/782-2811. **Terms:** Credit card guarantee; small pets only, $5. **Facility:** 40 rooms. Very neat, especially well kept units. 2 efficiencies, $65; 2 stories; exterior corridors; heated pool, whirlpool. **All Rooms:** no utensils, free movies, cable TV. **Some Rooms:** refrigerators. **Cards:** AE, CB, DI, DS, MC, VI.

THE WHALER
your oceanfront motel in Newport
Call Toll-Free for Reservations: 1-800-433-9444
155 SW Elizabeth St. • Newport, Oregon 97365 • (503) 265-9261
73 quiet, clean, comfortable rooms, each with a great ocean view!
• Queen-size beds • FREE Continental Breakfast • Guest Laundry Facilities
• Cable Color TV with FREE HBO – and FREE Fresh-Popped Popcorn
– Ask about our new Balcony Junior Suites –

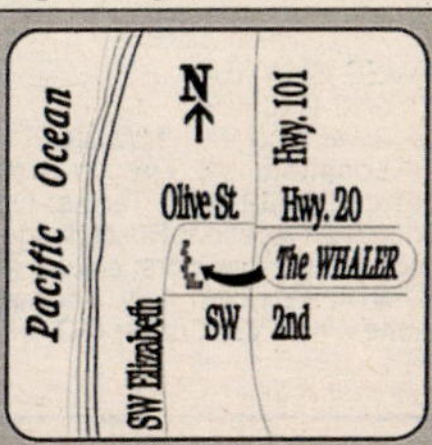

Checkout time
is noted in the listing if the required time
is before 10 a.m.

OCEANSIDE

LODGING

HOUSE ON THE HILL MOTEL — Rates Subject to Change — **Phone:** 503/842-6030

AAA ◆ Motel

5/1-10/31 1P: $75- 85 2P/1B: $75- 115 2P/2B: $95- 115 XP: $10
3/1-4/30 & 11/1-2/29 1P: $65- 75 2P/1B: $65- 90 2P/2B: $75- 100 XP: $10

Location: 9 mi w of Tillamook. Maxwell Point, Oceanside 97134 (PO Box 187). **Terms:** Credit card guarantee, 7 day notice, $10 cancellation fee; no pets. **Facility:** 16 rooms. On bluff overlooking ocean. Cozy 1 & 2-room units. 5 two-bedroom units. 1 bedroom suite with deck; 2 stories; exterior corridors; meeting rooms. **All Rooms:** combo & shower baths, cable TV, no A/C, no phones. **Some Rooms:** coffeemakers, 8 kitchens. **Cards:** MC, VI. *(See ad below)* (D) ⊗

RESTAURANT

ROSEANNA'S — **Dinner:** up to $10 — **Phone:** 503/842-7351

◆ American

Location: 1490 Pacific Ave 97134. **Hours:** 8 am-8 pm, Fri & Sat-9 pm. Closed: 1st 2 weeks in Dec. **Features:** No A/C; carryout; cocktails; a la carte. Small rustic restaurant overlooking ocean. Varied menu includes seafood, chicken, steaks, pasta dishes & salads. Smoke free premises. **Cards:** MC, VI. ⊗

ONTARIO—9,400

LODGINGS

BEST WESTERN INN — Rates Subject to Change — **Phone:** 503/889-2600

AAA ◆◆ Motel

All Year [CP] 1P: $56- 59 2P/1B: $59- 63 2P/2B: $69 XP: $4 F12

Location: E of I-84, exit 376. 251 Goodfellow St 97914. Fax: 503/889-2259. **Terms:** Sr. discount; reserv deposit, 30 day notice; small pets only, $20 dep req. **Facility:** 61 rooms. Nicely appointed units. 12 one-bedroom suites $80; 2 whirlpool units, $87; 2 stories; interior corridors; heated indoor pool, whirlpool; exercise room. **Dining:** Restaurant nearby. **Services:** Fee: coin laundry. **All Rooms:** free movies, cable TV. **Some Rooms:** coffeemakers, microwaves, refrigerators, VCP's. **Cards:** AE, CB, DI, DS, MC, VI. (D) ⊗

HOLIDAY MOTEL — Rates Subject to Change — **Phone:** 503/889-9188

◆ Motor Inn

All Year 1P: $29 2P/1B: $35 2P/2B: $39 XP: $5 F12

Location: On Hwy 30 business rt; 1 blk w of I-84 exit 376. 615 E Idaho 97914. Fax: 503/889-4303. **Terms:** Sr. discount; pets. **Facility:** 72 rooms. Many nicely furnished units. Truck stop facilities nearby. 2 stories; exterior corridors; heated pool. **Dining:** Restaurant; 6 am-midnight; $6-$12; wine/beer only. **All Rooms:** cable TV. **Cards:** AE, CB, DI, DS, MC, VI. (D) ⊗

HOWARD JOHNSON LODGE — AAA Special Value Rates — **Phone:** 503/889-8621

AAA ◆◆ Motor Inn

5/1-10/31 1P: $49- 57 2P/1B: $53- 61 2P/2B: $56 XP: $4 F17
3/1-4/30 & 11/1-2/29 1P: $47- 55 2P/1B: $51- 59 2P/2B: $54 XP: $4 F17

Location: On Hwy 30; 1 blk e of jct I-84 exit 376. 1249 Tapadera Ave 97914. Fax: 503/889-8023. **Terms:** Credit card guarantee; pets. **Facility:** 98 rooms. Very attractively furnished & decorated rooms. 2 stories; interior corridors; meeting rooms; heated pool. **Dining & Entertainment:** Restaurant; 6 am-midnight; $6-$11; cocktails/lounge. **All Rooms:** cable TV. **Some Rooms:** Fee: VCP's. **Cards:** AE, CB, DI, DS, MC, VI. (D) ⊗

SUPER 8 MOTEL — Rates Subject to Change — **Phone:** 503/889-8282

AAA ◆◆ Motel

3/1-10/31 [CP] 1P: $44- 47 2P/1B: $16- 52 2P/2B: $52- 56 XP: $5 F12
11/1-2/29 [CP] 1P: $41- 44 2P/1B: $43- 47 2P/2B: $48- 53 XP: $4 F12

Location: Off I-84, exit 376. 266 Goodfellow St 97914. Fax: 503/881-1400. **Terms:** Sr. discount; credit card guarantee; pets, $35, manager approval dep req. **Facility:** 41 rooms. Comfortably furnished & decorated rooms. 1 suite with wetbar, microwave & refrigerator, $64; 2 stories; interior corridors; heated indoor pool, whirlpool; exercise room. **Dining:** Restaurant nearby. **Services:** Fee: coin laundry. **All Rooms:** coffeemakers, free movies, cable TV. **Cards:** AE, CB, DI, DS, MC, VI. (D) (S) ⊗

OREGON CAVES NATIONAL MONUMENT

LODGING

OREGON CAVES CHATEAU — Rates Subject to Change — **Phone:** 503/592-3400

◆ Historic Lodge

5/22-9/10 [EP] 2P/1B: $79 2P/2B: $79 XP: $9 F6
3/1-5/21 & 9/11-12/31 [CP] 2P/1B: $59 2P/2B: $59 XP: $9 F6

Location: At Oregon Caves National Monument. 20000 Caves Hwy 97523 (PO Box 128, CAVE JUNCTION). Fax: 503/592-6654. **Terms:** Open 3/1-12/31; credit card guarantee; no pets. **Facility:** 22 rooms. On historic registry. Scenic mountain location. Rustic lodge rooms. Large and inviting lobby with stone fireplace. 4 two-bedroom units. 6 stories, no elevator; interior corridors; smoke free premises; meeting rooms. Fee: cave tours. **Dining:** Dining room, coffee shop; 7 am-9 pm; $7-$19; wine/beer only. **Services:** Fee: area transportation, to Cafe Jct. **All Rooms:** comb, shower & tub baths, no A/C, no phones, no TVs. **Cards:** MC, VI. (D) (S) ⊗

Beautiful, secluded Motel
with a SPECTACULAR VIEW of the Pacific Ocean.
Watch Sea Lions/Whales from your room.
Kitchens and Family rooms available.
HOUSE ON THE HILL MOTEL
Oceanside, OR (9 mi. West of Till.)
(503) 842-6030
Overlooking Bird and Sea Lion Sanctuary
M.C. and Visa

Check out our **bold** listings!

OREGON CITY—14,700 (See PORTLAND ACCOMMODATIONS spotting map page A47; see index starting on page A46)

LODGING

VAL-U INN Guaranteed Rates Phone: 503/655-7141 76

◆◆◆ Motor Inn

4/1-10/31 1P: $54- 58 2P/1B: $59- 64 2P/2B: $64- 69 XP: $5 F12
3/1-3/31 & 11/1-2/29 1P: $53 2P/1B: $59 2P/2B: $64 XP: $5 F12

Location: Off I-205, exit 9. 1900 Clackamette Dr 97045. Fax: 503/655-1927. **Terms:** Sr. discount; reserv deposit; small pets only, $5. **Facility:** 117 rooms. Some units with balcony overlooking Willamette River. 3 large very comfortably furnished units, each with refrigerator & microwave, $115; 3 stories; interior corridors; meeting rooms; heated pool, sauna, whirlpool. **Dining & Entertainment:** Restaurant; 6 am-10 pm, Sun 7 am-10 pm; $7-$13; cocktail lounge. **All Rooms:** free movies, cable TV. **Some Rooms:** coffeemakers, refrigerators. Fee: VCP's. **Cards:** AE, CB, DI, DS, MC, VI. *(See ad below)* D ⊗

PENDLETON—15,100

LODGINGS

BEST WESTERN PENDLETON INN Rates Subject to Change Phone: 503/276-2135

◆◆ Motel

5/1-9/30 [CP] 1P: $54- 69 2P/1B: $59- 75 2P/2B: $63- 69 XP: $8 F12
3/1-4/30 & 10/1-2/29 [CP] 1P: $50- 61 2P/1B: $54- 71 2P/2B: $58- 68 XP: $8 F12

Location: I-84, exit 210. 400 SE Nye Ave 97801. Fax: 503/278-2129. **Terms:** Sr. discount; reserv deposit, 5 day notice; no pets. **Facility:** 69 rooms. Neat, very nicely appointed & immaculately kept units. 19 new large very tastefully appointed units. 3 two-bedroom units. 2 two-bedroom units, from $75; 2 stories; interior corridors; heated pool, whirlpool; exercise room. **Dining:** Restaurant nearby. **Services:** data ports; airport transportation. Fee: coin laundry. **All Rooms:** free movies, cable TV. **Some Rooms:** refrigerators. **Cards:** AE, CB, DI, DS, MC, VI. D ⊗

CHAPARRAL MOTEL Guaranteed Rates Phone: 503/276-8654

◆ Motel

All Year 1P: $36 2P/1B: $43 2P/2B: $46 XP: $5 D12

Location: Off I-84 exit 209, 1 blk s on Hwy 395. 620 SW Tutuilla 97801 (PO Box 331). Fax: 503/276-5808. **Terms:** Credit card guarantee; small pets only, $5. **Facility:** 50 rooms. Attractively decorated units. 2 efficiencies, $50; 3 stories; exterior corridors. **Dining:** Restaurant nearby. **All Rooms:** free movies, cable TV. **Some Rooms:** coffeemakers, 2 efficiencies, refrigerators. **Cards:** AE, DI, DS, MC, VI.
(See ad below) D ⊗

RED LION INN/INDIAN HILLS AAA Special Value Rates Phone: 503/276-6111

◆◆◆ Motor Inn

All Year 1P: $84 2P/1B: $94 2P/2B: $94 XP: $10 F18

Location: I-84 exit 210. 304 SE Nye Ave 97801. Fax: 503/278-2413. **Terms:** Reserv deposit, 3 day notice; pets, $20 dep req. **Facility:** 170 rooms. Many large attractive rooms; some with scenic view & balcony. 3 two-bedroom units. 3 two-bedroom suites, 1 with whirlpool, refrigerator & wet bar from $109; 3 stories; interior/exterior corridors; conference facilities; heated pool, whirlpool; health club privileges, transportation provided. **Dining & Entertainment:** Dining room, coffee shop; 6 am-10:30 pm; $6-$17; cocktails; entertainment. **Services:** airport transportation. **All Rooms:** cable TV. Fee: movies. **Cards:** AE, CB, DI, DS, JCB, MC, VI. D ⊗

TAPADERA MOTOR INN Rates Subject to Change Phone: 503/276-3231

◆ Motor Inn

All Year 1P: $33 2P/1B: $38 2P/2B: $44 XP: $7 F13

Location: Center on Hwy 30 westbound; I-84 eastbound exit 207, westbound exit 213. 105 SE Court 97801. Fax: 503/276-0754. **Terms:** Sr. discount; reserv deposit, 3 day notice; pets, $5. **Facility:** 47 rooms. 2 stories; exterior corridors. **Dining:** Dining room; 6:30 am-9 pm, Fri & Sat-10 pm, Sun-2 pm; $5-$20; cocktails. **Services:** health club privileges; airport transportation. **All Rooms:** free movies, cable TV. **Cards:** AE, CB, DI, DS, MC, VI. D ⊗

RESTAURANTS

CIMMIYOTTI'S **Dinner:** $11-$20 **Phone:** 503/276-4314

◆◆ Steak and Seafood

Location: 137 S Main 97801. **Hours:** 4 pm-11 pm. Closed major holidays & Sun. **Reservations:** suggested; Fri & Sat. **Features:** children's menu; health conscious menu items; carryout; cocktails & lounge; a la carte. Long established. Relaxed atmosphere. Also popular Italian dishes. **Cards:** AE, MC, VI. ⊗

RAPHAEL'S **Dinner:** $21-$30 **Phone:** 503/276-8500

◆◆ American

Location: Center. 233 SE 4th 97801. **Hours:** 11:30 am-1:30 & 5-9 pm, Sat 5 pm-9 pm. Closed: 7/4-7/8, 11/21-11/25, Sun & Mon. **Reservations:** accepted. **Features:** No A/C; children's menu; early bird specials; carryout; cocktails. In converted historic house built in 1904. Emphasis on seafood; also prime rib & fettuccini dishes. **Cards:** AE, DS, MC, VI. ⊗

VAL-U INN MOTEL
OREGON CITY
•All River View Rooms
•Heated Outdoor Pool (seasonal) •Spa & Sauna
•Restaurant & Lounge •Small Pets Welcome
For Reservations, call: 1-800-443-7777
1900 Clackamette Drive. Oregon City, OR 97045 (503) 655-7141

CHAPARRAL MOTEL
Cleanliness & Friendliness Our Specialty
IN-ROOM COFFEE
NON-SMOKING ROOMS
620 S.W. TUTILLA
PENDLETON, OR 97801
(503) 276-8654

PORTLAND—437,300 (See DOWNTOWN PORTLAND ACCOMMODATION spotting map page A41; see index below)

To help you more easily locate accommodations in the Greater Portland area, the following two indexes and maps show lodgings and restaurants in multiple cities. Listings for these establishments are found under the heading for the city in which they are located. The Portland area comprises: Beaverton, Lake Oswego, Portland, Tigard, Tualatin, OR and Vancouver, WA.

Airport Accommodations

Listings for these establishments are found under the heading for the city in which they are located.

PORTLAND

- **Courtyard by Marriott, 2 mi e of airport terminal on Airport Way/PORTLAND**
- **Embassy Suites, 1/4 mi w/PORTLAND**
- **Howard Johnsons Airport Hotel, 1 3/4 mi s of airport terminal/PORTLAND**
- **Ramada Inn-Portland Airport, 1 1/4 mi s of airport/PORTLAND**
- **Sheraton Portland Airport Hotel, 3/4 mi e of terminal/PORTLAND**
- **Shilo Inn Portland Suites Hotel, 2 1/2 mi e of airport terminal/PORTLAND**

Index of Establishments on the DOWNTOWN PORTLAND ACCOMMODATION Spotting Map

Shilo Inn-Lloyd Center 1
Holiday Inn Portland-Dowtown 2
Travelodge Hotel 3
Comfort Inn-Lloyd Center 4
Red Lion Hotel/Lloyd Center 5
Best Western Inn at the Convention Center 6
Imperial Hotel 9
Mallory Hotel 10
Heathman Hotel 11
Portland Hilton 12
The Riverside Inn 13
Portland Marriott Hotel 14
The Portland Inn 15
RiverPlace Hotel 16
Red Lion Hotel/Downtown 17
Hotel Vintage Plaza 18
Best Western Inn at the Coliseum 19
Residence Inn by Marriott Portland Downtown ... 20
Governor Hotel 21

RESTAURANTS

London Grill 1
The Ringside 3
Jake's Famous Crawfish Restaurant 4
Couch Street Fish House 5
Dan & Louis Oyster Bar 6
McCormick & Schmick's Seafood Restaurant 7
Newport Bay Restaurant 8
Cafe des Amis 9
L'Auberge 10
Maxi's 11
Atwater's Restaurant & Lounge 13
Zefiro Restaurant & Bar 14

LODGINGS

BEST WESTERN INN AT THE COLISEUM Rates Subject to Change **Phone:** 503/287-9900 **19**

◆◆ Motor Inn

All Year 1P: $60- 70 2P/1B: $65- 75 2P/2B: $70- 75 XP: $5 F11

Location: From I-5, exit 302A; from I-84, Weidler exit. 10 N Weidler 97227. Fax: 503/287-3500. **Terms:** Sr. discount; reserv deposit, 3 day notice; no pets. **Facility:** 181 rooms. Opposite Memorial Coliseum. Especially well kept quest rooms. 5 stories; interior corridors; conference facilities; heated indoor pool. **Dining:** Dining room; 6:30 am-9 pm; $8-$15; cocktails. **Services:** data ports; airport transportation. Fee: coin laundry. **All Rooms:** free movies, cable TV. **Some Rooms:** microwaves, refrigerators. **Cards:** AE, CB, DI, DS, MC, VI. D

BEST WESTERN INN AT THE CONVENTION CENTER Rates Subject to Change **Phone:** 503/233-6331 **6**

◆◆ Motor Inn

All Year 1P: $60- 70 2P/1B: $65- 75 2P/2B: $67 XP: $5 F12

Location: On Hwy 99E; I-5 exit 302A to Weidler St, e to Martin Luther King Blvd; I-84W Lloyd Center exit 1. 420 NE Holladay 97232. Fax: 503/233-2677. **Terms:** Sr. discount; check-in 4 pm; reserv deposit, 3 day notice; small pets only, $6. **Facility:** 97 rooms. Comfortable units. Conveniently located opposite the Convention Center & next to the Max Lightrail System. 5 stories; interior corridors; meeting rooms. **Dining:** Coffee shop; 6 am-9 pm; $6-$7. **Services:** data ports. Fee: coin laundry. **All Rooms:** free movies, cable TV. **Some Rooms:** refrigerators. **Cards:** AE, CB, DI, DS, MC, VI. D

COMFORT INN-LLOYD CENTER Rates Subject to Change **Phone:** 503/233-7933 **4**

◆◆ Motel

6/11-9/5 [CP]	1P: $62- 68	2P/1B: $68- 75	2P/2B: $75- 82	XP: $10	F18
4/16-6/10 & 9/6-2/29 [CP]	1P: $58- 65	2P/1B: $65- 72	2P/2B: $71- 79	XP: $10	F18
3/1-4/15 [CP]	1P: $56- 63	2P/1B: $63- 69	2P/2B: $69- 75	XP: $10	F18

Location: From I-5 exit 302A to Weidler St, e to Martin Luther King Blvd; from I-84W Lloyd Center exit 1 to Holladay, n to Grand Ave. 431 NE Multnomah 97232. Fax: 503/233-6921. **Terms:** Sr. discount; pets. **Facility:** 79 rooms. Generous & attractively furnished units. 2 stories; interior corridors; meeting rooms; heated indoor pool. **Dining:** Restaurant nearby. **All Rooms:** free movies, combo & shower baths, cable TV. **Some Rooms:** Fee: whirlpools. **Cards:** AE, DI, DS, JCB, MC, VI. *(See color ad p A42)* D

GOVERNOR HOTEL Rates Subject to Change **Phone:** 503/224-3400 **21**

◆◆◆ Historic Hotel

All Year 1P: $145- 195 2P/1B: $165- 185 2P/2B: $165 XP: $20 F6

Location: 611 SW 10th 97205. Fax: 503/241-2122. **Terms:** Reserv deposit; no pets. **Facility:** 100 rooms. Authentically restored in classic 1909 design, blended with Lewis & Clark expedition theme. Stately, immaculately kept rooms & suites, some with fireplace or balcony. Suites with wet bar, $175-$205; 6 stories; interior corridors; business center, conference facilities; heated indoor pool, saunas, whirlpool; exercise room. Fee: parking; health club privileges restricted to children under 16. **Dining & Entertainment:** Restaurant, cafeteria; 6:30-1 am; $15-$28; cocktail lounge. **Services:** data ports, secretarial services; valet parking. **All Rooms:** honor bars, combo & shower baths, cable TV. Fee: movies. **Some Rooms:** whirlpools. Fee: VCP's. **Cards:** AE, CB, DI, DS, MC, VI. *(See color ad p A41)* D S

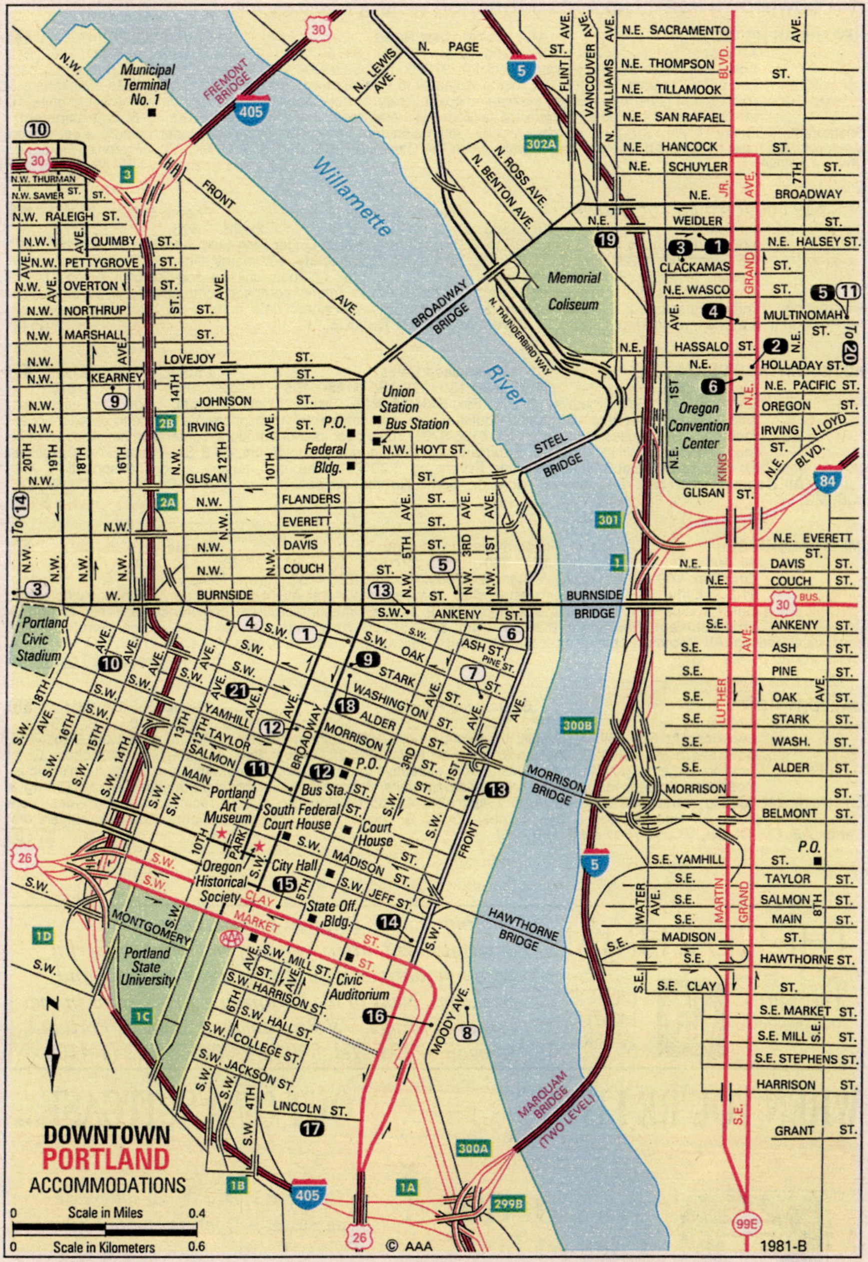

THE GOVERNOR HOTEL

Compromise Nothing

Portland's Historic Hotel

Creative cuisine, attentive service, full service athletic club and so much more. In the heart of downtown.
Special Offer: 50% off on Sunday Nights.

611 S.W. 10th at Alder, Portland, OR 97205 (503) 224-3400 1(800) 554-3456

(See DOWNTOWN PORTLAND ACCOMMODATION spotting map page A41)

HEATHMAN HOTEL AAA Special Value Rates **Phone:** 503/241-4100 **11**

AAA ◆◆◆◆ Historic Hotel

All Year 1P: $155- 200 2P/1B: $175- 220 2P/2B: $175 XP: $20 F12

Location: 1001 SW Broadway at Salmon 97205. Fax: 503/790-7110. **Terms:** Check-in 4 pm; credit card guarantee; no pets. **Facility:** 151 rooms. Adjacent to Portland Performing Arts Center. Dignified atmosphere & understated guest room decor, mezzanine guest library. Historic hotel built in 1927. 15 two-bedroom units. 10 stories; interior corridors; conference facilities; exercise room. Fee: health club. **Dining & Entertainment:** Restaurant; 6:30 am-11 pm; $15-$30; cocktails/lounge; entertainment. **Services:** data ports; valet laundry. Fee: airport transportation; valet parking. **All Rooms:** free movies, cable TV. **Cards:** AE, CB, DI, DS, JCB, MC, VI. A Preferred Hotel. *(See ad below)*

HOLIDAY INN PORTLAND-DOWTOWN Guaranteed Rates **Phone:** 503/235-2100 **2**

AAA ◆◆◆ Hotel

All Year 1P: $68 2P/1B: $78 2P/2B: $78

Location: On Hwy 99; I-5 exit 302A to Weidler St, e to Martin Luther King Blvd; I-84 w Lloyd Ctr exit. 1021 NE Grand Ave 97232. Fax: 503/238-0132. **Terms:** No pets. **Facility:** 166 rooms. Opposite Oregon Convention Center. Tastefully furnished & decorated guest rooms. 2 two-bedroom units. 4 one-bedroom suites $145; 2 two-bedroom suites with whirlpool & wetbar, $225; 6 stories; interior corridors; conference facilities; sauna; exercise room. **Dining:** Restaurant; 6:30 am-10 pm; $8-$12; cocktails. **Services:** data ports. Fee: airport transportation. **All Rooms:** free movies, refrigerators, cable TV. **Cards:** AE, CB, DI, DS, JCB, MC, VI.

HOTEL VINTAGE PLAZA Guaranteed Rates **Phone:** 503/228-1212 **18**

AAA ◆◆◆◆ Historic Hotel

All Year [CP] 1P: $145- 180 2P/1B: $165- 195 2P/2B: $165 XP: $15 F18

Location: 422 SW Broadway 97205. Fax: 503/228-3598. **Terms:** Check-in 4 pm; credit card guarantee; small pets only. **Facility:** 107 rooms. Boutique hotel with continental atmosphere. Very good to excellent guest rooms & 2-level suites. 9 parlor suites, $195-$205; 10 stories; interior corridors; conference facilities; exercise room. Fee: health club. **Dining & Entertainment:** Restaurant; 7 am-10 pm, Fri & Sat-11 pm; $7-$20; cocktail lounge. **Services:** data ports; complimentary evening beverages, 5:30-6:30. Fee: coin laundry, airport transportation; valet parking. **All Rooms:** honor bars, free movies, cable TV. **Some Rooms:** whirlpools. Fee: VCP's. **Cards:** AE, CB, DI, DS, JCB, MC, VI.

IMPERIAL HOTEL Rates Subject to Change **Phone:** 503/228-7221 **9**

AAA ◆◆ Historic Hotel

All Year 1P: $60- 75 2P/1B: $65- 85 2P/2B: $70- 80 XP: $5 F12

Location: 400 SW Broadway & Stark St 97205. Fax: 503/223-4551. **Terms:** Reserv deposit; small pets only, $10. **Facility:** 136 rooms. Long established & exceptionally well-maintained. Nicely furnished public areas. Guest rooms with distinctive appointments. 9 stories; interior corridors; conference facilities. **Dining & Entertainment:** Restaurant; 6:30 am-8 pm; $8-$15; cocktails/lounge; 24-hour room service. **Services:** data ports; valet parking. **All Rooms:** free movies, cable TV. **Some Rooms:** refrigerators. **Cards:** AE, CB, DI, DS, MC, VI. *(See color ad p A43)* Roll in showers.

MALLORY HOTEL Guaranteed Rates **Phone:** 503/223-6311 **10**

AAA ◆◆ Historic Hotel

All Year 1P: $60- 100 2P/1B: $65- 110 2P/2B: $65- 110 XP: $5

Location: At SW 15th & Yamhill; I-5 northbound, I-405, Salmon St exit; southbound exit 302B to I-405, Couch-Burnside exit. 729 SW 15th 97205. Fax: 503/223-0522. **Terms:** Pets, $10. **Facility:** 142 rooms. Quiet location. Exceptionally well kept guest rooms. Attractive lobby & public rooms with warm traditional historic atmosphere. Convenient parking. 14 two-bedroom units. 8 stories; interior corridors; meeting rooms. **Dining & Entertainment:** Dining room; 6:30 am-9 pm, Sun 7 am; $8-$14; cocktails/lounge; 24-hour room service. **Services:** data ports; valet laundry. **All Rooms:** free & pay movies, combo & shower baths, cable TV. **Some Rooms:** refrigerators. **Cards:** AE, CB, DI, DS, MC, VI. *(See color ad p A43)*

THE HEATHMAN

Preferred Hotels & Resorts Worldwide — Historic Hotels of America

Sublime dining, inspired service, evening entertainment, afternoon tea, perfectly wonderful accommodations with special weekend rates and packages. Next to the Performing Arts Center in the center of things. SW Broadway at Salmon, Portland, Oregon 97205 Tel. 800/551-0011 503/241-4100

WHEN YOU'RE LIVING OUT OF A SUITCASE...

Comfort Inn

In Portland

Comfort Inn Convention Center

431 N.E. Multnomah

Portland, OR 97232

I-5 Exit 302A-I84 Lloyd Center

• Covered Heated Pool • Private Spa Suites • Meeting Room • Free Deluxe Continental Breakfast • Free In-room Movies • 2 Blocks to Oregon Convention Center & Lloyd Center • Near Coliseum

For reservations call **503-233-7933** or toll free **800-4-CHOICE**

(See DOWNTOWN PORTLAND ACCOMMODATION spotting map page A41)

PORTLAND HILTON Rates Subject to Change **Phone:** 503/226-1611 **12**

AAA ◆◆◆◆ Hotel

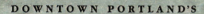

All Year 1P: $125- 145 2P/1B: $145- 165 2P/2B: $145- 165 XP: $20 F

Location: From I-5 to I-405, 6th Ave exit. 921 SW 6th Ave 97204. Fax: 503/220-2565. **Terms:** Reserv deposit, 3 day notice; no pets. **Facility:** 455 rooms. Convenient to Portland Performing Arts Center. Rooms in contemporary decor. 1 one-bedroom suite with whirlpool $600; 5 one-bedroom suites with wet bar & refrigerator, $575-$650, two-bedroom $750-$900; 22 stories; interior corridors; conference facilities, convention oriented; heated pool; exercise room. Fee: parking. **Dining & Entertainment:** 3 dining rooms, coffee shop; 6:30 am-11:30 pm; $9-$24; cocktails; entertainment. **Services:** data ports. Fee: airport transportation; valet parking. **All Rooms:** honor bars, coffeemakers, cable TV. Fee: movies. **Some Rooms:** refrigerators. **Cards:** AE, CB, DI, DS, JCB, MC, VI.

(See ad p 38)

THE PORTLAND INN Rates Subject to Change **Phone:** 503/221-1611 **15**

AAA ◆◆ Motor Inn

All Year 1P: $59- 75 2P/1B: $64- 79 2P/2B: $69- 85 XP: $10 F12

Location: I-5 City Center Rt, 6th Ave exit. 1414 SW 6th Ave 97201. Fax: 503/226-0447. **Terms:** Sr. discount; no pets. **Facility:** 173 rooms. Convenient downtown location. Comfortably equipped & nicely kept rooms. 5 stories; interior corridors; meeting rooms; heated pool. **Dining & Entertainment:** Dining room; 6:30 am-10 pm, Sat & Sun 7 am-10 pm; $7-$13; cocktails/lounge; 24-hour room service. **Services:** data ports; valet laundry. Fee: airport transportation. **All Rooms:** cable TV. **Cards:** AE, CB, DI, DS, MC, VI.

(See color ad p A44)

DOWNTOWN PORTLAND'S

IMPERIAL HOTEL

400 SOUTHWEST BROADWAY AT STARK

Beautifully Restored

Special Packages Available

FREE Covered, Secure Parking

In Room Movies

FREE SATV • FREE HBO

Fully Sprinklered

In Room Refrigerator and Safe Available

Meeting & Banquet Facilities For Up To 150

Excellent Dining Room & Cocktail Lounge

ADA Compliant

Walk To:

- Max Light Rail
- Downtown Shops and Entertainment
- Historic Old Town District
- Parks

RESERVATIONS

800-452-2323

MALLORY HOTEL

RESERVATIONS
1-800-228-8657

UPTOWN AT SW 15TH AVE & YAMHILL ST
EASY ACCESS FROM I-405, EXIT 2A

C/CATV, FREE HBO

Excellent Dining Room and Cocktail Lounge

FREE PARKING

Completely Air Conditioned

All Major Credit Cards

Guest Comment: "This is undoubtedly one of the finest small hotels we've stopped in and we've traveled considerably. It's attractive and immaculate."

(See DOWNTOWN PORTLAND ACCOMMODATION spotting map page A41)

PORTLAND MARRIOTT HOTEL Rates Subject to Change **Phone:** 503/226-7600 **14**

AAA ◆◆◆ Hotel

Sun-Thurs	1P: $125- 150	2P/1B: $135- 160	2P/2B: $135- 160	XP: $10	F18
Fri & Sat	1P: $99- 137	2P/1B: $99- 147	2P/2B: $99- 147	XP: $10	F18

Location: I-5 northbound 299B I-405 exit, then exit 1A to Front Ave; southbound 300B City Center exit to Morrison Bridge then s on Front Ave. 1401 SW Front Ave 97201. Fax: 503/221-1789. **Terms:** Check-in 4 pm; reserv deposit; pets. **Facility:** 503 rooms. Opposite waterfront park. Comfortably equipped guest rooms, many with view of Willamette River. Hair salon. 6 one- or two-bedroom suites, 1 with wet bar, $450; 15 stories; interior corridors; business center, conference facilities; heated indoor pool, saunas, whirlpool; 2 exercise rooms, hair salon. Fee: parking. **Dining & Entertainment:** Restaurant; 6:30 am-11 pm, Fri & Sat-midnight; $7-$20; cocktails/lounge; 24-hour room service; nightclub. **Services:** data ports; valet laundry. Fee: airport transportation; valet parking. **All Rooms:** free & pay movies, cable TV. **Some Rooms:** refrigerators, whirlpools. **Cards:** AE, CB, DI, DS, JCB, MC, VI.

RED LION HOTEL/DOWNTOWN Rates Subject to Change **Phone:** 503/221-0450 **17**

◆◆◆ Motor Inn

All Year	1P: $97- 107	2P/1B: $112- 122	2P/2B: $112- 122	XP: $15	F18

Location: Off I-5 to I-405; 4th Ave exit. 310 SW Lincoln 97201. Fax: 503/226-6260. **Terms:** Sr. discount; pets, $50 dep req. **Facility:** 235 rooms. Tastefully appointed & nicely maintained guest rooms. Attractive facilities. Suite with whirlpool & refrigerator, $350; 2 spacious & beautifully furnished units, $250; 3 stories; interior corridors; conference facilities; heated pool; exercise room. **Dining & Entertainment:** Restaurant; 6 am-2 & 5-11 pm; $13-$22; cocktails; entertainment. **Services:** airport transportation. Fee: coin laundry. **All Rooms:** coffeemakers, cable TV. Fee: movies. **Cards:** AE, CB, DI, DS, JCB, MC, VI.

RED LION HOTEL/LLOYD CENTER Rates Subject to Change **Phone:** 503/281-6111 **5**

◆◆◆ Hotel

All Year	1P: $120- 145	2P/1B: $135- 160	2P/2B: $145	XP: $15	F18

Location: Adjacent to Lloyd Center; I-5 exit 302A to Weidler St, e to 9th, s to Multnomah; I-84 westbound, Coliseum-Lloyd Center exit. 1000 NE Multnomah St 97232. Fax: 503/284-8553. **Terms:** Reserv deposit, 3 day notice; pets. **Facility:** 476 rooms. Opposite Lloyd Center shopping mall. Attractive building design & lobby. Very comfortably furnished guest rooms. Suites from $199, with whirlpool & wet bar from $435; 9-15 stories; interior corridors; conference facilities, convention oriented; luxury level rooms; heated pool; exercise room. Fee: parking. **Dining & Entertainment:** Dining room, restaurant, coffee shop; 6 am-midnight; $8-$25; cocktails/lounge. **Services:** data ports; valet laundry; airport transportation. Fee: valet parking. **All Rooms:** free movies, combo & shower baths, cable TV. **Some Rooms:** refrigerators. Fee: VCP's. **Cards:** AE, DI, DS, JCB, MC, VI.

RESIDENCE INN BY MARRIOTT PORTLAND DOWNTOWN Rates Subject to Change **Phone:** 503/288-1400 **20**

◆◆◆ Apartment Motel

All Year [CP]	1P: $130	2P/1B: $130- 160	2P/2B: $135- 175		

Location: From I-5 exit 302A, Weidler St s to Multnomah, e to 17th; from I-84, Lloyd Center exit 1, n on 13th St, then to Multnomah. 1710 NE Multnomah 97232. Fax: 503/288-0241. **Terms:** Sr. discount; check-in 4 pm; credit card guarantee; pets, $10. **Facility:** 168 rooms. Very comfortably furnished, 1 & 2-bedroom units, most with fireplace. Complimentary evening beverage & desert 6:30 pm-8 pm. 28 two-bedroom units. 3 stories, no elevator; exterior corridors; meeting rooms; heated pool, whirlpools; 1 tennis court; sports court. **Services:** data ports; airport transportation. Fee: coin laundry. **All Rooms:** kitchens, free movies, cable TV. **Cards:** AE, CB, DI, DS, MC, VI.

REST AND RELAX WITH SPECIAL WEEKEND RATES.

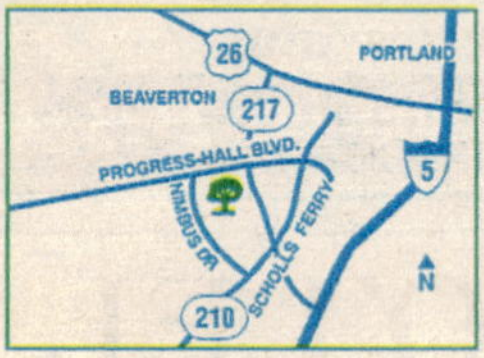

Spacious rooms, pool, whirlpool, exercise room, in-room coffee, cozy restaurant and lounge. AAA weekend rates, subject to availability.

BEAVERTON
8500 S.W. Nimbus Drive
503 641-3200

COURTYARD Marriott
800 443-6000

PORTLAND AIRPORT
11550 N.E. Airport Way
503 252-3200

DAYS INN CITY CENTER

Downtown Location
Portland Bar & Grill
Meeting facilities
Heated Pool

DAYS INN

Walk to attractions, shopping & restaurants
Free Parking
Cable TV

1414 SW 6th Ave., Portland, OR 97201
(503)221-1611 • (800)329-7466

(See DOWNTOWN PORTLAND ACCOMMODATION spotting map page A41)

RIVERPLACE HOTEL Rates Subject to Change **Phone:** 503/228-3233 16
◆◆◆◆ Hotel
All Year [CP] 1P: $155- 215 2P/1B: $175- 235 2P/2B: $195 XP: $20 F17
Location: I-5 northbound Front Ave exit 1A; southbound Morrison Bridge exit to Front Ave. 1510 SW Harbor Way 97201. Fax: 503/295-6161. **Terms:** Check-in 4 pm; credit card guarantee; pets. **Facility:** 84 rooms. Riverfront esplanade location. Guest rooms & suites with subdued decor. Many with fine Willamette River view. 5 suites with fireplace $325. 10 one- & two-bedroom apartments with fireplace & balcony, $275-$375. Junior suites & parlor suites, $180-$230; 4 stories; interior corridors; conference facilities; sauna, whirlpool. Fee: parking; health club privileges. **Dining & Entertainment:** Restaurant; 6:30 am-10:30 pm; $9-$25; cocktail lounge; entertainment. **Services:** data ports; valet laundry. Fee: valet parking. **All Rooms:** honor bars, free movies, combo & shower baths, cable TV. **Some Rooms:** whirlpools. **Cards:** AE, CB, DI, DS, JCB, MC, VI. Roll in showers. (D) (S)

THE RIVERSIDE INN Rates Subject to Change **Phone:** 503/221-0711 13
◆◆ Motor Inn
4/1-10/31 1P: $62- 75 2P/1B: $72- 87 2P/2B: $72- 87 XP: $10 F17
3/1-3/31 & 11/1-2/29 1P: $59- 72 2P/1B: $69- 85 2P/2B: $69- 85 XP: $10 F17
Location: From I-5 northbound take exit 299B, exit 1A to Front Ave & n 7 blks; southbound exit 300B, Morrison Street-City Center over Morrison Bridge & right on Front Ave. 50 SW Morrison at Front Ave 97204. Fax: 503/274-0312. **Terms:** Credit card guarantee; small pets only, $10. **Facility:** 140 rooms. Comfortably equipped units, some with river view. 1 bedroom suite, $150; 5 stories; interior corridors; meeting rooms. **Dining:** Dining room; 6:30 am-10 pm; $7-$15; cocktails; 24-hour room service. **Services:** health club privileges. Fee: airport transportation. **Some Rooms:** kitchen. **Cards:** AE, CB, DI, DS, MC, VI. *(See color ad below)* (D)

SHILO INN-LLOYD CENTER Rates Subject to Change **Phone:** 503/231-7665 1
◆ Motel
All Year [CP] 1P: $56- 64 2P/1B: $56- 64 2P/2B: $64- 76 XP: $8 F12
Location: 2 blks e of I-5 exit 302, e on Weidler to 2nd Ave; from I-84, Seattle-Coliseum Rt to exit 302A. 1506 NE 2nd Ave 97232. Fax: 503/236-6040. **Terms:** Sr. discount; pets, $7. **Facility:** 44 rooms. 2 stories; interior corridors; sauna. **Dining:** Restaurant nearby. **Services:** data ports; airport transportation. Fee: coin laundry. **All Rooms:** free movies. **Cards:** AE, CB, DI, DS, JCB, MC, VI. (D)

TRAVELODGE HOTEL AAA Special Value Rates **Phone:** 503/233-2401 3
◆◆◆ Hotel
All Year 1P: $65 2P/1B: $65 2P/2B: $70
Location: I-5 exit 302A, e on Weidler; from I-84W, Seattle-Coliseum rt, exit 302A. 1441 NE 2nd Ave 97232. Fax: 503/238-7016. **Terms:** Credit card guarantee; no pets. **Facility:** 236 rooms. Tastefully furnished & exceptionally maintained guest rooms. 1 suite with refrigerator, wet bar, kitchen & dining room, $250; 10 stories; interior corridors; conference facilities; heated pool; exercise room. **Dining & Entertainment:** Dining room; 6:30 am-10:30 pm; $10-$15; cocktails/lounge. **Services:** data ports; airport transportation. **All Rooms:** coffeemakers, cable TV. Fee: movies. **Cards:** AE, CB, DI, DS, JCB, MC, VI. (D)

RESTAURANTS

ATWATER'S RESTAURANT & LOUNGE **Dinner:** over $31 **Phone:** 503/275-3600 (13)
◆◆◆ Regional American
Location: On 30th floor of US Bancorp Tower. 111 SW 5th 97201. **Hours:** 5:30 pm-9:30 pm, Fri & Sat-10 pm, Sun 5 pm-9 pm. Closed: 1/1, 9/4 & 12/25. **Reservations:** suggested. **Features:** cocktails & lounge; entertainment; a la carte. Dignified dining room with panoramic view. Very attentive service. Emphasis on attractively presented northwest regional dishes; also, 4-course prix fixe meal, $35. Mother's Day & Easter Brunch 10 am-2 pm, $17-$22. Smoke free premises. **Cards:** AE, DI, DS, JCB, MC, VI.

CAFE DES AMIS **Dinner:** $11-$20 **Phone:** 503/295-6487 (9)
◆◆ French
Location: 1987 NW Kearney 97209. **Hours:** 5:30 pm-10 pm. Closed major holidays & Sun. **Reservations:** suggested. **Features:** cocktails. Small, dignified, bistro-style dining rooms with emphasis on excellently prepared Country French dishes. Seafood, poultry, lamb & beef entrees. Smoke free premises. **Cards:** AE, MC, VI.

COUCH STREET FISH HOUSE **Dinner:** $21-$30 **Phone:** 503/223-6173 (5)
◆◆◆ Regional Seafood
Location: 105 NW 3rd Ave 97209. **Hours:** 5 pm-10 pm, Fri & Sat-11 pm. Closed major holidays, 1/1, 7/4, 12/24, 12/25 & Sun. **Reservations:** suggested. **Features:** early bird specials; health conscious menu items; cocktails & lounge; valet parking; a la carte. In renovated historic building in Old Town. Warm intimate atmosphere & traditional service. Excellently prepared fresh northwest seafood specialties; also steaks, lamb, veal & chicken dishes. Smoke free premises. **Cards:** AE, CB, DI, MC, VI.

DAN & LOUIS OYSTER BAR Historical **Dinner:** up to $10 **Phone:** 503/227-5906 (6)
◆ Traditional Seafood
Location: 208 SW Ankeny St 97204. **Hours:** 11 am-10 pm, Fri & Sat-11 pm. Closed major holidays. **Reservations:** suggested. **Features:** children's menu; senior's menu; carryout; beer & wine only; a la carte. Popular, long-established seafood restaurant. Nautical atmosphere & memorabilia. Wide variety of shellfish & fish dishes, including fresh oysters & oyster stew. **Cards:** AE, CB, DI, DS, MC, VI.

JAKE'S FAMOUS CRAWFISH RESTAURANT Historical **Dinner:** $21-$30 **Phone:** 503/226-1419 (4)
◆◆◆ Seafood
Location: 401 SW 12th Ave 97205. **Hours:** 11:30 am-11 pm, Fri-midnight, Sat 5 pm-midnight, Sun 5 pm-10 pm. Closed major holidays. **Reservations:** suggested. **Features:** cocktails & lounge; a la carte. Popular long-established restaurant with original turn-of-the-century atmosphere. Extensive selection of very well prepared fresh entrees; also, steaks, salads & soups. **Cards:** AE, DI, DS, MC, VI.

L'AUBERGE **Dinner:** over $31 **Phone:** 503/223-3302 (10)
◆◆◆ Continental
Location: 2601 NW Vaughn 97210. **Hours:** 5:30 pm-10 pm. Closed major holidays & Sun. **Reservations:** suggested. **Features:** cocktails & lounge; a la carte. Dignified dining room. Entrees & prix fixe 6-course dinner using regional ingredients with choice of entrees, usually fish, poultry, beef, game & veal. Smoke free premises. **Cards:** AE, CB, DI, DS, MC, VI.

The Willamette River & Yamhill District At Your Doorstep
Riverside Inn
50 S.W. Morrison Street, Portland, OR 97204
(503) 221-0711 • (800) 648-6440
- Free Parking
- River Views
- Meeting Facilities
- Waterfront Location
- Riverside Cafe & Bar
- Near shopping & attractions

(See DOWNTOWN PORTLAND ACCOMMODATION spotting map page A41)

LONDON GRILL **Dinner:** $21-$30 **Phone:** 503/228-2000 (1)
◆◆◆ Regional American
Location: In The Benson Hotel. 309 SW Broadway 97205. **Hours:** 6:30 am-2 & 5-10 pm, Fri & Sat-11 pm, Sun 6:30 am-2 pm. **Reservations:** required. **Features:** Sunday brunch; health conscious menu items; cocktails; entertainment; valet parking; a la carte. Excellently prepared northwestern regional cuisines. Dignified atmosphere. **Cards:** AE, CB, DI, DS, MC, VI.

MAXI'S **Dinner:** $21-$30 **Phone:** 503/281-6111 (11)
◆◆◆ American
Location: In Red Lion Hotel/Lloyd Center. 1000 NE Multnomah 97232. **Hours:** 11:30 am-2:30 & 5-10 pm, Fri & Sat 5 pm-11 pm, Sun 9 am-2 & 5-10 pm. **Reservations:** suggested. **Features:** Sunday brunch; senior's menu; cocktails & lounge; entertainment; a la carte. Tastefully appointed dining room with relaxed atmosphere. Unique preparation of popular dishes, northwest ingredients. **Cards:** AE, DI, DS, MC, VI.

MCCORMICK & SCHMICK'S SEAFOOD RESTAURANT **Dinner:** $21-$30 **Phone:** 503/224-7522 (7)
◆◆◆ Seafood
Location: 235 SW 1st Ave 97204. **Hours:** 11:30 am-11 pm, Sat 5 pm-11 pm, Sun 5 pm-10 pm. Closed major holidays. **Reservations:** suggested. **Features:** early bird specials; carryout; cocktails & lounge; entertainment; a la carte. Historic building. Traditional early restaurant decor; lively atmosphere. Well-prepared dishes; emphasis on fresh seafood; also pasta, beef & poultry dishes. **Cards:** AE, DI, DS, MC, VI.

NEWPORT BAY RESTAURANT **Dinner:** $11-$20 **Phone:** 503/227-3474 (8)
◆◆ Seafood
Location: On Willamette Rivershore; I-5 northbound to Front Ave exit, southbound Morrison Bridge exit to Front Ave. 0425 SW Montgomery 97201. **Hours:** 11 am-11 pm, Fri & Sat-midnight; 10/1-3/31 to 10 pm, Sun 9 am-11 pm. Closed: 11/23 & 12/25. **Reservations:** suggested. **Features:** Sunday brunch; children's menu; carryout; cocktails & lounge; fee for parking; a la carte. Floating restaurant with picturesque rivershore view. Emphasis on fresh seafood, some pasta beef & chicken dishes & salads. **Cards:** AE, CB, DI, DS, MC, VI.

THE RINGSIDE **Dinner:** $21-$30 **Phone:** 503/223-1513 (3)
◆◆ American
Location: 3 1/2 blks w of Civic Stadium. 2165 W Burnside 97210. **Hours:** 5 pm-midnight, Sun 4 pm-11:30 pm. Closed: 12/24 & major holidays, except 1/1. **Reservations:** suggested. **Features:** carryout; cocktails & lounge; valet parking; a la carte. Long-established dinner house. Popular for steaks & onion rings. Emphasis on steaks, seafood, chicken & prime rib. Excellent service. **Cards:** AE, DI, DS, MC, VI.

ZEFIRO RESTAURANT & BAR **Dinner:** $21-$30 **Phone:** 503/226-3394 (14)
◆◆ Continental
Location: 500 NW 21st Ave 97210. **Hours:** 11:30 am-2:30 & 6-10:30 pm, Fri-11 pm, Sat 5:30 pm-11 pm. Closed major holidays & 2/1-2/10. **Reservations:** suggested. **Features:** cocktails & lounge; fee for valet parking; a la carte. Stylish, contemporary dining room. Selected creative entrees & appetizers with Mediteranian influence. Sidewalk seating, weather permitting. Smoke free premises. **Cards:** AE, DI, MC, VI.

GREATER PORTLAND (See PORTLAND ACCOMMODATIONS spotting map page A47; see index below)

Index of Establishments on the PORTLAND ACCOMMODATIONS Spotting Map

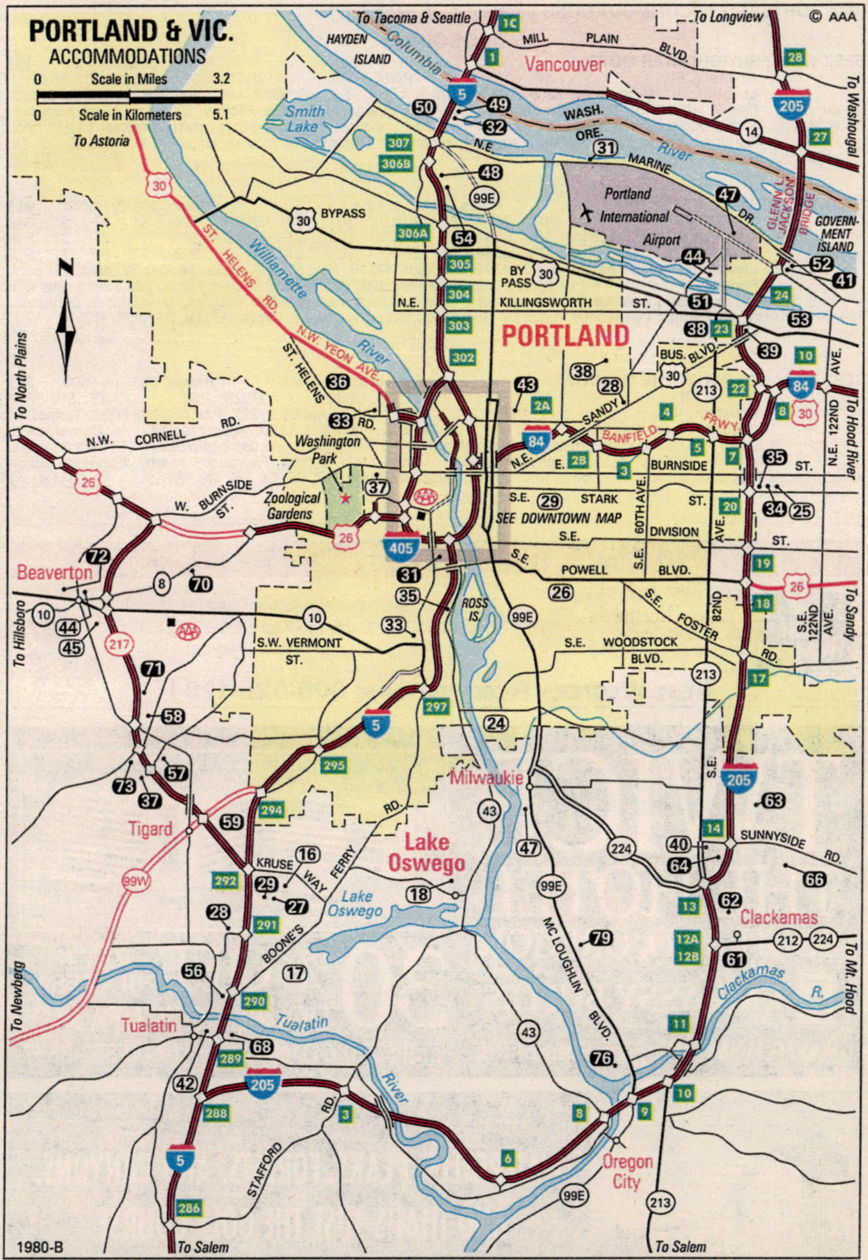

W E L C O M E

Just 15 min. south of downtown Portland, 100 rooms in beautiful garden setting. Features room service, swimming pool, nearby exercise facilities, cable TV, Restaurant and Lounge, Meeting & Banquet space for up to 400. Singles $55-$70. Doubles $63-$78.

7125 SW NYBERG RD. (EXIT 289)
TUALATIN, OR 97026

The Sweetbrier Inn

Member of Distinctive Inns & Resorts

1-800-551-9167
503-692-5800

(See PORTLAND ACCOMMODATIONS spotting map page A47)

LODGINGS

BEST WESTERN FORTNITER MOTEL — Guaranteed Rates — **Phone:** 503/255-9771 — 38

AAA ◆◆ Suite Motel

All Year [CP]	1P: $57	2P/1B: $62	2P/2B: $67	XP: $5

Location: 5 1/4 mi e on 82nd Ave; 1/2 mi n of jct I-84; exit 82nd Ave. 4911 NE 82nd Ave 97220. Fax: 503/255-9774. **Terms:** Sr. discount; credit card guarantee; no pets. **Facility:** 52 rooms. Nicely furnished 1- & 2-bedroom units with living room & efficiency. 2 stories; interior corridors; meeting rooms; heated pool. **Services:** airport transportation. Fee: coin laundry. **All Rooms:** free movies, cable TV. **Cards:** AE, CB, DI, DS, JCB, MC, VI. (D)

BEST WESTERN HERITAGE INN — Rates Subject to Change — **Phone:** 503/497-9044 — 36

AAA ◆◆ Motel

6/11-9/5 [CP]	1P: $60- 67	2P/1B: $67- 74	2P/2B: $74- 81	XP: $7	F18
4/16-6/10 & 9/6-2/29 [CP]	1P: $58- 65	2P/1B: $65- 71	2P/2B: $71- 77	XP: $7	F18
3/1-4/15 [CP]	1P: $58- 61	2P/1B: $61- 67	2P/2B: $69- 77	XP: $7	F18

Location: I-405 St Helens exit 3. 4319 NW Yeon 97210. Fax: 503/497-1030. **Terms:** Sr. discount; pets. **Facility:** 65 rooms. Nicely decorated units. 4 kitchen units, $85-$100; 6 efficiency units, $68-$76; 2 units with whirlpool $86-$115 in season; 2 stories; interior corridors; meeting rooms; heated indoor pool, sauna, whirlpool. **Services:** Fee: coin laundry. **All Rooms:** free movies, cable TV. **Some Rooms:** coffeemakers. **Cards:** AE, DI, DS, JCB, MC, VI.
(See color ad below) (D) (S)

BEST WESTERN INN AT THE MEADOWS — Rates Subject to Change — **Phone:** 503/286-9600 — 54

AAA ◆◆◆ Motel

All Year [CP]	1P: $70	2P/1B: $80	2P/2B: $80	XP: $10	F12

Location: 4 mi n from I-5, exit 306B. 1215 N Hayden Meadows Dr 97217. Fax: 503/286-8020. **Terms:** Sr. discount; reserv deposit; small pets only, $10. **Facility:** 146 rooms. Large, very attractive units. Convenient to Delta Park. 2 one-bedroom suites, $145; 42 rooms with refrigerator, wet bar & microwave $78-$98; 3 stories; interior corridors; meeting rooms; whirlpool; exercise room. **Dining:** Restaurant nearby. **Services:** airport transportation. Fee: coin laundry. **All Rooms:** free movies, cable TV. **Cards:** AE, CB, DI, DS, MC, VI. (D) (S)

IN PORTLAND, REQUEST THE BEST!
Best Western
Best Western Heritage Inn
Portland Northwest
4319 N.W. Yeon
Portland, OR 97210
503-497-9044
Located in the Northwest Industrial District • Indoor Pool, Sauna and Spa • Cable TV • Kitchenettes, Spa Suites • Meeting Rooms • Free Continental Breakfast
BEST WESTERN RESERVATIONS: 800-528-1234

TWICE THE HOTEL
PORTLAND, OREGON
EMBASSY SUITES
9000 S.W. Washington Square Rd.

30% OFF RACK RATES
DOUBLE OCCUPANCY
Call (503) 641-4000 or 1-800-772-3897

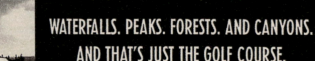

WATERFALLS. PEAKS. FORESTS. AND CANYONS.
AND THAT'S JUST THE GOLF COURSE.
Not to mention windsurfing, tennis, hiking, horseback riding, golfing, superb dining, spectacular views, soothing spa and crackling fireplaces. Call 800-221-7117.
In the Columbia Gorge–only 45 min. from Portland.
Skamania Lodge
Stevenson, WA

(See PORTLAND ACCOMMODATIONS spotting map page A47)

BEST WESTERN PONY SOLDIER MOTOR INN-AIRPORT Rates Subject to Change **Phone:** 503/256-1504 53
AAA ◆◆◆ Motel
All Year [CP] 1P: $86- 91 2P/1B: $86- 91 2P/2B: $81- 86 XP: $5 F12
Location: 3 mi e of Portland International Airport, 1 1/2 mi n of jct I-84 & I-205; from I-205, exit 23A to Sandy Blvd. 9901 NE Sandy Blvd 97220. Fax: 503/256-5928. **Terms:** Sr. discount; reserv deposit; no pets. **Facility:** 104 rooms. Very tastefully appointed guest rooms & public areas. Some units with balcony facing attractive central courtyard & swimming pool. 2 stories; interior corridors; meeting rooms; heated pool, whirlpool; exercise room. **Dining:** Restaurant nearby. **Services:** data ports; guest laundry; airport transportation. **All Rooms:** free movies, cable TV. **Some Rooms:** coffeemakers, 6 efficiencies, microwaves, refrigerators, whirlpools. **Cards:** AE, CB, DI, DS, JCB, MC, VI. (D) ⊗

CHESTNUT TREE INN Rates Subject to Change **Phone:** 503/255-4444 35
AAA ◆ Motel
All Year 1P: $36 2P/1B: $41 2P/2B: $43 XP: $2
Location: 1/2 mi s of jct I-205 & I-84. Off I-205, southbound exit 21A, northbound exit 20. 9699 SE Stark 97216. Fax: 503/255-4444. **Terms:** No pets. **Facility:** 58 rooms. Convenient access to I-205. Comfortably furnished units. 4 units with kitchen, $44-$50; 2 stories; exterior corridors. **Dining:** Restaurant nearby. **Services:** data ports. **All Rooms:** free movies, cable TV. **Some Rooms:** refrigerators. **Cards:** AE, CB, DI, MC, VI. (D) ⊗

COURTYARD BY MARRIOTT Rates Subject to Change **Phone:** 503/252-3200 41
AAA ◆◆◆ Motor Inn
All Year 1P: $73 2P/1B: $83 2P/2B: $95 XP: $10 F17
Location: 2 1/2 mi e of Airport terminal; from I-205 northbound take exit 24B, southbound take exit 24, to Airport Way; I-84 take exit 8 to I-205 n, then exit 24B. 11550 NE Airport Way 97220. Fax: 503/252-8921. **Terms:** Sr. discount; credit card guarantee; no pets. **Facility:** 150 rooms. 10 one-bedroom suites with wet bar, refrigerator, microwave & VCR, $100; 6 stories; interior corridors; conference facilities; heated pool, whirlpool; exercise room. **Dining & Entertainment:** Restaurant; 6 am-11:30 pm; $7-$15; cocktails/lounge. **Services:** data ports; airport transportation. **All Rooms:** free & pay movies, cable TV. **Some Rooms:** coffeemakers. **Cards:** AE, DI, DS, MC, VI.
(See color ad p A44) (D) (S) ⊗

CYPRESS INN-PORTLAND AAA Special Value Rates **Phone:** 503/252-8247 34
◆ Motel
All Year [CP] 1P: $65- 69 2P/1B: $72- 77 2P/2B: $72- 77 XP: $7 F13
Location: 5 mi ne off I-205, exit 20; 2 mi s of jct I-205 & I-84. 9707 SE Stark 97216. Fax: 503/254-8441. **Terms:** Reserv deposit; small pets only, $7. **Facility:** 78 rooms. Convenient freeway access. 2 efficiencies, $63-$70; 2 units with whirlpool, $92; 3 stories; interior corridors; meeting rooms; heated pool. **Dining:** Restaurant nearby. **Services:** data ports; airport transportation. **All Rooms:** free movies. **Some Rooms:** refrigerators. **Cards:** AE, CB, DI, DS, MC, VI. (D) ⊗

DELTA INN Rates Subject to Change **Phone:** 503/289-1800 48
AAA ◆◆ Motel
All Year 1P: $46 2P/1B: $51 2P/2B: $56 XP: $5 F12
Location: 4 mi n; off I-5 exit 306B. 9930 N Whitaker 97217. Fax: 503/289-3778. **Terms:** Reserv deposit, 3 day notice; pets, $10-$20. **Facility:** 214 rooms. Conveniently located to Delta Park. Large units. 14 efficiencies, $58; 4 stories; interior corridors; conference facilities. **Dining:** Restaurant nearby. **Services:** health club privileges; airport transportation. Fee: coin laundry. **All Rooms:** free movies, combo & shower baths, cable TV. **Cards:** AE, CB, DI, DS, MC, VI. (D) ⊗

GENERAL HOOKER'S BED & BREAKFAST Rates Subject to Change **Phone:** 503/222-4435 31
◆ Bed & Breakfast
All Year [CP] 1P: $65- 105 2P/1B: $70- 115 2P/2B: $80 XP: $20
Location: I-5N exit 298, n on Corbett merges with 1st St, w on Hooker 1/2 blk; I-5S to I-405N, 4th St exit 1B (do not take 302B), e on Lincoln, s 1st Ave, w on Hooker. 125 SW Hooker 97201. Fax: 503/295-6727. **Terms:** Check-in 4 pm; credit card guarantee; no pets. **Facility:** 4 rooms. 1888 Victorian home located in residential area. Casual modern decor. 2 rooms share a private deck with distant view of the city scape. Extensive video library. Resident cat. 2 stories; interior corridors; smoke free premises; street parking only; 1/2 price passes to the Metro YMCA. **Dining:** Extended continental breakfast (not full breakfast). **All Rooms:** free movies, cable TV, VCP's. **Some Rooms:** combo & shower baths, shared bathrooms. **Cards:** AE, MC, VI. (D) ⊗

HOLIDAY INN HAS A NEW NAME FOR SAAAVINGS.
Portland East/Gresham
2323 N.E.181st
I-84 Exit 13
Portland, OR 97230
503-492-4000
Indoor Pool • Sauna • Spa • Free Continental Breakfast & Local Calls • *Near Dog Track, Mt. Hood Festival of Jazz, Mt. Hood, Factory Outlet Mall.*
Holiday Inn EXPRESS
STAY WITH SOMEONE YOU KNOW.
FOR RESERVATIONS CALL 1-800-HOLIDAY OR THE HOTEL DIRECT.

The Greenwood Inn
A Northwest favorite in the heart of Washington county. Near wineries, shopping, zoo and downtown Portland. Affordable rooms, plenty of free parking, award winning restaurant and lounge, complimentary local shuttle and special early dinner selections.
25% discount off listed rates to AAA members.
Call toll free: 800/289-1300
Direct: 503/643-7444
10700 SW Allen Blvd
Just off Hwy 217
Beaverton, Oregon 97005

(See PORTLAND ACCOMMODATIONS spotting map page A47)

HOWARD JOHNSONS AIRPORT HOTEL Guaranteed Rates **Phone:** 503/255-6722 **44**
AAA ◆◆ Motor Inn
All Year [CP] 1P: $59- 66 2P/1B: $65- 70 2P/2B: $70 XP: $6 F12
Location: 82nd Ave; I-205 airport exit, s on 82nd 1/2 mi. 7101 NE 82nd Ave 97220. Fax: 503/254-3370. **Terms:** Sr. discount; credit card guarantee, 7 day notice; pets, $20 dep req. **Facility:** 137 rooms. Generous size, inviting units. 2 stories; interior corridors; conference facilities; heated pool, sauna, whirlpool. **Dining & Entertainment:** Restaurant; 5:30 am-11 pm; $8-$13; cocktail lounge. **Services:** airport transportation. **All Rooms:** free movies, cable TV. **Some Rooms:** refrigerators. **Cards:** AE, CB, DI, DS, MC, VI. (D) ⊗

THE LION AND THE ROSE VICTORIAN BED & BREAKFAST Rates Subject to Change **Phone:** 503/287-9245 **43**
◆◆◆ Historic Bed & Breakfast
6/1-9/30 [BP] 1P: $70- 110 2P/1B: $80- 120 2P/2B: $105
3/1-5/31 & 10/1-2/29 [BP] 1P: $60- 100 2P/1B: $70- 110 2P/2B: $95
Location: I-5 north or southbound exit 302A (Coliseum exit) to Weidler then e to 15th, n 2 blks. 1810 NE 15th 97212 (1517 NE Schuyler). Fax: 503/287-9247. **Terms:** Reserv deposit, 3 day notice, cancellation fee imposed; no pets. **Facility:** 6 rooms. Impressive 1906 Queen Anne-style home located in Portlands historical Irvington District. Located within walking distance to quaint shops & restaurants. Elegantly furnished rooms with period antiques & reproductions. 3 stories; interior corridors; smoke free premises; street parking only. **Dining:** Afternoon dessert tea 4-6 pm; breakfast served in dining room 7-9 am. **Services:** data ports. Fee: airport transportation. **Recreation:** Fee: bicycles. **All Rooms:** no A/C, no TVs. **Cards:** AE, MC, VI. (D) ⊗

OXFORD SUITES Rates Subject to Change **Phone:** 503/283-3030 **32**
AAA ◆◆◆ Motel
All Year [BP] 1P: $66- 96 2P/1B: $72- 102 2P/2B: $77 XP: $6 F10
Location: 4 mi n 1 blk e of I-5 exit 308. 12226 N Jantzen Dr 97217. Fax: 503/735-1661. **Terms:** Sr. discount; credit card guarantee, 14 day notice; small pets only, $10. **Facility:** 135 rooms. Comfortable guest rooms & suites. 2 two-bedroom units. 4 stories; interior corridors; meeting rooms; heated indoor pool, sauna, whirlpool. **Dining:** Complimentary breakfast 6 am-9 am, Sat & Sun 7-10 am; complimentary evening beverages & snacks. **Services:** data ports. Fee: coin laundry. **All Rooms:** microwaves, refrigerators, combo & shower baths, cable TV, VCP's. Fee: movies. **Some Rooms:** whirlpools. **Cards:** AE, CB, DI, DS, MC, VI. (D) (S) ⊗

QUALITY INN PORTLAND AIRPORT Rates Subject to Change **Phone:** 503/256-4111 **39**
AAA ◆◆ Motor Inn
6/1-8/31 1P: $60- 70 2P/1B: $65- 70 2P/2B: $70 XP: $5 F18
3/1-5/31 & 9/1-2/29 1P: $55- 60 2P/1B: $60- 65 2P/2B: $65 XP: $5 F18
Location: 5 mi e; northbound on I-205 (s of I-84) exit 23B to Sandy Blvd then w; southbound I-205 (north of I-84) exit 23A, w on Sandy Blvd. 8247 NE Sandy Blvd 97220. Fax: 503/254-1507. **Terms:** Sr. discount; reserv deposit, 3 day notice; pets. **Facility:** 120 rooms. Some guest rooms with balcony facing attractive courtyard. Few compact rooms. 2 two-bedroom units. 2 suites with fireplace, $100. 2 suites $70, off-season $65; 3 stories; interior corridors; conference facilities; heated pool. **Dining:** Restaurant; 7 am-2 & 5-10 pm; $7-$14; cocktails. **Services:** health club privileges; airport transportation. Fee: coin laundry. **All Rooms:** coffeemakers, free movies, cable TV. **Some Rooms:** refrigerators, whirlpools. **Cards:** AE, CB, DI, DS, JCB, MC, VI. (D) ⊗

RAMADA INN-PORTLAND AIRPORT AAA Special Value Rates **Phone:** 503/255-6511 **51**
AAA ◆◆ Motor Inn
All Year 2P/1B: $89- 140 2P/2B: $89- 130 XP: $10 F18
Location: 2 1/4 mi s of Portland International Airport on SR 213; from I-205 take exit 23B to Columbia Blvd, w to NE 80th Ave; from I-205N to Columbia Blvd. 6221 NE 82nd Ave 97220. Fax: 503/255-8417. **Terms:** Reserv deposit; no pets. **Facility:** 202 rooms. Attractively furnished units. Suites with whirlpool, microwave, refrigerator & wet bar, $250; 2 stories; interior corridors; business center, conference facilities; heated pool, sauna, whirlpool; exercise room. **Dining & Entertainment:** Restaurant; 6:30 am-10 pm, Fri & Sat-11 pm; $7-$14; cocktail lounge. **Services:** data ports; airport transportation. Fee: coin laundry. **All Rooms:** free movies, cable TV. **Cards:** AE, CB, DI, DS, JCB, MC, VI. (D) ⊗

RED LION HOTEL/COLUMBIA RIVER Rates Subject to Change **Phone:** 503/283-2111 **50**
◆◆◆ Motor Inn
All Year 1P: $105- 115 2P/1B: $120- 150 2P/2B: $120- 130 XP: $15 F18
Location: 4 mi n; off I-5, Jantzen Beach/Hayden Island, exit 308, near s end of Interstate Bridge. 1401 N Hayden Island Dr 97217. Fax: 503/283-4718. **Terms:** Reserv deposit, 3 day notice; small pets only, $15. **Facility:** 351 rooms. Mostly large units; many with a view of Columbia River. Spacious beautifully appointed suites. Balconies. 8 two-bedroom units. 1 bedroom suites with whirlpool, wet bar & refrigerator, $195-$300; 3 stories; interior corridors; conference facilities; luxury level rooms; putting green; heated pool, whirlpool; 2 lighted tennis courts; boat dock. **Dining & Entertainment:** Restaurant, coffee shop; 6 am-11 pm, Fri & Sat-midnight, Sun brunch; $8-$25; cocktail lounge; entertainment. **Services:** data ports; valet laundry; area transportation, to shopping mall & train, airport transportation. **All Rooms:** combo & shower baths, cable TV. Fee: movies. **Cards:** AE, CB, DI, DS, JCB, MC, VI. (D) ⊗

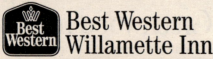

Best Western
Best Western Willamette Inn
"Affordable Luxury & Comfort"
Just minutes from downtown Portland, Washington Square, and Clackamas Mall • Comfortable, luxurious accommodations in a beautiful park-like setting. Free Continental Breakfast
HBO - 40 Ch. C/TV • Pool • Fitness Room • Spa • Recliner Easy Chairs • Guest Laundry • Kitchenettes & Microwaves • Free Local Calls • FAX
Interstate 5 & Exit 283 • Wilsonville, OR
(503) 682-2288 • TOLL FREE RESERVATIONS (800) 528-1234
See our listing under Wilsonville, OR
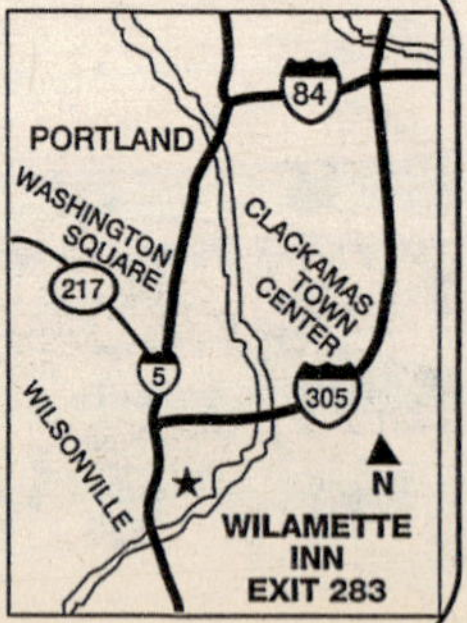

(See PORTLAND ACCOMMODATIONS spotting map page A47)

RED LION HOTEL-JANTZEN BEACH — Rates Subject to Change — **Phone:** 503/283-4466 — 49

◆◆◆ Motor Inn — All Year — 1P: $105- 125 2P/1B: $120- 140 2P/2B: $120- 140 XP: $15 F18

Location: 4 mi n off I-5, near Jantzen Beach/Hayden Island exit 308, near s end of Interstate Bridge. 909 N Hayden Island Dr 97217. Fax: 503/283-4743. **Terms:** Small pets only, $25 dep req. **Facility:** 320 rooms. Riverfront setting. Very attractive public rooms. Large, very comfortable guest rooms & beautifully appointed suites. 16 two-bedroom units. 8 one-bedroom suites with whirlpool, wet bar & refrigerator, $350-$450; 4 stories; interior corridors; conference facilities, convention oriented; heated pool, whirlpool; 2 lighted tennis courts; boat dock; exercise room. **Dining & Entertainment:** Dining room, coffee shop; 6 am-11:30 pm; $12-$20; cocktails/lounge; entertainment. **Services:** airport transportation. **All Rooms:** cable TV. Fee: movies. **Cards:** AE, CB, DI, DS, JCB, MC, VI.

SHERATON PORTLAND AIRPORT HOTEL — Rates Subject to Change — **Phone:** 503/281-2500 — 47

◆◆◆ Hotel — All Year — 1P: $108- 113 2P/1B: $125 2P/2B: $120 XP: $10 F18

Location: Northbound on I-205 take exit 24B, southbound take exit 24 east on Airport Way. 8235 NE Airport Way 97220-1398. Fax: 503/249-7602. **Terms:** Sr. discount; credit card guarantee, 7-10 days; no pets. **Facility:** 215 rooms. Well-equipped guest rooms. Tastefully appointed lobby & attractive guest facilities. 10 two-bedroom units. 10 suites, from $140; 5 stories; interior corridors; business center, conference facilities; heated indoor pool, saunas, whirlpool; exercise room, video game cartridges in each room. **Dining & Entertainment:** Dining room, coffee shop; 5:30 am-10 pm; $8-$18; cocktail lounge; 24-hour room service. **Services:** data ports, PC, secretarial services; valet laundry; airport transportation. **All Rooms:** honor bars, coffeemakers, free & pay movies, cable TV. **Some Rooms:** whirlpools. Fee: VCP's. **Cards:** AE, DI, DS, JCB, MC, VI.

SHILO INN PORTLAND SUITES HOTEL — Rates Subject to Change — **Phone:** 503/252-7500 — 52

AAA ◆◆◆ Suite Motor Inn — All Year [CP] — 1P: $114- 129 2P/1B: $114- 129 2P/2B: $114- 129 XP: $15 F12

Location: I-205 northbound exit 24B; southbound exit 24 to Airport Way; I-84 take exit 8 to I-205N then exit 24B. 11707 NE Airport Way 97220-1075. Fax: 503/254-0794. **Terms:** Sr. discount; no pets. **Facility:** 200 rooms. Comfortable units attractively decorated & well-equipped 1-bedroom suites. Large, very comfortable continental breakfast area. 4 stories; interior corridors; business center, conference facilities; heated indoor pool, sauna, steamroom, whirlpool; exercise room. **Dining & Entertainment:** Restaurant; 6 am-10 pm, Fri & Sat-11 pm; $10-$20; cocktails; entertainment. **Services:** data ports; airport transportation. Fee: coin laundry. **All Rooms:** microwaves, free movies, refrigerators, cable TV, VCP's. **Cards:** AE, CB, DI, DS, JCB, MC, VI.
(See ad below)

SILVER CLOUD INN — Rates Subject to Change — **Phone:** 503/242-2400 — 53

◆◆◆ Motel

6/15-9/30 [CP]	1P: $63	2P/1B: $69	2P/2B: $71	XP: $6 F12
3/1-6/14 & 10/1-2/29 [CP]	1P: $58	2P/1B: $64	2P/2B: $67	XP: $6 F12

Location: I-405 exit 3 to Vaughn St. 2426 NW Vaughn St 97210. Fax: 503/242-1770. **Terms:** Sr. discount; reserv deposit; no pets. **Facility:** 81 rooms. Generous, comfortably furnished guest rooms & suites. Outdoor patio seating area. 4 stories; interior corridors; meeting rooms; whirlpool; exercise room. **Services:** guest laundry. **All Rooms:** free movies, combo & shower baths, cable TV. **Some Rooms:** 11 efficiencies, microwaves, refrigerators, whirlpools. **Cards:** AE, DI, DS, MC, VI. Roll in showers.

RESTAURANTS

BRASSERIE MONTMARTRE — **Dinner:** $11-$20 — **Phone:** 503/224-5552 — 32

◆◆ American — **Location:** Downtown between SW Morrison & SW Alder at SW Park St. 626 SW Park Ave 97205. **Hours:** 11:30 am-2:30 am, Fri & Sat-3 am, Sat 10 am-3 am, Sun 10 am-2 am. Closed major holidays. **Reservations:** suggested. **Features:** cocktails & lounge; entertainment; street parking; a la carte. Parisian nightclub atmosphere. Very good selection of seafood, poultry, pasta & steak entrees. Also bistro menu avail from 2 pm. Nightly live jazz; strolling magician Tues-Sat 8:30 pm-12:30 am. **Cards:** AE, CB, DI, MC, VI.

THE CHART HOUSE — **Dinner:** $21-$30 — **Phone:** 503/246-6963 — 33

◆◆ American — **Location:** West Hills. 5700 SW Terwilliger Blvd 97219. **Hours:** 11:30 am-2 & 5-10 pm, Sun 5 pm-9 pm. **Reservations:** suggested. **Features:** children's menu; cocktails & lounge; valet parking; a la carte. Attractive restaurant with panoramic view of city & mountains. Seafood, steaks, prime rib & chicken dishes. Busy atmosphere. **Cards:** AE, DI, DS, MC, VI.

DER RHEINLANDER GERMAN RESTAURANT — **Dinner:** $11-$20 — **Phone:** 503/288-5503 — 28

◆◆◆ German — **Location:** 5035 NE Sandy Blvd 97213. **Hours:** 4:30 pm-10 pm, Sat 4 pm-11 pm, Sun 3:30 pm-9 pm. Closed: 7/4, 9/4, 12/24 & 12/25. **Reservations:** suggested. **Features:** children's menu; early bird specials; carryout; cocktails & lounge; entertainment. Popular, long-established restaurant. Colorful German decor & festive atmosphere with strolling musicians & singers. Some American dishes. **Cards:** AE, MC, VI.

GENOA — **Dinner:** over $31 — **Phone:** 503/238-1464 — 29

◆◆◆ Northern Italian — **Location:** 2832 SE Belmont 97214. **Hours:** 5:30 pm-9:30 pm. Closed major holidays & Sun. **Reservations:** required. **Features:** beer & wine only; street parking. Excellently prepared gourmet prix fixe 7-course dinners in intimate dining room, $45; also 4-course, $36. Classic beef, seafood & poultry entrees. Sitting room for pre or post dinner enjoyment. Smoke free premises. **Cards:** AE, CB, DI, DS, MC, VI.

Shilo Inns
"AFFORDABLE EXCELLENCE"

PORTLAND AIRPORT/I-205 SUITES HOTEL, RESTAURANT & CONVENTION CENTER
11707 N.E. Airport Way, Portland, OR 97220

(503) 252-7500

- 200 Ultra-Deluxe Suites featuring Wet Bar, Microwave & Refrigerator
- Fine Dining Restaurant & Lounge; Banquet/Convention Space for 500
- Indoor Pool, Spa, Sauna, Steam & Fitness Center
- Business Services available
- Complimentary Airport Shuttle

NATIONWIDE RESERVATIONS 1-800-222-2244

(See PORTLAND ACCOMMODATIONS spotting map page A47)

THE OLD SPAGHETTI FACTORY **Dinner:** up to $10 **Phone:** 503/222-5375 (35)
◆ Italian
Location: 0715 SW Bancroft 97201. **Hours:** 11:30 am-2 & 5-10 pm, Fri-11 pm, Sat 1 pm-11 pm, Sun noon-10 pm. Closed: 11/23, 12/24 & 12/25. **Features:** children's menu; carryout; cocktails & lounge; a la carte. Located along Willamette River. Family type restaurant with Rococo atmosphere & antique appointments. Serving spaghetti dishes with wide selection of sauces. Also, some popular Italian pasta & chicken dishes. **Cards:** DS, MC, VI. ⊗

PAPA HAYDN **Dinner:** $11-$20 **Phone:** 503/228-7317 (37)
◆◆ American
Location: 701 NW 23rd 97210. **Hours:** 11:30 am-11 pm, Fri & Sat-midnight, Sun brunch 10 am-3 pm. Closed: Mon. **Reservations:** suggested; for Sun brunch. **Features:** children's menu; cocktails; a la carte. Popular people watching restaurant, casual atmosphere. Entrees & light dishes. Northwest ingredients. Excellent pastry desserts. Sidewalk seating weather permitting. Daily special menu. Smoke free premises. **Cards:** AE, MC, VI. ⊗

SALTY'S ON THE COLUMBIA **Dinner:** $21-$30 **Phone:** 503/288-4444 (31)
◆◆ Seafood
Location: 4 mi n from I-5, exit 307 then Marine Dr e route. 3839 NE Marine Dr 97211. **Hours:** 11 am-10 pm, Sun 9:30 am-9 pm. Closed: 9/4 & 12/25. **Reservations:** suggested. **Features:** Sunday brunch; cocktails & lounge; valet parking; a la carte. Attractive riverfront restaurant with view of Columbia River. Emphasis on fresh seafood, also some steak & poultry selections. Some veranda dining. Smoke free premises. **Cards:** AE, CB, DI, MC, VI. ⊗

SAYLER'S OLD COUNTRY KITCHEN **Dinner:** $11-$20 **Phone:** 503/252-4171 (25)
AAA ◆◆ Steakhouse
Location: 10519 SE Stark St 97216. **Hours:** 4 pm-11 pm, Fri-midnight, Sat 3 pm-midnight, Sun noon-11 pm. Closed major holidays. **Features:** children's menu; senior's menu; cocktails & lounge. Very comfortable, casual atmosphere & very good service. Broad selection of complete steak dinners, also seafood & chicken. **Cards:** AE, DS, MC, VI. ⊗

WILLAMETTE ANCHORAGE **Dinner:** $21-$30 **Phone:** 503/231-8900 (24)
◆◆ American
Location: 6 blks s of Sellwood Bridge at foot of se Marion St. 513 SE Marion 97202. **Hours:** 11:30 am-2 & 5-9 pm, Fri & Sat 5 pm-10 pm, Sun 9:30 am-2 pm & 4:30-9 pm. Closed: 1/1 & 12/25. **Features:** Sunday brunch; children's menu; carryout; cocktails & lounge. Attractive restaurant overlooking Willamette river and boat moorage. Very tasteful dishes with emphasis on fresh seafood. Patio dining weather permitting. Also steak dishes. Sun seafood buffet brunch. Smoke free premises. **Cards:** AE, DI, DS, MC, VI. ⊗

WINTERBORNE RESTAURANT **Dinner:** $11-$20 **Phone:** 503/249-8489 (38)
◆◆ Continental
Location: 3520 NE 42nd Ave 97213. **Hours:** 5:30 pm-9:30 pm. Closed major holidays, Sun-Tues & 9/1-9/16. **Features:** beer & wine only; street parking. Long established. Small, neat dining room. Very well prepared Northwest regional dishes with classic influence. 1 prix-fixe, 5-course dinner, $18.50. Smoke free premises. **Cards:** AE, CB, DS, MC, VI. ⊗

YE OLDE TOWNE CRIER **Dinner:** $11-$20 **Phone:** 503/774-1822 (26)
AAA ◆ American
Location: 4515 SE 41st & Holgate Blvd 97202. **Hours:** 11:30 am-11 pm, Fri & Sat-midnight, Sun noon-10 pm. Closed major holidays. **Reservations:** suggested. **Features:** children's menu; cocktails & lounge; a la carte. Charming colonial atmosphere. Steaks, seafood, chicken & some Early American dishes. Also soups, sandwiches & salads. **Cards:** AE, DI, DS, MC, VI. ⊗

PORT ORFORD—1,000

LODGING

SEA CREST MOTEL Rates Subject to Change **Phone:** 503/332-3040
AAA ◆◆ Motel

6/20-9/20	1P: $43	2P/1B: $47	2P/2B: $55	XP: $3
3/1-6/19 & 9/21-2/29	1P: $36	2P/1B: $38	2P/2B: $45	XP: $3

Location: 1/2 mi s on Hwy 101. 97465 (PO Box C). **Terms:** No pets. **Facility:** 18 rooms. Attractive grounds. Immaculately kept units. 1 two-bedroom unit. 2 stories; exterior corridors; oceanview. **All Rooms:** coffeemakers, free movies, combo & shower baths, cable TV, no A/C. **Some Rooms:** phones. **Cards:** MC, VI. (D) ⊗

PRINEVILLE—5,400

LODGING

BEST WESTERN OF PRINEVILLE Rates Subject to Change **Phone:** 503/447-8080
AAA ◆◆◆ Motel

5/15-9/30 [CP]	1P: $55	2P/1B: $60	2P/2B: $65	XP: $5	F12
3/1-5/14 & 10/1-2/29 [CP]	1P: $45	2P/1B: $50	2P/2B: $55	XP: $5	F12

Location: 3/4 mi e on Hwy 26. 1475 E 3rd St 97754. Fax: 503/447-1011. **Terms:** Credit card guarantee, 3 day notice; no pets. **Facility:** 43 rooms. Inviting lobby. Comfortable units with pine furnishings & terra cotta accents. 2 stories; interior corridors; meeting rooms; heated indoor pool, whirlpool. **Services:** Fee: coin laundry. **All Rooms:** free movies, cable TV. **Some Rooms:** microwaves, refrigerators, whirlpools. **Cards:** AE, CB, DI, DS, MC, VI. ♿ (D) ⊗

Best Western Inn
Portland South
Best Western
Chateau 290
At Highways I-5 & I-205
Near 217 & 99W
Serving: Beaverton, Lake Oswego, Tualatin & Tigard
Near: Washington Square Mall, 1/2 hour to wine-country
Facilities: new mini-suites, pool, spa, sauna, meeting & office amenities
Local (503) 620-2030 • (800) 345-2030
Best Western Reservations: (800) 528-1234

REDMOND—7,200

LODGINGS

BEST WESTERN NEW REDMOND HOTEL Rates Subject to Change **Phone:** 503/923-7378

◆◆ Hotel

Fri & Sat 3/1-9/15 [CP]	1P: $47- 65	2P/1B: $52- 60	2P/2B: $57- 66	XP: $5 D12
Sun-Thurs 3/1-5/31, 6/1-9/15 & 9/16-2/29 [CP]	1P: $47- 57	2P/1B: $52	2P/2B: $57	XP: $5 D12

Location: 521 SW 6th St 97756. Fax: 503/923-3949. **Terms:** Sr. discount; credit card guarantee; no pets. **Facility:** 48 rooms. Renovated 1927 hotel. 15 parlor suites $65-$75, $89-$95 high season; 3 stories; interior corridors; meeting rooms; whirlpool; exercise room. **Dining:** Restaurant nearby. **Services:** data ports; airport transportation. Fee: coin laundry. **All Rooms:** free movies, cable TV. **Some Rooms:** refrigerators. Fee: VCP's. **Cards:** AE, CB, DI, DS, MC, VI.

BEST WESTERN RAMA INN Rates Subject to Change **Phone:** 503/548-8080

◆◆◆ Motel

6/1-8/31 [CP]	1P: $75	2P/1B: $75	2P/2B: $85	XP: $5 F12
3/1-5/31 & 9/1-2/29 [CP]	1P: $62	2P/1B: $67	2P/2B: $72	XP: $5 F12

Location: 1 mi s on Hwy 97. 2630 SW 17th Pl 97756. Fax: 503/548-3705. **Terms:** Sr. discount; reserv deposit; no pets. **Facility:** 49 rooms. Very attractively appointed units. 3 two-bedroom units. 1- bedroom suites, 4 with whirlpool, $75-$125; 2 honeymoon suites $125-$160; 2 stories; interior corridors; meeting rooms; heated indoor pool, sauna, whirlpool; exercise room. **Services:** data ports; airport transportation. Fee: coin laundry. **Recreation:** ski storage facilities. **All Rooms:** free movies, refrigerators, cable TV. **Some Rooms:** microwaves. Fee: VCP's. **Cards:** AE, CB, DI, DS, JCB, MC, VI.

THE INN AT EAGLE CREST AAA Special Value Rates **Phone:** 503/923-2453

◆◆◆ Resort Motor Inn

Fri & Sat 3/1-10/10	1P: $80- 114	2P/1B: $80- 114	2P/2B: $80- 114
Fri & Sat 10/11-2/29	1P: $72- 114	2P/1B: $72- 114	2P/2B: $72- 114
Sun-Thurs 10/11-2/29	1P: $67- 96	2P/1B: $67- 96	2P/2B: $67- 96
Sun-Thurs 3/1-10/10	1P: $60- 94	2P/1B: $60- 94	2P/2B: $60- 94

Location: 5 mi w on Hwy 126, then s on Cline Falls Rd. 1522 Cline Falls Rd 97756 (PO Box 1215). Fax: 503/923-1720. **Terms:** Check-in 4 pm; credit card guarantee; package plans; no pets. **Facility:** 119 rooms. In very attractive scenic setting. Large very attractive units, some with view, balcony or patio. 3 stories; interior corridors; meeting rooms; 36 holes golf, putting green; pool, whirlpool; 4 tennis courts; playground. Fee: golf instruction; wagon rides. **Dining & Entertainment:** Restaurant, coffee shop; 7 am-10 pm; in winter to 9 pm; $8-$21; cocktail lounge; Sun brunch. **Services:** data ports; airport transportation. Fee: coin laundry, area transportation, to Mt Bachelor. **Recreation:** recreation program, social program; fishing; hiking trails, jogging. Fee: horseback riding. Rental: bicycles. **All Rooms:** free movies, cable TV. **Some Rooms:** 49 efficiencies, whirlpools. Fee: VCP's. **Cards:** AE, DS, MC, VI.

REDMOND INN Rates Subject to Change **Phone:** 503/548-1091

◆◆ Motel

All Year	1P: $44- 46	2P/1B: $48- 50	2P/2B: $54- 58	XP: $5

Location: 1/2 mi s on Hwy 97. 1545 Hwy 97S 97756. **Terms:** Reserv deposit; pets, $5, in designated rooms. **Facility:** 46 rooms. Very well-kept & maintained units. 6 kitchens, $5 extra; 3 stories, no elevator; exterior corridors; heated pool, covered patio area. **Dining:** Restaurant nearby. **All Rooms:** free movies, refrigerators, cable TV. **Some Rooms:** radios. **Cards:** AE, DS, MC, VI. *(See ad below)*

VILLAGE SQUIRE MOTEL Rates Subject to Change **Phone:** 503/548-2105

◆◆ Motel

3/1-10/15	2P/1B: $55	2P/2B: $60	XP: $5
10/16-2/29	2P/1B: $40- 45	2P/2B: $45- 50	XP: $5

Location: 1 blk s on Hwy 97. 629 S 5th St 97756 (PO Box 81). **Terms:** Credit card guarantee; no pets. **Facility:** 24 rooms. Immaculately well-kept & maintained units. 2 stories; exterior corridors. **Services:** airport transportation. **All Rooms:** free movies, cable TV. **Some Rooms:** microwaves, refrigerators. Fee: VCP's. **Cards:** AE, DI, MC, VI. *(See ad below)*

RESTAURANT

SULLY'S ITALIAN RESTAURANT **Dinner:** $11-$20 **Phone:** 503/548-5483

◆◆ Italian

Location: On Hwy 97 southbound. 521 S Sixth 97756. **Hours:** 11 am-10 pm, Sat & Sun from 4 pm. Closed: 11/23 & 12/25. **Reservations:** suggested; for 6 or more. **Features:** children's menu; carryout; cocktails & lounge; street parking; a la carte. Popular, informal dining room with nice selection of well-prepared pasta, chicken, veal & sausage dishes. Also pizza, sandwiches, steaks & seafood. **Cards:** MC, VI.

REEDSPORT—4,800

LODGINGS

ANCHOR BAY INN Guaranteed Rates **Phone:** 503/271-2149

◆ Motel

5/15-10/31 [CP]	1P: $39	2P/1B: $46	2P/2B: $53	XP: $5 F10
3/1-5/14 & 11/1-2/29 [CP]	1P: $33	2P/1B: $38	2P/2B: $43	XP: $5 F10

Location: Center on Hwy 101. 1821 Winchester Ave 97467. Fax: 503/271-1802. **Terms:** Sr. discount; reserv deposit; pets, $5. **Facility:** 21 rooms. Pleasant units with simple decor. 1 two-bedroom unit. 4 efficiencies, $5 extra; 2 stories; exterior corridors; heated pool. **Services:** Fee: coin laundry. **All Rooms:** combo & shower baths, no A/C. **Some Rooms:** microwaves, refrigerators. Fee: VCP's. **Cards:** AE, CB, DI, DS, MC, VI. *(See ad p A54)*

REDMOND INN

1545 HWY 97 S., REDMOND, OREGON (503) 548-1091 OR TOLL FREE 1-800-833-3259

Heated pool *Kitchens* *Restaurant Adjacent* *Free HBO*

Village Squire Motel

North bound on Hwy 97 - Downtown
P.O. Box 81 Redmond
OR 97756

1-800-548-2102

- Direct Dial Phones
- Complimentary Coffee
- Courtesy Airport Shuttle
- Non-Smoking Rooms
- Cable TV/HBO
- Shopping and Restaurants Conveniently Located

Len & Florence Bradley
Your Hosts

BEST WESTERN SALBASGEON INN Rates Subject to Change **Phone:** 503/271-4831

◆◆◆ Motel

5/1-9/14 [CP] 1P: $66- 75 2P/1B: $71- 81 2P/2B: $76- 86 XP: $5
3/1-4/30 & 9/15-2/29 [CP] 1P: $56- 70 2P/1B: $61- 81 2P/2B: $71 XP: $5

Location: On Hwy 101. 1400 Hwy Ave 101 97467. Fax: 503/271-4832. **Terms:** Sr. discount; credit card guarantee; pets, $5, in designated rooms. **Facility:** 56 rooms. Well-furnished & immaculately kept units, some with river view. Suites with fireplace & kitchen $110-$115, $75-$80 off season; 2 stories; exterior corridors; meeting rooms; heated indoor pool, whirlpool; exercise room. **Dining:** Restaurant nearby. **Services:** Fee: coin laundry. **All Rooms:** free movies, cable TV. **Some Rooms:** coffeemakers, microwaves, refrigerators, whirlpools. **Cards:** AE, CB, DI, DS, MC, VI. (D) ⊗

SALBASGEON INN OF THE UMPQUA Rates Subject to Change **Phone:** 503/271-2025

◆◆ Motel

5/16-10/15 1P: $60 2P/1B: $65 2P/2B: $70 XP: $5
3/1-5/15 & 10/16-2/29 1P: $45 2P/1B: $50 2P/2B: $55 XP: $5

Location: 7 1/2 mi e on Hwy 38. 45209 Hwy 38 97467. **Terms:** Sr. discount; credit card guarantee, 3 day notice; pets, $5. **Facility:** 12 rooms. Neat, exceptionally maintained units in forested area next to Umpqua River. River view units. 4 kitchen units from $70, from $55 off season; 2 stories; exterior corridors. **All Rooms:** free movies, combo & shower baths, cable TV, no A/C. **Cards:** AE, CB, DI, DS, MC, VI. (D) ⊗

TROPICANA MOTEL Rates Subject to Change **Phone:** 503/271-3671

◆ Motel

5/1-9/30 1P: $35- 39 2P/1B: $40- 55 2P/2B: $42- 60 XP: $5 D12
3/1-4/30 & 10/1-2/29 1P: $29- 35 2P/1B: $35- 42 2P/2B: $38- 45 XP: $5 D12

Location: On Hwy 101. 1593 Highway Ave 101 97467. **Terms:** Sr. discount; credit card guarantee; small pets only, $3. **Facility:** 41 rooms. 1 spacious unit with king bed from $55, $50 off season; 2 stories; exterior corridors; small pool. **Dining:** Restaurant nearby. **All Rooms:** free movies, cable TV, no A/C. **Some Rooms:** kitchen, microwaves, refrigerators. **Cards:** AE, CB, DI, DS, MC, VI. *(See color ad below)* (D) ⊗

RESTAURANT

UNGER'S LANDING RESTAURANT & LOUNGE **Dinner:** $11-$20 **Phone:** 503/271-3328

◆ American

Location: Hwy 38 to 2nd Ave at Riverfront Way. 345 Riverfront Way 97467. **Hours:** 11:30 am-2:30 & 5-9 pm. Closed major holidays. **Reservations:** suggested; weekends. **Features:** cocktail lounge; a la carte. Moderate selection of seafood, beef & chicken dishes. Located in a wheel house of former research vessel. Comfortable booth seating. **Cards:** AE, MC, VI. ⊗

ROCKAWAY BEACH—1,000

LODGINGS

SILVER SANDS MOTEL Rates Subject to Change **Phone:** 503/355-2206

◆◆ Motel

5/20-9/15 2P/1B: $76 2P/2B: $81
3/1-5/19 & 9/16-2/29 2P/1B: $64 2P/2B: $69

Location: 1 blk w of Hwy 101, off S 2nd Ave. 97136 (PO Box 161). **Terms:** Credit card guarantee; small pets only. **Facility:** 64 rooms. Well-equipped and very well maintained 1- & 2-room units with ocean view. Some units with fireplace & balcony. 06 two-bedroom efficiencies, $86 for 2 persons. 23 one-bedroom efficiencies, 12 with fireplace & private balcony, $95-$108; 2 stories; exterior corridors; beachfront; heated indoor pool, sauna, whirlpool; playground. **All Rooms:** coffeemakers, free movies, refrigerators, cable TV, no A/C. **Some Rooms:** microwaves. **Cards:** AE, DI, DS, MC, VI. Roll in showers. (D)

TRADEWINDS MOTEL Rates Subject to Change **Phone:** 503/355-2112

◆◆ Motel

5/1-9/30 1P: $51- 87 2P/1B: $51- 87 2P/2B: $72- 87 XP: $5
3/1-4/30 & 10/1-2/29 1P: $45- 74 2P/1B: $45- 74 2P/2B: $60- 74

Location: 1 blk w of Hwy 101, off N 5th Ave. 523 N Pacific St 97136. Fax: 503/355-3840. **Terms:** Reserv deposit; pets, $10. **Facility:** 19 rooms. Attractively decorated units, most with balcony & fireplace. Beachfront. 5 two-bedroom units. 2- & 3-room suites with kitchen, one with whirlpool $125-$205; $115-$185 off-season; 2 stories; exterior corridors; oceanview; beach; playground. **All Rooms:** free movies, cable TV, no A/C. **Some Rooms:** 12 efficiencies, refrigerators. **Cards:** AE, CB, DI, DS, MC, VI. (D)

ROGUE RIVER—1,800

LODGING

BEST WESTERN INN AT THE ROGUE Rates Subject to Change **Phone:** 503/582-2200

◆◆◆ Motel

6/20-9/15 [CP] 1P: $65- 75 2P/1B: $65- 75 2P/2B: $75 XP: $5 F12
5/1-6/19 & 9/16-10/31 [CP] 1P: $60- 70 2P/1B: $60- 70 2P/2B: $70 XP: $5 F12
3/1-4/30 & 11/1-2/29 [CP] 1P: $50- 60 2P/1B: $50- 60 2P/2B: $60 XP: $5 F12

Location: W of I-5 exit 48; 7 mi s of Grants Pass, 14 mi n of Medford. 8959 Rogue River Hwy 97527. Fax: 503/582-1415. **Terms:** Sr. discount; reserv deposit; pets, $10, also $35 dep req. **Facility:** 54 rooms. Very attractively decorated units & well maintained guest facilities. 1-bedroom suite with wet bar & whirlpool, $150; $120 off season; 2 stories; interior corridors; meeting rooms; heated pool, whirlpool; exercise room. **Dining:** Restaurant nearby. **Services:** Fee: coin laundry. **All Rooms:** free movies, cable TV. **Some Rooms:** microwaves, refrigerators. Fee: VCP's. **Cards:** AE, CB, DI, DS, MC, VI. *(See ad p A26)* (D) (S) ⊗

10% Off posted rates*
Tropicana Motel
"GATEWAY TO THE OREGON DUNES"
"CENTER OF OREGON'S BEST SPORT FISHING"
• Enjoy your choice of 41 deluxe units • Pool
• HBO • Bridal Suite • Kitchenettes • N/S Units
• Senior Discount • Commercial rates • Renovated in 1991
1593 Hwy Ave. 101
Reedsport, Oregon
(503) 271-3671
1-800-799-9970
*not valid with any other offer

ANCHOR DOWN FOR THE NIGHT!
ANCHOR BAY INN
For Reservations Call: 503/271-2149
Gateway to the Oregon Dunes, Umpqua Discovery Center
Lighthouse Tours, Elk Viewing, Sport Fishing & Excellent Sea Food!

ROSEBURG—17,000

LODGINGS

BEST WESTERN GARDEN VILLA MOTEL Guaranteed Rates **Phone:** 503/672-1601

AAA ◆◆ Motel

6/1-9/30 [CP]	1P: $58	2P/1B: $58	2P/2B: $68	XP: $6
3/1-5/31 & 10/1-2/29 [CP]	1P: $45	2P/1B: $45	2P/2B: $48	XP: $6

Location: Off I-5 exit 125. 760 Garden Valley Blvd 97470. Fax: 503/672-1316. **Terms:** No pets. **Facility:** 122 rooms. Located next to the Garden Villa Shopping Center. Attractive units & lobby. 2 two-bedroom units. 2 suites $75, $70 off-season; 2 stories; exterior corridors; meeting rooms; 2 heated pools; exercise room. **Dining:** Restaurants nearby. **Services:** airport transportation. Fee: coin laundry. **All Rooms:** coffeemakers, free movies, combo & shower baths, cable TV. **Some Rooms:** microwaves, refrigerators. Fee: VCP's. **Cards:** AE, CB, DI, DS, MC, VI. Ⓓ ⊗

MOTEL ORLEANS Rates Subject to Change **Phone:** 503/673-5561

AAA ◆ Motel

All Year	1P: $40- 47	2P/1B: $40- 47	2P/2B: $46- 50	XP: $5 F12

Location: 1 blk e of I-5, exit 125. 427 NW Garden Valley Blvd 97470. **Terms:** Sr. discount; credit card guarantee; no pets. **Facility:** 72 rooms. Well kept units. Conveniently located off I-5. 6 two-bedroom units. 6 kitchens, $5 key deposit; 2 stories; exterior corridors; meeting rooms; pool. **Dining:** Restaurant nearby. **Services:** guest laundry. **All Rooms:** cable TV. **Some Rooms:** coffeemakers, microwaves, refrigerators. **Cards:** AE, CB, DI, DS, MC, VI. Ⓓ ⊗

ROSEBURG TRAVELODGE AAA Special Value Rates **Phone:** 503/672-4836

AAA ◆◆ Motel

6/1-9/30	1P: $57	2P/1B: $66	2P/2B: $78	XP: $5 F17
3/1-5/31 & 10/1-2/29	1P: $49	2P/1B: $55	2P/2B: $61	XP: $5 F17

Location: 1 blk e of I-5, exit 124. 315 W Harvard Blvd 97470. Fax: 503/672-4836. **Terms:** Reserv deposit; no pets. **Facility:** 40 rooms. Immaculately maintained units; some with balcony & river view. Attractively landscaped river shore area. 2 stories; exterior corridors; heated pool. **Dining:** Restaurant nearby. **All Rooms:** coffeemakers, free movies, combo & shower baths, cable TV. **Some Rooms:** refrigerators. **Cards:** AE, CB, DI, DS, JCB, MC, VI. *(See color ad below)* Ⓓ ⊗

SHADY OAKS MOTEL Rates Subject to Change **Phone:** 503/672-2608

AAA ◆◆ Motel

6/1-9/30	1P: $32	2P/1B: $37	2P/2B: $40	XP: $5 D
3/1-5/31 & 10/1-2/29	1P: $29	2P/1B: $32	2P/2B: $34	XP: $3 D

Location: Off I-5 exit 120, 1/2 mi n. 2954 Old 99S 97470. **Terms:** Credit card guarantee, 3 day notice; no pets. **Facility:** 12 rooms. Attractive tree-shaded lawn area. Large units with home-like atmosphere. 1 story; exterior corridors. **All Rooms:** coffeemakers, shower baths. **Cards:** DS, MC, VI. Ⓓ ⊗

AAA SPECIAL VALUE RATES
Travelodge
"Housekeeping" or "Room/Interior" Award Winners Last Four Years
ROSEBURG
315 West Harvard • Roseburg, OR 97470
Just off I-5 exit 124 on the S. Umpqua River
503/672-4836 or Call Toll Free 800/578-7878
• Senior Citizen Discount • Restaurant adjacent • Heated swimming pool
• Beautifully landscaped private park and picnic area
• Selected rooms have balconies with river views
• All rooms newly refurbished with 65% non-smoking
• Freshly brewed in-room coffee • Cable TV with HBO, ESPN, CNN, USA

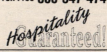

WINDMILL INN
of Roseburg
1450 Mulholland Drive
Roseburg, OR 97470
Toll Free 800-547-4747
Hospitality Guaranteed!
• Complimentary Morning Coffee, Muffin and Newspaper Delivered to Your Room
• Free Local Airport & Mall Shuttle
• Indoor Whirlpool, Sauna and Outdoor Pool
• Use of Guest Bicycles
• Use of "Best Seller" Lending Library
• Free Local Telephone Calls
• Children Under 18 Stay Free In An Adults Room
• Free Movie Channels
• Restaurant & Lounge Adjacent to Inn
• AAA Discount

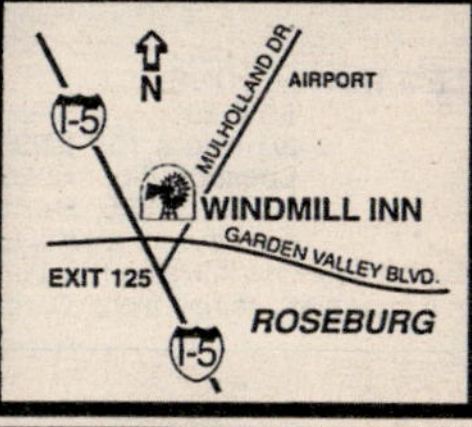

Towns under which AAA-approved lodging and dining facilities are listed are shown in red on AAA maps.

WINDMILL INN Guaranteed Rates **Phone:** 503/673-0901
AAA ◆◆◆ Motor Inn
6/1-9/30 1P: $54- 68 2P/1B: $64- 74 2P/2B: $67- 82 XP: $6 F17
3/1-5/31 & 10/1-2/29 1P: $52- 65 2P/1B: $58- 71 2P/2B: $61- 74 XP: $6 F17
Location: 1 blk e of I-5, exit 125. 1450 NW Mulholland Dr 97470. Fax: 503/673-0901. **Terms:** Sr. discount; reserv deposit, 3 day notice; pets. **Facility:** 128 rooms. Few balconies. Comfortably decorated rooms. 2 stories; interior corridors; meeting rooms; heated pool, sauna, whirlpool. **Dining & Entertainment:** Dining room, coffee shop; 6 am-midnight; $7-$18; cocktails/lounge. **Recreation:** bicycles. **All Rooms:** free movies, combo & shower baths, cable TV. **Some Rooms:** kitchen, microwaves, refrigerators. **Cards:** AE, DI, DS, MC, VI. *(See ad p A55)* (D) ⊗

RESTAURANT

BRUTKE'S WAGON WHEEL RESTAURANT & LOUNGE **Dinner:** $11-$20 **Phone:** 503/672-7555
AAA ◆ American
Location: 1 mi n; 2 blks e of I-5, off exit 125. 227 Garden Valley Blvd 97470. **Hours:** 7 am-10:30 pm, Fri & Sat-11 pm, Sun 7 am-10 pm. Closed: 12/25. **Features:** children's menu; senior's menu; carryout; cocktails & lounge. Casual attractive atmosphere. Prime rib, steak & seafood. Smoke free premises. **Cards:** AE, MC, VI. ⊗

SALEM—107,800

LODGINGS

BEST WESTERN MILL CREEK INN Guaranteed Rates **Phone:** 503/585-3332
AAA ◆◆◆ Motel
5/15-9/30 1P: $66- 79 2P/1B: $73- 82 2P/2B: $74 XP: $6 D
3/1-5/14 & 10/1-2/29 1P: $61- 63 2P/1B: $69 2P/2B: $69 XP: $6 D
Location: W of I-5, exit 253. 3125 Ryan Dr SE 97301. Fax: 503/375-9618. **Terms:** Sr. discount; credit card guarantee, 3 day notice; no pets. **Facility:** 109 rooms. Large very tastefully appointed & immaculately kept guest rooms. Comfortable guest lounge area. 6 spacious 1-bedroom suites, $80-$125; 3 stories; interior corridors; meeting rooms; heated indoor pool, saunas, whirlpool; exercise room. **Dining:** Restaurant nearby. **Services:** data ports; airport transportation. Fee: coin laundry. **All Rooms:** free movies, combo & shower baths, cable TV. **Some Rooms:** microwaves, refrigerators. **Cards:** AE, CB, DI, DS, MC, VI. (D) (S) ⊗

BEST WESTERN NEW KINGS INN AAA Special Value Rates **Phone:** 503/581-1559
AAA ◆◆◆ Motel
5/15-10/31 1P: $58 2P/1B: $61 2P/2B: $64 XP: $6
3/1-5/14 & 11/1-2/29 1P: $55 2P/1B: $58 2P/2B: $61 XP: $6
Location: On I-5 at Market St, exit 256. 3658 Market St NE 97301. Fax: 503/364-4272. **Terms:** Credit card guarantee; no pets. **Facility:** 101 rooms. Very convenient freeway location. Generous, well-furnished & very well-maintained units. 2 stories; exterior corridors; meeting rooms; heated indoor pool, wading pool, saunas, whirlpool; 2 tennis courts; exercise room, playground. **Dining:** Restaurant nearby. **Services:** data ports; airport transportation. Fee: coin laundry. **All Rooms:** free movies, refrigerators, cable TV. **Cards:** AE, CB, DI, DS, MC, VI. (D) ⊗

BEST WESTERN PACIFIC HWY INN Guaranteed Rates **Phone:** 503/390-3200
AAA ◆◆◆ Motel
5/15-10/31 [CP] 1P: $58 2P/1B: $65 2P/2B: $65 XP: $6
3/1-5/14 & 11/1-2/29 [CP] 1P: $53 2P/1B: $58 2P/2B: $58 XP: $6
Location: Northbound I-5 exit 258; southbound exit 258 make a U-turn at 1st light then n on Portland Rd. 4646 Portland Rd NE 97305. Fax: 503/393-7989. **Terms:** Credit card guarantee, 3 day notice; no pets. **Facility:** 52 rooms. Especially well-kept units. Inviting guest lounge area & recreation facilities. 2 stories; exterior corridors; meeting rooms; heated indoor pool, wading pool, whirlpool; exercise room. **Services:** data ports. Fee: coin laundry. **All Rooms:** free movies, refrigerators, cable TV. **Cards:** AE, CB, DI, DS, MC, VI. Roll in showers. (D) ⊗

PHOENIX INN Guaranteed Rates **Phone:** 503/588-9220
AAA ◆◆◆ Motel
All Year [CP] 1P: $49- 67 2P/1B: $54- 72 2P/2B: $60 XP: $5 F17
Location: I-5 exit 252 to Kuebler Rd, then n on Commercial. 4370 Commercial SE 97308. Fax: 503/585-3616. **Terms:** Small pets only, $10. **Facility:** 89 rooms. Tastefully decorated units. Comfortable continental breakfast area. 2 suites, $65-$90; 4 stories; interior corridors; meeting rooms; heated indoor pool, whirlpool; exercise room. **Services:** airport transportation. Fee: coin laundry. **All Rooms:** microwaves, free movies, refrigerators, cable TV. **Some Rooms:** whirlpools. **Cards:** AE, CB, DI, DS, MC, VI. (D) (S) ⊗

QUALITY INN AAA Special Value Rates **Phone:** 503/370-7888
AAA ◆◆ Motor Inn
All Year 1P: $66- 77 2P/1B: $73- 87 2P/2B: $78- 92 XP: $5 F18
Location: W of I-5 & Market St exit 256. 3301 Market St NE 97301. Fax: 503/370-6305. **Terms:** Pets, $10. **Facility:** 150 rooms. Very pleasant & attractively decorated guest rooms, some compact. 21 large rooms with whirlpools. 4 stories; interior corridors; conference facilities; heated indoor pool, saunas, whirlpool. **Dining & Entertainment:** Restaurant; 6:30 am-2 & 5-10 pm, Sat 7 am-12:30 & 5-10 pm, Sun 7 am-1 & 5-9 pm; $7-$15; cocktail lounge. **Services:** health club privileges. Fee: coin laundry. **All Rooms:** coffeemakers, free movies, combo & shower baths, cable TV. **Some Rooms:** microwaves, refrigerators. **Cards:** AE, CB, DI, DS, JCB, MC, VI. Roll in showers. (D) (S) ⊗

SALEM TRAVELODGE Rates Subject to Change **Phone:** 503/588-5423
AAA ◆ Motel
5/1-9/30 1P: $38- 40 2P/1B: $43- 46 2P/2B: $50- 53 XP: $5 F10
3/1-4/30 & 10/1-2/29 1P: $35- 38 2P/1B: $40- 45 2P/2B: $47- 50 XP: $5 F10
Location: I-5, exit 256; e on Market then n on Lancaster; w on Sunnyview then s on Fisher Rd. 1875 Fisher Rd NE 97305. Fax: 503/391-4781. **Terms:** Sr. discount; reserv deposit, 3 day notice; small pets only, $5. **Facility:** 72 rooms. Large, well-kept units. 3 stories; interior corridors. **Dining:** Restaurant nearby. **Services:** Fee: coin laundry. **All Rooms:** coffeemakers, combo & shower baths, cable TV. Fee: movies. **Some Rooms:** VCP's. Fee: microwaves, refrigerators. **Cards:** AE, CB, DI, DS, MC, VI. Roll in showers. (D) ⊗

SHILO INN Rates Subject to Change **Phone:** 503/581-4001
◆◆◆ Motel
6/1-9/30 [CP] 1P: $83- 88 2P/1B: $83- 88 2P/2B: $83- 88 XP: $10 F12
3/1-5/31 & 10/1-2/29 [CP] 1P: $79- 84 2P/1B: $79- 84 2P/2B: $79- 84 XP: $10 F12
Location: W of I-5 exit 256. 3304 Market St NE 97301. Fax: 503/399-9385. **Terms:** Sr. discount; credit card guarantee; no pets. **Facility:** 89 rooms. Spacious, especially well-equipped & very attractively decorated units. 4 stories; interior corridors; meeting rooms; heated indoor pool, sauna, steamroom, whirlpool; exercise room. **Dining:** Restaurant nearby. **Services:** data ports; airport transportation. Fee: coin laundry. **All Rooms:** microwaves, free movies, refrigerators, cable TV, VCP's. **Cards:** AE, CB, DI, DS, JCB, MC, VI. (D) (S) ⊗

RESTAURANT

THE INN AT ORCHARD HEIGHTS — **Dinner:** $11-$20 — **Phone:** 503/378-1780

AAA ◆◆ American

Location: W side; off SR 221 at Orchard Heights Rd; 3/4 mi n on SR 221 from w end of Marion St Bridge. 695 Orchard Heights NW 97304. **Hours:** 11 am-2 & 5-9 pm, Fri-10 pm, Sat 5 pm-10 pm, Sun-9 pm. Closed: 1/1, 7/4, 12/24 & 12/25. **Reservations:** suggested. **Features:** early bird specials; cocktails & lounge; a la carte. Attractive setting & charming dining rooms. Nice selection of seafood, beef, veal & poultry. Patio dining. Entertainment weekends. **Cards:** AE, DS, MC, VI. ⊗

SEASIDE—5,400

LODGINGS

BEACHWOOD BED & BREAKFAST — Rates Subject to Change — **Phone:** 503/738-9585

◆◆◆ Bed & Breakfast

6/15-9/30 [BP]	1P: $62- 107	2P/1B: $72- 117
3/1-6/14, 10/1-11/15 & 2/15-2/29 [BP]	1P: $60- 90	2P/1B: $70- 100

Location: Hwy 101; G Ave then west. 671 Beach Dr 97138. **Terms:** Open 3/1-11/15 & 2/15-2/29; check-in 4 pm; reserv deposit, 7 day notice; no pets. **Facility:** 3 rooms. Historic Craftsman-style house built in 1900. 1 blk from beach. Bright cheerful common areas & guest rooms. Large parlor suites with fireplace. Library nook. Outdoor tree-shaded patio. 2 stories; interior corridors; smoke free premises. **Dining:** Breakfast served 9 am. **Recreation:** bicycles. **All Rooms:** combo & shower baths, cable TV, no A/C, no phones. **Some Rooms:** radios, refrigerators, VCP's, whirlpools. **Cards:** MC, VI. (D) ⊗

BEST WESTERN OCEAN VIEW RESORT — AAA Special Value Rates — **Phone:** 503/738-3334

AAA ◆◆◆ Motor Inn

Fri & Sat 5/26-9/30	2P/1B: $80- 185	2P/2B: $114- 153
Sun-Thurs 5/26-9/30	2P/1B: $70- 185	2P/2B: $95- 153
3/1-5/25	2P/1B: $70- 185	2P/2B: $95- 147
10/1-2/29	2P/1B: $70- 165	2P/2B: $70- 137

Location: On 1st Ave, cross river; to Necanicum Dr, s on 4th to Ocean. 414 N Prom 97138. Fax: 503/738-3264. **Terms:** Reserv deposit; no pets. **Facility:** 84 rooms. Tastefully appointed units, many with deck & fireplace. 8 spacious units. 5 stories; exterior corridors; oceanfront; conference facilities; beach, heated indoor pool, whirlpool. **Dining & Entertainment:** Restaurant; 7 am-10 pm; 10/16-3/15, 7 am-1 & 5-10 pm; $8-$20; cocktails; entertainment 6/15-9/15. **Services:** data ports. Fee: coin laundry. **All Rooms:** combo & shower baths, cable TV, no A/C. Fee: movies. **Some Rooms:** coffeemakers, 54 efficiencies, microwaves, refrigerators, whirlpools. Fee: VCP's. **Cards:** AE, CB, DI, DS, MC, VI. (D) ⊗

COLONIAL MOTOR INN — Guaranteed Rates — **Phone:** 503/738-6295

AAA ◆◆ Motel

6/16-9/15	2P/1B: $68- 78	2P/2B: $78- 87
3/1-6/15 & 9/16-10/31	2P/1B: $65- 74	2P/2B: $74- 83
11/1-2/29	2P/1B: $51- 61	2P/2B: $61- 69

Location: 1/2 mi n; 1 blk w of jct Hwy 101 & 12th Ave. 1120 N Holladay 97138. Fax: 503/738-8437. **Terms:** Reserv deposit, 3 day notice; 7 night min stay, in suite; no pets. **Facility:** 9 rooms. Tastefully decorated units, most compact, in colonial motif. 2 two-bedroom units. Deluxe non-smoking king room with VCP, washer & dryer, $99. Large 1-bedroom suite with fireplace, kitchen, patio & river views, $265 in season; 1 story; exterior corridors. **All Rooms:** combo & shower baths, cable TV, VCP's, no A/C. **Cards:** AE, DS, MC, VI. *(See ad below)* (D) ⊗

EBB TIDE MOTEL — AAA Special Value Rates — **Phone:** 503/738-8371

AAA ◆◆ Motel

5/1-9/30	1P: $100- 115	2P/1B: $100- 115	2P/2B: $110- 120	XP: $5
3/1-4/30 & 10/1-2/29	1P: $80	2P/1B: $80- 90	2P/2B: $90- 100	XP: $5

Location: Broadway, n on Holladay, to 1st, then to Necanicum; 3rd to Ocean. 300 N Prom 97138. Fax: 503/738-0938. **Terms:** Check-in 4 pm; credit card guarantee; no pets. **Facility:** 83 rooms. 1- & 2-room units, most with ocean view & fireplace. 38 two-bedroom units. 3 stories; exterior corridors; oceanfront; beach, heated indoor pool, sauna, whirlpool. **All Rooms:** free movies, cable TV, no A/C. **Some Rooms:** coffeemakers, 61 efficiencies, kitchen, refrigerators, VCP's. **Cards:** AE, DI, DS, MC, VI. (D) ⊗

HI-TIDE MOTEL — AAA Special Value Rates — **Phone:** 503/738-8414

AAA ◆◆ Motel

5/1-9/30	1P: $80- 110	2P/1B: $85- 110	2P/2B: $85- 115	XP: $5	F6
3/1-4/30 & 10/1-2/29	1P: $60- 90	2P/1B: $60- 90	2P/2B: $65- 95	XP: $5	F6

Location: Ave G to ocean. 30 Ave G 97138. Fax: 503/738-0875. **Terms:** Credit card guarantee, 3 day notice; no pets. **Facility:** 64 rooms. Large, attractive units, many with ocean view. Gas burning fireplaces. 3 stories; exterior corridors; oceanfront; heated indoor pool, whirlpool. **All Rooms:** efficiencies, free movies, cable TV, no A/C. **Some Rooms:** Fee: VCP's. **Cards:** AE, CB, DI, DS, MC, VI. (D) ⊗

SEASHORE RESORT MOTEL — Rates Subject to Change — **Phone:** 503/738-6368

AAA ◆◆ Motel

5/16-9/30	2P/1B: $70- 88	2P/2B: $78- 96	XP: $10
3/1-5/15 & 10/1-2/29	2P/1B: $60- 78	2P/2B: $68- 86	XP: $10

Location: At 1st Ave & Ocean Beach. 60 N Prom 97138. Fax: 503/738-8314. **Terms:** No pets. **Facility:** 51 rooms. Very comfortable units. Most units with beach & ocean view. 5 efficiencies, $10 extra; 3 stories; interior/exterior corridors; oceanfront; heated indoor pool, sauna, whirlpool. **Dining:** Restaurant nearby. **All Rooms:** combo & shower baths, cable TV, no A/C. **Some Rooms:** coffeemakers. **Cards:** AE, CB, DI, DS, MC, VI. (D)

Colonial Motor Inn

Your "home away from home"

1120 NORTH HOLLADAY, SEASIDE, OREGON 97138

Welcome to Seaside, Oregon!

SHORT WALK TO PACIFIC OCEAN & BEACH
COMPLIMENTARY VIDEO CASSETTE PLAYERS
GAZEBO ON THE NECANICUM ESTUARY
KING ROOMS, TELEPHONES & FAX SERVICES

FOR RESERVATIONS CALL TOLL FREE 1-800-221-3804

SHILO INN Rates Subject to Change **Phone:** 503/738-9571
AAA ◆◆◆ Motor Inn
4/16-6/30 & 9/5-10/15 1P: $110- 194 2P/1B: $110- 194 2P/2B: $194- 289 XP: $15 F12
7/1-9/4 1P: $87- 160 2P/1B: $87- 160 2P/2B: $160- 210 XP: $15 F12
3/1-4/15 & 10/16-2/29 1P: $75- 139 2P/1B: $75- 139 2P/2B: $139- 184 XP: $15 F12
Location: At Broadway & Ocean Beach. 30 N Prom 97138. Fax: 503/738-0674. **Terms:** Sr. discount; check-in 4 pm; credit card guarantee; no pets. **Facility:** 113 rooms. Very attractive public areas. Well-equipped units, most with ocean view & balcony. Some with fireplace. 5 stories; exterior corridors; oceanfront; conference facilities; heated indoor pool, sauna, whirlpool; exercise room, steam room. **Dining & Entertainment:** Dining room, restaurant, coffee shop; 7 am-11 pm; $8-$18; cocktail lounge; restaurant, see separate listing. **Services:** data ports. Fee: coin laundry. **All Rooms:** free movies, cable TV, no A/C. **Some Rooms:** 61 kitchens, whirlpools. Fee: VCP's. **Cards:** AE, CB, DI, DS, JCB, MC, VI.

SUNDOWNER MOTOR INN Rates Subject to Change **Phone:** 503/738-8301
AAA ◆◆ Motel
3/1-10/30 2P/1B: $52 2P/2B: $69 XP: $5
10/31-2/29 2P/1B: $49 2P/2B: $59 XP: $5
Location: At Ocean Way & Columbia. 125 Ocean Way 97138. **Terms:** Reserv deposit, 10 day notice; no pets. **Facility:** 22 rooms. Neat units. 1 block from beach. 2 two-bedroom units. 2 one-bedroom efficiency suites, $89-$99; 2 stories; exterior corridors; sauna, small heated indoor pool. **All Rooms:** free movies, cable TV, VCP's. **Some Rooms:** refrigerators. **Cards:** AE, DS, MC, VI.

RESTAURANTS

DOOGER'S SEAFOOD & GRILL **Dinner:** $11-$20 **Phone:** 503/738-3773
AAA ◆ Seafood
Location: Center. 505 Broadway 97138. **Hours:** 11 am-9 pm; in winter 11 am-9:30 pm, Fri & Sat-10 pm. Closed: 11/23, 12/25 & 1st 2 weeks of Dec. **Features:** children's menu; senior's menu; carryout; beer & wine only. Popular, very pleasant family restaurant. Very good selection of seafood; also other popular dishes, salads & sandwiches. Smoke free premises. **Cards:** MC, VI.

SHILO INN RESTAURANT **Dinner:** $11-$20 **Phone:** 503/738-8481
◆◆ American
Location: At Shilo Inn. 30 N Prom 97138. **Hours:** 7 am-10 pm, Fri & Sat-11 pm. **Reservations:** suggested. **Features:** Sunday brunch; children's menu; early bird specials; senior's menu; health conscious menu; carryout; cocktails & lounge; a la carte. Attractive; beachfront. Seafood, popular beef & chicken dishes. **Cards:** AE, DI, DS, JCB, MC, VI.

SISTERS—700

LODGING

BEST WESTERN PONDEROSA LODGE Rates Subject to Change **Phone:** 503/549-1234
AAA ◆◆◆ Motel
All Year [CP] 1P: $60 2P/1B: $65 2P/2B: $65 XP: $5 F10
Location: On Hwy 20, 1/4 mi nw of jct Hwy 242. 505 W Hwy 20 97759 (PO Box 218). Fax: 503/549-0171. **Terms:** Reserv deposit; small pets only, $5, in designated rooms. **Facility:** 49 rooms. Spacious very well maintained grounds. Large units. 2 stories; exterior corridors; meeting rooms; heated pool, whirlpool. **Recreation:** jogging. **All Rooms:** cable TV. **Cards:** AE, DI, DS, MC, VI.

RESTAURANT

HOTEL SISTERS RESTAURANT Historical **Dinner:** $11-$20 **Phone:** 503/549-7427
AAA ◆ American
Location: Center, on SR 126. 101 Cascade St 97759. **Hours:** 11 am-9:30 pm, Fri & Sat-10 pm; winter hours vary. Closed: 12/25. **Reservations:** suggested; in summer. **Features:** children's menu; carryout; cocktails & lounge; a la carte. In Western setting of historic hotel. Popular steak, seafood, chicken & barbecue dishes. Also Mexican dishes. **Cards:** MC, VI.

SPRINGFIELD—44,700

LODGINGS

BEST WESTERN GRAND MANOR INN Rates Subject to Change **Phone:** 503/726-4769
AAA ◆◆◆ Motel
All Year [CP] 1P: $63 2P/1B: $69 2P/2B: $70 XP: $5 F12
Location: exit 195A south bound; exit 195 north bound; 2 mi n of Eugene off jct Beltline Hwy & I-5; North Springfield Gateway Mall exit. 971 Kruse Way 97477. Fax: 503/744-0745. **Terms:** Sr. discount; credit card guarantee; no pets. **Facility:** 65 rooms. Colonial style building with inviting lobby. Large units with traditional furnishings. Comfortable continental breakfast room. 3 one-bedroom suites; 1 with fireplace & balcony, $80-$125; 3 stories; interior corridors; meeting rooms; heated indoor pool, sauna; exercise room. **Services:** data ports. Fee: coin laundry. **All Rooms:** coffeemakers, refrigerators, cable TV. **Some Rooms:** microwaves. **Cards:** AE, CB, DI, DS, MC, VI. Roll in showers.

GATEWAY INN Rates Subject to Change **Phone:** 503/726-1212
◆ Motor Inn
All Year 1P: $40- 43 2P/1B: $51 2P/2B: $54 XP: $7 F17
Location: 2 mi n on I-5, off Beltline Rd, exit 195A southbound; exit 195 northbound. 3540 Gateway Rd 97477. Fax: 503/746-9504. **Terms:** Credit card guarantee; pets, $10. **Facility:** 91 rooms. Comfortable units with moderate decor. 2 stories; interior corridors; meeting rooms; heated pool. **Dining:** Restaurant; 6 am-10 pm, Sun 6 am-1:30 pm; $8-$14; cocktails. **Services:** Fee: coin laundry. **All Rooms:** free movies, cable TV. **Some Rooms:** refrigerators. **Cards:** AE, CB, DI, DS, VI.

MOTEL ORLEANS Rates Subject to Change **Phone:** 503/746-1314
AAA ◆◆ Motel
All Year 1P: $40 2P/1B: $45 2P/2B: $48 XP: $6 F12
Location: 2 mi n off Beltline Rd & I-5, southbound exit 195A,southbound exit 195 northbound. 3315 Gateway Rd 97477. **Terms:** Sr. discount; reserv deposit; no pets. **Facility:** 71 rooms. Nicely furnished rooms. 3 stories; interior corridors; whirlpool. **Services:** Fee: coin laundry. **All Rooms:** combo & shower baths, cable TV. **Cards:** AE, CB, DI, DS, MC, VI.

RED LION INN/EUGENE-SPRINGFIELD Guaranteed Rates **Phone:** 503/726-8181
◆◆◆ Motor Inn
6/1-9/5 1P: $59- 77 2P/1B: $74- 92 2P/2B: $92 XP: $15 F17
3/1-5/31 & 9/6-2/29 1P: $57- 76 2P/1B: $72- 90 2P/2B: $90 XP: $15 F17
Location: 2 mi n of Eugene on I-5, off Beltline Rd; exit 195A southbound; exit 195 northbound. 3280 Gateway Rd 97477. Fax: 503/747-1866. **Terms:** Sr. discount; credit card guarantee, 3 day notice; pets. **Facility:** 234 rooms. Large rooms, some with patio or balcony facing very attractive landscaped grounds. Beautifully appointed suites. 7 two-bedroom units. 4 suites, $200-$285; 2 stories; interior/exterior corridors; conference facilities; heated pool, whirlpool; 2 tennis courts. **Dining:** Dining room, restaurant, coffee shop; 6 am-10 pm, 5 pm-10 pm dinner only in The Grill; $8-$20; cocktails; Sun brunch 9 am-2 pm. **Services:** data ports; health club privileges; airport transportation. **All Rooms:** cable TV. Fee: movies. **Some Rooms:** refrigerators, whirlpools. **Cards:** AE, CB, DI, DS, MC, VI. Roll in showers.

RODEWAY INN Rates Subject to Change **Phone:** 503/746-8471
AAA ◆◆ Motor Inn
All Year [CP] 1P: $50 2P/1B: $56 2P/2B: $58 XP: $6 F18
Location: 2 mi n Eugene off I-5 exit 195A southbound; exit 195 northbound. 3480 Hutton St 97477. Fax: 503/747-1541. **Terms:** Sr. discount; credit card guarantee; pets, $10 dep req. **Facility:** 58 rooms. Attractive guest rooms. 3 stories; interior corridors; meeting rooms; heated indoor pool; exercise room. **Dining:** Restaurant nearby. **Services:** data ports. Fee: coin laundry. **All Rooms:** cable TV. Fee: movies. **Some Rooms:** coffeemakers. **Cards:** AE, CB, DI, DS, JCB, MC, VI. (D) (S) ⊗

VILLAGE INN MOTEL Rates Subject to Change **Phone:** 503/747-4546
AAA ◆◆ Motor Inn
All Year 1P: $42 2P/1B: $45- 49 2P/2B: $47- 57 XP: $5 F12
Location: 1 mi n at jct Hwy 126 & Mohawk Blvd; off I-5 exit 194A to Hwy 105 then to Mohawk Blvd. 1875 Mohawk Blvd 97477. Fax: 503/747-4452. **Terms:** Sr. discount; reserv deposit; small pets only. **Facility:** 70 rooms. Nicely landscaped grounds & attractive units. 1 spacious, very attractive unit, $65; 2 stories; exterior corridors; heated pool, whirlpool. **Dining:** Restaurant; 6 am-9:30 pm, Fri & Sat-10 pm, Sun 7 am-9 pm; $5-$14; cocktails. **Services:** Fee: coin laundry. **All Rooms:** free movies, cable TV. **Some Rooms:** 4 efficiencies, radios, whirlpools. **Cards:** AE, CB, DI, DS, MC, VI. (D) ⊗

THE DALLES—11,100

LODGINGS

BEST WESTERN TAPADERA MOTOR INN Rates Subject to Change **Phone:** 503/296-9107
AAA ◆◆ Motor Inn
All Year 1P: $45- 52 2P/1B: $53- 58 2P/2B: $56- 62 XP: $7 F12
Location: On Hwy 30; off I-84 eastbound exit 84, westbound exit 87 or 85. 112 W Second 97058. Fax: 503/296-3002. **Terms:** Sr. discount; credit card guarantee, 3 day notice; small pets only. **Facility:** 65 rooms. Downtown location. Tastefully furnished guest rooms. 2-4 stories; interior/exterior corridors; heated pool. **Dining:** Dining room; 6:30 am-10 pm, Sat & Sun 7 am-9 pm; $7-$15; cocktails. **Services:** data ports; health club privileges. **All Rooms:** free movies, combo & shower baths, cable TV. **Some Rooms:** microwaves, refrigerators, whirlpools. Fee: VCP's. **Cards:** AE, CB, DI, DS, MC, VI. (D) ⊗

DAYS INN Rates Subject to Change **Phone:** 503/296-1191
AAA ◆ Motel
All Year [CP] 1P: $45 2P/1B: $51 2P/2B: $63 XP: $6 F12
Location: 1 3/4 mi w off I-84; eastbound exit 83, westbound exit 84. 2500 W 6th 97058. Fax: 503/298-2455. **Terms:** Sr. discount; reserv deposit; pets, $10. **Facility:** 70 rooms. 2 stories; interior corridors; heated pool, whirlpool. **All Rooms:** free movies, cable TV. **Some Rooms:** radios, refrigerators. **Cards:** AE, CB, DI, DS, MC, VI. (D) (S) ⊗

LONE PINE MOTEL Rates Subject to Change **Phone:** 503/298-2800
AAA ◆◆◆ Motel
6/1-9/30 [BP] 1P: $52- 58 2P/1B: $52- 58 2P/2B: $65 XP: $6 F12
3/1-5/31 & 10/1-2/29 [BP] 1P: $42- 49 2P/1B: $42- 49 2P/2B: $55 XP: $6 F12
Location: 2 1/2 mi e at jct I-84 & Hwy 197, off exit 87. 351 Lone Pine Dr 97058. Fax: 503/298-8282. **Terms:** Sr. discount; credit card guarantee; pets, $6. **Facility:** 57 rooms. Attractively appointed, very quiet units. 1 one-bedroom apartment $109; off season $99; 2 stories; interior corridors; meeting rooms; heated indoor pool, whirlpool; exercise room. **Services:** data ports; airport transportation. Fee: coin laundry. **All Rooms:** free movies, cable TV. **Some Rooms:** kitchen, microwaves, whirlpools. **Cards:** AE, DI, DS, MC, VI. (D) (S) ⊗

QUALITY INN Rates Subject to Change **Phone:** 503/298-5161
◆◆ Motor Inn
6/1-9/30 1P: $54 2P/1B: $59 2P/2B: $69 XP: $4 F18
3/1-5/31 & 10/1-2/29 1P: $49 2P/1B: $54 2P/2B: $59 XP: $4 F18
Location: 1 1/2 mi w; off I-84 eastbound exit 83, westbound exit 84. 2114 W 6th 97058 (PO Box 723). Fax: 503/298-6411. **Terms:** Sr. discount; credit card guarantee; pets, $2. **Facility:** 85 rooms. Neatly furnished, very well maintained units. Unique farm theme restaurant. 2 stories; exterior corridors; meeting rooms; heated pool, whirlpool. **Dining & Entertainment:** Restaurant; 6 am-10 pm, Fri & Sat-11 pm; $7-$12; cocktail lounge. **Services:** data ports; health club privileges; airport transportation. Fee: coin laundry. **All Rooms:** free movies, cable TV. **Some Rooms:** refrigerators. **Cards:** AE, CB, DI, DS, MC, VI. (D) ⊗

SHILO INN Rates Subject to Change **Phone:** 503/298-5502
◆◆ Motor Inn
Fri & Sat 5/16-9/30 [CP] 1P: $58- 97 2P/1B: $58- 97 2P/2B: $68- 97 XP: $10 F12
Sun-Thurs 5/16-9/30 [CP] 1P: $51- 86 2P/1B: $51- 86 2P/2B: $63- 86 XP: $10 F12
3/1-5/15 & 10/1-2/29 [CP] 1P: $50- 76 2P/1B: $50- 76 2P/2B: $53- 76 XP: $10 F12
Location: 2 1/2 mi e at jct I-84 & Hwy 197, off exit 87. 3223 Bret Clodfelter Way 97058. Fax: 503/298-4673. **Terms:** Sr. discount; pets, $7. **Facility:** 112 rooms. Attractive facilities. Many large units, some with balcony. 2 two-bedroom units. 1- & 2-bedroom suites with whirlpool, $145-$165; 2 stories; interior corridors; meeting rooms; heated pool, sauna, whirlpool; exercise room. **Dining:** Dining room, restaurant; 6 am-2:30 & 4-10 pm, Fri & Sat-11 pm; $4-$18; cocktails. **Services:** area transportation, to bus & train depot. Fee: coin laundry. **All Rooms:** microwaves, free movies, refrigerators, cable TV. **Cards:** AE, CB, DI, DS, JCB, MC, VI. (D) ⊗

TIGARD—29,300 (See PORTLAND ACCOMMODATIONS spotting map page A47; see index starting on page A46)

LODGINGS

BEST WESTERN INN CHATEAU 290 Rates Subject to Change **Phone:** 503/620-2030 56
AAA ◆◆ Motel
5/15-9/15 [CP] 1P: $57 2P/1B: $62 2P/2B: $73 XP: $5 F12
3/1-5/14 & 9/16-2/29 [CP] 1P: $52 2P/1B: $57 2P/2B: $67 XP: $5 F12
Location: Off I-5 exit 290, 1 mi s of jct I-5 & SR 217; 10 mi s of Portland. 17993 Lower Boones Ferry Rd 97224. Fax: 503/620-2030. **Terms:** Sr. discount; credit card guarantee; small pets only, $10 credit card dep req. **Facility:** 68 rooms. Attractively landscaped grounds. Very tastefully decorated, especially well kept units. 1 large one-bedroom suite with wetbar, $78. 6 large units, $72; 2 stories; interior corridors; meeting rooms; sauna, whirlpool, small heated pool; exercise room. **Dining & Entertainment:** Cocktail lounge; restaurant nearby. **Services:** data ports. Fee: coin laundry. **All Rooms:** free movies, cable TV. **Some Rooms:** microwaves, refrigerators. Fee: VCP's. **Cards:** AE, CB, DI, DS, MC, VI. *(See color ad p A52)* (D) ⊗

EMBASSY SUITES HOTEL-PORTLAND WASHINGTON SQUARE Guaranteed Rates **Phone:** 503/644-4000 58
AAA ◆◆◆ Suite Hotel
All Year [BP] 1P: $137 2P/1B: $147 2P/2B: $147 XP: $10 F17
Location: At jct SR 217 & Scholls Ferry Rd; 2 1/4 mi nw of jct I-5 & SR 217. 9000 SW Washington Square Rd 97223. Fax: 503/641-4654. **Terms:** Sr. discount; credit card guarantee, 3 day notice; pets. **Facility:** 354 rooms. Very attractive atrium area with fountain & fish pond. Very comfortable 1-bedroom suites with living room. 4 two-bedroom suites, 2 with whirlpool & VCP $500; 9 stories; interior corridors; conference facilities; heated indoor pool, sauna, whirlpool. **Dining & Entertainment:** Dining room, restaurant; 11:30 am-2:30 & 5-10 pm, Sunday brunch 10 am-2 pm; $9-$20; cocktail lounge; entertainment. **Services:** data ports; complimentary evening beverages; health club privileges; area transportation, to mall & health club. Fee: airport transportation. **All Rooms:** coffeemakers, microwaves, free movies, refrigerators, cable TV. **Cards:** AE, CB, DI, DS, JCB, MC, VI. *(See ad p A48)* (D) (S) ⊗

(See PORTLAND ACCOMMODATIONS spotting map page A47)

PHOENIX INN/WASHINGTON SQUARE — Guaranteed Rates — **Phone:** 503/624-9000 — 57

Motel — All Year [CP] — 1P: $56 — 2P/1B: $62 — 2P/2B: $64 — XP: $5 — F17

Too new to rate; **Location:** Northbound or southbound Hwy 217, Greenburg Rd exit, n 2 blks. 9575 SW Locust 97223. **Terms:** no pets. **Facility:** 56 rooms. Rating withheld pending completion of construction. Scheduled to open May, 1995. 4 stories; interior corridors; meeting rooms; heated indoor pool, whirlpool. **Services:** data ports; guest laundry. **Recreation:** hiking trails. **All Rooms:** microwaves, free movies, refrigerators, cable TV. **Some Rooms:** whirlpools. **Cards:** AE, CB, DI, DS, MC, VI.

SHILO INN-WASHINGTON SQUARE — Rates Subject to Change — **Phone:** 503/620-4320 — 37

◆◆ Motel

7/1-9/5 [CP]	1P: $67- 78	2P/1B: $67- 78	2P/2B: $74- 95	XP: $8	F12
3/1-6/30 & 9/6-2/29 [CP]	1P: $62- 72	2P/1B: $62- 72	2P/2B: $68- 89	XP: $8	F12

Location: 1 blk w of jct SR 217 & Greenburg Rd. 10830 SW Greenburg Rd 97223. Fax: 503/620-8277. **Terms:** Sr. discount; pets, $7. **Facility:** 77 rooms. 1/2 mi from Washington Square. Very attractive & well-maintained guest rooms & facilities. 2 two-bedroom units. 4 stories; interior corridors; meeting rooms; sauna, whirlpool; exercise room. **Services:** airport transportation. Fee: coin laundry. **All Rooms:** free movies, combo & shower baths. **Some Rooms:** Fee: VCP's. **Cards:** AE, CB, DI, DS, JCB, MC, VI.

WAYSIDE MOTOR INN — Rates Subject to Change — **Phone:** 503/245-6421 — 59

AAA ◆◆ Motel

All Year — 1P: $50 — 2P/1B: $56 — 2P/2B: $62 — XP: $6 — F12

Location: 2 mi e on Hwy 99; s of I-5 exit 294. 8 mi sw of Portland. 11460 SW Pacific Hwy 97223. Fax: 503/245-6425. **Terms:** Sr. discount; reserv deposit, 3 day notice; no pets. **Facility:** 117 rooms. Generous, especially well-kept guest rooms & public areas. 4 stories; interior corridors; meeting rooms; heated pool, sauna. **Dining:** Restaurant nearby. **All Rooms:** free movies, cable TV. **Some Rooms:** Fee: VCP's. **Cards:** AE, CB, DI, DS, MC, VI.

TILLAMOOK—4,000

LODGINGS

MAR-CLAIR INN — Rates Subject to Change — **Phone:** 503/842-7571

AAA ◆◆ Motel

5/15-10/14	1P: $52	2P/1B: $58	2P/2B: $60	XP: $6
3/1-5/14 & 10/15-2/29	1P: $48	2P/1B: $52	2P/2B: $56	XP: $6

Location: On Hwy 101, 1/2 blk n of jct SR 6. 11 Main Ave 97141. **Terms:** Credit card guarantee; no pets. **Facility:** 47 rooms. Very tastefully decorated, especially well maintained units. 6 two-bedroom units. 6 very well furnished 1-bedroom apartments, $65-$95; 2 stories; exterior corridors; heated pool, sauna, whirlpool. **Dining:** Restaurant nearby. **All Rooms:** free movies, combo & shower baths, cable TV, no A/C. **Cards:** AE, DI, DS, MC, VI.

SHILO INN/TILLAMOOK — Rates Subject to Change — **Phone:** 503/842-7971

◆◆◆ Motor Inn

5/16-11/15	1P: $79- 93	2P/1B: $79- 93	2P/2B: $79- 93	XP: $10	F12
Fri & Sat 3/1-5/15 & 11/16-2/29	1P: $72- 79	2P/1B: $72- 79	2P/2B: $72- 79	XP: $10	F12
Sun-Thurs 3/1-5/15 & 11/16-2/29	1P: $62- 68	2P/1B: $62- 68	2P/2B: $62- 68	XP: $10	F12

Location: 1 mi n on Hwy 101. 2515 N Main 97141. Fax: 503/842-7960. **Terms:** Sr. discount; check-in 4 pm; credit card guarantee; no pets. **Facility:** 100 rooms. Generous, well-equipped units. 6 efficiencies, $80; 2 stories; interior corridors; meeting rooms; heated indoor pool, sauna, whirlpool; exercise room. **Dining & Entertainment:** Restaurant; 6 am-10 pm, Fri & Sat-11 pm; $8-$18; cocktail lounge. **Services:** data ports. Fee: coin laundry. **All Rooms:** free movies, cable TV. **Some Rooms:** microwaves, refrigerators. **Cards:** AE, CB, DI, DS, JCB, MC, VI.

WESTERN ROYAL INN — Rates Subject to Change — **Phone:** 503/842-8844

AAA ◆◆ Motel

7/1-10/31	1P: $65	2P/1B: $70	2P/2B: $75	XP: $5	F10
3/1-6/30 & 11/1-2/29	1P: $55	2P/1B: $60	2P/2B: $60	XP: $5	F10

Location: 1/2 mi n on Hwy 101. 1125 N Main 97141 (PO Box 136). Fax: 503/842-8876. **Terms:** Reserv deposit, 3 day notice; small pets only, $5. **Facility:** 42 rooms. Very well kept units. 12 two-bedroom units. 2 stories; exterior corridors; meeting rooms; whirlpool. **Dining:** Restaurant nearby. **Services:** Fee: coin laundry. **All Rooms:** microwaves, free movies, refrigerators, combo & shower baths, cable TV. **Cards:** AE, DI, DS, MC, VI.

In the time it takes to read this ad, we'll rescue eleven people.

Every year we save millions of motorists in distress. Call us and we'll send you service, usually at no charge, from a network of over 13,000 facilities throughout the U.S. and Canada. You can call no matter where you are, any time of the day and any day of the year. Call 24 hours a day, 365 days a year. Why not join us? Call your local AAA office.

AAA 1-800-AAA-HELP

TROUTDALE—7,900

LODGINGS

PHOENIX INN Guaranteed Rates **Phone:** 503/669-6500
◆◆◆ Motel
All Year [CP] 1P: $47 2P/1B: $52 2P/2B: $55 XP: $5 F17
Location: I-84 exit 17; 2 blks eastbound on Frontage Rd to Phoenix Dr. 477 NW Phoenix Dr 97060. Fax: 503/669-3500. **Terms:** Small pets only. **Facility:** 73 rooms. Tastefully decorated units. 2 one-bedroom suites with VCP, refrigerator & wet bar; 3 stories; interior corridors; smoke free premises; meeting rooms; heated indoor pool, whirlpool; exercise room. **Dining:** Restaurant nearby. **Services:** airport transportation. Fee: coin laundry. **All Rooms:** free movies. **Some Rooms:** microwaves, refrigerators, whirlpools. **Cards:** AE, CB, DI, DS, MC, VI.

TRAVELODGE Rates Subject to Change **Phone:** 503/666-6623
◆ Motel
6/1-10/31 [CP] 1P: $39 2P/1B: $46 2P/2B: $51 XP: $6 F17
3/1-5/31 & 11/1-2/29 [CP] 1P: $35 2P/1B: $42 2P/2B: $46 XP: $6 F17
Location: 2 mi ne; off I-84, exit 16A. 23705 NE Sandy Blvd 97060. Fax: 503/661-1308. **Terms:** Sr. discount; small pets only, $5. **Facility:** 44 rooms. In quiet area, well off highway. Well-kept units. 2 stories; interior corridors. **Dining:** Restaurant nearby. **Services:** Fee: coin laundry. **All Rooms:** free movies, cable TV. **Some Rooms:** coffeemakers, 3 efficiencies. **Cards:** AE, CB, DI, DS, JCB, MC, VI.

TUALATIN—15,000 (See PORTLAND ACCOMMODATIONS spotting map page A47; see index starting on page A46)

LODGING

SWEETBRIER INN Rates Subject to Change **Phone:** 503/692-5800 (68)
◆◆◆ Motor Inn
All Year 1P: $55- 70 2P/1B: $68- 78 2P/2B: $63- 68 XP: $8 F18
Location: Off I-5 exit 289, 12 mi s of Portland. 7125 SW Nyberg Rd 97062. Fax: 503/691-2894. **Terms:** Sr. discount; reserv deposit; pets, $25 dep req. **Facility:** 100 rooms. Traditionally appointed guest rooms. Attractively landscaped grounds. 2 stories; exterior corridors; conference facilities; heated pool; playground. **Dining & Entertainment:** Restaurant; 6:30 am-10 pm; $9-$15; cocktail lounge. **All Rooms:** free movies, cable TV. **Some Rooms:** efficiency. **Cards:** AE, DI, DS, JCB, MC, VI. *(See ad p A47)*

RESTAURANT

RICH'S **Dinner:** $11-$20 **Phone:** 503/692-1460 (42)
◆ Continental
Location: In Tualatin; 1 mi w of I-5 exit 289, w to Boones Ferry Rd, then 2 blks right. 18810 SW Boones Ferry Rd 97062. **Hours:** 11:30 am-2 & 5-9 pm, Fri-10 pm, Sat 5 pm-10 pm, Sun 10 am-2 & 5-9 pm. Closed major holidays. **Reservations:** suggested. **Features:** Sunday brunch; early bird specials; cocktails & lounge; a la carte. Cozy, intimate dining rooms in restored 1912 building. Dishes include seafood, steak & chicken. Also, ala cart bistro entrees. **Cards:** AE, DI, DS, MC, VI.

WALDPORT—1,600

LODGING

ALSEA MANOR MOTEL Rates Subject to Change **Phone:** 503/563-3249
◆ Motel
6/24-9/23 2P/1B: $45 2P/2B: $54 XP: $4
3/1-6/23 & 9/24-2/29 2P/1B: $35 2P/2B: $39 XP: $4
Location: Center on Hwy 101. 190 SW/Arrow (Hwy 101) 97394 (PO Box 446). **Terms:** Reserv deposit, 3 day notice; small pets only, dogs only. **Facility:** 16 rooms. Very well maintained units with attractive decor. 1 two-bedroom unit, $68; 2 stories; exterior corridors. **All Rooms:** coffeemakers, free movies, cable TV, no A/C. **Some Rooms:** refrigerators. **Cards:** AE, DI, DS, MC, VI.

WARM SPRINGS

LODGINGS

KAH-NEE-TA LODGE Rates Subject to Change **Phone:** 503/553-1112
◆◆◆ Resort Motor Inn
6/16-9/3 1P: $115- 130 2P/1B: $115- 130 2P/2B: $115- 130 XP: $14 F6
3/1-6/15 & 9/4-2/29 1P: $100- 120 2P/1B: $100- 120 2P/2B: $100- 120 XP: $14 F6
Location: 12 mi n of Hwy 26 in Warm Springs Indian Reservation. 100 Main St 97761 (PO Box K). Fax: 503/553-1071. **Terms:** Check-in 4 pm; reserv deposit, 3 day notice; no pets. **Facility:** 139 rooms. In quiet natural setting. Very attractive architecural style. Units with scenic views & balconies. 1- & 2-bedroom suites, $160 & $250; 3 with whirlpool & fireplace; 4 stories; exterior corridors; conference facilities; putting green; heated pool, saunas, steamroom, whirlpool; 2 tennis courts; exercise room, playground. Fee: 18 holes golf; tanning booths. **Dining:** Dining room, coffee shop; 7 am-10 pm; $12-$24; cocktails; pool side snack & beverage service in summer. **Recreation:** hiking trails, jogging. Fee: fishing; bicycles, horseback riding. **All Rooms:** coffeemakers, free & pay movies, cable TV. **Some Rooms:** Fee: VCP's. **Cards:** AE, CB, DI, DS, MC, VI.

KAH-NEE-TA VILLAGE Rates Subject to Change **Phone:** 503/553-1112
◆◆ Resort Complex
6/16-9/3 1P: $105- 125 2P/1B: $105- 125 2P/2B: $125 XP: $14 F6
3/1-6/15 & 9/4-2/29 1P: $90- 110 2P/1B: $90- 110 2P/2B: $110 XP: $14 F6
Location: 10 mi n, off Hwy 26, in Warm Springs Indian Reservation. 100 Main St 97761 (PO Box K). Fax: 503/553-1071. **Terms:** Check-in 4 pm; reserv deposit, 3 day notice; pets, $14. **Facility:** 25 rooms. Quiet natural setting along Warm Springs River. 1-bedroom units & 2-bedroom housekeeping apartments. 2-room units, $110; authentic Indian tepees, $50 for up to 5 persons; 1 story; exterior corridors; meeting rooms; wading pool, whirlpool, natural mineral baths, year-round naturally heated mineral water swimming pool; playground, horse shoe pits, vollyball court. Fee: miniature golf. **Dining:** Restaurant; 8 am-8 pm; $6-$24; snack bar in summer. **Services:** Fee: coin laundry; massage. **Recreation:** fishing. Fee: canoeing; horseback riding. Rental: bicycles. **All Rooms:** combo & shower baths, cable TV. Fee: movies. **Some Rooms:** coffeemakers, refrigerators, whirlpools. Fee: VCP's. **Cards:** AE, CB, DI, DS, MC, VI.

WARRENTON—2,700

LODGING

SHILO INN Rates Subject to Change **Phone:** 503/861-2181
◆◆◆ Motor Inn
Fri & Sat 6/2-10/15 1P: $101- 121 2P/1B: $101- 121 2P/2B: $101- 121 XP: $10 F12
Sun-Thurs 6/2-10/15 1P: $90- 103 2P/1B: $90- 103 2P/2B: $90- 103 XP: $10 F12
3/1-6/1 & 10/29-2/29 1P: $65- 84 2P/1B: $65- 84 2P/2B: $65- 84 XP: $10 F12
Location: On Hwy 26/101, near west end of Young's Bay Bridge. 1609 E Harbor Dr 97146. Fax: 503/861-2980. **Terms:** Sr. discount; check-in 4 pm; credit card guarantee; pets, $7. **Facility:** 62 rooms. Attractive units. 8 efficiencies, $20 extra Fri & Sat 6/2-10/15; 4 stories; interior corridors; meeting rooms; heated indoor pool, sauna, steamroom, whirlpool; exercise room. **Dining:** Restaurant; 7 am-9 pm, Fri & Sat-11 pm; $7-$18; cocktails. **Services:** Fee: coin laundry. **All Rooms:** cable TV. Fee: movies. **Some Rooms:** microwaves, refrigerators. Fee: VCP's. **Cards:** AE, CB, DI, DS, JCB, MC, VI.

WELCHES

LODGING

THE RESORT AT THE MOUNTAIN AAA Special Value Rates **Phone:** 503/622-3101

Fri & Sat 6/15-9/30 1P: $99- 155 2P/1B: $99- 155 2P/2B: $99- 155 XP: $20 F18
Sun-Thurs 6/15-9/30 1P: $95- 150 2P/1B: $95- 150 2P/2B: $95- 150 XP: $20 F18
3/1-6/14 & 10/1-2/29 1P: $87- 127 2P/1B: $87- 127 2P/2B: $87- 127 XP: $20 F18

◆◆◆ Resort Motor Inn

Location: 3/4 mi s of Hwy 26 on Welches Rd. 68010 E Fairway Ave 97067. Fax: 503/622-5677. **Terms:** Check-in 4 pm; credit card guarantee, 7 day notice, 3 days in winter; package plans; no pets. **Facility:** 160 rooms. Very attractively landscaped grounds in beautiful scenic mountain setting. Tastefully appointed units & 1- & 2-bedroom suites with balcony or patio. Many fireplaces. 6 two-bedroom units. 1- & 2-bedroom suites with kitchen, $155-$185; 2 stories; exterior corridors; meeting rooms; putting green; heated pool; 6 tennis courts (2 lighted); playground, volleyball, badmitten, horseshoes, recreation programs upon request. Fee: 27 holes golf. **Dining & Entertainment:** Dining room, coffee shop; 6:30 am-11 pm; $9-$18; cocktail lounge; 24-hour room service; entertainment. **Services:** Fee: coin laundry; massage. **Recreation:** fishing; hiking trails, jogging. Rental: bicycles. **All Rooms:** cable TV, no A/C. Fee: movies. **Some Rooms:** coffeemakers, 63 kitchens, refrigerators. **Cards:** AE, DI, DS, MC, VI. *(See ad below)* Ⓓ ⊗

RESTAURANT

CHALET SWISS **Dinner:** $11-$20 **Phone:** 503/622-3600

◆◆ Continental

Location: US 26 at Welches Rd. 24371 E Welches Rd 97067. **Hours:** 5 pm-10 pm, Sun-9 pm. Closed: Mon, Tues, 11/23, 12/24 & 12/25. **Reservations:** suggested. **Features:** children's menu; cocktails; a la carte. Swiss chalet atmosphere. Very good selection of Swiss specialties & fresh seafood dishes. **Cards:** AE, MC, VI. ⊗

WILSONVILLE—7,100

LODGINGS

BEST WESTERN WILLAMETTE INN Rates Subject to Change **Phone:** 503/682-2288

All Year [CP] 1P: $60- 65 2P/1B: $69- 75 2P/2B: $75 XP: $6 F12

◆◆◆ Motel

Location: Off I-5, exit 283. 30800 SW Parkway Ave 97070. Fax: 503/682-1088. **Terms:** No pets. **Facility:** 63 rooms. Attractively landscaped, tree-shaded grounds. Large very comfortably furnished units with balcony or patio. 2 stories; interior corridors; meeting rooms; heated pool, whirlpool; exercise room. **Services:** Fee: coin laundry. **All Rooms:** free movies, cable TV. **Some Rooms:** 7 efficiencies, refrigerators, VCP's. **Cards:** AE, DI, DS, MC, VI. *(See ad p A50)* Ⓓ ⊗

COMFORT INN Rates Subject to Change **Phone:** 503/682-9000

All Year [CP] 1P: $47- 55 2P/1B: $52- 56 2P/2B: $58 XP: $6 F18

◆◆ Motel

Location: Off I-5, exit 283. 8855 SW Citizens Dr 97070. Fax: 503/682-6874. **Terms:** Sr. discount; credit card guarantee; no pets. **Facility:** 63 rooms. Very neat, nicely equipped units. 2 stories; interior corridors; meeting rooms; heated indoor pool, whirlpool; exercise room. **Services:** data ports. Fee: coin laundry. **All Rooms:** microwaves, free movies, refrigerators, cable TV. **Some Rooms:** VCP's. Fee: whirlpools. Roll in showers. **Cards:** AE, CB, DI, DS, MC, VI. Ⓓ Ⓢ ⊗

HOLIDAY INN-PORTLAND SOUTH AAA Special Value Rates **Phone:** 503/682-2211

All Year 1P: $63- 74 2P/1B: $70- 81 2P/2B: $77 XP: $7 F19

◆◆ Motor Inn

Location: 2 1/2 mi n on I-5, exit 286. 25425 SW Boones Ferry Rd 97070. Fax: 503/682-2211. **Terms:** Credit card guarantee; pets, $25. **Facility:** 170 rooms. Very neat & completely refurbished units. 4 one-bedroom suites with refrigerator & microwave, $125; 5 stories; interior corridors; conference facilities; heated indoor pool, whirlpool; exercise room, central indoor recreation area. **Dining & Entertainment:** Dining room, coffee shop; 6:30 am-2 & 5-10 pm, Fri & Sat-11 pm; $6-$18; cocktails/lounge; nightclub. **Services:** data ports. Fee: coin laundry. **All Rooms:** free movies, cable TV. **Cards:** AE, DI, DS, MC, VI. Ⓓ ⊗

MOTEL ORLEANS Rates Subject to Change **Phone:** 503/682-3184

All Year 1P: $37- 42 2P/1B: $37- 42 2P/2B: $41 XP: $5

◆◆ Apartment Motel

Location: 2 mi n on I-5, exit 286. 8815 SW Sun Pl 97070. **Terms:** Reserv deposit, 3 day notice; no pets. **Facility:** 74 rooms. Large comfortable units. 3 suites, $68; 3 stories; interior corridors; meeting rooms; heated pool, whirlpool. **Dining:** Restaurant nearby. **Services:** Fee: coin laundry. **All Rooms:** refrigerators, cable TV. **Some Rooms:** microwaves. Fee: whirlpools. **Cards:** AE, CB, DI, MC, VI. Ⓓ Ⓢ ⊗

THE GATEWAY TO ADVENTURE ON MT. HOOD

The Resort at The Mountain features
- A 27 hole golf course in a forested setting
- 160 deluxe accommodations with patios; some with fireplaces
- 2 restaurants and lounges
- Pool, jacuzzi, and fitness center
- Hiking, biking, fishing and relaxing.

A perfect destination or a convenient overnight stay off Hwy. 26 on the west slope of Mt. Hood, just 55 minutes from Portland's International Airport.

The Resort at the Mountain

Call 1-800-669-ROOM (7666)

WINCHESTER BAY

LODGING

WINCHESTER BAY FRIENDSHIP INN AAA Special Value Rates **Phone:** 503/271-4871

AAA ◆◆ Motel

All Year [CP] 1P: $38 2P/1B: $50 2P/2B: $60 XP: $5 F18

Location: Northbound off Hwy 101 on Broadway 4 blks; southbound off Hwy 101 at motel sign (Salmon Harbor Dr) sharp turn n on Broadway 3 blks. 390 Broadway 97467 (PO Box 1037). Fax: 503/271-4871. **Terms:** Reserv deposit; pets, $2, no cats. **Facility:** 51 rooms. Established & comfortably appointed units. Located at north end of town. 6 two-bedroom units. 2 stories; exterior corridors. **Dining:** Coffee shop nearby. **All Rooms:** free movies, combo & shower baths, cable TV, no A/C. **Some Rooms:** 15 kitchens, microwaves, refrigerators, whirlpools. **Cards:** AE, CB, DI, DS, MC, VI. (D) ⊗

WOLF CREEK

RESTAURANT

WOLF CREEK TAVERN Historical **Dinner:** $11-$20 **Phone:** 503/866-2474

◆ American

Location: I-5 exit 76. 100 Front St 97497. **Hours:** 11 am-3:30 & 4-8:30 pm, Sun 10 am-2 & 3-8 pm. **Reservations:** suggested. **Features:** Sunday brunch; health conscious menu; beer & wine only; a la carte. Dining rooms in restored historic stage coach inn built in 1873. **Cards:** DS, MC, VI. ⊗

WOODBURN—13,400

LODGING

COMFORT INN WOODBURN Rates Subject to Change **Phone:** 503/982-1727

AAA ◆◆ Motel

6/11-9/5 [CP]	1P: $59- 69	2P/1B: $66- 76	2P/2B: $72- 82	XP: $7	F18
4/16-6/10 [CP]	1P: $57- 60	2P/1B: $64- 67	2P/2B: $71- 74	XP: $7	F18
3/1-4/15 & 9/6-2/29 [CP]	1P: $54- 57	2P/1B: $59- 63	2P/2B: $68- 71	XP: $7	F18

Location: I-5, exit 271. 120 NE Arney Rd 97071. Fax: 503/982-1727. **Terms:** Sr. discount; pets. **Facility:** 49 rooms. Attractive, especially well kept units. 2 large units with whirlpool & refrigerator, $98-$118; 3 stories; interior corridors; meeting rooms; heated pool, sauna, whirlpool; playground. **Services:** Fee: coin laundry. **All Rooms:** free movies, combo & shower baths, cable TV. **Cards:** AE, CB, DI, DS, JCB, MC, VI. *(See color ad below)* (D) ⊗

YACHATS—500

LODGINGS

THE ADOBE MOTEL AAA Special Value Rates **Phone:** 503/547-3141

AAA ◆◆◆ Motor Inn

All Year 2P/1B: $61- 95 2P/2B: $61- 95 XP: $5

Location: 1/2 mi n on Hwy 101. 1555 Hwy 101 97498 (PO Box 219). Fax: 503/547-4234. **Terms:** Reserv deposit; pets, $5, in designated rooms. **Facility:** 93 rooms. Many units with ocean view. Some with fireplace & balcony. Located back from highway. 2 two-bedroom housekeeping units, $100-$135. 6 whirlpool suites, $140; 2 kitchen units with view, $125; 2-3 stories; interior/exterior corridors; oceanfront; meeting rooms; sauna, whirlpool. **Dining:** Dining room; 8 am-2:30 & 5:30-9 pm; $10-$16; cocktails. **All Rooms:** cable TV, no A/C. Fee: movies. **Some Rooms:** coffeemakers, refrigerators. Fee: VCP's. **Cards:** AE, CB, DI, DS, MC, VI. *(See color ad below)* Roll in showers. (D) ⊗

WHEN YOU'RE LIVING OUT OF A SUITCASE...

Comfort Inn

In Portland/Salem

Comfort Inn
120 Arney Road N.E.
Woodburn, OR 97071

• Pool • Indoor Sauna & Spa • Playground • Laundry • Kitchenettes • Suites • Free Cable TV • Free Continental Breakfast • Near Museum, Golf & Drag Strip • Events Include Farmfest & Mexican Fiesta

For reservations call 503-982-1727 or toll free 800-4-CHOICE

The ADOBE YACHATS, OREGON

• Breathtaking Ocean Views • Sauna & Jacuzzi
• Many Rooms with Fireplaces • Refrigerators
• Romantic Spa/Fireplace Suites

Whale and Storm Watch from our Award-winning Restaurant and Lounge, or in your room. Explore tidepools and beach trails right outside our back door.

The ADOBE, A Resort Motel at the Ocean's Edge

YACHATS, OREGON AAA-◆◆◆ 1-800-52-ADOBE or 1-503-547-3141

THE DUBLIN HOUSE Rates Subject to Change **Phone:** 503/547-3200

◆ Motel

7/1-9/30	1P:	$55- 75	2P/1B:	$55- 75	2P/2B:	$65- 75	XP:	$2
3/1-6/30 & 10/1-2/29	1P:	$32	2P/1B:	$32	2P/2B:	$39	XP:	$2

Location: On Hwy 101 at 7th St. 251 W 7th St 97498 (PO Box 716). **Terms:** Reserv deposit; no pets. **Facility:** 26 rooms. Neat, very well-kept units. 1 bedroom suite, $125; $85 off-season; 2 stories; exterior corridors; heated indoor pool. **All Rooms:** free movies, combo & shower baths, cable TV, no A/C. **Some Rooms:** 2 kitchens. **Cards:** DS, MC, VI. *(See color ad below)* Ⓓ ⊗

FIRESIDE MOTEL AAA Special Value Rates **Phone:** 503/547-3636

◆◆ Motel

5/15-9/30	2P/1B:	$60- 83	2P/2B:	$62- 83	XP:	$5
10/1-2/29	2P/1B:	$55- 78	2P/2B:	$57- 78	XP:	$5
3/1-5/14	2P/1B:	$52- 74	2P/2B:	$54- 74	XP:	$5

Location: 1/4 mi n off Hwy 101. 1881 Hwy 101N 97498 (PO Box 313). Fax: 503/547-3152. **Terms:** Reserv deposit, 10 day notice; pets, $5. **Facility:** 43 rooms. Well back from the highway. Many large units overlooking ocean, few with fireplace. 2 one-bedroom suites, $129-$135 in season; 2 stories; exterior corridors; oceanfront; beach access; improved walking trail for nature enthusiast. **All Rooms:** coffeemakers, refrigerators, cable TV, no A/C. **Some Rooms:** Fee: VCP's, whirlpools. **Cards:** DS, MC, VI. *(See ad below)* Ⓓ ⊗

SHAMROCK LODGETTES Rates Subject to Change **Phone:** 503/547-3312

◆◆ Cottage

All Year	2P/1B:	$70- 100	2P/2B:	$67- 100	XP:	$7

Location: 1/4 mi s on Hwy 101. 105 Hwy 101S 97498 (PO Box 346). Fax: 503/547-3843. **Terms:** Reserv deposit; 2 night min stay, weekends; pets, $2, in cottages only. **Facility:** 19 rooms. On nicely landscaped grounds. Modern motel units with fireplace & deck or patio; also 1- & 2-bedroom rustic housekeeping cottages with fireplace. 2 two-bedroom units. 1 story; exterior corridors; beach, sauna, whirlpool; exercise room. **All Rooms:** free movies, combo & shower baths, cable TV, no A/C. **Some Rooms:** coffeemakers, 11 kitchens, microwaves, refrigerators, whirlpools. **Cards:** AE, CB, DI, MC, VI. Ⓓ

RESTAURANT

LA SERRE **Dinner:** $11-$20 **Phone:** 503/547-3420

◆◆ Seafood

Location: Off Hwy 101 at 2nd & Beach sts. 160 W 2nd 97498. **Hours:** Open 3/1-12/31; 5 pm-9 pm, Sun 9 am-noon & 5-9 pm; winter closing hours vary. Closed: Tues 10/1-6/30 & Jan. **Reservations:** suggested. **Features:** No A/C; children's menu; health conscious menu items; cocktails & lounge. Inviting dining room featuring varied menu specializing in shellfish dishes. **Cards:** AE, MC, VI. ⊗

The Dublin House Yachats Oregon

Indoor Heated Pool
- Big, Clean Rooms
- Ocean & Mountain Views
- Room Phones
- Coffee in rooms

The Dublin House
7th St & Hwy 101 Yachats, OR 97498

1/2 PRICE OFFER
October - June
Two Nights or More
Call for
Details, restrictions, availability

CALL (503) 547-3200

The Fireside MOTEL

43 OCEAN VIEW UNITS

Improved Walking Trail
Convenience Refrigerators
Direct Dial Phones
Cable Color TV
Fireplaces

P.O. Box 313 • **Yachats, Oregon** 97498
Phone (503) 547-3636

Reservations: (800) 336-3573

AAA Trip Interruption Protection
is designed to assist you
in reaching your destination
if your vehicle becomes disabled
as a result of a traffic collision.

WASHINGTON

ABERDEEN—16,600

LODGINGS

ABERDEEN MANSION INN BED & BREAKFAST Rates Subject to Change **Phone:** 360/533-7079

AAA ◆◆◆ Historic Bed & Breakfast

All Year [BP] 1P: $75- 95 2P/1B: $75- 95

Location: Westbound from US 101, 1/2 mi vie Williams & 5th; eastbound 1 mi n from Broadway to W 5th & M. 807 N M St 98520. **Terms:** Sr. discount; age restrictions may apply; reserv deposit; weekly/monthly rates; no pets. **Facility:** 4 rooms. 1905 Queen Anne mansion furnished with furniture of the period. 2 stories; interior corridors; smoke free premises. **All Rooms:** no A/C, no phones. **Some Rooms:** cable TV. **Cards:** MC, VI. (D) ⊗

NORDIC INN AAA Special Value Rates **Phone:** 360/533-0100

AAA ◆◆ Motor Inn

All Year [BP] 1P: $52- 72 2P/1B: $62- 77 2P/2B: $67- 82 XP: $10 F10

Location: 1 3/4 mi s on SR 105 (Westport Hwy). 1700 S Boone St 98520. Fax: 360/533-3229. **Terms:** Reserv deposit, 3 day notice; small pets only, $5. **Facility:** 66 rooms. 2 stories; exterior corridors; meeting rooms. **Dining:** Dining room, coffee shop; 24 hours; $6-$13; cocktails. **All Rooms:** shower baths, cable TV, no A/C. **Some Rooms:** refrigerators. Fee: VCP's. **Cards:** AE, CB, DI, DS, MC, VI. (D) ⊗

OLYMPIC INN Rates Subject to Change **Phone:** 360/533-4200

AAA ◆◆ Motel

All Year 1P: $40- 65 2P/1B: $50- 70 2P/2B: $55- 75 XP: $9

Location: 1/2 mi w on US 101 southbound. 616 W Heron St 98520. Fax: 360/533-6223. **Terms:** Small pets only, $5. **Facility:** 55 rooms. Exceptionally large units. 2 two-bedroom units. 3 efficiencies, $10-$25 extra; 2 stories; exterior corridors. **Dining:** Restaurant nearby. **Services:** Fee: coin laundry. **All Rooms:** free movies, cable TV, no A/C. **Some Rooms:** refrigerators. **Cards:** AE, CB, DI, DS, MC, VI. (D) ⊗

RED LION INN Rates Subject to Change **Phone:** 360/532-5210

AAA ◆◆ Motel

All Year 1P: $52- 72 2P/1B: $62- 77 2P/2B: $72 XP: $10

Location: 1/2 mi w on US 101 northbound. 521 W Wishkah 98520. Fax: 360/533-8483. **Terms:** Pets. **Facility:** 67 rooms. Commercial location. 2 stories; exterior corridors. **Dining:** Restaurant nearby. **All Rooms:** free movies, cable TV, no A/C. **Cards:** AE, DI, DS, MC, VI. ⊗

TRAVELURE MOTEL Rates Subject to Change **Phone:** 360/532-3280

AAA ◆◆ Motel

6/1-9/30 1P: $33- 37 2P/1B: $40- 45 2P/2B: $45- 50 XP: $6 D

3/1-5/31 & 10/1-2/29 1P: $31- 35 2P/1B: $39- 42 2P/2B: $42- 47 XP: $6 D

Location: 1/2 mi w on US 101 northbound. 623 W Wishkah 98520. Fax: 360/532-2472. **Terms:** Reserv deposit, 3 day notice; weekly rates; pets, $5. **Facility:** 24 rooms. Commercial location. 1 story; exterior corridors. **All Rooms:** free movies, cable TV, no A/C. **Some Rooms:** refrigerators. **Cards:** AE, CB, DI, DS, MC, VI. (D) ⊗

RESTAURANTS

BRIDGES RESTAURANT **Dinner:** up to $10 **Phone:** 360/532-6563

AAA ◆◆ American

Location: 1st & G St. 112 N G St 98520. **Hours:** 11 am-9 pm, Fri-10 pm, Sat noon-10 pm, Sun 4 pm-9 pm. Closed: 1/1, 7/4 & 12/25. **Reservations:** suggested. **Features:** children's menu; senior's menu; health conscious menu items; carryout; cocktails & lounge. Beef, chicken & fresh seafood in a multi-decor dining room. Smoke free premises. **Cards:** AE, DI, DS, MC, VI. ⊗

DUFFY'S RESTAURANT 1 **Dinner:** up to $10 **Phone:** 360/532-3842

AAA ◆◆ American

Location: 1 mi w on US 101. 1605 Simpson Ave 98520. **Hours:** 6 am-10:30 pm, Fri & Sat-11 pm, Sun 7 am-10:30 pm. **Features:** carryout; cocktails & lounge. Good sized portions & homemade pies. **Cards:** AE, DI, DS, MC, VI. ⊗

DUFFY'S RESTAURANT 2 **Dinner:** up to $10 **Phone:** 360/538-0606

AAA ◆ American

Location: 1/2 mi e on US 12. 1212 E Wishkah 98520. **Hours:** 6 am-9:30 pm, Fri & Sat-11 pm, Sun 7 am-9:30 pm. **Features:** carryout; cocktails. Good sized portions & tasty homemade pies. **Cards:** AE, DI, DS, MC, VI. ⊗

ANACORTES—11,500

LODGINGS

ALBATROSS BED & BREAKFAST Rates Subject to Change **Phone:** 360/293-0677

AAA ◆◆ Bed & Breakfast

6/1-10/15 [BP] 1P: $80 2P/1B: $85 XP: $15

3/1-5/31 & 10/16-2/29 [BP] 1P: $70 2P/1B: $75 XP: $15

Location: On Kingsway W; 1 mi sw from jct of Oakes & Sunset aves, 1 1/4 mi sw of Ferry. 5708 Kingsway W 98221. **Terms:** Check-in 4 pm; reserv deposit, 3 day notice; weekly rates; package plans; pets, by prior arrangement. **Facility:** 4 rooms. Cape Cod style home overlooking skyline marina. 1 story; interior corridors; smoke free premises. **Services:** airport transportation. **Recreation:** bicycles. **All Rooms:** no A/C, no phones, no TVs. **Cards:** AE, MC, VI. (D) ⊗

ANACORTES INN AAA Special Value Rates **Phone:** 360/293-3153

AAA ◆◆ Motel

5/1-10/15 1P: $55- 75 2P/1B: $60- 85 2P/2B: $65- 100 XP: $5

3/1-4/30 & 10/16-2/29 1P: $45- 65 2P/1B: $50- 80 2P/2B: $55- 95 XP: $5

Location: 1 3/4 mi s on SR 20. 3006 Commercial Ave 98221. Fax: 360/293-0209. **Terms:** Credit card guarantee, 14 day notice; pets, $10-$20, in designated rooms. **Facility:** 44 rooms. Commercial location. Some rooms offer view of Fidalgo Bay or Mt Baker. 5 efficiencies, $5 extra; 2 stories; exterior corridors. **Recreation:** heated pool open 5/30-9/5. **All Rooms:** coffeemakers, cable TV, no A/C. **Some Rooms:** microwaves, refrigerators. **Cards:** AE, CB, DI, DS, MC, VI. *(See color ad p A66)* (D) ⊗

PONY SOLDIER MOTOR INNS
Oregon • Washington • Idaho
1-800-634-PONY
Best Western
PONY SOLDIER MOTOR INNS

CAP SANTE INN — Guaranteed Rates — **Phone:** 360/293-0602

AAA ◆◆◆ Motel

Fri & Sat 3/1-3/31, 4/1-10/31 & Fri & Sat 11/1-2/29	1P:	$56	2P/1B:	$60	2P/2B:	$64	XP:	$4-5
Sun-Thurs 3/1-3/31 & 11/1-2/29	1P:	$42	2P/1B:	$46	2P/2B:	$50	XP:	$4

Location: E on 9th St. 906 9th St 98221. **Terms:** Reserv deposit; weekly rates; 2 night min stay; no pets. **Facility:** 34 rooms. 1 two-bedroom unit. 2 stories; exterior corridors. **Services:** Fee: coin laundry. **All Rooms:** combo & shower baths, cable TV, no A/C. **Cards:** AE, CB, DI, DS, MC, VI. *(See color ad below)* Ⓓ ⊗

HOLIDAY MOTEL — Guaranteed Rates — **Phone:** 360/293-6511

◆ Motel

5/1-10/15	1P:	$40- 50	2P/1B:	$44- 54	2P/2B:	$50- 58	XP:	$5
3/1-4/30 & 10/16-2/29	1P:	$28- 38	2P/1B:	$30- 40	2P/2B:	$38- 45	XP:	$5

Location: 1 3/4 mi s on SR 20. 2903 Commercial Ave 98221. **Terms:** Sr. discount; reserv deposit; weekly rates; no pets. **Facility:** 10 rooms. 3 two-bedroom units. 1 story; exterior corridors. **Dining:** Restaurant; 11 am-3 & 5-9 pm; $8-$10. **All Rooms:** cable TV, no A/C, no phones. **Cards:** DS, MC, VI. Ⓓ ⊗

ISLANDS INN — Rates Subject to Change — **Phone:** 360/293-4644

AAA ◆◆◆ Motor Inn

5/15-10/15 [CP]	1P:	$70- 110	2P/1B:	$70- 110	2P/2B:	$70- 80	XP:	$5
3/1-5/14 & 10/16-2/29 [CP]	1P:	$58- 85	2P/1B:	$58- 85	2P/2B:	$48- 55	XP:	$5

Location: 2 mi s on SR 20. 3401 Commercial Ave 98221. Fax: 360/293-4644. **Terms:** Reserv deposit, 3 day notice; small pets only, $5. **Facility:** 36 rooms. Beautiful view of Fidalgo Bay Islands & Mt Baker. Some balconies. Many fireplaces. 6 two-bedroom units. 2 stories; exterior corridors; meeting rooms; heated pool, whirlpool. **Dining:** Also, La Petite, see separate listing. **All Rooms:** coffeemakers, refrigerators, cable TV. **Some Rooms:** A/C, whirlpools. **Cards:** AE, CB, DI, DS, MC, VI. Ⓓ ⊗

MARINA INN — Rates Subject to Change — **Phone:** 360/293-1100

AAA ◆◆◆ Motel

5/15-9/30 [CP]	1P:	$65- 89	2P/1B:	$71- 95	2P/2B:	$71	XP:	$6	F12
3/1-5/14 & 10/1-2/29 [CP]	1P:	$48- 55	2P/1B:	$55- 70	2P/2B:	$55- 70	XP:	$6	F12

Location: In town. 3300 Commercial Ave 98221. Fax: 360/293-1100. **Terms:** Reserv deposit; no pets. **Facility:** 52 rooms. Commercial location. Charming contemporary rooms. 2 stories; interior corridors; indoor hot tub. **Services:** guest laundry. **All Rooms:** cable TV, no A/C. **Some Rooms:** coffeemakers, 4 efficiencies, microwaves, refrigerators. Fee: whirlpools. **Cards:** AE, CB, DI, DS, MC, VI. Ⓓ Ⓢ ⊗

SHIP HARBOR INN — AAA Special Value Rates — **Phone:** 360/293-5177

AAA ◆◆ Motel

5/1-9/30 [CP]	1P:	$59- 65	2P/1B:	$65- 75	2P/2B:	$75- 85	XP:	$4	F12
3/1-4/30 & 10/1-2/29 [CP]	1P:	$49- 59	2P/1B:	$52- 62	2P/2B:	$63- 72	XP:	$4	F12

Location: On Ferry Terminal Rd; 1/4 mi s of Ferry Landing. 5316 Ferry Terminal Rd 98221. Fax: 360/293-5177. **Terms:** Reserv deposit, 3 day notice; weekly rates; no pets. **Facility:** 26 rooms. Lodge & cabins on 7 acres of woodland overlooking ship harbor & ferry terminal. Balconies or lanais, some with fireplace. 2 stories; exterior corridors; meeting rooms; playground. **Services:** Fee: coin laundry. **Recreation:** Fee: bicycles. **All Rooms:** cable TV, no A/C. **Some Rooms:** coffeemakers, 6 kitchens, microwaves, refrigerators. **Cards:** AE, DI, DS, MC, VI. *(See color ad below)* Ⓓ ⊗

SUNSET BEACH BED & BREAKFAST — Guaranteed Rates — **Phone:** 360/293-5428

AAA ◆ Bed & Breakfast

6/1-9/30 [BP]	1P:	$69- 79	2P/1B:	$69- 79	XP:	$15-35
3/1-5/31 & 10/1-2/29 [BP]	1P:	$53- 63	2P/1B:	$53- 63	XP:	$15-35

Location: Across from Washington Park. 100 Sunset Beach 98221. **Terms:** Age restrictions may apply; check-in 4 pm; reserv deposit, 3 day notice; no pets. **Facility:** 3 rooms. 1 story; interior corridors; smoke free premises; whirlpool. **Recreation:** fishing. **All Rooms:** no A/C, no phones. **Some Rooms:** radios, cable TV. **Cards:** DS, MC, VI. Ⓓ ⊗

ANACORTES INN
On beautiful Fidalgo Island - The 1st of The San Juans
RESERVATIONS USA & CANADA 800-327-7976 3006 COMMERCIAL AVE

◆◆◆ CAP SANTE INN 206-293-0602
• View Rooms of Cap Sante Marina & Cape
• Queen Size Beds, Cable TV
• Courtesy Coffee & Laundry
• 10 Minutes to Ferry
• RSV. ONLY 1-800-852-0846.
• Non-Smoking Rooms Available
• Take "Scenic Route" – Ave. R
906 9th Street
Downtown Anacortes, WA 98221

SHIP HARBOR INN
"Best Value in the San Juans"
Spectacular View • Fireplaces • Coin Laundry • Kitchen Cabins
Balconies • Meeting Room • Continental Breakfast • Bike Rentals
800-852-8568 USA • 800-235-8568 Canada
LOCATED AT THE ANACORTES FERRY TERMINAL

Here Is Your Passport To A Free Night's Stay.

For each night you stay at a Red Lion Hotel or Inn and pay AAA rates, you'll receive a Red Lion passport stamp. Between now and March 31, 1996, collect three stamps and receive a 50% discount on AAA rates; collect six stamps and get one **free night**.

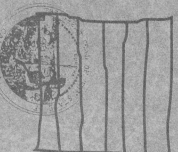

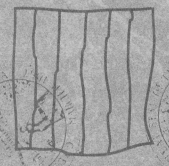

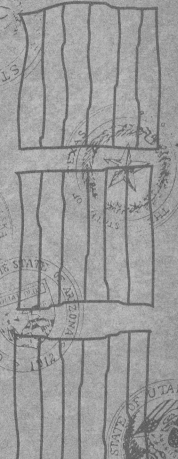

Either way, you'll want to start your collection today. Because when you consider that Red Lion offers large, comfortable guest rooms, exceptional dining and impeccable service—all in some of the West's best locations—this isn't just a passport to free accommodations, it's your ticket to some great hospitality.

Red Lion Hotels & Inns
800-RED LION

RED LION IS YOUR PASSPORT TO GREAT HOSPITALITY THROUGHOUT THE WEST.

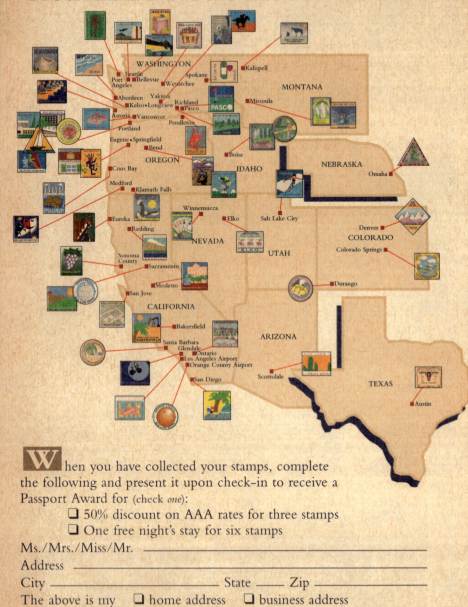

When you have collected your stamps, complete the following and present it upon check-in to receive a Passport Award for (check *one*):

- ❑ 50% discount on AAA rates for three stamps
- ❑ One free night's stay for six stamps

Ms./Mrs./Miss/Mr. ______________________________

Address ______________________________

City ____________________ State ____ Zip ____________

The above is my ❑ home address ❑ business address

RED LION HOTELS & INNS

800-RED LION

*Offer is subject to availability and advance reservations are required. Passport stamps will not be issued when redeeming Passport Awards. Guest must pay AAA rates to receive passport stamps. Guest accrues one passport stamp per paid night. Children 18 or under stay free when sharing adult's room. This offer may be combined with airlines mileage accrual and/or Frequent Guest Dividends benefits only. Not valid with any other discounts or promotions. Passport has no cash value. See Passport Award for additional terms and conditions. Expires 3/31/96.

RESTAURANTS

BOOMER'S LANDING ◆◆ Seafood — Dinner: $21-$30 — Phone: 360/293-5108

Location: On Guemes Channel next to Wyman's Marina; 4 blks e of Commercial Ave, 1 blk n of 4th St. 209 T Ave 98221. **Hours:** 11:30 am-9 pm, Fri-10 pm, Sat noon-10 pm, Sun 11 am-3 & 4-9 pm. Closed: 1/1, 11/23 & 12/25. **Reservations:** suggested. **Features:** Sunday brunch; children's menu; health conscious menu; carryout; cocktails & lounge. Pleasant terraced dining room overlooking Guemes Channel & Island. Also steaks, chicken, pasta & salads. Smoke free premises. **Cards:** AE, MC, VI. ⊗

THE COURTYARD BISTRO AAA ◆◆◆ French — Dinner: $11-$20 — Phone: 360/299-2923

Location: Downtown. 419 Commercial Ave 98221. **Hours:** 11:30 am-2:30 & 5:30-10 pm, Sun 10 am-3 & 5:30-10 pm. Closed: Tues 10/15-5/30. **Reservations:** suggested. **Features:** No A/C; Sunday brunch; children's menu; health conscious menu items; carryout; cocktails & lounge. Northwest food prepared bistro style, served with a classic touch. Smoke free premises. **Cards:** MC, VI. ⊗

LA PETITE AAA ◆◆ Ethnic — Dinner: $11-$20 — Phone: 360/293-4644

Location: At Islands Inn. 3401 Commercial Ave 98221. **Hours:** 5 pm-10 pm. Closed: Mon, 11/23 & 12/25. **Reservations:** suggested. **Features:** cocktails. Pleasant dining room overlooking Fidalgo Bay Islands. Menu varies. **Cards:** AE, DI, DS, MC, VI. ⊗

ARLINGTON—4,000

LODGING

ARLINGTON MOTOR INN AAA ◆◆◆ Motel — Rates Subject to Change — Phone: 360/652-9595

All Year	1P: $39- 44	2P/1B: $44- 49	2P/2B: $51- 56	XP: $5	F12

Location: 1 blk e of I-5, exit 208. 2214 SR 530 98223 (PO Box 3387). Fax: 360/652-9595. **Terms:** Reserv deposit, 4 day notice; small pets only, $10, $20 dep req. **Facility:** 41 rooms. Some rooms with view of Cascade Mountains. 2 stories; exterior corridors; whirlpool. **Dining:** Restaurant nearby. **All Rooms:** free movies, cable TV. **Some Rooms:** Fee: refrigerators. **Cards:** AE, DI, DS, MC, VI. (D) ⊗

RESTAURANT

PETOSA'S RESTAURANT ◆ American — Dinner: up to $10 — Phone: 360/652-8688

Location: W of I-5, exit 206. 17121 28th Dr NE 98223. **Hours:** 6 am-11 pm, Fri & Sat-midnight, Sun-10 pm. Closed: 12/25. **Features:** children's menu; salad bar; cocktails & lounge. Also Italian cuisine. **Cards:** MC, VI. ⊗

ASHFORD

LODGINGS

ALEXANDER'S COUNTRY INN AAA ◆◆◆ Historic Country Inn — Rates Subject to Change — Phone: 360/569-2300

5/1-10/31 [BP]	1P: $89- 125	2P/1B: $89- 125	2P/2B: $89- 125	XP: $15
3/1-4/30 & 11/1-2/29 [BP]	1P: $59- 95	2P/1B: $59- 95	2P/2B: $59- 95	XP: $15

Location: On SR 706; 1 mi w of Nisqually entrance to Mount Rainier National Park. 37515 SR 706 E 98304. **Terms:** Reserv deposit, 7 day notice; no pets. **Facility:** 13 rooms. Renovated 1912 historic inn with many period furnishings & appointments. Closed 12/25. 3-bedroom 2-bath house, $150-$195 for up to 4 persons; 3 stories; interior corridors; smoke free premises; whirlpool, hot tub. **Dining:** Dining room, see separate listing. **Services:** complimentary evening beverages. **Recreation:** nature trails; cross country skiing. **All Rooms:** no A/C, no phones, no TVs. **Cards:** MC, VI. (D) ⊗

MOUNTAIN MEADOWS INN BED & BREAKFAST ◆◆ Bed & Breakfast — Rates Subject to Change — Phone: 360/569-2788

6/1-9/30 [BP]	1P: $75	2P/1B: $95	2P/2B: $75	XP: $15
Sun-Thurs 3/1-5/31 & 10/1-2/29 [BP]	1P: $55	2P/1B: $75	2P/2B: $75	XP: $15
Fri & Sat 3/1-5/31 & 10/1-2/29 [BP]	1P: $55	2P/1B: $75	2P/2B: $65	XP: $15

Location: N end of town. 28912 SR 706E 98304. **Terms:** Check-in 4 pm; reserv deposit, 10 day notice; no pets. **Facility:** 5 rooms. Restored 1910 mill superintendent's home on acres of forest, fish ponds & nature trails. 2 stories; interior/exterior corridors; smoke free premises. **Recreation:** nature trails; fishing. **All Rooms:** comb, shower & tub baths, no A/C, no phones, no TVs. **Some Rooms:** 2 kitchens. **Cards:** MC, VI. (D) ⊗

THE NISQUALLY LODGE AAA ◆◆◆ Motel — Rates Subject to Change — Phone: 360/569-8804

5/1-9/30 [CP]	1P: $67	2P/1B: $67- 77	2P/2B: $77	XP:$5-10
3/1-4/30 & 10/1-2/29 [CP]	1P: $50	2P/1B: $50- 60	2P/2B: $60	XP:$5-10

Location: 1/2 mi e on SR 706. 31609 SR 706 98304. Fax: 360/569-2435. **Terms:** Reserv deposit; no pets. **Facility:** 24 rooms. Commercial rural location. Close to west entrance of Mt. Rainier National Park. 2 stories; interior corridors; smoke free premises; whirlpool. **Cards:** AE, CB, DI, MC, VI. (D) ⊗

RESTAURANT

ALEXANDER'S Historical ◆◆ American — Dinner: $11-$20 — Phone: 360/569-2300

Location: In Alexander's Country Inn. 37515 SR 706 E 98304. **Hours:** 8 am-10 & 11:30-8 pm; 11/1-6/1 Fri-Sun only. Closed: 12/25. **Reservations:** suggested. **Features:** children's menu; beer & wine only; a la carte. Relaxed country atmosphere. Homemade breads & desserts. Smoke free premises. **Cards:** MC, VI. ⊗

Budget Host
"Something *Better* At A Budget Rate" in **WASHINGTON...**
AAA
PORT ANGELES • 1006 E. Front St. (Hwy. 101) • 360 452-9255
For Reservations or a FREE Directory, Call: **1 800 BUD-HOST**

AUBURN—33,100

LODGINGS

BEST WESTERN PONY SOLDIER MOTOR INN Rates Subject to Change **Phone:** 206/939-5950

◆◆◆ Motel

All Year [CP] 1P: $66- 71 2P/1B: $69- 74 2P/2B: $74- 79 XP: $5 F12

Location: 1/4 mi e of SR 167, 15th St nw exit. 1521 D St NE 98002. Fax: 206/735-4197. **Terms:** Sr. discount; check-in 4 pm; reserv deposit, 7 day notice; small pets only. **Facility:** 66 rooms. 2 stories; exterior corridors; heated pool, sauna, whirlpool. **Dining:** Restaurant nearby. **All Rooms:** free movies, refrigerators, cable TV. **Cards:** AE, CB, DI, DS, JCB, MC, VI. *(See ad p A65)* (D) ⊗

NENDELS INN AUBURN Rates Subject to Change **Phone:** 206/833-8007

◆◆ Motel

All Year 1P: $46 2P/1B: $46 2P/2B: $54 XP: $10 F15

Location: 1/8 mi e of SR 167 at 15th St NW. 102 15th St NE 98002. Fax: 206/931-1113. **Terms:** Sr. discount; reserv deposit, 3 day notice; no pets. **Facility:** 35 rooms. 2 stories; interior corridors. **Dining:** Restaurant nearby. **All Rooms:** free movies, cable TV. **Some Rooms:** microwaves, refrigerators. **Cards:** AE, CB, DI, DS, MC, VI. (D) ⊗

VAL-U INN Rates Subject to Change **Phone:** 206/735-9600

◆◆◆ Motel

All Year [CP] 1P: $56 2P/1B: $66 2P/2B: $69 XP: $5 F12

Location: 1/8 mi e of SR 167, exit 15th St NW. 9 14th Ave NW 98001. Fax: 206/735-5228. **Terms:** Sr. discount; weekly rates; pets, $5. **Facility:** 66 rooms. 3 stories; interior corridors; meeting rooms; whirlpool. **Dining:** Restaurant nearby. **Services:** data ports. Fee: coin laundry. **All Rooms:** free movies, cable TV. **Some Rooms:** honor bars, refrigerators. Fee: VCP's. **Cards:** AE, DI, DS, MC, VI.

(See ad below) (D) (S) ⊗

BAINBRIDGE ISLAND

LODGINGS

BAINBRIDGE HOUSE BED & BREAKFAST Rates Subject to Change **Phone:** 206/842-1599

◆◆ Bed & Breakfast

All Year [BP] 1P: $65- 75 2P/1B: $65- 75 2P/2B: $65- 75 XP: $10

Location: 3 3/4 mi from ferry landing; on Hwy 305, 1/2 mi to N Madison, nw on N Madison, 1 mi to NE Valley, w 1/2 mi. 11301 Logg Rd NE 98110. **Terms:** Sr. discount; age restrictions may apply; reserv deposit, 7 day notice; weekly/monthly rates; no pets. **Facility:** 2 rooms. Cozy country-style cottage. 2 stories; interior corridors; smoke free premises. **All Rooms:** free movies, combo & shower baths, cable TV, no A/C. **Cards:** MC, VI. (D) ⊗

ISLAND COUNTRY INN Guaranteed Rates **Phone:** 206/842-6861

◆◆◆ Motel

All Year [CP] 1P: $55- 85 2P/1B: $65- 95 2P/2B: $65- 95 XP: $5 F14

Location: 3/4 mi n of ferry dock. 920 Hildebrand Ln NE 98110. Fax: 206/842-9808. **Terms:** Sr. discount; monthly rates; no pets. **Facility:** 46 rooms. 2 stories; exterior corridors; heated pool, whirlpool. **Services:** data ports. **All Rooms:** free movies, combo & shower baths, cable TV. **Some Rooms:** coffeemakers, 6 kitchens, refrigerators, whirlpools. **Cards:** AE, DI, DS, MC, VI.

(See color ad below) Roll in showers. (D) (S) ⊗

ROSE COTTAGE BED & BREAKFAST Rates Subject to Change **Phone:** 206/842-6248

◆◆ Bed & Breakfast

All Year [CP] 1P: $75 2P/1B: $75

Location: From SR 305, 2 mi via Koura Rd. 11744 Olympic Terr 98110. **Terms:** Sr. discount; reserv deposit, 7 day notice; no pets. **Facility:** 2 rooms. Suite with whirlpool avail; 1 story; interior/exterior corridors; smoke free premises. **All Rooms:** coffeemakers, refrigerators, combo & shower baths, no A/C. **Cards:** MC, VI. (D) ⊗

RESTAURANT

THE STREAMLINER DINER **Dinner:** up to $10 **Phone:** 206/842-8595

◆◆ American

Location: Downtown, 2 blks nw of ferry dock. 397 Winslow Way E 98110. **Hours:** 7 am-3 pm, Sat & Sun 8 am-2:30 pm. **Features:** carryout. Casual home-style decor. Open kitchen. Patio dining. Smoke free premises. ⊗

BELFAIR

LODGING

BELFAIR MOTEL Rates Subject to Change **Phone:** 206/275-4485

◆◆ Motel

6/1-10/31 1P: $42 2P/1B: $46 2P/2B: $51 XP: $5 F3

3/1-5/31 & 11/1-2/29 1P: $33 2P/1B: $38 2P/2B: $42 XP: $5 F3

Location: Downtown. NE 23322 Hwy 3 98528 (PO Box 1135). Fax: 206/275-5443. **Terms:** Sr. discount; reserv deposit, 7 day notice; weekly/monthly rates; no pets. **Facility:** 28 rooms. 6 efficiencies $10 extra; 2 stories; exterior corridors. **Dining:** Restaurant nearby. **Services:** Fee: coin laundry. **All Rooms:** cable TV. **Cards:** AE, DS, MC, VI. (D) ⊗

VAL-U INN MOTEL
AUBURN
•Spa
•Complimentary Continental Breakfast • Guest Laundry
•Remote Control Satellite TV • Non-Smoking Rooms
For Reservations, call: 1-800-443-7777
9-14th Avenue N.W. Auburn, WA 98001 (206) 735-9600

Island Country Inn
WELCOME TO BAINBRIDGE ISLAND.
• A new island retreat • 35 min. ferry from Seattle • 46 deluxe rooms
• Complimentary Continental Breakfast
• Non-smoking rooms • Pool/spa
920 Hildebrand Lane NE • Bainbridge, WA 98110
CALL 1-800-842-8429

BELLEVUE—86,900 (See SEATTLE & VICINITY ACCOMMODATIONS spotting map pages A136 & A137; see index starting on page A134)

LODGINGS

BELLEVUE HILTON INN — Rates Subject to Change — **Phone:** 206/455-3330 — 147
◆◆◆ Motor Inn
All Year — 1P: $79- 129 — 2P/1B: $89- 139 — 2P/2B: $89- 139 — XP: $10 — F
Location: Off I-405; northbound exit 12, southbound exit 13. 100 112th Ave NE 98004. Fax: 206/451-2473. **Terms:** Sr. discount; credit card guarantee; no pets. **Facility:** 180 rooms. 7 stories; interior corridors; business center, conference facilities; heated indoor pool, sauna, whirlpool; health club. **Dining:** 2 restaurants; 5:15 am-10:30 pm; $5-$12; cocktails; also, Sams Restaurant & Lounge, see separate listing. **Services:** secretarial services; valet laundry. Fee: PC, airport transportation. **All Rooms:** free & pay movies, cable TV. **Some Rooms:** Fee: refrigerators. **Cards:** AE, CB, DI, DS, JCB, MC, VI. *(See ad p 38)*

BELLEVUE TRAVELODGE — Rates Subject to Change — **Phone:** 206/454-4967 — 145
AAA ◆◆ Motel
All Year — 1P: $49 — 2P/1B: $54 — 2P/2B: $59 — XP: $5
Location: 1/4 mi w of I-405, northbound I-405, exit 13A-B to ne 8th W, southbound I-405, exit 13 to ne 8th W. 11011 NE 8th St 98004. Fax: 206/453-7160. **Terms:** Sr. discount; reserv deposit; no pets. **Facility:** 54 rooms. 1 two-bedroom unit, 1 three-bedroom unit. 3 kitchens, $65; 2 stories; exterior corridors; heated pool. **Dining:** Restaurant nearby. **Services:** Fee: coin laundry, airport transportation. **All Rooms:** coffeemakers, free movies, combo & shower baths, cable TV. **Some Rooms:** refrigerators. **Cards:** AE, CB, DI, DS, JCB, MC, VI.

BEST WESTERN BELLEVUE INN — AAA Special Value Rates — **Phone:** 206/455-5240 — 148
◆◆◆ Motor Inn
All Year — 1P: $80- 85 — 2P/1B: $90- 95 — 2P/2B: $90- 95
Location: Off I-405; northbound exit 12, southbound exit 12. 11211 Main St 98004. Fax: 206/455-0654. **Terms:** Check-in 4 pm; credit card guarantee, 4 day notice; weekly/monthly rates; pets, $30. **Facility:** 179 rooms. Many rooms with balcony, some with patio. 2 stories; interior corridors; conference facilities; heated pool; exercise room. **Dining:** Restaurant; 6:30 am-2:30 & 5-10 pm, Sun from 7 am; $7-$15. **Services:** data ports; valet laundry; area transportation. Fee: airport transportation. **All Rooms:** free movies, cable TV. **Some Rooms:** refrigerators. Fee: VCP's. **Cards:** AE, CB, DI, DS, JCB, MC, VI.

COURTYARD BY MARRIOTT — AAA Special Value Rates — **Phone:** 206/869-5300 — 154
◆◆◆ Motor Inn
All Year — 1P: $84 — 2P/1B: $94 — 2P/2B: $94 — XP: $10 — F18
Location: 2 1/4 mi e of I-405; off SR 520 at 148 Ave NE (north exit). 14615 NE 29th Pl 98007. Fax: 206/883-9122. **Terms:** Weekly rates; no pets. **Facility:** 152 rooms. 2 stories; interior corridors; meeting rooms; heated indoor pool, whirlpool. **Dining & Entertainment:** Dining room; 6:30 am-10:30 & 5-10 pm; $7-$15; cocktails/lounge. **Services:** data ports. Fee: coin laundry, airport transportation. **All Rooms:** free & pay movies, cable TV. **Some Rooms:** Fee: refrigerators. **Cards:** AE, CB, DI, DS, MC, VI. *(See color ad p A127)*

DAYS INN BELLEVUE — AAA Special Value Rates — **Phone:** 206/643-6644 — 151
AAA ◆◆◆ Motel
All Year [CP] — 1P: $44- 74 — 2P/1B: $49- 79 — 2P/2B: $59- 69 — XP: $5 — F18
Location: N of I-90, westbound exit 11, eastbound exit 11A. 3241 156th Ave SE 98007. Fax: 206/644-7279. **Terms:** Credit card guarantee; no pets. **Facility:** 110 rooms. Some small rooms. 2-3 stories; exterior corridors; meeting rooms; whirlpool. **Dining:** Restaurant nearby. **Services:** data ports. Fee: airport transportation. **All Rooms:** free movies, cable TV. **Some Rooms:** refrigerators. Fee: VCP's. **Cards:** AE, CB, DI, DS, MC, VI.

EASTGATE MOTEL — Rates Subject to Change — **Phone:** 206/746-4100 — 150
AAA ◆◆ Motel
All Year [CP] — 1P: $36 — 2P/1B: $42 — 2P/2B: $45 — XP: $6 — F12
Location: N of I-90; westbound exit 11, eastbound exit 11A; 1 1/4 mi e of I-405. 14632 SE Eastgate Way 98007. **Terms:** Reserv deposit; weekly rates; no pets. **Facility:** 29 rooms. 3 two-bedroom units. 4 kitchens, $5 extra; 1 story; exterior corridors. **All Rooms:** combo & shower baths. **Some Rooms:** microwaves, refrigerators. **Cards:** AE, CB, DI, DS, MC, VI.

EMBASSY SUITES HOTEL BELLEVUE — Rates Subject to Change — **Phone:** 206/644-2500 — 143
AAA ◆◆◆ Suite Hotel
6/16-8/18 [BP] — 1P: $129- 149 — 2P/1B: $149- 189 — 2P/2B: $159- 199 — XP: $15 — F18
3/1-6/15 & 8/19-2/29 [BP] — 1P: $129- 139 — 2P/1B: $139- 189 — 2P/2B: $149- 199 — XP: $15 — F18
Location: N of I-90; from I-90 westbound exit 11, eastbound exit 11A. 3225 158th Ave SE 98008. Fax: 206/644-2091. **Terms:** Sr. discount; reserv deposit, 3 day notice; no pets. **Facility:** 240 rooms. 5 stories; interior corridors; conference facilities; heated indoor pool, sauna, whirlpool; exercise room. **Dining & Entertainment:** Restaurant; 11:30 am-10 pm; $8-$25; cocktail lounge. **Services:** data ports, PC; childcare; complimentary evening beverages; area transportation. Fee: coin laundry, airport transportation. **All Rooms:** microwaves, free & pay movies, refrigerators, cable TV. **Some Rooms:** coffeemakers. Fee: whirlpools. **Cards:** AE, CB, DI, DS, MC, VI. *(See ad below)*

TWICE THE HOTEL
SEATTLE/BELLEVUE

- Off I-90, close to Bell Square Shopping Center & minutes from downtown Seattle
- 240, 2-room suites with refrigerator, microwave, coffee maker, 2 T.V.'s with free HBO and 2 phones
- Free, full cooked-to-order breakfast each morning and 2-hour guest reception each evening with light snacks and beverages of your choice
- Indoor pool, sauna, jacuzzi & rec center
- Free parking and kids under 18 stay free

EMBASSY SUITES®

20% OFF LISTED RATES 7 DAYS A WEEK

3225 158th Avenue,SE Bellevue, WA
Call (206) 644-2500 or 1-800-EMBASSY

(See SEATTLE & VICINITY ACCOMMODATIONS spotting map pages A136 & A137)

HYATT REGENCY BELLEVUE — Guaranteed Rates — **Phone:** 206/462-1234 — 153
◆◆◆◆ Hotel
Mon-Thurs 1P: $89- 145 2P/1B: $89- 170 2P/2B: $89- 170 XP: $25 F18
Fri-Sun 1P: $115 2P/1B: $115 2P/2B: $115 XP: $25 F18
Location: At jct I-405 & exit 13, 3 blks w on NE 8th St. 900 Bellevue Way NE 98004. Fax: 206/646-7567. **Terms:** Reserv deposit, 14 day notice; package plans; no pets. **Facility:** 382 rooms. 24 stories; interior corridors; business center, conference facilities. Fee: health club & indoor pool privileges. **Dining:** Also, Eques, see separate listing. **Services:** valet laundry. Fee: airport transportation; valet parking. **All Rooms:** free movies, cable TV. **Some Rooms:** coffeemakers, refrigerators, whirlpools. **Cards:** AE, DI, DS, JCB, MC, VI.

RED LION HOTEL — Rates Subject to Change — **Phone:** 206/455-1300 — 146
◆◆◆ Hotel
All Year 1P: $120- 140 2P/1B: $135- 155 2P/2B: $135- 155 XP: $15
Location: Off I-405 exit 12. 300 112th Ave SE 98004. Fax: 206/455-0466. **Terms:** Credit card guarantee; pets, in limited rooms, $25 dep req. **Facility:** 353 rooms. Very large units. Balconies. 10 stories; interior corridors; business center, conference facilities; heated pool, whirlpool; exercise room. **Dining & Entertainment:** Restaurant, coffee shop; 6 am-midnight; $5-$13; cocktail lounge; also, Velato's Ristorante, see separate listing; entertainment. **Services:** secretarial services; valet parking. Fee: airport transportation. **All Rooms:** cable TV. Fee: movies. **Some Rooms:** refrigerators, whirlpools. **Cards:** AE, CB, DI, DS, JCB, MC, VI.

RED LION INN/BELLEVUE CENTER — Rates Subject to Change — **Phone:** 206/455-1515 — 144
◆◆◆ Motor Inn
All Year 1P: $91- 120 2P/1B: $101- 131 2P/2B: $101- 131 XP: $10 F10
Location: 1/4 mi nw of I-405, exit 13B. 818 112th Ave NE 98004. Fax: 206/454-3964. **Terms:** Sr. discount; reserv deposit, 21 day notice; small pets only, $15, $30 dep req. **Facility:** 208 rooms. Most units with balcony. 3 two-bedroom units. 3 kitchens, $148; 2-3 stories, no elevator; interior/exterior corridors; meeting rooms; heated pool, whirlpool; exercise room. **Dining:** Dining room, coffee shop; 6 am-11 pm; $5-$14; cocktails. **Services:** data ports; valet laundry. Fee: airport transportation. **All Rooms:** cable TV. Fee: movies. **Some Rooms:** Fee: refrigerators. **Cards:** AE, CB, DI, DS, JCB, MC, VI. *(See color ad below)*

THE RESIDENCE INN BY MARRIOTT SEATTLE EAST — Rates Subject to Change — **Phone:** 206/882-1222 — 142
◆◆◆ Suite Hotel
7/1-10/31 [CP] 1P: $135- 195 2P/1B: $135- 195 2P/2B: $179- 195
3/1-6/30 & 11/1-2/29 [CP] 1P: $80- 129 2P/1B: $80- 129 2P/2B: $80- 129
Location: From I-405 at SR 520 exit, n at 148th N exit to 29th Pl. 14455 NE 29th Pl 98007. Fax: 206/885-9260. **Terms:** Sr. discount; reserv deposit, 3 day notice; weekly/monthly rates; pets, $10. **Facility:** 120 rooms. 1- & 2-bedroom suites with kitchen, fireplace, balcony or patio. Village setting of 8-plex units on terraced grounds. 2 stories; exterior corridors; meeting rooms; heated pool, whirlpools; sports court. **Dining:** Restaurant nearby. **Services:** area transportation. Fee: coin laundry, airport transportation. **All Rooms:** free movies, cable TV. **Some Rooms:** coffeemakers. Fee: VCP's. **Cards:** AE, DI, DS, JCB, MC, VI.

SILVER CLOUD — Rates Subject to Change — **Phone:** 206/637-7000 — 152
◆◆◆ Motel
6/15-9/30 [CP] 1P: $69 2P/1B: $75 2P/2B: $75 XP: $6 F12
3/1-6/14 & 10/1-2/29 [CP] 1P: $64 2P/1B: $70 2P/2B: $70 XP: $6 F12
Location: 1/2 mi nw of I-405, exit 13 via ne 8th & 106th sts. 10621 NE 12th St 98004. Fax: 206/455-0531. **Terms:** Sr. discount; reserv deposit, 3 day notice; no pets. **Facility:** 97 rooms. 4 stories; interior corridors; business center, meeting rooms; heated pool, whirlpool. **Dining:** Restaurant nearby. **Services:** Fee: airport transportation. **All Rooms:** free movies, combo & shower baths, cable TV. **Some Rooms:** honor bars, coffeemakers, 11 efficiencies, kitchen, microwaves, refrigerators, whirlpools. **Cards:** AE, DI, DS, MC, VI.

WEST COAST BELLEVUE HOTEL — Rates Subject to Change — **Phone:** 206/455-9444 — 149
AAA ◆◆◆ **Motor Inn**
All Year 1P: $58- 77 2P/1B: $68- 87 2P/2B: $68- 87 XP: $10 F18
Location: 1/4 mi se of I-405 exit 13. 625 116th Ave NE 98004. Fax: 206/455-2154. **Terms:** Sr. discount; small pets only. **Facility:** 176 rooms. All townhouse units with fireplace. 3-6 stories; interior/exterior corridors; conference facilities; heated pool; exercise room. **Dining:** Restaurant; 6 am-10 pm, Sat & Sun 7 am-10 pm; $5-$17; cocktails. **Services:** secretarial services; valet laundry. Fee: airport transportation. **All Rooms:** free & pay movies, cable TV. **Some Rooms:** coffeemakers, refrigerators. **Cards:** AE, CB, DI, DS, MC, VI.

RESTAURANTS

BILLY MCHALE'S — **Dinner:** $11-$20 — **Phone:** 206/746-1138 — 105
◆◆ American
Location: Off I-405 at Coalcreek exit, e to Newport, n to Factoria Square Mall. 4065 128th SE 98006. **Hours:** 11 am-10 pm, Fri-11 pm, Sat noon-11 pm, Sun noon-10 pm. Closed: 11/23 & 12/25. **Features:** children's menu; senior's menu; carryout; cocktails & lounge; a la carte. Famous for barbecue ribs, chicken, steaks, prime rib & fresh seafood. Family dining. **Cards:** AE, MC, VI.

THE BUTCHER IN BELLEVUE — **Dinner:** $11-$20 — **Phone:** 206/455-3930 — 111
◆◆ American
Location: 1 mi se of I-405 exit 13, via NE 8th St & 120th Ave NE. 300 120th Ave NE 98005. **Hours:** 11:30 am-2:30 & 4:30-9 pm, Fri & Sat-10 pm, Sun 4:30 pm-9 pm. Closed: 7/4, 11/23 & 12/25. **Features:** children's menu; early bird specials; carryout; salad bar; cocktails & lounge; a la carte. Full service steakhouse serving barbecue ribs, prime rib, seafood & fresh sourdough bread. **Cards:** AE, DI, DS, JCB, MC, VI.

SPECIAL AAA RATES
FALL—SPRING SUMMER SEASON*
$55 WEEKENDS $65 WEEKDAYS $69 WEEKENDS $79 WEEKDAYS
RED LION INN
BELLEVUE CENTER
818-112th Ave. N.E. • Bellevue, WA • Call 206-455-1515 or 800-RED LION
Single/Double Occupancy • Kids Free • Limited Availability • *Summer Season is 6/5-8/31/95
SEE OUR INSERT IN THIS ISSUE.

(See SEATTLE & VICINITY ACCOMMODATIONS spotting map pages A136 & A137)

CUCINA CUCINA **Dinner:** $11-$20 **Phone:** 206/637-1177 (100)
◆◆
Italian
Location: From I-405 exit 13, 3 blks w on NE 8th St. 800 Bellevue Way NE 98004. **Hours:** 11:30 am-10:30 pm. **Features:** children's menu; carryout; cocktails & lounge. Fun, lively, casual Italian cafe serving cutting edge as well as traditional Italian food. **Cards:** AE, DI, DS, MC, VI.

DANIEL'S BROILER, BELLEVUE PLACE **Dinner:** $21-$30 **Phone:** 206/462-4662 (103)
◆◆◆
Steakhouse
Location: At jct I-405 & exit 13; 3 blks w on NE 8th St. 10500 NE 8th St, Suite 2100 98004. **Hours:** 11:30 am-2 & 5:30-10 pm, Fri-11 pm, Sat 5:30 pm-11 pm, Sun 5 pm-10 pm. Closed: 12/25. **Reservations:** suggested. **Features:** children's menu; health conscious menu; carryout; cocktails & lounge; entertainment; valet parking; a la carte. Casually elegant dining with views of Seattle & the Olympic Range. Piano & oyster bar. **Cards:** AE, DI, DS, JCB, MC, VI.

EQUES **Dinner:** $11-$20 **Phone:** 206/451-3012 (104)
◆◆◆
American
Location: In Hyatt Regency Bellevue. 900 Bellevue Way 98004. **Hours:** 6:30 am-3 & 5-10 pm. **Features:** children's menu; health conscious menu; carryout; cocktails & lounge; fee for valet parking; a la carte. Fine cuisines in an airy garden cafe & an elegantly appointed dining room. **Cards:** AE, DI, DS, JCB, MC, VI.

SAMS RESTAURANT & LOUNGE **Dinner:** $11-$20 **Phone:** 206/455-1717 (110)
◆◆
American
Location: In Bellevue Hilton. 100 112th Ave NE 98004. **Hours:** 5:15 am-10:30 pm, Fri & Sat-11 pm. **Reservations:** suggested. **Features:** Sunday brunch; children's menu; early bird specials; senior's menu; health conscious menu; salad bar; cocktails & lounge; a la carte. Fresh seafood in season, steaks & salads. **Cards:** AE, CB, DI, DS, JCB, MC, VI.

SPAZZO MEDITERRANEAN GRILL **Dinner:** $11-$20 **Phone:** 206/454-8255 (107)
◆◆
Regional Ethnic
Location: 3/4 mi sw of I-405 exit 12; 2 blks e of Bellevue Square Shopping Center. 10655 NE 4th St, 9 flights up 98004. **Hours:** 11 am-10 pm, Fri-11 pm, Sat 4 pm-11 pm, Sun 4 pm-10 pm. Closed: 12/25. **Reservations:** suggested. **Features:** children's menu; cocktails & lounge; a la carte. Mediterranean cooking, casual dining that encourages passing, tasting, sharing & sampling of the large assortment of tapas. **Cards:** AE, DS, JCB, MC, VI.

VELATO'S RISTORANTE **Dinner:** $21-$30 **Phone:** 206/455-1300 (109)
◆◆◆
Italian
Location: In Red Lion Hotel. 300 112th Ave SE 98004. **Hours:** 11:30 am-2 & 5-10 pm, Fri & Sat-11 pm, Sun 10 am-2 & 5-10 pm. **Reservations:** suggested. **Features:** Sunday brunch; carryout; cocktails; valet parking; a la carte. Casual, lively dining with anti-pasta & wine tasting. **Cards:** AE, DI, DS, JCB, MC, VI.

THE YANKEE DINER **Dinner:** $11-$20 **Phone:** 206/643-1558 (101)
◆◆
American
Location: E of downtown, crossroads 140th & Bell Red Rd. 1645 140th Ave NE 98005. **Hours:** 7 am-10 pm, Sat 8 am-10 pm, Sun 8 am-9 pm. Closed: 12/25. **Features:** children's menu; carryout; cocktails. Old fashion cooking. Family dining. **Cards:** AE, DS, MC, VI.

BELLINGHAM—52,200

LODGINGS

ANDERSON CREEK LODGE Rates Subject to Change **Phone:** 360/966-2126
AAA ◆◆◆ Bed & Breakfast
All Year [BP] 1P: $70- 125 2P/1B: $70- 125 XP: $20 F10
Location: At exit 256 off I-5, 4 mi n to E Smith Rd; 6 mi e to Mission Rd N, 3/4 mi on Mission Rd. 5602 Mission Rd 98226. Fax: 360/734-9284. **Terms:** Sr. discount; reserv deposit, 7 day notice; weekly/monthly rates; no pets. **Facility:** 5 rooms. Adult romantic & rejuvenation in country setting. Elegance in theme rooms. 2 stories; interior corridors; smoke free premises. **Services:** airport transportation. **Recreation:** nature program. **All Rooms:** no A/C, no phones, no TVs. **Cards:** AE, MC, VI.

BAY CITY MOTOR INN AAA Special Value Rates **Phone:** 360/676-0332
AAA ◆◆◆ Motel

6/1-9/30 [CP]	1P: $45	2P/1B: $50	2P/2B: $55	XP: $5 F12
3/1-5/31 & 10/1-10/31 [CP]	1P: $43	2P/1B: $45	2P/2B: $47	XP: $5 F12
11/1-2/29 [CP]	1P: $39	2P/1B: $42	2P/2B: $45	XP: $5 F12

Location: 1/2 mi n of I-5, exit 252. 116 N Samish Way 98225. Fax: 360/676-0899. **Terms:** Reserv deposit; weekly/monthly rates; no pets. **Facility:** 51 rooms. Close to university. 4 stories; interior corridors; meeting rooms; exercise room. **All Rooms:** free movies, cable TV. **Some Rooms:** kitchen, refrigerators, whirlpools. **Cards:** AE, DI, DS, MC, VI.

BELLINGHAM TRAVELODGE Rates Subject to Change **Phone:** 360/734-1900
◆◆ Motel

5/1-10/15	1P: $45	2P/1B: $50	2P/2B: $55	XP: $4-5 F17
3/1-4/30 & 10/16-2/29	1P: $43	2P/1B: $47	2P/2B: $49- 52	XP: $4 F17

Location: 1/2 mi nw of I-5, exit 253; 1 mi sw of I-5, exit 254. 202 E Holly St 98225. Fax: 360/647-0709. **Terms:** Sr. discount; reserv deposit, 3 day notice; no pets. **Facility:** 49 rooms. 3 stories; exterior corridors. **Dining:** Restaurant nearby. **All Rooms:** coffeemakers, free movies, combo & shower baths, cable TV. **Some Rooms:** refrigerators. **Cards:** AE, CB, DI, DS, MC, VI.

BEST WESTERN HERITAGE INN Rates Subject to Change **Phone:** 360/647-1912
AAA ◆◆◆ Motel
All Year [CP] 1P: $64- 77 2P/1B: $69- 82 2P/2B: $74- 79 XP: $5
Location: At I-5 exit 256. 151 E McLeod Rd 98226. Fax: 360/671-3878. **Terms:** Credit card guarantee, 5/1-8/31; no pets. **Facility:** 91 rooms. Colonial design & furnishings. 3-4 stories, no elevator; interior corridors; meeting rooms; heated pool, whirlpool. **Dining:** Restaurant nearby. **Services:** airport transportation. Fee: coin laundry. **All Rooms:** free movies, combo & shower baths, cable TV. **Some Rooms:** 24 efficiencies, 2 kitchens. **Cards:** AE, CB, DI, DS, MC, VI.

Best Western
Lakeway Inn - Bellingham
FREE - HOT BREAKFAST BUFFET
Bellingham's Only Full Service Hotel
1-800-528-1234
714 Lakeway Dr.
206-671-1011

BEST WESTERN LAKEWAY INN — AAA Special Value Rates — **Phone:** 360/671-1011
AAA ◆◆◆ Hotel
All Year [BP] 1P: $61- 70 2P/1B: $72- 78 2P/2B: $69 XP: $10 F16
Location: 1/2 mi e off I-5 exit 253. 714 Lakeway Dr 98226. Fax: 360/676-8519. **Terms:** Reserv deposit, 3 day notice; no pets. **Facility:** 132 rooms. 4 stories; interior corridors; meeting rooms; sauna, whirlpool, small heated indoor pool; exercise room, domed recreation area. **Dining & Entertainment:** Dining room, coffee shop; 6 am-10 pm, Fri 6 am-11 pm, Sat 7 am-11 pm, Sun 7 am-10 pm; $8-$19; cocktails; 24-hour room service; entertainment. **Services:** airport transportation. Fee: coin laundry. **All Rooms:** free movies, cable TV. **Some Rooms:** Fee: VCP's. **Cards:** AE, CB, DI, DS, JCB, MC, VI. *(See color ad p A71)*

BIG TREES BED & BREAKFAST — Rates Subject to Change — **Phone:** 360/647-2850
◆◆◆ Historic Bed & Breakfast
All Year [BP] 2P/1B: $90- 110
Location: From I-5 at exit 253, 3 mi e via Lakeway Dr & Cable St, s on Geneva to Fremont. 4840 Fremont St 98226. Fax: 360/647-2850. **Terms:** Age restrictions may apply; check-in 4 pm; reserv deposit, 10 day notice; no pets. **Facility:** 3 rooms. Owner has pets on property. 1907 post Victorian home. 2 stories; interior corridors; smoke free premises. **All Rooms:** cable TV, no A/C. **Cards:** MC, VI.

COACHMAN INN — AAA Special Value Rates — **Phone:** 360/671-9000
AAA ◆◆ Motel
6/1-9/30 [CP] 1P: $45 2P/1B: $50 2P/2B: $55 XP: $3 F12
3/1-5/31 & 10/1-10/31 [CP] 1P: $42 2P/1B: $45 2P/2B: $48 XP: $3 F12
11/1-2/29 [CP] 1P: $39 2P/1B: $42 2P/2B: $45 XP: $3 F12
Location: 1/2 mi n of I-5 exit 252. 120 N Samish Way 98225. Fax: 360/738-1984. **Terms:** Reserv deposit; weekly/monthly rates; no pets. **Facility:** 60 rooms. 2 stories; interior corridors; heated pool, sauna, whirlpool. **Dining:** Restaurant nearby. **All Rooms:** free movies, cable TV. **Some Rooms:** refrigerators. **Cards:** AE, DI, DS, MC, VI.

COMFORT INN — Rates Subject to Change — **Phone:** 360/738-1100
AAA ◆◆◆ Motel
6/1-9/30 [CP] 1P: $55- 70 2P/1B: $60- 75 2P/2B: $65- 75 XP: $5 F18
3/1-5/31 & 10/1-2/29 [CP] 1P: $50- 65 2P/1B: $55- 70 2P/2B: $60- 70 XP: $5 F18
Location: From I-5 exit 256, 1 mi n. 4282 Meridian St 98226. Fax: 360/738-8123. **Terms:** Sr. discount; reserv deposit; weekly rates; no pets. **Facility:** 86 rooms. 3 stories; interior corridors; meeting rooms; heated indoor pool, sauna, whirlpool; exercise room. **Services:** area transportation, to ferry dock, airport transportation. Fee: coin laundry. **All Rooms:** free movies, cable TV. **Some Rooms:** 3 efficiencies, refrigerators, whirlpools. **Cards:** AE, CB, DI, DS, JCB, MC, VI.

DAYS INN — Rates Subject to Change — **Phone:** 360/671-6200
AAA ◆◆◆ Motel
5/15-9/2 [CP] 1P: $50- 55 2P/1B: $55- 60 2P/2B: $55- 60 XP: $5 F
3/1-5/14 & 9/3-2/29 [CP] 1P: $45- 50 2P/1B: $50- 55 2P/2B: $55- 60 XP: $5 F
Location: From I-5 exit 256, 4 blks n. 125 E Kellogg Rd 98226. Fax: 360/671-9491. **Terms:** Sr. discount; credit card guarantee; weekly/monthly rates; no pets. **Facility:** 70 rooms. Commercial location. Free 9 hole golf with room rate. 3 stories; interior corridors; meeting rooms; heated pool, whirlpool. **Services:** Fee: coin laundry. **All Rooms:** free movies, cable TV. **Some Rooms:** 10 efficiencies, utensils extra charge, whirlpools. **Cards:** AE, CB, DI, DS, MC, VI.

HAMPTON INN — Rates Subject to Change — **Phone:** 360/676-7700
AAA ◆◆◆ Motel
All Year [CP] 1P: $59- 64 2P/1B: $64- 74 2P/2B: $64- 74
Location: I-5 at exit 258. 3985 Bennett Dr 98225. Fax: 360/671-7557. **Terms:** Sr. discount; package plans; 2 night min stay; no pets. **Facility:** 133 rooms. Close to airport. 4 stories; interior corridors; business center, meeting rooms; heated pool; exercise room. **Services:** area transportation, airport transportation. **All Rooms:** coffeemakers, free movies, combo & shower baths, cable TV. **Some Rooms:** whirlpools. Fee: refrigerators. **Cards:** AE, CB, DI, DS, JCB, MC, VI. *(See ad below & color ad inside front cover)*

HOLIDAY INN EXPRESS-BELLINGHAM — AAA Special Value Rates — **Phone:** 360/671-4800
AAA ◆◆◆ Motel
All Year [CP] 1P: $61- 85 2P/1B: $67- 85 2P/2B: $67- 85 XP: $6 F19
Location: From I-5 exit 256, 3 blks n. 4160 Guide Meridian 98226. Fax: 360/671-9920. **Terms:** Reserv deposit, 14 day notice; monthly rates; package plans; no pets. **Facility:** 101 rooms. 3 stories; interior corridors; meeting rooms; heated indoor pool, whirlpool. **Dining:** Restaurant nearby. **Services:** data ports; area transportation, airport transportation. **All Rooms:** free movies, combo & shower baths, cable TV. **Some Rooms:** coffeemakers, 6 efficiencies, microwaves, refrigerators. Fee: VCP's. **Cards:** AE, CB, DI, DS, JCB, MC, VI. *(See color ad below)* Roll in showers.

LIONS INN MOTEL — Rates Subject to Change — **Phone:** 360/733-2330
AAA ◆◆ Motel
All Year 2P/1B: $38- 45 2P/2B: $40- 45 XP: $4 F16
Location: I-5 exit 257; 1 1/2 mi sw to Elm Ave via Northwest Ave. 2419 Elm St 98225. **Terms:** Sr. discount; reserv deposit; monthly rates, 10/1-3/31; pets, $10, in designated rooms. **Facility:** 15 rooms. Semi-residential location. Close to airport. Modest furnishings. 1 two-bedroom unit. 4 kitchens, $46-$50; 1 story; exterior corridors. **All Rooms:** cable TV, no A/C. **Some Rooms:** refrigerators. **Cards:** MC, VI.

Bellingham
10% off rack rates (not valid with any other offer)
• Easy I-5 access
• FREE 21 item breakfast buffet
• FREE local calls & in-room coffee
• Fitness room & heated pool
• 100% Satisfaction Guarantee
Hampton Inn
206-676-7700 or 1-800-HAMPTON
I-5 Exit 258 / 3985 Bennett Dr. Bellingham, WA 98225

SAAAVINGS IN BELLINGHAM
• Free Breakfast Buffet
• Indoor Pool & Spa
Holiday Inn EXPRESS®
4160 Guide Meridian
1-800-HOLIDAY
206-671-4800

NORTH GARDEN INN — AAA Special Value Rates — **Phone:** 360/671-7828
◆◆◆ Historic Bed & Breakfast
All Year [BP] 2P/1B: $59- 74 XP: $15 F10
Location: From I-5 at exit 253, sw via Lakeway & Holly to N Garden. 1014 N Garden 98225. **Terms:** Age restrictions may apply; reserv deposit; no pets. **Facility:** 8 rooms. Queen Anne Victorian home on National Register of Historic Places. Overlooking Bellingham Bay. 2 stories; interior corridors; smoke free premises. **All Rooms:** shower baths, no A/C, no phones, no TVs. **Cards:** DS, MC, VI. (D) ⊗

PARK MOTEL — Rates Subject to Change — **Phone:** 360/733-8280
◆◆◆ Motel

6/1-9/30 [CP]	1P: $54	2P/1B: $59	2P/2B: $64	XP: $5 F16
4/1-5/31 [CP]	1P: $50	2P/1B: $55	2P/2B: $60	XP: $5 F16
3/1-3/31 & 2/1-2/29 [CP]	1P: $45	2P/1B: $50	2P/2B: $55	XP: $5 F16
10/1-1/31 [CP]	1P: $40	2P/1B: $45	2P/2B: $50	XP: $5 F16

Location: 1 mi s on I-5 Business Rt; 1/2 mi n of I-5 exit 252. 101 N Samish Way 98225. Fax: 360/738-9186. **Terms:** Sr. discount; no pets. **Facility:** 56 rooms. Townhouse $85-$100; 2 stories; interior corridors; meeting rooms; sauna, whirlpool. **Dining:** Restaurant nearby. **Services:** airport transportation. **All Rooms:** free movies, cable TV. **Some Rooms:** refrigerators, whirlpools. **Cards:** AE, CB, DI, DS, MC, VI. (D) ⊗

QUALITY INN BARON SUITES — AAA Special Value Rates — **Phone:** 360/647-8000
◆◆◆ Motel

6/16-9/8 [CP]	1P: $66- 90	2P/1B: $72- 96	2P/2B: $72- 96	XP: $8 F18
3/1-6/15 & 9/9-2/29 [CP]	1P: $63- 85	2P/1B: $69- 91	2P/2B: $69- 91	XP: $8 F18

Location: From I-5, exit 256, 1 mi ne via Guide Meridian St. 100 E Kellogg Rd 98226. Fax: 360/647-8094. **Terms:** Small pets only, $25 dep req. **Facility:** 86 rooms. 3 stories; interior/exterior corridors; meeting rooms; heated pool, whirlpool; exercise room. **Services:** area transportation, airport transportation. Fee: coin laundry. **All Rooms:** free movies, cable TV. **Some Rooms:** coffeemakers, microwaves, refrigerators, whirlpools. Fee: VCP's. **Cards:** AE, CB, DI, DS, JCB, MC, VI. (D) (S) ⊗

RAMADA INN-BELLINGHAM — Rates Subject to Change — **Phone:** 360/734-8830
◆◆◆ Motel
All Year [CP] 1P: $90 2P/1B: $90 2P/2B: $96 XP: $6 F17
Location: 3/4 mi n of I-5, exit 252. 215 Samish Way 98225. Fax: 360/647-8956. **Terms:** Sr. discount; credit card guarantee; weekly rates; no pets. **Facility:** 66 rooms. Some rooms with balcony. Close to university. 3 stories, no elevator; interior corridors; meeting rooms; heated pool. **Dining:** Restaurant nearby. **All Rooms:** coffeemakers, free movies, refrigerators, cable TV. **Cards:** AE, DI, DS, JCB, MC, VI. (D) ⊗

RODEWAY INN — AAA Special Value Rates — **Phone:** 360/738-6000
◆◆◆ Motel
All Year [CP] 1P: $45 2P/1B: $45 2P/2B: $48 XP: $7 F18
Location: From I-5 at exit 256, 2 blks s. 3710 Meridian St 98225. Fax: 360/671-7005. **Terms:** Pets, $10. **Facility:** 75 rooms. 3 stories; interior corridors; whirlpool. **Dining:** Restaurant nearby. **All Rooms:** free movies, cable TV. **Some Rooms:** coffeemakers, radios, whirlpools. **Cards:** AE, DI, DS, MC, VI. (D) (S) ⊗

SUNRISE BAY BED & BREAKFAST — Rates Subject to Change — **Phone:** 360/647-0376
◆◆ Bed & Breakfast
All Year [BP] 1P: $80 2P/1B: $90 XP: $13
Location: From I-5 at exit 255, 2 1/2 mi to Briton Rd, 1 3/4 mi to N Shore Rd, 2 1/2 mi se on N Shore Rd. 2141 N Shore Rd 98226. **Terms:** Credit card guarantee, 3 day notice; no pets. **Facility:** 2 rooms. Contemporary lodging located on the north shore of Lake Whatcom. 1 story; exterior corridors; smoke free premises; beach, heated pool, whirlpool. **Recreation:** swimming, canoeing, fishing. **All Rooms:** cable TV, VCP's, no A/C. **Cards:** MC, VI. (D) ⊗

TRAVELERS INN — Rates Subject to Change — **Phone:** 360/671-4600
◆◆ Motel

3/1-4/30	1P: $45	2P/1B: $51	2P/2B: $51	XP: $4 F11
5/1-2/29	1P: $45	2P/1B: $51	2P/2B: $51	XP: $4 F11

Location: At I-5, exit 256; s on Meridian St. 3750 Meridian St 98225. Fax: 360/671-6487. **Terms:** Sr. discount; reserv deposit, 10 day notice; no pets. **Facility:** 124 rooms. 3 stories; exterior corridors; meeting rooms; heated pool, whirlpool. **Dining:** Restaurant nearby. **Services:** Fee: coin laundry. **All Rooms:** free movies, cable TV. **Some Rooms:** refrigerators. **Cards:** AE, CB, DI, DS, MC, VI. (D) (S) ⊗

VAL-U INN — Guaranteed Rates — **Phone:** 360/671-9600
◆◆◆ Motel

6/1-9/15 [CP]	1P: $50- 55	2P/1B: $55- 60	2P/2B: $60	XP: $5 F12
3/1-5/31 & 9/16-2/29 [CP]	1P: $45- 50	2P/1B: $50- 55	2P/2B: $55	XP: $5 F12

Location: Northbound 1 blk s off I-5; southbound 1 blk e off I-5, exit 253. 805 Lakeway Dr 98226. Fax: 206/671-8323. **Terms:** Sr. discount; weekly/monthly rates; pets, $5, small dogs only. **Facility:** 81 rooms. 3 stories; interior corridors; whirlpool. **Dining:** Restaurant nearby. **Services:** Fee: coin laundry. **All Rooms:** free movies, cable TV. **Some Rooms:** refrigerators. Fee: VCP's. **Cards:** AE, CB, DI, DS, MC, VI.
(See ad below) (D) ⊗

RESTAURANTS

BILLY MCHALE'S — **Dinner:** $11-$20 — **Phone:** 360/647-7763
◆◆ American
Location: From I-5 at exit 256, 1 mi n. 4301 Guide Meridian Rd 98226. **Hours:** 11 am-9 pm, Fri & Sat-11 pm, Sun 11 am-9 pm. Closed: 11/23 & 12/25. **Features:** children's menu; senior's menu; carryout; cocktails & lounge; a la carte. Famous for barbecue ribs, chicken, steaks, prime rib & fresh seafood. Family dining. **Cards:** AE, MC, VI. ⊗

THE CLIFF HOUSE — **Dinner:** $11-$20 — **Phone:** 360/734-8660
◆◆◆ American
Location: 2 mi w of I-5, exit 253. 331 N State 98225. **Hours:** 5 pm-10 pm. Closed: 11/23 & 12/25. **Reservations:** suggested. **Features:** No A/C; salad bar; cocktails & lounge; a la carte. Fresh seafood & steaks in attractive rooftop dining room overlooking Bellingham Bay. Smoke free premises. **Cards:** AE, DS, MC, VI. ⊗

DIRTY DAN HARRIS — **Dinner:** $11-$20 — **Phone:** 360/676-1011
◆◆◆ American
Location: In historic Fairhaven District; 1 1/2 mi w of I-5, exit 250. 1211 11th 98225. **Hours:** 5 pm-9:30 pm, Fri & Sat-10 pm. Closed: 11/23 & 12/25. **Reservations:** suggested. **Features:** salad bar; cocktails & lounge. Interesting 1890's saloon atmosphere. Specializing in prime rib & fresh local seafood. **Cards:** AE, DI, DS, MC, VI. ⊗

VAL-U INN MOTEL
BELLINGHAM
• Complimentary Continental Breakfast • Whirlpool
• Guest Laundry • Non-Smoking Rooms
• Listed AAA Rates Guaranteed • King & Queen Beds
• Airport & Ferry Terminal Free Transportation
For Reservations, call: 1-800-443-7777
805 Lakeway Drive. Bellingham, WA 98226 (206) 671-9600

PACIFIC CAFE **Dinner:** $11-$20 **Phone:** 360/647-0800
◆◆ Ethnic
Location: In Mt. Baker Theatre Bldg. 100 N Commercial St 98225. **Hours:** 11:30 am-2 & 5:30-9 pm, Sat from 5:30 pm. Closed major holidays & Sun. **Reservations:** suggested. **Features:** health conscious menu items; carryout; beer & wine only; a la carte. Eastwest/Northwest cuisine. Smoke free premises. **Cards:** MC, VI. ⊗

SADIGHI'S RESTAURANT **Dinner:** $11-$20 **Phone:** 360/647-1109
◆◆ Continental
Location: 2 blk e of I-5 at exit 253. 921 Lakeway Dr 98226. **Hours:** 11 am-2 & 5-9:30 pm, Fri & Sat-10:30 pm, Sat & Sun 4:30 pm-10:30 pm. Closed major holidays, Tue & 12/24-12/26. **Features:** carryout; cocktails. Open, airy dining area. Casual, relaxed. **Cards:** AE, DI, MC, VI. ⊗

TOP OF THE TOWERS **Dinner:** $11-$20 **Phone:** 360/733-3443
◆◆◆ Continental
Location: 1 mi sw of I-5, exit 254. 119 N Commercial 98225. **Hours:** 11:30 am-2 & 5-9:30 pm, Sat 5 pm-9:30 pm, Sun 5:30 pm-8:30 pm. Closed: 12/25. **Reservations:** suggested. **Features:** No A/C; children's menu; health conscious menu items; carryout; cocktails & lounge; a la carte. Elegant dining rooms offering panoramic dining from 15th floor of Bellingham Towers. **Cards:** AE, DI, MC, VI. ⊗

BLAINE—2,500

LODGING

INN AT SEMIAHMOO/ A WYNDHAM RESORT AAA Special Value Rates **Phone:** 360/371-2000

4/1-10/31	1P: $135- 273	2P/1B: $135- 273	2P/2B: $135- 273	XP: $20	F18
3/1-3/31 & 11/1-2/29	1P: $115- 215	2P/1B: $115- 215	2P/2B: $115- 215	XP: $20	F18

(AAA) ◆◆◆◆ Resort Motor Inn
Location: 10 mi w of I-5, exit 270 on Semiahmoo Spit. 9565 Semiahmoo Pkwy 98230. Fax: 360/371-5490. **Terms:** Check-in 4 pm; reserv deposit, 3 day notice; package plans; no pets. **Facility:** 198 rooms. Extensive resort of northwestern architecture in beautiful marine setting. Some balcony & patio views. 40 units with fireplace. 4 stories; interior corridors; conference facilities; beach, heated indoor/outdoor pool, saunas, whirlpool; marina; health club. Fee: 18 holes golf; racquetball courts, 1 indoor tennis court, squash 1-court. **Dining & Entertainment:** Dining room, restaurant; 11 am-10 pm; $5-$12; cocktails/lounge; also, Stars, see separate listing; entertainment. **Recreation:** children's program, nature trails, recreation program; charter fishing, fishing; jogging. Rental: bicycles. **All Rooms:** cable TV. **Some Rooms:** coffeemakers. Fee: VCP's. **Cards:** AE, CB, DI, DS, MC, VI.
(See ad below) Ⓓ Ⓢ ⊗

RESTAURANT

STARS **Dinner:** $11-$20 **Phone:** 360/371-2000
◆◆◆ Continental
Location: In the Inn at Semiahmoo. 9565 Semiahmoo Pkwy 98230. **Hours:** 6:30 am-2:30 & 5-10 pm. **Reservations:** suggested. **Features:** children's menu; early bird specials; health conscious menu items; cocktails & lounge; a la carte. Formal dining; specializing in Northwest cuisine. **Cards:** AE, DI, DS, MC, VI. ⊗

THE LATEST AAA BENEFIT:
WYNDHAM'S 50/50 OFFER.

1/1/95 - 3/1/95
$132
4/1/95 - 10/31/95
$155
11/1/95 - 2/29/96
$132
•
Rates are per room, per night, and based on single or double occupancy. Not applicable to conventions or groups. Limited availability.

50% Off Your Second Room
Or 50% Off Your Second Night.

With these savings off our regular rates, you can escape to the northwest region's premier waterfront resort. Enjoy a spacious cottage-style guest room. Go swimming and fishing, play tennis. Or golf on our Arnold Palmer-designed golf course. Dine at three fine restaurants and watch the area's best sunset. For reservations, call 206-371-0000 or 800-WYNDHAM. Or call your travel planner.

THE INN AT SEMI-AH-MOO
A WYNDHAM RESORT
THE RIGHT WAY. THE WYNDHAM WAY.
9565 Semiahmoo Parkway, Blaine, WA 98230 206-371-2000

BOTHELL—12,300 (See SEATTLE & VICINITY ACCOMMODATIONS spotting map pages A136 & A137; see index starting on page A134)

LODGINGS

RESIDENCE INN BY MARRIOTT SEATTLE NE Rates Subject to Change **Phone:** 206/485-3030 **170**

◆◆◆ Suite Motel

All Year [CP]	1P: $108	2P/1B: $108	2P/2B: $140

Location: At Hwy 405 exit 24. 11920 NE 195th St 98011. Fax: 206/485-2247. **Terms:** Check-in 4 pm; weekly/monthly rates; small pets only, $10, $100 dep req. **Facility:** 120 rooms. 24 two-bedroom units. 2 stories; exterior corridors; meeting rooms; heated pool, whirlpools. **Services:** secretarial services. Fee: coin laundry, airport transportation. **All Rooms:** kitchens, free movies, cable TV. **Some Rooms:** coffeemakers. Fee: VCP's. **Cards:** AE, CB, DI, DS, JCB, MC, VI.

WYNDHAM GARDEN Rates Subject to Change **Phone:** 206/485-5557 **171**

◆◆◆ Motor Inn

Fri & Sat 6/5-9/3 [EP]	1P: $79	2P/1B: $79	2P/2B: $89	XP: $10 F18
Sun-Thurs [BP]	1P: $74	2P/1B: $84	2P/2B: $84	XP: $10 F18
Fri & Sat 3/1-6/4 & 9/4-2/29 [EP]	1P: $54	2P/1B: $54	2P/2B: $64	XP: $10 F18

Location: On Northcreek Pkwy; at jct Hwy 405 & exit 24. 19333 Northcreek Pkwy 98011. Fax: 206/486-7314. **Terms:** No pets. **Facility:** 166 rooms. 2 stories; interior corridors; meeting rooms; heated pool, whirlpool; exercise room. **Dining:** Dining room; 6:30 am-2 & 5-10 pm; $7-$19; cocktails. **Services:** Fee: coin laundry, airport transportation. **All Rooms:** cable TV. Fee: movies. **Some Rooms:** coffeemakers, microwaves, refrigerators. **Cards:** AE, CB, DI, DS, JCB, MC, VI.
(See color ad p A138)

RESTAURANT

GERARD'S RELAIS DE LYON **Dinner:** over $31 **Phone:** 206/485-7600 **120**

◆◆◆ French

Location: Downtown on SR 522. 17121 Bothell Way NE 98041. **Hours:** 5 pm-9:30 pm. Closed: Mon, 1/1 & 12/25. **Reservations:** suggested. **Features:** No A/C; cocktails; a la carte. Bistro to 7-course menu. Relaxing dining. Patio avail. Smoke free premises. **Cards:** AE, DI, DS, MC, VI.

BOW

RESTAURANT

CHUCKANUT MANOR RESTAURANT Historical **Dinner:** $11-$20 **Phone:** 360/766-6191

◆◆ Seafood

Location: 9 1/2 mi nw of I-5 exit 231; 12 mi sw of I-5 exit 250. 302 Chuckanut Dr 98232. **Hours:** 4 pm-10 pm; 3/1-9/31 from 11:30 am, Fri-10:30 pm, Sat 11:30 am-10 pm, Sun 10:30 am-2:30 & 3-10 pm. Closed: Mon, 1/1, 7/4, 12/24 & 12/25. **Reservations:** suggested. **Features:** Sunday brunch; children's menu; carryout; cocktails & lounge; a la carte. Long-established dinner house overlooking Samish Bay. Also steak & prime rib. Seafood smorgasboard, Fri 5 pm-10:30 pm. Smoke free premises. **Cards:** AE, CB, DI, MC, VI.

BREMERTON—38,100

LODGINGS

BEST WESTERN BAYVIEW INN AAA Special Value Rates **Phone:** 360/373-9900

◆◆◆ Motor Inn

5/1-9/14 & 1/1-2/29	1P: $67	2P/1B: $73	2P/2B: $73	XP: $5 F18
3/1-4/30 & 9/15-12/31	1P: $62	2P/1B: $68	2P/2B: $68	XP: $5 F18

Location: 1/4 mi n of SR 3, Kitsap Way exit; 4 mi w of ferry terminal. 5640 Kitsap Way 98312. Fax: 360/377-8529. **Terms:** Credit card guarantee, 5 day notice; CP available; no pets. **Facility:** 143 rooms. Most rooms with balcony; views overlooking Oyster Bay. 5 stories; interior corridors; meeting rooms; heated indoor pool, whirlpool. **Dining:** Dining room, coffee shop; 7 am-2 & 5-9:30 pm, Fri & Sat-10 pm; $8-$15; cocktails. **All Rooms:** cable TV. **Some Rooms:** coffeemakers, microwaves, refrigerators, whirlpools. Fee: VCP's. **Cards:** AE, CB, DI, DS, JCB, MC, VI.

DUNES MOTEL AAA Special Value Rates **Phone:** 360/377-0093

◆◆ Motel

4/1-10/31 [CP]	1P: $38	2P/1B: $40	2P/2B: $44	XP: $3-4 F
3/1-3/31 & 11/1-2/29 [CP]	1P: $28- 36	2P/1B: $38	2P/2B: $42	XP: $4 F

Location: 2 mi w of ferry terminal; 1 mi e of SR 3, Kitsap Way exit. 3400 11th St 98312. Fax: 360/373-2864. **Terms:** Reserv deposit; weekly/monthly rates; small pets only, $20. **Facility:** 64 rooms. Convenient to ferry landing. 3 stories, no elevator; exterior corridors; whirlpool, swim spa. **Dining:** Restaurant nearby. **Services:** Fee: coin laundry. **All Rooms:** cable TV. Fee: movies. **Some Rooms:** 6 efficiencies, microwaves, refrigerators. Fee: VCP's. **Cards:** AE, CB, DI, DS, MC, VI.

CARS AREN'T OUR ONLY SPECIALTY

As the world's largest travel agency, with more than 800 full-service travel agency offices nationwide, we can help you plan your trip down to the smallest detail. Whether you're traveling overseas or close to home, we can arrange everything from airline tickets to tours to lodging. Don't just call us for car trouble, call us every time you want to travel.

AAA

FLAGSHIP INN Guaranteed Rates **Phone:** 360/479-6566
Motel ◆◆◆
All Year [CP] 1P: $50 2P/1B: $55 2P/2B: $60 XP: $6
Location: 3 1/2 mi w of ferry terminal; 1/2 mi e of SR 3, Kitsap Way exit. 4320 Kitsap Way 98312. Fax: 360/479-6745. **Terms:** Reserv deposit; small pets only, $6. **Facility:** 29 rooms. All rooms have view of Oyster Bay. 3 stories, no elevator; interior corridors; heated pool. **Dining:** Restaurant nearby. **All Rooms:** microwaves, free movies, refrigerators, cable TV. Fee: VCP's. **Cards:** AE, CB, DI, DS, JCB, MC, VI.

MIDWAY INN Rates Subject to Change **Phone:** 360/479-2909
Motel ◆◆◆
All Year [CP] 1P: $50 2P/1B: $50 2P/2B: $55 XP: $7 D8
Location: 2 mi n on SR 303, Wheaton Way in East Bremerton. 2909 Wheaton Way 98310. Fax: 360/479-1576. **Terms:** Sr. discount; reserv deposit; weekly rates; small pets only, $10. **Facility:** 60 rooms. 12 efficiencies, $10 extra; 3 stories; interior corridors; meeting rooms. **Dining:** Restaurant nearby. **Services:** Fee: coin laundry. **All Rooms:** cable TV. **Some Rooms:** microwaves, refrigerators. Fee: VCP's. **Cards:** AE, CB, DI, DS, MC, VI. *(See color ad below)*

QUALITY INN AT OYSTER BAY AAA Special Value Rates **Phone:** 360/405-1111
Apartment Motel ◆◆◆
All Year [CP] 1P: $55- 85 2P/1B: $60- 90 2P/2B: $65- 95 XP: $5 F18
Location: 3 1/2 mi w of ferry terminal; 1/2 mi e of SR 3, Kitsap Way exit. 4303 Kitsap Way 98312. Fax: 360/377-0597. **Terms:** Reserv deposit, 3 day notice; small pets only, $50 dep req. **Facility:** 102 rooms. Convenient access to ferry landing. 2 two-bedroom units. Suites with whirlpools avail; 2-3 stories; exterior corridors; conference facilities; heated pool, hot tub; playground. **Dining:** Restaurant nearby. **Services:** Fee: coin laundry. **All Rooms:** combo & shower baths, cable TV. **Some Rooms:** 10 efficiencies, 66 kitchens, refrigerators. Fee: microwaves. **Cards:** AE, CB, DI, DS, JCB, MC, VI. *(See color ad below)*

RESTAURANT

BOAT SHED **Dinner:** $11-$20 **Phone:** 360/377-2600
◆◆ American
Location: East side of Manette Bridge. 101 Shore Dr 98310. **Hours:** 11 am-midnight. Closed: 12/25. **Features:** No A/C; Sunday brunch; children's menu; carryout; cocktails & lounge. Casual, relaxed waterfront dining. **Cards:** MC, VI.

BUCKLEY

LODGING

MOUNTAIN VIEW INN AAA Special Value Rates **Phone:** 360/829-1100
Motel ◆◆◆
5/15-9/15 [CP] 1P: $55 2P/1B: $60 2P/2B: $65 XP: $5 F13
3/1-5/14 & 9/16-2/29 [CP] 2P/1B: $45 2P/2B: $50 XP: $5 F13
Location: 1/4 mi e on SR 410 at jct of SR 165. 100 410 Hwy 98321 (PO Box J). Fax: 360/829-9879. **Terms:** Credit card guarantee; package plans; pets, $10. **Facility:** 42 rooms. 2 stories; interior corridors; designated smoking area; meeting rooms; heated pool, whirlpool. **Dining:** Restaurant nearby. **Services:** Fee: coin laundry. **All Rooms:** free movies. **Some Rooms:** refrigerators, phones, cable TV, whirlpools. **Cards:** AE, DS, MC, VI.

Mid Way Inn

60 DELUXE ROOMS
ONE OF BREMERTON'S NEWEST MOTELS

"MIDWAY IN PRICE . . .
ALL THE WAY IN HOSPITALITY"

Fax: (206)479-1576
ON HWY. 303
2909 WHEATON WAY
EAST BREMERTON, WA 98310

- 24 HR. DESK/CR. CARDS
- KITCHENS W/MICROWAVES/AIR COND.
- WEEKLY RATES - COMMERCIAL RATES
- CONTINENTAL BREAKFAST - COFFEE BAR
- QUEEN & WATERBEDS - REFRIGERATORS
- CABLE TV MOVIES - VCRs, D.D. PHONES
- FAMILY UNITS - COIN LAUNDRY
- RESTAURANT & LOUNGE ADJACENT

Resv. 800-231-0575

THE HOME OF HOSPITALITY

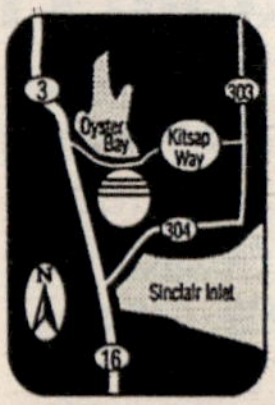

Comfortable, Spacious Rooms & Suites
Apartment Sized, Family Units
Available for extended stays or by the day
Heated Seasonal Pool & Spa
Free Continental Breakfast
Conference Facilities
Jacuzzi Suites
Fitness Room

Quality Inn
At Oyster Bay

1 Mile East of Hwy 3, Kitsap Way Exit
4303 Kitsap Way, Bremerton, WA 98312

(206) 405-1111 ❖ 1-800 4 CHOICE

BURLINGTON—4,300

LODGINGS

COCUSA MOTEL Rates Subject to Change **Phone:** 360/757-6044
AAA ◆◆◆ Motel
All Year 1P: $60 2P/1B: $60 2P/2B: $65 XP: $3
Location: I-5 exit 230. 370 W Rio Vista 98233. Fax: 360/757-8618. **Terms:** Reserv deposit; weekly rates; no pets. **Facility:** 61 rooms. 2 stories; exterior corridors; meeting rooms; heated pool, open 6/1-9/1. **Dining:** Restaurant nearby. **Services:** Fee: coin laundry. **All Rooms:** free movies, combo & shower baths, cable TV. **Some Rooms:** 6 efficiencies, refrigerators, whirlpools. **Cards:** AE, CB, DI, DS, MC, VI. (D) ⊗

STERLING MOTOR INN AAA Special Value Rates **Phone:** 360/757-0071
AAA ◆ Motor Inn
6/1-9/10 1P: $35 2P/1B: $40 2P/2B: $43 XP: $5 F12
3/1-5/31 & 9/11-2/29 1P: $30- 35 2P/1B: $33- 38 2P/2B: $36- 40 XP: $5 F12
Location: From I-5, exit 230, 1/2 mi se. 866 S Burlington Blvd 98233. **Terms:** Reserv deposit, 3 day notice; weekly/monthly rates; pets, $5. **Facility:** 35 rooms. Commercial highway setting. Large unpretentious rooms. 2 stories; exterior corridors. **Dining:** Restaurant; 7 am-10:30 pm; $10-$16; cocktails. **All Rooms:** free movies, cable TV. **Some Rooms:** 7 efficiencies. **Cards:** AE, DS, MC, VI. (D) ⊗

CASHMERE—2,500

LODGINGS

VILLAGE INN MOTEL Rates Subject to Change **Phone:** 509/782-3522
AAA ◆◆◆ Motel
Fri & Sat 5/1-12/31 1P: $48- 55 2P/1B: $50- 60 2P/2B: $57- 62 XP: $5-8
Sun-Thurs 5/1-12/31 2P/1B: $44- 48 2P/2B: $50- 55 XP: $5
3/1-4/30 & 1/1-2/29 1P: $36- 40 2P/1B: $40- 45 2P/2B: $45- 50 XP: $5
Location: Downtown on US 2-97 business rt. 229 Cottage Ave 98815. Fax: 509/782-2619. **Terms:** Sr. discount; reserv deposit, 3 day notice; weekly rates; small pets only, $20 dep req. **Facility:** 21 rooms. 2 stories; exterior corridors. **Services:** winter plug-ins. **All Rooms:** combo & shower baths, cable TV. **Some Rooms:** microwaves, refrigerators. **Cards:** AE, CB, DI, DS, MC, VI. (D) ⊗

WEDGE MOUNTAIN INN Rates Subject to Change **Phone:** 509/548-6694
AAA ◆◆◆ Motel
Fri & Sat 4/1-10/31 1P: $58 2P/1B: $58 2P/2B: $62 XP: $5 F
Sun-Thurs 4/1-10/31 1P: $49 2P/1B: $49 2P/2B: $54 XP: $5 F
3/1-3/31 & 11/1-2/29 1P: $49 2P/1B: $54 2P/2B: $54 XP: $5 F
Location: 6 mi w on US 2. (7335 Hwy 2, LEAVENWORTH). **Terms:** Sr. discount; reserv deposit; no pets. **Facility:** 28 rooms. 2 stories; interior corridors; mountain view; heated pool. **Services:** winter plug-ins. Fee: coin laundry. **All Rooms:** cable TV. **Cards:** AE, DS, MC, VI. (D) (S) ⊗

RESTAURANT

THE PEWTER POT **Dinner:** $11-$20 **Phone:** 509/782-2036
AAA ◆◆ American
Location: Downtown. 124 1/2 Cottage Ave 98815. **Hours:** 11 am-4 & 5-8 pm. Closed: Sun, Mon, 11/23 & 12/23-1/8. **Reservations:** suggested; for dinner. **Features:** carryout; salad bar; beer & wine only. Authentic European dinner specials prepared from scratch, served in a casual friendly atmosphere. Smoke free premises. **Cards:** MC, VI. ⊗

CASTLE ROCK—2,100

LODGING

TIMBERLAND MOTOR INN AAA Special Value Rates **Phone:** 360/274-6002
AAA ◆◆◆ Motel
4/16-11/30 1P: $38- 50 2P/1B: $45- 60 2P/2B: $48- 65 XP: $5
3/1-4/15 & 12/1-2/29 1P: $35- 45 2P/1B: $40- 55 2P/2B: $45- 60 XP: $5
Location: I-5, exit 49; 1/4 mi e on Mt St Helens Way. 1271 Mt St. Helens Way 98611. Fax: 360/274-6335. **Terms:** Reserv deposit; small pets only, $5. **Facility:** 40 rooms. Next to Mt St Helen Cinedome Theater. Family suite $88.60, for up to 6 persons; 2 stories; exterior corridors. **Services:** Fee: coin laundry. **All Rooms:** refrigerators, cable TV. **Some Rooms:** microwaves. Fee: whirlpools. **Cards:** AE, CB, DI, DS, MC, VI.
(See color ad below) (D) (S) ⊗

CATHLAMET—500

LODGING

COUNTRY KEEPER B & B/BRADLEY HOUSE Rates Subject to Change **Phone:** 360/795-3030
◆◆ Historic Bed & Breakfast
All Year [BP] 1P: $60- 75 2P/1B: $70- 85 2P/2B: $80 XP: $15
Location: On SR 409 2 blks s of SR 4. 61 Main St 98612 (PO Box 35). **Terms:** Age restrictions may apply; reserv deposit, 3 day notice; weekly rates; no pets. **Facility:** 4 rooms. 1907 Eastlake Victorian home resplendent with burnished wood & stained glass windows. Overlooking Puget Island & Columbia River. 2 stories; interior corridors; smoke free premises; street parking only. **All Rooms:** no A/C, no phones, no TVs. **Cards:** MC, VI. (D) ⊗

CENTRALIA—12,100

LODGINGS

FERRYMAN'S INN Rates Subject to Change **Phone:** 360/330-2094
AAA ◆◆◆ Motel
6/1-9/30 [CP] 1P: $43 2P/1B: $43 2P/2B: $52 XP: $5
3/1-5/31 & 10/1-2/29 [CP] 1P: $34 2P/1B: $37 2P/2B: $39 XP: $5
Location: E of I-5 exit 82. 1003 Eckerson Rd 98531. Fax: 360/330-5049. **Terms:** Credit card guarantee; pets, $5. **Facility:** 84 rooms. Some smaller rooms. 6 efficiencies, $6-$7 extra; 2 stories; interior/exterior corridors; meeting rooms; heated pool, whirlpool. **Dining:** Restaurant nearby. **Services:** Fee: coin laundry. **All Rooms:** free movies, cable TV. **Cards:** AE, CB, DI, MC, VI. (D) ⊗

TIMBERLAND INN & SUITES
360-274-6002
• 40 SPACIOUS ROOMS • 2 KING JACUZZI SUITES • FAMILY SUITES • CLOSE TO MT. ST. HELEN'S VISITOR CENTER & PARK • RESTAURANTS & SHOPPING NEARBY

HUNTLEY INN Guaranteed Rates **Phone:** 360/736-2875

AAA ◆◆ Motel

All Year [CP] 1P: $40 2P/1B: $48 2P/2B: $49 XP: $5 F12

Location: 2 blks e of I-5, exit 82. 702 W Harrison Ave 98531. Fax: 360/736-2651. **Terms:** Sr. discount; reserv deposit, 5 day notice; pets, $3. **Facility:** 87 rooms. Large rooms. 2 stories; exterior corridors; meeting rooms; heated pool. **Dining:** Restaurant nearby. **All Rooms:** free movies, combo & shower baths, cable TV. **Some Rooms:** refrigerators. Fee: VCP's, whirlpools. **Cards:** AE, CB, DI, DS, MC, VI.

PEPPERTREE WEST MOTOR INN & RV PARK Rates Subject to Change **Phone:** 360/736-1124

AAA ◆◆ Motor Inn

All Year 1P: $30- 33 2P/1B: $32- 35 2P/2B: $38 XP: $5

Location: Se of I-5 at exit 81. 1208 Alder St 98531. **Terms:** Reserv deposit, 3 day notice; weekly rates; pets, $5. **Facility:** 26 rooms. 1 two-bedroom unit. 1 story; exterior corridors; meeting rooms. **Dining:** Restaurant; 6 am-9 pm; $6-$13; cocktails. **Services:** Fee: coin laundry. **Some Rooms:** A/C, efficiency, refrigerators, phones, cable TV. **Cards:** MC, VI.

RESTAURANT

ANTIQUE MALL CAFE **Dinner:** $11-$20 **Phone:** 360/736-1183

◆◆ American

Location: In Centralia Square; 1/2 mi se of I-5, exit 82; 1 mi e of I-5, exit 81. 201 S Pearl St 98531. **Hours:** 7 am-9 pm, Sat from 8 am, Sun 8 am-5 pm. Closed: 4/16, 11/23 & 12/25. **Features:** salad bar; beer & wine only. Attractive relaxing dining room featuring well-prepared seafood, steaks, chicken, pasta & sandwiches. **Cards:** DS, MC, VI.

CHEHALIS—6,500

LODGINGS

CASCADE NON-SMOKERS' MOTEL Rates Subject to Change **Phone:** 360/748-8608

AAA ◆◆◆ Motel

All Year 2P/1B: $36- 40 2P/2B: $39- 42 XP: $4

Location: Off I-5, exit 76 (13th St). 550 SW Parkland Dr 98532. **Terms:** No pets. **Facility:** 29 rooms. 1 story; exterior corridors; smoke free premises. **Dining:** Restaurant nearby. **All Rooms:** free movies, cable TV. **Cards:** MC, VI.

PONY SOLDIER MOTOR INN Rates Subject to Change **Phone:** 360/748-0101

AAA ◆◆◆ Motel

All Year [CP] 1P: $38- 42 2P/1B: $42- 47 2P/2B: $44 XP: $4 F12

Location: 1 3/4 mi s on I-5, exit 76. 122 Interstate Ave 98532. Fax: 360/748-7591. **Terms:** Credit card guarantee; small pets only, $5. **Facility:** 69 rooms. 2 stories; exterior corridors; meeting rooms; heated pool, whirlpool. **Dining:** Restaurant nearby. **All Rooms:** free movies, cable TV. **Some Rooms:** microwaves, refrigerators. **Cards:** AE, CB, DI, DS, MC, VI.

RESTAURANT

HISTORIC MARY MCCRANKS RESTAURANT Country Inn **Dinner:** $11-$20 **Phone:** 360/748-3662

◆◆ American

Location: Northbound I-5 exit 72, e on Rush Rd, e on Bishop, n on Jackson, I-5S at exit 76 , 1 mi e on 13th, 4 mi s on Jackson. 2923 Jackson Hwy 98532. **Hours:** 11:30 am-2:30 & 5-8:30 pm, Sun noon-8 pm. Closed: Mon, 12/24 & 12/25. **Features:** children's menu; carryout; beer & wine only. Home-style cooking in roadside country inn, since 1935. Homemade breads & desserts. Smoke free premises. **Cards:** DS, MC, VI.

CHELAN—3,000

LODGINGS

APPLE INN MOTEL AAA Special Value Rates **Phone:** 509/682-4044

AAA ◆◆ Motel

5/27-9/10 1P: $49- 59 2P/1B: $49- 59 2P/2B: $49- 59 XP: $5
3/1-5/26 & 9/11-2/29 1P: $30- 34 2P/1B: $30- 34 2P/2B: $30- 34 XP: $5

Location: On US 97; 1/2 mi e of South Lake Shore. 1002 E Woodin Ave 98816 (PO Box 1450). **Terms:** No pets. **Facility:** 41 rooms. Complimentary coffee in lobby. 2 stories; interior/exterior corridors; heated pool, whirlpool. **All Rooms:** combo & shower baths, cable TV. **Some Rooms:** coffeemakers, 4 kitchens, refrigerators. **Cards:** AE, DI, DS, MC, VI.

CARAVEL RESORT Rates Subject to Change **Phone:** 509/682-2582

AAA ◆◆ Motel

6/15-10/15 1P: $92- 125 2P/1B: $92- 125 2P/2B: $100- 125
3/1-6/14 & 10/16-2/29 1P: $37- 95 2P/1B: $37- 95 2P/2B: $47- 110

Location: Downtown, by Lake Chelan. 322 W Woodin Ave 98816 (PO Box 1509). Fax: 509/682-3551. **Terms:** Sr. discount; check-in 4 pm; reserv deposit, 14 day notice, 30 days for weekly stays; weekly rates; package plans; no pets. **Facility:** 92 rooms. 6 two-bedroom units. 2-4 stories; exterior corridors; meeting rooms; beach, heated pool, whirlpool; boat dock. **Recreation:** swimming. **All Rooms:** coffeemakers, cable TV. **Some Rooms:** 45 kitchens, refrigerators, whirlpools. **Cards:** AE, DS, MC, VI. *(See color ad p 119)*

MARY KAY'S WHALEY MANSION Rates Subject to Change **Phone:** 509/682-5735

AAA ◆◆◆◆ Historic Bed & Breakfast

All Year [BP] 1P: $115- 125 2P/1B: $115- 125

Location: 1/2 blk n of US 97A. 415 3rd St 98816 (Rt 1, Box 693). Fax: 509/682-5385. **Terms:** Age restrictions may apply; reserv deposit, 3 day notice; no pets. **Facility:** 6 rooms. 1911 Whaley Mansion, Victorian decor. All rooms furnished with antiques. Outstanding breakfast presentation. 2 stories; interior corridors; smoke free premises. **All Rooms:** refrigerators, shower baths, cable TV, VCP's, no phones. **Cards:** MC, VI. *(See color ad below)*

Mary Kay's Romantic Whaley Mansion – Chelan, WA
• Elegant Rooms • Antique Furnishings • All Private Baths • Non-Smoking
• Air • Free Full Breakfast • Cable/TV • VCR-Movies
1-800-729-2408
415 3rd Street, Chelan, WA 98816 ◆◆◆◆ **Rating**

THE WESTVIEW RESORT MOTEL Guaranteed Rates **Phone:** 509/682-4396

AAA ◆◆◆ Motel

6/16-9/3	1P: $84	2P/1B: $88	2P/2B: $94	XP: $10
5/15-6/15 & 9/4-10/10	1P: $64	2P/1B: $68	2P/2B: $74	XP: $10
4/17-5/14	1P: $48	2P/1B: $52	2P/2B: $58	XP: $10
3/1-4/16 & 10/11-2/29	1P: $39	2P/1B: $43	2P/2B: $48	XP: $10

Location: W end of town. W 2312 Woodin Ave 98816. Fax: 509/682-2043. **Terms:** Reserv deposit, 7 day notice; no pets. **Facility:** 25 rooms. 2 stories; exterior corridors; lake view; meeting rooms; beach, heated pool, whirlpool; boat dock. **Dining:** Cafeteria nearby. **Services:** Fee: coin laundry. **Recreation:** swimming, waterskiing. **All Rooms:** coffeemakers, microwaves, refrigerators, combo & shower baths, cable TV. **Some Rooms:** 20 efficiencies, 5 kitchens, whirlpools. **Cards:** AE, CB, DI, DS, MC, VI. Ⓓ ⊗

RESTAURANTS

CAMPBELL HOUSE RESTAURANT Historical **Dinner:** $11-$20 **Phone:** 509/682-4250

◆◆ American

Location: In Campbell's Resort & Conference Center. 104 W Woodin Ave 98816. **Hours:** 6:45-11 am, 11:30-2 & 5-9 pm, Sun 6:45-noon, 12:30-2 & 5-9 pm. **Reservations:** suggested. **Features:** children's menu; health conscious menu; carryout; cocktails & lounge; a la carte. Northwest regional cuisine served in original 1901 Campbell Hotel. Smoke free premises. **Cards:** AE, DS, MC, VI. ⊗

GOOCHIS RESTAURANT Historical **Dinner:** $11-$20 **Phone:** 509/682-2436

AAA ◆◆ American

Location: Downtown. 104 E Woodin 98816. **Hours:** 11 am-10 pm. Closed: 11/23 & 12/25. **Features:** children's menu; carryout; cocktails & lounge. Creative American favorites served in a historical building; friendly atmosphere. **Cards:** AE, DS, MC, VI. ⊗

CHENEY—7,700

LODGING

WILLOW SPRINGS MOTEL Rates Subject to Change **Phone:** 509/235-5138

◆ Motel

All Year	1P: $35	2P/1B: $39	2P/2B: $41	XP: $4 D12

Location: 1 blk s of 1st St. 5 B St 99004. Fax: 509/235-4528. **Terms:** Credit card guarantee; small pets only, $5. **Facility:** 44 rooms. In the center of small rural college town. 12 efficiencies, $5 extra; 3 stories, no elevator; exterior corridors. **Dining:** Restaurant nearby. **Services:** Fee: coin laundry. **All Rooms:** cable TV. **Cards:** AE, DI, DS, MC, VI. Ⓓ ⊗

CHEWELAH—1,900

LODGING

NORDLIG MOTEL Guaranteed Rates **Phone:** 509/935-6704

AAA ◆◆ Motel

All Year	1P: $33	2P/1B: $39	2P/2B: $39	XP: $5

Location: US 395; n edge, across from City Park. 101 W Grant St 99109. **Terms:** Sr. discount; reserv deposit; weekly rates; pets, $3. **Facility:** 14 rooms. 2 stories; exterior corridors; meeting rooms. **All Rooms:** refrigerators, shower baths, cable TV. **Some Rooms:** coffeemakers. **Cards:** AE, DS, MC, VI. Ⓓ ⊗

CHINOOK

RESTAURANT

SANCTUARY RESTAURANT Historical **Dinner:** $11-$20 **Phone:** 360/777-8380

AAA ◆◆◆ American

Location: On US 101 at Hazel St. 98614. **Hours:** 5 pm-9 pm. Closed: 12/25, Mon & Tue 5/21-9/30 & Mon-Wed 10/1-5/20. **Reservations:** suggested. **Features:** No A/C; children's menu; cocktails; a la carte. Fresh local seafood & steaks in a refurbished 1906 church. Homemade desserts. **Cards:** AE, CB, DI, MC, VI. ⊗

CLARKSTON—6,800

LODGINGS

BEST WESTERN RIVERTREE INN Rates Subject to Change **Phone:** 509/758-9551

◆◆◆ Motel

All Year	1P: $55- 75	2P/1B: $60- 70	2P/2B: $60- 70	XP: $10

Location: On US 12; 6 blks w of jct SR 129. 1257 Bridge St 99403. Fax: 509/758-9551. **Terms:** Sr. discount; reserv deposit, 7 day notice; no pets. **Facility:** 47 rooms. Whirlpool suite $65-$90; 2 stories; exterior corridors; heated pool, sauna, whirlpool; exercise room. **Dining:** Cocktails; restaurant nearby. **Services:** data ports. **All Rooms:** free movies, refrigerators, cable TV. **Some Rooms:** 20 efficiencies, no utensils. **Cards:** AE, CB, DI, DS, MC, VI. Ⓓ ⊗

QUALITY INN-CLARKSTON Rates Subject to Change **Phone:** 509/758-9500

◆◆◆ Motor Inn

11/1-2/20	1P: $52- 75	2P/1B: $56- 75	2P/2B: $56- 75	XP: $5	F
5/1-10/31	1P: $57- 70	2P/1B: $60- 75	2P/2B: $62- 65	XP: $5	F
3/1-4/30 & 2/21-2/29	1P: $53- 66	2P/1B: $57- 71	2P/2B: $59- 62	XP: $5	F

Location: 1/4 mi w on SR 12, 2 blks n on 5th. 700 Port Dr 99403. Fax: 509/758-5580. **Terms:** Sr. discount; reserv deposit; no pets. **Facility:** 75 rooms. 2 stories; interior corridors; conference facilities; heated pool. **Dining & Entertainment:** Dining room, coffee shop; 6 am-10 pm; $8-$15; cocktail lounge; entertainment. **Services:** airport transportation. Fee: coin laundry. **All Rooms:** free movies, cable TV. **Some Rooms:** microwaves, refrigerators. **Cards:** AE, CB, DI, DS, JCB, MC, VI. Ⓓ ⊗

CLE ELUM—1,800

LODGINGS

CEDARS MOTEL Rates Subject to Change **Phone:** 509/674-5535

AAA ◆ Motel

All Year	1P: $30	2P/1B: $40	2P/2B: $44	XP: $4

Location: 1 mi e on I-90 business rt; 1 mi w of I-90 exit 85; on SR 903. 1001 E 1st St 98922. **Terms:** Reserv deposit; weekly rates, off-season; pets. **Facility:** 32 rooms. East end of town. 2 two-bedroom units. 2 stories; interior/exterior corridors. **Dining:** Restaurant nearby. **All Rooms:** combo & shower baths, cable TV. **Some Rooms:** microwaves, refrigerators, phones. **Cards:** AE, CB, DI, DS, MC, VI. Ⓓ

MOORE HOUSE BED & BREAKFAST COUNTRY INN Rates Subject to Change **Phone:** 509/674-5939

◆◆ Historic Bed & Breakfast

All Year [BP]	1P: $45- 105	2P/1B: $45- 105	2P/2B: $65- 105	XP: $10

Location: 1 1/2 mi ne of I-90 at exit 84 eastbound; 1 1/2 mi nw of I-90, exit 84 westbound; follow signs. 526 Marie St 98943 (PO Box 629, SOUTH CLE ELUM). **Terms:** Check-in 4 pm; reserv deposit, 7 day notice; 2 night min stay, weekends 12/15-3/1; no pets. **Facility:** 12 rooms. 1909 historical Chicago, Milwaukee, St. Paul & Pacific railroad bunkhouse. Adjacent to Ironhorse State Park Trail. 2 stories; interior/exterior corridors; designated smoking area; whirlpool; trail rides. **Recreation:** cross country skiing. **All Rooms:** no phones. **Some Rooms:** A/C, coffeemakers, refrigerators, cable TV, whirlpools. **Cards:** AE, MC, VI. Ⓓ ⊗

STEWART LODGE Guaranteed Rates **Phone:** 509/674-4548
AAA ◆◆◆ Motel
All Year 1P: $43 2P/1B: $48 2P/2B: $53- 58 XP: $5 D
Location: 805 W First St 98922. Fax: 509/674-5426. **Terms:** Reserv deposit; small pets only. **Facility:** 36 rooms. In country motif with unique pine furniture. 2 stories; exterior corridors; meeting rooms; whirlpool. **Dining:** Restaurant nearby. **Services:** winter plug-ins. Fee: coin laundry. **Recreation:** heated pool 4/1-11/30. **All Rooms:** combo & shower baths, cable TV. **Some Rooms:** refrigerators. **Cards:** AE, CB, DI, DS, MC, VI. (D) ⊗

TIMBER LODGE MOTEL Rates Subject to Change **Phone:** 509/674-5966
AAA ◆◆◆ Motel
All Year 1P: $42 2P/1B: $47 2P/2B: $52 XP: $3-5
Location: 1 mi ne of I-90 exit 84 eastbound, 2 1/2 mi nw of I-90 exit 85 westbound. 301 W First St 98922. Fax: 509/674-2737. **Terms:** Credit card guarantee, 3 day notice; weekly rates; small pets only, $10 dep req. **Facility:** 29 rooms. 2 stories; interior/exterior corridors; whirlpool. **Services:** Fee: coin laundry. **All Rooms:** cable TV. **Some Rooms:** Fee: microwaves, refrigerators, VCP's. **Cards:** AE, DI, MC, VI. (D) ⊗

RESTAURANTS

CAVALLINIS RESTAURANT INTERNATIONAL CUISINE **Dinner:** $11-$20 **Phone:** 509/674-2151
AAA ◆◆◆ Italian
Location: 1 1/2 blks w. 200 E First St 98922. **Hours:** 7:30 am-11 pm, Fri & Sat-midnight. **Reservations:** suggested. **Features:** Sunday brunch; children's menu; early bird specials; salad bar; cocktails & lounge; a la carte. Very well prepared dishes in pleasant natural cedar dining rooms. Also American cuisine. Smoke free premises. **Cards:** AE, MC, VI. ⊗

MA MA VALLONE'S STEAK HOUSE & INN **Dinner:** $11-$20 **Phone:** 509/674-5174
AAA ◆◆◆ Steakhouse
Location: 1 mi ne of I-90, exit 84 eastbound, 2 1/2 mi nw of I-90, exit 85 northbound. 302 W First St 98922. **Hours:** 4:30 pm-9:30 pm. Closed: Mon. **Reservations:** suggested. **Features:** carryout; cocktails; a la carte. Original Italian dishes & large selection of steaks. Smoke free premises. **Cards:** AE, CB, DI, DS, MC, VI. ⊗

COSMOPOLIS

LODGING

COONEY MANSION BED & BREAKFAST AAA Special Value Rates **Phone:** 206/533-0602
◆◆◆ Historic Bed & Breakfast
All Year [BP] 2P/1B: $65- 115 XP: $20
Location: 1/2 mi off Hwy 101 at C St. 1705 Fifth St 98537 (PO Box 54). Fax: 360/533-0602. **Terms:** Age restrictions may apply; check-in 4 pm; reserv deposit, 7 day notice; weekly/monthly rates; no pets. **Facility:** 5 rooms. Old fashioned warmth in a 1908 mansion. 3 stories, no elevator; interior corridors; smoke free premises; sauna, whirlpool; exercise room. **All Rooms:** combo & tub baths, no A/C, no phones. **Some Rooms:** radios, cable TV. **Cards:** AE, CB, DI, DS, MC, VI. (D) ⊗

COUGAR

LODGING

LONE FIR RESORT Rates Subject to Change **Phone:** 360/238-5210
◆◆ Motel
All Year 2P/1B: $38- 60 2P/2B: $40- 65 XP:$7-12
Location: Center. 16806 Lewis River Rd 98616. **Terms:** Sr. discount; reserv deposit, 5 day notice; weekly rates; no pets. **Facility:** 17 rooms. Motel units, duplexes & cabin in scenic mountain setting. 1 two-bedroom unit. 2 stories; exterior corridors; pool; Mt. St. Helens helicopter flights. **Services:** Fee: coin laundry. **All Rooms:** combo & shower baths, no phones. **Some Rooms:** A/C, 9 kitchens, refrigerators. Fee: VCP's. **Cards:** MC, VI. (D) ⊗

COULEE DAM—1,100

LODGING

COULEE HOUSE MOTEL Rates Subject to Change **Phone:** 509/633-1101
AAA ◆◆ Motel
All Year 1P: $48- 60 2P/1B: $48- 60 2P/2B: $68 XP: $5
Location: 1 blk from river bridge on SR 155. 110 Roosevelt Way 99116. **Terms:** Reserv deposit; pets. **Facility:** 61 rooms. Some rooms with scenic view of Grand Coulee Dam spillway, especially enjoyable during summer months lazer light show. 2 two-bedroom units. 2 stories; exterior corridors; heated pool, sauna, whirlpool. **Services:** Fee: coin laundry. **All Rooms:** free movies, combo & shower baths, cable TV. **Some Rooms:** 17 kitchens, radios, refrigerators. **Cards:** AE, DI, DS, MC, VI. (D) ⊗

COUPEVILLE—1,400

LODGINGS

ANCHORAGE INN Guaranteed Rates **Phone:** 360/678-5581
AAA ◆◆◆ Bed & Breakfast
4/1-12/20 [BP] 1P: $75- 90 2P/1B: $75- 90 XP: $10
2/10-3/31 [BP] 1P: $65- 80 2P/1B: $65- 80 XP: $10
Location: Downtown. 807 N Main St 98239 (PO Box 673). **Terms:** Open 2/10-12/20; age restrictions may apply; credit card guarantee, 3 day notice; no pets. **Facility:** 5 rooms. 3 stories, no elevator; interior corridors; smoke free premises. **All Rooms:** combo & shower baths, cable TV, no phones. **Cards:** AE, DS, MC, VI. (D) ⊗

CAPTAIN WHIDBEY INN Rates Subject to Change **Phone:** 360/678-4097
◆◆◆ Historic Country Inn
All Year [BP] 1P: $75- 185 2P/1B: $85- 125 2P/2B: $125 XP: $15
Location: 2 1/2 mi nw off Madrona Way. 2072 W Captain Whidbey Inn Rd 98239. Fax: 360/678-4110. **Terms:** Age restrictions may apply; check-in 4 pm; reserv deposit, 7 day notice; 2 night min stay, weekends; no pets. **Facility:** 32 rooms. 1907 Madrona log inn, quaint lodge rooms, rustic cottages & spacious rooms in 2 buildings overlooking lagoons. Outstanding marine vistas. On National Register of Historic Places. 2 two-bedroom units. 2 stories; interior/exterior corridors; designated smoking area; lakefront; meeting rooms; beach; boat dock. **Dining:** Dining room, see separate listing. **Recreation:** fishing, dock avail 5/1-10/31. **All Rooms:** no A/C, no TVs. **Some Rooms:** coffeemakers, 3 efficiencies, phones. **Cards:** AE, CB, DI, DS, MC, VI. (D) ⊗

COMPASS ROSE AAA Special Value Rates **Phone:** 360/678-5318
◆◆ Historic Bed & Breakfast
All Year [BP] 2P/1B: $65
Location: In town. 508 S Main St 98239. Fax: 360/678-5318. **Terms:** Check-in 4 pm; no pets. **Facility:** 2 rooms. Historical Queen Anne Victorian home, filled with antiques & beautiful woodwork. 2 stories; interior corridors; smoke free premises. **All Rooms:** no A/C, no phones, no TVs. (D) ⊗

THE COUPEVILLE INN Rates Subject to Change **Phone:** 360/678-6668
AAA 5/1-9/30 [CP] 1P: $54- 85 2P/1B: $54- 85 2P/2B: $54- 85 XP: $10
◆◆◆ 3/1-4/30 & 10/1-2/29 [CP] 1P: $54- 75 2P/1B: $54- 75 2P/2B: $54- 75 XP: $10
Motel **Location:** 2 blks w; 1/2 mi n of SR 20, off Main St. 200 Coveland St 98239 (PO Box 370). Fax: 360/678-3059. **Terms:** Reserv deposit; weekly rates; no pets. **Facility:** 24 rooms. Many units with balcony overlooking historic downtown & Penn Cove. 2 stories; interior corridors; meeting rooms. **Dining:** Restaurant nearby. **All Rooms:** combo & shower baths, no A/C. **Cards:** AE, CB, DI, DS, MC, VI. *(See color ad below)* D ⊗

GARDEN ISLE GUEST COTTAGES Guaranteed Rates **Phone:** 360/678-5641
◆◆ 6/1-9/30 [BP] 1P: $85- 95 2P/1B: $85- 95
Bed & Breakfast 3/1-5/31 & 10/1-2/29 [BP] 1P: $75- 85 2P/1B: $75- 85
Location: Downtown. 207 NW Coveland St 98239 (PO Box 1305). **Terms:** Reserv deposit, 10 day notice; no pets. **Facility:** 2 rooms. 1 story; exterior corridors; smoke free premises. **All Rooms:** coffeemakers, kitchens, shower baths, cable TV, no A/C, no phones. **Cards:** MC, VI. D ⊗

THE INN AT PENN COVE Rates Subject to Change **Phone:** 360/678-8000
◆◆◆ All Year [BP] 1P: $55- 120 2P/1B: $60- 125 XP: $15 F16
Historic Bed & Breakfast **Location:** Center of town. 702 N Main 98239 (PO Box 85). **Terms:** Age restrictions may apply; check-in 4 pm; reserv deposit, 7 day notice; no pets. **Facility:** 6 rooms. Elegance & grandeur of a bygone era in an Italiante home. 2 stories; interior corridors; smoke free premises; exercise room. **All Rooms:** no phones, no TVs. **Some Rooms:** A/C. **Cards:** AE, DS, MC, VI. D ⊗

THE VICTORIAN BED & BREAKFAST Guaranteed Rates **Phone:** 360/678-5305
◆◆◆ 6/1-9/30 [BP] 1P: $65 2P/1B: $80- 100 2P/2B: $100 XP: $15 F6
Historic Bed & Breakfast 3/1-5/31 & 10/1-2/29 [BP] 1P: $60 2P/1B: $65- 75 2P/2B: $85 XP: $15 F6
Location: Main St. 602 N Main St 98239 (PO Box 761). **Terms:** Reserv deposit, 7 day notice; small pets only, $50 dep req. **Facility:** 3 rooms. Italiante Victorian architecture. Restored house built in 1889; listed on National Registry of Historic Places. 1 two-bedroom unit. 2 stories; interior corridors; smoke free premises; street parking only. **All Rooms:** combo & shower baths, no A/C, no phones. **Some Rooms:** coffeemakers, radios, refrigerators. **Cards:** DS, MC, VI. D ⊗

RESTAURANT

CAPTAIN WHIDBEY INN **Dinner:** $21-$30 **Phone:** 360/678-4097
◆◆ Seafood **Location:** In Captain Whidbey Inn. 2072 W Captain Whidbey Inn Rd 98239. **Hours:** 6 pm-9:30 pm; 7/1-9/30 noon-9:30 pm lighter fare served in lounge. **Reservations:** suggested. **Features:** No A/C; cocktails & lounge; a la carte. Also fresh regional specialties in 1907 Madrona log inn overlooking Penn Cove; outdoor deck. Designated smoking areas. **Cards:** AE, DI, DS, MC, VI. ⊗

DAYTON—2,500

RESTAURANT

PATIT CREEK RESTAURANT **Dinner:** $11-$20 **Phone:** 509/382-2625
◆◆ Continental **Location:** On Hwy 12, n edge of town. 725 E Dayton Ave 99328. **Hours:** 11:30 am-1:30 & 4:30-8 pm, Fri-9 pm, Sat 4:30 pm-9 pm. Closed: Sun, Mon & 7/19-8/14. **Reservations:** suggested. **Features:** casual dress; beer & wine only. Not your typical continental restaurant, surprising dining experience in small agricultural town. Chef Heibert personally selects all ingredients and prepares all dishes. Smoke free premises. **Cards:** MC, VI. ⊗

DES MOINES—17,300 (See SEATTLE & VICINITY ACCOMMODATIONS spotting map pages A136 & A137; see index starting on page A134)

LODGING

RAMADA LIMITED SEA-TAC Guaranteed Rates **Phone:** 206/824-9920 (175)
AAA 7/1-9/30 [CP] 1P: $69 2P/1B: $75 2P/2B: $85 XP: $6 F
◆◆◆ 3/1-6/30 & 10/1-2/29 [CP] 1P: $59 2P/1B: $59 2P/2B: $69
Motor Inn **Location:** From I-5 exit 149, 2 mi w via Kent Des Moines Rd & Marine View Dr. 22300 7th Ave S 98198. Fax: 206/824-1372. **Terms:** Sr. discount; weekly/monthly rates; no pets. **Facility:** 41 rooms. 2 stories; interior corridors; meeting rooms; sauna, whirlpool. **Dining & Entertainment:** Restaurant; 7 am-3 & 5-10 pm; $7-$15; cocktail lounge. **Services:** data ports; airport transportation. Fee: coin laundry. **All Rooms:** refrigerators, combo & tub baths, cable TV. **Some Rooms:** microwaves, whirlpools. **Cards:** AE, CB, DI, DS, MC, VI. D ⊗

RESTAURANT

LE BONAPARTE **Dinner:** $11-$20 **Phone:** 206/878-4412 (124)
◆◆◆ Continental **Location:** S 216th & Marine View Dr. 21630 7th Pl S 98198. **Hours:** 11:30 am-2 & 4:30-9:30 pm, Fri & Sat-10:30 pm, Sun 11 am-2 & 4:30-9:30 pm. **Features:** Sunday brunch; children's menu; early bird specials; cocktails & lounge. Fresh, casual dining. Classic Continental menu. Deck dining, full bar service. **Cards:** AE, DI, DS, MC, VI. ⊗

EAST WENATCHEE—1,600

LODGINGS

FOUR SEASONS INN Rates Subject to Change **Phone:** 509/884-6611
◆◆ All Year 1P: $44- 52 2P/1B: $52- 58 2P/2B: $58- 62 XP: $5 F12
Motor Inn **Location:** 1/2 mi se; on SR 28 in East Wenatchee. 11 W Grant Rd 98802. Fax: 509/884-6611. **Terms:** Credit card guarantee; pets, $5 dep req. **Facility:** 101 rooms. Some with balcony, many rooms overlook Columbia River. 2 stories; interior corridors; meeting rooms; heated pool, sauna, whirlpool. **Dining & Entertainment:** Dining room, coffee shop; 24 hours; $4-$10; cocktails/lounge; also, Barney's Eatery, see separate listing. **All Rooms:** free movies, cable TV. **Some Rooms:** efficiency, refrigerators. **Cards:** AE, CB, DI, DS, MC, VI. D ⊗

WELCOME TO WHIDBEY ISLAND
And Our Country Inn, located in Ebey's National Historic Reserve.
A great retreat for 2 or 40, overlooking shops & beaches.
Nearby forts, trails, lighthouse & winery. AAA ◆◆◆

THE COUPEVILLE INN (206) 678-6668 • Box 370 • Coupeville, WA 98239

THE RIVER'S INN Rates Subject to Change **Phone:** 509/884-1474

◆◆◆ Motel

All Year [CP] 1P: $47 2P/1B: $52- 57 2P/2B: $62- 67 XP: $5 F11

Location: 1 1/2 mi se in East Wenatchee; across from Wenatchee Valley Mall. 580 Valley Mall Pkwy 98802. Fax: 509/884-9179. **Terms:** Weekly rates, 10/1-3/31; no pets. **Facility:** 54 rooms. On well-landscaped grounds overlooking lower Wenatchee Valley. Some units have balcony or patio. 2 stories; interior corridors; heated pool, whirlpool. **Dining:** Restaurant nearby. **All Rooms:** cable TV. **Some Rooms:** Fee: microwaves, refrigerators, VCP's. **Cards:** AE, DI, DS, MC, VI.

RESTAURANT

BARNEY'S EATERY **Dinner:** $11-$20 **Phone:** 509/884-6611

◆◆ American

Location: In Four Seasons Inn. 11 W Grant Rd 98802. **Hours:** 11 am-2 & 4:30-9 pm, Fri & Sat-10 pm, Sun 9 am-9 pm. **Features:** children's menu; early bird specials; health conscious menu items; carryout; cocktails & lounge; buffet. Casual family dining with view of Columbia River & snow capped mountains. **Cards:** AE, CB, DI, DS, MC, VI.

EATONVILLE—1,400

LODGING

MILL VILLAGE MOTEL Guaranteed Rates **Phone:** 360/832-3200

◆◆◆ Motel

6/1-9/30	1P: $49- 53	2P/1B: $53- 59	2P/2B: $59	XP: $5	F12
3/1-5/31 & 10/1-2/29	1P: $45- 49	2P/1B: $49- 55	2P/2B: $55	XP: $5	F12

Location: Downtown. 210 Center St E 98328 (PO Box 609). Fax: 360/832-3203. **Terms:** Reserv deposit, 3 day notice; no pets. **Facility:** 32 rooms. Close to Northwest Trek & Mt Rainier. 2 stories; exterior corridors. **All Rooms:** combo & shower baths, cable TV. **Some Rooms:** 11 efficiencies, no utensils. **Cards:** AE, DS, MC, VI.

EDMONDS—30,700 (See SEATTLE & VICINITY ACCOMMODATIONS spotting map pages A136 & A137; see index starting on page A134)

LODGINGS

EDMONDS HARBOR INN Rates Subject to Change **Phone:** 206/771-5021 119

◆◆◆ Motel

All Year [CP] 1P: $54 2P/1B: $64 2P/2B: $69 XP: $5 F12

Location: 3 blks s at Port of Edmonds; in Harbor Square Shopping Center. 130 W Dayton St 98020. Fax: 206/672-2880. **Terms:** Reserv deposit; AP available; no pets. **Facility:** 61 rooms. Located near waterfront & ferry terminal. 7 efficiencies, $75-$85; 2 stories; interior corridors; meeting rooms. Fee: health club. **Dining:** Restaurant nearby. **All Rooms:** free movies, cable TV. **Some Rooms:** refrigerators. **Cards:** AE, DI, DS, MC, VI. *(See color ad below)*

HOMEPORT INN Guaranteed Rates **Phone:** 206/771-8008 117

◆◆◆ Motel

All Year [CP] 1P: $42 2P/1B: $47 2P/2B: $52 XP: $5 F12

Location: From I-5 exit 177, 1 mi w; 1/4 mi n at jct SR 99 & 104. 23825 Hwy 99 98026. Fax: 206/771-8008. **Terms:** Sr. discount; reserv deposit; weekly rates; no pets. **Facility:** 58 rooms. 24 hour fax service. 8 efficiencies, $10 extra, no utensils; 3 stories, no elevator; exterior corridors; meeting rooms; whirlpool. **Dining:** Restaurant nearby. **Services:** Fee: coin laundry. **All Rooms:** free movies, cable TV. **Some Rooms:** refrigerators. Fee: whirlpools. **Cards:** AE, CB, DI, DS, MC, VI. *(See color ad below)*

K & E MOTOR INN Rates Subject to Change **Phone:** 206/778-2181 118

◆◆ Motel

All Year [CP] 1P: $39- 44 2P/1B: $44- 49 2P/2B: $49- 54 XP: $5 F12

Location: 1 mi w of I-5 exit 177; 1/4 mi n of jct SR 99 & 104. 23921 Hwy 99 98020. Fax: 206/778-1516. **Terms:** Sr. discount; reserv deposit; weekly rates; small pets only. **Facility:** 32 rooms. 2 stories; exterior corridors. **Dining:** Restaurant nearby. **Services:** Fee: coin laundry. **All Rooms:** free movies, cable TV. **Some Rooms:** A/C, 4 efficiencies, 4 kitchens, refrigerators. **Cards:** AE, DI, DS, MC, VI. *(See color ad below)*

EDMONDS HARBOR INN
5 Minutes to Beaches, Ferry, Restaurants, Sportfishing and Shopping
• 20 minutes north of Seattle • Color TV/HBO
• 61 Comfortable Rooms • Non-Smoking Rooms
• Complimentary Continental Breakfast • Health Club (fee)
130 W. Dayton, Edmonds, WA 98020 • (206) 771-5021
Call: 1-800-441-8033

SEATTLE/EDMONDS HOMEPORT Inn
PRIVATE JACUZZI SUITES
FAMILY SUITES
KITCHENETTE UNITS
RESTAURANTS/SHOPPING NEARBY
HOT TUB
FREE CONTINENTAL BREAKFAST
DIRECT DIAL PHONES (N/C LOCAL)
COMMERCIAL & SENIOR RATES
CLOSE TO FERRY
15 MIN. TO DOWNTOWN SEATTLE
1-800-771-8009
23825 HWY. 99, EDMONDS, WA 98026

AAA
K & E MOTOR INN
12 miles N of Downtown Seattle, 2.5 miles E of Kingston Ferry.
I-5 Exit 177 & follow the K&E Motor Inn signs.
• Local calls free • Cable TV & HBO
• Non-smoking rooms • Continental Breakfast
• 1 block N of new Home Depot & Costco stores.
23921 Hwy 99 Edmonds, WA 98020
Tel: 206-778-2181 FAX: 206-778-1516

(See SEATTLE & VICINITY ACCOMMODATIONS spotting map pages A136 & A137)

RESTAURANT

ARNIES AT EDMONDS Dinner: $11-$20 Phone: 206/771-5688 (84)
◆◆◆ American
Location: 2 blks s of ferry terminal; 6 mi w of I-5 exit 177 via SR 104. 300 Admiral Way 98020. **Hours:** 11:30 am-2:30 & 5-10:30 pm, Sat 11:30 am-3 & 5-10:30 pm, Sun 10 am-2 & 4-9 pm. Closed: 12/25. **Reservations:** suggested. **Features:** Sunday brunch; children's menu; early bird specials; health conscious menu; carryout; cocktails & lounge; a la carte. Picturesque view of Edmonds Bay. Specializing in fresh northwest seafood. **Cards:** AE, MC, VI.

ELLENSBURG—12,400

LODGINGS

BEST WESTERN ELLENSBURG INN Rates Subject to Change **Phone:** 509/925-9801
◆◆◆ Motor Inn

5/1-10/31	1P: $59	2P/1B: $64	2P/2B: $64	XP: $5 F12
3/1-4/30 & 11/1-2/29	1P: $49	2P/1B: $54	2P/2B: $54	XP: $5 F12

Location: At I-90 exit 109. 1700 Canyon Rd 98926. Fax: 509/925-2093. **Terms:** Sr. discount; pets. **Facility:** 105 rooms. 2 stories; interior corridors; meeting rooms; heated indoor pool, wading pool, sauna, whirlpools; exercise room, playground. **Dining:** Restaurant, see separate listing. **Services:** valet laundry; winter plug-ins. **All Rooms:** free movies, cable TV. **Some Rooms:** refrigerators. **Cards:** AE, DI, DS, MC, VI. (D)

HAROLDS MOTEL Rates Subject to Change **Phone:** 509/925-4141
◆ Motel

All Year	1P: $30- 45	2P/1B: $35- 50	2P/2B: $38- 55	XP: $6 F6

Location: Jct I-90 & Canyon Rd, exit 109; 1 1/2 mi n on Canyon Rd, then 1/4 mi w on 6th Ave. 601 N Water 98926. Fax: 509/925-4143. **Terms:** Sr. discount; reserv deposit; pets, $50 dep req. **Facility:** 40 rooms. 8 two-bedroom units. 2 stories; exterior corridors; heated pool. **Dining:** Restaurant nearby. **Services:** winter plug-ins. Fee: coin laundry. **All Rooms:** free movies, combo & shower baths, cable TV. **Some Rooms:** 8 efficiencies, refrigerators. **Cards:** AE, DI, DS, MC, VI. (D)

I-90 INN MOTEL Rates Subject to Change **Phone:** 509/925-9844
◆◆ Motel

5/15-10/15	1P: $36	2P/1B: $40	2P/2B: $42- 44	XP: $3
3/1-5/14 & 10/16-2/29	1P: $30	2P/1B: $36	2P/2B: $40	XP: $3

Location: I-90 exit 106. 1390 Dollar Way Rd 98926. **Terms:** Reserv deposit; small pets only, $3. **Facility:** 72 rooms. Alongside a small lake. 2 stories; exterior corridors; meeting rooms. **Dining:** Restaurant nearby. **Services:** winter plug-ins. Fee: coin laundry. **All Rooms:** free movies, cable TV. **Cards:** AE, DI, DS, MC, VI. (D)

MURPHYS COUNTRY BED & BREAKFAST Rates Subject to Change **Phone:** 509/925-7986
◆◆ Historic Bed & Breakfast

All Year [BP]	1P: $55	2P/1B: $60	XP: $15 D10

Location: I-90 at exit 106, 1 3/4 mi w on Thorp Hwy. 2830 Thorp Hwy S 98926. **Terms:** Check-in 4 pm; reserv deposit, 7 day notice; no pets. **Facility:** 2 rooms. A turn-of-the-century frontier home. 2 stories; interior corridors; smoke free premises. **All Rooms:** no A/C, no phones, no TVs. **Cards:** AE, MC, VI. (D)

NITES INN Rates Subject to Change **Phone:** 509/962-9600
◆◆◆ Motel

All Year	1P: $36	2P/1B: $39	2P/2B: $43	XP: $6 F10

Location: 1/4 mi n of I-90, exit 109. 1200 S Ruby 98926. **Terms:** Sr. discount; reserv deposit; pets, $6, small pets preferred. **Facility:** 32 rooms. Truck & RV parking. 2 stories; exterior corridors. **Dining:** Restaurant nearby. **Services:** Fee: coin laundry. **All Rooms:** free movies, cable TV. **Some Rooms:** microwaves. Fee: refrigerators. **Cards:** AE, DI, MC, VI. (D)

RESTAURANTS

BEST WESTERN ELLENSBURG RESTAURANT **Dinner:** $11-$20 **Phone:** 509/925-9801
◆◆ American
Location: In Best Western Ellensburg Inn. 1700 Canyon Rd 98926. **Hours:** 6:30 am-10 pm. **Features:** children's menu; carryout; salad bar; cocktails & lounge; a la carte. Family oriented dining with southwest decor. **Cards:** AE, DI, DS, JCB, MC, VI.

GIOVANNI'S ON PEARL Historical **Dinner:** $11-$20 **Phone:** 509/962-2260
◆◆◆ Italian
Location: Downtown in historic 1889 Davidson Bldg. 402 N Pearl St 98926. **Hours:** 11 am-10 pm, Sat 11 am-10 pm. Closed major holidays, Sun & Mon. **Features:** children's menu; cocktails & lounge; a la carte. Extremely attractive turn-of-the-century atmosphere. Fine & casual dining, seasonal menu. **Cards:** AE, CB, DI, DS, MC, VI.

VALLEY CAFE **Dinner:** $11-$20 **Phone:** 509/925-3050
◆◆ American
Location: 105 W Third 98926. **Hours:** 11 am-9 pm, Fri-10 pm, Sat 9 am-10 pm, Sun 9 am-9 pm. Closed: 7/4, 11/23 & 12/25. **Features:** children's menu; senior's menu; carryout; beer & wine only. Art Deco design. Casual relaxed dining. Smoke free premises. **Cards:** AE, DI, DS, MC, VI.

ELMA—2,400

RESTAURANT

PAPA'S PIZZA **Dinner:** up to $10 **Phone:** 360/482-5000
◆ Italian
Location: Downtown. 302 W Waldrup 98541. **Hours:** 11 am-9 pm, Fri & Sat-10 pm, Sun 1 pm-8 pm. Closed major holidays. **Features:** children's menu; carryout; salad bar; beer & wine only. Family oriented. Delivery avail. **Cards:** DI, DS, MC, VI.

EPHRATA—5,300

LODGINGS

EPHRATA TRAVELODGE Rates Subject to Change **Phone:** 509/754-4651
◆◆ Motel

All Year	1P: $45- 70	2P/1B: $55- 70	2P/2B: $60- 70	XP: $5

Location: Downtown; on SR 28. 31 Basin SW 98823. Fax: 509/754-0413. **Terms:** Sr. discount; reserv deposit; no pets. **Facility:** 28 rooms. 2 stories; exterior corridors; heated pool. **Services:** data ports. **All Rooms:** free movies, combo & shower baths, cable TV. **Some Rooms:** coffeemakers, microwaves, refrigerators. **Cards:** AE, CB, DI, DS, MC, VI. (D)

SHARLYN MOTEL Rates Subject to Change **Phone:** 509/754-3575
◆ Motel

All Year	1P: $35	2P/1B: $45	2P/2B: $50	XP: $8

Location: On SR 28. 848 Basin SW 98823. Fax: 509/754-0611. **Terms:** Credit card guarantee, 3 day notice; no pets. **Facility:** 17 rooms. 2 stories; exterior corridors. **All Rooms:** combo & shower baths, cable TV. **Some Rooms:** coffeemakers, refrigerators. **Cards:** AE, CB, DI, DS, MC, VI. (D)

EVERETT—70,000

LODGINGS

BEST WESTERN CASCADIA INN — AAA Special Value Rates — **Phone:** 206/258-4141

AAA ◆◆◆ Motor Inn

6/16-2/29 [CP]	1P: $69	2P/1B: $77	2P/2B: $77	XP: $8 F12
3/1-6/15 [CP]	1P: $61	2P/1B: $69	2P/2B: $69	XP: $8 F12

Location: I-5 northbound exit 193; I-5 southbound exit 194, then follow Everett Pacific Convention Center signs. 2800 Pacific Ave 98201. Fax: 206/258-4755. **Terms:** Reserv deposit, 3 day notice; no pets. **Facility:** 134 rooms. Modest rooms. 3 stories; interior corridors; conference facilities; heated pool, whirlpool; exercise room. **Dining:** Restaurant; 11 am-10 pm, Sat 5 pm-11 pm; $8-$14; cocktails. **Services:** Fee: coin laundry, airport transportation. **All Rooms:** coffeemakers, free movies, cable TV. **Some Rooms:** refrigerators. **Cards:** AE, CB, DI, DS, MC, VI. *(See color ad below)* Ⓓ ⊗

CYPRESS INN — AAA Special Value Rates — **Phone:** 206/347-9099

AAA ◆◆◆ Motel

All Year [CP]	1P: $59- 64	2P/1B: $66- 69	2P/2B: $66- 69	XP: $7 F13

Location: 8 mi s; on w side of I-5, exit 186W, on 128th St. 12619 4th Ave W 98208. Fax: 206/348-3048. **Terms:** Reserv deposit; monthly rates; small pets only, $7. **Facility:** 70 rooms. 3 stories; interior corridors; meeting rooms; heated pool. **Services:** valet laundry. **All Rooms:** free movies, refrigerators, cable TV. **Some Rooms:** Fee: VCP's, whirlpools. **Cards:** AE, CB, DI, DS, MC, VI. Ⓓ ⊗

DAYS INN — Rates Subject to Change — **Phone:** 206/252-8000

◆◆◆ Motel

6/15-9/30 [CP]	1P: $45	2P/1B: $50	2P/2B: $55	XP: $5 F12
3/1-6/14 [CP]	1P: $43	2P/1B: $45	2P/2B: $50	XP: $5 F12
10/1-11/30 [CP]	1P: $40	2P/1B: $40	2P/2B: $45	XP: $5 F12
12/1-2/29 [CP]	1P: $38	2P/1B: $38	2P/2B: $40	XP: $5 F12

Location: 3 1/4 mi n of northbound I-5 exit 192; 3 1/2 mi s of southbound I-5 exit 198. 1122 N Broadway N 98201. Fax: 206/252-8000. **Terms:** Sr. discount; no pets. **Facility:** 51 rooms. 24 hour fax service. 3 stories, no elevator; exterior corridors; whirlpool. **Dining:** Restaurant nearby. **Services:** Fee: coin laundry. **All Rooms:** free movies, cable TV. **Some Rooms:** microwaves, refrigerators. Fee: whirlpools. **Cards:** AE, CB, DI, DS, MC, VI. Ⓓ ⊗

EVERETT COMFORT INN — Guaranteed Rates — **Phone:** 206/355-1570

AAA ◆◆◆ Motel

5/15-9/2 [CP]	1P: $55- 60	2P/1B: $59- 64	2P/2B: $65- 70	XP: $5 F12
3/1-5/14 & 9/3-2/29 [CP]	1P: $45- 50	2P/1B: $49- 54	2P/2B: $55- 60	XP: $5 F12

Location: On w side of I-5, exit 189, at Everett Mall. 1602 SE Everett Mall Way 98208. Fax: 206/347-3381. **Terms:** Sr. discount; reserv deposit, 3 day notice; weekly rates; no pets. **Facility:** 72 rooms. Across from Everett Mall. 2 stories; exterior corridors; heated pool, whirlpool. **Dining:** Coffee shop nearby. **Services:** Fee: airport transportation. **All Rooms:** coffeemakers, free movies, refrigerators, cable TV. **Cards:** AE, DI, DS, MC, VI. Ⓓ ⊗

EVERETT TRAVELODGE — Rates Subject to Change — **Phone:** 206/259-6141

AAA ◆◆◆ Motel

6/1-9/7	1P: $44	2P/1B: $49	2P/2B: $59	XP: $5 F17
3/1-5/31 & 9/8-2/29	1P: $39	2P/1B: $44	2P/2B: $49	XP: $5 F17

Location: 1/4 mi s on SR 529; 1 1/4 mi n of northbound I-5 exit 192; 5 1/2 mi s of southbound I-5 exit 198. 3030 Broadway 98201. Fax: 206/339-5150. **Terms:** Sr. discount; pets, dogs only, $25. **Facility:** 29 rooms. Close to hospital. 2 two-bedroom units. 2 stories; exterior corridors. **All Rooms:** coffeemakers, free movies, combo & shower baths, cable TV. **Some Rooms:** microwaves, refrigerators. **Cards:** AE, CB, DI, DS, MC, VI. Ⓓ ⊗

FARWEST MOTEL — Rates Subject to Change — **Phone:** 206/355-3007

AAA ◆◆ Motel

All Year	1P: $32- 46	2P/1B: $37- 50	2P/2B: $42- 55	XP: $5 F5

Location: From I-5 exit 189, 2 1/2 mi nw on Evergreen Way. 6030 Evergreen Way 98203. **Terms:** Reserv deposit; weekly rates; no pets. **Facility:** 20 rooms. Modest furnishings. 1 two-bedroom unit. 2 stories; interior/exterior corridors. **All Rooms:** free movies, cable TV. **Some Rooms:** 12 efficiencies, no utensils, refrigerators. Fee: whirlpools. **Cards:** AE, MC, VI. Ⓓ ⊗

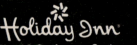

Best Western
Cascadia Inn
Just off I-5 in EVERETT
• FREE Gourmet Continental Breakfast
• Outdoor Pool and Spa
• Restaurants Nearby
206-258-4141 or 1-800-448-5544
15% Off Listed Rates

Seattle North/Everett
STAY WITH SOMEONE YOU KNOW.®
Holiday Inn®
Hotel & Conference Center
Seattle/Everett
1-800-HOLIDAY
or (206) 745-2555
✲ Great location adjacent to I-5 - close to Boeing, Alderwood & Everett malls
✲ FREE local phone calls, movie channel, & morning coffee
✲ 24 hour indoor pool & spa
✲ On-site restaurant & lounge
✲ 251 guest rooms & suites
15% Off listed rates
Not valid w/any other offer.
101 128th St. SE, Everett, WA 98208 / Exit 186 off I-5

HOLIDAY INN HOTEL & CONFERENCE CENTER SEATTLE/EVERETT Guaranteed Rates **Phone:** 206/745-2555
AAA ◆◆◆ Motor Inn
All Year 1P: $69- 95 2P/1B: $75- 101 2P/2B: $75- 101 XP: $10 F19
Location: 7 mi s at I-5 exit 186. 101 128th St SE 98208. Fax: 206/337-0707. **Terms:** Sr. discount; reserv deposit, 3 day notice; pets, $25. **Facility:** 251 rooms. 2-4 stories; interior corridors; business center, conference facilities; heated indoor pool, whirlpool; exercise room. **Dining:** Dining room; 6 am-2 & 5-10 pm, Fri & Sat-10:30 pm; $5-$15; cocktails. **Services:** PC, secretarial services; valet laundry; area transportation. Fee: airport transportation. **All Rooms:** free & pay movies, cable TV. **Some Rooms:** refrigerators. **Cards:** AE, DI, DS, JCB, MC, VI. *(See ad p A84)* (D) ⊗

MARINA VILLAGE INN Rates Subject to Change **Phone:** 206/259-4040
AAA ◆◆◆◆ Motel
All Year [CP] 1P: $82- 179 2P/1B: $82- 179 2P/2B: $82- 179 XP: $20 F16
Location: In Everett Marina Village; 3 mi nw of I-5 exit 193 northbound, exit 194 southbound. 1728 W Marine View Dr 98201. Fax: 206/252-8419. **Terms:** Sr. discount; reserv deposit, 7 day notice; no pets. **Facility:** 27 rooms. Upstairs inn; rooms overlook Port Gardner Bay or Marina Village. 2 stories; interior corridors; meeting rooms. **Dining:** Restaurant nearby. **Services:** valet laundry. **All Rooms:** coffeemakers, free movies, refrigerators, cable TV. **Some Rooms:** whirlpools. Fee: VCP's. **Cards:** AE, DI, DS, MC, VI. (D) ⊗

RAMADA INN-EVERETT Rates Subject to Change **Phone:** 206/337-9090
AAA ◆◆ Motel
6/15-9/14 [CP] 1P: $55- 65 2P/1B: $60- 70 2P/2B: $65- 70 XP: $5
3/1-6/14 & 9/15-2/29 [CP] 1P: $45- 55 2P/1B: $50- 60 2P/2B: $55- 60 XP: $5
Location: E of I-5 exit 189. 9602 19th Ave SE 98208. Fax: 206/337-9090. **Terms:** Sr. discount; reserv deposit, 3 day notice; small pets only, $25 dep req. **Facility:** 116 rooms. 2 stories; exterior corridors; meeting rooms; heated pool, whirlpool. **Dining:** Restaurant nearby. **Services:** Fee: coin laundry, airport transportation. **All Rooms:** free movies, cable TV. **Some Rooms:** 26 kitchens, microwaves, refrigerators. Fee: VCP's. **Cards:** AE, CB, DI, DS, MC, VI. (D) ⊗

WELCOME MOTOR INN Rates Subject to Change **Phone:** 206/252-8828
AAA ◆◆◆ Motel
All Year 1P: $37- 42 2P/1B: $42- 47 2P/2B: $47- 52 XP:$5-8 F12
Location: I-5 northbound, exit 192, 3 1/4 mi nw; I-5 southbound, exit 198, 3 1/2 mi sw. 1205 N Broadway 98201. Fax: 206/252-8880. **Terms:** Sr. discount; reserv deposit; no pets. **Facility:** 42 rooms. Comfortable, unpretentious rooms. 12 efficiencies, $10 extra, utensil deposit; 2 stories; exterior corridors. **Dining:** Restaurant nearby. **All Rooms:** free movies, cable TV. **Some Rooms:** microwaves, refrigerators. **Cards:** AE, DI, DS, MC, VI. (D) ⊗

WESTCOAST EVERETT PACIFIC HOTEL AAA Special Value Rates **Phone:** 206/339-3333
AAA ◆◆◆ Hotel
All Year 1P: $88- 98 2P/1B: $98- 108 2P/2B: $108- 118 XP: $10
Location: I-5 northbound exit 193; I-5 southbound exit 194. 3105 Pine St 98201. Fax: 206/259-1547. **Terms:** Reserv deposit; small pets only, $25 dep req. **Facility:** 247 rooms. Spacious rooms. 7 stories; interior corridors; conference facilities; heated indoor pool, sauna, whirlpool; exercise room. **Dining:** Dining room; 6 am-10 pm, Fri & Sat-11 pm; $9-$12; cocktails. **Services:** valet laundry; area transportation. Fee: airport transportation. **All Rooms:** cable TV. Fee: movies. **Some Rooms:** coffeemakers, microwaves, refrigerators. **Cards:** AE, CB, DI, DS, MC, VI. (D) (S) ⊗

RESTAURANTS

CONFETTI'S **Dinner:** $11-$20 **Phone:** 206/258-4000
◆◆ Steak and Seafood
Location: In Everett Marina Village; 3 mi nw of I-5 exit 193 northbound, exit 194 southbound. 1722 W Marina View Dr 98201. **Hours:** 4 pm-10 pm, Fri & Sat-11 pm, Sun 3:30 pm-10 pm; 9/1-5/31 4 pm-9:30 pm, Fri & Sat-10:30 pm, Sun 3:30 pm-10 pm.Closed: 11/23 & 12/25. **Features:** children's menu; early bird specials; carryout; cocktails & lounge; a la carte. Dockside dining. **Cards:** AE, DI, DS, MC, VI. ⊗

GERRY ANDAL'S RESTAURANT **Dinner:** $11-$20 **Phone:** 206/355-7999
◆◆ American
Location: From jct I-5, exit 189W; Everett Mall Way 1 1/2 mi. 620 SE Everett Mall Way 98204. **Hours:** 11 am-10 pm. Closed major holidays. **Reservations:** suggested; weekends. **Features:** children's menu; senior's menu; carryout; cocktails & lounge; entertainment; minimum charge-$4 weekends. Country western family fun oriented ranch house dining featuring steaks, barbecue ribs & weekend buffet. **Cards:** AE, DI, DS, MC, VI. ⊗

PASSPORT RESTAURANT **Dinner:** $11-$20 **Phone:** 206/259-5037
AAA ◆◆ Ethnic
Location: Downtown, cross sts Oakes & Lombard. 1507 Wall St 98201. **Hours:** 11 am-3 & 5:30-10 pm, Fri-11 pm, Sat 5:30 pm-11 pm. Closed major holidays & Sun. **Reservations:** suggested; weekends. **Features:** No A/C; carryout; cocktails & lounge. Your ticket to a culinary journey. Featuring Cajun, Korean, Greek, Japanese, Middle Eastern, Russian & several other cuisine types. Smoke free premises. **Cards:** MC, VI. ⊗

FEDERAL WAY—64,000

LODGINGS

BEST WESTERN FEDERAL WAY EXECUTEL AAA Special Value Rates **Phone:** 206/941-6000
AAA ◆◆◆ Motor Inn
6/16-9/15 1P: $93 2P/1B: $99 2P/2B: $99 XP: $6 F18
3/1-6/15 & 9/16-2/29 1P: $89 2P/1B: $95 2P/2B: $95 XP: $6 F18
Location: 1/2 mi w of I-5 exit 143; 1/4 mi n of S 320th across from Sea-Tac Mall. 31611 20th Ave S 98003. Fax: 206/941-9500. **Terms:** Credit card guarantee; small pets only, $50 dep req. **Facility:** 112 rooms. 3 stories; interior corridors; meeting rooms; heated pool, whirlpool. **Dining & Entertainment:** Restaurant; 6 am-2 & 5-10 pm; $7-$14; cocktails/lounge. **Services:** health club privileges; valet laundry; airport transportation. **All Rooms:** free movies, cable TV. **Some Rooms:** coffeemakers, refrigerators. **Cards:** AE, CB, DI, DS, JCB, MC, VI. (D) ⊗

HOLIDAY INN EXPRESS Rates Subject to Change **Phone:** 206/838-3164
Motel
4/1-9/30 1P: $59 2P/1B: $65 2P/2B: $65 XP: $6 F18
3/1-3/31 & 10/1-2/29 1P: $53 2P/1B: $59 2P/2B: $59 XP: $6 F18
Too new to rate; **Location:** From I-5 exit Hwy 18, w 1 mi. 34827 Pacific Hwy S 98003. Fax: 206/838-3168. **Terms:** credit card guarantee; no pets. **Facility:** 54 rooms. Rating withheld pending completion of construction. Scheduled to open fall of 1994. 2 stories; exterior corridors. **All Rooms:** free movies, cable TV. **Some Rooms:** whirlpools. **Cards:** AE, CB, DI, DS, JCB, MC, VI. (D) (S) ⊗

RESTAURANT

BILLY MCHALE'S **Dinner:** $11-$20 **Phone:** 206/839-4200
◆◆ American
Location: Off I-5 at exit S 320th w 3/4 mi. 1800 S 320th 98003. **Hours:** 11 am-10 pm, Fri-11 pm, Sat 11:30 am-11 pm, Sun 11:30 am-10 pm. Closed: 11/23 & 12/25. **Features:** children's menu; senior's menu; carryout; cocktails & lounge; a la carte. Barbecue ribs, chicken, steaks, prime rib & fresh seafood. **Cards:** AE, MC, VI. ⊗

FERNDALE—5,400

LODGING

SLATER HERITAGE HOUSE Guaranteed Rates **Phone:** 360/384-4273
◆◆ Bed & Breakfast
All Year [BP] 2P/1B: $60- 85 2P/2B: $60- 85 XP: $10 D4
Location: Off I-5 exit 262, 1 mi e. 1371 W Axton Rd 98248. Fax: 360/384-4273. **Terms:** Sr. discount; reserv deposit, 3 day notice; weekly rates; no pets. **Facility:** 4 rooms. Turn-of-the-century Victorian home. 2 stories; interior corridors; smoke free premises. **All Rooms:** shower & tub baths, no A/C, no phones, no TVs. **Some Rooms:** whirlpools. **Cards:** MC, VI. Ⓓ ⊗

RESTAURANT

SEA GALLEY **Dinner:** $11-$20 **Phone:** 360/384-1601
◆◆ Seafood
Location: I-5 exit 262 at Axton Rd. 5659 Barrett Rd 98248. **Hours:** 8 am-10 pm, Fri-11 pm, Sat 9 am-11 pm, Sun 9 am-10 pm. Closed: 11/23 & 12/25. **Features:** Sunday brunch; children's menu; senior's menu; health conscious menu items; carryout; salad bar; cocktails & lounge; a la carte. Dining room with view of farmlands & Mt Baker. **Cards:** AE, MC, VI. ⊗

FIFE—3,900

LODGINGS

BEST WESTERN EXECUTIVE INN Guaranteed Rates **Phone:** 206/922-0080
AAA ◆◆◆ Motor Inn
3/1-5/31 1P: $58- 68 2P/1B: $63- 73 2P/2B: $74- 79 XP: $8 F16
6/1-9/30 1P: $62- 73 2P/1B: $67- 78 XP: $8 F16
10/1-2/29 1P: $60- 72 2P/1B: $65- 77 XP: $8 F16
Location: I-5 exit 137. 5700 Pacific Hwy E 98424. Fax: 206/922-6439. **Terms:** Small pets only, $15, $25 dep req. **Facility:** 140 rooms. 4 stories; interior corridors; conference facilities; heated indoor pool, sauna, whirlpool. **Dining & Entertainment:** Dining room, coffee shop; 6 am-11 pm, Sun 7 am-10 pm; $6-$19; cocktails; entertainment. **Services:** secretarial services; valet laundry; area transportation, airport transportation. **All Rooms:** free & pay movies, cable TV. **Some Rooms:** honor bars, coffeemakers, microwaves, refrigerators. **Cards:** AE, CB, DI, DS, JCB, MC, VI. Ⓓ ⊗

DAYS INN Rates Subject to Change **Phone:** 206/922-3500
AAA ◆◆ Motor Inn
All Year 1P: $40- 55 2P/1B: $45- 55 2P/2B: $50- 70 XP: $5
Location: S I-5 at exit 136, n I-5 at exit 136B. 3021 Pacific Hwy E 98424. Fax: 206/922-0203. **Terms:** Sr. discount; reserv deposit; weekly/monthly rates; pets, $5. **Facility:** 186 rooms. 3 stories; interior corridors; meeting rooms; heated pool. **Dining:** Also, Fife City Bar & Grill, see separate listing. **Services:** Fee: coin laundry. **All Rooms:** free & pay movies, cable TV. **Some Rooms:** refrigerators. **Cards:** AE, DI, DS, JCB, MC, VI. Ⓓ ⊗

ECONO LODGE AAA Special Value Rates **Phone:** 206/922-0550
AAA ◆◆ Motel
5/1-9/30 1P: $33 2P/1B: $37 2P/2B: $42 XP: $4 F18
3/1-4/30 & 10/1-2/29 1P: $30 2P/1B: $34 2P/2B: $36 XP: $4 F18
Location: Off I-5 at exit 136. 3518 Pacific Hwy E 98424. Fax: 206/922-3203. **Terms:** Weekly/monthly rates; pets, $10. **Facility:** 81 rooms. Free local calls. 3 stories, no elevator; exterior corridors; heated pool. **Services:** Fee: coin laundry, airport transportation. **All Rooms:** free movies, cable TV. **Some Rooms:** refrigerators. Fee: VCP's. **Cards:** AE, CB, DI, DS, JCB, MC, VI. *(See ad p A157)* Ⓓ ⊗

HOMETEL INN Rates Subject to Change **Phone:** 206/922-0555
AAA ◆◆ Motor Inn
6/15-9/30 1P: $36 2P/1B: $40 2P/2B: $44 XP: $4 F12
3/1-6/14 & 10/1-2/29 1P: $30 2P/1B: $34 2P/2B: $42 XP: $4 F12
Location: I-5 at exit 136, 1/4 mi n. 3520 Pacific Hwy E 98424. Fax: 206/922-0690. **Terms:** Sr. discount; reserv deposit, 3 day notice; weekly rates; small pets only, $10, $50 dep req. **Facility:** 102 rooms. 2 stories; exterior corridors; heated pool. **Dining & Entertainment:** Dining room; 11 am-10 pm; $9-$15; cocktails/lounge. **Services:** Fee: coin laundry, airport transportation. **All Rooms:** free movies, cable TV. **Some Rooms:** microwaves, refrigerators. **Cards:** AE, DS, MC, VI. *(See color ad below)* Ⓓ ⊗

Travelodge Hotel
Enjoy HBO with our Remote Control Color TV's
• AAA, Senior, Entertainment, Military, Weekly Discount • Coin Laundry
• 100 A/C Rooms • Swimming Pool • HBO, CNN, ESPN • Microfridge
• 2 Miles from Tacoma Dome • Restaurant & Lounge • Free Local Call
3520 Pacific Hwy. E., Tacoma (Fife), WA 98424 • (206) 922-0555 • Fax: (206) 922-0690
Quality at Economical Prices • Reservations: 1-800-258-3520

GET THE ROYAL TREAT-MENT!
AAA Discount Rates

Custom decorated guest rooms (1/2 are non-smoking), cozy **Castle Fife Restaurant** serves cocktails, library room w/ fire-place, indoor spa or in-room private jac-uzzi, SHOWTIME & ESPN, free local calls, convenient to malls & Point Defiance Zoo & Aquarium. I-5 exit 137.
ROYAL COACHMAN MOTOR INN
5805 Pacific Hwy. E., Tacoma 98424 **Reservations:**
1-800-422-3051 or 206-922-2500

ROYAL COACHMAN INN Rates Subject to Change **Phone:** 206/922-2500
◆◆◆ Motor Inn
All Year 1P: $54- 59 2P/1B: $59- 67 2P/2B: $59- 67 XP: $6 F12
Location: 4 blks nw of I-5, exit 137; at Fife. 5805 Pacific Hwy E 98424. Fax: 206/922-6443. **Terms:** Sr. discount; reserv deposit; pets, $25 dep req. **Facility:** 94 rooms. 2 stories; exterior corridors; meeting rooms; whirlpools. **Dining:** Dining room; 6 am-8:30 pm, Fri-9:30 pm, Sat 7 am-9:30 pm, Sun 7 am-7 pm; $7-$21; cocktails. **Services:** Fee: coin laundry. **All Rooms:** free movies, cable TV. **Some Rooms:** 2 kitchens. Fee: microwaves, refrigerators, VCP's, whirlpools. **Cards:** AE, DI, DS, MC, VI. *(See color ad p A86)* (D)

TACOMA COMFORT INN Rates Subject to Change **Phone:** 206/926-2301
◆◆ Motel
All Year [CP] 1P: $51 2P/1B: $56 2P/2B: $56 XP: $5 F16
Location: Off I-5 at exit 137. 5601 Pacific Hwy E 98424. Fax: 206/922-1179. **Terms:** Sr. discount; pets, $15. **Facility:** 71 rooms. 2 stories; exterior corridors; whirlpool; exercise room. **Dining:** Restaurant nearby. **Services:** Fee: coin laundry. **All Rooms:** free movies, combo & shower baths, cable TV. **Some Rooms:** 5 efficiencies, no utensils. Fee: whirlpools. **Cards:** AE, DI, DS, JCB, MC, VI. (D) (S)

TRAVELERS INN Rates Subject to Change **Phone:** 206/922-9520
◆ Motel
All Year 1P: $32 2P/1B: $38 2P/2B: $38 XP: $4 F11
Location: I-5, exit 136. 3100 Pacific Hwy E 98424. Fax: 206/922-2002. **Terms:** Sr. discount; reserv deposit, 10 day notice; no pets. **Facility:** 116 rooms. 2 stories; exterior corridors; heated pool. **Dining:** Restaurant nearby. **All Rooms:** free movies, cable TV. **Some Rooms:** refrigerators. **Cards:** AE, CB, DI, DS, MC, VI. (D)

RESTAURANT

FIFE CITY BAR & GRILL **Dinner:** $11-$20 **Phone:** 206/922-9555
◆ American
Location: At Days Inn. 3025 Pacific Hwy E 98424. **Hours:** 6 am-9:30 pm, Sun 8 am-9 pm; in winter 7 am-9 pm, Sun-8 pm. Closed major holidays. **Features:** children's menu; early bird specials; cocktails & lounge. Very attractive casual dining room serving homestyle cooking. **Cards:** AE, MC, VI.

FORKS—2,900

LODGINGS

FORKS MOTEL Rates Subject to Change **Phone:** 360/374-6243
◆◆◆ Motel
All Year 1P: $38- 65 2P/1B: $42- 65 2P/2B: $45- 70 XP: $5 F12
Location: 4 blks s on US 101. 351 Forks Ave S 98331 (PO Box 510). Fax: 360/374-6760. **Terms:** Reserv deposit, 4 day notice; no pets. **Facility:** 73 rooms. Close to Hoh Rain Forest. Large rooms. 9 two-bedroom units. 8 kitchens, $5 extra. 37 units with 2 beds; 9 units with 3 beds; 2 stories; exterior corridors; meeting rooms; heated pool. **Dining:** Restaurant nearby. **Services:** Fee: coin laundry. **All Rooms:** combo & shower baths, cable TV. **Some Rooms:** A/C, coffeemakers, microwaves, refrigerators, whirlpools. **Cards:** AE, DI, DS, MC, VI. *(See color ad below)* (D)

MANITOU LODGE Rates Subject to Change **Phone:** 360/374-6295
◆◆ Bed & Breakfast
6/1-10/1 [BP] 1P: $57- 70 2P/1B: $57- 70 2P/2B: $57- 70 XP: $12
3/1-5/31 & 10/2-2/29 [BP] 1P: $35 2P/1B: $55- 65 2P/2B: $55- 65 XP: $12
Location: 8 mi w on Lapush Rd, then 1/2 mi n on Mora, follow signs, 1 mi. Kilmer Rd 98331 (PO Box 600). **Terms:** Reserv deposit, 3 day notice; no pets. **Facility:** 5 rooms. Within minutes of the Pacific Ocean, the Hoh Rain Forest & four rivers. 2 stories; interior corridors; smoke free premises. **Services:** airport transportation. **Recreation:** nature trails. **All Rooms:** combo & shower baths, no A/C, no phones, no TVs. **Cards:** MC, VI. (D)

MILLER TREE INN BED & BREAKFAST Guaranteed Rates **Phone:** 360/374-6806
◆ Historic Bed & Breakfast
All Year [BP] 1P: $35 2P/1B: $55 2P/2B: $55 XP: $10
Location: Downtown. 654 E Division 98331 (PO Box 953). **Terms:** Check-in 5 pm; reserv deposit; pets, $10. **Facility:** 6 rooms. 2 stories; interior corridors; smoke free premises; whirlpool. **All Rooms:** free movies, no A/C, no phones. **Some Rooms:** cable TV. **Cards:** MC, VI. (D)

OLYMPIC SUITES Rates Subject to Change **Phone:** 360/374-5400
◆ Apartment Motel
6/1-9/30 1P: $45 2P/1B: $55 2P/2B: $70 XP: $5 F12
3/1-5/31 & 10/1-2/29 1P: $40 2P/1B: $45 2P/2B: $60 XP: $5 F12
Location: 1/4 mi n; 1 blk n of US 101. 800 Olympic Dr 98331. **Terms:** Reserv deposit, 7 day notice; no pets. **Facility:** 30 rooms. 1- & 2-bedroom units with kitchen. Most with private balcony or patio. 2 stories; exterior corridors. **All Rooms:** coffeemakers, cable TV, no A/C, no phones. **Cards:** AE, DI, DS, MC, VI. *(See ad below)* (D)

PACIFIC INN MOTEL Guaranteed Rates **Phone:** 360/374-9400
◆◆ Motel
5/15-9/30 1P: $43 2P/1B: $48 2P/2B: $52 XP: $5 F12
3/1-5/14 & 10/1-2/29 1P: $38 2P/1B: $43 2P/2B: $47 XP: $5 F12
Location: 4 blks s on US 101. 352 Hwy 101 98331 (PO Box 1997). Fax: 360/374-9402. **Terms:** Credit card guarantee; no pets. **Facility:** 34 rooms. 2 stories; exterior corridors. **Services:** Fee: coin laundry. **All Rooms:** combo & shower baths, cable TV. **Cards:** AE, CB, DI, DS, MC, VI. (D)

FORKS MOTEL
P.O. Box 510
Forks, WA 98331

73 Deluxe Units, Queen/King Beds, Kitchenettes, Refrigerators, Microwaves, Handicap Rooms, Non-Smoking Rooms, some Air Conditioning, Cable TV, Heated Pool, Laundry Facility, D.D. Phones, Affordable Rates, On Hwy. 101, Major Credit Cards Welcome, (206) 374-6243.

RESERV TOLL FREE **1-800-544-3416**
FAX (206) 374-6760

QUIET OFF-HIWAY SETTING
Central to major attractions on the
BEAUTIFUL OLYMPIC PENINSULA
Your Hd'qrs while you hike the trails, comb the beaches, watch whales, dig clams, revel in the rain forest, soak in the hot springs or just plain sight-see.
"Enjoy a suite at motel rates."
(360) 374-5400 1-800-262-3433 (RESERVATIONS ONLY)

RESTAURANT

SMOKEHOUSE RESTAURANT — **Dinner:** $11-$20 — **Phone:** 360/374-6258

◆ Steak and Seafood

Location: 1 mi n on US 101 at LaPush jct. 193161 Hwy 101 98331. **Hours:** 11 am-10 pm, Fri & Sat-11 pm. Closed: 12/25. **Reservations:** suggested; weekends. **Features:** children's menu; carryout; salad bar; cocktails & lounge. Family restaurant specializing in seafood & prime rib. Senior discount portions. **Cards:** MC, VI. ⊗

FREELAND

LODGING

HARBOUR INN MOTEL — Rates Subject to Change — **Phone:** 360/331-6900

◆◆ Motel

All Year [CP] 1P: $47- 70 2P/1B: $53- 69 2P/2B: $69 XP: $5 D6

Location: 1 blk e of SR 525. 1606 Main St 98249 (PO Box 1350). **Terms:** Reserv deposit; weekly/monthly rates, 10/1-4/30; pets, $5.50, in selected rooms. **Facility:** 20 rooms. Commercial location. North end of town. Modest, clean, comfortable rooms. Kitchen units avail, $68.50-$75.50 for up 2 persons; 2 stories; exterior corridors. **Dining:** Restaurant nearby. **All Rooms:** cable TV, no A/C. **Some Rooms:** coffeemakers, 3 efficiencies, microwaves, refrigerators. **Cards:** AE, MC, VI. Ⓓ ⊗

GOLDENDALE—3,300

LODGINGS

FAR VUE MOTEL — Rates Subject to Change — **Phone:** 509/773-5881

AAA ◆◆◆ Motor Inn

All Year 1P: $43 2P/1B: $49 2P/2B: $49 XP: $6 D10

Location: 1 mi se at US 97. 808 E Simcoe Dr 98620. **Terms:** Sr. discount; credit card guarantee; weekly rates; no pets. **Facility:** 48 rooms. Rooms with view of Mt Adams & Mt Hood. 2 two-bedroom units. 2 stories; exterior corridors; heated pool. **Dining:** Restaurant; 6 am-11 pm; $3-$10; cocktails. **All Rooms:** cable TV. **Some Rooms:** coffeemakers, 2 kitchens, refrigerators. **Cards:** AE, CB, DI, DS, MC, VI. Ⓓ ⊗

PONDEROSA MOTEL — Rates Subject to Change — **Phone:** 509/773-5842

AAA ◆◆ Motel

All Year 1P: $36 2P/1B: $42 2P/2B: $47 XP: $5

Location: 1/2 mi w off US 97; off Klickitat & Goldendale exit 142. 775 E Broadway St 98620. Fax: 509/773-4049. **Terms:** Sr. discount; reserv deposit, 3 day notice; small pets only. **Facility:** 28 rooms. 2 two-bedroom units. 8 kitchens, $5 extra; 2 stories; exterior corridors. **Dining:** Restaurant nearby. **All Rooms:** cable TV. **Some Rooms:** coffeemakers, refrigerators. **Cards:** AE, DI, DS, MC, VI. Ⓓ ⊗

RESTAURANT

HIGHLAND CREEKS RESORT — **Dinner:** $11-$20 — **Phone:** 509/773-4026

AAA ◆◆◆ American

Location: At Three Creeks Lodge. 2120 Hwy 97 Satus Pass 98620. **Hours:** noon-8 pm, Fri & Sat 8 am-9 pm, Sun 8 am-8 pm. Closed: Mon-Thurs 11/1-3/31. **Reservations:** suggested. **Features:** carryout; cocktails & lounge. Terraced solarium over confluence of 2 creeks. Timbered dining room with handcrafted pine furnishings. **Cards:** AE, MC, VI. ⊗

GRAND COULEE—1,000

RESTAURANTS

THAT ITALIAN PLACE — **Dinner:** up to $10 — **Phone:** 509/633-1818

◆ Italian

Location: Hwy 174, 1 mi e of jct Hwy 155. 515 Grand Coulee Blvd 99133. **Hours:** 11 am-10 pm. Closed: Sun, 1/1, 11/23 & 12/25. **Features:** children's menu; beer & wine only; a la carte. Pastas, New York pizza & sandwiches. Casual family dining. Smoke free premises. **Cards:** AE, DI, DS, MC, VI. ⊗

WILDLIFE RESTAURANT — **Dinner:** up to $10 — **Phone:** 509/633-1160

◆◆ American

Location: 113 Midway, Box 47 99133. **Hours:** 7 am-9 pm. Closed: 11/23 & 12/25. **Features:** cocktails. Varied menu featuring steaks & seafood; relaxed family dining. **Cards:** MC, VI. ⊗

GREENBANK

LODGING

GUEST HOUSE BED & BREAKFAST COTTAGES — Rates Subject to Change — **Phone:** 360/678-3115

AAA ◆◆◆◆ Cottage

3/16-10/31 & Fri-Sun 11/1-2/29 [BP] 2P/1B: $135- 285 2P/2B: $210

3/1-3/15 & Mon-Thurs 11/1-2/29 [BP] 2P/1B: $115- 150 2P/2B: $180

Location: 1 mi s off SR 525. 3366 S Hwy 525 Rd 98253. **Terms:** Age restrictions may apply; check-in 4 pm; reserv deposit, 30 day notice; 2 night min stay, weekends; no pets. **Facility:** 7 rooms. Outstanding accommodations including 1920's farmhouse, 5 cottages & lodge at edge of Wildlife Conservation Pond. Most with fireplace, some with balcony. 1 two-bedroom unit. Exterior corridors; smoke free premises; heated pool, whirlpool; exercise room. **All Rooms:** coffeemakers, kitchens, cable TV, VCP's, whirlpools, no phones. **Some Rooms:** A/C. **Cards:** AE, DS, MC, VI. Ⓓ ⊗

HOODSPORT

LODGING

GLEN-AYR CANAL RESORT — Guaranteed Rates — **Phone:** 360/877-9522

AAA ◆◆◆ Motel

4/1-9/30 2P/1B: $55- 58 2P/2B: $63- 68 XP: $10

3/1-3/31 & 10/1-2/29 2P/1B: $50- 55 2P/2B: $58- 63 XP: $10

Location: 1 1/2 mi n on US 101. N 25381 Hwy 101 98548. **Terms:** Reserv deposit, 3 day notice; no pets. **Facility:** 16 rooms. 2 suites, $85; 2 stories; exterior corridors; whirlpool; boat dock. **Services:** Fee: coin laundry. **Recreation:** fishing, claming, crabbing, shrimp & oyster beds in season. **All Rooms:** free movies, cable TV, no A/C, no phones. **Some Rooms:** coffeemakers, 2 kitchens, microwaves, refrigerators. **Cards:** DS, MC, VI. Ⓓ ⊗

IT'S REFUNDABLE.

A security deposit on certain personal items may be required upon your entry into Canada. Read Border Information.

HOQUIAM—9,000

LODGINGS

LYTLE HOUSE BED & BREAKFAST AAA Special Value Rates **Phone:** 360/533-2320
◆◆ 5/1-9/30 [BP] 1P: $60 2P/1B: $75- 105 2P/2B: $75- 105 XP: $15
Historic Bed & Breakfast 3/1-4/30 & 10/1-2/29 [BP] 1P: $55 2P/1B: $65- 95 2P/2B: $65- 95 XP: $15
Location: On Chenault; 2 blks w of SR 101. 509 Chenault 98550. Fax: 360/533-4025. **Terms:** Age restrictions may apply; reserv deposit; weekly rates; no pets. **Facility:** 8 rooms. Very attractive historical home, circa late 1800's. Victorian with balcony overlooking bay. 3 stories; interior corridors; smoke free premises. **All Rooms:** no A/C. **Some Rooms:** phones, cable TV. **Cards:** MC, VI. *(See color ad below)* (D) (S) ⊗

SNORE & WHISKER MOTEL AAA Special Value Rates **Phone:** 360/532-5060
AAA ◆ Motel All Year 1P: $35 2P/1B: $40 2P/2B: $45 XP: $2-5
Location: On Hwy 101S; 1 mi s of town. 3031 Simpson Ave 98550. **Terms:** Credit card guarantee; weekly rates; pets, $2-$5. **Facility:** 11 rooms. 1 two-bedroom unit. 1 story; exterior corridors. **All Rooms:** shower baths, cable TV, no A/C. **Some Rooms:** 4 efficiencies, refrigerators. **Cards:** AE, DS, MC, VI. (D) ⊗

WESTWOOD INN Rates Subject to Change **Phone:** 360/532-8161
AAA ◆◆ Motel All Year 1P: $40- 65 2P/1B: $40- 65 2P/2B: $55- 75 XP: $7 D6
Location: On US 101 southbound. 910 Simpson Ave 98550. Fax: 360/533-6067. **Terms:** Sr. discount; credit card guarantee; weekly/monthly rates; small pets only, $5. **Facility:** 65 rooms. Extremely large rooms. 2 two-bedroom units. 2 stories; exterior corridors. **Dining:** Restaurant nearby. **Services:** Fee: coin laundry. **All Rooms:** free movies, cable TV, no A/C. **Some Rooms:** coffeemakers, 13 kitchens, refrigerators. **Cards:** AE, DI, MC, VI. *(See color ad below)* (D) ⊗

RESTAURANT

DUFFY'S RESTAURANT 3 **Dinner:** up to $10 **Phone:** 360/532-1519
AAA ◆◆ American
Location: 1 blk e on US 101. 825 Simpson Ave 98550. **Hours:** 6 am-10 pm, Fri & Sat-11 pm, Sun 7 am-10 pm. **Features:** children's menu; carryout; cocktails & lounge. Good sized portions. **Cards:** AE, DI, DS, MC, VI. ⊗

ISSAQUAH—7,800 (See SEATTLE & VICINITY ACCOMMODATIONS spotting map pages A136 & A137; see index starting on page A134)

RESTAURANT

JAY-BERRY'S GOURMET PIZZA & PASTA & LOUNGE **Dinner:** $11-$20 **Phone:** 206/392-0808 (133)
◆◆ Italian
Location: At jct I-90 & exit 17 se via Gilman Blvd; next to Gilman Village. 385 NW Gilman Blvd 98027. **Hours:** 11 am-10 pm, Fri-11 pm, Sat noon-11 pm, Sun 4 pm-10 pm. Closed: 4/9, 11/23 & 12/25. **Features:** children's menu; senior's menu; carryout; cocktails & lounge. Several creative & unique pork & vegetarian dishes. Served in a casual setting. **Cards:** DS, MC, VI. ⊗

KALALOCH

LODGING

KALALOCH LODGE Rates Subject to Change **Phone:** 360/962-2271
◆◆ 6/17-10/9 1P: $60- 105 2P/1B: $60- 105 2P/2B: $60- 105 XP: $10 F5
Lodge 4/30-6/16 & 10/10-10/30 1P: $60- 100 2P/1B: $60- 100 2P/2B: $60- 100 XP: $10 F5
3/1-4/29 & 10/31-2/29 1P: $59- 100 2P/1B: $59- 100 2P/2B: $59- 100 XP: $10 F5
Location: On Hwy 101. 98331 (HC 80 Box 1100). **Terms:** Check-in 4 pm; reserv deposit, 3 day notice; pets, $10. **Facility:** 58 rooms. 8 two-bedroom units. 2 stories; interior/exterior corridors; meeting rooms; beach. **Dining:** Restaurant; 7 am-8:30 pm; $9-$18; cocktails. **All Rooms:** coffeemakers, combo & shower baths, no A/C, no phones, no TVs. **Some Rooms:** 20 efficiencies, 14 kitchens, no utensils, refrigerators, whirlpools. **Cards:** AE, MC, VI. (D)

KELSO—11,800

LODGINGS

BEST WESTERN ALADDIN Rates Subject to Change **Phone:** 360/425-9660
AAA ◆◆◆ Motel 5/15-9/30 1P: $45- 50 2P/1B: $49- 55 2P/2B: $53- 60 XP: $5 F12
3/1-5/14 & 10/1-2/29 1P: $40- 45 2P/1B: $44- 50 2P/2B: $48- 55 XP: $5 F12
Location: E side of town at the foot of Cowlitz Bridge. 310 Long Ave 98626. Fax: 360/577-9436. **Terms:** Reserv deposit, 3 day notice; weekly/monthly rates; small pets only, $5. **Facility:** 78 rooms. 2 stories; interior corridors; meeting rooms; heated indoor pool, whirlpool. **All Rooms:** cable TV. **Some Rooms:** 20 efficiencies, microwaves, refrigerators. Fee: VCP's. **Cards:** AE, CB, DI, DS, JCB, MC, VI. (D) ⊗

Lytle House Bed & Breakfast
509 Chenault, Hoquiam, WA 98550
Don't you deserve the extraordinary?
Rooms $65-$95 double,
Evening Dessert & Full Breakfast
Near beach and rain forest.
800-677-2320

Westwood Inn
1-800-562-0994
910 SIMPSON AVE.
HOQUIAM, WA 98550
(206) 532-8161 ◆◆
65 SPACIOUS ROOMS • FREE CABLE HBO • SUITES • H/C
NON-SMOKER ROOMS • HONEYMOON SUITES
SOME ROOMS WITH KITCHENS • EXCEPTIONAL QUALITY
TWO PHONES PER ROOM • SENIOR DISCOUNTS
BUS PARKING • CONFERENCE ROOM WITH KITCHEN AVAILABLE

COMFORT INN Rates Subject to Change **Phone:** 360/425-4600
AAA ◆◆◆ Motel
All Year [CP] 1P: $55 2P/1B: $60 2P/2B: $60 XP: $5 F18
Location: I-5, exit 39. 440 Three Rivers Dr 98626. Fax: 360/423-0762. **Terms:** Sr. discount; no pets. **Facility:** 57 rooms. 5 rooms with whirlpool, $70 for 1 person; $75 for 2 persons; 2 stories; interior corridors; meeting rooms; heated indoor pool, whirlpool. **All Rooms:** free movies, cable TV. **Some Rooms:** microwaves, refrigerators. Fee: VCP's. **Cards:** AE, CB, DI, DS, JCB, MC, VI.

KELSO INN MOTEL Rates Subject to Change **Phone:** 360/636-4610
AAA ◆ Motel
All Year 1P: $29- 33 2P/1B: $34- 39 2P/2B: $38- 43 XP: $5 F13
Location: 1 blk n of SR 4; I-5 exit 40. 505 N Pacific 98626. **Terms:** Sr. discount; reserv deposit, 3 day notice; weekly rates; small pets only, $5, also $5 dep req. **Facility:** 51 rooms. 2 stories; interior/exterior corridors. **All Rooms:** cable TV. **Some Rooms:** 2 efficiencies, no utensils, refrigerators. **Cards:** AE, MC, VI.

RED LION INN Rates Subject to Change **Phone:** 360/636-4400
◆◆◆ Motor Inn
All Year 1P: $69- 79 2P/1B: $79- 89 2P/2B: $79- 89 XP: $10 F16
Location: I-5 exit 39. 510 Kelso Dr 98626. Fax: 360/425-3296. **Terms:** Reserv deposit, 3 day notice; pets. **Facility:** 163 rooms. 2 stories; exterior corridors; conference facilities; heated pool, whirlpool. **Dining & Entertainment:** Dining room, coffee shop; 6:30 am-10 pm, Fri & Sat-11 pm; $7-$12; cocktails/lounge; 24-hour room service. **Services:** data ports. **All Rooms:** cable TV. Fee: movies. **Some Rooms:** refrigerators. **Cards:** AE, DI, DS, MC, VI.

KENNEWICK—42,200

LODGINGS

CAVANAUGH'S AT COLUMBIA CENTER AAA Special Value Rates **Phone:** 509/783-0611
◆◆◆ Motor Inn
All Year 1P: $63- 73 2P/1B: $73- 83 2P/2B: $73- 83 XP: $5 F18
Location: 1/2 mi s of Columbia Center Blvd exit off SR 240. 1101 N Columbia Center Blvd 99336. Fax: 509/735-3087. **Terms:** Reserv deposit, 3 day notice; pets. **Facility:** 162 rooms. Fine cedar woodwork throughout facilities. 2 stories; interior corridors; conference facilities; heated pool, whirlpool. **Dining & Entertainment:** Dining room; 6:30 am-2 & 5-9 pm, Fri-10 pm, Sat & Sun 7 am-2 & 5-9 pm; $8-$18; cocktails/lounge; 24-hour room service; entertainment. **Services:** airport transportation. **All Rooms:** free movies, cable TV. **Some Rooms:** refrigerators. Fee: VCP's. **Cards:** AE, DI, DS, MC, VI. *(See color ad p A151)*

COMFORT INN Rates Subject to Change **Phone:** 509/783-8396
◆◆◆ Motel
All Year [CP] 1P: $47- 59 2P/1B: $52- 64 2P/2B: $64 XP: $5 F17
Location: 1/2 mi w off SR 240 on Columbia Center Blvd exit. 7801 W Quinault 99336. Fax: 509/783-8396. **Terms:** Sr. discount; credit card guarantee; pets, $11. **Facility:** 56 rooms. 2 stories; interior corridors; meeting rooms; heated indoor pool, whirlpool. **Services:** Fee: coin laundry. **All Rooms:** combo & shower baths, cable TV. **Some Rooms:** microwaves, refrigerators, whirlpools. **Cards:** AE, CB, DI, DS, JCB, MC, VI. Roll in showers.

KENNEWICK SILVER CLOUD INN Rates Subject to Change **Phone:** 509/735-6100
◆◆◆ Motel
6/15-9/30 [CP] 1P: $57 2P/1B: $63 2P/2B: $67 XP: $6 F18
3/1-6/14 & 10/1-2/29 [CP] 1P: $52 2P/1B: $58 2P/2B: $62 XP: $6 F18
Location: 1/2 mi s off SR 240 on Columbia Center Blvd exit. 7901 W Quinalt Ave 99336. Fax: 509/735-3084. **Terms:** Reserv deposit, 3 day notice; no pets. **Facility:** 125 rooms. 4 stories; interior corridors; meeting rooms; 2 pools (1 heated, 1 indoor), whirlpools. **Services:** data ports; guest laundry. **All Rooms:** free movies, refrigerators, cable TV. **Some Rooms:** microwaves, whirlpools. **Cards:** AE, DI, DS, MC, VI.

RAMADA INN CLOVER ISLAND AAA Special Value Rates **Phone:** 509/586-0541
AAA ◆◆◆ Motor Inn
3/1-10/31 1P: $68- 87 2P/1B: $73- 92 2P/2B: $83- 93 XP: $8 F
11/1-2/29 1P: $56- 75 2P/1B: $61- 80 2P/2B: $71- 81 XP: $8 F
Location: From SR 395, Port of Kennewick exit, 1 mi e on Columbia Dr, then left on Washington St. 99336 (435 Clover Island). Fax: 509/586-6956. **Terms:** Reserv deposit, 3 day notice; no pets. **Facility:** 149 rooms. View of Columbia River at Port of Kennewick on Clover Island. 4 stories; interior corridors; meeting rooms; heated pool, sauna, whirlpool; boat dock. **Dining & Entertainment:** Dining room; 24 hours; $6-$17; cocktails/lounge. **Services:** airport transportation. Fee: coin laundry. **Recreation:** fishing. **All Rooms:** coffeemakers, cable TV. **Some Rooms:** refrigerators, whirlpools. **Cards:** AE, CB, DI, DS, JCB, MC, VI.

SHANIKO INN Rates Subject to Change **Phone:** 509/735-6385
AAA ◆◆ Apartment Motel
All Year 1P: $45 2P/1B: $50 2P/2B: $53 XP: $5 F12
Location: 1/2 mi w of SR 395; 1 blk n of Clearwater Ave. 321 N Johnson St 99336. Fax: 509/736-6631. **Terms:** Sr. discount; reserv deposit; weekly/monthly rates; small pets only, $4. **Facility:** 47 rooms. 3 stories, no elevator; interior corridors; heated pool. **Dining:** Restaurant nearby. **Services:** winter plug-ins. Fee: coin laundry. **All Rooms:** kitchens, free movies, cable TV. **Some Rooms:** coffeemakers, microwaves. **Cards:** AE, CB, DI, DS, MC, VI.

TAPADERA BUDGET INN Rates Subject to Change **Phone:** 509/783-6191
AAA ◆◆ Motel
All Year 1P: $36- 46 2P/1B: $40- 54 2P/2B: $44- 60 XP: $7 F12
Location: On SR 14, 1 mi sw of jct SR 240 & SR 395. 300A N Ely 99336. Fax: 509/735-3854. **Terms:** Sr. discount; reserv deposit, 3 day notice; weekly rates; small pets only. **Facility:** 61 rooms. 2 stories; exterior corridors; heated pool. **Dining:** Restaurant nearby. **Services:** winter plug-ins. Fee: coin laundry. **All Rooms:** free movies, cable TV. **Some Rooms:** refrigerators. Fee: VCP's. **Cards:** AE, CB, DI, DS, MC, VI.

RESTAURANTS

BLACKBERRY'S RESTAURANT **Dinner:** up to $10 **Phone:** 509/735-7253
◆◆ American
Location: W end; off Clearwater Ave. 329 W Kellogg 99336. **Hours:** 7 am-9 pm, Mon-2 pm, Sat from 8 am, Sun 8 am-2 pm. Closed major holidays. **Features:** children's menu; carryout; wine only. Casual family dining, home-style meals. Smoke free premises. **Cards:** AE, DI, DS, MC, VI.

MA MA VALLONE'S ITALIAN GRILL **Dinner:** $21-$30 **Phone:** 509/736-1085
◆◆ Italian
Location: On Clearwater Ave; at jct SR 240 & SR 395 3/4 mi s. 2800 W Clearwater Ave 99336. **Hours:** 11 am-10 pm, Fri & Sat-11 pm, Sun noon-10 pm. Closed: 12/25. **Features:** children's menu; cocktails & lounge. Casual, Italian dining. Large selections of steaks. **Cards:** AE, MC, VI.

KENT—38,000 (See SEATTLE & VICINITY ACCOMMODATIONS spotting map pages A136 & A137; see index starting on page A134)

LODGINGS

BEST WESTERN CHOICELODGE Rates Subject to Change **Phone:** 206/854-8767 181
◆◆◆ Motel
4/1-8/31 [CP] 1P: $72- 82 2P/1B: $82- 92 2P/2B: $82- 92 XP: $6 F18
3/1-3/31 & 9/1-2/29 [CP] 1P: $60- 67 2P/1B: $65- 72 2P/2B: $65- 72 XP: $6 F18
Location: Off I-5 exit 149 southbound, 149A exit northbound e via Kent/Des Moines Rd to Meeker St. 24415 Russell Rd 98032. Fax: 206/850-7667. **Terms:** Sr. discount; no pets. **Facility:** 75 rooms. 2 stories; interior corridors; meeting rooms; sauna, whirlpool; exercise room. **Services:** data ports; airport transportation. **All Rooms:** coffeemakers, free movies, cable TV. **Some Rooms:** refrigerators, whirlpools. **Cards:** AE, CB, DI, DS, MC, VI.

BEST WESTERN PONY SOLDIER MOTOR INN Rates Subject to Change **Phone:** 206/852-7224 182
◆◆◆ Motel
All Year [CP] 1P: $66- 71 2P/1B: $69- 74 2P/2B: $74- 79 XP: $5 F12
Location: SR 167 N Central exit. 1233 N Central 98032. Fax: 206/854-9631. **Terms:** Sr. discount; reserv deposit; small pets only. **Facility:** 85 rooms. 2 stories; exterior corridors; heated pool, sauna, whirlpool; exercise room. **Dining:** Restaurant nearby. **Services:** data ports; guest laundry; airport transportation. **All Rooms:** free movies, refrigerators, cable TV. **Some Rooms:** microwaves. **Cards:** AE, CB, DI, DS, JCB, MC, VI.

CYPRESS INN AAA Special Value Rates **Phone:** 206/395-0219 183
◆◆◆ Motor Inn
All Year [CP] 1P: $67- 69 2P/1B: $74- 77 2P/2B: $74- 77 XP: $7 F13
Location: 1/4 mi n of SR 167, 84th Ave S exit. 22218 84th Ave S 98032. Fax: 206/395-0116. **Terms:** Reserv deposit; weekly/monthly rates; pets, $25 dep req. **Facility:** 120 rooms. 2 stories; interior/exterior corridors; meeting rooms; heated pool, whirlpool. **Dining & Entertainment:** Restaurant; 6 am-11 pm; $6-$11; cocktails/lounge. **Services:** airport transportation. Fee: coin laundry. **All Rooms:** free & pay movies, cable TV. **Some Rooms:** 24 kitchens, refrigerators, whirlpools. **Cards:** AE, CB, DI, DS, MC, VI.

DAYS INN OF KENT Rates Subject to Change **Phone:** 206/854-1950 184
◆◆ Motel
All Year [CP] 1P: $55 2P/1B: $60 2P/2B: $65 XP: $5 F16
Location: I-5 exit 149 via Kent/Des Moines Rd, 2 1/4 mi to Meeker St. 1711 W Meeker St 98032. Fax: 206/859-1018. **Terms:** Sr. discount; reserv deposit, 3 day notice; pets, $10. **Facility:** 82 rooms. 2 stories; interior corridors; heated pool. **Dining:** Restaurant nearby. **Services:** airport transportation. Fee: coin laundry. **All Rooms:** free movies. **Some Rooms:** 2 kitchens, refrigerators. **Cards:** AE, CB, DI, DS, JCB, MC, VI.

HOMECOURT ALL SUITE HOTEL Guaranteed Rates **Phone:** 206/395-3800 185
◆◆◆ Suite Motel
All Year [CP] 1P: $79 2P/1B: $79 2P/2B: $92
Location: Off I-5 at exit 152; follow Orilla Rd. 6329 S 212th 98032. Fax: 206/395-3022. **Terms:** Sr. discount; reserv deposit, 10 day notice; monthly rates; no pets. **Facility:** 152 rooms. Deluxe suites blended with traditional service. 76 two-bedroom units. 2 stories; exterior corridors; meeting rooms; heated pool, whirlpools; 1 tennis court; exercise room. **Services:** data ports; airport transportation. Fee: coin laundry. **All Rooms:** coffeemakers, kitchens, microwaves, refrigerators, cable TV. Fee: movies. **Some Rooms:** whirlpools. **Cards:** AE, DI, DS, MC, VI. Independent.

NEW BEST INN Rates Subject to Change **Phone:** 206/870-1280 180
◆◆ Motel
6/1-8/31 1P: $42 2P/1B: $50 2P/2B: $65 XP: $6
3/1-5/31 & 9/1-2/29 1P: $40 2P/1B: $45 2P/2B: $45 XP: $5
Location: At jct I-5, exit 149B. 23408 30th Ave 98032. **Terms:** Reserv deposit; pets, $5. **Facility:** 27 rooms. 2 stories; exterior corridors. **Services:** Fee: coin laundry. **All Rooms:** free movies, cable TV. **Some Rooms:** 4 efficiencies, microwaves, refrigerators. **Cards:** AE, CB, DI, DS, MC, VI.

VAL U INN Guaranteed Rates **Phone:** 206/872-5525 186
◆◆◆ Motel
All Year [CP] 1P: $51 2P/1B: $51 2P/2B: $57 XP: $5 F12
Location: 1/4 mi n of SR 167, exit 84th Ave S. 22420 84th Ave S 98032. Fax: 206/872-8458. **Terms:** Sr. discount; reserv deposit; weekly/monthly rates; small pets only, $5. **Facility:** 92 rooms. 3 stories; interior corridors; meeting rooms; whirlpool. **Dining:** Restaurant nearby. **Services:** airport transportation. Fee: coin laundry. **All Rooms:** free movies, cable TV. **Some Rooms:** microwaves, refrigerators. Fee: VCP's. **Cards:** AE, DI, DS, MC, VI. *(See ad below)*

RESTAURANTS

ROSE'S HIGHWAY INN **Dinner:** $11-$20 **Phone:** 206/839-7277 129
◆◆ American
Location: From I-5 at exit 147, 3/4 mi nw. 26915 Pacific Hwy S 98032. **Hours:** 11:30 am-2 & 4-9 pm, Sat 12:30 pm-9 pm, Sun 12:30 pm-8 pm. Closed: Mon & 12/25. **Features:** children's menu; senior's menu; carryout; cocktails & lounge; a la carte. Country hospitality, home cooking in an old farm house. Friendly feeling. **Cards:** MC, VI.

VELVET GOOSE **Dinner:** up to $10 **Phone:** 206/854-7706 130
◆ American
Location: In the Mad Hatter's Antique Mall. 25748 101st Ave SE 98031. **Hours:** 11 am-8 pm, Sat from 8 am, Sun 8 am-3 pm. Closed: Mon, 1/1, 11/23 & 12/25. **Features:** beer & wine only. American dining in a warm charming colonial setting with antique memorabilia. **Cards:** AE, DS, MC, VI.

VAL-U INN MOTEL
KENT
• Whirlpool • Complimentary Continental Breakfast
• Guest Laundry • Remote Control Satellite TV
• Non-Smoking Rooms
For Reservations, call: 1-800-443-7777
22420 84th South. Kent, WA 98032 (206) 872-5525

KIRKLAND—40,100 (See SEATTLE & VICINITY ACCOMMODATIONS spotting map pages A136 & A137; see index starting on page A134)

LODGINGS

BEST WESTERN ARNOLD'S MOTOR INN AAA Special Value Rates **Phone:** 206/822-2300 (134)
AAA ◆◆◆ Motel
6/1-9/1 [CP] 1P: $62- 78 2P/1B: $62- 81 2P/2B: $62- 81 XP: $6 F18
3/1-5/31 & 9/2-2/29 [CP] 1P: $56- 68 2P/1B: $62- 78 2P/2B: $62- 78 XP: $6 F18
Location: In Totem Lake area; I-405 exit 20 southbound, exit 20A northbound. 12223 NE 116th 98034. Fax: 206/889-9616. **Terms:** Reserv deposit; small pets only, $50 dep req. **Facility:** 110 rooms. Spacious rooms with natural wood, muted colors. 3 stories; exterior corridors; meeting rooms; heated pool, whirlpool. **Dining:** Restaurant nearby. **Services:** Fee: coin laundry, airport transportation. **All Rooms:** free movies, cable TV. **Some Rooms:** microwaves, refrigerators. Fee: VCP's, whirlpools. **Cards:** AE, CB, DI, DS, MC, VI. Roll in showers. (D) ⊗

CLARION INN Rates Subject to Change **Phone:** 206/821-2202 (131)
AAA ◆◆◆ Suite Motel
All Year [CP] 1P: $95 2P/1B: $105 2P/2B: $105 XP: $10 D
Location: Northbound I-405 exit 20B, southbound I-405 exit 20, 1 mi via 129th, Totem Lake Way 120th. 12233 NE Totem Lake Way 98034. Fax: 206/820-3457. **Terms:** Sr. discount; reserv deposit, 3 day notice; BP, MAP available; no pets. **Facility:** 59 rooms. Spacious suites. 2 stories; interior corridors; designated smoking area; meeting rooms; heated pool, sauna, whirlpool; exercise room. **Services:** valet laundry. Fee: airport transportation. **All Rooms:** free movies, refrigerators, safes, cable TV. **Cards:** AE, CB, DI, DS, MC, VI. (D) (S) ⊗

LA QUINTA INN Rates Subject to Change **Phone:** 206/828-6585 (135)
◆◆◆ Motel
5/27-10/14 [CP] 1P: $57- 63 2P/1B: $64- 70 2P/2B: $64 XP: $8 F18
3/1-5/26 & 10/15-2/29 [CP] 1P: $50- 56 2P/1B: $57- 63 2P/2B: $57 XP: $8 F18
Location: 1 blk ne of jct SR 520 & Bellevue Way. 10530 NE Northup Way 98033. Fax: 206/822-8722. **Terms:** Small pets only. **Facility:** 119 rooms. 4 stories; interior corridors; meeting rooms; small heated pool. **Dining:** Restaurant nearby. **Services:** valet laundry. Fee: airport transportation. **All Rooms:** free & pay movies, cable TV. **Some Rooms:** honor bars. Fee: microwaves, refrigerators, VCP's. **Cards:** AE, CB, DI, DS, MC, VI. (D) ⊗

SHUMWAY MANSION Guaranteed Rates **Phone:** 206/823-2303 (132)
◆◆◆ Historic Bed & Breakfast
All Year [BP] 2P/1B: $65- 95 XP: $10
Location: From I-405 southbound exit 20, 2 mi via ne 124 St & 98th Ave NE; northbound exit 20A, 1 1/2 mi via NE 16th St & 99th Pl. 11410 99th Pl NE 98033. Fax: 206/822-0421. **Terms:** Credit card guarantee; no pets. **Facility:** 8 rooms. A 1909 antique furnished 22 room mansion. 2 stories; interior corridors; smoke free premises; meeting rooms. **Services:** health club privileges. **All Rooms:** combo & shower baths, no A/C. **Cards:** AE, MC, VI. (D) ⊗

SILVER CLOUD INN AT KIRKLAND Rates Subject to Change **Phone:** 206/821-8300 (133)
◆◆◆ Motel
6/15-9/30 [CP] 1P: $53- 58 2P/1B: $59- 64 2P/2B: $63 XP: $6 F12
3/1-6/14 & 10/1-2/29 [CP] 1P: $48- 53 2P/1B: $54- 59 2P/2B: $58 XP: $6 F12
Location: 1 blk e of I-405, northbound exit 20B, southbound exit 20. 12202 NE 124th St 98034. Fax: 206/823-1218. **Terms:** Sr. discount; reserv deposit, 3 day notice; no pets. **Facility:** 99 rooms. 3 stories, no elevator; interior corridors; heated pool, whirlpool; exercise room. **Dining:** Restaurant nearby. **Services:** guest laundry. **All Rooms:** free movies, refrigerators, cable TV. **Some Rooms:** microwaves. **Cards:** AE, DI, DS, MC, VI. (D) ⊗

THE WOODMARK HOTEL ON LAKE WASHINGTON Rates Subject to Change **Phone:** 206/822-3700 (136)
AAA ◆◆◆◆ Hotel
All Year 1P: $110- 180 2P/1B: $120- 195 2P/2B: $120- 195 XP: $10 F18
Location: At Carillon Point on Lake Washington Blvd; from jct SR 520 & 908, 1 mi nw. 1200 Carillon Point 98033. Fax: 206/822-3699. **Terms:** Check-in 4 pm; credit card guarantee; no pets. **Facility:** 100 rooms. Many rooms provide view of Lake Washington. 3 stories; interior corridors; meeting rooms; boat dock. **Dining & Entertainment:** Carillon Room, see separate listing; entertainment. **Services:** valet laundry; area transportation; valet parking. Fee: airport transportation. **Recreation:** swimming. Rental: boats. **All Rooms:** honor bars, coffeemakers, cable TV, VCP's. **Some Rooms:** whirlpools. **Cards:** AE, DI, MC, VI. (D) ⊗

RESTAURANTS

BISTRO PROVENCAL **Dinner:** $11-$20 **Phone:** 206/827-3300 (93)
◆◆◆ French
Location: 1 mi w of I-405, exit 18. 212 Central Way 98033. **Hours:** 5:30 pm-10:30 pm. Closed major holidays. **Reservations:** suggested; weekends. **Features:** carryout; cocktails; a la carte. Fine dining in atmosphere of French countryside. Specialties include fresh seafood, rack of lamb, duck & filet Casanova. Prix fixe dinner. **Cards:** AE, CB, DI, MC, VI. ⊗

CAFE JUANITA **Dinner:** $11-$20 **Phone:** 206/823-1505 (92)
◆◆◆ Italian
Location: Southbound I-405 at exit 20, 1 1/2 mi via 124th to 100th Ave, s to 120th Pl; northbound I-405 at exit 20A, 1 1/2 mi via 116th to 97th Ave, n to 120th Pl. 9702 NE 120th Pl 98034. **Hours:** 6 pm-9:15 pm. Closed: 7/4, 11/23, 12/24 & 12/25. **Reservations:** suggested. **Features:** cocktails. Very popular restaurant with seasonal menu. Fresh pasta made daily. Fresh seafood. Extensive list of Italian wines. On-premise produced house wine. Smoke free premises. **Cards:** MC, VI. ⊗

CARILLON ROOM **Dinner:** $21-$30 **Phone:** 206/827-7733 (91)
◆◆◆ American
Location: In the Woodmark Hotel. 1200 Carillon Point 98033. **Hours:** 6:30 am-10 pm, Sat & Sun from 7 am. **Reservations:** suggested. **Features:** Sunday brunch; children's menu; health conscious menu; carryout; cocktails; valet parking; a la carte. Northwest cuisine. Elegant lakeside dining. Smoke free premises. **Cards:** AE, DI, MC, VI. ⊗

KIRKLAND ROASTER & ALE HOUSE **Dinner:** $11-$20 **Phone:** 206/827-4400 (96)
◆◆◆ American
Location: I-405, exit 18, 1 mi w. 111 Central Way 98033. **Hours:** 11:30 am-9 pm, Fri & Sat-10 pm, Sun-9 pm. **Reservations:** suggested. **Features:** No A/C; children's menu; health conscious menu; carryout; cocktails & lounge; a la carte. Comfortable, casual dining featuring a vertical spit roaster. **Cards:** AE, DI, MC, VI. ⊗

OLIVE GARDEN **Dinner:** $11-$20 **Phone:** 206/820-7740 (94)
◆◆ Italian
Location: From I-405 exit NE 124th St, 1/2 mi w. 11325 NE 124th St 98034. **Hours:** 11 am-10 pm, Fri & Sat-11 pm. Closed: 11/23 & 12/25. **Features:** children's menu; health conscious menu; carryout; cocktails & lounge. Popular trattoria, superb cuisine, warm decor. **Cards:** AE, DI, DS, MC, VI. ⊗

RISTORANTE PARADISO **Dinner:** $11-$20 **Phone:** 206/889-8601 (97)
◆◆◆ Regional Italian
Location: Downtown; from I-405 exit 18, 1 mi w. 120 A Park Ln 98033. **Hours:** 11 am-2:30 & 5-10:30 pm, Sun from 5 pm. Closed major holidays. **Reservations:** suggested. **Features:** No A/C; children's menu; beer & wine only. Nouvelle cuisine of Italian regions. **Cards:** AE, DI, MC, VI. ⊗

LACEY—19,300

LODGINGS

CAPITAL INN MOTEL AAA Special Value Rates **Phone:** 360/493-1991
◆◆◆ Motel
6/15-10/15 [CP] 2P/1B: $56 2P/2B: $66 XP: $5 F5
3/1-6/14 & 10/16-2/29 [CP] 2P/1B: $52 2P/2B: $62 XP: $5 F5
Location: Off I-5 at exit 109. 120 College St SE 98503. Fax: 360/493-1991. **Terms:** Weekly/monthly rates; small pets only, $5. **Facility:** 83 rooms. 3 stories, no elevator; interior corridors; meeting rooms; saunas; exercise room. **Dining:** Restaurant nearby. **Services:** Fee: coin laundry. **All Rooms:** free movies, combo & shower baths, cable TV. **Some Rooms:** microwaves, refrigerators. **Cards:** AE, DI, DS, MC, VI.
Roll in showers. (D) (S)

COMFORT INN Rates Subject to Change **Phone:** 360/456-6300
◆◆◆ Motel
All Year [CP] 1P: $65- 75 2P/1B: $75- 85 2P/2B: $75- 85 XP: $5 F18
Location: Off I-5 at exit 109; nw of interstate. 4700 Park Center Ave NE 98516. Fax: 360/456-7423. **Terms:** Sr. discount; reserv deposit, 60 day notice; no pets. **Facility:** 69 rooms. 3 stories; interior corridors; meeting rooms; heated indoor pool, whirlpool. **Services:** data ports. **All Rooms:** free movies, combo & shower baths, cable TV. **Some Rooms:** microwaves, refrigerators. Fee: VCP's. **Cards:** AE, CB, DI, DS, JCB, MC, VI.
Roll in showers. (D) (S)

RESTAURANT

THE RESTAURANT AT PANORAMA CITY **Dinner:** $11-$20 **Phone:** 360/456-0111
◆ American
Location: Off I-5 at exit 108, 1 1/4 mi s on Slater Kinney Rd. 150 Circle Dr 98503. **Hours:** 9-10 am, 11:30-3 & 4:30-7 pm, Fri & Sat-8 pm, Sun 11 am-4 pm. **Features:** children's menu; health conscious menu; cocktails. Inexpensive, relaxed casual family dining. **Cards:** MC, VI.

LA CONNER—700

LODGINGS

THE HERON IN LA CONNER Rates Subject to Change **Phone:** 360/466-4626
◆◆◆ Bed & Breakfast
All Year [CP] 1P: $65- 125 2P/1B: $65- 125
Location: Off Hwy 20, 4 mi s of Hwy 20 via La Conner-Whitney Rd at e edge of town. 117 Maple Ave 98257. **Terms:** Credit card guarantee; no pets. **Facility:** 12 rooms. A friendly Victorian style country inn. 2 stories; interior corridors; whirlpool. **All Rooms:** cable TV, no A/C. **Some Rooms:** Fee: whirlpools. **Cards:** MC, VI.
(D)

HOTEL PLANTER AAA Special Value Rates **Phone:** 360/466-4710
◆◆◆ Historic Hotel
All Year 1P: $70- 110 2P/1B: $70- 110 XP: $10
Location: Downtown; S 1st & Morris sts. 715 1st St 98257. Fax: 360/466-1320. **Terms:** Age restrictions may apply; reserv deposit, 3 day notice; no pets. **Facility:** 12 rooms. A historic inn built in early 1900's; modern ambiance. All rooms are located on 2nd floor. 2 stories; interior corridors; smoke free premises; street parking only; whirlpool. **All Rooms:** combo & shower baths, cable TV, no A/C. **Some Rooms:** Fee: whirlpools. **Cards:** AE, MC, VI.
(D)

LA CONNER CHANNEL LODGE AAA Special Value Rates **Phone:** 360/466-1500
◆◆◆ Motel
All Year [CP] 1P: $132- 199 2P/1B: $132- 199 2P/2B: $132- 199 XP: $20 F12
Location: On the Channel; downtown 1st & Morris sts. 205 N 1st St 98257. Fax: 360/466-1525. **Terms:** No pets. **Facility:** 41 rooms. Boat dock & deck for relaxing. 1 two-bedroom unit. 3 stories; interior corridors; designated smoking area; meeting rooms; boat ramp. **All Rooms:** coffeemakers, free movies, refrigerators, cable TV, no A/C. **Some Rooms:** Fee: whirlpools. **Cards:** AE, DI, MC, VI.
(D) (S)

LA CONNER COUNTRY INN AAA Special Value Rates **Phone:** 360/466-3101
◆◆◆ Motor Inn
All Year [CP] 1P: $81- 121 2P/1B: $81- 121 2P/2B: $81- 121 XP: $20 F12
Location: Downtown, 2nd & Morris sts. 107 S 2nd St 98257. Fax: 360/466-5902. **Terms:** Reserv deposit, 5 day notice; pets. **Facility:** 28 rooms. Turn-of-the-century decor. Fireplaces. 2 two-bedroom units. 2 stories; interior/exterior corridors; meeting rooms. **Dining & Entertainment:** Dining room; 11:30 am-2:30 & 5-9:30 pm, Fri & Sat-10 pm; $13-$18; cocktail lounge. **All Rooms:** free movies, combo & shower baths, cable TV, no A/C. **Some Rooms:** radios. **Cards:** AE, DI, MC, VI.
(D)

RIDGEWAY BED & BREAKFAST Rates Subject to Change **Phone:** 360/428-8068
◆◆◆ Historic Bed & Breakfast
All Year [BP] 1P: $70- 90 2P/1B: $75- 95 2P/2B: $95 XP: $25
Location: Southbound I-5 exit 230; 8 mi sw via Hwy 20 & Best Rd; northbound I-5 at exit 221 11 mi nw via Fir Island & Best rds. 1292 McLean Rd 98257 (PO Box 475). **Terms:** Age restrictions may apply; credit card guarantee, 5 day notice; weekly rates, 9/15-3/15; package plans; no pets. **Facility:** 5 rooms. A 1928 Dutch Colonial brick farmhouse in the Skagit tulip & daffodil country. 2 stories; interior corridors; smoke free premises. **Services:** complimentary evening beverages. **All Rooms:** no A/C, no phones, no TVs. **Cards:** AE, DS, MC, VI. (D)

RESTAURANTS

FARMHOUSE INN RESTAURANT **Dinner:** up to $10 **Phone:** 360/466-4411
◆◆ American
Location: 4 mi n on US 20. 1376 La Conner-Whitney Rd 98273. **Hours:** 7 am-10 pm, Fri & Sat-11 pm. Closed: 12/25. **Features:** children's menu; senior's menu; health conscious menu; carryout; cocktails & lounge; a la carte. Family restaurant with open oak finished country dining room serving home style cuisine. Daily specials. **Cards:** DS, MC, VI.

THE LIGHT HOUSE INN **Dinner:** $11-$20 **Phone:** 360/466-3147
◆◆ American
Location: Downtown. 512 S 1st 98257. **Hours:** 11:30 am-9 pm, Fri & Sat-10 pm. Closed: 1/1, 12/24 for dinner & 12/25. **Reservations:** suggested. **Features:** children's menu; health conscious menu; carryout; salad bar; cocktails & lounge. Dining with a view of the channel. Deck dining also avail. **Cards:** DS, MC, VI.

LANGLEY—800

LODGINGS

BOAT YARD INN Guaranteed Rates **Phone:** 360/221-5120
◆◆◆ Motel
5/30-10/1 1P: $145- 165 2P/1B: $145- 165 2P/2B: $145- 165 XP: $10 F12
3/1-5/29 & 10/2-2/29 1P: $125- 145 2P/1B: $125- 145 2P/2B: $125- 145 XP: $10 F12
Location: East end of town on the waterfront. 200 Wharf St 98260 (PO Box 866). Fax: 360/221-5124. **Terms:** Reserv deposit; 2 night min stay, weekends; no pets. **Facility:** 9 rooms. Studio & loft units. 4 two-bedroom units. 2 stories; exterior corridors. **Recreation:** fishing. **All Rooms:** coffeemakers, kitchens, free movies, combo & shower baths, cable TV, no A/C, no phones. **Some Rooms:** VCP's. **Cards:** AE, DI, MC, VI.
(D) (S)

EAGLES NEST INN Guaranteed Rates **Phone:** 360/221-5331

◆◆◆ Bed & Breakfast

All Year [BP] 1P: $85- 105 2P/1B: $95- 115 2P/2B: $105- 115 XP: $15

Location: 1 3/4 mi n. 3236 E Saratoga Rd 98260. Fax: 360/221-5331. **Terms:** Age restrictions may apply; reserv deposit, 7 day notice; no pets. **Facility:** 4 rooms. Excellent view of water & wooded hills. Breathtaking views of Mt Baker, Camano Island & Saratoge Passage. Closed Christmas week. 2 stories; interior/exterior corridors; smoke free premises; whirlpool. **All Rooms:** shower baths, cable TV, VCP's, no phones. **Cards:** DS, MC, VI. (D) ⊗

THE INN AT LANGLEY Rates Subject to Change **Phone:** 360/221-3033

◆◆◆ Motel

All Year [CP] 1P: $165- 245 2P/1B: $165- 245 XP: $25

Location: Center. 400 First St 98260 (PO Box 835). Fax: 360/221-3033. **Terms:** Age restrictions may apply; reserv deposit; 2 night min stay, weekends; no pets. **Facility:** 24 rooms. A northwest inn built into a bluff offering waterfront view. 4 stories, no elevator; exterior corridors; designated smoking area; meeting rooms. **All Rooms:** coffeemakers, free movies, refrigerators, cable TV, whirlpools, no A/C. **Some Rooms:** VCP's. **Cards:** AE, MC, VI. (D) (S) ⊗

TWICKENHAM HOUSE INN BED & BREAKFAST AAA Special Value Rates **Phone:** 360/221-2334

◆◆◆ Bed & Breakfast

All Year [BP] 2P/1B: $85- 120 2P/2B: $90 XP: $15

Location: 4 mi n from ferry landing at Clinton, to Maxwelton Rd, e to Langley Rd. 5023 Langley Rd 98206. **Terms:** Age restrictions may apply; reserv deposit, 14 day notice; no pets. **Facility:** 6 rooms. English-style country inn on 10 secluded pastoral acres with gourmet breakfast. 2 stories; interior corridors; smoke free premises. **All Rooms:** no A/C, no phones, no TVs. **Cards:** DS, MC, VI. (D) ⊗

LEAVENWORTH—1,700

LODGINGS

ALL SEASONS RIVER INN B & B Rates Subject to Change **Phone:** 509/548-1425

◆◆◆ Bed & Breakfast

Fri & Sat 3/1-5/15, 5/16-10/31, Fri & Sat 11/1-11/30 & 12/1-2/29 [BP]	1P: $85- 115	2P/1B: $95- 125	XP: $20
Sun-Thurs 3/1-5/15 & 11/1-11/30 [BP]	1P: $75- 105	2P/1B: $85- 115	XP: $20

Location: W; along Icicle River. 8751 Icicle Rd 98826 (PO Box 788). **Terms:** Age restrictions may apply; reserv deposit, 7 day notice; 2 night min stay, weekends; no pets. **Facility:** 5 rooms. Overlooking Icicle River. 2 stories; interior corridors; smoke free premises. **Recreation:** bicycles. **All Rooms:** comb, shower & tub baths, no phones, no TVs. **Some Rooms:** whirlpools. **Cards:** MC, VI. (D) ⊗

ALPEN INN Rates Subject to Change **Phone:** 509/548-4326

◆◆◆ Motel

All Year [CP] 1P: $55 2P/1B: $63 2P/2B: $66 XP: $6 D6

Location: W end. 405 W Hwy 2 98826. **Terms:** Sr. discount; reserv deposit; no pets. **Facility:** 40 rooms. 2 stories; exterior corridors; meeting rooms; heated pool, whirlpool. **Services:** winter plug-ins. **All Rooms:** cable TV. **Some Rooms:** 4 efficiencies, microwaves, refrigerators. **Cards:** AE, CB, DI, DS, MC, VI. (D) ⊗

It's more than a lodging, it's an experience!
• Authentic Bavarian elegance in a glorious Alpine setting
• 15 gracious rooms w/private baths, fireplaces, cable T.V., phones, private balconies & spas • Social room, dining room, spacious deck • Full complimentary breakfast
• Elevator • Meetings - Weddings - Receptions
Family owned & operated with the ambiance of a B & B and the privacy of a motor inn.
AlpenRose Inn
500 Alpine Place • Bavarian Village • Leavenworth, WA 98826 • 1-800-582-2474

Bayern on the River LEAVENWORTH *"The Bavarian Village"*

RESORT AND MOTOR INN - All rooms have private balconies overlooking the "musical" Wenatchee River with an incredible mountain view. Located in warm and cozy surroundings, just six blocks from the village for shopping. Featuring outdoor pool (May-Sept.); hot tub (all year); non-smoking rooms; cable TV; air-conditioning; phones; hospitality/conference rooms; complimentary coffee and tea; and fishing only steps away. Small pets ok. Senior and AAA member discounts.

COMING MAIFEST 1995 - EAGLE'S NEST HOFBRAU & GARDENS - outside food and entertainment at our location - families welcome. Listen to the new Bavarian Radio Station 101.1 FM KLVH.

1-800-873-3960 USA • 1-800-255-3151 CANADA SR2@ BRIDGE -E.LEAVENWORTH

GOING UP?

Expect elevators in establishments of four or more stories. We tell you in the listings if there are none.

ALPENROSE INN Rates Subject to Change **Phone:** 509/548-3000

◆◆◆ Bed & Breakfast

Fri & Sat 5/1-10/22 & 11/21-1/5 [BP] 1P: $80- 150 2P/1B: $80- 150 XP: $10
Sun-Thurs 5/1-10/22 & 11/21-1/5 [BP] 1P: $68- 125 2P/1B: $68- 125 XP: $10
Sun-Thurs 3/1-4/30, 10/23-11/20 & 1/6-2/29 [BP] 1P: $50- 98 2P/1B: $50- 98 XP: $10
Fri & Sat 3/1-4/30, 10/23-11/20 & 1/6-2/29 [BP] 1P: $60- 125 2P/1B: $60- 125 XP: $10

Location: W end of town. 500 Alpine Pl 98826. **Terms:** Reserv deposit, 3 day notice; weekly rates; no pets. **Facility:** 15 rooms. Rooms combine the ambience of the past with the present. 3 stories; interior corridors; smoke free premises; meeting rooms. **All Rooms:** combo & shower baths, cable TV. **Some Rooms:** whirlpools. **Cards:** AE, DS, MC, VI. *(See color ad p A94)* (D) (S) ⊗

BAYERN ON THE RIVER AAA Special Value Rates **Phone:** 509/548-5875

◆◆◆ Motel

3/1-12/31 1P: $59 2P/1B: $65- 75 2P/2B: $80 XP: $8 F6
1/1-2/29 1P: $49 2P/1B: $55- 65 2P/2B: $70 XP: $8 F6

Location: 6 blks e at Hwy 2 & Wenatchee River. 1505 Alpen See Strasse 98826 (PO Box 288). Fax: 509/782-4433. **Terms:** Reserv deposit, 3 day notice; small pets only, $10. **Facility:** 26 rooms. Private balconies overlooking Wenatchee River. 4 efficiencies, $79-$118; 3 stories, no elevator; exterior corridors; heated pool, whirlpool. **Recreation:** fishing. **All Rooms:** cable TV. **Cards:** AE, MC, VI. *(See color ad p A94)* (D) ⊗

BEST WESTERN ICICLE INN AAA Special Value Rates **Phone:** 509/548-7000

◆◆◆ Motel

Fri & Sat [CP] 1P: $89 2P/1B: $94 2P/2B: $94 XP: $10 F12
Sun-Thurs [CP] 1P: $79 2P/1B: $84 2P/2B: $84 XP: $10 F12

Location: W end of town. 505 W Hwy 2 98826. Fax: 509/548-7050. **Terms:** Reserv deposit; package plans; weekend rates available; no pets. **Facility:** 65 rooms. Expanded European Continental breakfast. 3 stories; interior corridors; meeting rooms; heated pool, whirlpool. **All Rooms:** combo & shower baths, cable TV. **Some Rooms:** refrigerators, whirlpools. Fee: VCP's. **Cards:** AE, DI, DS, JCB, MC, VI. Roll in showers. (D) (S) ⊗

BLACKBIRD LODGE AAA Special Value Rates **Phone:** 509/548-5800

◆◆◆ Motel

Fri & Sat 3/1-3/15 & 6/15-2/29 [CP] 1P: $79- 99 2P/1B: $79- 99 2P/2B: $79- 99 XP: $10 F12
Sun-Thurs 3/1-3/15, 3/16-6/14 & Sun-Thurs 6/15-2/29 [CP] 1P: $59- 79 2P/1B: $69- 89 2P/2B: $69- 89 XP: $10 F12

Location: Downtown. 305 8th 98826. Fax: 509/548-7134. **Terms:** Reserv deposit, 3 day notice; no pets. **Facility:** 16 rooms. Mountain view. Several rooms have a view deck & fireplace. 1 two-bedroom unit. 3 stories; interior corridors; smoke free premises. **Dining:** Restaurant nearby. **All Rooms:** cable TV. **Some Rooms:** efficiency, no utensils. (D) ⊗

BOSCH GARTEN AAA Special Value Rates **Phone:** 509/548-6900

◆◆◆ Bed & Breakfast

All Year [BP] 1P: $70 2P/1B: $85 2P/2B: $85 XP: $15

Location: E end of town. 9846 Dye Rd 98826. Fax: 509/548-6076. **Terms:** Age restrictions may apply; reserv deposit, 7 day notice; no pets. **Facility:** 3 rooms. 2 stories; interior corridors; smoke free premises; whirlpool. **All Rooms:** shower baths, cable TV, no phones. **Cards:** AE, MC, VI. (D) ⊗

CANYONS INN AAA Special Value Rates **Phone:** 509/548-7992

◆◆ Motel

All Year 1P: $61 2P/1B: $61 2P/2B: $75 XP: $10 F6

Location: 1/4 mi w on US 2. 185 Hwy 2 98826. **Terms:** Reserv deposit; pets, $10. **Facility:** 32 rooms. Commercial area. 3 two-bedroom units. 2 stories; exterior corridors; heated indoor pool, whirlpool. **All Rooms:** combo & shower baths, cable TV. **Some Rooms:** coffeemakers, whirlpools. **Cards:** AE, CB, DI, DS, MC, VI. *(See ad below)* (D) ⊗

DER RITTERHOF MOTOR INN Guaranteed Rates **Phone:** 509/548-5845

◆◆◆ Motel

All Year 2P/1B: $63 2P/2B: $69 XP: $8

Location: 1/4 mi w on US 2. 190 Hwy 2 98826. **Terms:** Sr. discount; reserv deposit, 7 day notice; pets. **Facility:** 52 rooms. 1 two-bedroom unit. 6 efficiencies, $6 extra; 2 stories; exterior corridors; meeting rooms; putting green; heated pool, whirlpools. **Dining:** Restaurant nearby. **All Rooms:** cable TV. **Some Rooms:** coffeemakers. **Cards:** AE, MC, VI. *(See color ad below)* (D) ⊗

ENZIAN MOTOR INN Rates Subject to Change **Phone:** 509/548-5269

◆◆◆ Motel

All Year [BP] 1P: $76- 165 2P/1B: $86- 165 2P/2B: $90 XP: $10 F5

Location: Downtown. 590 Hwy 2 98826. Fax: 509/548-5269. **Terms:** Reserv deposit, 7 day notice; no pets. **Facility:** 104 rooms. Very attractive Bavarian design & furnishing. Some rooms with balcony. City & mountain views. 9 rooms with fireplace & spa; 2-3 stories; interior corridors; meeting rooms; heated indoor pool, whirlpools. **Dining:** Restaurant nearby. **Recreation:** downhill skiing. **All Rooms:** combo & shower baths, cable TV. **Some Rooms:** whirlpools. **Cards:** AE, DI, DS, MC, VI. Roll in showers. (D) ⊗

The Canyons Inn of Leavenworth

1-800-693-1225 US & Canada

Indoor Heated Pool • Fireplace, Family and Jacuzzi Suites
Outdoor Hot Tub • 2 blocks to downtown
15% discount off guaranteed listed rates for AAA Menbers

Der Ritterhof MOTOR INN

US HIGHWAY 2 LEAVENWORTH, WA 98826
(509) 548-5845 - 1-(800)-255-5845 (RESERVATIONS)

B.B.Q PITS
HEATED POOL
AIR CONDITIONED
PUTTING GREEN
VOLLEYBALL
DIRECT DIAL PHONES
CABLE COLOR TV
HOT TUB

THE EVERGREEN INN — Rates Subject to Change — **Phone:** 509/548-5515
AAA ◆◆ Motel
All Year [CP] 1P: $40- 60 2P/1B: $50- 90 2P/2B: $55- 120 XP: $10
Location: 2 blks e; 1 blk s of US 2. 1117 Front St 98826. Fax: 509/548-6556. **Terms:** Reserv deposit, 14 day notice, 30 days in Dec; small pets only, $10, $20 dep req. **Facility:** 41 rooms. Bavarian decor in quiet setting. 22 two-bedroom units. 4 units with fireplace, $75-$125; 2 stories; interior/exterior corridors; meeting rooms; whirlpools; sun deck. Rental: bicycles. **All Rooms:** combo & shower baths, cable TV. **Some Rooms:** A/C, coffeemakers, 12 efficiencies, no utensils, microwaves, refrigerators, phones, whirlpools. **Cards:** AE, CB, DI, DS, MC, VI. (D) ⊗

HAUS ROHRBACH PENSION — AAA Special Value Rates — **Phone:** 509/548-7024
◆◆ Bed & Breakfast
All Year [BP] 1P: $55- 150 2P/1B: $65- 160 2P/2B: $80- 160 XP:$10-20D12
Location: N of Hwy 2, 1 1/3 mi via Skill Hill Dr. 12882 Ranger Rd 98826. Fax: 509/548-5038. **Terms:** Reserv deposit, 14 day notice, 30 days in Dec; weekly rates; no pets. **Facility:** 12 rooms. A little bit of the Austrian Alps. 3 stories; interior/exterior corridors; smoke free premises; heated pool, whirlpool. **All Rooms:** no phones, no TVs. **Some Rooms:** A/C, coffeemakers, 2 efficiencies, microwaves, radios, refrigerators, whirlpools. **Cards:** AE, DI, DS, MC, VI. (D) (S) ⊗

HOTEL-PENSION ANNA — Guaranteed Rates — **Phone:** 509/548-6273
AAA ◆◆◆ Hotel
All Year [CP] 1P: $65- 150 2P/1B: $75- 165
Location: Downtown. 926 Commercial St 98826 (PO Box 127). Fax: 509/548-4656. **Terms:** Reserv deposit, 3 day notice; weekly rates; no pets. **Facility:** 15 rooms. 1 two-bedroom unit. 3 stories, no elevator; interior/exterior corridors; smoke free premises. **All Rooms:** combo & shower baths, cable TV. **Some Rooms:** whirlpools. **Cards:** AE, DS, MC, VI. (D) ⊗

LINDERHOF MOTOR INN — Guaranteed Rates — **Phone:** 509/548-5283
AAA ◆◆◆ Motel
12/3-1/3 [CP] 1P: $80- 125 2P/1B: $80- 125 2P/2B: $80- 125 XP: $11 F6
3/1-12/2 & 1/4-2/29 [CP] 1P: $68- 105 2P/1B: $68- 105 2P/2B: $72- 105 XP: $10 F6
Location: West end of town. 690 Hwy 2 98826. Fax: 509/548-6616. **Terms:** Reserv deposit, 7 day notice; no pets. **Facility:** 26 rooms. 1 block to downtown. Some rooms with fireplace. 2 stories; interior/exterior corridors; meeting rooms; heated pool, whirlpool, sun deck; rafting. **Dining:** Restaurant nearby. **Recreation:** downhill & cross country skiing. **All Rooms:** free movies, cable TV. **Some Rooms:** coffeemakers, 10 efficiencies, refrigerators, whirlpools. **Cards:** AE, CB, DI, DS, MC, VI. *(See color ad below)* (D) ⊗

OBERTAL MOTOR INN — AAA Special Value Rates — **Phone:** 509/548-5204
AAA ◆◆◆ Motel
All Year 1P: $61 2P/1B: $61 2P/2B: $75 XP: $10 F6
Location: Off Hwy 2, 1 blk from center of city. 922 Commercial St 98826. Fax: 509/548-5992. **Terms:** Reserv deposit, 14 day notice; pets, $10. **Facility:** 25 rooms. Scenic view of mountains & city. 2 fireplace units, $99; 3 stories, no elevator; exterior corridors; meeting rooms; outdoor whirlpool all year. **Dining:** Restaurant nearby. **All Rooms:** free movies, cable TV. **Some Rooms:** coffeemakers, refrigerators. **Cards:** AE, DI, DS, MC, VI. (D) ⊗

RIVER'S EDGE MOTEL — Rates Subject to Change — **Phone:** 509/548-7612
AAA ◆◆ Motel
All Year 1P: $35- 55 2P/1B: $55- 75 2P/2B: $63- 68 XP: $6
Location: 3 1/2 mi e on US 2. 8401 Hwy 2 98826. **Terms:** Reserv deposit, 7 day notice; 2 night min stay; pets, in select units. **Facility:** 23 rooms. In park like setting along Wenatchee River; outstanding river views; many electric fireplaces. 2 stories; exterior corridors; beach, heated pool, whirlpool. **Services:** winter plug-ins. **Recreation:** fishing. **All Rooms:** combo & shower baths, cable TV. **Some Rooms:** 7 kitchens. **Cards:** DS, MC, VI. (D) ⊗

RUN OF THE RIVER — Guaranteed Rates — **Phone:** 509/548-7171
◆◆◆ Bed & Breakfast
All Year [BP] 1P: $85- 135 2P/1B: $95- 145
Location: 1 mi w on E Leavenworth off Hwy 2. 9308 E Leavenworth 98826 (PO Box 285). **Terms:** Age restrictions may apply; credit card guarantee, 10 day notice; 2 night min stay, weekends; no pets. **Facility:** 6 rooms. Log lodging with panoramic view of the Cascades. 2 stories; interior corridors; smoke free premises; whirlpool. **All Rooms:** combo & shower baths, cable TV, no A/C, no phones. **Some Rooms:** coffeemakers, refrigerators, whirlpools. **Cards:** AE, DS, MC, VI. (D) ⊗

TYROLEAN RITZ HOTEL — Rates Subject to Change — **Phone:** 509/548-5455
AAA ◆◆ Motel
All Year [CP] 1P: $40- 60 2P/1B: $50- 90 2P/2B: $50- 110 XP: $10
Location: Center. 633 Front St 98826. **Terms:** Reserv deposit, 14 day notice, 30 days in Dec; small pets only, $10, $20 dep req. **Facility:** 16 rooms. 3 two-bedroom units. 2 stories; interior corridors; smoke free premises; meeting rooms. **All Rooms:** coffeemakers, refrigerators, combo & shower baths, cable TV. **Some Rooms:** whirlpools. **Cards:** AE, CB, DI, DS, MC, VI. (D) ⊗

RESTAURANTS

CAFE CHRISTA — **Dinner:** $11-$20 — **Phone:** 509/548-5074
◆◆ German
Location: Downtown. 801 Front St 98826. **Hours:** 11 am-9 pm. Closed: 1/1, 7/4, 11/23 & 12/25. **Features:** No A/C; beer & wine only. Comfortable family dining, second floor location overlooking city square. **Cards:** MC, VI. ⊗

Leavenworth The Bavarian Village INVITES YOU TO SHARE

in our Fun Festival Celebrations and special events or, reflect in the majestic alpine setting and do nothing at all.
For a complete calendar of events, lodging and dining guide, write:
Leavenworth Chamber of Commerce, P.O. Box 327, Leavenworth, WA 98826 or call 509/548-5807.

Linderhof MOTOR INN
509-548-5283 1-800-828-5680 USA & CANADA
690 HIGHWAY 2 LEAVENWORTH, WA 98826
- Fireplace & In-Room Spas
- Family Suites With Kitchenettes
- Outdoor Swimming Pool & Hot Tub
- Color TV/Showtime & Air Conditioning
- Complimentary Continental Breakfast
- Close To Town, Restaurants, & Shopping

KATZENJAMMER Dinner: $11-$20 Phone: 509/548-5826
◆◆ Location: Downtown. 221 8th 98826. Hours: 5 pm-10 pm. Closed: 11/23 & 12/25.
Steak and Seafood Reservations: suggested; weekends. Features: children's menu; salad bar; cocktails & lounge; a la carte. Full range of quality steaks & fresh seafood. Smoke free premises. Cards: MC, VI.

LONG BEACH—1,200

LODGINGS

ANCHORAGE MOTOR COURT Rates Subject to Change **Phone:** 360/642-2351
◆◆ Apartment Motel
All Year 1P: $53- 84 2P/1B: $53- 98 2P/2B: $69- 98 XP: $10
Location: 1 mi n on SR 103. 22 NW Boulevard N 98631 (Rt 1, Box 581). **Terms:** Reserv deposit, 7 day notice; 5 night min stay, in August; pets, $10. **Facility:** 10 rooms. Most units with ocean view; 6 with fireplace, dry wood provided. 5 two-bedroom units. 1 story; exterior corridors; oceanfront; beach; playground. **All Rooms:** kitchens, combo & shower baths, cable TV, no A/C, no phones. **Some Rooms:** radios. **Cards:** AE, DS, MC, VI. (D)

NENDEL'S EDGEWATER INN Rates Subject to Change **Phone:** 360/642-2311
◆◆ Motel
5/15-9/30 1P: $60- 80 2P/1B: $60- 80 2P/2B: $68- 93
3/1-5/14 & 10/1-2/29 1P: $47- 75 2P/1B: $47- 75 2P/2B: $52- 80
Location: 1/4 mi s; 3 blks w of SR 103, on beach. 409 10th St SW 98631 (PO Box 793). Fax: 360/642-8018. **Terms:** Reserv deposit; pets, $3. **Facility:** 84 rooms. 2 structures, one with elevator. Many rooms with ocean view. 6 suite units, $80-$90; 10/1-5/14 $55-$65; 3 stories; interior/exterior corridors; beachfront; whirlpool. **Dining:** Also, The Lightship Restaurant, see separate listing. **All Rooms:** free movies, cable TV, no A/C. **Some Rooms:** microwaves, refrigerators. **Cards:** AE, CB, DI, DS, MC, VI. (D)

OUR PLACE AT THE BEACH Rates Subject to Change **Phone:** 360/642-3793
◆◆ Motel
7/1-9/3 1P: $45- 54 2P/1B: $45- 54 2P/2B: $59 XP: $5
5/15-6/30 & 9/4-9/30 1P: $45- 50 2P/1B: $45- 50 2P/2B: $55 XP: $5
3/1-5/14 & 10/1-2/29 1P: $37- 45 2P/1B: $37- 45 2P/2B: $50 XP: $5
Location: S end of town. 1309 S Blvd 98631 (PO Box 266). **Terms:** Sr. discount; reserv deposit, 3 day notice; pets, $5. **Facility:** 25 rooms. 3 two-bedroom units. 2 stories; exterior corridors; sauna, steamroom, whirlpools; exercise room. **All Rooms:** free movies, cable TV, no A/C. **Some Rooms:** coffeemakers, 21 kitchens, microwaves, refrigerators. **Cards:** AE, CB, DI, DS, MC, VI. (D)

SHAMAN MOTEL Rates Subject to Change **Phone:** 360/642-3714
◆◆ Motel
7/1-8/31 1P: $69- 89 2P/1B: $69- 89 2P/2B: $74- 84 XP: $5
6/1-6/30 & 9/1-10/31 1P: $49- 69 2P/1B: $49- 69 2P/2B: $54- 74 XP: $5
4/1-5/31 1P: $54- 64 2P/1B: $54- 64 2P/2B: $59- 69 XP: $5
3/1-3/31 & 11/1-2/29 1P: $44- 59 2P/1B: $44- 59 2P/2B: $49- 59 XP: $5
Location: Downtown. 115 3rd St SW 98631 (P O Box 235). Fax: 360/642-8599. **Terms:** Reserv deposit, 7 day notice; pets, $5. **Facility:** 42 rooms. Several ocean view rooms. Some rooms with fireplace. 2 stories; exterior corridors; heated pool. **Dining:** Restaurant nearby. **All Rooms:** cable TV, no A/C. **Some Rooms:** 20 efficiencies. **Cards:** AE, CB, DI, DS, MC, VI. (D)

SUPER 8 MOTEL AAA Special Value Rates **Phone:** 360/642-8988
◆◆◆ Motel
6/30-9/16 1P: $63 2P/1B: $68 2P/2B: $73 XP: $5 F12
5/12-6/29 & 9/17-10/28 1P: $55 2P/1B: $60 2P/2B: $64 XP: $5 F12
3/1-5/11 1P: $48 2P/1B: $51 2P/2B: $54 XP: $5 F12
10/29-2/29 1P: $45 2P/1B: $48 2P/2B: $51 XP: $5 F12
Location: Downtown; SR 103. 500 Ocean Beach Blvd 98631. Fax: 360/642-8986. **Terms:** Reserv deposit, 3 day notice; CP available; 2 night min stay, on weekends; no pets. **Facility:** 50 rooms. Close to beach. 3 stories; interior corridors; meeting rooms. **Services:** Fee: coin laundry. **All Rooms:** cable TV, no A/C. Fee: VCP's. **Some Rooms:** refrigerators. **Cards:** AE, CB, DI, DS, JCB, MC, VI. (D)

RESTAURANTS

THE LIGHTSHIP RESTAURANT **Dinner:** $11-$20 **Phone:** 360/642-3252
◆◆ American
Location: At Nendels Edgewater Inn. 410 SW 10th St 98644. **Hours:** 11 am-9 pm, Sat 8:30 am-10 pm, Sun 8:30 am-9:30 pm; Oct-May 8 pm closing. Closed: 12/25. **Features:** Sunday brunch; children's menu; senior's menu; health conscious menu items; carryout; cocktails & lounge; a la carte. **Cards:** AE, DI, MC, VI.

MILTON YORK **Dinner:** up to $10 **Phone:** 360/642-2352
◆◆ Seafood
Location: Downtown; on SR 103, 1st & Pacific St. 107 Pacific St 98631. **Hours:** 7:30 am-9 pm; 7/1-8/31, 7 am-10 pm. **Features:** carryout; beer & wine only; a la carte. Family restaurant specializing in breakfast, fresh seafood & steaks. Founded in 1882 as candy shop. Homemade candies & ice cream. Full fountain. **Cards:** AE, MC, VI.

LONGVIEW—31,500

LODGINGS

HUDSON MANOR MOTEL Rates Subject to Change **Phone:** 360/425-1100
◆ Motel
All Year 1P: $26- 30 2P/1B: $32- 36 2P/2B: $34- 38 XP: $4 F12
Location: Downtown. 1616 Hudson St 98632. Fax: 360/577-2037. **Terms:** Credit card guarantee; pets, $15 dep req. **Facility:** 25 rooms. 2 stories; exterior corridors. **All Rooms:** combo & shower baths, cable TV. **Some Rooms:** 4 efficiencies, utensil deposit, microwaves, refrigerators. **Cards:** AE, DI, DS, MC, VI. (D)

LEWIS & CLARK MOTOR INN AAA Special Value Rates **Phone:** 360/423-6460
◆◆ Motel
All Year 1P: $36- 39 2P/1B: $39- 44 2P/2B: $46 XP: $6 F18
Location: Opposite Medical Center. 838 15th Ave 98632. Fax: 360/425-6875. **Terms:** Reserv deposit, 3 day notice; weekly rates; small pets only, $5. **Facility:** 32 rooms. 2 stories; exterior corridors. **Dining:** Restaurant nearby. **All Rooms:** free movies, combo & shower baths, cable TV. **Some Rooms:** 2 efficiencies, refrigerators. **Cards:** AE, CB, DI, DS, MC, VI. (D)

THE TOWNHOUSE Rates Subject to Change **Phone:** 360/423-1100
◆◆ Motel
4/1-9/30 1P: $28 2P/1B: $34 2P/2B: $38 XP: $4
3/1-3/31 & 10/1-2/29 1P: $26 2P/1B: $34 2P/2B: $34 XP: $4
Location: Downtown. 744 Washington Way 98632. Fax: 360/578-1057. **Terms:** Credit card guarantee; pets, $20 dep req. **Facility:** 28 rooms. 1 two-bedroom unit. 2 stories; exterior corridors; heated pool. **Dining:** Restaurant nearby. **All Rooms:** combo & shower baths, cable TV. **Some Rooms:** A/C, refrigerators. **Cards:** AE, DS, MC, VI. (D)

RESTAURANT

HENRI'S Dinner: $11-$20 **Phone:** 360/425-7970

AAA ◆◆ American

Location: 5 1/2 mi w on SR 4. 4545 Ocean Beach Hwy 98632. **Hours:** 11 am-10 pm, Sat from 4:30 pm. Closed major holidays & Sun. **Reservations:** suggested; weekends. **Features:** children's menu; health conscious menu items; cocktails & lounge; a la carte. Smoke free premises. **Cards:** AE, DI, DS, MC, VI. ⊗

LYNDEN—5,700

LODGING

WINDMILL INN MOTEL Rates Subject to Change **Phone:** 360/354-3424

AAA ◆◆ Motel

All Year 1P: $34- 39 2P/1B: $39- 45 2P/2B: $41- 47 XP: $4

Location: 1 1/4 mi s of Lynden jct on SR 539. 8022 Guide Meridian 98264. **Terms:** Reserv deposit, 3 day notice; pets, small dogs only, $5. **Facility:** 15 rooms. Very attractive Dutch-Country designed rooms. Exceptionally well kept. 2 two-bedroom kitchen units, $42-$70; 1 story; exterior corridors. **All Rooms:** refrigerators, combo & shower baths. **Some Rooms:** coffeemakers. **Cards:** AE, DS, MC, VI. Ⓓ ⊗

LYNNWOOD—28,700 (See SEATTLE & VICINITY ACCOMMODATIONS spotting map pages A136 & A137; see index starting on page A134)

LODGINGS

BEST WESTERN LANDMARK HOTEL & CONVENTION CENTER Rates Subject to Change **Phone:** 206/775-7447 125

AAA ◆◆◆ Motor Inn

Fri & Sat 7/1-8/31 1P: $59 2P/1B: $63 2P/2B: $65 XP: $4 F18
Sun-Thurs 7/1-8/31 1P: $55 2P/1B: $59 2P/2B: $61 XP: $4 F18
3/1-6/30 & 9/1-2/29 1P: $51 2P/1B: $55 2P/2B: $57 XP: $4 F18

Location: W of I-5 exit 181 at 44th Ave W & 200th St SW. 4300 200th St SW 98036. Fax: 206/775-8063. **Terms:** Sr. discount; reserv deposit, 10 day notice; weekly/monthly rates; small pets only, $10, $30 dep req. **Facility:** 103 rooms. Unpretentious, modest decor. Sparkling cleanliness. 5 stories; interior corridors; conference facilities; heated indoor pool, whirlpool; exercise room. **Dining & Entertainment:** Dining room, coffee shop; 6 am-10 pm, Fri & Sat-11 pm; $6-$14; cocktails/lounge; entertainment. **Services:** valet laundry. Fee: airport transportation. **All Rooms:** free movies, cable TV. **Cards:** AE, CB, DI, DS, MC, VI. Ⓓ ⊗

EMBASSY SUITES Rates Subject to Change **Phone:** 206/775-2500 123

AAA ◆◆◆ Suite Hotel

All Year [BP] 1P: $89 2P/1B: $89 2P/2B: $89 XP: $10 F12

Location: I-5 exit 181; just e of I-5. 20610 44th Ave W 98036. Fax: 206/774-0485. **Terms:** Sr. discount; check-in 4 pm; monthly rates; no pets. **Facility:** 240 rooms. 5 stories; interior corridors; conference facilities; heated indoor pool, sauna, whirlpool; exercise room. **Dining:** Dining room; 11 am-10 pm; $9-$19. **Services:** data ports, secretarial services; complimentary evening beverages. Fee: coin laundry, airport transportation. **All Rooms:** coffeemakers, efficiencies, free & pay movies, combo & shower baths, cable TV. **Some Rooms:** Fee: whirlpools. **Cards:** AE, CB, DI, DS, MC, VI. *(See ad below)* Ⓓ Ⓢ ⊗

HOLIDAY INN EXPRESS Rates Subject to Change **Phone:** 206/775-8030 124

◆◆ Motel

6/1-9/30 [CP] 1P: $45 2P/1B: $50 2P/2B: $60 XP: $5 F19
3/1-5/31 & 10/1-2/29 [CP] 1P: $40 2P/1B: $45 2P/2B: $50 XP: $5 F19

Location: Northbound I-5 exit 181, 1 mi nw; southbound I-5 exit 181, 1 mi sw. 4117 196th St SW 98036. Fax: 206/774-0344. **Terms:** Sr. discount; reserv deposit, 3 day notice; weekly rates; no pets. **Facility:** 46 rooms. 2 stories; interior corridors; meeting rooms. **Dining:** Restaurant nearby. **Services:** Fee: coin laundry. **Recreation:** swim spa. **All Rooms:** free movies, cable TV. **Some Rooms:** refrigerators. Fee: whirlpools. **Cards:** AE, CB, DI, DS, JCB, MC, VI. Ⓓ Ⓢ ⊗

HOTEL INTERNATIONAL Guaranteed Rates **Phone:** 206/771-1777 122

AAA ◆◆◆ Motor Inn

All Year 1P: $46 2P/1B: $52 2P/2B: $56 XP: $8 F15

Location: Northbound I-5 exit 181 1/2 mi to 196th, 1/2 mi w; southbound I-5 exit 181, 1 1/2 mi w on 196th. 5621 196th SW 98036. Fax: 206/776-8520. **Terms:** Sr. discount; reserv deposit, 3 day notice; weekly/monthly rates; BP available; no pets. **Facility:** 53 rooms. Lounge & karaoke entertainment. 3 stories; interior corridors; meeting rooms; whirlpool. **Dining:** Dining room; 6:30-10 am, 11-2 & 5-9 pm, Sat & Sun 7 am-noon & 5-9 pm; $7-$13; cocktails. **Services:** valet laundry; area transportation, airport transportation. **All Rooms:** cable TV. **Some Rooms:** coffeemakers, 5 efficiencies, microwaves, refrigerators. **Cards:** AE, CB, DI, DS, JCB, MC, VI. Ⓓ Ⓢ ⊗

TWICE THE HOTEL
NO. SEATTLE/LYNNWOOD

EMBASSY SUITES®
20610 44TH AVE. W.

- off I-5 at exit 181, close to Alderwood Mall, Boeing Everett Plant and 15 minutes to downtown Seattle.
- Two-room suite, with refrigerator, wet bar, microwave, and coffee maker.
- Free, full cooked-to-order breakfast each morning and a 2-hour guest reception each evening with light snacks and beverages of your choice.
- Indoor pool, sauna, whirlpool and gym.
- Free parking and kids under 12 stay free.

$89.00 SINGLE/DOUBLE 7 DAYS A WEEK

CALL (206)775-2500 or 1-800-628-0611

(See SEATTLE & VICINITY ACCOMMODATIONS spotting map pages A136 & A137)

THE RESIDENCE INN BY MARRIOTT-SEATTLE NORTH AAA Special Value Rates **Phone:** 206/771-1100 (121)
◆◆◆ Apartment Motel
6/1-8/31 [CP] 1P: $120 2P/1B: $120 2P/2B: $150- 160
3/1-5/31 & 9/1-2/29 [CP] 1P: $85 2P/1B: $85 2P/2B: $120- 130
Location: 2 blks n of Alderwood Mall Shopping Center. 18200 Alderwood Mall Blvd 98037. Fax: 206/771-6602. **Terms:** Pets, $15. **Facility:** 120 rooms. Fully equipped kitchens & wood burning fireplaces. 30 two-bedroom units. Rates for 4 persons; 2 stories; exterior corridors; meeting rooms; whirlpools, heated pool open 5/31-9/6; sports court. **Dining:** Restaurant nearby. **Services:** area transportation, within 5 mi. Fee: coin laundry, airport transportation. **All Rooms:** coffeemakers, free movies, cable TV. **Some Rooms:** Fee: VCP's. **Cards:** AE, DI, DS, MC, VI. (D) (S) ⊗

SILVER CLOUD INN AT LYNNWOOD Rates Subject to Change **Phone:** 206/775-7600 (120)
◆◆◆ Motel
7/1-10/31 [CP] 1P: $53- 55 2P/1B: $59- 61 2P/2B: $61 XP: $6 F12
3/1-6/30 & 11/1-2/29 [CP] 1P: $48- 50 2P/1B: $54- 56 2P/2B: $56 XP: $6 F12
Location: 2 blks w of I-5 exit 181 southbound; 3/4 mi ne of I-5 exit 181 northbound via 200th St SW, then 1 blk n of 196th St SW near Alderwood Mall. 19332 36th Ave W 98036. Fax: 206/771-3087. **Terms:** Sr. discount; reserv deposit, 3 day notice; no pets. **Facility:** 167 rooms. 4 stories; interior corridors; meeting rooms; whirlpools, heated pool open 5/1-9/30; exercise room. **Dining:** Restaurant nearby. **Services:** Fee: airport transportation. **All Rooms:** free movies, combo & shower baths, cable TV. **Some Rooms:** 20 efficiencies, kitchen, microwaves, refrigerators. Fee: whirlpools. **Cards:** AE, CB, DI, DS, MC, VI. (D) (S) ⊗

RESTAURANTS

BILLY MCHALE'S **Dinner:** $11-$20 **Phone:** 206/775-8500 (89)
◆◆ American
Location: W of I-5, exit 181, across from Alterwood Mall. 18430 33 Ave W 98036. **Hours:** 11 am-9:30 pm, Mon-9 pm, Fri & Sat-11 pm, Sun 10 am-9 pm. **Features:** children's menu; senior's menu; carryout; cocktails & lounge. Famous for barbecue ribs, chicken, steaks, prime rib & fresh seafood. Family dining. **Cards:** AE, MC, VI. ⊗

CAFE 196 **Dinner:** $11-$20 **Phone:** 206/774-5701 (87)
◆◆◆ Ethnic
Location: Located in Hotel International. 5621 196th SW 98036. **Hours:** 6:30-10 am, 11-2 & 5-9 pm, Fri-10 pm, Sat 6:30 am-11 & 5-10 pm, Sun 7:30 am-1 & 5-9 pm. **Reservations:** suggested. **Features:** children's menu; carryout; cocktails. Euro-Asian cuisine. Nouvelle sauces. Oriental presentation with northwest ingredients. **Cards:** AE, DI, DS, JCB, MC, VI. ⊗

THE YANKEE DINER **Dinner:** $11-$20 **Phone:** 206/775-5485 (88)
◆◆ American
Location: Northbound I-5 exit 181, 1 mi nw; southbound I-5 exit 181, 1 mi sw. 4010 196th St SW 98107. **Hours:** 7 am-10 pm, Sat 8 am-10 pm, Sun 8 am-9 pm. Closed: 12/25. **Features:** children's menu; carryout; cocktails & lounge. Old fashioned cooking. Family dining. **Cards:** AE, DS, MC, VI. ⊗

MANSON

LODGING

MOUNTAIN VIEW LODGE Rates Subject to Change **Phone:** 509/687-9505
AAA ◆◆◆ Motel
6/16-9/15 1P: $75 2P/1B: $75 2P/2B: $88
5/16-6/15 1P: $61 2P/1B: $61 2P/2B: $69
9/16-10/15 1P: $58 2P/1B: $58 2P/2B: $65
3/1-5/15 & 10/16-2/29 1P: $48 2P/1B: $48 2P/2B: $54
Location: E edge on SR 150. 25 Wapato Point Pkwy 98831 (PO Box 337). Fax: 509/687-9505. **Terms:** Reserv deposit, 7 day notice, in season; no pets. **Facility:** 30 rooms. On the north shore of Lake Chelon. 1 two-bedroom unit. Sun-Thur & winter rates may be lower; 2 stories; exterior corridors; heated pool, whirlpool. **Dining:** Restaurant nearby. **All Rooms:** free movies, refrigerators, cable TV, no phones. **Some Rooms:** coffeemakers, kitchen. **Cards:** AE, DS, MC, VI. *(See color ad p 119)* (D) ⊗

RESTAURANT

THE QUAIL RESTAURANT AT WAPATO POINT **Dinner:** $11-$20 **Phone:** 509/687-9541
◆◆ American
Location: At Wapato Point. 200 N Wuetiloquasoon 98831. **Hours:** 5 pm-10 pm. Closed: 12/16-12/31 & Tues & Wed 10/1-3/31. **Reservations:** suggested. **Features:** children's menu; health conscious menu items; carryout; salad bar; cocktails & lounge. Smoke free premises. **Cards:** MC, VI. ⊗

MARYSVILLE—10,300

LODGINGS

BEST WESTERN TULALIP INN Rates Subject to Change **Phone:** 360/659-4488
AAA ◆◆◆ Motor Inn
All Year 1P: $63 2P/1B: $71 2P/2B: $71 XP: $8 F18
Location: W of I-5 exit 199. 6128 Marine Dr 98271-6801. Fax: 360/659-5688. **Terms:** Sr. discount; reserv deposit, 3 day notice; no pets. **Facility:** 69 rooms. Many rooms with sweeping mountain view. 3 stories; interior corridors; meeting rooms; heated indoor pool, whirlpool. **Dining:** Also, Henry's Lady, see separate listing. **Services:** valet laundry. Fee: airport transportation. **All Rooms:** free movies, combo & shower baths, cable TV. **Some Rooms:** microwaves, refrigerators. Fee: VCP's, whirlpools. **Cards:** AE, CB, DI, DS, MC, VI. Roll in showers. (D) ⊗

THE VILLAGE MOTOR INN Rates Subject to Change **Phone:** 360/659-0005
AAA ◆◆◆ Motor Inn
All Year 1P: $47- 54 2P/1B: $52- 59 2P/2B: $59 XP: $5 F17
Location: E of I-5, exit 199. 235 Beech St 98270. Fax: 360/658-0866. **Terms:** Sr. discount; monthly rates, in winter; CP available; small pets only, $10. **Facility:** 45 rooms. 3 stories; interior corridors; meeting rooms. **Dining & Entertainment:** Dining room, restaurant; 24 hours; $6-$13; cocktail lounge. **All Rooms:** coffeemakers, cable TV. **Some Rooms:** Fee: microwaves, refrigerators, whirlpools. **Cards:** AE, DI, DS, MC, VI. (D) (S) ⊗

RESTAURANTS

G A MAXWELLS RESTAURANT **Dinner:** $11-$20 **Phone:** 360/653-3581
◆◆◆ American
Location: E of I-5 at exit 199. 1204 3rd St 98270. **Hours:** 7 am-11 pm. **Reservations:** suggested. **Features:** children's menu; carryout; cocktails & lounge. Family dining in a unique log lodge. Fresh homemade soup, sandwiches, steaks & seafood. **Cards:** AE, DS, MC, VI. ⊗

HENRY'S LADY **Dinner:** $11-$20 **Phone:** 360/659-3434
◆◆ American
Location: In Best Western Tulalip Inn. 6128 Marine Dr 98271. **Hours:** 7 am-9 pm, Fri & Sat-10 pm. **Features:** children's menu; senior's menu; carryout; cocktails & lounge. Very attractive dining room emphasizing Northwest seafood, steaks & prime rib. Casual breakfast & lunch atmosphere. **Cards:** AE, CB, DI, DS, MC, VI. ⊗

MERCER ISLAND—20,800

LODGING

MERCER ISLAND TRAVELODGE Rates Subject to Change **Phone:** 206/232-8000
AAA ◆◆ Motel
All Year 1P: $47 2P/1B: $58 2P/2B: $65 XP: $6 F17
Location: Center of Mercer Island on I-90; exit 7. 7645 Sunset Hwy 98040. Fax: 206/236-5261. **Terms:** Sr. discount; reserv deposit, 5 day notice; no pets. **Facility:** 35 rooms. 5 two-bedroom units. 2 stories; exterior corridors; whirlpool. **Dining:** Restaurant nearby. **Services:** Fee: coin laundry. **All Rooms:** coffeemakers, free movies, combo & shower baths, cable TV. **Some Rooms:** refrigerators. **Cards:** AE, DS, MC, VI. D ⊗

RESTAURANTS

CAFFE ITALIA **Dinner:** $11-$20 **Phone:** 206/232-9009
◆◆ Italian
Location: From I-90, exit 7. 2448 76th Ave SE 98040. **Hours:** 11 am-3 & 5-9 pm, Fri-10 pm, Sat 5 pm-10 pm, Sun 4:30 pm-9 pm. Closed: Mon, 4/16, 11/23 & 12/25. **Reservations:** suggested. **Features:** children's menu; carryout; beer & wine only. Authentic, traditional dining in casual, relaxed atmosphere. Children welcome. **Cards:** MC, VI. ⊗

MI PUEBLO **Dinner:** up to $10 **Phone:** 206/232-8750
◆◆ Mexican
Location: From I-90 exit 7, center of island, cross street Island Crest Way. 7811 SE 27th St 98040. **Hours:** 11 am-10 pm, Fri-11 pm, Sat noon-10:30 pm, Sun 4 pm-9:30 pm. Closed: 7/4, 11/23 & 12/25. **Features:** children's menu; cocktails. Located in a strip mall. Family dining in a relaxed casual setting. **Cards:** AE, MC, VI. ⊗

RENE'S **Dinner:** up to $10 **Phone:** 206/232-6607
◆◆ American
Location: Downtown; from I-90 exit 7. 7660 SE 27th St 98040. **Hours:** 11 am-9 pm, Sat 10 am-3 pm, Sun 9 am-2 pm. Closed: 1/1 & 12/25. **Features:** No A/C; Sunday brunch; children's menu; early bird specials; carryout; beer & wine only. Casual family dining. **Cards:** AE, CB, DI, MC, VI. ⊗

THAI ON MERCER **Dinner:** $11-$20 **Phone:** 206/236-9990
AAA ◆◆◆ Ethnic
Location: From I-90 at exit 7, downtown. 7691 27th St SE 98040. **Hours:** 11:30 am-2 & 5-9 pm, Fri & Sat-10 pm, Sun 5 pm-9 pm. Closed: 1/1 & 12/25. **Features:** carryout; beer & wine only. Eddies contemporary Thai cuisine in relaxed atmosphere. Smoke free premises. **Cards:** MC, VI. ⊗

MILL CREEK—7,200 (See SEATTLE & VICINITY ACCOMMODATIONS spotting map pages A136 & A137; see index starting on page A134)

RESTAURANT

THE IMPERIAL GARDEN **Dinner:** $11-$20 **Phone:** 206/742-2288 (135)
◆◆◆ Chinese
Location: From I-5 at exit 183, 2 mi e on 164th St; 1 blk on Mill Creek Blvd. 16300 Mill Creek Blvd 98012. **Hours:** 5 pm-10 pm. Closed: 12/25. **Reservations:** suggested. **Features:** carryout; cocktails & lounge; entertainment; a la carte. Cantonese cuisine & some Mandarin dishes, live seafood. Setting over & fully surrounded by an award winning garden. **Cards:** AE, DI, DS, JCB, MC, VI. ⊗

MOCLIPS

LODGINGS

HI TIDE OCEAN BEACH RESORT Rates Subject to Change **Phone:** 360/276-4142
AAA ◆◆ Suite Motel
3/15-9/30 1P: $79- 89 2P/1B: $79- 89 2P/2B: $79- 159 XP: $10 F5
3/1-3/14 & 10/1-2/29 1P: $69- 79 2P/1B: $69- 79 2P/2B: $69- 149 XP: $10 F5
Location: 3/4 mi n; 4 blks nw of SR 109 on beach at 6th & Railroad sts. 4890 Railroad Ave 98562 (PO Box 308). **Terms:** Sr. discount; reserv deposit, 3 day notice; weekly rates; 2 night min stay, weekends; pets, $10, dogs only. **Facility:** 24 rooms. 1- & 2-bedroom suites with kitchen & balcony; most with fireplace. 2 stories; exterior corridors; oceanfront; beach. **All Rooms:** cable TV, no A/C, no phones. **Some Rooms:** Fee: VCP's. **Cards:** AE, MC, VI. D ⊗

OCEAN CREST RESORT Rates Subject to Change **Phone:** 360/276-4465
AAA ◆◆◆ Motor Inn
3/16-9/30 2P/1B: $54- 108 2P/2B: $85- 118 XP:$6-11 F3
3/1-3/15, 10/1-11/15 & 2/16-2/29 2P/1B: $46- 88 2P/2B: $73- 101 XP:$6-11 F3
11/16-2/15 2P/1B: $41- 78 2P/2B: $65- 90 XP:$6-11 F3
Location: 1 mi n of Pacific Beach bypass, jct SR 109. SR 109 98562 (PO Box 7). **Terms:** Sr. discount; reserv deposit, 7 day notice; package plans; 2 night min stay, weekends; no pets. **Facility:** 45 rooms. On bluff overlooking ocean. Some with fireplace; many balconies. 8 two-bedroom units. 3 stories, no elevator; interior/exterior corridors; beach, heated indoor pool, sauna, whirlpool. Fee: tanning booth. **Services:** Fee: coin laundry. **All Rooms:** combo & shower baths, cable TV, no A/C. **Some Rooms:** 4 efficiencies, 14 kitchens, refrigerators. Fee: VCP's. **Cards:** AE, DS, MC, VI. D

RESTAURANT

OCEAN CREST RESTAURANT **Dinner:** $11-$20 **Phone:** 360/276-4465
◆◆ American
Location: At Ocean Crest Resort. SR 109 98562. **Hours:** 8 am-2:30 & 5:30-9 pm, Fri & Sat-9:30 pm. **Reservations:** suggested. **Features:** children's menu; cocktails & lounge. Fresh seafood & Northwest Regional cuisine in a relaxed ocean view setting. Smoke free premises. **Cards:** AE, DS, MC, VI. ⊗

MONROE—4,300

LODGING

BEST WESTERN BARON INN Rates Subject to Change **Phone:** 360/794-3111
AAA ◆◆◆ Motel
6/1-9/30 [CP] 1P: $56- 64 2P/1B: $60 2P/2B: $68 XP: $6
3/1-5/31 & 10/1-2/29 [CP] 1P: $52- 60 2P/1B: $56 2P/2B: $64 XP: $6
Location: W end of town. 19233 Hwy 2 98272. Fax: 360/794-0179. **Terms:** Credit card guarantee, 3 day notice; small pets only, in limited rooms, $10. **Facility:** 58 rooms. 3 stories; interior corridors; meeting rooms; heated pool, whirlpool. **Services:** data ports. Fee: coin laundry. **All Rooms:** free movies, combo & shower baths, cable TV. **Some Rooms:** coffeemakers, 10 efficiencies, kitchen, whirlpools. **Cards:** AE, CB, DI, DS, MC, VI. Roll in showers. D S ⊗

MORTON—1,100

LODGINGS

THE SEASONS MOTEL Rates Subject to Change **Phone:** 360/496-6835
AAA ◆◆◆ Motel
All Year [CP] 1P: $50 2P/1B: $50 2P/2B: $60 XP: $5
Location: 1 blk nw of jct SR 7 & US 12. 200 Westlake 98356 (Box 567). Fax: 360/496-5127. **Terms:** Reserv deposit; small pets only. **Facility:** 50 rooms. Close to Mt St Helens & Mt Rainer. 2 stories; exterior corridors. **All Rooms:** combo & shower baths, cable TV. **Cards:** AE, DI, MC, VI. Ⓓ ⊗

ST HELENS MANORHOUSE AAA Special Value Rates **Phone:** 360/498-5243
◆◆ Historic Bed & Breakfast
All Year [BP] 1P: $59- 69 2P/1B: $59- 69 2P/2B: $69 XP: $10
Location: 5 3/4 mi e of Morton on US 12 at Fisher. 7476 US Hwy 12 98356. **Terms:** Age restrictions may apply; check-in 4 pm; reserv deposit; no pets. **Facility:** 4 rooms. 1910 mansion boasts original wavy, etched, stained & bevelled glasswork. Credit cards not accepted; 2 stories; interior corridors; smoke free premises. **All Rooms:** no A/C, no phones, no TVs. **Some Rooms:** radios. Ⓓ ⊗

MOSES LAKE—11,200

LODGINGS

BEST WESTERN HALLMARK INN AAA Special Value Rates **Phone:** 509/765-9211
AAA ◆◆◆ Motor Inn
5/16-9/15 1P: $69- 79 2P/1B: $73- 83 2P/2B: $77- 87 XP: $4 F12
3/1-5/15 & 9/16-2/29 1P: $59- 69 2P/1B: $63- 73 2P/2B: $67- 77 XP: $4 F12
Location: I-90 exit 176. 3000 Marina Dr 98837. Fax: 509/766-0493. **Terms:** Check-in 4 pm; reserv deposit; weekend rates available; pets, $2 dep req. **Facility:** 155 rooms. Located on the shores of Moses Lake. Spacious, well equipped rooms and enjoyable recreation facilities offer a very nice three diamond stay. Suites from $85-$120; 2 stories; interior corridors; conference facilities; heated pool, sauna, whirlpool; 2 tennis courts; boat dock. **Dining & Entertainment:** Dining room; 7 am-2 pm & 5 pm-10 pm; $9-$18; cocktails; entertainment. **Services:** airport transportation, 8 am-8 pm. Fee: coin laundry. **Recreation:** waterskiing. **All Rooms:** free movies, refrigerators, cable TV. **Some Rooms:** whirlpools. Fee: VCP's. **Cards:** AE, CB, DI, DS, JCB, MC, VI. Ⓓ ⊗

HOLIDAY INN EXPRESS Rates Subject to Change **Phone:** 509/766-2000
AAA ◆◆◆ Motel
All Year [CP] 1P: $63- 75 2P/1B: $68- 85 2P/2B: $68- 85 XP: $5 F19
Location: I-90, exit 179. 1735 E Kittleson 99337. Fax: 509/765-0466. **Terms:** Sr. discount; pets. **Facility:** 75 rooms. 3 stories; interior corridors; whirlpool, small heated indoor pool. **Dining:** Restaurant nearby. **Services:** data ports. **All Rooms:** coffeemakers, microwaves, refrigerators, comb, shower & tub baths, cable TV. Fee: movies. **Some Rooms:** whirlpools. Fee: VCP's. Roll in showers. Ⓓ Ⓢ ⊗

MOSES LAKE TRAVELODGE Rates Subject to Change **Phone:** 509/765-8631
AAA ◆◆ Motel
6/1-9/7 1P: $45 2P/1B: $55 2P/2B: $65 XP: $5 F18
3/1-5/31 & 9/8-2/29 1P: $39 2P/1B: $44 2P/2B: $49 XP: $5 F18
Location: Downtown on Business Loop 90. 316 S Pioneer Way 98837. Fax: 509/765-3685. **Terms:** Sr. discount; credit card guarantee, 7 day notice; pets, $25. **Facility:** 39 rooms. Comfortable accommodations in older yet well maintained city center property. 4 two-bedroom units. 2 stories; exterior corridors; heated pool, whirlpool. **All Rooms:** free movies, combo & shower baths, cable TV. **Some Rooms:** coffeemakers, microwaves, refrigerators. **Cards:** AE, CB, DI, DS, JCB, MC, VI. Ⓓ ⊗

SHILO INN Rates Subject to Change **Phone:** 509/765-9317
◆◆◆ Motel
5/1-9/30 1P: $78- 83 2P/1B: $78- 83 2P/2B: $78- 83 XP: $10 F12
3/1-4/30 & 10/1-2/29 1P: $67- 72 2P/1B: $67- 72 2P/2B: $67- 72 XP: $10 F12
Location: I-90 exit 179. 1819 E Kittleson 98837. Fax: 509/765-5058. **Terms:** Sr. discount; pets, $7. **Facility:** 100 rooms. "Fresh" contemporary highway property with relaxing pool & spa area. Snack bar & convienience store. Kitchen units, $88-$98; 2 stories; interior corridors; heated indoor pool, sauna, steamroom, whirlpool; exercise room. **Dining:** Restaurant nearby. **Services:** airport transportation. Fee: coin laundry. **All Rooms:** microwaves, free movies, refrigerators, cable TV. **Some Rooms:** 6 efficiencies. Fee: VCP's. **Cards:** AE, DI, DS, JCB, VI. Ⓓ Ⓢ ⊗

MOUNT VERNON—17,600

LODGINGS

BEST WESTERN COLLEGE WAY INN AAA Special Value Rates **Phone:** 360/424-4287
◆◆◆ Motel
6/15-10/14 [CP] 1P: $51- 61 2P/1B: $56- 66 2P/2B: $59- 69 XP: $5 F12
4/1-6/14 [CP] 1P: $47- 57 2P/1B: $52- 62 2P/2B: $55- 65 XP: $5 F12
3/1-3/31 & 10/15-2/29 [CP] 1P: $45- 55 2P/1B: $50- 60 2P/2B: $53- 63 XP: $5 F12
Location: W of I-5 exit 227. 300 W College Way 98273. Fax: 360/424-6036. **Terms:** Weekly rates; pets, $5. **Facility:** 66 rooms. Some lanais or balconies overlooking pool. 2 stories; exterior corridors; meeting rooms; heated pool, whirlpool. **Dining:** Restaurant nearby. **All Rooms:** combo & shower baths, cable TV. **Some Rooms:** A/C, 10 efficiencies, radios, refrigerators. **Cards:** AE, CB, DI, DS, MC, VI. Ⓓ ⊗

Best Western
COTTONTREE INN and Convention Center

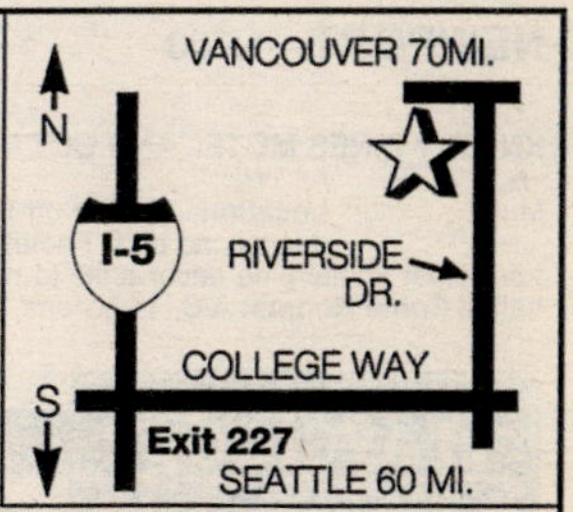

- 120 Oversized Rooms
- In-room Coffee
- Heated Pool
- Guest Laundry
- Restaurant & Lounge

Nearby Attractions
- Factory Outlet Mall
- San Juan Islands
- Scenic La Conner
- North Cascades Highway

For Reservations Call: (800) 662-6886 or (800) 528-1234
2300 Market Place (N. Riverside Dr.) Mt Vernon, WA 98273

BEST WESTERN COTTON TREE INN & CONVENTION CENTER Guaranteed Rates **Phone:** 360/428-5678

◆◆◆ Motel

All Year 1P: $64 2P/1B: $69 2P/2B: $69 XP: $5 F18

Location: Northbound I-5 at exit 227, southbound I-5 at exit 229; e of I-5. 2300 Market 98273. Fax: 360/428-1844. **Terms:** Sr. discount; weekly/monthly rates; small pets only. **Facility:** 120 rooms. 3 stories; interior corridors; conference facilities; heated pool open end of May to mid Sept. **Dining:** Restaurant nearby. **Services:** Fee: coin laundry, airport transportation. **All Rooms:** free movies, combo & shower baths, cable TV. **Some Rooms:** microwaves, refrigerators. Fee: VCP's. **Cards:** AE, CB, DI, DS, JCB, MC, VI.
(See ad p A101)

DAYS INN, MT VERNON Rates Subject to Change **Phone:** 360/424-4141

◆◆ Motor Inn

3/1-10/15	1P: $55	2P/1B: $60	2P/2B: $65	XP: $5 F13
10/16-2/29	1P: $50	2P/1B: $55	2P/2B: $60	XP: $5 F13

Location: 1/2 mi e of I-5 exit 227; 1 blk n of College Way. 2009 Riverside Dr 98273. Fax: 360/428-8661. **Terms:** Sr. discount; reserv deposit; weekly/monthly rates; no pets. **Facility:** 86 rooms. 2-3 stories; interior corridors; meeting rooms; heated pool. **Dining & Entertainment:** Dining room; 6 am-10 pm; $5-$10; cocktails/lounge; entertainment. **Services:** valet laundry. **All Rooms:** cable TV. **Some Rooms:** microwaves, refrigerators. Fee: whirlpools. **Cards:** AE, CB, DI, DS, MC, VI.

MOUNT VERNON TRAVELODGE Rates Subject to Change **Phone:** 360/428-7020

◆◆◆ Motel

4/1-4/30 [CP]	1P: $64	2P/1B: $64	2P/2B: $74	XP: $5 F16
7/1-9/30 [CP]	1P: $54	2P/1B: $54	2P/2B: $64	XP: $5 F16
3/1-3/31, 5/1-6/30 & 10/1-2/29 [CP]	1P: $44	2P/1B: $44	2P/2B: $49	XP: $5 F16

Location: 1/4 mi nw of I-5 exit 227, on College Way. 1910 Freeway Dr 98273. Fax: 360/428-7838. **Terms:** Sr. discount; weekly/monthly rates; pets, $5. **Facility:** 70 rooms. 3 two-bedroom units. 7 two-level suites with kitchen from $99; 3 stories; exterior corridors; heated indoor pool, whirlpool. **Dining:** Restaurant nearby. **Services:** Fee: coin laundry. **All Rooms:** coffeemakers, free movies, cable TV. **Some Rooms:** 6 efficiencies, refrigerators. Fee: whirlpools. **Cards:** AE, CB, DI, DS, MC, VI. *(See color ad below)*

RESTAURANTS

AUSTIN'S RIO CAFE **Dinner:** $11-$20 **Phone:** 360/424-5944

◆◆ Ethnic

Location: From northbound I-5, exit 227; southbound I-5, exit 229. 2401 Riverside Dr 98273. **Hours:** 7 am-9 pm, Fri & Sat-11 pm. Closed: 1/1 & 12/25. **Features:** casual dress; children's menu; carryout; cocktails & lounge. Casual, unpretentious family dining. Tex-mex meals with a Northwestern flare. **Cards:** AE, DI, DS, MC, VI.

LONGFELLOW CAFE **Dinner:** $11-$20 **Phone:** 360/336-6874

◆◆ American

Location: From I-5 at exit 226 at 3rd & 1st sts. 120 B 1st St 98273. **Hours:** 11:30 am-3 & 5-9:30 pm, Sun 11 am-4 pm. Closed major holidays, Sun & Mon for dinner. **Reservations:** suggested. **Features:** No A/C; children's menu; carryout; beer & wine only. Creative cuisine in a casual bistro atmosphere. Excellent selection of wine by the glass. Smoke free premises. **Cards:** MC, VI.

WILDFLOWERS RESTAURANT **Dinner:** $11-$20 **Phone:** 360/424-9724

◆◆◆ Continental

Location: 1 1/2 mi e of I-5 exit 227. 2001 E College Way 98273. **Hours:** 5 pm-9 pm, Fri & Sat-10 pm. Closed major holidays, Sun, Mon & 12/24. **Reservations:** suggested. **Features:** cocktails & lounge; a la carte. Intimate dining in renovated home. Breads & desserts made on premises. Smoke free premises. **Cards:** AE, MC, VI.

MUKILTEO—7,000

RESTAURANT

ARNIES RESTAURANT **Dinner:** $11-$20 **Phone:** 206/355-2181

◆◆ Seafood

Location: Downtown. 714 2nd St 98275. **Hours:** 11 am-2 & 4:30-9:30 pm, Fri 4:30 pm-10 pm, Sat 4 pm-10 pm, Sun 10 am-2:30 & 4-9 pm. Closed: 12/25. **Features:** Sunday brunch; children's menu; early bird specials; carryout; cocktails & lounge; a la carte. Specializing in Northwest seafood. Nautical atmosphere overlooking ferry dock, Puget Sound & Olympic Mountains. Smoke free premises. **Cards:** AE, MC, VI.

NAHCOTTA

RESTAURANT

THE ARK RESTAURANT AND BAKERY **Dinner:** $11-$20 **Phone:** 350/665-4133

◆◆◆ Seafood

Location: 3 blks n on Nahcotta Dock overlooking Willipa Bay. 98637. **Hours:** 5 pm-10 pm, Sun 11 am-8 pm, Thu-Sun 7/5-9/15 also 11 am-2:30 pm. Closed: Jan & Feb. **Reservations:** suggested. **Features:** No A/C; Sunday brunch; children's menu; senior's menu; cocktails & lounge; a la carte. Nationally known. Also daily & seasonal specialties. Homemade breads & desserts. Sun brunch 11 am-3 pm. Smoke free premises. **Cards:** DI, DS, MC, VI.

NEWPORT—1,700

LODGING

KNOTTY PINES MOTEL AND COTTAGES Rates Subject to Change **Phone:** 509/447-5427

◆ Motel

All Year 1P: $25- 50 2P/1B: $30- 80 2P/2B: $40- 80 XP: $5

Location: 10 mi s on US 2, at Diamond Lake. 324051 N Hwy 2 99156. Fax: 509/447-2455. **Terms:** Reserv deposit; no pets. **Facility:** 9 rooms. Small rural roadside motel nestled in pine studded setting. Room offerings from older knotty pine decor units to modern modular suites. Exterior corridors. **All Rooms:** refrigerators, combo & shower baths. **Some Rooms:** A/C, 4 kitchens, radios, phones, whirlpools. **Cards:** AE, MC, VI.

Travelodge
Mount Vernon
206-428-7020
1-800-578-7878
Mention this ad and receive a special gift!
• FREE continental breakfast
• FREE local calls, in-room coffee and HBO
• Near outlet shopping mall
• Shopping discounts
• Indoor pool & spa
10% off rack rates
1910 Freeway Dr. Mt. Vernon, WA 98273 / I-5 Exit #227
Not valid with any other offer

NORTH BEND—2,600

LODGINGS

EDGEWICK INN AAA Special Value Rates **Phone:** 206/888-9000
AAA ◆◆ Motel
All Year 1P: $50 2P/1B: $50 2P/2B: $56 XP: $6 F10
Location: 3 mi e at I-90 exit 34. 14600 468th Ave SE 98045. Fax: 206/888-9400. **Terms:** Credit card guarantee; no pets. **Facility:** 44 rooms. 2 stories; interior corridors; meeting rooms; whirlpool. **Dining:** Restaurant nearby. **Services:** Fee: coin laundry. **All Rooms:** free movies, cable TV. **Some Rooms:** radios. Fee: VCP's, whirlpools. **Cards:** AE, MC, VI. Ⓓ ⊗

NORTH BEND MOTEL Rates Subject to Change **Phone:** 206/888-1121
AAA ◆◆ Motel
5/1-9/30 1P: $36- 38 2P/1B: $38- 40 2P/2B: $46- 50 XP: $4 D10
3/1-4/30 & 10/1-2/29 1P: $34- 36 2P/1B: $36- 38 2P/2B: $42- 46 XP: $4 D10
Location: I-90, exit 31, 1/2 mi n on service road; then 3 blks e on E North Bend Way. 322 E North Bend Way 98045 (PO Box 1332). **Terms:** Reserv deposit; weekly rates, off season; no pets. **Facility:** 17 rooms. 1 story; exterior corridors. **All Rooms:** shower baths, cable TV, no A/C. **Some Rooms:** refrigerators. **Cards:** AE, CB, DI, DS, MC, VI. Ⓓ ⊗

OAK HARBOR—17,200

LODGINGS

ACORN MOTOR INN Guaranteed Rates **Phone:** 360/675-6646
AAA ◆◆ Motel
6/15-9/15 [CP] 1P: $48- 58 2P/1B: $52- 64 2P/2B: $52- 68 XP: $5 F12
3/1-6/14 & 9/16-2/29 [CP] 1P: $41- 52 2P/1B: $44- 56 2P/2B: $46- 60 XP: $5 F12
Location: Center on SR 20. 8066 State Hwy 20 98277. Fax: 360/679-1850. **Terms:** Sr. discount; age restrictions may apply; reserv deposit, 5 day notice; weekly/monthly rates; pets, $5. **Facility:** 26 rooms. 2 stories; interior corridors. **All Rooms:** refrigerators, cable TV. **Some Rooms:** A/C. **Cards:** AE, CB, DI, DS, MC, VI. Ⓓ ⊗

THE AULD HOLLAND INN Guaranteed Rates **Phone:** 360/675-2288
AAA ◆◆◆ Motor Inn
5/1-9/6 [CP] 1P: $55- 85 2P/1B: $55- 85 2P/2B: $55- 65 XP: $5
3/1-4/30 & 9/7-2/29 [CP] 1P: $45- 75 2P/1B: $45- 75 2P/2B: $45- 55 XP: $5
Location: N end of town. 5861 N SR 20 98277. Fax: 360/675-2817. **Terms:** Sr. discount; reserv deposit, 3 day notice; small pets only, in selected room, $120 dep req, $5-$10. **Facility:** 34 rooms. Attractive European decor, rooms with antique furnishings. 8 with fireplace. Romantic honeymoon suite located in windmill. Suites avail, $85-$135; 2 stories; interior/exterior corridors; heated pool, steamroom, whirlpool; 1 tennis court; exercise room, playground, basketball court. **Dining:** Also, Kasteel Franssen, see separate listing. **Services:** Fee: coin laundry. **All Rooms:** cable TV, no A/C. **Some Rooms:** 6 efficiencies, microwaves, refrigerators. Fee: VCP's, whirlpools. **Cards:** AE, CB, DI, DS, MC, VI. Ⓓ ⊗

BEST WESTERN HARBOR PLAZA Rates Subject to Change **Phone:** 360/679-4567
AAA ◆◆◆◆ Motel
5/1-9/30 [CP] 1P: $63- 94 2P/1B: $68- 102 2P/2B: $71- 95 XP: $5-8 F12
3/1-4/30 & 10/1-2/29 [CP] 1P: $60- 84 2P/1B: $65- 89 2P/2B: $65- 82 XP: $5 F12
Location: On SR 20 at n edge of town. 5691 SR 20 98277. Fax: 360/675-2543. **Terms:** Sr. discount; reserv deposit; no pets. **Facility:** 80 rooms. Very attractive rooms; some with balcony. 3 stories; interior corridors; meeting rooms; heated pool, whirlpool; exercise room. Fee: tanning bed. **Dining:** Restaurant nearby. **All Rooms:** coffeemakers, microwaves, free movies, refrigerators, cable TV. **Some Rooms:** Fee: VCP's. **Cards:** AE, CB, DI, DS. *(See color ad below)* Ⓓ ⊗

COACHMAN INN Guaranteed Rates **Phone:** 360/675-0727
AAA ◆◆◆◆ Motel
All Year [CP] 1P: $54- 100 2P/1B: $54- 100 2P/2B: $64- 84 XP: $5 F18
Location: N end of town, cross sts Goldie Rd & Hwy 20. 5563 Hwy 20 98277. Fax: 360/675-1419. **Terms:** Credit card guarantee; weekly/monthly rates; no pets. **Facility:** 102 rooms. A unique personal touch adds charm & hospitality to comfortable friendly rooms. Several studio & speciality suites. 3 two-bedroom units. Special units $110-$175; 2 stories; exterior corridors; meeting rooms; heated pool, whirlpool; exercise room. **Dining:** Restaurant nearby. **Services:** area transportation. Fee: coin laundry. **All Rooms:** coffeemakers, cable TV. **Some Rooms:** 48 efficiencies, microwaves, refrigerators, whirlpools. Fee: VCP's. **Cards:** AE, DI, DS, MC, VI. *(See color ad p A104)* Ⓓ ⊗

QUEEN ANN MOTEL Rates Subject to Change **Phone:** 360/675-2209
AAA ◆◆ Motor Inn
All Year 1P: $44- 49 2P/1B: $47- 53 2P/2B: $51- 55 XP: $5 F10
Location: Downtown. 1204 W Pioneer Way 98277. **Terms:** Reserv deposit; no pets. **Facility:** 21 rooms. 2 kitchens, $10 extra; 2 efficiencies, $8 extra; 1 story; exterior corridors; meeting rooms; heated indoor pool, whirlpool. **Dining:** Restaurant; 7 am-9 pm, Fri & Sat 8 am-10 pm, Sun 8 am-9 pm; $5-$15; cocktails. **All Rooms:** cable TV. **Some Rooms:** coffeemakers, refrigerators. **Cards:** AE, CB, DI, MC, VI. Ⓓ

Best Western
Best Western Harbor Plaza
Four Diamond Award
WHIDBEY ISLAND'S PREMIER HOTEL
• 80 Luxurious Rooms & Suites
• Restaurant & Lounge
• Heated Pool
• Banquet/Conv. Fac.
• Spa
• Special AAA Rate
• Exercise Room
• Room Service
For Reservations, Call: (206) 679-4567 or (800) 927-5478
5691 State Hwy 20 • Oak Harbor, WA 98277

RESTAURANT

KASTEEL FRANSSEN ◆◆◆ Continental — **Dinner:** $11-$20 — **Phone:** 360/675-0724

Location: In The Auld Holland Inn. 5861 N SR 20 98277. **Hours:** 5:30 pm-9 pm, Sat-9:30 pm. Closed: 1/1, 12/25 & Sun 11/1-7/4. **Reservations:** suggested. **Features:** carryout; cocktails & lounge; entertainment; a la carte. Classic European cuisine in an elegant Dutch atmosphere. **Cards:** AE, DI, DS, MC, VI. ⊗

OCEAN PARK

LODGING

OCEAN PARK RESORT — AAA Special Value Rates — **Phone:** 360/665-4585

◆ Motel

All Year 1P: $50- 55 2P/1B: $50- 55 2P/2B: $58 XP: $5

Location: In town; 2 blks e of SR 103. 25904 R St 98640 (PO Box 339). **Terms:** Reserv deposit, 10 day notice; pets, $5. **Facility:** 12 rooms. $6 surcharge for single night stay; 2 stories; exterior corridors; heated pool, whirlpool; playground, recreation room. **Services:** Fee: coin laundry. **All Rooms:** free movies, cable TV, no A/C, no phones. **Some Rooms:** coffeemakers, 8 kitchens, refrigerators. **Cards:** DS, MC, VI. (D)

OCEAN SHORES—2,300

LODGINGS

BEST WESTERN LIGHTHOUSE SUITES INN — Rates Subject to Change — **Phone:** 360/289-2311

◆◆◆ Suite Motel

4/1-10/15 [CP] 1P: $97- 157 2P/1B: $97- 157 2P/2B: $97- 157 XP: $10 F
3/1-3/31 & 10/16-2/29 [CP] 1P: $85- 157 2P/1B: $85- 157 2P/2B: $85- 157 XP: $10 F

Location: Off Ocean Shores Mall at Damon Rd. 491 Damon RD NW 98569 (PO Box 879). Fax: 360/289-0509. **Terms:** Check-in 4 pm; reserv deposit; no pets. **Facility:** 76 rooms. 4 stories; exterior corridors; meeting rooms; heated indoor pool, whirlpool; exercise room. **Services:** data ports. Fee: coin laundry. **All Rooms:** coffeemakers, microwaves, free movies, refrigerators, combo & shower baths, cable TV, VCP's, no A/C. **Some Rooms:** Fee: whirlpools. **Cards:** AE, DI, DS, MC, VI. *(See color ad below)* (D) (S) ⊗

THE CANTERBURY INN — Rates Subject to Change — **Phone:** 360/289-3317

◆◆◆ Suite Motel

Fri & Sat 3/1-3/31, 4/1-9/30 & Fri & Sat 10/1-2/29 1P: $78- 118 2P/1B: $78- 118 2P/2B: $104- 168 XP: $10 F13
Sun-Thurs 3/1-3/31 & 10/1-2/29 1P: $62- 94 2P/1B: $62- 94 2P/2B: $83- 134 XP: $10 F13

Location: Oceanfront; 2 1/2 blks s of Shores Mall. 643 Ocean Shores Blvd 98569 (PO Box 310). Fax: 360/289-3420. **Terms:** Reserv deposit; 2 night min stay, 7/1-8/31 & weekends; no pets. **Facility:** 44 rooms. Rooms with balcony or patio. Most with fireplace. 12 two-bedroom units. 3 stories; interior corridors; oceanview; meeting rooms; beach, heated indoor pool, whirlpool. **All Rooms:** coffeemakers, combo & shower baths, cable TV, no A/C. **Some Rooms:** 12 efficiencies, 32 kitchens. Fee: VCP's. **Cards:** AE, MC, VI. (D) ⊗

SO CLOSE TO THE OCEAN...
Best Western
Brand New!
Lighthouse Suites Inn
Call for your FREE Gateway Guide to beautiful Ocean Shores, Washington.
Call 1-800-757-SURF
YOU'LL SWEAR YOU'RE ON A CRUISE SHIP!

DISCOVERY INN — AAA Special Value Rates — **Phone:** 360/289-3371

◆◆ Motel

Fri & Sat 3/1-3/31, 4/1-9/30 & Fri & Sat 10/1-2/29	1P: $52- 78	2P/1B: $52- 78	2P/2B: $52- 78	XP: $5 F6
Sun-Thurs 3/1-3/31 & 10/1-2/29	1P: $42- 62	2P/1B: $42- 62	2P/2B: $42- 62	XP: $5 F6

Location: 5 mi s on Point Brown Ave. 1031 Discovery Ave SE 98569. **Terms:** Check-in 4 pm; reserv deposit; small pets only, $10. **Facility:** 22 rooms. Many rooms have fireplace. Close to beach & ocean. 2 stories; exterior corridors; heated pool, whirlpool. **All Rooms:** coffeemakers, cable TV, no A/C. **Some Rooms:** 5 efficiencies, 11 kitchens, microwaves, refrigerators. **Cards:** AE, DS, MC, VI. (D) ⊗

GITCHE GUMEE MOTEL — AAA Special Value Rates — **Phone:** 360/289-3323

AAA ◆◆ Motel

4/1-10/15	1P: $45- 85	2P/1B: $45- 85	2P/2B: $45- 85	XP: $5 F12
3/1-3/31 & 10/16-2/29	1P: $35- 65	2P/1B: $35- 65	2P/2B: $35- 65	XP: $5 F12

Location: 2 blks s of Shores Mall. 648 Ocean Shores Blvd NW 98569. **Terms:** Credit card guarantee; weekly rates; package plans; small pets only, $10 dep req. **Facility:** 80 rooms. 1 three-bedroom unit, 8 two-bedroom units. 3 stories; interior/exterior corridors; meeting rooms; 2 pools (2 heated, 1 indoor), saunas. **All Rooms:** cable TV, no A/C. **Some Rooms:** 20 efficiencies, 19 kitchens, refrigerators. **Cards:** AE, CB, DI, DS, JCB, MC, VI. *(See ad below)* (D)

GREY GULL — AAA Special Value Rates — **Phone:** 360/289-3381

AAA ◆◆◆ Apartment Motel

4/1-9/30 & Fri & Sat 12/24-1/1	2P/1B: $98- 129	2P/2B: $135- 150	XP: $5 F16
3/1-3/31, 10/1-12/23, Sun-Thurs 12/24-1/1 & 1/2-2/29	2P/1B: $78- 103	2P/2B: $108- 135	XP: $5 F16

Location: Oceanfront; 2 blks s of Shores Mall. 651 Ocean Shores Blvd SW 98569 (PO Box 1417). Fax: 360/289-3673. **Terms:** Check-in 4 pm; reserv deposit; 2 night min stay, weekends & 7/1-8/31; small pets only, in limited units. **Facility:** 36 rooms. All units have private patio or balcony & fireplace; wood provided. Most with ocean view. 1 two-bedroom unit, 1 three-bedroom unit. 3 stories; exterior corridors; oceanfront; beach, sauna, whirlpool, small heated pool. **Services:** Fee: coin laundry. **All Rooms:** cable TV, VCP's, no A/C. **Some Rooms:** 6 efficiencies, 30 kitchens. **Cards:** AE, DI, DS, MC, VI. (D) ⊗

THE POLYNESIAN CONDOMINIUM RESORT — Rates Subject to Change — **Phone:** 360/289-3361

AAA ◆◆◆ Apartment Motor Inn

Fri & Sat 3/1-3/31, 4/1-10/1 & Fri & Sat 10/2-2/29	1P: $69- 92	2P/1B: $69- 92	2P/2B: $104- 165	XP: $10
Sun-Thurs 3/1-3/31 & 10/2-2/29	1P: $45- 64	2P/1B: $45- 64	2P/2B: $74- 110	XP: $10

Location: Oceanfront; 3 blks s of Shores Mall. 615 Ocean Shores Blvd 98569 (PO Box 998). Fax: 360/289-0294. **Terms:** Check-in 4 pm; reserv deposit, 3 day notice; package plans; 2 night min stay, weekends & 7/1-8/31; no pets. **Facility:** 71 rooms. Many with fireplace, private balcony or patio. Most rooms with ocean view. 12 two-bedroom units, 2 three-bedroom units. 4 stories; interior/exterior corridors; conference facilities; beach, heated indoor pool, sauna, whirlpool. **Dining:** Restaurant; 4 pm-9 pm, Fri-10 pm, Sat 9 am-1 & 4-10 pm, Sun 9 am-1 & 4-9 pm; $9-$18; cocktails. **Services:** Fee: coin laundry. **All Rooms:** cable TV, no A/C. **Some Rooms:** coffeemakers, 13 efficiencies, 53 kitchens, VCP's, whirlpools. **Cards:** AE, CB, DI, DS, MC, VI. (D) ⊗

SHILO INN CONVENTION RESORT — **Phone:** 360/289-4600

Suite Motor Inn

Under construction; **Location:** Corner of Chance A Le Mer & the Pacific Ocean. 707 Ocean Shores Blvd NW 98569. **Terms:** sr. discount; check-in 4 pm; credit card guarantee; no pets. **Facility:** 113 rooms. Rating withheld pending completion of construction. Scheduled to open July, 1995. 4 stories; interior corridors; conference facilities; beach, heated indoor pool, sauna, steamroom, whirlpool; exercise room. **Dining & Entertainment:** Dining room; 6 am-10 pm, Fri & Sat-11 pm; $12-$20; cocktail lounge. **Services:** Fee: coin laundry. **All Rooms:** honor bars, microwaves, free movies, refrigerators, combo & shower baths, cable TV, VCP's, no A/C. **Some Rooms:** whirlpools. **Cards:** AE, DI, DS, JCB, MC, VI. Roll in showers. (D) (S) ⊗

RESTAURANT

HOME PORT RESTAURANT — **Dinner:** $11-$20 — **Phone:** 360/289-2600

◆◆ American

Location: 3 blks s of city entry gate. 857 Point Brown Ave 98569. **Hours:** 8 am-10 pm, Fri & Sat-11 pm. Closed: 12/25. **Reservations:** suggested. **Features:** children's menu; carryout; salad bar; cocktails & lounge. Very attractive family restaurant serving well-prepared seafood, steaks, burgers & breakfast. Smoke free premises. **Cards:** MC, VI. ⊗

OKANOGAN—2,400

LODGING

PONDEROSA MOTOR LODGE — Guaranteed Rates — **Phone:** 509/422-0400

AAA ◆ Motel

All Year	1P: $32	2P/1B: $35	2P/2B: $40

Location: 1/4 mi n on SR 215 from jct SR 20. 1034 S 2nd Ave 98840. Fax: 509/422-4206. **Terms:** Reserv deposit, 3 day notice; weekly/monthly rates; pets. **Facility:** 25 rooms. 6 two-bedroom units. 1 story; exterior corridors; pool. **Services:** winter plug-ins. Fee: coin laundry. **All Rooms:** coffeemakers, free movies, combo & shower baths, cable TV. **Some Rooms:** 7 kitchens, radios, refrigerators. **Cards:** AE, CB, DI, DS, MC, VI. (D) ⊗

AAA Approved

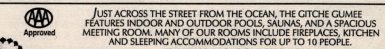

JUST ACROSS THE STREET FROM THE OCEAN, THE GITCHE GUMEE FEATURES INDOOR AND OUTDOOR POOLS, SAUNAS, AND A SPACIOUS MEETING ROOM. MANY OF OUR ROOMS INCLUDE FIREPLACES, KITCHEN AND SLEEPING ACCOMMODATIONS FOR UP TO 10 PEOPLE.

"FAMILY REUNIONS OUR SPECIALTY."

Gitche Gumee motel

CALL 1-800-448-2433 FOR RESERVATIONS

GITCHE GUMEE MOTEL, OCEAN SHORES, WA 98569

OLYMPIA—33,800

LODGINGS

BEST WESTERN-ALADDIN MOTOR INN — AAA Special Value Rates — **Phone:** 360/352-7200

◆◆◆ Motor Inn

6/1-9/15	1P: $60- 70	2P/1B: $65- 75	2P/2B: $70- 80	XP: $5	F12
1/1-2/29	1P: $58- 68	2P/1B: $63- 73	2P/2B: $68- 78	XP: $5	F12
3/1-5/31 & 9/16-12/31	1P: $56- 66	2P/1B: $61- 71	2P/2B: $66- 76	XP: $5	F12

Location: Downtown; from I-5 northbound exit 105; southbound exit 105A. 900 Capitol Way 98501. Fax: 360/352-0846. **Terms:** Small pets only, $5. **Facility:** 100 rooms. Close to state capitol. 3 stories; interior corridors; meeting rooms; heated pool. **Dining:** Dining room; 6:30 am-10 pm, Sat & Sun from 7 am; $9-$18; cocktails. **Services:** data ports. Fee: coin laundry. **All Rooms:** combo & shower baths, cable TV. **Some Rooms:** microwaves, refrigerators. Fee: VCP's. **Cards:** AE, CB, DI, DS, MC, VI. Roll in showers.

CARRIAGE INN MOTEL — Rates Subject to Change — **Phone:** 360/943-4710

◆◆ Motel

All Year	1P: $48	2P/1B: $51	2P/2B: $54	XP: $3	F16

Location: 1/4 mi n of I-5, southbound exit 105B, northbound exit 105B, Port of Olympia exit. 1211 S Quince 98501. Fax: 360/943-0804. **Terms:** Sr. discount; reserv deposit; no pets. **Facility:** 62 rooms. 2 stories; interior corridors; heated pool. **Dining:** Restaurant nearby. **All Rooms:** refrigerators, cable TV. **Cards:** AE, DI, DS, MC, VI.

GOLDEN GAVEL MOTOR HOTEL — Guaranteed Rates — **Phone:** 360/352-8533

◆◆ Motel

6/1-9/30	1P: $36	2P/1B: $39	2P/2B: $42	XP: $3
3/1-5/31 & 10/1-2/29	1P: $30	2P/1B: $33	2P/2B: $36	XP: $3

Location: I-5 exit 105. 909 Capitol Way 98501. **Terms:** Reserv deposit; weekly rates; no pets. **Facility:** 27 rooms. 3 two-bedroom units. 2 stories; exterior corridors. **Dining:** Restaurant nearby. **All Rooms:** cable TV, no A/C. **Cards:** AE, CB, DI, DS, JCB, MC, VI.

HARBINGER INN — AAA Special Value Rates — **Phone:** 360/754-0389

◆◆ Historic Bed & Breakfast

All Year [CP]	1P: $55- 90	2P/1B: $60- 95

Location: 1 1/4 mi n of I-5; southbound exit 105B, northbound exit 105, City Center exit. 1136 E Bay Dr 98506. **Terms:** Check-in 4 pm; reserv deposit, 3 day notice; no pets. **Facility:** 4 rooms. Turn-of-the-century inn. 2 stories; interior corridors; smoke free premises. **All Rooms:** no A/C, no phones, no TVs. **Cards:** AE, MC, VI.

QUALITY INN-WESTWATER — Rates Subject to Change — **Phone:** 360/943-4000

◆◆◆ Motor Inn

All Year	1P: $69- 79	2P/1B: $79- 89	2P/2B: $79- 89	XP: $10	F18

Location: 2 mi sw on US 101; 3/4 mi w of I-5, exit 104. 2300 Evergreen Park Dr 98502. Fax: 360/357-6604. **Terms:** Sr. discount; reserv deposit, 3 day notice; AP available; pets, $25. **Facility:** 191 rooms. Some rooms with balcony. Very attractive natural setting overlooking Capitol Lake & Capitol Dome. 3 stories; interior corridors; meeting rooms; whirlpool, 1 heated pool 5/31-9/31. **Dining:** Restaurant; 7 am-10 pm, Fri & Sat-11 pm, Sun-9 pm; $5-$19; cocktails. **Services:** secretarial services. Fee: coin laundry. **All Rooms:** free & pay movies, cable TV. **Some Rooms:** coffeemakers, refrigerators. Fee: whirlpools. **Cards:** AE, DI, DS, JCB, MC, VI.

RAMADA INN-GOVERNOR HOUSE — Rates Subject to Change — **Phone:** 360/352-7700

◆◆◆ Hotel

5/16-9/15	1P: $67- 77	2P/1B: $75- 88	XP: $8	F18
3/1-5/15 & 9/16-2/29	1P: $57- 67	2P/1B: $65- 78	XP: $8	F18

Location: Downtown. 621 S Capitol Way 98501. Fax: 360/943-9349. **Terms:** Sr. discount; reserv deposit, 15 day notice; weekly/monthly rates; no pets. **Facility:** 125 rooms. Rooms offer views of either City Park or Capitol Lake. 8 stories; interior corridors; meeting rooms; heated pool, sauna, whirlpool; exercise room. Fee: parking. **Dining & Entertainment:** Dining room; 7 am-9 pm, Fri & Sat-10 pm; $5-$14; cocktails/lounge. **Services:** Fee: coin laundry. **All Rooms:** cable TV. **Some Rooms:** coffeemakers, 34 efficiencies, refrigerators. **Cards:** AE, CB, DI, DS, JCB, MC, VI.

RESTAURANTS

BEN MOORE'S RESTAURANT — **Dinner:** $11-$20 — **Phone:** 360/357-7527

◆ American

Location: Downtown. 112 W 4th Ave 98501. **Hours:** 9 am-9 pm, Mon-8 pm, Fri-10 pm. Closed major holidays & Sun. **Features:** cocktails & lounge. Northwest regional cuisine emphasizing seasonal ingredients in casual dining room. **Cards:** AE, CB, DI, MC, VI.

GEONAS ON THE BAY — **Dinner:** $11-$20 — **Phone:** 360/943-7770

◆◆◆ Continental

Location: On the bay via Marine Dr. 1525 N Washington 98507. **Hours:** 11 am-10 pm, Sat from 4 pm, Sun 10 am-2:30 & 3-10 pm. Closed: 1/1, 11/23 & 12/25. **Reservations:** suggested. **Features:** Sunday brunch; children's menu; carryout; cocktails & lounge. Waterfront dining with fresh seafood & prime rib. **Cards:** AE, DI, DS, MC, VI.

OLYMPIC NATIONAL PARK

LODGING

LOG CABIN RESORT — Rates Subject to Change — **Phone:** 360/928-3325

◆ Complex

All Year	1P: $50- 86	2P/1B: $50- 86	2P/2B: $50- 86	XP: $11	F6

Location: 15 mi w of Port Angeles; 3 mi nw of US 101 at Piedmont recreation area on Lake Crescent. 3183 E Beach Rd 98363. Fax: 360/928-2088. **Terms:** Check-in 4 pm; reserv deposit; pets, in designated rooms. **Facility:** 24 rooms. Motel, chalet & very rustic cabins; most overlook lake. 14 two-bedroom units. Cabins, $38.40 for 2 persons; exterior corridors; beach; boat dock; playground. **Dining:** Restaurant; 8-10 am, 11:30-1:30 & 6-8:30 pm; $8-$15; beer only. **Services:** Fee: coin laundry. **Recreation:** nature program; swimming, fishing, waterskiing. Rental: boats, canoeing, paddleboats. **All Rooms:** shower & tub baths, no A/C, no phones, no TVs. **Some Rooms:** 3 kitchens, no utensils, refrigerators. **Cards:** DS, MC, VI.

West Coast Tyee Hotel
(800) 426-0670
(206) 352-0511
500 Tyee Drive, Olympia, WA 98502

- 145 Guest Rooms
- Restaurant & Lounge
- Tennis & Heated Pool
- Minutes to State Capital
- Meeting & Banquet Space
- 3-Diamond AAA Rating

OMAK—4,100

LODGINGS

LEISURE VILLAGE MOTEL Guaranteed Rates **Phone:** 509/826-4442
◆ Motel
All Year 1P: $33 2P/1B: $38 2P/2B: $44
Location: 3/4 mi s on SR 215 business route; 1 mi w, exit 215 from SR 97. 630 Okoma Dr 98841. **Terms:** Sr. discount; reserv deposit; small pets only, $5. **Facility:** 33 rooms. 3 two-bedroom units. 5 efficiencies, $5 extra; exterior corridors; heated indoor pool, sauna, whirlpool. **All Rooms:** refrigerators, cable TV. **Some Rooms:** coffeemakers, 2 kitchens, microwaves. **Cards:** AE, CB, DI, DS, MC, VI. (D) ⊗

MOTEL NICHOLAS Rates Subject to Change **Phone:** 509/826-4611
◆◆ Motel
All Year 1P: $35 2P/1B: $40 2P/2B: $43 XP: $4
Location: 3/4 mi n on SR 215 business route; 1/4 mi w of US 97 on n exit to Omak. 527 E Grape Av 98841 (Rt 3, Box 353). Fax: 509/826-4611. **Terms:** Reserv deposit, 3 day notice; no pets. **Facility:** 21 rooms. 1 two-bedroom unit. 1 story; exterior corridors. **Services:** winter plug-ins. **All Rooms:** refrigerators, combo & shower baths, cable TV. **Cards:** AE, CB, DI, DS, MC, VI. (D) ⊗

OROVILLE—1,500

LODGING

RED APPLE INN Rates Subject to Change **Phone:** 509/476-3694
◆◆ Motel
All Year 1P: $36 2P/1B: $44 2P/2B: $47 XP: $5 F5
Location: 1/4 mi n on US 97. 1815 Main St 98844 (PO Box 598). **Terms:** Credit card guarantee; small pets only, $1, no cats. **Facility:** 37 rooms. All rooms have murals depicting Okanagan scenes. 6 efficiencies, $2 extra; exterior corridors; heated pool. **Dining:** Restaurant nearby. **All Rooms:** free movies, cable TV. **Some Rooms:** coffeemakers, refrigerators. **Cards:** AE, DI, DS, MC, VI. (D) ⊗

OTHELLO—4,600

LODGING

ALADDIN MOTOR INN Rates Subject to Change **Phone:** 509/488-5671
◆ Motel
All Year 1P: $35- 39 2P/1B: $40- 44 2P/2B: $44- 49 XP: $5
Location: 1 blk off Main St at 10th & Cedar. 1020 E Cedar 99344. **Terms:** Reserv deposit; pets. **Facility:** 52 rooms. 11 efficiencies, $5 extra; 2 stories; interior corridors; pool. **All Rooms:** cable TV. **Cards:** AE, CB, DI, MC, VI. (D) ⊗

PACKWOOD

LODGINGS

THE COWLITZ RIVER LODGE Rates Subject to Change **Phone:** 360/494-4444
◆◆◆ Motel
All Year [CP] 1P: $50 2P/1B: $50 2P/2B: $60 XP: $5 F6
Location: E end. 13069 US Hwy 12 98361 (PO Box 488). Fax: 360/494-2075. **Terms:** Reserv deposit, 7 day notice; no pets. **Facility:** 32 rooms. Close to east entrance to Mt Rainier National Park. 2 stories; exterior corridors; whirlpool. **All Rooms:** free movies, cable TV. **Cards:** AE, DI, MC, VI. (D) ⊗

INN OF PACKWOOD Rates Subject to Change **Phone:** 360/494-5500
◆◆◆ Motor Inn
All Year [CP] 1P: $45 2P/1B: $53 2P/2B: $65 XP: $5
Location: Center of town. 13032 US Hwy 12 98361 (PO Box 390). **Terms:** Reserv deposit; weekly rates; 2 night min stay, 12/24-1/1; no pets. **Facility:** 33 rooms. Located between Mt St Helens & Mt Rainier National Parks. 2 stories; exterior corridors; meeting rooms. **Dining:** Restaurant; 11 am-8 pm; $6-$10. **All Rooms:** cable TV, no A/C. **Some Rooms:** coffeemakers, 3 efficiencies. **Cards:** DI, MC, VI. (D) ⊗

MOUNTAIN VIEW LODGE MOTEL Rates Subject to Change **Phone:** 360/494-5555
◆◆ Motel
All Year 1P: $31- 67 2P/1B: $34- 49 2P/2B: $45- 73 XP: $3
Location: 1/4 mi e on US 12; 12 mi sw of Stevens Canyon entrance to Mt Rainier National Park. 13163 Hwy 12 98361 (PO Box 525). **Terms:** Reserv deposit, 3 day notice; pets, $3, $10 dep req, on ground level only. **Facility:** 21 rooms. 2 stories; exterior corridors; heated pool, whirlpool. **All Rooms:** free movies, combo & shower baths. **Some Rooms:** 8 kitchens, refrigerators, B/W cable TV. **Cards:** AE, DI, MC, VI. (D)

TATOOSH MOTEL Rates Subject to Change **Phone:** 360/494-5321
◆◆◆ Motel
3/1-4/15, 5/21-10/15 & 12/23-2/29 1P: $45- 75 2P/1B: $45- 75 2P/2B: $48- 75 XP: $4 D
4/16-5/20 & 10/16-12/22 1P: $38- 50 2P/1B: $42- 50 2P/2B: $45- 50 XP: $3 D
Location: 3/4 mi w on US 12. 12880 Hwy 12 98361 (PO Box 677). **Terms:** Reserv deposit, 7 day notice; no pets. **Facility:** 14 rooms. 1950's home style country comfort. 1 three-bedroom unit, 3 two-bedroom units. Kitchen units, $65-$140; 1 story; exterior corridors; smoke free premises; whirlpool. **All Rooms:** combo & shower baths, cable TV, no phones. **Some Rooms:** coffeemakers, efficiency, radios. **Cards:** DS, MC, VI. (D) ⊗

WOODLAND MOTEL Rates Subject to Change **Phone:** 360/494-6766
◆◆ Motel
All Year 1P: $25- 35 2P/1B: $38- 42 2P/2B: $42- 45 XP: $4
Location: 4 1/2 mi w on Hwy 12. (11890 US 12, RANDLE). **Terms:** Reserv deposit, 10 day notice; small pets only, $4, also $4 dep req. **Facility:** 6 rooms. Rustic units in wooded mountain area. 4 efficiencies, $5 extra; 1 story; exterior corridors; smoke free premises. **All Rooms:** shower baths, no A/C, no phones. **Cards:** MC, VI. (D) ⊗

PASCO—20,300

LODGINGS

HALLMARK MOTEL Rates Subject to Change **Phone:** 509/547-7766
◆◆ Motel
All Year 1P: $32 2P/1B: $36 2P/2B: $41 XP: $4 F12
Location: 1 3/4 mi e of US 395 Lewis St exit, 1 1/2 mi sw of I-182, exit 13. 720 W Lewis St 99301. Fax: 509/545-5306. **Terms:** Sr. discount; reserv deposit, 3 day notice; weekly rates; small pets only, $10 dep req. **Facility:** 54 rooms. 3 two-bedroom units. 2 stories; exterior corridors; heated pool. **Dining:** Restaurant nearby. **All Rooms:** free movies, refrigerators, combo & shower baths, cable TV. **Cards:** DI, DS, MC, VI. (D) ⊗

KING CITY TRUCK STOP Rates Subject to Change **Phone:** 509/547-3475
◆◆◆ Motel
All Year 1P: $38 2P/1B: $43 2P/2B: $48 XP: $5 F12
Location: Northbound I-182, Hwy 12, Hwy 395 at exit Spokane 395N; go 1/2 mi on Hwy 395; southbound at Hillsboro Rd exit. 2100 E Hillsboro Rd 99301. Fax: 509/547-4004. **Terms:** Sr. discount; reserv deposit, 7 day notice; pets, $20 dep req. **Facility:** 36 rooms. Bright modern accommodations. 2 stories; exterior corridors. **Services:** Fee: coin laundry. **Cards:** AE, DI, DS, MC, VI. (D) (S)

RED LION INN Rates Subject to Change **Phone:** 509/547-0701

◆◆◆ Motor Inn

All Year [AP] 1P: $80- 90 2P/1B: $90- 100 2P/2B: $90- 100 XP: $10 F18

Location: N of I-182 exit 12B. 2525 N 20th Ave 99301. Fax: 509/547-4278. **Terms:** 2 night min stay, 7/23 & 7/24; pets. **Facility:** 279 rooms. Rooms with lanai or balcony. 2 two-bedroom units. 3 stories; interior corridors; conference facilities; 2 heated pools, whirlpool; exercise room. **Dining:** Coffee shop; 6 am-11 pm; $5-$11; cocktails; also, Rosso's Ristorante, see separate listing. **Services:** secretarial services; airport transportation. **All Rooms:** combo & shower baths, cable TV. Fee: movies. **Some Rooms:** refrigerators, whirlpools. **Cards:** AE, DI, DS, MC, VI. Ⓓ ⊗

STARLITE MOTEL Rates Subject to Change **Phone:** 509/547-7531

AAA ◆◆ Motel

All Year 1P: $28 2P/1B: $33 2P/2B: $35 XP: $5

Location: At jct I-182 & exit 13; 1/2 mi n. 2634 N 4th Ave 99301. Fax: 509/547-3935. **Terms:** Reserv deposit; weekly rates; small pets only, $5, $10 dep req. **Facility:** 19 rooms. Exterior corridors. **Services:** airport transportation. **All Rooms:** free movies, refrigerators, shower baths, cable TV. **Cards:** AE, DI, DS, MC, VI. Ⓓ ⊗

VINEYARD INN Rates Subject to Change **Phone:** 509/547-0791

AAA ◆◆ Motel

All Year [CP] 1P: $40- 45 2P/1B: $45- 55 2P/2B: $45- 55 XP: $10 F12

Location: 1 mi e of US 395 Lewis St exit, 1 1/4 mi s of I-182, exit 12B. 1800 W Lewis St 99301. Fax: 509/547-8632. **Terms:** Sr. discount; reserv deposit, 3 day notice; weekly/monthly rates; pets, $5. **Facility:** 165 rooms. 2-3 stories; interior corridors; meeting rooms; heated indoor pool, whirlpool. **Dining:** Restaurant nearby. **Services:** airport transportation. Fee: coin laundry. **All Rooms:** free movies, cable TV. **Some Rooms:** coffeemakers, 44 kitchens, radios. Fee: VCP's. **Cards:** AE, CB, DI, DS, MC, VI. *(See ad below)* Ⓓ ⊗

RESTAURANT

ROSSO'S RISTORANTE **Dinner:** $11-$20 **Phone:** 509/547-0701

◆◆ Italian

Location: In Red Lion Inn. 2525 N 20th Ave 99301. **Hours:** 11 am -2 & 5-10 pm, Fri-11 pm, Sat 5 pm-11 pm, Sun 9 am-2 pm. **Reservations:** suggested. **Features:** Sunday brunch; children's menu; carryout; cocktails; a la carte. Relaxed Italian dining, overlooking pool courtyard. **Cards:** AE, DI, DS, MC, VI. ⊗

PORT ANGELES—17,700

LODGINGS

AIRCREST MOTEL Rates Subject to Change **Phone:** 360/452-9255

AAA ◆◆ Motel

6/1-10/15	1P: $42	2P/1B: $48- 52	2P/2B: $58- 62	XP: $5
5/1-5/31	1P: $39	2P/1B: $39- 44	2P/2B: $48- 52	XP: $5
3/1-4/30 & 10/16-2/29	1P: $33	2P/1B: $39	2P/2B: $44	XP: $5

Location: 1 mi e on US 101 westbound. 1006 E Front St 98362. Fax: 360/452-9257. **Terms:** Reserv deposit, 3 day notice; no pets. **Facility:** 24 rooms. Minutes from ferry landing. 2 stories; exterior corridors; whirlpool. **Dining:** Restaurant nearby. **All Rooms:** free movies, combo & shower baths, cable TV. **Cards:** AE, CB, DI, DS, MC, VI. *(See color ad p A67 & ad below)* Ⓓ ⊗

BAVARIAN INN BED & BREAKFAST Rates Subject to Change **Phone:** 360/457-4098

◆◆ Bed & Breakfast

6/1-10/1 [BP]	1P: $80	2P/1B: $85- 95	2P/2B: $95
3/1-5/31 & 12/1-2/29 [BP]	1P: $70	2P/1B: $85- 90	2P/2B: $90

Location: 8 blks s of Hwy 101. 1126 E 7th 98362. **Terms:** Open 3/1-10/1 & 12/1-2/29; age restrictions may apply; check-in 4 pm; credit card guarantee, 5 day notice; 2 night min stay, weekends 7/1-8/30; no pets. **Facility:** 3 rooms. Cozy setting with panoramic view of the harbor. 2 stories; interior/exterior corridors; smoke free premises. **All Rooms:** combo & shower baths, no A/C, no phones, no TVs. **Cards:** MC, VI. Ⓓ ⊗

The VINEYARD INN
PASCO
• Heated Indoor Pool • Spa • Sauna • Restaurant & Lounge • Kitchen Units Available • Complimentary Continental Breakfast • Small Pets Are Welcome
For Reservations, call: 1-800-824-5457
1800 W. Lewis, Pasco, WA 99301 (509) 547-0791

10% Discount off Prevailing Rack Rates 10/1-5/31 for AAA Members
Budget Host
AIRCREST MOTEL
1006 E. Front St. on Hwy. 101
Port Angeles, WA 98362
• Spa • In-Room Coffee
• 20-Channel Satellite TV
Victoria Ferry Information
206/457-4491
AAA
206/452-9255 Toll-Free . . . Reservations Only 1-800/825-9255

HILL HAUS MOTEL
Water and Mt. View
• Close to Victoria
• Ferry, ELEVATOR
• Direct dial phones
• Remote C/CATV
RESERVATIONS
1-800-421-0706
FAX:
360-452-7935
PHONE:
360-452-9285
AAA ◆◆◆

BEST WESTERN OLYMPIC LODGE Rates Subject to Change **Phone:** 360/452-2993
AAA ◆◆◆ Motel
6/1-9/12 1P: $99- 129 2P/1B: $99- 139 2P/2B: $99- 139 XP: $10 F12
3/1-5/31 & 9/13-2/29 1P: $79- 109 2P/1B: $79- 109 2P/2B: $79- 109 XP: $10 F12
Location: E end. 140 Del Guzzi Dr 98362. Fax: 360/452-1497. **Terms:** Sr. discount; check-in 4 pm; credit card guarantee, 3 day notice; no pets. **Facility:** 106 rooms. Spectacular view of Olympic Mountains & Strait of Juan de Fuca. 3 stories; interior corridors; meeting rooms; heated pool, whirlpool; exercise room. **Dining:** Restaurant nearby. **All Rooms:** free movies, cable TV. **Some Rooms:** microwaves, refrigerators, whirlpools. **Cards:** AE, CB, DI, DS, MC, VI.
(D) (S) ⊗

DOMAINE MADELEINE Rates Subject to Change **Phone:** 360/457-4174
◆◆◆ Bed & Breakfast
5/1-9/30 [BP] 1P: $79 2P/1B: $105- 165 XP: $20
3/1-4/30 & 10/1-2/29 [BP] 1P: $69 2P/1B: $95- 145 XP: $20
Location: 9 mi e; 7 mi via Hwy 101, 1 1/2 mi n on Old Olympic Hwy, n on Gherke, then 1/2 mi e on Finn Hall Rd. 146 Wildflower Ln 98362. Fax: 360/457-3037. **Terms:** Age restrictions may apply; check-in 4 pm; credit card guarantee, 5 day notice; no pets. **Facility:** 4 rooms. Waterfront; replica Monet garden & picturesque views. Excellent furnishings, decor & ambience. Multi-course gourmet breakfast. 2 stories; interior/exterior corridors; smoke free premises; oceanview. **All Rooms:** combo & shower baths, cable TV, VCP's. **Some Rooms:** efficiency, whirlpools. **Cards:** MC, VI.
(D) ⊗

FLAGSTONE MOTEL AAA Special Value Rates **Phone:** 360/457-9494
AAA ◆◆ Motel
7/15-9/15 1P: $46 2P/1B: $52 2P/2B: $58 XP: $6
5/1-7/14 1P: $42 2P/1B: $49 2P/2B: $56 XP: $6
3/1-4/30 & 9/16-2/29 1P: $34 2P/1B: $40 2P/2B: $46 XP: $6
Location: Downtown. 415 E First St 98362. Fax: 360/457-9494. **Terms:** Reserv deposit, 3 day notice; weekly/monthly rates, in winter; no pets. **Facility:** 45 rooms. 2 two-bedroom units. 6 rooms with three beds $56-$70; 3 stories, no elevator; exterior corridors; heated indoor pool, sauna. **All Rooms:** cable TV, no A/C. **Some Rooms:** microwaves, refrigerators. **Cards:** AE, CB, DI, DS, MC, VI.
(D) ⊗

HILL HAUS MOTEL Rates Subject to Change **Phone:** 360/452-9285
AAA ◆◆◆ Motel
7/1-9/10 2P/1B: $48- 95 2P/2B: $48- 99 XP: $12
3/1-6/30 & 9/11-2/29 2P/1B: $39- 75 2P/2B: $42- 80 XP: $12
Location: 1 blk w of US 101 on bluff overlooking downtown. 111 E 2nd St 98362. Fax: 360/452-7935. **Terms:** Reserv deposit; no pets. **Facility:** 23 rooms. Most units with panoramic marine view. 2-3 stories; exterior corridors. **All Rooms:** cable TV, no A/C. **Cards:** DS, MC, VI. *(See color ad p A108)*
(D) ⊗

THE POND MOTEL Rates Subject to Change **Phone:** 360/452-8422
AAA ◆ Motel
6/15-9/15 1P: $34- 39 2P/1B: $39- 45 2P/2B: $49- 59 XP: $6 D
5/1-6/14 & 9/16-10/15 1P: $34 2P/1B: $35- 42 2P/2B: $39- 54 XP: $6 D
3/1-4/30 & 10/16-2/29 1P: $27- 33 2P/1B: $32- 37 2P/2B: $36- 42 XP: $6 D
Location: 2 mi w on US 101. 1425 W Hwy 101 98363. **Terms:** Credit card guarantee, 3 day notice; monthly rates; pets, $5. **Facility:** 10 rooms. Rural setting with exceptionally well landscaped grounds. Most units overlook pond. Kitchen units, $6 extra; 1 story; exterior corridors. **All Rooms:** combo & shower baths, cable TV, no A/C, no phones. **Some Rooms:** 6 efficiencies. **Cards:** MC, VI.
(D) ⊗

PORTSIDE INN Rates Subject to Change **Phone:** 360/452-4015
AAA ◆◆ Motel
5/13-10/31 1P: $53 2P/1B: $53 2P/2B: $60 XP: $4 F11
3/1-5/12 & 11/1-2/29 1P: $35 2P/1B: $35 2P/2B: $42 XP: $4 F11
Location: Front St at Alder, e end. 1510 E Front St 98362. Fax: 360/452-4364. **Terms:** Sr. discount; reserv deposit, 10 day notice; no pets. **Facility:** 109 rooms. Commercial location. East side of town. Comfortable clean rooms. 3 stories; exterior corridors; meeting rooms; heated pool, whirlpool. **Dining:** Restaurant nearby. **Services:** Fee: coin laundry. **All Rooms:** free movies, cable TV. **Some Rooms:** refrigerators. **Cards:** AE, CB, DI, DS, MC, VI.
(D) (S) ⊗

RED LION BAYSHORE INN Guaranteed Rates **Phone:** 360/452-9215
AAA ◆◆◆ Motor Inn
All Year 1P: $80- 110 2P/1B: $95- 125 2P/2B: $95- 125 XP: $15 F18
Location: On US 101 westbound. 221 N Lincoln St 98362. Fax: 360/452-4734. **Terms:** Pets. **Facility:** 187 rooms. Waterfront. Many units with view of harbor & Strait of Juan de Fuca; many with balcony. 1 two-bedroom unit. 2 stories; interior/exterior corridors; meeting rooms; heated pool, whirlpool. **Dining:** Dining room, coffee shop; 5:30 am-midnight; $9-$18; cocktails. **All Rooms:** combo & shower baths, cable TV. Fee: movies. **Some Rooms:** refrigerators. **Cards:** AE, CB, DI, DS, MC, VI.
Roll in showers. (D) ⊗

ROYAL VICTORIAN MOTEL Rates Subject to Change **Phone:** 360/452-2316
AAA ◆◆ Motel
5/15-10/14 1P: $34- 52 2P/1B: $40- 70 2P/2B: $44- 76 XP: $6-8 F12
3/1-5/14 & 10/15-2/29 1P: $29- 40 2P/1B: $34- 54 2P/2B: $38- 56 XP: $4 F12
Location: On US 101 eastbound. 521 E 1st St 98362. Fax: 206/452-4201. **Terms:** Reserv deposit; weekly rates; no pets. **Facility:** 20 rooms. 4 two-bedroom units. 2 stories; exterior corridors. **Dining:** Restaurant nearby. **All Rooms:** free movies, combo & shower baths, cable TV. **Some Rooms:** A/C, 3 efficiencies, microwaves, radios, refrigerators. **Cards:** AE, DS, MC, VI. *(See color ad below)*
(D) (S) ⊗

TUDOR INN BED & BREAKFAST Guaranteed Rates **Phone:** 360/452-3138
◆◆◆ Historic Bed & Breakfast
3/1-5/14 & 10/16-2/29 [BP] 1P: $55- 80 2P/1B: $55- 85
5/15-10/15 [BP] 1P: $55- 85 2P/1B: $58- 90
Location: 12 blks s of Ferry Terminal. 1108 S Oak 98362. **Terms:** Age restrictions may apply; reserv deposit, 5 day notice; package plans; 2 night min stay, weekends 7/1-9/30; no pets. **Facility:** 5 rooms. Located in a quiet residential area. Restored Tudor-style inn. View of Strait of Juan de Fuca. 2 stories; interior corridors; smoke free premises; mountain view. **Recreation:** Fee: cross country skiing. **All Rooms:** no A/C, no phones, no TVs. **Cards:** DS, MC, VI.
(D) ⊗

Royal Victorian
Royal Victorian Motel
521 E. First St., Port Angeles, WA
Direct Dial Phones · Newly Expanded in 1991 · Cable TV · Most Rooms have Air Conditioning, Microwave/Fridge
(206) 452-2316

RESTAURANTS

BUSHWHACKER RESTAURANT **Dinner:** $11-$20 **Phone:** 360/457-4113
◆◆ Seafood
Location: 1527 E 1st St 98362. **Hours:** 5 pm-11 pm; 10/1-5/30 to 10 pm, Sun-9 pm. Closed: 7/4, 11/23, 12/24 & 12/25. **Features:** children's menu; salad bar; cocktails & lounge; a la carte. Casual contemporary atmosphere. Smoke free premises. **Cards:** AE, MC, VI.

CAFE GARDEN **Dinner:** up to $10 **Phone:** 360/457-4611
◆◆ American
Location: E end of town on US 101. 1506 E 1st St 98362. **Hours:** 6:30 am-9:30 pm, Sat from 7 am, Sun 7 am-9 pm; Sun 11/1-4/30 7 am-2 pm. Closed: 11/23 & 12/25. **Features:** children's menu; carryout; beer & wine only; a la carte. Gourmet breakfast, extensive lunch menu, fresh seafood, pasta & steaks in charming English garden setting with patio seating. Smoke free premises. **Cards:** DS, MC, VI.

C'EST SI BON **Dinner:** $11-$20 **Phone:** 360/452-8888
◆◆◆ French
Location: 4 mi e of town on US 101 at Cedar Park Rd. 23 Cedar Park Rd 98362. **Hours:** 5 pm-midnight. Closed: Mon. **Reservations:** suggested. **Features:** cocktails & lounge. Dining room overlooking flower gardens & Olympic Mountains. **Cards:** AE, CB, DI, MC, VI.

CHESTNUT COTTAGE RESTAURANT **Dinner:** $11-$20 **Phone:** 360/452-8344
◆◆◆ American
Location: Cross street Washington. 929 E front st 98362. **Hours:** 7 am-3 & 5-9 pm, Fri & Sat-10 pm. Closed: 12/25. **Features:** children's menu; carryout; beer & wine only. Casual, relaxed, dining. Smoke free premises. **Cards:** MC, VI.

DOWNRIGGERS **Dinner:** $11-$20 **Phone:** 360/452-2700
◆◆ Steak and Seafood
Location: At the ferry landing. 115 E Railroad 98362. **Hours:** 11:30 am-9 pm, Sun from 11:30 am. **Reservations:** suggested. **Features:** children's menu; carryout; cocktails & lounge. Located at the Landing Mall. Across from ferry landing. Waterfront view. Casual dining. **Cards:** AE, DS, MC, VI.

EL AMIGO RESTAURANT **Dinner:** up to $10 **Phone:** 360/457-6477
◆ Mexican
Location: Downtown. 1017 E First St 98362. **Hours:** 11 am-10 pm, Sat from noon; 9/7-5/30, 11 am-10 pm, Sat noon-9 pm. Closed major holidays & Sun. **Reservations:** suggested; weekends. **Features:** children's menu; senior's menu; carryout; cocktails & lounge. Mexican-American dining in relaxed comfort. **Cards:** MC, VI.

THE GREENERY RESTAURANT **Dinner:** up to $10 **Phone:** 360/457-4112
◆◆ American
Location: Downtown; 1 blk w of US 101. 117 B East 1st 98362. **Hours:** 11 am-3 & 5-8:30 pm. Closed major holidays & Sun. **Reservations:** suggested. **Features:** children's menu; senior's menu; cocktails. Creative international cuisine emphasizing fresh local seafood, saute & fresh pasta served in an attractive dining room. **Cards:** AE, DI, MC, VI.

LA CASITA **Dinner:** $11-$20 **Phone:** 360/452-2289
◆◆ Mexican
Location: 203 E Front St 98362. **Hours:** 11 am-10 pm, Fri & Sat-11 pm, Sun from noon. Closed: 11/23 & 12/25. **Features:** children's menu; carryout; cocktails & lounge; a la carte. Waterview dining. A Taste of Mexico with fresh seafood. **Cards:** AE, DS, MC, VI.

ROSEWOOD'S FAMILY BUFFET **Dinner:** up to $10 **Phone:** 360/457-1400
◆ American
Location: On US 101. 1936 E 1st St 98362. **Hours:** 11 am-3:30 & 4-8 pm, Sun noon-7 pm. **Features:** children's menu; buffet. Cafeteria-style. One price dining for the family. **Cards:** DS, MC, VI.

PORT HADLOCK

LODGING

THE OLD ALCOHOL PLANT LODGE & MARINA — AAA Special Value Rates — **Phone:** 360/385-7030

◆◆	5/1-10/31	1P: $78	2P/1B: $80	2P/2B: $80	XP: $10 F
Motor Inn	3/1-4/30 & 11/1-2/29	1P: $60	2P/1B: $60	2P/2B: $60	

Location: 15 mi nw of Winslow Ferry, via SR 104 to Paradice Rd, Oak Bay Rd. 301 Alcohol Loop Rd 98339 (PO Box 1369). Fax: 360/385-6955. **Terms:** Reserv deposit; weekly rates; no pets. **Facility:** 25 rooms. Rural location. Spacious, comfortable rooms, many with marine or woodland view. 4 townhouses, 3 with fireplace; 2 stories; interior corridors; conference facilities; whirlpool; marina; fitness center, horseshoes, volleyball, pool room. **Dining:** Dining room; 7 am-10 pm; $10-$16; cocktails. **Recreation:** fishing, crabbing, clamming. **All Rooms:** combo & shower baths. **Some Rooms:** A/C, 5 kitchens. **Cards:** AE, DI, DS, MC, VI. *(See color ad below)*

PORT LUDLOW

LODGINGS

THE INN AT LUDLOW BAY — Rates Subject to Change — **Phone:** 360/437-0411

Lodge	All Year [CP]	1P: $165- 200	2P/1B: $165- 200	2P/2B: $185	XP: $35 F17

Too new to rate; **Location:** In town; 8 mi n of Hood Canal Floating Bridge. 1 Heron Rd 98365 (PO Box 65460). Fax: 360/437-0310. **Terms:** age restrictions may apply; credit card guarantee; BP available; package plans; 2 night min stay, weekends; small pets only, $100 dep req. **Facility:** 36 rooms. Rating withheld pendind completion of construction. 3 stories; interior corridors; mountain view; meeting rooms. **Dining & Entertainment:** Dining room; 5 pm-10 pm; $13-$25; cocktails/lounge; Sun brunch 9 am-noon. **All Rooms:** coffeemakers, refrigerators, cable TV, whirlpools, no A/C. Fee: VCP's. **Cards:** AE, MC, VI.

OLD ALCOHOL PLANT
LODGE & MARINA
310 ALCOHOL LOOP ROAD
TEL 360-385-7030
PORT HADLOCK, WA 98339
ON PORT TOWNSEND BAY

VISIT THE HISTORIC OLD ALCOHOL PLANT LODGE & MARINA THAT REALLY WAS AN ALCOHOL PLANT FROM 1911 TO 1913. NOW FEATURING 25 EXQUISITE UNIQUE SUITES & ROOMS • BEACH • MARINA • LOUNGE • RESTAURANT • SPA • FITNESS ROOM • GAME ROOM • ELEVATOR • TV • SAT. DISH • BEACH WALKING & MUCH MORE.

PORT LUDLOW RESORT & CONFERENCE CENTER AAA Special Value Rates **Phone:** 360/437-2222

AAA ◆◆◆ Resort Motor Inn

5/1-10/31	1P: $60- 150	2P/1B: $90- 150	2P/2B: $90- 150	XP: $10 F16
3/1-4/30 & 11/1-2/29	1P: $60- 120	2P/1B: $75- 120	2P/2B: $75- 120	XP: $10 F16

Location: In town; 8 mi n of Hood Canal Floating Bridge. 9483 Oak Bay Rd 98365. Fax: 360/437-2482. **Terms:** Check-in 4 pm; reserv deposit; weekly/monthly rates; package plans; no pets. **Facility:** 190 rooms. 1-to 4-bedroom suites in several buildings overlooking Port Ludlow Bay. Many rooms with balcony; some with fireplace. 2 stories; exterior corridors; conference facilities; beach, sauna, whirlpool, outdoor heated pool 5/31-9/6 & indoor heated pool 9/7-5/30; 5 tennis courts; marina; exercise room, playground. Fee: 27 holes golf. **Dining:** Also, Harbormaster, see separate listing. **Services:** Fee: coin laundry. **Recreation:** nature trails; charter fishing, fishing, windsurfing; hiking trails, jogging. Fee: boating, sailboats, driving range, aquatic equipment; bicycles. **All Rooms:** coffeemakers, cable TV, no A/C. **Some Rooms:** 60 kitchens. **Cards:** AE, MC, VI. (D) ⊗

RESTAURANT

HARBORMASTER **Dinner:** $21-$30 **Phone:** 360/437-2222

◆◆◆ Seafood

Location: In Port Ludlow Golf & Meeting Retreat. 98365. **Hours:** 7 am-2 & 5-10 pm. **Reservations:** suggested. **Features:** No A/C; children's menu; early bird specials; health conscious menu; carryout; cocktails & lounge; a la carte. Overlooking Port Ludlow Bay. Distinctive redesigned bistro style restaurant with attractive nautical decor. Boat moorage. **Cards:** AE, DI, DS, MC, VI. ⊗

PORT TOWNSEND—7,000

LODGINGS

ANN STARRETT MANSION Rates Subject to Change **Phone:** 360/385-3205

AAA ◆◆◆ Historic Bed & Breakfast

5/1-9/30 [BP]	2P/1B: $75- 185	2P/2B: $75- 185	XP: $25
3/1-4/30 & 10/1-2/29 [BP]	2P/1B: $70- 165	2P/2B: $70- 165	XP: $25

Location: On the Bluff. 744 Clay St 98368. Fax: 360/385-2976. **Terms:** Reserv deposit, 10 day notice; 2 night min stay, weekends in season; no pets. **Facility:** 10 rooms. Classic 1889 Victorian architecture. Frescoed ceilings & free hung three tiered spiral staircase leads to an unusual domed ceiling. 1 two-bedroom unit. 3 stories, no elevator; interior corridors; smoke free premises; street parking only. **All Rooms:** no A/C, no phones, no TVs. **Some Rooms:** combo & shower baths, shared bathrooms. **Cards:** AE, DS, MC, VI. (D) (S) ⊗

A ROSE COTTAGE Rates Subject to Change **Phone:** 360/385-6944

◆ Historic Bed & Breakfast

All Year [CP]	2P/1B: $75- 99	XP: $10

Location: On the Bluff. 1310 Clay 98368. **Terms:** Age restrictions may apply; check-in 4 pm; reserv deposit, 3 day notice; weekly/monthly rates; no pets. **Facility:** 4 rooms. A restored Victorian cottage. 2 stories; interior corridors; smoke free premises; street parking only. **All Rooms:** shower & tub baths, no A/C, no phones, no TVs. **Some Rooms:** whirlpools. **Cards:** MC, VI. (D) ⊗

BISHOP VICTORIAN GUEST SUITES Rates Subject to Change **Phone:** 360/385-6122

AAA ◆◆◆ Historic Hotel

4/1-10/14 [CP]	1P: $68	2P/1B: $83- 90	2P/2B: $98	XP: $10
3/1-3/31 & 10/15-2/29 [CP]	1P: $54	2P/1B: $68- 83	2P/2B: $89	XP: $10

Location: Corner of Washington & Quincy sts. 714 Washington St 98368. Fax: 360/385-5860. **Terms:** Sr. discount; reserv deposit; weekly/monthly rates; pets, $10-$15. **Facility:** 13 rooms. Units furnished in Victorian style. Stairway entry. 2 two-bedroom units. 2 stories; interior corridors. **All Rooms:** kitchens, shower baths, no A/C. **Cards:** AE, MC, VI. (D) ⊗

F.W. HASTINGS HOUSE OLD CONSULATE INN Rates Subject to Change **Phone:** 360/385-6753

AAA ◆◆◆◆ Historic Bed & Breakfast

Fri & Sat 4/1-5/31, 6/1-9/30 & Fri & Sat 10/1-11/30 [BP]	2P/1B: $79- 175	2P/2B: $102- 185	XP:$35-45
3/1-3/31, 10/1-11/30, & 12/1-2/29 [BP]	2P/1B: $69- 145	2P/2B: $92- 155	XP:$30-40

Location: The bluff, overlooking the bay, cross sts Walker & Washington. 313 Walker 98368. Fax: 360/385-2097. **Terms:** Age restrictions may apply; reserv deposit, 14 day notice; package plans; no pets. **Facility:** 8 rooms. 1889 Queen Anne Victorian mansion. Excellent view of Admiralty Inlet & the Olympics. 3 stories, no elevator; interior corridors; smoke free premises; street parking only; whirlpool. **Services:** area transportation, airport transportation. **All Rooms:** combo & shower baths, no A/C, no phones, no TVs. **Cards:** AE, MC, VI. *(See color ad below)* (D) (S) ⊗

HARBORSIDE INN Guaranteed Rates **Phone:** 360/385-7909

AAA ◆◆◆ Motel

5/1-10/14 [CP]	1P: $64- 84	2P/1B: $64- 84	2P/2B: $74- 94	XP: $5 F12
Fri & Sat 3/1-4/30 & 10/15-2/29 [CP]	1P: $54- 62	2P/1B: $54- 62	2P/2B: $62- 74	XP: $5 F12
Sun-Thurs 3/1-4/30 & 10/15-2/29 [CP]	1P: $45- 54	2P/1B: $45- 54	2P/2B: $55- 64	XP: $5 F12

Location: 1 blk e of SR 20 at Benedict St. 330 Benedict St 98368. Fax: 360/385-6984. **Terms:** Check-in 4 pm; credit card guarantee; small pets only, $5. **Facility:** 63 rooms. Commercial location. Private patio for each room. Close to marina & Fort Worden State Park. 3 stories; interior/exterior corridors; oceanview; meeting rooms; heated pool, whirlpool. **Services:** Fee: coin laundry. **All Rooms:** coffeemakers, cable TV, no A/C. **Some Rooms:** 3 efficiencies, microwaves, refrigerators, whirlpools. Fee: VCP's. **Cards:** AE, DI, DS, MC, VI. *(See color ad below)* (D) (S) ⊗

F.W. HASTINGS HOUSE
Old Consulate Inn
313 WALKER AT WASHINGTON, PORT TOWNSEND, WASHINGTON 98368
Port Townsend's founding family mansion
Banquet breakfasts • Afternoon tea
• Evening sherry • Kingbeds • Suites
• Private baths • Billiard room
Spectacular Water Views
1-800-300-6753
Four Diamond Award

Port Townsend's Newest & One Of The Finest Motels
63 Spectacular Rooms On The Waterfront ◆◆◆
In USA & Canada
1 - 800 - 942 - 5960
Harborside Inn

HOLLY HILL HOUSE Rates Subject to Change **Phone:** 360/385-5619

AAA ◆◆◆ Historic Bed & Breakfast

All Year [BP] 1P: $72 2P/1B: $72- 125 2P/2B: $86- 160

Location: 6 blks n of historic district. 611 Polk 98368. **Terms:** Age restrictions may apply; credit card guarantee; package plans; no pets. **Facility:** 5 rooms. Victorian charm amid holly trees & camperdown elm. 2 stories; interior/exterior corridors; smoke free premises. **All Rooms:** combo & shower baths, no A/C, no phones, no TVs. **Cards:** MC, VI. (D) (⊗)

THE JAMES HOUSE Rates Subject to Change **Phone:** 360/385-1238

◆◆◆ Historic Bed & Breakfast

Fri & Sat 3/1-4/30, 5/1-10/31 & Fri & Sat 11/1-2/29 [BP] 1P: $52- 75 2P/1B: $65- 145 2P/2B: $95- 120 XP: $20

Sun-Thurs 3/1-4/30 & 11/1-2/29 [BP] 1P: $47- 65 2P/1B: $60- 125 2P/2B: $80- 100 XP: $20

Location: On the bluff overlooking the sound. 1238 Washington St 98368. **Terms:** Age restrictions may apply; credit card guarantee, 7 day notice; no pets. **Facility:** 12 rooms. Victorian warmth & hospitality overlooking the bay. Built circa 1889. 2 two-bedroom units. 3 stories; interior corridors; smoke free premises; street parking only. **All Rooms:** no A/C, no phones, no TVs. **Cards:** AE, MC, VI. (D) (⊗)

MANRESA CASTLE Rates Subject to Change **Phone:** 360/385-5750

AAA ◆◆◆ Historic Hotel

6/1-10/31 [CP] 1P: $60- 90 2P/1B: $70- 100 2P/2B: $70- 100 XP: $10

3/1-5/31 & 11/1-2/29 [CP] 1P: $55- 75 2P/1B: $65- 85 2P/2B: $65- 85 XP: $10

Location: 1 1/4 mi s; 1 blk w of SR 20. 7th & Sheridan 98368 (PO Box 564). Fax: 360/385-5883. **Terms:** Check-in 4 pm; credit card guarantee, 3 day notice; no pets. **Facility:** 40 rooms. Restored 1892 hilltop Rhine-style castle with city, water & mountain views. 7 units have private bath down the hall. 4 two-bedroom units. 3 stories; interior corridors. **Dining & Entertainment:** 2 dining rooms; 5 pm-9 pm, Fri & Sat-10 pm in season; closed Mon & Tues off season; $12-$18; cocktail lounge. **All Rooms:** free movies, comb, shower & tub baths, cable TV, no A/C. **Some Rooms:** coffeemakers, radios, whirlpools. **Cards:** MC, VI. *(See ad below)* (D) (S)

PALACE HOTEL AAA Special Value Rates **Phone:** 360/385-0773

AAA ◆◆◆ Historic Hotel

Fri & Sat 3/1-4/30, 5/1-10/15 & Fri & Sat 10/16-2/29 [CP] 1P: $59- 119 2P/1B: $59- 119 2P/2B: $59- 119 XP: $10 F11

Sun-Thurs 3/1-4/30 & 10/16-2/29 [CP] 1P: $49- 99 2P/1B: $49- 99 2P/2B: $49- 99 XP: $10 F11

Location: Downtown. 1004 Water St 98368. **Terms:** Credit card guarantee, 3 day notice; no pets. **Facility:** 15 rooms. Beautifully restored 1889 building with harmonious Victorian furnishings. Stairway entry. Some views. 2 stories; interior corridors. **Dining:** Restaurant; 9 am-3 & 5-9 pm; $8-$13; afternoon tea. **Services:** Fee: coin laundry. **All Rooms:** coffeemakers, no A/C, no phones. **Some Rooms:** 4 efficiencies, 5 kitchens, refrigerators, B/W cable TV, whirlpools. **Cards:** AE, DS, MC, VI. (D) (⊗)

MANRESA CASTLE

- PRIVATE BATHS • CABLE TV
- FREE CONTINENTAL BREAKFAST
- EDWARDIAN COCKTAIL LOUNGE
- ELEGANT VICTORIAN RESTAURANT

7th & Sheridan • Port Townsend, WA 98368 (360)385-5750

PORT TOWNSEND
"Victorian Wonderland"
OLYMPIC HOST INNS
The Tides Inn and
Port Townsend Inn & Spa
Outstanding accommodations
for a truly wonderful visit.
Call for Package Information!
(Quiet Season Only)
RESERVATIONS 1-800-822-8696

Are you a Wheelchair traveler? Eat and sleep at the ♿ listings.

PORT TOWNSEND INN & SPA — Rates Subject to Change — **Phone:** 360/385-2211
◆◆ Motel
4/1-10/14 [CP] 1P: $58- 68 2P/1B: $68- 88 2P/2B: $78- 90
3/1-3/31 & 10/15-2/29 [CP] 1P: $48- 58 2P/1B: $58- 78 2P/2B: $68- 88
Location: 1/2 mi s on SR 20. 2020 Washington St 98368. Fax: 360/385-7370. **Terms:** Sr. discount; reserv deposit, 14 day notice; weekly/monthly rates; pets. **Facility:** 25 rooms. Commercial location. Close to marina, golf course & Fort Worden State Park. 2 two-bedroom units. 2 stories; exterior corridors; whirlpool. **All Rooms:** free movies, combo & shower baths, cable TV, no A/C. **Some Rooms:** 2 efficiencies, microwaves, refrigerators. Fee: VCP's. **Cards:** AE, CB, DI, DS, MC, VI. *(See color ad p A112)* Ⓓ ⊗

RAVENSCROFT — Rates Subject to Change — **Phone:** 360/385-2784
◆◆◆ Bed & Breakfast
5/15-10/15 [BP] 1P: $60- 148 2P/1B: $67- 165 2P/2B: $67- 165 XP: $25
3/1-5/14 & 10/16-2/29 [BP] 1P: $58- 123 2P/1B: $65- 135 2P/2B: $65- 135 XP: $25
Location: 6 blks n of historic district. 533 Quincy St 98368. Fax: 360/385-6724. **Terms:** Age restrictions may apply; reserv deposit, 7 day notice; no pets. **Facility:** 8 rooms. Southern colonial charm with a view of Mt. Ranier & The Cascades. 1 two-bedroom unit. 3 stories, no elevator; interior corridors; smoke free premises. **All Rooms:** combo & shower baths, no A/C, no phones, no TVs. **Cards:** AE, DS, MC, VI. Ⓓ ⊗

THE TIDES INN — Rates Subject to Change — **Phone:** 360/385-0595
AAA ◆◆◆ Motel
4/15-10/14 [CP] 1P: $68- 152 2P/1B: $68- 152 2P/2B: $68- 152
3/1-4/14 & 10/15-2/29 [CP] 1P: $58- 105 2P/1B: $58- 105 2P/2B: $58- 105
Location: 5 blks s, on SR 20; along waterfront. 1807 Water St 98368. Fax: 360/385-7370. **Terms:** Sr. discount; reserv deposit, 14 day notice; pets. **Facility:** 21 rooms. Most units overlook Port Townsend Bay; some with balcony. 2 stories; interior/exterior corridors; beach. **Recreation:** fishing. **All Rooms:** combo & shower baths, cable TV, no A/C. **Some Rooms:** coffeemakers, 5 efficiencies, refrigerators, VCP's, whirlpools. **Cards:** AE, CB, DI, DS, MC, VI. *(See color ad p A112)* Ⓓ ⊗

THE WATER STREET HOTEL — Rates Subject to Change — **Phone:** 360/385-5467
AAA ◆ Historic Hotel
5/1-10/31 [CP] 1P: $50- 125 2P/1B: $50- 125 2P/2B: $55- 125 XP: $8 F6
3/1-4/30 & 11/1-2/29 [CP] 1P: $45- 100 2P/1B: $45- 100 2P/2B: $50- 100 XP: $8 F6
Location: Downtown, historic district; cross street Quincy. 635 Water St 98368. **Terms:** Sr. discount; reserv deposit; weekly/monthly rates; pets, $25 dep req. **Facility:** 16 rooms. A panoramic view of Puget Sound & the Olympic Mountains from the balcony. 3 two-bedroom units. 3 stories, no elevator; interior corridors. **Services:** Fee: coin laundry. **All Rooms:** cable TV, no A/C, no phones. **Some Rooms:** coffeemakers, 5 efficiencies, refrigerators. **Cards:** AE, MC, VI. Ⓓ Ⓢ ⊗

RESTAURANTS

LANZA'S RISTORANTE/PIZZERIA — **Dinner:** up to $10 — **Phone:** 360/385-6221
AAA ◆◆ Italian
Location: 1/2 mi n in Uptown District. 1020 Lawrence St 98368. **Hours:** 5 pm-9 pm, Fri & Sat-10 pm. Closed major holidays & Sun. **Reservations:** suggested. **Features:** children's menu; carryout; beer & wine only; a la carte. Casual atmosphere. Smoke free premises. **Cards:** DI, MC, VI. ⊗

MANRESA CASTLE RESTAURANT — **Dinner:** $11-$20 — **Phone:** 360/385-5750
◆◆◆ Seafood
Location: In the Manresa Castle. 7th & Sheridan 98368. **Hours:** 5 pm-10 pm, Sun 9 am-2 & 5-10 pm; 10/18-4/30 4:30 pm-9:30 pm, Fri & Sat 5 pm-10 pm, Sun 9 am-2 pm. Closed: Mon & Tues 10/18-4/30. **Features:** children's menu; health conscious menu items; cocktails & lounge. Elegant Victorian decor. Edwardian cocktail lounge. Premium well drinks. Smoke free premises. **Cards:** MC, VI. ⊗

THE SILVERWATER CAFE — **Dinner:** up to $10 — **Phone:** 360/385-6448
◆ Seafood
Location: Downtown. 126 Quincy St 98368. **Hours:** 11:30 am-9 pm. Closed major holidays. **Features:** children's menu; carryout; beer & wine only. Featuring fresh local seafood & homemade desserts. Casual dining in a comfortable atmosphere. Locally grown produce, focus on healthy, flavorful cuisine. Smoke free premises. **Cards:** MC, VI. ⊗

POULSBO—4,800

LODGINGS

CYPRESS INN — AAA Special Value Rates — **Phone:** 360/697-2119
AAA ◆◆◆ Motel
All Year [CP] 1P: $54- 64 2P/1B: $64- 69 2P/2B: $64- 69 XP: $7 F13
Location: On SR 305 at Poulsbo Village. 19801 NE 7th 98370. Fax: 360/697-2707. **Terms:** Reserv deposit; monthly rates; small pets only, $8. **Facility:** 63 rooms. Commercial location. Close to shopping. 2-3 stories, no elevator; interior corridors; meeting rooms; small heated pool. **Dining:** Restaurant nearby. **Services:** Fee: coin laundry. **All Rooms:** free movies, cable TV. **Some Rooms:** 16 kitchens. Fee: VCP's, whirlpools. **Cards:** AE, CB, DI, DS, MC, VI. Ⓓ Ⓢ ⊗

EDGEWATER BEACH BED & BREAKFAST — Rates Subject to Change — **Phone:** 360/779-2525
◆◆ Bed & Breakfast
All Year [BP] 1P: $85- 125 2P/1B: $95- 135 2P/2B: $95- 135 XP: $25
Location: 3 mi nw of ferry landing via Hwy 305 & Hwy 3 to Pioneer Way, 2 mi to Edgewater Blvd N. 26818 Edgewater Blvd 98370. Fax: 360/779-6015. **Terms:** Check-in 4 pm; reserv deposit, 3 day notice; weekly rates; no pets. **Facility:** 3 rooms. Peaceful setting among English gardens, next to Hood Canal. 2 stories; interior corridors; smoke free premises; beach. **Recreation:** swimming. **All Rooms:** microwaves, free movies, refrigerators, shower baths. **Some Rooms:** cable TV. **Cards:** AE, DS, MC, VI. Ⓓ ⊗

POULSBO'S INN — Rates Subject to Change — **Phone:** 360/779-3921
AAA ◆◆◆ Motel
All Year 1P: $48- 65 2P/1B: $52- 75 2P/2B: $56- 85 XP: $4
Location: 1/2 mi e on Hwy 305. 18680 Hwy 305 98370. Fax: 360/779-9737. **Terms:** Reserv deposit, 3 day notice; weekly/monthly rates; pets, $5. **Facility:** 73 rooms. Commercial location. Close to beaches & water front. A few older, smaller units. 3 two-bedroom units. 22 housekeeping units, $65-$105; 2 stories; exterior corridors; heated pool, whirlpool; playground. **Dining:** Restaurant nearby. **Services:** Fee: coin laundry. **All Rooms:** combo & shower baths, cable TV. **Some Rooms:** coffeemakers, refrigerators. **Cards:** AE, CB, DI, DS, MC, VI. Ⓓ ⊗

PROSSER—4,500

LODGINGS

THE BARN MOTOR INN — Rates Subject to Change — **Phone:** 509/786-2121
AAA ◆◆◆ Motor Inn
All Year 1P: $38 2P/1B: $44 2P/2B: $44 XP: $6 F11
Location: Jct I-82 & Wine Country Rd, exit 80; 1/2 mi s on Wine Country Rd. 490 Wine Country Rd 99350 (PO Box 818). Fax: 509/786-4106. **Terms:** Sr. discount; reserv deposit, 3 day notice; no pets. **Facility:** 30 rooms. Commercial location. Close to airport. 10 minute drive to local golf club. 2 stories; exterior corridors; meeting rooms; pool. **Dining:** Dining room; 6 am-10 pm, Fri & Sat-11 pm; $6-$17; cocktails. **Services:** Fee: coin laundry. **All Rooms:** cable TV. **Some Rooms:** refrigerators, whirlpools. **Cards:** AE, DS, MC, VI. Ⓓ ⊗

BEST WESTERN PROSSER INN Rates Subject to Change **Phone:** 509/786-7977
◆◆◆ Motel
5/15-10/15 [CP] 1P: $49 2P/1B: $52 2P/2B: $52 XP: $8
10/16-2/29 [CP] 1P: $47 2P/1B: $50 2P/2B: $50 XP: $8
3/1-5/14 [CP] 1P: $45 2P/1B: $48 2P/2B: $48 XP: $7
Location: Off I-82 at exit 80. 225 Meriot Dr 99350. Fax: 509/786-7236. **Terms:** Reserv deposit; small pets only, $10, also $50 dep req. **Facility:** 49 rooms. 2 stories; interior corridors; meeting rooms; heated pool, whirlpool. **Services:** data ports. **All Rooms:** combo & shower baths, cable TV. **Some Rooms:** 2 efficiencies, no utensils, microwaves, refrigerators, whirlpools. **Cards:** AE, CB, DI, DS, JCB, MC, VI. Roll in showers. (D) (S) ⊗

PULLMAN—23,500

LODGINGS

AMERICAN TRAVEL INN Rates Subject to Change **Phone:** 509/334-3500
◆◆ Motel
All Year 1P: $34 2P/1B: $38 2P/2B: $44 XP: $4 F12
Location: 3 blks s on US 195 business rt. 515 S Grand 99163. **Terms:** Sr. discount; reserv deposit, 14 day notice; weekly rates; pets, limit 1, in designated rooms. **Facility:** 34 rooms. King suite, $52-$56. Family rooms, $56; 2 stories; exterior corridors; heated pool. **Dining:** Restaurant nearby. **Services:** winter plug-ins. **All Rooms:** combo & shower baths, cable TV. **Some Rooms:** refrigerators. **Cards:** AE, CB, DI, DS, MC, VI. (D) ⊗

HOLIDAY INN EXPRESS Rates Subject to Change **Phone:** 509/334-4437
◆◆◆ Motel
8/1-2/29 [CP] 1P: $64 2P/1B: $64 2P/2B: $64 XP: $5 F19
3/1-7/31 [CP] 1P: $59 2P/1B: $59 2P/2B: $59 XP: $5 F19
Location: 1 mi e on SR 270, then 1/2 mi s on Bishop Rd. SE 1190 Bishop Rd 99163. Fax: 509/334-4447. **Terms:** Sr. discount; **Facility:** 85 rooms. Engaging lobby & well-appointed rooms. 3 stories; interior corridors; meeting rooms; heated indoor pool, whirlpool; exercise room. **Services:** data ports; airport transportation. Fee: coin laundry. **All Rooms:** coffeemakers, free movies, combo & shower baths, cable TV. **Some Rooms:** microwaves, refrigerators, whirlpools. **Cards:** AE, DI, DS, JCB, MC, VI. *(See color ad below)* Roll in showers. (D) (S)

QUALITY INN PARADISE CREEK MOTOR INN Guaranteed Rates **Phone:** 509/332-0500
◆◆◆ Motel
All Year [CP] 1P: $52- 75 2P/1B: $60- 83 2P/2B: $60- 83 XP: $8 F18
Location: 1 mi e on SR 270, then 1/4 mi s on Bishop Blvd. SE 1050 Bishop Blvd 99163. Fax: 509/334-4271. **Terms:** Sr. discount; credit card guarantee; pets, $5. **Facility:** 66 rooms. Suites with whirlpool; 2 stories; interior corridors; conference facilities; heated pool, sauna, whirlpool. **Dining:** Restaurant nearby. **Services:** airport transportation. **All Rooms:** free movies, combo & shower baths, cable TV. **Some Rooms:** refrigerators. **Cards:** AE, CB, DI, DS, JCB, MC, VI. Roll in showers. (D) ⊗

RESTAURANT

SWILLY'S CAFE AND GATHERING PLACE **Dinner:** up to $10 **Phone:** 509/334-3395
◆◆ American
Location: Downtown. 200 Kamiaken 99163. **Hours:** 11 am-9:30 pm, Fri & Sat-10 pm. Closed: Sun, 7/4 & 12/25-1/1. **Features:** casual dress; health conscious menu; carryout; beer & wine only; street parking; a la carte. Upscale deli menu featuring calzones, fetuccini, salads & homemade desserts. Smoke free premises. **Cards:** AE, MC, VI. ⊗

PUYALLUP—23,900

LODGINGS

BEST WESTERN PARK PLAZA AAA Special Value Rates **Phone:** 206/848-1500
◆◆◆◆ Motel
6/1-2/29 [CP] 1P: $63- 67 2P/1B: $68- 73 2P/2B: $71- 76 XP: $5 F12
3/1-5/31 [CP] 1P: $60- 63 2P/1B: $65- 70 2P/2B: $68- 73 XP: $5 F12
Location: From Hwy 512, exit 161 (South Hill/Eatonville) w 1 blk. 9620 S Hill Park Pl E 98373. Fax: 206/848-1511. **Terms:** Monthly rates; no pets. **Facility:** 100 rooms. 3 stories; interior corridors; meeting rooms; heated pool, whirlpool. **Dining:** Restaurant nearby. **Services:** data ports. Fee: coin laundry. **All Rooms:** free movies, combo & shower baths, cable TV. **Some Rooms:** coffeemakers, 6 efficiencies, microwaves, refrigerators. Fee: whirlpools. **Cards:** AE, CB, DI, DS, MC, VI. Roll in showers. (D) (S) ⊗

NORTHWEST MOTOR INN Rates Subject to Change **Phone:** 206/841-2600
◆◆ Motel
All Year 1P: $39 2P/1B: $43 2P/2B: $47 XP: $4 F12
Location: 1/4 mi s of Meridian exit off SR 512. 1409 S Meridian 98371. Fax: 206/841-2600. **Terms:** Sr. discount; reserv deposit, 4 day notice; weekly/monthly rates; CP available; pets, $5. **Facility:** 51 rooms. Semi-rural location. Modest, comfortable rooms. 14 efficiencies, $3 extra; 3 stories, no elevator; exterior corridors; whirlpool. **Dining:** Restaurant nearby. **Services:** Fee: coin laundry. **All Rooms:** free movies, cable TV. Fee: VCP. **Some Rooms:** microwaves, refrigerators. **Cards:** AE, DI, DS, MC, VI. (D) (S) ⊗

RESTAURANTS

ANTON'S **Dinner:** $11-$20 **Phone:** 206/845-7569
◆◆ American
Location: 1 1/2 mi e on Puyallup-Summer Hwy; s of Puyallup River Bridge. 3207 E Main 98372. **Hours:** 11 am-10 pm, Sat 5 pm-11 pm, Fri-11 pm. Closed major holidays & Sun. **Reservations:** suggested. **Features:** children's menu; cocktails & lounge; entertainment. Steak & seafood. **Cards:** AE, MC, VI. ⊗

OLD COUNTRY BUFFET **Dinner:** up to $10 **Phone:** 206/840-2895
◆ American
Location: Jct SR 512 & 167; in South Hill Mall. 3500 S Meridian 98373. **Hours:** 7 am-8:30 pm, Fri-9 pm, Sat 8 am-9 pm, Sun 8 am-8:30 pm. Closed: 12/25. **Features:** salad bar; buffet. Family dining, menu varies daily. Farmhouse breakfast $5.39. Smoke free premises. ⊗

Holiday Inn EXPRESS
PULLMAN - Home of Washington State University
Come Home To Pullman's Newest Hotel & A Great Value!
1-800-HOLIDAY
or (509) 334-4437
S.E. 1190 Bishop Blvd., Pullman, WA 99163
5 min. from WSU / 10 min. from airport & UI
FREE Breakfast Buffet
FREE in-room coffee & local phone calls
Pullman's only hotel with indoor pool/spa
Guest laundry, gift shop & business center
10% off rack rates
(Not valid with any other offer.)

QUINAULT

LODGING

LAKE QUINAULT LODGE Rates Subject to Change **Phone:** 360/288-2900

◆◆	5/26-10/8	1P: $90- 125	2P/1B: $90- 125	XP: $10	F5
Historic Lodge	4/7-5/25 & 10/9-11/5	1P: $70- 115	2P/1B: $70- 115	XP: $10	F5
	3/1-4/6 & 11/6-2/29	1P: $59- 115	2P/1B: $59- 115	XP: $10	F5

Location: 2 mi e off US 101; on s shore of Lake Quinault. 98575 (PO Box 7). Fax: 360/288-2901. **Terms:** Reserv deposit, 3 day notice; 2 night min stay; pets, $10. **Facility:** 92 rooms. Historic lodge in beautiful lakefront setting next to rainforest. Some rooms with fireplace & balcony. 3 stories, no elevator; interior/exterior corridors; meeting rooms; heated indoor pool, sauna, whirlpool; boat dock. **Dining & Entertainment:** Dining room; 7 am-3 & 5-9:30 pm, Sun 7 am-9 pm; $10-$20; cocktails/lounge. **Recreation:** nature trails; swimming, fishing. Fee: canoeing. Rental: boats. **All Rooms:** comb, shower & tub baths, no A/C, no phones, no TVs. **Cards:** AE, MC, VI. *(See ad below)* Ⓓ ⊗

RAYMOND—2,900

LODGING

MAUNU'S MOUNTCASTLE MOTEL Rates Subject to Change **Phone:** 360/942-5571

All Year 1P: $36 2P/1B: $44 2P/2B: $50 XP: $4

AAA ◆◆ Motel

Location: 2 blks w of US 101, City Center exit. 524 3rd St 98577. **Terms:** Reserv deposit; weekly rates; pets, $4. **Facility:** 28 rooms. Very attractive landscaping. 2 two-bedroom units. 2 efficiencies, $4 extra; 2 stories; exterior corridors. **All Rooms:** combo & shower baths, cable TV, no A/C. **Some Rooms:** refrigerators. **Cards:** AE, CB, DI, DS, MC, VI. Ⓓ

REDMOND—35,800 (See SEATTLE & VICINITY ACCOMMODATIONS spotting map pages A136 & A137; see index starting on page A134)

LODGINGS

BEST WESTERN REDMOND INN Rates Subject to Change **Phone:** 206/883-4900 (164)

All Year 1P: $68- 91 2P/1B: $78- 101 2P/2B: $83 XP: $10

AAA ◆◆◆ Motor Inn

Location: 7 mi e of I-405, exit 14 on SR 520 to Redmond Way. 17601 Redmond Way 98052. Fax: 206/869-5838. **Terms:** Reserv deposit; no pets. **Facility:** 137 rooms. Tasteful, comfortable rooms. 3 stories; interior corridors; meeting rooms; heated pool, whirlpool. **Dining:** Restaurant; 5:30 am-10 pm; $5-$9; wine/beer only. **Services:** Fee: coin laundry, airport transportation. **All Rooms:** free movies, cable TV. **Some Rooms:** 4 efficiencies, refrigerators, whirlpools. **Cards:** AE, CB, DI, DS, MC, VI. Ⓓ Ⓢ ⊗

SILVER CLOUD INN AT REDMOND Rates Subject to Change **Phone:** 206/746-8200 (165)

◆◆◆	6/15-9/30 [CP]	1P: $59- 63	2P/1B: $65- 69	2P/2B: $69	XP: $6	F12
Motel	3/1-6/14 & 10/1-2/29 [CP]	1P: $54- 58	2P/1B: $60- 64	2P/2B: $63	XP: $6	F12

Location: 3 1/4 mi ne of I-405; off SR 520 via 148th Ave ne, South exit & ne 24th St to 152nd Ave. 15304 NE 21st St 98052. Fax: 206/747-2078. **Terms:** Sr. discount; reserv deposit, 3 day notice; no pets. **Facility:** 59 rooms. Some with city view. 4 stories; interior corridors; meeting rooms; whirlpool; exercise room. **Dining:** Restaurant nearby. **Services:** data ports; guest laundry. Fee: airport transportation. **All Rooms:** refrigerators, cable TV. **Some Rooms:** Fee: VCP's. **Cards:** AE, DI, DS, MC, VI. Ⓓ Ⓢ ⊗

RESTAURANTS

BILLY MCHALE'S **Dinner:** $11-$20 **Phone:** 206/881-0316 (115)

◆◆ American

Location: From I-405 exit 18 (Redmond/Kirkland) SR 905E, 2 1/2 mi on NE 85th to Redmond Way. 15210 Redmond Way 98052. **Hours:** 11 am-9 pm, Tues-Thurs to 10 pm, Fri-11 pm, Sat noon-11 pm, Sun 10 am-9 pm. Closed: 11/23 & 12/25. **Features:** children's menu; senior's menu; carryout; cocktails & lounge; a la carte. Barbecue ribs, chicken, steaks, prime rib & fresh seafood. **Cards:** AE, MC, VI. ⊗

NARA JAPANESE RESTAURANT **Dinner:** $11-$20 **Phone:** 206/885-0703 (114)

◆ Ethnic

Location: Downtown. 16564 Cleveland St #M 98052. **Hours:** Closed: Sun, 1/1, 11/23 & 12/25. **Features:** carryout; beer & wine only. Simple, comfortable, friendly Japanese dining. **Cards:** MC, VI. ⊗

RENTON—41,700 (See SEATTLE & VICINITY ACCOMMODATIONS spotting map pages A136 & A137; see index starting on page A134)

LODGINGS

HOLIDAY INN SEATTLE-RENTON Rates Subject to Change **Phone:** 206/226-7700 (116)

AAA	6/1-9/5	1P: $99	2P/1B: $109	2P/2B: $109	XP: $10
◆◆◆ Motor Inn	3/1-5/31 & 9/6-2/29	1P: $89	2P/1B: $99	2P/2B: $99	XP: $10

Location: I-405 exit 2B; at jct SR 167W. 800 Rainier Ave S 98055. Fax: 206/271-2315. **Terms:** Credit card guarantee; no pets. **Facility:** 188 rooms. Commercial location. Close to shopping. 3-6 stories; interior corridors; meeting rooms; whirlpool, heated pool open 5/1-10/31. **Dining:** Coffee shop; 6 am-11 pm, Fri & Sat-midnight; $5-$11; cocktails. **Services:** area transportation, airport transportation. **All Rooms:** free & pay movies, combo & shower baths, cable TV. **Some Rooms:** coffeemakers, refrigerators. **Cards:** AE, CB, DI, DS, MC, VI. Ⓓ ⊗

Before you read this, take a deep breath.

Now come to historic Lake Quinault Lodge and take a breather. You'll find the air fresh and your surroundings enchantingly beautiful. Nestled in the heart of Olympic National Forest on the Olympic Peninsula, Lake Quinault Lodge boasts spectacular rain forest scenery certain to take your breath away.

Call 360-288-2900 for more information.

Lake Quinault Lodge

The Rest Comes Easy.

Washington residents may phone 1-800-562-6672.

Lake Quinault Lodge is managed by ARAMARK and operates under special permit in Olympic National Forest.

(See SEATTLE & VICINITY ACCOMMODATIONS spotting map pages A136 & A137)

NENDEL'S INN RENTON Rates Subject to Change **Phone:** 206/251-9591 (115)

◆◆ Motel
All Year [CP] 1P: $58 2P/1B: $58 2P/2B: $63 XP: $5 F14
Location: 1 mi s of I-405 exit 2; off SR 167. 3700 E Valley Rd 98055. Fax: 206/251-0340. **Terms:** Sr. discount; reserv deposit; weekly/monthly rates; pets, $5. **Facility:** 130 rooms. Commercial location. Close to shopping. 4 stories; interior corridors; meeting rooms; whirlpool. **Dining:** Restaurant nearby. **Services:** area transportation, within 5 mi, airport transportation. Fee: coin laundry. **All Rooms:** free movies, cable TV. **Some Rooms:** 15 efficiencies, microwaves. **Cards:** AE, DI, DS, MC, VI. (D) (S) ⊗

SILVER CLOUD AT RENTON Rates Subject to Change **Phone:** 206/226-7600 (113)

◆◆◆ Motel
7/1-9/30 [CP] 1P: $54- 57 2P/1B: $60- 63 2P/2B: $64 XP: $6 F12
3/1-6/30 & 10/1-2/29 [CP] 1P: $49- 52 2P/1B: $55- 58 2P/2B: $58 XP: $6 F12
Location: Jct I-405 & Maple Valley Hwy, exit 4A northbound; southbound exit 4; then e at 2nd light. 1850 Maple Valley Hwy 98055. Fax: 206/271-1296. **Terms:** Sr. discount; reserv deposit, 3 day notice; no pets. **Facility:** 105 rooms. Commercial location. 1 two-bedroom unit. 4 stories; interior corridors; meeting rooms; whirlpool; exercise room. **Dining:** Restaurant nearby. **Services:** data ports; guest laundry. **All Rooms:** free movies, cable TV. **Some Rooms:** 15 efficiencies, kitchen, microwaves, refrigerators, whirlpools. **Cards:** AE, CB, DI, DS, MC, VI. (D) (S) ⊗

TRAVELERS INN Rates Subject to Change **Phone:** 206/228-2858 (114)

◆◆ Motel
All Year 1P: $35 2P/1B: $42 2P/2B: $42 XP: $4 F11
Location: 4 mi n at I-405, exit 7. 4710 Lake Washington NE 98056. Fax: 206/228-3055. **Terms:** Sr. discount; reserv deposit, 10 day notice; no pets. **Facility:** 116 rooms. Commercial location. 2-3 stories, no elevator; exterior corridors; heated pool. **Dining:** Restaurant nearby. **Services:** Fee: airport transportation. **All Rooms:** free movies, cable TV. **Some Rooms:** refrigerators. **Cards:** AE, CB, DI, DS, MC, VI. (D) ⊗

RESTAURANTS

BILLY MCHALE 'S **Dinner:** $11-$20 **Phone:** 206/271-7427 (82)

◆◆ American
Location: Off I-405 at exit Rainier Ave n, 1/2 mi to 7th. 241 SW 7th 98055. **Hours:** 11 am-9 pm, Fri-10:30 pm, Sat noon-10:30 pm, Sun noon-9 pm. Closed: 11/23 & 12/25. **Features:** children's menu; senior's menu; carryout; cocktails & lounge. Famous for barbecue ribs, chicken, steaks, prime rib & fresh seafood. **Cards:** AE, MC, VI. ⊗

GENE'S RISTORANTE **Dinner:** $11-$20 **Phone:** 206/271-7042 (81)

◆◆ Italian
Location: Downtown, at S 3rd & Shattuck sts. 212 S 3rd 98055. **Hours:** 11 am-3 & 5-9 pm, Fri & Sat-10 pm. Closed: Sun & 12/24-1/2. **Features:** No A/C; children's menu; carryout; beer & wine only. Smoke free premises. **Cards:** AE, MC, VI. ⊗

RICHLAND—32,300

LODGINGS

BALI HI MOTEL Rates Subject to Change **Phone:** 509/943-3101

◆◆ Motel
All Year 1P: $37- 38 2P/1B: $39- 42 2P/2B: $41- 44 XP: $5
Location: 1 3/4 mi n of I-182 exit 5B; on SR 240 business route. 1201 George Washington Way 99352. Fax: 509/943-6363. **Terms:** Credit card guarantee; pets, $5, also $10 dep req. **Facility:** 44 rooms. Attractively landscaped. 2 stories; exterior corridors; heated pool, whirlpool. **Dining:** Restaurant nearby. **All Rooms:** coffeemakers, microwaves, free movies, refrigerators, cable TV. **Cards:** AE, DI, DS, MC, VI. (D) ⊗

BEST WESTERN TOWER INN & CONFERENCE CENTER Rates Subject to Change **Phone:** 509/946-4121

◆◆◆ Motor Inn
All Year 1P: $70 2P/1B: $80 2P/2B: $80 XP: $10 F18
Location: 2 1/2 mi n of I-182 exit 5B; on SR 240 business route. 1515 George Washington Way 99352. Fax: 509/946-2222. **Terms:** Sr. discount; check-in 4 pm; reserv deposit, 3 day notice; 2 night min stay, 7/23-7/24; no pets. **Facility:** 195 rooms. Commercial area. Newly remodeled rooms, many with patio or balcony. 6 stories; interior corridors; conference facilities; heated indoor pool, wading pool, saunas, whirlpool. **Dining:** Dining room; 6 am-2 & 4:30-9 pm; $8-$22; cocktails. **Services:** airport transportation. Fee: coin laundry. **All Rooms:** free & pay movies, combo & shower baths, cable TV. **Some Rooms:** refrigerators. **Cards:** AE, DI, DS, MC, VI. Roll in showers. (D) ⊗

COLUMBIA CENTER DUNES Rates Subject to Change **Phone:** 509/783-8181

◆◆ Motel
All Year 1P: $33 2P/1B: $35- 37 2P/2B: $39 XP: $5
Location: 2 3/4 mi e of I-182, exit 5A; on SR 240 at Columbia Center Blvd-Columbia Park exit. 1751 Fowler Ave 99352. Fax: 509/783-2811. **Terms:** Reserv deposit; weekly rates; CP available; small pets only, $7. **Facility:** 90 rooms. Commercial area. Easy off state road. Modestly furnished. 2 efficiencies, $5 extra; 2 stories; exterior corridors; heated pool, sauna. **Dining:** Restaurant nearby. **Services:** Fee: coin laundry. **All Rooms:** combo & shower baths, cable TV. **Some Rooms:** refrigerators. Fee: VCP's. **Cards:** AE, CB, DI, DS, MC, VI.
(See color ad below) (D) ⊗

AAA **COLUMBIA CENTER DUNES MOTEL**

VALUE

1751 Fowler, Richland, WA 99352
(on SR 240, Columbia Center Blvd. Exit)

(509) 783-8181

- Clean, Friendly Affordable
- Queen Size Beds/Waterbeds
- Refrigerators - All Rooms
- Air Conditioned
- Sauna/Pool
- Coin Laundry
- C.T.V.-Cable-Movies-V.C R.s
- Cont. Breakfast
- Free Coffee in Rooms & Lobby
- Commercial Rates, Sr. Discount & AAA Discount
- Restaurant Adjacent
- Fast Food Closeby
- Columbia Center Mall - Nearby

FAX: (509) 783-2811 RES: 1-800-638-6168

NENDEL'S INN Rates Subject to Change **Phone:** 509/943-4611
◆◆ All Year 1P: $42- 47 2P/1B: $47- 52 2P/2B: $50- 55 XP: $5 F12
Motel **Location:** 1 mi n of I-182 exit 5B; 1 blk w of SR 240 business route. 615 Jadwin Ave 99352. Fax: 509/946-2271. **Terms:** Sr. discount; reserv deposit, 3 day notice; monthly rates; CP available; small pets only, $5. **Facility:** 98 rooms. Next to municipal park. Some small units. 15 efficiencies, $50-$53; 2 stories; exterior corridors; small heated pool. **Dining:** Restaurant nearby. **Services:** airport transportation; winter plug-ins. **All Rooms:** free movies, cable TV. **Some Rooms:** coffeemakers, microwaves, refrigerators. **Cards:** AE, CB, DI, DS, MC, VI. (D) ⊗

RED LION INN-HANFORD HOUSE Rates Subject to Change **Phone:** 509/946-7611
◆◆◆ All Year 1P: $69- 79 2P/1B: $79- 89 2P/2B: $79- 89 XP: $10
Motor Inn **Location:** 1 1/4 mi n of I-182 exit 5B; on SR 240 business route. 802 George Washington Way 99352. Fax: 509/943-8564. **Terms:** Credit card guarantee; pets. **Facility:** 150 rooms. On bank of Columbia River adjacent to municipal park. Poolside units have lanai or balcony. Some river view units. 1 two-bedroom unit. 2 stories; interior corridors; conference facilities; heated pool, whirlpool; boat dock. **Dining:** Also, Terrace Dining Room, see separate listing. **Services:** airport transportation. **Recreation:** fishing. **All Rooms:** cable TV. Fee: movies. **Some Rooms:** microwaves, refrigerators. **Cards:** AE, CB, DI, DS, JCB, MC, VI. (D) ⊗

SHILO INN-RIVERSHORE Rates Subject to Change **Phone:** 509/946-4661
◆◆◆ 5/16-9/15 1P: $53- 60 2P/1B: $53- 60 2P/2B: $71- 89 XP: $8 F12
Motor Inn 3/1-5/15 & 9/16-2/29 1P: $50- 58 2P/1B: $50- 58 2P/2B: $68- 79 XP: $8 F12
Location: Jct I-182 & George Washington Way, exit 5B, 1/2 mi n to Comstock St. 50 Comstock St 99352. Fax: 509/943-6741. **Terms:** Sr. discount; check-in 4 pm; weekly/monthly rates; pets, $7. **Facility:** 150 rooms. Rural lakeside location, next to golf course. 12 efficiencies, $85; 9/16-5/15, $75; 2 stories; exterior corridors; meeting rooms; heated pool, whirlpool. **Dining:** Dining room; 6 am-10 pm, Fri-11 pm, Sun 7 am-9 pm; $8-$14; cocktails. **Services:** airport transportation. Fee: coin laundry. **All Rooms:** free movies, cable TV. **Some Rooms:** microwaves, refrigerators. Fee: VCP's. **Cards:** AE, CB, DI, DS, JCB, MC, VI. (D) ⊗

RESTAURANTS

LAS MARGARITAS FAMILY MEXICAN RESTAURANT **Dinner:** $11-$20 **Phone:** 509/946-7755
◆◆ **Location:** Downtown. 627 Jadwin Ave 99352. **Hours:** 11 am-10:30 pm, Fri & Sat-11 pm. Closed: 7/4, 11/23
Mexican & 12/25. **Features:** children's menu; carryout; cocktails & lounge. Casual, lively family dining. Knowledgeable staff. **Cards:** AE, DI, DS, MC, VI. ⊗

TERRACE DINING ROOM **Dinner:** $11-$20 **Phone:** 509/946-7611
◆◆ **Location:** In Red Lion Hanford House. 802 George Washington Way 99352. **Hours:** 6 am-2 & 5-10 pm,
Seafood Fri-11 pm, Sat 7 am-2 & 5-11 pm, Sun 7 am-2 & 5-10 pm. **Reservations:** suggested. **Features:** Sunday brunch; children's menu; senior's menu; carryout; cocktails & lounge; a la carte. Also lamb, chicken & flambe served in circular terraced dining room with view of Columbia River. **Cards:** AE, DI, DS, JCB, MC, VI. ⊗

RITZVILLE—1,700

LODGINGS

BEST WESTERN HERITAGE INN Rates Subject to Change **Phone:** 509/659-1007
AAA 5/1-10/15 [CP] 1P: $51- 55 2P/1B: $58- 63 2P/2B: $63 XP: $7 F18
3/1-4/30 & 10/16-2/29 [CP] 1P: $45- 49 2P/1B: $58- 63 2P/2B: $63 XP: $7 F18
◆◆◆ **Location:** I-90 exit 221; 2 blks n, 1 blk e. 1405 Smitty's Blvd 99169. Fax: 509/659-1007. **Terms:** Sr.
Motel discount; pets, in designated rooms. **Facility:** 42 rooms. Comfortable, contemporary lodgings in small agricultural town. Easy interstate access. Suites with whirlpool; $90-$145; 2 stories; interior corridors; heated pool, whirlpool. **Dining:** Restaurant nearby. **Services:** Fee: coin laundry. **All Rooms:** free movies, combo & shower baths, cable TV. **Some Rooms:** kitchen, refrigerators, whirlpools. **Cards:** AE, DI, DS, MC, VI. *(See color ad below)* (D) ⊗

COLWELL MOTOR INN Guaranteed Rates **Phone:** 509/659-1620
AAA 5/1-10/31 2P/1B: $40- 50 2P/2B: $48- 56 XP: $4
3/1-4/30 & 11/1-2/29 2P/1B: $36- 45 2P/2B: $42- 48 XP: $3
◆◆◆ **Location:** Downtown; I-90 exit 220. 501 W 1st Ave 99169. Fax: 509/659-1620. **Terms:** Reserv deposit; pets,
Motel $4, also $25 dep req. **Facility:** 25 rooms. 3 two-bedroom units. Room with whirlpool, $60; 1 story; exterior corridors; heated pool, sauna. **Services:** Fee: coin laundry. **All Rooms:** coffeemakers, free movies, combo & shower baths, cable TV. **Some Rooms:** refrigerators. **Cards:** AE, CB, DI, DS, MC, VI. IMA. *(See color ad below)* (D) ⊗

SALKUM

LODGING

THE SHEPHERD'S INN BED & BREAKFAST Guaranteed Rates **Phone:** 360/985-2434
◆◆ 6/1-10/15 [BP] 1P: $55- 65 2P/1B: $60- 70 2P/2B: $55- 60 XP: $15
Bed & 3/1-5/31 & 10/16-2/29 [BP] 1P: $50- 55 2P/1B: $55- 60 2P/2B: $55 XP: $15
Breakfast **Location:** 13 mi e of I-5 off exit 68 on US Hwy 12, 3/4 mi off Hwy 12 via Fischer Rd. 168 Autumn Heights Dr. 98582. **Terms:** Age restrictions may apply; reserv deposit; no pets. **Facility:** 4 rooms. Old fashioned hospitality in a quiet country setting. 2 stories; interior corridors; smoke free premises. **All Rooms:** no A/C, no phones, no TVs. **Some Rooms:** whirlpools. **Cards:** AE, DS. (D) ⊗

RITZVILLE – A GREAT PLACE TO VISIT!

Best Western

Best Western Heritage Inn
1405 Smitty's Blvd.
Ritzville, WA 99169
I-90 Exit 221
509-659-1007

Pool & Spa (seasonal) • Cable TV
Kitchenettes • Spa Suites • Free
Continental Breakfast • Coin-op
Laundry • RV Park

Washington Ritzville

BEST WESTERN RESERVATIONS: 800-528-1234

COLWELL MOTOR INN

IMA America's Lodging Network

•Family Units •Outdoor Heated Pool •CATV-HBO
•King/Queen Beds •Direct Dial Phones •Laundry
•Jacuzzi King Suite •Non-Smoker's Rooms •A/C •Sauna

◆◆◆ AAA

1-800-341-8000 501 W 1st I-90 Exit 220 Ritzville

SAN JUAN ISLANDS

The San Juan Islands area is comprised of the following Islands: Deer Harbor, Eastsound, Friday Harbour, Lopez, Orcas Island and San Juan Island.

LODGINGS

DEER HARBOR INN — Rates Subject to Change — **Phone:** 360/376-4110
◆◆ Lodge
4/1-10/31 [CP] 2P/1B: $89 2P/2B: $89 XP: $15
3/1-3/31 & 11/1-2/29 [CP] 2P/1B: $65 2P/2B: $65 XP: $15
Location: On Orcas Island; on Deer Harbor Rd, 8 mi sw of Ferry Landing, 4 mi sw of West Sound. 98243 (PO Box 142, DEER HARBOR). **Terms:** Reserv deposit, 7 day notice; no pets. **Facility:** 8 rooms. Overlooking Deer Harbor Bay. 2 stories; interior corridors; smoke free premises. **Dining:** Restaurant; 5 pm-9 pm; $12-$18; wine/beer only. **All Rooms:** combo & shower baths, no A/C, no phones, no TVs. **Cards:** AE, MC, VI.

EDENWILD INN — Rates Subject to Change — **Phone:** 360/468-3238
◆◆ Bed & Breakfast
4/1-10/31 [CP] 1P: $85- 140 2P/1B: $85- 140 XP: $25
3/1-3/31 & 11/1-2/29 [CP] 1P: $75 2P/1B: $75 XP: $15
Location: In Lopez; downtown. Eads Ln 98261 (PO Box 271). **Terms:** Reserv deposit, 14 day notice; no pets. **Facility:** 8 rooms. Country elegance. 2 stories; interior corridors; smoke free premises; meeting rooms. **Dining:** Dining room nearby. **All Rooms:** combo & shower baths, no A/C, no phones, no TVs. **Cards:** MC, VI.

FRIDAY HARBOR HOUSE — Rates Subject to Change — **Phone:** 360/378-8455
Lodge
All Year [CP] 1P: $165- 185 2P/1B: $165- 185 2P/2B: $185 XP: $35 F17
Too new to rate; **Location:** In Friday Harbor; downtown. 130 West St 98250. Fax: 360/378-8453. **Terms:** credit card guarantee; BP available; 2 night min stay, weekends; small pets only, $100 dep req. **Facility:** 20 rooms. Rating withheld pending completion of construction. 3 stories; interior corridors; meeting rooms. **Dining:** Dining room; 5 pm-10 pm; $13-$25; cocktails; Sun brunch 9 am-noon. **All Rooms:** coffeemakers, refrigerators, cable TV, whirlpools, no A/C. Fee: VCP's. **Cards:** AE, MC, VI.

HILLSIDE HOUSE BED & BREAKFAST — Rates Subject to Change — **Phone:** 360/378-4730
◆◆ Bed & Breakfast
5/1-10/31 [BP] 1P: $75- 145 2P/1B: $85- 155 2P/2B: $85 XP: $25
3/1-4/30 & 11/1-2/29 [BP] 1P: $65- 120 2P/1B: $75- 130 2P/2B: $75 XP: $25
Location: In Friday Harbor; edge of town w. 365 Carter Ave 98250. **Terms:** Age restrictions may apply; reserv deposit, 3 day notice; no pets. **Facility:** 7 rooms. Rooms with a view of ferry crossings & Mt Baker. 2 stories; interior corridors; smoke free premises. **All Rooms:** combo & shower baths, no A/C. **Some Rooms:** phones, cable TV, whirlpools. **Cards:** AE, DS, MC, VI.

THE INN AT FRIDAY HARBOR — Rates Subject to Change — **Phone:** 360/378-4351
◆◆◆ Motel
5/21-9/30 1P: $75 2P/1B: $75 2P/2B: $85 XP: $5
3/1-5/20 & 10/1-2/29 1P: $55 2P/1B: $60 2P/2B: $70 XP: $5
Location: In Friday Harbor; 1/2 mi s of ferry dock. 410 Spring St W 98250 (PO Box 339). Fax: 360/378-5800. **Terms:** Credit card guarantee, 3 day notice; no pets. **Facility:** 72 rooms. 2 stories; exterior corridors; conference facilities; heated indoor pool, sauna, whirlpool; exercise room, rental cars, island tours. **Services:** data ports; area transportation, ferry pick-up, airport transportation. Fee: coin laundry. **All Rooms:** coffeemakers, cable TV, no A/C. **Some Rooms:** 2 efficiencies, refrigerators. **Cards:** AE, CB, DI, JCB, MC, VI.
(See color ad p A119)

INN AT FRIDAY HARBOR SUITES — Rates Subject to Change — **Phone:** 360/378-3031
◆◆◆ Suite Motor Inn
5/21-9/30 1P: $78- 108 2P/1B: $78- 108 2P/2B: $108- 188 XP: $10
3/1-5/20 & 10/1-2/29 1P: $68- 98 2P/1B: $68- 98 2P/2B: $98- 148 XP: $10
Location: In Friday Harbor; downtown. 680 Spring St 98250. Fax: 360/378-4228. **Terms:** Credit card guarantee, 3 day notice; 3 night min stay; pets, $50 dep req. **Facility:** 71 rooms. Easy access to ferry terminal. 4 two-bedroom units. 2 stories; interior corridors; meeting rooms. **Dining & Entertainment:** Restaurant; 7 am-midnight; $10-$20; cocktail lounge. **Services:** data ports; area transportation, airport transportation. Fee: coin laundry. **All Rooms:** coffeemakers, efficiencies, cable TV, no A/C. **Cards:** AE, DI, JCB, MC, VI. *(See color ad p A119)*

KANGAROO HOUSE BED & BREAKFAST — Rates Subject to Change — **Phone:** 360/376-2175
◆◆ Bed & Breakfast
Fri & Sat 3/1-4/30, 5/1-10/31 & Fri & Sat 11/1-2/29 [BP] 1P: $60- 100 2P/1B: $70- 110 2P/2B: $70- 110 XP: $20
Sun-Thurs 3/1-4/30 & 11/1-2/29 [BP] 1P: $45- 75 2P/1B: $55- 85 2P/2B: $55- 85 XP: $20
Location: On Orcas Island; 1 mi n of town via Prune Alley & N Beach Rd. N Beach Rd (PO Box 334, EASTSOUND). **Terms:** Reserv deposit, 7 day notice; no pets. **Facility:** 5 rooms. 2 stories; interior corridors; smoke free premises. **All Rooms:** no A/C, no phones, no TVs. **Cards:** MC, VI.

LANDMARK INN — Rates Subject to Change — **Phone:** 360/376-2423
◆◆ Apartment Motel
5/15-9/30 2P/1B: $100 2P/2B: $110 XP: $10
3/1-5/14 & 10/1-2/29 2P/1B: $60- 70 2P/2B: $90 XP: $10
Location: On Orcas Island; 11 mi n of Ferry Landing, on Main St. Main St 98245 (Rt 1, Box A-108, EASTSOUND). **Terms:** Reserv deposit, 7 day notice; weekly rates; 2 night min stay, 5/15-9/30; no pets. **Facility:** 15 rooms. Several units have view of the bay. 7 two-bedroom units. 3 stories, no elevator; exterior corridors. **Services:** Fee: coin laundry. **All Rooms:** coffeemakers, kitchens, cable TV, no A/C. **Cards:** AE, DS, MC, VI.

THE MEADOWS — Rates Subject to Change — **Phone:** 360/378-4004
◆ Bed & Breakfast
6/1-9/30 [BP] 1P: $75 2P/1B: $75 2P/2B: $75 XP: $20
3/1-5/31 & 10/1-2/29 [BP] 1P: $65 2P/1B: $65 2P/2B: $65 XP: $20
Location: In Friday Harbor, 2 1/2 mi s of town via Spring St, Mullis & Cattle Point Rd. 1980 Cattle Point Rd 98250. **Terms:** Age restrictions may apply; reserv deposit, 7 day notice; no pets. **Facility:** 2 rooms. Charming country setting surrounded by ancient oaks, firs & open fields. Exterior corridors; smoke free premises. **All Rooms:** no A/C, no phones, no TVs. **Cards:** MC, VI.

OUTLOOK INN ON ORCAS ISLAND — Rates Subject to Change — **Phone:** 360/376-2200
◆◆◆ Historic Country Inn
5/27-10/15 1P: $69- 225 2P/1B: $69- 225 2P/2B: $69- 225 XP: $10 F3
3/1-5/26 & 10/16-11/26 1P: $64- 175 2P/1B: $64- 175 2P/2B: $64- 175 XP: $10 F3
11/27-2/29 1P: $34- 110 2P/1B: $34- 110 2P/2B: $34- 110 XP: $10 F3
Location: On Orcas Island; downtown. Main St 98245 (Box 210, EASTSOUND). Fax: 360/376-2256. **Terms:** Sr. discount; credit card guarantee, 7 day notice; no pets. **Facility:** 41 rooms. Rustic turn-of-the century Victorian Inn. English & American antiques. Second building with Victorian decor & modern amenities. 8 shared half baths & 5 shared showers. 2 stories; interior/exterior corridors. **Dining & Entertainment:** Dining room; 8 am-9 pm, 5/1-10/31; $9-$14; cocktails/lounge. **Services:** airport transportation. **All Rooms:** no A/C. **Some Rooms:** refrigerators, cable TV, whirlpools. **Cards:** AE, MC, VI. *(See color ad p A120)*

ROSARIO RESORT Rates Subject to Change **Phone:** 360/376-2222

AAA ◆◆◆ Resort Complex

Fri & Sat	1P: $95- 195	2P/1B: $95- 195	2P/2B: $95- 195	XP: $10	F12
Sun-Thurs	1P: $63- 150	2P/1B: $63- 150	2P/2B: $63- 150	XP: $10	F12

Location: On Orcas Island; 16 1/2 mi n of Ferry Landing; 5 mi s of Eastsound Village on Cascade Bay. One Rosario Way 98245. Fax: 360/376-2289. **Terms:** Check-in 4 pm; reserv deposit, 7 day notice; package plans, off season; no pets. **Facility:** 179 rooms. 22 acre resort centered around historic 1906 Moran mansion. Waterfront & hillside villas overlooking Cascade Bay. Some rooms with fireplace & balcony. 2 stories; interior/exterior corridors; conference facilities; beach, 3 pools (3 heated, 1 indoor), sauna, whirlpool; 2 tennis courts; boat ramp, marina; health club, playground. **Dining & Entertainment:** Dining room, coffee shop; 7:30 am-2 & 6-9 pm, Fri & Sat-10 pm; $12-$25; cocktails; entertainment. **Services:** Fee: coin laundry, area transportation, airport transportation. **Recreation:** nature trails; charter fishing, fishing. Fee: kayaks. **All Rooms:** coffeemakers, free movies, combo & shower baths, cable TV, no A/C. **Some Rooms:** 14 kitchens, refrigerators. **Cards:** AE, DS, MC, VI. *(See ad p A120)* (D)

SPRING BAY INN Guaranteed Rates **Phone:** 360/376-5531

◆◆ Bed & Breakfast

All Year [BP]	1P: $135- 155	2P/1B: $155- 175	2P/2B: $175	XP: $25

Location: On Orcas Island; 20 mi e from Landing, via Horse Shoe Rd, at Lawrence & Obstruction Pass Rd, follow signs. (PO Box 97, OLGA). Fax: 360/376-2193. **Terms:** Reserv deposit, 14 day notice; weekly rates; no pets. **Facility:** 4 rooms. 2 stories; interior corridors; smoke free premises; whirlpool. **Recreation:** nature trails; fishing, kayak tour. **All Rooms:** no A/C, no TVs. **Cards:** MC, VI. (D) (S) ⊗

INNS AT FRIDAY HARBOR
SAN JUAN ISLAND

The perfect place . . .

- *THE ISLAND . . .* Is a natural paradise offering a wide variety of leisure pastimes, all water activities, golf, Whale Watch tours and a unique village with shops, galleries, and restaurants.
- Access to the island is by Anacortes and Victoria car ferry, Seattle and Vancouver airlines or by private boat. Arrival pick up service provided by the Inns.

The perfect choice . . .

INN AT FRIDAY HARBOR

INN AT FRIDAY HARBOR •SUITES•

- TWO beautiful Inns with a selection of spacious rooms or suites - one bedroom, one bath, & two bedroom, two baths - each with living room, sofabed, kitchenette and private patio or deck.
INDOOR POOL, remote cable TV, guest laundry, in-room coffee, exercise room, beauty shop, car rental, room data ports, "PAPA JOE'S" COCKTAIL lounge and restaurant.
- Outstanding meeting and unique banquet arrangements available for up to 120.

RESERVATIONS **1-800-752-5752**

- FRIDAY HARBOR INN POB 339 410 Spring St. 360-378-4000 FAX 360-378-5800
- FRIDAY HARBOR INN SUITES 680 Spring St. 360-378-3031 FAX 360-378-4228

—— FRIDAY HARBOR, WASHINGTON 98250 ——

STATES INN — AAA Special Value Rates — **Phone:** 360/378-6240

AAA ◆◆◆ Historic Bed & Breakfast

3/1-10/15 [BP]	1P: $80- 110	2P/1B: $80- 110	2P/2B: $90- 95	XP: $20
10/16-2/29 [BP]	1P: $70- 100	2P/1B: $70- 100	2P/2B: $80- 85	XP: $20

Location: In Friday Harbor; 7 mi nw via Guard St & Beaverton Valley Rd. 2039 W Valley Rd 98250. Fax: 360/378-6241. **Terms:** Age restrictions may apply; reserv deposit, 7 day notice; no pets. **Facility:** 9 rooms. Theme rooms set in a pastoral valley on a working ranch. 2 stories; interior corridors; smoke free premises. **All Rooms:** no A/C, no phones, no TVs. **Cards:** DS, MC, VI. Ⓓ ⊗

TRUMPETER INN — Rates Subject to Change — **Phone:** 360/378-3884

◆◆ Bed & Breakfast

6/1-10/31 [BP]	2P/1B: $90- 100	XP: $15
3/1-5/31 & 11/1-2/29 [BP]	2P/1B: $80- 90	XP: $15

Location: In Friday Harbor, 1 1/2 mi w via Spring St & San Juan Valley Rd. 420 Trumpeter Way 98250. **Terms:** Age restrictions may apply; credit card guarantee, 3 day notice; 2 night min stay; no pets. **Facility:** 5 rooms. Panoramic view of False Bay & the Olympic Mountains. 2 stories; interior corridors; smoke free premises. **All Rooms:** no A/C, no phones, no TVs. **Cards:** MC, VI. Ⓓ ⊗

TURTLEBACK FARM INN — Rates Subject to Change — **Phone:** 360/376-4914

AAA ◆◆◆ Historic Bed & Breakfast

4/1-10/31 [BP]	1P: $65- 145	2P/1B: $75- 155	XP: $25
3/1-3/31 & 11/1-2/29 [BP]	1P: $65- 100	2P/1B: $75- 110	XP: $25

Location: On Orcas Island; 6 mi n of Ferry Landing, 2 1/2 mi n of West Sound Marina on Crow Valley Rd; 4 mi sw of Eastsound Village. 98245 (Rt 1, Box 650, EASTSOUND). **Terms:** Reserv deposit, 10 day notice; 2 night min stay, 4/1-10/31; no pets. **Facility:** 7 rooms. Beautifully restored 1890's farmhouse on 80 acres of farm & forestland. 2 stories; interior corridors; smoke free premises; oceanfront. **Recreation:** nature trails; fishing. **All Rooms:** combo & shower baths, no A/C, no phones, no TVs. **Cards:** MC, VI. Ⓓ ⊗

RESTAURANTS

DOWNRIGGER — **Dinner:** $11-$20 — **Phone:** 360/378-2700

◆◆ Seafood

Location: In Friday Harbor; downtown at ferry landing. 10 Front St 98250. **Hours:** 11 am-10 pm, Sat-11 pm. **Reservations:** suggested. **Features:** Sunday brunch; children's menu; carryout; cocktails & lounge; a la carte. Next to ferry & marina; veranda dining. Smoke free premises. **Cards:** AE, MC, VI. ⊗

Outlook Inn *on Orcas Island*
Charming Fully Restored Country Inn
in the Heart of The San Juan Islands
• 41 Rooms • TV • Phone • Luxury Suites
(800)767-9506 (360)376-2200

Return To The Era Of The Tall Ships.

Visit historic Rosario Resort where gracious service and fine dining compliment the natural beauty of the San Juan Islands.

Discover a host of resort and island activities: hiking, biking, quaint shops, boating and whale watching. Resort amenities include spa, swimming pools, restaurants, marina and mansion tours.

For information and reservations
1-800-562-8820.

Rosario RESORT

Listed in the National Register of Historic Places.

One Rosario Way, Eastsound, WA 98245. 360-376-2222

MALOULA **Dinner:** $11-$20 **Phone:** 360/378-8485
◆◆ Ethnic **Location:** In Friday Harbor, downtown. 1 Front St 98250. **Hours:** Open 5/1-10/30; 11 am-10 pm, Fri & Sat-11 pm, Sun 11 am-8 pm. **Reservations:** required; summer. **Features:** No A/C; children's menu; health conscious menu items; carryout; beer & wine only. Casual family dining, with ocean view. Fresh cooked seafood, lamb, beef & chicken with Syrian spices. Smoke free premises. **Cards:** AE, MC, VI.

ORCAS HOTEL FIRESIDE LOUNGE **Dinner:** $21-$30 **Phone:** 360/376-4300
◆◆ American **Location:** On Orcas Island; in Orcas Hotel overlooking Orcas Island ferry landing. 98280. **Hours:** 8 am-9 pm, Sun from 7:30 am. Closed: 12/25 & 1/3-1/31. **Reservations:** suggested. **Features:** No A/C; Sunday brunch; health conscious menu items; carryout; cocktails & lounge; a la carte. Attractive Victorian dining room emphasizing fresh seafood & local ingredients. Smoke free premises. **Cards:** DS, MC, VI.

SPRINGTREE CAFE **Dinner:** $11-$20 **Phone:** 360/378-4848
◆◆ Seafood **Location:** In Friday Harbor; downtown. 310 Spring St 98250. **Hours:** 11:30 am-2:30 & 5-9 pm, Fri & Sat-10 pm, Sun 9 am-2 & 5-9 pm. Closed: 1/1, 11/23 & 12/25. **Reservations:** suggested. **Features:** Sunday brunch; children's menu; carryout; beer & wine only. Casual, family Eurobistro-style dining. Fresh seasonal ingredients. Smoke free premises. **Cards:** MC, VI.

SEA-TAC—24,000 (See SEATTLE & VICINITY ACCOMMODATIONS spotting map pages A136 & A137; see index starting on page A134)

LODGINGS

AIRPORT PLAZA HOTEL Rates Subject to Change **Phone:** 206/433-0400 46
AAA ◆◆ Motor Inn
All Year 1P: $44- 65 2P/1B: $50- 70 2P/2B: $50- 75 XP: $5 F12
Location: On SR 99. 18601 International Blvd 98188. Fax: 206/241-2222. **Terms:** Sr. discount; credit card guarantee; weekly rates; pets. **Facility:** 102 rooms. 4 suites with sauna & whirlpool; 3 stories; interior corridors; meeting rooms. **Dining:** Restaurant; 5 pm-10 pm; $6-$11; cocktails. **Services:** airport transportation. Fee: coin laundry. **All Rooms:** coffeemakers, cable TV. **Some Rooms:** refrigerators. **Cards:** AE, CB, DI, DS, JCB, MC, VI.

BEST WESTERN AIRPORT EXECUTEL AAA Special Value Rates **Phone:** 206/878-3300 58
AAA ◆◆◆ Motor Inn
6/16-9/15 1P: $95 2P/1B: $101 2P/2B: $101 XP: $6 F18
3/1-6/15 & 9/16-2/29 1P: $85 2P/1B: $91 2P/2B: $91 XP: $6 F18
Location: On SR 99. 20717 International Blvd 98198. Fax: 206/824-9000. **Terms:** Reserv deposit, 3 day notice; small pets only, $50 dep req, $30 refundable. **Facility:** 138 rooms. 3 stories; interior corridors; meeting rooms; heated indoor pool, sauna, whirlpool; exercise room. **Dining & Entertainment:** Restaurant; 5:30 am-10 pm; $7-$15; cocktails/lounge. **Services:** data ports; valet laundry; airport transportation. **All Rooms:** free movies, cable TV. **Some Rooms:** refrigerators. Fee: whirlpools. **Cards:** AE, CB, DI, DS, JCB, MC, VI.
(See color ad p A140)

COMFORT INN AT SEATAC Rates Subject to Change **Phone:** 206/878-1100 57
AAA ◆◆◆ Motel
6/1-9/30 [CP] 1P: $69- 75 2P/1B: $80 2P/2B: $85 XP: $10 F18
3/1-5/31 & 10/1-2/29 [CP] 1P: $65- 69 2P/1B: $75 2P/2B: $79 XP: $10 F18
Location: On SR 99. 19333 Pacific Hwy S 98188. Fax: 206/878-8678. **Terms:** Sr. discount; reserv deposit; small pets only, $25 dep req. **Facility:** 119 rooms. 4 stories; interior corridors; meeting rooms; whirlpool; exercise room. **Dining:** Restaurant nearby. **Services:** valet laundry; area transportation, within 5 mi, airport transportation. **All Rooms:** free & pay movies, cable TV. **Some Rooms:** microwaves, refrigerators. Fee: whirlpools. **Cards:** AE, DI, DS, JCB, MC, VI.

CONTINENTAL COURT ALL SUITES MOTEL Rates Subject to Change **Phone:** 206/241-1500 69
AAA ◆◆ Suite Motel
6/1-9/30 1P: $50 2P/1B: $55 2P/2B: $60 XP: $5 F5
3/1-5/31 & 10/1-2/29 1P: $40 2P/1B: $45 2P/2B: $50 XP: $5 F5
Location: 17223 32nd Ave S 98188. Fax: 206/244-2677. **Terms:** Sr. discount; reserv deposit, 7 day notice; weekly/monthly rates; pets, $20. **Facility:** 50 rooms. Commercial location. Most units with balcony & fireplace. 25 two-bedroom units. 2 stories; exterior corridors; heated pool. **Dining:** Restaurant nearby. **Services:** airport transportation. Fee: coin laundry. **All Rooms:** coffeemakers, kitchens, free movies, cable TV. **Cards:** AE, CB, DI, DS, JCB, MC, VI. *(See color ad p A139)*

DAYS INN SEATAC AIRPORT Rates Subject to Change **Phone:** 206/244-3600 60
◆◆◆ Motel
5/1-9/30 [CP] 1P: $69- 92 2P/1B: $79- 105 2P/2B: $89- 115 XP: $10 F18
3/1-4/30 & 10/1-2/28 [CP] 1P: $58- 85 2P/1B: $68- 93 2P/2B: $78- 100 XP: $10 F18
Location: Hwy 99. 19015 International Blvd 98188. Fax: 206/241-4556. **Terms:** Credit card guarantee; no pets. **Facility:** 86 rooms. 4 stories; interior corridors; meeting rooms. **Dining:** Restaurant nearby. **Services:** area transportation, airport transportation. Fee: coin laundry. **All Rooms:** free movies, cable TV. **Some Rooms:** 32 efficiencies. Fee: VCP's, whirlpools. **Cards:** AE, DI, DS, MC, VI.

HAMPTON INN HOTEL SEATTLE-AIRPORT Guaranteed Rates **Phone:** 206/878-1700 55
◆◆◆ Motel
6/1-2/29 [BP] 1P: $69- 71 2P/1B: $79- 81 2P/2B: $79- 81
3/1-5/31 [BP] 1P: $65- 67 2P/1B: $75- 77 2P/2B: $75- 77
Location: 14 mi s on SR 99, near Seattle-Tacoma International Airport. 19445 International Blvd 98188. Fax: 206/824-0720. **Terms:** CP available; no pets. **Facility:** 131 rooms. 4 stories; interior corridors; meeting rooms; heated pool; exercise room. **Services:** data ports; valet laundry; area transportation, airport transportation. **All Rooms:** free & pay movies, cable TV. **Some Rooms:** refrigerators. **Cards:** AE, CB, DI, DS, JCB, MC, VI.
(See color ad inside front cover)

HOLIDAY INN SEA-TAC Guaranteed Rates **Phone:** 206/248-1000 45
AAA ◆◆◆ Hotel
6/15-9/15 1P: $79 2P/1B: $79 2P/2B: $79 XP: $10 F18
3/1-6/14 & 9/16-2/29 1P: $59 2P/1B: $59 2P/2B: $59 XP: $10 F18
Location: On SR 99. 17338 International Blvd 98188. Fax: 206/242-7089. **Terms:** Sr. discount; no pets. **Facility:** 260 rooms. An excellent view of Mt Rainier. 12 stories; interior corridors; meeting rooms; heated indoor pool, whirlpool; exercise room. **Dining & Entertainment:** Revolving rooftop dining room; 6 am-2 & 5:30-10:30 pm; $12-$18; cocktails; entertainment. **Services:** area transportation, airport transportation. Fee: coin laundry. **All Rooms:** free & pay movies, cable TV. **Some Rooms:** refrigerators. **Cards:** AE, CB, DI, DS, JCB, MC, VI.
(See color ad p A141)

(See SEATTLE & VICINITY ACCOMMODATIONS spotting map pages A136 & A137)

HOWARD JOHNSON Rates Subject to Change **Phone:** 206/878-3310 59

AAA ◆◆ Motel

6/16-9/15 [CP] 1P: $50- 60 2P/1B: $55- 60 2P/2B: $60- 65 XP: $5 F18

3/1-6/15 & 9/16-2/29 [CP] 1P: $38- 48 2P/1B: $42- 52 2P/2B: $48- 58 XP: $5 F18

Location: On Hwy 99. 20045 International Blvd 98198. Fax: 206/824-8535. **Terms:** Credit card guarantee; weekly rates; small pets only, $5, also $25 dep req. **Facility:** 58 rooms. Spanish style exterior. 3 two-bedroom units. 3 stories; exterior corridors. **Services:** airport transportation. **All Rooms:** free movies, combo & shower baths, cable TV. **Some Rooms:** A/C, microwaves, radios, refrigerators. Fee: whirlpools. **Cards:** AE, CB, DI, DS, JCB, MC, VI.

JET MOTEL PARK' N FLY Rates Subject to Change **Phone:** 206/244-6255 68

AAA ◆ Motel

6/1-9/30 1P: $43- 50 2P/1B: $52- 56 2P/2B: $56- 61 XP: $5-7

3/1-5/31 & 10/1-2/29 1P: $35- 38 2P/1B: $44- 48 2P/2B: $48- 55 XP: $5-7

Location: SR 99. 17300 International Blvd 98188. Fax: 206/243-8951. **Terms:** Credit card guarantee; no pets. **Facility:** 51 rooms. Commercial location. Modest rooms. 3 stories; interior corridors; heated pool. **Dining:** Restaurant nearby. **Services:** airport transportation. **All Rooms:** free movies, combo & shower baths, cable TV. **Some Rooms:** refrigerators. **Cards:** AE, DI, DS, JCB, MC, VI. *(See color ad p A139)*

LA QUINTA INN-SEA TAC INTL Rates Subject to Change **Phone:** 206/241-5211 56

◆◆◆ Motel

5/27-9/30 [CP] 1P: $58- 64 2P/1B: $65- 71 2P/2B: $65- 71 XP: $8 F18

3/1-5/26 & 10/1-2/29 [CP] 1P: $53- 59 2P/1B: $60- 67 2P/2B: $60 XP: $8 F18

Location: SR 99. 2824 S 188th St 98188. Fax: 206/246-5596. **Terms:** Small pets only. **Facility:** 142 rooms. 6 stories; interior corridors; meeting rooms; heated pool, whirlpool; exercise room. **Dining:** Restaurant nearby. **Services:** airport transportation. Fee: coin laundry. **All Rooms:** free & pay movies, combo & shower baths, cable TV. **Cards:** AE, CB, DI, DS, MC, VI.

QUALITY INN-SEA-TAC AAA Special Value Rates **Phone:** 206/246-7000 61

◆◆◆ Motel

5/1-9/30 [CP] 1P: $79 2P/1B: $89 2P/2B: $89 XP: $10

3/1-4/30 & 10/1-2/29 [CP] 1P: $59 2P/1B: $69 2P/2B: $69 XP: $10

Location: SR 99. 17101 International Blvd 98188. Fax: 206/246-1715. **Terms:** No pets. **Facility:** 136 rooms. 3 stories; interior corridors; conference facilities. **Services:** guest laundry; airport transportation. **All Rooms:** combo & shower baths, cable TV. Fee: movies. **Some Rooms:** refrigerators. **Cards:** AE, CB, DI, DS, MC, VI.

RADISSON HOTEL SEATTLE AIRPORT Rates Subject to Change **Phone:** 206/244-6000 48

◆◆◆ Motor Inn

All Year 1P: $74 2P/1B: $82 2P/2B: $82

Location: On SR 99. 17001 International Blvd 98188. Fax: 206/246-6835. **Terms:** Credit card guarantee; package plans; no pets. **Facility:** 165 rooms. Somes rooms with balcony or patio. 2 stories; interior corridors; conference facilities; heated pool, sauna; exercise room. **Dining & Entertainment:** Restaurant; 6 am-11 pm; $8-$16; cocktails; entertainment. **Services:** valet laundry; massage; area transportation, within 5 mi, airport transportation. **All Rooms:** combo & shower baths. Fee: movies. **Some Rooms:** refrigerators, cable TV. **Cards:** AE, CB, DI, DS, JCB, MC, VI.

RED LION SEATTLE AIRPORT HOTEL AAA Special Value Rates **Phone:** 206/246-8600 65

◆◆◆ Motor Inn

All Year 1P: $120- 135 2P/1B: $125- 140 2P/2B: $125- 145 XP: $5-15 F18

Location: On SR 99. 18740 International Blvd 98188. Fax: 206/242-9727. **Terms:** Reserv deposit, 3 day notice; weekly rates; package plans; small pets only. **Facility:** 850 rooms. Commercial location. High rise tower. Many units with balcony. 3-13 stories; interior corridors; conference facilities; heated pool, whirlpool; exercise room. **Dining & Entertainment:** 2 dining rooms, coffee shop; 24 hours; $7-$15; cocktails; also, Maxi's, see separate listing; entertainment. **Services:** data ports, PC, secretarial services; valet laundry; area transportation, to Southcenter, airport transportation. **All Rooms:** cable TV. Fee: movies. **Some Rooms:** microwaves, refrigerators, whirlpools. **Cards:** AE, DI, DS, MC, VI. Roll in showers.

SANDSTONE INN Rates Subject to Change **Phone:** 206/824-1350 63

AAA ◆ Motor Inn

6/16-9/15 1P: $48- 58 2P/1B: $52- 62 2P/2B: $58- 68 XP: $4-5 F18

3/1-6/15 & 9/16-2/29 1P: $36- 48 2P/1B: $39- 52 2P/2B: $48- 58 XP: $4-5 F18

Location: On SR 99. 19225 International Blvd 98188. Fax: 206/824-8535. **Terms:** Credit card guarantee; weekly rates; small pets only, $5, $25 dep req. **Facility:** 98 rooms. 4 two-bedroom units. 2 stories; interior/exterior corridors; meeting rooms. **Dining & Entertainment:** Restaurant; 24 hours; $8-$17; cocktails/lounge. **Services:** airport transportation. **All Rooms:** free movies, combo & shower baths, cable TV. **Some Rooms:** A/C, 9 kitchens. **Cards:** AE, CB, DI, DS, MC, VI.

SEA-TAC AIRPORT TRAVELODGE Rates Subject to Change **Phone:** 206/241-9292 54

AAA ◆◆ Motel

7/7-9/3 1P: $45 2P/1B: $50 2P/2B: $55 XP: $5 F16

3/1-7/6 & 9/4-2/29 1P: $34 2P/1B: $39 2P/2B: $44 XP: $5 F16

Location: On SR 99. 2900 S 192nd St 98188. Fax: 206/242-0681. **Terms:** Sr. discount; reserv deposit; weekly rates; no pets. **Facility:** 104 rooms. 3 stories, no elevator; interior corridors; sauna. **Services:** airport transportation. Fee: coin laundry. **All Rooms:** coffeemakers, free movies, cable TV. **Some Rooms:** refrigerators. Fee: VCP's. **Cards:** AE, CB, DI, DS, JCB, MC, VI.

SEA-TAC CREST MOTOR INN Rates Subject to Change **Phone:** 206/433-0999 53

AAA ◆◆ Motel

All Year [CP] 1P: $42 2P/1B: $45 2P/2B: $48- 59

Location: On SR 99. 18845 International Blvd 98188. Fax: 206/248-7644. **Terms:** Sr. discount; credit card guarantee, 3 day notice; weekly rates; pets, $50 dep req. **Facility:** 46 rooms. 16 two-bedroom units. 4 stories; interior/exterior corridors. **Dining:** Restaurant nearby. **Services:** airport transportation. **All Rooms:** combo & shower baths, cable TV. **Some Rooms:** refrigerators. **Cards:** AE, CB, DI, DS, MC, VI.

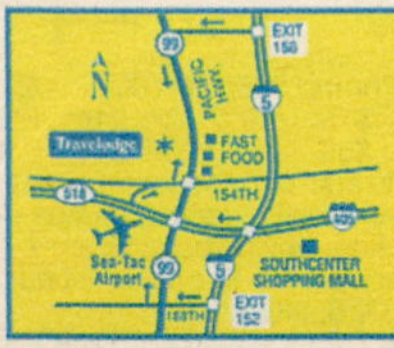

Travelodge

1-800-578-7878

14845 Pacific Hwy. South, Seattle, WA 98168

1 MILE NORTH OF SEA-TAC INTERNATIONAL AIRPORT-North

- 72 AIR CONDITIONED ROOMS
- FREE CONTINENTAL BREAKFAST
- 24 HR AIRPORT SHUTTLE, CABLE TV, HBO
- STAY 1 NIGHT & GET 7 DAYS FREE PARKING DISCOUNTS AAA & SENIORS

(206)242-1777 • FAX (206)248-4285

(See SEATTLE & VICINITY ACCOMMODATIONS spotting map pages A136 & A137)

SEATTLE AIRPORT HILTON AAA Special Value Rates **Phone:** 206/244-4800 51

AAA ◆◆◆ Motor Inn

All Year 1P: $105- 125 2P/1B: $105- 125 2P/2B: $105- 125

Location: On SR 99. 17620 International Blvd 98188. Fax: 206/439-7439. **Terms:** Reserv deposit, 14 day notice; small pets only. **Facility:** 173 rooms. Many rooms with patio. 3 stories; interior corridors; business center, conference facilities, convention oriented; heated pool, whirlpool; exercise room. **Dining & Entertainment:** Dining room; 6 am-11 pm; $7-$16; cocktails/lounge; 24-hour room service. **Services:** data ports, PC; valet laundry; area transportation, airport transportation. **All Rooms:** coffeemakers, free & pay movies, cable TV. **Some Rooms:** refrigerators. **Cards:** AE, DI, DS, MC, VI. *(See ad p 38)* Roll in showers. (D) (S) ⊗

SEATTLE MARRIOTT SEA-TAC AIRPORT Rates Subject to Change **Phone:** 206/241-2000 66

AAA ◆◆◆◆ Hotel

Mon-Thurs 1P: $114 2P/1B: $114 2P/2B: $114
Fri-Sun 1P: $89 2P/1B: $89 2P/2B: $89

Location: 2 blks e of SR 99. 3201 S 176th St 98188. Fax: 206/248-0789. **Terms:** Package plans; small pets only. **Facility:** 459 rooms. Commercial location. Rooms with view of Mt Rainier. 5-9 stories; interior corridors; conference facilities; luxury level rooms; heated indoor pool, saunas, whirlpools; exercise room. **Dining & Entertainment:** Dining room; 6 am-11 pm; $8-$15; cocktails/lounge. **Services:** data ports, PC, secretarial services; valet laundry; airport transportation. **All Rooms:** cable TV. Fee: movies. **Some Rooms:** Fee: refrigerators. **Cards:** AE, DI, DS, MC, VI. (D) (S) ⊗

TAC-SEA MOTEL PARK-FLY Guaranteed Rates **Phone:** 206/241-6511 62

AAA ◆ Motel

5/15-9/30 1P: $35 2P/1B: $41 2P/2B: $47 XP: $5 F5
3/1-5/14 & 10/1-2/29 1P: $30 2P/1B: $35 2P/2B: $40 XP: $5 F5

Location: 17024 International Blvd 98188. Fax: 206/635-0987. **Terms:** Reserv deposit; no pets. **Facility:** 29 rooms. 1 story; exterior corridors. **Dining:** Restaurant nearby. **Services:** airport transportation. **All Rooms:** free movies, combo & shower baths, cable TV. **Cards:** AE, CB, DI, MC, VI. (D) ⊗

THRIFTLODGE Rates Subject to Change **Phone:** 206/244-1230 47

AAA ◆◆ Motel

4/1-9/30 [CP] 1P: $49- 54 2P/1B: $54- 59 2P/2B: $56- 62 XP: $5
3/1-3/31 & 10/1-2/29 [CP] 1P: $34- 49 2P/1B: $37- 42 2P/2B: $37- 42 XP: $5

Location: On SR 99. 17108 International Blvd 98188. Fax: 206/241-0893. **Terms:** Sr. discount; credit card guarantee, 3 day notice; weekly rates; small pets only, $10 dep req. **Facility:** 74 rooms. 2 stories; exterior corridors; meeting rooms. **Dining:** Restaurant nearby. **Services:** airport transportation. Fee: coin laundry. **All Rooms:** free movies, combo & shower baths, cable TV. **Some Rooms:** kitchen, microwaves, refrigerators. **Cards:** AE, CB, DI, DS, MC, VI. (D) ⊗

WYNDHAM GARDEN HOTEL SEA-TAC Rates Subject to Change **Phone:** 206/244-6666 49

◆◆◆ Motor Inn

Sun-Thurs [BP] 1P: $110 2P/1B: $120 2P/2B: $120 XP: $10 F18
Fri & Sat 6/5-9/2 [EP] 1P: $89 2P/1B: $89 2P/2B: $89 XP: $10 F18
Fri & Sat 3/1-6/4 & 9/3-2/29 [EP] 1P: $64 2P/1B: $64 2P/2B: $64 XP: $10 F18

Location: On Hwy 99. 18118 International Blvd 98188. Fax: 206/244-6679. **Terms:** No pets. **Facility:** 204 rooms. Attractive, inviting library lounge. 6 stories; interior corridors; meeting rooms; heated indoor pool, whirlpool; exercise room. **Dining & Entertainment:** Dining room; 6:30 am-2 & 5-10 pm; $7-$18; cocktails/lounge. **Services:** airport transportation. Fee: coin laundry. **All Rooms:** coffeemakers, cable TV. Fee: movies. **Some Rooms:** Fee: refrigerators. **Cards:** AE, CB, DI, DS, JCB, MC, VI. *(See color ad p A138)* (D) (S) ⊗

RESTAURANTS

BAI TONG THAI RESTAURANT **Dinner:** up to $10 **Phone:** 206/431-0893 42

◆◆ Ethnic

Location: 1 mi n of airport on US 99. 15859 Pacific Hwy S 98188. **Hours:** 11 am-3 & 5-10 pm, Sat 5 pm-10 pm, Sun 5 pm-9 pm. **Features:** carryout; cocktail lounge; wine only; a la carte. Family-style Thai food. Casual relaxed dining. Smoke free premises. **Cards:** DS, MC, VI. ⊗

MAXI'S **Dinner:** $21-$30 **Phone:** 206/433-1892 45

◆◆ Steakhouse

Location: Atop Red Lion Seattle Airport Hotel. 18740 International Blvd 98188. **Hours:** 5:30 pm-10 pm, Sun 10 am-2 & 5:30-10 pm. **Reservations:** suggested. **Features:** Sunday brunch; children's menu; early bird specials; senior's menu; health conscious menu; carryout; cocktails & lounge; entertainment; a la carte. Also flambe dishes & exquisite desserts in dining room with attractive view. **Cards:** AE, DI, DS, JCB, MC, VI. ⊗

13 COINS RESTAURANT **Dinner:** $11-$20 **Phone:** 206/243-9500 44

AAA ◆◆◆ American

Location: Across from Sea-Tac Intl Airport. 18000 International Blvd 98188. **Hours:** 24 hours. **Features:** children's menu; carryout; cocktails & lounge; entertainment. Exhibition cooking, casual dining. **Cards:** AE, DI, DS, MC, VI.

SHARPS ROASTER & ALE HOUSE **Dinner:** $11-$20 **Phone:** 206/241-5744 46

◆◆ American

Location: On SR 99, adjacent to Sea-Tac Airport. 18427 International Blvd 98188. **Hours:** 11 am-10 pm, Sat & Sun from noon. Closed: 1/1 & 12/25. **Reservations:** required. **Features:** children's menu; carryout; cocktails & lounge. Casual relaxed family dining. Aldenwood roasting. **Cards:** AE, DI, MC, VI. ⊗

THREE MEN IN A TUB **Dinner:** $11-$20 **Phone:** 206/824-1765 43

◆◆ American

Location: On SR 99; near Seattle-Tacoma International Airport. 19204 International Blvd 98188. **Hours:** 6:30 am-11 pm, Sat from 7 am, Sun from 8 am. Closed: 11/23 & 12/25. **Features:** children's menu; carryout; salad bar; cocktails & lounge; a la carte. Family dining. Wide selection of home cooked meals. **Cards:** AE, CB, DI, DS, JCB, MC, VI. ⊗

Double your pleasure with AAA Plus.

SEATTLE—516,300 (See DOWNTOWN SEATTLE ACCOMMODATIONS spotting map page A125; see index below)

To help you more easily locate accommodations in the Greater Seattle area, the following two indexes and maps show lodgings and restaurants in multiple cities. Listings for these establishments are found under the heading for the city in which they are located. The Seattle area comprises: Bellevue, Bothell, Des Moines, Edmonds, Issaquah, Kent, Kirkland, Lynnwood, Redmond, Renton, Sea-Tac, Seattle, and Tukwila.

Airport Accommodations

Listings for these establishments are found under the heading for the city in which they are located.

SEATTLE

- **Airport Plaza Hotel, adjacent to airport/SEA-TAC**
- **Best Western Airport Executel, 2 mi s/SEA-TAC**
- **Comfort Inn at Seatac, 3/4 mi s of airport/SEA-TAC**
- **Continental Court All Suites Motel, 2 blks e of airport/SEA-TAC**
- **Days Inn Seatac Airport, 1/2 mi s of airport/SEA-TAC**
- **Econo Lodge-Sea Tac Airport, 2 mi n/TUKWILA**
- **Holiday Inn Sea-Tac, opposite airport/SEA-TAC**
- **Howard Johnson, 1 mi s of airport/SEA-TAC**
- **Jet Motel Park' N Fly, opposite airport/SEA-TAC**
- **La Quinta Inn-Sea Tac Intl, adjacent to airport/SEA-TAC**
- **Quality Inn-Sea-Tac, adjacent/SEA-TAC**
- **Radisson Hotel Seattle Airport, adjacent to airport/SEA-TAC**
- **Red Lion Seattle Airport Hotel, opposite airport/SEA-TAC**
- **Sandstone Inn, 1 mi s of airport/SEA-TAC**
- **Sea-Tac Airport North Travelodge, 2 mi n of airport/TUKWILA**
- **Sea-Tac Airport Travelodge, opposite airport/SEA-TAC**
- **Sea-Tac Crest Motor Inn, 1 blk s/SEA-TAC**
- **Seattle Airport Hilton, adjacent to terminal/SEA-TAC**
- **Seattle Marriott Sea-Tac Airport, opposite airport/SEA-TAC**
- **Tac-Sea Motel Park-Fly, 4 blks n of airport terminal/SEA-TAC**
- **Thriftlodge, opposite airport/SEA-TAC**
- **Wyndham Garden Hotel Sea-Tac, opposite airport/SEA-TAC**

Index of Establishments on the DOWNTOWN SEATTLE ACCOMMODATIONS Spotting Map

LODGINGS

THE ALEXIS HOTEL Rates Subject to Change **Phone:** 206/624-4844 24

◆◆◆◆ All Year [CP] 1P: $170- 335 2P/1B: $185- 350 2P/2B: $205 XP: $15 F17

Historic Hotel **Location:** Madison & First Ave cross sts. 1007 First Ave 98104. Fax: 206/621-9009. **Terms:** Reserv deposit; package plans; pets. **Facility:** 54 rooms. Downtown commercial location. Turn-of-the-century style building near the waterfront. Some rooms with fireplace. 3 stories; interior corridors; meeting rooms; steamroom; 2 tennis courts. **Dining & Entertainment:** 2 restaurants; 11:30 am-midnight, Sat 11:30-1 am, Sun noon-midnight; $9-$19; cocktails; 24-hour room service; also, The Painted Table, see separate listing; entertainment. **Services:** health club privileges; valet laundry. Fee: airport transportation; valet parking. **All Rooms:** honor bars, free & pay movies, cable TV. **Some Rooms:** coffeemakers, microwaves, whirlpools. **Cards:** AE, DI, DS, JCB, MC, VI. D S

(See DOWNTOWN SEATTLE ACCOMMODATIONS spotting map below)

B D WILLIAMS HOUSE BED & BREAKFAST — Guaranteed Rates — **Phone:** 206/285-0810 — 16

◆◆ Bed & Breakfast
3/1-4/30 & 10/1-2/29 [BP] 1P: $89 2P/1B: $99 2P/2B: $99 XP:$5-15
5/1-9/30 [BP] 1P: $95 2P/1B: $99 2P/2B: $99 XP:$5-15

Location: 4th Ave N & Galer St. 1505 4th Ave N 98109. Fax: 206/285-8526. **Terms:** Check-in 4 pm; reserv deposit, 7 day notice; weekly rates, off season; 2 night min stay, 6/1-9/30; no pets. **Facility:** 5 rooms. 2 stories; interior corridors; smoke free premises. **All Rooms:** no A/C, no phones, no TVs. **Some Rooms:** combo & shower baths, shared bathrooms. **Cards:** AE, CB, DI, MC, VI. (D) ⊗

BEST WESTERN EXECUTIVE INN — Rates Subject to Change — **Phone:** 206/448-9444 — 4

AAA ◆◆◆ Motor Inn
All Year 1P: $78- 116 2P/1B: $88- 126 2P/2B: $92- 113 XP: $10 F18

Location: 2 blks w of SR 99; 1 mi w of I-5 exit 166, near Seattle Center. 200 Taylor Ave N 98109. Fax: 206/441-7929. **Terms:** Sr. discount; reserv deposit, 14 day notice; small pets only, $10. **Facility:** 123 rooms. Commercial location, near Space Needle. 5 stories; interior corridors; conference facilities; whirlpool; exercise room. **Dining:** Dining room; 6:30 am-10 pm, Fri-Sun from 7 am; $6-$14; cocktails. **Services:** valet laundry; area transportation. Fee: airport transportation. **All Rooms:** cable TV. Fee: movies. **Some Rooms:** kitchen, no utensils, microwaves, refrigerators, whirlpools. **Cards:** AE, CB, DI, DS, JCB, MC, VI. (D) ⊗

BEST WESTERN LOYAL INN — Rates Subject to Change — **Phone:** 206/682-0200 — 5

AAA ◆◆◆ Motel
All Year 1P: $72- 96 2P/1B: $80- 105 2P/2B: $86- 96 XP: $6 F12

Location: 1/2 mi w of I-5 exit 166 to Denny Way W. 2301 8th Ave 98121. Fax: 206/467-8984. **Terms:** Sr. discount; reserv deposit; no pets. **Facility:** 91 rooms. Commercial location near Space Needle. 4 stories; interior corridors; designated smoking area; meeting rooms; sauna, whirlpool. **Dining:** Restaurant nearby. **Services:** data ports. **Some Rooms:** coffeemakers, microwaves, radios, cable TV. Fee: refrigerators. **Cards:** AE, CB, DI, DS, MC, VI. (D) ⊗

CAPITOL HILL INN — Rates Subject to Change — **Phone:** 206/323-1955 — 2

◆◆◆ Historic Bed & Breakfast
5/1-10/31 [BP] 1P: $85- 145 2P/1B: $90- 165 2P/2B: $90- 165 XP: $15
3/1-4/30 & 11/1-2/29 [BP] 1P: $75- 165 2P/1B: $85- 165 2P/2B: $85- 165 XP: $15

Location: Capitol Hill Area. 1713 Belmont Ave 98122. **Terms:** Age restrictions may apply; check-in 4 pm; reserv deposit, 7 day notice, 2-night dep req; 2 night min stay, 5/1-10/31; no pets. **Facility:** 5 rooms. European antiques. Brass beds, carved wood mouldings in a Victorian home. Owner's 2 small dogs roam the public areas. 2 stories; interior corridors; smoke free premises. **All Rooms:** no A/C, no phones, no TVs. **Some Rooms:** combo, shower & tub baths, shared bathrooms. **Cards:** AE, MC, VI. (D) ⊗

(See DOWNTOWN SEATTLE ACCOMMODATIONS map)

(See DOWNTOWN SEATTLE ACCOMMODATIONS spotting map page A125)

CROWNE PLAZA-SEATTLE Rates Subject to Change **Phone:** 206/464-1980 21
◆◆◆ All Year 1P: $140- 200 2P/1B: $140- 200 2P/2B: $140- 200 XP: $20 F19
Hotel **Location:** 6th Ave & Seneca St; Downtown at Freeway Park. 1113 6th Ave 98101. Fax: 206/340-1617. **Terms:** Sr. discount; check-in 4 pm; reserv deposit; AP, MAP available; package plans; no pets. **Facility:** 415 rooms. Commercial downtown location. Close to shopping & ferry terminal. 34 stories; interior corridors; conference facilities; luxury level rooms; sauna, whirlpool, hydrotherapy pool; exercise room. **Dining:** Dining room; 6 am-1 am; $10-$20; cocktails; 24-hour room service. **Services:** valet laundry. Fee: airport transportation; valet parking. **All Rooms:** cable TV. Fee: movies. **Some Rooms:** refrigerators. **Cards:** AE, CB, DI, DS, JCB, MC, VI. (D) (S)

DAYS INN TOWN CENTER Rates Subject to Change **Phone:** 206/448-3434 8

AAA	5/1-9/30	1P: $80	2P/1B: $85	2P/2B: $85	XP: $7 F18
	10/1-10/31	1P: $68	2P/1B: $70	2P/2B: $70	XP: $7 F18
◆◆◆	3/1-4/30 & 11/1-2/29	1P: $62	2P/1B: $65	2P/2B: $65	XP: $7 F18

Motor Inn **Location:** 2205 7th Ave 98121. Fax: 206/441-6976. **Terms:** Sr. discount; reserv deposit, 3 day notice; weekly/monthly rates; small pets only, $3. **Facility:** 90 rooms. 4 stories; interior corridors; designated smoking area. **Dining:** Coffee shop; 6:30 am-10 pm, Sun-9 pm; $8-$16; cocktails. **Services:** data ports; valet laundry. **All Rooms:** cable TV. **Cards:** AE, CB, DI, DS, JCB, MC, VI. (D)

ECONO LODGE BY THE SPACE NEEDLE AAA Special Value Rates **Phone:** 206/441-0400 28

◆◆	6/1-9/30	1P: $69	2P/1B: $69	2P/2B: $79	XP: $5 F18
Motel	3/1-5/31 & 10/1-2/29	1P: $59	2P/1B: $59	2P/2B: $69	XP: $5 F18

Location: SR 99. 325 Aurora N 98109. Fax: 206/448-3353. **Terms:** Pets, $10. **Facility:** 58 rooms. 3 stories; interior/exterior corridors; designated smoking area; meeting rooms; heated pool. **Dining:** Restaurant nearby. **Services:** Fee: coin laundry, airport transportation. **All Rooms:** cable TV. **Some Rooms:** 4 kitchens. Fee: microwaves, refrigerators, VCP's. **Cards:** AE, CB, DI, DS, MC, VI. (D)

EDGEWATER INN Guaranteed Rates **Phone:** 206/728-7000 11
◆◆◆ All Year 1P: $109- 170 2P/1B: $109- 195 2P/2B: $109- 195 XP: $15 F18
Motor Inn **Location:** On waterfront at Pier 67. 2411 Alaskan Way-Pier 67 98121. Fax: 206/441-4119. **Terms:** Sr. discount; package plans; no pets. **Facility:** 238 rooms. Seashore lodge ambience; very upscale rooms. Some rooms with balcony. Many units overlook Elliott Bay & Olympic Mountains. 4 stories; interior corridors; meeting rooms; exercise room. **Dining & Entertainment:** Dining room; 6 am-11 pm; $10-$20; cocktails/lounge; entertainment. **Services:** valet laundry; area transportation, within 3 mi; valet parking. **All Rooms:** honor bars, cable TV. Fee: movies. **Cards:** AE, CB, DI, DS, JCB, MC, VI. *(See color ad below)* (D) (S)

EXECUTIVE RESIDENCE ON ELLIOTT BAY PLAZA AAA Special Value Rates **Phone:** 206/329-8000 36
◆◆ All Year 1P: $69- 99 2P/1B: $69- 99 2P/2B: $69- 99 XP: $5
Condo Hotel **Location:** Downtown, 2 blks n of Pikes Pl Market. 2400 Elliott 98121. Fax: 206/382-0511. **Terms:** Reserv deposit, 3 day notice; weekly/monthly rates; 4 night min stay; small pets only, $150. **Facility:** 10 rooms. 1 two-bedroom unit. 4 stories; interior corridors; heated pool, sauna, whirlpool; exercise room. **Services:** guest laundry. **All Rooms:** coffeemakers, kitchens, cable TV, no A/C. **Cards:** AE, CB, DI, DS, JCB, MC, VI. (D) (S)

FOUR SEASONS OLYMPIC HOTEL Rates Subject to Change **Phone:** 206/621-1700 19

AAA	Mon-Thurs	1P: $195- 260	2P/1B: $225- 290	2P/2B: $225- 290	XP: $20 F18
	Fri-Sun	1P: $145- 205	2P/1B: $145- 205	2P/2B: $145- 205	XP: $20 F18

◆◆◆◆◆ Historic Hotel **Location:** 411 University St 98101. Fax: 206/682-9633. **Terms:** Reserv deposit, 7 day notice; package plans; pets. **Facility:** 450 rooms. Grand historic Italian Renaissance-style hotel. Beautiful lobby & room appointments. 11 stories; interior corridors; business center, conference facilities; heated indoor pool, saunas, whirlpool; exercise room. Fee: parking. **Dining & Entertainment:** Dining room, 2 restaurants; 11:30 am-11 pm; $11-$20; cocktails; 24-hour room service; also, Georgian Room, see separate listing; entertainment. **Services:** data ports, PC, secretarial services; valet laundry. Fee: massage, airport transportation; valet parking. **All Rooms:** honor bars, free & pay movies, combo & shower baths, cable TV. **Some Rooms:** refrigerators, whirlpools. **Cards:** AE, CB, DI, JCB, MC, VI. Roll in showers. (D) (S)

GASLIGHT INN Guaranteed Rates **Phone:** 206/325-3654 34
◆◆◆ All Year [CP] 2P/1B: $62- 98
Historic Bed & Breakfast **Location:** Northbound I-5 exit 165, 1/2 mi e via Madison to 15th Ave; southbound I-5 exit 166, 1/2 mi e via Denny & Olive to 15th Ave. 1727 15th Ave 98122. Fax: 206/324-3135. **Terms:** Age restrictions may apply; reserv deposit, 7 day notice; 2 night min stay, weekends; no pets. **Facility:** 9 rooms. 2 stories; interior corridors; designated smoking area; street parking only; heated pool. **All Rooms:** refrigerators, cable TV, no A/C, no phones. **Cards:** AE, MC, VI. (D) (S)

Waterfront Flavor, Northwest Tradition, & Downtown Excitement All In One Place.
10% DISCOUNT for AAA Members
the EDGEWATER
Seattle's Only Waterfront Hotel
Applies to regular rates only. Membership card must be shown upon check-in.
Pier 67 • Downtown Seattle • Reservations (206) 728-7000 or 1-800-624-0670

(See DOWNTOWN SEATTLE ACCOMMODATIONS spotting map page A125)

GEORGETOWN INN Rates Subject to Change **Phone:** 206/762-2233 **20**

Motel

All Year [CP] 1P: $59- 64 2P/1B: $67- 72 2P/2B: $74 XP: $8 F12

Location: From I-5 at exit 162. 6100 Corson Ave S 98108. Fax: 206/763-6708. **Terms:** Sr. discount; reserv deposit; no pets. **Facility:** 52 rooms. 3 stories; interior corridors; sauna; exercise room. **Services:** guest laundry. **All Rooms:** cable TV. **Some Rooms:** 8 efficiencies, whirlpools. **Cards:** AE, CB, DI, DS, MC, VI.

HILL HOUSE BED & BREAKFAST Rates Subject to Change **Phone:** 206/720-7161 **37**

Historic Bed & Breakfast

5/1-10/12 [BP] 2P/1B: $65- 95

3/1-4/30 & 10/13-2/29 [BP] 2P/1B: $60- 90

Location: Northbound I-5 at exit 166 Olive Way to John St; southbound I-5 via Roanoke to 10th Ave, 16 blks to John St. 1113 E John St 98102. Fax: 206/323-0772. **Terms:** Age restrictions may apply; check-in 5 pm; reserv deposit, 7 day notice; 2 night min stay, weekends in season; no pets. **Facility:** 5 rooms. Restored 1903 Victorian home. In historic Capitol Hill District. 2 stories; interior/exterior corridors; smoke free premises. **All Rooms:** no A/C. **Some Rooms:** radios, phones. **Cards:** AE, DS, MC, VI.

HOTEL VINTAGE PARK Rates Subject to Change **Phone:** 206/624-8000 **15**

Historic Hotel

All Year 1P: $170- 190 2P/1B: $185- 205 2P/2B: $185- 205 XP: $15 F12

Location: Downtown; at jct of Spring St at 5th Ave. 1100 5th Ave 98101. Fax: 206/623-0568. **Terms:** Reserv deposit; no pets. **Facility:** 129 rooms. Rich fabrics. Woodburning fireplace graces lobby. Regal room decor. 11 stories; interior corridors; meeting rooms. **Dining:** Tulio Restorante, see separate listing. **Services:** data ports; complimentary evening beverages; valet laundry. Fee: airport transportation; valet parking. **All Rooms:** honor bars, cable TV. Fee: movies. **Some Rooms:** Fee: whirlpools. **Cards:** AE, CB, DI, DS, JCB, MC, VI.

INN AT THE MARKET Rates Subject to Change **Phone:** 206/443-3600 **12**

Historic Hotel

All Year 1P: $115- 270 2P/1B: $125- 275 2P/2B: $175 XP: $15 F16

Location: At the historic Pike Place Market. 86 Pine St 98101. Fax: 206/448-0631. **Terms:** Check-in 4 pm; credit card guarantee; no pets. **Facility:** 65 rooms. French country design. 8 stories; interior/exterior corridors; meeting rooms; rooftop deck. **Dining:** Coffee shop; 7 am-4 pm; $4-$7; 24-hour room service. **Services:** valet laundry. Fee: valet parking. **All Rooms:** coffeemakers, refrigerators, combo & shower baths, cable TV. **Some Rooms:** microwaves. **Cards:** AE, CB, DI, DS, JCB, MC, VI. Roll in showers.

THE INN AT VIRGINIA MASON AAA Special Value Rates **Phone:** 206/583-6453 **27**

Historic Hotel

All Year 1P: $85- 100 2P/1B: $100- 125 2P/2B: $85- 135

Location: At 10th & Spring St; 3 blks ne of I-5 on First Hill. 1006 Spring St 98104. Fax: 206/223-7545. **Terms:** Credit card guarantee; no pets. **Facility:** 79 rooms. A European-style hotel attached to Virginia Mason Hospital. Maximum rate for up to 4 persons; 9 stories; interior corridors. **Dining:** Restaurant; 7-10 am, 11:30-2 & 5-9 pm; $10-$14; wine/beer only. **Services:** Fee: coin laundry. **All Rooms:** cable TV. **Some Rooms:** coffeemakers, microwaves, refrigerators, whirlpools. Fee: VCP's. **Cards:** AE, CB, DI, DS, JCB, MC, VI.

MAYFLOWER PARK HOTEL AAA Special Value Rates **Phone:** 206/623-8700 **13**

Historic Hotel

All Year 1P: $110- 140 2P/1B: $120- 150 2P/2B: $120- 155 XP: $10 F17

Location: 4th & Olive Way. 405 Olive Way 98101. Fax: 206/382-6997. **Terms:** Reserv deposit; no pets. **Facility:** 173 rooms. Elegant warmth with the Old World charm of a small European hotel. 12 stories; interior corridors; meeting rooms. Fee: parking. **Dining:** Dining room; 6:30 am-2:30 & 5-9:30 pm, Fri-10:30 pm, Sat 6:30 am-10:30 pm, Sun 6:30 am-9:30 pm; $10-$20; cocktails. **Services:** valet parking. **All Rooms:** free & pay movies, combo & shower baths, cable TV. **Some Rooms:** Fee: refrigerators, whirlpools. **Cards:** AE, CB, DI, DS, MC, VI.

PACIFIC PLAZA HOTEL

400 Spring Street, Seattle,
Washington 98104
206-623-3900 • 1-800-426-1165
"SEATTLE'S BEST LITTLE SECRET"

- Tastefully appointed guest rooms.
- Generous continental breakfast included.
- Convenient Downtown Seattle Location.
- Rooms from $68 to $97 (plus tax) per night
*single/double occupancy

REST AND RELAX WITH SPECIAL WEEKEND RATES.

Spacious rooms, pool, whirlpool, exercise room, in-room coffee, cozy restaurant and lounge. AAA weekend rates, subject to availability.

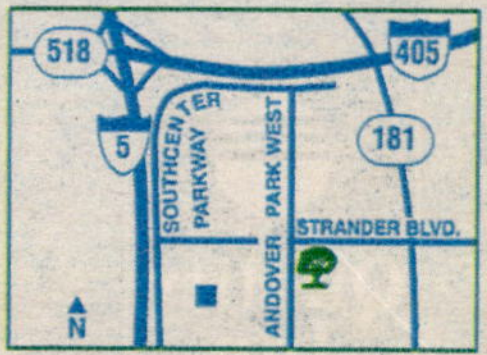

BELLEVUE
14615 N.E. 29th Place
206 869-5300

COURTYARD Marriott
800 443-6000

SOUTHCENTER
400 Andover Park West
206 575-2500

(See DOWNTOWN SEATTLE ACCOMMODATIONS spotting map page A125)

PACIFIC PLAZA HOTEL Rates Subject to Change **Phone:** 206/623-3900 **1**
◆◆ All Year [CP] 1P: $77- 97 2P/1B: $77- 97 2P/2B: $87
Historic Hotel **Location:** 4th Ave at Spring St. 400 Spring St 98104. Fax: 206/623-2059. **Terms:** Sr. discount; check-in 4 pm; reserv deposit; no pets. **Facility:** 160 rooms. 1928 vintage hotel. Off site public parking garage. 8 stories; interior corridors. Fee: parking. **Dining:** Dining room; 11 am-midnight; $5-$10. **Services:** valet laundry. **All Rooms:** combo & shower baths, cable TV, no A/C. Fee: movies. **Some Rooms:** refrigerators. **Cards:** AE, CB, DI, DS, JCB, MC, VI.
(See color ad p A127) Ⓓ

PLAZA PARK SUITES Rates Subject to Change **Phone:** 206/682-8282 **29**
AAA ◆◆◆ Hotel All Year [CP] 1P: $126- 238 2P/1B: $144- 280 2P/2B: $144- 280 XP: $20 F18
Location: I-5 northbound exit Seneca St to Pike St via 6th Ave; I-5 southbound exit Union St to Pike St. 1011 Pike St 98101. Fax: 206/682-5315. **Terms:** Credit card guarantee, 20 day notice; weekly/monthly rates; no pets. **Facility:** 191 rooms. Downtown commercial location. 26 two-bedroom units. 9 stories; interior corridors; conference facilities; heated pool, sauna, whirlpools; exercise room. **Services:** data ports; area transportation, to downtown. Fee: coin laundry, airport transportation; valet parking. **All Rooms:** Fee: movies. **Some Rooms:** whirlpools. **Cards:** AE, DI, DS, JCB, MC, VI. *(See ad p A129)* Ⓓ Ⓢ

QUALITY INN CITY CENTER AAA Special Value Rates **Phone:** 206/624-6820 **6**
AAA ◆◆◆ Motor Inn All Year [CP] 1P: $80- 165 2P/1B: $87- 175 2P/2B: $95- 175 XP: $10 F18
Location: Downtown, at 8th Ave & Blanchard. 2224 8th Ave 98121. Fax: 206/467-6926. **Terms:** Reserv deposit, 3 day notice; pets. **Facility:** 72 rooms. Commercial location. Close to downtown. Convenient to shopping & attractions. 5 two-bedroom units. 7 stories; interior corridors; meeting rooms; sauna, whirlpool. **Dining:** Dining room; 11 am-10 pm, Sat & Sun from 5 pm; $4-$10; cocktails. **Services:** valet laundry. Fee: airport transportation. **All Rooms:** free movies, cable TV. **Some Rooms:** coffeemakers, 5 efficiencies, microwaves, radios, refrigerators. **Cards:** AE, CB, DI, DS, JCB, MC, VI. *(See color ad below)* Ⓓ

RAMADA INN SEATTLE DOWNTOWN Rates Subject to Change **Phone:** 206/441-9785 **30**
AAA ◆◆◆ Hotel

6/1-9/25	1P: $150	2P/1B: $160	2P/2B: $150	XP: $10 F17
9/26-2/29	1P: $140	2P/1B: $150	2P/2B: $150	XP: $10 F17
3/1-5/31	1P: $130	2P/1B: $140	2P/2B: $140	XP: $10 F17

Location: Cross Road Blanchard & 5th Ave. 2200 5th Ave 98121. Fax: 206/448-0924. **Terms:** Sr. discount; reserv deposit, 5 day notice, in season; no pets. **Facility:** 110 rooms. Commercial location. 4 stories; interior corridors; meeting rooms. Fee: parking. **Dining:** Restaurant; 6:30 am-2 & 4:30-11 pm, Sat & Sun 6:30 am-noon & 4:30-11 pm; $7-$15; cocktails. **Services:** valet laundry. Fee: airport transportation. **All Rooms:** coffeemakers, combo & shower baths, cable TV. **Cards:** AE, CB, DI, DS, JCB, MC, VI. Ⓓ Ⓢ

RESIDENCE INN BY MARRIOTT SEATTLE DOWNTOWN Guaranteed Rates **Phone:** 206/624-6000 **33**
◆◆◆ Suite Hotel All Year [CP] 1P: $125 2P/1B: $125 2P/2B: $200
Location: From I-5 exit Fairview Ave, se end of Lake Union. 800 Fairview Ave N 98109. Fax: 206/223-8160. **Terms:** Check-in 4 pm; credit card guarantee; weekly/monthly rates; pets, $10. **Facility:** 234 rooms. 54 two-bedroom units. 7 stories; interior corridors; business center, meeting rooms; heated indoor pool, saunas, whirlpool; exercise room. **Services:** data ports, PC, secretarial services; complimentary evening beverages; area transportation. Fee: coin laundry, airport transportation. **All Rooms:** coffeemakers, kitchens, microwaves, free & pay movies, cable TV. **Cards:** AE, CB, DI, DS, MC, VI. Ⓓ Ⓢ

ROBERTA'S BED & BREAKFAST Rates Subject to Change **Phone:** 206/329-3326 **32**
◆◆ Historic Bed & Breakfast

3/1-6/30 & 10/1-2/29 [BP]	1P: $70- 85	2P/1B: $80- 100	XP: $10
7/1-9/30 [BP]	1P: $78- 98	2P/1B: $85- 105	XP: $10

Location: From I-5 northbound exit 166, southbound exit 168A, follow signs to Volunteer Park. 1147 16th Ave East 98112. Fax: 206/324-2149. **Terms:** Reserv deposit, 7 day notice; no pets. **Facility:** 5 rooms. Turn-of-the-century home. Owner's cat roams through the public area. 3 stories; smoke free premises; street parking only. **All Rooms:** combo & shower baths, no A/C, no phones, no TVs. **Cards:** MC, VI. Ⓓ

The Roosevelt
A WESTCOAST HOTEL
1531 7th Ave., Seattle, WA 98101 (206)621-1200 or (800)426-0670
151 Spacious guestrooms and suites • Fully equipped fitness center • Von's Grand City Cafe • Valet parking • 3 Diamond AAA rating.

WHEN YOU'RE LIVING OUT OF A SUITCASE...
Quality Inn
In Seattle
Quality Inn City Center
2224 Eighth Avenue
Seattle, WA 98121
• Indoor Spa & Sauna
• Free Movies, Sports and News
• Free Continental Breakfast
• Kitchenettes, Family and Executive Suites • Near Convention Center, Seattle Center and Pike Place Market • Free Parking
For reservations call 206-624-6820 or toll free 800-437-4867 or 800-4-CHOICE

(See DOWNTOWN SEATTLE ACCOMMODATIONS spotting map page A125)

ROOSEVELT HOTEL, A WESTCOAST HOTEL Rates Subject to Change **Phone:** 206/621-1200 **26**
◆◆◆ All Year 1P: $125- 160 2P/1B: $125- 170 2P/2B: $125- 170 XP: $10 F18
Hotel **Location:** Downtown at 7th Ave & Pine. 1531 7th Ave 98101. Fax: 206/233-0335. **Terms:** Sr. discount; AP available; no pets. **Facility:** 151 rooms. Business center location. 20 stories; interior corridors; conference facilities; exercise room. Fee: parking. **Services:** data ports; valet laundry. Fee: airport transportation. **All Rooms:** combo & shower baths, cable TV. Fee: movies. **Some Rooms:** honor bars. Fee: refrigerators, whirlpools. **Cards:** AE, CB, DI, DS, JCB, MC, VI. *(See ad p A128)* D S

SEATTLE HILTON Rates Subject to Change **Phone:** 206/624-0500 **18**
AAA 3/1-10/31 1P: $159- 184 2P/1B: $174- 199 XP: $10 F18
11/1-2/29 1P: $139- 164 2P/1B: $159- 179 XP: $10 F18
◆◆◆ Hotel **Location:** 6th Ave at University St. 1301 6th Ave 98101. Fax: 206/682-9029. **Terms:** Sr. discount; reserv deposit; package plans; no pets. **Facility:** 237 rooms. Downtown business area. 14 stories; interior corridors; meeting rooms. Fee: parking. **Dining:** Dining room, coffee shop; 6 am-10 pm, Fri & Sat-11 pm; $19-$25; cocktails; 24-hour room service. **Services:** valet laundry. Fee: airport transportation. **All Rooms:** free movies, cable TV. **Some Rooms:** Fee: refrigerators. **Cards:** AE, CB, DI, DS, JCB, MC, VI. *(See ad p 38)* D S

SHERATON SEATTLE HOTEL & TOWERS Rates Subject to Change **Phone:** 206/621-9000 **17**
◆◆◆◆ All Year 1P: $145- 214 2P/1B: $165- 234 2P/2B: $165- 234 XP: $20 F17
Hotel **Location:** 6th Ave & Pike. 1400 6th Ave 98101. Fax: 206/621-8441. **Terms:** Reserv deposit; package plans; no pets. **Facility:** 840 rooms. 35 stories; interior corridors; business center, conference facilities; luxury level rooms; heated indoor pool, sauna, whirlpool; exercise room. **Dining & Entertainment:** 2 restaurants; 6 am-midnight; $8-$15; cocktails/lounge; 24-hour room service; also, Fullers, see separate listing; entertainment. **Services:** data ports, PC, secretarial services; valet laundry. Fee: childcare, airport transportation; valet parking. **All Rooms:** honor bars, coffeemakers, free & pay movies, combo & shower baths, cable TV. **Some Rooms:** Fee: whirlpools. **Cards:** AE, CB, DI, DS, JCB, MC, VI. D S

SIXTH AVENUE INN Rates Subject to Change **Phone:** 206/441-8300 **9**
AAA All Year 1P: $48- 65 2P/1B: $58- 77 2P/2B: $68- 81 XP: $12 F16
◆◆◆ Motor Inn **Location:** 2000 6th Ave 98121. Fax: 206/441-9903. **Terms:** Credit card guarantee, 3 day notice; weekly/monthly rates; no pets. **Facility:** 166 rooms. 5 stories; interior corridors; meeting rooms. **Dining:** Dining room; 6:30 am-10 pm, Sat & Sun 7 am-10 pm; $7-$16; cocktails. **All Rooms:** combo & shower baths, cable TV. **Some Rooms:** refrigerators. **Cards:** AE, CB, DI, DS, MC, VI.
(See color ad below) D

THE SORRENTO HOTEL AAA Special Value Rates **Phone:** 206/622-6400 **22**
◆◆◆◆ All Year 1P: $135- 155 2P/1B: $145- 235 2P/2B: $185- 235 XP: $15 F16
Historic Hotel **Location:** 2 blks e of I-5 on First Hill at 9th & Madison St. 900 Madison St 98104. Fax: 206/343-6155. **Terms:** Check-in 4 pm; reserv deposit, 30 day notice; no pets. **Facility:** 76 rooms. European style. 6 stories; interior corridors; meeting rooms. **Dining:** Also, The Hunt Club, see separate listing. **Services:** data ports, secretarial services; valet laundry; area transportation. Fee: airport transportation; valet parking. **All Rooms:** honor bars, free movies, combo & shower baths, cable TV. **Cards:** AE, CB, DI, DS, JCB, MC, VI. A Preferred Hotel. D

Plaza Park Suites
DOWNTOWN SEATTLE'S ONLY ALL-SUITE
1011 Pike St. Seattle, WA 98101 (800)426-0670, (206)682-8282
Daily complimentary continental breakfast • Suites with separate bedrooms and full kitchens • City view, fireplace or jacuzzi tub available • Walk to downtown shopping & attractions • Year-round heated outdoor pool & fitness center • Complimentary downtown shuttle transportation. Call today!

GREAT ACCOMMODATIONS AT A VERY ACCOMMODATING RATE.

SPECIAL AAA RATES
$48 to $65 Sgl. Occupancy Plus Tax
Subject to availability

- Convenient Downtown location near Convention Center.
- Walking distance to Shopping, Waterfront, Sports and Major Attractions.
- Sixth Avenue Bar & Grill
- Non-smokers' Rooms
- Satellite TV
- Free Parking

SIXTH AVENUE INN
2000 Sixth Avenue • Seattle, WA 98121 • (206) 441-8300 • **(800) 648-6440**

(See DOWNTOWN SEATTLE ACCOMMODATIONS spotting map page A125)

STOUFFER MADISON HOTEL Guaranteed Rates **Phone:** 206/583-0300 25

AAA ◆◆◆◆ Hotel

4/1-11/15	1P: $119- 214	2P/1B: $129- 234	2P/2B: $129- 234	XP: $20	F18
3/1-3/31 & 11/16-2/29	1P: $99- 214	2P/1B: $109- 234	2P/2B: $109- 234	XP: $20	F18

Location: Cross streets 6th Ave & Madison. 515 Madison St 98104. Fax: 206/624-8125. **Terms:** Sr. discount; credit card guarantee; package plans; small pets only. **Facility:** 554 rooms. Outstanding views of the city & Puget Sound. 28 stories; interior corridors; conference facilities; heated indoor pool, whirlpool; exercise room. Fee: parking. **Dining:** Coffee shop; 6 am-10 pm; 9/6-5/29 6:30 am-10 pm; $7-$15; cocktails; also, Prego, see separate listing. **Services:** data ports, secretarial services; valet laundry. Fee: airport transportation. **All Rooms:** honor bars, cable TV. Fee: movies. **Some Rooms:** refrigerators, whirlpools. **Cards:** AE, CB, DI, DS, JCB, MC, VI.

(See ad below) Ⓓ Ⓢ ⊗

TRAVELODGE BY THE SPACE NEEDLE Rates Subject to Change **Phone:** 206/441-7878 3

◆◆◆ Motel

7/1-9/4	1P: $67- 83	2P/1B: $73- 89	2P/2B: $83- 109	XP: $6	F17
3/1-6/30 & 9/5-2/29	1P: $70- 77	2P/1B: $75- 83	2P/2B: $90- 98	XP: $6	F17

Location: 1 blk w of SR 99; 1 mi w of I-5, exit 166. 200 6th Ave N 98109. Fax: 206/448-4825. **Terms:** Sr. discount; CP available; pets, small dogs only, $25. **Facility:** 88 rooms. Commercial location. 4 stories; interior corridors; heated pool, whirlpool. **Services:** valet laundry. Fee: airport transportation. **All Rooms:** coffeemakers, free movies, combo & shower baths, cable TV. **Some Rooms:** microwaves, refrigerators. **Cards:** AE, CB, DI, DS, MC, VI. Ⓓ ⊗

TRAVELODGE DOWNTOWN Rates Subject to Change **Phone:** 206/624-6300 7

◆◆ Motel

5/1-9/30	1P: $60- 85	2P/1B: $75- 85	2P/2B: $85	XP: $6	F18
3/1-4/30 & 10/1-2/29	1P: $55- 70	2P/1B: $70	2P/2B: $70- 80	XP: $6	F18

Location: Downtown, at 8th Ave & Blanchard. 2213 8th Ave 98121. Fax: 206/233-0185. **Terms:** Sr. discount; no pets. **Facility:** 72 rooms. Some rooms with balcony. 3 stories; interior corridors. **Dining:** Restaurant nearby. **Services:** valet laundry. Fee: airport transportation. **All Rooms:** coffeemakers, free movies, combo & shower baths, cable TV. **Cards:** AE, CB, DI, DS, JCB, MC, VI. Ⓓ ⊗

WestCoast Vance Hotel

HISTORIC CHARM IN THE HEART OF THE CITY
620 Stewart St., Seattle, WA 98101
(206)441-4200 or (800)426-0670

- Located in the heart of downtown Seattle
- 165 charming guestrooms
- Covered valet parking
- Authentic Italian dining at Saluté in Citta
- ◆◆◆ Rating

Surround Yourself With Seattle.

$99* AAA Members

In Seattle, the Stouffer Madison Hotel is your all-around "best" choice. This AAA Four-Diamond hotel offers views of Puget Sound, the mountains, and downtown and is convenient to the waterfront, Pike Place Market, Pioneer Square, the Space Needle, and the Kingdome. You'll enjoy our fine restaurants, rooftop pool and fitness center, and complimentary coffee and newspaper delivered with your wake-up call. For reservations, call (206) 583-0300.

SEATTLE
STOUFFER
MADISON HOTEL

515 Madison Street, Seattle, WA 98104
*Rate $119 from 6/1/95 to 11/15/95. Limited rooms available at this rate.
AAA members only. Must present I.D. at check-in. Not applicable to groups.
May not be used in conjunction with any other special offer or discount.
Tax not included. Based on single or double occupancy.

Before you hit the open road,

tear along the dotted line.

Cut your travel expenses before you hit the road. Just clip the attached coupons and get $5 off the AAA room rate at participating Holiday Inn® hotels, where you'll always find a clean, comfortable room at an exceptional value.

Then relax. Enjoy the freedom of the open highway. And the extra savings in your pocket.

STAY WITH SOMEONE YOU KNOW.® Holiday Inn®

CALL 1-800-HOLIDAY OR YOUR TRAVEL AGENT.

SAVE $5

Save $5 off the already-reduced AAA room rate. See back for restrictions and participating hotels.

Holiday Inn®

SAVE $5

Save $5 off the already-reduced AAA room rate. See back for restrictions and participating hotels.

Holiday Inn®

SAVE $5

Save $5 off the already-reduced AAA room rate. See back for restrictions and participating hotels.

Holiday Inn®

Check out these participating Holiday Inn® hotels:

OREGON

Eugene
225 Coburg Road
(503) 342-5181

Grants Pass ◊
105 N.E. Agness Avenue
(503) 471-6144

Portland
Downtown
1021 NE Grand Avenue
(503) 235-2100

Lake Oswego †
14811 SW Kruse Oaks Blvd.
(503) 624-8400

South-I-5 (Wilsonville)
25425 SW Boones Ferry Road
(503) 682-2211

WASHINGTON

Pullman ◊
S.E. 1190 Bishop Blvd.
(509) 334-4437

Seattle
Boeing Field
11244 Pacific Hwy. South
(206) 762-0300

Everett
101 128th Street SE
(206) 745-2555

Lynnwood ◊
4117 196th Street S.W.
(206) 775-8030

WASHINGTON cont.
Renton
800 Rainier Avenue South
(206) 226-7700

Spokane-Downtown ◊
North 801 Division Street
(509) 328-8505

BRITISH COLUMBIA

Kelowna ◊
2429 Highway 97 North
(604) 763-0500

Vancouver
Abbotsford ◊
2073 Clearbrook Road
(604) 859-6211

Centre (Broadway)
711 West Broadway Avenue
(604) 879-0511

Coquitlam
631 Lougheed Highway
(604) 931-4433

Downtown Hotel & Tower Suites
1110 Howe Street
(604) 684-2151

Victoria
3020 Blanshard Street
(604) 382-4400

◊ Denotes Holiday Inn Express® hotel location. † Denotes Holiday Inn Crowne Plaza® hotel location.
This is a list of hotels participating in this promotion only. For a complete list of Holiday Inn hotel locations, see a Holiday Inn® Worldwide Directory available at any Holiday Inn hotel. © 1995, Holiday Inns, Inc. All rights reserved.

Valid at participating Oregon/Washington/British Columbia Holiday Inn® hotels (see list). One coupon per room, per single or multiple night stay; no copies or facsimiles accepted. Not valid for groups or in conjunction with any other discount, promotion or special event as established by each independent operator. Not valid with employee or travel industry discounts. Blackout dates apply. Rooms limited and subject to availability. Void where taxed, restricted or otherwise prohibited by law. Coupon has no cash value. Offer valid March 1, 1995 through February 29, 1996.

OR95AA

Valid at participating Oregon/Washington/British Columbia Holiday Inn® hotels (see list). One coupon per room, per single or multiple night stay; no copies or facsimiles accepted. Not valid for groups or in conjunction with any other discount, promotion or special event as established by each independent operator. Not valid with employee or travel industry discounts. Blackout dates apply. Rooms limited and subject to availability. Void where taxed, restricted or otherwise prohibited by law. Coupon has no cash value. Offer valid March 1, 1995 through February 29, 1996.

OR95AA

Valid at participating Oregon/Washington/British Columbia Holiday Inn® hotels (see list). One coupon per room, per single or multiple night stay; no copies or facsimiles accepted. Not valid for groups or in conjunction with any other discount, promotion or special event as established by each independent operator. Not valid with employee or travel industry discounts. Blackout dates apply. Rooms limited and subject to availability. Void where taxed, restricted or otherwise prohibited by law. Coupon has no cash value. Offer valid March 1, 1995 through February 29, 1996.

OR95AA

(See DOWNTOWN SEATTLE ACCOMMODATIONS spotting map page A125)

UNIVERSITY SILVER CLOUD INN — Rates Subject to Change — Phone: 206/526-5200 — 39

Motel	6/1-8/31 [CP]	1P: $69- 99	2P/1B: $75- 106	2P/2B: $77- 103	XP: $6	F12
	3/1-5/31 & 9/1-2/29 [CP]	1P: $64- 94	2P/1B: $70- 101	2P/2B: $72- 98	XP: $6	F12

Too new to rate; **Location:** From I-5 at exit 169, e 1 mi; across from university village. 5036 25th Ave NE 98105. **Terms:** no pets. **Facility:** 144 rooms. Rating withheld pending completion of construction. Scheduled to open Fall, 1994. 4 stories; interior corridors; meeting rooms; heated indoor pool, whirlpool; exercise room. **Services:** guest laundry. **All Rooms:** microwaves, free movies, refrigerators, combo & shower baths, cable TV. **Some Rooms:** 45 efficiencies, whirlpools. **Cards:** AE, CB, DI, DS, MC, VI. Roll in showers. (D) (S) ⊗

WARWICK HOTEL — Rates Subject to Change — Phone: 206/443-4300 — 10

AAA	5/1-10/31	1P: $175	2P/1B: $185	2P/2B: $185	XP: $10	F18
◆◆◆◆ Hotel	3/1-4/30 & 11/1-2/29	1P: $155	2P/1B: $165	2P/2B: $165	XP: $10	F18

Location: Downtown. 401 Lenora 98121. Fax: 206/448-1662. **Terms:** Sr. discount; credit card guarantee; package plans; small pets only. **Facility:** 229 rooms. Commercial location. City & Puget Sound views. Rooms with balcony. 1 two-bedroom unit, 1 three-bedroom unit. 19 stories; interior corridors; meeting rooms; heated indoor pool, sauna, whirlpool; exercise room. **Dining & Entertainment:** Dining room, coffee shop; 6:30 am-10 pm; $13-$18; cocktails; also, Liaison, see separate listing; entertainment. **Services:** data ports; valet laundry. Fee: valet parking. **All Rooms:** cable TV. Fee: movies. **Some Rooms:** honor bars, refrigerators, whirlpools. **Cards:** AE, CB, DI, DS, JCB, MC, VI. *(See ad below)* (D) (S) ⊗

WEST COAST VANCE HOTEL — AAA Special Value Rates — Phone: 206/441-4200 — 23

◆◆◆ Historic Hotel	All Year	1P: $85- 105	2P/1B: $95- 105	2P/2B: $115	XP: $10	F18

Location: Corner of 7th & Stewart St. 620 Stewart St 98101. Fax: 206/441-8612. **Terms:** Package plans; no pets. **Facility:** 165 rooms. Business center location. 10 stories; interior corridors. **Dining & Entertainment:** Dining room; 7 am-10 pm; $10-$16; cocktail lounge; entertainment. **Services:** valet laundry. Fee: valet parking. **All Rooms:** combo & shower baths. Fee: movies. **Some Rooms:** refrigerators, VCP's. **Cards:** AE, DI, DS, MC, VI. *(See ad p A130)* (D) (S) ⊗

WASHINGTON BED & BREAKFAST GUILD

Experience the Warm Welcome of Washington
*Licensed *Inspected *Approved* B & B's
Free Directory Call 1-800-647-2918 or
Write: WBBG-AAA, 2442 NW. Market, Seattle, WA 98107

AAA ◆◆◆◆

35% Off
Listed Rates*

Lenora and Fourth Avenue
Downtown Seattle
(206) 443-4300
Toll Free: **800-426-9280**

Affordable Elegance Downtown. Open the door to something special. Your room at the Warwick. Italian marble, fine woods, and carefully thought out necessities. Enjoy the indoor pool, sauna, exercise room and spa. The Liaison Restaurant will delightfully tempt you. The personal service will pamper you.

Step into our 24-hour complimentary van to be chauffeured to the Space Needle, Seattle Center Opera House, Pike Place Market, or Pioneer Square. Anywhere in the downtown area. Shopping, theatres and sporting events are just minutes away.

Call today for reservations. Commissionable.

*Limited number of rooms available at this special offer. AAA members only. Must present I.D. at check-in. Discount rates subject to availability and applicable only to hotel rack rates. Not applicable to groups. May not be used in conjunction with any other special offer or discount.

(See DOWNTOWN SEATTLE ACCOMMODATIONS spotting map page A125)

THE WESTIN HOTEL, SEATTLE Rates Subject to Change **Phone:** 206/728-1000 (14)

AAA ◆◆◆◆ Hotel

All Year 1P: $129- 195 2P/1B: $149- 215 2P/2B: $149- 215 XP: $25 F18

Location: 1900 5th Ave 98101. Fax: 206/728-2259. **Terms:** Reserv deposit; package plans; small pets only. **Facility:** 865 rooms. Twin cylindrical towers; outstanding city & water views. 47 stories; interior corridors; business center, conference facilities; heated indoor pool, saunas, whirlpool; exercise room, fitness center. Fee: parking. **Dining & Entertainment:** Coffee shop; 6:30 am-10 pm; $7-$18; cocktails/lounge; 24-hour room service; also, The Palm Court, Nikko, see separate listing; entertainment. **Services:** data ports, PC; valet laundry. Fee: airport transportation; valet parking. **All Rooms:** honor bars, free & pay movies, refrigerators, cable TV. **Some Rooms:** coffeemakers, microwaves, safes, whirlpools. **Cards:** AE, CB, DI, DS, JCB, MC, VI.

(See ad below)

RESTAURANTS

A JAY'S EATERY **Dinner:** $11-$20 **Phone:** 206/441-1511 (33)

◆◆ Italian

Location: Cross street Cedar. 2619 1st Ave 98121. **Hours:** 7 am-5 pm, Tue-Thurs to 10 pm, Fri & Sat to 11 pm. **Features:** children's menu; carryout; cocktails. Breakfast & lunch New York deli-style dining. Casual fine dining for dinner. **Cards:** MC, VI.

AL BOCCALINO RISTORANTE **Dinner:** $11-$20 **Phone:** 206/622-7688 (34)

◆◆◆ Italian

Location: In Pioneer Square; 1 blk w of 1st Ave. 1 Yesler Way 98104. **Hours:** 11:30 am-2 & 5-10 pm, Fri & Sat-10:30 pm, Sun 4:30 pm-9 pm. Closed: 1/1, 7/4, 9/4, 11/23 & 12/25. **Reservations:** suggested; weekends. **Features:** No A/C; children's menu; carryout; beer only. Innovative award winning classic Italian cuisine. **Cards:** AE, DI, MC, VI.

BENIHANA OF TOKYO **Dinner:** $21-$30 **Phone:** 206/682-4686 (9)

◆◆ Ethnic

Location: 5th Ave & University St; on Plaza Terrace of the IBM Bldg. 1200 5th Ave 98101. **Hours:** 11:30 am-2 & 5:30-10 pm, Fri-11 pm, Sat 5 pm-11 pm, Sun 5 pm-9:30 pm. Closed major holidays. **Reservations:** suggested. **Features:** cocktails & lounge; entertainment; a la carte. Tableside preparation Teppanyaki-style by Japanese chefs serving individual tables seating 8. Smoke free premises. **Cards:** AE, CB, DI, JCB, MC, VI.

THE BROOKLYN SEAFOOD, STEAK & OYSTER HOUSE **Dinner:** $11-$20 **Phone:** 206/224-7000 (15)

◆◆◆ Steak and Seafood

Location: Downtown; corner 2nd Ave & University. 1212 2nd Ave 98101. **Hours:** 11 am-3 & 5-10 pm, Sat 5 pm-11 pm, Sun 5 pm-9 pm. Closed: 1/1, 11/23 & 12/25. **Reservations:** suggested. **Features:** health conscious menu items; carryout; cocktails & lounge; valet parking; a la carte. Complimentary evening parking avail. **Cards:** AE, DI, DS, JCB, MC, VI.

CAMPAGNE **Dinner:** $21-$30 **Phone:** 206/728-2800 (19)

◆◆◆ French

Location: 1st Ave & Pine. 86 Pine St 98101. **Hours:** 5:30 pm-10 pm; 6/1-9/30 11:30 am-2 pm. Closed: 1/1, 5/29, 11/23, 12/24 & 12/25. **Reservations:** suggested. **Features:** No A/C; cocktails & lounge. Unpretentious French dining. View of Elliott Bay. Lounge dining until midnight. **Cards:** AE, CB, DI, MC, VI.

1900 FIFTH AVENUE

The Front Door To Seattle.

We're proud to be Seattle's grand entrance to the city's most inviting neighborhood. Visit the Pike Place Market, The Aquarium, Westlake Mall, ride the monorail to Seattle Center and the Space Needle or just relax in a panoramic view room. Scenic wonders. City pleasures. The Westin is the center of it all. Four restaurants, Room Service, Pool, Spa, Fitness Center, Ample Parking, Airport Transportation. 1-800-228-3000

$94* AAA MEMBERS single/double

THE WESTIN HOTEL
Seattle
1900 Fifth Avenue
Seattle, Washington 98101
1-206-728-1000 *Fax 206-728-2259*

***Per room except March 26 - November 19. $129. Limited number of rooms at this special offer. Other discounts not applicable. Call for availability.**

Off I-5 northbound, exit Seneca to 6th, turn right four blocks to hotel.
On I-5 southbound, exit Union Street to 6th, turn right two blocks to hotel.

(See DOWNTOWN SEATTLE ACCOMMODATIONS spotting map page A125)

CHANDLERS CRABHOUSE & FRESH FISH MARKET **Dinner:** $11-$20 **Phone:** 206/223-2722 (5)
AAA ◆◆◆ Seafood
Location: From I-5 exit Fairview Ave, se end of Lake Union. 901 Fairview Ave N 98109. **Hours:** 11:30 am-2 & 5-10 pm, Fri-11 pm, Sat 10:30 am-3 & 5-11 pm, Sun 10:30 am-3 & 4:30-10 pm. Closed: 12/25. **Reservations:** suggested. **Features:** children's menu; carryout; cocktails & lounge; a la carte. Fresh seafood, signature items with a view on the lake. **Cards:** AE, DI, DS, JCB, MC, VI. ⊗

DAHLIA LOUNGE **Dinner:** $11-$20 **Phone:** 206/682-4142 (20)
◆◆◆ American
Location: Crossroads 4th Ave & Stewart. 1904 4th Ave 98101. **Hours:** 11:30 am-2:30 & 5-10 pm, Fri & Sat to 11 pm, Sun 5 pm-9 pm. Closed major holidays. **Reservations:** suggested. **Features:** carryout; cocktails. Imaginative, exciting northwest dining in a warm atmosphere. Smoke free premises. **Cards:** AE, DI, DS, MC, VI. ⊗

ELLIOTT'S OYSTER HOUSE **Dinner:** $11-$20 **Phone:** 206/623-4340 (21)
◆◆ Seafood
Location: At Pier 56. Pier 56-Alaskan Way 98101. **Hours:** 11 am-11 pm. Closed: 11/24 & 12/25. **Reservations:** suggested. **Features:** children's menu; carryout; cocktails & lounge; a la carte. Contemporary setting, open kitchen & oyster bar. View of Elliott Bay. Smoke free premises. **Cards:** AE, DI, DS, JCB, MC, VI. ⊗

FULLERS **Dinner:** $21-$30 **Phone:** 206/621-9000 (7)
AAA ◆◆◆◆ Continental
Location: In Sheraton Seattle Hotel & Towers. 1400 6th Ave 98101. **Hours:** 11:30 am-2 & 5:30-10 pm, Sat from 5:30 pm. Closed: Sun & 1/1. **Reservations:** suggested. **Features:** children's menu; health conscious menu; cocktails & lounge; valet parking. Beautifully elegant artistic dining room. Leisurely service. Smoke free premises. **Cards:** AE, CB, DI, DS, JCB, MC, VI. ⊗

GEORGIAN ROOM Historical **Dinner:** $21-$30 **Phone:** 206/621-7889 (8)
AAA ◆◆◆◆ Continental
Location: In Four Seasons Olympic Hotel. 411 University St 98101. **Hours:** 6:30-11 am, 11:30-2:30 & 6-10 pm, Fri & Sat-10:30 pm, Sun 7-11 am. **Reservations:** suggested. **Features:** children's menu; health conscious menu; carryout; cocktails & lounge; fee for valet parking; a la carte. Grand elegant Renaissance dining room specializing in Northwest Regional cuisine & fresh seafood. Daily specials. Lavish desserts. **Cards:** AE, CB, DI, MC, VI. ⊗

THE HUNT CLUB **Dinner:** $21-$30 **Phone:** 206/343-6156 (17)
AAA ◆◆◆ American
Location: In The Sorrento Hotel. 900 Madison St 98104. **Hours:** 7 am-2:30 & 5:30-10 pm, Fri & Sat-11 pm. **Reservations:** suggested. **Features:** children's menu; health conscious menu; carryout; cocktails & lounge; valet parking; a la carte. Northwest cuisine. Sat & Sun brunch. Smoke free premises. **Cards:** AE, DI, DS, JCB, MC, VI. ⊗

KASPAR'S **Dinner:** $11-$20 **Phone:** 206/298-0123 (36)
◆◆◆ Seafood
Location: 2 blks w of Seattle Center. 19 W Harrison St 98119. **Hours:** 4:30 pm-9:30 pm, Fri 11:30 am-2 & 4:30-10:30 pm, Sat 4:30 pm-10:30 pm. Closed: Sun, Mon, 1/1 & 12/25. **Reservations:** suggested. **Features:** children's menu; early bird specials; cocktails & lounge; valet parking. Creative, contemporary cuisine. Casual & relaxed atmosphere. Smoke free premises. **Cards:** AE, MC, VI. ⊗

LABUZNIK **Dinner:** over $31 **Phone:** 206/441-8899 (3)
◆◆ Continental
Location: 1 blk n of Pike Place Market. 1924 First Ave 98101. **Hours:** 4:30 pm-midnight. Closed: Sun, Mon, 7/4, 11/23, 12/25 & 7/13-7/31. **Reservations:** suggested. **Features:** No A/C; cocktails & lounge; minimum charge-$10. No parking on premises. Smoke free premises. **Cards:** AE, CB, DI, DS, MC, VI. ⊗

LIAISON **Dinner:** $11-$20 **Phone:** 206/443-4300 (23)
AAA ◆◆◆ American
Location: In the Warwick Hotel. 401 Lenora 98121. **Hours:** 6:30 am-2:30 & 5:30-10 pm. **Reservations:** suggested. **Features:** Sunday brunch; children's menu; health conscious menu items; carryout; cocktails & lounge; valet parking. Northwest seafood. Piano music weekends. **Cards:** AE, DI, DS, JCB, MC, VI. *(See ad p A131)* ⊗

MANCA'S **Dinner:** $11-$20 **Phone:** 206/323-7686 (11)
◆◆◆ Continental
Location: E of I-5, 3 mi on Madison. 4000 E Madison St 98112. **Hours:** 11:30 am-2 & 5:30-10 pm, Sat 9 am-1 & 5:30-10 pm, Sun 9 am-1 & 5-9 pm. Closed: Mon, 1/1, 7/4, 11/23 & 12/25. **Reservations:** required. **Features:** children's menu; health conscious menu items; carryout; cocktails. Casual fine dining in Seattle's prestigious Madison Park area. Third generation restauranteur. Fresh seafood, lamb & NW cuisine. **Cards:** DI, MC, VI. ⊗

METROPOLITAN GRILL Historical **Dinner:** $21-$30 **Phone:** 206/624-3287 (6)
◆◆◆ Steakhouse
Location: Corner of 2nd Ave & Marion. 820 2nd Ave 98104. **Hours:** 11 am-3:30 & 5-11 pm, Sat from 5 pm, Sun 5 pm-10 pm. Closed: 11/23. **Reservations:** suggested. **Features:** children's menu; carryout; cocktails & lounge; a la carte. Lively dining. **Cards:** AE, DI, DS, JCB, MC, VI. ⊗

NIKKO **Dinner:** $21-$30 **Phone:** 206/727-5100 (24)
AAA ◆◆◆ Ethnic
Location: In the Westin Hotel, Seattle. 1900 5th Ave 98101. **Hours:** 11:30 am-2 & 5:30-10 pm, Sat & Sun from 5:30 pm. Closed: 12/25. **Features:** carryout; cocktails; valet parking; a la carte. Lively visual setting. A contemporary blend of symbolic Japanese architectural forms & nature. **Cards:** AE, DI, DS, JCB, MC, VI. ⊗

OLD SPAGHETTI FACTORY **Dinner:** up to $10 **Phone:** 206/441-7724 (2)
◆ Italian
Location: Across from Pier 70 on the waterfront at Broad St. 2801 Elliott Ave 98121. **Hours:** 11:30 am-2 & 5-10 pm, Fri-11 pm, Sat noon-11 pm, Sun noon-10 pm. Closed: 11/23, 12/24 & 12/25. **Features:** children's menu; carryout; cocktails & lounge. Popular family-type restaurant. **Cards:** DS, MC, VI. ⊗

THE PAINTED TABLE **Dinner:** $21-$30 **Phone:** 206/624-4844 (37)
◆◆◆ Continental
Location: In The Alexis Hotel. 1007 1st Ave 98104. **Hours:** 7-10:30 am, 11:30-2 & 5:30-10 pm. Closed: 12/25. **Reservations:** suggested. **Features:** children's menu; carryout; cocktails & lounge; fee for valet parking. Delightful dining, fresh food & pleasant atmosphere. Smoke free premises. **Cards:** AE, CB, DI, DS, MC, VI. ⊗

THE PALM COURT **Dinner:** $21-$30 **Phone:** 206/728-1000 (4)
AAA ◆◆◆◆ Regional American
Location: In The Westin Hotel, Seattle. 1900 5th Ave 98101. **Hours:** 11:30 am-2 & 5:30-10 pm, Fri-10:30 pm, Sat 5:30 pm-10:30 pm. Closed: Sun & 12/25. **Reservations:** suggested. **Features:** cocktails; valet parking; a la carte. Northwest regional cuisine in a casually elegant dining room with 4 glass pavilions. **Cards:** AE, CB, DI, DS, JCB, MC, VI. ⊗

PALOMINO EURO-SEATTLE BISTRO **Dinner:** $11-$20 **Phone:** 206/623-1300 (18)
◆◆◆ American
Location: 5th & Pike, Pacific First Center 3rd floor. 1420 5th Ave 98101. **Hours:** 11:15 am-3 & 5-10 pm, Fri-11 pm, Sat 11:15 am-2:30 & 5-11 pm, Sun 4 pm-9:30 pm. Closed: 11/23 & 12/25. **Features:** children's menu; carryout; cocktails & lounge. Mediterranean inspired Northwestern cuisines. Smoke free premises. **Cards:** AE, DS, MC, VI. ⊗

(See DOWNTOWN SEATTLE ACCOMMODATIONS spotting map page A125)

PREGO **Dinner:** $11-$20 **Phone:** 206/583-0300 (26)
◆◆◆ Italian
Location: In the Stouffer Madison Hotel. 515 Madison St 98104. **Hours:** 11 am-2 & 5:30-10 pm, Fri & Sat-11 pm. Closed major holidays. **Reservations:** required. **Features:** cocktails & lounge; a la carte. Casual Italian dining with Northwest flair. **Cards:** AE, DI, DS, JCB, MC, VI.

REINER'S **Dinner:** $11-$20 **Phone:** 206/624-2222 (27)
◆◆◆ Ethnic
Location: 1st hill between Spring & Seneca. 1106 8th Ave 98101. **Hours:** Open 3/1-1/8; 11:30 am-2 & 5:30-9 pm, Fri & Sat-9:30 pm. Closed: Sun & Mon. **Reservations:** suggested. **Features:** cocktails; a la carte. International cuisine. Smoke free premises. **Cards:** AE, DI, MC, VI.

RUTH'S CHRIS STEAK HOUSE **Dinner:** $21-$30 **Phone:** 206/624-8524 (14)
◆◆◆ Steakhouse
Location: 6th & Columbia. 800 5th Ave 98104. **Hours:** 5 pm-10 pm. Closed: 11/23 & 12/25. **Reservations:** suggested. **Features:** cocktails & lounge; valet parking; a la carte. **Cards:** AE, CB, DI, MC, VI.

SPACE NEEDLE RESTAURANT **Dinner:** over $31 **Phone:** 206/443-2100 (1)
◆◆ Seafood
Location: In Seattle Center. 219 4th Ave N 98109. **Hours:** 7 am-11 pm, Sun 8 am-3 & 4-11 pm. **Reservations:** suggested. **Features:** Sunday brunch; children's menu; health conscious menu; cocktails & lounge; a la carte. 2 revolving restaurants atop 600 foot symbol of the Northwest. Spectacular 360 degree view of the city & Puget Sound. Smoke free premises. **Cards:** AE, DI, DS, MC, VI. *(See ad p 166)*

13 COINS RESTAURANT **Dinner:** $11-$20 **Phone:** 206/682-2513 (30)
◆◆◆ American
Location: In the nw Furniture Mart. Corner of Boren & John. 125 Boren Ave N 98109. **Hours:** 24 hours. **Features:** children's menu; carryout; cocktails & lounge. National award winning restaurant. **Cards:** AE, DI, MC, VI.

TRATTORIA MITCHELLI **Dinner:** $11-$20 **Phone:** 206/623-3883 (12)
◆◆ Italian
Location: In Pioneer Square; 1 blk w of 1st Ave. 84 Yesler 98104. **Hours:** 7 am-4 am, Mon-11 pm, Sat 8 am-4 am, Sun 8 am-11 pm. Closed: 9/4, 11/23 & 12/25. **Reservations:** suggested. **Features:** No A/C; Sunday brunch; children's menu; carryout; cocktails & lounge. Popular people-watching, neighborhood cafe. Smoke free premises. **Cards:** AE, DS, MC, VI.

TULIO RESTORANTE **Dinner:** $21-$30 **Phone:** 206/624-5500 (31)
◆◆◆ Italian
Location: In the Hotel Vintage Park. 1100 5th Ave 98101. **Hours:** 7-10 am, 11:30-2:30 & 5-11 pm, Sat 8 am-11 & 5-11 pm, Sun-10 pm. Closed: 11/23 & 12/25. **Features:** carryout; cocktails & lounge; fee for valet parking; a la carte. Lively atmosphere, excellent service. Rustic & refined home-style cooking. Smoke free premises. **Cards:** AE, CB, DI, DS, JCB, MC, VI.

UMBERTO'S RISTORANTE **Dinner:** $11-$20 **Phone:** 206/621-0575 (16)
◆◆◆ Italian
Location: 1 blk s of Pioneer 59; 1 blk n of the Kingdome. 100 S King St 98104. **Hours:** 11:30 am-10 pm, Sat 5 pm-11 pm, Sun 4:30 pm-9 pm. Closed: 1/1, 11/23, 12/25. **Reservations:** suggested. **Features:** children's menu; carryout; cocktails & lounge; a la carte. Casual dining; featuring an Il Piccolo bar. **Cards:** AE, DI, DS, MC, VI.

UNION SQUARE GRILL **Dinner:** $21-$30 **Phone:** 206/224-4321 (32)
◆◆◆ Steakhouse
Location: 7th & Union. 621 Union St 98101. **Hours:** 11 am-3:30 & 5-11 pm, Fri-1 am, Sat 5 pm-1 am, Sun 5 pm-10 pm. Closed: 11/23 & 12/25. **Reservations:** suggested. **Features:** children's menu; carryout; cocktails & lounge; valet parking; a la carte. Steak & chop house in 1930's art deco surroundings. Valet parking avail after 5 pm. Smoke free premises. **Cards:** AE, DI, DS, JCB, MC, VI.

VON'S GRAND CITY CAFE **Dinner:** $11-$20 **Phone:** 206/621-8667 (10)
◆◆◆ American
Location: Downtown; corner of 7th Ave & Pine St. 619 Pine St 98101. **Hours:** 6:30-10:30 am, 11-3 & 5-10 pm. **Reservations:** suggested. **Features:** children's menu; carryout; cocktails & lounge. Merchant's & business memorabilia. Smoke free premises. **Cards:** AE, DI, MC, VI. *(See ad p A128)*

GREATER SEATTLE (See SEATTLE & VICINITY ACCOMMODATIONS spotting map pages A136 & A137; see index below)

Index of Establishments on the SEATTLE & VICINITY ACCOMMODATIONS Spotting Map

(See SEATTLE & VICINITY ACCOMMODATIONS spotting map pages A136 & A137)

Kayak Lakefront Grill 57
The Yankee Diner 58
Ray's Boathouse 59
Ray's Cafe 60
Rovers Restaurant 61
Salty's on Alki 63
Szmania's 64
Java Restaurant 65
Shilshole Broiler 66
Tillicum Village NW Coast Indian Cultural Center 68
Bush Garden 69
Four Seas Restaurant 70
Latitude 47o Restaurant 71
Canlis 73
India House 74
Hiram's at the Locks 75
Excaliburs 76
Palisade 77
Saleh al Lago 78

TUKWILA

Courtyard by Marriott 101
Doubletree Suites 102
Embassy Suites Southcenter 103
Hampton Inn Seattle Southcenter 104
Doubletree Inn 105
Econo Lodge-Sea Tac Airport 106
Holiday Inn Seattle-Boeing Field 107
Homewood Suites 108
The Marriott Residence Inn-Seattle South 109
Nendel's Inn-Seattle/Southcenter 110
Sea-Tac Airport North Travelodge 111
Silver Cloud Inn at Tukwila 112

RENTON

Silver Cloud At Renton 113
Travelers Inn 114
Nendel's Inn Renton 115
Holiday Inn Seattle-Renton 116

RESTAURANTS

Gene's Ristorante 81
Billy McHale's 82

EDMONDS

Homeport Inn 117
K & E Motor Inn 118
Edmonds Harbor Inn 119

RESTAURANT

Arnies at Edmonds 84

LYNNWOOD

Silver Cloud Inn at Lynnwood 120
The Residence Inn by Marriott-Seattle North 121
Hotel International 122
Embassy Suites 123
Holiday Inn Express 124
Best Western Landmark Hotel & Convention Center 125

RESTAURANTS

Cafe 196 87
The Yankee Diner 88
Billy McHale's 89

KIRKLAND

Clarion Inn 131
Shumway Mansion 132
Silver Cloud Inn at Kirkland 133
Best Western Arnold's Motor Inn 134
La Quinta Inn 135
The Woodmark Hotel on Lake Washington 136

RESTAURANTS

Carillon Room 91
Cafe Juanita 92
Bistro Provencal 93
Olive Garden 94
Kirkland Roaster & Ale House 96
Ristorante Paradiso 97

BELLEVUE

The Residence Inn By Marriott Seattle East 142
Embassy Suites Hotel Bellevue 143
Red Lion Inn/Bellevue Center 144
Bellevue Travelodge 145
Red Lion Hotel 146
Bellevue Hilton Inn 147
Best Western Bellevue Inn 148
West Coast Bellevue Hotel 149
Eastgate Motel 150
Days Inn Bellevue 151
Silver Cloud 152
Hyatt Regency Bellevue 153
Courtyard by Marriott 154

RESTAURANTS

Cucina Cucina 100
The Yankee Diner 101
Daniel's Broiler, Bellevue Place 103
Eques 104
Billy McHale's 105
Spazzo Mediterranean Grill 107
Velato's Ristorante 109
Sams Restaurant & Lounge 110
The Butcher in Bellevue 111

REDMOND

Best Western Redmond Inn 164
Silver Cloud Inn at Redmond 165

RESTAURANTS

Nara Japanese Restaurant 114
Billy McHale's 115

BOTHELL

Residence Inn by Marriott Seattle NE 170
Wyndham Garden 171

RESTAURANT

Gerard's Relais de Lyon 120

DES MOINES

Ramada Limited SEA-TAC 175

RESTAURANT

Le Bonaparte 124

KENT

New Best Inn 180
Best Western ChoiceLodge 181
Best Western Pony Soldier Motor Inn 182
Cypress Inn 183
Days Inn of Kent 184
Homecourt All Suite Hotel 185
Val U Inn 186

RESTAURANTS

Rose's Highway Inn 129
Velvet Goose 130

ISSAQUAH

RESTAURANT

Jay-Berry's Gourmet Pizza & Pasta & Lounge 133

MILL CREEK

RESTAURANT

The Imperial Garden 135

Fire precautions—These symbols note the warning device in each sleeping room:
(D)—smoke detector (S)—sprinkler system

SEATTLE
AND VICINITY
ACCOMMODATIONS
Scale in Miles
Scale in Kilometers
0
3.4
5.5
1982-B
To Monroe
To Snohomish
To Marysville
To Everett & Bellingham
To Fall City
To Victoria
TOLL
Mill Creek
Lynnwood
Edmonds
Bothell
Woodinville
Kirkland
Redmond
Bellevue
SEATTLE
SEE DOWNTOWN MAP
Kingston
Indianola
Port Madison
Rollingbay
Manitou Beach
Bainbridge Island
Port Blakely
Puget
Elliott Bay
Lake Washington
Lake Sammamish
Green L.
Lake Washington Ship Canal
Snoqualmie River
EVERGREEN PT. FLOATING BRIDGE
HIGH BRIDGE RD.
W. SNOQUALMIE VALLEY RD.
DUVALL RD.
PARADISE LAKE RD.
AVONDALE RD.
WOODINVILLE-REDMOND RD.
NOVELTY HILL RD.
UNION HILL RD.
FALL CITY RD.
REDMOND RD.
E. LAKE SAMMAMISH
INGLEWOOD HILL RD.
NORTHUP WAY
MALTBY RD.
JUANITA DR.
HOLMES POINT DR.
SAND POINT WAY
BRIER RD.
POPLAR WAY
AURORA AVE. N.
GREENWOOD AVE. N.
HOLMAN RD.
MARKET ST.
ROOSEVELT WAY
ELLIOTT AVE.
MADISON ST.
YESLER WAY
LAKE CITY WAY
RICHMOND BEACH RD.
PARK RD.
GROAT PT.

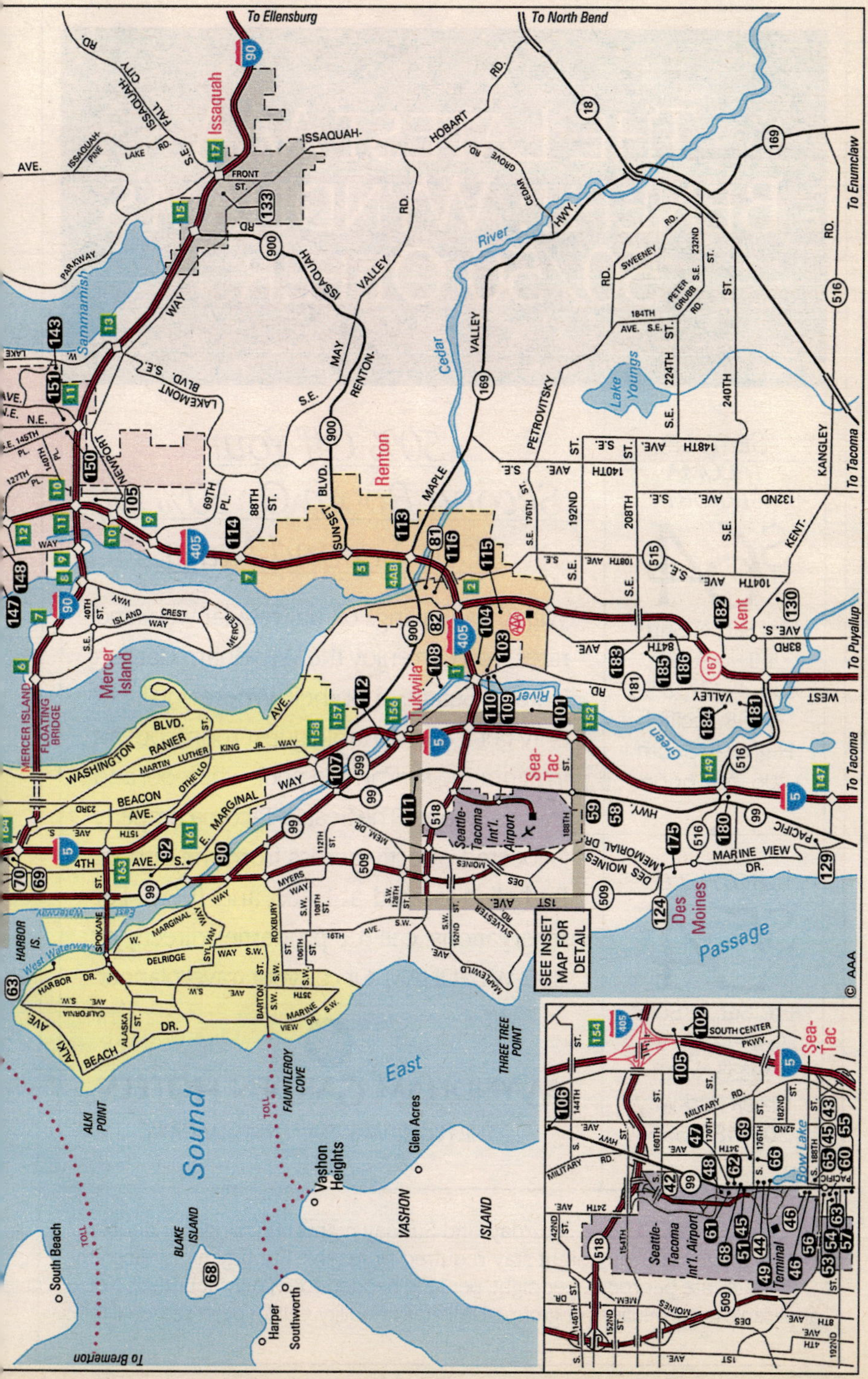
To Ellensburg
To North Bend
To Enumclaw
To Tacoma
To Puyallup
To Bremerton
Issaquah
Renton
Tukwila
Kent
Sea-Tac
Mercer Island
Des Moines
Seattle-Tacoma Int'l. Airport
Lake Youngs
Cedar River
Green River
Lake Sammamish
Harbor Is.
Alki Point
Fauntleroy Cove
Blake Island
Vashon Heights
Vashon Island
Glen Acres
Three Tree Point
South Beach
Harper
Southworth
Sound
East Passage
Mercer Island Floating Bridge
SEE INSET MAP FOR DETAIL
© AAA

THE LATEST AAA BENEFIT: WYNDHAM'S 50/50 OFFER.

SEATTLE-TACOMA AIRPORT

$64

Fri., Sat., & Sun.*
1/1 - 6/4/95
& 9/4 - 12/31/95
18118 Pacific
Highway South
206-244-6666

•

BOTHELL

$54**

Fri., Sat., & Sun.*
9/4 - 12/31/95
19333 North
Creek Parkway
206-485-5557

50% Off Your Second Room Or 50% Off Your Second Night.

With these savings off our regular weekend rates, you can enjoy the Wyndham Garden Hotel in Seattle or Bothell. Where you'll not only get a comfortable guest room, but an invigorating swimming pool, whirlpool and exercise room. The Seattle-Tacoma property is located directly across from the airport. Bothell is located at I-405 and 195th. For reservations, call the properties directly or 800-WYNDHAM. Or call your travel planner.

WYNDHAM GARDEN HOTELS

THE RIGHT WAY. THE WYNDHAM WAY.

Offer available Friday, Saturday, and Sunday nights only, single or double occupancy. *Saturday night stay required to receive Sunday night discount. **Rates are per room, per night, per king bedded room only at Bothell. Not applicable to conventions or groups. Limited availability. Call for other seasonal rates.

(See SEATTLE & VICINITY ACCOMMODATIONS spotting map pages A136 & A137)

LODGINGS

AURORA SEAFAIR INN Rates Subject to Change **Phone:** 206/522-3754 84

AAA ◆◆ Motel

7/1-9/5	1P: $55- 65	2P/1B: $58- 68	2P/2B: $68- 78	XP: $3
3/1-6/30 & 9/6-2/29	1P: $48- 58	2P/1B: $48- 58	2P/2B: $58- 68	XP: $3

Location: On SR 99, 2 mi w of I-5, exit 172. 9100 Aurora Ave N 98103. Fax: 206/523-2272. **Terms:** Reserv deposit; weekly rates; pets, $5. **Facility:** 53 rooms. 2-3 stories; exterior corridors. **Dining:** Restaurant nearby. **All Rooms:** free movies, cable TV. **Some Rooms:** 20 efficiencies, no utensils, refrigerators, whirlpools. **Cards:** AE, CB, DI, DS, MC, VI. (D) ⊗

BEST WESTERN CONTINENTAL PLAZA HOTEL Rates Subject to Change **Phone:** 206/284-1900 94

AAA ◆◆◆ Motel

6/15-9/30 [CP]	1P: $69- 79	2P/1B: $70- 80	2P/2B: $75- 90	XP: $8	F12
3/1-6/14 & 10/1-2/29 [CP]	1P: $55- 65	2P/1B: $58- 68	2P/2B: $60- 70	XP: $8	F12

Location: 2 mi n on SR 99, 2 mi nw of I-5 exit 167. 2500 Aurora Ave N 98109. Fax: 206/283-5298. **Terms:** Sr. discount; no pets. **Facility:** 94 rooms. Most with balcony, view of Lake Union & Cascade Mountains. 11 kitchens, $10 extra; 2-5 stories, no elevator; exterior corridors; heated pool. **Dining:** Restaurant nearby. **All Rooms:** free movies, combo & shower baths, cable TV. **Some Rooms:** refrigerators. Fee: whirlpools. **Cards:** AE, CB, DI, DS, JCB, MC, VI. (D) ⊗

BEST WESTERN EVERGREEN MOTOR INN Rates Subject to Change **Phone:** 206/361-3700 87

AAA ◆◆◆◆ Motel

6/1-9/30 [CP]	1P: $68	2P/1B: $74	2P/2B: $74	XP: $6	F
3/1-5/31 & 10/1-2/29 [CP]	1P: $60	2P/1B: $66	2P/2B: $66	XP: $6	F

Location: From I-5, exit 175; w 1 1/4 mi, s on (SR 99) Aurora Ave 1/4 mi. 13700 Aurora Ave N 98133. Fax: 206/361-0338. **Terms:** Sr. discount; credit card guarantee; weekly/monthly rates; no pets. **Facility:** 70 rooms. 4 stories; interior corridors; sauna, whirlpool; exercise room. **Dining:** Restaurant nearby. **Services:** Fee: coin laundry, airport transportation. **All Rooms:** free movies, cable TV. **Some Rooms:** 24 kitchens. Fee: VCP's. **Cards:** AE, CB, DI, DS, JCB, MC, VI. (D) (S)

EMERALD INN Guaranteed Rates **Phone:** 206/522-5000 80

AAA ◆◆ Motel

5/16-9/30	1P: $50- 60	2P/1B: $54- 65	2P/2B: $58- 70	XP: $4
3/1-5/15 & 10/1-2/29	1P: $44- 55	2P/1B: $46- 60	2P/2B: $52- 65	XP: $4

Location: N on SR 99; from I-5 exit 172, 1 mi w. 8512 Aurora Ave N 98103. **Terms:** Credit card guarantee; small pets only. **Facility:** 43 rooms. 4 two-bedroom units. 2 stories; exterior corridors. **Dining:** Restaurant nearby. **Services:** Fee: coin laundry. **All Rooms:** free movies, combo & shower baths, cable TV. **Some Rooms:** refrigerators. **Cards:** AE, DS, MC, VI. (D) ⊗

LA HACIENDA MOTEL Guaranteed Rates **Phone:** 206/762-2460 92

AAA ◆◆ Motel

All Year [CP]	1P: $42- 46	2P/1B: $45- 55	2P/2B: $55- 60	XP: $10

Location: 2 3/4 mi s of Kingdome; 2 blks e of SR 99, 1 1/2 mi w of I-5 exit 162. 5414 1st Ave S at Lucille St 98108. **Terms:** Reserv deposit, 3 day notice; no pets. **Facility:** 34 rooms. 11 efficiencies, $5 extra; 3 two-room suites with kitchen, $60-$80; 2 stories; exterior corridors. **Dining:** Restaurant nearby. **All Rooms:** free movies, combo & shower baths, cable TV. **Some Rooms:** A/C, refrigerators. **Cards:** AE, CB, DI, DS, MC, VI.
(See color ad p A141) (D) ⊗

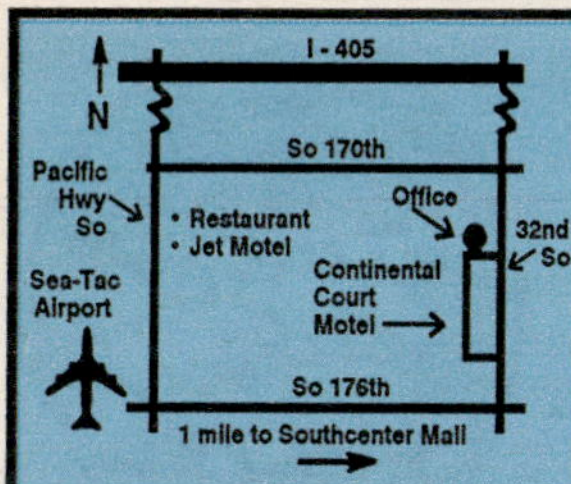

Reservations for Both Motels
1-800-233-1501
ECONOMY and DISCOUNT RATES

CONTINENTAL COURT ALL SUITE MOTEL
17223 32nd Ave. So.,
Seattle, Wa. 98188
(206)241-1500
Button #30,
Sea-Tac Courtesy Boards
3 BLOCKS from SEA-TAC AIRPORT • ADJACENT to MAJOR RESTAURANTS & LOUNGES • ONE & TWO BEDROOM SUITES with FULL KITCHENS • SOME with FIREPLACE & VIEW • A.C. • COLOR TV • POOL • FREE AIRPORT SHUTTLE 24 HRS • PARKING for FLYAWAY GUESTS

JET MOTEL
17300 Pacific Highway So.,
Seattle, Wa. 98188
(206)244-6255
Button #3,
Sea-Tac Courtesy Boards
ONE BLOCK from SEA-TAC AIPORT • AIR CONDITION • COLOR TV • POOL • IN-HOUSE JAPANESE RESTAURANT • NEXT to 24 HOUR RESTAURANT • FREE AIRPORT SHUTTLE 24 HRS • RENTAL CARS AVAILABLE • PARKING for FLYAWAY GUESTS

Need we mention the food?

With a setting like this, perhaps we needn't offer superb cuisine, crackling fireplaces and spa tubs. But we do. Call 1-800-826-6124.

Preferred Hotels & Resorts Worldwide

The Salish Lodge
At Snoqualmie Falls.

(See SEATTLE & VICINITY ACCOMMODATIONS spotting map pages A136 & A137)

MARCO POLO MOTEL Rates Subject to Change **Phone:** 206/633-4090 72

Motel

6/15-9/15	1P:	$40	2P/1B:	$44	2P/2B:	$46- 50	XP: $3	D
3/1-6/14 & 9/16-2/29	1P:	$38	2P/1B:	$40	2P/2B:	$40- 44	XP: $3	D

Location: 2 mi n on SR 99. 4114 Aurora Ave N 98103. **Terms:** Reserv deposit; weekly rates; no pets. **Facility:** 36 rooms. 2 stories; exterior corridors. **All Rooms:** free movies, combo & shower baths, no A/C. **Some Rooms:** 9 efficiencies, refrigerators. **Cards:** AE, DI, DS, MC, VI. *(See color ad p A141)* D

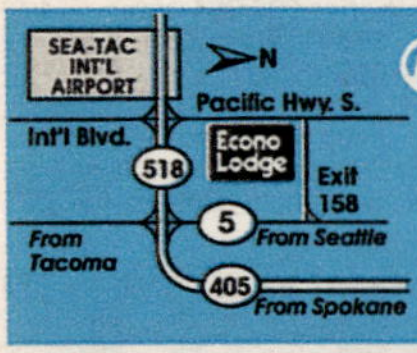

Econo Lodge

• Airport Shuttle • Whirlpool Suites • A/C • Refrigerator •
• Cable TV & Movies • Spa & Weight Room • Fresh Air Rooms •
• Continental Breakfast • Handicapped Facilities • On Bus Line •

Seattle Airport

13910 Pacific Highway South
Seattle, Washington 98168

(206) 244-0810
(800) 446-6661
Fax: (206) 431-9503

"YOUR BEST BET AT SEA-TAC"

Deluxe Guest Rooms & Suites
Indoor Pool, Sauna, & Whirlpool
Full Service Restaurant and Lounge

20% OFF *Listed Rates

Executel

BEST WESTERN AIRPORT EXECUTEL
20717 Pacific Hwy. South
Seattle, WA 98198
206-878-3300 or 1-800-648-3311
** Please mention "TourBook Discount" when calling.*
Discount subject to availability

Best Western

STAY WHERE THE SAVINGS ARE SWEETER.

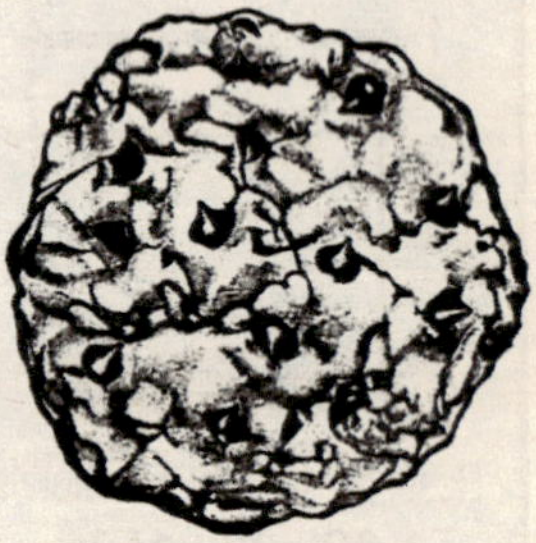

FOR AAA MEMBERS • $66-$89 • FOR AAA MEMBERS

We've got a treat in store for you. When you stay at any of the Doubletree Hotels in Seattle, you'll enjoy our warm, personal service and kids 18 and under stay free in your room. Shop 'til you drop at nearby Southcenter Mall. Or visit spectacular Puget Sound and the Space Needle. And our welcoming freshly baked chocolate chip cookies will make your AAA savings even sweeter. For reservations, call your travel agent.

DOUBLETREE
HOTELS·SEATTLE
1-800-222-TREE

Rates are based on single or double occupancy and subject to availability. Each additional person $10 per night (Inn) and $15 per night (Suites).

Inn at Southcenter
205 Strander Blvd.
$66

Seattle Suites
16500 Southcenter Parkway
$89

(See SEATTLE & VICINITY ACCOMMODATIONS spotting map pages A136 & A137)

MAX IVOR MOTEL AAA Special Value Rates **Phone:** 206/762-8194 (90)

AAA ◆ Motel

All Year 1P: $50- 100 2P/1B: $50- 100 2P/2B: $60- 120 XP: $4-6 F10

Location: 3 3/4 mi s; 1 blk e of SR 99; 1 mi w of I-5 exit 162. 6188 4th Ave S at S Michigan 98108. **Terms:** Reserv deposit; no pets. **Facility:** 42 rooms. 6 two-bedroom units. 2 stories; exterior corridors; meeting rooms. **Dining:** Restaurant nearby. **Services:** Fee: coin laundry. **All Rooms:** coffeemakers, free movies, combo & shower baths, cable TV. **Some Rooms:** A/C, 9 kitchens, refrigerators, whirlpools. **Cards:** AE, CB, DI, DS, MC, VI. (D)

Marco Polo MOTELS

Marco Polo MOTEL *3 minutes to Downtown*

• Close to UW • Non-smoking Rooms
• Free HBO and Parking

4114 Aurora Ave. N., Seattle, WA 98103 • (206) 633-4090

* SPECIAL AAA RATE $40
Based on single occupancy

1-800-295-4090

La Hacienda Motel

A

5414 First Ave., South, Seattle, Washington 98108

800-553-7531
206-762-2460

AAA

PHONES • KITCHENETTES • CABLE COLOR TV • ESPN
CLOSE TO KINGDOME, DOWNTOWN & PIONEER SQUARE
• HANDICAPPED ROOMS AVAILABLE

FIRST RATE.

Holiday Inn
SEA TAC
17338 Pacific Hwy. South
Seattle, Washington 98188

· Indoor, Olympic-sized pool
· Fitness center · Full-service, rooftop restaurant · Complimentary shuttle to airport and nearby shopping

$59* Sept-May
$79* June-Aug
*Single or double. Per night. Plus tax. Based on availability.

For reservations and information call (206) 248-1000 or 1-800-HOLIDAY.

In A Class By Itself Near University of Washington

- Panoramic Views of Seattle
- Walking Distance to University of Washington
- Minutes to downtown Seattle
- Convenient to Shopping
- Restaurant, Lounge & Meeting Facilities
- Non-smokers' Rooms
- Fitness Room

SPECIAL AAA RATES
$68-75* 5/1/95 - 10/31/95
$55-65* 11/1/95 - 4/30/96
*Single Occupancy, Plus Tax Based on availability

Meany Tower Hotel
IN THE UNIVERSITY DISTRICT
4507 Brooklyn Ave. N.E., Seattle, WA 98105 • (206) 634-2000 • **(800) 648-6440**

(See SEATTLE & VICINITY ACCOMMODATIONS spotting map pages A136 & A137)

MEANY TOWER HOTEL — Rates Subject to Change — **Phone:** 206/634-2000 — 74

AAA ◆◆◆ Hotel

5/1-10/31	1P: $68	2P/1B: $75	2P/2B: $75	XP: $10	F12
3/1-4/30 & 11/1-2/29	1P: $55	2P/1B: $65	2P/2B: $65	XP: $10	F12

Location: 3 mi ne in University District; 1/2 mi e of I-5, exit 169. 4507 Brooklyn Ave NE 98105. Fax: 206/634-2000. **Terms:** Reserv deposit, 3 day notice; weekly/monthly rates; no pets. **Facility:** 155 rooms. All corner rooms, excellent views of city, lakes & mountains. 14 stories; interior corridors; meeting rooms; exercise room. **Dining:** Dining room; 6:30 am-10 pm; $6-$13. **Services:** valet laundry. **All Rooms:** cable TV. **Cards:** AE, CB, DI, MC, VI. *(See color ad p A141)* (D) (⊗)

PARK PLAZA MOTEL — Rates Subject to Change — **Phone:** 206/632-2101 — 75

AAA ◆ Motel

All Year	1P: $27- 30	2P/1B: $30- 35	2P/2B: $33- 38	XP: $3	F12

Location: 4 mi n on SR 99 southbound; 1 1/4 mi w of I-5 exit 169. 4401 Aurora Ave N 98103. **Terms:** Reserv deposit, 3 day notice; no pets. **Facility:** 14 rooms. Commercial location. 1 two-bedroom unit. 1 story; exterior corridors. **All Rooms:** combo & shower baths, cable TV, no A/C. **Some Rooms:** refrigerators. **Cards:** MC, VI. (D)

QUEST INN — Guaranteed Rates — **Phone:** 206/367-7880 — 77

AAA ◆◆ Motel

All Year	1P: $45	2P/1B: $49	2P/2B: $55	XP: $4

Location: From I-5 exit 175, w 1 1/4 mi via ne 145th St. 14817 Aurora Ave N 98133. Fax: 206/368-8839. **Terms:** Sr. discount; credit card guarantee; weekly rates; no pets. **Facility:** 29 rooms. Cozy, pleasant rooms. Spectacular view of the Cascades from upper level rooms. 2 stories; exterior corridors. **All Rooms:** free movies, cable TV. **Some Rooms:** 2 efficiencies, no utensils, microwaves, refrigerators. Fee: whirlpools. **Cards:** DS, MC, VI. (D) (S) (⊗)

RAMADA INN SEATTLE AT NORTHGATE — AAA Special Value Rates — **Phone:** 206/365-0700 — 79

AAA ◆◆◆ Motel

7/12-10/31	1P: $99	2P/1B: $105	2P/2B: $105	XP: $6	F18
3/1-7/11 & 1/1-2/29	1P: $82	2P/1B: $92	2P/2B: $92	XP: $10	F18
11/1-12/31	1P: $85	2P/1B: $91	2P/2B: $91	XP: $6	F18

Location: 7 1/4 mi n; 1/4 mi w of I-5 exit 173. 2140 N Northgate Way 98133. Fax: 206/365-0750. **Terms:** Credit card guarantee; small pets only. **Facility:** 169 rooms. 4 stories; exterior corridors; meeting rooms; heated pool. **Dining:** Restaurant nearby. **Services:** valet laundry; area transportation. Fee: airport transportation. **All Rooms:** cable TV. **Some Rooms:** coffeemakers, 8 efficiencies, refrigerators. Fee: VCP's. **Cards:** AE, CB, DI, DS, JCB, MC, VI. (D) (⊗)

RODESIDE LODGE — Rates Subject to Change — **Phone:** 206/364-7771 — 82

◆◆ Motor Inn

6/1-9/30	1P: $40- 65	2P/1B: $40- 65	2P/2B: $42- 65	XP: $5	F18
3/1-5/31 & 10/1-2/29	1P: $40- 48	2P/1B: $40- 55	2P/2B: $40- 59	XP: $5	F18

Location: 8 1/2 mi n on SR 99; 1 mi w of I-5; northbound exit 174, southbound exit 175. 12501 Aurora Ave N 98133. Fax: 206/362-4169. **Terms:** Reserv deposit; weekly rates; pets, small dogs only, $3. **Facility:** 87 rooms. 4 two-bedroom units. 2 stories; interior/exterior corridors; heated pool, sauna, whirlpools; exercise room, 2 spas. **Dining:** Restaurant; 7 am-10 pm, Sun-2 pm; $5-$12; cocktails. **All Rooms:** free movies, cable TV. **Some Rooms:** microwaves, refrigerators. **Cards:** AE, CB, DI, DS, MC, VI. (D) (⊗)

UNIVERSITY INN — Guaranteed Rates — **Phone:** 206/632-5055 — 86

AAA ◆◆◆ Motel

All Year [CP]	1P: $68- 86	2P/1B: $77- 95	2P/2B: $77- 95	XP: $10	F

Location: 1/2 mi e of I-5, exit 169. 4140 Roosevelt Way NE 98105. Fax: 206/547-4937. **Terms:** Sr. discount; no pets. **Facility:** 102 rooms. 3 efficiencies, $10 extra; 4 stories; interior corridors; meeting rooms; whirlpool, heated pool, open 5/1-8/31; exercise room. **Services:** valet laundry. **All Rooms:** free movies, combo & shower baths, cable TV. **Some Rooms:** refrigerators. **Cards:** AE, CB, DI, DS, MC, VI. *(See color ad below)* (D) (⊗)

A small, neighborhood hotel.

- 5 minutes from downtown Seattle
- Easy access from I-5
- Walking distance to Univ. of Wash.
- Pool, spa and fitness room
- Complimentary continental breakfast
- Cable with Showtime and ESPN

4140 Roosevelt Way NE, Seattle, WA 98105 206/632-5055

UNIVERSITY INN

For reservations call 1-800-733-3855

UNIVERSITY MOTEL

"IN THE HEART OF THE UNIVERSITY DISTRICT"

4731 - 12TH AVENUE, N.E., SEATTLE, WA 98105

(206) 522-4724

1-800-522-4720

Large comfortable suites with cable TV; separate bedrooms, kitchens, laundry facilities, free parking garage. Quiet district, 5 blks. from University of Washington.

N.E. 50TH ST. EXIT OFF I-5

AAA

(See SEATTLE & VICINITY ACCOMMODATIONS spotting map pages A136 & A137)

UNIVERSITY MOTEL Rates Subject to Change **Phone:** 206/522-4724 (76)

5/1-9/30	1P: $49	2P/1B: $55	2P/2B: $58	XP: $6	
3/1-4/30 & 10/1-2/29	1P: $45	2P/1B: $50	2P/2B: $55	XP: $5	

◆◆ Apartment Motel

Location: 5 mi ne in University District; 1/2 mi e of I-5, exit 169. 4731 12th Ave NE 98105. **Terms:** Credit card guarantee; no pets. **Facility:** 21 rooms. Suburban location. 13 two-bedroom units. 3 stories, no elevator; interior corridors. **Services:** Fee: coin laundry, airport transportation. **All Rooms:** efficiencies, cable TV, no A/C. **Cards:** AE, CB, DI, DS, MC, VI. *(See color ad p A142)* Ⓓ

UNIVERSITY PLAZA HOTEL AAA Special Value Rates **Phone:** 206/634-0100 (73)

6/1-9/7	1P: $80	2P/1B: $88	2P/2B: $88	XP: $6	F12
3/1-5/31 & 9/8-2/29	1P: $72	2P/1B: $77	2P/2B: $77	XP: $6	F12

◆◆◆ Motor Inn

Location: In University District w of I-5, exit 169. 400 NE 45th St 98105. Fax: 206/633-2743. **Terms:** Credit card guarantee, 3 day notice; no pets. **Facility:** 135 rooms. Commercial location. 3 stories; interior corridors; conference facilities; heated pool; exercise room. **Dining:** Also, Excaliburs, see separate listing. **Services:** valet laundry. Fee: airport transportation. **All Rooms:** free movies, combo & shower baths, cable TV. **Some Rooms:** Fee: refrigerators. **Cards:** AE, DI, DS, MC, VI. *(See ad below)* Ⓓ ⊗

RESTAURANTS

BUSH GARDEN **Dinner:** $11-$20 **Phone:** 206/682-6830 (69)
◆◆ Ethnic
Location: In International District; 1/4 mi nw of I-5, exit 164. 614 Maynard Ave S 98104. **Hours:** 11:30 am-2 & 5-10 pm, Fri-10:30 pm, Sat 5 pm-10:30 pm, Sun 5 pm-9 pm. Closed major holidays. **Reservations:** suggested. **Features:** children's menu; carryout; cocktails & lounge; a la carte. Popular restaurant with Japanese decor & service. Private Tatami rooms, also sushi bar. **Cards:** AE, MC, VI. ⊗

CANLIS **Dinner:** over $31 **Phone:** 206/283-3313 (73)
◆◆◆ American
Location: Cross street Halladay, 1 1/2 mi n of The Space Needle. 2576 Aurora Ave N 98109. **Hours:** 5:30 pm-11:30 pm. Closed major holidays & Sun. **Reservations:** suggested. **Features:** carryout; cocktails & lounge; entertainment; valet parking; a la carte. Outstanding view of Lake Union & Cascade Mountains. Prime steak & fresh seafood prepared over Keawe-charcoal. Kimono clad waitresses. Excellent wine list. **Cards:** AE, CB, DI, MC, VI. ⊗

EXCALIBURS **Dinner:** $11-$20 **Phone:** 206/634-0100 (76)
◆◆ American
Location: In University Plaza Hotel. 400 NE 45th 98105. **Hours:** 6:30 am-2:30 & 5-10 pm. **Reservations:** suggested. **Features:** children's menu; senior's menu; health conscious menu items; carryout; cocktails & lounge; entertainment. Varied cuisine including Northwest favorites. Casually elegant dining in an English Tudor setting. **Cards:** AE, CB, DI, DS, MC, VI. ⊗

FOUR SEAS RESTAURANT **Dinner:** $11-$20 **Phone:** 206/682-4900 (70)
◆◆ Chinese
Location: In International District. 714 S King St 98104. **Hours:** 10:30 am-10 pm, Sun-midnight. **Reservations:** suggested. **Features:** cocktails & lounge; a la carte. Sophisticated modern Chinese restaurant serving full Cantonese menu with some hot & spicy dishes from Northern Chinese cuisine. **Cards:** AE, MC, VI. ⊗

HIRAM'S AT THE LOCKS **Dinner:** $11-$20 **Phone:** 206/784-1733 (75)
◆◆◆ Steak and Seafood
Location: From I-5 at exit 169, 4 mi w via N 45th St, NW Market. 5300 34th NW 98107. **Hours:** 11 am-3 & 4:30-10 pm, Sun 9 am-2 & 4:30-9:30 pm. **Reservations:** suggested. **Features:** Sunday brunch; children's menu; carryout; cocktails & lounge. Located at Historic Chittenden Locks. Dining room, lounge & patio provide superb view of canal. Smoke free premises. **Cards:** AE, DI, DS, JCB, MC, VI. ⊗

INDIA HOUSE **Dinner:** $11-$20 **Phone:** 206/632-5072 (74)
◆◆ Ethnic
Location: In University District; 4 blks e & 1/2 blk s of I-5, exit 169. 4737 Roosevelt Way NE 98105. **Hours:** 5 pm-9:45 pm, Fri & Sat-10:45 pm. **Reservations:** suggested; weekends. **Features:** cocktails & lounge. Authenic East Indian cuisine served in a villa atmosphere. **Cards:** AE, DI, MC, VI. ⊗

STAY CLOSE FOR COMFORT IN SEATTLE.

Plan to stay at the University Plaza Hotel for convenient home-away-from-home accommodations.

- 5 min. to Downtown, Seattle Center, Waterfront and Ferries. 1/2 mile to UW.
- Garden pool and Fitness room
- Fine dining and Piano bar
- I-5 at NE 45 St. • Free parking
- 10% Discount for AAA Members

For reservations call today toll free 800-203-3403 or 206-634-0100.

AAA ◆◆◆ **University Plaza Hotel**
400 NE 45th Street, Seattle, WA 98105

(See SEATTLE & VICINITY ACCOMMODATIONS spotting map pages A136 & A137)

JAVA RESTAURANT **Dinner:** $11-$20 **Phone:** 206/522-5282 (65)
◆◆◆
Ethnic
Location: 1 mi se of I-5, exit 173 northbound or southbound, e on Northgate 1 mi, s at Roosevelt 1 mi. 8929 Roosevelt Way NE 98115. **Hours:** 5 pm-10 pm. Closed: 11/23 & 12/25. **Reservations:** suggested. **Features:** beer & wine only. Indonesian cusine, served in a vintage home with Indonesian artifacts. **Cards:** AE, MC, VI. ⊗

KABUL AFGHAN CUISINE **Dinner:** $11-$20 **Phone:** 206/545-9000 (55)
◆
Ethnic
Location: 1 mi w of I-5 at exit 169. 2301 N 45th St 98103. **Hours:** 5:30 pm-10 pm. Closed major holidays & Sun. **Features:** carryout; wine only. A unique culinary experience, kebab's & vegetarian dishes. Smoke free premises. **Cards:** AE, DS, MC, VI. ⊗

KASPAR'S **Dinner:** $11-$20 **Phone:** 206/298-0123 (36)
◆◆◆
Seafood
Location: 2 blks w of Seattle Center. 19 W Harrison St 98119. **Hours:** 4:30 pm-9:30 pm, Fri 11:30 am-2 & 4:30-10:30 pm, Sat 4:30 pm-10:30 pm. Closed: Sun, Mon, 1/1 & 12/25. **Reservations:** suggested. **Features:** children's menu; early bird specials; cocktails & lounge; valet parking. Creative, contemporary cuisine. Casual & relaxed atmosphere. Smoke free premises. **Cards:** AE, MC, VI. ⊗

KAYAK LAKEFRONT GRILL **Dinner:** $11-$20 **Phone:** 206/284-2535 (57)
◆◆◆
American
Location: 1 3/4 mi n on sw shore of Lake Union. 1200 Westlake Ave N 98109. **Hours:** 11:30 am-2:30 & 5-10 pm, Sat & Sun 3:30 pm-10 pm. Closed: 11/23 & 12/25. **Features:** children's menu; carryout; cocktails & lounge. Comfortable, casual atmosphere. Patio dining. Diverse menu. Smoke free premises. **Cards:** AE, DI, DS, MC, VI. ⊗

LAKE WASHINGTON GRILL HOUSE **Dinner:** $11-$20 **Phone:** 206/486-3313 (52)
◆◆◆
American
Location: I-5 exit 171, 7 mi e via Lake City Way/Bothel Way (SR 522) to 61st Ave ne. 6161 NE 175th St 98155. **Hours:** 11:30 am-2:30 & 5-9:30 pm, Fri & Sat-10:30 pm, Sun 11:30 am-9 pm. **Reservations:** suggested. **Features:** No A/C; children's menu; carryout; cocktails & lounge; a la carte. Casual family dining, featuring meat, fish & poultry. Cooked over a cherrywood broiler grill. **Cards:** AE, DI, MC, VI. ⊗

LATITUDE 47O RESTAURANT **Dinner:** $11-$20 **Phone:** 206/284-1047 (71)
◆◆
Seafood
Location: 1 3/4 mi n on sw shore of Lake Union. 1232 Westlake Ave N 98109. **Hours:** 11:30 am-9:30 pm, Fri-10 pm, Sat 5 pm-10 pm, Sun 10 am-10 pm. Closed: 12/25. **Reservations:** suggested. **Features:** children's menu; carryout; cocktails & lounge; valet parking. View of Lake Union marinas. Fresh Atlantic & Northwest seafood. 32 item Sun buffet brunch. Valet parking for dinner. **Cards:** AE, DI, DS, MC, VI. ⊗

PALISADE **Dinner:** $21-$30 **Phone:** 206/285-1000 (77)
◆◆◆
Steak and Seafood
Location: Elliott Bay Marina. 2601 W Marina Pl 98199. **Hours:** 11:30 am-2:30 & 5-10 pm, Sat 4:30 pm-11 pm, Sun 10 am-2 & 4:30-9 pm. Closed: 11/23 & 12/25. **Reservations:** suggested. **Features:** semi-formal attire; Sunday brunch; children's menu; health conscious menu items; carryout; cocktails & lounge; valet parking; a la carte. Waterfront dining. Smoke free premises. **Cards:** AE, CB, DI, DS, MC, VI. ⊗

RAY'S BOATHOUSE **Dinner:** $11-$20 **Phone:** 206/789-3770 (59)
◆◆◆
Seafood
Location: From I-5 at exit 169, 4 1/2 mi w via n 45th St & NW Market. 6049 Seaview Ave NW 98107. **Hours:** 11:30 am-2 & 5-10 pm. Closed: 12/24 for dinner & 12/25. **Reservations:** suggested. **Features:** No A/C; children's menu; early bird specials; cocktails & lounge. Upscale, casual restaurant featuring large windows to highlight the view of Puget Sound. Smoke free premises. **Cards:** AE, DI, MC, VI. ⊗

RAY'S CAFE **Dinner:** $11-$20 **Phone:** 206/789-3770 (60)
◆◆
Seafood
Location: From I-5 exit 169, 4 1/2 mi w via N 45th St & NW Market. 6049 Seaview Ave NW 98107. **Hours:** 11:30 am-midnight. Closed: 12/25 & 1/1. **Features:** No A/C; children's menu; cocktails & lounge; valet parking. Casual bistro-style dining. Deck outdoor dining. **Cards:** AE, DI, DS, MC, VI. ⊗

ROVERS RESTAURANT **Dinner:** $21-$30 **Phone:** 206/325-7442 (61)
◆◆◆
French
Location: From I-5 at exit to Madison, 2 mi e. 2808 E Madison 98112. **Hours:** 5:30 pm-9:30 pm. Closed: Sun, Mon, 1/1, 9/4, 11/23 & 12/25. **Reservations:** suggested. **Features:** No A/C; beer & wine only. Smoke free premises. **Cards:** AE, DI, MC, VI. ⊗

SALEH AL LAGO **Dinner:** $11-$20 **Phone:** 206/524-4044 (78)
◆◆◆
Italian
Location: From I-5 at exit 170, 1 mi sw via Revenna. 6804 E Greenlake Way N 98115. **Hours:** 11:30 am-1:30 & 5:30-9:30 pm, Fri-10 pm, Sat 5:30 pm-10 pm. Closed major holidays & Sun. **Reservations:** suggested. **Features:** children's menu; cocktails; a la carte. Central Italian cuisine. Smoke free premises. **Cards:** AE, MC, VI. ⊗

SALTY'S ON ALKI **Dinner:** $11-$20 **Phone:** 206/937-1600 (63)
◆◆
Seafood
Location: From I-5 at exit 163 via W Seattle Frwy & Harbor Ave. 1936 Harbor Ave SW 98126. **Hours:** 11 am-2 & 5-10 pm, Fri & Sat-11 pm, Sun 9:30 am-2 & 5-10 pm. Closed: 12/25. **Reservations:** suggested; Fri & Sat. **Features:** Sunday brunch; children's menu; carryout; cocktails & lounge; a la carte. Flavors from around the world, fresh seafood. Waterfront dining. **Cards:** AE, DI, MC, VI. ⊗

SHILSHOLE BROILER **Dinner:** $11-$20 **Phone:** 206/789-0100 (66)
◆
American
Location: From I-5 exit 169, 3 1/2 mi w in Ballard. 2622 NW Market St 98107. **Hours:** 11 am-midnight, Sun noon-11 pm. Closed: 1/1, 7/4, 11/23 & 12/25. **Features:** children's menu; senior's menu; cocktails & lounge. Family dining. **Cards:** MC, VI. ⊗

SZMANIA'S **Dinner:** $11-$20 **Phone:** 206/284-7305 (64)
◆◆◆
Continental
Location: 3 1/2 mi nw of the Space Needle via Elliott Way, Montvale, McGraw. Over Magnolia Bridge. 3321 W McGraw 98199. **Hours:** 4:30 pm-9:30 pm, Fri & Sat-10 pm, Sun 4 pm-9 pm. Closed: Mon. **Reservations:** suggested; weekends. **Features:** children's menu; carryout; cocktails. Contemporary-style family dining. Pacific Rim Northwest flair menu. Smoke free premises. **Cards:** AE, DI, MC, VI. ⊗

TILLICUM VILLAGE NW COAST INDIAN CULTURAL CENTER **Dinner:** over $31 **Phone:** 206/443-1244 (68)
AAA
◆◆
Seafood
Location: Blake Island Marine State Park via charter vessel from Pier 55 & 56, Seattle central waterfront. 98121. **Hours:** 11:30 am, 4:30 pm & 6:30 pm, Sun 11:30 pm & 4:30 pm. Closed: 10/16-4/30. Call for schedule. **Reservations:** suggested. **Features:** No A/C; children's menu; senior's menu; entertainment; buffet, a la carte. Indian cultural center; includes narrated harbor tour, baked salmon dinner & native dance program in NW Coast Indian cedar longhouse. Reduced rates for children. Smoke free premises. **Cards:** AE, DS, MC, VI. ⊗

THE YANKEE DINER **Dinner:** $11-$20 **Phone:** 206/783-1964 (58)
◆◆
American
Location: In Ballard off Market St. 5300 24th Ave NW 98107. **Hours:** 7 am-10 pm, Sat 8 am-10 pm, Sun 8 am-9 pm. Closed: 12/25. **Features:** children's menu; carryout; cocktails & lounge. Old fashion cooking with a view of ship canal. Family dining. **Cards:** AE, DS, MC, VI. ⊗

SEAVIEW

LODGING

THE SHELBURNE INN Rates Subject to Change **Phone:** 360/642-2442

◆◆◆ Historic Bed & Breakfast

All Year [BP] 1P: $79- 159 2P/1B: $89- 160 XP: $10

Location: 1/2 mi n of jct US 101 on SR 103. 4415 Pacific Hwy 98644 (PO Box 250). Fax: 360/642-8904. **Terms:** Credit card guarantee, 5 day notice; package plans; 2 night min stay, weekends; no pets. **Facility:** 15 rooms. 1896 Victorian hotel featuring extensive antiques & turn-of-the-century charm. Some small rooms, many with balcony. 3 stories, no elevator; interior corridors; smoke free premises. **Dining:** Also, The Shoalwater Restaurant At The Shelburne Inn, see separate listing. **All Rooms:** combo & shower baths, no A/C, no phones, no TVs. **Cards:** AE, MC, VI. (D) ⊗

RESTAURANT

THE SHOALWATER RESTAURANT AT THE SHELBURNE INN Historical **Dinner:** $21-$30 **Phone:** 360/642-4142

◆◆◆ Continental

Location: In The Shelburne Inn. 4415 Pacific Way 98644. **Hours:** noon-9 pm. Closed: 12/25. **Reservations:** suggested. **Features:** No A/C; Sunday brunch; children's menu; health conscious menu items; carryout; cocktails & lounge; a la carte. Northwest regional cuisine emphasizing fresh seafood in casual yet elegant Victorian dining room. Extensive wine list. Summer Sun brunch 11 am-2 pm. Smoke free premises. **Cards:** AE, DI, MC, VI. ⊗

SEDRO-WOOLLEY—6,000

LODGING

THREE RIVERS INN AAA Special Value Rates **Phone:** 360/855-2626

◆◆◆ Motor Inn

6/1-9/4 [CP]	1P: $55	2P/1B: $61	2P/2B: $51- 63	XP: $6	F18
3/1-5/31 & 9/5-2/29 [CP]	1P: $45	2P/1B: $51	2P/2B: $47- 53	XP: $6	F18

Location: E end of town along SR 20. 210 Ball St 98284. Fax: 360/855-1333. **Terms:** Package plans; small pets only, $10 dep req. **Facility:** 40 rooms. 2 stories; exterior corridors; heated pool, whirlpool. **Dining & Entertainment:** Restaurant; 6 am-10 pm, Fri & Sat 7 am-11 pm; $9-$15; cocktails/lounge. **All Rooms:** free movies, cable TV. **Some Rooms:** refrigerators. **Cards:** AE, CB, DI, DS, JCB, MC, VI. *(See color ad below)* (D)(S) ⊗

SEQUIM—3,600

LODGINGS

BEST WESTERN SEQUIM BAY LODGE AAA Special Value Rates **Phone:** 360/683-0691

◆◆◆ Motor Inn

5/1-9/22	1P: $60- 140	2P/1B: $72- 140	2P/2B: $72- 140	XP: $6	F12
9/23-10/31	1P: $52- 130	2P/1B: $62- 130	2P/2B: $62- 130	XP: $6	F12
3/1-4/30 & 11/1-2/29	1P: $50- 125	2P/1B: $60- 125	2P/2B: $60- 125	XP: $6	F12

Location: 2 1/2 mi se of town on SR 101. 268522 Hwy 101 98382. Fax: 360/683-3748. **Terms:** Reserv deposit; package plans; pets, $25 dep req. **Facility:** 54 rooms. Convenient to Olympia National Park, Sequim Bay State Park & National Wildlife Refuge. 2 stories; exterior corridors; meeting rooms; putting green; heated pool. **Dining:** Dining room; 7 am-9 pm, Fri & Sat-9:30 pm; $10-$15. **All Rooms:** coffeemakers, free movies, combo & shower baths, cable TV. **Some Rooms:** A/C, microwaves, refrigerators, whirlpools. **Cards:** AE, CB, DI, DS, JCB, MC, VI. *(See ad below)* (D) ⊗

ECONO LODGE Guaranteed Rates **Phone:** 360/683-7113

◆◆◆ Motel

5/1-9/30 [CP]	1P: $59	2P/1B: $65	2P/2B: $65	XP: $6	F18
3/1-4/30 & 10/1-2/29 [CP]	1P: $49	2P/1B: $55	2P/2B: $55	XP: $6	F18

Location: E end on US 101. 801 E Washington St 98382 (PO Box 1570). Fax: 360/683-7343. **Terms:** Sr. discount; reserv deposit, 3 day notice; weekly/monthly rates; package plans; small pets only, $15. **Facility:** 43 rooms. 2 stories; interior corridors; putting green. **Services:** Fee: coin laundry. **All Rooms:** microwaves, refrigerators, cable TV. **Some Rooms:** Fee: VCP's. **Cards:** AE, CB, DI, DS, MC, VI. (D) ⊗

Three Rivers Inn & Restaurant is the perfect stop during your North Cascades or International Loop Tour.
• Restaurant & Lounge
• FREE Breakfast Vouchers
Three Rivers Inn & Restaurant
1-800-221-5122
Hwy 20 at Hwy 9 Sedro-Woolley, WA
• Children under 18 stay FREE
• Outdoor Pool & Spa
• Golf and other Outdoor Packages.
Call for today's low rate.

In The Middle Of Nowhere
In The Center Of Everything

Best Western
268522 Highway 101 ◆ Sequim, WA ◆ 98382
Sequim Bay
LODGE
Nestled on 17 forested acres in the Sequim-Dungeness sunbelt, midway between Port Townsend and Port Angeles, and near Olympic National Park, The Sequim Bay Lodge is a perfect basecamp for any getaway to the Olympic Peninsula. Conveniently located just minutes from The Seven Cedars Casino. Suites with fireplaces, in-room spas, or outdoor hot-tubs are available. Locally, call 206-683-0691 for brochures and information.
for reservations call
800-622-0691

GREYWOLF INN — AAA Special Value Rates — **Phone:** 360/683-5889
◆◆ Bed & Breakfast
6/1-9/6 [BP] 2P/1B: $65- 110 XP: $20
4/1-5/31 & 9/7-10/31 [BP] 2P/1B: $60- 99 XP: $20
3/1-3/31 & 11/1-2/29 [BP] 2P/1B: $55- 92 XP: $20
Location: 1 mi e of town on SR 101, then 1/2 mi n. 395 Keeler Rd 98382. **Terms:** Age restrictions may apply; reserv deposit, 3 day notice; package plans; no pets. **Facility:** 6 rooms. On a forest hilltop. Interior corridors; smoke free premises; whirlpool. **All Rooms:** combo & shower baths, no A/C. **Some Rooms:** phones. **Cards:** AE, MC, VI. Ⓓ ⊗

GROVELAND COTTAGE — Guaranteed Rates — **Phone:** 360/683-3565
◆ Historic Bed & Breakfast
6/1-10/15 [BP] 1P: $58- 80 2P/1B: $65- 90 2P/2B: $80 XP: $15
3/1-5/31 & 10/16-2/29 [BP] 1P: $55- 80 2P/1B: $60- 85 2P/2B: $75 XP: $15
Location: 5 mi n. 4861 Sequim-Dungeness Way 98382. Fax: 206/683-5181. **Terms:** Sr. discount; reserv deposit, 3 day notice; weekly rates; package plans; small pets only, in one room. **Facility:** 5 rooms. Turn-of-the-century charm. 2 stories; interior/exterior corridors; smoke free premises. **All Rooms:** cable TV, VCP's, no A/C. **Some Rooms:** phones, whirlpools. **Cards:** AE, DI, DS, MC, VI. Ⓓ ⊗

HIDDEN MEADOW INN — Guaranteed Rates — **Phone:** 360/681-2577
◆◆ Bed & Breakfast
5/1-10/31 [BP] 2P/1B: $79- 89 XP:$10-20 D11
Location: E of town 1 mi off US 101. 901 W Sequim Bay Rd 98382. Fax: 360/681-2070. **Terms:** Open 5/1-10/31; reserv deposit, 3 day notice; monthly rates; package plans; small pets only. **Facility:** 4 rooms. Suites $125; 1 story; interior/exterior corridors; smoke free premises. **All Rooms:** no A/C, no phones. **Some Rooms:** cable TV. **Cards:** MC, VI. Ⓓ ⊗

HOLIDAY INN EXPRESS — AAA Special Value Rates — **Phone:** 360/683-1775
Motel
5/1-9/22 [CP] 1P: $59- 135 2P/1B: $69- 135 2P/2B: $69- 135 XP: $10
3/1-4/30 & 9/23-2/29 [CP] 1P: $49- 120 2P/1B: $59- 120 2P/2B: $59- 120 XP: $10
Too new to rate; **Location:** E end of town on US 101. 1095 E Washington St 98382. Fax: 360/683-2698. **Terms:** reserv deposit; no pets. **Facility:** 61 rooms. Rating withheld pending completion of construction. Scheduled to open August, 1994. 2 stories; interior corridors; meeting rooms; heated indoor pool, whirlpool. **Dining:** Restaurant nearby. **All Rooms:** free movies, cable TV, no A/C. **Some Rooms:** whirlpools. **Cards:** AE, CB, DI, DS, MC, VI. Ⓓ Ⓢ ⊗

JUAN DE FUCA COTTAGES — Guaranteed Rates — **Phone:** 360/683-4433
◆◆◆ Cottage
All Year 2P/2B: $100- 105 XP: $7
Location: 7 mi n; via Sequim Ave & Sequim Dungeness Way. 182 Marine Dr 98382. **Terms:** Credit card guarantee, 7 day notice; weekly/monthly rates; 2 night min stay, weekends; no pets. **Facility:** 6 rooms. Charming, completely equipped housekeeping cottages. Overlooking Dungeness Spit & Strait of Juan de Fuca. 1 two-bedroom unit. Exterior corridors; beach access. **Recreation:** fishing, clamming. **All Rooms:** coffeemakers, kitchens, microwaves, cable TV, VCP's, whirlpools, no A/C, no phones. **Some Rooms:** radios. **Cards:** MC, VI. Ⓓ ⊗

MARGIE'S INN ON THE BAY — Rates Subject to Change — **Phone:** 360/683-7011
◆◆ Bed & Breakfast
5/1-9/30 [BP] 1P: $69- 114 2P/1B: $69- 114 2P/2B: $69 XP: $15
3/1-4/30 & 10/1-2/29 [BP] 1P: $59- 114 2P/1B: $59- 114 2P/2B: $59 XP: $15
Location: 2 mi ne of Hwy 101. 120 Forrest Rd 98382. **Terms:** Age restrictions may apply; check-in 4 pm; reserv deposit, 3 day notice; no pets. **Facility:** 5 rooms. Interior corridors; smoke free premises. **All Rooms:** combo & shower baths, no A/C, no phones. **Some Rooms:** B/W TV. **Cards:** MC, VI. Ⓓ ⊗

RED RANCH INN — Rates Subject to Change — **Phone:** 360/683-4195
◆◆ Motor Inn
4/1-10/31 1P: $60 2P/1B: $60 2P/2B: $66 XP: $6 F12
3/1-3/31 & 11/1-2/29 1P: $48 2P/1B: $48 2P/2B: $54 XP: $6 F12
Location: W end of town on SR 101. 830 W Washington 98382. Fax: 360/683-1546. **Terms:** Sr. discount; reserv deposit, 3 day notice; package plans; small pets only, $6. **Facility:** 55 rooms. 2 stories; exterior corridors; putting green. **Dining & Entertainment:** Restaurant; 6 am-10 pm; $9-$16; cocktail lounge. **All Rooms:** combo & shower baths, cable TV. **Some Rooms:** A/C, 2 efficiencies, microwaves, refrigerators. **Cards:** AE, CB, DI, DS, JCB, MC, VI. Ⓓ ⊗

SEQUIM WEST INN — Guaranteed Rates — **Phone:** 360/683-4144
AAA ◆◆◆ Motel
5/1-10/1 1P: $64 2P/1B: $64 2P/2B: $75
3/1-4/30 & 10/2-2/29 1P: $52 2P/1B: $52 2P/2B: $63
Location: 3/4 mi w on US 101. 740 W Washington St 98382. Fax: 360/683-6452. **Terms:** Credit card guarantee; weekly/monthly rates; no pets. **Facility:** 21 rooms. 4 two-bedroom units. 2 stories; exterior corridors. **Services:** Fee: coin laundry. **All Rooms:** coffeemakers, microwaves, free movies, refrigerators, cable TV. **Some Rooms:** A/C. **Cards:** AE, DI, DS, MC, VI. *(See color ad below)* Ⓓ ⊗

SUNDOWNER MOTEL — Guaranteed Rates — **Phone:** 360/683-5532
AAA ◆◆ Motel
5/15-10/15 1P: $59 2P/1B: $59 2P/2B: $69 XP: $5 F13
3/1-5/14 & 10/16-2/29 1P: $45 2P/1B: $45 2P/2B: $55 XP: $5 F13
Location: Center. 364 W Washington St 98382. **Terms:** Sr. discount; reserv deposit; weekly/monthly rates; small pets only, $4. **Facility:** 34 rooms. 1 two-bedroom unit. 2 stories; exterior corridors. **Dining:** Restaurant nearby. **All Rooms:** combo & shower baths, cable TV. **Some Rooms:** A/C, 7 efficiencies, no utensils, microwaves, refrigerators. **Cards:** AE. Ⓓ ⊗

"Escape from the Ordinary"

UNIQUE ROOMS

- King-Queen Beds - Suites
- C/CATV Movies - Phone
- Inn Room Coffee - Micro/Refrig.
- Non-Smoking Rooms - No Pets

740 W. Washington (Hwy 101)
Sequim, Wa. 98382
(Located in west Sequim)

1-800-528-4527
(360) 683-4144
AAA ◆◆◆

RESTAURANTS

CASONI'S AAA ◆◆◆ Italian — **Dinner:** $11-$20 — **Phone:** 360/683-2415
Location: 2 mi w on US 101 at Carlsborg Rd. 105 Hooker Rd 98324. **Hours:** 11:30 am-2:30 & 5-9 pm, Sun 4 pm-9 pm. Closed: 12/25. **Reservations:** suggested. **Features:** children's menu; health conscious menu items; carryout; cocktails. Mediterranean & Continental cuisine emphasizing seafood in pleasant airy dining room. Homemade pastas & desserts. **Cards:** MC, VI. ⊗

OAK TABLE CAFE ◆◆ American — **Dinner:** up to $10 — **Phone:** 360/683-2179
Location: 1 blk s of US 101, at 3rd Ave. 292 W Bell 98382. **Hours:** 7 am-3 pm, Fri & Sat 4 pm-8 pm. Closed: 11/23 & 12/25. **Features:** No A/C; children's menu. Handcrafted gourmet breakfasts served all day in an attractive, airy, oak dining room. Creative light lunches Mon-Fri, 11 am-3 pm. Smoke free premises. ⊗

THE 3 CRABS ◆◆ Seafood — **Dinner:** $11-$20 — **Phone:** 360/683-4264
Location: 5 1/2 mi n via Sequim Ave & Sequim Dungeness Way. 11 Three Crabs Rd 98382. **Hours:** 11:30 am-9 pm. Closed: 11/23, 12/24 & 12/25; call for winter hours. **Reservations:** suggested. **Features:** children's menu; cocktails & lounge. Well-known restaurant since 1958. Specializing in local seafood & Dungeness Crab. Casual dining along the strait of Juan de Fuca. **Cards:** MC, VI. ⊗

SHELTON—7,200

LODGING

SHELTON INN AAA ◆◆ Motel — Rates Subject to Change — **Phone:** 360/426-4468
All Year 1P: $38- 43 2P/1B: $43- 48 2P/2B: $48- 53 XP: $6 F12
Location: Downtown; 6 blks w of SR 3. 628 Railroad Ave 98584. Fax: 360/426-7927. **Terms:** Sr. discount; reserv deposit; monthly rates; small pets only, $5. **Facility:** 30 rooms. 2 kitchen units, $6 extra; 2 stories; exterior corridors; small heated pool. **Dining:** Restaurant nearby. **All Rooms:** coffeemakers, free movies, refrigerators, cable TV, no A/C. **Cards:** AE, DI, DS, MC, VI. Ⓓ ⊗

SILVERDALE

LODGINGS

CIMARRON MOTEL ◆◆ Motel — Rates Subject to Change — **Phone:** 360/692-7777
All Year 1P: $41- 50 2P/1B: $41- 50 2P/2B: $52
Location: Downtown. 9734 NW Silverdale Way 98383. Fax: 360/692-0961. **Terms:** Credit card guarantee, 3 day notice; weekly rates; no pets. **Facility:** 63 rooms. 9 efficiencies, $50; 3 stories, no elevator; interior corridors. **Services:** Fee: coin laundry. **All Rooms:** combo & shower baths, cable TV. **Some Rooms:** refrigerators. **Cards:** AE, CB, DI, DS, MC, VI. Ⓓ ⊗

SILVERDALE ON THE BAY ◆◆◆ Resort Motor Inn — Rates Subject to Change — **Phone:** 360/698-1000
5/1-10/31 1P: $75- 105 2P/1B: $85- 105 2P/2B: $85- 105 XP: $10 F17
3/1-4/30 & 11/1-2/29 1P: $65- 95 2P/1B: $75- 95 2P/2B: $75- 95 XP: $10 F17
Location: On the beach at n end of Dyes Inlet. 3073 Bucklin Hill Rd 98383. Fax: 360/692-0932. **Terms:** Sr. discount; reserv deposit; package plans; no pets. **Facility:** 151 rooms. Most units with balcony & marine view. 2 two-bedroom units, 2 three-bedroom units. 3 stories; interior corridors; conference facilities; putting green; heated indoor pool, sauna, whirlpool; 2 lighted tennis courts; exercise room. **Dining & Entertainment:** Dining room; 6 am-10 pm, Fri & Sat 7 am-11 pm, Sun 7 am-10 pm; $10-$21; cocktails/lounge. **Recreation:** fishing. **All Rooms:** cable TV. Fee: movies. **Some Rooms:** Fee: refrigerators. **Cards:** AE, CB, DI, DS, JCB, MC, VI. *(See ad below)* Ⓓ ⊗

WILLCOX HOUSE AAA ◆◆◆ Historic Bed & Breakfast — Guaranteed Rates — **Phone:** 360/830-4492
All Year [BP] 1P: $95- 155 2P/1B: $115- 175 2P/2B: $115 XP: $30
Location: 17 mi sw from Hwy 3 at the Newberry Hill Rd exit; w to Seabeck Hwy, right 13 mi, right on Old Holly Rd, follow signs. 2390 Tekiu Rd NW 98312 (2390 Tekiu Rd NW, BREMERTON). Fax: 360/830-0506. **Terms:** Reserv deposit; 2 night min stay, weekends; no pets. **Facility:** 6 rooms. In a secluded mansion with a beautiful view of Hood Canal & The Olympics. 1 two-bedroom unit. 2 stories; interior corridors; smoke free premises; beach, pool; boat dock. **Recreation:** swimming, boating, fishing. **All Rooms:** combo & shower baths, no A/C, no phones, no TVs. **Some Rooms:** whirlpools. **Cards:** MC, VI. Ⓓ ⊗

SNOHOMISH—6,500

LODGING

INN AT SNOHOMISH AAA ◆◆◆ Motel — Rates Subject to Change — **Phone:** 360/568-2208
All Year 1P: $51 2P/2B: $57 XP: $5 F17
Location: E end of town. 323 2nd St 98290. Fax: 360/568-6292. **Terms:** Sr. discount; reserv deposit; monthly rates; no pets. **Facility:** 21 rooms. 2 stories; exterior corridors. **All Rooms:** coffeemakers, cable TV. **Some Rooms:** whirlpools. **Cards:** DS, MC, VI. Ⓓ Ⓢ ⊗

RESTAURANT

COLLECTOR'S CHOICE AAA ◆◆ American — **Dinner:** up to $10 — **Phone:** 360/568-1277
Location: In Star Center Mall. 120 Glen Ave 98290. **Hours:** 7 am-9 pm, Sun-8 pm. Closed: 7/4, 11/23 & 12/25. **Reservations:** suggested; weekends. **Features:** children's menu; carryout; salad bar; cocktails; a la carte. Attractive dining room with historic photographs of local interest. Featuring seafood, steaks, chicken & pasta. Smoke free premises. **Cards:** DS, MC, VI. ⊗

Silverdale on the Bay
A WestCoast Hotel
3073 Bucklin Hill Rd. Silverdale, WA
(206)698-1000 or (800)426-0670

- Waterfront locale 1 hour from downtown Seattle by ferry
- Illuminated tennis and sport courts
- Glass enclosed year round swimming pool & spa
- Fully-equipped fitness center
- Waterfront dining at the Mariner Restaurant
- Cocktails and dancing at Salty Sam's Lounge

SNOQUALMIE—1,500

LODGINGS

THE OLD HONEY FARM COUNTRY INN Rates Subject to Change **Phone:** 360/888-9399
◆◆◆ All Year 1P: $75- 125 2P/1B: $75- 125 XP: $15
Country Inn **Location:** 1 1/2 mi ne of I-90, exit 27 eastbound, 4 mi nw of I-90, exit 31 westbound. 8910 384th Ave SE 98065. **Terms:** Reserv deposit, 3 day notice; BP available; no pets. **Facility:** 10 rooms. Country setting. Furnished with antiques & collectables; decor is country style. 2 stories; interior corridors; smoke free premises; mountain view. **Dining:** Dining room; 7 am-10:30 & 11-2 pm; closed Mon. **All Rooms:** combo & shower baths, no A/C, no phones, no TVs. **Cards:** DS, MC, VI. Roll in showers. (D) ⊗

THE SALISH LODGE AAA Special Value Rates **Phone:** 360/888-2556
AAA 3/1-5/31 & 11/1-2/29 [AP] 1P: $165- 245 2P/1B: $165- 245 2P/2B: $165- 245 XP: $25 F12
6/1-10/31 [AP] 1P: $180- 245 2P/1B: $180- 245 2P/2B: $180- 245 XP: $25 F12
◆◆◆◆ Lodge **Location:** 5 mi ne of I-90, exit 27 eastbound; 7 mi nw of I-90, exit 31 westbound. 37807 SE Falls City Snoqualmie Rd 98065 (PO Box 1109). Fax: 360/888-2533. **Terms:** Check-in 4 pm; reserv deposit, 7 day notice; package plans; small pets only, $25 dep req. **Facility:** 91 rooms. Very attractive rooms with fireplace. Above Snoqualmie Falls. 4 stories; interior corridors; conference facilities; sauna, whirlpool; exercise room. **Dining:** Restaurant, see separate listing. **Services:** data ports, secretarial services; valet laundry; valet parking. **Recreation:** nature program; fishing; bicycles. **All Rooms:** honor bars, free movies, cable TV, whirlpools. **Some Rooms:** Fee: VCP's. **Cards:** AE, CB, DI, DS, JCB, MC, VI. *(See ad p A139)* (D) (S) ⊗

RESTAURANT

THE SALISH LODGE **Dinner:** $21-$30 **Phone:** 360/888-2556
◆◆◆◆ American **Location:** In The Salish Lodge. 98065. **Hours:** 7 am-3 & 5-10 pm. **Reservations:** suggested. **Features:** children's menu; cocktails & lounge; valet parking; a la carte. Historic lodge overlooking Snoqualmie Falls. Famous 4-course country style breakfasts & dinner cuisine emphasizing fresh seafood & game. Smoke free premises. **Cards:** AE, DI, DS, MC, VI. *(See ad p A139)* ⊗

SNOQUALMIE PASS

LODGING

BEST WESTERN SNOQUALMIE SUMMITT INN Rates Subject to Change **Phone:** 360/434-6300
AAA Fri & Sat 1P: $79 2P/1B: $79 2P/2B: $79
Sun-Thurs 1P: $69 2P/1B: $69 2P/2B: $69
◆◆◆ Motor Inn **Location:** At jct I-90 eastbound & exit 52, 1/4 mi e on SR 906; I-90 westbound exit 53, 1/4 mi w on SR 906. 98068 (PO Box 163). Fax: 360/434-6396. **Terms:** Sr. discount; check-in 4 pm; reserv deposit, 3 day notice; weekly rates; package plans; 2 night min stay, 12/18-1/5; no pets. **Facility:** 82 rooms. Rural location atop the summit in a ski area. 2 stories; interior corridors; meeting rooms; heated pool, sauna, whirlpool; playground. **Dining:** Dining room; 6:30 am-9:30 pm, Fri & Sat-11 pm; $6-$12; cocktails. **Services:** Fee: coin laundry. **Recreation:** fishing. Fee: downhill skiing, snowmobiling, tobogganing; bicycles. **Some Rooms:** kitchen, phones, cable TV, whirlpools. Fee: VCP's. **Cards:** AE, DI, DS, MC, VI. (D) (S) ⊗

SOAP LAKE—1,100

LODGINGS

THE INN AT SOAP LAKE Rates Subject to Change **Phone:** 509/246-1132
AAA 4/1-9/30 1P: $45- 85 2P/1B: $50- 90 2P/2B: $50- 90 XP: $7
3/1-3/31 & 10/1-2/29 1P: $40- 80 2P/1B: $45- 85 2P/2B: $45- 85 XP: $7
◆◆◆ Motel **Location:** 1 blk w of SR 17 on Main. 226 E Main Ave 98851 (PO Box 98). **Terms:** Reserv deposit; no pets. **Facility:** 23 rooms. Country Victorian atmosphere in turn-of-the century inn. All rooms with Soap Lake mineral baths. 3 housekeeping cottages; 2 stories; interior corridors; beach, heated indoor pool, whirlpool. **Dining:** Restaurant nearby. **Recreation:** swimming. **All Rooms:** combo & shower baths, cable TV. **Some Rooms:** 3 kitchens, microwaves, refrigerators. **Cards:** MC, VI. (D) ⊗

NOTARAS LODGE Rates Subject to Change **Phone:** 509/246-0462
◆◆◆ All Year 1P: $38 2P/1B: $45 2P/2B: $45 XP: $7 F3
Motel **Location:** 1 blk w of SR 17 on Main. 236 E Main 98851 (PO Box 987). **Terms:** Reserv deposit, 3 day notice; pets, $10, also $50 dep req. **Facility:** 16 rooms. Unique, large, hand-hewn spruce log buildings. Individually appointed rooms depict the life & times of celebrities & local "characters". Mostly spacious rooms, all with Soap Lake mineral baths. Suites with whirlpool, $90-$125; 2 stories; exterior corridors. **Dining & Entertainment:** Restaurant nearby; entertainment, nightclub. **All Rooms:** microwaves, refrigerators, cable TV. **Cards:** MC, VI. (D) ⊗

SOUTH BEND—1,600

RESTAURANT

BOONDOCKS RESTAURANT **Dinner:** $11-$20 **Phone:** 360/875-5155
AAA ◆◆ Seafood **Location:** Downtown on Hwy 101. 1015 W Robert Bush Dr 98586. **Hours:** 8 am-9 pm. **Features:** No A/C; children's menu; cocktails & lounge; a la carte. International cuisine. Dining room overlooking Willapa River. Riverside deck dining. **Cards:** MC, VI. ⊗

SPOKANE—177,200 (See SPOKANE ACCOMMODATIONS spotting map page A150; see index below)

To help you more easily locate accommodations in the Spokane area, the following index and map show lodgings and restaurants within the Spokane area.

Airport Accommodations

Listings for these establishments are found under the heading for the city in which they are located.

SPOKANE

Ramada Inn, at the airport/SPOKANE

Index of Establishments on the SPOKANE ACCOMMODATIONS Spotting Map

(See SPOKANE ACCOMMODATIONS spotting map page A150)

LODGINGS

ALPINE MOTEL — Rates Subject to Change — **Phone:** 509/928-2700 — 28

◆◆ Motel

5/16-9/30	1P: $57	2P/1B: $60	2P/2B: $66	XP: $6
4/1-5/15	1P: $40	2P/1B: $44	2P/2B: $50	XP: $6
3/1-3/31 & 10/1-2/29	1P: $33	2P/1B: $40	2P/2B: $44	XP: $6

Location: 10 mi e on I-90, exit 293. 18815 E Cataldo 99016 (PO Box 363, GREENACRES). **Terms:** Reserv deposit; pets, $5. **Facility:** 14 rooms. 2 stories; exterior corridors; heated pool. **Services:** Fee: coin laundry. **All Rooms:** free movies, combo & shower baths, cable TV. **Cards:** MC, VI. (D) ⊗

APPLE TREE INN — Rates Subject to Change — **Phone:** 509/466-3020 — 12

◆◆ Motel

Fri & Sat 4/1-10/31	1P: $48	2P/1B: $51	2P/2B: $59	XP: $5
Sun-Thurs 4/1-10/31	1P: $46	2P/1B: $48	2P/2B: $54	XP: $5
3/1-3/31 & 11/1-2/29	1P: $42	2P/1B: $44	2P/2B: $52	XP: $5

Location: Jct US 395 (Division St) & I-90 exit 281, 7 mi n. 9508 N Division St 99218. Fax: 509/467-4377. **Terms:** Sr. discount; reserv deposit, 7 day notice; no pets. **Facility:** 71 rooms. 10 two-bedroom units, 8 three-bedroom units. 2 & 3-bedroom units with kitchen, $54-$81; 2 stories; interior/exterior corridors; heated pool. **Dining:** Restaurant nearby. **Services:** winter plug-ins. Fee: coin laundry. **All Rooms:** free movies, cable TV. **Some Rooms:** refrigerators. **Cards:** AE, DI, DS, MC, VI. (D) ⊗

BEL AIR-MOTEL 7 — Rates Subject to Change — **Phone:** 509/535-1677 — 2

AAA ◆ Motel

All Year	1P: $33- 37	2P/1B: $37- 39	2P/2B: $40- 49	XP: $5	F12

Location: I-90 exit 283A, 4 blks n on Altamonte St; 1 mi w on Sprague Ave. 1303 E Sprague Ave 99202. **Terms:** Pets, $6, small dogs only. **Facility:** 17 rooms. Neat older motel in semi commercial area on busy business route. 1 two-bedroom unit. 2 stories; exterior corridors. **All Rooms:** free movies, combo & shower baths, cable TV. **Some Rooms:** microwaves, refrigerators. **Cards:** AE, CB, DI, MC, VI. (D) ⊗

BEST WESTERN THUNDERBIRD INN — AAA Special Value Rates — **Phone:** 509/747-2011 — 8

AAA ◆◆◆ Motel

All Year	1P: $43- 46	2P/1B: $55- 60	2P/2B: $56- 66	XP: $5	F16

Location: I-90, exit 281 2 blks n, then 2 blks w on 2nd Ave. 120 W 3rd Ave 99204. Fax: 509/747-9170. **Terms:** Reserv deposit, 3 day notice; CP available; pets, $50. **Facility:** 90 rooms. 2 stories; exterior corridors; heated pool, whirlpool; exercise room. **Dining:** Restaurant nearby. **All Rooms:** free movies, cable TV. **Some Rooms:** coffeemakers, refrigerators. **Cards:** AE, CB, DI, DS, MC, VI. *(See ad below)* (D) ⊗

BEST WESTERN TRADE WINDS MOTEL — Guaranteed Rates — **Phone:** 509/838-2091 — 19

AAA ◆◆◆ Motel

5/1-10/15 [CP]	1P: $46- 60	2P/1B: $65	2P/2B: $65	XP: $5	F12
3/1-4/30 & 10/16-2/29 [CP]	1P: $36- 50	2P/1B: $44- 55	2P/2B: $44- 60	XP: $5	F12

Location: Eastbound exit 280 off I-90, e on 3rd; westbound exit 280B. 907 W 3rd Ave 99204. Fax: 509/838-2094. **Terms:** Sr. discount; no pets. **Facility:** 59 rooms. Most rooms with balcony. 4 stories; interior corridors; heated pool, sauna, whirlpool; exercise room. **Dining:** Restaurant nearby. **Services:** Fee: coin laundry. **All Rooms:** free movies, cable TV. **Some Rooms:** coffeemakers, refrigerators. **Cards:** AE, CB, DI, DS, MC, VI. (D) ⊗

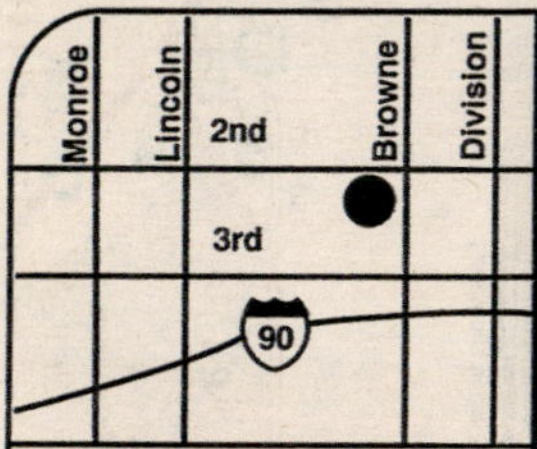

WEST 120 THIRD AVE.
SPOKANE, WA 99204
(509) 747-2011
Toll-Free: (800) 578-2473

BEST WESTERN
THUNDERBIRD INN
SPOKANE WASHINGTON

• Easy Access to Interstate 90 • Close to Downtown and Shopping
• Restaurant Adjacent to Property • 89 Spacious, Air-Conditioned Rooms • Heated pool - Whirlpool Spa • In-Room Coffee
• Non-Smoking Rooms • Handicap Equipped

A PACIFIC PLAZA HOTEL

Best Western

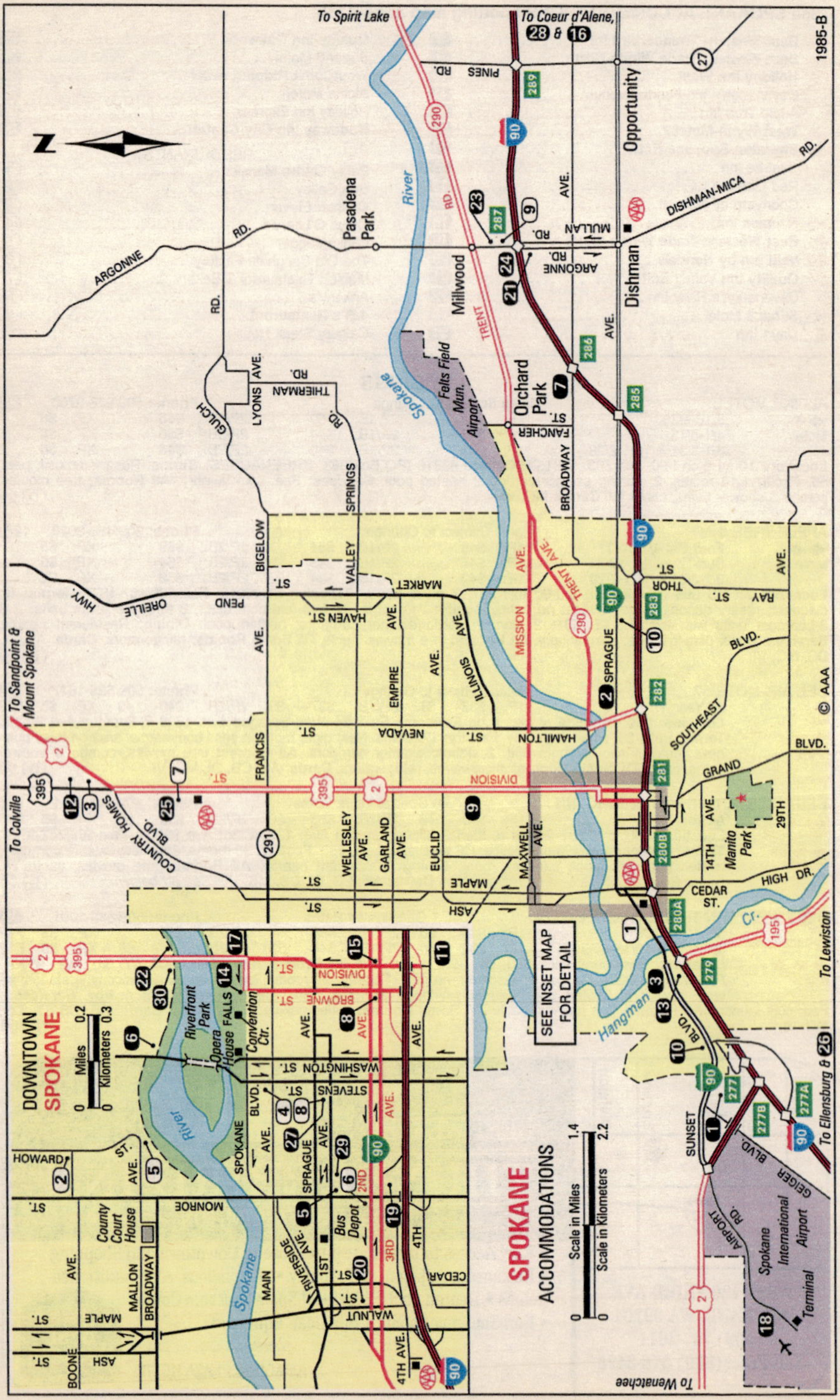
SPOKANE
ACCOMMODATIONS
Scale in Miles
Scale in Kilometers
0
1.4
2.2
DOWNTOWN
SPOKANE
Miles
Kilometers
0.2
0.3
SEE INSET MAP
FOR DETAIL
1985-B
© AAA
To Spirit Lake
To Coeur d'Alene,
28 & 16
To Sandpoint &
Mount Spokane
To Colville
To Lewiston
To Ellensburg & 26
To Wenatchee
Opportunity
Dishman
Millwood
Pasadena
Park
Orchard
Park
Felts Field
Mun.
Airport
Spokane
International
Airport
Terminal
Manito
Park
Spokane
River
Hangman
Cr.
Riverfront
Park
Opera
House
FALLS
Convention
Ctr.
County
Court
House
Bus
Depot
ARGONNE RD.
PINES RD.
DISHMAN-MICA RD.
MULLAN RD.
ARGONNE RD.
TRENT RD.
TRENT AVE.
MISSION AVE.
BROADWAY AVE.
FANCHER ST.
THIERMAN RD.
LYONS AVE.
GULCH RD.
SPRINGS RD.
BIGELOW
VALLEY
MARKET ST.
HAVEN ST.
PEND ORIELLE HWY.
EMPIRE AVE.
ILLINOIS AVE.
NEVADA ST.
FRANCIS AVE.
HAMILTON ST.
DIVISION ST.
COUNTRY HOMES BLVD.
WELLESLEY AVE.
GARLAND AVE.
EUCLID AVE.
MAXWELL AVE.
MAPLE ST.
ASH ST.
SPRAGUE
THOR ST.
RAY ST.
SOUTHEAST BLVD.
GRAND BLVD.
14TH AVE.
29TH
CEDAR ST.
HIGH DR.
SUNSET BLVD.
AIRPORT RD.
GEIGER BLVD.
HOWARD ST.
MONROE ST.
MALLON AVE.
BROADWAY
BOONE ST.
SPOKANE BLVD.
MAIN
RIVERSIDE AVE.
1ST
SPRAGUE AVE.
2ND AVE.
3RD AVE.
4TH
4TH AVE.
WALNUT ST.
CEDAR
STEVENS ST.
WASHINGTON ST.
BROWNE ST.
DIVISION ST.

© AAA

(See SPOKANE ACCOMMODATIONS spotting map page A150)

BEST WESTERN TRADE WINDS NORTH Guaranteed Rates **Phone:** 509/326-5500 9

AAA ◆◆◆ Motel

5/1-9/20 [CP] 1P: $58- 64 2P/1B: $60- 66 2P/2B: $68- 72 XP: $4 F12
3/1-4/30 & 9/21-2/29 [CP] 1P: $54- 60 2P/1B: $56- 62 2P/2B: $64- 68 XP: $4 F12

Location: 2 1/2 mi n on US 2 & 395 from jct I-90, exit 281. 3033 N Division 99207. Fax: 509/328-1357. **Terms:** Sr. discount; no pets. **Facility:** 63 rooms. Traditonal motel close to downtown & large suburban shopping center. 1 two-bedroom unit. 3 stories, no elevator; interior corridors; meeting rooms; heated indoor pool, saunas, whirlpool. **Dining:** Restaurant nearby. **All Rooms:** free movies, cable TV. **Cards:** AE, CB, DI, DS, JCB, MC, VI. Ⓓ ⊗

CAVANAUGH'S INN AT THE PARK AAA Special Value Rates **Phone:** 509/326-8000 6

◆◆◆◆ Hotel

All Year 1P: $84- 132 2P/1B: $94- 142 2P/2B: $117- 142 XP: $10 F17

Location: I-90 exit 281, 1 1/2 mi n on US 2, 195 & 395, then w on North River Dr. W 303 North River Dr 99201. Fax: 509/325-7329. **Terms:** Reserv deposit; pets. **Facility:** 402 rooms. Suites with private swimming pool, patio, lanai, fireplace & some balconies. Many overlook park. Suites from, $185; 5-11 stories; interior corridors; conference facilities, convention oriented; 2 pools (2 heated, 1 indoor), wading pool, sauna, whirlpools; exercise room. **Dining:** Dining room, coffee shop; 6:30 am-11 pm; $13-$22; cocktails. **Services:** data ports; airport transportation. Fee: valet parking. **All Rooms:** free movies, cable TV. **Some Rooms:** honor bars, 4 efficiencies, refrigerators, whirlpools. **Cards:** AE, DI, DS, MC, VI. *(See color ad below)* Ⓓ ⊗

CAVANAUGH'S INN-FOURTH AVENUE Rates Subject to Change **Phone:** 509/838-6101 11

◆◆ Motor Inn

All Year 1P: $45- 74 2P/1B: $51- 74 2P/2B: $53- 70 XP: $8 F18

Location: Downtown, I-90 exit 281. 110 E 4th Ave 99202. Fax: 509/624-0733. **Terms:** Sr. discount; small pets only. **Facility:** 153 rooms. Attractive brick & aggregate building near downtown & major medical facilities. Adjacent to busy interstate highway. 6 stories; interior corridors; heated pool. **Dining & Entertainment:** Dining room; 6 am-10 pm; $8-$15; cocktails/lounge. **Services:** airport transportation. **All Rooms:** free movies, cable TV. **Some Rooms:** refrigerators. **Cards:** AE, CB, DI, DS, MC, VI. Ⓓ ⊗

CAVANAUGH'S RIVER INN AAA Special Value Rates **Phone:** 509/326-5577 22

◆◆◆ Motor Inn

All Year 1P: $70- 94 2P/1B: $75- 99 2P/2B: $75- 99 XP: $10 F18

Location: I-90 exit 281, 1 1/2 mi n on US 2, 195 & 395. N 700 Division St 99202. Fax: 509/326-1120. **Terms:** Reserv deposit; CP available; small pets only, $50 dep req. **Facility:** 241 rooms. Rambling, downtown motor-inn located on the banks of the Spokane River. Enjoyable grounds, many rooms with relaxing view of river. Suites $130-$150; 2 stories; interior corridors; conference facilities; 2 pools (2 heated, 1 indoor/outdoor), wading pool, saunas, whirlpool; 1 tennis court; playground. **Dining & Entertainment:** Dining room; 6:30 am-10 pm; $8-$17; cocktails; entertainment. **Services:** airport transportation. **All Rooms:** free movies, cable TV. **Some Rooms:** refrigerators. Fee: VCP's. **Cards:** AE, DI, DS, MC, VI. *(See color ad below)* Ⓓ ⊗

COMFORT INN BROADWAY Rates Subject to Change **Phone:** 509/535-7185 7

AAA ◆◆ Motel

5/1-10/31 [CP] 1P: $60- 70 2P/1B: $65- 75 2P/2B: $75 XP: $7 F17
3/1-4/30 & 11/1-2/29 [CP] 1P: $51- 60 2P/1B: $56- 65 2P/2B: $65 XP: $7 F17

Location: I-90, exit 286, 3 blks w on Broadway. 6309 E Broadway 99212. Fax: 509/535-7185. **Terms:** Sr. discount; pets. **Facility:** 35 rooms. Pleasing property in busy commercial area. Easy off-on from interstate. 1 kitchen unit, $85; 2 stories; interior/exterior corridors; heated pool, whirlpool. **Services:** winter plug-ins. Fee: coin laundry. **All Rooms:** free movies, cable TV. **Some Rooms:** Fee: microwaves. **Cards:** AE, DI, DS, MC, VI. *(See color ad below)* Ⓓ ⊗

WHEN YOU'RE LIVING OUT OF A SUITCASE...

Comfort Inn

In Spokane
Comfort Inn
6309 E. Broadway, Spokane, WA 99212

- Pool • Spa • Free Continental Breakfast
- Free Cable TV • Truck Parking
- Restaurant Nearby • Near Fairgrounds

For reservations call **509-535-7185** or toll free **800-4-CHOICE**

CAVANAUGH'S INNS

HOSPITALITY ASSURED

Present your AAA Card and receive a 10% discount at all Cavanaugh's Inns locations. Call toll-free
1-800-THE-INNS

Spokane, WA • Kennewick, WA • Yakima, WA • Kalispell, MT

The best reservation is a *confirmed* reservation.

(See SPOKANE ACCOMMODATIONS spotting map page A150)

COURTYARD BY MARRIOTT — AAA Special Value Rates — **Phone:** 509/456-7600 — 17

◆◆◆ Motor Inn

Fri & Sat	1P: $79	2P/1B: $79	2P/2B: $79
Sun-Thurs	1P: $72	2P/1B: $72	2P/2B: $72

Location: I-90 exit 281, 6 blks n on Division St; then e 1 blk on Trent Ave. 401 N Riverpoint Blvd 99202. Fax: 509/456-0969. **Terms:** Check-in 4 pm; credit card guarantee; no pets. **Facility:** 149 rooms. Located along the Spokane river with convenient access to riverfront park & downtown. Comprehensive indoor recreational facilities. Suites from $99-$109; 3 stories; interior corridors; meeting rooms; heated indoor pool, whirlpool; exercise room. **Dining & Entertainment:** Restaurant; 6:30 am-10:30 & 4-10 pm; $5-$10; cocktails/lounge. **Services:** data ports. Fee: coin laundry. **All Rooms:** free movies, cable TV. **Some Rooms:** coffeemakers, refrigerators. **Cards:** AE, CB, DI, DS, MC, VI.
(See color ad below)

DAYS INN — AAA Special Value Rates — **Phone:** 509/926-5399 — 24

AAA ◆◆ Motel

All Year [CP]	1P: $45- 57	2P/1B: $50- 62	2P/2B: $62	XP: $5 F18

Location: I-90, exit 287, 1 blk n. 1919 N Hutchinson Rd 99212. Fax: 509/928-5974. **Terms:** Pets, $10. **Facility:** 92 rooms. Attractive property east of city in bustling retail area. Some compact, basic rooms. 2 stories; interior corridors. **Dining:** Restaurant nearby. **All Rooms:** combo & shower baths, cable TV. **Some Rooms:** refrigerators. Fee: VCP's. **Cards:** AE, CB, DI, DS, MC, VI. Roll in showers.

HAMPTON INN SPOKANE — Rates Subject to Change — **Phone:** 509/747-1100 — 1

AAA ◆◆◆ Motel

All Year [CP]	1P: $63	2P/1B: $73	2P/2B: $73

Location: I-90; eastbound exit 277A, Garden Springs Rd for 3/4 mi, n on Rustle 1/4 mi, w on Sunset Blvd 1 blk, then s on Assembly; westbound exit 277, n on Rustle 2 blks. 2010 S Assembly Rd 99204. Fax: 509/747-8722. **Terms:** Check-in 4 pm; no pets. **Facility:** 131 rooms. Spacious relaxing lobby & breakfast area. Nice rooms, near airport & interstate. Comprehensive indoor recreational facilities. 11 suites with whirlpool, $145-$185; 3 stories; interior corridors; meeting rooms; heated indoor pool, whirlpool; exercise room. **Dining:** Coffee shop, deli; 6 am-10 pm; limited menu; $6-$10. **Services:** airport transportation. Fee: coin laundry. **All Rooms:** free & pay movies, cable TV. **Some Rooms:** refrigerators. Fee: VCP's. **Cards:** AE, DI, DS, MC, VI.
(See ad below & color ad inside front cover)

HOLIDAY INN EXPRESS — Rates Subject to Change — **Phone:** 509/328-8505 — 29

◆◆◆ Motel

Fri & Sat [CP]	1P: $60- 75	2P/1B: $65- 80	2P/2B: $75- 85	XP: $5 F19
Sun-Thurs [CP]	1P: $50- 65	2P/1B: $55- 70	2P/2B: $65- 75	XP: $5 F19

Location: I-90 exit 281, 1 1/2 mi n on US 2. 801 N Division 99202. Fax: 509/325-9842. **Terms:** Sr. discount; no pets. **Facility:** 120 rooms. 3 stories, no elevator; interior corridors; smoke free premises; business center, meeting rooms. **Services:** data ports. **All Rooms:** combo & shower baths, cable TV. Fee: movies. **Some Rooms:** coffeemakers, refrigerators, whirlpools. **Cards:** AE, DI, DS, MC, VI. Roll in showers.

REST AND RELAX WITH SPECIAL WEEKEND RATES.
Spacious rooms, pool, whirlpool, exercise room, in-room coffee, cozy restaurant and lounge. AAA weekend rates, subject to availability.
SPOKANE
North 401 Riverpoint Boulevard 509 456-7600
COURTYARD Marriott
800 443-6000

Hampton Inn
Rated In Top 1% In Nation*
*By Hampton Inn
24-Hour Indoor Pool & Spa • FREE Local Phone Calls
FREE Deluxe Continental Breakfast • Hot Tub Suites
2010 S. Assembly • Spokane, WA 99204 • (509) 747-1100 • 1-800-HAMPTON

FIRST RATE.
Holiday Inn
WEST SPOKANE
4212 Sunset Blvd.
Spokane, Washington 99204
· Adjacent to golf course & riding stables
· On-site, full-service restaurant
· Inground pool
· Meeting facilities available
· Complimentary airport shuttle service
AAA Value Rates
$44* Weekdays
$59* Weekends
*Single or double. Per night. Plus tax. Based on availability.
For reservations and information call (509) 747-2021 or 1-800-HOLIDAY.

(See SPOKANE ACCOMMODATIONS spotting map page A150)

HOLIDAY INN WEST Rates Subject to Change **Phone:** 509/747-2021 **10**
AAA ◆◆ Motor Inn
All Year 1P: $52- 70 2P/1B: $60- 78 2P/2B: $70- 78 XP: $8 F18
Location: I-90; eastbound exit 277A, Garden Spring Rd for 3/4 mi, then n on Rustle 1/4 mi; westbound exit 277, n on Rustle 2 blks. 4212 W Sunset Blvd 99204. Fax: 509/747-5950. **Terms:** Sr. discount; pets. **Facility:** 136 rooms. 2 stories; exterior corridors; meeting rooms; heated pool; 1 tennis court. **Dining & Entertainment:** Dining room; 6 am-2 & 5-10 pm; $7-$16; cocktails/lounge. **Services:** airport transportation. Fee: coin laundry. **All Rooms:** free movies, cable TV. **Cards:** AE, DI, DS, JCB, MC, VI. *(See color ad p A152)*

QUALITY INN OAKWOOD Rates Subject to Change **Phone:** 509/467-4900 **25**
AAA ◆◆◆ Motel
All Year [CP] 1P: $63 2P/1B: $68 2P/2B: $68 XP: $5 F18
Location: Jct US 2 (Division St) & I-90 exit 281, 6 1/2 mi n. 7919 N Division St 99208. Fax: 509/467-4933. **Terms:** Sr. discount; check-in 4 pm; no pets. **Facility:** 96 rooms. Pleasing modern property in busy retail area. Inviting lobby gives way to attractive comfortable rooms. Light & airy pool & spa area. 7 suites with whirlpool, $125-$175; 3 stories; interior corridors; meeting rooms; heated indoor pool, whirlpool. **Dining:** Restaurant nearby. **Services:** winter plug-ins. Fee: coin laundry. **All Rooms:** free movies, cable TV. **Some Rooms:** refrigerators. **Cards:** AE, DI, DS, JCB, MC, VI. *(See ad below)*

QUALITY INN VALLEY SUITES AAA Special Value Rates **Phone:** 509/928-5218 **21**
AAA ◆◆◆ Motor Inn
All Year [CP] 1P: $79- 250 2P/1B: $89- 250 2P/2B: $89- 250 XP: $5 F18
Location: I-90 exit 287. 8923 E Mission 99212. Fax: 509/928-5218. **Terms:** Small pets only, credit card dep req. **Facility:** 91 rooms. A warm & inviting property located in a suburban, residental/business area. Light & airy, well appointed lobby & enjoyable recreational facilties. Variety of room offerings unique "Galaxy of Stars" rooms. Suites up to, $300; 3-4 stories; interior corridors; meeting rooms; heated indoor pool, sauna, whirlpool. **Dining:** Restaurant; 5 pm-10 pm; $6-$16. **Services:** data ports; airport transportation. Fee: coin laundry. **All Rooms:** microwaves, free movies, refrigerators, combo & shower baths, cable TV. **Some Rooms:** coffeemakers, kitchen. Fee: VCP's. **Cards:** AE, CB, DI, DS, JCB, MC, VI.

RAMADA INN AAA Special Value Rates **Phone:** 509/838-5211 **18**
◆◆◆ Motor Inn
6/1-8/31 1P: $75 2P/1B: $81 2P/2B: $81 XP: $8 F18
3/1-5/31 & 9/1-2/29 1P: $69 2P/1B: $75 2P/2B: $75
Location: At Spokane International Airport. 99219 (PO Box 19228). Fax: 509/838-1074. **Terms:** Reserv deposit; AP available; pets. **Facility:** 166 rooms. Contemporary motor-inn, offering upscale accomodations in somewhat remote airport location. 4 private pool suites, $125; 2 stories; interior corridors; conference facilities; 2 pools (2 heated, 1 indoor), whirlpool; exercise room. **Dining:** Dining room, coffee shop; 6 am-11 pm; $9-$17; cocktails. **Services:** airport transportation. **All Rooms:** cable TV. Fee: movies. **Some Rooms:** kitchen, refrigerators. Fee: VCP's, whirlpools. **Cards:** AE, CB, DI, DS, MC, VI.

RED LION INN Guaranteed Rates **Phone:** 509/924-9000 **16**
◆◆◆ Motor Inn
All Year 1P: $83- 93 2P/1B: $93- 103 2P/2B: $93- 103 XP: $10 F19
Location: I-90, exit 291. 1100 N Sullivan Rd 99220 (PO Box 3385). Fax: 509/922-4965. **Terms:** Credit card guarantee, 3 day notice; small pets only. **Facility:** 237 rooms. Large busy motor inn, in suburban light retail area. Offers carefully kept, mostly good sized rooms & enjoyable, well-tended grounds. 4 suites, $120; 2-3 stories; interior corridors; conference facilities; heated pool, whirlpool. **Dining & Entertainment:** Dining room, coffee shop; 6 am-11 pm; $9-$16; cocktails/lounge. **Services:** data ports; airport transportation. **All Rooms:** combo & shower baths, cable TV. Fee: movies. **Some Rooms:** refrigerators, whirlpools. **Cards:** AE, DI, DS, MC, VI.

RODEWAY INN CITY CENTER AAA Special Value Rates **Phone:** 509/456-8040 **30**
AAA ◆ Motel
6/15-8/31 [CP] 1P: $49- 54 2P/1B: $54- 67 2P/2B: $67 XP: $10 F18
3/1-6/14 & 9/1-2/29 [CP] 1P: $44- 49 2P/1B: $49- 54 2P/2B: $54 XP: $10 F18
Location: Downtown. 827 W First Ave 99204. Fax: 509/747-3574. **Terms:** Pets. **Facility:** 81 rooms. 4 stories; exterior corridors; heated pool, sauna, whirlpool. **Dining:** Dining room nearby. **Services:** data ports. **All Rooms:** cable TV. **Some Rooms:** coffeemakers, radios, refrigerators. **Cards:** AE, DI, DS, JCB, MC, VI. *(See color ad below)*

SHANGRI-LA MOTEL Rates Subject to Change **Phone:** 509/747-2066 **3**
AAA ◆ Motel
5/1-9/30 1P: $39 2P/1B: $41 2P/2B: $45 XP: $5
3/1-4/30 & 10/1-2/29 1P: $35 2P/1B: $37 2P/2B: $41 XP: $5
Location: I-90 eastbound exit 277A, westbound exit 277; Garden Springs Rd to Sunset Blvd, 1 mi e to Government Way, then 1 blk n to Hartson. 2922 W Government Way 99204. Fax: 509/456-8696. **Terms:** Reserv deposit; weekly rates; small pets only, no cats or young puppies. **Facility:** 19 rooms. Conventional older motel in out-of-the-way, quiet residental area. Varied room selection, some small units. 5 two-bedroom units, 3 three-bedroom units. 6 kitchen units, $40-$60; heated pool; playground. **Services:** airport transportation. **All Rooms:** cable TV. Fee: VCP. **Some Rooms:** coffeemakers, efficiency, refrigerators. **Cards:** AE, CB, DI, DS, MC, VI.

Quality Inn
Quality Inn OakwooD
Free Local Calls • 24-Hour Indoor Pool & Spa
Free Continental Breakfast • Hot Tub Suites
OAKWOOD
N. 7919 Division • Spokane, WA 99208 • (509) 467-4900 • 1-800-4-CHOICE

RODEWAY INN
WHEN YOU'RE LIVING OUT OF A SUITCASE...
In Spokane
Rodeway Inn
City Center
827 W. 1st
Spokane, WA 99204
Free deluxe continental breakfast and evening snack • heated pool (seasonal) • Indoor sauna and spa • Free local calls & cable TV • Spa Suite • Meeting Room • Coming soon: Restaurant & Lounge. Near Riverfront Park, museums, shopping, theater, Coliseum, Opera House. Events: Bloomsday, Lilac Festival, Neighbor Days
For reservations call **509-456-8040** or toll free **800-4-CHOICE**

(See SPOKANE ACCOMMODATIONS spotting map page A150)

SHERATON-SPOKANE HOTEL Rates Subject to Change **Phone:** 509/455-9600 **14**

AAA ◆◆◆◆ Hotel

All Year	1P: $98	2P/1B: $118	2P/2B: $118	XP: $10	F17

Location: I-90 exit 281, 6 blks n on Divison, then 1 blk w on Spokane Falls Blvd. 322 N Spokane Falls Court 99201. Fax: 509/455-6285. **Terms:** Sr. discount; pets. **Facility:** 370 rooms. High rise, city center hotel located along the Spokane river. Well equipped modernistic rooms, many with enjoyable view of riverfront park. Suites, $125-$450; 15 stories; interior corridors; conference facilities, convention oriented; heated indoor pool, sauna, whirlpool. **Dining & Entertainment:** Dining room, coffee shop; 6:30 am-10 pm, Sat-11 pm; $10-$30; cocktails; entertainment. **Services:** airport transportation; valet parking. **All Rooms:** free & pay movies, cable TV. **Some Rooms:** coffeemakers, refrigerators, whirlpools. Fee: VCP's. **Cards:** AE, DI, DS, JCB, MC, VI. Roll in showers. Ⓓ Ⓢ

SUNTREE INN Rates Subject to Change **Phone:** 509/838-6630 **15**

◆◆ Motel

6/1-10/15 [CP]	1P: $55	2P/1B: $60	2P/2B: $60	XP: $5	F14
10/16-2/29 [CP]	1P: $47	2P/1B: $52	2P/2B: $52	XP: $5	F14
3/1-5/31 [CP]	1P: $44	2P/1B: $49	2P/2B: $49	XP: $5	F14

Location: I-90, exit 281; 2 blks n at 2nd Ave & Division St. 211 S Division St 99202. Fax: 509/624-2147. **Terms:** Sr. discount; reserv deposit, 7 day notice; weekly rates; pets, $35 dep req. **Facility:** 80 rooms. Downtown motel 8 blks from retail area with pleasant, unpretentious rooms. 4 stories; interior corridors; whirlpool. **Dining:** Restaurant nearby. **All Rooms:** free movies, combo & shower baths, cable TV. **Some Rooms:** Fee: VCP's. **Cards:** AE, DI, DS, MC, VI. Ⓓ

SUPER 8 MOTEL Rates Subject to Change **Phone:** 509/838-8800 **26**

◆◆ Motel

6/1-9/30 [CP]	1P: $55	2P/1B: $61	2P/2B: $61	XP: $5	F14
3/1-5/31 & 10/1-10/31 [CP]	1P: $50	2P/1B: $56	2P/2B: $56	XP: $5	F14
11/1-2/29 [CP]	1P: $46	2P/1B: $51	2P/2B: $51	XP: $5	F14

Location: I-90, exit 272. 11102 W Westbow Blvd 99204. Fax: 509/624-3157. **Terms:** Sr. discount; reserv deposit, 7 day notice; weekly rates; pets, $35, dep req. **Facility:** 80 rooms. 3 stories; interior corridors; heated indoor pool, whirlpool. **All Rooms:** Fee: movies. **Some Rooms:** Fee: VCP's. **Cards:** AE, CB, DI, DS, JCB, MC, VI. Ⓓ Ⓢ

SUPER 8 MOTEL Rates Subject to Change **Phone:** 509/928-4888 **23**

◆ Motel

5/28-9/30	1P: $47	2P/1B: $55	2P/2B: $61		
4/1-5/27 & 10/1-10/31	1P: $41	2P/1B: $49	2P/2B: $55	XP: $5	F12
3/1-3/31 & 11/1-2/29	1P: $37	2P/1B: $43	2P/2B: $47	XP: $5	F12

Location: I-90, exit 287. N 2020 Argonne Rd 99212. **Terms:** Pets. **Facility:** 189 rooms. 3 stories; interior corridors. **Dining:** Restaurant nearby. **Services:** Fee: coin laundry. **All Rooms:** free movies, cable TV. **Some Rooms:** microwaves, radios, refrigerators. **Cards:** AE, DI, DS, MC, VI. Ⓓ

TOWNE CENTRE MOTOR INN Rates Subject to Change **Phone:** 509/747-1041 **5**

AAA ◆◆◆ Motel

All Year [CP]	1P: $44	2P/1B: $50	2P/2B: $60		

Location: Downtown. 901 W First Ave 99204. **Terms:** No pets. **Facility:** 36 rooms. 3 stories; exterior corridors; meeting rooms; steamroom; exercise room. **Services:** Fee: coin laundry. **All Rooms:** microwaves, free movies, refrigerators, cable TV. **Cards:** AE, DI, DS, MC, VI. *(See color ad below)* Ⓓ

VALU INN BY NENDELS Rates Subject to Change **Phone:** 509/838-2026 **20**

AAA ◆◆ Motel

All Year	1P: $38	2P/1B: $48	2P/2B: $52	XP: $5	

Location: I-90 eastbound exit 280, westbound exit 280A. 1420 W 2nd Ave 99204. Fax: 509/624-1420. **Terms:** Reserv deposit; pets. **Facility:** 54 rooms. 2 stories; exterior corridors; heated pool. **Dining:** Restaurant nearby. **Services:** winter plug-ins. **All Rooms:** free movies, combo & shower baths, cable TV. **Some Rooms:** microwaves, refrigerators. **Cards:** AE, CB, DI, DS, MC, VI. Roll in showers. Ⓓ

WESTCOAST RIDPATH HOTEL Rates Subject to Change **Phone:** 509/838-2711 **27**

AAA ◆◆◆ Hotel

All Year	1P: $65	2P/1B: $75	2P/2B: $85	XP: $10	F17

Location: Downtown. 515 W Sprague Ave 99204. Fax: 509/747-6970. **Terms:** Sr. discount; small pets only, $200 dep req. **Facility:** 350 rooms. Some lanai units surrounding pool. Suites $101-$125; 4-13 stories; interior corridors; conference facilities, convention oriented; heated pool. **Dining & Entertainment:** 2 restaurants; 6 am-9 pm; $12-$18; cocktails; also, Ankeny's, see separate listing; entertainment. **Services:** airport transportation; valet parking. **All Rooms:** cable TV. Fee: movies. **Some Rooms:** coffeemakers, refrigerators, whirlpools. Fee: VCP's. **Cards:** AE, CB, DI, DS, JCB, MC, VI. *(See ad below)* Ⓓ

Towne Centre Motor Inn
AAA
CAN. at PAR
WE ARE CENTRALLY LOCATED DOWNTOWN
S.W. CORNER OF FIRST & LINCOLN,
SPOKANE, WA 99204
Convenient walk to Shopping Mall, Convention Center, Hospitals, Federal Courthouse, Downtown Center
For Information 1-509-747-1041 24 hours
For Reservations: 1-800-247-1041
AAA SENIOR COMMERCIAL & HOSPITAL DISCOUNTS

WestCoast Ridpath Hotel
W. 515 Sprague, Spokane, WA 99204
(509)838-2711 or (800)426-0670

- Located in downtown Spokane
- 350 spacious guestrooms and suites
- Heated outdoor pool
- Fine dining & dancing at Ankeny's
- Silver Grill Restaurant & Lounge
- Three diamond AAA rating

(See SPOKANE ACCOMMODATIONS spotting map page A150)

WEST WYNN-MOTEL 7 Guaranteed Rates **Phone:** 509/747-3037 (13)
AAA ◆ Motel
All Year 1P: $35- 43 2P/1B: $35- 43 2P/2B: $35- 49 XP: $5
Location: I-90; eastbound exit 280, n 1 blk on Walnut, w 1/2 mi on 4th, w 1/2 mi on Sunset Blvd; westbound exit 280A, w 1/2 mi on 4th, w 1/2 mi on Sunset Blvd. 2701 W Sunset Blvd 99204. Fax: 509/747-9123. **Terms:** Credit card guarantee; no pets. **Facility:** 33 rooms. Older motel on edge of town. mixed room offerings, unpretentious but neat. 2 two-bedroom units. 2 kitchens, $42.90-$89.90; 2 stories; exterior corridors; heated indoor pool, sauna, whirlpool. **Dining:** Restaurant nearby. **Services:** winter plug-ins. Fee: coin laundry. **All Rooms:** no utensils, free movies, refrigerators, combo & shower baths, cable TV. **Some Rooms:** microwaves. **Cards:** AE, DS. (D) ⊗

RESTAURANTS

ANKENY'S **Dinner:** $11-$20 **Phone:** 509/838-2711 (8)
◆◆◆ American
Location: Downtown. 515 W Sprague Ave 99210. **Hours:** 11:30 am-1:30 & 5:30-10 pm, Fri-11 pm, Sat 5:30 pm-11 pm, Sun 9:30 am-1:30 pm. Closed: 1/1, 9/4 & 12/24. **Reservations:** suggested. **Features:** Sunday brunch; health conscious menu items; cocktails & lounge; entertainment; valet parking; a la carte. Fine dining atop the Ridpath Hotel with panoramic city view. A widely varied menu featuring beef & seafood specialties. The food & atmosphere are the strengths of this dining experience. **Cards:** AE, CB, DI, MC, VI. *(See ad p A154)* ⊗

CALGARY STEAK HOUSE **Dinner:** $11-$20 **Phone:** 509/535-7502 (10)
◆◆◆ Steakhouse
Location: 3 mi e on Sprague Ave. 3040 E Sprague 99202. **Hours:** 5 pm-10 pm, Fri & Sat-11 pm, Sun-9 pm. Closed: 7/4, 11/23 & 12/25. **Reservations:** suggested. **Features:** casual dress; children's menu; cocktails & lounge. Features generous portions of beef, chicken & seafood entrees with friendly, attentive service. **Cards:** AE, DI, DS, MC, VI. ⊗

CHAPTER ELEVEN **Dinner:** $11-$20 **Phone:** 509/467-7011 (3)
◆◆ American
Location: Jct US 2 (Division) & I-90 exit 281, 7 mi n; at jct US 2 & 395. 9304 N Division 99218. **Hours:** 11:30 am-10 pm, Fri-11 pm, Sat 4 pm-11 pm, Sun 4 pm-10 pm. Closed: 11/23 & 12/25. **Reservations:** suggested; Fri & Sat. **Features:** casual dress; children's menu; salad bar; cocktails & lounge. Prime rib, steak & seafood; casual family dining in rustic atmosphere. Smoke free premises. **Cards:** AE, DS, MC, VI. ⊗

CLINKERDAGGER **Dinner:** $11-$20 **Phone:** 509/328-5965 (5)
◆◆◆ American
Location: In the Old Flour Mill. 621 W Mallon St 99201. **Hours:** 11:30 am-2:30 & 5-9 pm, Fri & Sat-10 pm, Sun 4 pm-9 pm. Closed: 7/4, 11/23 & 12/25. **Reservations:** suggested. **Features:** casual dress; children's menu; health conscious menu items; salad bar; cocktails & lounge; fee for parking. 16th Century English Inn decor. Varied menu of meats, fish, poultry & pasta dishes. Some river-view seating. Great desserts. Relaxed dining. Smoke free premises. **Cards:** AE, CB, DI, DS, MC, VI. ⊗

CYRUS O'LEARY'S **Dinner:** up to $10 **Phone:** 509/624-9000 (4)
◆◆ American
Location: Downtown. 516 W Main 99201. **Hours:** 11:30 am-11 pm, Fri & Sat-midnight, Sat 11:30 am-midnight, Sun 11:30 am-10 pm. Closed: 11/23. **Reservations:** suggested; 8 or more. **Features:** casual dress; children's menu; cocktails & lounge; fee for parking; a la carte. Over 100 items on menu. Relaxed, casual costumed staff serve meals from extensive menu in bustling, uniquely & colorfully decorated fun atmosphere. **Cards:** MC, VI. ⊗

4 B'S RESTAURANT **Dinner:** up to $10 **Phone:** 509/924-2109 (9)
AAA ◆ American
Location: I-90 exit 287; westbound at exit, eastbound 2 blks n on Argonne. 2022 N Argonne Rd 99212. **Hours:** 24 hours. Closed: 11/23 & 12/25. **Features:** casual dress; children's menu; senior's menu; salad bar. Inexpensive family dining. **Cards:** AE, DI, DS, MC, VI. ⊗

MATTIE'S RESTAURANT & BAKERY **Dinner:** up to $10 **Phone:** 509/466-8800 (7)
◆◆ American
Location: Jcut US 2 (Division) & I-90 exit 281, 6 1/2 mi n. 7905 N Division 99208. **Hours:** 7 am-10 pm, Fri & Sat-11 pm, Sun 7 am-10 pm. Closed: 12/25. **Reservations:** accepted; for party of 5. **Features:** casual dress; Sunday brunch; children's menu; cocktails & lounge. Casual family dining with varied menu featuring homestyle pot pies. Wide selection of very tasty homemade pies & baked goods. **Cards:** AE, DI, DS, MC, VI. ⊗

THE OLD SPAGHETTI FACTORY **Dinner:** up to $10 **Phone:** 509/624-8916 (6)
◆◆ Italian
Location: Downtown. 152 S Monroe 99204. **Hours:** 5 pm-9:30 pm, Fri & Sat-11 pm, Sun 4 pm-9 pm. Closed: 11/23, 12/24 & 12/25. **Features:** casual dress; children's menu; cocktails & lounge; street parking. Offers good selection of non-traditional Italian dishes; enjoyable atmosphere. Smoke free premises. **Cards:** DI, MC, VI. ⊗

PATSY CLARK'S MANSION **Dinner:** $11-$20 **Phone:** 509/838-8300 (1)
◆◆◆ Continental
Location: Downtown. W 2208 2nd Ave 99204. **Hours:** 11:30 am-1:45 & 5-9 pm; Fri & Sat-10 pm, Sun 10 am-1:30 & 5-9 pm. **Reservations:** suggested. **Features:** cocktails; entertainment; street parking & valet parking. Casual elegance in original turn-of-the-century mansion. Varied menu featuring steaks, Duckling Amaretto, lamb, veal & seafood; changes seasonally. **Cards:** AE, CB, DI, MC, VI. ⊗

SEA GALLEY **Dinner:** $11-$20 **Phone:** 509/327-3361 (2)
◆◆ Seafood
Location: Downtown. 1221 N Howard St 99201. **Hours:** 11 am-10 pm, Fri & Sat-11 pm, Sun noon-10 pm. Closed: 11/23 & 12/25. **Reservations:** suggested. **Features:** children's menu; health conscious menu items; salad bar; cocktails & lounge. Popular family oriented regional seafood chain. Reasonable priced traditional seafood items, also offering steaks & prime rib. Cozy, nautical decor. Tempting dessert offerings. **Cards:** AE, MC, VI. ⊗

STEVENSON—1,100

LODGINGS

ECONO LODGE Rates Subject to Change **Phone:** 509/427-5628
AAA ◆◆ Motel
5/1-10/31 1P: $40- 45 2P/1B: $45- 50 2P/2B: $55- 60 XP: $5 F5
3/1-4/30 & 11/1-2/29 1P: $35- 40 2P/1B: $40- 45 2P/2B: $45- 50 XP: $5 F5
Location: 1/2 mi e on SR 14. MPO 02L Frank Johns Rd 98648. Fax: 509/427-4995. **Terms:** Sr. discount; reserv deposit, 7 day notice; weekly rates; small pets only, $5, $50 dep req. **Facility:** 29 rooms. 2 stories; exterior corridors. **All Rooms:** free movies, combo & shower baths, cable TV. **Some Rooms:** coffeemakers, 7 kitchens, microwaves, refrigerators, whirlpools. **Cards:** AE, DI, DS, MC, VI. Roll in showers. (D) ⊗

SKAMANIA LODGE Rates Subject to Change **Phone:** 509/427-7700
AAA ◆◆◆ Lodge
5/1-10/31 1P: $95- 160 2P/1B: $95- 160 2P/2B: $95- 160 XP: $15 F12
3/1-4/30 & 11/1-2/29 1P: $85- 135 2P/1B: $85- 135 2P/2B: $85- 135 XP: $15 F12
Location: W of town on SR 14. 1131 SW Skamania Lodge Dr 98648 (PO Box 189). Fax: 509/427-2547. **Terms:** Reserv deposit, 5 day notice; package plans; no pets. **Facility:** 195 rooms. A rustic mountain lodge. Panoramic vistas of the river, multi-hued canyons & dramatic mountain views. 4 stories; interior corridors; conference facilities; heated indoor pool, saunas, whirlpools; 2 tennis courts; exercise room, playground. Fee: 18 holes golf. **Dining & Entertainment:** Dining room; 7 am-10 pm; $12-$19; cocktails/lounge; entertainment. **Services:** secretarial services; valet laundry; area transportation. Fee: massage. **Recreation:** nature program; fishing, sailboats, windsurfing; hiking trails. Fee: white water rafting; cross country skiing; bicycles, horseback riding. **All Rooms:** coffeemakers, free & pay movies, combo & shower baths, cable TV. **Some Rooms:** microwaves, refrigerators, whirlpools. **Cards:** AE, CB, DI, DS, MC, VI. *(See ad p A48)* Roll in showers.

SULTAN—2,200

LODGING

DUTCH CUP MOTEL Rates Subject to Change **Phone:** 206/793-2215
AAA ◆◆ Motel
All Year 1P: $44 2P/1B: $52 2P/2B: $60 XP: $6 F15
Location: US 2 & Main St. 918 Main St 98294 (PO Box 369). Fax: 206/793-2216. **Terms:** Sr. discount; reserv deposit, 3 day notice; weekly/monthly rates; pets, $6. **Facility:** 21 rooms. Consistent friendly service. Free local calls. 2 stories; exterior corridors. **Dining:** Restaurant nearby. **All Rooms:** free movies, cable TV. **Some Rooms:** efficiency, refrigerators. **Cards:** AE, CB, DI, DS, MC, VI.

SUMNER—6,300

LODGING

SUMNER MOTOR INN AAA Special Value Rates **Phone:** 206/863-3250
AAA ◆◆ Motel
All Year 1P: $46- 49 2P/1B: $51- 54 2P/2B: $55 XP: $5 F14
Location: Downtown. 15506 E Main 98390. **Terms:** Reserv deposit, 3 day notice; weekly/monthly rates; no pets, except for dog shows. **Facility:** 39 rooms. Easy access to Mt Rainier & Crystal Mountains. Efficiencies, $5 extra; 2 stories; exterior corridors. **Dining:** Restaurant nearby. **All Rooms:** free movies, cable TV. **Cards:** AE, DS, MC, VI.

RESTAURANT

VIERTHALER WINERY & RESTAURANT **Dinner:** $21-$30 **Phone:** 206/863-1633
◆◆ German
Location: 2 mi e of town on Hwy 410. 17136 Hwy 410E 98390. **Hours:** 11 am-10 pm. **Features:** No A/C; children's menu; cocktails. Great view of the Puyallup Valley. German & American dishes. **Cards:** AE, DS, MC, VI.

SUNNYSIDE—11,200

LODGING

NENDEL'S MOTOR INN Rates Subject to Change **Phone:** 509/837-7878
AAA ◆◆ Motel
All Year [CP] 1P: $37 2P/1B: $41 2P/2B: $45 XP: $4 F13
Location: 4 mi e of I-82 exit 63; 2 1/2 mi w of I-82 exit 69. 408 Yakima Valley Hwy 98944. Fax: 509/837-5254. **Terms:** Sr. discount; reserv deposit, 3 day notice; weekly rates; pets. **Facility:** 73 rooms. 8 kitchens, $8 extra; 2 stories; exterior corridors; small heated pool. **Dining & Entertainment:** Cocktail lounge; restaurant nearby. **All Rooms:** free movies, cable TV. **Some Rooms:** microwaves, radios, refrigerators. **Cards:** AE, CB, DI, DS, MC, VI. *(See color ad below)*

SUQUAMISH

RESTAURANT

KARSTEN'S FINE DINING **Dinner:** $11-$20 **Phone:** 206/598-3080
◆◆ American
Location: 1 mi ne of SR 305. 18490 NE Suquamish Way 98392. **Hours:** 8 am-9 pm, Sun-8 pm. Closed: 12/25. **Features:** Sunday brunch; children's menu; carryout; salad bar; a la carte. Friendly, relaxed family dining. Smoke free premises. **Cards:** AE, DS, MC, VI.

TACOMA—176,700

LODGINGS

BEST WESTERN LAKEWOOD MOTOR INN AAA Special Value Rates **Phone:** 206/584-2212
AAA ◆◆◆ Motor Inn
All Year [CP] 1P: $50- 60 2P/1B: $57- 67 2P/2B: $59- 69 XP: $7 F18
Location: From I-5, exit 125, nw 2 mi via Bridgeport to Gravelly Lake Dr, left 1/4 blk to Motor Ave SW. 6125 Motor Ave SW 98499. Fax: 206/588-5546. **Terms:** Reserv deposit, 3 day notice; small pets only, $6. **Facility:** 78 rooms. 2 stories; exterior corridors; heated pool. **Dining:** Restaurant nearby. **Services:** Fee: coin laundry. **All Rooms:** cable TV. **Some Rooms:** coffeemakers, refrigerators. Fee: VCP's. **Cards:** AE, CB, DI, DS, JCB, MC, VI.

BEST WESTERN TACOMA INN AAA Special Value Rates **Phone:** 206/535-2880
AAA ◆◆◆ Motor Inn
All Year 1P: $58- 70 2P/1B: $64- 76 2P/2B: $64- 76 XP: $6 F12
Location: Southbound exit 129 on I-5 to 84th St, left to Hosmer; northbound exit 128 on I-5. 8726 S Hosmer St 98444. Fax: 206/537-8379. **Terms:** Reserv deposit, 6/1-9/30; small pets only, $20. **Facility:** 149 rooms. Most units have balcony or patio. 2 stories; exterior corridors; meeting rooms; putting green; heated pool, whirlpools; exercise room, playground. **Dining & Entertainment:** Restaurant; 6:30 am-11 pm; $6-$14; cocktails; entertainment. **Services:** Fee: coin laundry. **All Rooms:** coffeemakers, free movies, cable TV. **Some Rooms:** microwaves, refrigerators. Fee: whirlpools. **Cards:** AE, CB, DI, DS, MC, VI.

Reservations: 800-547-0106 / (509) 837-7878
Nendels INN
74 rooms featuring:
Color Cable TV * Free Local Calls * Heated Pool
A/C * Queen Beds * Restaurant Adjacent * HBO
* All Major Credit Cards * Senior discounts
* Kitchenettes * Conference Room
408 YAKIMA VALLEY HIGHWAY, Sunnyside, WA

COMMENCEMENT BAY BED & BREAKFAST Guaranteed Rates **Phone:** 206/752-8175
◆◆ 6/1-9/30 [BP] 2P/1B: $85- 105
Bed & Breakfast 3/1-5/31 & 10/1-2/29 [BP] 2P/1B: $75- 95
Location: From I-5 at exit 132 to Hwy 16, 2 1/2 mi via Union Ave N, w on 26th to Proctor, n to 34th, w to Union. 3312 N Union Ave 98407. **Terms:** Age restrictions may apply; check-in 4 pm; credit card guarantee, 7 day notice; weekly rates; no pets. **Facility:** 3 rooms. 2 stories; interior corridors; smoke free premises; street parking only. **All Rooms:** free movies, no A/C. **Some Rooms:** radios, phones, cable TV. **Cards:** AE, MC, VI. (D) ⊗

ECONO LODGE Rates Subject to Change **Phone:** 206/582-7550
AAA ◆◆ Motel All Year 1P: $32 2P/1B: $32 2P/2B: $44 XP: $5 F18
Location: From I-5, exit 127 n 1 mi on S Tacoma Way. 9325 S Tacoma Way 98499. **Terms:** Credit card guarantee; no pets. **Facility:** 77 rooms. Free local phone calls. 8 efficiencies, $36.40. 16 kitchens, $40.95, no utensils; 2 stories; interior/exterior corridors; whirlpool. **Services:** Fee: coin laundry. **All Rooms:** free movies, cable TV. **Some Rooms:** whirlpools. **Cards:** AE, CB, DI, DS, JCB, MC, VI. (D) ⊗

HOWARD JOHNSON AAA Special Value Rates **Phone:** 206/535-3100
AAA ◆◆ Motor Inn
7/1-9/30 1P: $69 2P/2B: $74
4/1-6/30 1P: $64 2P/2B: $69
3/1-3/31 & 10/1-2/29 1P: $59 2P/2B: $64
Location: Southbound on I-5, exit 129 to 84th St, left to Hosmer; northbound on I-5 exit 128. 8702 S Hosmer St 98444. Fax: 206/537-6497. **Terms:** Reserv deposit; weekly/monthly rates; CP available; small pets only, $5. **Facility:** 143 rooms. Close to military base. 2 stories; exterior corridors; meeting rooms; heated pool. **Dining:** Restaurant nearby. **Services:** data ports; valet laundry. **All Rooms:** coffeemakers, cable TV. **Cards:** AE, CB, DI, DS, JCB, MC, VI. (D) ⊗

LA QUINTA INN Rates Subject to Change **Phone:** 206/383-0146
◆◆◆ Motor Inn All Year [CP] 1P: $56- 62 2P/1B: $63- 69 2P/2B: $63 XP: $8 F18
Location: Off I-5 exit 135 southbound; n of I-5 exit 134 northbound. 1425 E 27th St 98421. Fax: 206/627-3280. **Terms:** Small pets only. **Facility:** 158 rooms. Free local calls. 7 stories; interior corridors; meeting rooms; heated pool, whirlpool. **Dining:** Restaurant; 6:30 am-10 pm; $6-$14; cocktails. **Services:** Fee: coin laundry. **All Rooms:** free & pay movies, cable TV. **Some Rooms:** Fee: refrigerators. **Cards:** AE, CB, DI, DS, MC, VI. (D) (S) ⊗

RAMADA HOTEL Rates Subject to Change **Phone:** 206/572-7272
◆◆◆ Hotel All Year 1P: $72 2P/1B: $77 2P/2B: $77 XP: $10 F12
Location: 1/4 mi nw of I-5 exit 133 at Tacoma Dome. 2611 East E St 98421. Fax: 206/572-9664. **Terms:** Credit card guarantee, 3 day notice; BP available; 2 night min stay, Feb, Mar, June & Sep; pets, must have pet cage. **Facility:** 160 rooms. 6 stories; interior corridors; meeting rooms; sauna; exercise room. **Dining & Entertainment:** Restaurant; 6 am-10 pm; $8-$15; cocktails/lounge. **Services:** valet laundry. **All Rooms:** free & pay movies, cable TV. **Some Rooms:** refrigerators, whirlpools. **Cards:** AE, CB, DI, DS, MC, VI. (D) ⊗

SHERATON-TACOMA HOTEL AAA Special Value Rates **Phone:** 206/572-3200
◆◆◆ Hotel All Year 1P: $105- 115 2P/1B: $115- 125 2P/2B: $115- 125 XP: $10 F
Location: Downtown, I-5 exit 705. 1320 Broadway Plaza 98402. Fax: 206/591-4105. **Terms:** Monthly rates; package plans; small pets only. **Facility:** 319 rooms. Rooms with panoramic views of Mt Rainier & Puget Sound. 26 stories; interior corridors; business center, conference facilities; sauna, whirlpool. Fee: parking. **Dining & Entertainment:** Dining room, coffee shop; 6:30 am-10:30 pm, Fri & Sat-11 pm; $5-$17; cocktails/lounge. **Services:** Fee: valet parking. **All Rooms:** honor bars, coffeemakers, free movies, cable TV. **Some Rooms:** refrigerators, whirlpools. **Cards:** AE, CB, DS, MC, VI. (D) (S) ⊗

SHERWOOD INN Rates Subject to Change **Phone:** 206/535-2800
AAA ◆◆ Motor Inn
6/15-9/25 [BP] 1P: $54- 59 2P/1B: $59- 64 2P/2B: $59- 64 XP: $5 F13
3/1-6/14 & 9/26-2/29 [BP] 1P: $44- 49 2P/1B: $49- 54 2P/2B: $49- 54 XP: $5 F13
Location: From I-5 at exit 129 southbound, from I-5 exit 128 northbound. 8402 S Hosmer St 98444. Fax: 206/535-2777. **Terms:** Reserv deposit, 3 day notice; weekly/monthly rates; AP available; pets, $6, $25 dep req. **Facility:** 113 rooms. 3 stories; interior corridors; meeting rooms; heated pool. **Dining:** Coffee shop; 6:30 am-9 pm; $6-$13; cocktails. **All Rooms:** coffeemakers, free movies, cable TV. **Some Rooms:** refrigerators. **Cards:** AE, DI, DS, MC, VI. (D) ⊗

SHILO INN Rates Subject to Change **Phone:** 206/475-4020
◆◆◆ Motel All Year [CP] 1P: $68- 79 2P/1B: $68- 79 2P/2B: $72- 79 XP: $10 F12
Location: Off I-5, southbound exit 129, northbound exit 128. 7414 S Hosmer St 98408. Fax: 206/475-1236. **Terms:** Sr. discount; weekly/monthly rates; pets, $7. **Facility:** 132 rooms. 4 stories; interior corridors; meeting rooms; heated indoor pool, sauna, whirlpool; exercise room. **Services:** area transportation, airport transportation. Fee: coin laundry. **All Rooms:** microwaves, free movies, refrigerators, combo & shower baths, cable TV. Fee: VCP's. **Some Rooms:** 11 kitchens. **Cards:** AE, CB, DI, DS, JCB, MC, VI. (D) ⊗

TACOMA TRAVELODGE Rates Subject to Change **Phone:** 206/539-1153
AAA ◆◆◆ Motel All Year [CP] 1P: $50- 55 2P/1B: $55- 60 2P/2B: $60- 65 XP: $5 F17
Location: Southbound exit 129 on I-5 to 84B St, left to Hosmer; northbound exit 128 on I-5. 8820 S Hosmer 98444. Fax: 206/539-1152. **Terms:** Reserv deposit; no pets. **Facility:** 108 rooms. Close to military bases. 2 stories; exterior corridors; meeting rooms; heated pool, whirlpool. **Services:** valet laundry. **All Rooms:** coffeemakers, free movies, cable TV. **Some Rooms:** 8 efficiencies, microwaves, refrigerators. **Cards:** AE, CB, DI, DS, MC, VI. (D) ⊗

WESTERN INN Rates Subject to Change **Phone:** 206/588-5241
AAA ◆◆ Motel All Year 1P: $36- 38 2P/1B: $42- 50 2P/2B: $42- 52 XP: $4 F12
Location: 1/4 mi off I-5 at exit 127 S Tacoma Way. 9920 S Tacoma Way 98499. Fax: 206/581-0652. **Terms:** Reserv deposit; pets, $4. **Facility:** 103 rooms. Some units have balcony or patio. Kitchens, $5 extra; 2 stories; exterior corridors; meeting rooms. **Dining:** Restaurant nearby. **All Rooms:** free movies, refrigerators, cable TV. **Cards:** AE, DI, DS, MC, VI. (D) ⊗

SPEND A NIGHT NOT A FORTUNE!
Econo Lodge
• Senior Discount
• Free HBO, local calls
• Kids stay free
• 1.5 mi from Tacoma Dome on Interstate 5
• Resv. 1-800-4CHOICE
TACOMA 3518 Pacific Hwy E. Tacoma(Fife), WA 98424 (206) 922-0550

RESTAURANTS

BILLY MCHALE'S — **Dinner:** $11-$20 — **Phone:** 206/582-6330
◆ American
Location: At jct I-5 & exit 127; 1 blk nw. 10115 S Tacoma Way 98499. **Hours:** 11 am-9 pm, Fri-10 pm, Sat 11:30 am-10 pm, Sun 11:30 am-9 pm. Closed: 11/23 & 12/25. **Features:** children's menu; senior's menu; carryout; cocktails & lounge; a la carte. Barbecue ribs a specialty. **Cards:** AE, MC, VI. ⊗

CLIFF HOUSE — **Dinner:** $21-$30 — **Phone:** 206/927-0400
AAA ◆◆◆ Continental
Location: 5 mi ne on SR 509; from I-5 exit 142B, w on SR 340, then w on Campus Dr, w on Northshore Pkwy, w on Slayden 8 1/2 mi. 6300 Marine View Dr NE 98422. **Hours:** 11:30 am-9 pm, Fri-10 pm, Sat 4 pm-10 pm, Sun 10:30 am-9 pm. Closed: 1/1, 12/24 & 12/25. **Reservations:** suggested. **Features:** Sunday brunch; cocktails & lounge; a la carte. Scenic view of Mt Rainier & Commencement Bay from dining area. Excellent food with northwest influence. **Cards:** AE, DI, MC, VI. ⊗

JOHNNY'S DOCK RESTAURANT — **Dinner:** $11-$20 — **Phone:** 206/627-3186
◆◆ Steak and Seafood
Location: 1/2 mi nw, at exit 133, on I-5; at Tacoma Dome. 1900 East D St 98421. **Hours:** 10 am-10 pm, Sun-9 pm. Closed: 1/1, 7/4 & 12/25. **Reservations:** suggested; weekends. **Features:** children's menu; carryout; cocktails & lounge. Famous for Dock Burger & Northwestern seafood. Smoke free premises. **Cards:** AE, DI, DS, MC, VI. ⊗

KNAPPS RESTAURANT — **Dinner:** $11-$20 — **Phone:** 206/759-9009
AAA ◆◆ American
Location: 3 mi nw; on Proctor St between N 27th & N 28th. 2707 N Proctor St 98407. **Hours:** 6 am-11 pm. Closed: 12/25. **Features:** children's menu; carryout; cocktails & lounge. Casual dining room. Homemade desserts. **Cards:** AE, MC, VI. ⊗

OLD COUNTRY BUFFET — **Dinner:** up to $10 — **Phone:** 206/584-0220
◆ American
Location: From I-5 exit 125, 1 1/2 mi nw via Bridgeport Way SW & Lakewood Dr SW; in Lakewood Mall I. 10121 Gravelly Lake Dr 98499. **Hours:** 7 am-10:30 & 11-8 pm, Fri-9 pm, Sat 8 am-9 pm, Sun 8 am-8 pm. Closed: 12/25. **Features:** children's menu; senior's menu. Varied menu daily. Smoke free premises. ⊗

OLD SPAGHETTI FACTORY — **Dinner:** up to $10 — **Phone:** 206/383-2214
◆◆ Italian
Location: Downtown, cross street 19th, by the Union Station Depot. 1735 Jefferson S 98402. **Hours:** 5 pm-10 pm, Fri-11 pm, Sat 3 pm-11 pm, Sun noon-9 pm. Closed: 11/23, 12/24 & 12/25. **Features:** children's menu; carryout; cocktails & lounge. Popular family restaurant; memorabilia of times past. Homemade pasta dishes. ⊗

THE OLIVE GARDEN — **Dinner:** up to $10 — **Phone:** 206/475-1772
◆◆ Italian
Location: 6 1/2 mi s off I-5; southbound exit 129, northbound exit 128. 1921 S 72nd 98404. **Hours:** 11 am-10 pm, Fri & Sat-11 pm. Closed: 11/23 & 12/25. **Features:** children's menu; carryout; cocktails & lounge. A popular trattoria. **Cards:** AE, DI, DS, MC, VI. ⊗

SHARI'S RESTAURANT — **Dinner:** up to $10 — **Phone:** 206/272-4837
◆◆ American
Location: From SR 16 exit Union Ave, or from I-5 exit 132 on SR 16 to Union Ave N. 2323 S Union Ave 98405. **Hours:** 24 hours. **Features:** children's menu; senior's menu; carryout. Family dining. **Cards:** AE, DI, DS, MC, VI. ⊗

STANLEY & SEAFORTS — **Dinner:** $11-$20 — **Phone:** 206/473-7300
◆◆◆ Steak and Seafood
Location: From I-5 City Center exit 133, W 38th & Pacific to 34th. 115 E 34th 98404. **Hours:** 11:15 am-3 & 5-10 pm, Sat 4:30 pm-11 pm, Sun 3 pm-10 pm. Closed: 7/4, 11/23 & 12/25. **Reservations:** accepted. **Features:** children's menu; health conscious menu items; carryout; cocktails & lounge. Traditional dining overlooking the city & Commencement Bay. **Cards:** AE, DI, DS, MC, VI. ♿ ⊗

TENINO—1,300

RESTAURANT

ALICE'S RESTAURANT & JOHNSON CREEK WINERY — **Dinner:** $21-$30 — **Phone:** 360/264-2887
◆◆◆ American
Location: From I-5 exit 88, 15 mi e via SR 507, then 5 mi s at Johnson Creek Rd. 19248 Johnson Creek Rd SE 98589. **Hours:** 5 pm-9 pm, Sun 2 pm-7 pm. Closed: Mon, Tues & 12/25. **Reservations:** suggested. **Features:** No A/C; children's menu; beer & wine only. 5-course country-style American & wild game dining in farmhouse restaurant; winery tours avail. Smoke free premises. **Cards:** AE, DI, DS, MC, VI. ⊗

TONASKET—800

LODGING

RED APPLE INN — Rates Subject to Change — **Phone:** 509/486-2119
AAA ◆◆ Motel
All Year 1P: $36- 40 2P/1B: $41- 44 2P/2B: $44- 47 XP: $5 F5
Location: 1/4 mi n on US 97 & 1st St. Hwy 97 & 1st St 98855 (PO Box 453). **Terms:** Credit card guarantee; small pets only, $2, no cats. **Facility:** 21 rooms. Each unit features historic Okanogan County wall murals. 2 two-bedroom units. 3 efficiencies, $6 extra; 1 story; exterior corridors. **Dining:** Restaurant nearby. **All Rooms:** combo & shower baths, cable TV. **Some Rooms:** refrigerators. **Cards:** AE, DI, DS, MC, VI. (D)

TOPPENISH—7,400

LODGING

TOPPENISH INN MOTEL — Rates Subject to Change — **Phone:** 509/865-7444
AAA ◆◆◆ Motel
All Year [CP] 1P: $39- 46 2P/1B: $39- 46 2P/2B: $56 XP: $5 F12
Location: Downtown. 515 S Elm St 98948. Fax: 509/865-7719. **Terms:** Sr. discount; credit card guarantee, 14 day notice; small pets only, $5. **Facility:** 41 rooms. Close to Yakima Indian Nation Center. 2 stories; interior corridors; meeting rooms; heated indoor pool, whirlpool; exercise room. **Services:** Fee: coin laundry. **All Rooms:** microwaves, refrigerators, cable TV. **Some Rooms:** whirlpools. **Cards:** AE, DI, DS, MC, VI. (D) (S) ⊗

TUKWILA—11,900 (See SEATTLE & VICINITY ACCOMMODATIONS spotting map pages A136 & A137; see index starting on page A134)

LODGINGS

COURTYARD BY MARRIOTT Rates Subject to Change **Phone:** 206/575-2500 101
◆◆◆ Sun-Thurs 1P: $87 2P/1B: $97 2P/2B: $97 XP: $10 F18
Motor Inn Fri & Sat 1P: $74 2P/1B: $74 2P/2B: $74 XP: $10 F18
Location: At jct I-5, exit 153; northbound exit Southcenter Pkwy to Strander Blvd, then 1/2 mi se; I-5 exit 154B southbound to Southcenter Blvd to Tukwila to Andover. 400 Andover Park W 98188. Fax: 206/575-0129. **Terms:** Sr. discount; reserv deposit, 7 day notice; weekly rates; weekend rates available; no pets. **Facility:** 149 rooms. 3 stories; interior corridors; meeting rooms; heated indoor pool; exercise room. **Dining:** Restaurant; 6:30 am-2 & 5-10 pm; $5-$8; cocktails. **Services:** data ports; airport transportation. Fee: coin laundry. **All Rooms:** free & pay movies, cable TV. **Some Rooms:** refrigerators. **Cards:** AE, CB, DI, DS, MC, VI. *(See color ad p A127)* (D) (S) ⊗

DOUBLETREE INN Rates Subject to Change **Phone:** 206/246-8220 105
AAA Mon-Thurs 1P: $88- 108 2P/1B: $88- 108 2P/2B: $108 XP: $10 F15
Fri-Sun 1P: $69- 89 2P/1B: $69- 89 2P/2B: $69- 89 XP: $10 F15
◆◆ Motor Inn **Location:** 12 3/4 mi s off I-5; northbound exit 153, southbound exit 154B; adjacent to Southcenter Shopping Mall. 205 Strander Blvd 98188. Fax: 206/575-4749. **Terms:** Sr. discount; credit card guarantee; package plans; small pets only, $100 dep req. **Facility:** 198 rooms. 2 stories; interior corridors; meeting rooms; heated pool; playground. **Dining:** Dining room; 6 am-11 pm; $9-$18; cocktails. **Services:** valet laundry; area transportation, airport transportation. **All Rooms:** cable TV. Fee: movies. **Some Rooms:** refrigerators. **Cards:** AE, CB, DI, DS, JCB, MC, VI. *(See ad p A140)* (D) ⊗

DOUBLETREE SUITES Rates Subject to Change **Phone:** 206/575-8220 102
AAA Mon-Thurs 1P: $123- 143 2P/1B: $123- 143 2P/2B: $123- 143 XP: $15 F15
Fri-Sun 1P: $89- 109 2P/1B: $89- 109 2P/2B: $89- 109 XP: $15 F15
◆◆◆ Suite Hotel **Location:** 12 3/4 mi s off I-5; northbound exit 153, southbound exit 154B; across from Southcenter Shopping Mall. 16500 Southcenter Pkwy 98188. Fax: 206/575-4743. **Terms:** Sr. discount; credit card guarantee; package plans; small pets only, $100 dep req. **Facility:** 221 rooms. Spacious 2 room suites with work space & wet bar. 8 stories; interior corridors; conference facilities; heated indoor pool, sauna, whirlpool; racquetball courts; exercise room. **Dining & Entertainment:** Dining room; 6:30 am-10 pm; $13-$20; cocktails/lounge. **Services:** data ports; valet laundry; area transportation, within 5 mi, airport transportation. **All Rooms:** refrigerators, cable TV. Fee: movies. **Some Rooms:** microwaves. Fee: whirlpools. **Cards:** AE, CB, DI, DS, JCB, MC, VI. *(See ad p A140)* (D) (S) ⊗

ECONO LODGE-SEA TAC AIRPORT Rates Subject to Change **Phone:** 206/244-0810 106
AAA 6/1-9/15 1P: $55- 60 2P/1B: $60- 65 2P/2B: $65- 70 XP: $5 F18
3/1-5/31 & 9/16-11/4 1P: $50 2P/1B: $55 2P/2B: $60 XP: $5 F18
◆◆ 11/5-2/29 1P: $45 2P/1B: $50 2P/2B: $55 XP: $5 F18
Motel **Location:** On SR 99. 13910 Pacific Hwy S 98168. Fax: 206/431-9503. **Terms:** Sr. discount; reserv deposit, 3 day notice, in high season; weekly rates; no pets. **Facility:** 47 rooms. 3 stories; interior corridors; whirlpool; exercise room. **Services:** airport transportation. **All Rooms:** free movies, refrigerators, cable TV. **Some Rooms:** whirlpools. **Cards:** AE, CB, DI, DS, MC, VI. *(See color ad p A140)* (D) ⊗

EMBASSY SUITES SOUTHCENTER Rates Subject to Change **Phone:** 206/227-8844 103
AAA Mon-Thurs 3/1-7/14, 2/16-2/29, Mon-Thurs
◆◆◆ 8/21-11/1 & [BP] 1P: $134 2P/1B: $134 2P/2B: $149 XP: $15
Suite Hotel Fri-Sun 3/1-7/14, 8/21-11/1 & 2/16-2/29 [BP] 1P: $119 2P/1B: $119 2P/2B: $134 XP: $15
11/2-2/15 [BP] 1P: $109 2P/1B: $109 2P/2B: $124 XP: $15
Location: From I-405, at exit 1; adjacent to Boeing Longacres Park. 15920 W Valley Hwy 98188. Fax: 206/227-9567. **Terms:** Reserv deposit, 3 day notice; package plans; no pets. **Facility:** 238 rooms. Suburban spacious rooms, well-lit dining/work table. Suites open on to glass covered atrium. 8 stories; interior corridors; business center, meeting rooms; heated indoor pool, sauna, whirlpool; exercise room. **Dining & Entertainment:** Dining room; 11 am-10 pm, Fri & Sat-11 pm; $8-$16; cocktails/lounge. **Services:** data ports, PC, secretarial services; complimentary evening beverages; valet laundry; area transportation, airport transportation. **All Rooms:** efficiencies, free & pay movies, cable TV. **Some Rooms:** coffeemakers. **Cards:** AE, CB, DI, DS, JCB, MC, VI. (D) (S) ⊗

HAMPTON INN SEATTLE SOUTHCENTER Rates Subject to Change **Phone:** 206/228-5800 104
AAA All Year [CP] 1P: $63- 71 2P/1B: $73- 81 2P/2B: $73- 81
◆◆◆ Motel **Location:** S of I-405 exit 1 on Hwy 181. 7200 S 156th St 98188. Fax: 206/228-6812. **Terms:** Sr. discount; pets. **Facility:** 154 rooms. 4 stories; interior corridors; meeting rooms; heated pool, whirlpool; exercise room. **Services:** data ports; valet laundry; airport transportation. **All Rooms:** free movies, cable TV. **Some Rooms:** refrigerators. **Cards:** AE, CB, DI, DS, MC, VI. *(See color ad inside front cover)* (D) (S) ⊗

HOLIDAY INN SEATTLE-BOEING FIELD Rates Subject to Change **Phone:** 206/762-0300 107
◆◆◆ All Year 1P: $72 2P/1B: $82 2P/2B: $82 XP: $8 F19
Motor Inn **Location:** On SR 99. 11244 Pacific Hwy S 98168. Fax: 206/762-8306. **Terms:** Sr. discount; reserv deposit; no pets. **Facility:** 118 rooms. 2 stories; interior corridors; meeting rooms; heated pool. **Dining & Entertainment:** Dining room; 6 am-2 & 5-10 pm; $11-$16; cocktails/lounge. **Services:** airport transportation. Fee: coin laundry. **All Rooms:** free & pay movies, cable TV. **Cards:** AE, CB, DI, DS, JCB, MC, VI. (D) ⊗

HOMEWOOD SUITES Rates Subject to Change **Phone:** 206/433-8000 108
◆◆◆ All Year [CP] 1P: $109- 129 2P/1B: $119- 139 2P/2B: $119- 139
Suite Hotel **Location:** I-405 at exit 1N. 6955 Southcenter Blvd 98188. Fax: 206/433-8994. **Terms:** Sr. discount; reserv deposit, 3 day notice; monthly rates; package plans; pets, $75. **Facility:** 106 rooms. Commercial area. Relaxed warm country-style decor. 8 two-bedroom units. 2-3 stories; interior/exterior corridors; business center, meeting rooms; heated pool, whirlpool; exercise room, sports court. **Services:** secretarial services; area transportation, within 5 mi, airport transportation. Fee: coin laundry. **All Rooms:** kitchens, cable TV, VCP's. **Some Rooms:** coffeemakers. **Cards:** AE, CB, DI, DS, JCB, MC, VI. (D) (S) ⊗

THE MARRIOTT RESIDENCE INN-SEATTLE SOUTH AAA Special Value Rates **Phone:** 206/226-5500 109
◆◆◆ All Year [CP] 1P: $124 2P/1B: $124 2P/2B: $185 XP: $15 F18
Apartment Motel **Location:** 1/4 mi s of I-405, exit 1 on Hwy 181; across from Boeing Longacre Park. 16201 W Valley Hwy 98188 (PO Box 88904, SEATTLE). Fax: 206/271-5023. **Terms:** Reserv deposit, 14 day notice; pets, $10. **Facility:** 144 rooms. Village-like complex on grassy setting along Green River; rooms with balcony or patio; fireplace. 36 two-bedroom units. 2 stories; exterior corridors; meeting rooms; heated pool, whirlpools; sports court. **Dining:** Restaurant nearby. **Services:** area transportation, airport transportation. Fee: coin laundry. **All Rooms:** kitchens, free movies, cable TV. **Some Rooms:** coffeemakers. Fee: VCP's. **Cards:** AE, CB, DI, DS, JCB, MC, VI. (D) (S) ⊗

(See SEATTLE & VICINITY ACCOMMODATIONS spotting map pages A136 & A137)

NENDEL'S INN-SEATTLE/SOUTHCENTER Rates Subject to Change **Phone:** 206/226-1812 **110**

6/15-9/15	1P: $75	2P/1B: $85	2P/2B: $85	XP: $6	F18
3/1-6/14 & 9/16-2/29	1P: $70	2P/1B: $80	2P/2B: $80	XP: $6	F18

◆◆ Motor Inn

Location: 1/4 mi s of I-405 exit 1 on Hwy 181, across from Boeing Longacres Park. 15901 W Valley Rd 98188. Fax: 206/255-7856. **Terms:** Sr. discount; 4 night min stay; no pets. **Facility:** 146 rooms. Many units overlook Green River. 3 stories; interior corridors; meeting rooms; heated pool, wading pool, sauna, whirlpool; exercise room. **Dining & Entertainment:** Restaurant; 6:30 am-10 pm; $9-$19; cocktails/lounge. **Services:** area transportation, airport transportation. Fee: coin laundry. **All Rooms:** coffeemakers, free movies, cable TV. **Some Rooms:** microwaves, refrigerators. Fee: whirlpools. **Cards:** AE, CB, DI, DS, MC, VI. *(See color ad below)* (D)

SEA-TAC AIRPORT NORTH TRAVELODGE Rates Subject to Change **Phone:** 206/242-1777 **111**

7/1-9/10	1P: $48	2P/1B: $53	2P/2B: $58	XP: $5	F17
3/1-6/30 & 9/11-2/29	1P: $38	2P/1B: $42	2P/2B: $47	XP: $5	F17

◆◆ Motel

Location: On SR 99 Pacific Hwy. 14845 Pacific Hwy S 98168. Fax: 206/248-4285. **Terms:** Sr. discount; credit card guarantee; weekly rates; no pets. **Facility:** 72 rooms. 2 stories; exterior corridors. **Dining:** Restaurant nearby. **Services:** airport transportation. **All Rooms:** free movies, cable TV. **Some Rooms:** coffeemakers, refrigerators. **Cards:** AE, DI, DS, JCB, MC, VI. *(See color ad p A122)* (D)

SILVER CLOUD INN AT TUKWILA Rates Subject to Change **Phone:** 206/241-2200 **112**

6/15-9/30 [CP]	1P: $49	2P/1B: $54	2P/2B: $58	XP: $6	F12
3/1-6/14 & 10/1-2/29 [CP]	1P: $44	2P/1B: $49	2P/2B: $53	XP: $6	F12

◆◆◆ Motel

Location: 11 mi s; 1 blk n of I-5, exit 156. 13050 48th Ave S 98168. Fax: 206/246-0222. **Terms:** Sr. discount; reserv deposit, 3 day notice; no pets. **Facility:** 120 rooms. 2 stories; exterior corridors; heated pool, whirlpool; exercise room. **Dining:** Restaurant nearby. **Services:** guest laundry. **All Rooms:** free movies, refrigerators, combo & shower baths, cable TV. **Some Rooms:** microwaves. **Cards:** AE, DI, DS, MC, VI. (D)

TUMWATER—10,000

LODGINGS

BEST WESTERN TUMWATER INN Rates Subject to Change **Phone:** 360/956-1235

3/1-5/31 & 10/1-2/29 [CP]	1P: $52	2P/1B: $56	2P/2B: $62	XP: $5	F5
6/1-9/30 [CP]	1P: $55- 60	2P/1B: $59	2P/2B: $62	XP: $5	F5

◆◆◆ Motel

Location: E of I-5 at exit 102, jct of Trosper Rd. 5188 Capitol Blvd 98501. Fax: 360/956-1235. **Terms:** Sr. discount; weekly/monthly rates; pets, $5. **Facility:** 89 rooms. 2 stories; interior corridors; meeting rooms; sauna, whirlpool; exercise room. **Dining:** Restaurant nearby. **Services:** Fee: coin laundry. **All Rooms:** free movies, combo & shower baths, cable TV. **Some Rooms:** 6 efficiencies, no utensils, microwaves, refrigerators. **Cards:** AE, CB, DI, DS, JCB, MC, VI. (D) (S)

TYEE HOTEL Rates Subject to Change **Phone:** 360/352-0511

All Year	1P: $71	2P/1B: $75	2P/2B: $78	XP: $4	F18

◆◆◆ Motor Inn

Location: From I-5, exit 102. 500 Tyee Dr 98512. Fax: 360/943-6448. **Terms:** Sr. discount; weekly/monthly rates; small pets only, $50 dep req. **Facility:** 146 rooms. Attractive rooms, some with balcony & fireplace. 2 stories; interior/exterior corridors; conference facilities; heated pool, 4 private indoor therapy pools; 1 tennis court. **Dining:** Dining room; 6:30 am-10 pm, Sat from 7 am, Sun 7 am-9 pm; $7-$16; cocktails; 24-hour room service. **Services:** data ports. **All Rooms:** combo & shower baths, cable TV. **Some Rooms:** Fee: refrigerators, whirlpools. **Cards:** AE, CB, DI, DS, MC, VI. *(See ad p A106)* (D) (S)

RESTAURANT

FALLS TERRACE RESTAURANT **Dinner:** $11-$20 **Phone:** 360/943-7830

◆◆ American

Location: From I-5 exit 103. 106 S Deschutes Way 98501. **Hours:** 11 am-9 pm, Sat 11:30 am-9 pm, Sun 11:30 am-8 pm. **Reservations:** suggested. **Features:** children's menu; early bird specials; health conscious menu; cocktails & lounge. Casual atmosphere; nice view of waterfalls. **Cards:** AE, DI, DS, MC, VI.

TWISP—900

LODGING

IDLE-A-WHILE MOTEL Rates Subject to Change **Phone:** 509/997-3222

All Year	1P: $36- 41	2P/1B: $40- 45	2P/2B: $43- 48	XP: $4

◆◆ Motel

Location: 1/4 mi n on SR 20. 505 N Hwy 20 98856 (PO Box 575). **Terms:** Reserv deposit, 4 day notice; pets, $1, dogs only. **Facility:** 25 rooms. 1 two-bedroom housekeeping cottage. Kitchenettes or cottages $5 extra; exterior corridors; sauna, whirlpool; 1 tennis court. **Dining:** Restaurant nearby. **Recreation:** cross country skiing. **All Rooms:** combo & shower baths. **Some Rooms:** refrigerators. Fee: VCP's. **Cards:** DS, MC, VI. (D)

Nendels® SEATTLE ✦ at Southcenter
(206) 226-1812
or 1-800-547-0106
15901 West Valley Rd. Tukwila, WA 98188

Seattle at Southcenter

- 5 miles from airport, near Southcenter Mall
- Vic's Broiler Restaurant & Lounge features mesquite wood-broiled specialties
- Free local phone calls & in-room coffee
- Fitness center, pool, sauna & spa

I-5 take I-405 N. then Exit #1

20% Off Rack Rates
(Not valid with any other offer.)

Choose an establishment with the AAA next to its listing!

UNION

LODGING

ALDERBROOK RESORT ON HOOD CANAL AAA Special Value Rates **Phone:** 360/898-2200

◆◆◆ Motor Inn

6/1-9/15	1P:	$75- 95	2P/1B:	$85- 99	2P/2B:	$85- 99	XP:$10-15 F17
9/16-11/15	1P:	$65- 85	2P/1B:	$75- 95	2P/2B:	$75- 95	XP:$10-15 F17
11/16-2/29	1P:	$65- 75	2P/1B:	$69- 85	2P/2B:	$69- 85	XP:$10-15 F17
3/1-5/31	1P:	$59- 75	2P/1B:	$69- 85	2P/2B:	$69- 85	XP:$10-15 F17

Location: 2 mi e on SR 106 along Hood Canal. E 7101 Hwy 106 98592. Fax: 360/898-4610. **Terms:** Reserv deposit, 5 day notice; pets, $7. **Facility:** 100 rooms. Rooms & 2-bedroom housekeeping cottages with fireplace. Many balconies. 18 two-bedroom cottages with fireplace, $99-$189, rates for up to 4 persons; 1-3 stories, no elevator; interior/exterior corridors; conference facilities; beach, heated indoor pool, whirlpool; 4 tennis courts; boat dock, marina; playground. Fee: 18 holes golf. **Dining & Entertainment:** Restaurant; 7 am-10 pm; $10-$16; cocktails/lounge; entertainment. **Services:** Fee: coin laundry. **Recreation:** swimming, fishing. Rental: boats. **All Rooms:** combo & shower baths, cable TV, no A/C. **Some Rooms:** microwaves, refrigerators. **Cards:** AE, CB, DI, DS, MC, VI. (D) ⊗

RESTAURANT

THE BEACHSIDE RESTAURANT & LOUNGE **Dinner:** $11-$20 **Phone:** 360/898-2200

◆◆◆◆ American

Location: In the Alderbrook Resort. E 7101 Hwy 106 98592. **Hours:** 7 am-10 pm, Sun & Mon-9 pm. **Features:** Sunday brunch; children's menu; health conscious menu; carryout; cocktails & lounge; entertainment. Waterfront dining with Northwest specialties. **Cards:** AE, DI, DS, MC, VI. ⊗

UNION GAP—3,100

LODGING

HUNTLEY INN Rates Subject to Change **Phone:** 509/248-6924

AAA ◆◆ Motel

5/1-9/5 [CP]	1P:	$48- 53	2P/1B:	$56- 64	2P/2B:	$61- 67	XP: $8 F12
3/1-4/30 & 9/6-2/29 [CP]	1P:	$45- 50	2P/1B:	$50- 58	2P/2B:	$50- 58	XP: $8 F12

Location: 3 1/4 mi s at I-82 & US 97 exit 36. 12 E Valley Mall Blvd 98903. Fax: 509/575-8470. **Terms:** Sr. discount; reserv deposit, 3 day notice; small pets only, $10. **Facility:** 85 rooms. Commercial location. Easy off interstate. Expanded continental breakfast. 2 stories; exterior corridors; meeting rooms; small heated pool. **Dining:** Restaurant nearby. **Services:** airport transportation. **All Rooms:** cable TV. **Some Rooms:** radios, refrigerators. **Cards:** AE, CB, DI, DS, MC, VI. (D) ⊗

VANCOUVER—46,500

LODGINGS

BEST WESTERN FERRYMAN'S INN Rates Subject to Change **Phone:** 360/574-2151

AAA ◆◆◆ Motel

4/5-4/10 & 6/1-9/15 [CP]	1P:	$59	2P/1B:	$59	2P/2B:	$68	XP: $5 F12
3/1-4/4, 4/11-5/31 & 9/16-2/29 [CP]	1P:	$54	2P/1B:	$59	2P/2B:	$63	XP: $5 F12

Location: At I-5; 78th St, exit 4. 7901 NE 6th Ave 98665. Fax: 360/574-9644. **Terms:** Sr. discount; check-in 4 pm; reserv deposit; pets, $45. **Facility:** 133 rooms. 10 kitchens, $50-$65; 2 stories; interior/exterior corridors; meeting rooms; heated pool. **Dining:** Restaurant nearby. **Services:** Fee: coin laundry. **All Rooms:** free movies, cable TV. **Some Rooms:** microwaves, radios, refrigerators. **Cards:** AE, CB, DI, DS, MC, VI. Best Western Motels. (D) ⊗

COMFORT INN Rates Subject to Change **Phone:** 360/574-6000

AAA ◆◆◆ Motel

6/1-9/30 [CP]	1P:	$52- 60	2P/1B:	$58- 70	2P/2B:	$65- 90	XP: $6 F18
3/1-5/31 & 10/1-2/29 [CP]	1P:	$45- 50	2P/1B:	$52- 60	2P/2B:	$60- 70	XP: $6 F18

Location: 1 blk e of I-5, exit 7 southbound; 1 blk w of I-205 exit 36 northbound. 13207 NE 20th Ave 98686. Fax: 360/573-3746. **Terms:** Sr. discount; credit card guarantee, 5 day notice; 4 night min stay; no pets. **Facility:** 58 rooms. 2 stories; interior/exterior corridors; meeting rooms; heated indoor pool, whirlpool. **Dining:** Restaurant nearby. **Services:** Fee: coin laundry, airport transportation. **All Rooms:** free movies, cable TV. **Some Rooms:** microwaves, refrigerators, whirlpools. Fee: VCP's. **Cards:** AE, CB, DI, DS, JCB, MC, VI. (D) ⊗

COMFORT SUITES Rates Subject to Change **Phone:** 360/253-3100

AAA ◆◆◆ Suite Motel

All Year [CP]	1P:	$65	2P/1B:	$70	2P/2B:	$70	XP: $5 F18

Location: I-205 southbound at exit SR 500 to Thurston Way; northbound on I-205 exit at SR 500 to Thurston Way. 4714 NE 94th Ave 98662. Fax: 360/253-7998. **Terms:** Sr. discount; reserv deposit, 3 day notice; no pets. **Facility:** 68 rooms. 2 stories; interior corridors; meeting rooms; heated indoor pool, whirlpool; exercise room. **Services:** valet laundry. **All Rooms:** microwaves, free movies, refrigerators, cable TV. **Some Rooms:** whirlpools. Fee: VCP's. **Cards:** AE, CB, DI, DS, JCB, MC, VI. (D) (S) ⊗

HOLIDAY INN EXPRESS Rates Subject to Change **Phone:** 360/253-5000

AAA ◆◆◆ Motel

All Year [CP]	1P:	$55	2P/1B:	$60	2P/2B:	$60	XP: $5 F18

Location: I-205 southbound at exit SR 30 to Vancouver Mall Way; exit 30 to Thurston Way. 9107 NE Vancouver Mall Dr 98662. Fax: 360/253-3137. **Terms:** Sr. discount; reserv deposit, 3 day notice; no pets. **Facility:** 56 rooms. 2 stories; interior corridors; meeting rooms; heated indoor pool. **All Rooms:** free movies, combo & shower baths, cable TV. **Some Rooms:** microwaves, refrigerators. Fee: VCP's. **Cards:** AE, CB, DI, DS, JCB, MC, VI. Roll in showers. (D) ⊗

MARK 205 INN Rates Subject to Change **Phone:** 360/256-7044

◆◆ Motel

All Year [CP]	1P:	$45- 55	2P/1B:	$50- 60	2P/2B:	$55- 65	XP: $5 F16

Location: 1 blk e, 1 blk n off I-205 Mill Plain, exit 28. 221 NE Chkalov Dr 98684. Fax: 360/256-1231. **Terms:** Sr. discount; reserv deposit, 3 day notice; weekly/monthly rates; pets, $15. **Facility:** 117 rooms. 2 stories; exterior corridors; meeting rooms; heated indoor pool, whirlpool. **Dining:** Restaurant nearby. **Services:** area transportation, airport transportation. **All Rooms:** free movies, cable TV. **Some Rooms:** coffeemakers, efficiency, microwaves, refrigerators, whirlpools. **Cards:** AE, CB, DI, DS, MC, VI. (D) ⊗

Quality Inn

All suites motel with newly renovated rooms

RESERVATIONS
1-800-228-5151
(206) 696-0516
7001 N.E. HIGHWAY 99
VANCOUVER, WA 98665

- Complimentary "Continental PLUS Breakfast"
- Full-sized Kitchens • Guest Laundries
- Outdoor Heated Pool and Spa
- Remote Control Color Cable TV • Free Local Calls
- Pets Allowed • Senior Discounts

I-5 Exit #4(78th. St.) 1 blk. E to 99 & 2 blks. S. - on left

QUALITY INN Rates Subject to Change **Phone:** 360/696-0516
AAA ◆◆◆ Apartment Motel
All Year [CP] 1P: $43- 48 2P/1B: $47- 53 2P/2B: $52- 58 XP: $5 F12
Location: 3/4 mi se of I-5, NE 78th St exit 4. 7001 NE Hwy 99 98665. Fax: 360/693-8343. **Terms:** Sr. discount; credit card guarantee; weekly/monthly rates; small pets only, $5. **Facility:** 72 rooms. 2 stories; interior/exterior corridors; heated pool, whirlpool. **Dining:** Restaurant nearby. **Services:** Fee: coin laundry. **All Rooms:** coffeemakers, kitchens, free movies, cable TV. **Cards:** AE, DI, DS, MC, VI.
(See color ad p A161) (D) (S) ⊗

RED LION INN AT THE QUAY Rates Subject to Change **Phone:** 360/694-8341
◆◆◆ Motor Inn
All Year 1P: $87- 107 2P/1B: $102- 122 2P/2B: $122 XP: $15 F18
Location: 1/2 mi s on dock at foot of Columbia St. 100 Columbia St 98660. Fax: 360/694-2023. **Terms:** Check-in 4 pm; reserv deposit; package plans; small pets only. **Facility:** 160 rooms. Waterfront setting overlooking Interstate Bridge & Columbia River. Many units with river or pool courtyard view. 3 stories; interior corridors; conference facilities; heated pool; boat dock. **Dining & Entertainment:** Dining room; 6 am-10 pm, Fri & Sat-11 pm; $7-$18; cocktails/lounge; Sun brunch 8 am-1:30 pm; entertainment. **Services:** airport transportation. **All Rooms:** combo & shower baths, cable TV. Fee: movies. **Some Rooms:** coffeemakers, efficiency, refrigerators, whirlpools. **Cards:** AE, CB, DI, DS, JCB, MC, VI. Roll in showers. (D) (S)

RESIDENCE INN-PORTLAND NORTH Rates Subject to Change **Phone:** 360/253-4800
◆◆◆ Suite Motel
All Year [CP] 1P: $119 2P/1B: $119 2P/2B: $145- 155 XP: $10 F18
Location: From jct I-205 & SR 500, 1/2 mi w on SR 500 to Thurston Way, 1 blk n to NE Parkway Dr, then 1 1/2 blks w. 8005 NE Parkway Dr 98662. Fax: 360/256-4758. **Terms:** Credit card guarantee; weekly/monthly rates; pets, $10. **Facility:** 120 rooms. Woodburning fireplaces. 30 two-bedroom units. 2 stories; exterior corridors; meeting rooms; heated pool, whirlpools; sports court. **Services:** airport transportation. Fee: coin laundry. **All Rooms:** coffeemakers, kitchens, free movies, cable TV. **Some Rooms:** Fee: VCP's. **Cards:** AE, CB, DI, DS, MC, VI. (D) ⊗

SALMON CREEK MOTEL Guaranteed Rates **Phone:** 360/573-0751
AAA ◆ Motel
All Year 1P: $40- 48 2P/1B: $45- 54 2P/2B: $50- 58 XP: $6
Location: 1 mi se of I-5 at exit 7 southbound; 3/4 mi se of SR 205 at exit 36 northbound. 11901 NE Hwy 99 98686. **Terms:** Sr. discount; reserv deposit; weekly rates; no pets. **Facility:** 18 rooms. 3 two-bedroom units. 2 stories; exterior corridors. **All Rooms:** free movies, cable TV. **Some Rooms:** 12 efficiencies, no utensils, radios. **Cards:** AE, CB, DI, DS, MC, VI. (D) ⊗

SHILO INN DOWNTOWN-VANCOUVER Rates Subject to Change **Phone:** 360/696-0411
◆◆◆ Motel
5/16-9/15 [CP] 1P: $68- 96 2P/1B: $68- 96 2P/2B: $79- 91 XP: $8 F12
3/1-5/15 & 9/16-2/29 [CP] 1P: $58- 70 2P/1B: $58- 70 2P/2B: $64- 70 XP: $8 F12
Location: 1 blk w off I-5, Mill Plain exit, then 2 blks s on D St. 401 E 13th St 98660. Fax: 360/750-0933. **Terms:** Sr. discount; reserv deposit; small pets only, $10. **Facility:** 120 rooms. 4 stories; interior corridors; meeting rooms; heated pool, sauna, whirlpool. **Dining:** Restaurant nearby. **Services:** airport transportation. Fee: coin laundry. **All Rooms:** free movies, cable TV. **Some Rooms:** microwaves, refrigerators. Fee: VCP's. **Cards:** AE, CB, DI, DS, MC, VI. (D) ⊗

SHILO INN-HAZEL DELL Rates Subject to Change **Phone:** 360/573-0511
◆◆◆ Motel
5/16-10/5 [CP] 1P: $62 2P/1B: $62 2P/2B: $65 XP: $8 F12
3/1-5/15 & 10/6-2/29 [CP] 1P: $52 2P/1B: $52 2P/2B: $55 XP: $8 F12
Location: 1 blk e of I-5, exit 7; 1 blk w of SR 205 at exit 36. 13206 Hwy 99 98686. Fax: 360/573-4644. **Terms:** Sr. discount; weekly/monthly rates; pets, $7. **Facility:** 66 rooms. 2 stories; interior corridors; meeting rooms; heated indoor pool, sauna, steamroom, whirlpool. **Dining:** Restaurant nearby. **Services:** airport transportation. Fee: coin laundry. **All Rooms:** free movies, cable TV. **Some Rooms:** 6 kitchens, microwaves, refrigerators. Fee: VCP's. **Cards:** AE, CB, DI, DS, JCB, MC, VI. (D) ⊗

TRAVELODGE VANCOUVER AAA Special Value Rates **Phone:** 360/254-4000
AAA ◆◆◆ Motel
All Year [CP] 1P: $45- 50 2P/1B: $53- 58 2P/2B: $58- 63 XP: $5 F17
Location: From I-205 at Mill Plain exit 28, 1 blk n then 1 blk e. 11506 NE 3rd St 98684. Fax: 360/254-8741. **Terms:** No pets. **Facility:** 59 rooms. 2 stories; exterior corridors; meeting rooms; heated indoor pool, whirlpool. **Dining:** Restaurant nearby. **Services:** Fee: coin laundry. **All Rooms:** coffeemakers, microwaves, free movies, refrigerators, cable TV. **Some Rooms:** whirlpools. **Cards:** AE, DI, DS, MC, VI. (D) (S) ⊗

VANCOUVER LODGE Rates Subject to Change **Phone:** 360/693-3668
AAA ◆◆ Motel
All Year 1P: $40- 50 2P/1B: $50- 55 2P/2B: $55- 60 XP: $5 F6
Location: Downtown. 601 Broadway 98660. **Terms:** Sr. discount; credit card guarantee; weekly rates; small pets only, $5. **Facility:** 48 rooms. 4 two-bedroom units. 2 stories; exterior corridors. **All Rooms:** free movies, refrigerators, combo & shower baths, cable TV. **Some Rooms:** microwaves, whirlpools. **Cards:** AE, DI, DS, MC, VI. *(See ad below)* (D) ⊗

RESTAURANTS

GRANT HOUSE CAFE Historical **Dinner:** $11-$20 **Phone:** 360/693-2391
◆◆ Continental
Location: In the Ft Vancouver National Historic Reserve, e on Evergreen Blvd. 1101 Officer's Row 98661. **Hours:** 11 am-3 pm, Thur-Sat 5:30 pm-9:30 pm. Closed: Sun, Mon, 11/23 & 12/25. **Reservations:** suggested. **Features:** No A/C; carryout; beer & wine only. Seasonally changing menu emphasizing Northwest cuisine served in a casual setting. Smoke free premises. **Cards:** AE, MC, VI. ⊗

THE HOLLAND RESTAURANT **Dinner:** up to $10 **Phone:** 360/694-7842
◆◆ American
Location: Downtown; corner of McLoughlin & Main sts. 1708 Main St 98660. **Hours:** 6 am-9 pm, Fri-10 pm, Sat 7 am-10 pm, Sun 8 am-9 pm. Closed major holidays. **Features:** children's menu; carryout; salad bar; wine only. Pleasant, casual family dining. **Cards:** MC, VI. ⊗

OLD COUNTRY BUFFET **Dinner:** up to $10 **Phone:** 360/256-9420
◆ American
Location: In Vancouver Plaza; crossroads, Thurston Way & Vancouver Plaza Dr. 7809-B NE Vancouver Plaza Dr 98662. **Hours:** 7:30 am-10:30 & 11-8:30 pm, Fri-9 pm, Sat 8 am-11:30 & 3:30-9 pm, Sun 8 am-8:30 pm. **Features:** Sunday brunch; children's menu; carryout; salad bar. Varied menu daily. Smoke free premises. ⊗

Our Facilities Include:
DD Phone, AC, HBO & ESPN,
Coffee, Refrig., & Microwaves.
Minutes to Portland Meadows &
Expo Center. Sr. Citizen Discount.
Hot Tubs Available.

VANCOUVER LODGE
(formerly Travel Lodge)

601 Broadway
Vancouver, WA 98660

☎ (206) 693-3668

AAA

Exit 1B off I-5 Northbound
Exit 1C off I-5 Southbound
2 Blocks West off exit to
Broadway & take a left

OLIVE GARDEN — **Dinner:** $11-$20 — **Phone:** 360/256-8174
◆◆ Italian
Location: From I-205, SR 500 exit, w to Thurston Way; in Vancouver Mall. 8101 NE Parkway Dr 98662. **Hours:** 11 am-10 pm, Fri & Sat-11 pm. Closed: 11/23 & 12/25. **Features:** children's menu; health conscious menu; carryout; cocktails & lounge. A popular trattoria. **Cards:** AE, DI, DS, MC, VI.

RED ROBIN BURGER & SPIRITS EMPORIUM — **Dinner:** up to $10 — **Phone:** 360/892-1121
◆◆ American
Location: 8311 NE Vancouver Mall Rd 98662. **Hours:** 11 am-midnight, Sun from 9 am, lounge to 2 am. Closed: 11/23 & 12/25. **Features:** Sunday brunch; children's menu; carryout; cocktails & lounge. Gourmet hamburgers served in casual, bright atmosphere. Smoke free premises. **Cards:** AE, DS, MC, VI.

WHO-SONG & LARRY'S — **Dinner:** $11-$20 — **Phone:** 360/695-1198
◆◆ Mexican
Location: 2 blks e of Columbia St; on the dock. 111 E Columbia River Way 98661. **Hours:** 11 am-10 pm, Fri & Sat-11 pm, Sun 10 am-10 pm. Closed: 11/23 & 12/25. **Reservations:** suggested. **Features:** Sunday brunch; children's menu; carryout; cocktails & lounge; buffet. South-of-the-border flair on the Columbia River. **Cards:** AE, DI, DS, MC, VI.

WALLA WALLA—26,500

LODGINGS

COMFORT INN — Rates Subject to Change — **Phone:** 509/525-2522
AAA ◆◆◆ Motel
All Year [CP] 1P: $62 2P/1B: $61- 68 2P/2B: $66- 73 XP: $8 F18
Location: US 12, 2nd Ave exit 1 blk s. 520 N 2nd Ave 99362. Fax: 509/522-2565. **Terms:** Sr. discount; reserv deposit, 14 day notice; pets. **Facility:** 61 rooms. 2 kitchen units, $74-$81; 3 stories; interior corridors; meeting rooms; heated pool, sauna, whirlpool. **Dining:** Restaurant nearby. **Services:** Fee: coin laundry. **All Rooms:** free movies, cable TV. **Some Rooms:** refrigerators. Fee: whirlpools. **Cards:** AE, CB, DI, DS, MC, VI. *(See color ad below)*

GREEN GABLES INN — Rates Subject to Change — **Phone:** 509/525-5501
◆◆◆ Bed & Breakfast
Fri-Sun [BP] 1P: $75- 100 2P/1B: $75- 100 XP: $15
Mon-Thurs [BP] 1P: $65- 90 2P/1B: $75- 100
Location: Hwy 12, Clinton St exit; 1/3 mi s then 1 blk w on Bonsella. 922 Bonsella 99362. **Terms:** Age restrictions may apply; reserv deposit, 7 day notice; no pets. **Facility:** 6 rooms. Enjoyable turn-of-the-century mansion with tastefully furnished rooms and large comfortable public rooms for guests use. Preferred check-in 3 to 8 pm. Housekeeping cottage, $160 for up to 4 persons; 2 stories; interior corridors; smoke free premises. **All Rooms:** refrigerators, cable TV, no phones. **Some Rooms:** whirlpools. **Cards:** DS, MC, VI.

NENDEL'S WHITMAN INN — Rates Subject to Change — **Phone:** 509/525-2200
AAA ◆◆ Motor Inn
5/1-10/31 1P: $55 2P/1B: $62 2P/2B: $65 XP: $7 F11
3/1-4/30 & 11/1-2/29 1P: $53 2P/1B: $58 2P/2B: $59 XP: $7 F11
Location: US 12, 2nd Ave exit, 1/4 mi s. 107 N 2nd Ave 99362. Fax: 509/522-1428. **Terms:** Sr. discount; no pets. **Facility:** 72 rooms. 3 stories; interior corridors; heated pool. **Services:** airport transportation. **All Rooms:** free movies, cable TV. **Some Rooms:** refrigerators. **Cards:** AE, DI, DS, MC, VI.

PONY SOLDIER MOTOR INN — Rates Subject to Change — **Phone:** 509/529-4360
AAA ◆◆◆ Motel
All Year [CP] 1P: $65- 70 2P/1B: $70- 75 2P/2B: $76- 81 XP: $5 F12
Location: US 12, 2nd Ave exit, 1/2 mi s then 1/4 mi e on Main St. 325 E Main 99362. Fax: 509/529-7463. **Terms:** Sr. discount; reserv deposit, 5 day notice; pets. **Facility:** 85 rooms. Relaxing common room for enjoyable continental breakfast, most rooms surround well landscaped courtyard with pool. Near City Center. 3 kitchen suites with whirlpool tub, from $95; 2 stories; interior/exterior corridors; business center, meeting rooms; heated pool, sauna, whirlpool; exercise room. **Services:** data ports; guest laundry. **All Rooms:** free movies, cable TV. **Some Rooms:** 3 kitchens, refrigerators. **Cards:** AE, CB, DI, DS, MC, VI.

WALLA WALLA TRAVELODGE — AAA Special Value Rates — **Phone:** 509/529-4940
AAA ◆◆ Motel
All Year 1P: $48 2P/1B: $56 2P/2B: $62 XP: $6 F17
Location: US 12, 2nd Ave exit, 1/2 mi s then 1/4 mi e on Main St. 421 E Main 99362. Fax: 509/529-4943. **Terms:** Reserv deposit, 3 day notice; no pets. **Facility:** 38 rooms. Comfortable accommodations in this near downtown motel. 2 stories; interior/exterior corridors; heated pool, whirlpool. **All Rooms:** free movies, refrigerators, combo & shower baths, cable TV. **Some Rooms:** coffeemakers. **Cards:** AE, CB, DI, DS, MC, VI.

RESTAURANTS

THE HOMESTEAD RESTAURANT — **Dinner:** $11-$20 — **Phone:** 509/522-0345
◆◆◆ American
Location: 1528 Isaacs 99362. **Hours:** 11:30 am-2:30 & 5-9 pm, Sat 5 pm-10 pm, Sun 8 am-8 pm. Closed: 1/1, 7/4 & 12/25. **Features:** casual dress; children's menu; health conscious menu; salad bar; cocktails. Casually elegant family dining, featuring varied menu of seafood, beef & pasta dishes & meatless entress. Home made desserts. Smoke free premises. **Cards:** AE, CB, DI, MC, VI.

MODERN RESTAURANT — **Dinner:** up to $10 — **Phone:** 509/525-8662
◆◆ Chinese
Location: 1 blk off Business Rt US 12, in Eastgate Plaza. 2200 Melrose 99362. **Hours:** 11 am-9 pm, Fri & Sat-9:30 pm. Closed: Mon, 7/4, 11/23 & 12/25. **Features:** casual dress; children's menu; early bird specials; senior's menu; carryout; cocktails & lounge. Long time family operated restaurant featuring cantonese and american dishes. **Cards:** DS, MC, VI.

SEA GALLEY — **Dinner:** up to $10 — **Phone:** 509/522-2030
◆◆ Seafood
Location: 1 mi s on SR 125 (9th Av S) at Plaza Shopping Center. 1500 Plaza Way 99362. **Hours:** 7 am-10 pm, Fri & Sat-11 pm, Sun 7 am-10 pm. Closed: 11/23 & 12/25. **Reservations:** suggested; Fri & Sat for dinner. **Features:** casual dress; children's menu; senior's menu; health conscious menu; carryout; salad bar; cocktails & lounge. Rustic shipboard atmosphere provides relaxed family dining. Beef & chicken selections also avail. **Cards:** AE, DS, MC, VI.

WHEN YOU'RE LIVING OUT OF A SUITCASE...
Comfort Inn
In Walla Walla
Comfort Inn
520 N. Second Ave.
Walla Walla, WA 99362
• Sauna • Spa • Pool • Laundry • Spa Suites
• Kitchenettes • Free Continental Breakfast
• Free Cable TV
For reservations call 509-525-2522 or toll-free
1-800-4-CHOICE

WASHOUGAL—4,800

LODGING

ECONO LODGE Rates Subject to Change **Phone:** 360/835-8591

AAA ◆◆ Motel

All Year	1P: $40	2P/1B: $45	2P/2B: $50	XP: $5 F12

Location: 1/4 mi n of SR 14, 6th St exit. 544 6th St 98671. Fax: 360/835-0240. **Terms:** Sr. discount; reserv deposit; weekly rates; pets, $5, $25 dep req. **Facility:** 26 rooms. 4 efficiencies, $7.50 extra; 2 stories; exterior corridors. **Dining:** Restaurant nearby. **All Rooms:** free movies, cable TV. **Some Rooms:** refrigerators. **Cards:** AE, DI, DS, MC, VI.

WENATCHEE—21,800

LODGINGS

AVENUE MOTEL Rates Subject to Change **Phone:** 509/663-7161

AAA ◆◆ Motel

7/1-8/31	1P: $45	2P/1B: $45	2P/2B: $55	XP: $5
5/1-6/30 & 9/1-9/30	1P: $40	2P/1B: $42	2P/2B: $47	XP: $5
3/1-4/30 & 10/1-2/29	1P: $38	2P/1B: $40	2P/2B: $45	XP: $5

Location: 3/4 mi n on US 2. 720 N Wenatchee Ave 98801. Fax: 509/663-7161. **Terms:** Reserv deposit, 5 day notice; pets. **Facility:** 39 rooms. Rustic oak furniture. Well-landscaped, park-like setting. 2 two-bedroom units. 12 efficiencies, $5 extra; 2 stories; interior/exterior corridors; heated pool, whirlpool. **Dining:** Restaurant nearby. **All Rooms:** free movies, combo & shower baths, cable TV. **Some Rooms:** Fee: microwaves, refrigerators, VCP's. **Cards:** AE, CB, DI, DS, MC, VI. *(See color ad below)*

ECONO LODGE Rates Subject to Change **Phone:** 509/663-8133

◆ Motel

5/1-10/31	1P: $40- 60	2P/1B: $40- 60	2P/2B: $50- 70	XP: $5 F18
3/1-4/30 & 11/1-2/29	1P: $30- 45	2P/1B: $30- 45	2P/2B: $40- 65	XP: $5 F18

Location: Center on US 2. 700 N Wenatchee Ave 98801. Fax: 509/662-0826. **Terms:** Sr. discount; reserv deposit, 3 day notice; small pets only, $5. **Facility:** 41 rooms. 2 stories; exterior corridors; pool. **All Rooms:** cable TV. **Some Rooms:** microwaves, refrigerators. Fee: VCP's. **Cards:** AE, DI, DS, MC, VI.

BEST WESTERN HERITAGE INN Rates Subject to Change **Phone:** 509/664-6565

AAA ◆◆◆ Motel

3/1-4/14 & 9/16-2/29 [CP]	1P: $60- 100	2P/1B: $69- 125	2P/2B: $62- 125	XP: $10 F18
4/15-9/15 [CP]	1P: $62- 125	2P/1B: $72- 125	2P/2B: $82- 125	XP: $10 F18

Location: W end of town. 1905 N Wenatchee Ave 98801. Fax: 509/664-0122. **Terms:** Sr. discount; reserv deposit, 3 day notice; monthly rates; small pets only. **Facility:** 65 rooms. 3 stories, no elevator; interior corridors; meeting rooms; heated indoor pool, sauna, whirlpool. **Services:** Fee: coin laundry. **All Rooms:** free movies, combo & shower baths, cable TV. **Some Rooms:** coffeemakers, 16 efficiencies, 2 kitchens, microwaves, refrigerators, whirlpools. **Cards:** AE, CB, DI, DS, JCB, MC, VI. *(See color ad below)* Roll in showers.

HOLIDAY LODGE Rates Subject to Change **Phone:** 509/663-8167

◆◆◆ Motel

5/1-10/15	1P: $40- 55	2P/1B: $42- 60	2P/2B: $48- 70
3/1-4/30 & 10/16-2/29	1P: $36- 40	2P/1B: $40- 46	2P/2B: $44- 50

Location: 1/2 mi n on US 2. 610 N Wenatchee Ave 98801. Fax: 509/663-8167. **Terms:** Reserv deposit; CP available; small pets only. **Facility:** 59 rooms. 2 stories; exterior corridors; heated pool, sauna, whirlpool. **Dining:** Restaurant nearby. **Services:** Fee: coin laundry. **All Rooms:** free movies, cable TV. **Some Rooms:** microwaves, refrigerators. **Cards:** AE, CB, DI, DS, MC, VI.

ORCHARD INN Rates Subject to Change **Phone:** 509/662-3443

AAA ◆◆◆ Motel

5/1-8/31	1P: $48	2P/1B: $53	2P/2B: $56	XP: $5 F12
3/1-4/30 & 9/1-10/31	1P: $45	2P/1B: $50	2P/2B: $53	XP: $5 F12
11/1-2/29	1P: $42	2P/1B: $47	2P/2B: $50	XP: $5 F12

Location: 1 1/2 mi n on US 2. 1401 N Miller St 98801. Fax: 509/662-3443. **Terms:** Sr. discount; reserv deposit, 7 day notice; small pets only. **Facility:** 103 rooms. 3 two-bedroom units. 3 stories; interior corridors; meeting rooms; heated pool, whirlpool. **Dining:** Restaurant nearby. **All Rooms:** free movies, cable TV. **Some Rooms:** microwaves, refrigerators. **Cards:** AE, CB, DI, DS, MC, VI.

AVENUE MOTEL
720 N. Wenatchee Ave.
Wenatchee, WA 98801 • (509)663-7161
RESERVATIONS
800-733-8981
"Your home away from home"
Come enjoy our parklike setting, outdoor pool, spa and much more.

IN WENATCHEE ... THE APPLE CAPITAL, YOUR BEST BET IS A BEST WESTERN

• 24 Hour Indoor Pool • Sauna • Spa • In-room Movies • Spa & Executive Suites • Free Continental Breakfast • Free Local Calls & Fax Service • Meeting Rooms • Coin-op Laundry • Kitchenettes • Corporate, Government, Senior & Family Rates

Near: OHME Gardens, Museums, Golf, Lake Wenatchee, Mission Ridge Ski Area, Leavenworth.

Best Western Heritage Inn
1905 N. Wenatchee Ave.
Wenatchee, WA 98801
509-664-6565
BEST WESTERN RESERVATIONS: 800-528-1234

RED LION HOTEL — Rates Subject to Change — **Phone:** 509/663-0711

◆◆◆ Motor Inn

All Year 1P: $65- 78 2P/1B: $75- 88 2P/2B: $75- 88 XP: $10

Location: 1 3/4 mi n on US 2. 1225 N Wenatchee Ave 98801. Fax: 509/662-8175. **Terms:** Credit card guarantee; pets. **Facility:** 149 rooms. Most with balcony. 3 stories; interior corridors; conference facilities; heated pool, whirlpool. **Dining & Entertainment:** Dining room, coffee shop; 6 am-10 pm, Fri & Sat-11 pm; $6-$17; cocktails/lounge; 24-hour room service. **Services:** data ports; valet laundry; airport transportation. **All Rooms:** combo & shower baths, cable TV. Fee: movies. **Some Rooms:** refrigerators. **Cards:** AE, CB, DI, DS, MC, VI. (D) ⊗

SCOTTY'S MOTEL — Rates Subject to Change — **Phone:** 509/662-8165

AAA ◆◆◆ Motel

5/1-10/14 1P: $43 2P/1B: $48 2P/2B: $55 XP: $5

3/1-4/30 & 10/15-2/29 1P: $35 2P/1B: $38 2P/2B: $45 XP: $5

Location: Nw end of town on US 97. 1004 N Wenatchee Ave 98801. Fax: 509/662-8165. **Terms:** Sr. discount; reserv deposit; weekly rates, 10/15-4/30; CP available; package plans; no pets. **Facility:** 50 rooms. 2 stories; exterior corridors; mountain view; heated pool, sauna, whirlpool. **Dining:** Restaurant nearby. **All Rooms:** cable TV. **Some Rooms:** microwaves, refrigerators, whirlpools. **Cards:** AE, CB, DI, DS, MC, VI. (D) ⊗

WESTCOAST WENATCHEE CENTER HOTEL — Rates Subject to Change — **Phone:** 509/662-1234

◆◆◆ Motor Inn

All Year 1P: $75 2P/1B: $85 2P/2B: $85 XP: $10 F18

Location: Center. 201 N Wenatchee Ave 98801. Fax: 509/662-0782. **Terms:** Sr. discount; check-in 4 pm; reserv deposit; BP available; package plans; pets, $50 dep req. **Facility:** 146 rooms. City & mountain views. Skybridge to convention center. 9 stories; interior corridors; conference facilities; heated indoor/outdoor pool, whirlpools; exercise room. **Dining & Entertainment:** Dining room; 6:30 am-10 pm, Sat & Sun from 7 am; $6-$10; cocktails; 24-hour room service; entertainment. **Services:** data ports; valet laundry; airport transportation. **All Rooms:** cable TV. Fee: movies. **Some Rooms:** refrigerators, whirlpools. **Cards:** AE, CB, DI, DS, JCB, MC, VI. *(See ad below)* (D) (S) ⊗

RESTAURANTS

EL ABUELO — **Dinner:** $11-$20 — **Phone:** 509/662-7331

◆◆ Mexican

Location: Downtown. 601 S Mission 98801. **Hours:** 11 am-10 pm, Fri & Sat-11 pm. Closed: 7/4, 11/23 & 12/25. **Reservations:** suggested; Mon-Thurs. **Features:** children's menu; cocktails. Friendly family setting with Mexican decor. **Cards:** MC, VI. ⊗

JOHN HORAN STEAK & SEAFOOD Historical — **Dinner:** $11-$20 — **Phone:** 509/663-0018

◆◆◆ Steak and Seafood

Location: Nw end of town off Hwy 2 along Wenatchee River. Two Horan Rd 98801. **Hours:** 5 pm-10 pm, Sun 11 am-2 & 5-10 pm. Closed: 12/25. **Reservations:** suggested; weekends. **Features:** Sunday brunch; cocktails; a la carte. Relaxed country dining in 1899 Pioneer farmhouse. Homemade pastry & breads. **Cards:** AE, DS, MC, VI. ⊗

PROSPECTOR PIES — **Dinner:** up to $10 — **Phone:** 509/662-1118

◆ American

Location: Downtown. 731 N Wenatchee Ave 98801. **Hours:** 6 am-11 pm. Closed: 12/25. **Features:** Sunday brunch; children's menu; senior's menu; carryout; salad bar; a la carte. Family atmosphere. The home of 26 varieties of fresh baked pies. **Cards:** DS, MC, VI. ⊗

VISCOUNTI'S ITALIAN RESTAURANT — **Dinner:** $11-$20 — **Phone:** 509/662-5013

AAA ◆◆ Italian

Location: Downtown. 1737 N Wenatchee Ave 98801. **Hours:** 11 am-2 & 5-10 pm, Sat from 5 pm, Sun 5 pm-9 pm. Closed: 11/23 & 12/25. **Reservations:** suggested. **Features:** children's menu; health conscious menu items; carryout; beer & wine only. Casual; several dining sections. Smoke free premises. **Cards:** AE, DI, DS, MC, VI. ⊗

WENATCHEE ROASTER & ALE HOUSE — **Dinner:** up to $10 — **Phone:** 509/662-1234

◆◆ American

Location: In the West Coast Wenatchee Center Hotel. 201 N Wenatchee Ave 98801. **Hours:** 6:30 am-10 pm, Fri-11 pm, Sat 7 am-11 pm, Sun 7 am-10 pm. **Reservations:** suggested; weekends. **Features:** Sunday brunch; children's menu; early bird specials; carryout; cocktails & lounge; entertainment. Horizontal spit roaster. Fresh & natural food. **Cards:** AE, CB, DI, DS, JCB, MC, VI. *(See ad below)* ⊗

WESTPORT—1,900

LODGINGS

CHATEAU WESTPORT — Rates Subject to Change — **Phone:** 360/268-9101

AAA ◆◆◆ Motel

5/1-9/30 [CP] 1P: $65- 70 2P/1B: $65- 70 2P/2B: $65- 70 XP: $7

3/1-4/30 & 10/1-2/29 [CP] 1P: $46- 50 2P/1B: $46- 50 2P/2B: $46- 50 XP: $7

Location: 1 mi sw; 1/4 mi w of SR 105 Alt & 1 1/2 mi n of Twin Harbors State Park. 710 W Hancock 98595 (PO Box 349). Fax: 360/268-1646. **Terms:** Reserv deposit; package plans; no pets. **Facility:** 108 rooms. Many with balcony & fireplace. 4 stories; interior corridors; oceanfront; meeting rooms; heated indoor pool, whirlpool; playground. **All Rooms:** cable TV, no A/C. **Some Rooms:** coffeemakers, 36 efficiencies, 10 kitchens. Fee: VCP's. **Cards:** AE, DI, DS, MC, VI. (D) ⊗

COHO MOTEL — Guaranteed Rates — **Phone:** 360/268-0111

◆◆ Motel

5/15-9/15 1P: $54 2P/1B: $56 2P/2B: $60 XP: $5

3/1-5/14 & 9/16-2/29 1P: $45 2P/1B: $48 2P/2B: $53 XP: $5

Location: 1 blk from boat basin. 2501 North NYHUS 98595 (PO Box 1087). Fax: 360/268-9425. **Terms:** Reserv deposit, 7 day notice; package plans; small pets only, $10. **Facility:** 28 rooms. Close to marina. Meeting hall with full kitchen avail. 8 two-bedroom units. 3 stories, no elevator; exterior corridors; beach. **Services:** Fee: coin laundry. **Recreation:** swimming, charter fishing, fishing. Fee: crabbing. **All Rooms:** cable TV, no A/C. **Cards:** AE, CB, DI, DS, MC, VI. (D) ⊗

◆ WestCoast ◆
Wenatchee Center Hotel
HOTEL AND CONVENTION CENTER
201 N. Wenatchee Ave.
(509)662-1234 or (800)426-0670

- Direct access to Wenatchee Convention Center
- 147 guestrooms and deluxe suites
- Fully-equipped fitness center
- Indoor/outdoor pool and jacuzzi
- Cable TV and in-room movies
- Wenatchee Roaster & Ale House

MARINERS COVE INN — Rates Subject to Change — **Phone:** 360/268-0531

◆◆ Motel

6/1-10/31	1P: $48	2P/1B: $48	2P/2B: $57	XP: $5
3/1-5/31 & 2/1-2/29	1P: $45	2P/1B: $45	2P/2B: $52	XP: $5
11/1-1/31	1P: $42	2P/1B: $42	2P/2B: $49	XP: $5

Location: Downtown. 303 Ocean Ave 98595 (PO Box 2079). **Terms:** Credit card guarantee; no pets. **Facility:** 9 rooms. 1 story; exterior corridors. **Dining:** Restaurant nearby. **All Rooms:** coffeemakers, refrigerators, combo & shower baths, cable TV, no A/C. **Some Rooms:** efficiency. **Cards:** AE, DI, MC, VI. (D) ⊗

WINDJAMMER MOTEL — Rates Subject to Change — **Phone:** 360/268-9351

AAA ◆◆ Motel

5/1-9/30	1P: $40- 45	2P/1B: $45- 50	2P/2B: $45- 50	XP: $5	F5
3/1-4/30 & 10/1-2/29	1P: $30- 35	2P/1B: $35- 40	2P/2B: $35- 40	XP: $5	F5

Location: Downtown. 461 E Pacific Ave 98595 (PO Box 655). **Terms:** Reserv deposit; no pets. **Facility:** 12 rooms. 3 two-bedroom units. 4 kitchens, $5 extra; 1 story; exterior corridors. **All Rooms:** shower baths, cable TV, no A/C, no phones. **Some Rooms:** refrigerators. **Cards:** MC, VI. (D) ⊗

WHITE PASS

LODGING

GAME RIDGE MOTEL-LODGE — AAA Special Value Rates — **Phone:** 509/672-2212

AAA ◆ Motel

All Year	1P: $37- 52	2P/1B: $47- 62	2P/2B: $55- 79	XP: $5

Location: 20 mi e on US 12. 27350 Hwy 12 98937 (27350 Hwy 12, RIMROCK). Fax: 509/672-2242. **Terms:** Reserv deposit, 7 day notice; weekly rates; pets, $5. **Facility:** 14 rooms. Nicely landscaped in a beautiful mountain setting on banks of the Tieton River. 4 two-bedroom units. Kitchen units, $5 extra; 1 story; exterior corridors; heated pool, whirlpool; playground, recreation room. **Recreation:** fishing, hunting, white water rafting; downhill skiing. **All Rooms:** free movies, shower baths, no A/C, no phones. **Some Rooms:** coffeemakers, 5 efficiencies, refrigerators, cable TV. **Cards:** AE, DS, MC, VI. (D) ⊗

WHITE SALMON—1,900

LODGING

INN OF THE WHITE SALMON — Rates Subject to Change — **Phone:** 509/493-2335

AAA ◆◆ Historic Bed & Breakfast

All Year [BP]	1P: $75	2P/1B: $89	2P/2B: $99	XP: $20

Location: Downtown on SR 141. 172 W Jewett 98672 (PO Box 1549). **Terms:** Reserv deposit, 3 day notice; small pets only. **Facility:** 16 rooms. Cozy atmosphere in a European style hotel. 3 two-bedroom units. Suites, $105-$115; 2 stories; interior corridors; street parking only; whirlpool. **All Rooms:** combo & shower baths, cable TV. **Cards:** AE, CB, DI, DS, MC, VI. (D)

WINTHROP—300

LODGINGS

HOTEL RIO VISTA — Rates Subject to Change — **Phone:** 509/996-3535

◆◆◆ Motel

5/1-10/31	1P: $80	2P/1B: $80	2P/2B: $85	XP: $5
Fri & Sat 3/1-4/30 & 11/1-2/29	1P: $65	2P/1B: $65	2P/2B: $70	XP: $5
Sun-Thurs 3/1-4/30 & 11/1-2/29	1P: $55	2P/1B: $55	2P/2B: $60	XP: $5

Location: Downtown. 285 Riverside 98862 (PO Box 815). **Terms:** Reserv deposit, 14 day notice; no pets. **Facility:** 16 rooms. Overlooking the Methow & Chewuch rivers. 3 stories; interior/exterior corridors; smoke free premises; whirlpool. **All Rooms:** cable TV. **Cards:** MC, VI. *(See ad below)* (D) ⊗

THE MARIGOT HOTEL — Guaranteed Rates — **Phone:** 509/996-3100

AAA ◆◆◆ Motel

Fri & Sat 4/16-10/31 [CP]	1P: $68	2P/1B: $75	2P/2B: $80	XP: $10	D5
Sun-Thurs 4/16-10/31 [CP]	1P: $53	2P/1B: $60	2P/2B: $65	XP: $10	D5
Fri & Sat 3/1-4/15 & 1/2-2/29 [CP]	1P: $45	2P/1B: $50	2P/2B: $55	XP: $10	D5
Sun-Thurs 3/1-4/15, 11/1-1/1 & Sun-Thurs 1/2-2/29 [CP]	1P: $46	2P/1B: $48	2P/2B: $53	XP: $10	D5

Location: On SR 20. 960 Hwy 20 98862 (PO Box 813). Fax: 509/996-3317. **Terms:** Reserv deposit, 5 day notice; pets, $15. **Facility:** 63 rooms. 2 stories; exterior corridors; whirlpool. **Services:** Fee: coin laundry. **Recreation:** Fee: bicycles. **All Rooms:** free movies, cable TV. **Some Rooms:** Fee: VCP's. **Cards:** AE, CB, DI, DS, MC, VI. (D) ⊗

SUN MOUNTAIN LODGE — AAA Special Value Rates — **Phone:** 509/996-2211

AAA ◆◆◆◆ Resort Lodge

6/30-9/3	1P: $125- 175	2P/1B: $125- 175	2P/2B: $125- 175	XP: $16	F12
5/26-6/29, 9/4-10/5 & 12/15-2/29	1P: $115- 160	2P/1B: $115- 160	2P/2B: $115- 160	XP: $16	F12
4/14-5/25 & 10/6-11/2	1P: $85- 130	2P/1B: $85- 130	2P/2B: $85- 130	XP: $16	F12
3/1-4/13 & 11/3-12/14	1P: $49- 90	2P/1B: $49- 90	2P/2B: $49- 90	XP: $16	F12

Location: 10 mi w off SR 20, on top of Sun Mountain. 98862 (PO Box 1000). Fax: 509/996-3133. **Terms:** Check-in 4 pm; reserv deposit, 30 day notice; package plans; 2 night min stay, weekends; weekend rates available; no pets. **Facility:** 78 rooms. Mountaintop setting, panoramic views. Rooms with balcony or patio. 2 stories; interior/exterior corridors; conference facilities; heated pool, whirlpools; exercise room, playground. **Dining:** Dining room, see separate listing. **Recreation:** nature trails; fishing; cross country skiing. Fee: white water rafting; horseback riding. Rental: boats, canoeing, paddleboats; bicycles. **All Rooms:** no TVs. **Some Rooms:** coffeemakers, refrigerators. **Cards:** AE, MC, VI. *(See ad p A167)* (D) (S) ⊗

HOTEL RIO VISTA
BOX815, WINTHROP, WA 98862 (509) 996-3535
"A River Lullaby"
The Methow River sings you to sleep every night at the Hotel Rio Vista.
Cozy rooms, each with a private deck on river's bank. In downtown Winthrop. Smoke free, hot tub, cable TV/AC, phones, minutes to hiking, skiing, horseback riding and lake swimming.

THE VIRGINIAN RESORT Rates Subject to Change **Phone:** 509/996-2535
◆◆ Motor Inn

6/1-10/31		2P/1B: $52- 75	2P/2B: $52- 75	XP: $10	F4
4/16-5/31 & 12/15-2/29	1P: $45	2P/1B: $52- 75	2P/2B: $52- 75	XP: $10	F4
3/1-4/15 & 11/1-12/14	1P: $40	2P/1B: $52- 65	2P/2B: $52- 65	XP: $10	F4

Location: S end of city limits on SR 20. 808 N Cascade Hwy 98862 (PO Box 237). **Terms:** Weekly rates; small pets only, in smoking rooms. **Facility:** 40 rooms. Housekeeping cabins, standard & deluxe motel units all constructed with cedar logs; some with fireplace; some with balcony overlooking Methow River. 1-bedroom house, $150; 3-bedroom fireplace unit, $225; 1-2 stories; exterior corridors; whirlpool, heated pool open 5/15-9/30. **Dining:** Restaurant, see separate listing. **Services:** winter plug-ins. **Recreation:** fishing; cross country skiing. **All Rooms:** combo & shower baths, no phones. **Some Rooms:** coffeemakers, kitchen, microwaves, refrigerators. **Cards:** AE, DS, MC, VI. Ⓓ ⊗

WINTHROP INN Rates Subject to Change **Phone:** 509/996-2217
◆◆ Motel

Fri & Sat 6/17-9/18	1P: $55	2P/1B: $60	2P/2B: $65	XP: $5
Sun-Thurs 6/17-9/18	1P: $49	2P/1B: $56	2P/2B: $61	XP: $5
3/1-6/16 & 9/19-2/29	1P: $38	2P/1B: $48	2P/2B: $53	XP: $5

Location: 1 mi e on SR 20. 950 Hwy 20 98862 (PO Box 265). **Terms:** Credit card guarantee, 3 day notice; no pets. **Facility:** 30 rooms. Along Methow River. Clean comfortable rooms. 2 stories; interior corridors; heated pool, whirlpool. **Recreation:** fishing; downhill skiing. **All Rooms:** shower baths, cable TV, no phones. **Cards:** MC, VI. Ⓓ ⊗

WINTHROP MTN VIEW CHALETS Guaranteed Rates **Phone:** 509/996-3113
AAA ◆◆◆ Cottage
All Year 2P/1B: $59
Location: S end of town. 1120 Hwy 20 Rd 98862 (PO Box 280). **Terms:** Sr. discount; reserv deposit, 30 day notice; weekly rates; no pets. **Facility:** 6 rooms. Delux cabins, modern amenities, overlooking the Methow River. Exterior corridors. **All Rooms:** coffeemakers, efficiencies, microwaves, refrigerators, no phones. **Cards:** MC, VI. Ⓓ ⊗

RESTAURANTS

DUCK BRAND RESTAURANT **Dinner:** $11-$20 **Phone:** 509/996-2192
◆ American
Location: Center. 248 Riverside 98862. **Hours:** 7 am-9:30 pm. Closed: 11/23. **Features:** carryout; beer & wine only; a la carte. Indoor & deck dining in an atmosphere of flowers & curios. Also offers steaks, homemade cheesecakes & pies. Imported beer & wine, expresso, in house bakery. **Cards:** AE, MC, VI. ⊗

SUN MOUNTAIN LODGE DINING ROOM **Dinner:** $21-$30 **Phone:** 509/996-2211
AAA ◆◆◆◆ Continental
Location: In Sun Mountain Lodge. 98862. **Hours:** 7-11 am, 11:30-2 & 5:30-10 pm. **Reservations:** suggested. **Features:** children's menu; cocktails & lounge; a la carte. Located above Methow Valley; scenic views of North Cascade Mountains. Smoke free premises. **Cards:** AE, MC, VI. ⊗

THE VIRGINIAN RESTAURANT **Dinner:** $11-$20 **Phone:** 509/996-2536
◆◆ American
Location: In The Virginian Resort. 816 N Cascade Hwy 98862. **Hours:** 7:30 am-9 pm. **Reservations:** suggested. **Features:** children's menu; carryout; cocktails & lounge. Northwest regional cuisine in cedar log dining rooms. Dining outdoors on deck. Smoke free premises. **Cards:** AE, DS, MC, VI. ⊗

WOODLAND—2,500

LODGINGS

GRANDMA'S HOUSE BED & BREAKFAST Rates Subject to Change **Phone:** 360/225-7002
◆◆ Bed & Breakfast

3/1-4/30 & 10/1-2/29 [BP]	1P: $37	2P/1B: $53
5/1-9/30 [BP]	1P: $39	2P/1B: $55

Location: 9 mi e on SR 503 & Fredrickson. 4551 Lewis River Rd 98674. **Terms:** Reserv deposit, 4 day notice; no pets. **Facility:** 2 rooms. 2 stories; interior corridors; smoke free premises. **All Rooms:** no A/C, no phones, no TVs. **Cards:** MC, VI. Ⓓ ⊗

LEWIS RIVER INN Rates Subject to Change **Phone:** 360/225-6257
AAA ◆◆◆ Motel
All Year 1P: $41- 56 2P/1B: $45- 56 2P/2B: $49- 59 XP: $4 F16
Location: From I-5 at exit 21, 1/4 mi e. 1100 Lewis River Rd 98674. Fax: 360/225-9515. **Terms:** Sr. discount; credit card guarantee, 3 day notice; small pets only, $5. **Facility:** 49 rooms. Along the Lewis River. Some rooms with balcony. 2 stories; exterior corridors. **Dining:** Restaurant nearby. **All Rooms:** cable TV. **Some Rooms:** microwaves, refrigerators. **Cards:** AE, CB, DI, DS, MC, VI. Ⓓ Ⓢ ⊗

SCANDIA MOTEL Rates Subject to Change **Phone:** 360/225-8006
AAA ◆◆ Motel

5/15-9/30	1P: $38	2P/1B: $40	2P/2B: $44	XP: $5
3/1-5/14 & 10/1-2/29	1P: $32	2P/1B: $34	2P/2B: $38	XP: $5

Location: W of I-5 exit 21. 1123 Hoffman St 98674. Fax: 360/225-7933. **Terms:** Reserv deposit, 4 day notice; pets, $5. **Facility:** 13 rooms. 9 two-bedroom units. 9 kitchens, $5; 1 story; exterior corridors; whirlpool. **Services:** Fee: coin laundry. **All Rooms:** utensils extra charge, free movies, cable TV. **Some Rooms:** microwaves, refrigerators. **Cards:** AE, DS, MC, VI. Ⓓ ⊗

Peak Experience

Sun Mountain Lodge near Winthrop is the ultimate getaway. Sumptuous rooms awarded Best in Hotel Design by *Interiors Magazine.* Stellar dining in our AAA Four Diamond restaurant. All with stunning views. Truly a peak experience! Call or write for a free brochure; 800-572-0493. P.O. Box 1000, Winthrop, WA 98862

Sun Mountain Lodge

WOODLANDER INN — AAA Special Value Rates — **Phone:** 360/225-6548

◆◆◆ Motel

All Year 1P: $42 2P/1B: $46 2P/2B: $50 XP: $5 D

Location: Off I-5 at exit 21. 1500 Atlantic St 98674. **Terms:** Reserv deposit; weekly rates; 3 night min stay, 7/20-7/24; pets, $3-$5. **Facility:** 61 rooms. 2 stories; exterior corridors; meeting rooms; heated indoor pool, whirlpool. **All Rooms:** cable TV. **Some Rooms:** refrigerators. Fee: microwaves. **Cards:** AE, CB, DI, DS, MC, VI.

YAKIMA—54,800

LODGINGS

BALI HAI MOTEL — Guaranteed Rates — **Phone:** 509/452-7178

◆◆ Motel

All Year 1P: $25- 28 2P/1B: $30- 32 2P/2B: $34- 36 XP: $5 D15

Location: 3/4 mi n on US 97 business route; 1 1/4 mi s of I-82, exit 31. 710 N 1st St 98901. **Terms:** Sr. discount; reserv deposit, 3 day notice; small pets only, $3. **Facility:** 28 rooms. Smaller rooms. 4 two-bedroom units. 1 story; exterior corridors; small pool. **All Rooms:** free movies, shower baths, cable TV. **Cards:** AE, DS, MC, VI.

BEST WESTERN RIO MIRADA MOTOR INN — Rates Subject to Change — **Phone:** 509/457-4444

◆◆◆ Motel

All Year 1P: $51 2P/1B: $56 2P/2B: $61 XP: $10 F6

Location: E of I-82 exit 33 along Yakima River. 1603 Terrace Heights Dr 98901. Fax: 509/453-7593. **Terms:** Reserv deposit, 4 day notice; no pets. **Facility:** 96 rooms. All rooms with river view & private balcony. 6 efficiencies, $5 extra; 4 stories; interior corridors; meeting rooms; heated pool, whirlpool; exercise room, Yakima River Greenway Recreation Trail. **Dining:** Restaurant nearby. **Services:** airport transportation. Fee: coin laundry. **Recreation:** fishing. **All Rooms:** free movies, combo & shower baths, cable TV. **Some Rooms:** coffeemakers, refrigerators. **Cards:** AE, CB, DI, DS, MC, VI. Roll in showers.

CAVANAUGH'S AT YAKIMA CENTER — Rates Subject to Change — **Phone:** 509/248-5900

◆◆◆ Motor Inn

All Year 1P: $57- 90 2P/1B: $67- 90 2P/2B: $67- 90 XP: $10 F18

Location: 3/4 mi w of I-82, exit 33. 607 E Yakima Ave 98901. Fax: 509/575-8975. **Terms:** Sr. discount; credit card guarantee; pets, $10. **Facility:** 152 rooms. Many private balconies or patios. 2 stories; interior/exterior corridors; conference facilities; seasonal pool. **Dining & Entertainment:** Dining room; 6:30 am-10 pm; $5-$18; cocktails/lounge; 24-hour room service; entertainment. **Services:** valet laundry; airport transportation. **All Rooms:** free movies, combo & shower baths, cable TV. **Some Rooms:** refrigerators, whirlpools. **Cards:** AE, CB, DI, DS, MC, VI.

(See color ad p A151)

ECONO LODGE — Rates Subject to Change — **Phone:** 509/457-6155

◆◆ Motel

All Year 1P: $40 2P/1B: $45 2P/2B: $50 XP: $5 F18

Location: 1/2 mi n on US 97 business route; 1 1/2 mi s of I-82 exit 31. 510 N 1st St 98901. Fax: 509/575-4653. **Terms:** Sr. discount; reserv deposit, 3 day notice; small pets only, $10. **Facility:** 36 rooms. 1 two-bedroom unit. 2 stories; exterior corridors; small heated pool. **Dining:** Restaurant nearby. **All Rooms:** cable TV. **Some Rooms:** refrigerators. **Cards:** AE, CB, DI, DS, MC, VI.

RED CARPET MOTOR INN — Rates Subject to Change — **Phone:** 509/457-1131

◆ Motel

All Year 1P: $34 2P/1B: $38 2P/2B: $45 XP: $5 F12

Location: From I-82, exit Hwy 12W to 16th Ave then 3/4 mi sw on 16th Ave. 1608 Fruitvale Blvd 98902. Fax: 509/457-1391. **Terms:** Sr. discount; reserv deposit, 3 day notice; weekly rates; pets, $6. **Facility:** 29 rooms. 4 two-bedroom units. 2 efficiencies, $6 extra; 1 story; exterior corridors; heated pool, sauna. **Services:** Fee: coin laundry. **All Rooms:** free movies, combo & shower baths, cable TV. **Some Rooms:** radios. Fee: microwaves, refrigerators. **Cards:** DS, MC, VI.

RED LION INN — AAA Special Value Rates — **Phone:** 509/453-0391

◆◆◆ Motel

All Year 1P: $59- 69 2P/1B: $69- 79 2P/2B: $69- 79 XP: $10

Location: 3/4 mi n on US 97 business route; 1 1/4 mi s of I-82 exit 31. 818 N 1st St 98901. Fax: 509/453-8348. **Terms:** Credit card guarantee; pets. **Facility:** 58 rooms. Large modest rooms. 2 two-bedroom units. 2 stories; exterior corridors; heated pool. **Dining:** Restaurant nearby. **Services:** data ports. **All Rooms:** free movies, cable TV. **Some Rooms:** microwaves, refrigerators. **Cards:** AE, CB, DI, DS, MC, VI.

RED LION INN/YAKIMA VALLEY — Rates Subject to Change — **Phone:** 509/248-7850

◆◆◆ Motor Inn

All Year 1P: $77- 84 2P/1B: $87- 94 2P/2B: $87- 94 XP: $10 F17

Location: On US 97 business route; 1/2 mi s of I-82 exit 31. 1507 N 1st St 98901. Fax: 509/575-1694. **Terms:** Package plans; small pets only. **Facility:** 209 rooms. Most with private balcony or patio. 3 two-bedroom units. 2 stories; interior corridors; conference facilities; 2 heated pools, whirlpool. **Dining:** Dining room, coffee shop; 6 am-11 pm; $6-$12; cocktails; 24-hour room service. **Services:** data ports; valet laundry; airport transportation. **All Rooms:** combo & shower baths, cable TV. Fee: movies. **Some Rooms:** coffeemakers. Fee: microwaves, refrigerators. **Cards:** AE, CB, DI, DS, JCB, MC, VI. Roll in showers.

SUN COUNTRY INN — Rates Subject to Change — **Phone:** 509/248-5650

◆◆◆ Motel

All Year [CP] 1P: $52- 66 2P/1B: $57- 67 2P/2B: $66- 71 XP: $5 F17

Location: 1 3/4 mi n on US 97 business route; 1/4 mi s of I-82 exit 31. 1700 N 1st St 98901. Fax: 509/457-6486. **Terms:** Sr. discount; reserv deposit, 3 day notice; 2 night min stay, weekends 3/1-11/30; no pets. **Facility:** 69 rooms. 2 stories; exterior corridors; heated pool, sauna. **Services:** Fee: coin laundry. **All Rooms:** free movies, cable TV. **Some Rooms:** 6 efficiencies. Fee: microwaves, refrigerators. **Cards:** AE, CB, DI, DS, JCB, MC, VI. *(See color ad below)*

SUN COUNTRY INN
1700 N. 1st. Street
Yakima, WA 98901

The sun never sets on exceptional service.
- Pool / Sauna • Free HBO
- Free Sunrise Breakfast • Kitchenettes
- Executive Suites • Senior Discounts
- Commercial / Govt. Rates

1 (800) 559-3675

AAA

RESTAURANTS

MARTI'S — **Dinner:** $11-$20 — **Phone:** 509/248-2062
◆◆ American
Location: E of I-82, exit 33. 1601 Terrace Heights 98901. **Hours:** 6 am-10 pm. Closed: 11/23, 12/25. **Reservations:** suggested. **Features:** Sunday brunch; children's menu; carryout; salad bar; cocktails & lounge. On Yakima River, offering family dining with an in house bakery. **Cards:** AE, DI, MC, VI.

THE MUSTARD SEED ORIENTAL CAFE — **Dinner:** $11-$20 — **Phone:** 509/576-8013
◆◆ Ethnic
Location: Across from Yakima Mall. E 402 Yakima Ave 98901. **Hours:** 11 am-9 pm, Fri & Sat-10 pm, Sun noon-9 pm. Closed major holidays. **Features:** carryout; cocktails & lounge. Asian cuisine; light sauces, lean meat, fresh vegetables blended for family dining. **Cards:** AE, DI, DS, MC, VI.

SANTIAGO'S GOURMET MEXICAN COOKING — **Dinner:** up to $10 — **Phone:** 509/453-1644
◆◆ Mexican
Location: Center. 111 E Yakima Ave 98901. **Hours:** 11 am-2:30 & 5-9:30 pm, Fri & Sat-10:30 pm, Sun 5 pm-9:30 pm. Closed major holidays. **Features:** children's menu; health conscious menu; carryout; cocktails & lounge; a la carte. Casual dining room with attractive southwestern decor. **Cards:** MC, VI.

Affordable Adventure
Make your next vacation an adventure – at a price that won't make paying the bill adventuresome. Travel consultants will help you plan a vacation that will meet all your needs. From a quiet getaway to a family gathering, AAA can arrange for the most economical or the most extravagant use of your vacation dollar. Come to your local AAA Travel Agency for the vacation adventure you can afford to enjoy.
AAA
The Most Trusted Name in Travel.®

Pull out the AAA state map to enhance navigation to your TourBook destination.

FOR YOUR INFORMATION

Four handy sections to help make your vacation planning easier.

AAA Clubs and Branch Offices

Need a sheet map or Triptik map? Run out of travelers checks? Want the latest update on local road conditions? All this information and more awaits you at more than 1,000 AAA and CAA clubs and offices across the United States and Canada— a boon for travelers in an unfamiliar state, province or city. Each listing provides the office address, phone number and hours of service.

Temperature Chart

Knowing what clothes to pack for a trip can make the difference between pleasant vacationing and unpleasant surprises. Use the temperature chart to help determine your on-the-road wardrobe. The chart, found in each TourBook, lists average monthly maximum and minimum temperatures for representative cities.

Driving Distances Map

For safety's sake, it makes sense to take regular breaks while driving on the open road. The driving distances map is a quick and useful reference for trip planning—from a 1-day excursion to a cross-country jaunt. It provides both the mileage and the average driving time (excluding stops) between towns and cities located throughout a state or province.

Border Information

Is it permissible to transport those bottles of fine wine or that treasured memento across international lines? Don't make an uninformed decision. Turn to the section on border information instead. It's a fact-packed assessment of just what and how much you can bring back.

Going somewhere?
AAA has already been, so ask us
how to get there, what to do,
where to stay and what to see. We know!

AAA OFFICES

Cities with main offices are listed in bold type with ALL CAPITAL letters. Toll-free member service number in italics. All are closed Saturdays, Sundays and holidays unless otherwise indicated.

The type of service provided is designated below the name of the city where the office is located:

- **Auto travel services, including books/maps, marked maps and on-demand Triptik maps +**
- **Auto travel services, including books/maps, marked maps, but no on-demand Triptik maps ●**
- **Provides books/maps only. No marked maps or on-demand Triptik maps available ■**
- **Travel agency services ▲**

OREGON

BEND—AAA Oregon, 20350 Empire Ave., #5, 97701. M-F 8-5. (503) 382-1303. *(800) 464-1303.*+▲

CLACKAMAS—AAA Oregon, 10365 S.E. Sunnyside Rd., 97015-9783. M-F 8-5. (503) 241-6800.+▲

COOS BAY—AAA Oregon, 1705 Ocean Blvd., S.E., 97420. M-F 8-5. (503) 269-7432.+

CORVALLIS—AAA Oregon, 815 N.W. 9th, #L105, 97330. M-F 8-5. (503) 757-2535.+▲

EUGENE—AAA Oregon, 983 Willagillespie Rd., 97401-6716. M-F 8-5. (503) 484-0661.+▲

KLAMATH FALLS—AAA Oregon, 2229 N. Eldorado, 97601. M-F 8-5. (503) 882-3439.+

MEDFORD—AAA Oregon, 1777 E. Barnett Rd., 97504. M-F 8-5. (503) 779-7170. *(800) 325-3089.*+▲

PENDLETON—AAA Oregon, 328 S.E. Emigrant St., 97801. M-F 8-5. (503) 276-2243.+

PORTLAND—AAA OREGON, 600 S.W. Market St., 97201. M-F 8-5. (503) 222-6734. *(800) 452-1643.*+▲

PORTLAND—AAA Oregon, 8555 S.W. Apple Way, 97225. M-F 8-5. (503) 243-6444. *(800) 452-1643.*+▲

SALEM—AAA Oregon, 2909 Ryan Dr., S.E., 97301. M-F 8-5. (503) 581-1608. *(800) 962-5855.*+▲

WARRENTON—AAA Oregon, 5 Hwy., 101, 97146. M-F 8-5. (503) 861-3118. *(800) 281-3118.*+

WASHINGTON

BELLEVUE—AAA Washington, 13201 Bellevue/Redmond Rd., 98005-2536; *Mailing Address: POB C-92000, 98009-2056.* M-F 8:30-5, W 8:30-6:30. (206) 455-3933. *(800) 562-2582.*+▲

BELLINGHAM—AAA Washington, 3600 Meridian St., 98225. M-F 8:30-5, W 8:30-6:30. (206) 733-2740. *(800) 562-2582.*+▲

BREMERTON—AAA Washington, 5700 Kitsap Way, 98312-2234; *Mailing Address: POB 1110, 98310-1110.* M-F 8:30-5, W 8:30-6:30. (206) 377-0081. *(800) 562-2582.*+▲

EVERETT—AAA Washington, 909 S.E. Everett Mall Way, 98208; *Mailing Address: POB 1126, 98206.* M-F 8:30-5, Phone Service W 8:30-6:30. (206) 353-7222. *(800) 562-2582.*+▲

KENNEWICK—AAA Washington, 6725 W. Clearwater Ave., #A, 99336-7698. M-F 8:30-5, W 8:30-6:30. (509) 735-6351. *(800) 562-2582.*+

LYNNWOOD—AAA Washington, 20000 68th Ave., W., 98036; *Mailing Address: POB 5230, 98046.* M-F 8:30-5. (206) 640-1204. *(800) 562-2582.*▲

LYNNWOOD—AAA Washington, 4100 200th St., S.W., 98036-6734; *Mailing Address: POB 1729, 98046-1729.* M-F 8:30-5, W 8:30-6:30. (206) 775-3571. *(800) 562-2582.*+▲

OLYMPIA—AAA Washington, 1000 E. Union Ave., 98501-1540; *Mailing Address: POB 2136, 98507-2136.* M-F 8:30-5, W 8:30-6:30. (206) 357-5561. *(800) 562-2582.*+

RENTON—AAA Washington, 3900 E. Valley Rd., #105, 98055-4805. M-F 8:30-5, W 8:30-6:30. (206) 251-6040. *(800) 562-2582.*+▲

SEATTLE—AAA Washington, 1420-5th Ave., Suite 450, 98101. M-F 8:30-5. (206) 623-6047.▲

SEATTLE—AAA Washington, 330 Sixth Ave., N., 98109-0628. M-F 8:30-5. (206) 448-5353. *(800) 562-2582.*+▲

SPOKANE—INLAND AUTO. ASSOCIATION, 1717 W. 4th Ave., 99204-1795; *Mailing Address: POB 2518, 99220-2518.* M-F 8-5. (509) 455-3400. *(800) 456-3222.*+▲

SPOKANE—Inland Auto. Association, 7307 N. Division St., #103, 99208. M-F 8:30-5. (509) 455-3433.+▲

SPOKANE—Inland Auto. Association, 9610 E. Sprague Ave., 99206-3671. M-F 8:45-5. (509) 455-3454.+▲

TACOMA—AAA Washington, 1801 S. Union Ave., 98405-1991. M-F 8:30-5, W 8:30-6:30. (206) 756-3050. *(800) 562-2582.*+▲

VANCOUVER—AAA Washington, 4301 E. 4th Plain Blvd., 98661-5651. M-F 8:30-5, W 8:30-6:30. (206) 696-4081. *(800) 562-2582.*+

WALLA WALLA—Inland Auto. Association, 229 E. Main St., 99362-2095. M-F 9-5:30. (509) 525-9213.+▲

WENATCHEE—AAA Washington, 221 N. Mission St., 98801-2003; *Mailing Address: POB 2025, 98807-2025.* M-F 8:30-5, W 8:30-6:30. (509) 662-8550. *(800) 562-2582.*+

YAKIMA—AAA Washington, 407 N. First St., 98901-2305; *Mailing Address: POB 1727, 98907-1727.* M-F 8:30-5, W 8:30-6:30. (509) 248-6520. *(800) 562-2582.*+▲

How Do You Get There From Here?

With AAA Triptik maps. They're complete routings made up of detailed strip maps tailored to your needs.Triptiks provide driving times, mileages, points of interest, and up-to-the-minute information on highway conditions and construction and detours.

Temperature Averages - Maximum/Minimum

From the records of the National Weather Service

	JAN.	FEB.	MAR.	APR.	MAY	JUNE	JULY	AUG.	SEPT.	OCT.	NOV.	DEC.
OREGON												
Eugene	45/33	50/35	55/37	62/40	68/44	74/48	82/51	82/50	76/47	64/42	53/38	47/36
Medford	44/29	51/32	58/34	65/38	72/43	79/49	89/55	88/53	82/47	68/40	53/34	45/32
Pendleton	38/25	44/29	53/35	62/40	71/47	78/53	88/59	85/57	77/51	64/43	48/33	42/30
Portland	44/33	49/35	54/38	62/42	67/47	72/52	79/56	78/55	74/51	63/45	52/38	46/36
WASHINGTON												
Seattle	46/37	49/38	53/40	59/44	66/49	70/53	75/56	74/56	69/53	60/48	52/42	48/39
Spokane	31/19	37/22	47/29	59/36	68/43	73/49	84/55	81/54	73/47	59/38	42/28	35/24
Walla Walla	39/27	45/32	54/38	65/44	72/50	79/56	89/63	87/61	78/54	65/46	49/36	44/32
Yakima	36/18	45/23	55/29	66/35	74/43	80/49	89/53	86/51	79/44	66/35	49/27	40/23

CONTACT YOUR LOCAL AAA OFFICE

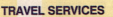

Thoughtful gift throughout the year
AAA GIFT MEMBERSHIPS–

TRAVEL SERVICES
- 1,000 full-service travel agencies
- AAA travel agencies offer domestic and international airline tickets, cruises and tours to anywhere in the world
- *Show Your Card & Save*SM program

FINANCIAL SERVICES
- Fee-free American Express Travelers Cheques®
- AAA/Visa • AAA/MasterCard

INSURANCE SERVICES
- Travel Accident Insurance, accidental death, term life, senior age and juvenile life products • Bail bond protection

AUTOMOTIVE ENGINEERING & ROAD SERVICE
- Members can receive road service and other information from AAA SUPERNUMBER ® - 24-hour toll-free service.

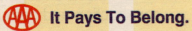

AAA **It Pays To Belong.**

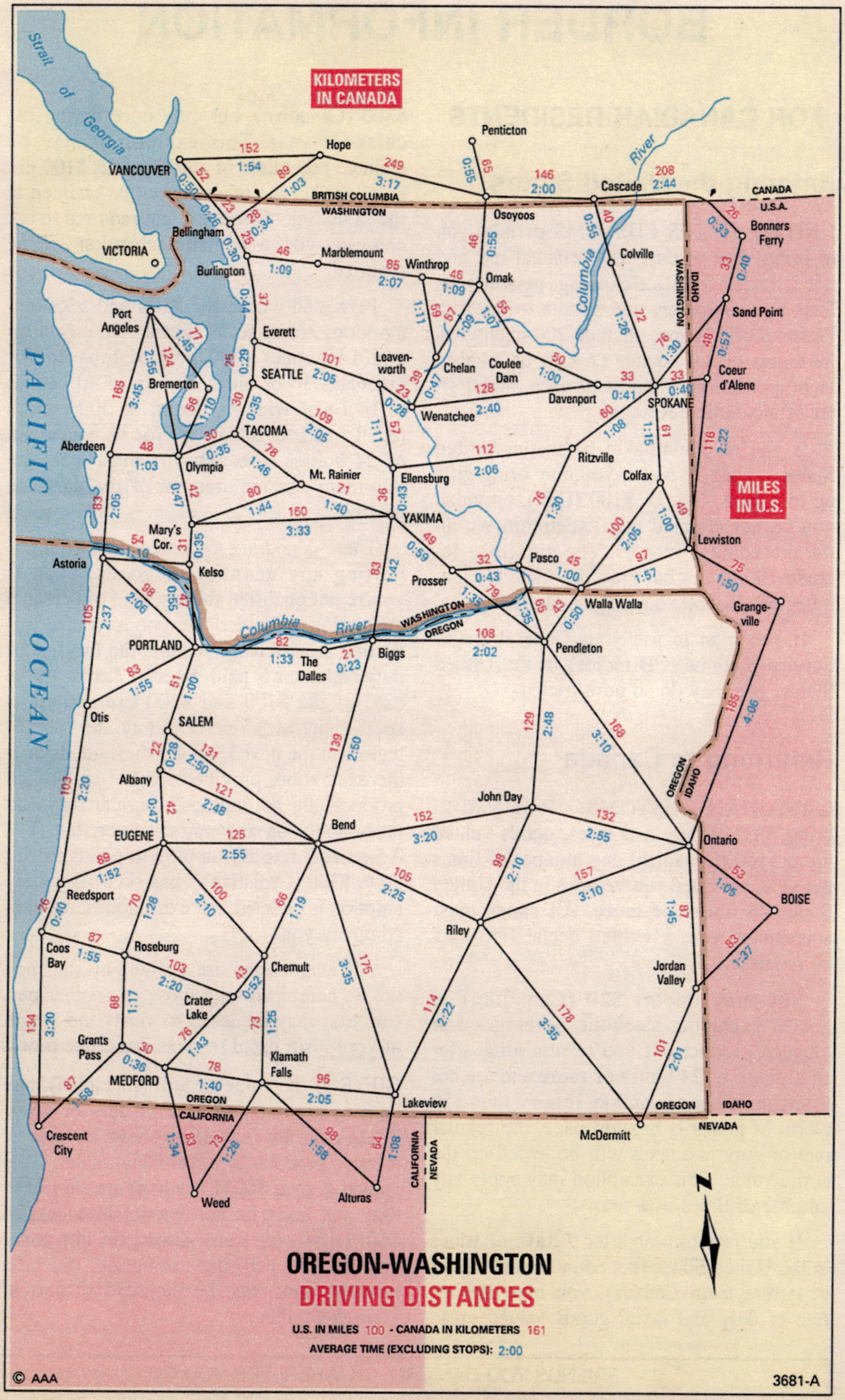
KILOMETERS IN CANADA
MILES IN U.S.
Strait of Georgia
PACIFIC OCEAN
Columbia River
BRITISH COLUMBIA
WASHINGTON
OREGON
IDAHO
CALIFORNIA
NEVADA
CANADA
U.S.A.
VANCOUVER
VICTORIA
Hope
Penticton
Osoyoos
Cascade
Bellingham
Burlington
Marblemount
Winthrop
Omak
Colville
Bonners Ferry
Sand Point
Port Angeles
Everett
SEATTLE
Bremerton
Leavenworth
Chelan
Coulee Dam
Davenport
SPOKANE
Coeur d'Alene
Wenatchee
Aberdeen
TACOMA
Olympia
Mt. Rainier
Ellensburg
Ritzville
Colfax
YAKIMA
Mary's Cor.
Astoria
Kelso
Prosser
Pasco
Walla Walla
Lewiston
Grangeville
PORTLAND
The Dalles
Biggs
Pendleton
Otis
SALEM
Albany
EUGENE
Bend
John Day
Ontario
Reedsport
Coos Bay
Roseburg
Chemult
Riley
BOISE
Jordan Valley
Crater Lake
Grants Pass
MEDFORD
Klamath Falls
Lakeview
McDermitt
Crescent City
Weed
Alturas
N
OREGON-WASHINGTON
DRIVING DISTANCES
U.S. IN MILES 100 - CANADA IN KILOMETERS 161
AVERAGE TIME (EXCLUDING STOPS): 2:00
© AAA
3681-A

BORDER INFORMATION

FOR CANADIAN RESIDENTS

Entering the United States

UNITED STATES CUSTOMS permits you to bring, free of duty, for personal use and not intended for sale: clothing, personal effects and equipment appropriate to the trip. Personal effects may include 200 cigarettes, 50 cigars or 4.4 pounds (2 kgs) of tobacco or proportionate amounts of each, and 1 liter of alcoholic beverage.

If you're planning to be in the United States at least 72 hours, you may bring gifts up to a total value of $100 (U.S.), provided you've not claimed this exemption within the preceding 6 months. The gifts may include 100 cigars but may *not* include cigarettes or alcoholic beverages.

If you plan to use your General Radio Service Stations (CB radios) in the United States, you may do so unrestricted.

Returning to Canada

CANADIAN CUSTOMS allows you to bring, free of duty and taxes, goods valued up to $100 (Canadian) any number of times per year, provided you've been in the United States **48 hours or more.** All goods must accompany you; a written declaration *may* be required.

You may import $20 (Canadian) in goods, excluding alcoholic beverages and tobacco products, if you're returning after an absence of **24 hours or more** and are not using any other exemption. If more than $20 worth of goods is brought back, the regular rate of duty and taxes will be levied on the entire value. This exemption may apply any number of times in a year.

If you're returning after **7 days or more** in the United States (not counting the day of departure from Canada), you may import, free of duty and taxes, goods valued up to $300 (Canadian), but only once during the calendar year. This exemption may be claimed regardless of any previous $100 exemption, but the two may not be claimed at the same time. Goods are not required to accompany you; a written declaration *will* be required.

Permitted within the $100 and $300 exemptions are up to 50 cigars, 200 cigarettes and 14 ounces (400 gm) of tobacco for claimants 16 or older, and up to 40 ounces (1.14 L) of wine or liquor, or 300 ounces (8.5 L) of beer and/or ale (or its equivalent of 24 bottles or cans). You must meet the minimum age requirement of the province entered.

There is nothing to prevent you from importing any quantity of goods, even if you're not qualified for any kind of personal exemption, provided the goods you're importing are not restricted and the full rate of duty and taxes is paid. **Special Tariff:** In the case of the $100 and $300 exemptions, a special rate of 3.5 percent duty and taxes is levied on the next $300 worth of goods over the exemption, provided alcohol or tobacco products are not included; regular duty and taxes apply on any amount over that. The 3.5-percent rate also applies to goods valued up to $300 (Canadian) when no personal exemption is claimed. All extra goods must accompany you.

All exemptions are individual and may not be combined with those of another person. You may be asked to verify the length of your visit; dated receipts constitute proof.

GIFTS to the value of $60 (Canadian) may be sent from abroad, free of duty or taxes. These may not include alcoholic beverages, tobacco products or advertising matter. Gifts valued at over $60 (Canadian) are subject to duty and taxes on the amount in excess of $60. Gifts *sent* from abroad do not count against your personal exemption, but gifts brought back *must* be included as part of your exemption.

POINTS OF INTEREST INDEX

INDEX ABBREVIATIONS

NB.......... national battlefield
NBP.......... national battlefield park
NC.......... national cemetery
NF.......... national forest
NHM.......... national historic(al) monument
NHP.......... national historic(al) park
NHS.......... national historic(al) site
NL.......... national lakeshore
NME.......... national memorial
NMO.......... national monument
NMP.......... national military park
NP.......... national park
NRA.......... national recreation area
NR.......... national river
NS.......... national seashore
NWR.......... national wildlife refuge
PHP.......... provincial historic(al) park
PHS.......... provincial historic(al) site
PP.......... provincial park
SF.......... state forest
SHM.......... state historic(al) monument
SHP.......... state historic(al) park
SHS.......... state historic(al) site
SME.......... state memorial
SP.......... state park
SRA.......... state recreation area

EVENTS-AVIATION

EVENTS-CARNIVAL & CIRCUSES

EVENTS-CRAFT SHOWS

EVENTS-DANCES

EVENTS-FAIRS

EVENTS-FESTIVALS

EVENTS-PAGEANTS, PARADES, DAYS

EVENTS-POWWOWS

EVENTS-RODEOS

EVENTS-SHOWS

EVENTS-SPORTS

EXHIBITS & COLLECTIONS-GENERAL

EXHIBITS & COLLECTIONS-ANIMALS & BIRDS

EXHIBITS & COLLECTIONS-AVIATION

EXHIBITS & COLLECTIONS-CLOCKS

EXHIBITS & COLLECTIONS-DOLLS & TOYS

... & COLLECTIONS-HISTORICAL

EXHIBITS & COLLECTIONS-INDIAN

EXHIBITS & COLLECTIONS-MUSIC

EXHIBITS & COLLECTIONS-SCIENCE

EXHIBITS & COLLECTIONS-VEHICLES

EXHIBITS & COLLECTIONS-WEAPONS

FARMS

FISH HATCHERIES

GRAVES & TOMBS

HALLS OF FAME

HISTORIC BUILDINGS & HOUSES

HISTORIC DOCUMENTS, MANUSCRIPTS & RARE BOOKS

HISTORIC SITES

INDIAN MOUNDS, REMAINS, RUINS

INDIAN PICTOGRAPHS & PETROGLYPHS

INDIAN RESERVATIONS & VILLAGES

INDUSTRIAL TOURS

ISLANDS

LAKES, PONDS & RESERVOIRS

LIBRARIES

LIGHTHOUSES

LOCKS

MARINE ATTRACTIONS

MARKETS

MEMORIALS

MILLS

MINES & MINERALS

MISSIONS

MONUMENTS-GENERAL

MONUMENTS, NATIONAL; STATE

MOUNTAINS

MURALS & MOSAICS

MUSEUMS

MUSIC EVENTS

MUSIC HALLS & OPERA HOUSES

NATURAL PHENOMENA

NATURE CENTERS

NATURE TRAILS

NAUTICAL TOURS

OBSERVATORIES

PARKS, CITY; STATE; PROVINCIAL

PARKS, NATIONAL

PETRIFIED FORESTS

PLANETARIUMS

PLAYS, DRAMAS & MUSICALS

RACETRACKS-AUTO

RACETRACKS-DOG

RACETRACKS-HORSE

RAILROADS

RAILROADS-LOCOMOTIVES & CARS

RAILWAYS & SKI LIFTS, CABLE; COG; INCLINE; NARROW GAUGE

RANCHES

SHIPS & BOATS

SHOPS, FIRMS & STORES

SIGHTSEEING-AIRCRAFT RIDES & TOURS

SIGHTSEEING TOURS

SIGHTSEEING TOURS-BOATS

SIGHTSEEING TOURS-HOUSE & GARDEN

SIGHTSEEING TOURS-RAFTING/CANOEING

SPORTS ARENAS

SPORTS EVENTS-AUTO & MOTORCYCLE RACES

SPORTS EVENTS-FISHING

SPORTS EVENTS-GENERAL

SPORTS EVENTS-WATER SPORTS

SPRINGS

STATUES

STREETS, PLAZAS, SQUARES, CITY AREAS

THEATERS

TOWERS

TREES

VIEWS

VISITOR CENTERS

VISITOR INFORMATION

WALKING TOURS

WATERFALLS

WATER PARKS

WAX MUSEUMS

WILDERNESS AREAS

WILDLIFE SANCTUARIES

WINERIES

ZOOLOGICAL PARKS & EXHIBITS

ZOOLOGICAL PARKS & EXHIBITS-CHILDREN'S ZOOS

ATTRACTION ADMISSION DISCOUNT INDEX

See individual attraction listings for details. Present your valid AAA or CAA card when purchasing tickets, whether or not a listing shows a discount; some attractions not formally enrolled in the program may still give members a discount.

OREGON

WASHINGTON

BED & BREAKFAST LODGINGS INDEX

Some bed and breakfasts listed below might have historical significance. Those properties are also referenced in the Historical index. The indication that continental [CP] or full breakfast [BP] is included in the room rate reflects whether a property is a Bed-and-Breakfast facility.

OREGON

Accommodations

WASHINGTON

Accommodations

COUNTRY INNS INDEX

Some of the following country inns can also be considered as bed-and-breakfast operations. The indication that continental [CP] or full breakfast [BP] is included in the room rate reflects whether a property is a Bed-and-Breakfast facility.

OREGON

Accommodation

WASHINGTON

Accommodations

Restaurant

Want to stay close to the stadium? The ocean? Convention center? Spotting maps of selected major metropolitan and resort areas will help you choose the best location.

HISTORICAL LODGINGS & RESTAURANTS INDEX

Some of the following historical lodgings can also be considered as bed-and-breakfast operations. The indication that continental [CP] or full breakfast [BP] is included in the room rate reflects whether a property is a Bed-and-Breakfast facility.

OREGON

Accommodations

Restaurants

WASHINGTON

Accommodations

Restaurants

RESORTS INDEX

Many establishments are located in resort areas; however, the following places have extensive on-premises recreational facilities:

OREGON

Accommodations

WASHINGTON

Accommodations

SHOW YOUR MEMBERSHIP CARD
WHEN YOU REGISTER
AT AAA APPROVED ESTABLISHMENTS.

"One phone call is all it takes to find a great room in any town worth singing about."

Whether you're traveling to Phoenix or Wichita or any other great American town, you'll find the right hotel at the right price at Quality, Comfort, Clarion and Sleep hotels, and Econo Lodge, Rodeway and Friendship inns. These hotels have many ways for AAA members to save, including a 10% AAA discount (more at some locations), and a family plan in which kids 18 and under stay free in their parent's or grandparent's room.

Plus they offer AT&T In-Room Long Distance Service for your AT&T Calling Card, AT&T Universal Card and operator-assisted calls (at most locations). For reservations at more than 2,200 North American locations, call 1-800-228-1AAA or your local AAA club. And get a deal that's worth singing about, too.

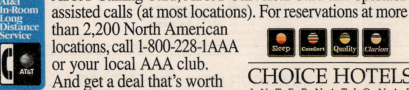

AT&T In-Room Long Distance Service

AT&T

Helping you along the way.™

Sleep Comfort Quality Clarion

CHOICE HOTELS INTERNATIONAL

Friendship Econo Lodge Rodeway

Call 1-800-228-1AAA

Only one discount per stay. All discounts subject to availability at participating hotels and do not apply to AAA Special Value Rates. Certain other restrictions apply.

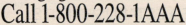